MILLENNIALS
in AMERICA

MILLENNIALS in AMERICA

Second Edition

2017

Robert L. Scardamalia

Bernan Press

Lanham, MD

Published in the United States of America
by Bernan Press, a wholly owned subsidary of
The Rowman & Littlefield Publishing Group, Inc.
4501 Forbes Boulevard, Suite 200
Lanham, Maryland 20706

Bernan Press
800-462-6420
www.rowman.com

ISBN-13: 978-1-59888-933-8
eISBN-13: 978-1-59888-934-5

♾™ The paper used in this publication meets the minimum requirements of
American National Standard for Information Sciences—Permanence of
Paper for Printed Library Materials, ANSI/NISO Z39.48-1992.
Manufactured in the United States of America.

Contents

Preface

Everyone ages. That's not a startling statement, but our national conversation on aging continues to be focused on the retirement, health, and service issues of the Baby Boom generation. The Baby Boom generation is commonly accepted to be those born between 1946 and 1964, and during those years some 76 million individuals were born. Today they are between the ages of 53 and 71. While the Boomers are swelling the ranks of the aging population, they are a declining proportion of the total U.S. population. Census estimates for July 1, 2015 report that Boomers accounted for 23 percent of the population, but by 2040 they will account for only half that, or 11 percent. Generation "X," or the Baby Bust generation, is markedly smaller, numbering only about 55 million people compared to the 76 million births in the Baby Boom years.

So why focus on the Millennial generation? The "echo" of the Baby Boom generation is made up of 78 million births between 1982 and 2001. The same Census estimates report the 2015 population of Millennials at almost 88 million people because this cohort of individuals is still growing due to foreign immigration. It is now our nation's largest generation and one that will continue to grow. Our national conversation on aging needs to shift and recognize that the Millennials will be the driving social and political force in the coming decades.

Unlike the commonly accepted period of birth for the Boomers, there is no common agreement on what birth years constitute the Millennial generation. We typically refer to the Millennials as those "coming of age" and born around the millennium but that can represent many different viewpoints. For the purposes of this portrait of the Millennials, I have defined the generation to be those born from 1982 through 2000. In the 2015 ACS used for this book, the Millennial generation is made up of those individuals between the ages of 15 (born in 2000) and 33 (born in 1982).

The Millennials are a generation who experienced the deepest recessionary period since the Great Depression while they were starting their careers. They continue to delay marriage and childbearing, are more supportive of gay rights, multi-racial marriage, have lower rates of home ownership than previous generations, and may not be able to attain as high a living standard as their parents.

It's natural to generalize about the characteristics and attitudes of any population sub-group, and outlining differences between generations is no different. However, large scale generalizations of youth, middle aged adults, seniors, low-income, high-income—you name it—completely misses the nuanced differences between our communities. The purpose of this compendium of statistics about the Millennial generation isn't a comparison with other generations but rather a comparison of characteristics across communities. Living arrangements, racial and ethnic diversity, migration patterns and many other characteristics simply aren't the same in all communities, and this volume will help to illustrate those differences.

There are a couple of important aspects of the data presented here that need explanation:

- As mentioned above, there is little agreement among demographers or in the media about what birth years constitute the Millennial generation. A search of the literature will find a number of definitions ranging from one of the earliest beginning years at 1976 to the latest year of 2004. It is unlikely that changing the definition by a year or two in either direction will have a large impact on area comparisons presented here. There is logic to maintaining a generational length of 18 to 20 years as that period when children move into adulthood, but there is also logic to lengthening that period to 25 or 28 years as delayed marriage and childbearing has extended the length of a generation. The years 1982 to 2000 were chosen to maintain a more traditional generation length yet capture the portion of the Millennials who have not quite reached the age of independence (15 to 17 years old) and also those generally completing their educations and moving into family and household formation (25 to 33 years old).

- The source of the data used here is the Census Bureau's American Community Survey. Subsequent chapters that describe many of the details of the survey will be helpful to data users in understanding some of the limitations of the ACS, but most important here is the use of the ACS microdata to define the Millennial generation. Typical Census Bureau summary data from the decennial census and the ACS is limited by predefined table structures that do not identify unique age ranges like that used to define the Millennials. The microdata provides the necessary flexibility to define specific age ranges but in that flexibility there is a limitation in terms of geography and the areas defined. This trade-off is described in much more detail in the section "Defining the Millennials" and readers are encouraged to pay special attention to how the geographic areas are defined.

- While the ACS is a very large survey of more than 3 million households each year, there are still significant concerns over the reliability of the estimates, especially for smaller areas. The Census Bureau continually advises users to focus on characteristic distributions rather than survey population counts, and that advice is reflected in this book. Population totals are provided to allow comparisons of area size, but the characteristics presented are percentages of the total rather than population counts. Comparisons of the percentages are less affected by relative population size and reduce misinterpretations due to sampling error.

This book is designed to include a sampling of key information about the Millennial generation but also help users understand the survey data and resources to access more detailed data available from the Census Bureau and the ACS. The 11 subject area tables in this book include data for each geographic area including all states and the District of Columbia and selected cities, counties, and metropolitan statistical areas meeting the required population threshold. This is a small sampling of the detailed data that could be presented.

The ACS survey estimates are different from the decennial census, as the Census Bureau surveys nearly 300,000 households every month as opposed to a single reference date of April 1 in the Census. The data in this book are from the 2015 ACS single year estimates, which are produced from 12 calendar months of survey data collection. They are period estimates with sample cases spread evenly throughout the 12-month survey time period.

Finally, it is always critical to remember that all estimates are subject to sampling error. On the Census Bureau's website, every ACS estimate is accompanied by its margin of error. In the interests of space and simplicity, this book does not include the margins of error, but all users are encouraged to consult the Census Bureau's website and to understand some basics: small differences are very likely to represent no difference at all; do not draw conclusions from small numbers; use these numbers as a starting point to explore the wealth of information from the ACS.

Introduction

The American Community Survey (ACS) has ushered in the most substantial change in the decennial census in more than 60 years. It replaced the decennial census long form in 2010, providing more current data throughout the decade by collecting long-form-type information annually rather than only once every 10 years. The ACS provides annual estimates for states, metropolitan areas, and large cities and counties based on 12-month periods of data collection. Estimates for midsize communities (20,000 to 65,000 population) were produced each year through 2013 based on 36-month periods of data collection but have been discontinued for budgetary reasons. Very small communities (under 20,000 population) and statistical areas like census tracts and zip code tabulation areas require 5 years (60 months) of survey responses.

The ACS gathers demographic, social, economic, housing, and financial information about the nation's people and communities as the survey is conducted on a continuing basis by the U.S. Census Bureau in every county, American Indian and Alaska Native Area, and Hawaiian Home Land in the United States. The Puerto Rican Community Survey is conducted in every municipality in Puerto Rico. As the largest survey in the United States, it is the only source of small-area data on a wide range of important social and economic characteristics for all communities in the country. After years of planning, development, and a demonstration period, the ACS began full nationwide implementation in 2005.

Information about the ACS are available on the Census Bureau's website. The ACS main page is http://www.census.gov/programs-surveys/acs. Data from the ACS is available from American FactFinder at http://factfinder.census.gov.

A vast amount of information is collected in the ACS. In this publication, selections of these data have been assembled in various tables by subject and geographic type.

VOLUME ORGANIZATION

The data tables in this book pertain to the population age 15 to 33 and include a selection of population and housing characteristics from the ACS in 11 subject areas:

- 1-Population summary
- 2-Race and ethnicity
- 3-Nativity and world region of birth
- 4-Household relationships and living arrangements
- 5-Educational attainment
- 6-Educational Field of Study
- 7-Language spoken at home and English ability
- 8-Employment and labor force status
- 9-Income and poverty status
- 10-Mobility
- 11-Housing summary

The 1-year estimates from the American Community Survey provide data for all areas of 65,000 population or more but the geographic comparisons here are limited by the minimum population threshold of the microdata which is 100,000. Each subject area includes data for the United States, the 50 states and the District of Columbia and the following:

- 633 counties, listed alphabetically within state,
- 344 cities, listed alphabetically within state, and
- 381 metropolitan areas and 34 micropolitan areas, listed alphabetically.

In addition, each part is preceded by highlights, maps and/or summary tables that show how areas diverge from the national norm, as well as the differences among areas. These research aids are invaluable for helping people understand what the census data tell us about who we are, what we do, and where we live.

In the following sections, information about the ACS and how to use the data is included, much of it excerpted from the wealth of information available on the Census Bureau's website. Especially helpful are the instructions, definitions, and guidelines on using the data in the sections on understanding and using the ACS. Readers are encouraged to explore the Census Bureau's website to expand on the information contained here and to keep up to date with this constantly changing dataset.

Robert Scardamalia is President of RLS Demographics, Inc. a firm providing data and analysis to private organizations, government agencies, and not-for-profits, especially in the areas of aging services and business development. He is an adjunct professor in the Sociology Department of the State University of New York at Albany. Prior to forming RLS Demographics, he was Chief Demographer of New York State and directed the Center for Research and Information Analysis in the New York Department of Economic Development. He also directed the New York State Data Center for

more than 20 years. Mr. Scardamalia is a past President of the Association of Public Data Users, has chaired the national State Data Center Steering Committee and served on numerous Census Bureau committees. He holds a Master of Arts in Demography from Georgetown University and Bachelor of Arts in Sociology from Penn State University.

Defining the Millennials

WHAT ARE MICRODATA FILES AND WHY USE THEM?

The Census Bureau produces a large number of data profiles and detailed tables in predefined tabular formats through American FactFinder and various reports. However, these predefined products cannot meet the unique research and analysis needs of every data user. To meet those needs, the Census Bureau produces the Public Use Microdata Sample (PUMS) files which allow data users to create custom tables and characteristics not available in the standard ACS products.

The PUMS files are a set of household and person records that provide the individual characteristics as they were reported on the ACS questionnaire. They differ from the ACS summary products which show data that have already been tabulated for specific geographic areas. For example, detailed tables on children will likely show the population tabulated for the population age 5 and under and 6 to 17. If a specific research task requires analysis of the population between the ages of 3 and 10, the standard products can't be used. With the PUMS files, the researcher can tabulate individuals within the specific ages of 3 and 10.

PUBLIC USE MICRODATA AREAS—RELATION TO POLITICAL GEOGRAPHY

The increased flexibility to tabulate characteristics from the PUMS files comes with the cost of reduced geographic detail. While summary data profiles and tables from the ACS can be obtained for every community and even small statistical areas like census tracts, the PUMS geography is limited to areas of 100,000 or more population size. This is necessary to protect the confidentiality of survey respondents. Even though 1-year estimates from the ACS are produced for areas of 65,000 or more population, it is not possible to tabulate data from the PUMS for areas under 100,000 population.

This volume presents data for all states and the District of Columbia because these areas are not affected by the 100,000 population threshold for the PUMS data. Also included are comparisons for counties, cities and metropolitan areas—most of which exceed the 100,000 population threshold but many that are between 90 and 100,000. The inclusion of areas below the 100,000 threshold is possible because of a statistical allocation model developed that creates an equivalency table between the PUMS geographic areas and the official boundaries of county, city and metropolitan areas. This allocation model is described below.

Figure 1: Manhattan, NY PUMA 03803

GEOGRAPHIC ALLOCATION METHOD

Understanding the allocation method first requires an understanding of the Census Bureau's PUMS geography and its relation to political and statistical geography. The following examples will help illustrate the problems and solutions.

The Census Bureau's PUMS geographic units are called Public Use Microdata Areas (PUMA's). PUMA's are constructed by the Census Bureau in cooperation with the individual states and are typically comprised of whole counties, county subdivisions and census tracts. The Census Bureau and states will aggregate the relevant statistical and political areas to make up a PUMA of at least 100,000 population. Individual counties that do not meet the 100,000 threshold are grouped with other counties until a PUMA of 100,000 or more can be identified. Counties with populations over 200,000 can theoretically have two PUMA's identified since each could potentially meet the 100,000 threshold.

In very large areas like New York City, numerous PUMA's can be created as long as each meets the required threshold. Figure 1 presents a PUMA in New York County (Manhattan - 03803) that is made up of 10 census tracts.

There are 55 PUMA's that make up the entire legal entity of New York City which represents an illustration of exact equivalency between the PUMA definitions and the legal/political boundaries of the city. The initial PUMA delineation by the New York City Department of City Planning was done in order to insure this exact equivalency.

Albany City, New York is an illustration of an area that is close to the 100,000 threshold but too small to be an individual PUMA. Albany's population in the 2010 census was only 97,856. In cases such as this, the population in adjacent census tracts can be added to the PUMA to meet the 100,000 threshold. In the case of Albany, two census tracts (140.01 and 140.02) from a contiguous

Figure 2: Albany, NY PUMA 02001

county sub-division were included in the Albany PUMA allowing it to be uniquely identified. Figure 2 illustrates this example.

Both of these cases illustrate very reasonable and workable PUMA definitions that equal or closely approximate legal/political entities. That is not the case for all PUMA definitions and in many cases counties and cities are split by multiple PUMA's and PUMA's can be split by multiple entities. These are the cases that required the development of a statistical allocation model so that cities, counties and metropolitan areas of over 100,000—but not defined as individual PUMA's—could be reported. Figures 3 and 4 illustrate this situation.

Concord, CA is a city of nearly 129,000 population as estimated for July 1, 2016. This city population in the 2010 Census was 122,000, clearly large enough to be defined as a single PUMA. Figure 3 shows that Concord is made up of portions of three separate PUMA's (black boundaries) and each PUMA includes lands outside of the city corporate limits (gray boundaries).

Atlanta, GA is a large city of nearly 473,000 in the 2016 Census estimates and could support the definition of four PUMA's that would be exactly equivalent to the legal boundaries of Atlanta. Instead, Atlanta is made up of six PUMA's, three of which are wholly contained within the city boundaries and three which extend beyond the city borders to include land area and population outside of Atlanta as seen in Figure 4.

In Concord, Atlanta and hundreds of other counties, cities and metropolitan areas, the PUMA boundaries and the legal/political boundaries to not match. In all of these cases, it is necessary to allocate a portion of

Figure 3: Concord, CA

Figure 4: Atlanta, GA

the person records in the affected PUMA's to the relevant county, city or metro area. However, due to confidentiality restrictions, there is no geographic identifier on the file that can be used to apportion records in the required fashion. An allocation method was developed that takes into account the proportional split of population between the PUMA and the legal entity and the proportion of the entity's population that is classified as the Millennial population.[1]

Based on the 2010 Census count, 46.5 percent of the population of PUMA 01306 resides within the City of Concord and 23.56 percent of the population of Concord is part of the Millennial generation, age 15 to 33. This results in an initial record allocation factor for PUMA

1. The author wishes to acknowledge the assistance of Mr. Doug Hilmer, formerly with the U.S. Census Bureau, for assistance in development of the allocation method; Dr. Hui Shien Tsu with the Center for Social and Demographic Analysis at SUNY Albany; and Dr. Florio Arguillas with the Cornell Institute for Social and Economic Research at Cornell University for assistance in SAS and SPSS programming of the method.

01306 of 8.203 percent. Since there are 1,094 person records in PUMA 01306, we will first sample 90 records (8.203 percent times 1,094) as Millennial records residing in the City of Concord. This initial sample allocation may not result in a sampled population equal to the estimated Millennial population of the area. This initial sample allocation may be increased or decreased in order to most closely approximate the estimated Millennial population.

This method assumes an even geographic distribution of records throughout the PUMA, which is obviously not always accurate. In some cases, this method attempts to allocate more records than the number of Millennial records in the PUMA, which case the record selection is limited to the maximum number of records available. In many other cases, like New York City, the PUMA allocation factor is 1.0, which means that all records will be selected and that the PUMA boundaries are wholly within the political/legal entity.

By applying this allocation method it is possible to approximate the characteristics of the defined Millennial population. It also allows for the reporting of estimates for some areas with populations below the PUMA threshold of 100,000. In addition to the standard cautions on the use of the American Community Survey data described in other sections, the user of these data should also understand that this allocation procedure may introduce additional error to the estimates.

Understanding the American Community Survey

Every 10 years since 1790, as required by the U.S. Constitution, Congress has authorized funds to conduct a national census of the U.S. population. From 1960 through 2000, censuses have consisted of:

- a "short form," which included basic questions about age, sex, race, Hispanic origin (since 1980), household relationship, and owner/renter status, and

- a "long form" used for a sample of approximately one of every six households that included not only the basic short-form questions but also detailed questions about socioeconomic and housing characteristics.

Beginning with the 2010 census, the American Community Survey (ACS) replaced the decennial census long form by collecting long-form-type information annually rather than only once every 10 years, providing more current data throughout the decade. The 2010 Census counted the population to support the constitutional mandate—to provide population counts needed to apportion the seats in the U.S. House of Representatives. The ACS data now provide, for the first time, a regular stream of updated information for states and local areas, revolutionizing the way we use data to understand our communities. It produces social, housing, and economic characteristics for demographic groups, even for geographic areas as small as census tracts and block groups.

SOME KEY FACTS ABOUT THE ACS

- The ACS annually provides the same kind of detailed information previously available only every 10 years from the census. The ACS is conducted under the authority of Title 13, United States Code, Sections 141 and 193.

- All answers are confidential. Any Census Bureau employee who violates that confidentiality is subject to a jail term, a fine, or both.

- The Census Bureau may use the information it collects only for statistical purposes.

- Addresses are selected at random from the Master Address File to represent similar households in the area. Approximately 290,000 addresses are selected each month and the survey is conducted by mail, telephone, and personal visit. Response to this survey is required by Section 221 of Title 13.

- Approximately 2.9 percent of U.S. households are surveyed each year. A sample of group quarters (nursing homes, college dormitories, etc.) is included in the ACS as well.

- While the ACS sample size approximates the traditional long-form census sample, it is a smaller sample resulting in somewhat larger margins of error.

The traditional long-form census each decade provided the socio-economic portrait of the nation and communities but that portrait was fixed in time for 10 years. Data from the ACS provides a regular update to that portrait which is used for a variety of purposes that include: monitoring the economic well-being of America's population, children and families, tracking trends in household living arrangements, analyzing the characteristics of the population, growth in the number of grandparents responsible for their grandchildren, determining the economic status of the working-poor, or tracking social, economic, and demographic changes in the general U.S. population.

The ACS provides critical information for communities on a current basis, when they need it most. But the ACS is still a sample survey. It is a different collection instrument and a different measure of the characteristics of the population and households than the traditional census data. It is good to be cautious in the interpretation of differences between areas and across time. Small differences may not be meaningful. On the other hand, the ACS provides annual estimates and the frequency of updates and currency of the data far outweighs waiting 10 years for new results.

NEW OPPORTUNITIES

The main benefits of the ACS are timeliness and access to annual data for states, local areas, and small population subgroups. The ACS will deliver useful, relevant data, similar to data from previous census long forms, but updated every year rather than every 10 years. The ACS provides comparable information across and within states for program evaluation and use in funding formulas.

- ACS information is often used to determine the placement of new schools, senior residential services, hospitals, and highways.

- ACS provides information for tracking the well-being of children, families, and the elderly allowing service providers to better target populations in need.

- The data will improve the distribution of aid through federal, state, and local governments. More than $400 billion in federal program funds are distributed each year based, in whole or in part, on census and ACS data.

- The data are used by community programs, such as those for the elderly, libraries, hospitals, banks, and other organizations.

- The data are used by transportation planners to evaluate peak volumes of traffic in order to reduce congestion, plan for parking, and develop plans for carpooling and flexible work schedules.

- Corporations, small businesses, and individuals use these data to develop business plans, to set strategies for expansion or starting a business, and to determine trends in their service areas to meet current and future needs.

- Small towns and rural communities have much to gain from the ACS. Lacking the staff and resources to conduct their own research, many local communities have relied on decennial census information that became increasingly outdated throughout the decade, or used local administrative records that are not comparable with information collected in neighboring areas.

- The ACS also provides tools for those who want to conduct their own research. The ACS includes a Public Use Microdata Sample (PUMS) file each year that enables researchers to create custom universes and tabulations from individual ACS records that have been stripped of personally identifiable information. It is this file that is the basis for the data presented here.

- Because the ACS data collection occurs every month, the Census Bureau uses professional, highly trained, permanent interviewers which have improved the accuracy of ACS data compared with those from the decennial census long-form sample. This strategy has effectively reduced the number of refusals to complete the ACS questionnaire and allows interviewers to obtain more complete information than decennial census interviewers.

NEW CHALLENGES

The main challenges for ACS data users are understanding and using multiyear estimates and the relatively large margins of error associated with ACS data for smaller geographic areas and subgroups of the population.

- ACS data will be produced every year, but the sample size of the ACS is smaller than that of the Census 2000 long form sample. Data users need to pay more attention to the margin of error, which is somewhat easier to do with the ACS products since the Census Bureau publishes the margin of error alongside the estimated characteristic.

- Data users have access to 5-year estimates of ACS data. The sample size based on 5-year period estimates of ACS data is still smaller than the long-form sample in the decennial census, resulting in larger margins of error in the ACS 5-year estimates.

- Because the ACS will produce 1-year and 5-year estimates, areas of 65,000 population or more will receive estimates of the same characteristics every year for each of the period estimates. For example, a large city will receive 1-year and a 5-year estimate of the number of persons 65 and over in poverty. Data users will have to decide which datasets are appropriate for their needs.

- Data users will need to be aware of the implications of multiyear estimates, particularly in analyzing employment and income data that will span a full year or even a 5-year period.

- Multiyear estimates, especially the 5-year estimates will not reflect short-term changes in the population or economy of an area. The recent recession is a good example because the 5-year ACS estimates span both the fall into recession and the resulting growth coming out.

The ACS includes several questions that are very similar to those collected in other federal surveys—especially the Current Population Survey (CPS), the American Housing Survey, and the Survey of Income and Program Participation. In some cases, there are clear guidelines about which data to use. For example, the CPS is the official source of income and poverty data. It includes detailed questions on these topics and should be used in reporting national trends in these subject areas. The Census Bureau recommends that ACS information on income and poverty be used to supplement CPS data for areas below the state level and for population subgroups (such as age, sex, race, Hispanic origin, type of household) at the state level. For an explanation of various income and poverty data sources, see the Census Bureau's guidelines at https://www.census.gov/topics/income-poverty/guidance.html For states, generally the Census Bureau recommends using the ACS, though the CPS is still valuable as a source for examining historical state income and poverty trends.

DATA COLLECTION VERSUS DATA REPORTING

Results from the ACS are reported each year which is a major advantage over the traditional long-form data from the decennial census. But unlike the decennial census release of data only once every 10 years, the annual release of data from the ACS can be quite confusing. The ACS sample size is such that the reliability of the data is greatly affected by the length of the data collection period and the size of geographic reporting areas. In survey sampling, it is well understood that larger samples yield more reliable estimates with smaller margins of error. In order to produce reliable estimates from the ACS, it is necessary to collect the data over differing periods of time in order to provide estimates for all areas, including small areas like census tracts.

Each set of period estimates is released each year, generally between September and December, and reflect data collection ending in the previous calendar year. Thus, the collection year 2015 1-year estimates for areas of 65,000 or more were released in September of 2016. The 2011–2015 5-year estimates follow as processing is completed.

THE ACS SAMPLE

The ACS is sent each month to a sample of roughly 290,000 addresses in the United States and Puerto Rico, or about 3.5 million a year, resulting in more than 2.2 million final interviews. The sample represents all housing units and group quarters in the United States and Puerto Rico. (Group quarters include places such as college dormitories, prisons, military barracks, and nursing homes.) The addresses are selected from the Census Bureau's Master Address File (MAF), which is also the basis for the decennial census.

The annual ACS sample is smaller than that of the Census 2000 long-form sample, which included about 18 million housing units. As a result, the ACS needs to combine population or housing data from multiple years to produce reliable numbers for small counties, neighborhoods, and other local areas. To provide information for communities each year, the ACS originally provided 1-, 3-, and 5-year estimates. Currently, estimates are provided for only 1-year and 5-year periods.

The ACS sample is not spread evenly across all areas but includes a larger proportion of addresses in sparsely populated rural communities and American Indian reservations and a lower proportion in densely populated areas. Over a 5-year period, the ACS will sample more than 17 million addresses and complete interviews for about 11 million. This sample is sufficient to produce estimates for small geographic areas, such as neighborhoods and sparsely-populated rural counties though the estimates will have larger margins of error than the census long-form data. In a 5-year period no address will be selected for the ACS more than once, and many addresses will never be selected for the survey. It's important to remember that the sample is address based so while a given address will not be in sample again for at least five years, it is possible that individuals who move or have a second home could be surveyed more than once.

Geography

The ACS data are tabulated for a variety of geographic areas ranging in size from broad geographic regions (Northeast, Midwest, South, and West) to cities, towns, neighborhoods, and census block groups. Before December 2008, the ACS data were only available for geographic areas with at least 65,000 people, including regions, divisions, states, the District of Columbia, Puerto Rico, congressional districts, Public Use Microdata Areas (PUMAs)—census-constructed geographic areas, each with approximately a population of 100,000—and many large counties, metropolitan areas, cities, school districts, and American Indian areas. Starting in December 2008, 3-year estimates became available for all areas with at least 20,000 residents, and in 2010, 5-year estimates for geographic areas down to the block group level became available. One- and five-year estimates—two sets of numbers—are now available and will be refreshed every year. Less populous areas will receive only 5-year estimates. The vast majority of areas will receive only 5-year estimates.

Data Product	Population Threshold	Year of Data Release							
		2009	2010	2011	2012	2013	2014	2015	2016
		Year(s) of Data Collection							
1-year Estimates	65,000+	2008	2009	2010	2011	2012	2013	2014	2015
3-year Estimates	20,000+	2006–2008	2007–2009	2008–2010	2009–2011	2010–2012	2011–2013	NA	NA
5-year Estimates	All Areas			2006–2010	2007–2011	2008–2012	2009–2013	2010–2014	2011–2015

Note that the 3-year estimates data products were eliminated due to budget cuts.

The data tables in this book contain data from the 1-year 2015 estimates. These tables are based on the current tabulation geography for political and statistical areas which are generally the same definitions as the 2010 Census. Changes in area boundaries can occur as a result of annexation, new incorporation or disincorporation of cities, towns, and places. For multiyear estimates, the Census Bureau reports the data based on the most current geographic boundaries incorporating any changes occurring in the multiyear period. More information about geography can be found in Appendix C.

DATA COMPARABILITY

Since the ACS data are collected continuously, they are not always comparable with data collected from the decennial census. For example, both surveys ask about employment status during the week prior to the survey. However, data from the decennial census are typically collected between March and July with a reference date of April 1st, whereas data from the ACS are collected nearly every day and reflect employment throughout the year. Other factors that may also have an impact on the data include seasonal variation in population and minor differences in question wording and question order.

While the categories of income by source are comparable with the decennial long-form data, the monthly collection of ACS data results in a significant difference in concept. In the decennial census, income refers to the previous calendar year whereas the ACS it refers to the previous 12-month period. Most people have a better understanding of what their calendar year income is, especially since the census is taken around tax time. With the ACS, individuals have to report income for a different period each month. A survey response in October of the year will report income from October of the previous year through September of the current year. This may require respondents to actually compute their 12-month income.

In 2006, the ACS began including samples of the population living in group quarters (e.g., jails, college dormitories, and nursing homes) for the first time. As a result, the ACS data from 2006 may not be comparable with data from earlier ACS surveys. This is especially true for estimates of young adults and the elderly, who are more likely than other groups to be living in group quarters facilities.

One of the most important uses of the ACS estimates is to make comparisons between estimates—over time or across areas. Several key types of comparisons are of general interest to users:

- Comparisons of estimates from different geographic areas within the same time period (e.g., comparing the

proportion of seniors below the poverty level in two counties).

- Comparisons of estimates for the same geographic area across time periods (e.g., comparing the proportion of people below the poverty level in a metropolitan area for 2014 and 2015).

- Comparisons of ACS estimates with the corresponding estimates from past decennial census samples (e.g., comparing the proportion of people below the poverty level in a county for 2015 and 2000).

A number of conditions must be met when comparing survey estimates.

- When comparing data for different geographic areas, always use the same period estimates. When comparing data for an area which only have 5-year estimates to an area with 1-, 3-, and 5-year estimates, it is important to compare only the 5-year estimates.

- When comparing over time for the same geographic area, again, only compare like-year period estimates. For example, it is not appropriate to compare a 1-year estimate for 2015 to a 5-year estimate for 2011–2015.

- Of primary importance is that the comparison takes into account the sampling error associated with each estimate, thus determining whether the observed differences between estimates are statistically significant. Statistical significance means that there is statistical evidence that a true difference exists within the full population, and that the observed difference is unlikely to have occurred by chance due to sampling. A method for determining statistical significance when making comparisons, as well as considerations associated with the various types of comparisons, can be found in Appendix 4 of the *ACS General Handbook*: https://census.gov/library/publications/2008/acs/general.html.

- The statistical properties of survey samples like the ACS are dependent upon independence of samples. In the ACS multiyear period estimates, the estimates are based on the sampled households for each year. That means that when comparing estimates for the period 2010–2014 to 2011–2015, four fifths of the sample cases are the same households—those surveyed in 2011 through 2014. The only different (independent) households are those from 2010 and 2015. When comparisons over time are made, it is best to compare non-overlapping samples. That is, compare estimates for 2006–2010 to the period 2011–2015 because both periods contain independent household samples. To meet this criteria for the use of 5-year estimates, data users had to wait for the 2011–2015 data to make time series comparisons.

Finally, the decennial census and the ACS have different residency rules. In the decennial census, population in tabulated by their "usual place of residence" typically where they spend six months or more of the year. This is subject to some seasonal variation due to persons with dual residences. In the ACS, there is a 2-month residency rule. That is, if the respondent has been in the sampled housing unit for 2 months or expects to be resident there for 2 months they are captured in the survey. This can have an impact on communities with highly seasonal populations and college communities.

SUBJECTS COVERED

The topics covered by the ACS focus on demographic, social, economic, and housing characteristics. These topics are virtually the same as those covered by the 2000 census long-form sample data.

Demographic Characteristics
Age, Sex, Hispanic Origin, Race, and Relationship to Householder (e.g., spouse).

Social Characteristics
Marital Status and Marital History; Fertility; Grandparents as Caregivers; Ancestry Place of Birth; Citizenship and Year of Entry; Language Spoken at Home; Educational Attainment and School Enrollment; Residence One Year Ago; Veteran Status, Period of Military Service, and VA Service-Connected Disability Rating; and Disability.

Economic Characteristics
Income, Food Stamps Benefit, Labor Force Status, Industry, Occupation, Class of Worker, Place of Work and Journey to Work, Work Status Last Year, Vehicles Available, and Health Insurance Coverage.

Housing Characteristics
Year Structure Built, Units in Structure, Year Moved Into Unit, Rooms, Bedrooms, Kitchen Facilities, Plumbing Facilities, House Heating Fuel, Telephone Service Available, and Farm Residence.

Financial Characteristics
Tenure (Owner/Renter), Housing Value, Rent, and Selected Monthly Owner Costs.

AVAILABILITY OF ACS ESTIMATES

The ACS began in 1996 and has expanded each subsequent year. From 2000 through 2004, the sample included between 740,000 and 900,000 addresses annually. In 2005, the ACS shifted from a demonstration program to the full sample size and design. It became the largest household survey in the United States, with an annual sample size of about 3 million addresses. Beginning with 2005, the ACS single-year estimates are available for geographic areas with a population of 65,000 or more. Three-year period estimates for areas of 20,000 or more were first released for the 2005–2007 time period while 5-year estimates for all areas were first released in 2010. The ACS will continue to accumulate samples over 5-year intervals to produce estimates for smaller geographic areas, including census tracts and block groups.

Annually, the ACS produces updated, single-year estimates of demographic, housing, social, and economic characteristics for all states, as well as for larger counties, cities, metropolitan and urban areas, and congressional districts. Geographic areas must have a minimum population of 65,000 to qualify for estimates based on a single year's sample. Every congressional district meets this threshold and therefore new single year estimates are released each year for every congressional district. Some school districts, townships, and American Indian and Alaska Native areas also meet this population threshold.

For areas with populations of at least 20,000, the Census Bureau produced estimates using data collected over a 3 year period but these estimates were discontinued due to budgetary reasons. For rural areas and city neighborhoods (including census tracts and block groups) with fewer than 20,000 people, the Census Bureau produces estimates using data collected over a 5-year period, with plans to update these multiyear estimates every year. ACS data are released annually, about 8 months after the end of each calendar year of data collection.

For some geographic areas—including three-quarters of all counties, most school districts, and most cities, towns, and American Indian reservations—only 5-year estimates are available because of their population size. Because some federal grant programs allocate funds directly to these areas, Congress can use the 5-year estimates to evaluate needs at the relevant geographic level, compare characteristics between areas within and among states, and analyze how various formulas distribute funds. The vast majority of areas will receive only 5-year estimates. In partnership with the states, the Census Bureau created *Public Use Microdata Areas (PUMAs)*, which are special, non-overlapping areas within a state, each with a population of about 100,000. These areas will have annual 1-year estimates.

Definitions of these geographic areas are at: http://www.census.gov/programs-surveys/acs/geography-acs.html.

Using the ACS

DIFFERENCES BETWEEN THE ACS AND THE DECENNIAL CENSUS

While the main function of the decennial census is to provide *counts* of people for the purpose of congressional apportionment and legislative redistricting, the primary purpose of the ACS is to measure the changing social and economic *characteristics* of the U.S. population. As a result, the ACS does not provide official counts of the population though users of the data will report the estimate results as though they were counts. In nondecennial census years, the Census Bureau's Population Estimates Program continues to be the official source for annual population totals, by age, race, Hispanic origin, and sex. The ACS sample estimates are controlled to match the decennial census and the Census Bureau's annual population estimates by selected age, sex, race, and Hispanic origin categories. For more information about population estimates, visit the Census Bureau's website at http://www.census.gov/programs-surveys/popest.html.

There are many similarities between the methods used in the past decennial census sample and the ACS but there are also a number of differences in collection method and concepts. Response to both the ACS and decennial census is required by law, a factor that helps improve overall response. Both the ACS and the decennial census sample data are based on information from a sample of the population. Sampled household addresses are drawn from the Master Address File for both collection processes. The data from the Census 2000 sample of about one-sixth of the population were collected using a "long-form" questionnaire, whose content was the model for the ACS. The sample for the ACS is somewhat smaller, approximately 1 in 7 households, resulting in larger margins of error.

While some differences exist in the specific Census 2000 question wording and that of the ACS, most questions are identical or nearly identical. Differences in the design and implementation of the two surveys are noted below with references provided to a series of evaluation studies that assess the degree to which these differences are likely to impact the estimates. The ACS produces period estimates and these estimates do not measure characteristics for the same time frame as the decennial census estimates, which are interpreted to be a snapshot as of April 1 of the census year.

Some data items were collected by both the ACS and the Census 2000 long form with slightly different definitions or reference periods that could affect the comparability of the estimates for these items. One example is annual costs for a mobile home. Census 2000 included installment loan costs in the total annual costs but the ACS does not. In this example, the ACS could be expected to yield smaller estimates than Census 2000.

While some differences were a part of the census and survey design objectives, other differences observed between ACS and census results were not by design, but due to nonsampling error—differences related to how well the surveys were conducted. The ACS and the census experience different levels and types of coverage error, different levels and treatment of housing unit and questionnaire item nonresponse, and different instances of measurement and processing error. Both Census 2000 and the ACS had similar high levels of survey coverage and low levels of unit nonresponse. Higher levels of unit nonresponse were found in the nonresponse follow-up stage of Census 2000 while lower levels of item nonresponse were found in the ACS due to a permanent staff of trained interviewers.

Census Bureau analysts have compared sample estimates from Census 2000 with 1-year ACS estimates based on data collected in 2000 and 3-year ACS estimates based on data collected in 1999–2001 in selected counties. In general, ACS estimates were found to be quite similar to those produced from decennial census data.

Detailed information about the ACS methodology can be found at: http://www.census.gov/programs-surveys/acs/methodology.html.

RESIDENCE RULES

The fundamentally different purposes of the ACS and the census, and their timing, led to important differences in the choice of data collection methods. For example, the residence rules for a census or survey determine the sample unit's occupancy status and household membership at the time of collection. Defining the rules in a dissimilar way can affect those two very important estimates. The 2010 census residence rules, which determined where people should be counted, were based on the principle of "usual residence" on April 1, 2010. This is in keeping with the focus of the census on the requirements of congressional apportionment and state redistricting. To accomplish this, the decennial census attempts to restrict and determine a principal place of residence on one specific date for everyone enumerated. The ACS residence rules are based on a "current residence" concept since data are collected continuously throughout the entire year with responses provided relative to the continuously changing survey interview dates. This method is consistent with the goal of the ACS to produce estimates that reflect annual averages of the characteristics of all areas.

Residence rules determine which individuals are considered to be residents of a particular housing unit or group quarters. While many people have definite ties to a single housing unit or group quarters, some people may stay in different places for significant periods of time over the course of the year. For example, "snow birds" can maintain two residences in different states and do not live in any one location for the entire year. In the decennial census, it is their residence on April 1, or their interpretation of their "usual place of residence," that is the basis for their location. Differences in treatment of these populations in the census and ACS can lead to differences in estimates of the characteristics of some areas.

For the past several censuses, decennial census residence rules were designed to produce an accurate count of the population as of Census Day, April 1, while the ACS residence rules were designed to collect representative information to produce annual average estimates of the characteristics of all types of areas. When interviewing the population living in housing units, the decennial census uses a "usual residence" rule to enumerate people at the place where they live or stay most of the time as of April 1. The ACS uses a "current residence" rule to interview people who are currently living or staying in the sample housing unit as long as their stay at that address has been, or will be, for at least 2 months. The residence rules governing the census enumerations of people in group quarters depend on the type of group quarter and, where permitted, whether people claim a "usual residence" elsewhere. The ACS applies a straight de facto residence rule to every type of group quarter. Everyone living or staying in a group quarter on the day it is visited by an ACS interviewer is eligible to be sampled and interviewed for the survey.

Further information on residence rules can be found at: https://www.census.gov/programs-surveys/acs/methodology/design-and-methodology.html.

The differences in the ACS and census data due to the different residence rules, are minimal for most areas and most characteristics. However, for certain segments of the population the usual and current residence concepts could result in different residence decisions. The older population is one of those segments as many retired and active seniors maintain dual residences. Appreciable differences may occur in areas where large proportions of the total population spend several months of the year in what would not be considered their residence under decennial census rules. In particular, data for seasonal and tourist vacation areas may differ appreciably between the census and the ACS if populations live there for more than 2 months. In addition, college students (hence Millennials) are to be counted at the location of the college rather than their parent's home in the decennial census. However, during summer months, college students can meet the 2-month residency rule for the ACS and be counted along with their parents rather than at the college.

REFERENCE PERIODS

Estimates produced by the ACS are measuring period averages. The ACS yearly samples, spread over 12 months, collect information that is anchored to the day on which the sampled unit was interviewed, whether it is the day that a mail questionnaire is completed or the day that an interview is conducted by telephone or personal visit. Individual questions with time references such as "last week" or "the last 12 months" all begin the reference period as of this interview date. Even the information on types and amounts of income refers to the 12 months prior to the day the question is answered. ACS mail returns and interviews occur every day of the year, and all of the estimates that the survey releases are considered to be averages for a specific time period. The 1-year estimates reflect the full calendar year; 3-year and 5-year estimates reflect the full 36- or 60-month period.

Most decennial census sample estimates are anchored in this same way, but to the reference date of April 1. The most obvious difference between the ACS and the census is the overall time frame in which they are conducted. The census enumeration time period is less than half the time period used to collect data for each single-year ACS estimate. But a more important difference is that the distribution of census enumeration dates are highly clustered in March and April (when most census mail returns were received) with additional, smaller clusters seen in May and June (when nonresponse follow-up activities took place).

This means that the data from the decennial census, intended to reflect the characteristics of the population and housing on April 1, tend to describe the characteristics in the March through June time period (with an overrepresentation of March/April). The ACS data describe the characteristics nearly every day over the full calendar year. For employment and income estimates, the decennial census referred to the prior calendar year for all respondents, while the ACS asks about the 12 months preceding the interview.

Those who are interested in more information about differences in reference periods should refer to the Census Bureau's guidance on comparisons that contrasts for each question the specific reference periods used in Census 2000 with those used in the ACS:

http://www.census.gov/programs-surveys/acs/guidance/comparing-acs-data.html.

Some specific differences in reference periods between the ACS and the decennial census are described below. Users should consider the potential impact these different reference periods could have on distributions when comparing ACS estimates with Census 2000.

Income Data

To estimate annual income, the Census 2000 long-form sample used the calendar year prior to Census Day as the reference period, and the ACS uses the 12 months prior to the interview date as the reference period. Thus, while Census 2000 collected income information for calendar year 1999, the ACS collects income information for the 12 months preceding the interview date. The annual responses are a mixture of the 12 reference periods ranging from, in the case of the 2015 ACS single-year estimates, the full calendar year 2014 through November 2015.

The ACS income responses for each of these reference periods are individually inflation-adjusted to represent dollar values for the ACS collection year. Further inflation adjustments are made to the 3- and 5-year estimates to reflect dollar values of the final year of the estimate. It's important to note that the rotating reference period for income can result in misreporting. The calendar year reference period of the decennial census coincides with an individual's annual salary and is also collected around tax time. Respondents will have a good idea of what their annual salary is. In the ACS, the respondent has to calculate their income for the previous 12 months, a figure which can vary considerably throughout the year.

School Enrollment

The school enrollment question on the ACS asks if a person had "at any time in the last 3 months attended a school or college." A consistent 3-month reference period is used for all interviews. In contrast, Census 2000 asked if a person had "at any time since February 1 attended a school or college." Since Census 2000 data were collected from mid-March to late-August, the reference period could have been as short as about 6 weeks or as long as 7 months.

Utility Costs

The reference periods for two utility cost questions—gas and electricity—differ between Census 2000 and the ACS. The census asked for annual costs, while the ACS asks for the utility costs in the previous month.

PERIOD ESTIMATES

The ACS produces period estimates of socioeconomic and housing characteristics. It is designed to provide estimates that describe the average characteristics of an area over a specific time period. In the case of ACS single-year estimates, the period is the calendar year (e.g., the 2015 ACS covers January through December 2015). In the case of ACS 5-year estimates for 2011–2015, the period of coverage includes January 2011 through December 2015. The ACS multiyear estimates are similar in many ways to the ACS single-year estimates, but they encompass a longer time period.

The differences in time periods between single-year and multiyear ACS estimates affect decisions about which set of estimates should be used for a particular analysis. While one may think of these estimates as representing average characteristics over a single calendar year or multiple calendar years, it must be remembered that the 1-year estimates are not calculated as an average of 12 monthly values and the multiyear estimates are not calculated as the average of either 36 or 60 monthly values, nor are the multiyear estimates calculated as the average of 3 or 5 single-year estimates. Rather, the ACS collects survey information continuously nearly every day of the year and then aggregates the results over a specific time period—1 year, 3 years, or 5 years. The data collection is spread evenly across the entire period represented so as not to over-represent any particular month or year within the period.

Because ACS estimates provide information about the characteristics of the population and housing for areas over the entire time frame, ACS single-year and multiyear estimates contrast with "point-in-time" estimates, such as those from the decennial census long-form samples or monthly employment estimates from the Current Population Survey (CPS), which are designed to measure characteristics as of a certain date or narrow time period. For example, Census 2000 was designed to measure the characteristics of the population and housing in the United States based upon data collected around April 1, 2000, thus its data reflect a narrower time frame than ACS data. The monthly CPS collects data for a more narrow time frame, the week containing the 12th of each month.

Most areas have consistent population characteristics throughout the calendar year, and their period estimates may not look much different from estimates that would be obtained from a "point-in-time" survey design. However, some areas (college towns and areas with high seasonal populations) may experience changes in the estimated characteristics of the population, depending on when in the calendar year the measurement occurred. For these areas, the ACS period estimates (even for a single year) may noticeably differ from "point-in-time" estimates. The impact will be more noticeable in smaller areas where changes such as a factory closing can have a large impact on population characteristics, and in areas with a large natural event such as Hurricane Katrina's impact on the New Orleans area. This logic can be extended to better interpret 3- and 5-year estimates where the periods involved are much longer. If, over the full period of time (for example, 36 months), there have been major or consistent changes in certain population or housing characteristics for an area, a period estimate for that area could differ markedly from estimates based on a "point-in-time" survey. For example, the 5-year estimates for 2009–2013 will be affected by the volatility in the economy and the housing market during those years and may mask shorter term fluctuations.

The tables in this book include 1-year estimates from 2015. Some areas will have shown more rapid recovery from the recession than others and experience stronger growth between the 2000 and 2010 censuses or the 2010 census and the 2015 ACS. The important thing to keep in mind is that ACS single-year estimates describe the population and characteristics of an area for the full year, not for any specific day or period within the year, while ACS multiyear estimates describe the population and characteristics of an area for the full 3- or 5-year period, not for any specific day, period, or year within the multiyear time period.

Single-year estimates provide more current information

Single-year estimates provide more current information about areas that have changing population and/or housing characteristics because they are based on the most current data—data from the past calendar year. In contrast, multiyear estimates provide less current information because they are based on both data from the previous year and data that are up to 5 years old. As noted earlier, for many areas with minimal change taking place, using the "less current" sample used to produce the multiyear estimates may not have a substantial influence on the estimates. However, in areas experiencing major changes over a given time period, the multiyear estimates may be quite different from the single-year estimates for any of the individual years. Single-year and multiyear estimates are not expected to be the same because they are based on data from two different time periods. This will be true even if the ACS single year is the midyear of the ACS multiyear period (e.g., 2013 single year, 2011–2015 multiyear).

Multiyear estimates are based on larger sample sizes and are therefore more reliable

The 5-year estimates are based on five times as many sample cases as the 1-year estimates. For some characteristics this increased sample is needed for the estimates to be reliable enough for use in certain applications. For other characteristics the increased sample may not be necessary.

Multiyear estimates are the only type of estimates available for geographic areas with populations of less than 65,000. Users may think that they only need to use multiyear estimates when they are working with small areas, but this isn't the case. Estimates for large geographic areas benefit from the increased sample, resulting in more precise estimates of population and housing characteristics, especially for subpopulations within those areas. In addition, users may determine that they want to use single-year estimates, despite their reduced reliability, as building blocks to produce estimates for meaningful higher levels of geography. These aggregations will similarly benefit from the increased sample sizes and gain reliability.

Currency	Reliability
1-year estimates provide information based on the most current year	Sample sizes producing estimates may be small and impact statistical reliability
3-year estimates provide information based on the last year and the 2 years before that	3-year estimates are based on 3 times as many sample cases as 1-year estimates
5-year estimates provide information based on the last year and the 4 years before that	5-year estimates are based on 5 times as many sample cases as 1-year estimates

DECIDING WHICH ACS ESTIMATE TO USE

Three primary uses of ACS estimates are:

- to understand the characteristics of the population of an area for local planning needs,

- to make comparisons across areas, and

- to assess change over time in an area.

Local planning could include making local decisions such as where to place schools or hospitals, determining the need for senior services or transportation, and carrying out other infrastructure analysis. In the past, decennial census sample data provided the most comprehensive information. However, the currency of those data suffered through the intercensal period, and the ability to assess change over time was limited. ACS estimates greatly improve the currency of data for understanding the characteristics of housing and population and enhance the ability to assess change over time. At the same time, small differences between ACS estimates can lead to misinterpretation due to larger margins of error.

Several key factors can help users decide whether to use single-year or multiyear ACS estimates for areas where both are available:

- intended use of the estimates

- required precision, or reliability, of the estimates

- currency of the estimates

All of these factors, along with an understanding of the differences between single-year and multiyear ACS estimates, should be taken into consideration when deciding which set of estimates to use.

For users interested in obtaining estimates for small geographic areas, multiyear ACS estimates are the only option. For the very smallest of these areas (like census tracts), the only option is to use the 5-year ACS estimates. Up until 2014, users had a choice of two sets of multiyear estimates when analyzing data for small geographic areas with populations of at least 20,000. Both 3- and 5-year ACS estimates were available. Only the largest areas with populations of 65,000 and more received all three data series. Since 2014 and the elimination of the 3-year estimates, areas of 65,000 or more receive both the 5-year and 1-year estimates.

The key trade-off to be made in deciding whether to use single-year or multiyear estimates is between currency and reliability. In general, the single-year estimates are preferred, as they will be more relevant to the current conditions. However, the user must take into account the level of uncertainty present in the single-year estimates, which may be large for small subpopulation groups and rare characteristics. While single-year estimates offer more current estimates, they also have higher sampling variability. One measure, the coefficient of variation (CV), can help you determine the fitness for use of a single-year estimate in order to assess if you should opt instead to use the multiyear estimate (or if you should use a 5-year estimate rather than a 3-year estimate). The CV is calculated as the ratio of the standard error of the estimate to the estimate, times 100. A single-year estimate with a small CV is usually preferable to a multiyear estimate as it is more up to date. However, multiyear estimates are an alternative option when a single-year estimate has an unacceptably high CV. Single-year estimates for small subpopulations (e.g., Millennials age 18 to 24 by income class) will typically have larger CVs. In general, multiyear estimates are preferable to single-year estimates when looking at estimates for small subpopulations.

For the complete discussion on deciding which estimates to use and on calculating the CV, see Appendix 1 of the *ACS General Handbook*: http://www.census.gov/library/publications/2008/acs/general.html.

Often users want to compare the characteristics of one area to those of another area. These comparisons can be in the form of rankings or of specific pairs of comparisons. Whenever you want to make a comparison between two different geographic areas you need to take the type of estimate into account. It is important that comparisons be made within the same estimate type. That is, 1-year estimates should only be compared with other 1-year estimates, 3-year estimates should only be compared with other 3-year estimates, and 5-year estimates should only be compared with other 5-year estimates.

You certainly can compare characteristics for areas with populations of 30,000 to areas with populations of 100,000 but you should use the data set that they have in common. In this example you could use the 5-year estimates because they are available for areas of 30,000 and areas of 100,000. You should NOT compare the single year estimate for the area of 100,000 to the 5-year estimate for the area of 30,000. This book includes only the 1-year estimates for 2015 so comparisons across geographic areas will be appropriate.

Users are encouraged to make comparisons between sequential single-year estimates. In American FactFinder (AFF), comparison profiles are available beginning with the 2007 single-year data. These profiles identify statistically significant differences between each year from 2007 through the most recently released year.

Caution is needed when using multiyear estimates for estimating year-to-year change in a particular characteristic. This is because roughly four-fifths of the respondents in a 5-year estimate overlap with the respondents in the next year's 5-year estimate period (the overlap is roughly two-thirds for 3-year estimates). When comparing 5-year estimates from 2010–2014 with those from 2011–2015, the differences in overlapping multiyear estimates are driven by differences in the non-overlapping years (i.e. 2010 and 2015). A more appropriate comparison of change over time would be comparing the 2006-2010 5-year estimate to the 2011–2015 5-year estimate because they include responses from totally independent samples. Comparison of overlapping periods should be made with caution.

Users who are interested in comparing overlapping multiyear period estimates should refer to Appendix 4 of the *ACS General Handbook* for more information: http://www.census.gov/library/publications/2008/acs/general.html.

Multiyear estimates are likely to confuse some data users, in part because of their statistical properties, and in part because this is a new product from the Census Bureau. The ACS will provide all states and communities that have at least 65,000 residents with single-year estimates of demographic, housing, social, and economic characteristics—a boon to government agencies that need to budget and plan for public services like transportation, medical care, and schools. For geographic areas with smaller populations, the ACS samples too few households to provide reliable single-year estimates. For these communities, several years of data will be pooled together to create reliable 3- or 5-year estimates.

Single-year, 3- and 5-year estimates from the ACS are all "period" estimates that represent data collected over a period of time as opposed to "point-in-time" estimates, such as the decennial census. A subtle but important change in how ACS estimates are referred to is needed. Since ACS estimates refer to a period of time, multiyear estimates should be labeled to indicate clearly the full period (e.g., "The poverty rate for persons age 25 to 31 in 2011–2015 was X percent"). It would be misleading to report the poverty rate data in this example as the beginning year 2011, the ending year 2015 or the mid-point year 2013.

Multiyear estimates should, in general, be used when single-year estimates have large CVs or when the precision of the estimates is more important than the currency of the data. Multiyear estimates should also be used when analyzing data for smaller geographies and smaller population subgroups in larger geographies. Multiyear estimates are also of value when examining change over non-overlapping time periods and for smoothing data trends over time.

Single-year estimates should, in general, be used for larger geographies and populations when currency is more important than the precision of the estimates. Single-year estimates should be used to examine year-to-year change for estimates with small CVs. Given the availability of a single-year estimate, calculating the CV provides useful information to determine if the single-year estimate should be used. For areas believed to be experiencing rapid changes in a characteristic, single-year estimates should generally be used rather than multiyear estimates as long as the CV for the single-year estimate is reasonable for the specific usage.

Local area variations may occur due to rapidly occurring changes. Multiyear estimates will tend to be insensitive to such changes when they first occur. Single-year estimates, if associated with sufficiently small CVs, can be very valuable in identifying and studying such phenomena.

Data users also need to use caution in looking at trends involving income or other measures that are adjusted for inflation, such as rental costs, home values, and energy costs. Note that inflation adjustment is based on a national-level consumer price index: it does not adjust for differences in costs of living across different geographic areas.

Appendix 5 of the *ACS General Handbook* provides information on the adjustment of single-year and multiyear ACS estimates for inflation: http://www.census.gov/library/publications/2008/acs/general.html.

MARGIN OF ERROR

All data that are based on samples, such as the ACS and the census long-form samples, include a range of uncertainty. Two broad types of error can occur: sampling error and nonsampling error. Nonsampling errors can result from mistakes in how the data are reported or coded, problems in the sampling frame or survey questionnaires, or problems related to nonresponse or interviewer bias. The Census Bureau tries to minimize nonsampling errors by using trained interviewers and by carefully reviewing the survey's sampling methods, data processing techniques, and questionnaire design.

Appendix 6 of the *ACS General Handbook* includes a more detailed description of different types of errors in the ACS and other measures of ACS quality: http://www.census.gov/library/publications/2008/acs/general.html.

Sampling error occurs when data are based on a sample of a population rather than the full population. Sampling error is easier to measure than nonsampling error and can be used to assess the statistical reliability of survey data. For any given area, the larger the sample and the more months included in the data, the greater the confidence in the estimate. The Census Bureau reports the 90-percent confidence interval on all ACS estimates produced for 2005 and later. Beginning with the release of the 2006 ACS data, *margins of error (MOE)* are now provided for every ACS estimate. Ninety percent confidence intervals define a range expected to contain the *true* value of an estimate with a level of confidence of 90 percent. Margins of error are easily converted into these confidence ranges. By adding and subtracting the margin of error from the point estimate, we can calculate the 90-percent confidence interval for an estimate. Therefore, we can be 90 percent confident that the true number falls between the lower-bound interval and the upper-bound interval. For example, the 2015 1-year estimate of the poverty rate for the United States is 14.7 percent with a +/- 0.1 margin of error. With these reported figures, the user can say with 90 percent confidence that the *true* poverty rate in the United States is between 14.6 percent and 14.8 percent.

Detailed information about sampling error and instructions for calculating confidence intervals and margins of error are included in Appendix 3 of the *ACS General Handbook*: http://www.census.gov/library/publications/2008/acs/general.html.

The margin of error around an estimate is important because it helps one draw conclusions about the data. Small differences between two estimates may not be statistically significant if the confidence intervals of those estimates overlap. However, the Census Bureau cautions data users not to rely on overlapping confidence intervals as a test for statistical significance, because this method will not always produce accurate results. Instead, the Census Bureau recommends following the detailed instructions for conducting statistical significance tests in Appendix 4 of the *ACS General Handbook*.

In some cases, data users will need to construct custom ACS estimates by combining data across multiple geographic areas or population subgroups or it may be necessary to derive a new percentage, proportion, or ratio from published ACS data. In such cases, additional calculations are needed to produce confidence intervals and margins of error for the derived estimates. Appendix 3 of the *ACS General Handbook* provides detailed instructions on how to make these calculations. Note that these error measures do not tell us about the magnitude of nonsampling errors.

Some advanced data users will also want to construct custom ACS estimates from the Census Bureau's Public Use Microdata Samples (PUMS). There are separate instructions for conducting significance tests for PUMS estimates, available on the Census Bureau's American FactFinder (AFF) website at: https://www2.census.gov/programs-surveys/acs/tech_docs/statistical_testing/2015 StatisticalTesting1year.pdf.

Accessing ACS Data Online

All ACS data are available through the Census Bureau's American FactFinder (AFF) website at http://factfinder.census.gov. However, American FactFinder is the dissemination tool for all Census Bureau data sources so it's important to make note of the source information to verify that the ACS is the source of the data presented. From the AFF home page, there are three paths to accessing the data:

- Community Facts—this will provide summary data profiles for a single geographic area. It's useful for obtaining quick demographic and economic indicators for states, cities, counties, towns or zip codes.

- Guided Search—this "wizard" leads the user through six steps to select the characteristics and geography of interest. Guided Search is available for all Census datasets so it is still important to verify the source of the data presented.

- Advanced Search—this path provides the most flexibility for data selection by the user but also requires a basic level of knowledge about Census datasets and characteristics. Clicking on the "Topics" button will allow the user to view and select "Datasets." For each year of available ACS data through 2013 there are three datasets shown—the 1-year, 3-year and 5-year estimates. For years after 2013 there are only two datasets shown—the 1-year and 5-year estimates. The tables in this book were produced from the 1-year estimates for 2015. It is important for all users to understand that once a data set is selected, the accessed tables will all correspond to this specific data set and period of estimate. All tables are clearly labeled, identifying the data set.

Basic help information on using the functions and features of American FactFinder can be found at http://factfinder.census.gov/help/en/index.htm#. The *American FactFinder* main page provides information about available data and guidance on using FactFinder, under the headings *Using American* FactFinder and *What We Provide*.

The various ACS data products are described below.

- **Data profiles, quick tables and ranking tables.** The *data profiles, quick tables* and *ranking tables* are good places to start for novice data users. *Data profiles and quick tables* provide separate fact sheets on the social, economic, demographic, and housing characteristics for different geographic areas, while *ranking tables* provide state-level rankings of key ACS variables.

- **Geographic comparison tables.** Those interested in geographic comparisons for areas other than states may be interested in the *geographic comparison tables*, which allow comparison of ACS data across a variety of geographic areas including metropolitan areas, cities, counties, and congressional districts.

- **Subject tables.** These are similar to *data profiles* but are specific to a more detailed characteristic or topic (e.g., employment, education, and income). *Subject tables* provide pre-tabulated numbers and percentages for a wide variety of topics, often available separately by age (for example, 60 and over and 65 and over), gender, or race/ethnicity.

- **Selected population profiles.** The most detailed race/ethnic data are available through the *selected population profiles*, which provide summary tables separately for more than 400 detailed race, ethnic, tribal, ancestry, and country of birth groups.

- **Comparison profiles.** The *comparison profiles* show data side-by-side from multiple years, indicating where there is a statistically significant difference between the two sets of estimates. Comparison profiles are only available for 1-year estimates which limits the profiles to geographic areas of 65,000 or more population.

- **Detailed tables and summary files.** The *detailed tables* are the best source for advanced data users or those who want access to the most comprehensive ACS tables. For more advanced users, *detailed tables* are also available for download through the ACS *Summary File*: http://www.census.gov/programs-surveys/acs/technical-documentation/summary-file-documentation.html

- **Thematic maps.** The *thematic maps* provide graphic displays of the data available through the various tables. Different shades of color are used to display variations in the data across geographic areas. Data users can also highlight areas with statistically different values from a selected state, county, or metropolitan area of interest. If a mapping option is available, it will display as an option when you view a table.

- **Public Use Microdata Sample files.** Those with expertise in using SAS, SPSS, or STATA may also be interested in the *Public Use Microdata Sample (PUMS) files*, which contain a sample of individual records of people and households that responded to the survey (stripped of all identifying information). The PUMS files permit analysis of specific population groups and custom variables that are not available through the summary tables in American FactFinder. The data presented in this book was produced using the 2015 1-year micro-data files and will be explained in more detail in the chapter "Defining the Millennials." Briefly, the age definition of the millennial population used here is age 13 through 31. This age group simply isn't tabulated in the Census Bureau's summary files and requires the more detailed characteristics identified in the PUMS file. This flexibility is not provided by the pre-tabulated detailed tables provided in American FactFinder. Data users can also combine multiple years of PUMS data to produce data for relatively small population subgroups (e.g., female physicians over age 55). More information about the PUMS is available on the technical documentation page at: http://www.census.gov/programs-surveys/acs/technical-documentation/pums.html.

For readers who are used to data from the traditional decennial census long-form, it is important to note that there are many conceptual and data collection differences in the ACS. The following is a summary of some of these differences which are described more fully in the chapter "Using the ACS."

The ACS data are complex and cover a broad range of topics and geographic areas. Because this is a relatively new survey, many people do not fully understand how to interpret and use the ACS data. The key points are summarized below.

- Use caution in comparing ACS data with data from the decennial census or other sources. Every survey uses different methods, which could affect the comparability of the numbers.

- The ACS was designed to provide estimates of the characteristics of the population, not to provide counts of the population in different geographic areas or population subgroups. However, counts of the population are often what is required by grant applications and researchers.

- Be careful in drawing conclusions about small differences between two estimates because they may not be statistically different. Statistical testing should always be considered based on the sensitivity of conclusions to differences in the data results.

- Data users need to be careful not to interpret annual fluctuations in the data as long-term trends. Again, statistical testing is necessary to determine if annual fluctuations are real or merely a result of the sample.

- Use caution in comparing data from 2006 and later surveys with data from the 2000–2005 surveys. Unlike the earlier surveys, the 2006 and later ACS surveys include samples of the population living in group quarters (e.g., college dorms and nursing homes), so the data may not be comparable. This is especially important for young adults and the elderly who are more likely than other age groups to be living in group quarters facilities.

- The questionnaire series to define disability changed in 2008 making it impossible to compare disability status for periods before that date.

- Data users should not interpret or refer to 3- year or 5-year period estimates as estimates of the middle year or last year in the series. For example, a 2008–2010 estimate is not a "2009 average."

- Data users should always be consistent in comparing similar period estimates over time or between geographic areas. Compare 1-year to 1-year, 3-year to 3-year and 5-year to 5-year estimates. Since geographic areas of different population size have different period estimates available, always compare make comparisons using the same period estimate. Do not compare a 1-year estimate for a large population size are to a 5-year estimate for a small area or census tract.

- Data users should *not* rely on overlapping confidence intervals as a test for statistical significance because this method will not always provide an accurate result.

More ACS Resources

There is a wealth of information about the ACS on the Web with new information made available on a regular basis. Each year, the ACS data release represents a new stage in the process. Consequently, many new documents are required to explain the survey, year-to-year changes, and how to use it. These resources cover many of the topics discussed in this book, but in greater detail.

The best place to start is the Census Bureau's ACS main page: http://www.census.gov/programs-surveys/acs/.

BACKGROUND AND OVERVIEW INFORMATION

About the Survey provides background and general information about the importance of the ACS, how sampled households are selected, response options, privacy protections and questionnaire information.
http://www.census.gov/programs-surveys/acs/about.html

News & Updates provides the latest information on data releases, ACS news and events such as the ACS Data Users Conference and other presentations using ACS data.
https://www.census.gov/programs-surveys/acs/news.html

Data provides access to the latest data releases and various tables and tools. This will often lead the user to American FactFinder for accessing specific tables and characteristics.
https://www.census.gov/programs-surveys/acs/data.html

Guidance for Data Users provides detailed information that helps users understand the geographic coverage of the survey data, how and when to use the multi-year estimates and handbooks for users of various types.
http://www.census.gov/programs-surveys/acs/guidance.html

Geography & ACS provides descriptions of geographic concepts and definitions, lists of areas with published ACS data and updates on geographic boundary changes.
https://www.census.gov/programs-surveys/acs/geography-acs.html

Technical Documentation is critical for users who need to understand the details of the data that's available, research and detailed documentation for the various data file products.
http://www.census.gov/programs-surveys/acs/technical-documentation.html

Methodology provides the most detailed information about the survey sample size, response rates and data quality.
http://www.census.gov/programs-surveys/acs/methodology.html

Library is a link to volumes of research and papers describing aspects of survey methodology, research, and analytical reports categorized by year.
http://www.census.gov/programs-surveys/acs/library.html

Accuracy of the Data (2013)
Provides a basic understanding of the sample design, estimation methodology, and accuracy of the 2015 ACS data.
https://www2.census.gov/programs-surveys/acs/tech_docs/accuracy/MultiyearACSAccuracyofData2015.pdf

ACS Sample Size and Data Quality Measures
Provides sample size information for each state for each year of the ACS. The initial sample size, the final completed response and coverage rates, as well as, item allocation rates are provided. Sample sizes for all published geographic entities starting with the 2007 ACS are available in the B98 series of detailed tables on American FactFinder.
http://www.census.gov/acs/www/methodology/sample-size-and-data-quality/

ACS Multiyear Estimates and Census Comparison
Multiyear estimates were an entirely new product of Census Bureau ACS operations and their use can be confusing to data users. The ACS "Methodology" page provides content and documentation of the multiyear estimates which are helpful to understanding the uses of multiyear estimates and making appropriate comparisons to traditional decennial census data.
http://www.census.gov/programs-surveys/acs/methodology.html

GUIDANCE ON DATA PRODUCTS AND USING THE DATA

How to Use the Data:
Includes links to many documents and materials that explain the ACS data products.
http://www.census.gov/programs-surveys/acs/guidance.html

Comparing ACS Data to Other Sources:
Guidance on comparing the ACS data products to other years of ACS data and to Census 2000 long-form data.
http://www.census.gov/programs-surveys/acs/guidance/comparing-acs-data.html

When to Use 1-year, 3-year, or 5-year Estimates
The availability of multiple characteristic estimates for a given geographic area for different period estimates can be confusing for users of ACS data. Guidance on comparing across geographies and time periods.
http://www.census.gov/programs-surveys/acs/guidance/estimates.html

Information on Using Different Sources of Data for Income and Poverty:
Highlights various measures of economic well-being and provides access links to the latest news, data and publications.
https://www.census.gov/topics/income-poverty.html

Poverty: 2014 and 2015 American Community Survey brief on poverty.
https://census.gov/library/publications/2016/acs/acsbr15-01.html

Public Use Microdata Sample (PUMS):
Provides guidance on accessing ACS microdata.
http://www.census.gov/programs-surveys/acs/data/pums.html

ACS Data Users Group
In partnership with the U.S. Census Bureau, the Population Reference Bureau (PRB) maintains the American Community Survey (ACS) Data Users Group. The purpose of the ACS Data Users Group is to improve understanding of the value and utility of ACS data and to promote information sharing among data users about key ACS data issues and applications. Membership in the group is free and open to all interested ACS data users. You can join this online community at:
https://acsdatacommunity.prb.org

OTHER DATA RESOURCES

- FactFinder Help (online help, census data information, glossary, and tutorial)
http://factfinder.census.gov/help/en/index.htm#

- *A Compass for Understanding and Using American Community Survey Data: What General Data Users Need to Know* provides a complete overview:
http://www.census.gov/programs-surveys/acs/guidance/handbooks.html

- Other Compass handbooks are available for the business community, media, Congress and many other user groups at:
http://www.census.gov/programs-surveys/acs/guidance/handbooks.html

- *Using the American Community Survey: Benefits and Challenges*, edited by Constance F. Citro and Graham Kalton (The National Academies Press, 2007). An excellent overview of the ACS, complete with several chapters of useful information for data users. The book is available for purchase and is also available to read online at no charge.
http://www.nap.edu/catalog/11901/using-the-american-community-survey-benefits-and-challenges

PART A
POPULATION SUMMARY

In 1982, the population of the United States stood at 232.6 million. The Baby Boomers (age 18 to 36 at that time) represented 32.9 percent of the country's population, and their numbers pressured employment and housing opportunities. In 2015, Baby Boomers (now age 51 to 69) represented only 23.1 percent of the population and their numbers are declining. In 1982 they were also in the process of giving birth to the Millennial generation, which has now become the largest generation in the nation's history. Between the years of 1982 and 2001 more than 78 million children were born, compared to about 76 million births in the Baby Boom years.

While the aging of the Baby Boom generation captures a lot of national attention, the Millennial generation is the new economic and cultural force in the country. But it's important to note that, just as with any other demographic or economic characteristic, the portrait is not uniform. As the geographic level of analysis gets smaller, the variation across our communities grows with some areas following national trends while others outpace or lag the nation. Analyzing population change is like telling a story of our communities. It's important to look at population change over time, the varying demographic composition of our communities, and how each compares to other areas. The text and tables in this volume are intended to provide the basic demographic portrait of the Millennial generation at the state, county, city, and metropolitan/micropolitan area levels and allow planners, researchers, and interested individuals to tell their own stories.

The tables in this book provide data for calendar year 2015 from the Census Bureau's 1-year American Community Survey (ACS). Users are encouraged to read the introductory sections describing the ACS and Public Use Microdata Sample (PUMS) and the important aspects of data collection and use that impact the interpretation of these data. In general, the book provides summaries for counties, cities, metropolitan areas, and selected micropolitan areas of approximately 100,000 population, because 100,000 is the population threshold for defining a Census Public Use Microdata Area (PUMA). However, PUMAs do not always follow the boundaries of counties and cities. The algorithm described in the section "Defining the Millennials" sometimes allowed for the definition of areas smaller than 100,000 and sometimes required eliminating areas larger than 100,000.

THE MILLENNIALS

In 2015 the Millennials, now age 15 to 33, numbered 83.5 million individuals and comprised 26.0 percent of the population. Unlike the Baby Boomer generation which is aging and shrinking, the Millennial generation continues to increase due to foreign immigration, which explains why there are more Millennials in 2015 than those born during their birth years. There are slightly more males (50.9 percent) than females (49.1 percent), and this difference is also influenced by the higher number of male births and the higher proportion of foreign immigrants that are male.

In this book, the Millennial generation is categorized by age into three groups: 15 to 17 representing the pre-college ages, 18 to 24 representing those in college or early in their employment years, and 25 to 33 representing those fully into the labor force years and beginning to establish households. Unlike the Baby Boomers who were fully invested in the labor force and establishing households before their 30th birthday, the Millennials have delayed many of the traditional life cycle stages like marriage, childbearing, and family formation. Of the 83.5 million Millennials, 15.0 percent were age 15 to 17 while the 18 to 24 population accounts for 37.5 percent and 25 to 33 population makes up nearly half of all Millennials at 47.4 percent.

Millennials range from a low of 22.5 percent in Maine to a high of 35.1 percent in the District of Columbia. Thirty-eight states have between 25 and 30 percent of the population between the ages of 15 and 33. Nine other states have less than 25 percent. Aside from the District of Columbia, Alaska is the second highest at just 30.0 percent.

The District of Columbia also stands out with respect to the age distribution of Millennials. It has the lowest percentage age 15 to 17 (6.4 percent) and the highest percentage age 25 to 33 at 58.9 percent. North Dakota has the second lowest percentage of 15 to 17 year olds at 11.7 percent. Colorado (50.7 percent), Hawaii (50.9 percent) and Washington (50.6 percent) all have just over half of their Millennial population in the 25 to 33 age group. The 15 to 17 year olds fall in a tight range with 42 states having between 14 and 17 percent of the total Millennial population. For the 25 to 33 year olds there

Millennials Age 15 to 33 as a Percent of the Total Population

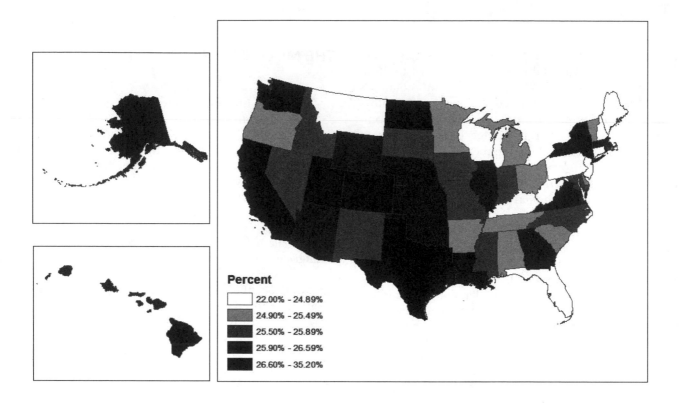

Percent

	22.00% – 24.89%
	24.90% – 25.49%
	25.50% – 25.89%
	25.90% – 26.59%
	26.60% – 35.20%

is a similarly tight range with 32 states falling between 44 and 48 percent.

There are 633 counties meeting the population size criteria to be included. At the county level there is much more variation in the composition of the Millennial population. Sumter County, FL has the lowest percentage of Millennials at 9.1 percent, while Story County, IA has the highest at 47.2 percent. In Story, home to Iowa State University in Ames, fully 67 percent of the Millennial population is between the ages of 18 and 24. Nine counties have a Millennial population greater than 40 percent of the total, and all are counties with large college populations such as the University of Georgia in Clark County, Cornell University in Tompkins County, NY, Penn State in Centre County, PA, Virginia Tech in Montgomery County, VA, and West Virginia University in Monongalia County, WV. These are good illustrations of the need to understand important community characteristics that influence their demographic compositions.

The distribution of the Millennial population by sex varies much more for counties than at the state level, with males comprising the lowest percentage in Dougherty County, GA (42.1 percent) and the highest percentage

in Onslow County, NC at 61.5 percent. Clark County, GA, home of the University of Georgia had the lowest percentage of 15 to 17 year olds at only 4.7 percent and Arlington County, VA had the highest percentage of 25 to 33 year olds with 71.6 percent. This is easily understood as Arlington is an easy commute to Washington, DC. Tompkins County, NY has the lowest percentage of 25 to 33 year olds (where Cornell University is located) at 25.4 percent because it also has the highest percentage of 18 to 24 year olds with 68.8 percent. Williamson County, TN has the highest percentage of Millennials 15 to 17 years old at 28.0 percent, likely influenced by its close proximity to Nashville, TN.

More than one-third (34.1 percent) of the nation's Millennial population lives in the 344 cities identified here. Meridian City, ID, has the smallest number with 17,705 and also the lowest percentage of the city's population at 19.5 percent. Not surprisingly, New York City has the than the national average of 26.0 percent. College Station City, TX home to Texas A&M University in Brazos County, TX, has the highest percentage at 55.1 percent. The Millennial population is higher than 50 percent in only three cities: College Station City, TX, Gainesville City, FL, and Provo City, UT, and is between

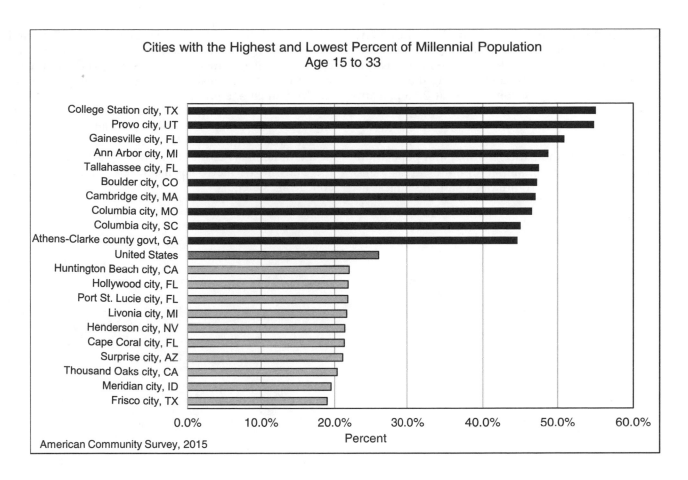

Cities with the Highest and Lowest Percent of Millennial Population
Age 15 to 33

American Community Survey, 2015

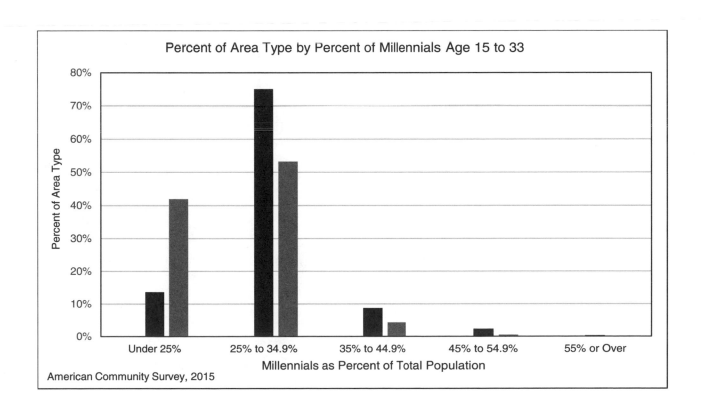

Percent of Area Type by Percent of Millennials Age 15 to 33

American Community Survey, 2015

40 and 50 percent in another 14 cities. Cambridge City, MA, has the lowest percentage of Millennials age 15 to 17 at 4.1 percent, while West Jordan City, UT, has the highest percentage at 25.8 percent. Among the 25 to 33 age group, Athens-Clarke County, GA, at 28.6 percent has the lowest percentage, and Alexandria City, VA, has the highest at 76.8 percent.

Fully 87.3 percent of the nation's Millennial population lives in the 415 metropolitan/micropolitan areas identified. The New York metro area is again the largest at 5.2 million followed by Los Angeles at 3.6 million and Chicago at 2.5 million. As a percentage, however, the college dominated metro of Ames, IA (Iowa State University) has the largest percentage of its population in the Millennial age groups at 47.4 percent. The Villages, FL, is lowest at 9.3 percent. Ithaca, NY (Cornell University) has the largest proportion of population in the 18 to 24 age group with more than two-thirds (68.2 percent) of the Millennials in that age category. At 28.7 percent, the Danville, IL, metro has the lowest percentage in the college age category.

Table A-1: States—Summary Population Characteristics

	Total 2015 ACS Population	Millennial Population Age 15 to 33	Millennials as Percent of Total	Millennial Percentage by Gender		Millennial Percentage by Age		
				Male	Female	15 to 17	18 to 24	25 to 33
United States......................	321,418,821	83,504,484	26.0%	50.9%	49.1%	15.0%	37.5%	47.4%
Alabama..............................	4,858,979	1,228,275	25.3%	49.6%	50.4%	15.9%	38.2%	45.9%
Alaska	738,432	221,416	30.0%	55.6%	44.4%	13.4%	38.0%	48.5%
Arizona...............................	6,828,065	1,768,256	25.9%	51.6%	48.4%	15.6%	38.0%	46.4%
Arkansas.............................	2,978,204	751,127	25.2%	50.3%	49.7%	15.7%	37.6%	46.6%
California............................	39,144,818	10,739,063	27.4%	51.4%	48.6%	14.3%	36.8%	48.9%
Colorado.............................	5,456,574	1,481,249	27.1%	52.4%	47.6%	13.9%	35.4%	50.7%
Connecticut.........................	3,590,886	892,841	24.9%	50.8%	49.2%	16.0%	39.8%	44.2%
Delaware.............................	945,934	237,360	25.1%	49.7%	50.3%	14.7%	36.9%	48.4%
District of Columbia	672,228	236,132	35.1%	47.0%	53.0%	6.4%	34.7%	58.9%
Florida................................	20,271,272	4,841,980	23.9%	50.8%	49.2%	14.8%	36.8%	48.4%
Georgia	10,214,860	2,694,824	26.4%	50.6%	49.4%	15.8%	38.2%	46.0%
Hawaii	1,431,603	371,354	25.9%	54.6%	45.4%	12.3%	36.8%	50.9%
Idaho..................................	1,654,930	426,778	25.8%	50.7%	49.3%	16.8%	36.9%	46.3%
Illinois................................	12,859,995	3,334,874	25.9%	50.5%	49.5%	15.3%	37.1%	47.6%
Indiana...............................	6,619,680	1,706,914	25.8%	50.4%	49.6%	16.0%	39.7%	44.3%
Iowa...................................	3,123,899	804,927	25.8%	51.2%	48.8%	15.4%	39.9%	44.7%
Kansas	2,911,641	763,691	26.2%	51.9%	48.1%	15.6%	38.8%	45.6%
Kentucky	4,425,092	1,102,117	24.9%	50.9%	49.1%	15.8%	38.5%	45.7%
Louisiana	4,670,724	1,253,683	26.8%	49.9%	50.1%	14.9%	36.6%	48.4%
Maine	1,329,328	298,983	22.5%	50.6%	49.4%	16.1%	38.5%	45.4%
Maryland.............................	6,006,401	1,532,505	25.5%	49.8%	50.2%	14.8%	36.4%	48.7%
Massachusetts.....................	6,794,422	1,806,926	26.6%	50.1%	49.9%	13.9%	38.7%	47.5%
Michigan.............................	9,922,576	2,494,156	25.1%	50.7%	49.3%	16.1%	39.5%	44.4%
Minnesota...........................	5,489,594	1,390,845	25.3%	50.5%	49.5%	15.5%	36.2%	48.2%
Mississippi..........................	2,992,333	769,119	25.7%	50.3%	49.7%	16.1%	40.7%	43.2%
Missouri..............................	6,083,672	1,561,298	25.7%	50.5%	49.5%	15.4%	38.3%	46.3%
Montana..............................	1,032,949	251,820	24.4%	52.1%	47.9%	14.7%	40.3%	45.0%
Nebraska.............................	1,896,190	496,505	26.2%	51.3%	48.7%	15.1%	39.3%	45.6%
Nevada...............................	2,890,845	738,080	25.5%	50.8%	49.2%	14.8%	34.5%	50.8%
New Hampshire....................	1,330,608	316,827	23.8%	51.6%	48.4%	16.1%	40.9%	43.0%
New Jersey	8,958,013	2,182,669	24.4%	51.1%	48.9%	16.1%	36.3%	47.6%
New Mexico	2,085,109	534,063	25.6%	51.6%	48.4%	15.3%	39.1%	45.7%
New York............................	19,795,791	5,267,039	26.6%	50.3%	49.7%	13.7%	36.8%	49.5%
North Carolina.....................	10,042,802	2,561,562	25.5%	50.8%	49.2%	15.2%	38.7%	46.1%
North Dakota.......................	756,928	222,346	29.4%	54.1%	45.9%	11.7%	42.1%	46.2%
Ohio	11,613,423	2,898,493	25.0%	50.6%	49.4%	16.1%	37.6%	46.2%
Oklahoma............................	3,911,338	1,026,095	26.2%	50.8%	49.2%	15.0%	38.2%	46.8%
Oregon...............................	4,028,977	1,008,523	25.0%	50.7%	49.3%	14.8%	36.3%	49.0%
Pennsylvania.......................	12,802,503	3,172,455	24.8%	50.7%	49.3%	15.0%	38.2%	46.8%
Rhode Island.......................	1,056,298	280,625	26.6%	49.7%	50.3%	13.2%	40.7%	46.1%
South Carolina	4,896,146	1,248,377	25.5%	51.3%	48.7%	15.2%	39.1%	45.7%
South Dakota	858,469	221,860	25.8%	51.4%	48.6%	15.3%	38.0%	46.6%
Tennessee	6,600,299	1,676,588	25.4%	49.9%	50.1%	15.4%	37.8%	46.8%
Texas.................................	27,469,114	7,561,743	27.5%	51.2%	48.8%	15.7%	36.8%	47.5%
Utah...................................	2,995,919	885,542	29.6%	50.9%	49.1%	16.4%	39.0%	44.6%
Vermont..............................	626,042	156,472	25.0%	51.5%	48.5%	14.7%	43.2%	42.2%
Virginia...............................	8,382,993	2,193,469	26.2%	50.8%	49.2%	14.3%	37.7%	48.1%
Washington..........................	7,170,351	1,885,191	26.3%	51.6%	48.4%	14.2%	35.2%	50.6%
West Virginia.......................	1,844,128	426,279	23.1%	50.7%	49.3%	15.7%	38.4%	45.9%
Wisconsin	5,771,337	1,426,801	24.7%	50.6%	49.4%	15.6%	38.9%	45.5%
Wyoming	586,107	154,367	26.3%	51.2%	48.8%	13.6%	37.9%	48.5%

Table A-2: Counties—Summary Population Characteristics

	Total 2015 ACS Population	Millennial Population Age 15 to 33	Millennials as Percent of Total	Millennial Percentage by Gender		Millennial Percentage by Age		
				Male	Female	15 to 17	18 to 24	25 to 33
Alabama								
Baldwin County	203,709	41,881	20.6%	49.7%	50.3%	17.8%	34.3%	47.9%
Calhoun County	115,620	30,590	26.5%	49.1%	50.9%	15.5%	42.3%	42.2%
Etowah County	103,057	22,502	21.8%	51.1%	48.9%	17.1%	40.3%	42.6%
Houston County	104,173	24,905	23.9%	49.4%	50.6%	18.3%	35.1%	46.6%
Jefferson County	660,367	168,431	25.5%	48.5%	51.5%	14.8%	34.8%	50.3%
Lauderdale County	92,596	23,069	24.9%	47.9%	52.1%	22.2%	38.7%	39.1%
Lee County	156,993	54,789	34.9%	49.8%	50.2%	9.7%	56.0%	34.3%
Madison County	353,089	90,891	25.7%	48.7%	51.3%	15.4%	36.1%	48.5%
Marshall County	94,725	21,899	23.1%	48.1%	51.9%	17.6%	40.6%	41.8%
Mobile County	415,395	108,104	26.0%	48.5%	51.5%	15.8%	34.7%	49.6%
Montgomery County	226,519	63,386	28.0%	48.7%	51.3%	14.2%	38.7%	47.1%
Morgan County	119,565	29,027	24.3%	54.5%	45.5%	19.8%	32.9%	47.3%
Shelby County	208,713	49,471	23.7%	51.0%	49.0%	17.7%	36.2%	46.0%
Tuscaloosa County	203,976	72,277	35.4%	49.3%	50.7%	10.7%	50.1%	39.2%
Alaska								
Anchorage Municipality	298,695	92,794	31.1%	53.0%	47.0%	12.6%	37.3%	50.1%
Fairbanks North Star Borough	99,631	34,834	35.0%	56.5%	43.5%	12.0%	43.5%	44.5%
Matanuska-Susitna Borough	101,095	27,889	27.6%	55.9%	44.1%	16.0%	38.3%	45.6%
Arizona								
Cochise County	126,427	29,422	23.3%	53.0%	47.0%	17.1%	32.5%	50.4%
Coconino County	139,097	51,771	37.2%	47.4%	52.6%	9.6%	57.3%	33.1%
Maricopa County	4,167,947	1,083,464	26.0%	51.2%	48.8%	15.9%	35.8%	48.2%
Mohave County	204,737	39,552	19.3%	53.0%	47.0%	17.4%	32.2%	50.4%
Navajo County	108,277	26,103	24.1%	49.6%	50.4%	18.1%	37.4%	44.5%
Pima County	1,010,025	267,442	26.5%	50.7%	49.3%	13.9%	44.6%	41.4%
Pinal County	406,584	92,776	22.8%	56.0%	44.0%	17.8%	33.4%	48.8%
Yavapai County	222,255	39,793	17.9%	52.9%	47.1%	16.3%	38.4%	45.3%
Yuma County	204,275	57,750	28.3%	56.1%	43.9%	15.8%	39.9%	44.3%
Arkansas								
Benton County	249,672	63,010	25.2%	49.9%	50.1%	17.0%	31.8%	51.3%
Craighead County	104,354	31,552	30.2%	54.8%	45.2%	16.3%	42.1%	41.7%
Faulkner County	121,552	40,148	33.0%	49.0%	51.0%	16.1%	43.5%	40.4%
Garland County	97,177	21,044	21.7%	47.5%	52.5%	16.0%	38.0%	46.0%
Pulaski County	392,664	103,489	26.4%	49.0%	51.0%	13.6%	34.4%	51.9%
Saline County	117,460	26,931	22.9%	49.0%	51.0%	17.4%	31.8%	50.8%
Sebastian County	127,780	32,407	25.4%	52.3%	47.7%	19.3%	35.6%	45.1%
Washington County	225,477	72,894	32.3%	51.2%	48.8%	11.1%	45.6%	43.4%
California								
Alameda County	1,638,215	433,320	26.5%	49.6%	50.4%	12.3%	32.5%	55.2%
Butte County	225,411	66,344	29.4%	50.6%	49.4%	11.4%	50.6%	38.0%
Contra Costa County	1,126,745	264,278	23.5%	50.8%	49.2%	17.3%	36.4%	46.4%
El Dorado County	184,452	38,085	20.6%	52.8%	47.2%	20.4%	36.1%	43.5%
Fresno County	974,861	280,870	28.8%	51.5%	48.5%	15.9%	37.8%	46.2%
Humboldt County	135,727	38,052	28.0%	50.9%	49.1%	9.5%	47.9%	42.6%
Imperial County	180,191	49,645	27.6%	52.5%	47.5%	16.6%	40.2%	43.2%
Kern County	882,176	255,273	28.9%	53.3%	46.7%	15.6%	37.8%	46.6%
Kings County	150,965	46,492	30.8%	58.8%	41.2%	13.5%	36.1%	50.4%
Los Angeles County	10,170,292	2,815,660	27.7%	50.7%	49.3%	13.7%	36.0%	50.3%
Madera County	154,998	41,540	26.8%	48.8%	51.2%	16.0%	37.8%	46.3%
Marin County	261,221	47,166	18.1%	55.0%	45.0%	18.2%	34.9%	46.8%
Merced County	268,455	78,357	29.2%	53.0%	47.0%	16.0%	41.7%	42.3%
Monterey County	433,898	120,053	27.7%	52.2%	47.8%	14.7%	38.5%	46.8%
Napa County	142,456	33,408	23.5%	51.6%	48.4%	16.0%	39.1%	44.9%
Nevada County	98,877	18,893	19.1%	51.5%	48.5%	16.9%	32.5%	50.6%
Orange County	3,169,776	823,644	26.0%	51.2%	48.8%	15.0%	36.6%	48.4%
Placer County	375,391	81,509	21.7%	51.0%	49.0%	18.8%	35.3%	45.9%
Riverside County	2,361,026	623,922	26.4%	51.2%	48.8%	17.2%	38.2%	44.7%
Sacramento County	1,501,335	400,317	26.7%	50.5%	49.5%	14.7%	34.2%	51.1%
San Bernardino County	2,128,133	622,075	29.2%	51.4%	48.6%	15.9%	37.8%	46.2%
San Diego County	3,299,521	944,277	28.6%	52.9%	47.1%	12.5%	37.3%	50.1%
San Francisco County	864,816	256,915	29.7%	49.8%	50.2%	6.6%	24.4%	69.0%
San Joaquin County	726,106	194,976	26.9%	52.1%	47.9%	17.2%	37.2%	45.6%
San Luis Obispo County	281,401	81,571	29.0%	53.3%	46.7%	10.5%	51.8%	37.8%
San Mateo County	765,135	177,686	23.2%	52.3%	47.7%	14.2%	32.2%	53.5%
Santa Barbara County	444,769	136,421	30.7%	52.2%	47.8%	11.8%	52.2%	36.0%
Santa Clara County	1,918,044	491,230	25.6%	51.9%	48.1%	13.7%	33.3%	52.9%
Santa Cruz County	274,146	81,439	29.7%	50.4%	49.6%	11.0%	51.8%	37.2%
Shasta County	179,533	41,748	23.3%	51.4%	48.6%	16.4%	32.9%	50.6%
Solano County	436,092	112,131	25.7%	52.1%	47.9%	14.7%	35.9%	49.4%
Sonoma County	502,146	118,618	23.6%	51.0%	49.0%	14.8%	36.9%	48.3%
Stanislaus County	538,388	150,344	27.9%	50.5%	49.5%	17.0%	36.0%	47.0%
Sutter County	96,463	25,161	26.1%	49.9%	50.1%	12.0%	32.7%	55.3%
Tulare County	459,863	131,238	28.5%	51.1%	48.9%	17.7%	36.9%	45.4%
Ventura County	850,536	220,516	25.9%	51.2%	48.8%	15.9%	37.9%	46.2%
Yolo County	213,016	73,824	34.7%	48.0%	52.0%	9.9%	54.6%	35.5%

Table A-2: Counties—Summary Population Characteristics—*Continued*

	Total 2015 ACS Population	Millennial Population Age 15 to 33	Millennials as Percent of Total	Millennial Percentage by Gender		Millennial Percentage by Age		
				Male	Female	15 to 17	18 to 24	25 to 33
Colorado								
Adams County	491,337	137,531	28.0%	52.1%	47.9%	16.7%	31.2%	52.0%
Arapahoe County	631,096	166,327	26.4%	49.2%	50.8%	15.5%	32.6%	51.9%
Boulder County	319,372	99,882	31.3%	55.2%	44.8%	12.0%	50.4%	37.6%
Denver County	682,545	212,964	31.2%	50.3%	49.7%	7.7%	26.8%	65.4%
Douglas County	322,387	67,516	20.9%	48.1%	51.9%	23.6%	36.0%	40.4%
El Paso County	674,471	197,064	29.2%	53.3%	46.7%	13.5%	36.9%	49.6%
Jefferson County	565,524	139,577	24.7%	53.0%	47.0%	14.4%	35.3%	50.3%
Larimer County	333,577	101,823	30.5%	51.9%	48.1%	11.1%	44.3%	44.5%
Mesa County	148,513	38,715	26.1%	53.1%	46.9%	14.3%	39.4%	46.3%
Pueblo County	163,591	40,596	24.8%	52.4%	47.6%	16.0%	37.7%	46.3%
Weld County	285,174	77,770	27.3%	50.9%	49.1%	17.7%	37.3%	45.0%
Connecticut								
Fairfield County	948,053	223,389	23.6%	51.2%	48.8%	18.1%	38.1%	43.8%
Hartford County	895,841	219,321	24.5%	50.6%	49.4%	15.6%	37.8%	46.5%
Litchfield County	183,603	36,755	20.0%	51.7%	48.3%	18.2%	36.9%	44.9%
Middlesex County	164,063	37,415	22.8%	49.7%	50.3%	18.5%	40.6%	40.9%
New Haven County	859,470	219,820	25.6%	49.3%	50.7%	15.2%	39.6%	45.2%
New London County	271,863	71,058	26.1%	55.7%	44.3%	14.9%	40.3%	44.8%
Tolland County	151,420	48,690	32.2%	50.4%	49.6%	10.8%	57.6%	31.6%
Windham County	116,573	29,791	25.6%	48.3%	51.7%	14.7%	39.9%	45.3%
Delaware								
Kent County	173,533	46,169	26.6%	50.2%	49.8%	14.9%	40.6%	44.5%
New Castle County	556,779	148,800	26.7%	49.5%	50.5%	14.5%	35.3%	50.1%
Sussex County	215,622	41,781	19.4%	50.0%	50.0%	15.5%	37.5%	47.0%
Florida								
Alachua County	259,964	99,489	38.3%	48.8%	51.2%	7.6%	56.5%	35.8%
Bay County	181,635	44,374	24.4%	51.5%	48.5%	13.7%	33.4%	52.9%
Brevard County	568,088	120,364	21.2%	51.7%	48.3%	16.7%	37.4%	45.8%
Broward County	1,896,425	454,842	24.0%	50.3%	49.7%	15.4%	34.2%	50.4%
Charlotte County	173,115	23,149	13.4%	49.3%	50.7%	18.9%	41.2%	39.9%
Citrus County	141,058	20,619	14.6%	52.4%	47.6%	19.0%	37.4%	43.6%
Clay County	203,967	47,909	23.5%	50.5%	49.5%	19.3%	36.7%	44.1%
Collier County	357,305	67,976	19.0%	51.0%	49.0%	16.6%	38.1%	45.3%
Duval County	913,010	249,721	27.4%	50.5%	49.5%	13.4%	34.6%	52.0%
Escambia County	311,003	92,108	29.6%	53.8%	46.2%	11.8%	43.9%	44.3%
Flagler County	105,392	18,726	17.8%	54.8%	45.2%	19.8%	42.1%	38.0%
Hernando County	178,439	34,015	19.1%	51.1%	48.9%	19.8%	33.7%	46.5%
Highlands County	99,491	17,486	17.6%	48.4%	51.6%	21.6%	34.7%	43.7%
Hillsborough County	1,349,050	357,315	26.5%	50.4%	49.6%	14.6%	34.5%	50.9%
Indian River County	147,919	26,890	18.2%	47.8%	52.2%	14.9%	42.8%	42.3%
Lake County	325,875	63,518	19.5%	50.4%	49.6%	19.2%	33.9%	47.0%
Lee County	701,982	139,414	19.9%	49.7%	50.3%	15.6%	35.5%	48.9%
Leon County	286,272	109,230	38.2%	48.5%	51.5%	8.0%	59.7%	32.3%
Manatee County	363,369	71,745	19.7%	49.8%	50.2%	17.3%	36.7%	46.1%
Marion County	343,254	70,359	20.5%	50.0%	50.0%	16.2%	35.8%	48.0%
Martin County	156,283	27,863	17.8%	52.8%	47.2%	17.1%	40.9%	42.0%
Miami-Dade County	2,693,117	678,428	25.2%	51.1%	48.9%	14.1%	34.9%	51.0%
Okaloosa County	198,664	54,676	27.5%	54.0%	46.0%	11.8%	34.7%	53.5%
Orange County	1,288,126	381,877	29.6%	49.6%	50.4%	12.9%	37.7%	49.4%
Osceola County	323,993	85,749	26.5%	52.5%	47.5%	16.9%	36.4%	46.7%
Palm Beach County	1,422,789	305,192	21.5%	51.6%	48.4%	16.2%	35.7%	48.1%
Pasco County	497,909	102,294	20.5%	49.7%	50.3%	18.2%	36.0%	45.8%
Pinellas County	949,827	192,338	20.2%	49.7%	50.3%	14.4%	34.2%	51.4%
Polk County	650,092	157,735	24.3%	50.3%	49.7%	16.1%	35.5%	48.4%
Santa Rosa County	226,640	49,046	21.6%	50.8%	49.2%	20.7%	35.8%	43.5%
Sarasota County	298,563	64,135	21.5%	47.1%	52.9%	16.0%	34.5%	49.5%
Seminole County	167,040	40,873	24.5%	52.6%	47.4%	16.0%	32.1%	51.9%
St. Johns County	405,549	66,167	16.3%	49.9%	50.1%	16.5%	35.5%	48.0%
St. Lucie County	449,144	113,327	25.2%	51.3%	48.7%	16.0%	34.7%	49.3%
Sumter County	118,891	10,799	9.1%	54.7%	45.3%	20.2%	43.8%	36.0%
Volusia County	517,887	112,669	21.8%	50.3%	49.7%	14.6%	37.6%	47.8%
Georgia								
Bartow County	102,747	24,596	23.9%	50.9%	49.1%	17.8%	37.8%	44.4%
Bibb County	153,721	40,873	26.6%	45.9%	54.1%	14.9%	39.7%	45.4%
Carroll County	114,545	34,092	29.8%	48.7%	51.3%	15.0%	45.3%	39.7%
Chatham County	286,956	85,554	29.8%	49.9%	50.1%	10.7%	39.3%	50.0%
Cherokee County	235,900	55,192	23.4%	51.5%	48.5%	19.9%	34.6%	45.6%
Clarke County	123,912	55,559	44.8%	47.2%	52.8%	4.7%	65.8%	29.5%
Clayton County	273,955	75,687	27.6%	48.6%	51.4%	15.8%	36.5%	47.7%
Cobb County	741,334	190,361	25.7%	50.5%	49.5%	15.7%	34.8%	49.6%
Columbia County	144,052	38,305	26.6%	49.5%	50.5%	16.6%	32.9%	50.5%
Coweta County	138,427	33,183	24.0%	49.7%	50.3%	19.8%	34.7%	45.5%
DeKalb County	734,871	200,382	27.3%	48.1%	51.9%	12.3%	32.7%	54.9%
Dougherty County	91,332	25,148	27.5%	42.1%	57.9%	15.4%	45.0%	39.6%
Douglas County	140,733	35,335	25.1%	53.0%	47.0%	19.1%	37.2%	43.8%

Table A-2: Counties—Summary Population Characteristics—*Continued*

	Total 2015 ACS Population	Millennial Population Age 15 to 33	Millennials as Percent of Total	Millennial Percentage by Gender		Millennial Percentage by Age		
				Male	Female	15 to 17	18 to 24	25 to 33
Georgia—Cont.								
Fayette County	110,714	23,415	21.1%	52.6%	47.4%	27.0%	44.6%	28.4%
Floyd County	96,504	24,395	25.3%	47.6%	52.4%	15.7%	37.6%	46.7%
Forsyth County	212,438	44,097	20.8%	50.4%	49.6%	23.7%	34.2%	42.1%
Fulton County	1,010,562	286,250	28.3%	49.3%	50.7%	13.6%	34.6%	51.8%
Gwinnett County	895,823	228,875	25.5%	50.9%	49.1%	18.8%	36.2%	45.0%
Hall County	193,535	48,649	25.1%	51.5%	48.5%	18.0%	37.6%	44.4%
Henry County	217,739	56,794	26.1%	49.1%	50.9%	22.3%	40.7%	37.0%
Houston County	150,033	38,791	25.9%	50.6%	49.4%	16.2%	37.8%	46.0%
Lowndes County	112,865	39,082	34.6%	51.4%	48.6%	11.0%	46.6%	42.4%
Muscogee County	200,579	60,678	30.3%	55.9%	44.1%	11.2%	39.9%	48.9%
Newton County	105,473	26,592	25.2%	49.8%	50.2%	22.8%	30.7%	46.5%
Paulding County	152,238	38,745	25.5%	50.2%	49.8%	19.9%	37.0%	43.2%
Richmond County	201,793	61,312	30.4%	52.4%	47.6%	12.0%	38.7%	49.3%
Whitfield County	104,216	28,290	27.1%	48.8%	51.2%	16.1%	36.7%	47.2%
Hawaii								
Hawaii County	196,428	44,356	22.6%	48.4%	51.6%	14.4%	36.8%	48.9%
Honolulu County	998,714	273,410	27.4%	56.1%	43.9%	11.3%	38.1%	50.6%
Maui County	164,593	39,215	23.8%	53.6%	46.4%	14.6%	32.1%	53.3%
Idaho								
Ada County	434,211	112,757	26.0%	51.6%	48.4%	16.0%	33.1%	50.9%
Bonneville County	110,089	27,468	25.0%	52.4%	47.6%	15.1%	32.5%	52.4%
Canyon County	207,478	53,108	25.6%	46.2%	53.8%	19.9%	35.9%	44.2%
Kootenai County	150,346	35,105	23.3%	53.6%	46.4%	16.0%	33.4%	50.6%
Illinois								
Champaign County	208,861	80,297	38.4%	52.0%	48.0%	6.7%	63.3%	30.0%
Cook County	5,238,216	1,420,119	27.1%	49.6%	50.4%	13.6%	33.7%	52.8%
DeKalb County	104,352	37,893	36.3%	52.5%	47.5%	9.0%	57.7%	33.4%
DuPage County	933,736	225,783	24.2%	50.5%	49.5%	16.8%	37.5%	45.7%
Kane County	530,847	127,899	24.1%	51.3%	48.7%	19.0%	37.8%	43.2%
Kankakee County	110,879	28,451	25.7%	50.9%	49.1%	16.2%	40.6%	43.2%
Kendall County	123,355	32,579	26.4%	43.8%	56.2%	20.2%	34.8%	45.0%
Lake County	703,910	174,597	24.8%	53.6%	46.4%	19.7%	40.8%	39.5%
LaSalle County	111,333	25,216	22.6%	53.5%	46.5%	17.6%	35.2%	47.2%
Macon County	307,343	68,743	22.4%	51.9%	48.1%	21.6%	38.3%	40.1%
Madison County	173,166	57,011	32.9%	51.0%	49.0%	11.2%	53.9%	34.9%
McHenry County	107,303	24,600	22.9%	47.3%	52.7%	16.1%	41.4%	42.5%
McLean County	266,209	64,921	24.4%	49.1%	50.9%	15.5%	35.4%	49.1%
Peoria County	186,221	49,723	26.7%	46.8%	53.2%	14.5%	35.3%	50.2%
Rock Island County	146,133	32,689	22.4%	47.6%	52.4%	15.7%	39.2%	45.0%
Sangamon County	264,052	63,031	23.9%	49.0%	51.0%	16.0%	35.0%	49.0%
St. Clair County	198,712	47,979	24.1%	49.3%	50.7%	17.5%	36.5%	46.0%
Tazewell County	134,800	30,206	22.4%	53.9%	46.1%	16.9%	31.7%	51.4%
Will County	687,263	164,849	24.0%	50.9%	49.1%	19.8%	37.5%	42.7%
Winnebago County	287,078	68,339	23.8%	48.7%	51.3%	16.7%	36.2%	47.1%
Indiana								
Allen County	368,450	94,493	25.6%	49.6%	50.4%	16.4%	38.0%	45.7%
Clark County	115,371	26,766	23.2%	51.9%	48.1%	16.0%	32.4%	51.6%
Delaware County	116,852	37,184	31.8%	46.3%	53.7%	10.5%	61.7%	27.8%
Elkhart County	203,474	51,393	25.3%	49.3%	50.7%	19.2%	36.8%	44.1%
Hamilton County	309,697	70,348	22.7%	48.0%	52.0%	22.5%	31.5%	46.0%
Hendricks County	158,192	38,770	24.5%	49.3%	50.7%	17.7%	33.0%	49.3%
Johnson County	149,633	35,533	23.7%	49.3%	50.7%	18.3%	35.6%	46.1%
Lake County	487,865	115,765	23.7%	49.9%	50.1%	19.1%	36.9%	44.0%
LaPorte County	110,884	25,919	23.4%	57.2%	42.8%	16.9%	33.6%	49.5%
Madison County	129,723	31,647	24.4%	51.4%	48.6%	16.9%	37.7%	45.3%
Marion County	939,020	265,530	28.3%	48.5%	51.5%	12.8%	33.1%	54.1%
Monroe County	144,705	64,077	44.3%	50.9%	49.1%	6.3%	63.2%	30.5%
Porter County	167,688	40,152	23.9%	51.7%	48.3%	18.1%	40.6%	41.4%
St. Joseph County	268,441	71,602	26.7%	50.3%	49.7%	15.8%	41.9%	42.3%
Tippecanoe County	185,826	74,144	39.9%	54.5%	45.5%	7.3%	61.5%	31.2%
Vanderburgh County	181,877	47,427	26.1%	47.7%	52.3%	12.6%	38.4%	49.0%
Vigo County	107,896	33,172	30.7%	55.1%	44.9%	11.8%	52.4%	35.8%
Iowa								
Black Hawk County	133,455	41,294	30.9%	47.9%	52.1%	11.0%	49.0%	40.0%
Dubuque County	97,125	25,302	26.1%	55.8%	44.2%	17.8%	42.0%	40.2%
Johnson County	144,251	55,180	38.3%	49.4%	50.6%	8.3%	55.2%	36.5%
Linn County	219,916	56,398	25.6%	47.5%	52.5%	15.8%	36.4%	47.8%
Polk County	467,711	124,068	26.5%	48.4%	51.6%	14.4%	34.1%	51.4%
Pottawattamie County	93,671	21,863	23.3%	50.0%	50.0%	16.2%	34.9%	48.9%
Scott County	172,126	42,538	24.7%	50.4%	49.6%	14.9%	35.1%	50.0%
Story County	96,021	45,309	47.2%	57.2%	42.8%	5.8%	67.3%	26.8%
Woodbury County	102,782	28,317	27.6%	49.4%	50.6%	17.9%	36.1%	46.0%
Kansas								
Douglas County	118,053	46,763	39.6%	54.1%	45.9%	6.4%	58.4%	35.2%
Johnson County	580,159	142,925	24.6%	49.6%	50.4%	17.7%	31.8%	50.5%

Table A-2: Counties—Summary Population Characteristics—*Continued*

	Total 2015 ACS Population	Millennial Population Age 15 to 33	Millennials as Percent of Total	Millennial Percentage by Gender		Millennial Percentage by Age		
				Male	Female	15 to 17	18 to 24	25 to 33
Kansas—Cont.								
Sedgwick County	511,574	133,877	26.2%	48.7%	51.3%	16.4%	31.4%	52.2%
Shawnee County	178,725	44,074	24.7%	54.7%	45.3%	17.3%	35.4%	47.3%
Wyandotte County	163,369	43,648	26.7%	49.4%	50.6%	16.8%	36.6%	47.6%
Kentucky								
Boone County	127,712	29,906	23.4%	50.1%	49.9%	17.5%	35.5%	47.0%
Campbell County	92,066	25,040	27.2%	48.6%	51.4%	10.9%	40.5%	48.6%
Daviess County	99,259	23,244	23.4%	50.6%	49.4%	17.6%	35.6%	46.8%
Fayette County	314,488	97,769	31.1%	51.6%	48.4%	10.2%	44.1%	45.7%
Hardin County	106,439	27,726	26.0%	54.7%	45.3%	21.1%	31.4%	47.5%
Jefferson County	763,623	192,549	25.2%	50.2%	49.8%	14.6%	35.0%	50.4%
Kenton County	165,012	40,933	24.8%	50.9%	49.1%	15.4%	32.3%	52.4%
Warren County	122,851	38,963	31.7%	48.7%	51.3%	13.2%	52.0%	34.9%
Louisiana								
Ascension Parish	119,455	31,170	26.1%	49.4%	50.6%	19.2%	31.9%	48.9%
Bossier Parish	125,175	34,599	27.6%	55.0%	45.0%	15.6%	30.0%	54.4%
Caddo Parish	251,460	64,036	25.5%	47.4%	52.6%	15.4%	35.8%	48.7%
Calcasieu Parish	198,788	53,237	26.8%	51.3%	48.7%	15.5%	36.0%	48.5%
East Baton Rouge Parish	446,753	141,766	31.7%	49.9%	50.1%	11.8%	45.7%	42.5%
Jefferson Parish	436,275	109,416	25.1%	49.2%	50.8%	12.9%	32.7%	54.3%
Lafayette Parish	240,098	69,964	29.1%	50.5%	49.5%	13.8%	35.9%	50.3%
Lafourche Parish	98,325	25,238	25.7%	55.3%	44.7%	15.6%	35.7%	48.7%
Livingston Parish	137,788	35,503	25.8%	49.5%	50.5%	13.9%	35.0%	51.1%
Orleans Parish	389,617	113,293	29.1%	48.2%	51.8%	10.5%	32.6%	56.9%
Ouachita Parish	156,761	43,846	28.0%	47.3%	52.7%	15.0%	37.1%	47.9%
Rapides Parish	132,141	32,779	24.8%	49.8%	50.2%	17.0%	37.1%	45.8%
St. Tammany Parish	250,088	56,023	22.4%	48.9%	51.1%	19.3%	31.9%	48.8%
Tangipahoa Parish	128,755	36,570	28.4%	51.1%	48.9%	14.4%	41.6%	44.0%
Terrebonne Parish	113,972	27,572	24.2%	45.1%	54.9%	14.2%	32.8%	53.0%
Maine								
Androscoggin County	107,233	24,352	22.7%	48.1%	51.9%	16.4%	38.7%	44.9%
Cumberland County	289,977	71,428	24.6%	51.1%	48.9%	16.0%	38.4%	45.6%
Kennebec County	119,980	25,926	21.6%	52.2%	47.8%	15.8%	40.2%	44.0%
Penobscot County	152,692	40,856	26.8%	49.8%	50.2%	12.7%	42.6%	44.7%
York County	201,169	44,517	22.1%	52.2%	47.8%	18.4%	33.5%	48.1%
Maryland								
Anne Arundel County	564,195	142,073	25.2%	52.0%	48.0%	14.4%	34.9%	50.8%
Baltimore County	831,128	208,008	25.0%	48.3%	51.7%	14.1%	36.4%	49.5%
Carroll County	167,627	38,124	22.7%	51.0%	49.0%	19.9%	39.6%	40.5%
Cecil County	102,382	24,753	24.2%	52.2%	47.8%	16.5%	40.9%	42.6%
Charles County	156,118	39,543	25.3%	51.9%	48.1%	18.6%	37.0%	44.4%
Frederick County	245,322	59,201	24.1%	50.1%	49.9%	17.0%	39.9%	43.1%
Harford County	250,290	58,548	23.4%	48.4%	51.6%	17.2%	36.2%	46.6%
Howard County	313,414	74,617	23.8%	50.4%	49.6%	19.4%	33.1%	47.5%
Montgomery County	1,040,116	242,582	23.3%	49.8%	50.2%	16.5%	33.2%	50.3%
Prince George's County	909,535	244,582	26.9%	50.3%	49.7%	13.3%	37.7%	49.0%
St. Mary's County	111,413	28,580	25.7%	45.4%	54.6%	16.3%	39.1%	44.6%
Washington County	149,585	36,398	24.3%	54.0%	46.0%	16.8%	35.6%	47.6%
Wicomico County	102,370	30,106	29.4%	51.6%	48.4%	12.4%	51.6%	36.0%
Massachusetts								
Barnstable County	214,333	38,001	17.7%	48.9%	51.1%	18.6%	38.1%	43.3%
Berkshire County	127,828	28,645	22.4%	51.2%	48.8%	15.7%	46.6%	37.6%
Bristol County	556,772	138,908	24.9%	50.7%	49.3%	14.5%	38.7%	46.8%
Essex County	776,043	188,868	24.3%	50.1%	49.9%	16.8%	37.3%	45.9%
Hampden County	470,690	122,400	26.0%	50.1%	49.9%	15.3%	41.7%	43.0%
Hampshire County	161,292	57,803	35.8%	48.1%	51.9%	13.1%	52.7%	34.3%
Middlesex County	1,585,139	424,674	26.8%	50.6%	49.4%	13.3%	35.6%	51.1%
Norfolk County	696,023	162,312	23.3%	49.6%	50.4%	19.4%	34.8%	45.8%
Plymouth County	510,393	114,104	22.4%	51.4%	48.6%	18.3%	42.0%	39.7%
Suffolk County	778,121	293,994	37.8%	48.8%	51.2%	6.9%	37.2%	55.9%
Worcester County	818,963	200,721	24.5%	51.2%	48.8%	17.3%	39.6%	43.1%
Michigan								
Allegan County	114,625	26,922	23.5%	48.8%	51.2%	19.2%	36.4%	44.4%
Bay County	105,659	24,229	22.9%	55.9%	44.1%	16.9%	36.1%	47.0%
Berrien County	154,636	34,168	22.1%	50.2%	49.8%	16.8%	36.4%	46.7%
Calhoun County	134,314	31,922	23.8%	49.5%	50.5%	17.8%	33.7%	48.5%
Eaton County	108,801	25,668	23.6%	51.6%	48.4%	16.6%	40.2%	43.2%
Genesee County	410,849	98,458	24.0%	50.6%	49.4%	17.1%	38.2%	44.7%
Ingham County	286,085	103,204	36.1%	49.6%	50.4%	10.2%	54.2%	35.7%
Jackson County	159,494	38,015	23.8%	51.8%	48.2%	15.4%	36.5%	48.1%
Kalamazoo County	260,263	80,525	30.9%	51.0%	49.0%	11.4%	50.5%	38.1%
Kent County	636,369	172,733	27.1%	48.8%	51.2%	15.6%	34.2%	50.2%
Lenawee County	98,573	23,269	23.6%	55.0%	45.0%	16.4%	45.2%	38.4%
Livingston County	187,316	41,203	22.0%	51.9%	48.1%	21.1%	39.3%	39.6%
Macomb County	864,840	205,742	23.8%	50.3%	49.7%	17.4%	35.4%	47.1%
Monroe County	149,568	33,502	22.4%	52.4%	47.6%	18.9%	35.7%	45.4%

Table A-2: Counties—Summary Population Characteristics—*Continued*

	Total 2015 ACS Population	Millennial Population Age 15 to 33	Millennials as Percent of Total	Millennial Percentage by Gender		Millennial Percentage by Age		
				Male	Female	15 to 17	18 to 24	25 to 33
Michigan—Cont.								
Muskegon County	172,790	41,707	24.1%	52.7%	47.3%	15.9%	35.6%	48.5%
Oakland County	1,242,304	287,890	23.2%	50.7%	49.3%	17.4%	34.5%	48.1%
Ottawa County	279,955	79,401	28.4%	50.3%	49.7%	15.7%	47.5%	36.8%
Saginaw County	193,307	48,370	25.0%	51.2%	48.8%	14.5%	41.4%	44.1%
St. Clair County	159,875	35,117	22.0%	47.2%	52.8%	19.9%	36.8%	43.3%
Washtenaw County	358,880	123,278	34.4%	51.2%	48.8%	9.7%	53.5%	36.8%
Wayne County	1,759,335	444,288	25.3%	49.5%	50.5%	16.4%	36.3%	47.3%
Minnesota								
Anoka County	344,151	80,904	23.5%	52.2%	47.8%	18.7%	35.3%	46.1%
Carver County	98,741	21,899	22.2%	45.2%	54.8%	17.0%	40.3%	42.7%
Dakota County	414,686	98,765	23.8%	49.0%	51.0%	18.2%	33.0%	48.8%
Hennepin County	1,223,149	332,438	27.2%	50.1%	49.9%	13.0%	30.7%	56.3%
Olmsted County	151,436	36,745	24.3%	48.3%	51.7%	14.2%	35.5%	50.3%
Ramsey County	538,133	152,482	28.3%	48.9%	51.1%	12.3%	35.1%	52.6%
Scott County	200,431	54,619	27.3%	52.7%	47.3%	12.3%	43.6%	44.1%
St. Louis County	141,660	32,848	23.2%	48.0%	52.0%	20.7%	30.6%	48.7%
Stearns County	154,708	47,263	30.5%	50.5%	49.5%	12.4%	49.4%	38.2%
Washington County	251,597	57,531	22.9%	52.2%	47.8%	19.4%	32.1%	48.5%
Wright County	131,311	27,686	21.1%	49.9%	50.1%	20.9%	32.9%	46.2%
Mississippi								
DeSoto County	173,323	42,966	24.8%	48.2%	51.8%	20.8%	37.2%	42.0%
Harrison County	201,410	55,153	27.4%	52.4%	47.6%	14.9%	37.2%	48.0%
Hinds County	242,891	71,084	29.3%	45.0%	55.0%	13.9%	38.9%	47.3%
Jackson County	141,425	33,350	23.6%	52.0%	48.0%	17.8%	35.0%	47.2%
Madison County	103,465	25,688	24.8%	50.1%	49.9%	17.7%	37.1%	45.3%
Rankin County	149,039	37,036	24.8%	48.8%	51.2%	19.0%	30.9%	50.1%
Missouri								
Boone County	174,974	65,947	37.7%	49.8%	50.2%	9.1%	53.1%	37.9%
Cass County	101,603	22,570	22.2%	47.0%	53.0%	17.7%	34.6%	47.6%
Clay County	235,637	58,001	24.6%	50.2%	49.8%	16.7%	32.8%	50.5%
Franklin County	102,426	23,013	22.5%	50.2%	49.8%	18.9%	33.4%	47.7%
Greene County	288,072	87,400	30.3%	48.7%	51.3%	11.5%	45.0%	43.5%
Jackson County	687,623	176,621	25.7%	48.0%	52.0%	14.5%	33.2%	52.3%
Jasper County	118,596	31,672	26.7%	52.0%	48.0%	18.6%	39.7%	41.7%
Jefferson County	224,124	52,895	23.6%	50.1%	49.9%	18.4%	32.1%	49.5%
Platte County	96,096	24,357	25.3%	48.4%	51.6%	15.8%	33.2%	51.0%
St. Charles County	385,590	93,881	24.3%	50.3%	49.7%	17.0%	36.2%	46.7%
St. Louis County	1,003,362	242,954	24.2%	49.7%	50.3%	16.7%	37.7%	45.7%
Montana								
Flathead County	96,165	19,915	20.7%	52.3%	47.7%	19.6%	35.7%	44.7%
Gallatin County	100,739	34,706	34.5%	55.6%	44.4%	11.0%	50.9%	38.0%
Missoula County	114,181	35,981	31.5%	56.1%	43.9%	12.2%	41.0%	46.8%
Yellowstone County	157,048	38,872	24.8%	52.6%	47.4%	12.3%	39.3%	48.4%
Nebraska								
Douglas County	550,064	149,220	27.1%	50.3%	49.7%	14.6%	32.2%	53.1%
Lancaster County	306,468	94,646	30.9%	50.7%	49.3%	9.7%	47.3%	43.0%
Sarpy County	175,692	45,405	25.8%	52.9%	47.1%	16.4%	35.2%	48.4%
Nevada								
Clark County	2,114,801	548,876	26.0%	50.3%	49.7%	14.7%	33.8%	51.5%
Washoe County	446,903	115,819	25.9%	51.6%	48.4%	14.3%	35.0%	50.7%
New Hampshire								
Hillsborough County	406,678	96,735	23.8%	52.7%	47.3%	16.6%	37.6%	45.8%
Merrimack County	147,994	35,723	24.1%	53.5%	46.5%	17.4%	43.0%	39.6%
Rockingham County	301,777	66,202	21.9%	53.8%	46.2%	17.7%	37.5%	44.8%
Strafford County	126,825	39,197	30.9%	49.0%	51.0%	11.8%	51.9%	36.4%
New Jersey								
Atlantic County	274,219	66,570	24.3%	51.7%	48.3%	15.1%	39.7%	45.2%
Bergen County	938,506	207,884	22.2%	50.6%	49.4%	18.0%	36.7%	45.2%
Burlington County	450,226	107,421	23.9%	53.2%	46.8%	16.8%	37.4%	45.7%
Camden County	510,923	128,390	25.1%	49.6%	50.4%	15.5%	35.2%	49.3%
Cape May County	94,727	19,149	20.2%	50.2%	49.8%	20.0%	33.7%	46.3%
Cumberland County	155,854	39,803	25.5%	55.2%	44.8%	14.8%	31.5%	53.7%
Essex County	797,434	199,329	25.0%	49.3%	50.7%	15.7%	37.0%	47.3%
Gloucester County	291,479	69,545	23.9%	49.2%	50.8%	17.0%	36.0%	47.0%
Hudson County	674,836	204,390	30.3%	51.7%	48.3%	9.8%	28.1%	62.1%
Hunterdon County	125,488	27,170	21.7%	55.8%	44.2%	23.4%	41.5%	35.1%
Mercer County	371,398	96,122	25.9%	50.5%	49.5%	14.8%	44.6%	40.6%
Middlesex County	840,900	214,716	25.5%	51.4%	48.6%	14.9%	37.3%	47.8%
Monmouth County	628,715	140,826	22.4%	50.8%	49.2%	18.9%	37.2%	43.9%
Morris County	499,509	114,443	22.9%	49.9%	50.1%	18.9%	36.7%	44.4%
Ocean County	588,721	122,446	20.8%	50.8%	49.2%	17.1%	35.1%	47.8%
Passaic County	510,916	131,980	25.8%	50.6%	49.4%	15.5%	38.0%	46.5%
Somerset County	333,654	72,159	21.6%	52.0%	48.0%	18.5%	37.2%	44.4%
Sussex County	143,673	30,701	21.4%	53.8%	46.2%	20.0%	39.7%	40.4%
Union County	555,786	133,055	23.9%	52.4%	47.6%	16.5%	36.9%	46.5%

Table A-2: Counties—Summary Population Characteristics—*Continued*

	Total 2015 ACS Population	Millennial Population Age 15 to 33	Millennials as Percent of Total	Millennial Percentage by Gender		Millennial Percentage by Age		
				Male	Female	15 to 17	18 to 24	25 to 33
New Jersey—Cont.								
Warren County	106,869	22,864	21.4%	50.8%	49.2%	19.6%	38.2%	42.2%
New Mexico								
Bernalillo County	676,685	182,851	27.0%	50.6%	49.4%	15.0%	36.0%	49.1%
Doña Ana County	214,295	64,094	29.9%	51.8%	48.2%	14.0%	47.4%	38.5%
San Juan County	139,394	32,797	23.5%	49.9%	50.1%	18.4%	32.3%	49.3%
Sandoval County	118,737	30,632	25.8%	50.7%	49.3%	16.3%	37.9%	45.8%
Santa Fe County	148,686	30,994	20.8%	49.6%	50.4%	15.8%	35.6%	48.6%
New York								
Albany County	309,381	90,605	29.3%	49.7%	50.3%	11.7%	48.6%	39.6%
Bronx County	1,455,444	420,540	28.9%	50.3%	49.7%	14.0%	37.7%	48.3%
Broome County	196,567	54,933	27.9%	51.9%	48.1%	14.1%	51.6%	34.3%
Chautauqua County	130,779	31,756	24.3%	53.7%	46.3%	16.5%	43.0%	40.5%
Dutchess County	295,754	75,653	25.6%	51.2%	48.8%	15.1%	44.6%	40.2%
Erie County	922,578	239,874	26.0%	49.9%	50.1%	14.2%	37.4%	48.4%
Jefferson County	117,635	35,425	30.1%	58.4%	41.6%	11.8%	42.7%	45.5%
Kings County	2,636,735	753,015	28.6%	48.9%	51.1%	12.0%	31.1%	56.9%
Monroe County	749,600	201,722	26.9%	50.5%	49.5%	13.8%	39.5%	46.7%
Nassau County	1,361,350	314,680	23.1%	51.3%	48.7%	17.5%	38.6%	43.9%
New York County	1,644,518	520,283	31.6%	46.8%	53.2%	6.2%	28.6%	65.2%
Niagara County	212,652	49,427	23.2%	51.7%	48.3%	15.8%	39.5%	44.7%
Oneida County	232,500	57,337	24.7%	49.1%	50.9%	13.8%	39.0%	47.3%
Onondaga County	468,463	123,197	26.3%	49.2%	50.8%	15.9%	39.3%	44.8%
Ontario County	109,561	26,317	24.0%	46.2%	53.8%	16.2%	43.7%	40.1%
Orange County	377,647	96,177	25.5%	54.6%	45.4%	18.6%	42.8%	38.5%
Oswego County	120,146	32,086	26.7%	51.5%	48.5%	16.2%	43.3%	40.5%
Putnam County	99,042	21,543	21.8%	53.8%	46.2%	20.9%	42.9%	36.2%
Queens County	2,339,150	608,419	26.0%	50.7%	49.3%	12.0%	32.3%	55.6%
Rensselaer County	160,266	42,660	26.6%	53.8%	46.2%	12.4%	41.0%	46.6%
Richmond County	474,558	118,607	25.0%	49.4%	50.6%	16.0%	35.8%	48.2%
Rockland County	326,037	78,832	24.2%	51.2%	48.8%	18.7%	40.2%	41.1%
Saratoga County	111,007	32,089	28.9%	53.3%	46.7%	12.1%	49.5%	38.4%
Schenectady County	226,249	50,020	22.1%	49.5%	50.5%	17.4%	35.4%	47.2%
St. Lawrence County	154,604	38,446	24.9%	53.3%	46.7%	16.2%	36.0%	47.8%
Steuben County	97,631	22,675	23.2%	52.4%	47.6%	19.6%	38.1%	42.3%
Suffolk County	1,501,587	350,920	23.4%	51.6%	48.4%	17.4%	38.7%	44.0%
Tompkins County	104,926	44,550	42.5%	49.6%	50.4%	5.8%	68.8%	25.4%
Ulster County	180,143	43,352	24.1%	50.8%	49.2%	12.9%	45.2%	41.9%
Wayne County	91,446	20,592	22.5%	49.9%	50.1%	18.4%	34.9%	46.6%
Westchester County	976,396	227,429	23.3%	51.1%	48.9%	18.4%	39.0%	42.6%
North Carolina								
Alamance County	158,276	37,828	23.9%	46.6%	53.4%	17.0%	39.0%	44.0%
Brunswick County	122,765	21,327	17.4%	49.6%	50.4%	17.7%	39.2%	43.1%
Buncombe County	253,170	62,054	24.5%	48.8%	51.2%	14.2%	34.1%	51.8%
Cabarrus County	196,762	45,207	23.0%	50.9%	49.1%	19.0%	35.1%	45.9%
Catawba County	155,056	36,359	23.4%	51.0%	49.0%	19.1%	37.2%	43.7%
Cleveland County	96,879	22,228	22.9%	49.5%	50.5%	15.9%	42.6%	41.5%
Craven County	103,451	28,641	27.7%	57.9%	42.1%	10.2%	44.9%	44.9%
Cumberland County	323,838	101,310	31.3%	53.2%	46.8%	12.3%	40.3%	47.5%
Davidson County	164,622	36,326	22.1%	50.0%	50.0%	19.4%	34.6%	46.0%
Durham County	300,952	89,780	29.8%	48.3%	51.7%	11.0%	33.3%	55.7%
Forsyth County	369,019	92,421	25.0%	47.5%	52.5%	15.4%	37.7%	46.9%
Gaston County	213,442	50,930	23.9%	50.7%	49.3%	16.0%	34.4%	49.6%
Guilford County	517,600	137,587	26.6%	48.0%	52.0%	15.1%	39.2%	45.7%
Harnett County	128,140	35,903	28.0%	50.5%	49.5%	15.1%	37.3%	47.6%
Henderson County	112,655	20,521	18.2%	48.5%	51.5%	14.6%	35.5%	49.9%
Iredell County	169,866	39,135	23.0%	53.9%	46.1%	21.2%	37.6%	41.2%
Johnston County	185,660	41,911	22.6%	49.3%	50.7%	19.5%	35.2%	45.2%
Mecklenburg County	1,034,070	285,842	27.6%	49.1%	50.9%	13.1%	33.2%	53.6%
Moore County	94,352	19,495	20.7%	54.2%	45.8%	19.9%	33.0%	47.1%
Nash County	93,919	21,537	22.9%	51.5%	48.5%	17.8%	37.1%	45.1%
New Hanover County	220,358	62,467	28.3%	46.9%	53.1%	12.4%	45.3%	42.4%
Onslow County	186,311	76,563	41.1%	61.5%	38.5%	7.7%	48.8%	43.5%
Orange County	141,354	49,316	34.9%	46.4%	53.6%	10.0%	55.0%	35.0%
Pitt County	175,842	61,542	35.0%	46.4%	53.6%	10.3%	53.0%	36.7%
Randolph County	142,799	32,208	22.6%	51.3%	48.7%	17.0%	37.4%	45.6%
Robeson County	134,197	34,806	25.9%	52.0%	48.0%	16.3%	43.9%	39.8%
Rockingham County	91,758	19,131	20.8%	51.8%	48.2%	18.9%	34.2%	46.9%
Rowan County	139,142	32,505	23.4%	52.4%	47.6%	16.3%	38.5%	45.2%
Union County	222,742	51,248	23.0%	50.0%	50.0%	22.8%	40.7%	36.5%
Wake County	1,024,198	269,495	26.3%	50.5%	49.5%	15.2%	34.4%	50.4%
Wayne County	124,132	32,804	26.4%	53.0%	47.0%	13.0%	37.0%	50.1%
North Dakota								
Cass County	171,512	57,528	33.5%	49.8%	50.2%	8.4%	49.6%	42.0%
Ohio								
Allen County	104,425	25,254	24.2%	52.7%	47.3%	15.9%	38.4%	45.7%

Table A-2: Counties—Summary Population Characteristics—*Continued*

	Total 2015 ACS Population	Millennial Population Age 15 to 33	Millennials as Percent of Total	Millennial Percentage by Gender		Millennial Percentage by Age		
				Male	Female	15 to 17	18 to 24	25 to 33
Ohio—Cont.								
Ashtabula County	98,632	22,614	22.9%	51.0%	49.0%	22.1%	34.6%	43.3%
Butler County	376,353	100,977	26.8%	49.1%	50.9%	15.8%	44.7%	39.5%
Clark County	135,959	31,343	23.1%	47.9%	52.1%	17.9%	38.3%	43.9%
Clermont County	201,973	47,651	23.6%	48.5%	51.5%	18.9%	31.7%	49.4%
Columbiana County	104,806	21,390	20.4%	50.9%	49.1%	18.7%	35.1%	46.2%
Cuyahoga County	1,255,921	307,066	24.4%	49.6%	50.4%	15.1%	36.8%	48.1%
Delaware County	193,013	40,687	21.1%	50.5%	49.5%	22.5%	36.0%	41.5%
Fairfield County	151,408	33,757	22.3%	50.5%	49.5%	19.6%	36.4%	44.0%
Franklin County	1,251,722	368,067	29.4%	49.6%	50.4%	12.3%	32.8%	54.9%
Geauga County	94,102	19,169	20.4%	54.2%	45.8%	22.6%	41.2%	36.1%
Greene County	164,427	45,617	27.7%	49.6%	50.4%	13.0%	45.3%	41.7%
Hamilton County	807,598	210,833	26.1%	49.1%	50.9%	14.7%	34.5%	50.8%
Lake County	229,245	49,316	21.5%	52.9%	47.1%	19.1%	37.1%	43.9%
Licking County	170,570	40,615	23.8%	51.1%	48.9%	18.0%	39.3%	42.8%
Lorain County	305,147	69,817	22.9%	52.2%	47.8%	19.2%	37.4%	43.4%
Lucas County	433,689	112,127	25.9%	49.7%	50.3%	15.0%	36.6%	48.4%
Mahoning County	231,900	54,236	23.4%	49.2%	50.8%	15.4%	37.4%	47.2%
Medina County	176,395	38,688	21.9%	50.2%	49.8%	19.4%	35.0%	45.6%
Miami County	104,224	23,293	22.3%	50.1%	49.9%	21.2%	33.4%	45.3%
Montgomery County	532,258	131,048	24.6%	50.2%	49.8%	14.8%	36.2%	48.9%
Portage County	162,275	49,657	30.6%	47.3%	52.7%	12.7%	54.7%	32.7%
Richland County	121,707	27,953	23.0%	53.9%	46.1%	16.7%	38.7%	44.7%
Stark County	375,165	88,128	23.5%	51.9%	48.1%	16.9%	36.9%	46.2%
Summit County	541,968	128,898	23.8%	52.0%	48.0%	15.4%	37.0%	47.7%
Trumbull County	203,751	44,176	21.7%	53.7%	46.3%	19.1%	38.7%	42.2%
Tuscarawas County	92,916	20,822	22.4%	51.2%	48.8%	20.3%	34.0%	45.7%
Warren County	224,469	49,951	22.3%	52.9%	47.1%	23.0%	34.6%	42.4%
Wayne County	116,063	28,015	24.1%	52.1%	47.9%	19.8%	40.1%	40.1%
Wood County	129,730	43,113	33.2%	53.6%	46.4%	15.8%	41.7%	42.5%
Oklahoma								
Canadian County	133,378	32,644	24.5%	52.5%	47.5%	15.0%	32.9%	52.1%
Cleveland County	274,458	88,250	32.2%	49.8%	50.2%	12.2%	45.1%	42.7%
Comanche County	124,648	39,557	31.7%	56.6%	43.4%	12.0%	37.9%	50.1%
Oklahoma County	776,864	208,662	26.9%	49.0%	51.0%	12.8%	33.7%	53.5%
Tulsa County	639,242	166,034	26.0%	47.8%	52.2%	15.9%	35.1%	49.0%
Oregon								
Clackamas County	401,515	91,377	22.8%	51.8%	48.2%	19.6%	35.6%	44.9%
Deschutes County	175,268	37,506	21.4%	51.0%	49.0%	14.3%	33.4%	52.3%
Douglas County	107,685	21,869	20.3%	50.0%	50.0%	15.1%	34.7%	50.2%
Jackson County	212,567	48,007	22.6%	49.0%	51.0%	15.3%	33.9%	50.9%
Lane County	362,895	101,413	27.9%	50.5%	49.5%	12.7%	45.9%	41.5%
Linn County	120,547	28,340	23.5%	50.5%	49.5%	14.9%	45.3%	39.9%
Marion County	330,700	85,650	25.9%	50.7%	49.3%	17.2%	37.4%	45.4%
Multnomah County	790,294	217,351	27.5%	49.2%	50.8%	10.3%	29.9%	59.8%
Washington County	574,326	148,421	25.8%	50.4%	49.6%	16.1%	31.1%	52.8%
Yamhill County	102,659	26,349	25.7%	55.5%	44.5%	16.6%	43.9%	39.4%
Pennsylvania								
Adams County	102,295	23,400	22.9%	50.4%	49.6%	17.9%	36.6%	45.6%
Allegheny County	1,230,459	317,665	25.8%	51.3%	48.7%	13.0%	34.7%	52.3%
Beaver County	168,871	37,432	22.2%	54.7%	45.3%	16.8%	33.9%	49.3%
Berks County	415,271	102,383	24.7%	49.7%	50.3%	16.2%	40.3%	43.4%
Blair County	125,593	28,645	22.8%	50.4%	49.6%	18.2%	34.4%	47.4%
Bucks County	627,367	134,522	21.4%	51.1%	48.9%	18.6%	36.9%	44.5%
Butler County	186,818	43,323	23.2%	50.9%	49.1%	16.7%	37.6%	45.8%
Cambria County	136,411	30,779	22.6%	53.1%	46.9%	17.8%	40.3%	41.9%
Centre County	160,580	67,059	41.8%	55.3%	44.7%	5.7%	61.2%	33.1%
Chester County	515,939	118,752	23.0%	51.6%	48.4%	17.1%	39.3%	43.6%
Cumberland County	246,338	60,812	24.7%	51.2%	48.8%	15.1%	40.5%	44.4%
Dauphin County	272,983	65,894	24.1%	50.9%	49.1%	15.7%	40.1%	44.2%
Delaware County	563,894	143,127	25.4%	50.3%	49.7%	15.5%	40.2%	44.3%
Erie County	278,045	71,032	25.5%	48.2%	51.8%	16.1%	40.0%	43.8%
Fayette County	133,628	28,056	21.0%	52.4%	47.6%	17.6%	34.4%	48.0%
Franklin County	153,638	34,699	22.6%	53.0%	47.0%	15.7%	40.5%	43.8%
Lackawanna County	211,917	50,772	24.0%	50.4%	49.6%	16.1%	38.6%	45.2%
Lancaster County	536,624	129,595	24.2%	48.7%	51.3%	17.0%	38.2%	44.8%
Lebanon County	137,067	29,746	21.7%	52.4%	47.6%	14.8%	41.7%	43.4%
Lehigh County	360,685	91,016	25.2%	50.2%	49.8%	17.8%	36.3%	45.9%
Luzerne County	318,449	75,606	23.7%	49.6%	50.4%	15.3%	41.3%	43.4%
Lycoming County	116,048	28,105	24.2%	49.2%	50.8%	13.1%	42.8%	44.2%
Mercer County	114,234	26,023	22.8%	54.4%	45.6%	19.6%	39.2%	41.2%
Monroe County	166,397	42,076	25.3%	48.0%	52.0%	17.5%	43.4%	39.2%
Montgomery County	819,264	186,127	22.7%	49.8%	50.2%	15.8%	35.3%	48.9%
Northampton County	300,813	72,627	24.1%	53.2%	46.8%	15.3%	43.7%	41.0%
Northumberland County	93,246	20,330	21.8%	52.3%	47.7%	15.3%	32.7%	52.1%
Philadelphia County	1,567,442	485,276	31.0%	48.6%	51.4%	11.0%	34.1%	54.9%
Schuylkill County	144,590	30,373	21.0%	52.7%	47.3%	17.6%	33.5%	48.9%
Washington County	208,261	45,987	22.1%	51.4%	48.6%	14.9%	40.0%	45.1%

Table A-2: Counties—Summary Population Characteristics—*Continued*

	Total 2015 ACS Population	Millennial Population Age 15 to 33	Millennials as Percent of Total	Millennial Percentage by Gender		Millennial Percentage by Age		
				Male	Female	15 to 17	18 to 24	25 to 33
Pennsylvania—Cont.								
Westmoreland County	357,956	74,211	20.7%	51.4%	48.6%	18.2%	39.0%	42.8%
York County	442,867	101,242	22.9%	50.3%	49.7%	16.4%	33.8%	49.8%
Rhode Island								
Kent County	164,801	37,771	22.9%	49.4%	50.6%	15.2%	30.8%	54.0%
Providence County	633,473	177,530	28.0%	49.2%	50.8%	12.4%	39.7%	47.9%
Washington County	126,517	32,522	25.7%	48.7%	51.3%	13.4%	54.2%	32.4%
South Carolina								
Aiken County	165,829	39,663	23.9%	52.4%	47.6%	16.3%	37.7%	45.9%
Anderson County	194,692	44,484	22.8%	50.3%	49.7%	20.0%	39.7%	40.3%
Beaufort County	179,589	42,199	23.5%	53.3%	46.7%	11.6%	39.1%	49.3%
Berkeley County	202,786	55,285	27.3%	53.6%	46.4%	15.7%	32.2%	52.1%
Charleston County	389,262	110,362	28.4%	49.7%	50.3%	13.1%	35.2%	51.6%
Dorchester County	152,478	39,833	26.1%	53.3%	46.7%	13.1%	30.6%	56.2%
Florence County	138,900	34,104	24.6%	47.2%	52.8%	16.2%	38.4%	45.3%
Greenville County	491,863	127,063	25.8%	50.4%	49.6%	15.4%	37.3%	47.3%
Horry County	309,199	69,260	22.4%	52.3%	47.7%	15.6%	35.9%	48.4%
Lexington County	281,833	69,290	24.6%	50.4%	49.6%	16.3%	34.2%	49.5%
Pickens County	121,691	39,215	32.2%	54.2%	45.8%	12.7%	47.6%	39.7%
Richland County	407,051	133,553	32.8%	53.1%	46.9%	12.5%	48.1%	39.3%
Spartanburg County	297,302	74,202	25.0%	49.5%	50.5%	15.9%	38.7%	45.5%
Sumter County	107,400	29,989	27.9%	58.7%	41.3%	14.7%	44.7%	40.7%
York County	251,195	61,013	24.3%	47.7%	52.3%	17.9%	37.3%	44.8%
South Dakota								
Minnehaha County	185,197	51,061	27.6%	51.2%	48.8%	12.7%	30.4%	56.9%
Pennington County	108,702	27,812	25.6%	52.6%	47.4%	15.6%	30.6%	53.8%
Tennessee								
Blount County	127,253	28,362	22.3%	47.6%	52.4%	17.4%	37.8%	44.8%
Bradley County	104,091	27,347	26.3%	49.6%	50.4%	18.0%	36.7%	45.3%
Davidson County	678,889	207,280	30.5%	49.1%	50.9%	10.1%	33.7%	56.3%
Hamilton County	354,098	89,012	25.1%	48.9%	51.1%	13.8%	36.7%	49.5%
Knox County	451,324	126,547	28.0%	49.3%	50.7%	14.1%	44.6%	41.3%
Madison County	97,610	25,119	25.7%	45.3%	54.7%	15.1%	42.0%	42.9%
Montgomery County	193,479	64,486	33.3%	54.2%	45.8%	11.4%	34.2%	54.4%
Rutherford County	298,612	90,154	30.2%	51.9%	48.1%	14.0%	44.0%	42.0%
Sevier County	95,946	21,355	22.3%	46.6%	53.4%	20.2%	39.7%	40.1%
Shelby County	938,069	254,967	27.2%	49.0%	51.0%	15.7%	35.9%	48.3%
Sullivan County	156,791	34,048	21.7%	52.1%	47.9%	21.9%	36.2%	41.9%
Sumner County	175,989	41,241	23.4%	50.1%	49.9%	16.7%	35.4%	47.9%
Washington County	126,302	33,607	26.6%	50.2%	49.8%	12.8%	46.1%	41.1%
Williamson County	211,672	42,103	19.9%	49.5%	50.5%	28.0%	37.0%	35.0%
Wilson County	128,911	28,214	21.9%	48.2%	51.8%	18.3%	38.9%	42.8%
Texas								
Bell County	334,941	105,325	31.4%	53.0%	47.0%	13.2%	38.0%	48.8%
Bexar County	1,897,753	542,377	28.6%	51.1%	48.9%	15.0%	36.0%	49.0%
Bowie County	93,389	23,025	24.7%	56.7%	43.3%	15.4%	37.5%	47.2%
Brazoria County	346,312	88,816	25.6%	50.9%	49.1%	19.4%	33.0%	47.6%
Brazos County	215,037	97,285	45.2%	52.8%	47.2%	6.7%	60.4%	32.9%
Cameron County	422,156	114,476	27.1%	50.3%	49.7%	20.3%	39.3%	40.4%
Collin County	914,127	217,272	23.8%	50.8%	49.2%	19.9%	32.8%	47.3%
Comal County	129,048	28,645	22.2%	49.0%	51.0%	19.5%	36.5%	44.0%
Dallas County	2,553,385	713,204	27.9%	50.3%	49.7%	14.5%	34.7%	50.8%
Denton County	780,612	210,431	27.0%	48.8%	51.2%	15.9%	34.4%	49.7%
Ector County	159,436	49,508	31.1%	52.0%	48.0%	15.0%	36.4%	48.5%
El Paso County	163,632	40,687	24.9%	52.6%	47.4%	20.7%	35.7%	43.6%
Ellis County	835,593	242,594	29.0%	52.9%	47.1%	15.7%	38.8%	45.5%
Fort Bend County	716,087	174,314	24.3%	50.8%	49.2%	19.9%	34.6%	45.5%
Galveston County	322,225	79,208	24.6%	49.7%	50.3%	17.1%	36.3%	46.6%
Grayson County	125,467	30,076	24.0%	53.3%	46.7%	16.4%	40.9%	42.7%
Gregg County	124,108	31,707	25.5%	48.0%	52.0%	15.5%	38.1%	46.4%
Guadalupe County	151,249	37,951	25.1%	51.4%	48.6%	19.5%	34.2%	46.3%
Harris County	4,538,028	1,272,358	28.0%	50.6%	49.4%	15.0%	33.9%	51.0%
Hays County	194,739	66,615	34.2%	49.8%	50.2%	10.9%	51.5%	37.6%
Hidalgo County	842,304	236,165	28.0%	50.9%	49.1%	18.9%	39.6%	41.5%
Jefferson County	254,308	67,989	26.7%	52.1%	47.9%	15.1%	35.2%	49.7%
Johnson County	159,990	39,272	24.5%	50.9%	49.1%	18.7%	36.2%	45.0%
Kaufman County	114,690	27,740	24.2%	50.0%	50.0%	17.1%	34.2%	48.7%
Lubbock County	299,453	102,399	34.2%	51.5%	48.5%	11.2%	49.5%	39.3%
McLennan County	245,671	74,841	30.5%	49.4%	50.6%	14.3%	48.1%	37.6%
Midland County	161,077	48,875	30.3%	52.2%	47.8%	15.2%	33.1%	51.7%
Montgomery County	537,559	128,604	23.9%	50.7%	49.3%	18.6%	35.8%	45.6%
Nueces County	359,715	100,540	27.9%	50.1%	49.9%	15.9%	36.3%	47.8%
Parker County	126,042	27,518	21.8%	53.2%	46.8%	21.7%	37.9%	40.3%
Potter County	121,802	32,293	26.5%	51.9%	48.1%	13.9%	34.9%	51.2%
Randall County	130,269	36,250	27.8%	50.3%	49.7%	14.4%	37.2%	48.4%

Table A-2: Counties—Summary Population Characteristics—*Continued*

	Total 2015 ACS Population	Millennial Population Age 15 to 33	Millennials as Percent of Total	Millennial Percentage by Gender		Millennial Percentage by Age		
				Male	Female	15 to 17	18 to 24	25 to 33
Texas—Cont.								
Smith County	222,936	60,703	27.2%	49.8%	50.2%	14.7%	38.5%	46.8%
Tarrant County	1,982,498	531,633	26.8%	50.1%	49.9%	16.5%	34.5%	49.0%
Taylor County	136,051	43,310	31.8%	49.4%	50.6%	12.4%	48.2%	39.4%
Tom Green County	118,105	35,765	30.3%	53.9%	46.1%	12.5%	41.8%	45.7%
Travis County	1,176,558	364,058	30.9%	51.5%	48.5%	10.9%	30.8%	58.4%
Webb County	269,721	76,206	28.3%	49.6%	50.4%	19.4%	40.0%	40.6%
Wichita County	131,705	41,345	31.4%	56.6%	43.4%	11.8%	46.0%	42.3%
Williamson County	508,514	122,798	24.1%	50.1%	49.9%	18.8%	32.4%	48.8%
Utah								
Cache County	120,783	44,550	36.9%	51.0%	49.0%	14.1%	47.2%	38.7%
Davis County	336,043	92,284	27.5%	51.5%	48.5%	18.8%	35.1%	46.1%
Salt Lake County	1,107,314	315,750	28.5%	51.7%	48.3%	15.7%	33.9%	50.4%
Utah County	575,205	196,901	34.2%	49.9%	50.1%	15.4%	47.9%	36.7%
Washington County	155,602	39,437	25.3%	50.1%	49.9%	19.0%	42.4%	38.7%
Weber County	243,645	68,284	28.0%	50.9%	49.1%	16.1%	34.8%	49.1%
Vermont								
Chittenden County	161,382	51,415	31.9%	51.7%	48.3%	12.5%	48.9%	38.6%
Virginia								
Albemarle County	105,703	29,197	27.6%	47.2%	52.8%	8.2%	46.4%	45.4%
Arlington County	229,164	77,494	33.8%	49.6%	50.4%	6.0%	22.4%	71.6%
Chesterfield County	335,687	81,100	24.2%	49.6%	50.4%	19.5%	38.8%	41.7%
Fairfax County	1,142,234	282,006	24.7%	50.2%	49.8%	15.7%	33.9%	50.4%
Hanover County	103,227	22,860	22.1%	45.6%	54.4%	21.2%	42.9%	35.9%
Henrico County	325,155	79,300	24.4%	47.7%	52.3%	15.5%	33.4%	51.1%
Loudoun County	375,629	84,610	22.5%	49.2%	50.8%	20.0%	28.8%	51.2%
Montgomery County	97,653	43,081	44.1%	54.1%	45.9%	5.9%	63.9%	30.2%
Prince William County	451,721	116,795	25.9%	52.2%	47.8%	17.8%	34.4%	47.8%
Roanoke County	94,409	21,530	22.8%	49.9%	50.1%	19.7%	33.3%	47.0%
Spotsylvania County	130,475	31,802	24.4%	52.3%	47.7%	19.9%	38.0%	42.1%
Stafford County	142,003	38,069	26.8%	51.4%	48.6%	15.8%	40.3%	43.9%
Washington								
Benton County	190,309	48,145	25.3%	47.1%	52.9%	19.7%	36.1%	44.3%
Clark County	459,495	114,195	24.9%	51.1%	48.9%	18.1%	34.5%	47.4%
Cowlitz County	103,468	23,053	22.3%	54.6%	45.4%	14.9%	28.9%	56.2%
Grant County	93,259	24,728	26.5%	58.0%	42.0%	12.5%	46.9%	40.6%
King County	2,117,125	568,084	26.8%	50.9%	49.1%	12.0%	30.3%	57.7%
Kitsap County	260,131	69,919	26.9%	54.5%	45.5%	14.0%	39.2%	46.8%
Pierce County	843,954	225,257	26.7%	52.1%	47.9%	14.6%	35.0%	50.4%
Skagit County	121,846	27,287	22.4%	51.8%	48.2%	17.1%	32.8%	50.1%
Snohomish County	772,501	192,324	24.9%	51.5%	48.5%	15.9%	33.5%	50.6%
Spokane County	490,945	135,628	27.6%	51.6%	48.4%	14.1%	35.8%	50.2%
Thurston County	269,536	67,330	25.0%	52.4%	47.6%	13.8%	37.0%	49.2%
Whatcom County	212,284	64,215	30.2%	50.2%	49.8%	11.3%	47.7%	41.0%
Yakima County	248,830	64,342	25.9%	51.6%	48.4%	17.6%	39.5%	42.9%
West Virginia								
Berkeley County	111,901	26,822	24.0%	52.9%	47.1%	15.2%	37.2%	47.6%
Cabell County	96,844	26,637	27.5%	46.3%	53.7%	16.0%	42.9%	41.2%
Kanawha County	188,332	40,670	21.6%	47.6%	52.4%	15.3%	34.7%	50.0%
Monongalia County	104,236	43,034	41.3%	51.5%	48.5%	7.7%	50.3%	42.1%
Wisconsin								
Brown County	258,718	65,276	25.2%	51.2%	48.8%	14.2%	35.7%	50.1%
Dane County	523,643	159,007	30.4%	50.8%	49.2%	11.1%	42.4%	46.5%
Eau Claire County	102,105	32,420	31.8%	51.0%	49.0%	13.8%	47.0%	39.2%
Fond du Lac County	101,973	24,162	23.7%	48.0%	52.0%	21.2%	35.2%	43.6%
Kenosha County	168,437	42,022	24.9%	49.9%	50.1%	17.0%	40.8%	42.2%
La Crosse County	118,212	35,803	30.3%	47.7%	52.3%	11.2%	53.7%	35.0%
Marathon County	135,868	29,492	21.7%	49.8%	50.2%	18.8%	32.9%	48.3%
Milwaukee County	957,735	267,550	27.9%	47.6%	52.4%	13.3%	35.9%	50.9%
Outagamie County	183,245	45,906	25.1%	51.1%	48.9%	15.8%	33.5%	50.7%
Racine County	195,080	45,504	23.3%	52.3%	47.7%	17.6%	39.2%	43.2%
Rock County	161,448	36,704	22.7%	51.7%	48.3%	18.0%	40.4%	41.6%
Sheboygan County	115,569	24,958	21.6%	51.5%	48.5%	18.7%	34.1%	47.2%
Walworth County	102,804	27,201	26.5%	52.1%	47.9%	14.2%	48.8%	37.0%
Washington County	133,674	27,605	20.7%	43.6%	56.4%	17.3%	37.5%	45.2%
Waukesha County	396,488	82,793	20.9%	51.4%	48.6%	21.2%	36.1%	42.7%
Winnebago County	169,546	46,787	27.6%	50.4%	49.6%	13.5%	41.2%	45.3%
Wyoming								
Laramie County	97,121	26,622	27.4%	57.2%	42.8%	12.3%	52.3%	35.4%

Table A-3: Places—Summary Population Characteristics

	Total 2015 ACS Population	Millennial Population Age 15 to 33	Millennials as Percent of Total	Millennial Percentage by Gender		Millennial Percentage by Age		
				Male	Female	15 to 17	18 to 24	25 to 33
Alabama								
Birmingham city	214,911	65,276	30.4%	50.1%	49.9%	12.1%	37.9%	49.9%
Huntsville city	189,114	50,582	26.7%	50.5%	49.5%	13.8%	38.2%	48.0%
Mobile city	194,305	54,926	28.3%	46.2%	53.8%	14.3%	36.7%	49.1%
Montgomery city	200,586	56,640	28.2%	48.0%	52.0%	14.1%	38.5%	47.4%
Tuscaloosa city	98,338	43,300	44.0%	48.4%	51.6%	8.6%	59.7%	31.7%
Alaska								
Anchorage municipality	298,695	92,449	31.0%	52.4%	47.6%	12.7%	37.4%	49.9%
Arizona								
Chandler city	260,833	68,912	26.4%	50.9%	49.1%	16.9%	30.7%	52.4%
Glendale city	240,114	67,526	28.1%	47.1%	52.9%	17.3%	35.8%	46.8%
Mesa city	471,833	128,122	27.2%	54.2%	45.8%	14.8%	35.3%	49.8%
Peoria city	171,242	42,034	24.5%	47.8%	52.2%	17.1%	32.7%	50.2%
Phoenix city	1,563,001	432,935	27.7%	51.1%	48.9%	15.0%	36.1%	48.9%
Scottsdale city	236,844	52,609	22.2%	54.5%	45.5%	13.2%	29.3%	57.5%
Surprise city	128,442	27,081	21.1%	48.1%	51.9%	21.9%	28.1%	50.0%
Tempe city	175,826	78,172	44.5%	52.7%	47.3%	7.1%	56.7%	36.2%
Tucson city	531,674	169,695	31.9%	51.2%	48.8%	12.0%	48.9%	39.1%
Yuma city	94,145	27,585	29.3%	51.5%	48.5%	19.3%	40.9%	39.8%
Arkansas								
Little Rock city	197,986	53,598	27.1%	50.0%	50.0%	12.8%	33.2%	53.9%
California								
Anaheim city	350,738	104,887	29.9%	53.0%	47.0%	14.2%	36.7%	49.2%
Antioch city	110,542	31,157	28.2%	47.2%	52.8%	16.9%	44.4%	38.7%
Bakersfield city	373,627	116,248	31.1%	50.1%	49.9%	14.5%	39.1%	46.4%
Berkeley city	120,971	49,498	40.9%	49.0%	51.0%	7.3%	52.1%	40.6%
Burbank city	105,314	27,930	26.5%	45.7%	54.3%	14.3%	25.3%	60.4%
Carlsbad city	113,466	25,879	22.8%	50.7%	49.3%	18.0%	33.8%	48.2%
Chico city	90,336	35,558	39.4%	53.0%	47.0%	10.1%	56.8%	33.0%
Carson city	93,296	26,003	27.9%	51.3%	48.7%	18.2%	38.4%	43.4%
Chula Vista city	265,754	73,367	27.6%	55.7%	44.3%	15.4%	40.0%	44.6%
Clovis city	104,172	26,306	25.3%	53.2%	46.8%	15.3%	31.5%	53.2%
Compton city	98,448	30,522	31.0%	51.4%	48.6%	15.4%	43.0%	41.6%
Concord city	128,668	30,735	23.9%	60.3%	39.7%	13.8%	32.7%	53.5%
Corona city	164,242	42,345	25.8%	47.1%	52.9%	15.7%	34.9%	49.4%
Costa Mesa city	113,186	36,378	32.1%	52.0%	48.0%	16.1%	29.8%	54.1%
Daly City city	106,574	29,604	27.8%	49.9%	50.1%	6.9%	35.0%	58.1%
Downey city	114,211	33,813	29.6%	45.5%	54.5%	13.6%	41.4%	45.0%
El Cajon city	103,688	30,072	29.0%	58.4%	41.6%	13.0%	36.8%	50.2%
Elk Grove city	166,890	41,650	25.0%	50.9%	49.1%	16.9%	41.8%	41.3%
El Monte city	116,745	33,568	28.8%	53.4%	46.6%	15.5%	37.0%	47.6%
Escondido city	151,458	47,202	31.2%	50.8%	49.2%	11.3%	37.4%	51.3%
Fairfield city	112,972	31,243	27.7%	51.1%	48.9%	14.9%	33.9%	51.2%
Fontana city	207,472	63,986	30.8%	50.7%	49.3%	14.0%	36.6%	49.4%
Fremont city	232,191	58,826	25.3%	48.9%	51.1%	14.4%	32.9%	52.7%
Fresno city	520,072	160,820	30.9%	51.3%	48.7%	14.9%	38.1%	47.0%
Fullerton city	140,849	43,980	31.2%	51.5%	48.5%	14.1%	41.8%	44.1%
Garden Grove city	175,384	47,042	26.8%	51.0%	49.0%	14.4%	37.2%	48.4%
Glendale city	201,026	49,189	24.5%	55.2%	44.8%	10.7%	30.5%	58.7%
Hayward city	158,300	47,670	30.1%	49.6%	50.4%	11.7%	31.5%	56.8%
Hesperia city	93,286	27,100	29.1%	47.6%	52.4%	19.6%	32.7%	47.7%
Huntington Beach city	201,927	44,399	22.0%	50.6%	49.4%	11.1%	32.5%	56.4%
Inglewood city	111,656	31,703	28.4%	51.6%	48.4%	13.9%	36.4%	49.7%
Irvine city	256,927	83,108	32.3%	49.4%	50.6%	12.6%	43.3%	44.1%
Jurupa Valley city	100,314	29,976	29.9%	47.2%	52.8%	15.3%	41.2%	43.5%
Lancaster city	161,113	49,208	30.5%	49.2%	50.8%	18.2%	30.2%	51.6%
Long Beach city	474,172	137,426	29.0%	49.3%	50.7%	14.1%	34.9%	51.0%
Los Angeles city	3,971,896	1,208,578	30.4%	50.8%	49.2%	11.8%	35.5%	52.7%
Mission Viejo city	97,163	22,309	23.0%	55.3%	44.7%	15.8%	42.5%	41.7%
Modesto city	211,257	57,185	27.1%	49.0%	51.0%	14.5%	40.2%	45.2%
Moreno Valley city	204,181	66,439	32.5%	47.3%	52.7%	17.8%	40.7%	41.5%
Murrieta city	109,816	30,451	27.7%	52.1%	47.9%	22.3%	31.6%	46.1%
Norwalk city	107,145	30,689	28.6%	55.1%	44.9%	10.9%	44.7%	44.4%
Oakland city	419,278	122,337	29.2%	48.6%	51.4%	10.9%	28.0%	61.1%
Oceanside city	175,714	45,355	25.8%	63.3%	36.7%	10.7%	51.0%	38.3%
Ontario city	171,200	51,531	30.1%	52.1%	47.9%	15.9%	36.7%	47.4%
Orange city	140,995	44,072	31.3%	49.7%	50.3%	11.4%	39.4%	49.2%
Oxnard city	207,252	62,289	30.1%	49.8%	50.2%	14.0%	34.6%	51.4%
Palmdale city	158,350	42,360	26.8%	48.7%	51.3%	18.2%	38.5%	43.3%
Pasadena city	142,246	36,762	25.8%	46.4%	53.6%	7.3%	32.1%	60.6%
Pomona city	153,252	48,713	31.8%	51.2%	48.8%	13.7%	41.6%	44.7%
Rancho Cucamonga city	175,232	50,125	28.6%	56.1%	43.9%	13.8%	42.3%	43.9%
Redding city	91,579	24,840	27.1%	48.5%	51.5%	18.6%	28.7%	52.7%
Rialto city	103,137	32,854	31.9%	51.3%	48.7%	16.1%	38.6%	45.3%
Richmond city	109,715	32,546	29.7%	51.1%	48.9%	7.9%	41.1%	51.0%

Table A-3: Places—Summary Population Characteristics—Continued

	Total 2015 ACS Population	Millennial Population Age 15 to 33	Millennials as Percent of Total	Millennial Percentage by Gender		Millennial Percentage by Age		
				Male	Female	15 to 17	18 to 24	25 to 33
California—Cont.								
Riverside city	322,423	108,944	33.8%	50.7%	49.3%	11.1%	43.3%	45.6%
Roseville city	130,282	32,596	25.0%	49.9%	50.1%	17.8%	38.4%	43.9%
Sacramento city	490,715	142,256	29.0%	49.8%	50.2%	13.7%	31.2%	55.0%
Salinas city	157,386	45,235	28.7%	53.4%	46.6%	15.7%	36.1%	48.1%
San Bernardino city	216,137	68,511	31.7%	51.1%	48.9%	15.0%	40.4%	44.6%
San Buenaventura (Ventura) city	109,717	27,629	25.2%	51.8%	48.2%	13.8%	32.5%	53.8%
San Diego city	1,394,907	445,012	31.9%	50.9%	49.1%	10.8%	36.8%	52.4%
San Francisco city	864,816	258,717	29.9%	49.8%	50.2%	6.6%	24.6%	68.9%
San Jose city	1,026,919	269,874	26.3%	52.0%	48.0%	13.8%	34.5%	51.7%
San Leandro city	90,711	22,760	25.1%	52.6%	47.4%	14.3%	29.6%	56.1%
San Marcos city	92,934	24,402	26.3%	49.8%	50.2%	16.0%	38.2%	45.8%
San Mateo city	103,524	24,437	23.6%	52.1%	47.9%	18.0%	30.4%	51.7%
Santa Ana city	335,423	101,668	30.3%	50.9%	49.1%	15.1%	34.0%	50.9%
Santa Clara city	126,216	39,593	31.4%	50.2%	49.8%	7.0%	33.7%	59.3%
Santa Clarita city	182,367	47,773	26.2%	49.8%	50.2%	14.6%	38.7%	46.7%
Santa Maria city	105,082	30,556	29.1%	53.6%	46.4%	19.6%	40.9%	39.5%
Santa Monica city	93,219	24,672	26.5%	48.8%	51.2%	11.3%	23.8%	64.9%
Santa Rosa city	174,989	44,446	25.4%	51.2%	48.8%	13.0%	35.2%	51.8%
Simi Valley city	126,766	32,740	25.8%	56.4%	43.6%	19.4%	38.3%	42.3%
South Gate city	96,399	28,277	29.3%	44.5%	55.5%	15.4%	39.8%	44.8%
Stockton city	305,650	91,948	30.1%	53.7%	46.3%	17.0%	37.0%	46.0%
Sunnyvale city	151,760	41,801	27.5%	54.9%	45.1%	9.9%	21.2%	68.9%
Temecula city	112,026	30,276	27.0%	51.0%	49.0%	22.6%	33.4%	44.1%
Thousand Oaks city	129,329	26,301	20.3%	47.8%	52.2%	22.5%	39.7%	37.9%
Torrance city	148,468	35,250	23.7%	48.5%	51.5%	12.9%	42.8%	44.3%
Vacaville city	96,794	26,462	27.3%	55.3%	44.7%	15.8%	36.0%	48.2%
Vallejo city	121,269	33,732	27.8%	51.4%	48.6%	12.9%	33.9%	53.2%
Victorville city	122,236	36,736	30.1%	50.3%	49.7%	22.4%	31.4%	46.1%
Visalia city	130,094	33,963	26.1%	52.9%	47.1%	14.3%	37.5%	48.2%
Vista city	100,884	31,575	31.3%	49.8%	50.2%	11.2%	37.7%	51.1%
West Covina city	108,489	29,341	27.0%	50.0%	50.0%	15.7%	32.3%	52.0%
Westminster city	92,111	21,766	23.6%	53.8%	46.2%	13.1%	30.4%	56.5%
Colorado								
Arvada city	115,035	25,827	22.5%	45.9%	54.1%	19.1%	27.6%	53.3%
Aurora city	358,870	102,094	28.4%	48.0%	52.0%	16.1%	33.3%	50.7%
Boulder city	107,342	50,704	47.2%	59.2%	40.8%	5.0%	63.8%	31.2%
Centennial city	109,726	24,786	22.6%	46.1%	53.9%	22.0%	30.7%	47.3%
Colorado Springs city	456,562	132,077	28.9%	50.7%	49.3%	13.0%	34.2%	52.7%
Denver city	682,545	217,281	31.8%	50.1%	49.9%	7.7%	26.8%	65.5%
Fort Collins city	161,181	64,784	40.2%	51.6%	48.4%	8.2%	49.4%	42.3%
Greeley city	100,883	32,325	32.0%	53.9%	46.1%	16.2%	38.2%	45.6%
Lakewood city	152,589	44,017	28.8%	56.2%	43.8%	13.8%	37.2%	48.9%
Longmont city	92,221	21,632	23.5%	50.0%	50.0%	20.7%	35.3%	44.0%
Pueblo city	109,419	29,065	26.6%	56.6%	43.4%	17.3%	34.6%	48.1%
Thornton city	133,459	34,916	26.2%	51.0%	49.0%	18.3%	32.5%	49.2%
Westminster city	113,117	30,054	26.6%	52.9%	47.1%	16.1%	31.1%	52.8%
Connecticut								
Bridgeport city	147,619	43,968	29.8%	49.4%	50.6%	12.0%	40.5%	47.5%
Hartford city	124,014	44,108	35.6%	48.1%	51.9%	11.5%	47.8%	40.7%
New Haven city	130,310	52,463	40.3%	52.8%	47.2%	9.6%	41.8%	48.6%
Stamford city	128,877	38,194	29.6%	57.2%	42.8%	13.3%	32.6%	54.1%
Waterbury city	108,807	28,106	25.8%	48.3%	51.7%	15.7%	36.9%	47.4%
District of Columbia								
Washington city	672,228	236,132	35.1%	47.0%	53.0%	6.4%	34.7%	58.9%
Florida								
Boca Raton city	93,226	21,653	23.2%	46.6%	53.4%	17.2%	42.2%	40.6%
Cape Coral city	175,230	37,325	21.3%	46.2%	53.8%	20.2%	27.2%	52.6%
Clearwater city	112,979	25,001	22.1%	49.3%	50.7%	11.7%	31.5%	56.8%
Coral Springs city	129,502	32,839	25.4%	52.0%	48.0%	25.5%	35.7%	38.8%
Fort Lauderdale city	178,587	40,875	22.9%	54.2%	45.8%	13.8%	25.7%	60.5%
Gainesville city	130,133	66,238	50.9%	50.0%	50.0%	5.3%	63.1%	31.5%
Hialeah city	237,082	54,580	23.0%	53.3%	46.7%	12.9%	34.7%	52.4%
Hollywood city	149,721	32,699	21.8%	54.2%	45.8%	8.6%	34.8%	56.5%
Jacksonville city	868,031	236,574	27.3%	50.2%	49.8%	12.7%	35.1%	52.2%
Lakeland city	104,410	27,759	26.6%	47.3%	52.7%	14.1%	37.8%	48.1%
Miami city	440,989	110,351	25.0%	48.9%	51.1%	10.8%	30.4%	58.8%
Miami Beach city	92,311	21,815	23.6%	55.9%	44.1%	12.0%	25.8%	62.2%
Miami Gardens city	113,199	30,931	27.3%	50.0%	50.0%	14.0%	36.8%	49.2%
Miramar city	137,115	34,640	25.3%	48.9%	51.1%	14.1%	36.8%	49.1%
Orlando city	270,917	91,969	33.9%	48.2%	51.8%	10.5%	30.7%	58.8%
Palm Bay city	107,895	23,931	22.2%	48.4%	51.6%	17.7%	39.5%	42.8%
Pembroke Pines city	166,624	41,693	25.0%	51.4%	48.6%	15.8%	38.9%	45.3%
Plantation city	92,555	21,871	23.6%	47.4%	52.6%	12.9%	28.3%	58.7%
Pompano Beach city	107,771	24,729	22.9%	56.5%	43.5%	15.1%	35.8%	49.0%
Port St. Lucie city	179,410	39,093	21.8%	49.4%	50.6%	15.9%	36.7%	47.3%

Table A-3: Places—Summary Population Characteristics—*Continued*

	Total 2015 ACS Population	Millennial Population Age 15 to 33	Millennials as Percent of Total	Millennial Percentage by Gender		Millennial Percentage by Age		
				Male	Female	15 to 17	18 to 24	25 to 33
Florida—Cont.								
St. Petersburg city	257,088	62,378	24.3%	50.0%	50.0%	14.5%	33.2%	52.3%
Sunrise city	92,706	25,017	27.0%	47.8%	52.2%	13.0%	27.9%	59.1%
Tallahassee city	189,894	90,224	47.5%	48.1%	51.9%	6.4%	64.1%	29.5%
Tampa city	369,028	109,385	29.6%	49.2%	50.8%	12.0%	35.8%	52.3%
West Palm Beach city	106,782	27,920	26.1%	53.8%	46.3%	14.5%	32.3%	53.2%
Georgia								
Athens-Clarke County unified govt (balance)	122,563	54,663	44.6%	46.7%	53.3%	4.8%	66.6%	28.6%
Atlanta city	463,875	160,144	34.5%	50.1%	49.9%	6.7%	37.2%	56.1%
Augusta-Richmond County consolidated govt (balance)	196,579	59,362	30.2%	52.5%	47.5%	12.4%	39.2%	48.3%
Columbus city	200,579	61,108	30.5%	55.9%	44.1%	11.5%	39.9%	48.6%
Macon-Bibb county	153,459	40,814	26.6%	46.0%	54.0%	14.9%	39.8%	45.3%
Roswell city	94,496	20,927	22.1%	53.2%	46.8%	23.6%	34.5%	41.9%
Sandy Springs city	105,347	30,066	28.5%	50.8%	49.2%	15.0%	26.6%	58.4%
Savannah city	145,684	55,172	37.9%	50.0%	50.0%	10.8%	44.8%	44.4%
Hawaii								
Urban Honolulu CDP	352,766	84,598	24.0%	54.7%	45.3%	11.0%	36.4%	52.7%
Idaho								
Boise City city	218,280	62,159	28.5%	52.9%	47.1%	14.6%	32.6%	52.7%
Meridian city	90,753	17,705	19.5%	51.4%	48.6%	14.8%	33.3%	51.9%
Illinois								
Aurora city	203,715	55,022	27.0%	52.6%	47.4%	15.3%	37.1%	47.7%
Chicago city	2,720,556	861,024	31.6%	49.4%	50.6%	10.9%	33.1%	56.0%
Elgin city	111,076	26,488	23.8%	48.9%	51.1%	12.6%	42.1%	45.2%
Joliet city	150,025	39,858	26.6%	49.8%	50.2%	18.9%	40.2%	40.9%
Naperville city	147,159	33,918	23.0%	45.7%	54.3%	18.8%	38.2%	43.1%
Peoria city	118,661	34,871	29.4%	47.0%	53.0%	14.3%	33.6%	52.1%
Rockford city	149,346	40,012	26.8%	48.9%	51.1%	16.1%	36.0%	47.9%
Springfield city	117,809	31,951	27.1%	50.6%	49.4%	16.9%	34.7%	48.4%
Indiana								
Evansville city	117,679	32,735	27.8%	46.5%	53.5%	12.5%	39.0%	48.5%
Fort Wayne city	258,144	70,772	27.4%	48.4%	51.6%	13.7%	38.8%	47.5%
Indianapolis city (balance)	848,423	244,048	28.8%	48.7%	51.3%	12.8%	33.0%	54.2%
South Bend city	103,757	29,483	28.4%	53.3%	46.7%	12.1%	47.0%	40.9%
Iowa								
Cedar Rapids city	130,405	35,359	27.1%	47.1%	52.9%	16.8%	36.7%	46.5%
Davenport city	102,577	27,789	27.1%	49.1%	50.9%	15.4%	34.0%	50.6%
Des Moines city	210,317	62,827	29.9%	48.9%	51.1%	11.9%	36.0%	52.0%
Kansas								
Kansas City city	151,261	40,363	26.7%	50.4%	49.6%	15.6%	35.4%	49.0%
Olathe city	134,316	33,638	25.0%	52.5%	47.5%	24.4%	33.4%	42.2%
Overland Park city	186,511	45,901	24.6%	46.5%	53.5%	17.6%	28.3%	54.1%
Topeka city	127,257	33,790	26.6%	54.1%	45.9%	16.7%	38.9%	44.4%
Wichita city	389,955	105,291	27.0%	50.4%	49.6%	16.1%	31.2%	52.7%
Kentucky								
Lexington-Fayette urban county	314,488	99,204	31.5%	51.3%	48.7%	10.1%	44.2%	45.7%
Louisville/Jefferson County metro govt (balance)	615,389	158,771	25.8%	50.7%	49.3%	15.3%	35.7%	48.9%
Louisiana								
Baton Rouge city	228,596	81,142	35.5%	49.8%	50.2%	10.5%	46.3%	43.2%
Lafayette city	127,661	44,471	34.8%	53.1%	46.9%	15.4%	33.1%	51.6%
New Orleans city	389,617	116,032	29.8%	47.8%	52.2%	10.5%	32.2%	57.3%
Shreveport city	196,994	54,837	27.8%	47.5%	52.5%	16.6%	34.6%	48.8%
Maryland								
Baltimore city	621,849	191,864	30.9%	47.8%	52.2%	10.3%	33.7%	56.1%
Massachusetts								
Boston city	669,469	266,782	39.8%	49.0%	51.0%	6.6%	37.8%	55.7%
Brockton city	95,314	27,045	28.4%	51.5%	48.5%	16.7%	41.0%	42.3%
Cambridge city	110,402	51,938	47.0%	53.7%	46.3%	4.1%	39.4%	56.4%
Lowell city	110,720	35,014	31.6%	51.9%	48.1%	8.5%	44.5%	47.1%
Lynn city	92,459	25,352	27.4%	48.0%	52.0%	13.4%	33.2%	53.4%
New Bedford city	94,959	25,304	26.6%	47.3%	52.7%	12.4%	43.9%	43.7%
Quincy city	93,629	24,780	26.5%	49.2%	50.8%	12.2%	29.1%	58.7%
Springfield city	154,336	46,972	30.4%	50.3%	49.7%	14.8%	44.1%	41.1%
Worcester city	184,806	62,036	33.6%	48.8%	51.2%	10.9%	44.5%	44.6%
Michigan								
Ann Arbor city	117,070	57,080	48.8%	51.1%	48.9%	4.7%	63.7%	31.6%
Dearborn city	95,180	25,414	26.7%	51.7%	48.3%	14.8%	43.3%	41.9%
Detroit city	677,124	189,160	27.9%	47.4%	52.6%	15.4%	38.3%	46.3%
Flint city	98,297	25,633	26.1%	48.7%	51.3%	15.6%	39.9%	44.5%
Grand Rapids city	195,099	64,132	32.9%	48.5%	51.5%	8.6%	36.9%	54.5%
Lansing city	114,110	38,419	33.7%	51.9%	48.1%	12.4%	37.6%	50.0%

Table A-3: Places—Summary Population Characteristics—*Continued*

	Total 2015 ACS Population	Millennial Population Age 15 to 33	Millennials as Percent of Total	Millennial Percentage by Gender		Millennial Percentage by Age		
				Male	Female	15 to 17	18 to 24	25 to 33
Michigan—Cont.								
Livonia city	94,633	20,481	21.6%	51.9%	48.1%	16.0%	37.2%	46.8%
Sterling Heights city	132,062	32,628	24.7%	53.4%	46.6%	8.5%	38.4%	53.1%
Warren city	135,356	31,442	23.2%	50.8%	49.2%	19.9%	35.2%	44.9%
Minnesota								
Minneapolis city	410,935	147,877	36.0%	49.8%	50.2%	8.4%	35.1%	56.5%
Rochester city	112,216	30,983	27.6%	44.0%	56.0%	15.0%	35.3%	49.6%
St. Paul city	300,840	99,544	33.1%	48.9%	51.1%	10.8%	37.0%	52.2%
Mississippi								
Jackson city	170,811	52,989	31.0%	45.3%	54.7%	12.1%	39.2%	48.7%
Missouri								
Columbia city	119,098	55,488	46.6%	50.7%	49.3%	9.5%	51.8%	38.7%
Independence city	117,255	28,662	24.4%	47.2%	52.8%	13.2%	38.0%	48.8%
Kansas City city	475,361	128,225	27.0%	49.0%	51.0%	13.5%	34.0%	52.5%
Lee's Summit city	95,068	22,012	23.2%	46.5%	53.5%	19.9%	31.6%	48.5%
St. Louis city	315,685	98,295	31.1%	48.4%	51.6%	9.7%	32.6%	57.7%
Springfield city	166,798	60,490	36.3%	49.2%	50.8%	8.8%	48.3%	42.9%
Montana								
Billings city	110,270	30,086	27.3%	50.4%	49.6%	11.7%	38.5%	49.8%
Nebraska								
Lincoln city	277,346	90,424	32.6%	50.9%	49.1%	9.9%	48.5%	41.6%
Omaha city	443,887	129,660	29.2%	50.3%	49.7%	14.0%	33.2%	52.8%
Nevada								
Henderson city	285,658	61,057	21.4%	51.1%	48.9%	15.6%	31.3%	53.1%
Las Vegas city	623,769	158,295	25.4%	50.0%	50.0%	15.1%	32.3%	52.6%
North Las Vegas city	234,793	67,041	28.6%	49.7%	50.3%	19.1%	36.7%	44.2%
Reno city	241,443	68,801	28.5%	53.5%	46.5%	12.7%	39.1%	48.3%
Sparks city	96,098	24,437	25.4%	54.2%	45.8%	16.3%	34.3%	49.5%
New Hampshire								
Manchester city	110,223	30,293	27.5%	49.8%	50.2%	9.2%	42.0%	48.7%
New Jersey								
Elizabeth city	129,012	34,801	27.0%	52.0%	48.0%	13.9%	36.0%	50.1%
Jersey City city	264,277	82,952	31.4%	50.4%	49.6%	9.7%	27.6%	62.7%
Newark city	281,913	79,653	28.3%	50.7%	49.3%	12.5%	38.2%	49.3%
Paterson city	147,757	41,192	27.9%	48.2%	51.8%	15.3%	38.2%	46.5%
New Mexico								
Albuquerque city	559,131	151,120	27.0%	51.9%	48.1%	14.5%	34.9%	50.6%
Las Cruces city	101,644	30,485	30.0%	50.3%	49.7%	7.6%	52.8%	39.6%
Rio Rancho city	94,155	23,555	25.0%	51.4%	48.6%	19.7%	30.5%	49.9%
New York								
Albany city	98,452	37,519	38.1%	50.3%	49.7%	7.3%	53.5%	39.3%
Buffalo city	258,066	81,428	31.6%	49.2%	50.8%	11.2%	37.3%	51.5%
New York city	8,550,405	2,469,069	28.9%	49.1%	50.9%	11.3%	32.2%	56.5%
Rochester city	209,808	71,818	34.2%	49.2%	50.8%	10.0%	43.3%	46.6%
Syracuse city	144,152	53,473	37.1%	45.4%	54.6%	10.3%	48.8%	40.9%
Yonkers city	201,118	50,984	25.4%	53.5%	46.5%	16.0%	34.7%	49.3%
North Carolina								
Charlotte city	827,121	239,744	29.0%	49.3%	50.7%	11.8%	33.6%	54.6%
Durham city	257,598	81,450	31.6%	48.9%	51.1%	11.1%	32.4%	56.5%
Fayetteville city	201,965	69,316	34.3%	53.5%	46.5%	13.6%	37.8%	48.6%
Greensboro city	285,344	83,708	29.3%	47.4%	52.6%	13.4%	41.6%	45.0%
High Point city	109,828	29,830	27.2%	46.1%	53.9%	18.4%	38.3%	43.3%
Raleigh city	451,949	149,042	33.0%	51.5%	48.5%	10.9%	40.8%	48.3%
Wilmington city	115,947	37,892	32.7%	46.3%	53.7%	10.6%	48.4%	41.0%
Winston-Salem city	241,232	69,003	28.6%	46.4%	53.6%	13.0%	40.4%	46.5%
North Dakota								
Fargo city	119,250	44,861	37.6%	54.5%	45.5%	7.3%	52.0%	40.8%
Ohio								
Akron city	197,553	54,257	27.5%	52.5%	47.5%	12.4%	40.0%	47.6%
Cincinnati city	298,537	102,382	34.3%	49.4%	50.6%	11.3%	38.4%	50.3%
Cleveland city	388,059	110,836	28.6%	50.0%	50.0%	14.5%	38.3%	47.2%
Columbus city	849,067	281,922	33.2%	50.1%	49.9%	10.8%	36.5%	52.7%
Dayton city	140,597	45,452	32.3%	51.0%	49.0%	11.7%	41.5%	46.7%
Toledo city	279,778	80,265	28.7%	50.1%	49.9%	12.1%	39.3%	48.7%
Oklahoma								
Broken Arrow city	107,595	25,634	23.8%	52.3%	47.7%	18.4%	33.3%	48.3%
Edmond city	90,090	27,188	30.2%	52.8%	47.2%	13.9%	40.2%	46.0%
Lawton city	96,659	30,368	31.4%	56.8%	43.2%	10.4%	36.5%	53.1%
Norman city	120,297	46,393	38.6%	47.4%	52.6%	11.6%	45.0%	43.4%
Oklahoma City city	631,263	171,575	27.2%	49.5%	50.5%	12.3%	34.2%	53.5%
Tulsa city	403,091	112,612	27.9%	48.2%	51.8%	15.0%	35.0%	50.0%

Table A-3: Places—Summary Population Characteristics—*Continued*

	Total 2015 ACS Population	Millennial Population Age 15 to 33	Millennials as Percent of Total	Millennial Percentage by Gender		Millennial Percentage by Age		
				Male	Female	15 to 17	18 to 24	25 to 33
Oregon								
Beaverton city	96,577	28,218	29.2%	48.4%	51.6%	13.8%	30.9%	55.3%
Eugene city	163,448	57,375	35.1%	49.7%	50.3%	10.7%	49.2%	40.1%
Gresham city	110,582	27,972	25.3%	47.4%	52.6%	17.4%	30.8%	51.8%
Hillsboro city	102,360	27,426	26.8%	49.6%	50.4%	15.9%	27.1%	57.0%
Portland city	632,187	180,671	28.6%	48.6%	51.4%	9.1%	29.5%	61.4%
Salem city	164,543	46,098	28.0%	52.6%	47.4%	15.0%	43.9%	41.0%
Pennsylvania								
Allentown city	120,207	34,851	29.0%	50.8%	49.2%	15.4%	35.8%	48.8%
Erie city	99,470	28,758	28.9%	47.3%	52.7%	14.3%	39.1%	46.7%
Philadelphia city	1,567,442	485,771	31.0%	48.6%	51.4%	11.0%	34.0%	55.0%
Pittsburgh city	304,385	118,026	38.8%	52.6%	47.4%	5.8%	45.9%	48.3%
Rhode Island								
Providence city	179,204	66,314	37.0%	46.6%	53.4%	9.9%	46.4%	43.7%
South Carolina								
Charleston city	135,524	45,908	33.9%	49.4%	50.6%	10.0%	37.7%	52.3%
Columbia city	133,393	60,087	45.0%	51.8%	48.2%	7.9%	52.3%	39.9%
North Charleston city	111,864	36,486	32.6%	53.7%	46.3%	11.1%	42.5%	46.5%
South Dakota								
Sioux Falls city	171,530	48,646	28.4%	53.2%	46.8%	11.9%	31.3%	56.9%
Tennessee								
Chattanooga city	176,597	50,693	28.7%	47.8%	52.2%	10.7%	39.9%	49.4%
Clarksville city	149,190	53,597	35.9%	52.0%	48.0%	10.7%	34.3%	55.0%
Knoxville city	185,312	65,226	35.2%	50.9%	49.1%	7.5%	54.0%	38.5%
Memphis city	655,760	187,750	28.6%	48.5%	51.5%	13.6%	37.3%	49.1%
Murfreesboro city	126,121	45,897	36.4%	52.2%	47.8%	10.6%	50.3%	39.1%
Nashville-Davidson metropolitan govt (balance)	654,596	204,893	31.3%	49.3%	50.7%	10.0%	33.9%	56.1%
Texas								
Abilene city	125,876	43,601	34.6%	49.4%	50.6%	12.8%	48.5%	38.7%
Allen city	98,138	22,320	22.7%	49.2%	50.8%	24.0%	29.7%	46.3%
Amarillo city	199,651	53,022	26.6%	53.3%	46.7%	15.4%	35.3%	49.2%
Arlington city	388,122	117,582	30.3%	50.9%	49.1%	15.4%	37.1%	47.5%
Austin city	931,840	318,545	34.2%	50.9%	49.1%	9.1%	32.8%	58.2%
Beaumont city	118,110	34,816	29.5%	52.7%	47.3%	15.5%	38.7%	45.8%
Brownsville city	183,888	53,320	29.0%	49.0%	51.0%	21.1%	39.6%	39.4%
Carrollton city	133,146	34,297	25.8%	50.6%	49.4%	14.2%	33.8%	52.0%
College Station city	107,899	59,465	55.1%	52.9%	47.1%	6.1%	62.6%	31.3%
Corpus Christi city	324,082	91,539	28.2%	50.1%	49.9%	14.9%	37.8%	47.3%
Dallas city	1,300,082	383,991	29.5%	50.1%	49.9%	12.7%	33.9%	53.5%
Denton city	131,047	53,139	40.5%	50.8%	49.2%	8.4%	51.4%	40.2%
El Paso city	681,136	191,550	28.1%	53.4%	46.0%	14.9%	39.8%	45.4%
Fort Worth city	836,969	234,187	28.0%	50.8%	49.2%	14.2%	33.7%	52.0%
Frisco city	154,388	29,311	19.0%	47.7%	52.3%	24.9%	27.2%	48.0%
Garland city	236,836	62,780	26.5%	49.9%	50.1%	16.9%	34.5%	48.5%
Grand Prairie city	187,755	53,813	28.7%	53.0%	47.0%	19.9%	37.5%	42.6%
Houston city	2,298,628	694,760	30.2%	51.6%	48.4%	13.5%	34.6%	51.8%
Irving city	236,617	71,697	30.3%	48.3%	51.7%	13.2%	35.7%	51.1%
Killeen city	140,809	47,750	33.9%	51.0%	49.0%	13.3%	32.9%	53.8%
Laredo city	255,789	73,722	28.8%	49.9%	50.1%	19.8%	39.8%	40.3%
Lewisville city	104,808	33,171	31.6%	53.1%	46.9%	13.7%	26.1%	60.2%
Lubbock city	249,051	90,665	36.4%	50.2%	49.8%	10.4%	51.1%	38.5%
McAllen city	140,253	39,474	28.1%	48.9%	51.1%	17.3%	41.2%	41.5%
McKinney city	162,887	38,625	23.7%	51.7%	48.3%	24.0%	31.5%	44.5%
Mesquite city	145,124	38,987	26.9%	50.6%	49.4%	14.8%	34.5%	50.7%
Midland city	132,950	40,199	30.2%	51.6%	48.4%	15.4%	34.5%	50.0%
Odessa city	118,980	36,951	31.1%	51.2%	48.8%	14.5%	35.3%	50.3%
Pasadena city	153,786	41,599	27.0%	54.6%	45.4%	15.2%	31.2%	53.6%
Pearland city	111,665	28,993	26.0%	41.1%	58.9%	16.9%	28.5%	54.6%
Plano city	283,619	70,607	24.9%	50.2%	49.8%	15.9%	32.1%	52.0%
Richardson city	110,827	31,827	28.7%	51.7%	48.3%	9.1%	37.3%	53.6%
Round Rock City	115,839	31,178	26.9%	52.4%	47.6%	21.2%	35.6%	43.3%
San Angelo city	100,413	32,118	32.0%	53.9%	46.1%	12.7%	42.5%	44.9%
San Antonio city	1,469,824	435,615	29.6%	51.5%	48.5%	14.1%	35.9%	50.0%
Tyler city	103,705	31,668	30.5%	50.5%	49.5%	11.9%	44.2%	43.9%
Waco city	132,342	45,423	34.3%	48.6%	51.4%	8.8%	53.6%	37.6%
Wichita Falls city	104,709	33,545	32.0%	55.1%	44.9%	12.4%	44.0%	43.5%
Utah								
Orem city	94,457	34,882	36.9%	48.1%	51.9%	14.5%	44.9%	40.6%
Provo city	115,258	63,221	54.9%	49.6%	50.4%	5.7%	64.7%	29.6%
Salt Lake City city	192,660	70,936	36.8%	51.7%	48.3%	9.2%	37.0%	53.8%
Sandy city	93,612	23,301	24.9%	51.5%	48.5%	20.3%	32.8%	46.9%
West Jordan city	111,942	32,488	29.0%	58.4%	41.6%	25.8%	27.2%	47.0%
West Valley City city	136,224	41,728	30.6%	53.5%	46.5%	16.0%	37.6%	46.4%

Table A-3: Places—Summary Population Characteristics—*Continued*

	Total 2015 ACS Population	Millennial Population Age 15 to 33	Millennials as Percent of Total	Millennial Percentage by Gender		Millennial Percentage by Age		
				Male	Female	15 to 17	18 to 24	25 to 33
Virginia								
Alexandria city	153,511	43,452	28.3%	47.5%	52.5%	6.9%	16.3%	76.8%
Chesapeake city	235,429	63,149	26.8%	50.2%	49.8%	15.3%	34.5%	50.2%
Hampton city	136,454	40,233	29.5%	51.0%	49.0%	10.8%	40.0%	49.3%
Newport News city	182,385	58,525	32.1%	50.4%	49.6%	11.1%	41.0%	48.0%
Norfolk city	246,393	95,849	38.9%	56.8%	43.2%	6.8%	48.9%	44.2%
Portsmouth city	96,201	29,069	30.2%	51.7%	48.3%	13.1%	35.2%	51.6%
Richmond city	220,289	76,850	34.9%	48.0%	52.0%	6.5%	38.9%	54.6%
Roanoke city	99,897	26,140	26.2%	41.5%	58.5%	8.4%	38.9%	52.6%
Virginia Beach city	452,745	132,947	29.4%	51.8%	48.2%	13.0%	35.0%	52.0%
Washington								
Bellevue city	139,814	37,913	27.1%	52.4%	47.6%	14.1%	27.3%	58.6%
Everett city	108,012	30,503	28.2%	53.5%	46.5%	16.1%	35.3%	48.6%
Federal Way city	95,188	26,673	28.0%	52.3%	47.7%	16.6%	25.4%	57.9%
Kent city	126,962	40,119	31.6%	52.1%	47.9%	15.8%	30.9%	53.3%
Renton city	100,247	24,731	24.7%	49.4%	50.6%	17.0%	23.9%	59.1%
Seattle city	684,443	236,331	34.5%	51.0%	49.0%	5.8%	32.0%	62.2%
Spokane city	213,267	61,887	29.0%	48.6%	51.4%	11.3%	35.2%	53.5%
Spokane Valley city	94,908	24,796	26.1%	50.0%	50.0%	15.9%	28.3%	55.8%
Tacoma city	207,950	58,809	28.3%	48.9%	51.1%	13.8%	33.0%	53.3%
Vancouver city	172,853	44,929	26.0%	53.1%	46.9%	16.3%	34.5%	49.3%
Yakima city	93,700	25,386	27.1%	49.0%	51.0%	13.9%	45.3%	40.8%
Wisconsin								
Green Bay city	105,221	30,607	29.1%	49.2%	50.8%	9.2%	42.7%	48.1%
Kenosha city	99,856	25,028	25.1%	49.7%	50.3%	15.2%	43.2%	41.6%
Madison city	248,956	101,061	40.6%	50.7%	49.3%	9.4%	51.3%	39.3%
Milwaukee city	600,154	186,306	31.0%	46.3%	53.7%	14.7%	37.1%	48.2%

Table A-4: Metropolitan/Micropolitan Statistical Areas—Summary Population Characteristics

	Total 2015 ACS Population	Millennial Population Age 15 to 33	Millennials as Percent of Total	Millennial Percentage by Gender		Millennial Percentage by Age		
				Male	Female	15 to 17	18 to 24	25 to 33
Abilene, TX.................................	168,922	50,234	29.7%	50.5%	49.5%	13.8%	46.9%	39.3%
Adrian, MI micro..........................	98,573	22,899	23.2%	54.7%	45.3%	15.9%	45.0%	39.0%
Akron, OH..................................	704,243	178,555	25.4%	50.7%	49.3%	14.6%	41.9%	43.5%
Albany, GA.................................	156,997	39,484	25.1%	45.3%	54.7%	16.5%	41.0%	42.5%
Albany, OR.................................	120,547	28,485	23.6%	50.8%	49.2%	14.8%	45.0%	40.2%
Albany-Schenectady-Troy, NY......	881,830	232,952	26.4%	51.2%	48.8%	13.9%	42.1%	44.0%
Albertville, AL micro....................	94,725	21,899	23.1%	48.1%	51.9%	17.6%	40.6%	41.8%
Albuquerque, NM........................	906,209	233,207	25.7%	50.5%	49.5%	15.2%	36.3%	48.6%
Alexandria, LA............................	154,484	38,875	25.2%	51.0%	49.0%	17.4%	36.6%	46.0%
Allentown-Bethlehem-Easton, PA-NJ.........	832,327	194,803	23.4%	51.9%	48.1%	17.2%	39.2%	43.6%
Altoona, PA................................	125,593	29,180	23.2%	50.6%	49.4%	17.9%	35.1%	47.0%
Amarillo, TX...............................	263,258	71,925	27.3%	51.2%	48.8%	14.6%	35.6%	49.8%
Ames, IA...................................	96,021	45,468	47.4%	57.1%	42.9%	5.8%	67.4%	26.8%
Anchorage, AK............................	399,790	123,015	30.8%	54.9%	45.1%	13.4%	37.2%	49.4%
Ann Arbor, MI.............................	358,880	123,278	34.4%	51.2%	48.8%	9.7%	53.5%	36.8%
Anniston-Oxford-Jacksonville, AL....	115,620	30,590	26.5%	49.1%	50.9%	15.5%	42.3%	42.2%
Appleton, WI..............................	233,007	58,416	25.1%	51.2%	48.8%	17.4%	32.7%	49.9%
Asheville, NC..............................	446,840	92,784	20.8%	49.5%	50.5%	15.4%	36.1%	48.5%
Ashtabula, OH micro....................	98,632	22,614	22.9%	51.0%	49.0%	22.1%	34.6%	43.3%
Athens-Clarke County, GA.............	201,813	72,553	36.0%	47.8%	52.2%	9.6%	56.2%	34.3%
Atlanta-Sandy Springs-Roswell, GA....	5,709,731	1,464,745	25.7%	50.0%	50.0%	17.0%	35.8%	47.2%
Atlantic City-Hammonton, NJ........	274,219	66,498	24.2%	52.3%	47.7%	14.9%	40.6%	44.4%
Auburn-Opelika, AL.....................	156,993	54,789	34.9%	49.8%	50.2%	9.7%	56.0%	34.3%
Augusta-Richmond County, GA-SC....	590,772	159,165	26.9%	51.3%	48.7%	15.1%	36.4%	48.5%
Augusta-Waterville, ME micro........	119,980	25,926	21.6%	52.2%	47.8%	15.8%	40.2%	44.0%
Austin-Round Rock, TX.................	2,000,860	586,533	29.3%	51.0%	49.0%	13.2%	34.4%	52.4%
Bakersfield, CA...........................	882,176	255,273	28.9%	53.3%	46.7%	15.6%	37.8%	46.6%
Baltimore-Columbia-Towson, MD....	2,797,407	713,900	25.5%	49.2%	50.8%	14.3%	35.3%	50.5%
Bangor, ME................................	152,692	40,856	26.8%	49.8%	50.2%	12.7%	42.6%	44.7%
Barnstable Town, MA...................	214,333	37,022	17.3%	48.9%	51.1%	18.9%	38.4%	42.7%
Baton Rouge, LA.........................	830,480	239,352	28.8%	50.1%	49.9%	13.8%	41.2%	45.0%
Battle Creek, MI..........................	134,314	31,922	23.8%	49.5%	50.5%	17.8%	33.7%	48.5%
Bay City, MI...............................	105,659	24,229	22.9%	55.9%	44.1%	16.9%	36.1%	47.0%
Beaumont-Port Arthur, TX.............	408,216	107,613	26.4%	53.5%	46.5%	16.2%	35.0%	48.8%
Beckley, WV...............................	122,507	26,400	21.5%	50.8%	49.2%	14.8%	36.1%	49.1%
Bellingham, WA...........................	212,284	64,215	30.2%	50.2%	49.8%	11.3%	47.7%	41.0%
Bend-Redmond, OR......................	175,268	37,506	21.4%	51.0%	49.0%	14.3%	33.4%	52.3%
Billings, MT................................	169,329	40,628	24.0%	51.7%	48.3%	10.9%	40.1%	49.0%
Binghamton, NY...........................	246,020	66,508	27.0%	50.9%	49.1%	14.3%	49.6%	36.1%
Birmingham-Hoover, AL.................	1,145,647	285,663	24.9%	49.8%	50.2%	16.6%	34.8%	48.6%
Bismarck, ND..............................	129,640	34,187	26.4%	53.2%	46.8%	13.0%	32.1%	54.9%
Blacksburg-Christiansburg-Radford, VA.......	179,904	65,831	36.6%	53.3%	46.7%	7.3%	62.0%	30.7%
Bloomington, IL...........................	188,725	61,716	32.7%	50.2%	49.8%	11.6%	52.6%	35.8%
Bloomington, IN..........................	165,577	67,026	40.5%	51.6%	48.4%	7.2%	61.6%	31.2%
Bloomsburg-Berwick, PA...............	85,229	23,536	27.6%	48.8%	51.2%	9.6%	44.2%	46.3%
Boise City, ID.............................	675,800	173,741	25.7%	51.2%	48.8%	17.4%	33.5%	49.1%
Boston-Cambridge-Newton, MA-NH....	4,774,321	1,270,242	26.6%	50.1%	49.9%	13.6%	37.5%	48.9%
Boulder, CO...............................	319,372	98,666	30.9%	55.3%	44.7%	11.7%	50.2%	38.1%
Bowling Green, KY.......................	166,890	48,473	29.0%	49.7%	50.3%	13.9%	47.1%	39.0%
Bremerton-Silverdale, WA.............	260,131	69,919	26.9%	54.5%	45.5%	14.0%	39.2%	46.8%
Bridgeport-Stamford-Norwalk, CT....	948,053	223,389	23.6%	51.2%	48.8%	18.1%	38.1%	43.8%
Brownsville-Harlingen, TX.............	422,156	113,745	26.9%	50.2%	49.8%	20.4%	39.5%	40.1%
Brunswick, GA............................	117,771	26,627	22.6%	60.1%	39.9%	16.9%	35.3%	47.8%
Buffalo-Cheektowaga-Niagara Falls, NY.......	1,135,230	286,861	25.3%	50.2%	49.8%	14.4%	37.8%	47.8%
Burlington, NC............................	158,276	37,828	23.9%	46.6%	53.4%	17.0%	39.0%	44.0%
Burlington-South Burlington, VT......	216,661	64,031	29.6%	49.0%	51.0%	11.5%	47.7%	40.8%
California-Lexington Park, MD........	111,413	28,974	26.0%	45.2%	54.8%	16.3%	38.6%	45.1%
Canton-Massillon, OH...................	402,976	93,640	23.2%	51.1%	48.9%	17.4%	36.9%	45.7%
Cape Coral-Fort Myers, FL............	701,982	142,244	20.3%	49.7%	50.3%	15.5%	35.4%	49.1%
Cape Girardeau, MO-IL.................	96,542	25,928	26.9%	47.8%	52.2%	12.7%	41.4%	45.9%
Carbondale-Marion, IL.................	126,828	39,218	30.9%	51.9%	48.1%	14.6%	47.5%	37.9%
Carson City, NV..........................	54,521	11,558	21.2%	53.4%	46.6%	17.5%	45.2%	37.3%
Casper, WY................................	82,178	20,678	25.2%	49.7%	50.3%	13.4%	34.4%	52.2%
Cedar Rapids, IA.........................	266,040	65,970	24.8%	48.1%	51.9%	16.0%	37.3%	46.6%
Chambersburg-Waynesboro, PA......	153,638	34,854	22.7%	53.8%	46.2%	16.4%	39.2%	44.4%
Champaign-Urbana, IL..................	239,672	89,066	37.2%	52.1%	47.9%	8.2%	59.4%	32.4%
Charleston, WV...........................	219,236	46,810	21.4%	48.4%	51.6%	16.0%	33.7%	50.2%
Charleston-North Charleston, SC....	744,526	204,724	27.5%	50.5%	49.5%	12.9%	34.0%	53.2%
Charlotte-Concord-Gastonia, NC-SC....	2,426,363	604,040	24.9%	49.8%	50.2%	16.8%	35.4%	47.8%
Charlottesville, VA......................	230,602	67,057	29.1%	51.6%	48.4%	10.5%	44.4%	45.1%
Chattanooga, TN-GA....................	546,351	137,823	25.2%	49.2%	50.8%	15.2%	37.1%	47.7%
Cheyenne, WY............................	97,121	27,461	28.3%	57.9%	42.1%	12.4%	52.7%	34.9%
Chicago-Naperville-Elgin, IL-IN-WI....	9,550,108	2,504,124	26.2%	50.3%	49.7%	15.5%	35.8%	48.7%
Chico, CA..................................	225,411	66,585	29.5%	50.8%	49.2%	11.4%	50.6%	38.0%
Cincinnati, OH-KY-IN...................	2,159,329	542,779	25.1%	49.8%	50.2%	16.5%	36.5%	47.0%
Clarksburg, WV micro..................	91,756	19,685	21.5%	46.0%	54.0%	16.9%	38.8%	44.3%
Clarksville, TN-KY.......................	279,887	91,109	32.6%	55.6%	44.4%	11.0%	35.9%	53.1%

Table A-4: Metropolitan/Micropolitan Statistical Areas—Summary Population Characteristics—*Continued*

	Total 2015 ACS Population	Millennial Population Age 15 to 33	Millennials as Percent of Total	Millennial Percentage by Gender		Millennial Percentage by Age		
				Male	Female	15 to 17	18 to 24	25 to 33
Cleveland, TN	121,678	30,847	25.4%	50.5%	49.5%	17.7%	39.0%	43.3%
Cleveland-Elyria, OH	2,060,810	484,581	23.5%	50.4%	49.6%	16.7%	36.8%	46.5%
Coeur d'Alene, ID	150,346	35,105	23.3%	53.6%	46.4%	16.0%	33.4%	50.6%
College Station-Bryan, TX	250,145	100,404	40.1%	52.7%	47.3%	7.5%	58.9%	33.6%
Colorado Springs, CO	697,856	202,070	29.0%	53.8%	46.2%	13.6%	37.4%	49.0%
Columbia, MO	174,974	65,947	37.7%	49.8%	50.2%	9.1%	53.1%	37.9%
Columbia, SC	810,574	228,727	28.2%	51.8%	48.2%	14.2%	43.5%	42.2%
Columbus, GA-AL	312,936	93,090	29.7%	55.4%	44.6%	13.6%	38.8%	47.6%
Columbus, IN	81,162	20,841	25.7%	57.0%	43.0%	17.2%	35.0%	47.8%
Columbus, OH	2,021,632	545,703	27.0%	50.2%	49.8%	14.7%	33.9%	51.4%
Concord, NH micro	147,994	26,150	17.7%	56.1%	43.9%	16.3%	40.2%	43.5%
Cookeville, TN micro	107,851	30,681	28.4%	51.5%	48.5%	14.9%	46.7%	38.3%
Corpus Christi, TX	450,436	119,621	26.6%	51.3%	48.7%	15.8%	37.4%	46.8%
Corvallis, OR	87,572	32,589	37.2%	51.6%	48.4%	15.2%	46.9%	37.9%
Crestview-Fort Walton Beach-Destin, FL	262,172	69,335	26.4%	54.6%	45.4%	10.8%	34.6%	54.7%
Cumberland, MD-WV	99,979	26,249	26.3%	52.5%	47.5%	14.6%	45.4%	40.1%
Dallas-Fort Worth-Arlington, TX	7,102,165	1,874,485	26.4%	50.2%	49.8%	16.5%	34.8%	48.8%
Dalton, GA	143,781	37,337	26.0%	50.0%	50.0%	16.0%	36.7%	47.3%
Danville, IL	79,282	18,480	23.3%	54.0%	46.0%	18.2%	28.7%	53.1%
Danville, VA micro	104,276	22,276	21.4%	53.0%	47.0%	18.7%	35.1%	46.2%
Daphne-Fairhope-Foley, AL	203,709	41,881	20.6%	49.7%	50.3%	17.8%	34.3%	47.9%
Davenport-Moline-Rock Island, IA-IL	384,584	91,165	23.7%	49.5%	50.5%	14.6%	38.3%	47.1%
Dayton, OH	800,909	198,327	24.8%	49.9%	50.1%	15.2%	37.7%	47.1%
Decatur, AL	152,680	35,433	23.2%	52.4%	47.6%	17.6%	34.3%	48.1%
Decatur, IL	107,303	24,600	22.9%	47.3%	52.7%	16.1%	41.4%	42.5%
Deltona-Daytona Beach-Ormond Beach, FL	623,279	132,761	21.3%	50.5%	49.5%	15.8%	38.6%	45.6%
Denver-Aurora-Lakewood, CO	2,814,330	745,375	26.5%	51.3%	48.7%	14.6%	31.4%	54.0%
Des Moines-West Des Moines, IA	622,899	164,874	26.5%	50.4%	49.6%	16.0%	32.6%	51.4%
Detroit-Warren-Dearborn, MI	4,302,043	1,027,782	23.9%	49.9%	50.1%	17.3%	35.9%	46.8%
Dothan, AL	148,171	34,274	23.1%	50.0%	50.0%	17.5%	35.4%	47.1%
Dover, DE	173,533	46,169	26.6%	50.2%	49.8%	14.9%	40.6%	44.5%
Dubuque, IA	97,125	25,588	26.3%	55.6%	44.4%	17.6%	42.1%	40.3%
Duluth, MN-WI	279,601	72,709	26.0%	51.5%	48.5%	12.6%	43.3%	44.1%
Dunn, NC micro	128,140	35,041	27.3%	50.6%	49.4%	15.0%	37.3%	47.7%
Durham-Chapel Hill, NC	552,493	161,733	29.3%	49.0%	51.0%	11.7%	40.4%	47.9%
East Stroudsburg, PA	166,397	42,076	25.3%	48.0%	52.0%	17.5%	43.4%	39.2%
Eau Claire, WI	165,636	47,724	28.8%	49.2%	50.8%	12.2%	46.4%	41.4%
El Centro, CA	180,191	49,791	27.6%	52.6%	47.4%	16.5%	40.4%	43.1%
El Paso, TX	838,019	243,628	29.1%	53.0%	47.0%	15.7%	38.8%	45.5%
Elizabethtown-Fort Knox, KY	147,877	37,272	25.2%	53.6%	46.4%	18.3%	35.2%	46.5%
Elkhart-Goshen, IN	203,474	51,393	25.3%	49.3%	50.7%	19.2%	36.8%	44.1%
Elmira, NY	87,071	20,951	24.1%	55.9%	44.1%	12.3%	35.0%	52.6%
Erie, PA	278,045	71,032	25.5%	48.2%	51.8%	16.1%	40.0%	43.8%
Eugene, OR	362,895	101,020	27.8%	50.4%	49.6%	12.6%	45.9%	41.5%
Eureka-Arcata-Fortuna, CA micro	135,727	38,052	28.0%	50.9%	49.1%	9.5%	47.9%	42.6%
Evansville, IN-KY	315,693	77,662	24.6%	47.4%	52.6%	15.4%	36.4%	48.1%
Fairbanks, AK	99,631	34,834	35.0%	56.5%	43.5%	12.0%	43.5%	44.5%
Fargo, ND-MN	233,836	76,111	32.5%	52.6%	47.4%	9.7%	48.2%	42.1%
Farmington, NM	118,737	30,632	25.8%	50.7%	49.3%	16.3%	37.9%	45.8%
Fayetteville, NC	376,509	114,794	30.5%	53.6%	46.4%	12.6%	39.6%	47.7%
Fayetteville-Springdale-Rogers, AR-MO	515,403	145,133	28.2%	50.3%	49.7%	14.0%	39.3%	46.7%
Flagstaff, AZ	139,097	51,771	37.2%	47.4%	52.6%	9.6%	57.3%	33.1%
Flint, MI	410,849	96,273	23.4%	50.7%	49.3%	17.1%	38.2%	44.7%
Florence, SC	206,448	49,298	23.9%	50.7%	49.3%	17.1%	38.6%	44.3%
Florence-Muscle Shoals, AL	146,950	34,708	23.6%	47.9%	52.1%	20.1%	40.0%	39.9%
Fond du Lac, WI	101,973	24,678	24.2%	47.9%	52.1%	21.6%	34.4%	43.9%
Fort Collins, CO	333,577	103,634	31.1%	51.7%	48.3%	10.9%	44.5%	44.6%
Fort Smith, AR-OK	280,241	68,405	24.4%	52.5%	47.5%	15.0%	35.2%	49.8%
Fort Wayne, IN	429,820	110,786	25.8%	48.9%	51.1%	16.7%	38.7%	44.6%
Fresno, CA	974,861	280,870	28.8%	51.5%	48.5%	15.9%	37.8%	46.2%
Gadsden, AL	103,057	22,502	21.8%	51.1%	48.9%	17.1%	40.3%	42.6%
Gainesville, FL	276,881	102,661	37.1%	48.6%	51.4%	8.2%	55.5%	36.4%
Gainesville, GA	193,535	48,649	25.1%	51.5%	48.5%	18.0%	37.6%	44.4%
Gettysburg, PA	102,295	23,400	22.9%	50.4%	49.6%	17.9%	36.6%	45.6%
Glens Falls, NY	126,918	26,846	21.2%	51.7%	48.3%	17.9%	36.4%	45.7%
Goldsboro, NC	124,132	32,804	26.4%	53.0%	47.0%	13.0%	37.0%	50.1%
Grand Forks, ND-MN	102,449	36,405	35.5%	53.8%	46.2%	10.1%	52.3%	37.6%
Grand Island, NE	84,942	20,619	24.3%	52.6%	47.4%	17.4%	38.4%	44.2%
Grand Junction, CO	148,513	38,770	26.1%	53.5%	46.5%	14.1%	40.0%	45.9%
Grand Rapids-Wyoming, MI	1,038,583	282,938	27.2%	49.3%	50.7%	15.9%	38.2%	45.9%
Grants Pass, OR	84,745	16,859	19.9%	51.1%	48.9%	23.6%	37.5%	38.9%
Great Falls, MT	82,278	20,486	24.9%	54.6%	45.4%	11.2%	41.3%	47.5%
Greeley, CO	285,174	79,145	27.8%	50.8%	49.2%	17.6%	37.6%	44.7%
Green Bay, WI	316,519	78,353	24.8%	51.3%	48.7%	15.5%	35.0%	49.6%
Greensboro-High Point, NC	752,157	187,158	24.9%	48.8%	51.2%	16.1%	38.2%	45.7%
Greenville, NC	175,842	60,468	34.4%	46.1%	53.9%	10.3%	52.6%	37.1%

Table A-4: Metropolitan/Micropolitan Statistical Areas—Summary Population Characteristics—*Continued*

	Total 2015 ACS Population	Millennial Population Age 15 to 33	Millennials as Percent of Total	Millennial Percentage by Gender		Millennial Percentage by Age		
				Male	Female	15 to 17	18 to 24	25 to 33
Greenville-Anderson-Mauldin, SC	874,869	220,414	25.2%	51.3%	48.7%	15.8%	39.0%	45.2%
Greenwood, SC micro	94,211	22,832	24.2%	51.7%	48.3%	15.8%	45.7%	38.5%
Gulfport-Biloxi-Pascagoula, MS	389,255	99,689	25.6%	52.3%	47.7%	16.3%	37.0%	46.6%
Hagerstown-Martinsburg, MD-WV	261,486	61,867	23.7%	53.4%	46.6%	15.2%	36.8%	48.0%
Hammond, LA	128,755	35,483	27.6%	49.7%	50.3%	13.8%	40.9%	45.3%
Hanford-Corcoran, CA	150,965	46,492	30.8%	58.8%	41.2%	13.5%	36.1%	50.4%
Harrisburg-Carlisle, PA	565,006	136,047	24.1%	51.6%	48.4%	15.4%	40.2%	44.3%
Harrisonburg, VA	131,131	44,407	33.9%	47.7%	52.3%	9.8%	58.0%	32.2%
Hartford-West Hartford-East Hartford, CT	1,211,324	287,773	23.8%	50.6%	49.4%	15.5%	40.1%	44.4%
Hattiesburg, MS	148,610	42,138	28.4%	47.9%	52.1%	12.1%	47.6%	40.3%
Hickory-Lenoir-Morganton, NC	362,510	81,844	22.6%	53.0%	47.0%	18.3%	38.9%	42.8%
Hilo, HI micro	196,428	44,356	22.6%	48.4%	51.6%	14.4%	36.8%	48.9%
Hilton Head Island-Bluffton-Beaufort, SC	207,413	48,455	23.4%	53.7%	46.3%	12.2%	37.9%	50.0%
Hinesville, GA	78,811	27,109	34.4%	61.1%	38.9%	10.9%	48.2%	40.9%
Holland, MI micro	114,625	26,922	23.5%	48.8%	51.2%	19.2%	36.4%	44.4%
Homosassa Springs, FL	141,058	20,619	14.6%	52.4%	47.6%	19.0%	37.4%	43.6%
Hot Springs, AR	97,177	21,426	22.0%	47.8%	52.2%	15.9%	37.4%	46.7%
Houma-Thibodaux, LA	212,297	54,143	25.5%	50.3%	49.7%	15.2%	33.7%	51.1%
Houston-The Woodlands-Sugar Land, TX	6,656,946	1,795,490	27.0%	50.5%	49.5%	16.2%	34.3%	49.5%
Huntington-Ashland, WV-KY-OH	361,580	84,689	23.4%	49.9%	50.1%	17.5%	39.4%	43.2%
Huntsville, AL	444,752	116,099	26.1%	50.3%	49.7%	15.6%	35.0%	49.4%
Idaho Falls, ID	139,849	34,928	25.0%	49.2%	50.8%	18.2%	32.4%	49.4%
Indianapolis Carmel Anderson, IN	1,988,152	506,665	25.5%	49.4%	50.6%	15.7%	34.5%	49.8%
Iowa City, IA	166,498	60,642	36.4%	49.0%	51.0%	9.7%	52.1%	38.2%
Ithaca, NY	104,926	45,449	43.3%	49.4%	50.6%	5.9%	68.2%	25.9%
Jackson, MI	159,494	38,466	24.1%	51.8%	48.2%	15.4%	36.2%	48.4%
Jackson, MS	578,561	150,950	26.1%	47.9%	52.1%	16.8%	36.0%	47.2%
Jackson, TN	129,682	33,924	26.2%	47.5%	52.5%	14.0%	41.0%	45.1%
Jacksonville, FL	1,449,481	373,861	25.8%	50.5%	49.5%	15.5%	34.9%	49.6%
Jacksonville, NC	186,311	75,308	40.4%	61.2%	38.8%	7.8%	48.4%	43.8%
Jamestown-Dunkirk-Fredonia, NY micro	130,779	31,756	24.3%	53.7%	46.3%	16.5%	43.0%	40.5%
Janesville-Beloit, WI	161,448	36,704	22.7%	51.7%	48.3%	18.0%	40.4%	41.6%
Jefferson City, MO	151,357	38,312	25.3%	52.4%	47.6%	16.5%	38.3%	45.2%
Johnson City, TN	200,264	48,247	24.1%	48.7%	51.3%	13.8%	42.6%	43.6%
Johnstown, PA	136,411	30,779	22.6%	53.1%	46.9%	17.8%	40.3%	41.9%
Jonesboro, AR	128,394	36,893	28.7%	54.3%	45.7%	16.0%	42.4%	41.6%
Joplin, MO	177,211	43,861	24.8%	53.8%	46.2%	17.8%	39.6%	42.6%
Kahului-Wailuku-Lahaina, HI	164,726	39,215	23.8%	53.6%	46.4%	14.6%	32.1%	53.3%
Kalamazoo-Portage, MI	335,340	97,259	29.0%	51.7%	48.3%	12.8%	49.5%	37.6%
Kalispell, MT micro	96,165	20,702	21.5%	50.3%	49.7%	18.9%	34.3%	46.8%
Kankakee, IL	110,879	28,451	25.7%	50.9%	49.1%	16.2%	40.6%	43.2%
Kansas City, MO-KS	2,088,260	522,562	26.1%	49.4%	50.6%	16.1%	34.5%	49.4%
Kennewick-Richland, WA	279,116	75,872	27.2%	51.2%	48.8%	17.3%	36.2%	46.5%
Killeen-Temple, TX	430,642	139,806	32.5%	53.7%	46.3%	13.4%	38.6%	48.0%
Kingsport-Bristol-Bristol, TN-VA	305,929	66,770	21.8%	50.5%	49.5%	10.9%	35.0%	46.1%
Kingston, NY	180,143	41,944	23.3%	51.1%	48.9%	13.1%	46.2%	40.7%
Knoxville, TN	861,679	212,739	24.7%	49.5%	50.5%	15.1%	41.4%	43.5%
Kokomo, IN	82,556	17,889	21.7%	51.3%	48.7%	18.6%	33.8%	47.6%
La Crosse-Onalaska, WI-MN	136,985	40,654	29.7%	49.2%	50.8%	11.5%	53.6%	34.9%
Lafayette, LA	490,488	134,345	27.4%	48.5%	51.5%	16.2%	35.5%	48.3%
Lafayette-West Lafayette, IN	214,997	80,391	37.4%	55.0%	45.0%	8.1%	60.1%	31.8%
Lake Charles, LA	205,493	54,900	26.7%	50.6%	49.4%	15.2%	35.5%	49.2%
Lake Havasu City-Kingman, AZ	204,737	38,567	18.8%	52.9%	47.1%	16.7%	32.9%	50.4%
Lakeland-Winter Haven, FL	650,092	157,735	24.3%	50.3%	49.7%	16.1%	35.5%	48.4%
Lancaster, PA	536,624	133,315	24.8%	49.1%	50.9%	16.6%	38.6%	44.8%
Lansing-East Lansing, MI	472,276	145,575	30.8%	50.3%	49.7%	12.4%	48.9%	38.7%
Laredo, TX	269,721	76,206	28.3%	49.6%	50.4%	19.4%	40.0%	40.6%
Las Cruces, NM	214,295	64,094	29.9%	51.8%	48.2%	14.0%	47.4%	38.5%
Las Vegas-Henderson-Paradise, NV	2,114,801	551,377	26.1%	50.3%	49.7%	14.7%	33.8%	51.5%
Lawrence, KS	118,053	46,763	39.6%	54.1%	45.9%	6.4%	58.4%	35.2%
Lawton, OK	130,581	40,304	30.9%	56.8%	43.2%	12.0%	37.8%	50.3%
Lebanon, PA	137,067	29,746	21.7%	52.4%	47.6%	14.8%	41.7%	43.4%
Lewiston, ID-WA	62,153	14,434	23.2%	56.4%	43.6%	12.9%	44.1%	42.9%
Lewiston-Auburn, ME	107,233	24,352	22.7%	48.1%	51.9%	16.4%	38.7%	44.9%
Lexington-Fayette, KY	500,535	144,801	28.9%	50.4%	49.6%	13.0%	40.6%	46.4%
Lima, OH	104,425	25,254	24.2%	52.7%	47.3%	15.9%	38.4%	45.7%
Lincoln, NE	323,557	99,230	30.7%	51.4%	48.6%	9.9%	46.7%	43.4%
Little Rock-North Little Rock-Conway, AR	730,250	197,454	27.0%	49.9%	50.1%	14.6%	36.1%	49.3%
Logan, UT-ID	133,821	48,158	36.0%	51.0%	49.0%	13.6%	46.2%	40.3%
Longview, TX	217,781	52,337	24.0%	50.5%	49.5%	15.5%	37.9%	46.6%
Longview, WA	103,468	22,743	22.0%	54.7%	45.3%	15.0%	28.8%	56.2%
Los Angeles-Long Beach-Anaheim, CA	13,340,068	3,649,069	27.4%	50.8%	49.2%	14.0%	36.2%	49.8%
Louisville/Jefferson County, KY-IN	1,279,335	310,933	24.3%	50.3%	49.7%	16.4%	34.9%	48.6%
Lubbock, TX	312,433	108,228	34.6%	51.8%	48.2%	11.4%	49.0%	39.6%
Lumberton, NC micro	134,197	32,547	24.3%	50.9%	49.1%	16.5%	42.6%	41.0%
Lynchburg, VA	260,504	71,290	27.4%	51.0%	49.0%	15.1%	46.2%	38.7%
Macon, GA	231,448	57,298	24.8%	47.6%	52.4%	15.3%	44.4%	40.3%

Table A-4: Metropolitan/Micropolitan Statistical Areas—Summary Population Characteristics—*Continued*

	Total 2015 ACS Population	Millennial Population Age 15 to 33	Millennials as Percent of Total	Millennial Percentage by Gender		Millennial Percentage by Age		
				Male	Female	15 to 17	18 to 24	25 to 33
Madera, CA	154,998	41,540	26.8%	48.8%	51.2%	16.0%	37.8%	46.3%
Madison, WI	641,385	192,036	29.9%	51.6%	48.4%	12.3%	41.6%	46.1%
Manchester-Nashua, NH	406,678	98,967	24.3%	52.5%	47.5%	16.2%	37.8%	46.1%
Manhattan, KS	98,545	44,533	45.2%	54.5%	45.5%	8.7%	53.2%	38.1%
Mankato-North Mankato, MN	99,134	34,477	34.8%	49.1%	50.9%	11.2%	54.3%	34.5%
Mansfield, OH	121,707	27,953	23.0%	53.9%	46.1%	16.7%	38.7%	44.7%
McAllen-Edinburg-Mission, TX	842,304	231,675	27.5%	51.0%	49.0%	18.8%	39.7%	41.6%
Medford, OR	212,567	48,007	22.6%	49.0%	51.0%	15.3%	33.9%	50.9%
Memphis, TN-MS-AR	1,343,572	357,724	26.6%	49.0%	51.0%	16.9%	36.1%	47.0%
Merced, CA	268,455	78,357	29.2%	53.0%	47.0%	16.0%	41.7%	42.3%
Meridian, MS micro	104,782	27,324	26.1%	49.6%	50.4%	17.2%	37.7%	45.1%
Miami-Fort Lauderdale-West Palm Beach, FL	6,012,331	1,441,011	24.0%	50.9%	49.1%	14.9%	34.8%	50.2%
Michigan City-La Porte, IN	110,884	25,919	23.4%	57.2%	42.8%	16.9%	33.6%	49.5%
Midland, MI	83,632	20,208	24.2%	55.4%	44.6%	19.5%	33.2%	47.3%
Midland, TX	165,427	50,504	30.5%	52.0%	48.0%	15.1%	33.7%	51.2%
Milwaukee-Waukesha-West Allis, WI	1,575,747	397,142	25.2%	48.8%	51.2%	15.7%	36.1%	48.1%
Minneapolis-St. Paul-Bloomington, MN-WI	3,524,583	893,153	25.3%	50.0%	50.0%	15.8%	32.6%	51.5%
Missoula, MT	114,181	36,592	32.0%	55.2%	44.8%	12.8%	40.4%	46.8%
Mobile, AL	415,395	108,104	26.0%	48.5%	51.5%	15.8%	34.7%	49.6%
Modesto, CA	538,388	113,568	21.1%	50.2%	49.8%	18.0%	36.1%	45.9%
Monroe, LA	179,238	48,731	27.2%	49.9%	50.1%	15.4%	36.9%	47.7%
Monroe, MI	149,568	33,502	22.4%	52.4%	47.6%	18.9%	35.7%	45.4%
Montgomery, AL	375,435	98,811	26.3%	49.6%	50.4%	15.4%	37.3%	47.3%
Morgantown, WV	138,176	51,218	37.1%	52.7%	47.3%	7.6%	50.5%	41.8%
Morristown, TN	116,642	26,778	23.0%	52.9%	47.1%	23.7%	36.6%	39.7%
Mount Vernon-Anacortes, WA	121,846	27,287	22.4%	51.8%	48.2%	17.1%	32.8%	50.1%
Muncie, IN	116,852	37,184	31.8%	46.3%	53.7%	10.5%	61.7%	27.8%
Muskegon, MI	172,790	41,707	24.1%	52.7%	47.3%	15.9%	35.6%	48.5%
Myrtle Beach-Conway-North Myrtle Beach, SC-NC	431,964	90,587	21.0%	51.7%	48.3%	16.1%	36.7%	47.2%
Napa, CA	142,456	33,408	23.5%	51.6%	48.4%	16.0%	39.1%	44.9%
Naples-Immokalee-Marco Island, FL	357,305	67,976	19.0%	51.0%	49.0%	16.6%	38.1%	45.3%
Nashville-Davidson–Murfreesboro–Franklin, TN	1,830,298	487,986	26.7%	49.8%	50.2%	15.1%	36.0%	49.0%
New Bern, NC	125,066	34,596	27.7%	57.0%	43.0%	11.6%	43.5%	44.9%
New Castle, PA micro	88,082	18,906	21.5%	49.0%	51.0%	17.6%	35.3%	47.1%
New Haven-Milford, CT	859,470	220,739	25.7%	49.3%	50.7%	15.2%	39.5%	45.3%
New Orleans-Metairie, LA	1,262,888	328,881	26.0%	48.7%	51.3%	14.5%	32.6%	52.9%
New Philadelphia-Dover, OH micro	92,916	20,822	22.4%	51.2%	48.8%	20.3%	34.0%	45.7%
New York-Newark-Jersey City, NY-NJ-PA	20,182,305	5,196,245	25.7%	50.3%	49.7%	14.2%	35.1%	50.7%
Niles-Benton Harbor, MI	154,636	34,168	22.1%	50.2%	49.8%	16.8%	36.4%	46.7%
North Port-Sarasota-Bradenton, FL	768,918	138,244	18.0%	49.8%	50.2%	17.0%	36.1%	46.9%
Norwich-New London, CT	271,863	71,058	26.1%	55.7%	44.3%	14.9%	40.3%	44.8%
Ocala, FL	343,254	70,359	20.5%	50.0%	50.0%	16.2%	35.8%	48.0%
Ocean City, NJ	94,727	18,811	19.9%	50.5%	49.5%	20.3%	33.3%	46.4%
Odessa, TX	159,436	49,508	31.1%	52.0%	48.0%	15.0%	36.4%	48.5%
Ogden-Clearfield, UT	644,030	175,789	27.3%	51.7%	48.3%	17.5%	35.0%	47.5%
Ogdensburg-Massena, NY micro	111,007	32,089	28.9%	53.3%	46.7%	12.1%	49.5%	38.4%
Oklahoma City, OK	1,358,452	375,784	27.7%	50.1%	49.9%	13.7%	37.1%	49.2%
Olympia-Tumwater, WA	269,536	67,330	25.0%	52.4%	47.6%	13.8%	37.0%	49.2%
Omaha-Council Bluffs, NE-IA	915,557	238,509	26.1%	51.0%	49.0%	15.8%	33.6%	50.6%
Orangeburg, SC micro	89,208	22,898	25.7%	50.7%	49.3%	16.4%	33.2%	50.3%
Orlando-Kissimmee-Sanford, FL	2,387,138	647,918	27.1%	50.3%	49.7%	14.7%	36.4%	48.9%
Oshkosh-Neenah, WI	169,546	46,787	27.6%	50.4%	49.6%	13.5%	41.2%	45.3%
Ottawa-Peru, IL micro	151,595	25,216	16.6%	53.5%	46.5%	17.6%	35.2%	47.2%
Owensboro, KY	117,967	27,255	23.1%	50.3%	49.7%	17.0%	34.8%	48.2%
Oxnard-Thousand Oaks-Ventura, CA	850,536	217,504	25.6%	51.2%	48.8%	15.9%	37.7%	46.4%
Palm Bay-Melbourne-Titusville, FL	568,088	120,364	21.2%	51.7%	48.3%	16.7%	37.4%	45.8%
Panama City, FL	197,723	48,956	24.8%	51.3%	48.7%	14.5%	33.2%	52.2%
Parkersburg-Vienna, WV	92,776	20,168	21.7%	50.9%	49.1%	17.1%	36.3%	46.6%
Pensacola-Ferry Pass-Brent, FL	478,043	132,104	27.6%	53.5%	46.5%	12.9%	40.4%	46.7%
Peoria, IL	376,987	90,607	24.0%	49.7%	50.3%	16.0%	34.6%	49.4%
Philadelphia-Camden-Wilmington, PA-NJ-DE-MD	6,069,875	1,554,689	25.6%	50.1%	49.9%	14.7%	35.9%	49.4%
Phoenix-Mesa-Scottsdale, AZ	4,574,531	1,190,960	26.0%	51.5%	48.5%	16.0%	35.9%	48.1%
Pine Bluff, AR	94,489	22,491	23.8%	46.3%	53.7%	15.7%	40.2%	44.1%
Pittsburgh, PA	2,353,045	559,661	23.8%	51.9%	48.1%	14.8%	36.1%	49.1%
Pittsfield, MA	127,828	28,289	22.1%	51.3%	48.7%	15.5%	46.7%	37.8%
Pocatello, ID	83,744	24,466	29.2%	51.1%	48.9%	14.0%	40.5%	45.5%
Port St. Lucie, FL	454,846	91,998	20.2%	48.8%	51.2%	16.3%	36.5%	47.2%
Portland-South Portland, ME	526,295	121,993	23.2%	50.9%	49.1%	15.8%	38.0%	46.1%
Portland-Vancouver-Hillsboro, OR-WA	2,390,244	614,186	25.7%	50.6%	49.4%	15.0%	32.8%	52.2%
Pottsville, PA micro	144,590	30,373	21.0%	52.7%	47.3%	17.6%	33.5%	48.9%
Prescott, AZ	222,255	39,793	17.9%	52.9%	47.1%	16.3%	38.4%	45.3%
Providence-Warwick, RI-MA	1,613,070	414,862	25.7%	49.8%	50.2%	13.7%	39.9%	46.4%
Provo-Orem, UT	585,257	198,288	33.9%	50.2%	49.8%	15.4%	47.7%	36.9%

Table A-4: Metropolitan/Micropolitan Statistical Areas—Summary Population Characteristics—*Continued*

	Total 2015 ACS Population	Millennial Population Age 15 to 33	Millennials as Percent of Total	Millennial Percentage by Gender		Millennial Percentage by Age		
				Male	Female	15 to 17	18 to 24	25 to 33
Pueblo, CO	163,591	40,672	24.9%	54.2%	45.8%	16.1%	36.9%	47.1%
Punta Gorda, FL	173,115	23,149	13.4%	49.3%	50.7%	18.9%	41.2%	39.9%
Racine, WI	195,080	45,504	23.3%	52.3%	47.7%	17.6%	39.2%	43.2%
Raleigh, NC	1,273,568	328,403	25.8%	50.0%	50.0%	15.8%	34.4%	49.8%
Rapid City, SD	145,457	36,640	25.2%	54.7%	45.3%	16.6%	30.7%	52.7%
Reading, PA	415,271	103,746	25.0%	49.9%	50.1%	16.5%	39.9%	43.6%
Redding, CA	179,533	40,454	22.5%	51.6%	48.4%	16.9%	32.1%	51.0%
Reno, NV	451,138	115,549	25.6%	51.3%	48.7%	14.6%	35.0%	50.4%
Richmond, VA	1,271,142	331,236	26.1%	49.5%	50.5%	15.0%	36.9%	48.1%
Riverside-San Bernardino-Ontario, CA	4,489,159	1,242,971	27.7%	51.4%	48.6%	16.5%	38.1%	45.4%
Roanoke, VA	311,901	72,916	23.4%	46.6%	53.4%	14.6%	37.4%	47.9%
Rochester, MN	213,873	51,703	24.2%	50.4%	49.6%	14.0%	40.1%	45.9%
Rochester, NY	1,081,954	279,031	25.8%	50.3%	49.7%	14.6%	39.6%	45.8%
Rockford, IL	340,663	80,061	23.5%	49.0%	51.0%	18.1%	35.6%	46.2%
Rocky Mount, NC	148,069	33,841	22.9%	48.2%	51.8%	18.6%	39.5%	41.9%
Rome, GA	96,504	24,685	25.6%	48.2%	51.8%	15.5%	37.2%	47.3%
Roseburg, OR micro	107,685	21,577	20.0%	50.4%	49.6%	15.3%	34.1%	50.6%
Sacramento–Roseville–Arden-Arcade, CA	2,274,194	592,077	26.0%	50.4%	49.6%	15.0%	36.8%	48.1%
Saginaw, MI	193,307	48,370	25.0%	51.2%	48.8%	14.5%	41.4%	44.1%
Salem, OH micro	104,806	21,390	20.4%	50.9%	49.1%	18.7%	35.1%	46.2%
Salem, OR	410,091	106,365	25.9%	51.8%	48.2%	17.5%	38.5%	44.1%
Salinas, CA	433,898	118,338	27.3%	51.6%	48.4%	14.2%	38.5%	47.3%
Salisbury, MD-DE	395,300	89,917	22.7%	49.7%	50.3%	14.7%	43.5%	41.8%
Salt Lake City, UT	1,170,266	338,055	28.9%	51.6%	48.4%	15.7%	34.0%	50.3%
San Angelo, TX	120,106	36,639	30.5%	54.5%	45.5%	12.3%	42.0%	45.7%
San Antonio-New Braunfels, TX	2,381,828	674,563	28.3%	51.4%	48.6%	15.6%	36.6%	47.9%
San Diego-Carlsbad, CA	3,299,521	944,397	28.6%	52.9%	47.1%	12.5%	37.4%	50.2%
San Francisco-Oakland-Hayward, CA	4,656,132	1,181,069	25.4%	50.5%	49.5%	12.7%	31.8%	55.6%
San Jose-Sunnyvale-Santa Clara, CA	1,976,836	508,745	25.7%	51.9%	48.1%	13.7%	33.7%	52.6%
San Luis Obispo-Paso Robles-Arroyo Grande, CA	281,401	81,571	29.0%	53.3%	46.7%	10.5%	51.8%	37.8%
Santa Cruz-Watsonville, CA	274,146	81,439	29.7%	50.4%	49.6%	11.0%	51.8%	37.2%
Santa Fe, NM	148,686	30,994	20.8%	49.6%	50.4%	15.8%	35.6%	48.6%
Santa Maria-Santa Barbara, CA	444,769	136,421	30.7%	52.2%	47.8%	11.8%	52.2%	36.0%
Santa Rosa, CA	502,146	118,618	23.6%	51.0%	49.0%	14.8%	36.9%	48.3%
Savannah, GA	379,199	110,241	29.1%	49.7%	50.3%	10.5%	42.8%	46.7%
Scranton–Wilkes-Barre–Hazleton, PA	558,166	130,840	23.4%	49.4%	50.6%	15.9%	39.6%	44.5%
Seattle-Tacoma-Bellevue, WA	3,733,580	993,581	26.6%	51.1%	48.9%	13.3%	31.9%	54.7%
Sebastian-Vero Beach, FL	147,919	26,890	18.2%	47.8%	52.2%	14.9%	42.8%	42.3%
Sebring, FL	99,491	17,160	17.2%	47.7%	52.3%	18.6%	36.5%	45.0%
Sheboygan, WI	115,569	24,958	21.6%	51.5%	48.5%	18.7%	34.1%	47.2%
Sherman-Denison, TX	125,467	29,792	23.7%	53.1%	46.9%	16.3%	41.0%	42.7%
Show Low, AZ micro	108,277	26,103	24.1%	49.6%	50.4%	18.1%	37.4%	44.5%
Shreveport-Bossier City, LA	443,708	115,714	26.1%	49.6%	50.4%	14.7%	35.4%	49.9%
Sierra Vista-Douglas, AZ	126,427	29,422	23.3%	53.0%	47.0%	17.1%	32.5%	50.4%
Sioux City, IA-NE-SD	165,491	40,932	24.7%	48.8%	51.2%	18.6%	36.6%	44.8%
Sioux Falls, SD	252,234	66,928	26.5%	49.7%	50.3%	13.1%	34.1%	52.9%
South Bend-Mishawaka, IN-MI	320,098	84,142	26.3%	51.0%	49.0%	17.0%	41.7%	41.3%
Spartanburg, SC	325,079	79,956	24.6%	49.3%	50.7%	17.0%	39.1%	43.9%
Spokane-Spokane Valley, WA	546,807	144,143	26.4%	50.9%	49.1%	14.3%	35.8%	49.8%
Springfield, IL	211,598	51,217	24.2%	48.6%	51.4%	17.8%	36.1%	46.1%
Springfield, MA	631,982	179,075	28.3%	49.3%	50.7%	14.2%	45.5%	40.3%
Springfield, MO	455,074	127,743	28.1%	49.0%	51.0%	13.3%	43.0%	43.7%
Springfield, OH	135,959	31,343	23.1%	47.9%	52.1%	17.9%	38.3%	43.9%
St. Cloud, MN	194,418	58,133	29.9%	50.1%	49.9%	14.3%	44.5%	41.2%
St. George, UT	155,602	39,437	25.3%	50.1%	49.9%	19.0%	42.4%	38.7%
St. Joseph, MO-KS	127,421	33,339	26.2%	52.7%	47.3%	15.4%	33.9%	50.7%
St. Louis, MO-IL	2,812,313	695,032	24.7%	49.7%	50.3%	16.0%	35.7%	48.3%
State College, PA	160,580	67,059	41.8%	55.3%	44.7%	5.7%	61.2%	33.1%
Staunton-Waynesboro, VA	120,221	28,708	23.9%	51.5%	48.5%	12.3%	46.6%	41.1%
Stockton-Lodi, CA	726,106	194,976	26.9%	52.1%	47.9%	17.2%	37.2%	45.6%
Sumter, SC	107,480	29,989	27.9%	58.7%	41.3%	14.7%	44.7%	40.7%
Sunbury, PA micro	93,246	20,330	21.8%	52.3%	47.7%	15.3%	32.7%	52.1%
Syracuse, NY	660,458	172,604	26.1%	50.1%	49.9%	15.8%	41.4%	42.8%
Tallahassee, FL	378,593	131,206	34.7%	49.3%	50.7%	9.5%	54.1%	36.5%
Tampa-St. Petersburg-Clearwater, FL	2,975,225	687,275	23.1%	50.1%	49.9%	15.2%	34.8%	49.9%
Terre Haute, IN	172,107	47,389	27.5%	51.8%	48.2%	15.5%	45.9%	38.6%
Texarkana, TX-AR	151,316	36,299	24.0%	54.0%	46.0%	16.2%	37.2%	46.5%
The Villages, FL	118,891	11,009	9.3%	54.6%	45.4%	19.8%	45.2%	34.9%
Toledo, OH	605,956	163,570	27.0%	49.9%	50.1%	15.0%	41.0%	43.9%
Topeka, KS	233,791	54,373	23.3%	55.2%	44.8%	16.9%	35.4%	47.7%
Torrington, CT micro	183,603	36,755	20.0%	51.7%	48.3%	18.2%	36.9%	44.9%
Traverse City, MI micro	148,334	31,729	21.4%	53.3%	46.7%	18.6%	36.6%	44.8%
Trenton, NJ	371,398	96,611	26.0%	50.6%	49.4%	14.8%	44.5%	40.7%
Truckee-Grass Valley, CA micro	98,877	18,893	19.1%	51.5%	48.5%	16.9%	32.5%	50.6%
Tucson, AZ	1,010,025	265,127	26.2%	50.7%	49.3%	14.0%	44.6%	41.4%
Tullahoma-Manchester, TN micro	102,576	23,694	23.1%	46.4%	53.6%	17.2%	41.7%	41.2%
Tulsa, OK	980,794	248,733	25.4%	48.6%	51.4%	16.0%	36.2%	47.8%

Table A-4: Metropolitan/Micropolitan Statistical Areas—Summary Population Characteristics—*Continued*

	Total 2015 ACS Population	Millennial Population Age 15 to 33	Millennials as Percent of Total	Millennial Percentage by Gender		Millennial Percentage by Age		
				Male	Female	15 to 17	18 to 24	25 to 33
Tupelo, MS micro	139,817	33,847	24.2%	50.7%	49.3%	17.3%	39.3%	43.4%
Tuscaloosa, AL	241,851	80,383	33.2%	50.2%	49.8%	11.1%	50.2%	38.8%
Tyler, TX	222,936	59,464	26.7%	49.3%	50.7%	14.7%	38.0%	47.3%
Urban Honolulu, HI	998,714	273,410	27.4%	56.1%	43.9%	11.3%	38.1%	50.6%
Utica-Rome, NY	295,600	69,188	23.4%	49.6%	50.4%	15.3%	39.1%	45.6%
Valdosta, GA	142,202	46,199	32.5%	51.0%	49.0%	11.8%	46.0%	42.2%
Vallejo-Fairfield, CA	436,092	112,131	25.7%	52.1%	47.9%	14.7%	35.9%	49.4%
Victoria, TX	99,040	25,601	25.8%	52.8%	47.2%	17.0%	37.7%	45.3%
Vineland-Bridgeton, NJ	155,854	40,801	26.2%	54.4%	45.6%	15.2%	31.1%	53.6%
Virginia Beach-Norfolk-Newport News, VA-NC	1,723,351	507,885	29.5%	51.6%	48.4%	12.9%	38.6%	48.4%
Visalia-Porterville, CA	459,863	131,238	28.5%	51.1%	48.9%	17.7%	36.9%	45.4%
Waco, TX	262,425	78,233	29.8%	49.0%	51.0%	14.7%	47.7%	37.6%
Walla Walla, WA	64,056	17,618	27.5%	56.5%	43.5%	12.9%	37.4%	49.7%
Warner Robins, GA	187,953	49,429	26.3%	49.9%	50.1%	15.0%	41.5%	43.4%
Washington-Arlington-Alexandria, DC-VA-MD-WV	6,098,283	1,605,799	26.3%	49.9%	50.1%	14.1%	34.1%	51.8%
Waterloo-Cedar Falls, IA	170,612	50,906	29.8%	50.3%	49.7%	11.4%	46.7%	41.8%
Watertown-Fort Drum, NY	117,635	35,878	30.5%	58.6%	41.4%	11.7%	42.3%	46.0%
Wausau, WI	135,868	29,492	21.7%	49.8%	50.2%	18.8%	32.9%	48.3%
Weirton-Steubenville, WV-OH	121,403	27,390	22.6%	48.3%	51.7%	14.7%	40.5%	44.9%
Wenatchee, WA	116,178	25,938	22.3%	54.9%	45.1%	16.7%	35.7%	47.6%
Wheeling, WV-OH	144,198	31,989	22.2%	46.8%	53.2%	14.9%	42.9%	42.2%
Whitewater-Elkhorn, WI micro	102,804	27,201	26.5%	52.1%	47.9%	14.2%	48.8%	37.0%
Wichita Falls, TX	150,780	44,916	29.8%	56.0%	44.0%	12.3%	45.6%	42.1%
Wichita, KS	644,502	169,912	26.4%	50.5%	49.5%	17.3%	32.6%	50.1%
Williamsport, PA	116,048	28,105	24.2%	49.2%	50.8%	13.1%	42.8%	44.2%
Wilmington, NC	277,969	75,894	27.3%	50.6%	49.4%	14.3%	42.5%	43.3%
Winchester, VA-WV	133,621	29,424	22.0%	49.2%	50.8%	14.9%	41.5%	43.6%
Winston-Salem, NC	659,330	159,220	24.1%	48.5%	51.5%	16.9%	37.5%	45.6%
Wooster, OH micro	116,063	28,015	24.1%	52.1%	47.9%	19.8%	40.1%	40.1%
Worcester, MA-CT	935,536	232,320	24.8%	50.7%	49.3%	16.9%	39.7%	43.4%
Yakima, WA	248,830	64,342	25.9%	51.6%	48.4%	17.6%	39.5%	42.9%
York-Hanover, PA	442,867	102,477	23.1%	50.2%	49.8%	16.4%	34.1%	49.5%
Youngstown-Warren-Boardman, OH-PA	549,885	120,714	22.0%	51.5%	48.5%	17.6%	38.5%	44.0%
Yuba City, CA	170,955	45,459	26.6%	50.8%	49.2%	14.5%	34.2%	51.4%
Yuma, AZ	204,275	57,750	28.3%	56.1%	43.9%	15.8%	39.9%	44.3%

PART B
RACE AND ETHNICITY

PART B. RACE AND ETHNICITY

The nation's population continues to grow more diverse, but that diversity isn't just in the large cities and metropolitan areas. Diversity is not uniform across the country, and large differences occur at smaller geographic levels.

Racial and ethnic identification in the Census is obtained in a number of different ways, including direct questions on race and Hispanic Origin. Other questions obtain data on ancestry, language spoken at home, and place of birth. The Census and American Community Survey also allow for respondents to identify with more than one racial group. The term race "Alone" means the respondent identifies with that single racial group. Those who identify with two or more racial groups are identified as "Multi-race." Hispanic Origin is obtained in a separate question, and a relatively small number of individuals identify themselves as "Some Other Race."

Some of these categories are not included in these tables because of their small sample sizes. The tables in this section present only selected major response categories—White, Non-Hispanic; Black, Non-Hispanic; Asian, Non-Hispanic; and Hispanic. The race categories, American Indian and Alaskan Native, Multi-race and Some Other Race are excluded because of the small population size. However, the counties, cities, and metropolitan/micropolitan areas with large populations of Native American Millennials are identified in the table below.

Unlike many other tables in this volume, some of the ACS sample population counts by race and Hispanic Origin are often too small to be reported for all geographies. This can be due to the small sample sizes noted above, but it can also be due to the geographic allocation methods described in the section "Defining the Millennials." In these cases, the random sample record allocation method simply did not select any records of the Hispanic Origin group. This certainly does not mean that there are no individuals in those groups, simply that the method did not select any records. As a result, some geographic areas will have these categories indicated by "na." Part B—Race and Ethnicity presents data only for the Millennial ages of 15 to 33 and therefore may exhibit different distributions of the racial and Hispanic Origin population than that for the general population. For example, of the total U.S. Millennial population, 55.4 percent are White, Non-Hispanic, compared to 61.5 percent of the general population. The Asian, Non-Hispanic population represents 5.8 percent of Millennials much like the 5.3 percent in the general population.

White, Non-Hispanic

As noted above, 55.9 percent of the nation's Millennials are White, Non-Hispanic, but the proportion by state shows considerable variation ranging from a low of

Percent Native American for Areas with 5 Percent or More Native American Population

Area Name	Millennials as Percent of Population		Area Name	Millennials as Percent of Population
Counties			**Counties**	
Coconino County, Arizona	23.5%		Robeson County, North Carolina	36.0%
Flathead County, Montana	6.5%		San Juan County, New Mexico	39.1%
Missoula County, Montana	10.4%		Sandoval County, New Mexico	12.0%
Navajo County, Arizona	64.2%		Terrebonne Parish, Louisiana	5.0%
Pennington County, South Dakota	6.2%		Tulsa County, Oklahoma	5.3%
Pinal County, Arizona	7.8%		Yellowstone County, Montana	10.8%
Places			**Places**	
Billings city, Montana	6.4%		Rio Rancho city, New Mexico	9.2%
Broken Arrow city, Oklahoma	5.1%			
Metropolitan Statistical Areas			**Metropolitan Statistical Areas**	
Albuquerque, New Mexico	5.5%		Kalispell, Montana micro	6.3%
Billings, Montana	8.9%		Lumberton, North Carolina micro	37.9%
Farmington, New Mexico	39.1%		Missoula, Montana	11.1%
Flagstaff, Arizona	23.5%		Pocatello, Idaho	6.4%
Fort Smith, Arkansas-Oklahoma	7.0%		Show Low, Arizona micro	64.2%
Great Falls, Montana	11.1%		Tulsa, Oklahoma	7.9%

Minority Millennials as a Percent of the Millennial Population

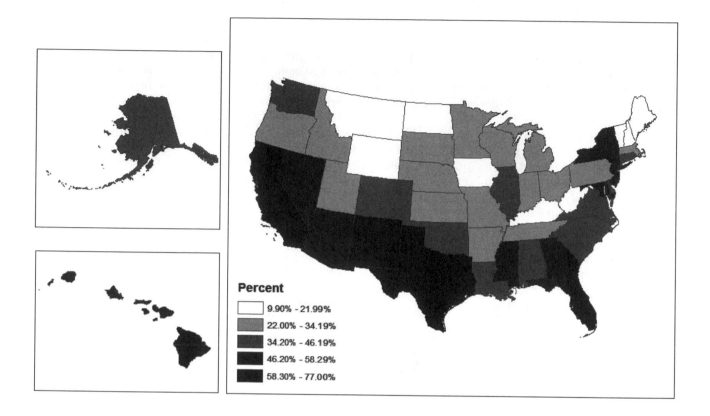

Percent

☐	9.90% - 21.99%
☐	22.00% - 34.19%
☐	34.20% - 46.19%
☐	46.20% - 58.29%
☐	58.30% - 77.00%

23.5 percent in Hawaii to a high of 90.1 percent in Maine. In 41 of the states and District of Columbia more than half of the Millennial population is White, Non-Hispanic, and in only two states (Hawaii and New Mexico) is it below 30 percent. By age, the percentage of Millennials in the 15 to 17 and 25 to 33 age groups show the greatest variation. In the 15 to 17 category, the District of Columbia is lowest at only 2.1 percent and New Jersey is highest at 17.2 percent. The District of Columbia is the real outlier, as the only other state below 10 percent is Hawaii (5.8 percent). Among the 25 to 33 age group, DC has the highest percentage at 67.3 percent with Hawaii as the second highest at 58.0 percent. Just under 40 percent of the Millennial population is 25 to 33 in Vermont. In the 18 to 24 age group, all states fall between 30 and 44 percent.

There is increasing variation as the geographic area of analysis gets smaller. For counties, the percentage of their Millennial population that is White, Non-Hispanic varies from lows of 3.8 percent in Hidalgo County, TX, and 4.0 percent in Webb County, TX, to a high of 96.5 percent in Wright County, MN. Only six counties are below 10 percent White, Non-Hispanic while 25 counties are above 90 percent. By age, counties show the widest range in the 18 to 24 with a low of 26.0 percent in Fayette County, GA, to the high of 69.3 percent in Clarke County GA. The 25 to 33 category, ranges from lows of less than 1 percent to a high of 79.5 percent.

The cities of Compton and South Gate, CA have the lowest percentage of Millennials who are White, Non-Hispanic, with values of 2.0 percent and 2.9 percent, respectively. Inglewood, CA is a close third at 3.0 percent. Eighteen cities are below 10 percent. However, 26 cities have greater than 75 percent, with Fargo, ND, the highest at 85.2 percent. At the metropolitan area level, McAllen-Edinburg-Mission, TX, has the lowest percentage with 3.9 percent, followed closely by Laredo, TX, at 4.0 percent. Clarksburg, WV, is highest at 95.0 percent. In 18 metros, the percentage of Millennials who are White, Non-Hispanic is greater than 90 percent.

Black, Non-Hispanic

Nationwide, 13.8 percent of Millennials are Black, Non-Hispanic. The percentage is highest in the state of

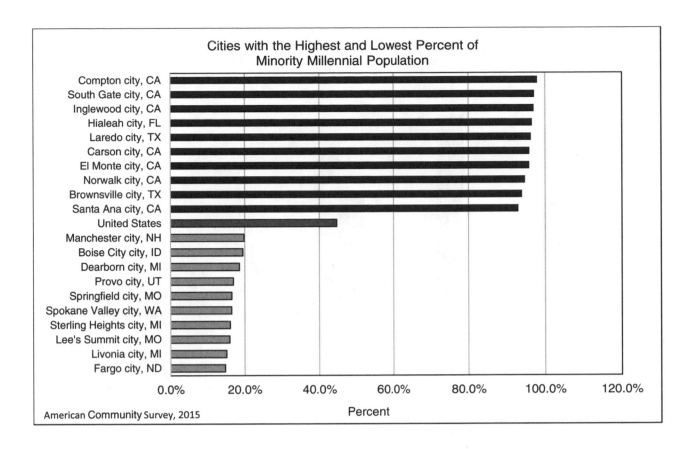

Cities with the Highest and Lowest Percent of Minority Millennial Population

American Community Survey, 2015

Percent

Mississippi at 42.6 percent and lowest in Montana at 0.5 percent. Idaho follows closely as the second lowest percentage Black, Non-Hispanic at 0.7 percent. The District of Columbia is second highest at 37.4 percent, and the third highest state is Louisiana at 35.5 percent. Thirty-four states are below the national average of 13.8 percent Black, Non-Hispanic.

Each of the Millennial age groups shows wide variation. Among the 15 to 17 population, states range from a low of zero percent in Montana (though that low level is probably due to sampling variability) to a high of 35.2 percent in Idaho. The 18 to 24 age group varies between the low of 13.6 percent (South Dakota) and the high of 79.3 percent in Montana. While those are the extremes for the 18 to 24 population, 28 states are in a tight range from 35 to 45 percent. Idaho has the lowest percentage of Millennials in the 25 to 33 age group at 7.0 percent while South Dakota is highest at 71.1 percent.

In 35 counties the percentage of Millennials who are Black, Non-Hispanic is less than 1 percent, and 205 are below 5 percent. In Hinds County, MS, three of every four (74.7 percent) Millennials is Black, Non-Hispanic, and in 28 counties the percentage is greater than 50 percent.

Similar to the county distribution, in 15 cities the Black, Non-Hispanic population have below 1 percent of the total Millennials and 172 are below 10 percent. Jackson, MS (76.9 percent) and Detroit City, MI (76.1 percent) have the highest percentages, and 14 cities have over 50 percent. Thirteen metro/micro areas have too small of a Black, Non-Hispanic population to be reported. And 25 additional metro/micros have less than one percent while 231 are less than 10 percent. Six metropolitan/micropolitan areas have over 50 percent, with the Orangeburg, SC micro highest at 63.1 percent.

Asian, Non-Hispanic

Hawaii's Millennial population is the highest percentage at 27.2 percent, more than twice that of the second highest state (California) at 13.5 percent. Mississippi has the lowest percentage of Asian, Non-Hispanics at 1.2 percent but fully 36 states have less than 5 percent and 15 states have less than 2 percent.

There is wide variation by age among the Asian, Non-Hispanic population, especially among the 18 to 24 and 25 to 33 age groups. Wyoming at 1.9 percent has the lowest proportion of 15 to 17 year olds. The Western states of

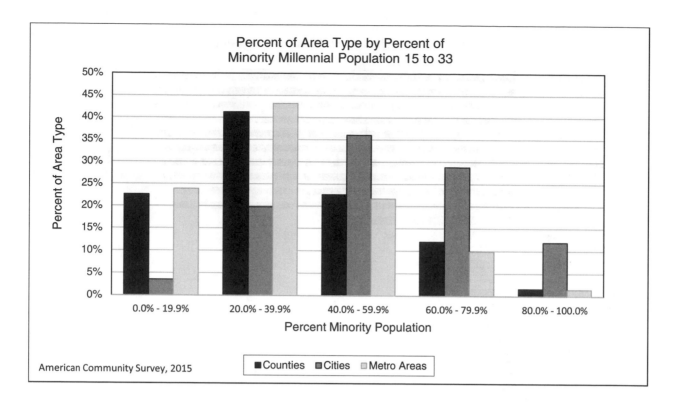

Percent of Area Type by Percent of
Minority Millennial Population 15 to 33

American Community Survey, 2015

■ Counties ▣ Cities ▢ Metro Areas

Montana and North Dakota are also quite low (5.4 percent and 5.7 percent, respectively), but the District of Columbia is also in that low category at only 4.6 percent. New Mexico has the highest percentage of 15 to 17 year olds at 19.4 percent. Wyoming's Millennials are concentrated in the 18 to 24 age group with the highest figure of 73.3 percent, while North Dakota has the highest percentage in the 25 to 33 age group at 82.1 percent.

The smaller Asian, Non-Hispanic population results in no data for 24 counties, and for an additional 71 counties the percentage of the Millennial population is less than 1 percent. In 450 of the 633 counties less than five percent of the Millennial population is Asian, Non-Hispanic. This minority category is highest in Santa Clara County, CA at 33.6 percent.

Among cities, the percentage of Millennials is less than one percent Asian, Non-Hispanic in 23 cities and less than 10 percent in 242 cities. Three California cities have the highest percentages: Fremont (54.8 percent), Santa Clara (48.8 percent) and Sunnyvale (44.5 percent) along with Urban Honolulu CDP, HI at 43.5 percent. Metro/micros with less than one percent Asian, Non-Hispanic number 60, with 378 having fewer than 10 percent. The San Jose-Sunnyvale metro, known for its high-technology sector, is highest with 32.5 percent followed by the

Urban Honolulu metro at 29.2 percent and San Francisco-Oakland-Hayward, CA at 25.1 percent.

Hispanic

The Hispanic Millennials are the largest percentage of the population in New Mexico at 54.9 percent, followed by the other Southern and Western states of California (44.9 percent), Texas (43.3 percent), Arizona (38.1 percent), and Nevada (34.8 percent). West Virginia is lowest at 2.1 percent, and 23 states are below 10 percent.

Among the 15 to 17 year olds, the District of Columbia is lowest at 6.4 percent and West Virginia is highest at 20.1 percent. West Virginia's Millennials are also the lowest percentage in the 18 to 24 age group at 20.8 percent, while 56.6 percent of the Maine's Millennials are in that age group. Among the 25 to 33 year olds, Maine has the lowest percentage at 24.6 percent, while the District of Columbia is highest at 60.6 percent.

Hispanics make up less than one percent of the Millennial population in six counties, with Fairfield, OH and Trumbull counties in Ohio lowest at 0.2 and 0.5 percent, respectively. There are 84 counties at less than five percent and 215 less than 10 percent. Webb County, TX is highest at 95.3 percent, followed closely by two other Texas counties—Hidalgo (94.4 percent) and Cameron

(92.0 percent). The Millennial population is more than 50 percent Hispanic in 25 counties.

Flint, MI (0.5 percent) has the lowest percentage of Millennials who are Hispanic, though 77 cities are below 10 percent. Four cities are greater than 90 percent: Hialeah, FL (92.9 percent), Brownsville, TX (93.2 percent), South Gate, CA (93.1 percent), and Laredo, TX (95.5 percent). The Laredo, TX metro area is also the highest metro area at 95.3 percent, with two other Texas metro areas close behind: McAllen-Edinburg-Mission (94.3 percent) and Brownsville-Harlingen (92.1 percent).

Table B-1: States—Race and Hispanic Origin by Age

	White, Non-Hispanic					Black, Non-Hispanic				
	Millennial Population		Percent by Age			Millennial Population		Percent by Age		
	Number	Percent	15 to 17	18 to 24	25 to 33	Number	Percent	15 to 17	18 to 24	25 to 33
United States	46,269,102	55.4%	14.7%	36.8%	48.5%	11,545,363	13.8%	15.2%	39.8%	45.1%
Alabama	749,648	61.0%	15.8%	37.7%	46.5%	372,634	30.3%	15.2%	40.3%	44.6%
Alaska	124,869	56.4%	12.0%	34.5%	53.4%	8,965	4.0%	13.4%	47.9%	38.8%
Arizona	806,638	45.6%	14.3%	35.9%	49.8%	89,943	5.1%	15.5%	36.7%	47.8%
Arkansas	511,828	68.1%	15.5%	36.8%	47.7%	135,097	18.0%	16.4%	40.9%	42.7%
California	3,381,369	31.5%	12.7%	34.4%	52.9%	637,601	5.9%	13.4%	38.9%	47.6%
Colorado	936,151	63.2%	12.7%	34.6%	52.7%	65,673	4.4%	13.7%	32.6%	53.7%
Connecticut	534,669	59.9%	16.5%	39.6%	43.9%	106,289	11.9%	16.8%	42.0%	41.2%
Delaware	133,195	56.1%	14.0%	34.9%	51.1%	57,045	24.0%	16.4%	42.1%	41.5%
District of Columbia	103,675	43.9%	2.1%	30.6%	67.3%	88,308	37.4%	12.0%	40.7%	47.2%
Florida	2,244,694	46.4%	14.4%	35.6%	50.0%	941,787	19.5%	15.5%	39.2%	45.3%
Georgia	1,295,152	48.1%	15.5%	37.4%	47.1%	926,027	34.4%	15.7%	39.9%	44.4%
Hawaii	87,228	23.5%	5.8%	36.3%	58.0%	11,198	3.0%	3.1%	49.1%	47.9%
Idaho	331,315	77.6%	16.9%	36.3%	46.8%	2,812	0.7%	35.2%	57.8%	7.0%
Illinois	1,870,743	56.1%	14.8%	35.8%	49.5%	521,157	15.6%	15.6%	42.2%	42.2%
Indiana	1,289,048	75.5%	15.9%	38.9%	45.2%	179,933	10.5%	16.2%	38.9%	44.9%
Iowa	658,488	81.8%	15.3%	39.6%	45.1%	36,601	4.5%	17.6%	42.1%	40.3%
Kansas	549,234	71.9%	15.2%	38.3%	46.6%	48,851	6.4%	15.2%	42.5%	42.3%
Kentucky	906,751	82.3%	15.7%	38.1%	46.2%	103,383	9.4%	16.4%	40.5%	43.1%
Louisiana	679,279	54.2%	14.6%	35.0%	50.4%	444,561	35.5%	16.2%	39.6%	44.2%
Maine	269,342	90.1%	16.0%	37.0%	47.0%	4,332	1.4%	12.8%	70.9%	16.3%
Maryland	725,256	47.3%	14.7%	35.8%	49.5%	470,053	30.7%	14.8%	37.6%	47.6%
Massachusetts	1,203,606	66.6%	14.0%	38.5%	47.6%	142,130	7.9%	15.0%	39.0%	46.1%
Michigan	1,758,489	70.5%	16.0%	39.0%	45.1%	401,066	16.1%	15.6%	41.8%	42.7%
Minnesota	1,048,009	75.4%	15.2%	36.1%	48.7%	99,784	7.2%	14.9%	35.1%	50.0%
Mississippi	393,314	51.1%	15.5%	39.7%	44.7%	327,366	42.6%	16.9%	42.6%	40.5%
Missouri	1,178,954	75.5%	15.3%	37.3%	47.4%	213,588	13.7%	15.5%	40.8%	43.7%
Montana	207,668	82.5%	14.6%	39.4%	46.1%	1,382	0.5%	0.0%	79.3%	20.7%
Nebraska	373,729	75.3%	14.6%	38.7%	46.6%	33,298	6.7%	12.9%	42.7%	44.4%
Nevada	309,528	41.9%	13.7%	31.2%	55.1%	68,941	9.3%	11.6%	37.9%	50.5%
New Hampshire	278,778	88.0%	15.9%	40.9%	43.2%	5,210	1.6%	10.0%	56.6%	33.4%
New Jersey	1,074,458	49.2%	17.2%	36.6%	46.3%	317,912	14.6%	14.6%	39.3%	46.1%
New Mexico	157,831	29.6%	12.7%	37.0%	50.3%	10,545	2.0%	18.5%	42.7%	38.8%
New York	2,676,558	50.8%	13.9%	36.5%	49.6%	806,419	15.3%	14.2%	38.2%	47.6%
North Carolina	1,494,943	58.4%	14.7%	38.1%	47.2%	590,297	23.0%	15.1%	40.8%	44.1%
North Dakota	183,884	82.7%	11.6%	42.6%	45.8%	7,744	3.5%	2.2%	48.6%	49.2%
Ohio	2,189,262	75.5%	16.0%	36.9%	47.1%	395,242	13.6%	16.3%	40.2%	43.6%
Oklahoma	615,910	60.0%	14.2%	36.9%	48.9%	87,336	8.5%	12.4%	42.7%	44.9%
Oregon	707,591	70.2%	14.0%	35.1%	50.9%	23,544	2.3%	12.9%	34.9%	52.2%
Pennsylvania	2,276,102	71.7%	14.9%	37.3%	47.7%	395,772	12.5%	15.4%	40.4%	44.2%
Rhode Island	184,385	65.7%	13.2%	41.0%	45.8%	18,206	6.5%	10.3%	39.2%	50.5%
South Carolina	728,510	58.4%	14.7%	38.0%	47.4%	372,937	29.9%	16.3%	39.9%	43.8%
South Dakota	170,180	76.7%	14.9%	38.7%	46.4%	5,546	2.5%	15.3%	13.6%	71.1%
Tennessee	1,162,881	69.4%	15.3%	37.0%	47.7%	331,932	19.8%	15.2%	39.8%	45.0%
Texas	2,809,408	37.2%	14.4%	35.5%	50.1%	957,796	12.7%	15.2%	38.4%	46.4%
Utah	672,892	76.0%	16.3%	38.4%	45.3%	16,204	1.8%	13.9%	39.9%	46.3%
Vermont	139,300	89.0%	14.7%	43.7%	41.6%	4,771	3.0%	7.7%	30.9%	61.5%
Virginia	1,279,046	58.3%	14.0%	37.1%	48.9%	448,529	20.4%	14.7%	39.7%	45.6%
Washington	1,197,100	63.5%	13.7%	34.3%	52.0%	78,936	4.2%	13.5%	37.8%	48.7%
West Virginia	381,867	89.6%	15.6%	38.5%	45.9%	19,807	4.6%	12.6%	42.9%	44.5%
Wisconsin	1,103,902	77.4%	15.3%	39.1%	45.6%	109,629	7.7%	16.3%	43.4%	40.4%
Wyoming	122,445	79.3%	13.9%	36.8%	49.3%	1,244	0.8%	20.1%	33.9%	46.0%

Table B-1: States—Race and Hispanic Origin by Age—*Continued*

	Asian, Non-Hispanic					Hispanic				
	Millennial Population		Percent by Age			Millennial Population		Percent by Age		
	Number	Percent	15 to 17	18 to 24	25 to 33	Number	Percent	15 to 17	18 to 24	25 to 33
United States	4,878,158	5.8%	11.6%	34.4%	54.0%	17,528,602	21.0%	16.1%	38.4%	45.5%
Alabama	16,212	1.3%	6.5%	35.9%	57.7%	58,023	4.7%	19.1%	34.4%	46.6%
Alaska	14,052	6.3%	15.4%	30.8%	53.9%	20,820	9.4%	12.1%	49.8%	38.1%
Arizona	62,562	3.5%	9.6%	36.8%	53.6%	672,850	38.1%	17.3%	40.8%	42.0%
Arkansas	13,918	1.9%	13.2%	37.9%	48.9%	67,611	9.0%	16.4%	38.3%	45.3%
California	1,448,317	13.5%	11.6%	33.7%	54.8%	4,820,257	44.9%	16.1%	38.9%	45.0%
Colorado	49,016	3.3%	11.4%	36.6%	52.1%	367,174	24.8%	16.3%	37.7%	46.0%
Connecticut	45,322	5.1%	12.8%	34.3%	52.8%	177,487	19.9%	14.7%	39.5%	45.8%
Delaware	10,852	4.6%	10.8%	33.4%	55.8%	28,167	11.9%	15.7%	35.3%	49.1%
District of Columbia	12,474	5.3%	4.6%	29.9%	65.5%	23,877	10.1%	6.4%	33.0%	60.6%
Florida	143,735	3.0%	11.1%	37.0%	51.9%	1,370,531	28.3%	15.0%	36.6%	48.4%
Georgia	111,672	4.1%	12.8%	34.8%	52.4%	292,359	10.8%	17.7%	36.6%	45.7%
Hawaii	101,074	27.2%	13.6%	36.5%	49.9%	49,355	13.3%	10.8%	40.1%	49.2%
Idaho	6,728	1.6%	8.0%	36.6%	55.4%	70,175	16.4%	16.7%	38.1%	45.2%
Illinois	194,765	5.8%	10.3%	32.7%	57.0%	669,282	20.1%	17.2%	37.5%	45.3%
Indiana	50,201	2.9%	10.6%	44.9%	44.5%	138,597	8.1%	17.4%	41.5%	41.1%
Iowa	28,213	3.5%	6.0%	41.2%	52.8%	60,738	7.5%	18.2%	39.6%	42.2%
Kansas	28,067	3.7%	10.4%	40.9%	48.7%	106,626	14.0%	18.3%	37.4%	44.3%
Kentucky	16,435	1.5%	9.3%	37.4%	53.3%	48,089	4.4%	18.3%	37.8%	43.9%
Louisiana	28,420	2.3%	9.4%	39.2%	51.4%	71,853	5.7%	11.0%	33.2%	55.8%
Maine	4,091	1.4%	9.9%	30.0%	60.1%	9,965	3.3%	18.8%	56.6%	24.6%
Maryland	100,340	6.5%	12.0%	34.2%	53.8%	174,632	11.4%	14.3%	35.7%	50.0%
Massachusetts	142,207	7.9%	8.9%	36.1%	54.9%	258,484	14.3%	14.7%	40.3%	45.0%
Michigan	95,992	3.8%	13.0%	37.5%	49.5%	153,270	6.1%	16.8%	42.8%	40.4%
Minnesota	99,866	7.2%	13.4%	33.4%	53.2%	85,481	6.1%	18.8%	40.1%	41.1%
Mississippi	9,611	1.2%	17.2%	31.1%	51.7%	26,943	3.5%	14.0%	36.5%	49.5%
Missouri	38,097	2.4%	9.3%	42.5%	48.2%	77,829	5.0%	16.3%	42.3%	41.4%
Montana	3,436	1.4%	5.4%	59.4%	35.2%	10,979	4.4%	17.2%	43.5%	39.2%
Nebraska	14,789	3.0%	8.1%	38.0%	53.9%	60,542	12.2%	18.7%	41.9%	39.4%
Nevada	58,603	7.9%	11.4%	30.8%	57.9%	256,880	34.8%	16.9%	37.6%	45.5%
New Hampshire	11,137	3.5%	18.4%	30.4%	51.2%	14,506	4.6%	17.1%	36.6%	46.4%
New Jersey	213,232	9.8%	14.0%	31.1%	54.9%	518,452	23.8%	15.2%	35.9%	48.9%
New Mexico	7,592	1.4%	19.4%	18.1%	62.5%	293,065	54.9%	16.5%	40.3%	43.2%
New York	494,165	9.4%	10.8%	33.9%	55.3%	1,134,490	21.5%	13.8%	37.4%	48.8%
North Carolina	81,656	3.2%	13.8%	33.8%	52.4%	291,399	11.4%	10.1%	30.0%	45.9%
North Dakota	3,198	1.4%	5.7%	12.3%	82.1%	10,240	4.6%	12.3%	40.0%	47.8%
Ohio	80,149	2.8%	11.2%	34.1%	54.7%	131,579	4.5%	15.9%	38.1%	46.0%
Oklahoma	28,212	2.7%	9.6%	32.1%	58.3%	134,801	13.1%	15.5%	40.8%	43.7%
Oregon	49,896	4.9%	12.4%	38.1%	49.5%	164,695	16.3%	17.6%	40.6%	41.8%
Pennsylvania	137,276	4.3%	11.3%	39.9%	48.8%	276,258	8.7%	15.4%	39.7%	44.9%
Rhode Island	15,244	5.4%	6.5%	38.2%	55.3%	51,612	18.4%	14.3%	41.4%	44.3%
South Carolina	20,307	1.6%	11.8%	35.6%	52.6%	88,179	7.1%	15.8%	40.9%	43.3%
South Dakota	3,372	1.5%	11.9%	57.6%	30.5%	11,062	5.0%	11.7%	40.8%	47.5%
Tennessee	31,491	1.9%	14.6%	39.5%	45.9%	101,734	6.1%	15.5%	36.6%	48.0%
Texas	355,682	4.7%	12.3%	32.1%	55.6%	3,272,752	43.3%	17.1%	37.9%	45.0%
Utah	24,210	2.7%	11.9%	30.1%	58.1%	129,376	14.6%	14.6%	41.3%	40.5%
Vermont	2,702	1.7%	14.7%	64.2%	21.1%	5,198	3.3%	14.8%	50.0%	35.2%
Virginia	145,082	6.6%	13.8%	34.0%	52.1%	232,710	10.6%	14.1%	38.3%	47.6%
Washington	163,851	8.7%	10.5%	32.5%	57.0%	292,197	15.5%	15.8%	37.6%	46.5%
West Virginia	5,695	1.3%	8.2%	26.2%	65.6%	8,946	2.1%	20.1%	20.8%	59.1%
Wisconsin	52,773	3.7%	13.6%	32.8%	53.7%	116,882	8.2%	17.6%	37.3%	45.1%
Wyoming	2,169	1.4%	1.9%	73.3%	24.9%	19,593	12.7%	15.4%	41.1%	43.4%

Table B-2: Counties—Race and Hispanic Origin by Age

| | White, Non-Hispanic | | | | | Black, Non-Hispanic | | | | |
| | Millennial Population | | Percent by Age | | | Millennial Population | | Percent by Age | | |
	Number	Percent	15 to 17	18 to 24	25 to 33	Number	Percent	15 to 17	18 to 24	25 to 33
Alabama										
Baldwin County	33,898	80.9%	18.4%	34.6%	47.1%	5,821	13.9%	19.3%	41.7%	39.0%
Calhoun County	19,700	64.4%	16.4%	35.4%	48.2%	7,181	23.5%	9.3%	51.4%	39.3%
Etowah County	17,469	77.6%	17.9%	35.4%	46.7%	3,732	16.6%	9.1%	61.2%	29.6%
Houston County	15,254	61.2%	19.3%	32.7%	48.0%	7,334	29.4%	17.2%	41.3%	41.5%
Jefferson County	79,677	47.3%	13.7%	34.2%	52.1%	76,523	45.4%	15.8%	36.2%	48.0%
Lauderdale County	16,081	69.7%	16.8%	39.9%	43.3%	3,673	15.9%	20.4%	48.5%	31.1%
Lee County	39,103	71.4%	9.2%	58.4%	32.4%	11,013	20.1%	12.8%	41.6%	45.7%
Madison County	51,860	57.1%	17.1%	34.0%	48.9%	27,163	29.9%	10.6%	41.4%	48.1%
Marshall County	16,910	77.2%	15.5%	41.5%	43.0%	1,086	5.0%	21.9%	22.7%	55.4%
Mobile County	56,872	52.6%	15.0%	35.1%	49.9%	41,514	38.4%	17.3%	38.1%	44.6%
Montgomery County	21,120	33.3%	12.4%	37.6%	50.0%	38,346	60.5%	14.3%	39.4%	46.3%
Morgan County	19,532	67.3%	19.2%	33.7%	47.1%	4,883	16.8%	15.7%	37.9%	46.4%
Shelby County	37,475	75.8%	18.9%	33.7%	47.4%	7,802	15.8%	17.2%	49.7%	33.1%
Tuscaloosa County	43,364	60.0%	9.2%	49.9%	40.9%	22,715	31.4%	13.6%	50.9%	35.5%
Alaska										
Anchorage Municipality	50,469	54.4%	9.6%	33.3%	57.1%	7,015	7.6%	16.4%	49.8%	33.8%
Fairbanks North Star Borough	22,436	64.4%	12.5%	37.6%	50.0%	824	2.4%	0.0%	74.9%	25.1%
Matanuska-Susitna Borough	21,472	77.0%	18.0%	36.5%	45.5%	373	1.3%	13.1%	0.0%	86.9%
Arizona										
Cochise County	10,331	35.1%	16.5%	32.5%	51.0%	1,158	3.9%	10.8%	0.0%	89.2%
Coconino County	27,337	52.8%	7.1%	60.3%	32.7%	717	1.4%	0.0%	100.0%	0.0%
Maricopa County	516,373	47.7%	14.9%	33.0%	52.2%	68,065	6.3%	16.6%	37.3%	46.2%
Mohave County	24,865	62.9%	17.1%	32.2%	50.8%	883	2.2%	35.6%	0.0%	64.4%
Navajo County	5,798	22.2%	11.4%	35.9%	52.6%	115	0.4%	0.0%	0.0%	100.0%
Pima County	112,519	42.1%	12.2%	44.8%	43.0%	9,724	3.6%	11.9%	44.5%	43.6%
Pinal County	39,923	43.0%	18.6%	29.7%	51.7%	3,851	4.2%	15.0%	26.8%	58.2%
Yavapai County	28,693	72.1%	16.6%	35.0%	48.4%	341	0.9%	0.0%	27.9%	72.1%
Yuma County	12,306	21.3%	10.7%	41.1%	48.2%	1,820	3.2%	0.0%	11.6%	88.4%
Arkansas										
Benton County	43,377	68.8%	17.1%	29.9%	53.0%	1,269	2.0%	14.2%	5.2%	80.6%
Craighead County	23,742	75.2%	15.7%	36.2%	48.1%	4,639	14.7%	9.8%	66.2%	23.9%
Faulkner County	31,479	78.4%	14.9%	44.5%	40.6%	5,243	13.1%	21.1%	42.5%	36.4%
Garland County	15,684	74.5%	17.0%	38.8%	44.1%	4,048	19.2%	12.2%	34.7%	53.1%
Pulaski County	48,818	47.2%	12.5%	30.6%	56.9%	41,741	40.3%	16.7%	36.8%	46.5%
Saline County	21,879	81.2%	18.0%	31.8%	50.3%	2,036	7.6%	25.5%	14.8%	59.7%
Sebastian County	21,496	66.3%	21.4%	33.1%	45.5%	3,209	9.9%	18.1%	41.9%	40.0%
Washington County	50,946	69.9%	10.8%	47.4%	41.8%	1,711	2.3%	1.7%	65.8%	32.5%
California										
Alameda County	119,216	27.5%	10.3%	29.7%	60.1%	47,221	10.9%	12.6%	38.0%	49.4%
Butte County	44,159	66.6%	10.7%	48.8%	40.5%	1,632	2.5%	21.7%	56.5%	21.8%
Contra Costa County	97,096	36.7%	17.2%	35.9%	46.9%	26,418	10.0%	18.8%	32.9%	48.2%
El Dorado County	27,066	71.1%	19.8%	37.4%	42.8%	90	0.2%	53.3%	0.0%	46.7%
Fresno County	64,861	23.1%	14.6%	34.9%	50.6%	14,525	5.2%	14.7%	48.0%	37.3%
Humboldt County	26,072	68.5%	10.6%	44.6%	44.8%	1,023	2.7%	0.0%	80.7%	19.3%
Imperial County	4,008	8.1%	21.7%	39.4%	38.9%	1,233	2.5%	0.0%	69.3%	30.7%
Kern County	73,880	28.9%	14.2%	33.0%	52.8%	16,338	6.4%	12.1%	45.3%	42.6%
Kings County	13,592	29.2%	11.1%	33.3%	55.6%	2,822	6.1%	0.7%	35.0%	64.2%
Los Angeles County	632,448	22.5%	10.6%	30.8%	58.6%	222,895	7.9%	13.4%	37.6%	49.0%
Madera County	9,975	24.0%	17.2%	32.8%	50.0%	985	2.4%	0.0%	7.8%	92.2%
Marin County	28,118	59.6%	20.8%	35.2%	44.0%	2,306	4.9%	7.8%	16.9%	75.3%
Merced County	17,342	22.1%	13.3%	33.2%	53.5%	2,651	3.4%	5.4%	75.4%	19.2%
Monterey County	29,322	24.4%	12.3%	40.1%	47.6%	2,961	2.5%	1.9%	31.7%	66.4%
Napa County	14,131	42.3%	14.7%	35.7%	49.6%	1,093	3.3%	13.6%	24.1%	62.3%
Nevada County	14,741	78.0%	18.1%	32.4%	49.5%	392	2.1%	0.0%	0.0%	100.0%
Orange County	289,199	35.1%	14.3%	34.9%	50.8%	14,065	1.7%	8.5%	36.0%	55.5%
Placer County	56,320	69.1%	18.5%	35.0%	46.5%	1,921	2.4%	13.6%	42.0%	44.4%
Riverside County	172,351	27.6%	15.9%	33.6%	50.5%	36,114	5.8%	17.0%	43.9%	39.1%
Sacramento County	155,708	38.9%	13.7%	31.7%	54.7%	42,450	10.6%	15.4%	40.5%	44.1%
San Bernardino County	147,973	23.8%	13.8%	35.2%	51.0%	51,302	8.2%	16.3%	40.0%	43.6%
San Diego County	379,612	40.2%	10.6%	36.2%	53.1%	53,176	5.6%	12.6%	38.4%	49.0%
San Francisco County	109,597	42.7%	3.7%	16.8%	79.5%	11,656	4.5%	11.5%	31.8%	56.7%
San Joaquin County	52,310	26.8%	16.2%	35.2%	48.6%	13,106	6.7%	15.7%	42.1%	42.2%
San Luis Obispo County	49,932	61.2%	10.0%	55.1%	34.9%	2,107	2.6%	6.7%	49.5%	43.8%
San Mateo County	57,270	32.2%	14.6%	30.3%	55.1%	3,540	2.0%	12.4%	35.8%	51.8%
Santa Barbara County	53,823	39.5%	9.0%	55.7%	35.4%	2,586	1.9%	1.5%	69.9%	28.6%
Santa Clara County	136,538	27.8%	12.9%	33.1%	53.9%	13,781	2.8%	12.0%	34.4%	53.6%
Santa Cruz County	39,461	48.5%	9.9%	51.3%	38.8%	1,475	1.8%	10.3%	20.7%	69.0%
Shasta County	30,741	73.6%	15.8%	32.0%	52.1%	1,073	2.6%	0.0%	34.2%	65.8%
Solano County	36,794	32.8%	12.7%	33.7%	53.5%	13,542	12.1%	14.3%	34.1%	51.6%
Sonoma County	64,392	54.3%	13.9%	35.3%	50.8%	2,482	2.1%	1.8%	42.7%	55.5%
Stanislaus County	53,256	35.4%	15.2%	32.5%	52.3%	4,622	3.1%	30.1%	33.9%	35.9%
Sutter County	11,438	45.5%	13.6%	27.5%	58.9%	587	2.3%	4.4%	11.6%	84.0%
Tulare County	29,830	22.7%	16.0%	33.1%	50.9%	1,857	1.4%	22.4%	57.3%	20.3%
Ventura County	82,029	37.2%	15.9%	38.0%	46.1%	5,346	2.4%	1.2%	42.5%	56.3%
Yolo County	30,065	40.7%	9.8%	53.6%	36.6%	1,445	2.0%	0.0%	69.8%	30.2%

Table B-2: Counties—Race and Hispanic Origin by Age—*Continued*

	Asian, Non-Hispanic					Hispanic				
	Millennial Population		Percent by Age			Millennial Population		Percent by Age		
	Number	Percent	15 to 17	18 to 24	25 to 33	Number	Percent	15 to 17	18 to 24	25 to 33
Alabama										
Baldwin County	62	0.1%	100.0%	0.0%	0.0%	1,459	3.5%	0.0%	16.0%	84.0%
Calhoun County	451	1.5%	0.0%	56.8%	43.2%	1,598	5.2%	37.0%	63.0%	0.0%
Etowah County	na	na	na	na	na	1,163	5.2%	29.3%	47.5%	23.2%
Houston County	209	0.8%	0.0%	0.0%	100.0%	1,368	5.5%	19.7%	33.3%	46.9%
Jefferson County	2,926	1.7%	10.9%	25.0%	64.1%	6,218	3.7%	14.8%	31.8%	53.4%
Lauderdale County	200	0.9%	0.0%	71.5%	28.5%	2,682	11.6%	62.0%	17.3%	20.7%
Lee County	1,023	1.9%	0.0%	41.2%	58.8%	1,932	3.5%	0.0%	100.0%	0.0%
Madison County	2,288	2.5%	12.1%	37.8%	50.2%	5,860	6.4%	17.6%	37.0%	45.4%
Marshall County	483	2.2%	57.1%	42.9%	0.0%	2,740	12.5%	13.5%	41.9%	44.5%
Mobile County	2,544	2.4%	9.4%	14.3%	76.2%	4,164	3.9%	22.6%	8.5%	68.9%
Montgomery County	579	0.9%	17.4%	14.0%	68.6%	1,405	2.2%	10.9%	30.5%	58.6%
Morgan County	273	0.9%	0.0%	0.0%	100.0%	2,964	10.2%	28.5%	33.3%	38.1%
Shelby County	791	1.6%	0.0%	0.0%	100.0%	3,300	6.7%	10.9%	42.5%	46.5%
Tuscaloosa County	2,067	2.9%	0.0%	81.7%	18.3%	3,240	4.5%	9.4%	39.3%	51.3%
Alaska										
Anchorage Municipality	8,453	9.1%	22.1%	36.0%	41.9%	11,450	12.3%	15.3%	42.7%	42.0%
Fairbanks North Star Borough	1,737	5.0%	9.2%	0.0%	90.8%	3,621	10.4%	4.5%	82.7%	12.8%
Matanuska-Susitna Borough	392	1.4%	0.0%	41.8%	58.2%	1,828	6.6%	9.5%	49.8%	40.8%
Arizona										
Cochise County	409	1.4%	31.5%	0.0%	68.5%	16,329	55.5%	17.2%	36.7%	46.2%
Coconino County	1,556	3.0%	4.9%	78.6%	16.5%	7,184	13.9%	8.5%	60.7%	30.8%
Maricopa County	45,395	4.2%	10.0%	32.9%	57.2%	401,716	37.1%	17.8%	39.6%	42.6%
Mohave County	513	1.3%	0.0%	0.0%	100.0%	10,584	26.8%	18.6%	34.6%	46.8%
Navajo County	32	0.1%	18.8%	81.3%	0.0%	2,742	10.5%	19.7%	38.8%	41.5%
Pima County	10,300	3.9%	6.2%	50.0%	43.7%	118,148	44.2%	16.1%	44.1%	39.8%
Pinal County	1,133	1.2%	28.2%	3.4%	68.4%	37,899	40.9%	18.2%	38.8%	43.0%
Yavapai County	541	1.4%	0.0%	55.5%	44.5%	8,396	21.1%	15.4%	45.4%	39.1%
Yuma County	919	1.6%	23.6%	8.1%	68.3%	40,796	70.6%	16.6%	42.1%	41.3%
Arkansas										
Benton County	3,024	4.8%	11.0%	40.8%	48.2%	12,661	20.1%	18.8%	39.3%	41.9%
Craighead County	571	1.8%	0.0%	100.0%	0.0%	1,957	6.2%	22.9%	45.8%	31.3%
Faulkner County	670	1.7%	7.3%	61.9%	30.7%	2,546	6.3%	23.9%	32.2%	43.9%
Garland County	na	na	na	na	na	716	3.4%	28.9%	29.7%	41.3%
Pulacki County	2,641	2.5%	10.0%	32.0%	48.1%	6,998	6.0%	1.5%	39.3%	59.1%
Saline County	397	1.5%	16.1%	0.0%	83.9%	2,106	7.8%	0.0%	52.2%	47.8%
Sebastian County	1,426	4.4%	5.4%	37.0%	57.6%	4,123	12.7%	15.4%	45.2%	39.4%
Washington County	2,660	3.6%	11.0%	48.2%	40.9%	12,188	16.7%	16.8%	43.8%	39.4%
California										
Alameda County	124,088	28.6%	11.0%	30.3%	58.7%	114,150	26.3%	14.6%	35.3%	50.1%
Butte County	4,011	6.0%	9.7%	63.4%	26.9%	13,160	19.8%	14.4%	54.3%	31.3%
Contra Costa County	38,759	14.7%	17.3%	34.5%	48.2%	83,840	31.7%	17.3%	38.8%	43.9%
El Dorado County	1,862	4.9%	11.3%	25.9%	62.8%	7,405	19.4%	21.6%	37.5%	40.9%
Fresno County	32,672	11.6%	12.9%	33.3%	53.8%	161,608	57.5%	17.2%	38.5%	44.3%
Humboldt County	1,421	3.7%	14.6%	21.8%	63.5%	5,146	13.5%	3.8%	52.7%	43.5%
Imperial County	184	0.4%	0.0%	0.0%	100.0%	43,290	87.2%	17.0%	38.8%	44.1%
Kern County	11,183	4.4%	13.8%	32.7%	53.5%	149,248	58.5%	16.9%	39.5%	43.6%
Kings County	1,663	3.6%	19.5%	18.4%	62.1%	26,550	57.1%	15.9%	38.0%	46.1%
Los Angeles County	367,408	13.0%	11.1%	33.1%	55.7%	1,510,266	53.6%	15.5%	38.7%	45.8%
Madera County	1,099	2.6%	0.0%	79.4%	20.6%	27,957	67.3%	17.3%	38.4%	44.3%
Marin County	2,527	5.4%	13.0%	16.4%	70.6%	10,739	22.8%	12.1%	41.6%	46.3%
Merced County	5,975	7.6%	12.3%	59.2%	28.5%	50,041	63.9%	18.2%	40.1%	41.7%
Monterey County	5,773	4.8%	17.1%	31.4%	51.5%	77,360	64.4%	15.5%	37.9%	46.6%
Napa County	2,687	8.0%	7.4%	71.2%	21.4%	14,767	44.2%	18.0%	39.1%	42.9%
Nevada County	243	1.3%	43.2%	0.0%	56.8%	2,519	13.3%	0.0%	47.5%	52.5%
Orange County	150,178	18.2%	12.9%	35.0%	52.1%	337,686	41.0%	16.3%	38.9%	44.8%
Placer County	6,374	7.8%	13.8%	38.5%	47.7%	13,997	17.2%	19.0%	35.3%	45.7%
Riverside County	37,687	6.0%	15.5%	40.4%	44.2%	354,985	56.9%	18.1%	39.3%	42.6%
Sacramento County	64,534	16.1%	12.8%	30.8%	56.4%	109,093	27.3%	15.9%	37.1%	47.0%
San Bernardino County	38,558	6.2%	12.9%	32.6%	54.5%	362,660	58.3%	17.1%	39.2%	43.7%
San Diego County	102,183	10.8%	10.1%	33.2%	56.7%	360,053	38.1%	14.9%	39.3%	45.7%
San Francisco County	81,678	31.8%	8.2%	30.9%	60.9%	41,597	16.2%	10.3%	29.7%	59.9%
San Joaquin County	29,923	15.3%	13.4%	33.9%	52.7%	91,032	46.7%	18.4%	37.8%	43.7%
San Luis Obispo County	4,060	5.0%	3.4%	60.4%	36.2%	22,634	27.7%	12.9%	45.9%	41.2%
San Mateo County	48,344	27.2%	10.9%	26.6%	62.5%	55,736	31.4%	14.7%	36.2%	49.1%
Santa Barbara County	10,440	7.7%	5.7%	67.5%	26.8%	65,414	48.0%	15.1%	46.0%	38.9%
Santa Clara County	165,178	33.6%	12.8%	29.3%	57.9%	150,882	30.7%	15.0%	37.7%	47.3%
Santa Cruz County	6,147	7.5%	0.0%	58.6%	41.4%	29,919	36.7%	14.4%	49.6%	36.0%
Shasta County	1,796	4.3%	17.8%	47.5%	34.7%	5,365	12.9%	18.7%	45.0%	36.3%
Solano County	15,775	14.1%	14.8%	32.9%	52.3%	36,003	32.1%	16.7%	38.2%	45.1%
Sonoma County	4,964	4.2%	11.0%	32.1%	56.9%	40,184	33.9%	17.5%	39.2%	43.3%
Stanislaus County	8,138	5.4%	13.7%	30.0%	56.3%	76,951	51.2%	17.6%	37.9%	44.4%
Sutter County	3,247	12.9%	5.9%	33.1%	61.0%	8,179	32.5%	11.5%	40.5%	48.0%
Tulare County	4,356	3.3%	13.2%	32.9%	53.9%	93,066	70.9%	18.2%	38.1%	43.7%
Ventura County	14,769	6.7%	11.9%	33.1%	55.0%	112,031	50.8%	16.4%	38.4%	45.2%
Yolo County	16,218	22.0%	4.9%	67.9%	27.2%	22,858	31.0%	13.1%	46.0%	40.9%

Table B-2: Counties—Race and Hispanic Origin by Age—*Continued*

	White, Non-Hispanic					Black, Non-Hispanic				
	Millennial Population		Percent by Age			Millennial Population		Percent by Age		
	Number	Percent	15 to 17	18 to 24	25 to 33	Number	Percent	15 to 17	18 to 24	25 to 33
Colorado										
Adams County	65,573	47.7%	13.3%	27.1%	59.6%	4,728	3.4%	22.1%	27.1%	50.8%
Arapahoe County	91,698	55.1%	14.0%	30.2%	55.8%	14,394	8.7%	15.4%	32.2%	52.4%
Boulder County	75,079	75.2%	11.2%	50.4%	38.4%	1,281	1.3%	0.0%	57.3%	42.7%
Denver County	113,383	53.2%	3.4%	20.5%	76.0%	18,354	8.6%	9.4%	35.1%	55.6%
Douglas County	54,312	80.4%	24.0%	35.8%	40.2%	1,313	1.9%	30.5%	16.8%	52.7%
El Paso County	128,485	65.2%	13.6%	37.4%	48.9%	13,757	7.0%	10.4%	30.1%	59.6%
Jefferson County	99,410	71.2%	14.3%	35.0%	50.7%	2,824	2.0%	7.5%	9.3%	83.1%
Larimer County	80,344	78.9%	10.8%	46.5%	42.7%	1,088	1.1%	0.0%	51.8%	48.2%
Mesa County	28,393	73.3%	14.5%	36.4%	49.2%	749	1.9%	21.0%	11.7%	67.3%
Pueblo County	18,042	44.4%	14.0%	36.7%	49.3%	394	1.0%	0.0%	60.9%	39.1%
Weld County	44,221	56.9%	13.9%	38.7%	47.4%	3,147	4.0%	35.8%	29.6%	34.6%
Connecticut										
Fairfield County	120,058	53.7%	20.6%	38.8%	40.6%	29,251	13.1%	17.6%	39.8%	42.7%
Hartford County	118,809	54.2%	16.0%	36.8%	47.2%	32,660	14.9%	16.1%	40.7%	43.2%
Litchfield County	32,453	88.3%	19.2%	36.4%	44.3%	745	2.0%	7.8%	2.0%	90.2%
Middlesex County	29,133	77.9%	17.1%	39.3%	43.6%	2,428	6.5%	28.8%	34.6%	36.6%
New Haven County	122,705	55.8%	14.7%	38.2%	47.2%	32,327	14.7%	16.5%	45.7%	37.8%
New London County	49,162	69.2%	14.1%	39.4%	46.5%	4,263	6.0%	15.9%	39.0%	45.2%
Tolland County	38,467	79.0%	12.1%	58.3%	29.6%	2,313	4.8%	1.0%	50.9%	48.0%
Windham County	22,118	74.2%	15.8%	39.7%	44.5%	708	2.4%	21.0%	68.2%	10.7%
Delaware										
Kent County	27,024	58.5%	14.3%	34.9%	50.8%	12,676	27.5%	15.0%	49.1%	35.9%
New Castle County	78,874	53.0%	13.4%	35.3%	51.3%	36,421	24.5%	17.1%	37.0%	45.9%
Sussex County	27,180	65.1%	15.7%	33.7%	50.6%	7,584	18.2%	16.3%	51.9%	31.8%
Florida										
Alachua County	59,668	60.0%	6.9%	57.1%	36.1%	18,106	18.2%	12.8%	50.1%	37.1%
Bay County	32,542	73.3%	13.3%	32.1%	54.7%	6,043	13.6%	18.0%	39.2%	42.8%
Brevard County	80,284	66.7%	16.3%	35.1%	48.6%	14,918	12.4%	13.3%	45.2%	41.5%
Broward County	133,532	29.4%	15.5%	32.6%	52.0%	149,590	32.9%	15.8%	36.0%	48.2%
Charlotte County	17,421	75.3%	18.1%	37.5%	44.4%	2,074	9.0%	27.3%	41.9%	30.8%
Citrus County	17,880	86.7%	18.0%	37.1%	44.9%	662	3.2%	40.5%	11.5%	48.0%
Clay County	33,976	70.9%	19.8%	34.1%	46.1%	5,202	10.9%	26.2%	47.0%	26.8%
Collier County	29,561	43.5%	16.9%	36.7%	46.3%	6,030	8.9%	15.7%	47.5%	36.9%
Duval County	124,554	49.9%	11.3%	32.7%	56.0%	78,151	31.3%	15.6%	37.2%	47.1%
Escambia County	54,429	59.1%	10.1%	43.7%	46.2%	20,690	22.5%	17.2%	44.7%	38.1%
Flagler County	12,156	64.9%	18.6%	36.4%	45.0%	2,546	13.6%	12.1%	62.3%	25.6%
Hernando County	24,773	72.8%	18.3%	33.5%	48.2%	2,153	6.3%	13.3%	35.9%	50.8%
Highlands County	8,960	51.2%	15.6%	24.6%	59.8%	2,975	17.0%	18.7%	63.6%	17.8%
Hillsborough County	159,942	44.8%	13.3%	32.6%	54.1%	62,538	17.5%	16.6%	36.7%	46.6%
Indian River County	16,266	60.5%	18.1%	37.2%	44.7%	4,476	16.6%	1.4%	44.1%	54.5%
Lake County	38,129	60.0%	17.0%	32.7%	50.3%	8,480	13.4%	24.7%	30.3%	45.0%
Lee County	76,451	54.8%	14.9%	34.9%	50.2%	17,322	12.4%	19.2%	34.7%	46.1%
Leon County	57,188	52.4%	8.3%	58.5%	33.2%	36,656	33.6%	9.1%	59.6%	31.3%
Manatee County	41,261	57.5%	16.9%	35.3%	47.8%	8,672	12.1%	18.1%	35.4%	46.5%
Marion County	41,893	59.5%	15.9%	32.8%	51.3%	13,953	19.8%	18.6%	40.2%	41.2%
Martin County	19,089	68.5%	18.6%	35.2%	46.2%	2,956	10.6%	5.3%	69.7%	25.0%
Miami-Dade County	95,854	14.1%	14.9%	31.6%	53.5%	130,934	19.3%	14.4%	37.1%	48.5%
Okaloosa County	37,455	68.5%	12.4%	34.2%	53.4%	7,123	13.0%	11.9%	31.0%	57.1%
Orange County	149,837	39.2%	10.1%	35.5%	54.5%	80,582	21.1%	15.2%	38.3%	46.5%
Osceola County	23,922	27.9%	16.0%	33.7%	50.3%	9,299	10.8%	16.6%	38.3%	45.1%
Palm Beach County	133,094	43.6%	15.5%	35.7%	48.8%	72,711	23.8%	17.6%	36.9%	45.5%
Pasco County	69,646	68.1%	17.9%	33.8%	48.3%	7,461	7.3%	9.9%	52.6%	37.4%
Pinellas County	124,607	64.8%	13.9%	33.4%	52.7%	26,133	13.6%	18.3%	36.5%	45.2%
Polk County	81,315	51.6%	15.3%	34.3%	50.4%	27,082	17.2%	14.3%	39.5%	46.2%
Santa Rosa County	37,593	76.6%	20.5%	35.2%	44.3%	3,529	7.2%	21.7%	25.8%	52.5%
Sarasota County	30,975	48.3%	14.4%	31.8%	53.7%	15,373	24.0%	16.3%	46.2%	37.5%
Seminole County	32,778	80.2%	16.6%	32.4%	51.0%	2,682	6.6%	11.1%	32.3%	56.6%
St. Johns County	47,704	72.1%	16.4%	35.1%	48.5%	5,791	8.8%	19.3%	37.9%	42.8%
St. Lucie County	64,507	56.9%	16.2%	33.8%	50.0%	14,664	12.9%	18.1%	32.6%	49.3%
Sumter County	6,299	58.3%	15.1%	49.9%	35.1%	2,231	20.7%	39.2%	19.1%	41.7%
Volusia County	71,682	63.6%	14.0%	35.4%	50.6%	17,059	15.1%	13.1%	41.3%	45.5%
Georgia										
Bartow County	18,194	74.0%	18.1%	35.8%	46.2%	2,610	10.6%	19.0%	31.3%	49.6%
Bibb County	14,179	34.7%	12.2%	39.6%	48.2%	23,844	58.3%	16.6%	40.5%	42.9%
Carroll County	21,282	62.4%	13.4%	43.5%	43.1%	9,712	28.5%	14.8%	59.9%	25.3%
Chatham County	39,047	45.6%	8.8%	33.7%	57.6%	34,655	40.5%	13.4%	44.0%	42.6%
Cherokee County	41,271	74.8%	18.8%	33.8%	47.4%	3,780	6.8%	19.3%	43.1%	37.6%
Clarke County	34,900	62.8%	1.3%	69.3%	29.4%	11,638	20.9%	12.0%	59.3%	28.7%
Clayton County	6,064	8.0%	9.4%	28.3%	62.3%	54,338	71.8%	15.9%	37.9%	46.2%
Cobb County	86,930	45.7%	14.6%	34.7%	50.7%	58,225	30.6%	14.7%	36.0%	49.3%
Columbia County	23,988	62.6%	18.0%	32.0%	50.0%	6,611	17.3%	17.3%	36.8%	45.9%
Coweta County	22,802	68.7%	18.9%	34.0%	47.1%	6,630	20.0%	19.4%	42.4%	38.2%
DeKalb County	51,246	25.6%	7.9%	28.3%	63.7%	110,238	55.0%	14.7%	35.8%	49.5%
Dougherty County	7,797	31.0%	18.2%	38.7%	43.1%	16,196	64.4%	15.1%	47.0%	37.9%
Douglas County	12,838	36.3%	17.7%	36.8%	45.5%	18,063	51.1%	20.7%	37.9%	41.4%

Table B-2: Counties—Race and Hispanic Origin by Age—*Continued*

	Asian, Non-Hispanic					Hispanic				
	Millennial Population		Percent by Age			Millennial Population		Percent by Age		
	Number	Percent	15 to 17	18 to 24	25 to 33	Number	Percent	15 to 17	18 to 24	25 to 33
Colorado										
Adams County	5,672	4.1%	8.7%	33.8%	57.5%	56,377	41.0%	20.1%	36.4%	43.6%
Arapahoe County	8,808	5.3%	16.6%	29.7%	53.6%	42,107	25.3%	17.7%	37.9%	44.4%
Boulder County	4,143	4.1%	3.7%	55.2%	41.1%	15,538	15.6%	16.7%	47.7%	35.6%
Denver County	8,631	4.1%	1.3%	36.0%	62.7%	64,047	30.1%	15.0%	33.6%	51.5%
Douglas County	2,168	3.2%	9.2%	28.8%	61.9%	6,139	9.1%	23.2%	56.2%	20.6%
El Paso County	4,652	2.4%	15.1%	39.1%	45.8%	38,427	19.5%	12.9%	36.4%	50.7%
Jefferson County	4,326	3.1%	11.4%	47.2%	41.4%	27,959	20.0%	17.3%	36.1%	46.6%
Larimer County	3,438	3.4%	22.7%	42.3%	35.0%	13,815	13.6%	12.0%	37.0%	51.0%
Mesa County	432	1.1%	0.0%	100.0%	0.0%	7,408	19.1%	12.7%	44.2%	43.1%
Pueblo County	377	0.9%	30.0%	70.0%	0.0%	20,795	51.2%	17.5%	38.1%	44.5%
Weld County	1,262	1.6%	6.7%	44.9%	48.4%	27,088	34.8%	20.9%	35.8%	43.3%
Connecticut										
Fairfield County	12,585	5.6%	15.5%	24.9%	59.6%	54,684	24.5%	14.2%	37.7%	48.1%
Hartford County	11,968	5.5%	11.6%	28.3%	60.1%	49,005	22.3%	15.3%	38.5%	46.2%
Litchfield County	1,011	2.8%	38.8%	40.9%	20.3%	2,116	5.8%	0.2%	51.7%	48.2%
Middlesex County	1,168	3.1%	0.0%	81.6%	18.4%	2,970	7.9%	16.4%	50.7%	32.9%
New Haven County	10,601	4.8%	13.4%	34.6%	52.1%	47,864	21.8%	16.2%	38.9%	44.9%
New London County	3,576	5.0%	13.6%	34.3%	52.1%	9,109	12.8%	15.2%	49.9%	34.9%
Tolland County	3,545	7.3%	2.2%	67.9%	30.0%	3,383	6.9%	15.8%	44.0%	40.1%
Windham County	660	2.2%	16.5%	50.6%	32.9%	5,484	18.4%	10.1%	32.6%	57.3%
Delaware										
Kent County	1,082	2.3%	22.2%	64.6%	13.2%	3,533	7.7%	17.0%	46.4%	36.5%
New Castle County	9,367	6.3%	9.1%	30.1%	60.8%	18,734	12.6%	16.3%	32.7%	51.0%
Sussex County	403	1.0%	18.6%	26.1%	55.3%	5,900	14.1%	12.8%	36.8%	50.4%
Florida										
Alachua County	7,614	7.7%	5.5%	61.9%	32.6%	11,714	11.8%	5.4%	61.7%	32.9%
Bay County	921	2.1%	8.8%	11.4%	79.8%	2,589	5.8%	15.9%	42.6%	41.4%
Brevard County	1,703	1.4%	23.5%	50.8%	25.7%	16,607	13.8%	18.0%	37.7%	44.3%
Broward County	16,241	3.6%	8.3%	34.7%	57.0%	143,291	31.5%	14.6%	34.4%	51.0%
Charlotte County	974	4.2%	0.0%	38.8%	61.2%	1,730	7.5%	31.5%	53.5%	15.0%
Citrus County	341	1.7%	50.1%	49.9%	0.0%	1,211	5.9%	14.1%	50.9%	35.0%
Clay County	957	2.0%	0.0%	60.0%	40.0%	5,101	10.6%	7.1%	38.4%	54.4%
Collier County	1,151	1.7%	14.8%	19.3%	65.9%	28,493	41.9%	14.8%	37.3%	48.0%
Duval County	12,271	4.9%	13.7%	24.5%	61.8%	26,607	10.7%	14.4%	39.4%	46.2%
Escambia County	2,872	3.1%	0.0%	40.3%	59.7%	7,741	8.4%	11.4%	44.8%	43.8%
Flagler County	348	1.9%	0.0%	26.7%	73.3%	2,844	15.2%	32.0%	53.4%	14.5%
Hernando County	474	1.4%	0.0%	49.8%	50.2%	5,693	16.7%	23.0%	32.2%	44.8%
Highlands County	na	na	na	na	na	5,006	28.6%	36.5%	31.2%	32.3%
Hillsborough County	13,886	3.9%	12.0%	31.5%	56.5%	107,674	30.1%	15.7%	35.9%	48.4%
Indian River County	87	0.3%	0.0%	0.0%	100.0%	5,312	19.8%	18.8%	51.4%	29.8%
Lake County	951	1.5%	35.9%	16.5%	47.6%	13,697	21.6%	19.9%	42.4%	37.7%
Lee County	2,551	1.8%	17.0%	32.3%	50.6%	30,016	27.8%	16.5%	35.3%	48.2%
Leon County	3,164	2.9%	2.0%	56.8%	41.2%	8,311	7.6%	2.7%	69.0%	28.3%
Manatee County	1,715	2.4%	15.7%	46.6%	37.7%	17,982	25.1%	18.9%	39.7%	41.4%
Marion County	2,257	3.2%	5.3%	61.7%	33.0%	11,270	16.0%	17.4%	38.2%	44.5%
Martin County	98	0.4%	0.0%	68.4%	31.6%	5,712	20.5%	18.5%	44.8%	36.7%
Miami-Dade County	11,008	1.6%	11.1%	30.7%	58.2%	434,686	64.1%	13.8%	35.0%	51.2%
Okaloosa County	1,336	2.4%	3.1%	57.7%	39.1%	6,736	12.3%	11.3%	37.1%	51.0%
Orange County	20,595	5.4%	10.8%	41.1%	48.0%	119,171	31.2%	15.1%	38.8%	46.2%
Osceola County	1,370	1.6%	0.0%	39.1%	60.9%	49,256	57.4%	17.8%	36.9%	45.3%
Palm Beach County	8,873	2.9%	10.5%	33.3%	56.2%	81,321	26.6%	16.1%	35.4%	48.5%
Pasco County	2,080	2.0%	21.5%	43.6%	34.9%	19,597	19.2%	19.5%	37.8%	42.7%
Pinellas County	7,251	3.8%	10.8%	29.2%	60.0%	26,167	13.6%	15.2%	33.6%	51.2%
Polk County	3,736	2.4%	15.5%	32.3%	52.3%	41,460	26.3%	17.9%	35.1%	47.0%
Santa Rosa County	2,434	5.0%	8.0%	39.2%	52.8%	3,953	8.1%	20.1%	40.9%	39.0%
Sarasota County	1,509	2.4%	5.2%	21.5%	73.2%	14,656	22.9%	15.6%	30.2%	54.2%
Seminole County	1,293	3.2%	0.0%	39.0%	61.0%	2,287	5.6%	26.0%	22.4%	51.6%
St. Johns County	1,543	2.3%	0.0%	37.8%	62.2%	8,940	13.5%	14.9%	34.0%	51.0%
St. Lucie County	3,458	3.1%	25.3%	59.2%	15.4%	27,327	24.1%	11.9%	34.1%	54.0%
Sumter County	108	1.0%	46.3%	0.0%	53.7%	1,813	16.8%	12.4%	54.4%	33.2%
Volusia County	2,660	2.4%	22.3%	38.5%	39.2%	18,653	16.6%	17.4%	40.3%	42.3%
Georgia										
Bartow County	81	0.3%	100.0%	0.0%	0.0%	3,323	13.5%	10.4%	56.6%	33.0%
Bibb County	776	1.9%	28.0%	41.1%	30.9%	1,550	3.8%	11.7%	31.6%	56.6%
Carroll County	na	na	na	na	na	2,642	7.7%	30.7%	8.4%	60.9%
Chatham County	2,688	3.1%	2.1%	59.0%	38.9%	6,982	8.2%	10.0%	41.8%	48.3%
Cherokee County	362	0.7%	27.6%	47.0%	25.4%	7,552	13.7%	21.3%	36.3%	42.5%
Clarke County	3,166	5.7%	2.6%	72.9%	24.5%	4,674	8.4%	15.1%	55.8%	29.0%
Clayton County	3,376	4.5%	15.3%	33.4%	51.3%	10,313	13.6%	17.3%	36.5%	46.2%
Cobb County	11,166	5.9%	11.9%	25.6%	62.6%	27,223	14.3%	17.7%	35.7%	46.6%
Columbia County	893	2.3%	17.1%	82.9%	0.0%	3,400	8.9%	8.2%	35.4%	56.4%
Coweta County	344	1.0%	8.7%	91.3%	0.0%	3,114	9.4%	22.8%	18.8%	58.4%
DeKalb County	14,414	7.2%	6.9%	25.4%	67.7%	17,565	8.8%	13.0%	31.3%	55.7%
Dougherty County	341	1.4%	0.0%	0.0%	100.0%	814	3.2%	0.0%	84.3%	15.7%
Douglas County	117	0.3%	0.0%	0.0%	100.0%	3,650	10.3%	19.9%	43.2%	36.9%

Table B-2: Counties—Race and Hispanic Origin by Age—*Continued*

	White, Non-Hispanic					Black, Non-Hispanic				
	Millennial Population		Percent by Age			Millennial Population		Percent by Age		
	Number	Percent	15 to 17	18 to 24	25 to 33	Number	Percent	15 to 17	18 to 24	25 to 33
Georgia—Cont.										
Fayette County	14,164	60.5%	24.7%	49.3%	26.0%	5,573	23.8%	28.0%	34.9%	37.1%
Floyd County	16,929	69.4%	17.5%	36.4%	46.1%	3,599	14.8%	1.2%	44.8%	54.0%
Forsyth County	32,628	74.0%	26.1%	35.6%	38.3%	982	2.2%	8.7%	66.4%	24.9%
Fulton County	105,049	36.7%	12.2%	31.1%	56.7%	130,984	45.8%	14.6%	37.5%	48.0%
Gwinnett County	77,463	33.8%	18.4%	37.0%	44.6%	66,699	29.1%	20.1%	37.2%	42.6%
Hall County	26,177	53.8%	16.8%	35.5%	47.7%	4,667	9.6%	15.8%	45.0%	39.2%
Henry County	24,152	42.5%	19.8%	35.5%	44.8%	23,781	41.9%	24.3%	43.7%	32.1%
Houston County	19,391	50.0%	18.3%	35.3%	46.4%	14,359	37.0%	18.0%	37.6%	44.4%
Lowndes County	20,602	52.7%	9.9%	42.6%	47.5%	14,326	36.7%	12.5%	51.1%	36.4%
Muscogee County	23,933	39.4%	8.9%	40.9%	50.2%	25,899	42.7%	13.2%	38.2%	48.7%
Newton County	9,429	35.5%	12.7%	38.6%	48.7%	13,762	51.8%	25.1%	26.3%	48.5%
Paulding County	26,633	68.7%	19.5%	33.9%	46.6%	6,890	17.8%	24.3%	31.1%	44.6%
Richmond County	20,472	33.4%	9.1%	38.0%	52.9%	34,206	55.8%	14.0%	38.7%	47.3%
Whitfield County	13,545	47.9%	17.7%	37.0%	45.3%	1,412	5.0%	0.0%	41.4%	58.6%
Hawaii										
Hawaii County	9,981	22.5%	10.8%	38.8%	50.4%	10,951	24.7%	3.1%	50.2%	46.7%
Honolulu County	65,323	23.9%	4.6%	38.0%	57.4%	247	0.1%	0.0%	0.0%	100.0%
Maui County	8,980	22.9%	7.4%	27.1%	65.5%	1,777	4.5%	34.0%	57.3%	8.6%
Idaho										
Ada County	86,785	77.0%	15.6%	32.3%	52.1%	1,347	1.2%	28.5%	71.5%	0.0%
Bonneville County	22,296	81.2%	15.8%	31.5%	52.7%	9,492	34.6%	5.3%	74.6%	20.1%
Canyon County	34,305	64.6%	19.5%	33.3%	47.2%	328,141	617.9%	16.3%	40.1%	43.7%
Kootenai County	31,408	89.5%	16.5%	34.1%	49.4%	4,503	12.8%	4.5%	75.1%	20.4%
Illinois										
Champaign County	49,926	62.2%	7.6%	58.9%	33.5%	13,349	16.6%	19.8%	41.5%	38.6%
Cook County	548,662	38.6%	10.5%	28.6%	60.9%	7,941	0.6%	17.1%	51.1%	31.9%
DeKalb County	26,689	70.4%	10.0%	53.2%	36.8%	5,594	14.8%	17.7%	27.5%	54.7%
DuPage County	140,408	62.2%	17.1%	37.0%	46.0%	2,553	1.1%	8.9%	65.0%	26.0%
Kane County	63,584	49.7%	19.6%	35.6%	44.8%	14,074	11.0%	17.9%	44.6%	37.5%
Kankakee County	18,822	66.2%	16.0%	41.2%	42.8%	979	3.4%	0.0%	20.7%	79.3%
Kendall County	22,614	69.4%	22.5%	31.6%	45.9%	585	1.8%	25.5%	61.4%	13.2%
Lake County	97,236	55.7%	19.6%	42.1%	38.4%	3,255	1.9%	23.5%	54.7%	21.9%
LaSalle County	20,424	81.0%	18.2%	35.7%	46.1%	4,449	17.6%	16.6%	44.1%	39.3%
Macon County	55,166	80.2%	21.0%	37.7%	41.3%	7,175	10.4%	16.8%	46.4%	36.8%
Madison County	44,314	77.7%	10.2%	56.2%	33.7%	9,848	17.3%	16.8%	49.0%	34.1%
McHenry County	16,515	67.1%	16.0%	38.9%	45.1%	3,259	13.2%	9.8%	50.1%	40.1%
McLean County	52,567	81.0%	15.3%	34.1%	50.6%	22,984	35.4%	18.3%	40.1%	41.6%
Peoria County	31,986	64.3%	13.4%	34.1%	52.6%	7,137	14.4%	16.3%	36.5%	47.2%
Rock Island County	22,097	67.6%	15.1%	36.7%	48.2%	782	2.4%	12.1%	10.0%	77.9%
Sangamon County	35,037	55.6%	16.2%	34.2%	49.7%	22,439	35.6%	20.3%	40.3%	39.4%
St. Clair County	34,330	71.6%	15.8%	33.5%	50.6%	9,934	20.7%	13.9%	40.5%	45.6%
Tazewell County	28,026	92.8%	17.2%	32.5%	50.4%	11,428	37.8%	12.6%	36.6%	50.8%
Will County	98,331	59.6%	20.1%	37.0%	42.9%	1,668	1.0%	22.2%	25.2%	52.5%
Winnebago County	41,203	60.3%	14.8%	36.6%	48.6%	2,349	3.4%	4.4%	78.7%	16.9%
Indiana										
Allen County	66,368	70.2%	16.2%	35.1%	48.6%	4,020	4.3%	15.1%	16.8%	68.0%
Clark County	22,702	84.8%	15.8%	32.0%	52.1%	3,660	13.7%	13.5%	43.4%	43.1%
Delaware County	33,048	88.9%	10.1%	60.0%	29.9%	3,187	8.6%	15.3%	12.0%	72.7%
Elkhart County	35,581	69.2%	18.2%	34.7%	47.1%	452	0.9%	13.9%	39.2%	46.9%
Hamilton County	58,616	83.3%	22.8%	30.3%	46.8%	29,003	41.2%	21.8%	39.2%	39.1%
Hendricks County	30,678	79.1%	19.8%	33.4%	46.8%	4,169	10.8%	17.5%	21.7%	60.9%
Johnson County	32,108	90.4%	18.7%	36.4%	44.9%	2,941	8.3%	25.8%	32.9%	41.3%
Lake County	56,070	48.4%	16.8%	34.3%	48.9%	73,517	63.5%	16.0%	37.0%	47.0%
LaPorte County	19,065	73.6%	16.9%	36.3%	46.8%	2,250	8.7%	0.0%	66.4%	33.6%
Madison County	25,449	80.4%	16.7%	35.7%	47.6%	2,103	6.6%	17.5%	32.0%	50.4%
Marion County	143,392	54.0%	10.9%	32.2%	56.9%	10,409	3.9%	19.0%	43.9%	37.2%
Monroe County	49,883	77.8%	6.4%	61.7%	32.0%	3,652	5.7%	0.3%	75.6%	24.1%
Porter County	31,550	78.6%	17.7%	38.0%	44.3%	4,848	12.1%	11.6%	31.9%	56.5%
St. Joseph County	48,501	67.7%	14.5%	43.0%	42.4%	3,118	4.4%	7.4%	47.3%	45.3%
Tippecanoe County	54,882	74.0%	7.6%	59.2%	33.2%	3,883	5.2%	10.5%	27.3%	62.2%
Vanderburgh County	38,614	81.4%	12.6%	37.1%	50.3%	1,013	2.1%	7.2%	36.1%	56.7%
Vigo County	25,901	78.1%	10.6%	50.7%	38.7%	1,896	5.7%	18.3%	52.6%	29.1%
Iowa										
Black Hawk County	32,301	78.2%	9.9%	50.6%	39.5%	3,754	9.1%	13.1%	69.9%	17.0%
Dubuque County	22,678	89.6%	17.3%	43.9%	38.8%	9,667	38.2%	21.1%	42.9%	36.0%
Johnson County	43,138	78.2%	7.5%	54.3%	38.3%	92	0.2%	10.9%	89.1%	0.0%
Linn County	45,014	79.8%	16.1%	35.9%	48.0%	3,680	6.5%	9.9%	28.1%	62.0%
Polk County	94,299	76.0%	14.1%	32.8%	53.2%	775	0.6%	33.3%	53.9%	12.8%
Pottawattamie County	18,875	86.3%	16.7%	35.4%	47.9%	2,439	11.2%	48.5%	24.5%	27.0%
Scott County	32,986	77.5%	14.8%	34.2%	51.0%	2,042	4.8%	0.0%	72.0%	28.0%
Story County	35,847	79.1%	6.2%	65.4%	28.4%	7,554	16.7%	18.1%	35.1%	46.8%
Woodbury County	19,059	67.3%	15.4%	37.7%	46.9%	12,295	43.4%	18.9%	30.0%	51.0%
Kansas										
Douglas County	35,778	76.5%	7.2%	58.8%	34.0%	2,402	5.1%	12.3%	22.2%	65.5%

Table B-2: Counties—Race and Hispanic Origin by Age—*Continued*

	Asian, Non-Hispanic					Hispanic				
	Millennial Population		Percent by Age			Millennial Population		Percent by Age		
	Number	Percent	15 to 17	18 to 24	25 to 33	Number	Percent	15 to 17	18 to 24	25 to 33
Georgia—Cont.										
Fayette County	1,489	6.4%	22.0%	49.2%	28.9%	1,605	6.9%	53.2%	28.7%	18.1%
Floyd County	na	na	na	na	na	3,155	12.9%	17.6%	34.1%	48.3%
Forsyth County	3,655	8.3%	18.7%	12.8%	68.5%	5,473	12.4%	20.4%	27.9%	51.7%
Fulton County	22,885	8.0%	11.0%	34.6%	54.5%	21,494	7.5%	17.2%	29.5%	53.2%
Gwinnett County	25,622	11.2%	16.4%	34.5%	49.1%	53,773	23.5%	18.4%	34.8%	46.7%
Hall County	947	1.9%	20.9%	21.5%	57.6%	16,152	33.2%	19.7%	39.2%	41.1%
Henry County	2,586	4.6%	21.8%	25.1%	53.2%	4,506	7.9%	30.3%	47.0%	22.6%
Houston County	629	1.6%	0.0%	42.0%	58.0%	3,067	7.9%	5.4%	51.2%	43.4%
Lowndes County	1,132	2.9%	0.0%	49.6%	50.4%	2,259	5.8%	11.9%	53.2%	34.9%
Muscogee County	1,909	3.1%	15.7%	23.2%	61.1%	5,909	9.7%	7.3%	47.0%	45.7%
Newton County	na	na	na	na	na	1,684	6.3%	40.6%	21.3%	38.1%
Paulding County	727	1.9%	0.0%	30.9%	69.1%	3,370	8.7%	21.9%	69.7%	8.4%
Richmond County	1,223	2.0%	0.0%	31.4%	68.6%	3,969	6.5%	12.8%	43.0%	44.3%
Whitfield County	402	1.4%	0.0%	36.1%	63.9%	12,534	44.3%	16.5%	36.3%	47.2%
Hawaii										
Hawaii County	6,604	14.9%	10.5%	37.5%	52.0%	7,256	16.4%	11.4%	36.7%	51.9%
Honolulu County	79,882	29.2%	13.2%	37.7%	49.2%	34,270	12.5%	9.4%	44.1%	46.5%
Maui County	9,647	24.6%	19.4%	29.0%	51.7%	5,826	14.9%	19.4%	24.1%	56.5%
Idaho										
Ada County	1,579	1.4%	0.0%	33.1%	66.9%	18,225	16.2%	16.4%	34.6%	49.0%
Bonneville County	719	2.6%	15.3%	27.4%	57.3%	3,909	14.2%	11.6%	31.4%	56.9%
Canyon County	462	0.9%	60.2%	26.2%	13.6%	16,402	30.9%	19.5%	37.9%	42.5%
Kootenai County	383	1.1%	0.0%	0.0%	100.0%	2,188	6.2%	8.9%	27.4%	63.7%
Illinois										
Champaign County	13,645	17.0%	2.3%	68.6%	29.1%	4,891	6.1%	13.7%	55.9%	30.4%
Cook County	109,365	7.7%	8.2%	28.5%	63.2%	401,287	28.3%	16.6%	36.6%	46.8%
DeKalb County	1,141	3.0%	0.0%	80.8%	19.2%	4,854	12.8%	8.7%	58.9%	32.5%
DuPage County	25,356	11.2%	15.9%	37.2%	46.8%	40,461	17.9%	15.8%	37.3%	47.0%
Kane County	4,167	3.3%	21.0%	20.3%	58.7%	49,510	38.7%	17.8%	39.4%	42.8%
Kankakee County	220	0.8%	0.0%	0.0%	100.0%	3,015	10.6%	19.5%	50.6%	29.9%
Kendall County	1,417	4.3%	5.2%	0.0%	94.8%	5,207	16.0%	22.8%	34.3%	43.0%
Lake County	11,036	6.3%	18.4%	31.9%	49.7%	47,352	27.1%	19.7%	39.4%	40.9%
LaSalle County	439	1.7%	0.0%	79.0%	21.0%	3,166	12.6%	19.2%	31.0%	49.8%
Macon County	858	1.2%	39.5%	7.6%	52.9%	10,710	15.6%	22.3%	39.5%	38.2%
Madison County	2,971	5.2%	0.0%	1.6%	98.4%	4,696	8.2%	21.9%	56.6%	21.5%
McHenry County	562	2.3%	28.6%	38.1%	33.3%	954	3.9%	0.0%	26.5%	73.5%
McLean County	1,184	1.8%	0.0%	63.4%	36.6%	2,961	4.6%	15.3%	23.0%	61.7%
Peoria County	2,166	6.0%	3.0%	29.0%	68.0%	2,945	5.9%	19.0%	29.9%	51.1%
Rock Island County	871	2.7%	12.1%	28.9%	59.0%	5,479	16.8%	19.3%	45.8%	35.0%
Sangamon County	1,401	2.2%	0.0%	0.0%	100.0%	1,992	3.2%	2.3%	16.5%	81.2%
St. Clair County	2,025	4.2%	21.4%	67.8%	10.8%	1,549	3.2%	26.8%	31.1%	42.1%
Tazewell County	703	2.3%	27.0%	39.1%	33.9%	459	1.5%	0.0%	0.0%	100.0%
Will County	6,379	3.9%	17.3%	25.3%	57.4%	34,448	20.9%	18.4%	39.4%	42.1%
Winnebago County	1,580	2.3%	20.0%	9.2%	70.8%	13,263	19.4%	17.3%	35.9%	46.9%
Indiana										
Allen County	4,644	4.9%	14.5%	55.7%	29.8%	8,348	8.8%	18.7%	47.6%	33.7%
Clark County	348	1.3%	0.0%	0.0%	100.0%	2,048	7.7%	15.7%	47.9%	36.4%
Delaware County	346	0.9%	83.5%	0.0%	16.5%	846	2.3%	0.0%	100.0%	0.0%
Elkhart County	653	1.3%	0.0%	54.1%	45.9%	8,934	17.4%	21.4%	48.2%	30.4%
Hamilton County	3,427	4.9%	34.3%	10.4%	55.3%	2,707	3.8%	21.4%	33.9%	44.7%
Hendricks County	1,548	4.0%	15.5%	44.3%	40.2%	1,833	4.7%	0.0%	0.0%	100.0%
Johnson County	1,381	3.9%	9.9%	29.0%	61.0%	1,230	3.5%	16.5%	14.6%	68.9%
Lake County	2,059	1.8%	17.1%	28.4%	54.5%	25,141	21.7%	20.2%	40.6%	39.2%
LaPorte County	19	0.1%	0.0%	100.0%	0.0%	2,087	8.1%	17.1%	31.7%	51.2%
Madison County	na	na	na	na	na	1,544	4.9%	14.4%	41.1%	44.4%
Marion County	9,706	3.7%	5.5%	23.0%	71.5%	29,595	11.1%	15.1%	32.5%	52.3%
Monroe County	6,518	10.2%	1.8%	84.6%	13.6%	3,464	5.4%	11.1%	61.7%	27.2%
Porter County	590	1.5%	25.8%	63.2%	11.0%	5,021	12.5%	19.9%	58.7%	21.4%
St. Joseph County	2,490	3.5%	8.4%	46.5%	45.1%	7,406	10.3%	17.9%	34.9%	47.2%
Tippecanoe County	9,103	12.3%	4.9%	68.4%	26.7%	4,856	6.5%	9.2%	64.4%	26.4%
Vanderburgh County	524	1.1%	33.6%	41.8%	24.6%	1,884	4.0%	15.2%	51.7%	33.1%
Vigo County	188	0.6%	0.0%	100.0%	0.0%	770	2.3%	13.4%	40.4%	46.2%
Iowa										
Black Hawk County	1,204	2.9%	0.0%	59.2%	40.8%	2,858	6.9%	24.8%	54.1%	21.2%
Dubuque County	580	2.3%	45.3%	27.1%	27.6%	534	2.1%	46.1%	29.2%	24.7%
Johnson County	4,625	8.4%	6.6%	59.4%	34.0%	3,863	7.0%	17.6%	61.2%	21.2%
Linn County	2,581	4.6%	0.0%	0.0%	100.0%	2,158	3.8%	30.8%	10.1%	59.1%
Polk County	5,191	4.2%	12.6%	26.1%	61.3%	12,285	9.9%	12.8%	41.4%	45.8%
Pottawattamie County	342	1.6%	0.0%	0.0%	100.0%	2,156	9.9%	6.7%	33.3%	60.0%
Scott County	885	2.1%	19.2%	42.6%	38.2%	3,343	7.9%	25.5%	40.3%	34.2%
Story County	5,653	12.5%	0.0%	69.0%	31.0%	956	2.1%	17.5%	69.2%	13.3%
Woodbury County	901	3.2%	0.0%	61.2%	38.8%	4,767	16.8%	17.7%	34.4%	47.8%
Kansas										
Douglas County	2,632	5.6%	4.8%	77.6%	17.6%	3,210	6.9%	0.0%	33.6%	66.4%

Table B-2: Counties—Race and Hispanic Origin by Age—*Continued*

	White, Non-Hispanic					Black, Non-Hispanic				
	Millennial Population		Percent by Age			Millennial Population		Percent by Age		
	Number	Percent	15 to 17	18 to 24	25 to 33	Number	Percent	15 to 17	18 to 24	25 to 33
Kansas—Cont.										
Johnson County	108,922	76.2%	17.3%	31.8%	50.8%	9,748	6.8%	19.3%	46.1%	34.7%
Sedgwick County	88,585	66.2%	15.0%	32.7%	52.3%	1,399	1.0%	0.0%	66.6%	33.4%
Shawnee County	32,660	74.1%	17.1%	33.3%	49.6%	699	1.6%	36.1%	48.1%	15.9%
Wyandotte County	16,405	37.6%	12.1%	28.3%	59.6%	928	2.1%	0.0%	25.3%	74.7%
Kentucky										
Boone County	25,768	86.2%	20.1%	33.8%	46.1%	14,217	47.5%	15.7%	38.7%	45.6%
Campbell County	22,535	90.0%	10.9%	37.4%	51.6%	3,210	12.8%	18.5%	25.2%	56.3%
Daviess County	20,843	89.7%	18.6%	37.3%	44.1%	43,503	187.2%	16.3%	40.9%	42.7%
Fayette County	69,668	71.3%	9.2%	45.6%	45.3%	2,716	2.8%	15.9%	37.6%	46.5%
Hardin County	20,872	75.3%	22.0%	32.5%	45.5%	3,901	14.1%	19.8%	50.4%	29.7%
Jefferson County	126,305	65.6%	13.6%	33.4%	53.0%	7,434	3.9%	23.1%	32.0%	45.0%
Kenton County	36,295	88.7%	15.4%	32.1%	52.6%	9,299	22.7%	16.5%	33.2%	50.3%
Warren County	30,223	77.6%	11.3%	51.5%	37.2%	33,886	87.0%	16.4%	39.7%	43.9%
Louisiana										
Ascension Parish	19,326	62.0%	17.4%	31.8%	50.8%	13,288	42.6%	18.2%	39.0%	42.8%
Bossier Parish	19,439	56.2%	15.3%	31.1%	53.6%	64,760	187.2%	14.7%	44.9%	40.5%
Caddo Parish	26,174	40.9%	13.7%	32.0%	54.3%	31,267	48.8%	13.4%	36.2%	50.4%
Calcasieu Parish	35,398	66.5%	15.5%	33.9%	50.6%	20,180	37.9%	16.4%	42.0%	41.6%
East Baton Rouge Parish	61,394	43.3%	9.4%	47.8%	42.8%	5,104	3.6%	22.8%	34.2%	43.0%
Jefferson Parish	53,541	48.9%	13.1%	31.3%	55.6%	2,196	2.0%	13.6%	46.0%	40.4%
Lafayette Parish	43,514	62.2%	12.8%	31.8%	55.4%	63,963	91.4%	14.2%	37.8%	48.0%
Lafourche Parish	17,690	70.1%	14.8%	37.6%	47.5%	18,495	73.3%	16.7%	40.2%	43.1%
Livingston Parish	30,548	86.0%	15.2%	32.5%	52.4%	8,631	24.3%	18.4%	35.9%	45.7%
Orleans Parish	36,629	32.3%	5.0%	25.2%	69.8%	7,677	6.8%	21.2%	34.4%	44.4%
Ouachita Parish	22,812	52.0%	14.7%	36.0%	49.3%	11,807	26.9%	16.0%	47.6%	36.4%
Rapides Parish	20,250	61.8%	17.0%	34.5%	48.4%	4,992	15.2%	17.8%	40.0%	42.2%
St. Tammany Parish	41,439	74.0%	17.7%	33.6%	48.8%	414	0.7%	59.7%	30.2%	9.9%
Tangipahoa Parish	22,115	60.5%	14.1%	34.1%	51.9%	1,022	2.8%	0.0%	45.0%	55.0%
Terrebonne Parish	18,457	66.9%	15.8%	33.1%	51.0%	351	1.3%	0.0%	100.0%	0.0%
Maine										
Androscoggin County	21,063	86.5%	16.0%	38.7%	45.3%	976	4.0%	0.0%	100.0%	0.0%
Cumberland County	63,314	88.6%	15.6%	35.9%	48.5%	56	0.1%	0.0%	0.0%	100.0%
Kennebec County	24,372	94.0%	16.8%	38.1%	45.1%	23,849	92.0%	13.3%	32.3%	54.4%
Penobscot County	36,391	89.1%	12.9%	41.3%	45.8%	62,967	154.1%	16.0%	36.7%	47.2%
York County	41,678	93.6%	18.0%	32.9%	49.1%	1,455	3.3%	26.9%	50.0%	23.1%
Maryland										
Anne Arundel County	91,996	64.8%	14.7%	34.1%	51.2%	1,094	0.8%	7.3%	51.4%	41.3%
Baltimore County	111,116	53.4%	13.2%	35.7%	51.1%	16,910	8.1%	19.2%	39.0%	41.8%
Carroll County	33,745	88.5%	19.8%	38.4%	41.8%	4,779	12.5%	8.2%	49.6%	42.1%
Cecil County	20,000	80.8%	18.4%	34.7%	46.9%	8,078	32.6%	18.7%	35.9%	45.4%
Charles County	15,755	39.8%	16.0%	33.9%	50.0%	14,370	36.3%	18.3%	29.1%	52.6%
Frederick County	42,641	72.0%	17.4%	35.5%	47.1%	46,285	78.2%	16.0%	35.2%	48.7%
Harford County	43,072	73.6%	17.9%	35.2%	46.9%	142,966	244.2%	14.5%	36.8%	48.7%
Howard County	37,839	50.7%	18.2%	35.4%	46.4%	4,761	6.4%	2.4%	50.7%	46.8%
Montgomery County	92,643	38.2%	17.8%	33.8%	48.4%	6,396	2.6%	17.8%	38.9%	43.3%
Prince George's County	33,185	13.6%	5.4%	43.8%	50.7%	9,012	3.7%	10.6%	50.8%	38.6%
St. Mary's County	20,617	72.1%	16.3%	35.2%	48.6%	105,460	369.0%	14.2%	37.6%	48.3%
Washington County	25,814	70.9%	17.3%	34.5%	48.2%	2,372	6.5%	9.7%	12.3%	78.0%
Wicomico County	17,304	57.5%	11.0%	53.2%	35.9%	1,532	5.1%	8.6%	87.1%	4.3%
Massachusetts										
Barnstable County	32,235	84.8%	16.7%	40.8%	42.5%	6,039	15.9%	24.0%	42.7%	33.4%
Berkshire County	23,973	83.7%	15.6%	43.0%	41.4%	10,348	36.1%	18.0%	47.9%	34.1%
Bristol County	109,557	78.9%	14.3%	37.9%	47.8%	2,250	1.6%	13.0%	31.6%	55.4%
Essex County	121,628	64.4%	16.6%	37.2%	46.2%	22,499	11.9%	13.8%	37.7%	48.4%
Hampden County	68,197	55.7%	13.5%	41.9%	44.6%	16,135	13.2%	22.3%	29.9%	47.8%
Hampshire County	46,970	81.3%	13.5%	51.6%	34.9%	12,180	21.1%	19.4%	40.4%	40.2%
Middlesex County	292,399	68.9%	14.2%	35.3%	50.6%	49,625	11.7%	13.7%	39.3%	47.0%
Norfolk County	112,320	69.2%	19.8%	35.2%	45.0%	10,340	6.4%	12.9%	43.4%	43.7%
Plymouth County	88,295	77.4%	19.2%	41.5%	39.3%	723	0.6%	8.9%	1.0%	90.2%
Suffolk County	144,803	49.3%	3.2%	34.3%	62.5%	6,315	2.1%	10.6%	36.7%	52.8%
Worcester County	147,435	73.5%	17.1%	39.2%	43.8%	2,622	1.3%	8.0%	27.2%	64.8%
Michigan										
Allegan County	22,261	82.7%	19.3%	34.3%	46.4%	1,931	7.2%	17.2%	39.6%	43.2%
Bay County	21,614	89.2%	17.7%	34.7%	47.5%	20,529	84.7%	18.1%	43.9%	38.0%
Berrien County	23,735	69.5%	17.1%	35.9%	47.1%	11,837	34.6%	6.8%	55.7%	37.5%
Calhoun County	26,490	83.0%	18.5%	33.7%	47.7%	4,081	12.8%	17.1%	35.3%	47.6%
Eaton County	20,252	78.9%	16.8%	38.0%	45.2%	9,105	35.5%	17.2%	57.9%	24.9%
Genesee County	68,377	69.4%	17.3%	36.0%	46.6%	19,027	19.3%	16.6%	43.1%	40.3%
Ingham County	67,750	65.6%	8.3%	55.1%	36.6%	729	0.7%	8.4%	29.9%	61.7%
Jackson County	30,505	80.2%	16.7%	37.1%	46.2%	81	0.2%	0.0%	32.1%	67.9%
Kalamazoo County	60,502	75.1%	11.1%	50.2%	38.6%	29,875	37.1%	17.7%	40.5%	41.8%
Kent County	121,245	70.2%	14.1%	33.3%	52.5%	1,439	0.8%	16.2%	83.8%	0.0%
Lenawee County	19,635	84.4%	18.8%	41.7%	39.6%	7,887	33.9%	12.2%	35.6%	52.2%
Livingston County	38,035	92.3%	21.6%	37.0%	41.3%	45,788	111.1%	17.3%	41.0%	41.7%

Table B-2: Counties—Race and Hispanic Origin by Age—*Continued*

| | Asian, Non-Hispanic | | | | | Hispanic | | | | |
| | Millennial Population | | Percent by Age | | | Millennial Population | | Percent by Age | | |
	Number	Percent	15 to 17	18 to 24	25 to 33	Number	Percent	15 to 17	18 to 24	25 to 33
Kansas—Cont.										
Johnson County	8,159	5.7%	16.5%	25.0%	58.4%	12,683	8.9%	18.7%	28.6%	52.7%
Sedgwick County	6,603	4.9%	13.5%	25.7%	60.8%	20,576	15.4%	19.4%	28.1%	52.5%
Shawnee County	193	0.4%	44.6%	55.4%	0.0%	6,414	14.6%	19.3%	50.9%	29.8%
Wyandotte County	2,501	5.7%	10.3%	39.0%	50.7%	13,791	31.6%	18.7%	35.2%	46.1%
Kentucky										
Boone County	na	na	na	na	na	2,268	7.6%	2.2%	22.0%	75.7%
Campbell County	466	1.9%	0.0%	99.1%	0.9%	861	3.4%	0.0%	100.0%	0.0%
Daviess County	341	1.5%	0.0%	26.4%	73.6%	546	2.3%	38.8%	31.3%	29.9%
Fayette County	3,157	3.2%	2.7%	25.8%	71.6%	6,587	6.7%	13.0%	37.6%	49.3%
Hardin County	962	3.5%	0.0%	0.0%	100.0%	1,749	6.3%	24.0%	45.5%	30.6%
Jefferson County	4,891	2.5%	14.4%	22.2%	63.4%	11,725	6.1%	13.0%	32.7%	54.3%
Kenton County	324	0.8%	66.4%	33.6%	0.0%	1,243	3.0%	0.0%	26.5%	73.5%
Warren County	1,288	3.3%	18.9%	50.9%	30.1%	2,511	6.4%	25.3%	53.8%	20.8%
Louisiana										
Ascension Parish	431	1.4%	0.0%	0.0%	100.0%	3,036	9.7%	16.0%	35.6%	48.4%
Bossier Parish	1,108	3.2%	28.5%	24.6%	46.8%	3,721	10.8%	15.7%	17.3%	67.0%
Caddo Parish	951	1.5%	19.5%	21.5%	59.1%	1,985	3.1%	10.3%	29.8%	59.9%
Calcasieu Parish	962	1.8%	0.0%	49.1%	50.9%	2,272	4.3%	0.0%	39.3%	60.7%
East Baton Rouge Parish	6,563	4.6%	7.9%	58.2%	33.9%	6,388	4.5%	4.7%	37.2%	58.0%
Jefferson Parish	4,170	3.8%	14.8%	29.7%	55.5%	17,569	16.1%	10.0%	32.5%	57.5%
Lafayette Parish	1,866	2.7%	19.0%	26.1%	54.9%	3,269	4.7%	3.8%	61.1%	35.1%
Lafourche Parish	103	0.4%	0.0%	0.0%	100.0%	1,199	4.8%	12.9%	22.7%	64.4%
Livingston Parish	na	na	na	na	na	1,449	4.1%	0.0%	13.3%	86.7%
Orleans Parish	4,291	3.8%	6.3%	32.5%	61.2%	7,195	6.4%	7.8%	25.0%	67.2%
Ouachita Parish	817	1.9%	0.0%	32.8%	67.2%	904	2.1%	8.7%	0.0%	91.3%
Rapides Parish	526	1.6%	0.0%	75.3%	24.7%	2,208	6.7%	19.6%	52.2%	28.2%
St. Tammany Parish	1,168	2.1%	0.0%	18.1%	81.9%	3,583	6.4%	33.8%	3.8%	62.4%
Tangipahoa Parish	285	0.8%	0.0%	100.0%	0.0%	1,993	5.4%	10.1%	77.8%	12.1%
Terrebonne Parish	395	1.4%	0.0%	51.6%	48.4%	871	3.2%	0.0%	0.0%	100.0%
Maine										
Androscoggin County	447	1.8%	0.0%	22.1%	77.9%	1,465	6.0%	15.6%	56.0%	28.5%
Cumberland County	936	1.3%	8.2%	45.9%	45.8%	3,529	4.9%	19.9%	62.7%	17.5%
Kennebec County	582	2.2%	0.0%	36.4%	63.6%	582	2.2%	0.0%	100.0%	0.0%
Penobscot County	1,028	2.5%	0.0%	10.1%	89.9%	961	2.4%	26.7%	73.3%	0.0%
York County	300	0.7%	9.3%	90.7%	0.0%	1,132	2.5%	36.1%	8.8%	55.0%
Maryland										
Anne Arundel County	6,894	4.9%	8.3%	37.4%	54.3%	13,554	9.5%	14.4%	38.1%	47.5%
Baltimore County	13,864	6.7%	13.2%	37.5%	49.3%	13,403	6.4%	11.1%	25.8%	63.1%
Carroll County	820	2.2%	8.5%	58.1%	33.4%	1,683	4.4%	20.0%	39.0%	41.1%
Cecil County	249	1.0%	0.0%	100.0%	0.0%	1,719	6.9%	0.0%	63.0%	37.0%
Charles County	1,479	3.7%	4.4%	28.1%	67.5%	2,593	6.6%	26.0%	57.2%	16.8%
Frederick County	3,063	5.2%	8.7%	38.8%	52.5%	6,009	10.2%	18.9%	62.7%	18.4%
Harford County	1,722	2.9%	0.0%	50.8%	49.2%	3,752	6.4%	12.3%	31.2%	56.5%
Howard County	12,460	16.7%	17.2%	28.6%	54.1%	5,668	7.6%	18.0%	39.9%	42.1%
Montgomery County	34,269	14.1%	15.4%	30.4%	54.2%	56,630	23.3%	13.7%	33.0%	53.3%
Prince George's County	12,484	5.1%	7.7%	38.8%	53.6%	46,619	19.1%	14.4%	34.6%	50.9%
St. Mary's County	585	2.0%	19.5%	46.0%	34.5%	1,245	4.4%	25.1%	60.3%	14.6%
Washington County	789	2.2%	14.8%	46.4%	38.8%	2,250	6.2%	10.3%	28.7%	61.0%
Wicomico County	942	3.1%	0.0%	39.0%	61.0%	2,094	7.0%	32.0%	53.0%	15.0%
Massachusetts										
Barnstable County	443	1.2%	44.7%	55.3%	0.0%	1,089	2.9%	49.8%	32.0%	18.2%
Berkshire County	743	2.6%	20.5%	47.6%	31.9%	1,468	5.1%	14.5%	62.9%	22.6%
Bristol County	3,561	2.6%	11.0%	47.3%	41.7%	13,820	9.9%	18.0%	40.6%	41.5%
Essex County	7,508	4.0%	14.5%	36.8%	48.7%	47,552	25.2%	16.2%	38.6%	45.2%
Hampden County	3,336	2.7%	4.4%	17.4%	78.1%	37,219	30.4%	18.1%	42.0%	40.0%
Hampshire County	2,516	4.4%	0.0%	97.4%	2.6%	4,346	7.5%	7.9%	51.1%	41.0%
Middlesex County	54,855	12.9%	8.2%	35.0%	56.8%	40,069	9.4%	11.6%	38.0%	50.4%
Norfolk County	18,204	11.2%	13.2%	27.2%	59.6%	10,328	6.4%	17.2%	44.5%	38.4%
Plymouth County	2,089	1.8%	0.0%	40.2%	59.8%	6,115	5.4%	7.7%	51.8%	40.5%
Suffolk County	28,890	9.8%	5.8%	43.0%	51.3%	61,680	21.0%	11.6%	38.1%	50.4%
Worcester County	10,910	5.4%	15.5%	37.0%	47.5%	26,016	13.0%	17.7%	42.3%	40.1%
Michigan										
Allegan County	105	0.4%	0.0%	0.0%	100.0%	3,103	11.5%	13.3%	56.7%	30.1%
Bay County	132	0.5%	0.0%	18.9%	81.1%	847	3.5%	22.1%	53.7%	24.2%
Berrien County	1,350	4.0%	22.3%	57.2%	20.5%	1,702	5.0%	24.0%	43.5%	32.5%
Calhoun County	742	2.3%	0.0%	42.9%	57.1%	1,348	4.2%	12.6%	53.6%	33.8%
Eaton County	930	3.6%	0.0%	61.5%	38.5%	1,254	4.9%	33.2%	50.3%	16.5%
Genesee County	1,699	1.7%	0.0%	12.1%	87.9%	2,728	2.8%	19.0%	48.7%	32.3%
Ingham County	9,291	9.0%	8.2%	53.1%	38.7%	8,130	7.9%	24.4%	42.8%	32.8%
Jackson County	843	2.2%	0.0%	16.7%	83.3%	1,815	4.8%	0.0%	41.5%	58.5%
Kalamazoo County	2,771	3.4%	9.1%	23.0%	68.0%	5,164	6.4%	2.7%	55.7%	41.7%
Kent County	6,029	3.5%	18.9%	27.7%	53.4%	21,787	12.6%	19.4%	35.0%	45.6%
Lenawee County	na	na	na	na	na	1,674	7.2%	1.4%	55.4%	43.1%
Livingston County	285	0.7%	20.4%	58.9%	20.7%	1,502	3.6%	10.8%	69.4%	19.8%

Table B-2: Counties—Race and Hispanic Origin by Age—*Continued*

| | White, Non-Hispanic | | | | | Black, Non-Hispanic | | | | |
| | Millennial Population | | Percent by Age | | | Millennial Population | | Percent by Age | | |
	Number	Percent	15 to 17	18 to 24	25 to 33	Number	Percent	15 to 17	18 to 24	25 to 33
Michigan—Cont.										
Macomb County	153,087	74.4%	17.0%	34.9%	48.1%	1,484	0.7%	6.9%	93.1%	0.0%
Monroe County	30,665	91.5%	18.7%	34.7%	46.6%	8,054	24.0%	17.5%	45.8%	36.7%
Muskegon County	29,610	71.0%	16.8%	36.0%	47.2%	1,707	4.1%	5.5%	16.9%	77.6%
Oakland County	199,478	69.3%	17.3%	34.3%	48.4%	16,258	5.6%	11.4%	57.4%	31.2%
Ottawa County	62,513	78.7%	14.9%	48.1%	37.0%	188,075	236.9%	16.3%	38.7%	45.0%
Saginaw County	31,017	64.1%	15.0%	38.8%	46.2%	2,828	5.8%	16.8%	26.4%	56.8%
St. Clair County	30,390	86.5%	19.5%	37.3%	43.1%	364	1.0%	0.0%	56.3%	43.7%
Washtenaw County	81,733	66.3%	9.6%	52.1%	38.4%	2,683	2.2%	23.3%	24.0%	52.7%
Wayne County	199,288	44.9%	16.1%	34.3%	49.5%	47,183	10.6%	14.3%	32.2%	53.5%
Minnesota										
Anoka County	63,512	78.5%	18.1%	33.1%	48.7%	3,402	4.2%	13.4%	78.0%	8.6%
Carver County	19,547	89.3%	19.0%	37.2%	43.7%	18,654	85.2%	14.0%	32.2%	53.8%
Dakota County	76,678	77.6%	17.2%	33.5%	49.3%	1,066	1.1%	0.8%	29.0%	70.2%
Hennepin County	210,705	63.4%	11.5%	29.8%	58.7%	1,438	0.4%	34.8%	48.2%	17.0%
Olmsted County	28,306	77.0%	15.3%	31.3%	53.4%	1,908	5.2%	11.5%	42.1%	46.4%
Ramsey County	86,428	56.7%	9.9%	34.7%	55.4%	4,522	3.0%	17.7%	2.6%	79.6%
Scott County	47,684	87.3%	13.2%	42.9%	43.9%	44	0.1%	100.0%	0.0%	0.0%
St. Louis County	24,631	75.0%	18.6%	30.8%	50.7%	11,778	35.9%	23.1%	42.0%	34.9%
Stearns County	40,278	85.2%	12.6%	49.5%	38.0%	13,612	28.8%	17.2%	37.9%	44.9%
Washington County	44,524	77.4%	20.3%	35.4%	44.3%	53,116	92.3%	14.9%	40.3%	44.7%
Wright County	26,730	96.5%	20.9%	32.5%	46.6%	8,105	29.3%	17.6%	39.0%	43.4%
Mississippi										
DeSoto County	26,709	62.2%	19.0%	33.9%	47.1%	13,258	30.9%	17.4%	40.9%	41.7%
Harrison County	32,983	59.8%	13.4%	35.6%	51.0%	9,291	16.8%	21.3%	33.0%	45.6%
Hinds County	15,114	21.3%	12.5%	36.6%	50.9%	7,436	10.5%	10.0%	50.1%	40.0%
Jackson County	21,509	64.5%	17.2%	33.5%	49.3%	844	2.5%	0.0%	91.6%	8.4%
Madison County	11,024	42.9%	18.3%	32.4%	49.4%	2,677	10.4%	19.7%	19.2%	61.2%
Rankin County	25,667	69.3%	18.3%	31.2%	50.4%	432	1.2%	73.8%	26.2%	0.0%
Missouri										
Boone County	50,821	77.1%	7.7%	54.5%	37.8%	4,643	7.0%	11.5%	37.5%	51.1%
Cass County	20,612	91.3%	18.9%	34.0%	47.1%	41,276	182.9%	16.5%	37.9%	45.7%
Clay County	46,463	80.1%	16.3%	32.0%	51.7%	329	0.6%	0.0%	74.2%	25.8%
Franklin County	21,894	95.1%	18.4%	34.0%	47.6%	1,029	4.5%	58.8%	39.2%	2.0%
Greene County	73,770	84.4%	11.7%	45.0%	43.3%	656	0.8%	0.0%	32.6%	67.4%
Jackson County	106,444	60.3%	13.2%	30.1%	56.7%	3,598	2.0%	7.1%	32.7%	60.3%
Jasper County	24,700	78.0%	17.4%	36.2%	46.3%	71,033	224.3%	17.5%	39.4%	43.1%
Jefferson County	49,737	94.0%	17.3%	32.2%	50.5%	42,443	80.2%	14.3%	38.4%	47.3%
Platte County	18,239	74.9%	15.3%	35.2%	49.4%	143	0.6%	0.0%	84.6%	15.4%
St. Charles County	79,746	84.9%	17.6%	34.7%	47.7%	18,952	20.2%	16.1%	31.8%	52.1%
St. Louis County	144,804	59.6%	16.4%	35.9%	47.7%	4,845	2.0%	0.0%	77.7%	22.3%
Montana										
Flathead County	16,916	84.9%	18.0%	35.9%	46.1%	64,746	325.1%	12.0%	37.4%	50.6%
Gallatin County	30,248	87.2%	12.1%	47.4%	40.5%	3,378	9.7%	7.8%	36.7%	55.6%
Missoula County	29,860	83.0%	12.7%	41.6%	45.7%	2,879	8.0%	3.1%	57.1%	39.8%
Yellowstone County	29,584	76.1%	12.2%	38.1%	49.6%	286	0.7%	0.0%	89.5%	10.5%
Nebraska										
Douglas County	98,590	66.1%	12.7%	31.7%	55.6%	154	0.1%	0.0%	100.0%	0.0%
Lancaster County	74,384	78.6%	10.3%	49.3%	40.3%	303	0.3%	0.0%	100.0%	0.0%
Sarpy County	35,804	78.9%	16.9%	31.8%	51.4%	10,502	23.1%	11.2%	47.8%	41.0%
Nevada										
Clark County	196,855	35.9%	13.4%	29.6%	57.0%	12,709	2.3%	16.1%	40.5%	43.4%
Washoe County	65,539	56.6%	12.7%	33.1%	54.1%	18,612	16.1%	14.8%	40.8%	44.4%
New Hampshire										
Hillsborough County	79,978	82.7%	16.8%	36.7%	46.5%	25,339	26.2%	16.9%	38.4%	44.7%
Merrimack County	32,693	91.5%	17.5%	42.7%	39.7%	1,529	4.3%	36.6%	44.7%	18.6%
Rockingham County	58,839	88.9%	17.3%	38.3%	44.4%	7,874	11.9%	15.1%	27.7%	57.2%
Strafford County	34,709	88.6%	11.8%	51.7%	36.4%	83,172	212.2%	14.7%	37.0%	48.3%
New Jersey										
Atlantic County	33,069	49.7%	14.0%	41.1%	44.9%	6,406	9.6%	11.7%	34.2%	54.2%
Bergen County	105,899	50.9%	19.7%	38.7%	41.6%	22,189	10.7%	12.7%	35.0%	52.3%
Burlington County	67,144	62.5%	17.1%	35.4%	47.5%	1,879	1.7%	32.0%	60.4%	7.6%
Camden County	65,661	51.1%	15.2%	32.5%	52.3%	21,165	16.5%	15.2%	40.8%	43.9%
Cape May County	14,682	76.7%	15.6%	38.5%	45.9%	23,361	122.0%	15.7%	40.5%	43.8%
Cumberland County	17,873	44.9%	15.2%	31.6%	53.2%	12,152	30.5%	14.1%	41.7%	44.2%
Essex County	49,348	24.8%	17.4%	38.6%	43.9%	4,196	2.1%	6.6%	47.0%	46.4%
Gloucester County	53,043	76.3%	17.5%	35.8%	46.7%	4,806	6.9%	1.7%	20.4%	77.9%
Hudson County	59,124	28.9%	6.2%	20.9%	72.9%	17,484	8.6%	14.0%	41.3%	44.7%
Hunterdon County	21,228	78.1%	24.7%	40.0%	35.3%	6,992	25.7%	4.8%	49.0%	46.2%
Mercer County	44,375	46.2%	14.0%	45.8%	40.1%	718	0.7%	46.8%	22.8%	30.4%
Middlesex County	82,948	38.6%	14.5%	38.0%	47.5%	30,066	14.0%	16.6%	43.4%	40.0%
Monmouth County	98,879	70.2%	19.9%	38.1%	42.0%	611	0.4%	50.6%	44.5%	4.9%
Morris County	75,558	66.0%	20.5%	37.8%	41.7%	3,939	3.4%	10.3%	46.5%	43.2%
Ocean County	96,771	79.0%	17.6%	35.0%	47.4%	825	0.7%	0.0%	100.0%	0.0%
Passaic County	47,095	35.7%	15.5%	40.0%	44.5%	392	0.3%	0.0%	0.0%	100.0%

Table B-2: Counties—Race and Hispanic Origin by Age—*Continued*

	Asian, Non-Hispanic					Hispanic				
	Millennial Population		Percent by Age			Millennial Population		Percent by Age		
	Number	Percent	15 to 17	18 to 24	25 to 33	Number	Percent	15 to 17	18 to 24	25 to 33
Michigan—Cont.										
Macomb County	9,198	4.5%	21.9%	34.5%	43.6%	6,196	3.0%	13.1%	36.6%	50.4%
Monroe County	289	0.9%	0.0%	0.0%	100.0%	436	1.3%	0.0%	20.4%	79.6%
Muskegon County	115	0.3%	0.0%	3.5%	96.5%	2,706	6.5%	17.8%	51.4%	30.8%
Oakland County	20,990	7.3%	15.7%	29.9%	54.4%	14,480	5.0%	16.7%	32.2%	51.1%
Ottawa County	3,070	3.9%	13.4%	15.3%	71.3%	10,042	12.6%	17.9%	53.8%	28.3%
Saginaw County	1,716	3.5%	0.0%	36.9%	63.1%	4,818	10.0%	11.6%	39.6%	48.8%
St. Clair County	764	2.2%	73.2%	0.0%	26.8%	1,176	3.3%	2.8%	71.3%	25.9%
Washtenaw County	13,610	11.0%	4.8%	61.8%	33.4%	6,041	4.9%	11.5%	57.9%	30.6%
Wayne County	15,839	3.6%	15.1%	37.1%	47.8%	29,933	6.7%	20.1%	35.6%	44.3%
Minnesota										
Anoka County	5,848	7.2%	24.7%	27.9%	47.4%	4,218	5.2%	20.3%	63.3%	16.5%
Carver County	1,015	4.6%	0.0%	76.0%	24.0%	699	3.2%	0.0%	43.8%	56.2%
Dakota County	6,871	7.0%	12.5%	13.3%	74.2%	9,001	9.1%	18.7%	47.9%	33.4%
Hennepin County	34,905	10.5%	11.3%	28.7%	60.0%	22,746	6.8%	21.6%	36.1%	42.3%
Olmsted County	2,622	7.1%	0.0%	39.7%	60.3%	978	2.7%	26.2%	1.6%	72.2%
Ramsey County	28,919	19.0%	14.1%	39.6%	46.3%	12,426	8.1%	17.7%	29.3%	53.0%
Scott County	1,462	2.7%	10.4%	60.5%	29.1%	971	1.8%	0.0%	70.3%	29.7%
St. Louis County	3,536	10.8%	24.0%	15.0%	61.1%	2,164	6.6%	26.8%	31.9%	41.3%
Stearns County	1,843	3.9%	0.0%	50.7%	49.3%	2,224	4.7%	15.3%	49.3%	35.4%
Washington County	4,767	8.3%	15.2%	38.3%	46.6%	2,092	3.6%	20.4%	14.4%	65.2%
Wright County	na	na	na	na	na	769	2.8%	19.2%	54.5%	26.3%
Mississippi										
DeSoto County	924	2.2%	29.3%	54.0%	16.7%	2,988	7.0%	22.3%	43.6%	34.1%
Harrison County	1,943	3.5%	9.0%	39.9%	51.1%	4,623	8.4%	18.0%	45.0%	36.9%
Hinds County	1,178	1.7%	0.0%	22.5%	77.5%	1,281	1.8%	0.0%	15.9%	84.1%
Jackson County	427	1.3%	80.8%	19.2%	0.0%	2,313	6.9%	12.5%	44.5%	43.0%
Madison County	617	2.4%	32.4%	54.5%	13.1%	645	2.5%	0.0%	31.3%	68.7%
Rankin County	741	2.0%	30.6%	0.0%	69.4%	324	0.9%	41.7%	0.0%	58.3%
Missouri										
Boone County	3,738	5.7%	3.1%	52.1%	44.9%	2,463	3.7%	25.1%	52.9%	22.0%
Cass County	na	na	na	na	na	802	3.6%	14.3%	0.0%	85.7%
Clay County	958	1.7%	17.5%	53.2%	29.2%	3,458	6.0%	27.9%	30.7%	41.4%
Franklin County	238	1.0%	0.0%	0.0%	100.0%	140	0.6%	0.0%	0.0%	100.0%
Greene County	1,924	2.2%	0.0%	63.9%	36.1%	3,750	4.3%	12.7%	39.6%	47.7%
Jackson County	4,218	2.4%	7.4%	32.5%	60.1%	17,066	9.7%	17.0%	34.6%	48.4%
Jasper County	256	0.8%	73.0%	27.0%	0.0%	3,720	11.7%	24.7%	47.9%	27.4%
Jefferson County	411	0.8%	29.2%	48.4%	22.4%	456	0.9%	0.0%	21.9%	78.1%
Platte County	889	3.6%	0.0%	20.0%	80.0%	2,216	9.1%	1.2%	32.5%	66.2%
St. Charles County	2,047	2.2%	8.4%	23.8%	67.8%	4,081	4.3%	8.4%	65.8%	25.8%
St. Louis County	12,506	5.2%	17.5%	39.7%	43.0%	8,780	3.6%	14.1%	48.0%	37.6%
Montana										
Flathead County	25	0.1%	0.0%	0.0%	100.0%	344	1.7%	16.9%	46.8%	36.3%
Gallatin County	1,528	4.4%	0.0%	100.0%	0.0%	1,918	5.5%	9.3%	63.0%	27.7%
Missoula County	na	na	na	na	na	604	1.7%	24.3%	14.6%	61.1%
Yellowstone County	1,338	3.4%	11.2%	0.3%	88.5%	2,958	7.6%	1.5%	63.2%	35.4%
Nebraska										
Douglas County	6,706	4.5%	15.5%	38.2%	46.3%	20,203	13.5%	19.4%	30.6%	50.0%
Lancaster County	6,325	6.7%	0.0%	34.1%	65.9%	7,299	7.7%	14.2%	26.9%	58.9%
Sarpy County	750	1.7%	17.6%	28.4%	54.0%	4,679	10.3%	15.6%	51.6%	32.8%
Nevada										
Clark County	51,515	9.4%	11.9%	29.5%	58.6%	203,356	37.0%	17.0%	36.5%	46.5%
Washoe County	6,152	5.3%	8.3%	40.8%	50.9%	33,813	29.2%	16.6%	38.6%	44.9%
New Hampshire										
Hillsborough County	4,285	4.4%	19.4%	29.3%	51.2%	8,215	8.5%	19.7%	37.9%	42.4%
Merrimack County	645	1.8%	14.0%	17.1%	69.0%	1,461	4.1%	0.0%	58.3%	41.7%
Rockingham County	1,657	2.5%	18.2%	26.1%	55.8%	3,371	5.1%	15.8%	25.0%	59.2%
Strafford County	2,014	5.1%	13.7%	45.0%	41.3%	695	1.8%	0.0%	100.0%	0.0%
New Jersey										
Atlantic County	4,472	6.7%	15.5%	37.9%	46.6%	15,888	23.9%	17.7%	33.6%	48.6%
Bergen County	34,109	16.4%	15.7%	29.4%	55.0%	50,950	24.5%	16.8%	36.6%	46.6%
Burlington County	5,236	4.9%	15.1%	40.0%	45.0%	11,197	10.4%	17.6%	38.4%	44.0%
Camden County	7,994	6.2%	11.7%	31.6%	56.8%	26,200	20.4%	15.0%	40.0%	45.0%
Cape May County	189	1.0%	100.0%	0.0%	0.0%	2,645	13.8%	26.8%	3.6%	69.6%
Cumberland County	343	0.9%	29.2%	36.2%	34.7%	11,573	29.1%	13.9%	29.7%	56.4%
Essex County	9,811	4.9%	15.6%	36.4%	48.0%	50,989	25.6%	13.6%	36.3%	50.0%
Gloucester County	2,397	3.4%	29.5%	50.9%	19.5%	4,898	7.0%	15.5%	20.2%	64.4%
Hudson County	34,919	17.1%	5.1%	22.9%	71.9%	82,913	40.6%	13.3%	34.5%	52.3%
Hunterdon County	944	3.5%	0.0%	41.1%	58.9%	2,597	9.6%	17.6%	38.9%	43.4%
Mercer County	10,231	10.6%	18.1%	50.4%	31.5%	18,687	19.4%	12.6%	43.4%	44.0%
Middlesex County	51,872	24.2%	12.9%	31.4%	55.7%	51,049	23.8%	17.0%	39.9%	43.1%
Monmouth County	6,202	4.4%	19.7%	44.8%	35.5%	18,881	13.4%	15.5%	33.8%	50.7%
Morris County	12,892	11.3%	16.1%	31.2%	52.7%	19,628	17.2%	16.2%	34.3%	49.5%
Ocean County	2,543	2.1%	38.5%	19.2%	42.3%	15,150	12.4%	15.0%	37.3%	47.6%
Passaic County	8,054	6.1%	15.0%	29.2%	55.8%	57,851	43.8%	16.3%	36.9%	46.8%

Table B-2: Counties—Race and Hispanic Origin by Age—*Continued*

	White, Non-Hispanic					Black, Non-Hispanic				
	Millennial Population		Percent by Age			Millennial Population		Percent by Age		
	Number	Percent	15 to 17	18 to 24	25 to 33	Number	Percent	15 to 17	18 to 24	25 to 33
New Jersey—Cont.										
Somerset County	38,929	53.9%	21.1%	38.9%	40.0%	104	0.1%	0.0%	100.0%	0.0%
Sussex County	26,307	85.7%	20.4%	39.3%	40.3%	379	1.2%	0.0%	13.2%	86.8%
Union County	43,899	33.0%	19.4%	35.2%	45.4%	11,131	8.4%	12.1%	43.3%	44.6%
Warren County	18,887	82.6%	18.3%	38.1%	43.6%	117,235	512.7%	14.0%	36.6%	49.3%
New Mexico										
Bernalillo County	56,519	30.9%	12.0%	34.8%	53.2%	4,233	2.3%	13.1%	54.1%	32.8%
Doña Ana County	15,347	23.9%	10.7%	45.5%	43.8%	1,468	2.3%	16.8%	69.3%	13.9%
San Juan County	11,258	34.3%	20.1%	29.8%	50.1%	8,589	26.2%	10.7%	49.7%	39.6%
Sandoval County	10,164	33.2%	15.2%	33.0%	51.8%	37,260	121.6%	16.1%	40.6%	43.3%
Santa Fe County	8,572	27.7%	13.8%	32.1%	54.1%	3,219	10.4%	0.0%	46.0%	54.0%
New York										
Albany County	61,122	67.5%	11.3%	51.0%	37.7%	218,375	241.0%	14.1%	34.8%	51.0%
Bronx County	30,553	7.3%	12.7%	38.9%	48.4%	33,973	8.1%	14.8%	41.8%	43.4%
Broome County	40,994	74.6%	13.8%	49.1%	37.1%	39,823	72.5%	12.9%	39.8%	47.3%
Chautauqua County	25,703	80.9%	15.7%	41.9%	42.4%	55,866	175.9%	11.6%	36.1%	52.3%
Dutchess County	50,550	66.8%	15.7%	45.4%	38.9%	4,025	5.3%	19.7%	59.2%	21.2%
Erie County	168,019	70.0%	14.1%	35.1%	50.8%	4,725	2.0%	12.1%	43.4%	44.4%
Jefferson County	27,678	78.1%	12.4%	40.3%	47.3%	15,030	42.4%	17.4%	42.1%	40.5%
Kings County	267,646	35.5%	10.0%	26.0%	64.0%	558	0.1%	45.0%	0.0%	55.0%
Monroe County	132,037	65.5%	13.1%	38.2%	48.7%	10,163	5.0%	18.3%	44.0%	37.7%
Nassau County	174,751	55.5%	18.9%	39.5%	41.6%	305	0.1%	0.0%	50.5%	49.5%
New York County	244,953	47.1%	3.7%	23.5%	72.8%	866	0.2%	55.5%	20.3%	24.1%
Niagara County	41,255	83.5%	15.8%	36.7%	47.5%	107,413	217.3%	14.4%	36.2%	49.4%
Oneida County	43,507	75.9%	13.3%	40.2%	46.5%	3,359	5.9%	3.7%	44.9%	51.4%
Onondaga County	88,419	71.8%	14.8%	38.4%	46.8%	13,606	11.0%	15.3%	35.9%	48.8%
Ontario County	23,151	88.0%	15.2%	44.8%	40.0%	10,609	40.3%	20.3%	47.1%	32.6%
Orange County	57,480	59.8%	18.4%	42.2%	39.4%	1,746	1.8%	0.4%	56.9%	42.7%
Oswego County	28,806	89.8%	15.2%	41.9%	42.9%	582	1.8%	0.0%	44.8%	55.2%
Putnam County	17,194	79.8%	20.3%	40.2%	39.5%	4,780	22.2%	23.7%	28.3%	48.0%
Queens County	134,852	22.2%	9.7%	27.0%	63.4%	827	0.1%	9.9%	14.9%	75.2%
Rensselaer County	33,003	77.4%	13.5%	39.6%	46.9%	28,913	67.8%	18.0%	40.7%	41.3%
Richmond County	65,428	55.2%	15.3%	35.6%	49.1%	1,525	1.3%	2.6%	88.5%	8.9%
Rockland County	45,778	58.1%	21.6%	39.5%	38.9%	3,617	4.6%	21.8%	44.5%	33.6%
Saratoga County	27,660	86.2%	12.7%	48.3%	39.0%	1,047	3.3%	39.8%	37.3%	22.8%
Schenectady County	46,287	92.5%	17.3%	36.2%	46.5%	33,801	67.6%	16.0%	39.9%	44.1%
St. Lawrence County	25,211	65.6%	14.5%	35.2%	50.3%	6,236	16.2%	20.2%	40.9%	38.9%
Steuben County	19,903	87.8%	19.5%	39.5%	41.0%	2,037	9.0%	38.5%	28.0%	33.5%
Suffolk County	216,180	61.6%	18.7%	39.2%	42.1%	4,318	1.2%	9.0%	43.1%	47.9%
Tompkins County	28,913	64.9%	7.0%	64.1%	28.9%	7,282	16.3%	27.0%	34.1%	38.9%
Ulster County	31,404	72.4%	12.9%	39.7%	47.3%	2,987	6.9%	11.3%	51.5%	37.1%
Wayne County	16,991	82.5%	18.7%	34.2%	47.0%	4,175	20.3%	9.5%	37.9%	52.6%
Westchester County	102,933	45.3%	20.3%	40.4%	39.3%	6,951	3.1%	10.2%	44.3%	45.5%
North Carolina										
Alamance County	23,247	61.5%	15.7%	39.4%	45.0%	34,236	90.5%	14.1%	40.0%	45.9%
Brunswick County	15,162	71.1%	16.7%	34.0%	49.3%	3,916	18.4%	34.1%	14.2%	51.7%
Buncombe County	48,989	78.9%	12.7%	33.5%	53.8%	33,002	53.2%	12.9%	39.4%	47.7%
Cabarrus County	31,468	69.6%	16.6%	33.7%	49.7%	26,289	58.2%	14.3%	46.0%	39.7%
Catawba County	24,616	67.7%	17.4%	38.0%	44.6%	9,377	25.8%	19.0%	30.2%	50.8%
Cleveland County	14,123	63.5%	16.3%	42.6%	41.1%	53,395	240.2%	12.8%	44.8%	42.3%
Craven County	18,471	64.5%	11.1%	44.7%	44.2%	7,481	26.1%	14.6%	45.3%	40.2%
Cumberland County	43,728	43.2%	10.0%	38.3%	51.7%	1,258	1.2%	0.0%	25.4%	74.6%
Davidson County	28,215	77.7%	18.6%	35.2%	46.2%	5,193	14.3%	20.7%	45.9%	33.5%
Durham County	34,655	38.6%	6.6%	27.9%	65.5%	5,934	6.6%	16.5%	49.1%	34.4%
Forsyth County	47,665	51.6%	14.7%	36.8%	48.4%	90,717	98.2%	14.5%	37.6%	47.9%
Gaston County	35,313	69.3%	16.3%	35.8%	47.9%	3,171	6.2%	21.3%	26.6%	52.1%
Guilford County	60,621	44.1%	14.4%	38.8%	46.8%	10,877	7.9%	18.1%	37.4%	44.5%
Harnett County	20,388	56.8%	13.2%	35.1%	51.7%	9,829	27.4%	14.5%	29.6%	55.8%
Henderson County	15,482	75.4%	12.4%	37.9%	49.7%	10,935	53.3%	15.7%	46.1%	38.3%
Iredell County	27,329	69.8%	22.0%	36.6%	41.5%	6,276	16.0%	2.6%	58.6%	38.8%
Johnston County	27,411	65.4%	19.6%	31.7%	48.7%	19,983	47.7%	14.6%	46.5%	38.9%
Mecklenburg County	125,344	43.9%	11.6%	30.5%	57.9%	2,129	0.7%	4.4%	63.7%	31.9%
Moore County	13,142	67.4%	17.1%	33.9%	49.1%	10,411	53.4%	15.6%	46.4%	38.0%
Nash County	8,242	38.3%	14.4%	40.0%	45.6%	2,169	10.1%	19.7%	35.3%	45.0%
New Hanover County	47,012	75.3%	10.7%	48.7%	40.6%	6,405	10.3%	15.3%	52.5%	32.2%
Onslow County	49,820	65.1%	6.2%	49.2%	44.6%	8,347	10.9%	20.0%	36.4%	43.6%
Orange County	33,151	67.2%	10.1%	57.7%	32.2%	57,377	116.3%	15.0%	38.7%	46.3%
Pitt County	35,565	57.8%	7.3%	58.4%	34.3%	9,619	15.6%	15.3%	36.6%	48.1%
Randolph County	24,811	77.0%	18.2%	35.0%	46.7%	3,517	10.9%	2.3%	82.9%	14.7%
Robeson County	6,722	19.3%	12.4%	45.5%	42.1%	3,463	9.9%	11.0%	30.2%	58.9%
Rockingham County	14,635	76.5%	18.1%	32.8%	49.1%	1,466	7.7%	39.7%	46.6%	13.7%
Rowan County	21,939	67.5%	16.5%	34.2%	49.3%	8,412	25.9%	20.2%	36.2%	43.6%
Union County	34,193	66.7%	24.6%	40.1%	35.3%	3,494	6.8%	18.4%	33.7%	47.9%
Wake County	155,824	57.8%	14.6%	33.2%	52.2%	408	0.2%	0.0%	0.0%	100.0%
Wayne County	17,203	52.4%	13.3%	35.7%	51.0%	225	0.7%	40.4%	0.0%	59.6%
North Dakota										
Cass County	48,965	85.1%	9.2%	48.8%	42.0%	91,578	159.2%	15.7%	42.6%	41.7%

Table B-2: Counties—Race and Hispanic Origin by Age—*Continued*

	Asian, Non-Hispanic					Hispanic				
	Millennial Population		Percent by Age			Millennial Population		Percent by Age		
	Number	Percent	15 to 17	18 to 24	25 to 33	Number	Percent	15 to 17	18 to 24	25 to 33
New Jersey—Cont.										
Somerset County	12,880	17.8%	19.2%	28.4%	52.4%	12,591	17.4%	17.9%	34.8%	47.3%
Sussex County	69	0.2%	0.0%	0.0%	100.0%	2,494	8.1%	16.2%	37.9%	45.9%
Union County	5,964	4.5%	15.6%	27.1%	57.4%	48,340	36.3%	14.3%	35.3%	50.4%
Warren County	530	2.3%	36.6%	18.1%	45.3%	2,438	10.7%	15.9%	41.0%	43.1%
New Mexico										
Bernalillo County	4,585	2.5%	25.5%	24.3%	50.3%	103,478	56.6%	16.1%	36.5%	47.4%
Doña Ana County	1,135	1.8%	0.0%	19.7%	80.3%	45,572	71.1%	15.7%	47.4%	36.9%
San Juan County	508	1.5%	24.8%	0.0%	75.2%	15,581	47.5%	17.2%	34.4%	48.4%
Sandoval County	26	0.1%	0.0%	0.0%	100.0%	7,994	26.1%	14.8%	46.6%	38.5%
Santa Fe County	325	1.0%	13.8%	0.0%	86.2%	20,006	64.5%	17.3%	36.5%	46.2%
New York										
Albany County	7,758	8.6%	14.8%	40.4%	44.8%	5,805	6.4%	10.6%	40.0%	49.4%
Bronx County	16,732	4.0%	14.9%	29.1%	56.0%	247,320	58.8%	14.5%	38.5%	47.1%
Broome County	4,705	8.6%	8.5%	72.5%	19.0%	3,251	5.9%	21.7%	55.3%	23.0%
Chautauqua County	408	1.3%	33.1%	24.0%	42.9%	3,593	11.3%	20.2%	40.5%	39.3%
Dutchess County	2,834	3.7%	26.9%	29.5%	43.6%	11,146	14.7%	14.3%	42.0%	43.7%
Erie County	12,743	5.3%	7.1%	45.9%	47.0%	16,021	6.7%	15.0%	42.2%	42.8%
Jefferson County	245	0.7%	0.0%	35.9%	64.1%	3,014	8.5%	5.1%	73.5%	21.4%
Kings County	95,014	12.6%	10.4%	30.8%	58.8%	154,633	20.6%	13.8%	35.7%	50.5%
Monroe County	10,819	5.4%	11.4%	46.2%	42.4%	20,656	10.2%	15.9%	41.0%	43.1%
Nassau County	28,750	9.1%	17.4%	34.4%	48.1%	61,492	19.5%	15.7%	36.5%	47.7%
New York County	74,401	14.3%	3.4%	26.6%	70.0%	128,840	24.8%	9.7%	34.7%	55.5%
Niagara County	947	1.9%	33.3%	37.1%	29.7%	1,627	3.3%	7.1%	39.6%	53.3%
Oneida County	3,263	5.7%	8.9%	42.9%	48.2%	4,475	7.8%	16.0%	22.4%	61.5%
Onondaga County	6,042	4.9%	14.0%	45.2%	40.8%	7,716	6.3%	20.8%	48.0%	31.1%
Ontario County	858	3.3%	31.6%	60.7%	7.7%	1,539	5.8%	15.7%	32.1%	52.2%
Orange County	2,521	2.6%	4.9%	60.3%	34.7%	23,125	24.0%	20.3%	39.8%	39.9%
Oswego County	621	1.9%	33.3%	66.7%	0.0%	1,223	3.8%	16.6%	71.1%	12.3%
Putnam County	199	0.9%	54.3%	45.7%	0.0%	3,077	14.3%	13.6%	60.3%	26.0%
Queens County	153,658	25.3%	11.6%	31.0%	57.4%	187,224	30.8%	12.8%	33.8%	53.4%
Rensselaer County	2,839	6.7%	4.2%	59.0%	36.8%	3,110	7.3%	15.1%	36.9%	48.0%
Richmond County	10,101	8.5%	18.0%	33.2%	48.8%	26,654	22.5%	16.5%	37.6%	46.0%
Rockland County	4,358	5.5%	12.3%	28.2%	59.6%	16,282	20.7%	11.9%	42.2%	45.8%
Saratoga County	560	1.7%	33.0%	21.4%	45.5%	973	3.0%	6.7%	73.7%	19.6%
Schenectady County	874	1.7%	0.0%	49.5%	50.5%	1,541	3.1%	18.3%	8.0%	73.7%
St. Lawrence County	2,320	6.0%	16.5%	33.3%	50.3%	3,028	7.9%	5.2%	58.0%	36.9%
Steuben County	296	1.3%	0.0%	48.3%	51.7%	867	3.8%	8.4%	27.8%	63.8%
Suffolk County	19,349	5.5%	17.0%	38.9%	44.1%	79,448	22.6%	13.6%	36.8%	40.0%
Tompkins County	7,771	17.4%	0.0%	79.7%	20.3%	3,325	7.5%	3.5%	75.2%	21.3%
Ulster County	1,349	3.1%	15.4%	69.6%	15.0%	5,785	13.3%	9.2%	66.9%	23.9%
Wayne County	292	1.4%	49.7%	25.3%	25.0%	1,685	8.2%	2.0%	38.0%	60.0%
Westchester County	11,678	5.1%	16.6%	27.5%	55.9%	70,342	30.9%	16.5%	38.2%	45.3%
North Carolina										
Alamance County	316	0.8%	10.1%	0.0%	89.9%	6,107	16.1%	19.6%	30.7%	49.8%
Brunswick County	207	1.0%	0.0%	0.0%	100.0%	2,053	9.6%	4.2%	75.2%	20.6%
Buncombe County	1,459	2.4%	11.4%	65.7%	22.9%	5,066	8.2%	14.7%	27.7%	57.6%
Cabarrus County	792	1.8%	18.6%	30.6%	50.9%	4,926	10.9%	21.1%	43.5%	35.4%
Catawba County	3,002	8.3%	27.9%	44.4%	27.6%	4,787	13.2%	21.5%	16.3%	62.2%
Cleveland County	362	1.6%	0.0%	100.0%	0.0%	2,913	13.1%	11.6%	48.8%	39.6%
Craven County	965	3.4%	0.0%	17.5%	82.5%	2,041	7.1%	3.4%	66.5%	30.1%
Cumberland County	1,267	1.3%	19.3%	61.1%	19.6%	13,583	13.4%	10.1%	39.0%	50.9%
Davidson County	356	1.0%	0.0%	61.2%	38.8%	3,205	8.8%	12.3%	51.4%	36.3%
Durham County	6,506	7.2%	2.9%	41.9%	55.2%	13,189	14.7%	19.2%	27.0%	53.7%
Forsyth County	3,450	3.7%	5.0%	39.0%	56.0%	13,322	14.4%	22.5%	25.0%	52.4%
Gaston County	690	1.4%	0.0%	94.1%	5.9%	4,779	9.4%	11.2%	20.0%	68.8%
Guilford County	7,436	5.4%	22.9%	31.0%	46.1%	12,390	9.0%	17.2%	24.1%	58.7%
Harnett County	489	1.4%	21.5%	78.5%	0.0%	5,340	14.9%	17.2%	34.0%	48.8%
Henderson County	176	0.9%	65.9%	0.0%	34.1%	3,034	14.8%	16.5%	35.7%	47.8%
Iredell County	1,752	4.5%	13.1%	13.0%	74.0%	4,135	10.6%	20.4%	46.2%	33.4%
Johnston County	74	0.2%	100.0%	0.0%	0.0%	6,797	16.2%	16.1%	33.0%	50.9%
Mecklenburg County	18,915	6.6%	8.6%	25.1%	66.2%	40,752	14.3%	15.3%	37.0%	47.7%
Moore County	221	1.1%	0.0%	100.0%	0.0%	2,700	13.8%	35.5%	29.5%	35.0%
Nash County	na	na	na	na	na	2,093	9.7%	32.0%	22.1%	45.9%
New Hanover County	615	1.0%	36.1%	16.3%	47.6%	4,356	7.0%	18.5%	45.1%	36.4%
Onslow County	1,176	1.5%	24.1%	50.1%	25.8%	10,586	13.8%	2.4%	54.5%	43.1%
Orange County	3,994	8.1%	12.4%	31.5%	56.0%	3,979	8.1%	18.7%	45.8%	35.5%
Pitt County	788	1.3%	21.4%	69.2%	9.4%	3,743	6.1%	7.9%	35.8%	56.3%
Randolph County	113	0.4%	0.0%	0.0%	100.0%	4,130	12.8%	12.1%	41.5%	46.4%
Robeson County	196	0.6%	0.0%	33.2%	66.8%	3,356	9.6%	18.3%	51.4%	30.2%
Rockingham County	na	na	na	na	na	2,027	10.6%	26.6%	47.3%	26.1%
Rowan County	253	0.8%	0.0%	98.8%	1.2%	3,028	9.3%	19.0%	31.0%	50.0%
Union County	631	1.2%	25.0%	47.2%	27.7%	6,542	12.8%	16.5%	43.3%	40.2%
Wake County	18,715	6.9%	17.8%	27.0%	55.3%	29,626	11.0%	15.1%	37.7%	47.2%
Wayne County	548	1.7%	0.0%	20.3%	79.7%	4,631	14.1%	10.6%	41.4%	48.0%
North Dakota										
Cass County	1,903	3.3%	9.6%	2.6%	87.9%	2,086	3.6%	3.0%	53.1%	43.9%

Table B-2: Counties—Race and Hispanic Origin by Age—*Continued*

	White, Non-Hispanic					Black, Non-Hispanic				
	Millennial Population		Percent by Age			Millennial Population		Percent by Age		
	Number	Percent	15 to 17	18 to 24	25 to 33	Number	Percent	15 to 17	18 to 24	25 to 33
Ohio										
Allen County	19,914	78.9%	16.4%	41.3%	42.4%	2,334	9.2%	17.8%	41.3%	40.9%
Ashtabula County	18,570	82.1%	18.8%	35.3%	45.9%	3,069	13.6%	21.5%	40.2%	38.3%
Butler County	80,012	79.2%	15.5%	45.4%	39.2%	75,299	74.6%	14.1%	36.1%	49.8%
Clark County	25,603	81.7%	17.3%	36.5%	46.2%	351	1.1%	50.4%	29.6%	19.9%
Clermont County	44,740	93.9%	18.7%	32.7%	48.6%	4,721	9.9%	6.7%	72.1%	21.1%
Columbiana County	20,247	94.7%	18.9%	35.6%	45.5%	56,016	261.9%	18.9%	36.1%	44.9%
Cuyahoga County	168,469	54.9%	14.4%	34.3%	51.3%	2,947	1.0%	22.2%	35.7%	42.1%
Delaware County	34,196	84.0%	23.2%	35.8%	41.0%	1,436	3.5%	0.0%	70.0%	30.0%
Fairfield County	29,816	88.3%	19.7%	35.2%	45.1%	7,220	21.4%	23.7%	24.1%	52.2%
Franklin County	232,650	63.2%	10.8%	31.0%	58.2%	23,896	6.5%	18.0%	39.5%	42.5%
Geauga County	18,324	95.6%	22.7%	41.3%	36.0%	10,023	52.3%	18.4%	45.7%	35.9%
Greene County	34,875	76.5%	14.0%	39.1%	46.9%	1,082	2.4%	2.1%	70.1%	27.8%
Hamilton County	133,994	63.6%	13.5%	33.9%	52.6%	839	0.4%	91.3%	0.0%	8.7%
Lake County	42,629	86.4%	19.2%	35.8%	45.0%	28,624	58.0%	12.9%	42.7%	44.4%
Licking County	35,315	87.0%	18.3%	36.3%	45.4%	3,126	7.7%	11.5%	52.7%	35.7%
Lorain County	49,333	70.7%	18.0%	37.7%	44.4%	2,477	3.5%	0.0%	64.7%	35.3%
Lucas County	71,681	63.9%	14.2%	33.7%	52.1%	7,299	6.5%	18.8%	31.3%	49.9%
Mahoning County	37,713	69.5%	15.9%	36.2%	47.9%	21,320	39.3%	17.3%	42.0%	40.7%
Medina County	35,415	91.5%	20.7%	35.2%	44.1%	3,947	10.2%	11.8%	50.4%	37.8%
Miami County	20,860	89.6%	18.8%	34.2%	47.0%	61	0.3%	100.0%	0.0%	0.0%
Montgomery County	90,042	68.7%	14.6%	35.0%	50.3%	1,882	1.4%	3.1%	37.1%	59.8%
Portage County	41,974	84.5%	12.8%	53.4%	33.8%	410	0.8%	0.0%	72.0%	28.0%
Richland County	22,500	80.5%	17.7%	36.6%	45.7%	1,917	6.9%	14.0%	33.0%	52.9%
Stark County	73,687	83.6%	16.7%	36.4%	46.9%	2,122	2.4%	16.4%	46.6%	37.0%
Summit County	94,842	73.6%	14.7%	36.3%	48.9%	6,125	4.8%	17.8%	58.5%	23.8%
Trumbull County	38,387	86.9%	18.6%	37.1%	44.3%	4,612	10.4%	14.0%	34.4%	51.6%
Tuscarawas County	19,390	93.1%	20.4%	35.1%	44.5%	32,910	158.1%	12.1%	31.9%	56.0%
Warren County	41,567	83.2%	22.8%	33.1%	44.1%	18,378	36.8%	13.9%	38.5%	47.6%
Wayne County	25,994	92.8%	17.9%	39.6%	42.5%	872	3.1%	27.6%	46.7%	25.7%
Wood County	36,834	85.4%	15.4%	42.8%	41.9%	247	0.6%	0.0%	0.0%	100.0%
Oklahoma										
Canadian County	23,105	70.8%	17.3%	29.2%	53.5%	299	0.9%	0.0%	30.1%	69.9%
Cleveland County	58,960	66.8%	11.2%	45.6%	43.2%	1,787	2.0%	1.1%	62.7%	36.1%
Comanche County	22,310	56.4%	9.4%	36.3%	54.3%	1,508	3.8%	58.2%	32.3%	9.5%
Oklahoma County	109,682	52.6%	11.5%	32.2%	56.3%	13,115	6.3%	10.0%	31.3%	58.7%
Tulsa County	93,005	56.0%	15.1%	33.6%	51.3%	2,759	1.7%	14.3%	29.7%	56.0%
Oregon										
Clackamas County	70,902	77.6%	18.4%	34.3%	47.3%	327	0.4%	0.0%	62.4%	37.6%
Deschutes County	32,937	87.8%	16.1%	29.7%	54.2%	848	2.3%	99.4%	0.6%	0.0%
Douglas County	17,925	82.0%	17.4%	34.0%	48.6%	49,224	225.1%	17.8%	41.2%	41.0%
Jackson County	35,682	74.3%	15.8%	33.9%	50.3%	4,085	8.5%	23.5%	25.4%	51.1%
Lane County	76,638	75.6%	11.8%	45.0%	43.2%	5,714	5.6%	15.9%	57.1%	27.0%
Linn County	22,697	80.1%	15.8%	44.3%	40.0%	1,206	4.3%	20.8%	36.4%	42.8%
Marion County	50,537	59.0%	14.5%	34.1%	51.4%	5,863	6.8%	24.1%	36.1%	39.8%
Multnomah County	143,690	66.1%	8.9%	27.7%	63.4%	561	0.3%	6.6%	25.1%	68.3%
Washington County	89,052	60.0%	15.0%	31.1%	53.8%	970	0.7%	6.6%	62.2%	31.2%
Yamhill County	19,068	72.4%	15.8%	46.1%	38.1%	3,450	13.1%	0.0%	63.9%	36.1%
Pennsylvania										
Adams County	19,715	84.3%	14.5%	40.8%	44.7%	7,458	31.9%	10.7%	63.1%	26.2%
Allegheny County	233,972	73.7%	12.4%	32.8%	54.8%	2,047	0.6%	0.0%	48.7%	51.3%
Beaver County	31,272	83.5%	16.4%	35.4%	48.2%	12,443	33.2%	18.2%	52.3%	29.5%
Berks County	67,064	65.5%	15.6%	39.7%	44.8%	35,742	34.9%	16.7%	40.6%	42.6%
Blair County	25,764	89.9%	18.1%	35.6%	46.3%	5,247	18.3%	15.2%	36.5%	48.3%
Bucks County	111,937	83.2%	18.8%	36.8%	44.5%	964	0.7%	0.0%	0.0%	100.0%
Butler County	40,110	92.6%	16.9%	38.0%	45.1%	1,511	3.5%	2.9%	51.0%	46.1%
Cambria County	27,476	89.3%	15.6%	40.8%	43.5%	1,319	4.3%	27.1%	22.2%	50.6%
Centre County	52,246	77.9%	6.8%	58.0%	35.2%	4,976	7.4%	15.5%	53.4%	31.1%
Chester County	90,634	76.3%	18.7%	38.1%	43.2%	737	0.6%	0.0%	37.9%	62.1%
Cumberland County	51,675	85.0%	14.5%	39.5%	46.1%	5,486	9.0%	22.2%	36.5%	41.2%
Dauphin County	40,859	62.0%	15.3%	31.7%	53.0%	3,856	5.9%	18.6%	44.0%	37.4%
Delaware County	89,385	62.5%	14.8%	39.9%	45.3%	1,069	0.7%	15.3%	49.0%	35.6%
Erie County	57,461	80.9%	14.8%	39.8%	45.4%	1,288	1.8%	32.8%	23.3%	43.9%
Fayette County	25,309	90.2%	17.1%	35.1%	47.8%	5,819	20.7%	27.4%	39.1%	33.5%
Franklin County	29,161	84.0%	17.1%	34.7%	48.2%	17,985	51.8%	11.6%	46.9%	41.5%
Lackawanna County	42,570	83.8%	14.3%	37.8%	47.9%	2,540	5.0%	5.0%	74.9%	20.1%
Lancaster County	100,694	77.7%	16.6%	35.9%	47.5%	986	0.8%	18.9%	48.7%	32.5%
Lebanon County	23,848	80.2%	17.1%	38.1%	44.8%	182,525	613.6%	14.6%	36.7%	48.6%
Lehigh County	53,433	58.7%	16.0%	36.9%	47.1%	1,881	2.1%	28.2%	2.8%	69.0%
Luzerne County	59,146	78.2%	14.8%	39.7%	45.5%	1,841	2.4%	6.2%	48.1%	45.7%
Lycoming County	24,924	88.7%	13.6%	42.7%	43.7%	2,466	8.8%	10.3%	56.7%	33.1%
Mercer County	22,840	87.8%	17.0%	40.7%	42.4%	7,102	27.3%	23.5%	28.0%	48.5%
Monroe County	25,341	60.2%	16.2%	46.6%	37.2%	1,714	4.1%	0.0%	0.0%	100.0%
Montgomery County	133,751	71.9%	17.2%	34.8%	48.0%	14,352	7.7%	11.6%	41.6%	46.9%
Northampton County	52,084	71.7%	14.7%	39.7%	45.6%	535	0.7%	0.0%	95.7%	4.3%
Northumberland County	18,439	90.7%	13.9%	31.6%	54.5%	10,799	53.1%	12.8%	44.8%	42.4%
Philadelphia County	175,973	36.3%	6.5%	29.8%	63.6%	8,074	1.7%	20.9%	51.2%	27.9%

Table B-2: Counties—Race and Hispanic Origin by Age—*Continued*

	Asian, Non-Hispanic					Hispanic				
	Millennial Population		Percent by Age			Millennial Population		Percent by Age		
	Number	Percent	15 to 17	18 to 24	25 to 33	Number	Percent	15 to 17	18 to 24	25 to 33
Ohio										
Allen County	380	1.5%	0.0%	0.0%	100.0%	732	2.9%	15.2%	20.6%	64.2%
Ashtabula County	299	1.3%	16.1%	0.0%	83.9%	1,891	8.4%	34.2%	26.3%	39.6%
Butler County	4,082	4.0%	4.4%	55.6%	40.0%	5,428	5.4%	19.5%	36.9%	43.6%
Clark County	na	na	na	na	na	481	1.5%	64.2%	35.8%	0.0%
Clermont County	523	1.1%	0.0%	0.0%	100.0%	na	na	na	na	na
Columbiana County	na	na	na	na	na	547	2.6%	1.5%	21.0%	77.5%
Cuyahoga County	13,607	4.4%	10.9%	29.9%	59.2%	22,258	7.2%	16.1%	39.2%	44.8%
Delaware County	2,307	5.7%	14.7%	33.8%	51.5%	1,164	2.9%	17.7%	28.5%	53.8%
Fairfield County	45	0.1%	0.0%	100.0%	0.0%	62	0.2%	100.0%	0.0%	0.0%
Franklin County	20,334	5.5%	13.3%	27.2%	59.5%	21,470	5.8%	13.2%	33.1%	53.8%
Geauga County	na	na	na	na	na	265	1.4%	0.0%	0.0%	100.0%
Greene County	1,664	3.6%	14.7%	46.0%	39.4%	1,876	4.1%	4.5%	59.2%	36.4%
Hamilton County	7,037	3.3%	10.9%	27.5%	61.6%	6,518	3.1%	11.0%	29.3%	59.7%
Lake County	921	1.9%	6.6%	0.0%	93.4%	1,950	4.0%	15.4%	69.3%	15.3%
Licking County	751	1.8%	0.0%	53.9%	46.1%	1,216	3.0%	6.0%	74.2%	19.8%
Lorain County	1,556	2.2%	17.9%	65.6%	16.5%	8,664	12.4%	20.5%	41.5%	38.0%
Lucas County	2,584	2.3%	8.7%	72.3%	19.0%	9,327	8.3%	15.2%	39.5%	45.3%
Mahoning County	308	0.6%	0.0%	22.7%	77.3%	4,523	8.3%	2.4%	22.9%	74.7%
Medina County	438	1.1%	0.0%	0.0%	100.0%	1,158	3.0%	6.5%	12.4%	81.1%
Miami County	521	2.2%	0.0%	41.8%	58.2%	661	2.8%	16.3%	64.9%	18.8%
Montgomery County	2,918	2.2%	8.1%	23.5%	68.3%	4,194	3.2%	6.0%	31.0%	63.1%
Portage County	1,739	3.5%	0.0%	63.7%	36.3%	1,564	3.1%	24.7%	60.1%	15.2%
Richland County	542	1.9%	0.0%	42.1%	57.9%	988	3.5%	14.0%	46.2%	39.9%
Stark County	884	1.0%	15.0%	23.2%	61.8%	2,335	2.6%	9.5%	58.2%	32.2%
Summit County	4,391	3.4%	19.4%	32.9%	47.7%	3,188	2.5%	11.3%	22.3%	66.4%
Trumbull County	320	0.7%	80.0%	20.0%	0.0%	201	0.5%	61.7%	38.3%	0.0%
Tuscarawas County	591	2.8%	0.0%	0.0%	100.0%	780	3.7%	26.3%	35.6%	38.1%
Warren County	2,867	5.7%	22.3%	43.8%	33.9%	1,550	3.1%	20.1%	42.0%	37.9%
Wayne County	27	0.1%	0.0%	100.0%	0.0%	731	2.6%	22.0%	68.4%	9.6%
Wood County	895	2.1%	12.6%	24.7%	62.7%	2,133	4.9%	35.4%	39.1%	25.5%
Oklahoma										
Canadian County	1,176	3.6%	7.7%	53.8%	38.5%	2,384	7.3%	9.7%	66.2%	24.1%
Cleveland County	6,635	7.5%	3.4%	20.3%	76.3%	9,339	10.6%	19.4%	44.4%	36.2%
Comanche County	1,152	2.9%	0.0%	41.2%	58.8%	6,840	17.3%	16.6%	51.6%	31.8%
Oklahoma County	7,357	3.5%	8.7%	37.9%	53.4%	41,059	19.7%	15.2%	39.7%	45.1%
Tulsa County	6,306	3.8%	16.9%	28.1%	55.0%	24,475	14.7%	15.5%	34.6%	49.9%
Oregon										
Clackamas County	5,234	5.7%	21.1%	27.4%	51.6%	10,533	11.5%	23.8%	41.9%	34.3%
Deschutes County	393	1.0%	0.0%	44.8%	55.2%	3,385	9.0%	1.5%	59.7%	38.8%
Douglas County	na	na	na	na	na	1,677	7.7%	4.1%	49.4%	46.5%
Jackson County	937	2.0%	11.0%	15.2%	73.9%	8,254	17.2%	18.5%	33.9%	47.6%
Lane County	3,847	3.8%	3.4%	64.1%	32.5%	11,504	11.3%	15.3%	44.5%	40.1%
Linn County	1,868	6.6%	5.2%	76.9%	17.9%	3,172	11.2%	17.0%	33.2%	49.8%
Marion County	1,558	1.8%	47.9%	24.6%	27.4%	26,636	31.1%	19.6%	45.5%	34.8%
Multnomah County	16,283	7.5%	11.7%	36.8%	51.5%	28,818	13.3%	13.4%	38.6%	48.0%
Washington County	15,745	10.6%	11.8%	28.3%	59.9%	31,378	21.1%	18.8%	31.1%	50.1%
Yamhill County	545	2.1%	40.9%	21.3%	37.8%	5,045	19.1%	19.1%	41.2%	39.7%
Pennsylvania										
Adams County	170	0.7%	50.0%	0.0%	50.0%	2,355	10.1%	17.0%	21.3%	61.7%
Allegheny County	15,545	4.9%	4.3%	38.1%	57.6%	8,832	2.8%	5.7%	43.9%	50.4%
Beaver County	363	1.0%	20.1%	0.0%	79.9%	475	1.3%	28.2%	43.2%	28.6%
Berks County	2,162	2.1%	23.2%	52.7%	24.1%	25,744	25.1%	16.8%	38.4%	44.7%
Blair County	372	1.3%	0.0%	14.2%	85.8%	524	1.8%	0.0%	12.4%	87.6%
Bucks County	5,459	4.1%	14.8%	28.9%	56.4%	8,079	6.0%	15.8%	41.6%	42.6%
Butler County	436	1.0%	0.0%	34.4%	65.6%	1,266	2.9%	7.0%	20.3%	72.7%
Cambria County	695	2.3%	48.3%	51.7%	0.0%	819	2.7%	59.3%	19.0%	21.6%
Centre County	6,425	9.6%	0.0%	76.8%	23.2%	2,845	4.2%	2.6%	82.5%	14.9%
Chester County	6,685	5.6%	11.6%	26.1%	62.3%	10,415	8.8%	8.7%	38.4%	52.9%
Cumberland County	3,403	5.6%	15.2%	46.1%	38.7%	2,588	4.3%	23.9%	51.7%	24.4%
Dauphin County	3,373	5.1%	4.4%	72.8%	22.9%	7,101	10.8%	20.8%	51.7%	27.5%
Delaware County	7,474	5.2%	19.1%	37.9%	43.1%	5,731	4.0%	9.3%	51.0%	39.7%
Erie County	1,940	2.7%	8.6%	60.2%	31.2%	3,865	5.4%	28.5%	42.6%	28.9%
Fayette County	111	0.4%	100.0%	0.0%	0.0%	255	0.9%	9.4%	90.6%	0.0%
Franklin County	732	2.1%	53.1%	44.7%	2.2%	2,455	7.1%	1.1%	89.7%	9.2%
Lackawanna County	1,575	3.1%	15.4%	23.3%	61.3%	3,977	7.8%	30.2%	49.3%	20.6%
Lancaster County	3,426	2.6%	14.6%	62.1%	23.2%	17,675	13.6%	18.7%	40.9%	40.4%
Lebanon County	366	1.2%	0.0%	100.0%	0.0%	4,413	14.8%	7.7%	56.9%	35.3%
Lehigh County	3,542	3.9%	17.0%	29.6%	53.4%	25,348	27.9%	19.2%	32.5%	48.3%
Luzerne County	1,264	1.7%	0.0%	67.6%	32.4%	10,090	13.3%	18.0%	47.9%	34.1%
Lycoming County	576	2.0%	10.2%	28.8%	60.9%	992	3.5%	0.0%	36.4%	63.6%
Mercer County	185	0.7%	77.3%	22.7%	0.0%	676	2.6%	69.2%	28.6%	2.2%
Monroe County	1,893	4.5%	0.0%	64.1%	35.9%	7,557	18.0%	19.0%	28.8%	52.1%
Montgomery County	16,995	9.1%	13.4%	28.4%	58.2%	12,215	6.6%	8.8%	31.5%	59.7%
Northampton County	2,999	4.1%	8.4%	64.3%	27.3%	10,918	15.0%	15.7%	50.1%	34.2%
Northumberland County	na	na	na	na	na	741	3.6%	32.1%	40.1%	27.8%
Philadelphia County	41,706	8.6%	9.3%	35.2%	55.4%	71,068	14.6%	14.3%	36.6%	49.1%

Table B-2: Counties—Race and Hispanic Origin by Age—*Continued*

| | White, Non-Hispanic | | | | | Black, Non-Hispanic | | | | |
| | Millennial Population | | Percent by Age | | | Millennial Population | | Percent by Age | | |
	Number	Percent	15 to 17	18 to 24	25 to 33	Number	Percent	15 to 17	18 to 24	25 to 33
Pennsylvania—Cont.										
Schuylkill County	26,057	85.8%	17.6%	35.4%	47.0%	12,225	40.2%	11.8%	30.3%	57.8%
Washington County	40,379	87.8%	15.6%	38.9%	45.5%	15,509	33.7%	21.2%	29.1%	49.7%
Westmoreland County	66,606	89.8%	17.3%	37.7%	45.0%	25,961	35.0%	21.4%	32.2%	46.4%
York County	81,017	80.0%	16.4%	34.4%	49.2%	13,661	13.5%	14.5%	31.1%	54.4%
Rhode Island										
Kent County	31,519	83.4%	16.0%	32.7%	51.3%	16,845	44.6%	12.9%	40.7%	46.4%
Providence County	97,403	54.9%	11.5%	38.6%	49.9%	26,897	15.2%	17.2%	38.3%	44.4%
Washington County	29,546	90.8%	13.9%	54.0%	32.1%	11,360	34.9%	16.5%	43.6%	39.9%
South Carolina										
Aiken County	23,692	59.7%	16.9%	35.5%	47.7%	12,603	31.8%	17.0%	39.5%	43.5%
Anderson County	33,004	74.2%	17.9%	36.3%	45.8%	3,482	7.8%	27.5%	18.7%	53.8%
Beaufort County	22,068	52.3%	11.1%	44.1%	44.8%	55,982	132.7%	14.6%	47.9%	37.4%
Berkeley County	34,942	63.2%	14.1%	32.9%	53.1%	16,956	30.7%	13.9%	37.9%	48.2%
Charleston County	72,611	65.8%	11.2%	34.7%	54.1%	16,441	14.9%	13.2%	42.1%	44.6%
Dorchester County	22,273	55.9%	14.0%	30.5%	55.5%	14,141	35.5%	16.9%	39.9%	43.2%
Florence County	15,371	45.1%	17.8%	37.4%	44.8%	3,530	10.4%	13.9%	3.1%	83.0%
Greenville County	81,384	64.1%	15.3%	37.0%	47.8%	1,118	0.9%	0.0%	48.4%	51.6%
Horry County	48,159	69.5%	13.5%	33.8%	52.7%	1,260	1.8%	5.6%	91.0%	3.4%
Lexington County	46,443	67.0%	16.6%	32.6%	50.9%	1,499	2.2%	24.9%	39.4%	35.7%
Pickens County	31,546	80.4%	10.8%	49.9%	39.2%	57,316	146.2%	13.0%	41.9%	45.1%
Richland County	59,787	44.8%	10.5%	49.2%	40.2%	19,253	14.4%	17.6%	39.6%	42.8%
Spartanburg County	47,207	63.6%	16.4%	37.3%	46.3%	11,579	15.6%	15.0%	54.4%	30.7%
Sumter County	11,228	37.4%	19.0%	46.2%	34.8%	8,624	28.8%	17.3%	38.5%	44.2%
York County	39,728	65.1%	18.5%	35.2%	46.4%	13,392	21.9%	12.7%	39.1%	48.1%
South Dakota										
Minnehaha County	42,102	82.5%	13.3%	30.9%	55.7%	14,505	28.4%	11.4%	50.2%	38.3%
Pennington County	22,171	79.7%	16.8%	33.7%	49.6%	122	0.4%	0.0%	93.4%	6.6%
Tennessee										
Blount County	24,794	87.4%	17.6%	36.3%	46.1%	143,741	506.8%	16.7%	37.6%	45.8%
Bradley County	22,335	81.7%	17.5%	34.9%	47.7%	1,770	6.5%	57.6%	30.5%	12.0%
Davidson County	112,503	54.3%	6.9%	28.7%	64.4%	2,765	1.3%	12.9%	42.3%	44.8%
Hamilton County	59,945	67.3%	12.8%	33.9%	53.3%	1,916	2.2%	8.5%	49.5%	42.0%
Knox County	101,965	80.6%	13.6%	43.3%	43.1%	2,627	2.1%	46.7%	34.1%	19.1%
Madison County	14,072	56.0%	14.1%	42.7%	43.2%	1,792	7.1%	11.8%	69.3%	19.0%
Montgomery County	38,493	59.7%	11.7%	34.9%	53.4%	21,922	34.0%	14.5%	34.9%	50.6%
Rutherford County	62,988	69.9%	13.0%	42.5%	44.4%	41,798	46.4%	17.1%	37.6%	45.4%
Sevier County	18,302	85.7%	20.0%	38.4%	41.5%	5,508	25.8%	19.1%	43.5%	37.4%
Shelby County	80,412	31.5%	14.5%	33.4%	52.2%	11,128	4.4%	24.3%	23.8%	51.9%
Sullivan County	30,595	89.9%	20.5%	35.3%	44.2%	8,036	23.6%	11.1%	42.1%	46.8%
Sumner County	34,236	83.0%	18.4%	33.2%	48.3%	272	0.7%	59.6%	0.0%	40.4%
Washington County	29,247	87.0%	13.0%	45.4%	41.6%	23,765	70.7%	17.7%	35.0%	47.3%
Williamson County	36,729	87.2%	26.2%	36.7%	37.1%	916	2.2%	20.0%	65.8%	14.2%
Wilson County	23,965	84.9%	19.3%	33.9%	46.7%	158,035	560.1%	15.3%	36.4%	48.3%
Texas										
Bell County	45,863	43.5%	11.1%	38.2%	50.6%	24,385	23.2%	11.4%	36.8%	51.8%
Bexar County	136,354	25.1%	11.7%	34.9%	53.4%	2,211	0.4%	16.0%	25.3%	58.7%
Bowie County	14,214	61.7%	13.3%	37.2%	49.5%	3,534	15.3%	33.2%	33.6%	33.2%
Brazoria County	38,458	43.3%	16.0%	32.7%	51.2%	8,774	9.9%	10.7%	46.2%	43.2%
Brazos County	58,037	59.7%	4.9%	66.3%	28.7%	37,822	38.9%	22.0%	35.2%	42.8%
Cameron County	7,859	6.9%	21.4%	26.1%	52.5%	9,534	8.3%	17.9%	47.5%	34.7%
Collin County	117,832	54.2%	20.5%	33.2%	46.3%	1,804	0.8%	11.8%	69.1%	19.2%
Comal County	16,403	57.3%	20.4%	34.9%	44.7%	7,095	24.8%	17.7%	36.6%	45.7%
Dallas County	182,140	25.5%	10.2%	30.3%	59.6%	2,950	0.4%	23.7%	37.3%	39.0%
Denton County	116,297	55.3%	16.4%	33.3%	50.2%	247,257	117.5%	14.7%	35.1%	50.3%
Ector County	14,219	28.7%	12.3%	33.5%	54.1%	2,927	5.9%	0.0%	77.6%	22.4%
El Paso County	22,875	56.2%	19.0%	35.6%	45.5%	1,994	4.9%	14.3%	41.3%	44.4%
Ellis County	29,365	12.1%	9.8%	40.0%	50.2%	23,357	9.6%	16.5%	35.9%	47.6%
Fort Bend County	51,833	29.7%	19.7%	32.4%	47.8%	1,353	0.8%	16.6%	68.8%	14.6%
Galveston County	41,257	52.1%	16.5%	32.6%	50.9%	2,981	3.8%	11.6%	29.2%	59.2%
Grayson County	21,040	70.0%	13.3%	40.3%	46.4%	6,264	20.8%	15.9%	52.8%	31.4%
Gregg County	17,264	54.4%	14.1%	36.8%	49.1%	11,247	35.5%	16.4%	43.3%	40.3%
Guadalupe County	17,073	45.0%	18.5%	31.1%	50.4%	3,194	8.4%	41.1%	23.3%	35.6%
Harris County	331,899	26.1%	13.4%	30.6%	56.0%	7,468	0.6%	8.5%	47.8%	43.7%
Hays County	35,389	53.1%	9.8%	53.5%	36.7%	4,631	7.0%	19.5%	39.0%	41.5%
Hidalgo County	9,004	3.8%	16.7%	42.4%	40.8%	329	0.1%	0.0%	68.4%	31.6%
Jefferson County	23,995	35.3%	13.5%	36.6%	49.9%	2,272	3.3%	11.4%	43.4%	45.2%
Johnson County	26,650	67.9%	18.6%	32.5%	48.9%	700	1.8%	0.0%	66.1%	33.9%
Kaufman County	17,538	63.2%	19.1%	30.9%	50.0%	12,718	45.8%	11.5%	48.5%	40.0%
Lubbock County	54,780	53.5%	8.5%	53.9%	37.6%	90,145	88.0%	17.2%	35.8%	47.0%
McLennan County	40,201	53.7%	11.9%	52.1%	36.0%	4,434	5.9%	7.1%	55.1%	37.8%
Midland County	19,818	40.5%	12.3%	30.3%	57.4%	2,436	5.0%	10.8%	58.2%	31.0%
Montgomery County	77,414	60.2%	19.7%	34.9%	45.3%	30,513	23.7%	12.1%	41.4%	46.5%
Nueces County	26,286	26.1%	13.0%	31.6%	55.4%	4,965	4.9%	7.4%	61.2%	31.4%
Parker County	21,858	79.4%	20.2%	37.5%	42.4%	7,325	26.6%	17.1%	42.3%	40.6%

Table B-2: Counties—Race and Hispanic Origin by Age—*Continued*

	Asian, Non-Hispanic					Hispanic				
	Millennial Population		Percent by Age			Millennial Population		Percent by Age		
	Number	Percent	15 to 17	18 to 24	25 to 33	Number	Percent	15 to 17	18 to 24	25 to 33
Pennsylvania—Cont.										
Schuylkill County	na	na	na	na	na	2,143	7.1%	10.4%	42.7%	46.9%
Washington County	917	2.0%	12.8%	44.9%	42.3%	1,827	4.0%	2.5%	48.8%	48.7%
Westmoreland County	1,192	1.6%	81.1%	7.8%	11.1%	1,902	2.6%	25.5%	49.6%	24.9%
York County	1,698	1.7%	5.8%	55.7%	38.5%	8,031	7.9%	13.0%	21.9%	65.1%
Rhode Island										
Kent County	946	2.5%	15.1%	17.1%	67.8%	2,683	7.1%	8.9%	30.8%	60.2%
Providence County	12,434	7.0%	4.3%	39.6%	56.1%	43,847	24.7%	14.9%	42.1%	42.9%
Washington County	702	2.2%	8.7%	32.5%	58.8%	1,391	4.3%	8.0%	55.7%	36.3%
South Carolina										
Aiken County	435	1.1%	26.0%	0.0%	74.0%	3,939	9.9%	20.3%	37.2%	42.5%
Anderson County	296	0.7%	0.0%	100.0%	0.0%	2,530	5.7%	48.8%	37.6%	13.6%
Beaufort County	397	0.9%	0.0%	2.5%	97.5%	6,182	14.6%	14.6%	33.8%	51.6%
Berkeley County	598	1.1%	0.0%	86.0%	14.0%	2,215	4.0%	17.1%	14.7%	68.2%
Charleston County	1,927	1.7%	5.3%	64.1%	30.6%	6,609	6.0%	9.5%	44.7%	45.9%
Dorchester County	301	0.8%	0.0%	100.0%	0.0%	1,947	4.9%	6.2%	7.2%	86.6%
Florence County	535	1.6%	0.0%	0.0%	100.0%	851	2.5%	33.6%	53.6%	12.8%
Greenville County	2,946	2.3%	11.5%	35.0%	53.5%	12,874	10.1%	13.7%	34.8%	51.5%
Horry County	1,174	1.7%	15.2%	10.1%	74.7%	5,430	7.8%	16.2%	45.9%	37.9%
Lexington County	1,378	2.0%	4.1%	39.6%	56.3%	6,039	8.7%	16.9%	28.6%	54.5%
Pickens County	867	2.2%	20.8%	33.1%	46.1%	2,510	6.4%	17.4%	65.5%	17.1%
Richland County	4,707	3.5%	14.1%	39.4%	46.5%	7,799	5.8%	11.2%	41.0%	47.7%
Spartanburg County	1,494	2.0%	23.1%	26.7%	50.2%	5,372	7.2%	20.3%	36.4%	43.4%
Sumter County	255	0.9%	0.0%	32.2%	67.8%	1,432	4.8%	6.9%	61.5%	31.6%
York County	2,046	3.4%	12.6%	32.0%	55.4%	3,706	6.1%	19.1%	49.4%	31.5%
South Dakota										
Minnehaha County	1,170	2.3%	0.0%	55.4%	44.6%	2,166	4.2%	13.1%	40.9%	46.0%
Pennington County	na	na	na	na	na	1,643	5.9%	6.6%	26.3%	67.1%
Tennessee										
Blount County	209	0.7%	0.0%	20.1%	79.9%	1,192	4.2%	7.7%	24.5%	67.8%
Bradley County	331	1.2%	39.0%	61.0%	0.0%	2,440	8.9%	9.5%	47.3%	43.2%
Davidson County	8,508	4.1%	14.0%	36.8%	49.2%	20,861	10.1%	15.6%	34.5%	49.9%
Hamilton County	2,820	3.2%	7.8%	60.7%	31.6%	5,360	6.0%	10.5%	37.5%	52.0%
Knox County	2,062	1.6%	8.6%	39.2%	52.2%	5,868	4.6%	15.6%	42.6%	41.8%
Madison County	394	1.6%	0.0%	0.0%	100.0%	1,032	4.1%	30.7%	26.0%	43.3%
Montgomery County	1,479	2.3%	15.8%	0.0%	84.2%	7,684	11.9%	6.6%	31.8%	61.6%
Rutherford County	3,079	3.4%	24.5%	41.6%	34.0%	6,403	7.1%	26.1%	33.9%	40.0%
Sevier County	527	2.5%	0.0%	100.0%	0.0%	1,040	8.3%	40.9%	17.0%	42.1%
Shelby County	6,443	2.5%	18.4%	36.3%	45.3%	17,440	6.8%	15.1%	30.6%	54.2%
Sullivan County	123	0.4%	0.0%	58.5%	41.5%	966	2.8%	10.8%	53.9%	35.3%
Sumner County	640	1.6%	0.0%	36.6%	63.4%	2,304	5.6%	2.2%	53.1%	44.7%
Washington County	350	1.0%	0.0%	23.4%	76.6%	1,228	3.7%	28.1%	43.4%	28.5%
Williamson County	986	2.3%	47.2%	31.9%	20.9%	1,598	3.8%	30.0%	53.4%	16.5%
Wilson County	432	1.5%	0.0%	51.6%	48.4%	1,436	5.1%	5.9%	83.3%	10.8%
Texas										
Bell County	2,408	2.3%	1.9%	29.1%	69.1%	28,124	26.7%	14.4%	38.1%	47.5%
Bexar County	15,917	2.9%	11.6%	35.4%	52.9%	337,752	62.3%	16.3%	36.2%	47.5%
Bowie County	na	na	na	na	na	2,120	9.2%	4.8%	24.2%	71.0%
Brazoria County	5,756	6.5%	39.1%	35.8%	25.1%	32,012	36.0%	17.6%	36.8%	45.6%
Brazos County	6,674	6.9%	3.9%	54.1%	42.0%	22,600	23.2%	10.0%	53.1%	36.9%
Cameron County	842	0.7%	13.1%	53.8%	33.1%	105,338	92.0%	20.2%	40.2%	39.6%
Collin County	29,097	13.4%	16.5%	27.5%	56.0%	39,240	18.1%	20.1%	33.9%	46.0%
Comal County	387	1.4%	0.0%	75.5%	24.5%	10,357	36.2%	18.3%	37.1%	44.5%
Dallas County	45,289	6.4%	9.2%	27.3%	63.5%	311,137	43.6%	17.2%	37.5%	45.4%
Denton County	17,008	8.1%	13.0%	34.0%	53.0%	46,010	21.9%	17.5%	36.5%	46.0%
Ector County	1,047	2.1%	18.3%	81.7%	0.0%	31,286	63.2%	15.0%	37.1%	47.9%
El Paso County	395	1.0%	30.1%	38.2%	31.6%	13,256	32.6%	19.5%	36.8%	43.6%
Ellis County	2,920	1.2%	6.4%	21.9%	71.7%	197,082	81.2%	17.0%	38.8%	44.2%
Fort Bend County	32,775	18.8%	18.9%	29.1%	52.0%	48,812	28.0%	19.5%	39.4%	41.1%
Galveston County	3,444	4.3%	20.4%	44.8%	34.8%	23,263	29.4%	17.7%	39.0%	43.3%
Grayson County	209	0.7%	0.0%	100.0%	0.0%	5,398	17.9%	19.6%	38.8%	41.6%
Gregg County	185	0.6%	0.0%	40.0%	60.0%	6,703	21.1%	18.1%	38.8%	43.0%
Guadalupe County	752	2.0%	18.4%	12.5%	69.1%	16,332	43.0%	19.5%	38.5%	42.0%
Harris County	87,143	6.8%	11.8%	30.8%	57.4%	581,025	45.7%	16.5%	35.9%	47.6%
Hays County	1,286	1.9%	0.0%	35.5%	64.5%	25,928	38.9%	14.3%	47.4%	38.3%
Hidalgo County	1,603	0.7%	23.1%	43.5%	33.4%	222,885	94.4%	19.0%	39.4%	41.6%
Jefferson County	2,428	3.6%	12.6%	31.7%	55.7%	16,635	24.5%	16.4%	33.3%	50.3%
Johnson County	182	0.5%	0.0%	0.0%	100.0%	10,120	25.8%	19.2%	39.3%	41.5%
Kaufman County	869	3.1%	0.0%	38.1%	61.9%	5,972	21.5%	17.8%	45.0%	37.2%
Lubbock County	2,910	2.8%	7.5%	40.4%	52.2%	36,679	35.8%	14.7%	43.1%	42.2%
McLennan County	1,858	2.5%	26.2%	42.2%	31.6%	20,767	27.7%	16.4%	43.3%	40.3%
Midland County	1,392	2.8%	14.9%	14.9%	70.3%	23,214	47.5%	15.0%	35.8%	49.3%
Montgomery County	3,744	2.9%	5.7%	22.8%	71.6%	37,529	29.2%	19.9%	37.0%	43.2%
Nueces County	2,135	2.1%	12.9%	38.2%	48.9%	66,081	65.7%	17.1%	37.9%	45.0%
Parker County	296	1.1%	54.4%	45.6%	0.0%	3,916	14.2%	32.9%	31.5%	35.5%

Table B-2: Counties—Race and Hispanic Origin by Age—*Continued*

| | White, Non-Hispanic | | | | | Black, Non-Hispanic | | | | |
| | Millennial Population | | Percent by Age | | | Millennial Population | | Percent by Age | | |
	Number	Percent	15 to 17	18 to 24	25 to 33	Number	Percent	15 to 17	18 to 24	25 to 33
Texas—Cont.										
Potter County	12,200	37.8%	13.8%	32.3%	53.9%	440	1.4%	0.0%	33.2%	66.8%
Randall County	23,926	66.0%	14.5%	35.3%	50.2%	2,680	7.4%	10.9%	45.4%	43.6%
Smith County	31,555	52.0%	14.4%	34.9%	50.7%	8,768	14.4%	17.8%	32.2%	50.0%
Tarrant County	223,286	42.0%	15.4%	32.8%	51.9%	1,456	0.3%	24.6%	29.9%	45.5%
Taylor County	26,244	60.6%	10.7%	47.1%	42.2%	1,032	2.4%	0.0%	100.0%	0.0%
Tom Green County	16,725	46.8%	11.8%	39.5%	48.7%	1,093	3.1%	0.6%	54.6%	44.7%
Travis County	166,688	45.8%	8.7%	27.2%	64.2%	1,532	0.4%	3.3%	11.0%	85.8%
Webb County	3,024	4.0%	23.1%	19.4%	57.4%	2,121	2.8%	8.9%	45.1%	46.0%
Wichita County	24,893	60.2%	10.8%	43.8%	45.5%	5,623	13.6%	9.5%	20.8%	69.7%
Williamson County	68,121	55.5%	18.1%	31.1%	50.8%	22,679	18.5%	21.3%	49.4%	29.3%
Utah										
Cache County	36,028	80.9%	13.9%	49.6%	36.6%	25,244	56.7%	14.4%	30.9%	54.7%
Davis County	74,707	81.0%	19.5%	32.9%	47.6%	3,052	3.3%	7.6%	56.6%	35.8%
Salt Lake County	212,699	67.4%	14.7%	31.8%	53.5%	26,662	8.4%	17.0%	36.6%	46.4%
Utah County	163,179	82.9%	15.2%	48.6%	36.2%	6,118	3.1%	21.3%	24.5%	54.2%
Washington County	30,576	77.5%	19.7%	35.6%	44.6%	2,804	7.1%	7.9%	69.4%	22.7%
Weber County	50,309	73.7%	16.2%	32.1%	51.7%	26,448	38.7%	19.5%	34.5%	46.0%
Vermont										
Chittenden County	45,146	87.8%	12.6%	49.3%	38.1%	2,907	5.7%	24.4%	25.5%	50.2%
Virginia										
Albemarle County	21,556	73.8%	8.6%	43.3%	48.1%	6,978	23.9%	15.7%	41.5%	42.8%
Arlington County	48,742	62.9%	5.4%	19.3%	75.3%	5,974	7.7%	10.9%	39.5%	49.5%
Chesterfield County	45,013	55.5%	19.1%	34.4%	46.4%	8,332	10.3%	8.6%	24.6%	66.8%
Fairfax County	134,259	47.6%	15.9%	33.2%	50.9%	17,524	6.2%	8.9%	42.5%	48.6%
Hanover County	17,524	76.7%	23.4%	39.0%	37.6%	20,864	91.3%	13.6%	42.3%	44.1%
Henrico County	38,169	48.1%	16.1%	32.2%	51.7%	22,118	27.9%	15.7%	35.7%	48.7%
Loudoun County	45,127	53.3%	21.8%	32.7%	45.6%	39,060	46.2%	10.0%	48.4%	41.7%
Montgomery County	34,097	79.1%	6.5%	62.3%	31.2%	13,756	31.9%	15.8%	39.2%	44.9%
Prince William County	46,733	40.0%	17.6%	31.3%	51.1%	31,239	26.7%	12.0%	42.3%	45.7%
Roanoke County	17,334	80.5%	19.9%	33.4%	46.7%	6,695	31.1%	8.9%	40.6%	50.5%
Spotsylvania County	20,512	64.5%	20.1%	36.6%	43.3%	28,279	88.9%	14.4%	41.2%	44.4%
Stafford County	25,264	66.4%	13.9%	40.2%	45.9%	137	0.4%	0.0%	44.5%	55.5%
Washington										
Benton County	28,331	58.8%	17.2%	30.2%	52.5%	3,361	7.0%	4.7%	48.0%	47.4%
Clark County	84,289	73.8%	17.8%	33.2%	49.0%	52	0.0%	0.0%	0.0%	100.0%
Cowlitz County	18,329	79.5%	15.9%	33.3%	50.8%	366	1.6%	30.6%	69.4%	0.0%
Grant County	15,644	63.3%	14.9%	48.3%	36.8%	1,753	7.1%	15.2%	59.4%	25.4%
King County	319,746	56.3%	11.3%	28.9%	59.7%	883	0.2%	16.6%	16.5%	66.8%
Kitsap County	49,389	70.6%	13.3%	37.6%	49.1%	3,992	5.7%	10.8%	33.2%	55.9%
Pierce County	140,804	62.5%	13.5%	34.2%	52.4%	1,003	0.4%	0.0%	54.3%	45.7%
Skagit County	19,754	72.4%	14.5%	33.1%	52.4%	1,750	6.4%	0.0%	26.8%	73.2%
Snohomish County	128,249	66.7%	15.3%	32.8%	51.9%	7,344	3.8%	19.7%	32.9%	47.4%
Spokane County	107,462	79.2%	13.7%	35.8%	50.5%	999	0.7%	0.0%	70.6%	29.4%
Thurston County	47,175	70.1%	14.4%	32.9%	52.8%	943	1.4%	71.2%	23.2%	5.6%
Whatcom County	47,751	74.4%	10.9%	48.7%	40.4%	3,146	4.9%	10.6%	70.3%	19.1%
Yakima County	22,424	34.9%	16.3%	34.1%	49.7%	485	0.8%	0.0%	100.0%	0.0%
West Virginia										
Berkeley County	22,788	85.0%	14.0%	38.1%	47.9%	528	2.0%	56.6%	20.1%	23.3%
Cabell County	24,643	92.5%	15.7%	43.2%	41.1%	76,099	285.7%	16.9%	42.1%	41.0%
Kanawha County	34,094	83.8%	15.4%	35.0%	49.7%	990	2.4%	0.0%	78.7%	21.3%
Monongalia County	36,371	84.5%	7.6%	51.9%	40.5%	6,517	15.1%	16.5%	46.0%	37.5%
Wisconsin										
Brown County	49,664	76.1%	15.6%	36.6%	47.8%	771	1.2%	21.1%	46.6%	32.3%
Dane County	124,239	78.1%	9.8%	44.1%	46.1%	148	0.1%	23.6%	44.6%	31.8%
Eau Claire County	28,732	88.6%	14.2%	45.6%	40.2%	170	0.5%	0.0%	81.8%	18.2%
Fond du Lac County	20,236	83.8%	19.9%	31.8%	48.3%	245	1.0%	0.0%	100.0%	0.0%
Kenosha County	30,087	71.6%	17.0%	37.1%	45.9%	1,125	2.7%	9.6%	70.8%	19.6%
La Crosse County	32,621	91.1%	10.7%	53.9%	35.4%	967	2.7%	0.0%	0.0%	100.0%
Marathon County	26,210	88.9%	18.0%	34.5%	47.6%	260	0.9%	0.0%	70.4%	29.6%
Milwaukee County	129,481	48.4%	10.1%	32.4%	57.5%	129,481	48.4%	10.1%	32.4%	57.5%
Outagamie County	37,895	82.5%	16.9%	35.0%	48.1%	37,895	82.5%	16.9%	35.0%	48.1%
Racine County	28,693	63.1%	18.3%	34.9%	46.8%	28,693	63.1%	18.3%	34.9%	46.8%
Rock County	29,806	81.2%	17.3%	36.9%	45.8%	29,806	81.2%	17.3%	36.9%	45.8%
Sheboygan County	19,431	77.9%	19.1%	37.6%	43.4%	19,431	77.9%	19.1%	37.6%	43.4%
Walworth County	21,580	79.3%	14.9%	51.5%	33.5%	21,580	79.3%	14.9%	51.5%	33.5%
Washington County	25,358	91.9%	15.7%	37.6%	46.6%	25,358	91.9%	15.7%	37.6%	46.6%
Waukesha County	71,762	86.7%	20.3%	36.6%	43.2%	71,762	86.7%	20.3%	36.6%	43.2%
Winnebago County	40,556	86.7%	12.5%	44.9%	42.6%	40,556	86.7%	12.5%	44.9%	42.6%
Wyoming										
Laramie County	19,989	75.1%	12.9%	45.1%	42.0%	19,989	75.1%	12.9%	45.1%	42.0%

Table B-2: Counties—Race and Hispanic Origin by Age—*Continued*

	Asian, Non-Hispanic					Hispanic				
	Millennial Population		Percent by Age			Millennial Population		Percent by Age		
	Number	Percent	15 to 17	18 to 24	25 to 33	Number	Percent	15 to 17	18 to 24	25 to 33
Texas—Cont.										
Potter County	1,272	3.9%	3.4%	53.5%	43.1%	14,957	46.3%	15.5%	35.8%	48.7%
Randall County	1,073	3.0%	0.0%	38.4%	61.6%	9,588	26.4%	15.4%	41.0%	43.6%
Smith County	1,214	2.0%	13.8%	75.5%	10.6%	13,990	23.0%	17.6%	32.9%	49.5%
Tarrant County	30,027	5.6%	9.6%	35.9%	54.5%	172,691	32.5%	17.8%	35.9%	46.3%
Taylor County	1,011	2.3%	19.8%	80.2%	0.0%	10,703	24.7%	16.8%	46.1%	37.1%
Tom Green County	721	2.0%	0.0%	36.2%	63.8%	15,117	42.3%	14.2%	40.5%	45.3%
Travis County	25,574	7.0%	8.0%	31.3%	60.7%	133,203	36.6%	13.3%	32.6%	54.0%
Webb County	550	0.7%	50.0%	40.4%	9.6%	72,632	95.3%	19.1%	40.8%	40.1%
Wichita County	964	2.3%	0.0%	53.6%	46.4%	8,818	21.3%	13.6%	44.1%	42.2%
Williamson County	6,423	5.2%	17.5%	8.9%	73.5%	35,783	29.1%	19.1%	36.7%	44.3%
Utah										
Cache County	1,251	2.8%	0.0%	11.1%	88.9%	5,275	11.8%	12.2%	39.5%	48.3%
Davis County	1,808	2.0%	36.1%	23.7%	40.2%	10,397	11.3%	13.9%	49.3%	36.8%
Salt Lake County	13,907	4.4%	9.2%	28.6%	62.2%	63,068	20.0%	20.6%	39.2%	40.2%
Utah County	4,176	2.1%	14.9%	39.3%	45.8%	20,569	10.4%	15.8%	43.2%	40.9%
Washington County	213	0.5%	0.0%	27.2%	72.8%	3,684	9.3%	16.1%	61.0%	22.9%
Weber County	993	1.5%	13.8%	67.3%	18.9%	13,466	19.7%	18.1%	43.0%	38.9%
Vermont										
Chittenden County	1,482	2.9%	23.9%	62.3%	13.8%	2,100	4.1%	6.5%	56.8%	36.7%
Virginia										
Albemarle County	1,875	6.4%	16.3%	57.5%	26.2%	2,723	9.3%	0.0%	64.3%	35.7%
Arlington County	8,610	11.1%	10.1%	27.6%	62.3%	11,207	14.5%	4.8%	28.7%	66.5%
Chesterfield County	2,495	3.1%	20.5%	24.8%	54.7%	8,255	10.2%	17.9%	35.7%	46.4%
Fairfax County	52,875	18.7%	16.0%	29.8%	54.2%	53,171	18.9%	15.4%	36.2%	48.4%
Hanover County	462	2.0%	0.0%	34.8%	65.2%	870	3.8%	37.2%	40.6%	22.2%
Henrico County	6,960	8.8%	11.9%	15.7%	72.4%	5,338	6.7%	6.5%	53.2%	40.2%
Loudoun County	13,735	16.2%	18.7%	20.1%	61.2%	12,848	15.2%	17.3%	29.8%	52.9%
Montgomery County	2,865	6.7%	0.0%	63.0%	37.0%	2,591	6.0%	0.4%	83.1%	16.5%
Prince William County	9,561	8.2%	16.1%	30.5%	53.3%	28,974	24.8%	17.7%	38.9%	43.4%
Roanoke County	291	1.4%	0.0%	21.6%	78.4%	761	3.5%	9.6%	52.4%	38.0%
Spotsylvania County	336	1.1%	72.3%	0.0%	27.7%	1,958	6.2%	17.7%	46.5%	35.9%
Stafford County	841	2.2%	23.9%	22.1%	54.0%	4,397	11.6%	26.3%	51.6%	22.1%
Washington										
Denton County	755	1.6%	14.7%	2.1%	83.2%	14,723	30.6%	19.6%	52.3%	28.1%
Clark County	4,582	4.0%	16.8%	31.4%	51.8%	13,749	12.0%	16.8%	37.6%	45.7%
Cowlitz County	321	1.4%	0.0%	33.3%	66.7%	3,183	13.8%	9.2%	6.2%	84.7%
Grant County	868	3.5%	0.0%	100.0%	0.0%	7,682	31.1%	9.7%	38.5%	51.8%
King County	103,875	18.3%	9.2%	31.0%	59.8%	63,681	11.2%	12.7%	31.4%	55.9%
Kitsap County	2,187	3.1%	14.4%	28.2%	57.4%	7,402	10.6%	9.2%	45.0%	45.8%
Pierce County	12,978	5.8%	12.2%	34.0%	53.8%	29,180	13.0%	17.7%	35.7%	46.6%
Skagit County	649	2.4%	63.3%	23.3%	13.4%	5,155	18.9%	15.3%	36.4%	48.3%
Snohomish County	18,394	9.6%	14.8%	33.3%	51.8%	23,025	12.0%	16.5%	31.1%	52.4%
Spokane County	4,192	3.1%	8.8%	19.7%	71.5%	10,284	7.6%	17.0%	32.5%	50.6%
Thurston County	4,111	6.1%	12.6%	30.8%	56.5%	7,834	11.6%	15.0%	48.0%	37.0%
Whatcom County	2,733	4.3%	6.0%	59.0%	35.0%	6,639	10.3%	16.2%	43.7%	40.1%
Yakima County	126	0.2%	0.0%	0.0%	100.0%	37,736	58.6%	19.1%	42.1%	38.7%
West Virginia										
Berkeley County	1,627	6.1%	22.6%	4.9%	72.6%	1,627	6.1%	22.6%	4.9%	72.6%
Cabell County	89	0.3%	0.0%	67.4%	32.6%	363	1.4%	0.0%	46.0%	54.0%
Kanawha County	686	1.7%	16.2%	6.3%	77.6%	725	1.8%	16.8%	39.9%	43.3%
Monongalia County	1,590	3.7%	1.5%	2.7%	95.8%	1,637	3.8%	0.0%	21.7%	78.3%
Wisconsin										
Brown County	2,920	4.5%	3.3%	14.0%	82.7%	7,486	11.5%	9.3%	40.8%	49.9%
Dane County	14,903	9.4%	13.1%	43.9%	43.0%	9,096	5.7%	17.1%	25.8%	57.1%
Eau Claire County	1,707	5.3%	12.9%	41.4%	45.7%	803	2.5%	1.2%	88.0%	10.7%
Fond du Lac County	854	3.5%	0.0%	77.0%	23.0%	1,591	6.6%	20.3%	68.2%	11.5%
Kenosha County	659	1.6%	0.5%	0.0%	99.5%	7,306	17.4%	21.0%	47.0%	32.0%
La Crosse County	1,889	5.3%	10.7%	43.1%	46.2%	580	1.6%	36.2%	63.8%	0.0%
Marathon County	1,706	5.8%	22.6%	1.9%	75.4%	760	2.6%	19.5%	41.4%	39.1%
Milwaukee County	10,233	3.8%	10.6%	29.8%	59.6%	41,967	15.7%	16.4%	38.8%	44.8%
Outagamie County	2,700	5.9%	9.4%	17.4%	73.2%	1,682	3.7%	0.0%	5.6%	94.4%
Racine County	1,277	2.8%	18.5%	78.4%	3.1%	8,173	18.0%	15.5%	42.1%	42.4%
Rock County	422	1.1%	7.6%	54.5%	37.9%	3,780	10.3%	19.6%	49.9%	30.6%
Sheboygan County	2,073	8.3%	4.2%	25.0%	70.8%	2,820	11.3%	23.0%	17.9%	59.0%
Walworth County	363	1.3%	38.0%	50.7%	11.3%	4,395	16.2%	10.3%	34.9%	54.8%
Washington County	404	1.5%	0.0%	49.8%	50.2%	651	2.4%	94.3%	5.7%	0.0%
Waukesha County	3,534	4.3%	26.2%	16.8%	57.0%	4,291	5.2%	36.0%	25.1%	39.0%
Winnebago County	1,749	3.7%	0.0%	7.1%	92.9%	2,920	6.2%	42.3%	17.6%	40.1%
Wyoming										
Laramie County	1,043	3.9%	3.9%	94.1%	2.0%	3,910	14.7%	17.1%	62.6%	20.3%

Table B-3: Places—Race and Hispanic Origin by Age

	White, Non-Hispanic					Black, Non-Hispanic				
	Millennial Population		Percent by Age			Millennial Population		Percent by Age		
	Number	Percent	15 to 17	18 to 24	25 to 33	Number	Percent	15 to 17	18 to 24	25 to 33
Alabama										
Birmingham city	19,977	30.6%	4.0%	43.1%	52.9%	41,810	64.1%	16.1%	36.6%	47.3%
Huntsville city	27,589	54.5%	15.2%	35.3%	49.5%	16,634	32.9%	12.7%	43.7%	43.6%
Mobile city	22,093	40.2%	9.5%	34.8%	55.8%	27,602	50.3%	18.7%	40.7%	40.5%
Montgomery city	17,584	31.0%	12.1%	37.7%	50.2%	35,443	62.6%	14.2%	39.3%	46.6%
Tuscaloosa city	23,666	54.7%	5.4%	64.7%	29.9%	15,638	36.1%	13.9%	52.9%	33.2%
Alaska										
Anchorage municipality	50,011	54.1%	10.3%	33.1%	56.6%	6,763	7.3%	13.3%	52.1%	34.5%
Arizona										
Chandler city	36,537	53.0%	17.8%	32.4%	49.8%	2,754	4.0%	28.9%	22.6%	48.5%
Glendale city	31,354	46.4%	14.3%	35.9%	49.8%	4,707	7.0%	22.1%	31.4%	46.5%
Mesa city	66,648	52.0%	14.4%	35.3%	50.2%	6,673	5.2%	18.2%	33.1%	48.7%
Peoria city	24,540	58.4%	17.8%	32.5%	49.7%	1,971	4.7%	5.5%	36.8%	57.7%
Phoenix city	151,900	35.1%	11.8%	31.1%	57.1%	33,576	7.8%	13.5%	38.8%	47.7%
Scottsdale city	38,119	72.5%	11.4%	26.2%	62.4%	1,824	3.5%	19.5%	5.9%	74.6%
Surprise city	15,552	57.4%	18.2%	24.5%	57.2%	2,037	7.5%	26.5%	33.8%	39.7%
Tempe city	40,825	52.2%	5.2%	58.2%	36.6%	3,938	5.0%	13.5%	53.4%	33.1%
Tucson city	68,016	40.1%	9.5%	50.8%	39.7%	7,926	4.7%	13.7%	42.9%	43.4%
Yuma city	6,792	24.6%	14.0%	42.8%	43.1%	298	1.1%	0.0%	27.2%	72.8%
Arkansas										
Little Rock city	20,064	37.4%	12.2%	24.5%	63.3%	24,245	45.2%	16.9%	39.7%	43.4%
California										
Anaheim city	23,092	22.0%	10.0%	40.9%	49.0%	738	0.7%	0.0%	64.9%	35.1%
Antioch city	8,648	27.8%	9.3%	50.5%	40.2%	6,824	21.9%	24.0%	40.1%	35.9%
Bakersfield city	31,913	27.5%	12.7%	36.2%	51.2%	6,197	5.3%	17.0%	48.3%	34.6%
Berkeley city	22,352	45.2%	5.2%	45.1%	49.6%	2,954	6.0%	32.5%	28.5%	39.0%
Burbank city	15,658	56.1%	16.5%	24.4%	59.1%	968	3.5%	0.0%	12.0%	88.0%
Carlsbad city	17,764	68.6%	16.3%	36.9%	46.8%	42	0.2%	0.0%	100.0%	0.0%
Chico city	24,087	67.7%	9.2%	56.3%	34.4%	760	2.1%	46.6%	53.4%	0.0%
Carson city	1,083	4.2%	33.4%	24.6%	42.0%	4,304	16.6%	12.4%	53.3%	34.3%
Chula Vista city	9,699	13.2%	16.3%	30.6%	53.0%	3,839	5.2%	8.5%	44.1%	47.4%
Clovis city	13,755	52.3%	20.1%	29.8%	50.1%	981	3.7%	0.0%	87.4%	12.6%
Compton city	631	2.1%	17.7%	55.2%	27.1%	6,061	19.9%	17.1%	58.5%	24.5%
Concord city	12,308	40.0%	15.0%	27.3%	57.7%	1,895	6.2%	22.5%	22.9%	54.6%
Corona city	14,247	33.6%	16.4%	37.5%	46.2%	2,446	5.8%	20.0%	45.6%	34.5%
Costa Mesa city	20,487	56.3%	13.5%	24.2%	62.3%	1,313	3.6%	0.0%	10.2%	89.8%
Daly City city	6,525	22.0%	5.2%	26.8%	68.0%	874	3.0%	0.0%	51.0%	49.0%
Downey city	2,597	7.7%	8.5%	44.6%	46.9%	1,600	4.7%	26.9%	26.6%	46.6%
El Cajon city	16,747	55.7%	13.4%	32.9%	53.7%	882	2.9%	11.1%	38.1%	50.8%
Elk Grove city	13,499	32.4%	12.6%	49.2%	38.2%	4,618	11.1%	7.0%	47.3%	45.7%
El Monte city	1,414	4.2%	23.6%	38.9%	37.6%	na	na	na	na	na
Escondido city	16,441	34.8%	8.0%	37.9%	54.1%	595	1.3%	0.0%	25.4%	74.6%
Fairfield city	9,335	29.9%	13.9%	26.4%	59.7%	2,824	9.0%	19.8%	38.7%	41.5%
Fontana city	4,943	7.7%	12.7%	32.0%	55.3%	3,940	6.2%	11.8%	47.9%	40.4%
Fremont city	9,835	16.7%	15.3%	35.5%	49.3%	3,002	5.1%	3.4%	65.6%	31.0%
Fresno city	35,084	21.8%	10.9%	36.3%	52.8%	12,452	7.7%	14.4%	45.0%	40.6%
Fullerton city	12,259	27.9%	11.9%	40.1%	48.0%	698	1.6%	0.9%	81.4%	17.8%
Garden Grove city	7,122	15.1%	11.7%	23.0%	65.4%	105	0.2%	0.0%	0.0%	100.0%
Glendale city	28,508	58.0%	9.9%	31.1%	59.1%	1,089	2.2%	0.0%	2.3%	97.7%
Hayward city	5,613	11.8%	10.7%	19.8%	69.5%	4,253	8.9%	9.7%	44.7%	45.6%
Hesperia city	8,365	30.9%	10.7%	35.6%	53.7%	2,327	8.6%	33.5%	39.8%	26.7%
Huntington Beach city	24,788	55.8%	13.4%	28.7%	57.8%	742	1.7%	13.7%	46.6%	39.6%
Inglewood city	952	3.0%	0.0%	11.7%	88.3%	9,805	30.9%	15.4%	36.5%	48.1%
Irvine city	31,061	37.4%	13.0%	42.9%	44.0%	3,720	4.5%	6.4%	54.0%	39.6%
Jurupa Valley city	5,576	18.6%	10.1%	41.0%	48.9%	1,451	4.8%	0.0%	52.4%	47.6%
Lancaster city	15,148	30.8%	20.0%	29.3%	50.6%	11,695	23.8%	16.9%	23.2%	60.0%
Long Beach city	28,873	21.0%	9.6%	30.5%	59.9%	16,500	12.0%	12.4%	34.6%	53.0%
Los Angeles city	303,404	25.1%	7.6%	29.5%	63.0%	105,597	8.7%	13.1%	36.6%	50.3%
Mission Viejo city	13,076	58.6%	13.6%	43.9%	42.5%	89	0.4%	100.0%	0.0%	0.0%
Modesto city	22,525	39.4%	12.0%	32.9%	55.0%	2,065	3.6%	26.2%	49.9%	23.8%
Moreno Valley city	10,573	15.9%	12.2%	31.6%	56.2%	10,120	15.2%	19.8%	47.3%	32.9%
Murrieta city	13,101	43.0%	22.3%	28.4%	49.3%	1,170	3.8%	26.3%	43.9%	29.7%
Norwalk city	1,638	5.3%	5.3%	42.7%	52.0%	1,703	5.5%	12.8%	52.0%	35.2%
Oakland city	32,865	26.9%	6.3%	21.8%	71.9%	25,710	21.0%	11.7%	37.0%	51.2%
Oceanside city	19,261	42.5%	8.1%	54.7%	37.1%	3,300	7.3%	6.2%	53.7%	40.1%
Ontario city	6,203	12.0%	13.1%	30.0%	56.9%	3,607	7.0%	12.5%	34.2%	53.3%
Orange city	20,191	45.8%	13.4%	42.0%	44.6%	729	1.7%	1.0%	16.9%	82.2%
Oxnard city	9,546	15.3%	9.4%	28.9%	61.7%	1,355	2.2%	3.8%	31.1%	65.1%
Palmdale city	8,831	20.8%	17.5%	29.0%	53.5%	6,904	16.3%	12.5%	56.3%	31.2%
Pasadena city	10,924	29.7%	4.9%	25.7%	69.4%	3,213	8.7%	2.4%	43.9%	53.7%
Pomona city	5,596	11.5%	6.4%	38.1%	55.5%	2,069	4.2%	0.4%	47.2%	52.3%
Rancho Cucamonga city	16,773	33.5%	15.4%	35.3%	49.3%	6,929	13.8%	12.2%	51.0%	36.8%
Redding city	18,296	73.7%	19.1%	27.8%	53.1%	412	1.7%	0.0%	0.0%	100.0%
Rialto city	3,027	9.2%	13.7%	52.9%	33.4%	1,311	4.0%	25.2%	40.2%	34.6%

Table B-3: Places—Race and Hispanic Origin by Age—*Continued*

| | Asian, Non-Hispanic | | | | | Hispanic | | | | |
| | Millennial Population | | Percent by Age | | | Millennial Population | | Percent by Age | | |
	Number	Percent	15 to 17	18 to 24	25 to 33	Number	Percent	15 to 17	18 to 24	25 to 33
Alabama										
Birmingham city	774	1.2%	22.9%	12.3%	64.9%	1,893	2.9%	9.1%	32.4%	58.5%
Huntsville city	872	1.7%	0.0%	65.7%	34.3%	3,443	6.8%	5.0%	34.7%	60.3%
Mobile city	1,975	3.6%	12.2%	18.5%	69.4%	1,962	3.6%	9.5%	18.0%	72.5%
Montgomery city	447	0.8%	11.2%	0.0%	88.8%	1,284	2.3%	11.9%	26.3%	61.8%
Tuscaloosa city	1,908	4.4%	0.0%	80.2%	19.8%	1,933	4.5%	6.3%	39.0%	54.7%
Alaska										
Anchorage municipality	8,453	9.1%	22.1%	36.0%	41.9%	11,450	12.4%	15.3%	42.7%	42.0%
Arizona										
Chandler city	7,988	11.6%	3.9%	25.0%	71.0%	18,542	26.9%	18.6%	31.2%	50.2%
Glendale city	3,808	5.6%	8.6%	23.6%	67.8%	25,200	37.3%	20.1%	36.9%	43.0%
Mesa city	3,006	2.3%	7.9%	39.7%	52.5%	42,466	33.1%	17.5%	34.5%	47.9%
Peoria city	1,245	3.0%	10.4%	7.6%	82.1%	12,816	30.5%	18.2%	34.3%	47.5%
Phoenix city	11,086	2.6%	11.2%	21.0%	67.8%	216,105	49.9%	17.4%	40.6%	42.1%
Scottsdale city	2,547	4.8%	13.2%	43.9%	42.9%	7,407	14.1%	19.7%	42.5%	37.8%
Surprise city	214	0.8%	67.3%	0.0%	32.7%	8,309	30.7%	25.0%	33.7%	41.3%
Tempe city	9,847	12.6%	3.0%	59.8%	37.1%	20,685	26.5%	11.8%	53.0%	35.2%
Tucson city	8,232	4.9%	3.1%	54.7%	42.1%	77,047	45.4%	14.2%	48.1%	37.7%
Yuma city	281	1.0%	61.2%	26.3%	12.5%	19,848	72.0%	20.7%	40.6%	38.7%
Arkansas										
Little Rock city	1,596	3.0%	14.1%	20.7%	65.2%	5,680	10.6%	1.9%	35.5%	62.6%
California										
Anaheim city	12,790	12.2%	8.5%	30.8%	60.7%	65,684	62.6%	16.1%	36.1%	47.8%
Antioch city	3,125	10.0%	6.5%	47.9%	45.6%	9,832	31.6%	21.2%	41.9%	36.9%
Bakersfield city	7,223	6.2%	14.5%	29.6%	55.9%	68,643	59.0%	15.6%	39.8%	44.6%
Berkeley city	14,497	29.3%	2.3%	64.4%	33.2%	6,430	13.0%	5.4%	61.1%	33.5%
Burbank city	3,060	11.0%	6.0%	29.2%	64.8%	6,724	24.1%	17.0%	26.5%	56.5%
Carlsbad city	1,962	7.6%	44.0%	6.1%	49.9%	4,737	18.3%	16.6%	34.7%	48.7%
Chico city	958	2.7%	0.0%	61.4%	38.6%	8,451	23.8%	12.2%	56.9%	31.0%
Carson city	8,480	32.6%	9.5%	37.1%	53.4%	9,591	36.9%	19.9%	38.1%	42.0%
Chula Vista city	11,368	15.5%	11.1%	56.6%	32.4%	44,813	61.1%	16.9%	38.0%	45.1%
Clovis city	2,525	9.6%	8.0%	32.2%	59.7%	8,328	31.7%	9.9%	28.1%	61.9%
Compton city	101	0.3%	0.0%	0.0%	100.0%	22,638	74.2%	15.5%	37.8%	46.7%
Concord city	3,909	12.7%	14.1%	24.4%	61.5%	10,875	35.4%	12.7%	40.0%	47.3%
Corona city	3,192	7.5%	11.0%	24.5%	64.4%	22,061	52.1%	15.8%	33.4%	50.8%
Costa Mesa city	4,044	11.1%	17.6%	36.1%	46.3%	8,909	24.5%	21.9%	41.5%	36.6%
Daly City city	13,068	44.1%	4.0%	31.5%	64.5%	7,781	26.3%	9.4%	44.3%	46.2%
Downey city	2,637	7.8%	8.8%	26.0%	65.2%	26,561	78.6%	14.0%	43.3%	42.7%
El Cajon city	607	2.0%	8.9%	26.9%	64.3%	8,969	29.8%	14.6%	42.9%	42.5%
Elk Grove city	11,973	28.7%	15.4%	35.3%	49.3%	7,912	19.0%	25.6%	44.3%	30.2%
El Monte city	7,377	22.0%	12.8%	31.1%	56.1%	24,578	73.2%	16.0%	38.4%	45.7%
Escondido city	3,098	6.6%	2.0%	22.4%	75.7%	23,782	50.4%	15.6%	36.4%	48.0%
Fairfield city	5,042	16.1%	14.5%	28.9%	56.6%	10,421	33.4%	18.2%	30.6%	51.2%
Fontana city	2,039	3.2%	2.9%	30.6%	66.6%	52,702	82.4%	14.5%	36.3%	49.2%
Fremont city	32,248	54.8%	13.0%	23.7%	63.3%	10,647	18.1%	15.8%	42.7%	41.5%
Fresno city	24,616	15.3%	12.6%	32.7%	54.7%	83,889	52.2%	17.2%	38.8%	43.9%
Fullerton city	8,489	19.3%	13.8%	30.3%	55.9%	20,688	47.0%	15.3%	46.4%	38.3%
Garden Grove city	17,213	36.6%	14.1%	38.1%	47.8%	21,661	46.0%	16.1%	40.5%	43.3%
Glendale city	8,140	16.5%	16.4%	30.3%	53.3%	9,201	18.7%	8.4%	32.0%	59.6%
Hayward city	12,201	25.6%	10.2%	28.2%	61.6%	21,568	45.2%	14.0%	33.2%	52.8%
Hesperia city	421	1.6%	0.0%	0.0%	100.0%	15,107	55.7%	23.5%	32.2%	44.3%
Huntington Beach city	5,118	11.5%	7.6%	20.3%	72.1%	11,326	25.5%	7.5%	40.7%	51.8%
Inglewood city	173	0.5%	32.4%	67.6%	0.0%	20,295	64.0%	13.5%	37.6%	49.0%
Irvine city	32,187	38.7%	12.7%	39.5%	47.8%	12,139	14.6%	9.8%	53.4%	36.8%
Jurupa Valley city	2,932	9.8%	32.7%	14.1%	53.3%	19,368	64.6%	15.8%	44.0%	40.2%
Lancaster city	1,710	3.5%	6.8%	15.6%	77.7%	19,702	40.0%	17.9%	36.7%	45.4%
Long Beach city	15,954	11.6%	9.9%	30.5%	59.6%	70,414	51.2%	16.9%	37.2%	46.0%
Los Angeles city	141,893	11.7%	7.9%	36.6%	55.6%	625,215	51.7%	14.7%	38.1%	47.2%
Mission Viejo city	2,730	12.2%	9.6%	31.1%	59.3%	5,972	26.8%	18.0%	47.7%	34.4%
Modesto city	3,861	6.8%	10.9%	42.5%	46.6%	26,208	45.8%	15.7%	43.5%	40.9%
Moreno Valley city	3,163	4.8%	13.4%	43.5%	43.1%	41,124	61.9%	19.4%	41.3%	39.3%
Murrieta city	1,929	6.3%	20.7%	42.4%	36.9%	11,872	39.0%	21.8%	32.4%	45.8%
Norwalk city	2,765	9.0%	6.2%	31.0%	62.8%	24,274	79.1%	11.9%	45.4%	42.7%
Oakland city	17,950	14.7%	9.5%	29.0%	61.6%	37,407	30.6%	13.7%	28.1%	58.2%
Oceanside city	2,709	6.0%	17.5%	31.0%	51.5%	16,588	36.6%	15.7%	48.3%	36.0%
Ontario city	4,266	8.3%	12.5%	34.0%	53.5%	36,239	70.3%	17.1%	38.3%	44.6%
Orange city	4,335	9.8%	4.3%	42.1%	53.6%	17,823	40.4%	11.3%	37.0%	51.8%
Oxnard city	3,103	5.0%	21.4%	23.0%	55.5%	46,444	74.6%	14.4%	35.5%	50.1%
Palmdale city	1,807	4.3%	26.5%	40.6%	32.9%	24,144	57.0%	19.4%	36.7%	43.9%
Pasadena city	5,309	14.4%	2.5%	26.5%	71.0%	15,801	43.0%	11.4%	36.9%	51.7%
Pomona city	6,229	12.8%	5.0%	35.9%	59.0%	34,066	69.9%	17.1%	42.6%	40.3%
Rancho Cucamonga city	4,923	9.8%	10.8%	39.9%	49.3%	20,009	39.9%	14.5%	46.4%	39.1%
Redding city	898	3.6%	6.6%	23.9%	69.5%	3,074	12.4%	21.4%	52.7%	25.9%
Rialto city	1,452	4.4%	18.6%	18.0%	63.4%	26,297	80.0%	16.2%	36.6%	47.2%

Table B-3: Places—Race and Hispanic Origin by Age—*Continued*

| | White, Non-Hispanic | | | | | Black, Non-Hispanic | | | | |
| | Millennial Population | | Percent by Age | | | Millennial Population | | Percent by Age | | |
	Number	Percent	15 to 17	18 to 24	25 to 33	Number	Percent	15 to 17	18 to 24	25 to 33
California—Cont.										
Richmond city	2,893	8.9%	7.1%	36.5%	56.4%	5,630	17.3%	7.7%	30.7%	61.6%
Riverside city	31,312	28.7%	9.3%	38.2%	52.5%	5,927	5.4%	22.7%	44.3%	33.0%
Roseville city	20,024	61.4%	16.5%	35.5%	48.0%	803	2.5%	32.6%	19.8%	47.6%
Sacramento city	38,258	26.9%	11.5%	25.1%	63.4%	15,316	10.8%	17.8%	40.1%	42.1%
Salinas city	5,008	11.1%	13.0%	45.1%	41.9%	959	2.1%	4.4%	27.1%	68.5%
San Bernardino city	8,492	12.4%	12.6%	41.1%	46.3%	5,369	7.8%	5.1%	35.4%	59.5%
San Buenaventura (Ventura) city...	12,831	46.4%	16.2%	28.7%	55.1%	484	1.8%	0.0%	100.0%	0.0%
San Diego city	177,005	39.8%	8.7%	35.1%	56.2%	30,107	6.8%	10.2%	36.8%	53.0%
San Francisco city	110,083	42.5%	3.7%	16.8%	79.6%	11,846	4.6%	11.3%	32.0%	56.7%
San Jose city	64,712	24.0%	11.9%	31.4%	56.7%	7,963	3.0%	6.7%	33.9%	59.4%
San Leandro city	5,171	22.7%	6.4%	28.5%	65.0%	1,248	5.5%	0.0%	34.5%	65.5%
San Marcos city	9,969	40.9%	6.5%	37.8%	55.7%	1,383	5.7%	58.1%	41.9%	0.0%
San Mateo city	8,948	36.6%	18.4%	31.1%	50.4%	159	0.7%	100.0%	0.0%	0.0%
Santa Ana city	7,201	7.1%	3.6%	29.0%	67.4%	1,155	1.1%	38.6%	17.8%	43.5%
Santa Clara city	10,823	27.3%	5.5%	39.6%	54.9%	1,828	4.6%	0.0%	50.4%	49.6%
Santa Clarita city	20,847	43.6%	14.0%	35.8%	50.1%	2,663	5.6%	0.0%	52.2%	47.8%
Santa Maria city	5,410	17.7%	13.8%	43.8%	42.5%	81	0.3%	0.0%	0.0%	100.0%
Santa Monica city	14,179	57.5%	7.8%	15.2%	77.0%	2,170	8.8%	17.6%	29.5%	52.9%
Santa Rosa city	22,048	49.6%	9.7%	34.0%	56.3%	674	1.5%	3.9%	45.1%	51.0%
Simi Valley city	16,447	50.2%	21.8%	41.7%	36.5%	1,102	3.4%	0.5%	0.0%	99.5%
South Gate city	808	2.9%	19.2%	29.5%	51.4%	789	2.8%	0.0%	57.3%	42.7%
Stockton city	17,616	19.2%	13.7%	39.1%	47.2%	8,829	9.6%	15.3%	44.5%	40.2%
Sunnyvale city	10,629	25.4%	9.7%	26.1%	64.2%	1,964	4.7%	26.5%	22.4%	51.1%
Temecula city	14,691	48.5%	23.2%	31.8%	45.0%	1,159	3.8%	16.3%	13.2%	70.5%
Thousand Oaks city	14,241	54.1%	24.3%	44.9%	30.8%	1,312	5.0%	0.0%	67.8%	32.2%
Torrance city	9,176	26.0%	15.6%	31.1%	53.2%	2,352	6.7%	14.0%	48.3%	37.7%
Vacaville city	11,883	44.9%	14.1%	39.8%	46.1%	1,988	7.5%	18.7%	38.4%	42.9%
Vallejo city	8,663	25.7%	6.3%	28.0%	65.7%	5,013	14.9%	7.9%	27.6%	64.6%
Victorville city	7,697	21.0%	26.6%	32.8%	40.6%	5,681	15.5%	33.7%	31.4%	34.9%
Visalia city	12,457	36.7%	15.0%	34.0%	51.1%	669	2.0%	0.0%	83.1%	16.9%
Vista city	13,314	42.2%	7.7%	33.6%	58.7%	1,487	4.7%	18.0%	56.2%	25.9%
West Covina city	2,305	7.9%	9.7%	21.5%	68.8%	1,082	3.7%	0.0%	43.9%	56.1%
Westminster city	4,489	20.6%	7.8%	21.8%	70.3%	85	0.4%	0.0%	100.0%	0.0%
Colorado										
Arvada city	19,621	76.0%	20.4%	27.4%	52.2%	1,258	4.9%	2.9%	7.6%	89.6%
Aurora city	41,160	40.3%	13.1%	26.8%	60.1%	13,404	13.1%	17.1%	37.0%	46.0%
Boulder city	40,642	80.2%	4.4%	62.6%	33.0%	948	1.9%	0.0%	77.4%	22.6%
Centennial city	18,577	74.9%	21.9%	33.8%	44.4%	614	2.5%	0.0%	20.7%	79.3%
Colorado Springs city	85,537	64.8%	13.5%	34.4%	52.1%	9,206	7.0%	4.5%	25.3%	70.1%
Denver city	115,993	53.4%	3.6%	20.4%	76.0%	18,184	8.4%	9.9%	35.4%	54.7%
Fort Collins city	51,439	79.4%	8.1%	50.1%	41.7%	705	1.1%	0.0%	80.0%	20.0%
Greeley city	19,471	60.2%	13.5%	36.8%	49.7%	1,169	3.6%	45.3%	54.7%	0.0%
Lakewood city	28,738	65.3%	11.0%	39.3%	49.7%	662	1.5%	11.5%	0.0%	88.5%
Longmont city	14,208	65.7%	21.8%	34.7%	43.5%	83	0.4%	0.0%	0.0%	100.0%
Pueblo city	12,712	43.7%	16.9%	29.7%	53.3%	174	0.6%	0.0%	43.1%	56.9%
Thornton city	14,901	42.7%	14.5%	32.5%	53.0%	415	1.2%	0.0%	40.7%	59.3%
Westminster city	18,112	60.3%	14.8%	26.4%	58.8%	838	2.8%	0.0%	38.9%	61.1%
Connecticut										
Bridgeport city	10,558	24.0%	4.5%	38.9%	56.6%	11,939	27.2%	17.8%	34.8%	47.4%
Hartford city	8,575	19.4%	0.6%	65.1%	34.3%	13,836	31.4%	17.8%	40.5%	41.7%
New Haven city	16,641	31.7%	4.5%	38.5%	57.1%	12,324	23.5%	17.7%	43.2%	39.1%
Stamford city	18,655	48.8%	12.1%	32.1%	55.8%	3,793	9.9%	18.2%	26.6%	55.2%
Waterbury city	8,913	31.7%	13.0%	35.6%	51.3%	6,842	24.3%	12.7%	36.7%	50.6%
District of Columbia										
Washington city	103,675	43.9%	2.1%	30.6%	67.3%	88,308	37.4%	12.0%	40.7%	47.2%
Florida										
Boca Raton city	13,175	60.8%	19.3%	41.6%	39.1%	2,121	9.8%	5.1%	76.1%	18.8%
Cape Coral city	22,665	60.7%	19.2%	28.3%	52.5%	2,583	6.9%	27.3%	15.1%	57.6%
Clearwater city	14,925	59.7%	11.3%	28.6%	60.1%	3,352	13.4%	12.1%	29.9%	58.1%
Coral Springs city	12,869	39.2%	23.8%	40.2%	36.0%	6,862	20.9%	29.8%	31.9%	38.3%
Fort Lauderdale city	13,421	32.8%	8.6%	19.2%	72.2%	16,100	39.4%	17.5%	35.1%	47.3%
Gainesville city	37,423	56.5%	2.4%	68.6%	29.0%	12,224	18.5%	14.1%	47.3%	38.6%
Hialeah city	1,889	3.5%	15.0%	35.5%	49.6%	1,895	3.5%	16.8%	31.1%	52.1%
Hollywood city	12,878	39.4%	5.2%	29.1%	65.7%	7,114	21.8%	11.8%	29.3%	58.9%
Jacksonville city	116,311	49.2%	10.6%	33.5%	55.9%	76,538	32.4%	15.2%	36.9%	47.9%
Lakeland city	15,919	57.3%	13.3%	36.3%	50.4%	5,901	21.3%	14.6%	46.4%	39.0%
Miami city	14,961	13.6%	11.5%	18.3%	70.2%	20,429	18.5%	7.1%	39.3%	53.6%
Miami Beach city	7,387	33.9%	12.6%	26.2%	61.2%	2,513	11.5%	15.4%	16.2%	68.4%
Miami Gardens city	2,584	8.4%	13.0%	51.6%	35.3%	19,791	64.0%	13.5%	34.7%	51.7%
Miramar city	5,261	15.2%	12.0%	46.1%	41.9%	12,872	37.2%	10.6%	35.6%	53.8%
Orlando city	31,233	34.0%	4.0%	25.2%	70.7%	24,803	27.0%	16.1%	38.5%	45.4%
Palm Bay city	12,791	53.4%	16.2%	35.3%	48.5%	4,875	20.4%	17.9%	64.8%	17.3%
Pembroke Pines city	11,528	27.6%	21.3%	44.7%	34.0%	8,310	19.9%	6.2%	34.6%	59.3%
Plantation city	5,209	23.8%	9.9%	43.0%	47.0%	8,736	39.9%	19.1%	24.6%	56.2%

Table B-3: Places—Race and Hispanic Origin by Age—*Continued*

	Asian, Non-Hispanic					Hispanic				
	Millennial Population		Percent by Age			Millennial Population		Percent by Age		
	Number	Percent	15 to 17	18 to 24	25 to 33	Number	Percent	15 to 17	18 to 24	25 to 33
California—Cont.										
Richmond city	7,220	22.2%	9.0%	45.5%	45.5%	15,478	47.6%	7.2%	43.9%	48.9%
Riverside city	9,960	9.1%	1.8%	64.7%	33.5%	57,589	52.9%	12.7%	41.8%	45.6%
Roseville city	3,207	9.8%	16.0%	41.0%	43.1%	7,047	21.6%	18.6%	46.7%	34.7%
Sacramento city	28,001	19.7%	9.5%	30.6%	59.9%	50,925	35.8%	15.3%	33.2%	51.5%
Salinas city	1,752	3.9%	18.5%	22.7%	58.8%	36,372	80.4%	15.6%	35.5%	48.9%
San Bernardino city	3,944	5.8%	8.5%	44.1%	47.4%	47,122	68.8%	16.8%	40.7%	42.5%
San Buenaventura (Ventura) city...	1,196	4.3%	0.0%	37.5%	62.5%	11,908	43.1%	12.7%	34.7%	52.6%
San Diego city	68,243	15.3%	8.9%	31.3%	59.8%	148,231	33.3%	13.5%	40.9%	45.6%
San Francisco city	82,430	31.9%	8.1%	31.1%	60.8%	41,888	16.2%	10.3%	30.2%	59.5%
San Jose city	81,320	30.1%	14.1%	32.6%	53.3%	102,601	38.0%	15.0%	38.0%	46.9%
San Leandro city	9,077	39.9%	18.5%	17.7%	63.9%	5,122	22.5%	13.1%	45.0%	41.9%
San Marcos city	3,072	12.6%	16.0%	30.9%	53.0%	9,520	39.0%	20.6%	38.8%	40.6%
San Mateo city	7,206	29.5%	12.3%	25.0%	62.7%	6,098	25.0%	21.3%	35.7%	43.0%
Santa Ana city	9,961	9.8%	9.4%	32.5%	58.1%	81,737	80.4%	16.6%	34.9%	48.5%
Santa Clara city	19,310	48.8%	4.8%	27.4%	67.8%	6,464	16.3%	15.9%	41.6%	42.6%
Santa Clarita city	5,143	10.8%	14.7%	38.5%	46.8%	17,004	35.6%	15.6%	39.5%	44.9%
Santa Maria city	705	2.3%	11.5%	41.4%	47.1%	23,315	76.3%	21.4%	41.3%	37.3%
Santa Monica city	1,800	7.3%	14.6%	34.6%	50.8%	5,164	20.9%	16.0%	38.2%	45.8%
Santa Rosa city	2,488	5.6%	9.0%	16.8%	74.2%	16,569	37.3%	18.2%	36.9%	44.9%
Simi Valley city	3,100	9.5%	4.6%	32.1%	63.3%	10,863	33.2%	20.7%	40.9%	38.4%
South Gate city	208	0.7%	0.0%	48.6%	51.4%	26,331	93.1%	15.9%	39.7%	44.3%
Stockton city	17,765	19.3%	17.9%	34.8%	47.3%	43,852	47.7%	17.4%	34.6%	47.9%
Sunnyvale city	18,620	44.5%	5.0%	11.5%	83.5%	7,364	17.6%	8.3%	36.2%	55.5%
Temecula city	1,785	5.9%	45.5%	30.5%	24.0%	10,916	36.1%	18.6%	38.2%	43.2%
Thousand Oaks city	2,747	10.4%	23.6%	16.0%	60.4%	7,585	28.8%	19.0%	35.7%	45.3%
Torrance city	11,815	33.5%	12.3%	42.3%	45.5%	8,307	23.6%	10.7%	49.5%	39.8%
Vacaville city	1,209	4.6%	9.0%	8.5%	82.5%	9,023	34.1%	16.4%	32.8%	50.7%
Vallejo city	7,426	22.0%	11.8%	41.5%	46.7%	10,017	29.7%	19.1%	38.9%	42.0%
Victorville city	367	1.0%	55.0%	23.7%	21.3%	21,016	57.2%	18.6%	31.9%	49.6%
Visalia city	1,538	4.5%	19.2%	22.6%	58.2%	18,810	55.4%	13.3%	38.9%	47.8%
Vista city	1,345	4.3%	5.2%	40.2%	54.6%	14,400	45.6%	12.7%	39.2%	48.1%
West Covina city	4,513	15.4%	16.6%	22.9%	60.5%	20,690	70.5%	17.1%	34.8%	48.1%
Westminster city	6,653	30.6%	13.2%	29.4%	57.4%	9,299	42.7%	14.9%	33.7%	51.4%
Colorado										
Arvada city	141	0.5%	0.0%	0.0%	100.0%	4,118	15.9%	19.2%	33.6%	47.3%
Aurora city	5,481	5.4%	16.1%	27.1%	56.8%	36,464	35.7%	19.4%	40.9%	39.7%
Boulder city	2,781	5.5%	3.1%	54.5%	42.4%	5,083	10.0%	9.8%	71.9%	18.4%
Centennial city	1,871	7.5%	23.2%	32.7%	44.1%	2,986	12.0%	18.9%	16.1%	65.0%
Colorado Springs city	3,390	2.6%	18.3%	41.9%	39.8%	26,203	19.8%	12.3%	36.2%	51.4%
Denver city	8,327	3.8%	1.4%	34.2%	64.4%	66,163	30.5%	14.7%	33.8%	51.5%
Fort Collins city	2,171	3.4%	24.6%	53.7%	21.6%	8,343	12.9%	5.2%	47.6%	47.2%
Greeley city	341	1.1%	0.0%	18.2%	81.8%	10,668	33.0%	17.0%	42.0%	41.0%
Lakewood city	1,456	3.3%	15.7%	56.9%	27.4%	11,985	27.2%	21.1%	30.0%	49.0%
Longmont city	307	1.4%	0.0%	32.2%	67.8%	6,295	29.1%	20.4%	34.6%	45.0%
Pueblo city	342	1.2%	33.0%	67.0%	0.0%	15,549	53.5%	17.0%	38.0%	45.1%
Thornton city	1,304	3.7%	9.4%	37.2%	53.4%	16,626	47.6%	21.2%	31.7%	47.1%
Westminster city	1,983	6.6%	12.5%	26.2%	61.3%	8,492	28.3%	20.6%	41.0%	38.4%
Connecticut										
Bridgeport city	1,955	4.4%	3.7%	50.1%	46.1%	17,831	40.6%	14.0%	44.0%	42.0%
Hartford city	1,812	4.1%	5.8%	39.7%	54.4%	19,222	43.6%	12.8%	45.4%	41.8%
New Haven city	3,894	7.4%	4.8%	39.4%	55.8%	17,448	33.3%	10.5%	44.1%	45.3%
Stamford city	4,736	12.4%	10.8%	24.8%	64.4%	10,492	27.5%	14.7%	40.1%	45.1%
Waterbury city	274	1.0%	23.4%	66.8%	9.9%	11,185	39.8%	16.9%	38.2%	44.9%
District of Columbia										
Washington city	12,474	5.3%	4.6%	29.9%	65.5%	23,877	10.1%	6.4%	33.0%	60.6%
Florida										
Boca Raton city	674	3.1%	17.8%	29.8%	52.4%	5,004	23.1%	17.8%	34.0%	48.2%
Cape Coral city	467	1.3%	34.5%	65.5%	0.0%	10,085	27.0%	23.1%	21.8%	55.1%
Clearwater city	78	0.3%	0.0%	0.0%	100.0%	6,004	24.0%	13.5%	41.6%	44.8%
Coral Springs city	1,005	3.1%	25.4%	39.2%	35.4%	11,665	35.5%	24.0%	33.2%	42.8%
Fort Lauderdale city	176	0.4%	19.3%	0.0%	80.7%	10,448	25.6%	13.0%	21.7%	65.3%
Gainesville city	6,383	9.6%	5.8%	61.4%	32.8%	8,352	12.6%	5.1%	65.3%	29.6%
Hialeah city	79	0.1%	0.0%	100.0%	0.0%	50,717	92.9%	12.7%	34.7%	52.6%
Hollywood city	1,141	3.5%	0.0%	22.8%	77.2%	10,983	33.6%	11.9%	45.9%	42.1%
Jacksonville city	10,898	4.6%	10.5%	25.5%	64.0%	25,010	10.6%	13.7%	39.6%	46.7%
Lakeland city	1,005	3.6%	30.5%	33.2%	36.2%	4,157	15.0%	11.5%	32.1%	56.4%
Miami city	642	0.6%	0.0%	0.0%	100.0%	73,826	66.9%	11.8%	30.7%	57.6%
Miami Beach city	370	1.7%	0.0%	17.3%	82.7%	11,421	52.4%	11.4%	28.1%	60.5%
Miami Gardens city	48	0.2%	0.0%	0.0%	100.0%	7,897	25.5%	14.5%	35.0%	50.5%
Miramar city	3,368	9.7%	6.5%	45.1%	48.3%	11,958	34.5%	16.6%	33.8%	49.6%
Orlando city	3,130	3.4%	1.6%	35.2%	63.2%	30,604	33.3%	11.8%	28.7%	59.5%
Palm Bay city	139	0.6%	0.0%	23.7%	76.3%	5,077	21.2%	18.2%	21.0%	60.8%
Pembroke Pines city	4,129	9.9%	5.3%	40.3%	54.3%	16,870	40.5%	18.7%	37.3%	44.0%
Plantation city	703	3.2%	0.0%	17.2%	82.8%	6,261	28.6%	10.3%	19.8%	70.0%

Table B-3: Places—Race and Hispanic Origin by Age—*Continued*

	White, Non-Hispanic					Black, Non-Hispanic				
	Millennial Population		Percent by Age			Millennial Population		Percent by Age		
	Number	Percent	15 to 17	18 to 24	25 to 33	Number	Percent	15 to 17	18 to 24	25 to 33
Florida—Cont.										
Pompano Beach city	8,239	33.3%	19.7%	31.8%	48.5%	8,118	32.8%	10.5%	46.9%	42.6%
Port St. Lucie city	21,928	56.1%	18.1%	30.8%	51.1%	6,826	17.5%	14.1%	55.5%	30.4%
St. Petersburg city	32,223	51.7%	12.2%	34.2%	53.5%	18,772	30.1%	19.7%	34.6%	45.7%
Sunrise city	6,602	26.4%	11.0%	34.9%	54.0%	8,972	35.9%	20.5%	24.8%	54.8%
Tallahassee city	45,735	50.7%	6.2%	65.0%	28.8%	31,981	35.4%	8.4%	60.7%	30.9%
Tampa city	48,678	44.5%	8.6%	34.5%	56.9%	24,701	22.6%	16.1%	34.6%	49.3%
West Palm Beach city	7,242	25.9%	10.3%	32.0%	57.7%	10,521	37.7%	17.3%	22.2%	60.5%
Georgia										
Athens-Clarke County unified govt (balance)	34,677	63.4%	1.3%	69.5%	29.2%	11,048	20.2%	12.6%	62.4%	24.9%
Atlanta city	64,697	40.4%	3.7%	32.9%	63.4%	70,763	44.2%	10.4%	36.7%	52.9%
Augusta-Richmond County consolidated govt (balance)	19,755	33.3%	9.5%	38.5%	52.1%	33,055	55.7%	14.5%	39.6%	45.9%
Columbus city	24,062	39.4%	9.1%	40.9%	49.9%	26,200	42.9%	13.5%	38.1%	48.4%
Macon-Bibb county	14,179	34.7%	12.2%	39.6%	48.2%	23,785	58.3%	16.6%	40.6%	42.8%
Roswell city	9,962	47.6%	21.1%	32.3%	46.6%	5,473	26.2%	30.2%	41.5%	28.3%
Sandy Springs city	16,999	56.5%	16.0%	29.0%	55.0%	5,082	16.9%	9.0%	33.8%	57.2%
Savannah city	20,374	36.9%	7.0%	41.7%	51.2%	26,733	48.5%	14.2%	43.1%	42.7%
Hawaii										
Urban Honolulu CDP	16,892	20.0%	6.5%	31.3%	62.2%	1,504	1.8%	0.0%	0.0%	100.0%
Idaho										
Boise City city	50,059	80.5%	14.1%	32.5%	53.4%	827	1.3%	73.2%	26.8%	0.0%
Meridian city	13,649	77.1%	18.7%	23.7%	57.6%	797	4.5%	0.0%	100.0%	0.0%
Illinois										
Aurora city	21,595	39.2%	14.2%	37.1%	48.7%	4,473	8.1%	11.8%	56.2%	32.0%
Chicago city	300,136	34.9%	4.6%	25.4%	70.1%	232,824	27.0%	15.6%	39.6%	44.8%
Elgin city	11,646	44.0%	12.2%	38.5%	49.3%	1,737	6.6%	9.7%	43.4%	46.9%
Joliet city	18,697	46.9%	19.7%	39.5%	40.9%	7,060	17.7%	11.2%	47.1%	41.7%
Naperville city	22,718	67.0%	19.9%	37.8%	42.4%	3,407	10.0%	18.1%	37.1%	44.8%
Peoria city	22,901	65.7%	15.6%	31.1%	53.3%	5,975	17.1%	12.7%	51.3%	36.0%
Rockford city	21,467	53.7%	11.1%	35.8%	53.1%	6,796	17.0%	9.5%	44.6%	45.9%
Springfield city	22,932	71.8%	14.5%	32.9%	52.5%	4,249	13.3%	11.9%	31.7%	56.4%
Indiana										
Evansville city	26,198	80.0%	12.7%	36.7%	50.7%	3,606	11.0%	7.1%	39.2%	53.7%
Fort Wayne city	45,694	64.6%	12.4%	34.5%	53.1%	10,115	14.3%	12.8%	38.5%	48.7%
Indianapolis city (balance)	131,932	54.1%	11.6%	32.2%	56.2%	66,581	27.3%	16.2%	36.8%	47.0%
South Bend city	17,363	58.9%	11.0%	48.4%	40.6%	5,729	19.4%	13.9%	53.8%	32.3%
Iowa										
Cedar Rapids city	27,970	79.1%	18.2%	39.6%	42.2%	1,827	5.2%	19.5%	45.6%	34.9%
Davenport city	21,821	78.5%	14.6%	35.1%	50.3%	2,349	8.5%	7.4%	24.6%	67.9%
Des Moines city	42,462	67.6%	9.4%	33.7%	56.9%	7,678	12.2%	18.8%	55.2%	25.9%
Kansas										
Kansas City city	15,073	37.3%	12.4%	26.1%	61.6%	9,482	23.5%	19.8%	44.6%	35.6%
Olathe city	25,816	76.7%	22.9%	34.6%	42.5%	1,502	4.5%	41.5%	21.8%	36.7%
Overland Park city	36,069	78.6%	19.5%	27.2%	53.3%	1,046	2.3%	23.9%	23.5%	52.6%
Topeka city	22,773	67.4%	16.9%	36.2%	46.9%	1,953	5.8%	25.5%	25.9%	48.6%
Wichita city	70,751	67.2%	15.3%	32.5%	52.2%	10,536	10.0%	18.9%	33.8%	47.2%
Kentucky										
Lexington-Fayette urban county	70,857	71.4%	9.0%	45.7%	45.3%	14,355	14.5%	15.5%	38.6%	45.9%
Louisville/Jefferson County metro govt (balance)	102,996	64.9%	14.6%	33.3%	52.1%	36,616	23.1%	16.6%	43.8%	39.6%
Louisiana										
Baton Rouge city	33,450	41.2%	7.9%	43.4%	48.7%	38,487	47.4%	14.3%	46.8%	38.9%
Lafayette city	28,123	63.2%	15.5%	28.1%	56.4%	12,127	27.3%	18.3%	39.0%	42.6%
New Orleans city	38,091	32.8%	5.4%	24.7%	69.9%	64,988	56.0%	14.1%	37.4%	48.6%
Shreveport city	21,974	40.1%	14.1%	29.4%	56.4%	29,141	53.1%	18.5%	39.5%	42.0%
Maryland										
Baltimore city	59,027	30.8%	4.0%	27.2%	68.8%	107,507	56.0%	14.2%	37.8%	48.0%
Massachusetts										
Boston city	134,756	50.5%	2.7%	34.3%	63.0%	48,879	18.3%	13.7%	39.4%	46.8%
Brockton city	8,353	30.9%	14.8%	35.9%	49.3%	10,799	39.9%	23.3%	38.6%	38.1%
Cambridge city	31,567	60.8%	2.9%	36.1%	61.0%	2,850	5.5%	33.6%	36.8%	29.5%
Lowell city	13,649	39.0%	7.7%	41.8%	50.6%	2,384	6.8%	7.3%	35.5%	57.3%
Lynn city	9,730	38.4%	15.5%	39.2%	45.3%	1,696	6.7%	27.7%	26.1%	46.2%
New Bedford city	14,847	58.7%	7.8%	40.9%	51.3%	1,863	7.4%	24.8%	55.3%	19.9%
Quincy city	13,333	53.8%	8.5%	42.0%	49.5%	2,476	10.0%	21.6%	20.4%	58.0%
Springfield city	12,464	26.5%	9.8%	51.8%	38.4%	9,094	19.4%	17.3%	46.2%	36.5%
Worcester city	32,239	52.0%	9.4%	47.9%	42.7%	6,361	10.3%	9.0%	37.4%	53.6%
Michigan										
Ann Arbor city	38,202	66.9%	3.9%	62.6%	33.5%	3,404	6.0%	0.0%	73.1%	26.9%
Dearborn city	20,695	81.4%	15.6%	40.4%	43.9%	2,447	9.6%	11.7%	70.8%	17.4%

Table B-3: Places—Race and Hispanic Origin by Age—*Continued*

	Asian, Non-Hispanic					Hispanic				
	Millennial Population		Percent by Age			Millennial Population		Percent by Age		
	Number	Percent	15 to 17	18 to 24	25 to 33	Number	Percent	15 to 17	18 to 24	25 to 33
Florida—Cont.										
Pompano Beach city	772	3.1%	4.4%	5.6%	90.0%	6,400	25.9%	8.7%	36.3%	55.1%
Port St. Lucie city	1,268	3.2%	0.0%	25.6%	74.4%	7,833	20.0%	5.1%	40.1%	54.7%
St. Petersburg city	3,378	5.4%	7.8%	27.1%	65.1%	5,558	8.9%	18.7%	24.6%	56.7%
Sunrise city	775	3.1%	0.0%	24.9%	75.1%	7,706	30.8%	8.8%	23.5%	67.7%
Tallahassee city	2,864	3.2%	2.2%	62.8%	35.0%	6,683	7.4%	1.7%	73.0%	25.3%
Tampa city	3,290	3.0%	15.6%	30.4%	54.0%	29,260	26.7%	13.9%	39.7%	46.4%
West Palm Beach city	1,202	4.3%	2.3%	40.0%	57.7%	8,600	30.8%	15.7%	43.5%	40.8%
Georgia										
Athens-Clarke County unified govt (balance)	3,083	5.6%	2.6%	72.2%	25.2%	4,674	8.6%	15.1%	55.8%	29.0%
Atlanta city	12,492	7.8%	5.3%	47.9%	46.8%	8,356	5.2%	2.3%	46.0%	51.7%
Augusta-Richmond County consolidated govt (balance)	1,223	2.1%	0.0%	31.4%	68.6%	3,969	6.7%	12.8%	43.0%	44.3%
Columbus city	1,909	3.1%	15.7%	23.2%	61.1%	5,909	9.7%	7.3%	47.0%	45.7%
Macon-Bibb county	776	1.9%	28.0%	41.1%	30.9%	1,550	3.8%	11.7%	31.6%	56.6%
Roswell city	1,568	7.5%	0.0%	21.8%	78.2%	3,318	15.9%	30.0%	29.2%	40.8%
Sandy Springs city	3,393	11.3%	12.0%	17.6%	70.4%	3,897	13.0%	16.7%	19.1%	64.2%
Savannah city	2,017	3.7%	2.8%	67.5%	29.6%	4,612	8.4%	7.8%	58.7%	33.5%
Hawaii										
Urban Honolulu CDP	36,802	43.5%	12.1%	38.7%	49.2%	8,476	10.0%	4.8%	51.5%	43.7%
Idaho										
Boise City city	934	1.5%	0.0%	56.0%	44.0%	6,949	11.2%	9.7%	31.1%	59.2%
Meridian city	na	na	na	na	na	2,508	14.2%	2.9%	44.2%	53.0%
Illinois										
Aurora city	1,505	2.7%	23.1%	21.9%	55.0%	26,383	47.9%	16.7%	33.5%	49.7%
Chicago city	66,327	7.7%	5.6%	30.0%	64.4%	242,966	28.2%	15.5%	37.2%	47.3%
Elgin city	1,668	6.3%	0.0%	65.5%	34.5%	11,359	42.9%	15.5%	42.5%	42.0%
Joliet city	284	0.7%	43.7%	56.3%	0.0%	12,718	31.9%	22.5%	35.8%	41.7%
Naperville city	3,289	9.7%	27.8%	24.6%	47.6%	3,955	11.7%	6.5%	53.6%	39.9%
Peoria city	2,087	6.0%	0.0%	35.0%	65.0%	1,854	5.3%	13.6%	31.3%	55.1%
Rockford city	1,458	3.6%	21.7%	9.9%	68.4%	8,485	21.2%	21.5%	36.2%	42.3%
Springfield city	1,327	4.2%	18.8%	64.8%	16.4%	1,039	3.3%	39.9%	24.1%	36.0%
Indiana										
Evansville city	502	1.5%	35.1%	39.2%	25.7%	1,116	3.4%	20.8%	57.3%	22.0%
Fort Wayne city	4,398	6.2%	15.3%	54.8%	29.9%	7,089	10.0%	15.3%	52.3%	32.4%
Indianapolis city (balance)	9,621	3.9%	5.5%	22.3%	72.2%	27,391	11.2%	13.0%	32.7%	54.3%
South Bend city	992	3.4%	7.8%	75.8%	16.4%	4,756	16.1%	14.6%	28.9%	56.5%
Iowa										
Cedar Rapids city	2,581	7.3%	0.0%	0.0%	100.0%	1,681	4.7%	10.1%	13.1%	76.0%
Davenport city	432	1.6%	39.4%	28.5%	32.2%	2,211	8.0%	34.1%	36.5%	29.4%
Des Moines city	3,236	5.2%	9.6%	39.3%	51.1%	7,866	12.5%	17.8%	28.1%	54.1%
Kansas										
Kansas City city	2,293	5.7%	11.2%	33.4%	55.3%	12,312	30.5%	17.0%	35.6%	47.4%
Olathe city	967	2.9%	36.3%	9.4%	54.3%	4,281	12.7%	28.4%	29.0%	42.7%
Overland Park city	3,992	8.7%	9.0%	21.5%	69.5%	3,225	7.0%	1.3%	39.4%	59.3%
Topeka city	193	0.6%	44.6%	55.4%	0.0%	6,796	20.1%	15.7%	51.1%	33.2%
Wichita city	4,103	3.9%	7.9%	12.2%	79.9%	16,978	16.1%	19.7%	28.3%	52.0%
Kentucky										
Lexington-Fayette urban county	3,157	3.2%	2.7%	25.8%	71.6%	6,587	6.6%	13.0%	37.6%	49.3%
Louisville/Jefferson County metro govt (balance)	4,264	2.7%	16.5%	25.5%	58.0%	10,624	6.7%	12.4%	34.8%	52.9%
Louisiana										
Baton Rouge city	3,848	4.7%	4.1%	75.5%	20.4%	4,079	5.0%	3.0%	46.6%	50.4%
Lafayette city	1,400	3.1%	0.0%	26.9%	73.1%	2,453	5.5%	5.0%	65.5%	29.5%
New Orleans city	4,291	3.7%	6.3%	32.5%	61.2%	7,447	6.4%	7.9%	26.2%	65.9%
Shreveport city	951	1.7%	19.5%	21.5%	59.1%	1,950	3.6%	8.7%	30.4%	61.0%
Maryland										
Baltimore city	8,121	4.2%	8.1%	32.0%	59.8%	10,581	5.5%	8.9%	26.1%	65.0%
Massachusetts										
Boston city	26,809	10.0%	6.0%	44.1%	49.8%	47,747	17.9%	11.4%	40.7%	48.0%
Brockton city	734	2.7%	0.0%	12.9%	87.1%	4,296	15.9%	5.3%	51.4%	43.2%
Cambridge city	10,121	19.5%	1.1%	42.8%	56.1%	5,254	10.1%	3.2%	54.5%	42.3%
Lowell city	10,577	30.2%	5.6%	54.0%	40.4%	7,236	20.7%	15.9%	37.4%	46.7%
Lynn city	3,148	12.4%	12.4%	29.9%	57.7%	9,893	39.0%	10.4%	32.5%	57.1%
New Bedford city	1,339	5.3%	11.9%	50.9%	37.2%	5,318	21.0%	19.7%	43.4%	36.9%
Quincy city	8,459	34.1%	16.0%	11.1%	72.9%	414	1.7%	0.0%	24.4%	75.6%
Springfield city	1,679	3.6%	4.9%	18.0%	77.1%	22,237	47.3%	18.1%	40.7%	41.2%
Worcester city	6,627	10.7%	9.5%	38.6%	51.9%	14,590	23.5%	17.0%	43.6%	39.4%
Michigan										
Ann Arbor city	9,961	17.5%	2.6%	69.6%	27.8%	2,779	4.9%	16.1%	58.5%	25.4%
Dearborn city	824	3.2%	8.0%	24.5%	67.5%	702	2.8%	12.0%	43.6%	44.4%

Table B-3: Places—Race and Hispanic Origin by Age—*Continued*

	White, Non-Hispanic					Black, Non-Hispanic				
	Millennial Population		Percent by Age			Millennial Population		Percent by Age		
	Number	Percent	15 to 17	18 to 24	25 to 33	Number	Percent	15 to 17	18 to 24	25 to 33
Michigan—Cont.										
Detroit city	19,486	10.3%	6.3%	29.5%	64.3%	143,949	76.1%	16.3%	40.3%	43.4%
Flint city	10,966	42.8%	11.7%	35.6%	52.7%	13,551	52.9%	19.3%	41.5%	39.3%
Grand Rapids city	40,405	63.0%	5.7%	34.8%	59.5%	8,020	12.5%	14.3%	53.7%	32.0%
Lansing city	20,854	54.3%	7.8%	38.6%	53.5%	8,216	21.4%	5.6%	44.8%	49.6%
Livonia city	17,382	84.9%	13.3%	37.8%	48.9%	2,539	12.4%	30.7%	38.1%	31.2%
Sterling Heights city	27,374	83.9%	8.4%	40.8%	50.8%	1,218	3.7%	39.2%	45.9%	14.9%
Warren city	18,538	59.0%	16.5%	36.2%	47.3%	7,263	23.1%	19.5%	29.2%	51.3%
Minnesota										
Minneapolis city	86,042	58.2%	3.6%	34.6%	61.9%	24,984	16.9%	16.5%	40.2%	43.3%
Rochester city	23,194	74.9%	16.2%	31.3%	52.5%	3,173	10.2%	14.3%	76.4%	9.2%
St. Paul city	48,858	49.1%	6.3%	37.4%	56.3%	14,404	14.5%	13.0%	33.6%	53.4%
Mississippi										
Jackson city	9,745	18.4%	9.6%	32.4%	58.0%	40,760	76.9%	13.5%	42.1%	44.4%
Missouri										
Columbia city	42,704	77.0%	7.5%	52.4%	40.1%	6,855	12.4%	10.8%	54.2%	35.0%
Independence city	19,441	67.8%	14.0%	34.5%	51.5%	4,509	15.7%	10.2%	46.0%	43.8%
Kansas City city	68,970	53.8%	10.7%	33.6%	55.7%	34,437	26.9%	17.9%	35.1%	47.1%
Lee's Summit city	18,498	84.0%	20.5%	29.4%	50.1%	1,360	6.2%	16.6%	22.8%	60.6%
St. Louis city	42,584	43.3%	4.5%	25.3%	70.2%	42,931	43.7%	14.2%	38.8%	47.0%
Springfield city	50,481	83.5%	8.9%	49.0%	42.1%	3,691	6.1%	9.3%	37.7%	53.0%
Montana										
Billings city	23,672	78.7%	12.5%	36.5%	51.0%	121	0.4%	0.0%	100.0%	0.0%
Nebraska										
Lincoln city	71,810	79.4%	10.4%	50.5%	39.1%	4,047	4.5%	0.0%	81.4%	18.6%
Omaha city	81,524	62.9%	11.5%	32.6%	55.9%	17,599	13.6%	16.7%	34.8%	48.4%
Nevada										
Henderson city	34,982	57.3%	16.0%	32.9%	51.1%	3,134	5.1%	7.1%	22.8%	70.2%
Las Vegas city	54,330	34.3%	14.1%	28.4%	57.5%	18,034	11.4%	8.5%	36.3%	55.2%
North Las Vegas city	15,896	23.7%	15.2%	35.1%	49.7%	12,203	18.2%	17.4%	47.3%	35.3%
Reno city	40,057	58.2%	11.1%	36.1%	52.8%	1,751	2.5%	9.1%	42.7%	48.2%
Sparks city	11,264	46.1%	17.9%	25.9%	56.2%	1,261	5.2%	8.2%	41.2%	50.7%
New Hampshire										
Manchester city	24,298	80.2%	8.7%	41.6%	49.6%	1,723	5.7%	0.0%	40.4%	59.6%
New Jersey										
Elizabeth city	3,444	9.9%	13.1%	37.3%	49.6%	6,380	18.3%	17.5%	44.9%	37.6%
Jersey City city	17,426	21.0%	4.8%	21.2%	74.0%	15,035	18.1%	15.2%	34.5%	50.3%
Newark city	7,925	9.9%	6.2%	44.2%	49.6%	38,691	48.6%	12.8%	40.6%	46.6%
Paterson city	4,732	11.5%	7.9%	39.7%	52.3%	10,644	25.8%	10.5%	46.3%	43.1%
New Mexico										
Albuquerque city	51,702	34.2%	12.0%	35.9%	52.1%	3,786	2.5%	10.8%	44.3%	45.0%
Las Cruces city	8,147	26.7%	4.7%	54.4%	40.9%	686	2.3%	0.0%	100.0%	0.0%
Rio Rancho city	8,929	37.9%	25.3%	23.5%	51.2%	35	0.1%	0.0%	0.0%	100.0%
New York										
Albany city	19,135	51.0%	4.9%	58.0%	37.1%	8,280	22.1%	14.5%	45.7%	39.9%
Buffalo city	38,562	47.4%	6.4%	33.8%	59.8%	26,644	32.7%	15.3%	42.1%	42.5%
New York city	762,279	30.9%	8.3%	26.5%	65.2%	519,724	21.0%	13.9%	35.7%	50.4%
Rochester city	26,775	37.3%	2.2%	41.4%	56.4%	25,489	35.5%	15.1%	44.8%	40.2%
Syracuse city	26,767	50.1%	5.8%	51.0%	43.3%	13,781	25.8%	14.4%	46.3%	39.3%
Yonkers city	16,057	31.5%	14.8%	41.1%	44.1%	7,854	15.4%	18.7%	23.7%	57.6%
North Carolina										
Charlotte city	101,067	42.2%	10.1%	31.6%	58.3%	76,338	31.8%	13.3%	36.8%	49.8%
Durham city	31,564	38.8%	6.8%	26.2%	67.1%	29,597	36.3%	12.4%	39.5%	48.2%
Fayetteville city	27,668	39.9%	11.8%	34.5%	53.7%	26,285	37.9%	14.7%	38.4%	46.9%
Greensboro city	34,210	40.9%	12.6%	40.7%	46.6%	35,985	43.0%	11.4%	47.5%	41.1%
High Point city	13,308	44.6%	17.8%	39.7%	42.5%	10,286	34.5%	16.8%	41.9%	41.3%
Raleigh city	81,208	54.5%	9.7%	40.3%	49.9%	39,906	26.8%	11.8%	42.7%	45.5%
Wilmington city	27,575	72.8%	8.6%	51.3%	40.1%	6,906	18.2%	16.5%	34.1%	49.4%
Winston-Salem city	30,549	44.3%	11.5%	40.3%	48.2%	24,620	35.7%	13.3%	47.6%	39.1%
North Dakota										
Fargo city	38,210	85.2%	7.8%	52.1%	40.1%	2,288	5.1%	2.5%	74.9%	22.6%
Ohio										
Akron city	31,906	58.8%	9.9%	39.7%	50.4%	16,303	30.0%	16.0%	41.7%	42.2%
Cincinnati city	54,469	53.2%	6.7%	41.3%	52.0%	35,535	34.7%	18.9%	31.9%	49.2%
Cleveland city	38,095	34.4%	10.2%	35.4%	54.4%	49,984	45.1%	16.4%	40.4%	43.2%
Columbus city	176,842	62.7%	9.0%	35.5%	55.5%	60,878	21.6%	12.4%	37.5%	50.1%
Dayton city	27,550	60.6%	8.6%	44.7%	46.7%	13,135	28.9%	15.7%	37.8%	46.5%
Toledo city	43,139	53.7%	8.6%	36.1%	55.3%	22,816	28.4%	18.8%	40.3%	40.9%
Oklahoma										
Broken Arrow city	15,167	59.2%	19.2%	31.5%	49.3%	1,712	6.7%	21.6%	45.4%	33.0%
Edmond city	19,047	70.1%	13.1%	38.4%	48.5%	2,327	8.6%	39.5%	20.8%	39.7%

Table B-3: Places—Race and Hispanic Origin by Age—*Continued*

	Asian, Non-Hispanic					Hispanic				
	Millennial Population		Percent by Age			Millennial Population		Percent by Age		
	Number	Percent	15 to 17	18 to 24	25 to 33	Number	Percent	15 to 17	18 to 24	25 to 33
Michigan—Cont.										
Detroit city	4,246	2.2%	14.0%	32.3%	53.7%	15,784	8.3%	17.8%	33.9%	48.3%
Flint city	307	1.2%	0.0%	0.0%	100.0%	138	0.5%	0.0%	100.0%	0.0%
Grand Rapids city	2,679	4.2%	0.0%	25.9%	74.1%	11,021	17.2%	13.1%	38.8%	48.0%
Lansing city	1,930	5.0%	29.4%	0.0%	70.6%	4,555	11.9%	21.5%	34.7%	43.8%
Livonia city	163	0.8%	52.8%	47.2%	0.0%	397	1.9%	26.2%	0.0%	73.8%
Sterling Heights city	3,013	9.2%	0.0%	22.1%	77.9%	742	2.3%	0.0%	17.4%	82.6%
Warren city	3,296	10.5%	36.3%	46.5%	17.1%	861	2.7%	0.0%	26.2%	73.8%
Minnesota										
Minneapolis city	15,141	10.2%	5.4%	38.7%	56.0%	12,323	8.3%	18.4%	25.6%	56.1%
Rochester city	2,364	7.6%	0.0%	33.1%	66.9%	978	3.2%	26.2%	1.6%	72.2%
St. Paul city	22,589	22.7%	13.9%	42.5%	43.6%	9,510	9.6%	18.3%	25.5%	56.2%
Mississippi										
Jackson city	952	1.8%	0.0%	11.4%	88.6%	1,281	2.4%	0.0%	15.9%	84.1%
Missouri										
Columbia city	2,780	5.0%	4.1%	55.3%	40.5%	1,910	3.4%	32.3%	47.4%	20.3%
Independence city	904	3.2%	0.0%	41.2%	58.8%	2,622	9.1%	20.7%	35.2%	44.1%
Kansas City city	3,480	2.7%	2.8%	42.8%	54.4%	13,607	10.6%	16.3%	31.6%	52.0%
Lee's Summit city	217	1.0%	0.0%	0.0%	100.0%	1,381	6.3%	18.5%	65.5%	16.1%
St. Louis city	4,169	4.2%	2.9%	47.0%	50.1%	5,766	5.9%	8.0%	36.0%	56.0%
Springfield city	1,632	2.7%	0.0%	63.1%	36.9%	2,350	3.9%	8.6%	34.0%	57.4%
Montana										
Billings city	1,330	4.4%	11.0%	0.0%	89.0%	2,500	8.3%	0.0%	58.7%	41.3%
Nebraska										
Lincoln city	5,791	6.4%	0.0%	37.3%	62.7%	6,983	7.7%	14.8%	28.2%	57.0%
Omaha city	5,322	4.1%	16.9%	39.9%	43.2%	20,994	16.2%	18.9%	29.8%	51.3%
Nevada										
Henderson city	7,440	12.2%	10.6%	30.7%	58.7%	12,238	20.0%	19.5%	29.5%	51.0%
Las Vegas city	11,277	7.1%	8.4%	24.0%	67.6%	65,300	41.3%	17.5%	33.9%	48.6%
North Las Vegas city	2,990	4.5%	22.9%	31.5%	45.6%	31,522	47.0%	22.0%	34.3%	43.8%
Reno city	4,203	6.1%	10.7%	50.2%	39.1%	18,629	27.1%	16.5%	43.6%	39.8%
Sparks city	1,299	5.3%	0.0%	19.5%	80.5%	9,157	37.5%	11.8%	47.1%	41.2%
New Hampshire										
Manchester city	910	3.0%	12.1%	37.7%	50.2%	3,055	10.1%	15.3%	46.5%	38.2%
New Jersey										
Elizabeth city	238	0.7%	0.0%	0.0%	100.0%	24,411	70.1%	13.1%	33.5%	53.4%
Jersey City city	24,416	29.4%	3.4%	24.6%	72.0%	23,071	27.8%	15.2%	33.5%	51.4%
Newark city	2,227	2.8%	10.7%	28.6%	60.8%	28,222	35.4%	12.8%	35.1%	52.1%
Paterson city	3,119	7.6%	24.6%	29.0%	46.4%	22,390	54.4%	18.0%	34.5%	47.6%
New Mexico										
Albuquerque city	4,472	3.0%	26.1%	24.9%	49.0%	77,747	51.4%	15.3%	33.9%	50.7%
Las Cruces city	1,012	3.3%	0.0%	22.1%	77.9%	19,482	63.9%	9.0%	51.5%	39.5%
Rio Rancho city	398	1.7%	31.7%	0.0%	68.3%	11,113	47.2%	15.6%	33.9%	50.6%
New York										
Albany city	3,708	9.9%	3.9%	48.4%	47.7%	3,771	10.1%	12.2%	40.6%	47.2%
Buffalo city	4,274	5.2%	16.1%	29.9%	54.0%	9,869	12.1%	16.7%	39.4%	43.9%
New York city	355,710	14.4%	9.8%	30.0%	60.2%	759,090	30.7%	13.2%	36.0%	50.7%
Rochester city	4,637	6.5%	4.1%	58.4%	37.5%	12,847	17.9%	13.8%	42.4%	43.8%
Syracuse city	4,620	8.6%	4.5%	61.6%	33.9%	5,069	9.5%	14.4%	47.0%	38.6%
Yonkers city	2,562	5.0%	22.8%	36.2%	41.1%	23,345	45.8%	14.7%	33.8%	51.6%
North Carolina										
Charlotte city	16,381	6.8%	6.1%	24.8%	69.1%	36,946	15.4%	14.6%	37.4%	47.9%
Durham city	6,355	7.8%	3.0%	40.5%	56.5%	11,759	14.4%	20.8%	27.2%	52.0%
Fayetteville city	749	1.1%	22.8%	56.6%	20.6%	8,793	12.7%	12.2%	33.7%	54.0%
Greensboro city	3,882	4.6%	22.8%	34.8%	42.4%	7,811	9.3%	17.3%	22.4%	60.2%
High Point city	1,733	5.8%	32.5%	38.6%	28.9%	3,174	10.6%	10.8%	28.4%	60.8%
Raleigh city	8,617	5.8%	15.4%	32.6%	52.0%	15,226	10.2%	10.4%	42.8%	46.8%
Wilmington city	369	1.0%	20.6%	0.0%	79.4%	2,636	7.0%	16.6%	54.4%	29.0%
Winston-Salem city	2,617	3.8%	3.0%	26.5%	70.5%	10,516	15.2%	19.2%	27.4%	53.4%
North Dakota										
Fargo city	1,431	3.2%	12.7%	0.0%	87.3%	1,875	4.2%	3.4%	59.0%	37.6%
Ohio										
Akron city	2,499	4.6%	22.3%	34.5%	43.2%	1,322	2.4%	0.0%	42.1%	57.9%
Cincinnati city	4,387	4.3%	6.0%	39.0%	55.0%	3,968	3.9%	16.0%	39.0%	45.0%
Cleveland city	4,619	4.2%	5.0%	57.0%	38.0%	12,863	11.6%	15.7%	36.0%	48.3%
Columbus city	16,144	5.7%	10.5%	33.3%	56.2%	16,335	5.8%	14.7%	36.2%	49.1%
Dayton city	1,397	3.1%	0.0%	32.6%	67.4%	1,582	3.5%	6.8%	36.9%	56.4%
Toledo city	2,124	2.6%	5.2%	71.6%	23.2%	8,872	11.1%	14.6%	39.0%	46.4%
Oklahoma										
Broken Arrow city	1,057	4.1%	15.9%	31.5%	52.6%	3,971	15.5%	22.5%	24.3%	53.2%
Edmond city	1,277	4.7%	14.6%	85.4%	0.0%	1,855	6.8%	5.8%	24.7%	69.4%

Table B-3: Places—Race and Hispanic Origin by Age—*Continued*

| | White, Non-Hispanic | | | | | Black, Non-Hispanic | | | | |
| | Millennial Population | | Percent by Age | | | Millennial Population | | Percent by Age | | |
	Number	Percent	15 to 17	18 to 24	25 to 33	Number	Percent	15 to 17	18 to 24	25 to 33
Oklahoma—Cont.										
Lawton city	15,690	51.7%	6.3%	35.3%	58.4%	4,444	14.6%	14.5%	33.2%	52.3%
Norman city	31,118	67.1%	10.5%	43.9%	45.6%	4,034	8.7%	18.7%	67.9%	13.4%
Oklahoma City city	88,212	51.4%	11.2%	34.6%	54.2%	23,150	13.5%	10.8%	31.5%	57.7%
Tulsa city	66,205	58.8%	14.8%	33.7%	51.5%	12,324	10.9%	11.8%	41.1%	47.2%
Oregon										
Beaverton city	16,862	59.8%	8.7%	31.1%	60.1%	430	1.5%	0.0%	32.3%	67.7%
Eugene city	41,376	72.1%	9.3%	49.3%	41.4%	952	1.7%	0.0%	88.8%	11.2%
Gresham city	15,502	55.4%	16.5%	27.9%	55.6%	763	2.7%	28.4%	18.9%	52.7%
Hillsboro city	14,626	53.3%	16.5%	26.8%	56.8%	648	2.4%	16.4%	38.4%	45.2%
Portland city	122,399	67.7%	7.9%	26.6%	65.5%	11,424	6.3%	9.1%	33.6%	57.3%
Salem city	27,247	59.1%	11.7%	42.9%	45.4%	1,210	2.6%	61.4%	26.7%	11.9%
Pennsylvania										
Allentown city	8,715	25.0%	9.4%	42.2%	48.4%	4,401	12.6%	24.5%	37.4%	38.0%
Erie city	19,778	68.8%	10.5%	38.6%	50.9%	4,216	14.7%	18.6%	29.0%	52.4%
Philadelphia city	176,188	36.3%	6.5%	29.8%	63.6%	182,549	37.6%	14.6%	36.7%	48.6%
Pittsburgh city	75,611	64.1%	3.9%	46.2%	49.9%	23,346	19.8%	14.2%	42.7%	43.1%
Rhode Island										
Providence city	25,111	37.9%	4.9%	52.9%	42.2%	6,652	10.0%	13.2%	38.2%	48.5%
South Carolina										
Charleston city	32,606	71.0%	7.7%	37.6%	54.7%	9,855	21.5%	17.3%	33.9%	48.8%
Columbia city	26,235	43.7%	6.6%	56.3%	37.1%	24,125	40.2%	9.1%	47.3%	43.6%
North Charleston city	17,944	49.2%	12.0%	40.6%	47.4%	11,056	30.3%	15.2%	39.1%	45.7%
South Dakota										
Sioux Falls city	38,035	78.2%	13.5%	32.4%	54.1%	3,530	7.3%	13.9%	3.1%	83.0%
Tennessee										
Chattanooga city	29,617	58.4%	8.1%	35.7%	56.2%	14,626	28.9%	16.8%	41.4%	41.8%
Clarksville city	31,694	59.1%	11.1%	34.7%	54.2%	10,735	20.0%	9.8%	40.0%	50.3%
Knoxville city	48,392	74.2%	6.4%	52.6%	41.0%	9,603	14.7%	10.8%	59.1%	30.2%
Memphis city	47,617	25.4%	12.0%	30.2%	57.9%	117,404	62.5%	14.2%	39.5%	46.3%
Murfreesboro city	31,183	67.9%	10.5%	48.4%	41.1%	9,198	20.0%	6.0%	56.1%	37.9%
Nashville-Davidson metropolitan govt (balance)	111,158	54.3%	7.0%	29.2%	63.8%	56,740	27.7%	12.4%	41.5%	46.1%
Texas										
Abilene city	26,394	60.5%	10.7%	48.0%	41.3%	4,502	10.3%	7.0%	54.3%	38.7%
Allen city	11,238	50.3%	19.6%	32.4%	48.0%	4,684	21.0%	32.0%	33.3%	34.7%
Amarillo city	27,565	52.0%	15.6%	34.4%	50.0%	2,197	4.1%	11.8%	37.1%	51.0%
Arlington city	36,917	31.4%	13.2%	32.8%	54.0%	28,591	24.3%	17.5%	36.1%	46.4%
Austin city	146,138	45.9%	6.9%	28.6%	64.5%	24,287	7.6%	7.7%	49.0%	43.3%
Beaumont city	9,500	27.3%	8.8%	44.5%	46.7%	15,220	43.7%	16.0%	41.1%	42.9%
Brownsville city	3,267	6.1%	26.0%	32.7%	41.3%	118	0.2%	6.8%	0.0%	93.2%
Carrollton city	13,340	38.9%	14.6%	26.0%	59.3%	4,830	14.1%	3.1%	32.8%	64.1%
College Station city	35,115	59.1%	4.2%	68.2%	27.6%	4,733	8.0%	10.3%	46.8%	42.9%
Corpus Christi city	21,531	23.5%	8.6%	33.7%	57.7%	4,433	4.8%	17.7%	40.7%	41.6%
Dallas city	109,551	28.5%	9.7%	27.9%	62.4%	79,008	20.6%	11.3%	35.6%	53.1%
Denton city	28,939	54.5%	5.8%	45.9%	48.3%	7,708	14.5%	11.8%	70.6%	17.6%
El Paso city	24,084	12.6%	7.4%	40.5%	52.1%	8,427	4.4%	11.1%	44.5%	44.4%
Fort Worth city	93,307	39.8%	11.7%	33.4%	54.9%	38,594	16.5%	15.6%	35.5%	48.9%
Frisco city	16,513	56.3%	25.0%	31.2%	43.8%	2,333	8.0%	20.3%	20.8%	58.9%
Garland city	18,724	29.8%	8.5%	33.5%	58.0%	9,746	15.5%	20.9%	33.2%	45.9%
Grand Prairie city	7,775	14.4%	13.1%	43.5%	43.4%	12,457	23.1%	24.0%	28.9%	47.0%
Houston city	158,014	22.7%	10.0%	28.3%	61.7%	140,166	20.2%	13.2%	37.7%	49.1%
Irving city	15,677	21.9%	10.1%	40.7%	49.2%	8,276	11.5%	5.2%	31.9%	62.9%
Killeen city	18,481	38.7%	7.3%	32.8%	59.9%	12,368	25.9%	16.2%	31.5%	52.4%
Laredo city	2,793	3.8%	25.1%	18.5%	56.4%	na	na	na	na	na
Lewisville city	13,926	42.0%	9.8%	24.2%	66.1%	4,446	13.4%	6.2%	22.9%	70.9%
Lubbock city	48,436	53.4%	8.1%	55.2%	36.7%	5,934	6.5%	14.6%	58.7%	26.6%
McAllen city	4,600	11.7%	17.4%	41.8%	40.8%	992	2.5%	0.0%	76.2%	23.8%
McKinney city	21,498	55.7%	25.2%	29.8%	45.0%	3,571	9.2%	28.4%	26.4%	45.2%
Mesquite city	9,135	23.4%	9.1%	25.5%	65.3%	10,284	26.4%	15.2%	47.8%	37.0%
Midland city	16,250	40.4%	15.0%	32.8%	52.3%	2,364	5.9%	46.2%	27.1%	26.7%
Odessa city	10,087	27.3%	12.2%	34.1%	53.6%	2,204	6.0%	26.1%	25.4%	48.5%
Pasadena city	8,698	20.9%	11.3%	36.1%	52.6%	1,653	4.0%	23.6%	14.6%	61.8%
Pearland city	12,445	42.9%	17.1%	28.6%	54.3%	5,260	18.1%	14.6%	8.8%	76.5%
Plano city	35,681	50.5%	15.6%	34.3%	50.0%	7,046	10.0%	5.9%	44.7%	49.4%
Richardson city	10,861	34.1%	12.4%	32.4%	55.3%	4,134	13.0%	4.7%	35.8%	59.4%
Round Rock City	14,948	47.9%	20.0%	35.1%	45.0%	2,597	8.3%	20.1%	39.6%	40.3%
San Angelo city	15,002	46.7%	10.4%	41.6%	48.0%	2,262	7.0%	11.6%	55.6%	32.8%
San Antonio city	102,418	23.5%	11.2%	34.8%	54.0%	29,307	6.7%	12.8%	35.1%	52.1%
Tyler city	15,541	49.1%	9.0%	43.0%	48.0%	7,640	24.1%	10.5%	47.2%	42.3%
Waco city	21,261	46.8%	5.4%	59.1%	35.5%	8,225	18.1%	9.8%	48.2%	41.9%
Wichita Falls city	20,293	60.5%	12.3%	41.4%	46.2%	3,922	11.7%	5.0%	60.3%	34.7%
Utah										
Orem city	25,680	73.6%	14.1%	47.3%	38.6%	1,105	3.2%	32.4%	24.1%	43.5%

Table B-3: Places—Race and Hispanic Origin by Age—*Continued*

	Asian, Non-Hispanic					Hispanic				
	Millennial Population		Percent by Age			Millennial Population		Percent by Age		
	Number	Percent	15 to 17	18 to 24	25 to 33	Number	Percent	15 to 17	18 to 24	25 to 33
Oklahoma—Cont.										
Lawton city	1,152	3.8%	0.0%	41.2%	58.8%	5,691	18.7%	18.6%	51.3%	30.1%
Norman city	3,376	7.3%	0.0%	31.2%	68.8%	4,444	9.6%	17.6%	35.3%	47.1%
Oklahoma City city	6,984	4.1%	8.6%	36.8%	54.6%	38,073	22.2%	15.6%	38.6%	45.8%
Tulsa city	5,542	4.9%	14.9%	29.2%	55.9%	14,725	13.1%	17.0%	33.3%	49.8%
Oregon										
Beaverton city	2,895	10.3%	8.9%	38.7%	52.4%	5,827	20.6%	29.0%	23.8%	47.2%
Eugene city	2,488	4.3%	5.2%	62.7%	32.0%	7,721	13.5%	9.9%	45.8%	44.2%
Gresham city	1,363	4.9%	20.2%	41.2%	38.7%	8,979	32.1%	20.3%	37.1%	42.6%
Hillsboro city	4,232	15.4%	5.0%	12.0%	83.0%	6,168	22.5%	14.6%	37.5%	48.0%
Portland city	14,730	8.2%	11.1%	37.0%	51.9%	19,146	10.6%	10.3%	41.0%	48.7%
Salem city	1,284	2.8%	59.7%	16.4%	24.0%	14,050	30.5%	15.5%	50.4%	34.0%
Pennsylvania										
Allentown city	684	2.0%	0.0%	41.5%	58.5%	20,139	57.8%	17.0%	29.8%	53.2%
Erie city	1,024	3.6%	16.3%	48.4%	35.3%	2,564	8.9%	25.1%	56.4%	18.6%
Philadelphia city	41,962	8.6%	9.3%	35.0%	55.7%	71,068	14.6%	14.3%	36.6%	49.1%
Pittsburgh city	10,934	9.3%	0.8%	50.5%	48.6%	4,080	3.5%	6.3%	54.9%	38.8%
Rhode Island										
Providence city	6,354	9.6%	2.2%	52.9%	44.9%	25,973	39.2%	15.6%	41.4%	43.0%
South Carolina										
Charleston city	504	1.1%	0.0%	40.3%	59.7%	2,410	5.2%	15.3%	61.0%	23.8%
Columbia city	2,445	4.1%	16.3%	45.4%	38.2%	4,557	7.6%	4.3%	45.1%	50.6%
North Charleston city	1,393	3.8%	7.3%	75.1%	17.6%	3,550	9.7%	1.0%	43.1%	55.9%
South Dakota										
Sioux Falls city	1,193	2.5%	0.0%	56.2%	43.8%	2,318	4.8%	6.2%	43.4%	50.5%
Tennessee										
Chattanooga city	2,131	4.2%	0.0%	71.0%	29.0%	3,558	7.0%	10.4%	43.1%	46.5%
Clarksville city	1,479	2.8%	15.8%	0.0%	84.2%	6,690	12.5%	7.6%	32.7%	59.7%
Knoxville city	907	1.4%	0.0%	52.9%	47.1%	3,553	5.4%	9.4%	46.3%	44.3%
Memphis city	4,379	2.3%	8.5%	44.8%	46.8%	14,380	7.7%	17.6%	34.6%	47.9%
Murfreesboro city	926	2.0%	65.2%	6.5%	28.3%	2,639	5.7%	5.3%	43.3%	51.4%
Nashville-Davidson metropolitan govt (balance)	8,508	4.2%	14.0%	36.8%	49.2%	20,321	9.9%	16.0%	34.7%	49.3%
Texas										
Abilene city	1,011	2.3%	19.8%	80.2%	0.0%	10,723	24.6%	18.0%	46.0%	36.0%
Allen city	2,482	11.1%	36.1%	10.9%	53.0%	3,478	15.6%	22.2%	20.5%	57.3%
Amarillo city	2,215	4.2%	1.9%	49.3%	48.7%	19,119	36.1%	16.9%	35.7%	47.3%
Arlington city	9,843	8.4%	6.4%	39.1%	54.5%	38,161	32.5%	17.9%	40.3%	41.9%
Austin city	25,383	8.0%	6.5%	32.3%	61.2%	115,724	36.3%	11.6%	34.7%	53.6%
Beaumont city	1,310	3.8%	2.2%	24.9%	72.9%	7,531	21.6%	26.4%	29.1%	44.5%
Brownsville city	53	0.1%	0.0%	0.0%	100.0%	49,717	93.2%	20.9%	40.0%	39.2%
Carrollton city	4,931	14.4%	10.7%	25.6%	63.8%	9,836	28.7%	20.2%	45.8%	34.0%
College Station city	4,213	7.1%	1.8%	52.6%	45.6%	14,522	24.4%	10.2%	55.9%	33.9%
Corpus Christi city	2,135	2.3%	12.9%	38.2%	48.9%	62,259	68.0%	17.1%	39.0%	43.9%
Dallas city	19,849	5.2%	9.8%	32.7%	57.5%	167,265	43.6%	15.3%	36.8%	47.9%
Denton city	4,603	8.7%	14.8%	61.4%	23.9%	10,229	19.2%	10.3%	48.7%	40.9%
El Paso city	2,284	1.2%	8.2%	14.3%	77.5%	153,218	80.0%	16.3%	40.1%	43.6%
Fort Worth city	11,018	4.7%	7.7%	42.5%	49.9%	86,103	36.8%	16.9%	32.7%	50.4%
Frisco city	2,610	8.9%	32.1%	14.1%	53.7%	7,274	24.8%	22.6%	22.6%	54.9%
Garland city	7,322	11.7%	19.3%	32.7%	48.0%	24,342	38.8%	21.2%	37.9%	41.0%
Grand Prairie city	3,343	6.2%	10.6%	32.7%	56.7%	29,084	54.0%	19.9%	39.8%	40.3%
Houston city	53,234	7.7%	8.4%	31.9%	59.7%	331,085	47.7%	16.2%	36.9%	46.9%
Irving city	11,283	15.7%	5.8%	20.4%	73.7%	34,645	48.3%	18.4%	39.5%	42.1%
Killeen city	1,401	2.9%	3.2%	25.2%	71.6%	11,173	23.4%	15.8%	30.8%	53.4%
Laredo city	550	0.7%	50.0%	40.4%	9.6%	70,379	95.5%	19.4%	40.7%	39.9%
Lewisville city	3,699	11.2%	7.5%	26.4%	66.1%	10,009	30.2%	22.4%	31.3%	46.4%
Lubbock city	2,607	2.9%	8.3%	33.9%	57.7%	32,135	35.4%	13.3%	44.7%	42.0%
McAllen city	1,298	3.3%	18.2%	40.5%	41.3%	32,296	81.8%	18.0%	40.3%	41.8%
McKinney city	1,822	4.7%	15.3%	16.8%	67.9%	10,536	27.3%	19.3%	40.8%	39.9%
Mesquite city	1,058	2.7%	17.3%	25.2%	57.5%	18,099	46.4%	17.1%	32.1%	50.7%
Midland city	684	1.7%	30.3%	30.3%	39.5%	19,716	49.0%	12.6%	34.4%	53.0%
Odessa city	581	1.6%	0.0%	100.0%	0.0%	23,610	63.9%	13.7%	35.2%	51.1%
Pasadena city	627	1.5%	4.6%	16.9%	78.5%	30,254	72.7%	16.1%	31.0%	52.8%
Pearland city	3,349	11.6%	25.6%	41.1%	33.4%	7,632	26.3%	15.0%	37.1%	47.9%
Plano city	15,012	21.3%	18.9%	23.9%	57.2%	10,629	15.1%	15.5%	29.8%	54.7%
Richardson city	5,947	18.7%	11.1%	38.7%	50.3%	8,504	26.7%	6.6%	44.2%	49.2%
Round Rock City	1,871	6.0%	24.2%	28.2%	47.7%	10,679	34.3%	19.8%	36.9%	43.3%
San Angelo city	691	2.2%	0.0%	33.4%	66.6%	13,447	41.9%	16.0%	40.3%	43.7%
San Antonio city	13,021	3.0%	9.0%	35.8%	55.1%	284,553	65.3%	15.6%	36.5%	47.9%
Tyler city	1,071	3.4%	7.8%	85.6%	6.5%	7,113	22.5%	20.4%	36.3%	43.3%
Waco city	1,022	2.2%	0.0%	72.4%	27.6%	14,497	31.9%	13.2%	46.8%	40.0%
Wichita Falls city	964	2.9%	0.0%	53.6%	46.4%	7,211	21.5%	16.1%	42.6%	41.3%
Utah										
Orem city	1,791	5.1%	5.4%	45.8%	48.8%	5,241	15.0%	15.8%	33.9%	50.3%

Table B-3: Places—Race and Hispanic Origin by Age—*Continued*

	White, Non-Hispanic					Black, Non-Hispanic				
	Millennial Population		Percent by Age			Millennial Population		Percent by Age		
	Number	Percent	15 to 17	18 to 24	25 to 33	Number	Percent	15 to 17	18 to 24	25 to 33
Utah—Cont.										
Provo city	52,495	83.0%	4.9%	67.5%	27.6%	351	0.6%	0.0%	48.1%	51.9%
Salt Lake City city	48,854	68.9%	9.1%	37.0%	53.9%	876	1.2%	11.3%	15.6%	73.1%
Sandy city	16,754	71.9%	18.6%	36.1%	45.3%	401	1.7%	0.0%	0.0%	100.0%
West Jordan city	24,942	76.8%	22.4%	27.5%	50.0%	384	1.2%	44.3%	55.7%	0.0%
West Valley City city	23,463	56.2%	16.8%	31.6%	51.6%	266	0.6%	18.8%	21.8%	59.4%
Virginia										
Alexandria city	21,373	49.2%	5.6%	15.2%	79.2%	8,332	19.2%	8.6%	24.6%	66.8%
Chesapeake city	34,686	54.9%	16.1%	33.1%	50.7%	17,524	27.8%	8.9%	42.5%	48.6%
Hampton city	15,090	37.5%	9.2%	33.8%	57.0%	20,864	51.9%	13.6%	42.3%	44.1%
Newport News city	26,291	44.9%	7.7%	45.0%	47.3%	22,118	37.8%	15.7%	35.7%	48.7%
Norfolk city	40,470	42.2%	4.0%	47.8%	48.2%	39,672	41.4%	9.8%	48.3%	41.9%
Portsmouth city	10,656	36.7%	10.9%	28.5%	60.7%	13,756	47.3%	15.8%	39.2%	44.9%
Richmond city	33,949	44.2%	3.2%	31.9%	64.9%	31,239	40.6%	12.0%	42.3%	45.7%
Roanoke city	16,350	62.5%	6.7%	36.1%	57.2%	6,695	25.6%	8.9%	40.6%	50.5%
Virginia Beach city	77,200	58.1%	12.0%	33.0%	55.1%	28,279	21.3%	14.4%	41.2%	44.4%
Washington										
Bellevue city	16,545	43.6%	22.2%	24.7%	53.0%	1,131	3.0%	4.2%	62.6%	33.2%
Everett city	20,584	67.5%	14.3%	31.0%	54.8%	920	3.0%	37.5%	35.8%	26.7%
Federal Way city	12,573	47.1%	17.7%	28.4%	53.9%	2,161	8.1%	25.3%	23.8%	50.9%
Kent city	14,449	36.0%	10.8%	38.3%	50.8%	6,225	15.5%	16.3%	22.1%	61.7%
Renton city	10,450	42.3%	11.8%	24.9%	63.3%	2,075	8.4%	16.8%	18.1%	65.1%
Seattle city	147,336	62.3%	5.1%	29.3%	65.6%	16,682	7.1%	10.3%	31.2%	58.5%
Spokane city	47,304	76.4%	9.6%	34.6%	55.8%	1,199	1.9%	0.0%	50.5%	49.5%
Spokane Valley city	20,705	83.5%	15.9%	29.7%	54.4%	4	0.0%	100.0%	0.0%	0.0%
Tacoma city	36,904	62.8%	10.6%	32.2%	57.2%	4,870	8.3%	10.8%	37.7%	51.5%
Vancouver city	30,089	67.0%	14.6%	31.9%	53.5%	1,125	2.5%	16.7%	56.4%	26.9%
Yakima city	10,854	42.8%	8.6%	38.8%	52.6%	295	1.2%	13.9%	86.1%	0.0%
Wisconsin										
Green Bay city	18,829	61.5%	9.0%	43.3%	47.7%	1,392	4.5%	0.0%	25.8%	74.2%
Kenosha city	16,991	67.9%	12.7%	39.1%	48.3%	1,850	7.4%	18.1%	69.5%	12.4%
Madison city	79,410	78.6%	7.4%	53.1%	39.6%	5,236	5.2%	24.6%	35.8%	39.6%
Milwaukee city	72,216	38.8%	8.9%	36.1%	55.0%	69,960	37.6%	18.2%	40.1%	41.7%

Table B-3: Places—Race and Hispanic Origin by Age—*Continued*

	Asian, Non-Hispanic					Hispanic				
	Millennial Population		Percent by Age			Millennial Population		Percent by Age		
	Number	Percent	15 to 17	18 to 24	25 to 33	Number	Percent	15 to 17	18 to 24	25 to 33
Utah—Cont.										
Provo city	900	1.4%	27.0%	17.0%	56.0%	5,947	9.4%	11.8%	51.9%	36.4%
Salt Lake City city	4,216	5.9%	2.5%	32.8%	64.8%	14,614	20.6%	12.2%	37.4%	50.4%
Sandy city	1,899	8.1%	8.7%	12.4%	78.8%	3,077	13.2%	32.1%	29.5%	38.3%
West Jordan city	1,220	3.8%	10.0%	9.6%	80.4%	5,384	16.6%	46.2%	26.6%	27.2%
West Valley City city	2,063	4.9%	2.2%	39.2%	58.7%	12,667	30.4%	20.1%	40.0%	39.8%
Virginia										
Alexandria city	3,686	8.5%	7.5%	11.0%	81.5%	7,479	17.2%	9.3%	13.5%	77.2%
Chesapeake city	1,915	3.0%	16.0%	34.1%	49.9%	5,340	8.5%	16.6%	26.5%	56.9%
Hampton city	863	2.1%	0.0%	24.9%	75.1%	2,472	6.1%	0.0%	58.2%	41.8%
Newport News city	2,307	3.9%	11.7%	30.6%	57.7%	5,016	8.6%	12.4%	49.2%	38.4%
Norfolk city	3,211	3.4%	12.1%	42.9%	44.9%	10,028	10.5%	4.9%	54.0%	41.1%
Portsmouth city	636	2.2%	21.9%	14.8%	63.4%	2,588	8.9%	13.4%	39.9%	46.7%
Richmond city	2,868	3.7%	0.0%	72.1%	27.9%	5,279	6.9%	3.5%	41.9%	54.6%
Roanoke city	1,380	5.3%	37.2%	57.6%	5.2%	890	3.4%	0.0%	0.0%	100.0%
Virginia Beach city	7,715	5.8%	13.4%	33.2%	53.4%	13,972	10.5%	13.5%	34.9%	51.5%
Washington										
Bellevue city	16,162	42.6%	7.7%	28.4%	63.9%	3,006	7.9%	4.4%	18.2%	77.4%
Everett city	2,141	7.0%	31.2%	28.9%	39.9%	3,671	12.0%	13.9%	34.2%	51.8%
Federal Way city	3,708	13.9%	10.2%	22.0%	67.8%	5,827	21.8%	11.8%	20.4%	67.8%
Kent city	6,459	16.1%	11.8%	39.8%	48.4%	9,230	23.0%	19.3%	22.8%	57.9%
Renton city	5,003	20.2%	7.8%	16.3%	75.9%	4,039	16.3%	17.2%	45.4%	37.4%
Seattle city	39,582	16.7%	5.1%	41.1%	53.8%	17,467	7.4%	5.9%	30.3%	63.8%
Spokane city	2,655	4.3%	6.9%	25.9%	67.2%	4,246	6.9%	13.6%	37.5%	48.9%
Spokane Valley city	339	1.4%	54.9%	0.0%	45.1%	2,484	10.0%	16.5%	20.8%	62.7%
Tacoma city	2,828	4.8%	7.7%	41.2%	51.1%	7,806	13.3%	24.6%	36.8%	38.6%
Vancouver city	1,703	3.0%	0.0%	45.0%	55.0%	7,262	16.2%	14.6%	38.7%	46.7%
Yakima city	126	0.5%	0.0%	0.0%	100.0%	13,358	52.6%	18.4%	47.8%	33.8%
Wisconsin										
Green Bay city	1,884	6.2%	5.1%	21.7%	73.1%	6,024	19.7%	11.5%	49.2%	39.3%
Kenosha city	659	2.6%	0.5%	0.0%	99.5%	4,932	19.7%	24.2%	56.2%	19.6%
Madison city	10,819	10.7%	9.5%	52.8%	37.8%	3,987	3.9%	22.7%	40.8%	36.4%
Milwaukee city	7,658	4.1%	13.8%	28.7%	57.5%	31,917	17.1%	18.4%	35.7%	45.9%

Table B-4: Metropolitan/Micropolitan Statistical Areas—Race and Hispanic Origin by Age

| | White, Non-Hispanic | | | | | Black, Non-Hispanic | | | | |
| | Millennial Population | | Percent by Age | | | Millennial Population | | Percent by Age | | |
	Number	Percent	15 to 17	18 to 24	25 to 33	Number	Percent	15 to 17	18 to 24	25 to 33
Abilene, TX	30,972	61.7%	12.9%	46.6%	40.5%	4,745	9.4%	6.6%	51.5%	41.9%
Adrian, MI micro	19,265	84.1%	18.3%	41.4%	40.3%	729	3.2%	8.4%	29.9%	61.7%
Akron, OH	136,816	76.6%	14.1%	41.6%	44.3%	24,446	13.7%	16.5%	43.4%	40.0%
Albany, GA	13,161	33.3%	20.8%	30.7%	48.4%	24,091	61.0%	15.6%	45.1%	39.3%
Albany, OR	22,697	79.7%	15.8%	44.3%	40.0%	na	na	na	na	na
Albany-Schenectady-Troy, NY	175,890	75.5%	14.0%	42.5%	43.5%	20,009	8.6%	13.0%	40.4%	46.6%
Albertville, AL micro	16,910	77.2%	15.5%	41.5%	43.0%	1,086	5.0%	21.9%	22.7%	55.4%
Albuquerque, NM	73,334	31.4%	13.7%	33.9%	52.3%	4,556	2.0%	8.9%	45.1%	46.0%
Alexandria, LA	23,955	61.6%	17.3%	35.5%	47.3%	11,088	28.5%	18.6%	33.7%	47.7%
Allentown-Bethlehem-Easton, PA-NJ	131,002	67.2%	16.3%	38.1%	45.6%	9,125	4.7%	18.1%	51.2%	30.7%
Altoona, PA	26,299	90.1%	17.8%	36.4%	45.9%	1,206	4.1%	20.8%	36.4%	42.8%
Amarillo, TX	37,398	52.0%	15.0%	33.7%	51.3%	3,062	4.3%	8.5%	47.3%	44.2%
Ames, IA	36,006	79.2%	6.2%	65.5%	28.3%	775	1.7%	33.3%	53.9%	12.8%
Anchorage, AK	73,282	59.6%	12.1%	33.5%	54.4%	7,366	6.0%	16.3%	46.0%	37.8%
Ann Arbor, MI	81,733	66.3%	9.6%	52.1%	38.4%	16,258	13.2%	11.4%	57.4%	31.2%
Anniston-Oxford-Jacksonville, AL	19,700	64.4%	16.4%	35.4%	48.2%	7,181	23.5%	9.3%	51.4%	39.3%
Appleton, WI	49,486	84.7%	18.9%	33.4%	47.8%	1,111	1.9%	0.0%	76.2%	23.8%
Asheville, NC	72,095	77.7%	13.7%	35.8%	50.5%	5,622	6.1%	6.9%	39.6%	53.5%
Ashtabula, OH micro	18,570	82.1%	18.8%	35.3%	45.9%	1,466	6.5%	39.7%	46.6%	13.7%
Athens-Clarke County, GA	46,745	64.4%	8.4%	58.1%	33.4%	16,236	22.4%	11.4%	49.1%	39.5%
Atlanta-Sandy Springs-Roswell, GA	628,209	42.9%	16.7%	34.7%	48.7%	536,634	36.6%	16.8%	38.0%	45.2%
Atlantic City-Hammonton, NJ	33,402	50.2%	13.8%	42.4%	43.8%	10,358	15.6%	12.5%	48.5%	39.1%
Auburn-Opelika, AL	39,103	71.4%	9.2%	58.4%	32.4%	11,013	20.1%	12.8%	41.6%	45.7%
Augusta-Richmond County, GA-SC	76,862	48.3%	15.3%	33.8%	50.9%	61,551	38.7%	15.3%	40.0%	44.6%
Augusta-Waterville, ME micro	24,372	94.0%	16.8%	38.1%	45.1%	351	1.4%	0.0%	100.0%	0.0%
Austin-Round Rock, TX	284,161	48.4%	11.6%	32.2%	56.2%	44,352	7.6%	13.7%	45.8%	40.6%
Bakersfield, CA	73,880	28.9%	14.2%	33.0%	52.8%	16,338	6.4%	12.1%	45.3%	42.6%
Baltimore-Columbia-Towson, MD	380,419	53.3%	14.1%	34.3%	51.6%	216,019	30.3%	14.6%	36.4%	49.0%
Bangor, ME	36,391	89.1%	12.9%	41.3%	45.8%	976	2.4%	0.0%	100.0%	0.0%
Barnstable Town, MA	31,352	84.7%	16.9%	41.4%	41.8%	2,372	6.4%	9.7%	12.3%	78.0%
Baton Rouge, LA	127,311	53.2%	13.3%	39.7%	47.0%	88,521	37.0%	15.7%	43.4%	40.9%
Battle Creek, MI	26,490	83.0%	18.5%	33.7%	47.7%	2,622	8.2%	8.0%	27.2%	64.8%
Bay City, MI	21,614	89.2%	17.7%	34.7%	47.5%	723	3.0%	8.9%	1.0%	90.2%
Beaumont-Port Arthur, TX	54,648	50.8%	16.0%	35.8%	48.2%	28,483	26.5%	16.9%	35.4%	47.8%
Beckley, WV	23,393	88.6%	16.0%	37.3%	46.7%	2,077	7.9%	7.6%	24.7%	67.8%
Bellingham, WA	47,751	74.4%	10.9%	48.7%	40.4%	52	0.1%	0.0%	0.0%	100.0%
Bend-Redmond, OR	32,937	87.8%	16.1%	29.7%	54.2%	247	0.7%	0.0%	0.0%	100.0%
Billings, MT	31,773	78.2%	11.6%	38.8%	49.7%	143	0.4%	0.0%	84.6%	15.4%
Binghamton, NY	52,110	78.4%	14.2%	46.9%	38.9%	4,319	6.5%	12.9%	55.0%	32.2%
Birmingham-Hoover, AL	170,863	59.8%	16.8%	33.2%	50.0%	93,196	32.6%	16.1%	38.8%	45.1%
Bismarck, ND	31,710	92.8%	13.7%	31.7%	54.6%	na	na	na	na	na
Blacksburg-Christiansburg-Radford, VA	53,574	81.4%	7.9%	60.3%	31.8%	3,811	5.8%	5.8%	71.0%	23.2%
Bloomington, IL	49,058	79.5%	10.6%	53.8%	35.6%	3,317	5.4%	23.0%	55.5%	21.5%
Bloomington, IN	52,563	78.4%	7.4%	60.1%	32.6%	2,250	3.4%	0.0%	66.4%	33.6%
Bloomsburg-Berwick, PA	20,853	88.6%	10.2%	41.8%	48.1%	1,443	6.1%	0.0%	55.0%	45.0%
Boise City, ID	130,520	75.1%	16.8%	32.4%	50.8%	2,327	1.3%	42.5%	50.9%	6.6%
Boston-Cambridge-Newton, MA-NH	840,503	66.2%	14.0%	37.5%	48.5%	104,669	8.2%	15.4%	37.4%	47.1%
Boulder, CO	74,232	75.2%	10.9%	50.8%	38.3%	1,281	1.3%	0.0%	57.3%	42.7%
Bowling Green, KY	38,516	79.5%	11.1%	45.8%	43.0%	4,315	8.9%	20.0%	53.1%	26.9%
Bremerton-Silverdale, WA	49,389	70.6%	13.3%	37.6%	49.1%	1,293	1.8%	11.0%	29.6%	59.4%
Bridgeport-Stamford-Norwalk, CT	120,058	53.7%	20.6%	38.8%	40.6%	29,251	13.1%	17.6%	39.8%	42.7%
Brownsville-Harlingen, TX	7,859	6.9%	21.4%	26.1%	52.5%	162	0.1%	100.0%	0.0%	0.0%
Brunswick, GA	18,902	71.0%	16.2%	33.6%	50.2%	4,988	18.7%	21.1%	29.2%	49.7%
Buffalo-Cheektowaga-Niagara Falls, NY	207,430	72.3%	14.4%	35.4%	50.2%	41,206	14.4%	16.5%	42.3%	41.2%
Burlington, NC	23,247	61.5%	15.7%	39.4%	45.0%	6,236	16.5%	20.2%	40.9%	38.9%
Burlington-South Burlington, VT	55,717	87.0%	11.8%	48.9%	39.4%	2,465	3.8%	2.0%	7.7%	90.2%
California-Lexington Park, MD	21,011	72.5%	16.2%	34.5%	49.3%	4,761	16.4%	2.4%	50.7%	46.8%
Canton-Massillon, OH	78,944	84.3%	17.0%	36.7%	46.3%	7,475	8.0%	18.4%	31.3%	50.3%
Cape Coral-Fort Myers, FL	78,069	54.9%	14.7%	34.6%	50.7%	17,637	12.4%	18.9%	35.3%	45.8%
Cape Girardeau, MO-IL	22,538	86.9%	11.9%	43.5%	44.7%	2,656	10.2%	19.4%	24.3%	56.3%
Carbondale-Marion, IL	29,205	74.5%	13.9%	45.8%	40.3%	6,057	15.4%	12.7%	53.4%	33.9%
Carson City, NV	6,656	57.6%	20.4%	38.4%	41.2%	230	2.0%	0.0%	100.0%	0.0%
Casper, WY	17,534	84.8%	14.1%	32.5%	53.4%	72	0.3%	0.0%	0.0%	100.0%
Cedar Rapids, IA	52,815	80.1%	15.6%	37.9%	46.5%	3,914	5.9%	14.2%	69.5%	16.3%
Chambersburg-Waynesboro, PA	29,236	83.9%	17.0%	32.9%	50.0%	1,519	4.4%	23.5%	50.7%	25.8%
Champaign-Urbana, IL	57,924	65.0%	9.7%	54.0%	36.3%	10,061	11.3%	5.0%	72.5%	22.5%
Charleston, WV	39,723	84.9%	16.2%	34.2%	49.6%	4,396	9.4%	9.8%	30.2%	60.0%
Charleston-North Charleston, SC	126,441	61.8%	11.8%	32.6%	55.6%	54,091	26.4%	16.2%	34.9%	48.9%
Charlotte-Concord-Gastonia, NC-SC	346,169	57.3%	16.9%	33.7%	49.4%	149,102	24.7%	16.8%	38.6%	44.7%
Charlottesville, VA	45,275	67.5%	11.1%	42.0%	46.9%	10,522	15.7%	11.2%	37.8%	51.0%
Chattanooga, TN-GA	100,808	73.1%	14.7%	35.2%	50.1%	21,510	15.6%	16.0%	38.8%	45.2%
Cheyenne, WY	20,681	75.3%	12.4%	46.3%	41.3%	260	0.9%	0.0%	70.4%	29.6%
Chicago-Naperville-Elgin, IL-IN-WI	1,207,292	48.2%	14.6%	33.5%	51.9%	433,193	17.3%	16.7%	41.0%	42.2%
Chico, CA	44,245	66.4%	10.7%	48.9%	40.4%	1,632	2.5%	21.7%	56.5%	21.8%
Cincinnati, OH-KY-IN	422,418	77.8%	16.4%	36.2%	47.4%	71,295	13.1%	18.7%	36.6%	44.8%
Clarksburg, WV micro	18,709	95.0%	16.7%	39.2%	44.1%	97	0.5%	0.0%	100.0%	0.0%

Table B-4: Metropolitan/Micropolitan Statistical Areas—Race and Hispanic Origin by Age—*Continued*

	Asian, Non-Hispanic					Hispanic				
	Millennial Population		Percent by Age			Millennial Population		Percent by Age		
	Number	Percent	15 to 17	18 to 24	25 to 33	Number	Percent	15 to 17	18 to 24	25 to 33
Abilene, TX.................	1,065	2.1%	18.8%	81.2%	0.0%	12,233	24.4%	17.2%	45.0%	37.7%
Adrian, MI micro.................	na	na	na	na	na	1,674	7.3%	1.4%	55.4%	43.1%
Akron, OH.................	6,130	3.4%	13.9%	41.6%	44.5%	4,752	2.7%	15.7%	34.7%	49.5%
Albany, GA.................	341	0.9%	0.0%	0.0%	100.0%	1,529	3.9%	0.0%	69.5%	30.5%
Albany, OR.................	1,868	6.6%	5.2%	76.9%	17.9%	3,317	11.6%	16.3%	31.7%	52.0%
Albany-Schenectady-Troy, NY.................	13,773	5.9%	11.0%	43.6%	45.4%	14,314	6.1%	10.9%	38.9%	50.1%
Albertville, AL micro.................	483	2.2%	57.1%	42.9%	0.0%	2,740	12.5%	13.5%	41.9%	44.5%
Albuquerque, NM.................	5,093	2.2%	25.4%	21.8%	52.7%	129,433	55.5%	15.4%	37.8%	46.8%
Alexandria, LA.................	479	1.2%	0.0%	72.9%	27.1%	2,189	5.6%	19.8%	51.3%	28.9%
Allentown-Bethlehem-Easton, PA-NJ.................	7,266	3.7%	14.4%	43.3%	42.3%	39,794	20.4%	17.8%	37.4%	44.9%
Altoona, PA.................	372	1.3%	0.0%	14.2%	85.8%	524	1.8%	0.0%	12.4%	87.6%
Amarillo, TX.................	2,568	3.6%	1.7%	45.2%	53.1%	26,298	36.6%	15.6%	37.4%	47.0%
Ames, IA.................	5,653	12.4%	0.0%	69.0%	31.0%	956	2.1%	17.5%	69.2%	13.3%
Anchorage, AK.................	8,684	7.1%	19.7%	36.9%	43.4%	13,280	10.8%	13.8%	45.8%	40.4%
Ann Arbor, MI.................	13,610	11.0%	4.8%	61.8%	33.4%	6,041	4.9%	11.5%	57.9%	30.6%
Anniston-Oxford-Jacksonville, AL.................	451	1.5%	0.0%	56.8%	43.2%	1,598	5.2%	37.0%	63.0%	0.0%
Appleton, WI.................	2,748	4.7%	9.2%	18.9%	71.9%	2,172	3.7%	1.3%	17.1%	81.5%
Asheville, NC.................	1,713	1.8%	15.9%	56.0%	28.1%	8,275	8.9%	16.3%	37.3%	46.4%
Ashtabula, OH micro.................	299	1.3%	16.1%	0.0%	83.9%	1,891	8.4%	34.2%	26.3%	39.6%
Athens-Clarke County, GA.................	2,758	3.8%	2.9%	68.9%	28.2%	5,498	7.6%	19.6%	56.6%	23.8%
Atlanta-Sandy Springs-Roswell, GA.................	86,698	5.9%	13.7%	30.6%	55.7%	173,824	11.9%	18.9%	34.4%	46.7%
Atlantic City-Hammonton, NJ.................	4,472	6.7%	15.5%	37.9%	46.6%	15,642	23.5%	16.7%	34.2%	49.1%
Auburn-Opelika, AL.................	1,023	1.9%	0.0%	41.2%	58.8%	1,932	3.5%	0.0%	100.0%	0.0%
Augusta-Richmond County, GA-SC.................	2,860	1.8%	12.3%	43.2%	44.5%	12,132	7.6%	12.4%	37.3%	50.3%
Augusta-Waterville, ME micro.................	582	2.2%	0.0%	36.4%	63.6%	582	2.2%	0.0%	100.0%	0.0%
Austin-Round Rock, TX.................	33,322	5.7%	9.6%	27.1%	63.3%	209,635	35.7%	15.1%	36.1%	48.8%
Bakersfield, CA.................	11,183	4.4%	13.8%	32.7%	53.5%	149,248	58.5%	16.9%	39.5%	43.6%
Baltimore-Columbia-Towson, MD.................	43,140	6.0%	11.8%	34.5%	53.7%	48,672	6.8%	13.1%	34.4%	52.6%
Bangor, ME.................	1,028	2.5%	0.0%	10.1%	89.9%	961	2.4%	26.7%	73.3%	0.0%
Barnstable Town, MA.................	353	1.0%	56.1%	43.9%	0.0%	1,083	2.9%	49.5%	32.2%	18.3%
Baton Rouge, LA.................	7,044	2.9%	7.4%	54.2%	38.4%	11,303	4.7%	7.0%	35.0%	58.0%
Battle Creek, MI.................	742	2.3%	0.0%	42.9%	57.1%	1,348	4.2%	12.6%	53.6%	33.8%
Bay City, MI.................	132	0.5%	0.0%	18.9%	81.1%	847	3.5%	22.1%	53.7%	24.2%
Beaumont-Port Arthur, TX.................	3,027	2.8%	10.1%	33.2%	56.7%	19,777	18.4%	16.8%	33.2%	50.0%
Beckley, WV.................	496	1.9%	0.0%	6.7%	93.3%	434	1.6%	0.0%	59.2%	40.8%
Bellingham, WA.................	2,733	4.3%	6.0%	59.0%	36.0%	6,630	10.3%	16.2%	43.7%	40.1%
Bend-Redmond, OR.................	303	1.0%	0.0%	44.8%	55.2%	3,385	9.0%	1.5%	59.7%	38.8%
Billings, MT.................	1,338	3.3%	11.2%	0.3%	88.5%	3,089	7.6%	5.6%	60.5%	33.9%
Binghamton, NY.................	4,814	7.2%	8.3%	73.1%	18.6%	3,434	5.2%	21.7%	53.7%	24.6%
Birmingham-Hoover, AL.................	4,679	1.6%	6.8%	21.8%	71.3%	11,691	4.1%	16.5%	30.8%	52.6%
Bismarck, ND.................	na	na	na	na	na	887	2.6%	9.6%	32.5%	57.9%
Blacksburg-Christiansburg-Radford, VA.................	3,962	6.0%	0.0%	61.9%	38.1%	3,293	5.0%	1.8%	83.1%	14.9%
Bloomington, IL.................	2,624	4.3%	0.0%	1.8%	98.2%	4,887	7.9%	21.7%	57.6%	20.7%
Bloomington, IN.................	6,518	9.7%	1.8%	84.6%	13.6%	3,652	5.4%	10.6%	58.5%	30.9%
Bloomsburg-Berwick, PA.................	386	1.6%	0.0%	66.6%	33.4%	612	2.6%	21.6%	73.0%	5.4%
Boise City, ID.................	2,336	1.3%	14.3%	27.6%	58.1%	32,798	18.9%	18.0%	36.4%	45.6%
Boston-Cambridge-Newton, MA-NH.................	113,573	8.9%	9.2%	34.3%	56.6%	169,391	13.3%	13.1%	38.9%	48.0%
Boulder, CO.................	4,184	4.2%	3.6%	54.7%	41.7%	15,409	15.6%	16.5%	44.7%	38.8%
Bowling Green, KY.................	1,288	2.7%	18.9%	50.9%	30.1%	3,138	6.5%	40.2%	43.1%	16.7%
Bremerton-Silverdale, WA.................	2,187	3.1%	14.4%	28.2%	57.4%	7,402	10.6%	9.2%	45.0%	45.8%
Bridgeport-Stamford-Norwalk, CT.................	12,585	5.6%	15.5%	24.9%	59.6%	54,684	24.5%	14.2%	37.7%	48.1%
Brownsville-Harlingen, TX.................	842	0.7%	13.1%	53.8%	33.1%	104,717	92.1%	20.3%	40.3%	39.4%
Brunswick, GA.................	393	1.5%	0.0%	92.1%	7.9%	1,404	5.3%	21.2%	27.9%	50.9%
Buffalo-Cheektowaga-Niagara Falls, NY.................	13,597	4.7%	9.0%	44.9%	46.1%	17,422	6.1%	13.8%	42.5%	43.7%
Burlington, NC.................	316	0.8%	10.1%	0.0%	89.9%	6,107	16.1%	19.6%	30.7%	49.8%
Burlington-South Burlington, VT.................	1,683	2.6%	21.0%	62.4%	16.6%	2,434	3.8%	8.7%	59.7%	31.6%
California-Lexington Park, MD.................	585	2.0%	19.5%	46.0%	34.5%	1,245	4.3%	25.1%	60.3%	14.6%
Canton-Massillon, OH.................	884	0.9%	15.0%	23.2%	61.8%	2,543	2.7%	16.9%	53.5%	29.6%
Cape Coral-Fort Myers, FL.................	2,551	1.8%	17.0%	32.3%	50.6%	39,713	27.9%	16.7%	35.3%	48.0%
Cape Girardeau, MO-IL.................	304	1.2%	0.0%	19.7%	80.3%	232	0.9%	0.0%	100.0%	0.0%
Carbondale-Marion, IL.................	1,290	3.3%	28.2%	14.7%	57.1%	2,012	5.1%	8.7%	80.1%	11.2%
Carson City, NV.................	na	na	na	na	na	3,862	33.4%	11.9%	49.6%	38.6%
Casper, WY.................	288	1.4%	0.0%	100.0%	0.0%	2,504	12.1%	11.9%	33.9%	54.2%
Cedar Rapids, IA.................	2,835	4.3%	2.4%	0.0%	97.6%	3,205	4.9%	28.7%	9.6%	61.7%
Chambersburg-Waynesboro, PA.................	732	2.1%	53.1%	44.7%	2.2%	2,527	7.3%	0.0%	91.1%	8.9%
Champaign-Urbana, IL.................	13,645	15.3%	2.3%	68.6%	29.1%	4,950	5.6%	14.1%	55.3%	30.6%
Charleston, WV.................	765	1.6%	24.8%	5.6%	69.5%	725	1.5%	16.8%	39.9%	43.3%
Charleston-North Charleston, SC.................	2,880	1.4%	3.5%	53.1%	43.4%	14,936	7.3%	14.0%	35.3%	50.8%
Charlotte-Concord-Gastonia, NC-SC.................	24,252	4.0%	11.3%	30.4%	58.3%	67,935	11.2%	16.4%	38.3%	45.3%
Charlottesville, VA.................	4,474	6.7%	7.2%	74.4%	18.4%	4,718	7.0%	4.4%	59.5%	36.2%
Chattanooga, TN-GA.................	3,811	2.8%	6.2%	53.2%	40.6%	7,670	5.6%	16.0%	36.2%	47.7%
Cheyenne, WY.................	1,043	3.8%	3.9%	94.1%	2.0%	4,041	14.7%	19.8%	60.6%	19.6%
Chicago-Naperville-Elgin, IL-IN-WI.................	165,760	6.6%	10.9%	29.8%	59.3%	639,387	25.5%	17.2%	37.7%	45.1%
Chico, CA.................	4,035	6.1%	9.7%	63.0%	27.3%	13,182	19.8%	14.4%	54.3%	31.3%
Cincinnati, OH-KY-IN.................	15,006	2.8%	12.0%	40.5%	47.5%	18,145	3.3%	11.3%	33.4%	55.3%
Clarksburg, WV micro.................	300	1.5%	48.3%	48.0%	3.7%	349	1.8%	0.0%	0.0%	100.0%

Table B-4: Metropolitan/Micropolitan Statistical Areas—Race and Hispanic Origin by Age—*Continued*

	White, Non-Hispanic					Black, Non-Hispanic				
	Millennial Population		Percent by Age			Millennial Population		Percent by Age		
	Number	Percent	15 to 17	18 to 24	25 to 33	Number	Percent	15 to 17	18 to 24	25 to 33
Clarksville, TN-KY	57,156	62.7%	11.7%	36.0%	52.3%	18,098	19.9%	10.4%	42.2%	47.3%
Cleveland, TN	25,120	81.4%	17.7%	36.5%	45.8%	1,780	5.8%	21.0%	49.0%	30.1%
Cleveland-Elyria, OH	313,632	64.7%	16.7%	35.5%	47.8%	103,292	21.3%	16.6%	41.3%	42.2%
Coeur d'Alene, ID	31,408	89.5%	16.5%	34.1%	49.4%	na	na	na	na	na
College Station-Bryan, TX	58,538	58.3%	6.5%	63.5%	30.0%	8,728	8.7%	10.1%	43.7%	46.3%
Colorado Springs, CO	132,224	65.4%	13.7%	38.1%	48.2%	14,343	7.1%	12.2%	29.1%	58.7%
Columbia, MO	50,821	77.1%	7.7%	54.5%	37.8%	7,436	11.3%	10.0%	50.1%	40.0%
Columbia, SC	119,339	52.2%	13.6%	42.1%	44.3%	79,345	34.7%	15.6%	45.6%	38.8%
Columbus, GA-AL	38,484	41.3%	11.5%	39.0%	49.6%	41,117	44.2%	16.5%	36.9%	46.6%
Columbus, IN	16,546	79.4%	17.3%	36.1%	46.6%	271	1.3%	17.0%	13.3%	69.7%
Columbus, OH	388,066	71.1%	14.5%	32.7%	52.7%	85,326	15.6%	14.2%	37.1%	48.8%
Concord, NH micro	23,996	91.8%	15.7%	41.3%	43.0%	286	1.1%	0.0%	89.5%	10.5%
Cookeville, TN micro	26,675	86.9%	14.5%	47.3%	38.2%	743	2.4%	1.5%	58.4%	40.1%
Corpus Christi, TX	31,991	26.7%	12.4%	35.0%	52.6%	5,730	4.8%	16.3%	37.9%	45.8%
Corvallis, OR	25,585	78.5%	16.9%	44.4%	38.7%	na	na	na	na	na
Crestview-Fort Walton Beach-Destin, FL	48,180	69.5%	11.3%	33.5%	55.2%	8,916	12.9%	10.8%	32.3%	56.9%
Cumberland, MD-WV	21,470	81.8%	15.7%	40.2%	44.1%	2,360	9.0%	2.8%	82.6%	14.7%
Dallas-Fort Worth-Arlington, TX	779,125	41.6%	15.8%	33.0%	51.2%	306,442	16.3%	15.9%	36.5%	47.6%
Dalton, GA	20,450	54.8%	16.9%	38.5%	44.5%	1,746	4.7%	0.0%	37.3%	62.7%
Danville, IL	15,298	82.8%	19.4%	28.6%	52.0%	2,156	11.7%	12.4%	38.6%	49.0%
Danville, VA micro	13,046	58.6%	22.0%	30.0%	48.0%	7,382	33.1%	15.1%	40.8%	44.1%
Daphne-Fairhope-Foley, AL	33,898	80.9%	18.4%	34.6%	47.1%	5,821	13.9%	19.3%	41.7%	39.0%
Davenport-Moline-Rock Island, IA-IL	68,851	75.5%	14.5%	36.9%	48.6%	8,304	9.1%	8.2%	42.0%	49.8%
Dayton, OH	144,492	72.9%	15.1%	35.6%	49.3%	33,864	17.1%	14.1%	45.2%	40.7%
Decatur, AL	24,590	69.4%	16.4%	34.9%	48.7%	5,446	15.4%	16.9%	37.4%	45.7%
Decatur, IL	16,515	67.1%	16.0%	38.9%	45.1%	4,449	18.1%	16.6%	44.1%	39.3%
Deltona-Daytona Beach-Ormond Beach, FL	84,083	63.3%	15.2%	35.8%	49.0%	19,907	15.0%	13.9%	43.7%	42.3%
Denver-Aurora-Lakewood, CO	442,358	59.3%	13.2%	28.9%	57.9%	40,517	5.4%	14.8%	30.4%	54.8%
Des Moines-West Des Moines, IA	129,498	78.5%	16.0%	32.1%	52.0%	10,122	6.1%	20.1%	41.4%	38.5%
Detroit-Warren-Dearborn, MI	636,309	61.9%	17.3%	35.0%	47.7%	261,944	25.5%	16.8%	39.1%	44.1%
Dothan, AL	22,156	64.6%	18.5%	32.5%	49.0%	9,393	27.4%	15.4%	43.7%	40.9%
Dover, DE	27,024	58.5%	14.3%	34.9%	50.8%	12,676	27.5%	15.0%	49.1%	35.9%
Dubuque, IA	22,964	89.7%	17.1%	43.9%	39.0%	1,013	4.0%	7.2%	36.1%	56.7%
Duluth, MN-WI	63,257	87.0%	12.3%	43.1%	44.5%	1,248	1.7%	4.2%	32.0%	63.8%
Dunn, NC micro	19,932	56.9%	13.5%	35.6%	50.9%	7,239	20.7%	15.0%	43.5%	41.5%
Durham-Chapel Hill, NC	81,510	50.4%	9.6%	40.7%	49.7%	44,992	27.8%	12.5%	43.0%	44.5%
East Stroudsburg, PA	25,341	60.2%	16.2%	46.6%	37.2%	5,819	13.8%	27.4%	39.1%	33.5%
Eau Claire, WI	43,501	91.2%	12.2%	45.4%	42.4%	1,285	2.7%	0.0%	77.1%	22.9%
El Centro, CA	4,008	8.0%	21.7%	39.4%	38.9%	1,233	2.5%	0.0%	69.3%	30.7%
El Paso, TX	29,472	12.1%	9.8%	39.8%	50.4%	8,952	3.7%	10.5%	45.3%	44.3%
Elizabethtown-Fort Knox, KY	27,623	74.1%	19.3%	35.3%	45.4%	4,189	11.2%	17.7%	39.2%	43.2%
Elkhart-Goshen, IN	35,581	69.2%	18.2%	34.7%	47.1%	4,020	7.8%	15.1%	16.8%	68.0%
Elmira, NY	17,223	82.2%	13.8%	37.0%	49.1%	2,342	11.2%	3.8%	33.1%	63.1%
Erie, PA	57,461	80.9%	14.8%	39.8%	45.4%	5,247	7.4%	15.2%	36.5%	48.3%
Eugene, OR	76,324	75.6%	11.9%	45.0%	43.1%	1,787	1.8%	1.1%	62.7%	36.1%
Eureka-Arcata-Fortuna, CA micro	26,072	68.5%	10.6%	44.6%	44.8%	1,023	2.7%	0.0%	80.7%	19.3%
Evansville, IN-KY	66,027	85.0%	15.4%	35.6%	49.0%	5,666	7.3%	9.9%	36.6%	53.5%
Fairbanks, AK	22,436	64.4%	12.5%	37.6%	50.0%	824	2.4%	0.0%	74.9%	25.1%
Fargo, ND-MN	64,307	84.5%	9.7%	47.5%	42.8%	4,011	5.3%	2.0%	80.2%	17.8%
Farmington, NM	10,164	33.2%	15.2%	33.0%	51.8%	104	0.3%	0.0%	100.0%	0.0%
Fayetteville, NC	50,347	43.9%	10.9%	36.4%	52.7%	39,004	34.0%	14.4%	39.9%	45.7%
Fayetteville-Springdale-Rogers, AR-MO	102,770	70.8%	14.1%	39.3%	46.6%	3,150	2.2%	6.6%	43.2%	50.1%
Flagstaff, AZ	27,337	52.8%	7.1%	60.3%	32.7%	717	1.4%	0.0%	100.0%	0.0%
Flint, MI	66,066	68.6%	17.3%	35.9%	46.8%	20,509	21.3%	18.1%	43.8%	38.1%
Florence, SC	23,045	46.7%	17.4%	37.3%	45.4%	23,619	47.9%	16.1%	40.3%	43.6%
Florence-Muscle Shoals, AL	26,038	75.0%	17.0%	41.6%	41.4%	4,468	12.9%	19.4%	48.5%	32.1%
Fond du Lac, WI	20,614	83.5%	19.9%	31.2%	48.8%	943	3.8%	71.2%	23.2%	5.6%
Fort Collins, CO	81,844	79.0%	10.6%	46.7%	42.6%	1,213	1.2%	0.0%	46.5%	53.5%
Fort Smith, AR-OK	44,996	65.8%	14.0%	35.1%	50.9%	4,250	6.2%	17.6%	37.5%	44.9%
Fort Wayne, IN	81,919	73.9%	16.7%	36.4%	46.9%	11,558	10.4%	12.5%	36.9%	50.6%
Fresno, CA	64,861	23.1%	14.6%	34.9%	50.6%	14,525	5.2%	14.7%	48.0%	37.3%
Gadsden, AL	17,469	77.6%	17.9%	35.4%	46.7%	3,732	16.6%	9.1%	61.2%	29.6%
Gainesville, FL	62,038	60.4%	7.9%	55.6%	36.5%	18,912	18.4%	12.2%	50.5%	37.3%
Gainesville, GA	26,177	53.8%	16.8%	35.5%	47.7%	4,667	9.6%	15.8%	45.0%	39.2%
Gettysburg, PA	19,715	84.3%	14.5%	40.8%	44.7%	848	3.6%	99.4%	0.6%	0.0%
Glens Falls, NY	24,699	92.0%	17.2%	36.7%	46.2%	763	2.8%	6.7%	33.3%	60.0%
Goldsboro, NC	17,203	52.4%	13.3%	35.7%	51.0%	9,619	29.3%	15.3%	36.6%	48.1%
Grand Forks, ND-MN	28,159	77.3%	8.6%	53.1%	38.3%	2,117	5.8%	0.0%	20.3%	79.7%
Grand Island, NE	15,502	75.2%	19.1%	34.8%	46.1%	711	3.4%	12.1%	0.0%	87.9%
Grand Junction, CO	28,330	73.1%	14.2%	37.0%	48.8%	749	1.9%	21.0%	11.7%	67.3%
Grand Rapids-Wyoming, MI	210,653	74.5%	14.7%	38.1%	47.2%	21,658	7.7%	15.0%	46.4%	38.5%
Grants Pass, OR	13,446	79.8%	21.5%	34.6%	43.9%	na	na	na	na	na
Great Falls, MT	16,661	81.3%	12.2%	37.2%	50.6%	462	2.3%	0.0%	87.2%	12.8%
Greeley, CO	45,146	57.0%	14.0%	38.7%	47.2%	3,264	4.1%	34.5%	28.6%	36.9%
Green Bay, WI	62,086	79.2%	16.7%	35.7%	47.7%	2,115	2.7%	9.5%	29.9%	60.6%
Greensboro-High Point, NC	101,704	54.3%	16.6%	37.0%	46.4%	56,349	30.1%	13.2%	43.9%	42.9%

Table B-4: Metropolitan/Micropolitan Statistical Areas—Race and Hispanic Origin by Age—*Continued*

	Asian, Non-Hispanic					Hispanic				
	Millennial Population		Percent by Age			Millennial Population		Percent by Age		
	Number	Percent	15 to 17	18 to 24	25 to 33	Number	Percent	15 to 17	18 to 24	25 to 33
Clarksville, TN-KY	1,630	1.8%	17.9%	5.6%	76.4%	9,149	10.0%	6.9%	30.1%	63.0%
Cleveland, TN	331	1.1%	39.0%	61.0%	0.0%	2,818	9.1%	8.2%	50.3%	41.5%
Cleveland-Elyria, OH	16,484	3.4%	11.1%	30.9%	58.0%	34,577	7.1%	16.9%	38.3%	44.8%
Coeur d'Alene, ID	383	1.1%	0.0%	0.0%	100.0%	2,168	6.2%	8.9%	27.4%	63.7%
College Station-Bryan, TX	6,255	6.2%	4.2%	55.5%	40.4%	24,653	24.6%	9.4%	53.7%	36.9%
Colorado Springs, CO	4,682	2.3%	15.0%	38.8%	46.1%	38,991	19.3%	12.7%	37.0%	50.2%
Columbia, MO	3,738	5.7%	3.1%	52.1%	44.9%	2,463	3.7%	25.1%	52.9%	22.0%
Columbia, SC	6,179	2.7%	11.7%	39.3%	49.0%	15,360	6.7%	12.8%	40.1%	47.1%
Columbus, GA-AL	2,373	2.5%	17.2%	29.8%	53.0%	7,992	8.6%	7.2%	47.4%	45.4%
Columbus, IN	1,459	7.0%	0.0%	14.3%	85.7%	2,229	10.7%	27.9%	45.3%	26.9%
Columbus, OH	23,505	4.3%	13.1%	28.3%	58.6%	24,901	4.6%	13.9%	34.3%	51.8%
Concord, NH micro	620	2.4%	14.5%	13.7%	71.8%	610	2.3%	0.0%	19.5%	80.5%
Cookeville, TN micro	563	1.8%	0.0%	64.8%	35.2%	2,172	7.1%	20.2%	34.8%	45.1%
Corpus Christi, TX	2,572	2.2%	14.8%	31.7%	53.5%	77,527	64.8%	17.5%	38.3%	44.2%
Corvallis, OR	1,988	6.1%	4.9%	78.3%	16.8%	4,206	12.9%	12.8%	46.2%	41.0%
Crestview-Fort Walton Beach-Destin, FL	1,448	2.1%	2.9%	43.6%	53.5%	7,989	11.5%	11.0%	39.4%	49.6%
Cumberland, MD-WV	350	1.3%	0.0%	37.1%	62.9%	709	2.7%	29.6%	55.7%	14.7%
Dallas-Fort Worth-Arlington, TX	123,510	6.6%	11.7%	30.6%	57.7%	615,379	32.8%	17.9%	37.0%	45.0%
Dalton, GA	485	1.3%	0.0%	35.5%	64.5%	14,124	37.8%	17.2%	34.5%	48.2%
Danville, IL	29	0.2%	100.0%	0.0%	0.0%	670	3.6%	16.0%	14.6%	69.4%
Danville, VA micro	147	0.7%	0.0%	100.0%	0.0%	1,366	6.1%	0.0%	48.2%	51.8%
Daphne-Fairhope-Foley, AL	62	0.1%	100.0%	0.0%	0.0%	1,459	3.5%	0.0%	16.0%	84.0%
Davenport-Moline-Rock Island, IA-IL	1,809	2.0%	15.2%	34.8%	50.0%	9,373	10.3%	20.9%	43.2%	35.9%
Dayton, OH	5,077	2.6%	9.5%	32.9%	57.6%	6,731	3.4%	6.6%	42.2%	51.3%
Decatur, AL	273	0.8%	0.0%	0.0%	100.0%	3,374	9.5%	25.1%	41.4%	33.5%
Decatur, IL	562	2.3%	28.6%	38.1%	33.3%	954	3.9%	0.0%	26.5%	73.5%
Deltona-Daytona Beach-Ormond Beach, FL	3,114	2.3%	19.1%	39.3%	41.7%	22,152	16.7%	18.8%	43.3%	38.0%
Denver-Aurora-Lakewood, CO	31,855	4.3%	10.7%	30.8%	58.4%	197,512	26.5%	17.5%	36.9%	45.6%
Des Moines-West Des Moines, IA	6,448	3.9%	10.2%	24.8%	65.0%	14,639	8.9%	12.6%	34.9%	52.4%
Detroit-Warren-Dearborn, MI	48,096	4.7%	17.1%	32.2%	50.7%	53,234	5.2%	18.0%	36.9%	45.1%
Dothan, AL	209	0.6%	0.0%	0.0%	100.0%	1,598	4.7%	21.5%	28.5%	50.0%
Dover, DE	1,082	2.3%	22.2%	64.6%	13.2%	3,533	7.7%	17.0%	46.4%	36.5%
Dubuque, IA	580	2.3%	45.3%	27.1%	27.6%	534	2.1%	46.1%	29.2%	24.7%
Duluth, MN-WI	1,598	2.2%	9.5%	57.4%	33.1%	1,756	2.4%	25.4%	50.5%	24.1%
Dunn, NC micro	489	1.4%	21.5%	78.5%	0.0%	5,215	14.9%	15.2%	34.9%	49.9%
Durham-Chapel Hill, NC	10,021	6.0%	6.4%	30.3%	55.3%	19,040	12.3%	20.1%	31.5%	48.4%
East Stroudsburg, PA	1,893	4.5%	0.0%	64.1%	35.9%	7,557	18.0%	19.0%	28.8%	52.1%
Eau Claire, WI	1,805	3.8%	15.7%	39.1%	45.2%	927	1.9%	1.1%	76.3%	22.7%
El Centro, CA	184	0.4%	0.0%	0.0%	100.0%	43,436	87.2%	17.0%	39.0%	44.0%
El Paso, TX	2,920	1.2%	6.4%	21.9%	71.7%	197,751	81.2%	17.0%	38.8%	44.1%
Elizabethtown-Fort Knox, KY	1,256	3.4%	0.0%	0.0%	100.0%	2,859	7.7%	14.7%	49.5%	35.9%
Elkhart-Goshen, IN	653	1.3%	0.0%	54.1%	45.9%	8,934	17.4%	21.4%	48.2%	30.4%
Elmira, NY	220	1.1%	0.0%	18.2%	81.8%	719	3.4%	0.0%	0.0%	100.0%
Erie, PA	1,940	2.7%	8.6%	60.2%	31.2%	3,865	5.4%	28.5%	42.6%	28.9%
Eugene, OR	3,847	3.8%	3.4%	64.1%	32.5%	11,504	11.4%	15.3%	44.5%	40.1%
Eureka-Arcata-Fortuna, CA micro	1,421	3.7%	14.6%	21.8%	63.5%	5,146	13.5%	3.8%	52.7%	43.5%
Evansville, IN-KY	1,444	1.9%	24.9%	21.8%	53.3%	2,525	3.3%	26.0%	49.3%	24.7%
Fairbanks, AK	1,737	5.0%	9.2%	0.0%	90.8%	3,621	10.4%	4.5%	82.7%	12.8%
Fargo, ND-MN	2,163	2.8%	8.4%	12.5%	79.1%	3,800	5.0%	17.1%	44.9%	38.0%
Farmington, NM	26	0.1%	0.0%	0.0%	100.0%	7,994	26.1%	14.8%	46.6%	38.5%
Fayetteville, NC	1,400	1.2%	17.5%	47.5%	35.0%	14,212	12.4%	11.7%	39.1%	49.3%
Fayetteville-Springdale-Rogers, AR-MO	5,770	4.0%	10.8%	43.6%	45.6%	25,635	17.7%	17.5%	42.2%	40.3%
Flagstaff, AZ	1,556	3.0%	4.9%	78.6%	16.5%	7,184	13.9%	8.5%	60.7%	30.8%
Flint, MI	1,699	1.8%	0.0%	12.1%	87.9%	2,874	3.0%	18.1%	51.3%	30.7%
Florence, SC	539	1.1%	0.0%	0.7%	99.3%	1,339	2.7%	21.4%	45.3%	33.4%
Florence-Muscle Shoals, AL	200	0.6%	0.0%	71.5%	28.5%	3,277	9.4%	50.8%	14.4%	34.8%
Fond du Lac, WI	854	3.5%	0.0%	77.0%	23.0%	1,729	7.0%	26.7%	62.8%	10.6%
Fort Collins, CO	3,438	3.3%	22.7%	42.3%	35.0%	14,001	13.5%	11.8%	36.5%	51.7%
Fort Smith, AR-OK	1,851	2.7%	11.7%	28.5%	59.8%	8,180	12.0%	16.2%	35.3%	48.5%
Fort Wayne, IN	4,644	4.2%	14.5%	55.7%	29.8%	8,817	8.0%	19.0%	48.5%	32.5%
Fresno, CA	32,672	11.6%	12.9%	33.3%	53.8%	161,608	57.5%	17.2%	38.5%	44.3%
Gadsden, AL	na	na	na	na	na	1,163	5.2%	29.3%	47.5%	23.2%
Gainesville, FL	7,710	7.5%	5.4%	60.4%	34.1%	11,593	11.3%	5.5%	60.8%	33.7%
Gainesville, GA	947	1.9%	20.9%	21.5%	57.6%	16,152	33.2%	19.7%	39.2%	41.1%
Gettysburg, PA	170	0.7%	50.0%	0.0%	50.0%	2,355	10.1%	17.0%	21.3%	61.7%
Glens Falls, NY	312	1.2%	0.0%	81.4%	18.6%	539	2.0%	44.9%	17.6%	37.5%
Goldsboro, NC	548	1.7%	0.0%	20.3%	79.7%	4,631	14.1%	10.6%	41.4%	48.0%
Grand Forks, ND-MN	716	2.0%	0.0%	78.9%	21.1%	2,444	6.7%	29.3%	51.9%	18.7%
Grand Island, NE	44	0.2%	13.6%	86.4%	0.0%	4,066	19.7%	13.4%	58.7%	28.0%
Grand Junction, CO	432	1.1%	0.0%	100.0%	0.0%	7,526	19.4%	12.5%	45.1%	42.4%
Grand Rapids-Wyoming, MI	9,332	3.3%	16.6%	25.4%	58.0%	33,559	11.9%	19.0%	41.2%	39.7%
Grants Pass, OR	na	na	na	na	na	2,044	12.1%	29.1%	59.3%	11.6%
Great Falls, MT	na	na	na	na	na	776	3.8%	0.0%	55.4%	44.6%
Greeley, CO	1,262	1.6%	6.7%	44.9%	48.4%	27,421	34.6%	20.6%	36.9%	42.5%
Green Bay, WI	3,396	4.3%	2.4%	12.0%	85.5%	7,586	9.7%	10.1%	41.3%	48.6%
Greensboro-High Point, NC	6,618	3.5%	21.3%	34.9%	43.8%	17,635	9.4%	15.6%	30.4%	53.9%

Table B-4: Metropolitan/Micropolitan Statistical Areas—Race and Hispanic Origin by Age—*Continued*

| | White, Non-Hispanic | | | | | Black, Non-Hispanic | | | | |
| | Millennial Population | | Percent by Age | | | Millennial Population | | Percent by Age | | |
	Number	Percent	15 to 17	18 to 24	25 to 33	Number	Percent	15 to 17	18 to 24	25 to 33
Greenville, NC	35,070	58.0%	7.4%	57.8%	34.8%	19,568	32.4%	14.3%	46.7%	39.0%
Greenville-Anderson-Mauldin, SC	151,754	68.8%	14.9%	39.2%	45.9%	40,699	18.5%	18.5%	37.6%	43.9%
Greenwood, SC micro	12,268	53.7%	15.5%	41.1%	43.5%	7,609	33.3%	19.5%	44.5%	36.0%
Gulfport-Biloxi-Pascagoula, MS	63,363	63.6%	15.6%	36.0%	48.4%	23,102	23.2%	17.8%	37.8%	44.4%
Hagerstown-Martinsburg, MD-WV	47,636	77.0%	15.3%	36.6%	48.2%	8,129	13.1%	17.0%	43.4%	39.5%
Hammond, LA	22,074	62.2%	14.1%	33.9%	52.0%	10,761	30.3%	14.1%	45.9%	39.9%
Hanford-Corcoran, CA	13,592	29.2%	11.1%	33.3%	55.6%	2,822	6.1%	0.7%	35.0%	64.2%
Harrisburg-Carlisle, PA	101,279	74.4%	14.9%	36.1%	49.0%	14,022	10.3%	16.6%	49.9%	33.5%
Harrisonburg, VA	35,288	79.5%	8.9%	56.9%	34.2%	1,819	4.1%	19.5%	70.0%	10.5%
Hartford-West Hartford-East Hartford, CT	177,069	61.5%	15.6%	40.4%	43.9%	34,470	12.0%	16.0%	40.4%	43.6%
Hattiesburg, MS	24,506	58.2%	9.7%	45.7%	44.6%	14,834	35.2%	16.5%	51.3%	32.2%
Hickory-Lenoir-Morganton, NC	62,960	76.9%	17.9%	38.5%	43.6%	4,943	6.0%	11.5%	51.0%	37.5%
Hilo, HI micro	9,981	22.5%	10.8%	38.8%	50.4%	na	na	na	na	na
Hilton Head Island-Bluffton-Beaufort, SC	25,350	52.3%	10.8%	42.5%	46.7%	13,371	27.6%	12.8%	28.0%	59.1%
Hinesville, GA	12,266	45.2%	7.4%	50.2%	42.4%	9,108	33.6%	14.7%	47.7%	37.6%
Holland, MI micro	22,261	82.7%	19.3%	34.3%	46.4%	na	na	na	na	na
Homosassa Springs, FL	17,880	86.7%	18.0%	37.1%	44.9%	662	3.2%	40.5%	11.5%	48.0%
Hot Springs, AR	15,920	74.3%	17.0%	38.4%	44.6%	4,194	19.6%	11.7%	33.5%	54.7%
Houma-Thibodaux, LA	36,626	67.6%	15.4%	34.9%	49.8%	10,585	19.6%	21.9%	35.3%	42.7%
Houston-The Woodlands-Sugar Land, TX	563,789	31.4%	15.6%	31.8%	52.6%	325,301	18.1%	15.6%	36.0%	48.4%
Huntington-Ashland, WV-KY-OH	78,556	92.8%	17.6%	39.0%	43.4%	2,709	3.2%	15.0%	30.7%	54.2%
Huntsville, AL	70,099	60.4%	16.2%	33.5%	50.3%	30,564	26.3%	12.3%	41.3%	46.4%
Idaho Falls, ID	27,561	78.9%	18.4%	30.7%	50.9%	na	na	na	na	na
Indianapolis-Carmel-Anderson, IN	348,228	68.7%	16.1%	33.9%	50.0%	86,455	17.1%	16.0%	36.8%	47.2%
Iowa City, IA	48,209	79.5%	9.4%	50.5%	40.1%	1,945	3.2%	17.8%	51.3%	30.8%
Ithaca, NY	29,387	64.7%	7.3%	63.9%	28.8%	1,525	3.4%	2.6%	88.5%	8.9%
Jackson, MI	30,956	80.5%	16.7%	36.7%	46.6%	4,081	10.6%	17.1%	35.3%	47.6%
Jackson, MS	58,532	38.8%	17.2%	33.2%	49.7%	84,282	55.8%	16.7%	39.2%	44.2%
Jackson, TN	20,062	59.1%	12.6%	42.2%	45.1%	11,246	33.2%	16.8%	37.5%	45.7%
Jacksonville, FL	218,531	58.5%	14.8%	33.3%	51.9%	89,443	23.9%	17.0%	37.6%	45.4%
Jacksonville, NC	48,986	65.0%	6.3%	48.5%	45.2%	10,712	14.2%	16.0%	47.0%	37.0%
Jamestown-Dunkirk-Fredonia, NY micro	25,703	80.9%	15.7%	41.9%	42.4%	1,468	4.6%	16.8%	69.3%	13.9%
Janesville-Beloit, WI	29,806	81.2%	17.3%	36.9%	45.8%	771	2.1%	21.1%	46.6%	32.3%
Jefferson City, MO	31,473	82.1%	15.8%	38.7%	45.5%	4,053	10.6%	18.8%	40.3%	40.9%
Johnson City, TN	43,128	89.4%	14.5%	41.2%	44.3%	2,044	4.2%	2.1%	54.3%	43.6%
Johnstown, PA	27,476	89.3%	15.6%	40.8%	43.5%	970	3.2%	6.6%	62.2%	31.2%
Jonesboro, AR	27,016	73.2%	16.0%	36.6%	47.4%	6,590	17.9%	8.0%	63.0%	29.1%
Joplin, MO	35,284	80.4%	17.1%	36.1%	46.8%	487	1.1%	0.0%	64.5%	35.5%
Kahului-Wailuku-Lahaina, HI	8,980	22.9%	7.4%	27.1%	65.5%	247	0.6%	0.0%	0.0%	100.0%
Kalamazoo-Portage, MI	72,538	74.6%	13.1%	48.3%	38.7%	9,534	9.8%	16.9%	58.8%	24.3%
Kalispell, MT micro	17,703	85.5%	17.2%	34.3%	48.5%	na	na	na	na	na
Kankakee, IL	18,822	66.2%	16.0%	41.2%	42.8%	5,594	19.7%	17.7%	27.5%	54.7%
Kansas City, MO-KS	364,289	69.6%	15.7%	32.9%	51.5%	66,276	12.7%	16.2%	39.6%	44.2%
Kennewick-Richland, WA	40,553	53.4%	15.6%	32.3%	52.0%	466	0.6%	0.0%	31.1%	68.9%
Killeen-Temple, TX	65,252	46.7%	12.8%	37.5%	49.6%	25,295	18.1%	13.9%	35.7%	50.5%
Kingsport-Bristol-Bristol, TN-VA	60,507	90.6%	18.2%	33.6%	48.2%	2,598	3.9%	40.2%	37.2%	22.6%
Kingston, NY	30,264	72.2%	13.1%	40.4%	46.5%	3,423	8.2%	23.0%	47.1%	29.9%
Knoxville, TN	180,083	84.6%	15.3%	40.9%	43.8%	13,884	6.5%	13.4%	52.2%	34.4%
Kokomo, IN	14,228	79.5%	21.8%	33.5%	44.8%	496	2.8%	37.3%	23.6%	39.1%
La Crosse-Onalaska, WI-MN	36,658	90.2%	10.7%	54.3%	35.0%	609	1.5%	0.0%	100.0%	0.0%
Lafayette, LA	84,397	62.8%	15.0%	33.7%	51.3%	39,107	29.1%	17.5%	39.9%	42.5%
Lafayette-West Lafayette, IN	59,572	74.1%	8.9%	57.2%	33.9%	3,926	4.9%	0.3%	77.3%	22.4%
Lake Charles, LA	36,423	66.3%	15.7%	33.4%	50.9%	13,862	25.2%	16.9%	38.6%	44.5%
Lake Havasu City-Kingman, AZ	24,288	63.0%	15.7%	32.7%	51.6%	560	1.5%	56.1%	0.0%	43.9%
Lakeland-Winter Haven, FL	81,315	51.6%	15.3%	34.3%	50.4%	27,082	17.2%	14.3%	39.5%	46.2%
Lancaster, PA	104,010	78.0%	16.1%	36.4%	47.5%	4,989	3.7%	15.5%	53.4%	31.0%
Lansing-East Lansing, MI	102,086	70.1%	11.7%	47.9%	40.4%	14,662	10.1%	8.4%	54.9%	36.7%
Laredo, TX	3,024	4.0%	23.1%	19.4%	57.4%	na	na	na	na	na
Las Cruces, NM	15,347	23.9%	10.7%	45.5%	43.8%	825	1.3%	0.0%	100.0%	0.0%
Las Vegas-Henderson-Paradise, NV	197,729	35.9%	13.5%	29.6%	57.0%	64,825	11.8%	11.9%	37.5%	50.6%
Lawrence, KS	35,778	76.5%	7.2%	58.8%	34.0%	2,042	4.4%	0.0%	72.0%	28.0%
Lawton, OK	22,849	56.7%	9.2%	35.8%	55.0%	4,612	11.4%	14.0%	34.4%	51.6%
Lebanon, PA	23,848	80.2%	17.1%	38.1%	44.8%	737	2.5%	0.0%	37.9%	62.1%
Lewiston, ID-WA	11,143	77.2%	11.4%	47.2%	41.4%	56	0.4%	0.0%	100.0%	0.0%
Lewiston-Auburn, ME	21,063	86.5%	16.0%	38.7%	45.3%	414	1.7%	59.9%	30.2%	9.9%
Lexington-Fayette, KY	112,421	77.6%	12.7%	40.8%	46.5%	14,816	10.2%	18.9%	34.7%	46.3%
Lima, OH	19,914	78.9%	16.4%	41.3%	42.4%	3,463	13.7%	11.0%	30.2%	58.9%
Lincoln, NE	78,301	78.9%	10.4%	48.3%	41.3%	5,212	5.3%	0.0%	79.3%	20.7%
Little Rock-North Little Rock-Conway, AR	121,751	61.7%	13.8%	35.8%	50.4%	54,064	27.4%	17.3%	35.6%	47.1%
Logan, UT-ID	39,271	81.5%	12.9%	48.2%	38.9%	440	0.9%	0.0%	33.2%	66.8%
Longview, TX	30,080	57.5%	15.0%	37.6%	47.4%	11,422	21.8%	15.6%	36.8%	47.6%
Longview, WA	18,086	79.5%	16.0%	33.4%	50.6%	131	0.6%	42.0%	58.0%	0.0%
Los Angeles-Long Beach-Anaheim, CA	923,935	25.3%	11.8%	32.0%	56.2%	237,313	6.5%	13.0%	37.7%	49.3%
Louisville/Jefferson County, KY-IN	230,879	74.3%	16.0%	33.6%	50.4%	45,615	14.7%	16.6%	40.2%	43.1%
Lubbock, TX	57,033	52.7%	8.7%	53.5%	37.7%	6,804	6.3%	14.6%	55.8%	29.6%
Lumberton, NC micro	6,075	18.7%	13.7%	41.6%	44.7%	9,270	28.5%	14.8%	45.0%	40.2%

Table B-4: Metropolitan/Micropolitan Statistical Areas—Race and Hispanic Origin by Age—*Continued*

	Asian, Non-Hispanic				Hispanic				
	Millennial Population		Percent by Age			Millennial Population		Percent by Age		
	Number	Percent	15 to 17	18 to 24	25 to 33	Number	Percent	15 to 17	18 to 24	25 to 33
Greenville, NC	788	1.3%	21.4%	69.2%	9.4%	3,666	6.1%	8.1%	34.4%	57.5%
Greenville-Anderson-Mauldin, SC	4,109	1.9%	12.6%	39.3%	48.1%	18,956	8.6%	19.3%	38.3%	42.4%
Greenwood, SC micro	87	0.4%	0.0%	0.0%	100.0%	1,597	7.0%	0.0%	67.3%	32.7%
Gulfport-Biloxi-Pascagoula, MS	2,370	2.4%	21.9%	36.2%	41.9%	7,866	7.9%	14.9%	45.8%	39.3%
Hagerstown-Martinsburg, MD-WV	789	1.3%	14.8%	46.4%	38.8%	3,510	5.7%	6.6%	20.6%	72.8%
Hammond, LA	285	0.8%	0.0%	100.0%	0.0%	1,993	5.6%	10.1%	77.8%	12.1%
Hanford-Corcoran, CA	1,663	3.6%	19.5%	18.4%	62.1%	26,550	57.1%	15.9%	38.0%	46.1%
Harrisburg-Carlisle, PA	6,816	5.0%	9.7%	59.6%	30.7%	10,061	7.4%	20.8%	52.8%	26.4%
Harrisonburg, VA	1,413	3.2%	7.7%	82.0%	10.3%	4,442	10.0%	13.4%	45.5%	41.1%
Hartford-West Hartford-East Hartford, CT	15,869	5.5%	9.2%	38.1%	52.6%	50,885	17.7%	15.9%	37.8%	46.3%
Hattiesburg, MS	164	0.4%	0.0%	0.0%	100.0%	1,489	3.5%	20.4%	39.2%	40.4%
Hickory-Lenoir-Morganton, NC	4,430	5.4%	17.9%	51.9%	30.2%	8,483	10.4%	22.6%	26.3%	51.1%
Hilo, HI micro	6,604	14.9%	10.5%	37.5%	52.0%	7,256	16.4%	11.4%	36.7%	51.9%
Hilton Head Island-Bluffton-Beaufort, SC	397	0.8%	0.0%	2.5%	97.5%	7,978	16.5%	16.8%	35.8%	47.4%
Hinesville, GA	786	2.9%	6.0%	26.7%	67.3%	3,450	12.7%	13.4%	53.2%	33.4%
Holland, MI micro	105	0.4%	0.0%	0.0%	100.0%	3,103	11.5%	13.3%	56.7%	30.1%
Homosassa Springs, FL	341	1.7%	50.1%	49.9%	0.0%	1,211	5.9%	14.1%	50.9%	35.0%
Hot Springs, AR	na	na	na	na	na	716	3.3%	28.9%	29.7%	41.3%
Houma-Thibodaux, LA	617	1.1%	0.0%	52.4%	47.6%	2,244	4.1%	6.9%	12.1%	81.0%
Houston-The Woodlands-Sugar Land, TX	133,713	7.4%	14.7%	30.7%	54.6%	738,378	41.1%	17.2%	36.1%	46.7%
Huntington-Ashland, WV-KY-OH	321	0.4%	8.1%	51.1%	40.8%	1,662	2.0%	19.9%	42.2%	38.0%
Huntsville, AL	2,441	2.1%	11.3%	35.4%	53.3%	8,411	7.2%	19.0%	32.8%	48.3%
Idaho Falls, ID	813	2.3%	25.1%	24.2%	50.7%	5,933	17.0%	16.9%	35.7%	47.4%
Indianapolis-Carmel-Anderson, IN	16,016	3.2%	13.0%	23.0%	64.0%	38,649	7.6%	14.0%	31.9%	54.1%
Iowa City, IA	4,638	7.6%	6.6%	59.5%	33.9%	4,165	6.9%	16.3%	61.6%	22.1%
Ithaca, NY	7,842	17.3%	0.0%	79.9%	20.1%	3,679	8.1%	3.2%	68.0%	28.9%
Jackson, MI	843	2.2%	0.0%	16.7%	83.3%	1,815	4.7%	0.0%	41.5%	58.5%
Jackson, MS	2,700	1.8%	19.9%	23.2%	57.0%	3,866	2.6%	15.6%	16.2%	68.2%
Jackson, TN	587	1.7%	0.0%	0.0%	100.0%	1,032	3.0%	30.7%	26.0%	43.3%
Jacksonville, FL	16,613	4.4%	11.9%	29.3%	58.8%	36,900	9.9%	13.8%	38.8%	47.4%
Jacksonville, NC	1,123	1.5%	25.3%	52.4%	22.3%	10,538	14.0%	2.4%	54.3%	43.3%
Jamestown-Dunkirk-Fredonia, NY micro	408	1.3%	33.1%	24.0%	42.9%	3,593	11.3%	20.2%	40.5%	39.3%
Janesville-Beloit, WI	422	1.1%	7.6%	54.5%	37.9%	3,780	10.3%	19.6%	49.9%	30.6%
Jefferson City, MO	567	1.5%	0.0%	0.0%	100.0%	1,333	3.5%	39.1%	30.9%	30.0%
Johnson City, TN	487	1.0%	0.0%	37.0%	63.0%	1,492	3.1%	23.1%	46.2%	30.7%
Johnstown, PA	695	2.3%	48.3%	51.7%	0.0%	819	2.7%	59.3%	19.0%	21.6%
Jonesboro, AR	571	1.5%	0.0%	100.0%	0.0%	1,968	5.3%	20.5%	45.8%	25.7%
Joplin, MO	559	1.3%	33.5%	64.4%	2.1%	4,357	9.9%	21.8%	50.3%	27.8%
Kahului-Wailuku-Lahaina, HI	9,647	24.6%	19.4%	29.0%	51.7%	5,826	14.9%	19.4%	24.1%	56.5%
Kalamazoo-Portage, MI	3,106	3.2%	8.1%	23.3%	68.6%	7,847	8.1%	4.6%	57.3%	38.1%
Kalispell, MT micro	25	0.1%	0.0%	0.0%	100.0%	344	1.7%	16.9%	46.8%	36.3%
Kankakee, IL	220	0.8%	0.0%	0.0%	100.0%	3,015	10.6%	19.5%	50.6%	29.9%
Kansas City, MO-KS	17,762	3.4%	11.7%	33.1%	55.1%	52,870	10.1%	17.7%	33.6%	48.7%
Kennewick-Richland, WA	1,720	2.3%	6.5%	5.8%	87.8%	28,224	37.2%	17.5%	45.4%	37.1%
Killeen-Temple, TX	3,711	2.7%	5.8%	32.1%	62.2%	36,671	26.2%	14.1%	41.9%	44.0%
Kingsport-Bristol-Bristol, TN-VA	216	0.3%	0.0%	33.3%	66.7%	1,782	2.7%	19.8%	61.1%	19.1%
Kingston, NY	1,349	3.2%	15.4%	69.6%	15.0%	5,711	13.6%	9.3%	67.7%	22.9%
Knoxville, TN	2,546	1.2%	7.0%	33.4%	59.6%	9,514	4.5%	12.7%	35.1%	52.2%
Kokomo, IN	356	2.0%	0.0%	34.6%	65.4%	2,118	11.8%	2.3%	46.6%	51.1%
La Crosse-Onalaska, WI-MN	2,364	5.8%	17.6%	34.5%	47.9%	616	1.5%	34.1%	60.1%	5.8%
Lafayette, LA	3,078	2.3%	21.9%	22.7%	55.4%	4,694	3.5%	18.0%	42.6%	39.4%
Lafayette-West Lafayette, IN	9,088	11.3%	4.9%	68.5%	26.6%	5,997	7.5%	7.4%	63.9%	28.7%
Lake Charles, LA	1,127	2.1%	0.0%	47.6%	52.4%	2,272	4.1%	0.0%	39.3%	60.7%
Lake Havasu City-Kingman, AZ	513	1.3%	0.0%	0.0%	100.0%	10,529	27.3%	18.7%	34.8%	46.5%
Lakeland-Winter Haven, FL	3,736	2.4%	15.5%	32.3%	52.3%	41,460	26.3%	17.9%	35.1%	47.0%
Lancaster, PA	3,470	2.6%	14.4%	62.6%	22.9%	17,859	13.4%	18.5%	40.5%	41.0%
Lansing-East Lansing, MI	10,122	7.0%	7.5%	53.4%	39.1%	11,051	7.6%	23.2%	42.0%	34.8%
Laredo, TX	550	0.7%	50.0%	40.4%	9.6%	72,632	95.3%	19.1%	40.8%	40.1%
Las Cruces, NM	1,135	1.8%	0.0%	19.7%	80.3%	45,572	71.1%	15.7%	47.4%	36.9%
Las Vegas-Henderson-Paradise, NV	51,795	9.4%	11.8%	29.4%	58.7%	204,235	37.0%	16.9%	36.4%	46.6%
Lawrence, KS	2,632	5.6%	4.8%	77.6%	17.6%	3,210	6.9%	0.0%	33.6%	66.4%
Lawton, OK	1,152	2.9%	0.0%	41.2%	58.8%	7,048	17.5%	17.3%	51.9%	30.9%
Lebanon, PA	366	1.2%	0.0%	100.0%	0.0%	4,413	14.8%	7.7%	56.9%	35.3%
Lewiston, ID-WA	319	2.2%	18.5%	23.2%	58.3%	2,255	15.6%	23.1%	37.9%	39.0%
Lewiston-Auburn, ME	447	1.8%	0.0%	22.1%	77.9%	1,465	6.0%	15.6%	56.0%	28.5%
Lexington-Fayette, KY	3,991	2.8%	2.1%	36.1%	61.7%	7,899	5.5%	13.9%	35.5%	50.6%
Lima, OH	380	1.5%	0.0%	0.0%	100.0%	732	2.9%	15.2%	20.6%	64.2%
Lincoln, NE	6,325	6.4%	0.0%	34.1%	65.9%	7,487	7.5%	14.3%	27.7%	58.0%
Little Rock-North Little Rock-Conway, AR	4,169	2.1%	23.4%	31.9%	44.7%	13,183	6.7%	6.7%	39.4%	53.8%
Logan, UT-ID	1,297	2.7%	0.0%	10.7%	89.3%	5,275	11.0%	12.2%	39.5%	48.3%
Longview, TX	185	0.4%	0.0%	40.0%	60.0%	9,922	19.0%	18.4%	38.1%	43.4%
Longview, WA	321	1.4%	0.0%	33.3%	66.7%	3,116	13.7%	9.4%	4.1%	86.5%
Los Angeles-Long Beach-Anaheim, CA	518,564	14.2%	11.6%	33.7%	54.7%	1,853,849	50.8%	15.6%	38.8%	45.6%
Louisville/Jefferson County, KY-IN	6,461	2.1%	22.5%	21.6%	55.9%	18,433	5.9%	17.1%	36.1%	46.8%
Lubbock, TX	2,996	2.8%	7.2%	40.5%	52.3%	39,601	36.6%	15.0%	41.9%	43.1%
Lumberton, NC micro	196	0.6%	0.0%	33.2%	66.8%	3,070	9.4%	18.3%	48.7%	33.1%

Table B-4: Metropolitan/Micropolitan Statistical Areas—Race and Hispanic Origin by Age—*Continued*

| | White, Non-Hispanic | | | | | Black, Non-Hispanic | | | | |
| | Millennial Population | | Percent by Age | | | Millennial Population | | Percent by Age | | |
	Number	Percent	15 to 17	18 to 24	25 to 33	Number	Percent	15 to 17	18 to 24	25 to 33
Lynchburg, VA	52,933	74.3%	12.5%	48.0%	39.5%	11,666	16.4%	18.3%	37.8%	43.9%
Macon, GA	24,689	43.1%	13.9%	43.7%	42.4%	29,235	51.0%	16.3%	45.8%	37.9%
Madera, CA	9,975	24.0%	17.2%	32.8%	50.0%	985	2.4%	0.0%	7.8%	92.2%
Madison, WI	155,064	80.7%	11.7%	42.6%	45.7%	7,983	4.2%	18.1%	35.9%	46.1%
Manchester-Nashua, NH	82,095	83.0%	16.3%	37.0%	46.7%	2,879	2.9%	3.1%	57.1%	39.8%
Manhattan, KS	34,868	78.3%	7.5%	56.1%	36.3%	1,921	4.3%	5.4%	74.0%	20.6%
Mankato-North Mankato, MN	30,354	88.0%	10.5%	51.3%	38.2%	2,540	7.4%	13.3%	75.0%	11.6%
Mansfield, OH	22,500	80.5%	17.7%	36.6%	45.7%	2,477	8.9%	0.0%	64.7%	35.3%
McAllen-Edinburg-Mission, TX	9,004	3.9%	16.7%	42.4%	40.8%	1,994	0.9%	14.3%	41.3%	44.4%
Medford, OR	35,682	74.3%	15.8%	33.9%	50.3%	299	0.6%	0.0%	30.1%	69.9%
Memphis, TN-MS-AR	143,038	40.0%	16.7%	34.8%	48.5%	176,634	49.4%	17.4%	37.3%	45.3%
Merced, CA	17,342	22.1%	13.3%	33.2%	53.5%	2,651	3.4%	5.4%	75.4%	19.2%
Meridian, MS micro	12,967	47.5%	18.1%	35.9%	46.0%	12,919	47.3%	15.8%	38.8%	45.4%
Miami-Fort Lauderdale-West Palm Beach, FL	364,967	25.3%	15.2%	33.4%	51.4%	353,660	24.5%	15.7%	36.6%	47.7%
Michigan City-La Porte, IN	19,065	73.6%	16.9%	36.3%	46.8%	4,169	16.1%	17.5%	21.7%	60.9%
Midland, MI	18,154	89.8%	20.4%	31.7%	47.9%	723	3.6%	8.9%	1.0%	90.2%
Midland, TX	20,577	40.7%	11.8%	31.6%	56.6%	3,194	6.3%	41.1%	23.3%	35.6%
Milwaukee-Waukesha-West Allis, WI	243,204	61.2%	14.8%	34.6%	50.6%	77,867	19.6%	16.6%	42.7%	40.7%
Minneapolis-St. Paul-Bloomington, MN-WI	640,200	71.7%	15.3%	32.6%	52.1%	77,403	8.7%	15.6%	30.2%	54.1%
Missoula, MT	30,134	82.4%	12.6%	41.3%	46.1%	na	na	na	na	na
Mobile, AL	56,872	52.6%	15.0%	35.1%	49.9%	41,514	38.4%	17.3%	38.1%	44.6%
Modesto, CA	45,365	39.9%	15.1%	33.1%	51.8%	3,072	2.7%	27.1%	46.1%	26.8%
Monroe, LA	24,806	50.9%	16.6%	36.1%	47.2%	21,214	43.5%	15.3%	39.7%	44.9%
Monroe, MI	30,665	91.5%	18.7%	34.7%	46.6%	1,439	4.3%	16.2%	83.8%	0.0%
Montgomery, AL	41,916	42.4%	15.5%	35.0%	49.4%	51,217	51.8%	14.2%	39.5%	46.3%
Morgantown, WV	43,428	84.8%	7.7%	51.7%	40.6%	1,291	2.5%	0.0%	64.5%	35.5%
Morristown, TN	22,317	83.3%	25.4%	38.3%	36.3%	132	0.5%	93.9%	0.0%	6.1%
Mount Vernon-Anacortes, WA	19,754	72.4%	14.5%	33.1%	52.4%	1,232	4.5%	44.7%	20.8%	34.5%
Muncie, IN	33,048	88.9%	10.1%	60.0%	29.9%	2,349	6.3%	4.4%	78.7%	16.9%
Muskegon, MI	29,610	71.0%	16.8%	36.0%	47.2%	7,887	18.9%	12.2%	35.6%	52.2%
Myrtle Beach-Conway-North Myrtle Beach, SC-NC	63,321	69.9%	14.3%	33.9%	51.9%	13,397	14.8%	19.8%	41.2%	38.9%
Napa, CA	14,131	42.3%	14.7%	35.7%	49.6%	1,093	3.3%	13.6%	24.1%	62.3%
Naples-Immokalee-Marco Island, FL	29,561	43.5%	16.9%	36.7%	46.3%	6,030	8.9%	15.7%	47.5%	36.9%
Nashville-Davidson–Murfreesboro–Franklin, TN	341,745	70.0%	14.7%	34.0%	51.3%	79,629	16.3%	13.7%	42.1%	44.2%
New Bern, NC	23,319	67.4%	11.4%	43.6%	45.0%	7,890	22.8%	13.2%	42.3%	44.5%
New Castle, PA micro	16,559	87.6%	17.2%	35.2%	47.6%	1,805	9.5%	22.2%	36.8%	40.9%
New Haven-Milford, CT	122,938	55.7%	14.6%	38.2%	47.2%	32,558	14.7%	16.8%	45.8%	37.5%
New Orleans-Metairie, LA	155,304	47.2%	13.9%	30.4%	55.7%	121,965	37.1%	16.0%	36.2%	47.8%
New Philadelphia-Dover, OH micro	19,390	93.1%	20.4%	35.1%	44.5%	61	0.3%	100.0%	0.0%	0.0%
New York-Newark-Jersey City, NY-NJ-PA	2,169,118	41.7%	14.9%	34.3%	50.7%	865,353	16.7%	14.3%	37.6%	48.1%
Niles-Benton Harbor, MI	23,735	69.5%	17.1%	35.9%	47.1%	6,315	18.5%	10.6%	36.7%	52.8%
North Port-Sarasota-Bradenton, FL	89,164	64.5%	16.7%	35.2%	48.1%	14,596	10.6%	18.4%	37.0%	44.6%
Norwich-New London, CT	49,162	69.2%	14.1%	39.4%	46.5%	4,263	6.0%	15.9%	39.0%	45.2%
Ocala, FL	41,893	59.5%	15.9%	32.8%	51.3%	13,953	19.8%	18.6%	40.2%	41.2%
Ocean City, NJ	14,344	76.3%	15.9%	38.1%	46.0%	1,529	8.1%	36.6%	44.7%	18.6%
Odessa, TX	14,219	28.7%	12.3%	33.5%	54.1%	2,211	4.5%	16.0%	25.3%	58.7%
Ogden-Clearfield, UT	137,218	78.1%	18.0%	32.9%	49.1%	3,920	2.2%	7.7%	46.3%	46.0%
Ogdensburg-Massena, NY micro	27,660	86.2%	12.7%	48.3%	39.0%	1,746	5.4%	0.4%	56.9%	42.7%
Oklahoma City, OK	223,548	59.5%	13.2%	35.9%	50.9%	44,805	11.9%	12.9%	40.5%	46.7%
Olympia-Tumwater, WA	47,175	70.1%	14.4%	32.9%	52.8%	3,361	5.0%	4.7%	48.0%	47.4%
Omaha-Council Bluffs, NE-IA	173,225	72.6%	15.0%	32.7%	52.3%	21,888	9.2%	14.3%	35.4%	50.4%
Orangeburg, SC micro	8,002	34.9%	22.6%	25.9%	51.6%	14,443	63.1%	13.6%	36.5%	49.9%
Orlando-Kissimmee-Sanford, FL	280,447	43.3%	13.3%	34.2%	52.5%	113,556	17.5%	16.4%	36.6%	47.0%
Oshkosh-Neenah, WI	40,556	86.7%	12.5%	44.9%	42.6%	967	2.1%	0.0%	0.0%	100.0%
Ottawa-Peru, IL micro	20,424	81.0%	18.2%	35.7%	46.1%	979	3.9%	0.0%	20.7%	79.3%
Owensboro, KY	24,086	88.4%	18.4%	35.5%	46.1%	1,331	4.9%	0.0%	33.3%	66.7%
Oxnard-Thousand Oaks-Ventura, CA	81,785	37.6%	15.8%	38.1%	46.1%	5,085	2.3%	1.3%	39.5%	59.2%
Palm Bay-Melbourne-Titusville, FL	80,284	66.7%	16.3%	35.1%	48.6%	14,918	12.4%	13.3%	45.2%	41.5%
Panama City, FL	35,074	71.6%	14.6%	31.0%	54.5%	7,713	15.8%	16.5%	42.3%	41.3%
Parkersburg-Vienna, WV	18,718	92.8%	17.0%	34.8%	48.2%	328	1.6%	3.7%	96.3%	0.0%
Pensacola-Ferry Pass-Brent, FL	86,731	65.7%	12.4%	39.6%	48.0%	23,035	17.4%	16.2%	43.4%	40.4%
Peoria, IL	69,684	76.9%	15.8%	34.0%	50.2%	10,948	12.1%	12.8%	47.3%	40.0%
Philadelphia-Camden-Wilmington, PA-NJ-DE-MD	890,932	57.3%	14.8%	34.8%	50.4%	337,511	21.7%	15.2%	38.6%	46.2%
Phoenix-Mesa-Scottsdale, AZ	562,953	47.3%	15.0%	33.1%	51.9%	73,071	6.1%	16.3%	36.9%	46.8%
Pine Bluff, AR	11,828	52.6%	15.9%	45.0%	39.1%	10,214	45.4%	15.3%	34.8%	49.9%
Pittsburgh, PA	452,313	80.8%	14.5%	35.2%	50.3%	58,063	10.4%	17.5%	39.8%	42.8%
Pittsfield, MA	23,617	83.5%	15.4%	43.0%	41.6%	1,532	5.4%	8.6%	87.1%	4.3%
Pocatello, ID	18,729	76.6%	16.0%	34.7%	49.3%	244	1.0%	0.0%	100.0%	0.0%
Port St. Lucie, FL	50,064	54.4%	16.0%	33.1%	50.9%	18,329	19.9%	14.5%	50.0%	35.5%
Portland-South Portland, ME	107,859	88.4%	15.7%	35.2%	49.0%	1,782	1.5%	0.0%	62.7%	37.3%
Portland-Vancouver-Hillsboro, OR-WA	419,792	68.3%	14.2%	31.8%	54.0%	19,831	3.2%	11.7%	36.8%	51.5%
Pottsville, PA micro	26,057	85.8%	17.6%	35.4%	47.0%	1,881	6.2%	28.2%	2.8%	69.0%
Prescott, AZ	28,693	72.1%	16.6%	35.0%	48.4%	341	0.9%	0.0%	27.9%	72.1%
Providence-Warwick, RI-MA	293,566	70.8%	13.7%	39.7%	46.6%	23,476	5.7%	10.7%	38.9%	50.4%
Provo-Orem, UT	164,733	83.1%	15.3%	48.5%	36.2%	1,456	0.7%	24.6%	29.9%	45.5%
Pueblo, CO	19,037	46.8%	13.6%	36.3%	50.2%	394	1.0%	0.0%	60.9%	39.1%

Table B-4: Metropolitan/Micropolitan Statistical Areas—Race and Hispanic Origin by Age—*Continued*

	Asian, Non-Hispanic					Hispanic				
	Millennial Population		Percent by Age			Millennial Population		Percent by Age		
	Number	Percent	15 to 17	18 to 24	25 to 33	Number	Percent	15 to 17	18 to 24	25 to 33
Lynchburg, VA............................	1,553	2.2%	37.1%	49.0%	13.9%	2,790	3.9%	27.1%	49.2%	23.7%
Macon, GA..................................	776	1.4%	28.0%	41.1%	30.9%	2,055	3.6%	15.0%	38.6%	46.4%
Madera, CA................................	1,099	2.6%	0.0%	79.4%	20.6%	27,957	67.3%	17.3%	38.4%	44.3%
Madison, WI...............................	14,703	7.7%	11.4%	47.2%	41.4%	10,634	5.5%	16.7%	23.9%	59.4%
Manchester-Nashua, NH..............	4,285	4.3%	19.4%	29.3%	51.2%	8,330	8.4%	19.5%	37.5%	43.0%
Manhattan, KS...........................	1,336	3.0%	0.0%	70.2%	29.8%	4,354	9.8%	13.0%	30.6%	56.4%
Mankato-North Mankato, MN........	246	0.7%	0.0%	100.0%	0.0%	825	2.4%	34.1%	65.9%	0.0%
Mansfield, OH............................	542	1.9%	0.0%	42.1%	57.9%	988	3.5%	14.0%	46.2%	39.9%
McAllen-Edinburg-Mission, TX.......	1,603	0.7%	23.1%	43.5%	33.4%	218,395	94.3%	18.9%	39.5%	41.6%
Medford, OR..............................	937	2.0%	11.0%	15.2%	73.9%	8,254	17.2%	18.5%	33.9%	47.6%
Memphis, TN-MS-AR....................	7,422	2.1%	19.6%	38.2%	42.1%	22,589	6.3%	15.5%	31.3%	53.3%
Merced, CA................................	5,975	7.6%	12.3%	59.2%	28.5%	50,041	63.9%	18.2%	40.1%	41.7%
Meridian, MS micro....................	634	2.3%	0.0%	63.4%	36.6%	267	1.0%	68.5%	0.0%	31.5%
Miami-Fort Lauderdale-West Palm Beach, FL.......	36,218	2.5%	9.9%	33.0%	57.1%	658,839	45.7%	14.3%	34.9%	50.9%
Michigan City-La Porte, IN...........	19	0.1%	0.0%	100.0%	0.0%	2,087	8.1%	17.1%	31.7%	51.2%
Midland, MI...............................	25	0.1%	0.0%	100.0%	0.0%	704	3.5%	26.6%	44.3%	29.1%
Midland, TX...............................	1,392	2.8%	14.9%	14.9%	70.3%	24,084	47.7%	15.2%	35.8%	48.9%
Milwaukee-Waukesha-West Allis, WI..................	14,748	3.7%	15.5%	27.4%	57.1%	48,235	12.1%	18.7%	36.7%	44.6%
Minneapolis-St. Paul-Bloomington, MN-WI........	81,881	9.2%	13.8%	29.7%	56.4%	58,095	6.5%	20.0%	37.4%	42.6%
Missoula, MT.............................	na	na	na	na	na	604	1.7%	24.3%	14.6%	61.1%
Mobile, AL.................................	2,544	2.4%	9.4%	14.3%	76.2%	4,164	3.9%	22.6%	8.5%	68.9%
Modesto, CA..............................	6,292	5.5%	17.7%	31.9%	50.3%	53,037	46.7%	19.7%	37.7%	42.5%
Monroe, LA................................	817	1.7%	0.0%	32.8%	67.2%	1,122	2.3%	7.0%	0.0%	93.0%
Monroe, MI................................	289	0.9%	0.0%	0.0%	100.0%	436	1.3%	0.0%	20.4%	79.6%
Montgomery, AL..........................	651	0.7%	15.5%	12.4%	72.0%	1,943	2.0%	18.2%	24.3%	57.4%
Morgantown, WV.........................	2,359	4.6%	2.0%	19.3%	78.7%	1,707	3.3%	0.0%	20.9%	79.1%
Morristown, TN...........................	113	0.4%	0.0%	100.0%	0.0%	3,017	11.3%	13.4%	21.7%	64.9%
Mount Vernon-Anacortes, WA........	649	2.4%	63.3%	23.3%	13.4%	5,155	18.9%	15.3%	36.4%	48.3%
Muncie, IN................................	346	0.9%	83.5%	0.0%	16.5%	846	2.3%	0.0%	100.0%	0.0%
Muskegon, MI.............................	115	0.3%	0.0%	3.5%	96.5%	2,706	6.5%	17.8%	51.4%	30.8%
Myrtle Beach-Conway-North Myrtle Beach, SC-NC.......	1,381	1.5%	13.0%	8.5%	78.5%	7,483	8.3%	12.9%	54.0%	33.2%
Napa, CA...................................	2,687	8.0%	7.4%	71.2%	21.4%	14,767	44.2%	18.0%	39.1%	42.9%
Naples-Immokalee-Marco Island, FL..................	1,151	1.7%	14.8%	19.3%	65.9%	28,493	41.9%	14.8%	37.3%	48.0%
Nashville-Davidson–Murfreesboro–Franklin, TN...	13,446	2.8%	19.2%	34.6%	46.2%	37,320	7.6%	18.0%	38.1%	44.0%
New Bern, NC.............................	965	2.8%	0.0%	17.5%	82.5%	2,209	6.4%	10.8%	61.4%	27.8%
New Castle, PA micro..................	73	0.4%	100.0%	0.0%	0.0%	na	na	na	na	na
New Haven-Milford, CT................	10,601	4.8%	13.4%	34.6%	52.1%	48,181	21.8%	16.1%	38.6%	45.3%
New Orleans-Metairie, LA..............	11,736	3.6%	8.3%	31.4%	60.3%	31,730	9.6%	12.8%	30.0%	57.2%
New Philadelphia-Dover, OH micro..................	591	2.8%	0.0%	0.0%	100.0%	780	3.7%	26.3%	35.6%	38.1%
New York-Newark-Jersey City, NY-NJ-PA............	597,779	11.5%	11.7%	30.5%	57.8%	1,421,287	27.4%	14.1%	36.5%	49.4%
Niles-Benton Harbor, MI...............	1,350	4.0%	22.3%	57.2%	20.5%	1,702	5.0%	24.0%	43.5%	32.5%
North Port-Sarasota-Bradenton, FL..................	3,258	2.4%	0.3%	42.4%	49.3%	26,922	10.5%	17.6%	37.8%	44.6%
Norwich-New London, CT..............	3,576	5.0%	13.6%	34.3%	52.1%	9,109	12.8%	15.2%	49.9%	34.9%
Ocala, FL..................................	2,257	3.2%	5.3%	61.7%	33.0%	11,270	16.0%	17.4%	38.2%	44.5%
Ocean City, NJ...........................	189	1.0%	100.0%	0.0%	0.0%	2,645	14.1%	26.8%	3.6%	69.6%
Odessa, TX................................	1,047	2.1%	18.3%	81.7%	0.0%	31,286	63.2%	15.0%	37.1%	47.9%
Ogden-Clearfield, UT...................	3,160	1.8%	25.0%	34.7%	40.3%	25,961	14.8%	15.5%	45.8%	38.7%
Ogdensburg-Massena, NY micro.....	560	1.7%	33.0%	21.4%	45.5%	973	3.0%	6.7%	73.7%	19.6%
Oklahoma City, OK.....................	15,274	4.1%	6.3%	31.2%	62.5%	57,089	15.2%	15.5%	43.2%	41.4%
Olympia-Tumwater, WA................	4,111	6.1%	12.6%	30.8%	56.5%	7,834	11.6%	15.0%	48.0%	37.0%
Omaha-Council Bluffs, NE-IA.........	7,798	3.3%	15.0%	35.6%	49.4%	28,346	11.9%	18.5%	35.7%	45.8%
Orangeburg, SC micro..................	86	0.4%	0.0%	100.0%	0.0%	320	1.4%	0.0%	56.3%	43.8%
Orlando-Kissimmee-Sanford, FL......	25,888	4.0%	13.5%	41.8%	44.7%	208,237	32.1%	15.7%	37.9%	46.4%
Oshkosh-Neenah, WI...................	1,749	3.7%	0.0%	7.1%	92.9%	2,920	6.2%	42.3%	17.6%	40.1%
Ottawa-Peru, IL micro..................	439	1.7%	0.0%	79.0%	21.0%	3,166	12.6%	19.2%	31.0%	49.8%
Owensboro, KY...........................	341	1.3%	0.0%	26.4%	73.6%	748	2.7%	28.3%	49.9%	21.8%
Oxnard-Thousand Oaks-Ventura, CA...................	14,636	6.7%	12.0%	33.0%	55.1%	109,797	50.5%	16.4%	38.2%	45.4%
Palm Bay-Melbourne-Titusville, FL..................	1,703	1.4%	23.5%	50.8%	25.7%	16,607	13.8%	18.0%	37.7%	44.3%
Panama City, FL.........................	921	1.9%	8.8%	11.4%	79.8%	2,774	5.7%	16.3%	40.8%	42.9%
Parkersburg-Vienna, WV...............	41	0.2%	100.0%	0.0%	0.0%	403	2.0%	54.1%	0.0%	45.9%
Pensacola-Ferry Pass-Brent, FL......	4,101	3.1%	0.0%	38.9%	61.1%	10,028	7.6%	14.7%	39.7%	45.6%
Peoria, IL..................................	3,043	3.4%	9.1%	28.3%	62.5%	4,204	4.6%	23.3%	30.5%	46.2%
Philadelphia-Camden-Wilmington, PA-NJ-DE-MD	102,283	6.6%	12.3%	33.0%	54.7%	173,732	11.2%	14.1%	36.6%	49.3%
Phoenix-Mesa-Scottsdale, AZ.........	47,982	4.0%	10.1%	33.5%	56.4%	444,950	37.4%	17.8%	39.5%	42.7%
Pine Bluff, AR............................	57	0.3%	0.0%	0.0%	100.0%	277	1.2%	0.0%	59.6%	40.4%
Pittsburgh, PA............................	17,710	3.2%	10.8%	36.3%	52.8%	14,811	2.6%	8.7%	45.0%	46.4%
Pittsfield, MA............................	743	2.6%	20.5%	47.6%	31.9%	1,468	5.2%	14.5%	62.9%	22.6%
Pocatello, ID.............................	422	1.7%	0.0%	89.1%	10.9%	3,237	13.2%	6.4%	57.9%	35.7%
Port St. Lucie, FL.......................	1,607	1.7%	4.9%	24.4%	70.7%	20,368	22.1%	16.4%	34.3%	49.3%
Portland-South Portland, ME..........	1,902	1.6%	18.6%	42.4%	39.1%	5,543	4.5%	19.9%	54.5%	25.6%
Portland-Vancouver-Hillsboro, OR-WA................	42,664	6.9%	14.1%	31.8%	54.1%	91,545	14.9%	17.2%	37.1%	45.7%
Pottsville, PA micro.....................	na	na	na	na	na	2,143	7.1%	10.4%	42.7%	46.9%
Prescott, AZ..............................	541	1.4%	0.0%	55.5%	44.5%	8,396	21.1%	15.4%	45.4%	39.1%
Providence-Warwick, RI-MA...........	17,799	4.3%	7.8%	39.1%	53.1%	62,749	15.1%	14.8%	41.1%	44.2%
Provo-Orem, UT.........................	4,105	2.1%	13.4%	40.0%	46.6%	20,732	10.5%	16.1%	42.5%	41.5%
Pueblo, CO................................	377	0.9%	30.0%	70.0%	0.0%	19,876	48.9%	18.1%	36.9%	45.0%

Table B-4: Metropolitan/Micropolitan Statistical Areas—Race and Hispanic Origin by Age—*Continued*

	White, Non-Hispanic					Black, Non-Hispanic				
	Millennial Population		Percent by Age			Millennial Population		Percent by Age		
	Number	Percent	15 to 17	18 to 24	25 to 33	Number	Percent	15 to 17	18 to 24	25 to 33
Punta Gorda, FL	17,421	75.3%	18.1%	37.5%	44.4%	2,074	9.0%	27.3%	41.9%	30.8%
Racine, WI	28,693	63.1%	18.3%	34.9%	46.8%	6,517	14.3%	16.5%	46.0%	37.5%
Raleigh, NC	191,405	58.3%	15.6%	32.7%	51.7%	70,063	21.3%	14.7%	39.8%	45.5%
Rapid City, SD	28,297	77.2%	14.9%	36.0%	49.1%	1,130	3.1%	1.1%	47.9%	51.1%
Reading, PA	67,352	64.9%	15.7%	39.5%	44.9%	5,763	5.6%	15.8%	56.6%	27.7%
Redding, CA	29,532	73.0%	16.4%	30.7%	52.9%	1,073	2.7%	0.0%	34.2%	65.8%
Reno, NV	65,401	56.6%	13.3%	33.1%	53.6%	3,378	2.9%	7.8%	36.7%	55.6%
Richmond, VA	175,187	52.9%	15.3%	33.6%	51.1%	105,994	32.0%	15.3%	41.7%	43.0%
Riverside-San Bernardino-Ontario, CA	319,898	25.7%	14.9%	34.4%	50.7%	87,478	7.0%	16.5%	41.1%	42.4%
Roanoke, VA	51,918	71.2%	14.2%	35.6%	50.2%	13,068	17.9%	16.2%	42.0%	41.7%
Rochester, MN	40,685	78.7%	14.6%	37.6%	47.9%	4,609	8.9%	11.9%	81.0%	7.1%
Rochester, NY	203,212	72.8%	14.0%	39.1%	46.9%	34,057	12.2%	15.8%	38.6%	45.6%
Rockford, IL	51,301	64.1%	17.2%	35.9%	47.0%	9,934	12.4%	13.9%	40.5%	45.6%
Rocky Mount, NC	13,146	38.8%	18.4%	42.1%	39.5%	16,920	50.0%	17.6%	37.3%	45.1%
Rome, GA	17,219	69.8%	17.2%	35.8%	47.0%	3,599	14.6%	1.2%	44.8%	54.0%
Roseburg, OR micro	17,757	82.3%	17.5%	33.8%	48.7%	na	na	na	na	na
Sacramento–Roseville–Arden-Arcade, CA	268,982	45.4%	14.9%	35.0%	50.1%	45,631	7.7%	14.6%	41.5%	44.0%
Saginaw, MI	31,017	64.1%	15.0%	38.8%	46.2%	8,054	16.7%	17.5%	45.8%	36.7%
Salem, OH micro	20,247	94.7%	18.9%	35.6%	45.5%	225	1.1%	40.4%	0.0%	59.6%
Salem, OR	65,184	61.3%	15.3%	36.8%	47.9%	1,835	1.7%	47.8%	37.7%	14.6%
Salinas, CA	29,371	24.8%	12.2%	39.8%	48.0%	2,850	2.4%	2.0%	29.6%	68.4%
Salisbury, MD-DE	56,200	62.5%	14.2%	42.1%	43.7%	21,535	23.9%	13.5%	49.7%	36.8%
Salt Lake City, UT	230,360	68.1%	15.0%	32.1%	53.0%	8,894	2.6%	17.5%	31.8%	50.7%
San Angelo, TX	17,158	46.8%	11.5%	40.0%	48.5%	2,436	6.6%	10.8%	58.2%	31.0%
San Antonio-New Braunfels, TX	197,066	29.2%	13.6%	35.3%	51.1%	48,283	7.2%	17.5%	38.4%	44.0%
San Diego-Carlsbad, CA	377,730	40.0%	10.7%	36.2%	53.1%	52,589	5.6%	12.0%	38.3%	49.7%
San Francisco-Oakland-Hayward, CA	412,599	34.9%	11.4%	28.2%	60.3%	90,903	7.7%	14.2%	35.2%	50.6%
San Jose-Sunnyvale-Santa Clara, CA	139,221	27.4%	12.9%	33.2%	53.8%	14,259	2.8%	11.6%	33.3%	55.1%
San Luis Obispo-Paso Robles-Arroyo Grande, CA	49,932	61.2%	10.0%	55.1%	34.9%	2,107	2.6%	6.7%	49.5%	43.8%
Santa Cruz-Watsonville, CA	39,461	48.5%	9.9%	51.3%	38.8%	1,475	1.8%	10.3%	20.7%	69.0%
Santa Fe, NM	8,572	27.7%	13.8%	32.1%	54.1%	379	1.2%	0.0%	13.2%	86.8%
Santa Maria-Santa Barbara, CA	53,823	39.5%	9.0%	55.7%	35.4%	2,586	1.9%	1.5%	69.9%	28.6%
Santa Rosa, CA	64,392	54.3%	13.9%	35.3%	50.8%	2,482	2.1%	1.8%	42.7%	55.5%
Savannah, GA	54,630	49.6%	8.7%	37.5%	53.8%	41,215	37.4%	12.6%	48.0%	39.5%
Scranton–Wilkes-Barre–Hazleton, PA	105,231	80.4%	14.8%	38.3%	46.9%	5,161	3.9%	20.8%	38.3%	40.9%
Seattle-Tacoma-Bellevue, WA	593,933	59.8%	12.7%	31.1%	56.2%	62,668	6.3%	14.4%	35.5%	50.1%
Sebastian-Vero Beach, FL	16,266	60.5%	18.1%	37.2%	44.7%	4,476	16.6%	1.4%	44.1%	54.5%
Sebring, FL	9,260	54.0%	15.1%	26.3%	58.6%	2,975	17.3%	18.7%	63.6%	17.8%
Sheboygan, WI	19,431	77.9%	19.1%	37.6%	43.4%	148	0.6%	23.6%	44.6%	31.8%
Sherman-Denison, TX	20,970	70.4%	13.3%	40.5%	46.2%	1,726	5.8%	12.3%	72.2%	15.5%
Show Low, AZ micro	5,798	22.2%	11.4%	35.9%	52.6%	115	0.4%	0.0%	0.0%	100.0%
Shreveport-Bossier City, LA	56,018	48.4%	13.8%	33.7%	52.5%	48,772	42.1%	15.6%	39.7%	44.7%
Sierra Vista-Douglas, AZ	10,331	35.1%	16.5%	32.5%	51.0%	1,158	3.9%	10.8%	0.0%	89.2%
Sioux City, IA-NE-SD	29,924	73.1%	16.1%	38.2%	45.7%	2,473	6.0%	47.9%	24.1%	28.0%
Sioux Falls, SD	54,211	81.0%	14.4%	33.8%	51.8%	3,686	5.5%	13.3%	3.0%	83.7%
South Bend-Mishawaka, IN-MI	57,472	68.3%	16.6%	41.2%	42.2%	10,554	12.5%	18.3%	44.9%	36.8%
Spartanburg, SC	50,956	63.7%	17.5%	37.3%	45.2%	18,528	23.2%	14.7%	40.8%	44.5%
Spokane-Spokane Valley, WA	113,332	78.6%	14.0%	35.8%	50.3%	2,682	1.9%	0.1%	42.4%	57.4%
Springfield, IL	37,483	73.2%	16.3%	33.3%	50.5%	7,167	14.0%	16.2%	36.7%	47.0%
Springfield, MA	113,555	63.4%	13.1%	46.5%	40.4%	12,669	7.1%	17.0%	45.3%	37.7%
Springfield, MO	111,539	87.3%	13.5%	42.3%	44.2%	5,324	4.2%	10.3%	44.5%	45.2%
Springfield, OH	25,603	81.7%	17.3%	36.5%	46.2%	3,494	11.1%	18.4%	33.7%	47.9%
St. Cloud, MN	49,792	85.7%	13.6%	45.1%	41.3%	2,962	5.1%	22.9%	27.1%	49.9%
St. George, UT	30,576	77.5%	19.7%	35.6%	44.6%	1,032	2.6%	0.0%	100.0%	0.0%
St. Joseph, MO-KS	25,301	75.9%	15.2%	33.6%	51.2%	3,753	11.3%	25.4%	8.2%	66.3%
St. Louis, MO-IL	484,230	69.7%	15.9%	34.2%	49.9%	146,059	21.0%	17.1%	39.1%	43.8%
State College, PA	52,246	77.9%	6.8%	58.0%	35.2%	3,450	5.1%	0.0%	63.9%	36.1%
Staunton-Waynesboro, VA	23,902	83.3%	12.7%	46.7%	40.7%	2,684	9.3%	5.2%	33.8%	61.0%
Stockton-Lodi, CA	52,310	26.8%	16.2%	35.2%	48.6%	13,106	6.7%	15.7%	42.1%	42.2%
Sumter, SC	11,228	37.4%	19.0%	46.2%	34.8%	16,441	54.8%	13.2%	42.1%	44.6%
Sunbury, PA micro	18,439	90.7%	13.9%	31.6%	54.5%	986	4.8%	18.9%	48.7%	32.5%
Syracuse, NY	134,870	78.1%	14.8%	40.6%	44.6%	15,286	8.9%	17.5%	43.1%	39.4%
Tallahassee, FL	70,569	53.8%	10.3%	51.5%	38.1%	42,822	32.6%	9.6%	56.3%	34.1%
Tampa-St. Petersburg-Clearwater, FL	379,609	55.2%	14.6%	33.4%	52.0%	99,117	14.4%	16.1%	37.9%	46.0%
Terre Haute, IN	40,423	85.3%	15.3%	43.8%	40.9%	2,804	5.9%	8.3%	52.8%	38.9%
Texarkana, TX-AR	22,826	62.9%	14.4%	36.8%	48.8%	9,334	25.7%	17.3%	43.8%	38.9%
The Villages, FL	6,509	59.1%	14.6%	52.1%	33.3%	2,231	20.3%	39.2%	19.1%	41.7%
Toledo, OH	113,758	69.5%	14.5%	40.1%	45.4%	25,280	15.5%	17.9%	40.5%	41.6%
Topeka, KS	41,170	75.7%	16.8%	34.4%	48.9%	3,268	6.0%	9.0%	30.0%	60.9%
Torrington, CT micro	32,453	88.3%	19.2%	36.4%	44.3%	745	2.0%	7.8%	2.0%	90.2%
Traverse City, MI micro	26,900	84.8%	18.6%	36.1%	45.3%	1,411	4.4%	0.5%	26.0%	73.5%
Trenton, NJ	44,419	46.0%	14.0%	45.9%	40.1%	21,284	22.0%	15.7%	40.6%	43.7%
Truckee-Grass Valley, CA micro	14,741	78.0%	18.1%	32.4%	49.5%	392	2.1%	0.0%	0.0%	100.0%
Tucson, AZ	111,574	42.1%	12.2%	44.7%	43.1%	9,478	3.6%	12.2%	45.7%	42.2%
Tullahoma-Manchester, TN micro	20,890	88.2%	17.1%	40.7%	42.2%	350	1.5%	0.0%	90.3%	9.7%
Tulsa, OK	146,109	58.7%	15.1%	35.0%	49.9%	21,470	8.6%	13.0%	42.4%	44.6%

Table B-4: Metropolitan/Micropolitan Statistical Areas—Race and Hispanic Origin by Age—*Continued*

	Asian, Non-Hispanic					Hispanic				
	Millennial Population		Percent by Age			Millennial Population		Percent by Age		
	Number	Percent	15 to 17	18 to 24	25 to 33	Number	Percent	15 to 17	18 to 24	25 to 33
Punta Gorda, FL	974	4.2%	0.0%	38.8%	61.2%	1,730	7.5%	31.5%	53.5%	15.0%
Racine, WI	1,277	2.8%	18.5%	78.4%	3.1%	8,173	18.0%	15.5%	42.1%	42.4%
Raleigh, NC	18,922	5.8%	18.0%	26.7%	55.4%	38,147	11.6%	15.2%	36.8%	48.0%
Rapid City, SD	na	na	na	na	na	2,308	6.3%	4.7%	18.7%	76.6%
Reading, PA	2,162	2.1%	23.2%	52.7%	24.1%	26,428	25.5%	17.8%	37.9%	44.3%
Redding, CA	1,796	4.4%	17.8%	47.5%	34.7%	5,280	13.1%	19.0%	45.7%	35.3%
Reno, NV	5,697	4.9%	9.0%	38.1%	52.9%	33,888	29.3%	16.5%	38.5%	45.0%
Richmond, VA	13,920	4.2%	9.6%	31.9%	58.4%	24,129	7.3%	13.8%	40.4%	45.9%
Riverside-San Bernardino-Ontario, CA	76,460	6.2%	14.1%	36.3%	49.6%	715,037	57.5%	17.5%	39.4%	43.1%
Roanoke, VA	2,631	3.6%	19.5%	50.7%	29.8%	3,613	5.0%	11.1%	23.9%	65.1%
Rochester, MN	3,097	6.0%	6.9%	33.6%	59.5%	1,696	3.3%	21.6%	4.8%	73.5%
Rochester, NY	11,030	4.0%	15.0%	45.8%	39.2%	24,984	9.0%	15.3%	41.5%	43.2%
Rockford, IL	1,580	2.0%	20.0%	9.2%	70.8%	14,366	17.9%	18.4%	34.6%	47.0%
Rocky Mount, NC	187	0.6%	0.0%	100.0%	0.0%	2,514	7.4%	31.7%	19.9%	48.4%
Rome, GA	na	na	na	na	na	3,155	12.8%	17.6%	34.1%	48.3%
Roseburg, OR micro	na	na	na	na	na	1,553	7.2%	4.4%	45.4%	50.2%
Sacramento–Roseville–Arden-Arcade, CA	88,343	14.9%	11.5%	38.2%	50.3%	152,883	25.8%	16.0%	38.2%	45.8%
Saginaw, MI	1,716	3.5%	0.0%	36.9%	63.1%	4,818	10.0%	11.6%	39.6%	48.8%
Salem, OH micro	na	na	na	na	na	547	2.6%	1.5%	21.0%	77.5%
Salem, OR	2,103	2.0%	46.1%	23.8%	30.1%	30,660	28.8%	19.7%	44.3%	35.9%
Salinas, CA	5,958	5.0%	16.6%	30.4%	53.0%	75,522	63.8%	14.8%	38.1%	47.1%
Salisbury, MD-DE	1,561	1.7%	4.8%	44.1%	51.1%	8,193	9.1%	19.0%	40.9%	40.1%
Salt Lake City, UT	14,609	4.3%	8.7%	27.6%	63.7%	66,309	19.6%	20.2%	39.1%	40.7%
San Angelo, TX	721	2.0%	0.0%	36.2%	63.8%	15,558	42.5%	14.0%	40.5%	45.5%
San Antonio-New Braunfels, TX	17,894	2.7%	13.3%	33.7%	53.0%	399,081	59.2%	16.4%	37.2%	46.4%
San Diego-Carlsbad, CA	104,662	11.1%	9.8%	33.0%	57.2%	360,150	38.1%	14.9%	39.5%	45.6%
San Francisco-Oakland-Hayward, CA	296,908	25.1%	11.0%	30.5%	58.5%	305,046	25.8%	14.7%	36.0%	49.3%
San Jose-Sunnyvale-Santa Clara, CA	165,488	32.5%	12.7%	29.8%	57.5%	164,349	32.3%	15.0%	38.1%	46.9%
San Luis Obispo-Paso Robles-Arroyo Grande, CA	4,060	5.0%	3.4%	60.4%	36.2%	22,634	27.7%	12.9%	45.9%	41.2%
Santa Cruz-Watsonville, CA	6,147	7.5%	0.0%	58.6%	41.4%	29,919	36.7%	14.4%	49.6%	36.0%
Santa Fe, NM	325	1.0%	13.8%	0.0%	86.2%	20,006	64.5%	17.3%	36.5%	46.2%
Santa Maria-Santa Barbara, CA	10,440	7.7%	5.7%	67.5%	26.8%	65,414	48.0%	15.1%	46.0%	38.9%
Santa Rosa, CA	4,964	4.2%	11.0%	32.1%	56.9%	40,184	33.9%	17.5%	39.2%	43.3%
Savannah, GA	3,302	3.0%	5.4%	56.3%	38.3%	8,477	7.7%	12.8%	48.4%	38.7%
Scranton–Wilkes-Barre–Hazleton, PA	2,984	2.3%	8.1%	45.2%	46.7%	14,816	11.3%	23.1%	46.3%	30.6%
Seattle-Tacoma-Bellevue, WA	136,213	13.7%	10.3%	31.3%	58.4%	116,402	11.7%	14.6%	32.3%	53.0%
Sebastian-Vero Beach, FL	87	0.3%	0.0%	0.0%	100.0%	5,312	19.8%	18.8%	51.4%	29.8%
Sebring, FL	na	na	na	na	na	4,380	25.5%	28.3%	34.8%	36.9%
Sheboygan, WI	2,073	8.3%	4.2%	25.0%	70.8%	2,820	11.3%	23.0%	17.9%	59.0%
Sherman-Denison, TX	209	0.7%	0.0%	100.0%	0.0%	5,262	17.7%	18.8%	38.5%	42.7%
Show Low, AZ micro	32	0.1%	18.8%	81.3%	0.0%	2,742	10.5%	19.7%	38.8%	41.5%
Shreveport-Bossier City, LA	2,263	2.0%	22.1%	24.7%	53.1%	6,412	5.5%	12.3%	22.3%	65.5%
Sierra Vista-Douglas, AZ	409	1.4%	31.5%	0.0%	68.5%	16,329	55.5%	17.2%	36.7%	46.2%
Sioux City, IA-NE-SD	1,053	2.6%	0.0%	52.3%	47.7%	5,796	14.2%	23.8%	33.3%	42.9%
Sioux Falls, SD	1,462	2.2%	0.0%	64.3%	35.7%	3,731	5.6%	7.6%	61.0%	31.4%
South Bend-Mishawaka, IN-MI	2,375	2.8%	8.8%	43.9%	47.3%	9,694	11.5%	16.0%	40.2%	43.8%
Spartanburg, SC	1,494	1.9%	23.1%	26.7%	50.2%	5,641	7.1%	21.3%	36.1%	42.7%
Spokane-Spokane Valley, WA	3,716	2.6%	9.9%	22.3%	67.8%	11,998	8.3%	16.7%	34.5%	48.8%
Springfield, IL	2,025	4.0%	21.4%	67.8%	10.8%	1,549	3.0%	26.8%	31.1%	42.1%
Springfield, MA	6,559	3.7%	2.3%	51.7%	46.1%	41,186	23.0%	17.0%	41.9%	41.1%
Springfield, MO	2,138	1.7%	5.4%	60.1%	34.5%	5,224	4.1%	15.0%	45.1%	39.9%
Springfield, OH	na	na	na	na	na	481	1.5%	64.2%	35.8%	0.0%
St. Cloud, MN	1,811	3.1%	0.0%	49.8%	50.2%	2,241	3.9%	15.2%	48.9%	35.9%
St. George, UT	213	0.5%	0.0%	27.2%	72.8%	3,684	9.3%	16.1%	61.0%	22.9%
St. Joseph, MO-KS	971	2.9%	0.0%	59.3%	40.7%	2,662	8.0%	12.7%	57.7%	29.6%
St. Louis, MO-IL	22,105	3.2%	11.5%	37.4%	51.1%	24,223	3.5%	10.6%	42.4%	47.0%
State College, PA	6,425	9.6%	0.0%	76.8%	23.2%	2,845	4.2%	2.6%	82.5%	14.9%
Staunton-Waynesboro, VA	523	1.8%	44.6%	46.3%	9.2%	1,152	4.0%	0.0%	65.5%	34.5%
Stockton-Lodi, CA	29,923	15.3%	13.4%	33.9%	52.7%	91,032	46.7%	18.4%	37.8%	43.7%
Sumter, SC	255	0.9%	0.0%	32.2%	67.8%	1,432	4.8%	6.9%	61.5%	31.6%
Sunbury, PA micro	na	na	na	na	na	741	3.6%	32.1%	40.1%	27.8%
Syracuse, NY	6,537	3.8%	16.1%	46.9%	37.0%	8,550	5.0%	19.3%	56.6%	24.1%
Tallahassee, FL	3,164	2.4%	2.0%	56.8%	41.2%	10,170	7.8%	4.8%	60.9%	34.4%
Tampa-St. Petersburg-Clearwater, FL	23,811	3.5%	12.2%	32.3%	55.5%	158,820	23.1%	16.4%	35.9%	47.8%
Terre Haute, IN	52	0.1%	0.0%	100.0%	0.0%	969	2.0%	10.6%	28.2%	61.2%
Texarkana, TX-AR	41	0.1%	0.0%	0.0%	100.0%	2,709	7.5%	18.2%	19.0%	62.8%
The Villages, FL	108	1.0%	46.3%	0.0%	53.7%	1,813	16.5%	12.4%	54.4%	33.2%
Toledo, OH	4,085	2.5%	5.5%	57.2%	37.3%	13,627	8.3%	18.4%	41.2%	40.4%
Topeka, KS	445	0.8%	19.3%	24.0%	56.6%	6,536	12.0%	20.2%	45.6%	34.2%
Torrington, CT micro	1,011	2.8%	38.8%	40.9%	20.3%	2,116	5.8%	0.2%	51.7%	48.2%
Traverse City, MI micro	512	1.6%	0.0%	28.5%	71.5%	1,967	6.2%	10.2%	58.9%	30.9%
Trenton, NJ	10,231	10.6%	18.1%	50.4%	31.5%	19,013	19.7%	12.4%	42.9%	44.7%
Truckee-Grass Valley, CA micro	243	1.3%	43.2%	0.0%	56.8%	2,519	13.3%	0.0%	47.5%	52.5%
Tucson, AZ	10,300	3.9%	6.2%	50.0%	43.7%	117,103	44.2%	16.2%	43.9%	39.9%
Tullahoma-Manchester, TN micro	555	2.3%	0.0%	100.0%	0.0%	862	3.6%	58.0%	42.0%	0.0%
Tulsa, OK	7,855	3.2%	16.7%	28.2%	55.1%	30,596	12.3%	16.4%	35.9%	47.7%

Table B-4: Metropolitan/Micropolitan Statistical Areas—Race and Hispanic Origin by Age—*Continued*

	White, Non-Hispanic					Black, Non-Hispanic				
	Millennial Population		Percent by Age			Millennial Population		Percent by Age		
	Number	Percent	15 to 17	18 to 24	25 to 33	Number	Percent	15 to 17	18 to 24	25 to 33
Tupelo, MS micro	22,210	65.6%	19.7%	36.6%	43.8%	10,236	30.2%	13.8%	42.6%	43.7%
Tuscaloosa, AL	46,362	57.7%	9.6%	49.2%	41.1%	27,744	34.5%	13.4%	52.1%	34.5%
Tyler, TX	31,357	52.7%	14.4%	35.0%	50.6%	12,091	20.3%	11.2%	46.7%	42.1%
Urban Honolulu, HI	65,323	23.9%	4.6%	38.0%	57.4%	10,951	4.0%	3.1%	50.2%	46.7%
Utica-Rome, NY	54,669	79.0%	15.0%	39.9%	45.1%	4,343	6.3%	13.2%	47.0%	39.8%
Valdosta, GA	25,764	55.8%	11.0%	44.2%	44.7%	15,902	34.4%	13.4%	48.8%	37.8%
Vallejo-Fairfield, CA	36,794	32.8%	12.7%	33.7%	53.5%	13,542	12.1%	14.3%	34.1%	51.6%
Victoria, TX	9,484	37.0%	15.4%	35.2%	49.5%	1,503	5.9%	14.6%	69.9%	15.5%
Vineland-Bridgeton, NJ	18,447	45.2%	15.6%	31.1%	53.3%	8,007	19.6%	16.5%	27.2%	56.3%
Virginia Beach-Norfolk-Newport News, VA-NC	264,435	52.1%	11.7%	37.2%	51.2%	160,879	31.7%	14.4%	41.5%	44.1%
Visalia-Porterville, CA	29,830	22.7%	16.0%	33.1%	50.9%	1,857	1.4%	22.4%	57.3%	20.3%
Waco, TX	42,441	54.2%	11.8%	51.6%	36.6%	11,576	14.8%	18.8%	42.1%	39.1%
Walla Walla, WA	11,027	62.6%	11.2%	30.9%	57.9%	307	1.7%	0.0%	51.5%	48.5%
Warner Robins, GA	27,463	55.6%	16.7%	38.7%	44.6%	16,847	34.1%	15.9%	43.9%	40.2%
Washington-Arlington-Alexandria, DC-VA-MD-WV	708,503	44.1%	13.5%	32.7%	53.8%	396,626	24.7%	14.3%	36.7%	49.0%
Waterloo-Cedar Falls, IA	41,194	80.9%	10.8%	47.2%	42.0%	4,181	8.2%	10.1%	31.7%	58.2%
Watertown-Fort Drum, NY	28,048	78.2%	12.3%	40.0%	47.7%	3,219	9.0%	0.0%	46.0%	54.0%
Wausau, WI	26,210	88.9%	18.0%	34.5%	47.6%	528	1.8%	56.6%	20.1%	23.3%
Weirton-Steubenville, WV-OH	25,510	93.1%	13.7%	40.8%	45.5%	835	3.0%	21.2%	45.0%	33.8%
Wenatchee, WA	16,080	62.0%	16.6%	33.0%	50.4%	na	na	na	na	na
Wheeling, WV-OH	29,709	92.9%	14.2%	43.5%	42.3%	1,008	3.2%	18.5%	37.3%	44.2%
Whitewater-Elkhorn, WI micro	21,580	79.3%	14.9%	51.5%	33.5%	170	0.6%	0.0%	81.8%	18.2%
Wichita Falls, TX	27,587	61.4%	11.9%	43.0%	45.1%	4,914	10.9%	7.5%	60.8%	31.7%
Wichita, KS	115,442	67.9%	16.0%	33.3%	50.7%	14,500	8.5%	20.6%	32.0%	47.4%
Williamsport, PA	24,924	88.7%	13.6%	42.7%	43.7%	1,069	3.8%	15.3%	49.0%	35.6%
Wilmington, NC	56,483	74.4%	11.5%	44.6%	43.9%	11,557	15.2%	21.4%	27.4%	51.2%
Winchester, VA-WV	23,207	78.9%	15.2%	38.2%	46.6%	799	2.7%	15.9%	65.7%	18.4%
Winston-Salem, NC	101,047	63.5%	16.7%	37.1%	46.2%	31,952	20.1%	17.6%	41.1%	41.3%
Wooster, OH micro	25,994	92.8%	17.9%	39.6%	42.5%	410	1.5%	0.0%	72.0%	28.0%
Worcester, MA-CT	170,430	73.4%	16.9%	39.3%	43.9%	11,150	4.8%	13.3%	45.5%	41.2%
Yakima, WA	22,424	34.9%	16.3%	34.1%	49.7%	366	0.6%	30.6%	69.4%	0.0%
York-Hanover, PA	82,166	80.2%	16.4%	34.8%	48.9%	7,102	6.9%	23.5%	28.0%	48.5%
Youngstown-Warren-Boardman, OH-PA	95,060	78.7%	17.2%	37.8%	45.0%	15,421	12.8%	18.3%	44.6%	37.2%
Yuba City, CA	20,553	45.2%	15.0%	33.0%	51.9%	634	1.4%	4.1%	10.7%	85.2%
Yuma, AZ	12,306	21.3%	10.7%	41.1%	48.2%	1,820	3.2%	0.0%	11.6%	88.4%

Table B-4: Metropolitan/Micropolitan Statistical Areas—Race and Hispanic Origin by Age—*Continued*

	Asian, Non-Hispanic					Hispanic				
	Millennial Population		Percent by Age			Millennial Population		Percent by Age		
	Number	Percent	15 to 17	18 to 24	25 to 33	Number	Percent	15 to 17	18 to 24	25 to 33
Tupelo, MS micro..................................	71	0.2%	0.0%	100.0%	0.0%	1,131	3.3%	0.0%	56.0%	44.0%
Tuscaloosa, AL......................................	2,067	2.6%	0.0%	81.7%	18.3%	3,240	4.0%	9.4%	39.3%	51.3%
Tyler, TX..	1,214	2.0%	13.8%	75.5%	10.6%	13,718	23.1%	17.4%	32.9%	49.6%
Urban Honolulu, HI	79,882	29.2%	13.2%	37.7%	49.2%	34,270	12.5%	9.4%	44.1%	46.5%
Utica-Rome, NY	3,301	4.8%	8.8%	42.4%	48.8%	5,185	7.5%	14.3%	26.1%	59.5%
Valdosta, GA	1,350	2.9%	0.0%	41.6%	58.4%	2,353	5.1%	11.4%	51.0%	37.5%
Vallejo-Fairfield, CA.............................	15,775	14.1%	14.8%	32.9%	52.3%	36,003	32.1%	16.7%	38.2%	45.1%
Victoria, TX	318	1.2%	0.0%	0.0%	100.0%	14,015	54.7%	18.2%	36.4%	45.4%
Vineland-Bridgeton, NJ	343	0.8%	29.2%	36.2%	34.7%	11,864	29.1%	13.6%	29.8%	56.6%
Virginia Beach-Norfolk-Newport News, VA-NC	17,809	3.5%	13.3%	39.4%	47.3%	43,863	8.6%	13.2%	38.5%	48.3%
Visalia-Porterville, CA...........................	4,356	3.3%	13.2%	32.9%	53.9%	93,066	70.9%	18.2%	38.1%	43.7%
Waco, TX..	1,858	2.4%	26.2%	42.2%	31.6%	21,476	27.5%	17.0%	43.1%	39.9%
Walla Walla, WA....................................	282	1.6%	0.0%	35.1%	64.9%	4,785	27.2%	13.3%	44.3%	42.3%
Warner Robins, GA	629	1.3%	0.0%	42.0%	58.0%	3,126	6.3%	5.3%	52.1%	42.5%
Washington-Arlington-Alexandria, DC-VA-MD-WV	156,584	9.8%	13.7%	29.5%	56.8%	266,735	16.6%	14.2%	35.6%	50.2%
Waterloo-Cedar Falls, IA........................	1,274	2.5%	0.0%	56.0%	44.0%	3,130	6.1%	22.6%	54.1%	23.3%
Watertown-Fort Drum, NY	245	0.7%	0.0%	35.9%	64.1%	3,014	8.4%	5.1%	73.5%	21.4%
Wausau, WI	1,706	5.8%	22.6%	1.9%	75.4%	760	2.6%	19.5%	41.4%	39.1%
Weirton-Steubenville, WV-OH	69	0.3%	0.0%	0.0%	100.0%	536	2.0%	29.1%	33.8%	37.1%
Wenatchee, WA	na	na	na	na	na	9,824	37.9%	16.8%	40.0%	43.1%
Wheeling, WV-OH	117	0.4%	0.0%	17.9%	82.1%	715	2.2%	21.8%	42.2%	35.9%
Whitewater-Elkhorn, WI micro	363	1.3%	38.0%	50.7%	11.3%	4,395	16.2%	10.3%	34.9%	54.8%
Wichita Falls, TX	964	2.1%	0.0%	53.6%	46.4%	9,746	21.7%	12.7%	46.0%	41.4%
Wichita, KS	7,720	4.5%	11.6%	24.8%	63.6%	25,631	15.1%	20.8%	31.8%	47.4%
Williamsport, PA	576	2.0%	10.2%	28.8%	60.9%	992	3.5%	0.0%	36.4%	63.6%
Wilmington, NC	871	1.1%	25.5%	40.9%	33.6%	5,469	7.2%	18.0%	49.0%	33.0%
Winchester, VA-WV	419	1.4%	0.0%	34.1%	65.9%	3,583	12.2%	13.2%	51.4%	35.4%
Winston-Salem, NC	3,796	2.4%	4.6%	38.4%	57.1%	19,722	12.4%	19.7%	34.4%	46.0%
Wooster, OH micro................................	27	0.1%	0.0%	100.0%	0.0%	731	2.6%	22.0%	68.4%	9.6%
Worcester, MA-CT..................................	11,808	5.1%	15.2%	37.0%	47.8%	31,903	13.7%	16.1%	41.3%	42.5%
Yakima, WA...	126	0.2%	0.0%	0.0%	100.0%	37,736	58.6%	19.1%	42.1%	38.7%
York-Hanover, PA...................................	1,698	1.7%	5.8%	55.7%	38.5%	8,117	7.9%	12.9%	21.6%	65.5%
Youngstown-Warren-Boardman, OH-PA	749	0.6%	53.3%	15.0%	31.8%	5,600	4.6%	14.7%	24.7%	60.6%
Yuba City, CA	6,008	13.2%	5.3%	30.2%	64.5%	15,354	33.8%	18.1%	38.2%	43.7%
Yuma, AZ	919	1.6%	23.6%	0.1%	00.3%	40,790	70.6%	16.6%	42.1%	41.3%

PART C
NATIVITY AND WORLD REGION OF BIRTH

The U.S. Department of Homeland Security publishes the annual *Yearbook of Immigration Statistics*, which is a compendium of data on legal permanent admissions as well as many other categories of entry for foreign nationals. Between 2008 and 2015, legal permanent admissions averaged just over 1 million per year. During that same period, the number of persons age 15 to 34 averaged nearly 450,000 or more than 40 percent of all legal permanent admissions.[1] This high percentage of foreign immigrants in the Millennial age categories implies two important trends: the Millennial generation will continue to grow as a result of foreign immigration, and it will grow more diverse than it already is.

Nativity in the American Community Survey is based on the answers to the question on place of birth—either in the United States or outside the United States. If born outside of the United States, respondents then indicate their foreign country of birth or U.S. territory (Puerto

Rico, Guam, etc.). Persons are classified as either native or foreign born based on this and the question on citizenship. The foreign born population includes anyone who was not a U.S. citizen at birth and is shown by country or region of birth. These data are useful in understanding immigration patterns, policy, and assimilation.

Nearly 10.7 million Millennials, or 12.8 percent, are foreign born. By world region of birth, Latin America is the origin for 51.7 percent of the foreign born, followed by Asia (30.2 percent), Europe (10.1 percent), Africa (5.7 percent), North America (1.6 percent) and Oceania (0.6 percent). This distribution shows the clear shift in immigration from European origins to Latin America and Asia among more recent immigrants.

California (21.0 percent) and New Jersey (20.8 percent) have the highest foreign born concentrations of Millennials and are closely followed by New York at 19.7 percent. Montana and West Virginia are tied for is lowest at only 2.3 percent. Ten states are less than five percent foreign born while seven states are over 15 percent. Latin America is the foreign origin for 14.9 percent of Florida's

---

1 US Department of Homeland Security, *Yearbook of Immigration Statistics: 2008–2015*, Table 8.

Percent of Millennials Who are Foreign Born

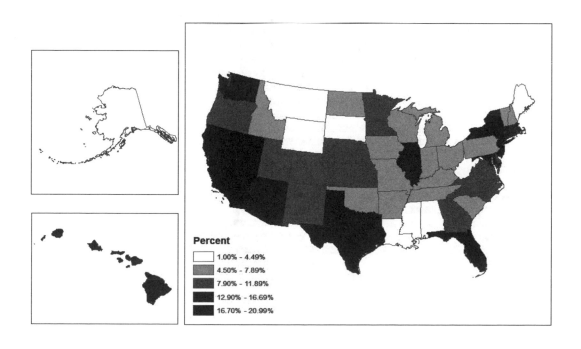

Percent

- 1.00% - 4.49%
- 4.50% - 7.89%
- 7.90% - 11.89%
- 12.90% - 16.69%
- 16.70% - 20.99%

Millennial population, and Texas is the second highest at 12.2 percent. In North Dakota, the Latin origin population is only 0.4 and Montana (0.8 percent) and West Virginia (0.6 percent) are also low. Hawaii has the highest percentage of Millennials who are of Asian origin at 10.5 percent. Less than two percent of Millennials in 14 states are of Asian origin, and European origins are highest in the District of Columbia (2.8 percent) and Connecticut (2.7 percent). Maryland and Minnesota's percentage of African origin Millennials are highest but only at 2.7 percent and 2.6 percent, respectively. Hawaii is the only state with more than a fraction of Millennials from Oceania, at 2.1 percent.

Queens County, NY has the highest percentage of Millennials who are of foreign birth at 41.7 percent, followed closely by Miami-Dade County, FL, at 41.1 percent. Thirty-one counties are above 25 percent. Counties with less and five percent foreign born number 156. Miami-Dade County, FL, has the largest percentage of Millennials who are of Latin American birth at 37.7 percent, and Collier County, FL, is the next highest with 27.3 percent. Almost two-thirds of all counties (410) have less than five percent of Millennials who originated in Latin America. Millennials of Asian origin are most prevalent (20.9 percent) in Santa Clara County, CA. St. Johns County, FL, has 7.0 percent of European origin and Prince George's County, MD, is highest for population of African origin at 6.5 percent. North American

and Oceania origins both represent small percentages, with York County, ME (1.8 percent) highest for North America and Marion County, OR, highest for Oceania (2.6 percent).

In 38 cities more than 30 percent of Millennials are of foreign birth. Hialeah City, FL is highest at 62.2 percent followed by Sunnyvale, CA (49.1 percent) and Bellevue, WA (46.4 percent). The majority of Hialeah's Millennials who are foreign born have Latin American origins with 62.7 percent from that region. In 14 cities, Latin America is the origin of more than 25 percent of Millennials. Persons of Asian origin make up 37.2 percent in Santa Clara, CA, and only five other cities are above 30 percent: Santa Clara, CA (37.2 percent), Fremont, CA (36.2 percent), Sunnyvale, CA (34.7 percent), Glendale, CA (34.3 percent), and Bellevue, WA (32.9 percent). In Brockton, MA Millennials of African origin make up 19.6 percent of the total. North American origins make up 2.4 percent in Everett, WA, and Everett is also highest for Oceania at 3.7 percent, followed closely by the Urban Honolulu CDP at 3.3 percent.

The Miami-Fort Lauderdale-West Palm Beach metropolitan area has the highest percentage of foreign born Millennials at 33.2 percent but is followed closely by the San Jose-Sunnyvale-Santa Clara, CA metro at 32.1 percent. Only 20 metro/micros are above 20 percent, while 153 are below 5 percent. In the Miami-Fort Lauderdale,

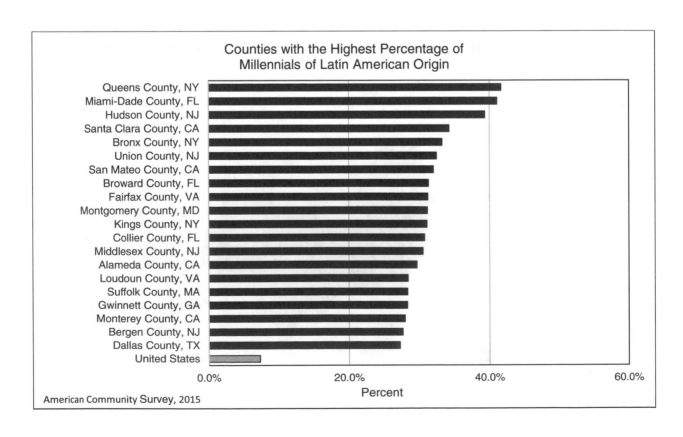

Counties with the Highest Percentage of Millennials of Latin American Origin

American Community Survey, 2015

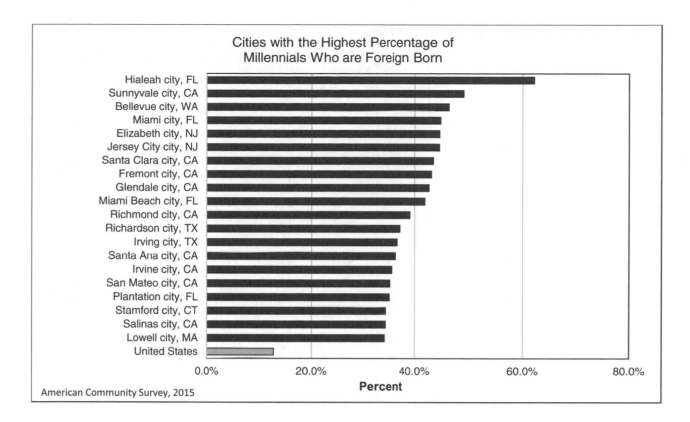

Cities with the Highest Percentage of
Millennials Who are Foreign Born

American Community Survey, 2015

FL metro area Latin American Millennials make up 30.6 percent of the total. Latin America is the origin for more than 25 percent of Millennials in six metros. Those of Asian origin make up 20.2 percent of the total in the San Jose-Sunnyvale-Santa Clara, CA metro. In the Kalispell, MT micropolitan area, European origins are highest at 5.8 percent, and at 3.8 percent, African origins are highest in the Burlington-South Burlington, VT metro area. Other North American and Oceania origins are again the lowest groups at 1.6 percent in the Bellingham, WA metro and 2.4 percent in Urban Honolulu, HI, respectively.

Table C-1: States—Nativity and World Region of Birth

	Total Millennial Population	Percent		Total Foreign Born	Percent of All Millennials by Region of Birth					
		Native	Foreign Born		Latin America	Asia	Europe	Africa	North America	Oceania
United States	83,504,484	87.2%	12.8%	10,684,536	7.2%	4.2%	1.4%	0.8%	0.2%	0.1%
Alabama	1,228,275	95.8%	4.2%	51,449	2.6%	1.1%	0.7%	0.4%	0.2%	0.0%
Alaska	221,416	91.8%	8.2%	18,116	1.2%	4.3%	2.8%	1.1%	0.2%	0.0%
Arizona	1,768,256	87.4%	12.6%	223,336	9.0%	3.2%	1.0%	0.7%	0.2%	0.1%
Arkansas	751,127	93.5%	6.5%	48,490	4.6%	1.7%	0.6%	0.2%	0.1%	0.3%
California	10,739,063	79.0%	21.0%	2,257,910	11.9%	8.1%	1.4%	0.5%	0.3%	0.2%
Colorado	1,481,249	89.9%	10.1%	149,312	6.6%	2.7%	1.4%	0.7%	0.3%	0.1%
Connecticut	892,841	85.4%	14.6%	129,939	7.8%	4.2%	2.7%	0.9%	0.2%	0.1%
Delaware	237,360	89.0%	11.0%	26,143	5.8%	3.7%	0.6%	1.3%	0.2%	0.0%
District of Columbia	236,132	85.7%	14.3%	33,759	4.7%	5.1%	2.8%	1.9%	0.7%	0.2%
Florida	4,841,980	82.0%	18.0%	871,283	14.9%	2.4%	1.6%	0.4%	0.3%	0.0%
Georgia	2,694,824	89.4%	10.6%	284,453	5.9%	3.0%	1.4%	1.3%	0.2%	0.0%
Hawaii	371,354	87.0%	13.0%	48,220	1.6%	10.5%	1.2%	0.0%	0.1%	2.1%
Idaho	426,778	92.8%	7.2%	30,783	4.1%	2.2%	1.3%	0.2%	0.2%	0.0%
Illinois	3,334,874	86.7%	13.3%	443,244	6.5%	4.5%	2.4%	0.8%	0.1%	0.0%
Indiana	1,706,914	93.9%	6.1%	104,176	3.0%	2.4%	0.6%	0.5%	0.2%	0.1%
Iowa	804,927	92.7%	7.3%	58,443	3.0%	3.1%	0.9%	0.8%	0.1%	0.0%
Kansas	763,691	91.1%	8.9%	68,260	4.8%	3.1%	0.8%	0.7%	0.1%	0.0%
Kentucky	1,102,117	95.0%	5.0%	54,935	2.3%	2.0%	1.0%	0.3%	0.1%	0.1%
Louisiana	1,253,683	95.5%	4.5%	56,784	2.5%	1.7%	0.6%	0.2%	0.1%	0.0%
Maine	298,983	97.2%	2.8%	8,389	0.6%	1.6%	1.2%	0.5%	0.6%	0.0%
Maryland	1,532,505	85.2%	14.8%	227,263	7.1%	4.7%	1.6%	2.8%	0.1%	0.1%
Massachusetts	1,806,926	83.8%	16.2%	292,855	6.6%	5.9%	2.4%	1.9%	0.5%	0.1%
Michigan	2,494,156	93.0%	7.0%	174,396	1.6%	4.2%	1.2%	0.4%	0.4%	0.0%
Minnesota	1,390,845	89.3%	10.7%	148,804	2.9%	4.5%	1.1%	2.7%	0.3%	0.1%
Mississippi	769,119	97.2%	2.8%	21,412	1.7%	0.7%	0.6%	0.2%	0.1%	0.0%
Missouri	1,561,298	94.9%	5.1%	80,357	2.0%	2.2%	1.0%	0.6%	0.1%	0.1%
Montana	251,820	97.7%	2.3%	5,754	0.8%	0.4%	1.0%	0.1%	0.7%	0.0%
Nebraska	496,505	91.2%	8.8%	43,546	4.3%	3.5%	0.5%	1.5%	0.1%	0.0%
Nevada	738,080	82.4%	17.6%	129,781	11.1%	5.6%	1.2%	1.0%	0.2%	0.1%
New Hampshire	316,827	94.0%	6.0%	19,060	2.1%	3.0%	1.1%	0.5%	0.3%	0.0%
New Jersey	2,182,669	79.2%	20.8%	454,425	11.4%	6.9%	2.0%	1.4%	0.2%	0.0%
New Mexico	534,063	91.2%	8.8%	47,166	7.1%	1.5%	1.0%	0.5%	0.2%	0.0%
New York	5,267,039	80.3%	19.7%	1,040,136	10.4%	6.9%	2.6%	1.0%	0.4%	0.2%
North Carolina	2,561,562	90.2%	9.8%	249,886	6.3%	2.4%	1.2%	0.6%	0.1%	0.0%
North Dakota	222,346	95.1%	4.9%	10,836	0.4%	1.5%	1.5%	1.6%	0.4%	0.0%
Ohio	2,898,493	94.9%	5.1%	147,347	1.2%	2.6%	0.9%	0.8%	0.1%	0.0%
Oklahoma	1,026,095	92.2%	7.8%	80,523	5.6%	2.3%	0.4%	0.3%	0.1%	0.0%
Oregon	1,008,523	89.1%	10.9%	109,593	5.8%	3.5%	1.4%	0.5%	0.4%	0.5%
Pennsylvania	3,172,455	93.1%	6.9%	218,922	2.4%	3.2%	1.2%	0.8%	0.1%	0.0%
Rhode Island	280,625	86.1%	13.9%	38,882	6.7%	4.3%	1.5%	1.6%	0.4%	0.2%
South Carolina	1,248,377	94.4%	5.6%	70,145	3.3%	1.6%	1.4%	0.2%	0.2%	0.1%
South Dakota	221,860	95.4%	4.6%	10,133	1.4%	1.8%	0.9%	0.7%	0.1%	0.0%
Tennessee	1,676,588	93.6%	6.4%	107,133	3.3%	2.0%	1.0%	0.8%	0.1%	0.0%
Texas	7,561,743	83.3%	16.7%	1,264,189	12.2%	3.7%	1.0%	0.9%	0.2%	0.0%
Utah	885,542	91.7%	8.3%	73,647	5.3%	2.3%	0.8%	0.7%	0.3%	0.2%
Vermont	156,472	94.3%	5.7%	8,991	1.3%	1.5%	1.4%	2.1%	0.6%	0.1%
Virginia	2,193,469	88.1%	11.9%	260,597	5.0%	5.5%	1.8%	1.3%	0.2%	0.0%
Washington	1,885,191	85.3%	14.7%	277,842	5.7%	6.3%	2.8%	0.8%	0.5%	0.3%
West Virginia	426,279	97.7%	2.3%	9,699	0.6%	1.4%	0.7%	0.1%	0.1%	0.0%
Wisconsin	1,426,801	93.9%	6.1%	87,361	3.0%	2.4%	0.9%	0.3%	0.1%	0.0%
Wyoming	154,367	95.8%	4.2%	6,431	3.0%	0.6%	0.8%	0.2%	0.2%	0.0%

Table C-2: Counties—Nativity and World Region of Birth

	Total Millennial	Percent		Total Foreign Born	Percent of All Millennials by Region of Birth					
		Native	Foreign Born		Latin America	Asia	Europe	Africa	North America	Oceania
Alabama										
Baldwin County	39,966	95.4%	4.6%	1,915	3.5%	0.1%	0.5%	0.0%	0.5%	0.0%
Calhoun County	29,374	96.0%	4.0%	1,216	0.0%	1.5%	2.1%	0.3%	0.0%	0.0%
Etowah County	21,971	97.6%	2.4%	531	1.7%	0.6%	0.0%	0.1%	0.0%	0.0%
Houston County	23,542	94.5%	5.5%	1,363	3.5%	1.1%	0.8%	0.0%	0.1%	0.0%
Jefferson County	157,532	93.5%	6.5%	10,899	3.1%	1.6%	0.7%	0.9%	0.2%	0.0%
Lauderdale County	22,380	97.0%	3.0%	689	1.1%	1.3%	0.0%	0.6%	0.0%	0.0%
Lee County	52,103	95.1%	4.9%	2,686	2.8%	1.8%	0.2%	0.1%	0.0%	0.0%
Madison County	83,380	91.7%	8.3%	7,511	3.5%	2.2%	1.6%	0.9%	0.0%	0.0%
Marshall County	19,865	90.7%	9.3%	2,034	7.4%	0.9%	0.9%	0.0%	0.0%	0.0%
Mobile County	102,658	95.0%	5.0%	5,446	1.3%	1.7%	0.6%	1.4%	0.0%	0.0%
Montgomery County	61,632	97.2%	2.8%	1,754	1.0%	0.8%	0.6%	0.1%	0.3%	0.0%
Morgan County	27,757	95.6%	4.4%	1,270	3.4%	0.9%	0.0%	0.0%	0.0%	0.0%
Shelby County	46,219	93.4%	6.6%	3,252	4.2%	1.0%	1.3%	0.0%	0.0%	0.0%
Tuscaloosa County	68,432	94.7%	5.3%	3,845	1.8%	2.5%	0.8%	0.1%	0.1%	0.0%
Alaska										
Anchorage Municipality	80,320	86.6%	13.4%	12,474	2.0%	5.8%	2.6%	2.6%	0.4%	0.0%
Fairbanks North Star Borough	31,248	89.7%	10.3%	3,586	0.4%	4.7%	4.8%	0.4%	0.0%	0.0%
Matanuska-Susitna Borough	26,800	96.1%	3.9%	1,089	1.2%	0.8%	1.9%	0.0%	0.0%	0.0%
Arizona										
Cochise County	25,276	85.9%	14.1%	4,146	12.0%	1.4%	0.6%	0.0%	0.0%	0.1%
Coconino County	49,261	95.2%	4.8%	2,510	0.6%	3.0%	0.8%	0.2%	0.2%	0.0%
Maricopa County	916,084	84.6%	15.4%	167,380	9.5%	3.8%	1.1%	0.8%	0.2%	0.1%
Mohave County	36,545	92.4%	7.6%	3,007	3.8%	1.9%	1.8%	0.0%	0.1%	0.0%
Navajo County	25,885	99.2%	0.8%	218	0.5%	0.4%	0.0%	0.0%	0.0%	0.0%
Pima County	228,188	85.3%	14.7%	39,254	9.0%	3.3%	1.2%	0.8%	0.1%	0.2%
Pinal County	82,700	89.1%	10.9%	10,076	9.1%	0.6%	0.8%	0.1%	0.0%	0.2%
Yavapai County	37,643	94.6%	5.4%	2,150	3.8%	1.3%	0.0%	0.2%	0.0%	0.0%
Yuma County	45,805	79.3%	20.7%	11,945	18.6%	0.6%	0.5%	0.2%	0.8%	0.0%
Arkansas										
Benton County	51,823	82.2%	17.8%	11,187	12.3%	3.6%	0.6%	0.4%	0.2%	0.6%
Craighead County	30,469	96.6%	3.4%	1,083	0.6%	1.2%	0.0%	0.9%	0.8%	0.0%
Faulkner County	38,506	95.9%	4.1%	1,642	1.9%	2.2%	0.0%	0.0%	0.0%	0.0%
Garland County	20,269	96.3%	3.7%	775	0.7%	1.2%	0.7%	1.1%	0.0%	0.0%
Pulaski County	94,853	91.7%	8.3%	8,636	4.3%	3.2%	0.7%	0.1%	0.0%	0.0%
Saline County	25,069	93.1%	6.9%	1,862	2.9%	1.5%	2.5%	0.0%	0.0%	0.0%
Sebastian County	28,441	87.8%	12.2%	3,966	8.3%	2.3%	0.4%	1.2%	0.0%	0.0%
Washington County	61,985	85.0%	15.0%	10,909	9.2%	2.9%	0.4%	0.0%	0.0%	2.5%
California										
Alameda County	304,975	70.4%	29.6%	128,345	9.1%	16.4%	2.0%	0.9%	0.4%	0.7%
Butte County	61,585	92.8%	7.2%	4,759	2.5%	3.9%	0.6%	0.0%	0.2%	0.0%
Contra Costa County	201,888	76.4%	23.6%	62,390	11.5%	9.2%	1.8%	0.6%	0.3%	0.3%
El Dorado County	35,155	92.3%	7.7%	2,930	4.2%	3.2%	0.4%	0.0%	0.0%	0.0%
Fresno County	225,427	80.3%	19.7%	55,443	13.7%	4.9%	0.8%	0.0%	0.3%	0.0%
Humboldt County	36,415	95.7%	4.3%	1,637	2.5%	0.7%	0.6%	0.0%	0.5%	0.0%
Imperial County	38,272	77.1%	22.9%	11,373	22.2%	0.4%	0.3%	0.0%	0.0%	0.0%
Kern County	212,463	83.2%	16.8%	42,810	12.7%	3.6%	0.3%	0.1%	0.1%	0.1%
Kings County	38,548	82.9%	17.1%	7,944	12.1%	3.1%	1.5%	0.0%	0.0%	0.4%
Los Angeles County	2,118,370	75.2%	24.8%	697,290	14.2%	8.4%	1.4%	0.4%	0.2%	0.1%
Madera County	32,366	77.9%	22.1%	9,174	18.6%	3.2%	0.2%	0.0%	0.0%	0.0%
Marin County	38,647	81.9%	18.1%	8,519	12.4%	3.0%	2.6%	0.0%	0.1%	0.0%
Merced County	58,458	74.6%	25.4%	19,899	19.2%	4.1%	2.0%	0.0%	0.1%	0.0%
Monterey County	86,527	72.1%	27.9%	33,526	23.6%	2.7%	0.8%	0.5%	0.3%	0.1%
Napa County	27,097	81.1%	18.9%	6,311	14.0%	3.6%	0.8%	0.0%	0.5%	0.0%
Nevada County	17,447	92.3%	7.7%	1,446	1.7%	0.7%	4.0%	0.6%	0.6%	0.0%
Orange County	614,508	74.6%	25.4%	209,136	12.6%	10.5%	1.0%	0.6%	0.3%	0.2%
Placer County	72,008	88.3%	11.7%	9,501	4.5%	5.0%	1.7%	0.1%	0.2%	0.1%
Riverside County	522,306	83.7%	16.3%	101,616	12.1%	3.1%	0.6%	0.4%	0.0%	0.1%
Sacramento County	319,303	79.8%	20.2%	81,014	6.6%	8.8%	3.3%	1.0%	0.1%	0.5%
San Bernardino County	533,772	85.8%	14.2%	88,303	9.4%	4.0%	0.5%	0.1%	0.1%	0.1%
San Diego County	756,957	80.2%	19.8%	187,320	9.6%	7.2%	1.8%	0.7%	0.3%	0.2%
San Francisco County	191,539	74.6%	25.4%	65,376	4.8%	15.1%	3.2%	1.0%	1.0%	0.2%
San Joaquin County	152,021	78.0%	22.0%	42,955	13.2%	8.0%	0.3%	0.6%	0.0%	0.0%
San Luis Obispo County	73,337	89.9%	10.1%	8,234	6.3%	2.7%	0.9%	0.0%	0.2%	0.0%
San Mateo County	120,845	68.0%	32.0%	56,841	13.2%	14.8%	2.8%	0.3%	0.8%	0.2%
Santa Barbara County	107,255	78.6%	21.4%	29,166	14.4%	4.5%	2.0%	0.3%	0.2%	0.0%
Santa Clara County	323,221	65.8%	34.2%	168,009	9.7%	20.9%	2.2%	0.6%	0.6%	0.2%
Santa Cruz County	67,550	82.9%	17.1%	13,889	11.0%	4.1%	1.0%	0.3%	0.4%	0.2%
Shasta County	38,848	93.1%	6.9%	2,900	0.4%	1.8%	3.8%	0.0%	0.0%	0.9%
Solano County	91,968	82.0%	18.0%	20,163	9.7%	7.1%	0.6%	0.0%	0.3%	0.3%
Sonoma County	97,164	81.9%	18.1%	21,454	12.7%	3.1%	1.8%	0.3%	0.2%	0.0%
Stanislaus County	126,237	84.0%	16.0%	24,107	10.5%	4.1%	0.6%	0.3%	0.0%	0.5%
Sutter County	20,932	83.2%	16.8%	4,229	6.7%	8.2%	1.3%	0.3%	0.0%	0.4%
Tulare County	103,419	78.8%	21.2%	27,819	18.7%	1.9%	0.1%	0.1%	0.2%	0.2%
Ventura County	175,785	79.7%	20.3%	44,731	15.2%	4.3%	0.6%	0.2%	0.1%	0.1%
Yolo County	56,663	76.8%	23.2%	17,161	8.0%	12.2%	1.5%	0.6%	0.6%	0.4%

Table C-2: Counties—Nativity and World Region of Birth—*Continued*

	Total Millennial	Percent		Total Foreign Born	Percent of All Millennials by Region of Birth					
		Native	Foreign Born		Latin America	Asia	Europe	Africa	North America	Oceania
Colorado										
Adams County	115,221	83.8%	16.2%	22,310	12.0%	2.6%	1.0%	0.6%	0.0%	0.0%
Arapahoe County	138,954	83.5%	16.5%	27,373	7.6%	4.7%	1.8%	2.0%	0.2%	0.1%
Boulder County	87,426	87.5%	12.5%	12,456	5.8%	3.1%	1.8%	0.4%	0.9%	0.4%
Denver County	174,289	81.8%	18.2%	38,675	10.7%	4.2%	1.5%	1.2%	0.5%	0.1%
Douglas County	62,964	93.3%	6.7%	4,552	1.3%	3.7%	0.7%	0.7%	0.4%	0.0%
El Paso County	179,875	91.3%	8.7%	17,189	3.6%	2.0%	2.3%	0.6%	0.1%	0.2%
Jefferson County	128,872	92.3%	7.7%	10,705	3.4%	1.6%	1.7%	0.4%	0.5%	0.0%
Larimer County	93,080	91.4%	8.6%	8,743	2.5%	2.7%	2.8%	0.0%	0.5%	0.0%
Mesa County	36,722	94.9%	5.1%	1,993	2.8%	1.1%	0.8%	0.0%	0.0%	0.4%
Pueblo County	39,351	96.9%	3.1%	1,245	2.0%	0.2%	0.9%	0.0%	0.0%	0.0%
Weld County	67,346	86.6%	13.4%	10,424	10.6%	1.1%	0.4%	0.8%	0.1%	0.5%
Connecticut										
Fairfield County	172,587	77.3%	22.7%	50,802	14.5%	4.7%	3.0%	0.2%	0.3%	0.1%
Hartford County	182,905	83.4%	16.6%	36,416	5.8%	4.6%	4.3%	1.6%	0.2%	0.1%
Litchfield County	33,427	90.9%	9.1%	3,328	4.1%	1.7%	2.5%	0.8%	0.0%	0.0%
Middlesex County	34,634	92.6%	7.4%	2,781	1.5%	2.5%	2.6%	0.8%	0.0%	0.0%
New Haven County	185,921	84.6%	15.4%	33,899	7.6%	4.1%	2.0%	1.4%	0.3%	0.1%
New London County	64,349	90.6%	9.4%	6,709	3.7%	3.9%	1.2%	0.5%	0.1%	0.1%
Tolland County	45,118	92.7%	7.3%	3,572	0.5%	4.9%	1.5%	0.3%	0.3%	0.0%
Windham County	27,155	91.2%	8.8%	2,636	6.0%	2.1%	0.4%	0.0%	0.0%	0.3%
Delaware										
Kent County	43,415	94.0%	6.0%	2,754	3.5%	1.3%	1.0%	0.2%	0.0%	0.0%
New Castle County	127,615	85.8%	14.2%	21,185	6.0%	5.2%	0.6%	2.1%	0.3%	0.0%
Sussex County	38,085	91.2%	8.8%	3,696	7.8%	1.0%	0.1%	0.0%	0.0%	0.0%
Florida										
Alachua County	86,750	87.2%	12.8%	12,739	4.2%	5.4%	2.1%	0.5%	0.5%	0.1%
Bay County	40,612	91.5%	8.5%	3,762	2.4%	2.7%	2.7%	0.6%	0.1%	0.0%
Brevard County	107,356	89.2%	10.8%	13,008	5.4%	2.9%	1.9%	0.1%	0.3%	0.2%
Broward County	312,503	68.7%	31.3%	142,339	26.2%	2.9%	1.7%	0.3%	0.2%	0.0%
Charlotte County	21,346	92.2%	7.8%	1,803	0.3%	6.4%	0.0%	0.0%	1.2%	0.0%
Citrus County	19,630	95.2%	4.8%	989	2.8%	0.7%	1.4%	0.0%	0.0%	0.0%
Clay County	45,084	94.1%	5.9%	2,825	4.7%	0.4%	0.9%	0.0%	0.0%	0.0%
Collier County	47,094	69.3%	30.7%	20,882	27.3%	1.6%	1.2%	0.0%	0.7%	0.0%
Duval County	220,554	88.3%	11.7%	29,167	4.2%	4.3%	2.6%	0.2%	0.4%	0.1%
Escambia County	85,791	93.1%	6.9%	6,317	1.7%	3.4%	1.5%	0.2%	0.1%	0.0%
Flagler County	17,246	92.1%	7.9%	1,480	2.4%	3.3%	2.2%	0.0%	0.0%	0.0%
Hernando County	32,544	95.7%	4.3%	1,471	2.3%	1.5%	0.0%	0.0%	0.5%	0.0%
Highlands County	15,914	91.0%	9.0%	1,572	6.6%	0.0%	1.8%	0.5%	0.0%	0.0%
Hillsborough County	294,088	82.3%	17.7%	63,227	11.9%	3.1%	1.4%	0.8%	0.4%	0.1%
Indian River County	24,770	92.1%	7.9%	2,120	3.8%	0.3%	2.7%	0.6%	0.4%	0.0%
Lake County	59,814	94.2%	5.8%	3,704	5.4%	0.0%	0.1%	0.1%	0.2%	0.0%
Lee County	110,806	79.5%	20.5%	28,608	17.1%	1.1%	1.1%	0.5%	0.8%	0.0%
Leon County	99,605	91.2%	8.8%	9,625	3.7%	2.5%	1.3%	0.8%	0.5%	0.0%
Manatee County	60,008	83.6%	16.4%	11,737	12.9%	1.8%	1.6%	0.0%	0.1%	0.0%
Marion County	64,886	92.2%	7.8%	5,473	6.8%	0.5%	0.5%	0.0%	0.0%	0.0%
Martin County	25,932	93.1%	6.9%	1,931	5.6%	0.1%	0.0%	1.2%	0.0%	0.0%
Miami-Dade County	399,615	58.9%	41.1%	278,813	37.7%	1.3%	1.6%	0.3%	0.2%	0.0%
Okaloosa County	48,981	89.6%	10.4%	5,695	2.9%	2.1%	5.0%	0.0%	0.2%	0.1%
Orange County	306,383	80.2%	19.8%	75,494	13.8%	3.7%	1.1%	0.6%	0.5%	0.1%
Osceola County	69,123	80.6%	19.4%	16,626	16.1%	1.9%	0.7%	0.6%	0.0%	0.0%
Palm Beach County	224,560	73.6%	26.4%	80,632	21.9%	2.6%	1.2%	0.4%	0.3%	0.0%
Pasco County	94,750	92.6%	7.4%	7,544	3.5%	1.4%	1.8%	0.4%	0.2%	0.0%
Pinellas County	164,412	85.5%	14.5%	27,926	7.5%	3.1%	2.9%	0.8%	0.3%	0.0%
Polk County	139,525	88.5%	11.5%	18,210	9.9%	0.9%	0.5%	0.1%	0.1%	0.0%
Santa Rosa County	43,211	88.1%	11.9%	5,835	1.0%	3.6%	7.0%	0.1%	0.2%	0.0%
Sarasota County	53,440	83.3%	16.7%	10,695	13.8%	2.0%	0.4%	0.5%	0.0%	0.0%
Seminole County	37,943	92.8%	7.2%	2,930	2.0%	2.2%	2.2%	0.0%	0.0%	0.7%
St. Johns County	59,323	89.7%	10.3%	6,844	5.8%	0.8%	3.4%	0.1%	0.1%	0.1%
St. Lucie County	100,996	89.1%	10.9%	12,331	5.4%	3.2%	1.3%	0.5%	0.5%	0.0%
Sumter County	10,581	98.0%	2.0%	218	0.0%	0.0%	0.0%	0.5%	1.5%	0.0%
Volusia County	102,211	90.7%	9.3%	10,458	3.2%	3.4%	1.7%	0.2%	0.7%	0.0%
Georgia										
Bartow County	23,731	96.5%	3.5%	865	2.6%	0.0%	0.1%	0.2%	0.0%	0.6%
Bibb County	38,322	93.8%	6.2%	2,551	2.3%	1.6%	1.4%	0.9%	0.0%	0.0%
Carroll County	31,470	92.3%	7.7%	2,622	4.6%	1.3%	1.8%	0.0%	0.0%	0.0%
Chatham County	77,404	90.5%	9.5%	8,150	4.2%	2.4%	1.7%	1.2%	0.0%	0.0%
Cherokee County	48,460	87.8%	12.2%	6,732	8.2%	0.7%	2.8%	0.3%	0.2%	0.0%
Clarke County	49,599	89.3%	10.7%	5,960	5.5%	3.8%	1.2%	0.2%	0.0%	0.1%
Clayton County	64,734	85.5%	14.5%	10,953	7.9%	3.1%	1.1%	2.3%	0.0%	0.0%
Cobb County	154,309	81.1%	18.9%	36,052	11.0%	3.9%	1.6%	2.3%	0.1%	0.0%
Columbia County	36,727	95.9%	4.1%	1,578	1.3%	1.2%	1.7%	0.0%	0.0%	0.0%
Coweta County	31,075	93.6%	6.4%	2,108	3.0%	0.9%	2.2%	0.0%	0.2%	0.0%
DeKalb County	160,071	79.9%	20.1%	40,311	8.2%	6.1%	1.1%	4.5%	0.3%	0.0%
Dougherty County	24,351	96.8%	3.2%	797	0.5%	2.5%	0.0%	0.0%	0.1%	0.0%
Douglas County	32,431	91.8%	8.2%	2,904	5.8%	0.3%	0.9%	1.2%	0.0%	0.0%
Fayette County	21,973	93.8%	6.2%	1,442	2.7%	3.4%	0.0%	0.0%	0.0%	0.0%

Table C-2: Counties—Nativity and World Region of Birth—Continued

| | Total Millennial | Percent | | Total Foreign Born | Percent of All Millennials by Region of Birth | | | | | |
		Native	Foreign Born		Latin America	Asia	Europe	Africa	North America	Oceania
Georgia—Cont.										
Floyd County	22,522	92.3%	7.7%	1,873	6.2%	0.5%	1.0%	0.0%	0.0%	0.0%
Forsyth County	36,595	83.0%	17.0%	7,502	7.7%	6.8%	2.1%	0.2%	0.3%	0.0%
Fulton County	242,839	84.8%	15.2%	43,411	4.4%	6.1%	2.4%	1.7%	0.5%	0.1%
Gwinnett County	164,162	71.7%	28.3%	64,713	14.4%	7.0%	2.3%	4.0%	0.6%	0.0%
Hall County	37,863	77.8%	22.2%	10,786	19.8%	1.5%	0.4%	0.4%	0.0%	0.0%
Henry County	53,628	94.4%	5.6%	3,166	2.2%	1.8%	0.1%	0.2%	1.3%	0.0%
Houston County	37,191	95.9%	4.1%	1,600	1.6%	2.0%	0.3%	0.0%	0.0%	0.2%
Lowndes County	37,401	95.7%	4.3%	1,681	1.2%	1.9%	1.1%	0.0%	0.0%	0.0%
Muscogee County	55,708	91.8%	8.2%	4,970	3.6%	3.2%	1.4%	0.1%	0.0%	0.0%
Newton County	23,795	89.5%	10.5%	2,797	5.6%	0.0%	2.5%	2.4%	0.1%	0.0%
Paulding County	37,254	96.2%	3.8%	1,491	0.5%	2.6%	0.7%	0.0%	0.0%	0.0%
Richmond County	57,457	93.7%	6.3%	3,855	0.9%	2.0%	3.4%	0.0%	0.0%	0.0%
Whitfield County	21,813	77.1%	22.9%	6,477	20.9%	1.6%	0.0%	0.4%	0.0%	0.0%
Hawaii										
Hawaii County	38,702	87.3%	12.7%	5,654	2.8%	6.9%	1.5%	0.0%	0.2%	1.4%
Honolulu County	231,812	84.8%	15.2%	41,598	1.0%	10.3%	1.3%	0.1%	0.1%	2.4%
Maui County	32,225	82.2%	17.8%	6,990	3.8%	12.0%	0.6%	0.0%	0.0%	1.4%
Idaho										
Ada County	102,251	90.7%	9.3%	10,506	3.3%	3.3%	2.3%	0.1%	0.3%	0.0%
Bonneville County	25,911	94.3%	5.7%	1,557	4.5%	0.0%	0.6%	0.5%	0.0%	0.0%
Canyon County	49,743	93.7%	6.3%	3,365	5.3%	0.2%	0.8%	0.0%	0.0%	0.0%
Kootenai County	34,441	98.1%	1.9%	664	0.2%	0.1%	1.0%	0.0%	0.6%	0.0%
Illinois										
Champaign County	65,798	81.9%	18.1%	14,499	2.1%	12.6%	2.6%	0.5%	0.2%	0.0%
Cook County	1,138,630	80.2%	19.8%	281,489	8.5%	6.3%	3.6%	1.3%	0.2%	0.0%
DeKalb County	35,637	94.0%	6.0%	2,256	4.1%	1.0%	0.8%	0.0%	0.0%	0.0%
DuPage County	184,398	81.7%	18.3%	41,385	5.4%	6.8%	5.2%	0.6%	0.3%	0.0%
Kane County	103,240	80.7%	19.3%	24,659	15.7%	1.8%	0.7%	1.0%	0.0%	0.0%
Kankakee County	26,563	93.4%	6.6%	1,888	3.9%	1.0%	1.8%	0.0%	0.0%	0.0%
Kendall County	29,782	91.4%	8.6%	2,797	4.4%	4.1%	0.0%	0.1%	0.0%	0.1%
Lake County	146,076	83.7%	16.3%	28,521	10.4%	3.3%	2.4%	0.1%	0.1%	0.1%
LaSalle County	24,817	98.4%	1.6%	399	1.2%	0.4%	0.0%	0.0%	0.0%	0.0%
Macon County	61,984	90.2%	9.8%	6,759	8.0%	0.6%	0.6%	0.7%	0.0%	0.0%
Madison County	52,829	92.7%	7.3%	4,182	1.9%	4.7%	0.5%	0.0%	0.2%	0.0%
McHenry County	23,565	95.8%	4.2%	1,035	2.5%	1.6%	0.1%	0.0%	0.0%	0.0%
McLean County	61,561	94.8%	5.2%	3,360	2.5%	2.1%	0.3%	0.3%	0.0%	0.0%
Peoria County	47,001	94.5%	5.5%	2,722	1.4%	2.9%	1.0%	0.2%	0.0%	0.0%
Rock Island County	29,492	90.2%	9.8%	3,197	2.9%	3.4%	0.0%	3.4%	0.0%	0.0%
Sangamon County	58,881	93.4%	6.6%	4,150	1.2%	3.8%	1.4%	0.1%	0.0%	0.0%
St. Clair County	44,889	93.6%	6.4%	3,090	1.4%	4.1%	0.6%	0.1%	0.3%	0.0%
Tazewell County	29,475	97.6%	2.4%	731	0.0%	1.5%	1.0%	0.0%	0.0%	0.0%
Will County	147,428	89.4%	10.6%	17,421	6.3%	2.1%	1.7%	0.1%	0.2%	0.0%
Winnebago County	59,531	87.1%	12.9%	8,808	9.4%	2.3%	0.7%	0.6%	0.0%	0.0%
Indiana										
Allen County	86,252	91.3%	8.7%	8,241	4.4%	3.5%	0.3%	0.0%	0.3%	0.1%
Clark County	26,575	99.3%	0.7%	191	0.5%	0.3%	0.0%	0.0%	0.0%	0.0%
Delaware County	37,017	99.6%	0.4%	167	0.0%	0.2%	0.0%	0.0%	0.3%	0.0%
Elkhart County	47,541	92.5%	7.5%	3,852	6.8%	0.4%	0.3%	0.0%	0.0%	0.0%
Hamilton County	65,511	93.1%	6.9%	4,837	1.0%	3.7%	0.7%	0.2%	1.3%	0.0%
Hendricks County	35,844	92.5%	7.5%	2,926	0.0%	2.6%	0.4%	4.6%	0.0%	0.0%
Johnson County	33,162	93.3%	6.7%	2,371	2.4%	2.9%	0.2%	0.1%	0.0%	0.9%
Lake County	107,395	92.8%	7.2%	8,370	3.5%	1.9%	1.1%	0.7%	0.1%	0.0%
LaPorte County	25,758	99.4%	0.6%	161	0.5%	0.1%	0.0%	0.0%	0.0%	0.0%
Madison County	30,445	96.2%	3.8%	1,202	2.6%	0.0%	0.9%	0.3%	0.0%	0.0%
Marion County	235,235	88.6%	11.4%	30,295	6.3%	2.8%	0.7%	1.0%	0.3%	0.2%
Monroe County	57,057	89.0%	11.0%	7,020	0.8%	8.2%	1.2%	0.1%	0.6%	0.0%
Porter County	39,167	97.5%	2.5%	985	0.5%	0.5%	1.4%	0.0%	0.2%	0.0%
St. Joseph County	64,837	90.6%	9.4%	6,765	2.9%	3.1%	0.6%	2.8%	0.0%	0.0%
Tippecanoe County	61,624	83.1%	16.9%	12,520	3.7%	11.7%	0.8%	0.3%	0.4%	0.0%
Vanderburgh County	45,807	96.6%	3.4%	1,620	0.9%	1.0%	1.0%	0.1%	0.1%	0.3%
Vigo County	32,583	98.2%	1.8%	589	0.9%	0.5%	0.1%	0.2%	0.0%	0.0%
Iowa										
Black Hawk County	38,265	92.7%	7.3%	3,029	5.6%	0.6%	0.9%	0.0%	0.0%	0.2%
Dubuque County	24,260	95.9%	4.1%	1,042	0.0%	2.3%	0.9%	0.0%	0.0%	0.9%
Johnson County	48,683	88.2%	11.8%	6,497	1.9%	7.5%	1.8%	0.5%	0.0%	0.0%
Linn County	52,328	92.8%	7.2%	4,070	1.0%	4.8%	0.8%	0.6%	0.0%	0.0%
Polk County	108,834	87.7%	12.3%	15,234	3.1%	3.9%	2.2%	3.1%	0.0%	0.0%
Pottawattamie County	20,612	94.3%	5.7%	1,251	4.2%	1.6%	0.0%	0.0%	0.0%	0.0%
Scott County	41,374	97.3%	2.7%	1,164	0.4%	2.3%	0.0%	0.0%	0.0%	0.0%
Story County	39,860	88.0%	12.0%	5,449	0.0%	11.1%	0.2%	0.3%	0.4%	0.0%
Woodbury County	24,404	86.2%	13.8%	3,913	10.9%	0.2%	0.2%	2.5%	0.0%	0.0%
Kansas										
Douglas County	40,692	87.0%	13.0%	6,071	5.3%	5.3%	1.4%	0.4%	0.7%	0.0%
Johnson County	128,656	90.0%	10.0%	14,269	2.8%	5.2%	0.6%	1.4%	0.1%	0.0%
Sedgwick County	120,055	89.7%	10.3%	13,822	4.9%	3.5%	0.8%	0.9%	0.2%	0.0%

Table C-2: Counties—Nativity and World Region of Birth—*Continued*

	Total Millennial	Percent		Total Foreign Born	Percent of All Millennials by Region of Birth					
		Native	Foreign Born		Latin America	Asia	Europe	Africa	North America	Oceania
Kansas—Cont.										
Shawnee County	43,340	98.3%	1.7%	734	0.2%	0.7%	0.4%	0.3%	0.0%	0.0%
Wyandotte County	34,666	79.4%	20.6%	8,982	13.8%	4.0%	0.6%	2.0%	0.2%	0.0%
Kentucky										
Boone County	27,127	90.7%	9.3%	2,779	6.1%	0.0%	1.8%	1.4%	0.0%	0.0%
Campbell County	23,433	93.6%	6.4%	1,607	3.4%	1.7%	0.5%	0.0%	0.8%	0.0%
Daviess County	22,611	97.3%	2.7%	633	0.7%	1.5%	0.5%	0.0%	0.0%	0.0%
Fayette County	86,978	89.0%	11.0%	10,791	4.7%	5.0%	1.0%	0.1%	0.2%	0.0%
Hardin County	26,275	94.8%	5.2%	1,451	0.6%	1.6%	3.1%	0.0%	0.0%	0.0%
Jefferson County	170,741	88.7%	11.3%	21,808	4.2%	3.3%	2.1%	1.1%	0.2%	0.4%
Kenton County	39,868	97.4%	2.6%	1,065	1.3%	0.3%	1.0%	0.0%	0.0%	0.0%
Warren County	34,490	88.5%	11.5%	4,473	3.9%	5.7%	1.7%	0.2%	0.0%	0.0%
Louisiana										
Ascension Parish	30,222	97.0%	3.0%	948	2.5%	0.2%	0.0%	0.3%	0.0%	0.0%
Bossier Parish	32,276	93.3%	6.7%	2,323	3.3%	3.0%	0.4%	0.0%	0.0%	0.0%
Caddo Parish	61,273	95.7%	4.3%	2,763	2.1%	1.0%	1.1%	0.0%	0.0%	0.0%
Calcasieu Parish	50,043	94.0%	6.0%	3,194	2.4%	2.7%	0.8%	0.0%	0.0%	0.0%
East Baton Rouge Parish	129,583	91.4%	8.6%	12,183	3.4%	4.6%	0.5%	0.0%	0.0%	0.0%
Jefferson Parish	95,344	87.1%	12.9%	14,072	8.4%	2.9%	0.8%	0.5%	0.3%	0.0%
Lafayette Parish	67,071	95.9%	4.1%	2,893	1.2%	2.5%	0.4%	0.0%	0.0%	0.0%
Lafourche Parish	24,659	97.7%	2.3%	579	2.0%	0.3%	0.0%	0.0%	0.0%	0.0%
Livingston Parish	35,503	100.0%	0.0%	0	0.0%	0.0%	0.0%	0.0%	0.0%	0.0%
Orleans Parish	107,189	94.6%	5.4%	6,104	2.0%	2.0%	0.8%	0.3%	0.3%	0.1%
Ouachita Parish	42,543	97.0%	3.0%	1,303	0.9%	2.1%	0.0%	0.0%	0.0%	0.0%
Rapides Parish	31,692	96.7%	3.3%	1,087	0.5%	1.1%	0.9%	0.7%	0.0%	0.0%
St. Tammany Parish	54,149	96.7%	3.3%	1,874	2.1%	0.4%	0.6%	0.3%	0.0%	0.0%
Tangipahoa Parish	35,149	96.1%	3.9%	1,421	2.1%	1.1%	0.6%	0.0%	0.0%	0.0%
Terrebonne Parish	26,155	94.9%	5.1%	1,417	3.4%	1.4%	0.0%	0.3%	0.0%	0.0%
Maine										
Androscoggin County	22,598	92.8%	7.2%	1,754	3.3%	2.1%	0.6%	0.8%	0.3%	0.0%
Cumberland County	67,160	94.0%	6.0%	4,268	0.6%	1.3%	2.9%	1.1%	0.0%	0.0%
Kennebec County	24,934	96.2%	3.8%	992	0.0%	2.2%	0.2%	1.4%	0.0%	0.0%
Penobscot County	38,988	95.4%	4.6%	1,868	0.0%	2.3%	1.0%	0.3%	1.0%	0.0%
York County	42,616	95.7%	4.3%	1,901	0.8%	0.9%	0.6%	0.1%	1.8%	0.0%
Maryland										
Anne Arundel County	126,646	89.1%	10.9%	15,427	5.2%	3.4%	1.2%	1.0%	0.0%	0.1%
Baltimore County	176,826	85.0%	15.0%	31,182	5.1%	5.8%	1.7%	2.3%	0.0%	0.1%
Carroll County	36,039	94.5%	5.5%	2,085	1.7%	2.7%	1.0%	0.2%	0.0%	0.0%
Cecil County	24,226	97.9%	2.1%	527	2.1%	0.0%	0.1%	0.0%	0.0%	0.0%
Charles County	37,712	95.4%	4.6%	1,831	0.4%	3.8%	0.5%	0.0%	0.0%	0.0%
Frederick County	53,298	90.0%	10.0%	5,903	4.3%	2.0%	1.8%	1.4%	0.4%	0.0%
Harford County	54,106	92.4%	7.6%	4,442	3.5%	1.3%	1.4%	1.2%	0.1%	0.0%
Howard County	59,244	79.4%	20.6%	15,373	4.5%	10.7%	2.4%	2.4%	0.6%	0.0%
Montgomery County	167,060	68.9%	31.1%	75,522	13.0%	9.0%	2.7%	6.0%	0.3%	0.2%
Prince George's County	181,808	74.3%	25.7%	62,774	14.4%	3.9%	0.7%	6.5%	0.2%	0.0%
St. Mary's County	26,731	93.5%	6.5%	1,849	3.7%	2.3%	0.2%	0.3%	0.0%	0.0%
Washington County	34,055	93.6%	6.4%	2,343	2.6%	1.8%	1.7%	0.2%	0.0%	0.1%
Wicomico County	27,668	91.9%	8.1%	2,438	4.1%	0.5%	1.9%	1.6%	0.0%	0.0%
Massachusetts										
Barnstable County	34,150	89.9%	10.1%	3,851	3.9%	1.2%	1.9%	3.1%	0.0%	0.0%
Berkshire County	26,559	92.7%	7.3%	2,086	1.6%	2.8%	2.9%	0.0%	0.0%	0.0%
Bristol County	127,998	92.1%	7.9%	10,910	3.1%	1.9%	1.8%	0.8%	0.2%	0.0%
Essex County	155,355	82.3%	17.7%	33,513	11.2%	3.4%	1.7%	1.0%	0.4%	0.0%
Hampden County	110,655	90.4%	9.6%	11,745	3.1%	2.7%	2.9%	0.5%	0.4%	0.0%
Hampshire County	53,246	92.1%	7.9%	4,557	1.5%	3.1%	1.9%	1.0%	0.0%	0.3%
Middlesex County	332,318	78.3%	21.7%	92,356	6.4%	10.1%	2.9%	1.6%	0.8%	0.0%
Norfolk County	134,342	82.8%	17.2%	27,970	4.2%	7.9%	2.5%	2.1%	0.4%	0.1%
Plymouth County	100,673	88.2%	11.8%	13,431	4.0%	1.7%	1.4%	4.6%	0.1%	0.0%
Suffolk County	210,797	71.7%	28.3%	83,197	13.1%	7.4%	3.2%	3.5%	0.8%	0.3%
Worcester County	180,604	90.0%	10.0%	20,117	2.7%	3.9%	1.5%	1.9%	0.1%	0.0%
Michigan										
Allegan County	25,553	94.9%	5.1%	1,369	4.1%	0.4%	0.6%	0.0%	0.0%	0.0%
Bay County	23,453	96.8%	3.2%	776	2.0%	0.4%	0.8%	0.0%	0.0%	0.0%
Berrien County	30,788	90.1%	9.9%	3,380	2.7%	3.8%	0.8%	2.2%	0.1%	0.2%
Calhoun County	30,741	96.3%	3.7%	1,181	1.0%	2.3%	0.3%	0.0%	0.0%	0.0%
Eaton County	24,503	95.5%	4.5%	1,165	0.6%	3.8%	0.1%	0.0%	0.0%	0.0%
Genesee County	94,350	95.8%	4.2%	4,108	0.4%	2.0%	0.7%	0.8%	0.4%	0.0%
Ingham County	91,392	88.6%	11.4%	11,812	0.9%	9.1%	0.6%	0.4%	0.4%	0.1%
Jackson County	36,522	96.1%	3.9%	1,493	0.8%	2.4%	0.8%	0.0%	0.0%	0.0%
Kalamazoo County	75,302	93.5%	6.5%	5,223	1.8%	2.4%	1.5%	0.3%	0.4%	0.0%
Kent County	152,965	88.6%	11.4%	19,768	4.1%	3.3%	1.2%	1.9%	0.8%	0.1%
Lenawee County	22,865	98.3%	1.7%	404	0.7%	0.5%	0.0%	0.0%	0.6%	0.0%
Livingston County	39,915	96.9%	3.1%	1,288	2.2%	0.7%	0.0%	0.0%	0.3%	0.0%
Macomb County	182,227	88.6%	11.4%	23,515	1.3%	5.7%	3.2%	0.4%	0.7%	0.0%
Monroe County	32,695	97.6%	2.4%	807	1.1%	0.9%	0.5%	0.0%	0.0%	0.0%
Muskegon County	40,525	97.2%	2.8%	1,182	1.3%	0.6%	0.0%	0.6%	0.3%	0.0%

Table C-2: Counties—Nativity and World Region of Birth—*Continued*

| | Total Millennial | Percent | | Total Foreign Born | Percent of All Millennials by Region of Birth | | | | | |
		Native	Foreign Born		Latin America	Asia	Europe	Africa	North America	Oceania
Michigan—Cont.										
Oakland County	254,168	88.3%	11.7%	33,722	1.7%	7.2%	2.3%	0.2%	0.3%	0.0%
Ottawa County	73,403	92.4%	7.6%	5,998	2.7%	3.5%	1.1%	0.0%	0.2%	0.0%
Saginaw County	44,758	92.5%	7.5%	3,612	1.0%	5.7%	0.4%	0.0%	0.3%	0.0%
St. Clair County	34,060	97.0%	3.0%	1,057	0.6%	1.8%	0.3%	0.0%	0.3%	0.0%
Washtenaw County	109,500	88.8%	11.2%	13,778	0.4%	7.2%	2.3%	0.5%	0.8%	0.0%
Wayne County	400,726	90.2%	9.8%	43,562	2.4%	5.6%	1.0%	0.5%	0.4%	0.0%
Minnesota										
Anoka County	74,777	92.4%	7.6%	6,127	2.2%	4.3%	0.5%	0.6%	0.1%	0.0%
Carver County	20,145	92.0%	8.0%	1,754	2.7%	2.4%	2.4%	0.6%	0.0%	0.0%
Dakota County	86,324	87.4%	12.6%	12,441	5.1%	4.5%	1.6%	0.5%	0.9%	0.0%
Hennepin County	270,051	81.2%	18.8%	62,387	3.4%	6.8%	1.8%	6.5%	0.2%	0.1%
Olmsted County	31,857	86.7%	13.3%	4,888	1.8%	7.0%	1.7%	1.3%	0.9%	0.5%
Ramsey County	124,118	81.4%	18.6%	28,364	2.9%	11.7%	0.5%	3.5%	0.0%	0.0%
Scott County	53,170	97.3%	2.7%	1,449	0.6%	1.3%	0.5%	0.0%	0.2%	0.0%
St. Louis County	28,179	85.8%	14.2%	4,669	7.2%	2.9%	2.7%	0.0%	1.5%	0.0%
Stearns County	43,319	91.7%	8.3%	3,944	2.3%	3.2%	0.1%	2.8%	0.0%	0.0%
Washington County	51,508	89.5%	10.5%	6,023	2.9%	3.5%	2.1%	2.0%	0.0%	0.0%
Wright County	27,004	97.5%	2.5%	682	1.4%	0.0%	0.9%	0.2%	0.0%	0.0%
Mississippi										
DeSoto County	40,960	95.3%	4.7%	2,006	3.7%	0.8%	0.0%	0.0%	0.2%	0.0%
Harrison County	50,118	90.9%	9.1%	5,035	3.8%	2.2%	1.8%	1.4%	0.0%	0.0%
Hinds County	69,233	97.4%	2.6%	1,851	0.3%	0.8%	0.6%	0.6%	0.2%	0.0%
Jackson County	31,552	94.6%	5.4%	1,798	4.6%	0.0%	0.8%	0.0%	0.0%	0.0%
Madison County	24,658	96.0%	4.0%	1,030	2.1%	0.5%	0.0%	1.5%	0.0%	0.0%
Rankin County	36,174	97.7%	2.3%	862	0.1%	1.9%	0.4%	0.0%	0.0%	0.0%
Missouri										
Boone County	60,788	92.2%	7.8%	5,159	0.6%	3.9%	1.1%	2.3%	0.0%	0.0%
Cass County	21,861	96.9%	3.1%	709	1.7%	1.3%	0.2%	0.0%	0.0%	0.0%
Clay County	54,164	93.4%	6.6%	3,837	2.5%	1.1%	2.2%	0.3%	0.1%	0.4%
Franklin County	22,635	98.4%	1.6%	378	0.6%	1.0%	0.0%	0.0%	0.0%	0.0%
Greene County	82,327	94.2%	5.8%	5,073	1.5%	2.1%	1.2%	0.7%	0.2%	0.1%
Jackson County	164,273	93.0%	7.0%	12,348	3.8%	2.2%	0.5%	0.4%	0.1%	0.0%
Jasper County	30,222	95.4%	4.6%	1,450	3.7%	0.2%	0.2%	0.0%	0.0%	0.5%
Jefferson County	52,191	98.7%	1.3%	704	0.1%	0.2%	0.2%	0.0%	0.8%	0.0%
Platte County	22,326	91.7%	8.3%	2,031	0.0%	5.4%	2.8%	0.1%	0.0%	0.1%
St. Charles County	88,130	93.9%	6.1%	5,751	3.1%	1.8%	0.5%	0.7%	0.1%	0.0%
St. Louis County	221,489	91.2%	8.8%	21,465	1.7%	4.1%	2.3%	0.7%	0.1%	0.0%
Montana										
Flathead County	18,512	93.0%	7.0%	1,403	0.0%	0.1%	6.0%	0.0%	0.9%	0.0%
Gallatin County	34,100	98.3%	1.7%	606	0.5%	0.0%	0.8%	0.4%	0.0%	0.0%
Missoula County	35,968	100.0%	0.0%	13	0.0%	0.0%	0.0%	0.0%	0.0%	0.0%
Yellowstone County	37,546	96.6%	3.4%	1,326	1.8%	1.5%	0.0%	0.0%	0.1%	0.0%
Nebraska										
Douglas County	128,946	86.4%	13.6%	20,274	6.0%	4.6%	0.7%	2.1%	0.0%	0.1%
Lancaster County	83,230	87.9%	12.1%	11,416	2.3%	7.6%	0.2%	1.8%	0.0%	0.1%
Sarpy County	42,142	92.8%	7.2%	3,263	3.0%	3.2%	0.9%	0.0%	0.0%	0.0%
Nevada										
Clark County	427,623	77.9%	22.1%	121,253	12.6%	6.5%	1.5%	1.2%	0.2%	0.1%
Washoe County	101,463	87.6%	12.4%	14,356	7.1%	4.4%	0.4%	0.4%	0.0%	0.1%
New Hampshire										
Hillsborough County	86,704	89.6%	10.4%	10,031	4.1%	2.9%	1.6%	1.2%	0.5%	0.0%
Merrimack County	34,274	95.9%	4.1%	1,449	0.6%	2.9%	0.5%	0.0%	0.0%	0.0%
Rockingham County	61,444	92.8%	7.2%	4,758	2.7%	2.1%	2.0%	0.1%	0.3%	0.0%
Strafford County	35,997	91.8%	8.2%	3,200	0.4%	6.4%	1.1%	0.3%	0.0%	0.0%
New Jersey										
Atlantic County	54,614	82.0%	18.0%	11,956	9.5%	6.0%	1.4%	1.1%	0.0%	0.0%
Bergen County	150,459	72.4%	27.6%	57,425	9.1%	12.5%	4.4%	1.3%	0.3%	0.0%
Burlington County	97,699	90.9%	9.1%	9,722	4.0%	3.2%	1.0%	0.8%	0.2%	0.0%
Camden County	112,012	87.2%	12.8%	16,378	6.3%	4.7%	0.8%	0.9%	0.0%	0.0%
Cape May County	17,366	90.7%	9.3%	1,783	7.6%	1.0%	0.2%	0.5%	0.0%	0.0%
Cumberland County	35,220	88.5%	11.5%	4,583	9.9%	0.9%	0.5%	0.3%	0.0%	0.0%
Essex County	151,288	75.9%	24.1%	48,041	17.1%	2.7%	1.0%	3.0%	0.2%	0.1%
Gloucester County	66,613	95.8%	4.2%	2,932	1.6%	1.1%	0.7%	0.9%	0.0%	0.0%
Hudson County	123,962	60.6%	39.4%	80,428	19.2%	14.4%	2.0%	3.4%	0.3%	0.0%
Hunterdon County	25,034	92.1%	7.9%	2,136	3.1%	2.4%	2.1%	0.2%	0.0%	0.0%
Mercer County	72,663	75.6%	24.4%	23,459	11.0%	7.6%	4.1%	1.6%	0.0%	0.1%
Middlesex County	149,233	69.5%	30.5%	65,483	11.0%	15.6%	2.1%	1.8%	0.1%	0.0%
Monmouth County	121,528	86.3%	13.7%	19,298	8.5%	3.1%	1.6%	0.5%	0.0%	0.1%
Morris County	95,025	83.0%	17.0%	19,418	8.2%	5.8%	2.2%	0.8%	0.0%	0.0%
Ocean County	110,115	89.9%	10.1%	12,331	5.4%	2.1%	1.2%	0.4%	0.9%	0.0%
Passaic County	98,032	74.3%	25.7%	33,948	17.4%	4.6%	2.7%	1.0%	0.1%	0.0%
Somerset County	57,270	79.4%	20.6%	14,889	7.4%	10.3%	2.1%	0.6%	0.2%	0.0%
Sussex County	29,733	96.8%	3.2%	968	2.7%	0.0%	0.4%	0.0%	0.1%	0.0%
Union County	89,908	67.6%	32.4%	43,147	24.5%	3.7%	3.2%	0.6%	0.4%	0.0%
Warren County	21,048	92.1%	7.9%	1,816	4.7%	2.1%	1.2%	0.0%	0.0%	0.0%

Table C-2: Counties—Nativity and World Region of Birth—*Continued*

	Total Millennial	Percent		Total Foreign Born	Percent of All Millennials by Region of Birth					
		Native	Foreign Born		Latin America	Asia	Europe	Africa	North America	Oceania
New Mexico										
Bernalillo County	156,500	85.6%	14.4%	26,351	9.2%	3.1%	1.1%	0.6%	0.4%	0.0%
Doña Ana County	56,930	88.8%	11.2%	7,164	8.8%	1.8%	0.0%	0.6%	0.0%	0.0%
San Juan County	30,715	93.7%	6.3%	2,082	4.4%	1.8%	0.0%	0.0%	0.2%	0.0%
Sandoval County	29,475	96.2%	3.8%	1,157	2.4%	0.1%	1.1%	0.0%	0.0%	0.2%
Santa Fe County	26,699	86.1%	13.9%	4,295	8.8%	0.7%	4.2%	0.0%	0.0%	0.1%
New York										
Albany County	80,117	88.4%	11.6%	10,488	0.6%	7.1%	2.3%	1.3%	0.4%	0.0%
Bronx County	280,872	66.8%	33.2%	139,668	25.5%	3.0%	1.1%	3.6%	0.0%	0.0%
Broome County	50,403	91.8%	8.2%	4,530	0.7%	5.9%	1.5%	0.0%	0.1%	0.0%
Chautauqua County	30,580	96.3%	3.7%	1,176	1.8%	0.8%	1.1%	0.1%	0.0%	0.0%
Dutchess County	68,875	91.0%	9.0%	6,778	5.7%	2.0%	0.8%	0.3%	0.2%	0.0%
Erie County	217,789	90.8%	9.2%	22,085	1.1%	5.3%	1.7%	0.7%	0.3%	0.0%
Jefferson County	34,000	96.0%	4.0%	1,425	1.6%	0.8%	0.9%	0.0%	0.1%	0.5%
Kings County	519,016	68.9%	31.1%	233,999	14.0%	10.3%	5.2%	1.1%	0.4%	0.1%
Monroe County	180,630	89.5%	10.5%	21,092	1.6%	5.6%	2.2%	0.9%	0.2%	0.0%
Nassau County	257,869	81.9%	18.1%	56,811	10.3%	5.0%	1.5%	0.8%	0.3%	0.1%
New York County	379,490	72.9%	27.1%	140,793	8.8%	9.5%	4.7%	1.5%	1.7%	1.0%
Niagara County	47,627	96.4%	3.6%	1,800	2.1%	0.3%	0.5%	0.2%	0.6%	0.0%
Oneida County	51,089	89.1%	10.9%	6,248	2.1%	5.3%	2.0%	1.4%	0.0%	0.0%
Onondaga County	110,181	89.4%	10.6%	13,016	2.2%	5.2%	1.5%	1.1%	0.5%	0.0%
Ontario County	24,937	94.8%	5.2%	1,380	0.3%	2.9%	2.0%	0.0%	0.0%	0.0%
Orange County	86,028	89.4%	10.6%	10,149	6.9%	0.7%	1.6%	1.2%	0.1%	0.0%
Oswego County	30,934	96.4%	3.6%	1,152	0.8%	1.8%	0.7%	0.0%	0.4%	0.0%
Putnam County	20,599	95.6%	4.4%	944	2.8%	0.9%	0.7%	0.0%	0.0%	0.0%
Queens County	354,850	58.3%	41.7%	253,569	20.1%	17.1%	2.9%	1.2%	0.2%	0.2%
Rensselaer County	39,460	92.5%	7.5%	3,200	2.6%	3.6%	0.6%	0.3%	0.5%	0.0%
Richmond County	97,435	82.1%	17.9%	21,172	4.6%	6.0%	5.6%	1.7%	0.0%	0.0%
Rockland County	64,911	82.3%	17.7%	13,921	12.3%	3.5%	1.0%	0.1%	0.8%	0.0%
Saratoga County	30,147	93.9%	6.1%	1,942	0.5%	2.2%	2.7%	0.1%	0.6%	0.0%
Schenectady County	47,821	95.6%	4.4%	2,199	1.9%	1.2%	0.9%	0.0%	0.4%	0.0%
St. Lawrence County	33,849	88.0%	12.0%	4,597	4.3%	4.7%	1.4%	1.6%	0.0%	0.0%
Steuben County	22,377	98.7%	1.3%	298	0.2%	1.0%	0.1%	0.0%	0.0%	0.0%
Suffolk County	294,276	83.9%	16.1%	56,644	10.8%	4.2%	1.0%	0.2%	0.0%	0.0%
Tompkins County	35,692	80.1%	19.9%	8,858	2.0%	14.6%	3.2%	0.0%	0.0%	0.0%
Ulster County	39,984	92.2%	7.8%	3,368	3.6%	3.2%	0.8%	0.2%	0.0%	0.0%
Wayne County	20,158	97.9%	2.1%	434	0.1%	1.4%	0.2%	0.2%	0.1%	0.0%
Westchester County	175,288	77.1%	22.9%	52,141	15.9%	3.5%	2.9%	0.4%	0.2%	0.0%
North Carolina										
Alamance County	32,765	86.6%	13.4%	5,063	11.3%	0.8%	1.0%	0.0%	0.3%	0.0%
Brunswick County	20,130	94.4%	5.6%	1,197	3.8%	1.8%	0.0%	0.0%	0.0%	0.0%
Buncombe County	54,881	88.4%	11.6%	7,173	5.8%	1.8%	3.9%	0.0%	0.0%	0.0%
Cabarrus County	42,005	92.9%	7.1%	3,202	5.7%	0.9%	0.0%	0.5%	0.0%	0.0%
Catawba County	32,160	88.5%	11.5%	4,199	10.4%	0.8%	0.3%	0.0%	0.0%	0.0%
Cleveland County	19,708	88.7%	11.3%	2,520	10.2%	0.0%	1.1%	0.0%	0.0%	0.0%
Craven County	26,975	94.2%	5.8%	1,666	1.3%	3.7%	0.9%	0.0%	0.0%	0.0%
Cumberland County	91,710	90.5%	9.5%	9,600	2.9%	1.3%	4.1%	0.8%	0.1%	0.3%
Davidson County	33,308	91.7%	8.3%	3,018	6.3%	0.6%	1.4%	0.0%	0.0%	0.0%
Durham County	71,189	79.3%	20.7%	18,591	10.7%	5.9%	1.3%	2.6%	0.1%	0.0%
Forsyth County	80,186	86.8%	13.2%	12,235	8.0%	3.5%	0.4%	1.1%	0.2%	0.0%
Gaston County	46,891	92.1%	7.9%	4,039	5.0%	1.6%	1.3%	0.0%	0.0%	0.0%
Guilford County	121,482	88.3%	11.7%	16,105	6.3%	3.6%	1.1%	0.5%	0.1%	0.2%
Harnett County	32,264	89.9%	10.1%	3,639	6.8%	0.7%	2.3%	0.3%	0.0%	0.0%
Henderson County	17,939	87.4%	12.6%	2,582	10.2%	2.0%	0.0%	0.4%	0.0%	0.0%
Iredell County	34,846	89.0%	11.0%	4,289	5.9%	4.8%	0.0%	0.3%	0.0%	0.0%
Johnston County	38,885	92.8%	7.2%	3,026	6.8%	0.0%	0.4%	0.0%	0.0%	0.0%
Mecklenburg County	235,993	82.6%	17.4%	49,849	9.0%	5.0%	1.7%	1.4%	0.3%	0.0%
Moore County	18,504	94.9%	5.1%	991	3.5%	0.7%	0.9%	0.0%	0.0%	0.0%
Nash County	20,772	96.4%	3.6%	765	1.9%	0.6%	1.0%	0.0%	0.0%	0.0%
New Hanover County	58,477	93.6%	6.4%	3,990	2.9%	0.9%	1.7%	0.7%	0.2%	0.0%
Onslow County	71,808	93.8%	6.2%	4,755	3.5%	1.3%	1.4%	0.0%	0.0%	0.0%
Orange County	41,243	83.6%	16.4%	8,073	4.9%	7.3%	0.2%	3.2%	0.3%	0.5%
Pitt County	58,273	94.7%	5.3%	3,269	3.6%	0.4%	0.8%	0.4%	0.0%	0.0%
Randolph County	30,046	93.3%	6.7%	2,162	6.1%	0.0%	0.1%	0.0%	0.5%	0.0%
Robeson County	33,074	95.0%	5.0%	1,732	4.3%	0.2%	0.0%	0.5%	0.0%	0.0%
Rockingham County	18,030	94.2%	5.8%	1,101	4.5%	0.7%	0.5%	0.0%	0.0%	0.0%
Rowan County	30,178	92.8%	7.2%	2,327	4.7%	0.4%	1.1%	0.0%	1.0%	0.0%
Union County	45,547	88.9%	11.1%	5,701	7.1%	1.4%	2.3%	0.2%	0.2%	0.0%
Wake County	229,537	85.2%	14.8%	39,958	6.5%	5.3%	1.7%	0.9%	0.3%	0.1%
Wayne County	28,732	87.6%	12.4%	4,072	8.0%	2.0%	1.5%	0.0%	0.9%	0.0%
North Dakota										
Cass County	52,424	91.1%	8.9%	5,104	1.0%	3.2%	1.0%	3.3%	0.3%	0.0%
Ohio										
Allen County	25,155	99.6%	0.4%	99	0.0%	0.0%	0.4%	0.0%	0.0%	0.0%
Ashtabula County	22,363	98.9%	1.1%	251	0.0%	1.1%	0.0%	0.0%	0.0%	0.0%
Butler County	91,414	90.5%	9.5%	9,563	3.2%	3.6%	2.1%	0.5%	0.0%	0.0%
Clark County	30,905	98.6%	1.4%	438	0.8%	0.0%	0.0%	0.6%	0.0%	0.0%

Table C-2: Counties—Nativity and World Region of Birth—*Continued*

| | Total Millennial | Percent | | Total Foreign Born | Percent of All Millennials by Region of Birth | | | | | |
		Native	Foreign Born		Latin America	Asia	Europe	Africa	North America	Oceania
Ohio—Cont.										
Clermont County	46,669	97.9%	2.1%	982	0.2%	1.1%	0.6%	0.0%	0.2%	0.0%
Columbiana County	20,767	97.1%	2.9%	623	1.5%	0.0%	1.0%	0.4%	0.0%	0.0%
Cuyahoga County	279,492	91.0%	9.0%	27,574	1.4%	5.0%	2.1%	0.3%	0.2%	0.0%
Delaware County	37,706	92.7%	7.3%	2,981	0.8%	3.3%	1.7%	1.5%	0.0%	0.0%
Fairfield County	32,819	97.2%	2.8%	938	0.0%	1.3%	1.2%	0.3%	0.0%	0.0%
Franklin County	322,878	87.7%	12.3%	45,189	2.9%	4.9%	1.0%	3.4%	0.1%	0.0%
Geauga County	18,677	97.4%	2.6%	492	0.0%	0.0%	2.6%	0.0%	0.0%	0.0%
Greene County	43,326	95.0%	5.0%	2,291	0.0%	3.6%	0.4%	0.5%	0.5%	0.1%
Hamilton County	194,042	92.0%	8.0%	16,791	1.6%	3.3%	1.3%	1.5%	0.2%	0.0%
Lake County	47,239	95.8%	4.2%	2,077	1.0%	3.0%	0.0%	0.2%	0.0%	0.0%
Licking County	39,622	97.6%	2.4%	993	0.0%	1.3%	0.9%	0.0%	0.3%	0.0%
Lorain County	67,518	96.7%	3.3%	2,299	0.8%	1.8%	0.5%	0.0%	0.0%	0.2%
Lucas County	108,017	96.3%	3.7%	4,110	0.2%	2.3%	0.2%	1.0%	0.0%	0.0%
Mahoning County	52,871	97.5%	2.5%	1,365	1.4%	1.0%	0.1%	0.0%	0.0%	0.0%
Medina County	37,744	97.6%	2.4%	944	0.2%	1.1%	0.7%	0.0%	0.4%	0.0%
Miami County	22,037	98.0%	2.0%	456	0.0%	1.4%	0.6%	0.0%	0.0%	0.0%
Montgomery County	121,656	92.8%	7.2%	9,392	1.4%	2.8%	1.6%	1.4%	0.0%	0.0%
Portage County	46,180	93.0%	7.0%	3,477	1.8%	3.8%	1.2%	0.1%	0.0%	0.1%
Richland County	27,787	99.4%	0.6%	166	0.0%	0.5%	0.1%	0.0%	0.0%	0.0%
Stark County	85,565	97.1%	2.9%	2,563	1.4%	0.7%	0.2%	0.0%	0.5%	0.0%
Summit County	121,411	94.2%	5.8%	7,487	1.2%	3.1%	1.5%	0.0%	0.0%	0.0%
Trumbull County	44,088	99.8%	0.2%	88	0.0%	0.1%	0.1%	0.0%	0.0%	0.0%
Tuscarawas County	20,200	97.0%	3.0%	622	0.0%	2.8%	0.1%	0.0%	0.0%	0.0%
Warren County	46,349	92.8%	7.2%	3,602	0.5%	5.8%	0.4%	0.0%	0.4%	0.0%
Wayne County	27,703	98.9%	1.1%	312	0.2%	0.1%	0.0%	0.4%	0.0%	0.3%
Wood County	41,821	97.0%	3.0%	1,292	0.5%	2.0%	0.4%	0.0%	0.0%	0.0%
Oklahoma										
Canadian County	31,821	97.5%	2.5%	823	2.1%	0.2%	0.2%	0.0%	0.0%	0.0%
Cleveland County	79,719	90.3%	9.7%	8,531	2.2%	5.7%	0.3%	1.4%	0.0%	0.0%
Comanche County	37,480	94.7%	5.3%	2,077	2.2%	1.6%	1.4%	0.0%	0.0%	0.0%
Oklahoma County	179,527	86.0%	14.0%	29,135	9.8%	3.2%	0.5%	0.4%	0.0%	0.0%
Tulsa County	144,452	87.0%	13.0%	21,582	9.0%	2.9%	0.6%	0.4%	0.2%	0.0%
Oregon										
Clackamas County	83,697	91.6%	8.4%	7,680	2.4%	3.3%	1.9%	0.2%	0.3%	0.3%
Deschutes County	35,492	94.6%	5.4%	2,014	1.7%	2.9%	0.6%	0.0%	0.2%	0.0%
Douglas County	20,973	95.9%	4.1%	896	2.5%	0.0%	1.6%	0.0%	0.0%	0.0%
Jackson County	44,923	93.6%	6.4%	3,084	4.3%	0.6%	0.2%	0.0%	1.2%	0.3%
Lane County	95,137	93.8%	6.2%	6,276	2.9%	2.3%	0.3%	0.0%	0.3%	0.4%
Linn County	25,306	89.3%	10.7%	3,034	5.9%	3.9%	1.0%	0.0%	0.0%	0.0%
Marion County	71,007	82.9%	17.1%	14,643	11.5%	1.4%	0.6%	0.6%	0.5%	2.6%
Multnomah County	181,937	83.7%	16.3%	35,414	5.3%	5.3%	3.7%	1.0%	0.4%	0.6%
Washington County	118,768	80.0%	20.0%	29,653	9.3%	8.0%	1.3%	0.7%	0.5%	0.1%
Yamhill County	23,799	90.3%	9.7%	2,550	7.5%	1.9%	0.0%	0.3%	0.0%	0.0%
Pennsylvania										
Adams County	22,609	96.6%	3.4%	791	2.3%	0.4%	0.0%	0.0%	0.7%	0.0%
Allegheny County	291,122	91.6%	8.4%	26,543	0.7%	3.9%	1.5%	1.9%	0.3%	0.0%
Beaver County	36,914	98.6%	1.4%	518	0.5%	0.8%	0.1%	0.0%	0.0%	0.0%
Berks County	93,850	91.7%	8.3%	8,533	5.9%	1.5%	0.5%	0.4%	0.0%	0.0%
Blair County	28,310	98.8%	1.2%	335	0.0%	0.6%	0.6%	0.0%	0.0%	0.0%
Bucks County	121,756	90.5%	9.5%	12,766	3.1%	3.0%	2.4%	0.8%	0.2%	0.0%
Butler County	41,846	96.6%	3.4%	1,477	1.3%	1.0%	1.1%	0.0%	0.0%	0.0%
Cambria County	30,012	97.5%	2.5%	767	0.2%	2.1%	0.2%	0.0%	0.0%	0.0%
Centre County	58,951	87.9%	12.1%	8,108	1.3%	8.6%	1.5%	0.0%	0.7%	0.0%
Chester County	104,876	88.3%	11.7%	13,876	4.9%	4.8%	1.7%	0.2%	0.0%	0.1%
Cumberland County	56,604	93.1%	6.9%	4,208	0.4%	3.8%	1.9%	0.8%	0.0%	0.0%
Dauphin County	60,803	92.3%	7.7%	5,091	2.5%	3.7%	1.0%	0.5%	0.0%	0.0%
Delaware County	129,205	90.3%	9.7%	13,922	2.6%	2.9%	1.0%	3.0%	0.2%	0.1%
Erie County	66,510	93.6%	6.4%	4,522	0.9%	3.7%	1.0%	0.8%	0.0%	0.0%
Fayette County	27,481	98.0%	2.0%	575	0.8%	0.8%	0.1%	0.0%	0.3%	0.0%
Franklin County	33,639	96.9%	3.1%	1,060	0.7%	0.0%	2.2%	0.0%	0.1%	0.0%
Lackawanna County	48,442	95.4%	4.6%	2,330	1.5%	2.8%	0.3%	0.0%	0.0%	0.0%
Lancaster County	122,063	94.2%	5.8%	7,532	2.5%	1.6%	1.6%	0.0%	0.1%	0.0%
Lebanon County	28,949	97.3%	2.7%	797	1.1%	0.0%	0.6%	0.9%	0.0%	0.0%
Lehigh County	80,792	88.8%	11.2%	10,224	6.8%	3.9%	0.3%	0.2%	0.0%	0.0%
Luzerne County	71,813	95.0%	5.0%	3,793	2.9%	1.6%	0.2%	0.4%	0.0%	0.0%
Lycoming County	27,315	97.2%	2.8%	790	0.0%	1.7%	0.4%	0.0%	0.7%	0.0%
Mercer County	25,439	97.8%	2.2%	584	1.4%	0.5%	0.2%	0.0%	0.0%	0.0%
Monroe County	37,636	89.4%	10.6%	4,440	4.2%	1.3%	3.5%	0.5%	1.0%	0.0%
Montgomery County	164,542	88.4%	11.6%	21,585	3.4%	6.0%	1.5%	0.5%	0.1%	0.1%
Northampton County	66,243	91.2%	8.8%	6,384	1.8%	3.7%	3.2%	0.0%	0.1%	0.0%
Northumberland County	20,117	99.0%	1.0%	213	0.0%	0.0%	1.0%	0.0%	0.0%	0.0%
Philadelphia County	419,273	86.4%	13.6%	66,003	4.1%	5.6%	1.9%	1.7%	0.2%	0.0%
Schuylkill County	29,965	98.7%	1.3%	408	1.3%	0.0%	0.0%	0.1%	0.0%	0.0%
Washington County	44,283	96.3%	3.7%	1,704	1.5%	1.8%	0.3%	0.2%	0.0%	0.0%
Westmoreland County	72,525	97.7%	2.3%	1,686	0.4%	1.5%	0.3%	0.1%	0.0%	0.0%
York County	97,619	96.4%	3.6%	3,623	1.3%	1.0%	0.7%	0.5%	0.0%	0.0%

Table C-2: Counties—Nativity and World Region of Birth—*Continued*

	Total Millennial	Percent		Total Foreign Born	Percent of All Millennials by Region of Birth					
		Native	Foreign Born		Latin America	Asia	Europe	Africa	North America	Oceania
Rhode Island										
Kent County	35,870	95.0%	5.0%	1,901	1.7%	0.7%	2.4%	0.0%	0.3%	0.0%
Providence County	142,607	80.3%	19.7%	34,923	9.2%	5.6%	1.6%	2.5%	0.6%	0.2%
Washington County	31,465	96.7%	3.3%	1,057	0.8%	2.0%	0.4%	0.0%	0.0%	0.0%
South Carolina										
Aiken County	37,101	93.5%	6.5%	2,562	3.1%	1.3%	2.1%	0.0%	0.0%	0.0%
Anderson County	42,213	94.9%	5.1%	2,271	3.9%	0.8%	0.4%	0.0%	0.0%	0.0%
Beaufort County	37,207	88.2%	11.8%	4,992	9.4%	2.0%	0.5%	0.0%	0.0%	0.0%
Berkeley County	52,782	95.5%	4.5%	2,503	1.6%	1.2%	1.4%	0.2%	0.2%	0.0%
Charleston County	103,643	93.9%	6.1%	6,719	2.7%	1.6%	1.1%	0.2%	0.4%	0.1%
Dorchester County	38,565	96.8%	3.2%	1,268	0.8%	0.9%	1.3%	0.0%	0.2%	0.0%
Florence County	33,174	97.3%	2.7%	930	0.2%	1.4%	0.4%	0.0%	0.2%	0.6%
Greenville County	112,612	88.6%	11.4%	14,451	6.6%	2.8%	1.0%	0.2%	0.2%	0.5%
Horry County	62,503	90.2%	9.8%	6,757	3.5%	2.9%	3.0%	0.1%	0.3%	0.0%
Lexington County	62,392	90.0%	10.0%	6,898	6.6%	2.2%	1.1%	0.1%	0.0%	0.0%
Pickens County	37,639	96.0%	4.0%	1,576	2.0%	1.2%	0.6%	0.0%	0.2%	0.0%
Richland County	123,794	92.7%	7.3%	9,759	1.7%	2.5%	2.4%	0.5%	0.1%	0.0%
Spartanburg County	68,803	92.7%	7.3%	5,399	3.2%	0.7%	3.3%	0.1%	0.0%	0.0%
Sumter County	29,248	97.5%	2.5%	741	0.8%	1.0%	0.4%	0.0%	0.3%	0.0%
York County	56,574	92.7%	7.3%	4,439	2.7%	2.8%	1.1%	0.0%	0.6%	0.0%
South Dakota										
Minnehaha County	46,045	90.2%	9.8%	5,016	1.6%	4.1%	1.1%	2.7%	0.3%	0.0%
Pennington County	26,974	97.0%	3.0%	838	0.6%	0.0%	2.4%	0.0%	0.0%	0.0%
Tennessee										
Blount County	27,121	95.6%	4.4%	1,241	2.2%	1.2%	0.0%	1.0%	0.0%	0.0%
Bradley County	25,062	91.6%	8.4%	2,285	4.8%	1.2%	2.4%	0.0%	0.0%	0.0%
Davidson County	171,373	82.7%	17.3%	35,907	7.5%	4.3%	1.1%	4.2%	0.3%	0.0%
Hamilton County	82,611	92.8%	7.2%	6,401	3.7%	2.9%	0.5%	0.0%	0.0%	0.0%
Knox County	120,114	94.9%	5.1%	6,433	2.3%	1.6%	0.7%	0.0%	0.1%	0.3%
Madison County	23,829	94.9%	5.1%	1,290	2.5%	2.3%	0.3%	0.0%	0.0%	0.0%
Montgomery County	60,174	93.3%	6.7%	4,312	1.3%	2.7%	2.7%	0.1%	0.0%	0.0%
Rutherford County	81,193	90.1%	9.9%	8,961	4.6%	4.3%	0.7%	0.4%	0.0%	0.0%
Sevier County	19,565	91.6%	8.4%	1,790	4.1%	2.5%	1.4%	0.0%	0.4%	0.0%
Shelby County	231,758	90.9%	9.1%	23,209	4.2%	2.4%	1.2%	1.2%	0.1%	0.0%
Sullivan County	33,626	98.8%	1.2%	422	0.5%	0.1%	0.3%	0.3%	0.0%	0.0%
Sumner County	37,320	90.5%	9.5%	3,921	2.5%	1.7%	4.8%	0.5%	0.0%	0.0%
Washington County	30,843	91.8%	8.2%	2,764	3.7%	2.5%	1.8%	0.0%	0.2%	0.0%
Williamson County	40,504	96.2%	3.8%	1,599	1.0%	0.8%	1.6%	0.0%	0.5%	0.0%
Wilson County	26,961	95.6%	4.4%	1,253	1.7%	1.0%	1.1%	0.4%	0.2%	0.0%
Texas										
Bell County	92,148	87.5%	12.5%	13,177	6.7%	2.6%	3.1%	0.1%	0.1%	0.0%
Bexar County	469,166	86.5%	13.5%	73,211	8.7%	2.8%	1.7%	0.2%	0.1%	0.0%
Bowie County	22,715	98.7%	1.3%	310	1.3%	0.0%	0.0%	0.0%	0.0%	0.0%
Brazoria County	76,285	85.9%	14.1%	12,531	8.8%	3.9%	0.8%	0.3%	0.3%	0.0%
Brazos County	82,564	84.9%	15.1%	14,721	7.0%	7.4%	0.3%	0.1%	0.3%	0.1%
Cameron County	93,900	82.0%	18.0%	20,576	17.2%	0.6%	0.1%	0.0%	0.1%	0.0%
Collin County	168,085	77.4%	22.6%	49,187	7.0%	9.2%	2.2%	3.3%	0.8%	0.2%
Comal County	25,184	87.9%	12.1%	3,461	8.8%	0.7%	2.7%	0.0%	0.0%	0.0%
Dallas County	519,118	72.8%	27.2%	194,086	19.1%	5.4%	0.6%	1.9%	0.2%	0.0%
Denton County	178,786	85.0%	15.0%	31,645	7.3%	5.5%	0.8%	1.2%	0.2%	0.0%
Ector County	43,191	87.2%	12.8%	6,317	8.8%	1.7%	1.1%	1.2%	0.0%	0.0%
El Paso County	35,569	87.4%	12.6%	5,118	11.4%	0.9%	0.1%	0.2%	0.0%	0.0%
Ellis County	200,232	82.5%	17.5%	42,362	15.4%	1.2%	0.8%	0.0%	0.0%	0.0%
Fort Bend County	131,277	75.3%	24.7%	43,037	9.4%	11.6%	1.3%	2.0%	0.4%	0.0%
Galveston County	71,445	90.2%	9.8%	7,763	5.7%	2.8%	1.3%	0.0%	0.0%	0.0%
Grayson County	26,993	89.7%	10.3%	3,083	7.8%	1.0%	1.5%	0.0%	0.0%	0.0%
Gregg County	28,893	91.1%	8.9%	2,814	7.0%	0.2%	0.0%	1.6%	0.1%	0.0%
Guadalupe County	33,945	89.4%	10.6%	4,006	4.0%	1.8%	4.2%	0.0%	0.5%	0.0%
Harris County	927,833	72.9%	27.1%	344,525	18.1%	5.9%	1.1%	1.7%	0.2%	0.1%
Hays County	60,655	91.1%	8.9%	5,960	8.1%	0.3%	0.5%	0.0%	0.0%	0.0%
Hidalgo County	181,110	76.7%	23.3%	55,055	22.7%	0.4%	0.2%	0.0%	0.0%	0.1%
Jefferson County	58,126	85.5%	14.5%	9,863	10.5%	3.2%	0.6%	0.2%	0.0%	0.0%
Johnson County	35,922	91.5%	8.5%	3,350	7.0%	0.0%	0.3%	1.0%	0.0%	0.1%
Kaufman County	24,485	88.3%	11.7%	3,255	10.6%	0.8%	0.3%	0.0%	0.0%	0.0%
Lubbock County	93,774	91.6%	8.4%	8,625	2.8%	2.6%	2.1%	0.9%	0.0%	0.0%
McLennan County	66,771	89.2%	10.8%	8,070	7.9%	1.4%	0.4%	0.4%	0.6%	0.1%
Midland County	41,606	85.1%	14.9%	7,269	11.0%	3.2%	0.4%	0.0%	0.3%	0.0%
Montgomery County	110,228	85.7%	14.3%	18,376	10.4%	2.4%	0.8%	0.1%	0.6%	0.0%
Nueces County	91,876	91.4%	8.6%	8,664	5.2%	2.2%	0.7%	0.1%	0.1%	0.2%
Parker County	25,890	94.1%	5.9%	1,628	3.5%	0.2%	1.9%	0.0%	0.3%	0.0%
Potter County	26,835	83.1%	16.9%	5,458	12.8%	3.3%	0.8%	0.0%	0.0%	0.0%
Randall County	33,048	91.2%	8.8%	3,202	5.9%	2.6%	0.3%	0.0%	0.0%	0.0%
Smith County	57,392	94.5%	5.5%	3,311	4.6%	0.8%	0.1%	0.0%	0.0%	0.0%
Tarrant County	439,696	82.7%	17.3%	91,937	10.9%	3.6%	1.0%	1.7%	0.1%	0.0%
Taylor County	40,178	92.8%	7.2%	3,132	2.3%	2.2%	1.8%	0.8%	0.1%	0.0%
Tom Green County	33,539	93.8%	6.2%	2,226	3.3%	1.8%	0.5%	0.3%	0.0%	0.3%

Table C-2: Counties—Nativity and World Region of Birth—*Continued*

	Total Millennial	Percent		Total Foreign Born	Percent of All Millennials by Region of Birth					
		Native	Foreign Born		Latin America	Asia	Europe	Africa	North America	Oceania
Texas—Cont.										
Travis County	290,793	79.9%	20.1%	73,265	12.8%	5.0%	1.2%	0.8%	0.3%	0.0%
Webb County	56,380	74.0%	26.0%	19,826	25.7%	0.1%	0.0%	0.0%	0.2%	0.0%
Wichita County	37,145	89.8%	10.2%	4,200	7.0%	1.5%	0.9%	0.7%	0.0%	0.0%
Williamson County	107,588	87.6%	12.4%	15,210	6.6%	3.2%	1.6%	0.7%	0.2%	0.1%
Utah										
Cache County	40,828	91.6%	8.4%	3,722	4.8%	2.4%	0.4%	0.8%	0.0%	0.0%
Davis County	87,306	94.6%	5.4%	4,978	3.6%	0.4%	0.6%	0.3%	0.2%	0.2%
Salt Lake County	273,532	86.6%	13.4%	42,218	6.6%	3.6%	1.1%	1.2%	0.6%	0.3%
Utah County	180,063	91.4%	8.6%	16,838	5.1%	2.0%	0.9%	0.2%	0.1%	0.2%
Washington County	37,175	94.3%	5.7%	2,262	2.4%	0.1%	0.7%	2.2%	0.4%	0.0%
Weber County	60,601	88.7%	11.3%	7,683	8.7%	1.8%	0.6%	0.0%	0.1%	0.0%
Vermont										
Chittenden County	45,439	88.4%	11.6%	5,976	1.4%	3.2%	2.8%	3.0%	1.2%	0.0%
Virginia										
Albemarle County	24,960	85.5%	14.5%	4,237	4.2%	8.1%	1.8%	0.3%	0.0%	0.0%
Arlington County	58,481	75.5%	24.5%	19,013	10.4%	8.3%	3.4%	2.0%	0.1%	0.3%
Chesterfield County	74,380	91.7%	8.3%	6,720	4.1%	1.3%	2.3%	0.2%	0.3%	0.0%
Fairfax County	193,960	68.8%	31.2%	88,046	10.0%	15.2%	2.5%	3.3%	0.2%	0.0%
Hanover County	21,846	95.6%	4.4%	1,014	1.1%	1.9%	1.5%	0.0%	0.0%	0.0%
Henrico County	66,765	84.2%	15.8%	12,535	3.0%	8.5%	0.9%	3.0%	0.3%	0.0%
Loudoun County	60,601	71.6%	28.4%	24,009	8.6%	13.6%	2.2%	3.9%	0.1%	0.0%
Montgomery County	37,830	87.8%	12.2%	5,251	2.8%	5.9%	2.6%	1.0%	0.0%	0.0%
Prince William County	88,609	75.9%	24.1%	28,186	12.1%	6.9%	3.4%	1.4%	0.2%	0.1%
Roanoke County	19,952	92.7%	7.3%	1,578	2.7%	1.1%	2.2%	0.0%	1.4%	0.0%
Spotsylvania County	30,687	96.5%	3.5%	1,115	0.9%	0.4%	0.4%	1.7%	0.0%	0.0%
Stafford County	34,674	91.1%	8.9%	3,395	3.0%	3.9%	1.3%	0.3%	0.4%	0.0%
Washington										
Benton County	41,553	86.3%	13.7%	6,592	8.7%	3.1%	1.8%	0.0%	0.2%	0.0%
Clark County	99,768	87.4%	12.6%	14,427	4.9%	2.5%	4.5%	0.3%	0.1%	0.4%
Cowlitz County	20,269	87.9%	12.1%	2,784	10.7%	0.0%	1.0%	0.3%	0.0%	0.0%
Grant County	19,357	78.3%	21.7%	5,371	16.4%	3.5%	1.4%	0.4%	0.0%	0.0%
King County	426,032	75.0%	25.0%	142,052	5.6%	13.0%	3.6%	1.8%	0.8%	0.3%
Kitsap County	66,837	95.6%	4.4%	3,082	1.5%	2.3%	0.5%	0.0%	0.0%	0.1%
Pierce County	197,854	87.8%	12.2%	27,403	3.8%	4.1%	3.5%	0.5%	0.1%	0.2%
Skagit County	24,986	91.6%	8.4%	2,301	4.9%	2.2%	0.9%	0.0%	0.3%	0.1%
Snohomish County	156,323	81.3%	18.7%	36,001	5.5%	7.7%	3.1%	0.6%	0.9%	1.0%
Spokane County	123,042	90.7%	9.3%	12,586	0.8%	2.8%	3.4%	0.9%	0.7%	0.7%
Thurston County	60,356	89.6%	10.4%	6,974	3.6%	3.8%	2.8%	0.0%	0.2%	0.0%
Whatcom County	58,684	91.4%	8.6%	5,531	3.3%	2.4%	1.4%	0.0%	1.6%	0.0%
Yakima County	51,562	80.1%	19.9%	12,780	18.9%	0.0%	0.2%	0.3%	0.4%	0.0%
West Virginia										
Berkeley County	25,965	96.8%	3.2%	857	2.5%	0.0%	0.7%	0.0%	0.0%	0.0%
Cabell County	26,548	99.7%	0.3%	89	0.0%	0.3%	0.0%	0.0%	0.0%	0.0%
Kanawha County	39,465	97.0%	3.0%	1,205	0.4%	1.4%	0.0%	1.1%	0.0%	0.0%
Monongalia County	38,794	90.1%	9.9%	4,240	0.7%	8.7%	0.5%	0.0%	0.0%	0.0%
Wisconsin										
Brown County	59,484	91.1%	8.9%	5,792	7.7%	1.1%	0.0%	0.0%	0.0%	0.1%
Dane County	137,996	86.8%	13.2%	21,011	2.6%	7.3%	2.2%	0.6%	0.5%	0.0%
Eau Claire County	30,547	94.2%	5.8%	1,873	0.0%	5.5%	0.3%	0.0%	0.0%	0.0%
Fond du Lac County	23,659	97.9%	2.1%	503	1.8%	0.2%	0.1%	0.0%	0.0%	0.0%
Kenosha County	38,243	91.0%	9.0%	3,779	7.3%	1.3%	0.4%	0.0%	0.0%	0.0%
La Crosse County	34,364	96.0%	4.0%	1,439	0.8%	1.8%	1.4%	0.0%	0.0%	0.0%
Marathon County	27,279	92.5%	7.5%	2,213	2.2%	4.4%	0.9%	0.0%	0.0%	0.0%
Milwaukee County	240,163	89.8%	10.2%	27,387	5.3%	2.5%	1.5%	0.8%	0.1%	0.0%
Outagamie County	42,437	92.4%	7.6%	3,469	0.8%	6.6%	0.2%	0.0%	0.0%	0.0%
Racine County	44,450	97.7%	2.3%	1,054	1.4%	0.4%	0.0%	0.0%	0.5%	0.0%
Rock County	36,136	98.5%	1.5%	568	0.6%	0.4%	0.0%	0.5%	0.0%	0.0%
Sheboygan County	21,467	86.0%	14.0%	3,491	7.7%	3.9%	2.4%	0.0%	0.0%	0.0%
Walworth County	24,612	90.5%	9.5%	2,589	8.7%	0.0%	0.3%	0.1%	0.4%	0.0%
Washington County	26,975	97.7%	2.3%	630	0.0%	0.7%	1.2%	0.3%	0.0%	0.0%
Waukesha County	78,763	95.1%	4.9%	4,030	1.5%	2.6%	0.7%	0.0%	0.0%	0.0%
Winnebago County	44,963	96.1%	3.9%	1,824	0.3%	2.0%	1.6%	0.0%	0.0%	0.0%
Wyoming										
Laramie County	25,582	96.1%	3.9%	1,040	1.5%	1.2%	0.4%	0.7%	0.0%	0.0%

Table C-3: Places—Nativity and World Region of Birth

	Total Millennial	Percent		Total Foreign Born	Percent of All Millennials by Region of Birth					
		Native	Foreign Born		Latin America	Asia	Europe	Africa	North America	Oceania
Alabama										
Birmingham city	65,276	94.5%	5.5%	3,561	2.5%	1.8%	0.8%	0.6%	0.0%	0.0%
Huntsville city	50,582	92.9%	7.1%	3,596	4.3%	1.6%	2.0%	0.6%	0.1%	0.0%
Mobile city	54,926	95.6%	4.4%	2,396	1.4%	2.7%	0.8%	0.8%	0.0%	0.0%
Montgomery city	56,640	97.7%	2.3%	1,299	1.1%	0.6%	0.7%	0.0%	0.3%	0.0%
Tuscaloosa city	43,300	95.3%	4.7%	2,054	0.7%	3.7%	1.0%	0.2%	0.2%	0.0%
Alaska										
Anchorage municipality	92,449	89.1%	10.9%	10,083	2.0%	5.8%	2.6%	2.6%	0.5%	0.0%
Arizona										
Chandler city	68,912	86.3%	13.7%	9,416	3.9%	9.5%	0.9%	0.0%	0.4%	0.0%
Glendale city	67,526	82.6%	17.4%	11,749	9.9%	5.3%	1.8%	1.2%	0.1%	0.1%
Mesa city	128,122	88.4%	11.6%	14,823	8.9%	1.8%	0.6%	0.8%	0.5%	0.1%
Peoria city	42,034	92.5%	7.5%	3,162	4.6%	1.4%	2.4%	0.0%	0.0%	0.0%
Phoenix city	432,935	81.8%	18.2%	78,589	15.0%	2.7%	1.0%	1.1%	0.0%	0.2%
Scottsdale city	52,609	91.5%	8.5%	4,475	3.6%	3.4%	1.1%	0.6%	0.9%	0.0%
Surprise city	27,081	91.9%	8.1%	2,202	5.9%	3.2%	1.4%	0.2%	0.0%	0.0%
Tempe city	78,172	83.7%	16.3%	12,759	5.5%	10.3%	2.2%	0.7%	0.5%	0.0%
Tucson city	169,695	84.8%	15.2%	25,739	10.0%	3.9%	0.7%	1.2%	0.2%	0.3%
Yuma city	27,585	78.9%	21.1%	5,827	22.0%	0.3%	1.0%	0.5%	0.3%	0.0%
Arkansas										
Little Rock city	53,598	90.9%	9.1%	4,901	5.4%	3.7%	1.1%	0.2%	0.0%	0.0%
California										
Anaheim city	104,887	70.6%	29.4%	30,862	21.8%	7.3%	0.6%	0.2%	0.2%	0.0%
Antioch city	31,157	83.4%	16.6%	5,181	8.3%	8.3%	1.3%	0.5%	0.0%	0.0%
Bakersfield city	116,248	82.0%	18.0%	20,945	12.5%	5.6%	0.1%	0.2%	0.2%	0.1%
Berkeley city	49,498	75.5%	24.5%	12,126	3.3%	17.3%	4.6%	0.7%	0.6%	0.2%
Burbank city	27,930	75.5%	24.5%	6,833	4.8%	13.5%	4.5%	2.6%	0.0%	0.6%
Carlsbad city	25,879	88.1%	11.9%	3,082	4.1%	6.8%	0.0%	0.7%	0.5%	0.0%
Chico city	35,558	91.8%	8.2%	2,911	4.2%	3.9%	0.5%	0.0%	0.0%	0.0%
Carson city	26,003	81.0%	19.0%	4,943	6.4%	12.3%	0.8%	0.6%	0.0%	0.0%
Chula Vista city	73,367	81.2%	18.8%	13,817	15.4%	5.4%	0.2%	0.0%	0.0%	0.2%
Clovis city	26,306	89.4%	10.6%	2,776	3.3%	6.2%	1.7%	0.0%	0.0%	0.0%
Compton city	30,522	80.7%	19.3%	5,901	19.7%	0.3%	0.0%	0.4%	0.0%	0.0%
Concord city	30,735	79.0%	21.0%	6,455	12.9%	9.0%	2.5%	0.0%	0.3%	1.1%
Corona city	42,345	81.9%	18.1%	7,658	13.1%	3.2%	0.9%	2.0%	0.0%	0.0%
Costa Mesa city	36,378	85.0%	15.0%	5,449	8.0%	5.6%	0.0%	1.7%	0.6%	0.4%
Daly City city	29,604	68.8%	31.2%	9,248	9.5%	20.7%	1.6%	0.0%	1.0%	0.3%
Downey city	33,813	81.7%	18.3%	6,191	14.6%	4.3%	0.0%	0.0%	0.0%	0.0%
El Cajon city	30,072	76.9%	23.1%	6,958	4.5%	18.1%	0.0%	0.7%	0.0%	0.4%
Elk Grove city	41,650	84.3%	15.7%	6,522	1.7%	13.8%	0.6%	0.2%	0.0%	0.2%
El Monte city	33,568	69.1%	30.9%	10,379	18.5%	12.8%	0.4%	0.0%	0.0%	0.0%
Escondido city	47,202	74.2%	25.8%	12,170	20.6%	4.8%	0.9%	1.5%	0.4%	0.1%
Fairfield city	31,243	75.9%	24.1%	7,528	15.2%	10.9%	0.0%	0.0%	0.7%	0.9%
Fontana city	63,986	84.0%	16.0%	10,251	14.4%	2.9%	0.0%	0.0%	0.0%	0.0%
Fremont city	58,826	56.8%	43.2%	25,403	4.2%	36.2%	1.3%	0.3%	0.3%	1.7%
Fresno city	160,820	82.2%	17.8%	28,646	10.6%	6.4%	1.0%	0.1%	0.4%	0.0%
Fullerton city	43,980	76.3%	23.7%	10,441	13.4%	10.7%	0.3%	0.2%	0.0%	0.0%
Garden Grove city	47,042	69.9%	30.1%	14,175	10.2%	19.6%	0.5%	0.6%	0.4%	0.0%
Glendale city	49,189	57.3%	42.7%	21,012	4.9%	34.3%	3.6%	0.0%	0.4%	0.1%
Hayward city	47,670	68.6%	31.4%	14,962	16.4%	12.5%	1.2%	0.1%	0.6%	1.6%
Hesperia city	27,100	91.4%	8.6%	2,341	7.4%	1.3%	0.0%	0.0%	0.0%	0.0%
Huntington Beach city	44,399	83.0%	17.0%	7,567	8.8%	6.3%	1.1%	2.2%	0.0%	0.0%
Inglewood city	31,703	81.5%	18.5%	5,871	16.7%	0.3%	0.0%	2.1%	0.0%	0.0%
Irvine city	83,108	64.5%	35.5%	29,472	3.3%	27.3%	2.2%	1.8%	1.6%	1.1%
Jurupa Valley city	29,976	86.1%	13.9%	4,153	8.3%	5.5%	1.4%	0.2%	0.0%	0.0%
Lancaster city	49,208	94.7%	5.3%	2,632	3.7%	1.3%	0.2%	0.4%	0.0%	0.0%
Long Beach city	137,426	79.8%	20.2%	27,787	14.2%	5.7%	0.6%	0.3%	0.3%	0.0%
Los Angeles city	1,208,578	71.8%	28.2%	341,366	17.6%	8.7%	2.2%	0.5%	0.4%	0.1%
Mission Viejo city	22,309	89.0%	11.0%	2,450	3.9%	5.8%	2.6%	0.0%	0.0%	0.0%
Modesto city	57,185	89.4%	10.6%	6,075	6.2%	3.7%	0.7%	0.8%	0.0%	0.5%
Moreno Valley city	66,439	86.5%	13.5%	8,964	9.8%	4.0%	0.2%	0.5%	0.0%	0.1%
Murrieta city	30,451	91.2%	8.8%	2,692	3.8%	7.1%	0.5%	0.0%	0.0%	0.2%
Norwalk city	30,689	78.9%	21.1%	6,471	15.3%	5.8%	0.0%	0.0%	0.0%	0.0%
Oakland city	122,337	74.9%	25.1%	30,672	14.9%	7.7%	1.3%	1.8%	0.3%	0.3%
Oceanside city	45,355	89.2%	10.8%	4,896	6.1%	5.0%	0.4%	0.8%	0.0%	0.0%
Ontario city	51,531	80.3%	19.7%	10,145	13.8%	6.0%	0.5%	0.0%	0.0%	0.0%
Orange city	44,072	80.1%	19.9%	8,766	13.5%	5.4%	1.5%	0.0%	0.2%	0.1%
Oxnard city	62,289	72.5%	27.5%	17,160	24.8%	3.0%	0.3%	0.0%	0.0%	0.0%
Palmdale city	42,360	85.5%	14.5%	6,161	13.1%	1.2%	0.3%	0.7%	0.0%	0.0%
Pasadena city	36,762	77.3%	22.7%	8,327	13.7%	6.1%	1.9%	0.0%	1.4%	0.0%
Pomona city	48,713	76.7%	23.3%	11,367	13.4%	10.0%	0.0%	0.1%	0.0%	0.0%
Rancho Cucamonga city	50,125	92.4%	7.6%	3,834	1.6%	4.3%	1.7%	0.2%	0.6%	0.3%
Redding city	24,840	91.0%	9.0%	2,228	0.7%	2.0%	5.4%	0.0%	0.0%	1.4%
Rialto city	32,854	76.3%	23.7%	7,776	20.5%	4.1%	0.0%	0.0%	0.3%	0.0%
Richmond city	32,546	60.9%	39.1%	12,731	23.5%	17.2%	1.6%	0.2%	0.2%	0.0%

Table C-3: Places—Nativity and World Region of Birth—*Continued*

	Total Millennial	Percent		Total Foreign Born	Percent of All Millennials by Region of Birth					
		Native	Foreign Born		Latin America	Asia	Europe	Africa	North America	Oceania
California—Cont.										
Riverside city	108,944	83.2%	16.8%	18,259	13.0%	3.7%	0.7%	0.2%	0.0%	0.0%
Roseville city	32,596	89.7%	10.3%	3,367	2.2%	8.7%	1.0%	0.0%	0.4%	0.3%
Sacramento city	142,256	77.8%	22.2%	31,545	9.7%	10.1%	2.3%	1.4%	0.2%	0.9%
Salinas city	45,235	65.9%	34.1%	15,426	31.7%	2.3%	0.1%	0.0%	0.5%	0.0%
San Bernardino city	68,511	76.3%	23.7%	16,256	18.9%	5.4%	0.0%	0.2%	0.0%	0.0%
San Buenaventura (Ventura) city	27,629	84.9%	15.1%	4,173	13.0%	1.2%	0.0%	0.0%	0.4%	0.4%
San Diego city	445,012	80.0%	20.0%	89,076	8.4%	8.7%	2.9%	0.9%	0.4%	0.2%
San Francisco city	258,717	76.2%	23.8%	61,455	4.9%	15.1%	3.2%	1.0%	1.0%	0.2%
San Jose city	269,874	70.9%	29.1%	78,536	12.2%	16.8%	1.3%	0.5%	0.2%	0.1%
San Leandro city	22,760	78.4%	21.6%	4,911	2.2%	18.8%	2.4%	0.0%	0.4%	0.0%
San Marcos city	24,402	77.7%	22.3%	5,431	16.9%	7.8%	0.5%	0.0%	0.0%	0.0%
San Mateo city	24,437	65.0%	35.0%	8,561	12.5%	19.5%	4.0%	0.5%	0.0%	0.6%
Santa Ana city	101,668	63.8%	36.2%	36,851	31.1%	4.8%	0.0%	0.5%	0.0%	0.1%
Santa Clara city	39,593	56.5%	43.5%	17,228	4.6%	37.2%	1.8%	0.9%	0.4%	0.3%
Santa Clarita city	47,773	82.2%	17.8%	8,487	8.5%	7.9%	1.5%	1.4%	0.1%	0.0%
Santa Maria city	30,556	69.3%	30.7%	9,383	29.4%	1.2%	0.1%	0.0%	0.2%	0.0%
Santa Monica city	24,672	89.4%	10.6%	2,627	1.8%	3.5%	4.7%	0.0%	1.0%	0.0%
Santa Rosa city	44,446	78.8%	21.2%	9,439	14.0%	5.2%	1.6%	0.6%	0.0%	0.0%
Simi Valley city	32,740	89.4%	10.6%	3,466	3.6%	7.5%	0.2%	0.0%	0.0%	0.0%
South Gate city	28,277	76.9%	23.1%	6,528	22.5%	0.7%	0.0%	0.0%	0.0%	0.0%
Stockton city	91,948	78.4%	21.6%	19,817	12.7%	9.0%	0.4%	0.7%	0.0%	0.0%
Sunnyvale city	41,801	50.9%	49.1%	20,527	8.7%	34.7%	3.0%	1.2%	1.5%	0.8%
Temecula city	30,276	93.6%	6.4%	1,927	3.0%	2.6%	2.0%	0.0%	0.0%	0.4%
Thousand Oaks city	26,301	84.1%	15.9%	4,177	9.0%	6.9%	2.1%	0.0%	0.0%	0.0%
Torrance city	35,250	81.0%	19.0%	6,685	4.3%	13.5%	0.2%	0.9%	0.0%	0.0%
Vacaville city	26,462	90.5%	9.5%	2,523	7.2%	2.3%	1.5%	0.0%	0.5%	0.0%
Vallejo city	33,732	83.2%	16.8%	5,678	7.4%	9.5%	0.3%	0.0%	0.0%	0.0%
Victorville city	36,736	91.6%	8.4%	3,075	7.1%	1.3%	0.7%	0.0%	0.0%	0.0%
Visalia city	33,963	86.9%	13.1%	4,453	9.8%	2.1%	0.2%	0.3%	0.4%	0.7%
Vista city	31,575	84.2%	15.8%	4,984	13.7%	3.2%	0.4%	0.4%	0.0%	0.3%
West Covina city	29,341	84.1%	15.9%	4,670	9.6%	6.7%	0.0%	0.0%	0.7%	0.0%
Westminster city	21,766	70.9%	29.1%	6,338	11.4%	17.3%	0.0%	0.9%	0.0%	0.3%
Colorado										
Arvada city	25,827	95.0%	5.0%	1,281	4.4%	0.3%	1.4%	0.2%	0.2%	0.0%
Aurora city	102,094	82.3%	17.7%	18,095	10.5%	4.6%	1.5%	3.2%	0.3%	0.1%
Boulder city	50,704	90.5%	9.5%	4,042	3.0%	4.3%	2.5%	0.0%	1.4%	0.0%
Centennial city	24,786	90.3%	9.7%	2,416	1.4%	7.7%	2.3%	1.1%	0.7%	0.0%
Colorado Springs city	132,077	92.8%	7.2%	9,547	3.9%	2.1%	2.2%	0.9%	0.2%	0.1%
Denver city	217,281	83.8%	16.2%	35,186	10.7%	4.0%	1.5%	1.2%	0.5%	0.1%
Fort Collins city	64,784	93.2%	6.8%	4,411	2.8%	2.9%	3.0%	0.1%	0.3%	0.0%
Greeley city	32,325	92.0%	8.0%	2,580	7.3%	1.1%	0.4%	0.6%	0.2%	0.0%
Lakewood city	44,017	93.0%	7.0%	3,075	3.4%	1.1%	1.9%	0.6%	0.7%	0.0%
Longmont city	21,632	90.1%	9.9%	2,140	12.1%	1.0%	1.5%	0.0%	0.0%	1.8%
Pueblo city	29,065	97.6%	2.4%	707	1.7%	0.3%	1.1%	0.0%	0.0%	0.0%
Thornton city	34,916	81.9%	18.1%	6,331	16.0%	1.7%	0.4%	0.0%	0.0%	0.0%
Westminster city	30,054	91.0%	9.0%	2,694	5.6%	3.3%	1.3%	0.2%	0.0%	0.1%
Connecticut										
Bridgeport city	43,968	70.4%	29.6%	13,035	20.8%	7.1%	2.3%	0.0%	0.3%	0.0%
Hartford city	44,108	76.3%	23.7%	10,465	16.4%	5.1%	2.5%	0.7%	0.3%	0.0%
New Haven city	52,463	78.5%	21.5%	11,302	15.9%	4.3%	1.1%	0.8%	0.9%	0.3%
Stamford city	38,194	65.9%	34.1%	13,038	17.9%	11.7%	4.4%	0.8%	0.7%	0.2%
Waterbury city	28,106	81.0%	19.0%	5,344	14.7%	0.4%	3.9%	2.8%	0.5%	0.0%
District of Columbia										
Washington city	236,132	85.7%	14.3%	33,759	4.7%	5.1%	2.8%	1.9%	0.7%	0.2%
Florida										
Boca Raton city	21,653	77.3%	22.7%	4,926	18.7%	3.6%	1.8%	0.5%	0.0%	0.0%
Cape Coral city	37,325	87.6%	12.4%	4,617	11.8%	0.0%	1.4%	1.0%	0.0%	0.0%
Clearwater city	25,001	84.1%	15.9%	3,970	11.9%	2.9%	2.7%	0.9%	0.0%	0.0%
Coral Springs city	32,839	75.9%	24.1%	7,911	19.6%	3.0%	1.6%	0.2%	0.2%	0.0%
Fort Lauderdale city	40,875	69.0%	31.0%	12,669	27.8%	1.6%	1.5%	1.1%	0.2%	0.0%
Gainesville city	66,238	88.2%	11.8%	7,844	5.7%	5.3%	2.3%	0.3%	0.2%	0.0%
Hialeah city	54,580	37.8%	62.2%	33,922	62.7%	0.0%	0.1%	0.0%	0.0%	0.0%
Hollywood city	32,699	69.1%	30.9%	10,088	24.6%	5.7%	2.4%	0.2%	0.0%	0.0%
Jacksonville city	236,574	90.2%	9.8%	23,111	4.4%	4.0%	2.5%	0.2%	0.4%	0.1%
Lakeland city	27,759	90.5%	9.5%	2,631	7.4%	2.1%	0.5%	0.0%	0.0%	0.0%
Miami city	110,351	55.1%	44.9%	49,511	43.1%	0.4%	2.1%	0.2%	0.4%	0.0%
Miami Beach city	21,815	58.0%	42.0%	9,154	28.5%	3.1%	11.8%	0.1%	0.0%	0.0%
Miami Gardens city	30,931	76.3%	23.7%	7,320	25.7%	0.5%	0.7%	0.0%	0.0%	0.0%
Miramar city	34,640	71.8%	28.2%	9,764	26.3%	3.7%	0.4%	0.0%	0.0%	0.0%
Orlando city	91,969	80.5%	19.5%	17,959	14.8%	2.8%	1.7%	1.2%	0.4%	0.0%
Palm Bay city	23,931	92.4%	7.6%	1,828	5.8%	2.3%	0.0%	0.0%	0.0%	0.0%
Pembroke Pines city	41,693	69.7%	30.3%	12,638	26.0%	4.2%	1.1%	0.2%	0.0%	0.0%
Plantation city	21,871	65.1%	34.9%	7,635	30.3%	5.1%	1.1%	0.8%	0.0%	0.0%
Pompano Beach city	24,729	73.1%	26.9%	6,659	23.5%	2.7%	0.8%	0.2%	0.3%	0.0%
Port St. Lucie city	39,093	84.5%	15.5%	6,058	12.6%	2.1%	0.4%	0.4%	0.0%	0.0%

Table C-3: Places—Nativity and World Region of Birth—Continued

	Total Millennial	Percent		Total Foreign Born	Percent of All Millennials by Region of Birth					
		Native	Foreign Born		Latin America	Asia	Europe	Africa	North America	Oceania
California—Cont.										
St. Petersburg city	62,378	90.4%	9.6%	5,986	4.5%	4.0%	1.8%	0.4%	0.2%	0.0%
Sunrise city	25,017	66.6%	33.4%	8,351	27.2%	5.0%	2.6%	0.7%	0.0%	0.0%
Tallahassee city	90,224	92.2%	7.8%	7,064	3.7%	2.7%	1.3%	1.0%	0.6%	0.0%
Tampa city	109,385	85.5%	14.5%	15,852	11.0%	2.6%	1.0%	0.8%	0.7%	0.1%
West Palm Beach city	27,920	74.7%	25.3%	7,060	21.4%	4.1%	0.8%	0.2%	0.0%	0.0%
Georgia										
Athens-Clarke County unified govt (balance)	54,663	90.9%	9.1%	4,976	5.6%	3.7%	1.2%	0.2%	0.0%	0.1%
Atlanta city	160,144	90.2%	9.8%	15,733	2.4%	5.2%	2.0%	0.6%	0.5%	0.0%
Augusta-Richmond County consolidated govt (balance)	59,362	97.5%	2.5%	1,468	0.4%	2.0%	3.2%	0.0%	0.0%	0.0%
Columbus city	61,108	93.2%	6.8%	4,142	3.5%	3.2%	1.4%	0.1%	0.0%	0.0%
Macon-Bibb county	40,814	95.7%	4.3%	1,773	2.3%	1.6%	1.4%	0.9%	0.0%	0.0%
Roswell city	20,927	81.1%	18.9%	3,947	7.8%	4.2%	1.4%	4.7%	1.5%	0.0%
Sandy Springs city	30,066	75.5%	24.5%	7,376	6.3%	10.7%	6.5%	1.8%	0.6%	0.0%
Savannah city	55,172	94.0%	6.0%	3,310	3.6%	1.8%	1.3%	0.7%	0.1%	0.0%
Hawaii										
Urban Honolulu CDP	84,598	79.4%	20.6%	17,394	1.2%	17.9%	0.8%	0.1%	0.1%	3.3%
Idaho										
Boise City city	62,159	91.4%	8.6%	5,356	2.8%	3.6%	2.6%	0.0%	0.3%	0.0%
Meridian city	17,705	86.6%	13.4%	2,366	3.7%	4.6%	4.4%	0.0%	0.7%	0.0%
Illinois										
Aurora city	55,022	72.7%	27.3%	15,016	21.3%	2.2%	1.3%	3.2%	0.0%	0.0%
Chicago city	861,024	82.1%	17.9%	154,525	8.4%	6.2%	2.9%	1.3%	0.2%	0.0%
Elgin city	26,488	69.0%	31.0%	8,213	24.5%	5.5%	1.6%	0.0%	0.0%	0.0%
Joliet city	39,858	87.7%	12.3%	4,903	11.4%	0.5%	0.7%	0.2%	0.0%	0.0%
Naperville city	33,918	88.0%	12.0%	4,069	3.8%	5.7%	1.8%	1.1%	0.0%	0.0%
Peoria city	34,871	95.7%	4.3%	1,485	0.5%	3.1%	0.6%	0.2%	0.0%	0.0%
Rockford city	40,012	85.5%	14.5%	5,784	8.7%	3.6%	1.2%	0.9%	0.0%	0.0%
Springfield city	31,951	94.1%	5.9%	1,884	1.4%	3.9%	0.2%	0.2%	0.4%	0.0%
Indiana										
Evansville city	32,735	97.1%	2.9%	943	0.7%	1.0%	1.0%	0.2%	0.1%	0.0%
Fort Wayne city	70,772	90.8%	9.2%	6,493	4.8%	4.4%	0.1%	0.0%	0.2%	0.1%
Indianapolis city (balance)	244,048	89.1%	10.9%	26,536	6.6%	2.9%	0.8%	0.8%	0.4%	0.2%
South Bend city	29,483	92.3%	7.7%	2,277	5.0%	2.3%	0.8%	1.5%	0.0%	0.0%
Iowa										
Cedar Rapids city	35,359	89.4%	10.6%	3,734	1.7%	7.7%	1.2%	0.4%	0.0%	0.0%
Davenport city	27,789	98.4%	1.6%	433	0.6%	2.9%	0.0%	0.0%	0.0%	0.0%
Des Moines city	62,827	87.9%	12.1%	7,619	4.4%	5.1%	2.2%	2.8%	0.0%	0.1%
Kansas										
Kansas City city	40,363	78.9%	21.1%	8,513	14.6%	3.8%	0.7%	2.1%	0.2%	0.0%
Olathe city	33,638	90.8%	9.2%	3,099	5.3%	2.8%	0.0%	1.1%	0.3%	0.0%
Overland Park city	45,901	89.2%	10.8%	4,971	1.7%	9.0%	0.3%	1.3%	0.0%	0.0%
Topeka city	33,790	97.6%	2.4%	799	1.6%	1.0%	0.6%	0.5%	0.0%	0.0%
Wichita city	105,291	91.7%	8.3%	8,713	4.4%	2.6%	0.8%	1.0%	0.0%	0.0%
Kentucky										
Lexington-Fayette urban county	99,204	89.8%	10.2%	10,151	4.6%	5.0%	1.0%	0.2%	0.2%	0.0%
Louisville/Jefferson County metro govt (balance)	158,771	88.9%	11.1%	17,643	4.9%	3.6%	2.5%	1.1%	0.1%	0.2%
Louisiana										
Baton Rouge city	81,142	90.7%	9.3%	7,560	4.3%	5.2%	0.7%	0.1%	0.1%	0.0%
Lafayette city	44,471	95.6%	4.4%	1,964	1.4%	3.0%	0.0%	0.0%	0.0%	0.0%
New Orleans city	116,032	95.2%	4.8%	5,625	2.0%	1.9%	1.0%	0.3%	0.3%	0.1%
Shreveport city	54,837	96.4%	3.6%	1,992	2.4%	1.2%	1.2%	0.0%	0.0%	0.0%
Maryland										
Baltimore city	191,864	90.6%	9.4%	17,951	3.9%	3.6%	2.2%	0.9%	0.1%	0.0%
Massachusetts										
Boston city	266,782	75.8%	24.2%	64,616	10.8%	7.5%	3.4%	3.2%	0.9%	0.3%
Brockton city	27,045	68.1%	31.9%	8,620	9.9%	2.4%	0.9%	19.6%	0.0%	0.0%
Cambridge city	51,938	72.3%	27.7%	14,390	5.1%	14.0%	7.5%	1.8%	1.5%	0.0%
Lowell city	35,014	66.1%	33.9%	11,868	7.8%	19.1%	2.2%	5.5%	0.7%	0.0%
Lynn city	25,352	66.9%	33.1%	8,399	24.2%	4.1%	3.3%	2.5%	0.4%	0.0%
New Bedford city	25,304	84.7%	15.3%	3,881	7.1%	5.3%	2.1%	1.5%	0.0%	0.0%
Quincy city	24,780	72.1%	27.9%	6,915	3.1%	22.3%	3.0%	0.2%	0.0%	0.0%
Springfield city	46,972	90.7%	9.3%	4,354	5.9%	3.2%	0.7%	0.3%	0.2%	0.0%
Worcester city	62,036	81.2%	18.8%	11,651	4.7%	7.1%	2.5%	5.2%	0.3%	0.0%
Michigan										
Ann Arbor city	57,080	86.0%	14.0%	7,977	0.6%	10.6%	3.7%	0.3%	0.7%	0.0%
Dearborn city	25,414	76.6%	23.4%	5,948	0.4%	23.4%	0.7%	3.0%	0.4%	0.0%
Detroit city	189,160	92.9%	7.1%	13,481	3.6%	3.2%	0.8%	0.6%	0.4%	0.0%
Flint city	25,633	96.4%	3.6%	913	0.5%	1.2%	0.0%	2.4%	0.0%	0.0%
Grand Rapids city	64,132	88.2%	11.8%	7,585	6.6%	4.2%	1.1%	0.9%	0.8%	0.2%
Lansing city	38,419	94.8%	5.2%	1,995	0.4%	5.0%	0.2%	0.1%	0.2%	0.0%

Table C-3: Places—Nativity and World Region of Birth—*Continued*

	Total Millennial	Percent		Total Foreign Born	Percent of All Millennials by Region of Birth					
		Native	Foreign Born		Latin America	Asia	Europe	Africa	North America	Oceania
Michigan—Cont.										
Livonia city	20,481	98.6%	1.4%	280	0.0%	2.3%	0.8%	0.0%	0.0%	0.0%
Sterling Heights city	32,628	78.0%	22.0%	7,193	0.4%	15.2%	6.5%	0.0%	1.2%	0.0%
Warren city	31,442	93.3%	6.7%	2,097	1.5%	7.2%	0.4%	0.0%	0.3%	0.0%
Minnesota										
Minneapolis city	147,877	80.5%	19.5%	28,874	4.8%	6.3%	2.5%	6.6%	0.3%	0.2%
Rochester city	30,983	87.6%	12.4%	3,847	2.1%	7.5%	1.2%	0.9%	1.1%	0.6%
St. Paul city	99,544	78.6%	21.4%	21,337	4.3%	13.5%	0.2%	3.9%	0.0%	0.0%
Mississippi										
Jackson city	52,989	98.0%	2.0%	1,056	0.4%	1.0%	0.5%	0.9%	0.0%	0.0%
Missouri										
Columbia city	55,488	93.1%	6.9%	3,801	0.5%	3.1%	1.0%	2.7%	0.0%	0.0%
Independence city	28,662	94.2%	5.8%	1,656	1.5%	3.5%	0.0%	0.3%	0.4%	0.0%
Kansas City city	128,225	91.2%	8.8%	11,347	5.3%	2.5%	1.4%	0.6%	0.1%	0.2%
Lee's Summit city	22,012	98.0%	2.0%	450	0.5%	1.0%	0.0%	0.5%	0.0%	0.0%
St. Louis city	98,295	89.8%	10.2%	10,000	2.9%	5.1%	0.5%	2.1%	0.3%	0.0%
Springfield city	60,490	94.5%	5.5%	3,355	1.9%	2.7%	1.6%	0.4%	0.2%	0.0%
Montana										
Billings city	30,086	95.7%	4.3%	1,285	2.3%	1.9%	0.0%	0.0%	0.2%	0.0%
Nebraska										
Lincoln city	90,424	88.1%	11.9%	10,742	2.4%	7.4%	0.0%	1.9%	0.0%	0.1%
Omaha city	129,660	86.4%	13.6%	17,611	7.4%	3.9%	0.7%	2.3%	0.0%	0.1%
Nevada										
Henderson city	61,057	87.7%	12.3%	7,537	4.6%	8.6%	1.1%	0.8%	0.0%	0.0%
Las Vegas city	158,295	80.5%	19.5%	30,940	14.3%	5.0%	0.9%	0.3%	0.3%	0.0%
North Las Vegas city	67,041	83.0%	17.0%	11,387	15.2%	3.1%	0.7%	0.1%	0.1%	0.2%
Reno city	68,801	88.4%	11.6%	7,951	6.6%	5.0%	0.6%	0.3%	0.0%	0.2%
Sparks city	24,437	88.1%	11.9%	2,901	8.8%	3.0%	0.0%	1.2%	0.0%	0.0%
New Hampshire										
Manchester city	30,293	85.5%	14.5%	4,394	6.0%	3.4%	3.6%	3.2%	0.0%	0.0%
New Jersey										
Elizabeth city	34,801	55.3%	44.7%	15,545	44.8%	0.7%	0.9%	1.5%	0.5%	0.0%
Jersey City city	82,952	55.4%	44.6%	37,030	13.2%	24.7%	1.2%	6.5%	0.3%	0.0%
Newark city	79,653	72.5%	27.5%	21,924	20.2%	2.5%	1.5%	4.8%	0.1%	0.0%
Paterson city	41,192	72.3%	27.7%	11,400	23.0%	4.7%	0.0%	1.9%	0.0%	0.0%
New Mexico										
Albuquerque city	151,120	88.1%	11.9%	17,937	8.4%	3.5%	1.3%	0.8%	0.5%	0.0%
Las Cruces city	30,485	91.2%	8.8%	2,684	6.3%	3.3%	0.0%	1.3%	0.0%	0.0%
Rio Rancho city	23,555	94.2%	5.0%	1,376	5.4%	2.0%	0.0%	0.0%	0.3%	0.0%
New York										
Albany city	37,519	87.1%	12.9%	4,832	0.9%	7.9%	2.1%	2.5%	0.0%	0.0%
Buffalo city	81,428	89.6%	10.4%	8,456	1.8%	5.8%	1.9%	1.6%	0.3%	0.0%
New York city	2,469,069	69.5%	30.5%	752,984	15.9%	10.4%	3.8%	1.7%	0.5%	0.3%
Rochester city	71,818	90.3%	9.7%	6,963	2.6%	5.4%	1.6%	1.3%	0.2%	0.0%
Syracuse city	53,473	85.0%	15.0%	8,000	3.2%	9.5%	0.8%	2.6%	0.5%	0.0%
Yonkers city	50,984	77.0%	23.0%	11,703	20.0%	2.6%	3.3%	0.0%	0.5%	0.0%
North Carolina										
Charlotte city	239,744	82.7%	17.3%	41,514	9.9%	5.0%	1.6%	1.5%	0.4%	0.0%
Durham city	81,450	79.1%	20.9%	17,008	10.6%	6.5%	1.3%	2.9%	0.2%	0.0%
Fayetteville city	69,316	95.7%	4.3%	2,998	3.3%	1.4%	4.1%	0.9%	0.1%	0.0%
Greensboro city	83,708	89.1%	10.9%	9,115	7.1%	2.3%	1.4%	0.7%	0.1%	0.4%
High Point city	29,830	87.0%	13.0%	3,872	7.2%	5.3%	0.6%	0.0%	0.0%	0.0%
Raleigh city	149,042	86.5%	13.5%	20,052	6.2%	4.5%	1.9%	1.0%	0.1%	0.1%
Wilmington city	37,892	94.2%	5.8%	2,216	3.4%	1.1%	2.1%	1.1%	0.1%	0.0%
Winston-Salem city	69,003	86.3%	13.7%	9,439	8.7%	3.3%	0.2%	1.6%	0.3%	0.0%
North Dakota										
Fargo city	44,861	93.1%	6.9%	3,078	1.3%	3.1%	0.9%	1.8%	0.4%	0.0%
Ohio										
Akron city	54,257	96.0%	4.0%	2,154	0.0%	3.7%	0.3%	0.1%	0.0%	0.0%
Cincinnati city	102,382	92.2%	7.8%	7,973	1.6%	3.9%	1.4%	1.3%	0.2%	0.1%
Cleveland city	110,836	93.6%	6.4%	7,113	0.9%	4.9%	0.4%	0.4%	0.0%	0.0%
Columbus city	281,922	87.2%	12.8%	36,191	3.4%	5.0%	1.0%	3.9%	0.1%	0.1%
Dayton city	45,452	92.0%	8.0%	3,657	2.1%	3.1%	2.5%	0.3%	0.0%	0.0%
Toledo city	80,265	95.4%	4.6%	3,664	0.1%	2.9%	0.3%	1.4%	0.0%	0.0%
Oklahoma										
Broken Arrow city	25,634	87.8%	12.2%	3,123	10.8%	1.3%	0.5%	0.0%	0.8%	0.0%
Edmond city	27,188	93.4%	6.6%	1,807	1.5%	5.2%	0.0%	0.0%	0.0%	0.0%
Lawton city	30,368	96.1%	3.9%	1,180	2.0%	2.1%	1.8%	0.0%	0.0%	0.0%
Norman city	46,393	90.9%	9.1%	4,243	2.3%	4.4%	0.3%	2.4%	0.0%	0.0%
Oklahoma City city	171,575	86.2%	13.8%	23,606	10.5%	3.3%	0.7%	0.3%	0.0%	0.0%
Tulsa city	112,612	87.8%	12.2%	13,761	7.4%	4.4%	0.7%	0.5%	0.3%	0.0%

Table C-3: Places—Nativity and World Region of Birth—*Continued*

	Total Millennial	Percent		Total Foreign Born	Percent of All Millennials by Region of Birth					
		Native	Foreign Born		Latin America	Asia	Europe	Africa	North America	Oceania
Oregon										
Beaverton city	28,218	78.5%	21.5%	6,063	12.2%	10.6%	1.7%	0.0%	0.0%	0.0%
Eugene city	57,375	93.5%	6.5%	3,732	3.1%	3.0%	0.6%	0.0%	0.5%	0.3%
Gresham city	27,972	77.7%	22.3%	6,251	13.0%	3.4%	4.1%	0.8%	0.0%	1.6%
Hillsboro city	27,426	75.7%	24.3%	6,662	10.5%	12.8%	1.8%	0.0%	0.0%	0.6%
Portland city	180,671	85.9%	14.1%	25,504	4.3%	5.7%	3.4%	1.1%	0.5%	0.8%
Salem city	46,098	81.1%	18.9%	8,704	14.7%	2.7%	0.3%	0.5%	0.0%	1.7%
Pennsylvania										
Allentown city	34,851	84.9%	15.1%	5,256	14.4%	0.9%	0.1%	0.0%	0.0%	0.0%
Erie city	28,758	93.1%	6.9%	1,997	1.0%	4.1%	1.9%	1.6%	0.0%	0.0%
Philadelphia city	485,771	87.4%	12.6%	61,021	4.1%	5.6%	1.9%	1.7%	0.2%	0.0%
Pittsburgh city	118,026	88.1%	11.9%	13,987	1.3%	6.9%	2.3%	1.7%	0.7%	0.0%
Rhode Island										
Providence city	66,314	69.4%	30.6%	20,259	17.4%	8.9%	1.7%	2.6%	0.5%	0.5%
South Carolina										
Charleston city	45,908	95.9%	4.1%	1,881	1.3%	1.3%	0.7%	0.1%	0.9%	0.2%
Columbia city	60,087	92.3%	7.7%	4,633	2.2%	3.8%	3.2%	1.0%	0.3%	0.0%
North Charleston city	36,486	91.5%	8.5%	3,115	6.2%	2.3%	1.7%	0.2%	0.2%	0.0%
South Dakota										
Sioux Falls city	48,646	87.9%	12.1%	5,909	2.3%	4.8%	2.3%	2.8%	0.3%	0.0%
Tennessee										
Chattanooga city	50,693	93.9%	6.1%	3,105	3.5%	3.7%	0.4%	0.0%	0.0%	0.0%
Clarksville city	53,597	95.6%	4.4%	2,348	1.4%	3.2%	2.5%	0.1%	0.0%	0.0%
Knoxville city	65,226	94.1%	5.9%	3,836	3.1%	1.8%	0.6%	0.0%	0.2%	0.7%
Memphis city	187,750	92.9%	7.1%	13,415	4.8%	1.7%	1.1%	1.1%	0.1%	0.0%
Murfreesboro city	45,897	94.7%	5.3%	2,416	4.5%	1.6%	0.2%	0.3%	0.0%	0.0%
Nashville-Davidson metropolitan govt (balance)	204,893	83.8%	16.2%	33,144	7.3%	4.2%	1.1%	4.2%	0.3%	0.0%
Texas										
Abilene city	43,601	95.4%	4.6%	2,024	2.3%	2.2%	1.7%	0.8%	0.1%	0.0%
Allen city	22,320	80.7%	19.3%	4,307	5.3%	7.4%	3.2%	3.5%	0.0%	0.0%
Amarillo city	53,022	88.6%	11.4%	6,056	8.3%	3.5%	0.7%	0.0%	0.0%	0.0%
Arlington city	117,582	81.2%	18.8%	22,141	10.6%	5.8%	0.7%	2.5%	0.1%	0.0%
Austin city	318,545	80.2%	19.8%	62,923	13.0%	5.6%	1.2%	0.5%	0.4%	0.0%
Beaumont city	34,816	88.1%	11.9%	4,143	7.1%	4.3%	0.7%	0.3%	0.0%	0.0%
Brownsville city	53,320	81.2%	18.8%	10,044	19.1%	0.1%	0.2%	0.0%	0.0%	0.0%
Carrollton city	34,297	73.2%	26.8%	9,193	12.7%	10.8%	1.5%	2.9%	0.2%	0.0%
College Station city	59,465	85.1%	14.9%	8,889	7.5%	8.1%	0.4%	0.1%	0.3%	0.0%
Corpus Christi city	91,539	92.7%	7.3%	6,641	4.7%	2.2%	0.8%	0.1%	0.2%	0.2%
Dallas city	383,991	71.7%	28.3%	108,634	21.9%	3.9%	0.8%	2.4%	0.2%	0.0%
Denton city	53,139	87.5%	12.5%	6,657	4.7%	5.9%	0.6%	2.1%	0.4%	0.0%
El Paso city	191,550	85.0%	15.0%	28,725	14.5%	1.3%	0.9%	0.0%	0.0%	0.0%
Fort Worth city	234,187	83.3%	16.7%	39,052	13.1%	2.4%	0.7%	1.3%	0.1%	0.0%
Frisco city	29,311	82.4%	17.6%	5,150	9.7%	3.8%	3.1%	2.4%	0.8%	0.0%
Garland city	62,780	76.0%	24.0%	15,086	15.1%	7.5%	0.7%	1.8%	0.1%	0.0%
Grand Prairie city	53,813	73.0%	27.0%	14,539	22.1%	4.2%	0.3%	1.5%	0.0%	0.0%
Houston city	694,760	69.5%	30.5%	211,711	20.1%	7.3%	1.2%	2.4%	0.3%	0.1%
Irving city	71,697	63.4%	36.6%	26,251	19.9%	14.2%	0.3%	2.3%	0.8%	0.0%
Killeen city	47,750	90.0%	10.0%	4,797	6.6%	3.5%	3.0%	0.1%	0.0%	0.0%
Laredo city	73,722	76.1%	23.9%	17,616	25.5%	0.1%	0.0%	0.0%	0.2%	0.0%
Lewisville city	33,171	76.0%	24.0%	7,951	14.4%	10.4%	1.0%	0.0%	0.0%	0.0%
Lubbock city	90,665	92.6%	7.4%	6,749	3.0%	2.7%	2.4%	0.9%	0.0%	0.0%
McAllen city	39,474	82.0%	18.0%	7,111	17.1%	2.1%	0.2%	0.0%	0.0%	0.4%
McKinney city	38,625	84.2%	15.8%	6,106	11.6%	2.8%	1.8%	0.0%	1.4%	0.0%
Mesquite city	38,987	73.2%	26.8%	10,438	20.5%	4.1%	0.5%	2.2%	0.0%	0.0%
Midland city	40,199	85.6%	14.4%	5,770	12.4%	2.2%	0.5%	0.0%	0.2%	0.0%
Odessa city	36,951	88.5%	11.5%	4,266	8.9%	1.5%	1.0%	1.3%	0.0%	0.0%
Pasadena city	41,599	75.2%	24.8%	10,328	24.7%	1.3%	0.7%	0.0%	0.0%	0.0%
Pearland city	28,993	90.2%	9.8%	2,855	3.1%	9.1%	0.8%	0.0%	0.0%	0.0%
Plano city	70,607	72.2%	27.8%	19,655	6.8%	14.4%	2.0%	4.7%	1.2%	0.3%
Richardson city	31,827	62.8%	37.2%	11,841	15.9%	12.7%	0.8%	7.1%	1.4%	0.0%
Round Rock City	31,178	89.9%	10.1%	3,155	6.6%	2.0%	2.3%	1.4%	0.6%	0.0%
San Angelo city	32,118	94.4%	5.6%	1,795	3.7%	1.9%	0.6%	0.3%	0.0%	0.3%
San Antonio city	435,615	88.0%	12.0%	52,431	9.7%	2.6%	1.2%	0.3%	0.1%	0.0%
Tyler city	31,668	92.2%	7.8%	2,469	6.8%	1.1%	0.0%	0.0%	0.0%	0.0%
Waco city	45,423	88.7%	11.3%	5,124	9.9%	1.5%	0.0%	0.7%	0.0%	0.0%
Wichita Falls city	33,545	91.3%	8.7%	2,930	6.5%	1.9%	0.8%	0.9%	0.0%	0.0%
Utah										
Orem city	34,882	86.0%	14.0%	4,879	7.1%	6.1%	1.0%	1.2%	0.0%	1.0%
Provo city	63,221	93.8%	6.2%	3,912	5.2%	1.1%	1.1%	0.0%	0.2%	0.2%
Salt Lake City city	70,936	86.7%	13.3%	9,457	6.4%	4.8%	1.6%	0.7%	1.0%	0.4%
Sandy city	23,301	89.7%	10.3%	2,396	3.8%	5.3%	2.8%	0.0%	0.8%	0.0%
West Jordan city	32,488	90.9%	9.1%	2,956	2.8%	4.1%	0.0%	1.2%	1.5%	0.0%
West Valley City city	41,728	86.5%	13.5%	5,616	10.1%	3.5%	0.3%	0.6%	0.2%	0.4%

Table C-3: Places—Nativity and World Region of Birth—*Continued*

| | Total Millennial | Percent | | Total Foreign Born | Percent of All Millennials by Region of Birth | | | | | |
		Native	Foreign Born		Latin America	Asia	Europe	Africa	North America	Oceania
Virginia										
Alexandria city	43,452	66.5%	33.5%	14,572	12.3%	10.2%	4.2%	9.6%	0.0%	0.0%
Chesapeake city	63,149	93.3%	6.7%	4,261	5.8%	1.2%	0.2%	0.1%	0.2%	0.2%
Hampton city	40,233	96.6%	3.4%	1,361	0.3%	2.2%	1.1%	1.3%	0.4%	0.0%
Newport News city	58,525	94.5%	5.5%	3,210	2.7%	3.3%	2.6%	0.4%	0.0%	0.0%
Norfolk city	95,849	94.7%	5.3%	5,054	2.5%	2.6%	1.2%	0.4%	0.0%	0.1%
Portsmouth city	29,069	98.5%	1.5%	424	0.6%	0.9%	0.2%	0.0%	0.0%	0.0%
Richmond city	76,850	91.5%	8.5%	6,547	4.7%	3.0%	1.5%	0.8%	0.4%	0.0%
Roanoke city	26,140	92.1%	7.9%	2,077	3.2%	2.3%	0.2%	2.3%	0.0%	0.0%
Virginia Beach city	132,947	93.6%	6.4%	8,448	2.0%	4.4%	3.0%	0.1%	0.4%	0.0%
Washington										
Bellevue city	37,913	53.6%	46.4%	17,584	5.3%	32.9%	6.5%	2.1%	1.8%	0.3%
Everett city	30,503	82.9%	17.1%	5,230	6.3%	4.8%	2.9%	0.0%	2.4%	3.7%
Federal Way city	26,673	76.3%	23.7%	6,312	14.0%	7.6%	2.9%	0.6%	0.0%	0.0%
Kent city	40,119	68.1%	31.9%	12,801	15.1%	10.7%	2.3%	4.7%	0.0%	0.1%
Renton city	24,731	70.0%	30.0%	7,429	9.7%	12.9%	4.1%	2.6%	0.2%	1.8%
Seattle city	236,331	82.1%	17.9%	42,324	2.9%	11.3%	2.8%	1.6%	0.7%	0.4%
Spokane city	61,887	93.6%	6.4%	3,934	0.8%	3.0%	2.1%	0.8%	1.4%	1.2%
Spokane Valley city	24,796	91.3%	8.7%	2,157	0.4%	0.7%	9.6%	0.0%	0.5%	0.0%
Tacoma city	58,809	90.9%	9.1%	5,328	4.0%	3.6%	3.1%	0.4%	0.1%	0.0%
Vancouver city	44,929	83.9%	16.1%	7,235	9.1%	2.7%	4.5%	0.6%	0.1%	0.2%
Yakima city	25,386	80.8%	19.2%	4,876	18.8%	0.0%	0.6%	0.4%	0.4%	0.0%
Wisconsin										
Green Bay city	30,607	86.1%	13.9%	4,255	12.2%	1.7%	0.0%	0.0%	0.0%	0.0%
Kenosha city	25,028	91.9%	8.1%	2,032	6.6%	1.5%	0.7%	0.0%	0.0%	0.0%
Madison city	101,061	87.2%	12.8%	12,972	1.7%	8.0%	2.9%	0.6%	0.3%	0.0%
Milwaukee city	186,306	90.5%	9.5%	17,695	6.4%	2.8%	0.8%	0.8%	0.1%	0.0%

Table C-4: Metropolitan/Micropolitan Statistical Areas—Nativity and World Region of Birth

	Total Millennial	Percent		Total Foreign Born	Percent of All Millennials by Region of Birth					
		Native	Foreign Born		Latin America	Asia	Europe	Africa	North America	Oceania
Abilene, TX	50,234	93.2%	6.8%	3,425	2.5%	2.0%	1.5%	0.7%	0.1%	0.0%
Adrian, MI	22,899	98.2%	1.8%	404	0.7%	0.5%	0.0%	0.0%	0.6%	0.0%
Akron, OH	178,555	93.9%	6.1%	10,964	1.4%	3.3%	1.4%	0.0%	0.0%	0.0%
Albany, GA	39,484	97.7%	2.3%	904	0.6%	1.6%	0.0%	0.0%	0.1%	0.0%
Albany, OR	28,485	88.8%	11.2%	3,179	6.3%	3.8%	1.0%	0.0%	0.0%	0.0%
Albany-Schenectady-Troy, NY	232,952	91.2%	8.8%	20,516	1.9%	4.3%	1.4%	0.8%	0.3%	0.0%
Albertville, AL	21,899	90.7%	9.3%	2,034	7.4%	0.9%	0.9%	0.0%	0.0%	0.0%
Albuquerque, NM	233,207	87.3%	12.7%	29,703	8.2%	2.6%	0.9%	0.6%	0.4%	0.0%
Alexandria, LA	38,875	97.3%	2.7%	1,040	0.5%	0.8%	0.7%	0.6%	0.0%	0.0%
Allentown-Bethlehem-Easton, PA-NJ	194,803	90.6%	9.4%	18,382	4.4%	3.5%	1.4%	0.1%	0.0%	0.0%
Altoona, PA	29,180	98.9%	1.1%	335	0.0%	0.6%	0.6%	0.0%	0.0%	0.0%
Amarillo, TX	71,925	87.0%	13.0%	9,378	9.4%	2.9%	0.7%	0.0%	0.0%	0.0%
Ames, IA	45,468	88.0%	12.0%	5,449	0.0%	11.1%	0.2%	0.3%	0.4%	0.0%
Anchorage, AK	123,015	89.1%	10.9%	13,463	1.7%	4.4%	2.6%	1.9%	0.3%	0.0%
Ann Arbor, MI	123,278	88.8%	11.2%	13,778	0.4%	7.2%	2.3%	0.5%	0.8%	0.0%
Anniston-Oxford-Jacksonville, AL	30,590	96.0%	4.0%	1,216	0.0%	1.5%	2.1%	0.3%	0.0%	0.0%
Appleton, WI	58,416	93.4%	6.6%	3,832	1.1%	5.3%	0.2%	0.0%	0.0%	0.0%
Asheville, NC	92,784	89.8%	10.2%	9,432	5.7%	1.7%	2.7%	0.1%	0.1%	0.0%
Ashtabula, OH	22,614	98.9%	1.1%	251	0.0%	1.1%	0.0%	0.0%	0.0%	0.0%
Athens-Clarke County, GA	72,553	91.5%	8.5%	6,162	4.7%	2.7%	0.8%	0.1%	0.1%	0.1%
Atlanta-Sandy Springs-Roswell, GA	1,464,745	84.3%	15.7%	229,436	7.3%	4.2%	1.7%	2.1%	0.3%	0.0%
Atlantic City-Hammonton, NJ	66,498	82.1%	17.9%	11,914	9.5%	6.0%	1.4%	1.1%	0.0%	0.0%
Auburn-Opelika, AL	54,789	95.1%	4.9%	2,686	2.8%	1.8%	0.2%	0.1%	0.0%	0.0%
Augusta-Richmond County, GA-SC	159,165	94.7%	5.3%	8,412	1.7%	1.4%	2.2%	0.0%	0.0%	0.0%
Augusta-Waterville, ME	25,926	96.2%	3.8%	992	0.0%	2.2%	0.2%	1.4%	0.0%	0.0%
Austin-Round Rock, TX	586,533	83.3%	16.7%	97,819	10.8%	3.8%	1.2%	0.6%	0.3%	0.0%
Bakersfield, CA	255,273	83.2%	16.8%	42,810	12.7%	3.6%	0.3%	0.1%	0.1%	0.1%
Baltimore-Columbia-Towson, MD	713,900	87.7%	12.3%	88,067	4.4%	4.6%	1.7%	1.5%	0.1%	0.0%
Bangor, ME	40,856	95.4%	4.6%	1,868	0.0%	2.3%	1.0%	0.3%	1.0%	0.0%
Barnstable Town, MA	37,022	89.8%	10.2%	3,761	4.0%	1.0%	1.9%	3.2%	0.0%	0.0%
Baton Rouge, LA	239,352	94.4%	5.6%	13,411	2.4%	2.8%	0.3%	0.1%	0.0%	0.0%
Battle Creek, MI	31,922	96.3%	3.7%	1,181	1.0%	2.3%	0.3%	0.0%	0.0%	0.0%
Bay City, MI	24,229	96.8%	3.2%	776	2.0%	0.4%	0.8%	0.0%	0.0%	0.0%
Beaumont-Port Arthur, TX	107,613	89.7%	10.3%	11,096	7.1%	2.5%	0.6%	0.1%	0.0%	0.0%
Beckley, WV	26,400	98.1%	1.9%	510	0.4%	1.1%	0.4%	0.0%	0.0%	0.0%
Bellingham, WA	64,215	91.4%	8.6%	5,531	3.3%	2.4%	1.4%	0.0%	1.6%	0.0%
Bend-Redmond, OR	37,506	94.6%	5.4%	2,014	1.7%	2.9%	0.6%	0.0%	0.2%	0.0%
Billings, MT	40,628	96.5%	3.5%	1,435	1.7%	1.4%	0.3%	0.0%	0.1%	0.0%
Binghamton, NY	66,508	92.8%	7.2%	4,817	1.0%	4.9%	1.3%	0.0%	0.1%	0.0%
Birmingham-Hoover, AL	285,663	94.3%	5.7%	16,154	2.9%	1.5%	0.6%	0.6%	0.1%	0.0%
Bismarck, ND	34,187	96.3%	3.7%	1,249	0.0%	0.2%	2.9%	0.0%	0.6%	0.0%
Blacksburg-Christiansburg-Radford, VA	65,831	89.4%	10.6%	6,979	1.8%	5.7%	2.1%	0.8%	0.2%	0.0%
Bloomington, IL	61,716	93.8%	6.2%	3,812	1.7%	3.8%	0.4%	0.0%	0.2%	0.0%
Bloomington, IN	67,026	89.5%	10.5%	7,020	0.8%	7.8%	1.2%	0.1%	0.6%	0.0%
Bloomsburg-Berwick, PA	23,536	97.3%	2.7%	636	0.3%	2.1%	0.2%	0.0%	0.0%	0.0%
Boise City, ID	173,741	91.9%	8.1%	13,993	3.6%	2.4%	1.8%	0.1%	0.2%	0.0%
Boston-Cambridge-Newton, MA-NH	1,270,242	80.1%	19.9%	252,586	7.8%	6.9%	2.4%	2.1%	0.6%	0.1%
Boulder, CO	98,666	88.1%	11.9%	11,700	5.2%	3.2%	1.8%	0.4%	1.0%	0.4%
Bowling Green, KY	48,473	90.8%	9.2%	4,473	3.1%	4.5%	1.4%	0.2%	0.0%	0.0%
Bremerton-Silverdale, WA	69,919	95.6%	4.4%	3,082	1.5%	2.3%	0.5%	0.0%	0.0%	0.1%
Bridgeport-Stamford-Norwalk, CT	223,389	77.3%	22.7%	50,802	14.5%	4.7%	3.0%	0.2%	0.3%	0.1%
Brownsville-Harlingen, TX	113,745	82.0%	18.0%	20,466	17.2%	0.7%	0.1%	0.0%	0.1%	0.0%
Brunswick, GA	26,627	95.1%	4.9%	1,301	3.1%	1.5%	0.3%	0.0%	0.0%	0.0%
Buffalo-Cheektowaga-Niagara Falls, NY	286,861	91.7%	8.3%	23,753	1.3%	4.5%	1.5%	0.7%	0.3%	0.0%
Burlington, NC	37,828	86.6%	13.4%	5,063	11.3%	0.8%	1.0%	0.0%	0.3%	0.0%
Burlington-South Burlington, VT	64,031	88.8%	11.2%	7,198	1.1%	2.9%	2.5%	3.8%	1.0%	0.0%
California-Lexington Park, MD	28,974	93.6%	6.4%	1,849	3.6%	2.3%	0.2%	0.3%	0.0%	0.0%
Canton-Massillon, OH	93,640	97.2%	2.8%	2,630	1.4%	0.7%	0.2%	0.0%	0.5%	0.0%
Cape Coral-Fort Myers, FL	142,244	79.7%	20.3%	28,943	17.0%	1.1%	1.1%	0.5%	0.8%	0.0%
Cape Girardeau, MO-IL	25,928	97.6%	2.4%	624	0.0%	1.1%	1.3%	0.0%	0.0%	0.0%
Carbondale-Marion, IL	39,218	95.2%	4.8%	1,889	1.1%	3.6%	0.0%	0.0%	0.1%	0.0%
Carson City, NV	11,558	90.6%	9.4%	1,084	9.4%	0.0%	0.0%	0.0%	0.0%	0.0%
Casper, WY	20,678	98.8%	1.2%	240	1.2%	0.0%	0.0%	0.0%	0.0%	0.0%
Cedar Rapids, IA	65,970	92.9%	7.1%	4,663	1.4%	4.3%	0.8%	0.5%	0.0%	0.0%
Chambersburg-Waynesboro, PA	34,854	96.7%	3.3%	1,158	1.0%	0.0%	2.2%	0.0%	0.1%	0.0%
Champaign-Urbana, IL	89,066	83.7%	16.3%	14,499	1.9%	11.4%	2.3%	0.5%	0.2%	0.0%
Charleston, WV	46,810	97.4%	2.6%	1,205	0.4%	1.2%	0.0%	1.0%	0.0%	0.0%
Charleston-North Charleston, SC	204,724	93.5%	6.5%	13,234	3.2%	1.4%	1.4%	0.2%	0.3%	0.1%
Charlotte-Concord-Gastonia, NC-SC	604,040	88.0%	12.0%	72,226	6.6%	3.1%	1.2%	0.7%	0.3%	0.0%
Charlottesville, VA	67,057	87.5%	12.5%	8,404	3.5%	6.3%	1.9%	0.8%	0.0%	0.0%
Chattanooga, TN-GA	137,823	93.7%	6.3%	8,692	3.2%	2.1%	0.5%	0.2%	0.2%	0.0%
Cheyenne, WY	27,461	96.2%	3.8%	1,056	1.5%	1.2%	0.4%	0.7%	0.0%	0.1%
Chicago-Naperville-Elgin, IL-IN-WI	2,504,124	83.1%	16.9%	422,890	8.0%	4.9%	2.9%	0.9%	0.2%	0.0%
Chico, CA	66,585	92.9%	7.1%	4,759	2.5%	3.9%	0.6%	0.0%	0.2%	0.0%
Cincinnati, OH-KY-IN	542,779	93.3%	6.7%	36,139	1.9%	2.6%	1.2%	0.8%	0.3%	0.0%
Clarksburg, WV	19,685	99.6%	0.4%	74	0.0%	0.1%	0.3%	0.0%	0.0%	0.0%
Clarksville, TN-KY	91,109	94.2%	5.8%	5,314	1.0%	2.1%	2.6%	0.0%	0.1%	0.0%

Table C-4: Metropolitan/Micropolitan Statistical Areas—Nativity and World Region of Birth—*Continued*

	Total Millennial	Percent		Total Foreign Born	Percent of All Millennials by Region of Birth					
		Native	Foreign Born		Latin America	Asia	Europe	Africa	North America	Oceania
Cleveland, TN	30,847	91.7%	8.3%	2,547	5.0%	1.0%	2.2%	0.0%	0.0%	0.0%
Cleveland-Elyria, OH	484,581	93.1%	6.9%	33,471	1.1%	3.9%	1.6%	0.2%	0.2%	0.0%
Coeur d'Alene, ID	35,105	98.1%	1.9%	664	0.2%	0.1%	1.0%	0.0%	0.6%	0.0%
College Station-Bryan, TX	100,404	85.4%	14.6%	14,616	7.0%	6.8%	0.3%	0.1%	0.3%	0.1%
Colorado Springs, CO	202,070	91.5%	8.5%	17,252	3.5%	1.9%	2.2%	0.6%	0.1%	0.2%
Columbia, MO	65,947	92.2%	7.8%	5,159	0.6%	3.9%	1.1%	2.3%	0.0%	0.0%
Columbia, SC	228,727	92.5%	7.5%	17,185	3.0%	2.2%	1.8%	0.3%	0.1%	0.0%
Columbus, GA-AL	93,090	92.6%	7.4%	6,852	3.7%	2.4%	1.2%	0.0%	0.0%	0.0%
Columbus, IN	20,841	87.5%	12.5%	2,596	6.4%	6.1%	0.0%	0.0%	0.0%	0.0%
Columbus, OH	545,703	90.6%	9.4%	51,210	2.1%	3.8%	1.0%	2.4%	0.1%	0.0%
Concord, NH	26,150	94.9%	5.1%	1,322	0.4%	3.9%	0.7%	0.0%	0.0%	0.0%
Cookeville, TN	30,681	89.3%	10.7%	3,281	3.9%	5.3%	1.1%	0.4%	0.0%	0.0%
Corpus Christi, TX	119,621	91.5%	8.5%	10,213	5.4%	2.2%	0.6%	0.1%	0.1%	0.2%
Corvallis, OR	32,589	88.6%	11.4%	3,709	6.5%	3.4%	1.1%	0.0%	0.4%	0.0%
Crestview-Fort Walton Beach-Destin, FL	69,335	89.8%	10.2%	7,088	2.7%	2.6%	4.7%	0.0%	0.2%	0.1%
Cumberland, MD-WV	26,249	97.9%	2.1%	563	0.2%	0.8%	0.9%	0.2%	0.0%	0.0%
Dallas-Fort Worth-Arlington, TX	1,874,485	79.5%	20.5%	385,044	12.8%	4.8%	0.9%	1.7%	0.2%	0.0%
Dalton, GA	37,337	79.4%	20.6%	7,706	18.6%	1.7%	0.0%	0.3%	0.0%	0.0%
Danville, IL	18,480	97.3%	2.7%	501	1.7%	1.0%	0.0%	0.0%	0.0%	0.0%
Danville, VA	22,276	96.6%	3.4%	749	2.0%	0.3%	1.1%	0.0%	0.0%	0.0%
Daphne-Fairhope-Foley, AL	41,881	95.4%	4.6%	1,915	3.5%	0.1%	0.5%	0.0%	0.5%	0.0%
Davenport-Moline-Rock Island, IA IL	91,165	94.4%	5.6%	5,141	1.6%	2.5%	0.2%	1.3%	0.0%	0.0%
Dayton, OH	198,327	93.9%	6.1%	12,113	1.0%	2.8%	1.2%	1.0%	0.1%	0.0%
Decatur, AL	35,433	95.7%	4.3%	1,535	3.6%	0.8%	0.0%	0.0%	0.0%	0.0%
Decatur, IL	24,600	95.8%	4.2%	1,035	2.5%	1.6%	0.1%	0.0%	0.0%	0.0%
Deltona-Daytona Beach-Ormond Beach, FL	132,761	91.2%	8.8%	11,644	3.0%	3.4%	1.5%	0.2%	0.6%	0.0%
Denver-Aurora-Lakewood, CO	745,375	86.0%	14.0%	104,481	7.6%	3.5%	1.4%	1.1%	0.4%	0.0%
Des Moines-West Des Moines, IA	164,874	89.0%	11.0%	18,078	3.4%	3.5%	1.8%	2.2%	0.0%	0.0%
Detroit-Warren-Dearborn, MI	1,027,782	90.0%	10.0%	103,205	1.8%	5.7%	1.7%	0.4%	0.4%	0.0%
Dothan, AL	34,274	95.6%	4.4%	1,524	2.9%	0.8%	0.6%	0.0%	0.1%	0.0%
Dover, DE	46,169	94.0%	6.0%	2,754	3.5%	1.3%	1.0%	0.2%	0.0%	0.0%
Dubuque, IA	25,588	95.7%	4.3%	1,096	0.0%	2.3%	1.1%	0.0%	0.0%	0.9%
Duluth, MN-WI	72,709	97.8%	2.2%	1,626	0.7%	1.0%	0.4%	0.1%	0.1%	0.0%
Dunn, NC	35,041	90.0%	10.0%	3,514	6.6%	0.7%	2.4%	0.3%	0.0%	0.0%
Durham-Chapel Hill, NC	161,733	82.4%	17.6%	28,451	8.4%	5.6%	0.8%	2.4%	0.2%	0.1%
East Stroudsburg, PA	42,076	89.4%	10.6%	4,440	4.2%	1.3%	3.5%	0.5%	1.0%	0.0%
Eau Claire, WI	47,724	95.8%	4.2%	2,016	0.0%	3.8%	0.2%	0.2%	0.0%	0.0%
El Centro, CA	49,791	76.9%	23.1%	11,519	22.4%	0.4%	0.3%	0.0%	0.0%	0.0%
El Paso, TX	37,272	95.0%	5.0%	1,849	0.4%	2.0%	2.6%	0.0%	0.0%	0.0%
Elizabethtown-Fort Knox, KY	51,393	92.5%	7.5%	3,852	6.8%	0.4%	0.3%	0.0%	0.0%	0.0%
Elkhart-Goshen, IN	20,951	96.7%	3.3%	701	1.9%	1.4%	0.0%	0.0%	0.0%	0.0%
Elmira, NY	243,628	82.5%	17.5%	42,655	15.5%	1.2%	0.8%	0.0%	0.0%	0.0%
Erie, PA	71,032	93.6%	6.4%	4,522	0.9%	3.7%	1.0%	0.8%	0.0%	0.0%
Eugene, OR	101,020	93.8%	6.2%	6,276	2.9%	2.3%	0.3%	0.0%	0.3%	0.4%
Eureka-Arcata-Fortuna, CA	38,052	95.7%	4.3%	1,637	2.5%	0.7%	0.6%	0.0%	0.5%	0.0%
Evansville, IN-KY	77,662	96.5%	3.5%	2,730	0.6%	2.0%	0.6%	0.1%	0.0%	0.2%
Fairbanks, AK	34,834	89.7%	10.3%	3,586	0.4%	4.7%	4.8%	0.4%	0.0%	0.0%
Fargo, ND-MN	76,111	91.3%	8.7%	6,610	1.2%	3.1%	1.4%	2.7%	0.3%	0.0%
Farmington, NM	30,632	96.2%	3.8%	1,157	2.4%	0.1%	1.1%	0.0%	0.0%	0.2%
Fayetteville, NC	114,794	91.8%	8.2%	9,379	2.9%	1.0%	3.3%	0.7%	0.1%	0.2%
Fayetteville-Springdale-Rogers, AR-MO	145,133	84.4%	15.6%	22,570	10.1%	3.1%	0.6%	0.2%	0.1%	1.5%
Flagstaff, AZ	51,771	95.2%	4.8%	2,510	0.6%	3.0%	0.8%	0.2%	0.2%	0.0%
Flint, MI	96,273	95.7%	4.3%	4,108	0.4%	2.0%	0.7%	0.8%	0.4%	0.0%
Florence, SC	49,298	98.1%	1.9%	930	0.1%	1.0%	0.3%	0.0%	0.1%	0.4%
Florence-Muscle Shoals, AL	34,708	96.5%	3.5%	1,220	2.2%	0.9%	0.0%	0.4%	0.0%	0.0%
Fond du Lac, WI	24,678	98.0%	2.0%	503	1.7%	0.2%	0.1%	0.0%	0.0%	0.0%
Fort Collins, CO	103,634	91.6%	8.4%	8,743	2.4%	2.7%	2.7%	0.0%	0.5%	0.0%
Fort Smith, AR-OK	68,405	89.6%	10.4%	7,143	7.9%	1.5%	0.2%	0.7%	0.0%	0.1%
Fort Wayne, IN	110,786	92.4%	7.6%	8,454	3.9%	3.0%	0.3%	0.1%	0.3%	0.1%
Fresno, CA	280,870	80.3%	19.7%	55,443	13.7%	4.9%	0.8%	0.0%	0.3%	0.0%
Gadsden, AL	22,502	97.6%	2.4%	531	1.7%	0.6%	0.0%	0.1%	0.0%	0.0%
Gainesville, FL	102,661	87.6%	12.4%	12,679	4.2%	5.2%	2.0%	0.5%	0.5%	0.1%
Gainesville, GA	48,649	77.8%	22.2%	10,786	19.8%	1.5%	0.4%	0.4%	0.0%	0.0%
Gettysburg, PA	23,400	96.6%	3.4%	791	2.3%	0.4%	0.0%	0.0%	0.7%	0.0%
Glens Falls, NY	26,846	96.4%	3.6%	967	1.2%	0.4%	1.0%	0.2%	0.9%	0.0%
Goldsboro, NC	32,804	87.6%	12.4%	4,072	8.0%	2.0%	1.5%	0.0%	0.9%	0.0%
Grand Forks, ND-MN	36,405	90.4%	9.6%	3,479	0.7%	2.4%	2.7%	2.9%	1.0%	0.0%
Grand Island, NE	20,619	91.8%	8.2%	1,696	5.0%	0.0%	0.2%	3.0%	0.0%	0.0%
Grand Junction, CO	38,770	94.9%	5.1%	1,993	2.8%	1.1%	0.8%	0.0%	0.0%	0.4%
Grand Rapids-Wyoming, MI	282,938	90.6%	9.4%	26,606	3.4%	3.1%	1.1%	1.2%	0.6%	0.0%
Grants Pass, OR	16,859	95.5%	4.5%	754	4.5%	0.0%	0.0%	0.0%	0.0%	0.0%
Great Falls, MT	20,486	99.9%	0.1%	21	0.0%	0.0%	0.1%	0.0%	0.0%	0.0%
Greeley, CO	79,145	86.4%	13.6%	10,737	10.8%	1.1%	0.3%	0.8%	0.1%	0.5%
Green Bay, WI	78,353	92.7%	7.3%	5,712	6.0%	0.9%	0.3%	0.0%	0.0%	0.1%
Greensboro-High Point, NC	187,158	90.0%	10.0%	18,694	6.1%	2.5%	1.0%	0.3%	0.2%	0.0%
Greenville, NC	60,468	94.6%	5.4%	3,269	3.7%	0.4%	0.8%	0.4%	0.0%	0.0%
Greenville-Anderson-Mauldin, SC	220,414	91.5%	8.5%	18,737	5.2%	2.1%	0.7%	0.1%	0.1%	0.3%

Table C-4: Metropolitan/Micropolitan Statistical Areas—Nativity and World Region of Birth—*Continued*

	Total Millennial	Percent		Total Foreign Born	Percent of All Millennials by Region of Birth					
		Native	Foreign Born		Latin America	Asia	Europe	Africa	North America	Oceania
Greenwood, SC	22,832	98.7%	1.3%	297	0.1%	0.4%	0.8%	0.0%	0.0%	0.0%
Gulfport-Biloxi-Pascagoula, MS	99,689	92.4%	7.6%	7,529	3.6%	1.2%	2.0%	0.8%	0.0%	0.0%
Hagerstown-Martinsburg, MD-WV	61,867	94.8%	5.2%	3,200	2.7%	1.0%	1.3%	0.1%	0.0%	0.1%
Hammond, LA	35,483	96.0%	4.0%	1,421	2.2%	1.2%	0.6%	0.0%	0.0%	0.0%
Hanford-Corcoran, CA	46,492	82.9%	17.1%	7,944	12.1%	3.1%	1.5%	0.0%	0.0%	0.4%
Harrisburg-Carlisle, PA	136,047	93.0%	7.0%	9,478	1.5%	3.5%	1.4%	0.6%	0.0%	0.0%
Harrisonburg, VA	44,407	88.0%	12.0%	5,314	5.3%	3.3%	2.1%	1.2%	0.0%	0.0%
Hartford-West Hartford-East Hartford, CT	287,773	86.1%	13.9%	39,977	4.1%	4.5%	3.7%	1.4%	0.2%	0.0%
Hattiesburg, MS	42,138	94.5%	5.5%	2,320	3.0%	0.5%	1.6%	0.2%	0.2%	0.0%
Hickory-Lenoir-Morganton, NC	81,844	92.9%	7.1%	5,844	6.3%	0.6%	0.3%	0.0%	0.0%	0.0%
Hilo, HI	44,356	87.3%	12.7%	5,654	2.8%	6.9%	1.5%	0.0%	0.2%	1.4%
Hilton Head Island-Bluffton-Beaufort, SC	48,455	88.1%	11.9%	5,755	9.4%	1.7%	0.4%	0.3%	0.0%	0.0%
Hinesville, GA	27,109	91.0%	9.0%	2,427	3.2%	2.2%	3.6%	0.0%	0.0%	0.0%
Holland, MI	26,922	94.9%	5.1%	1,369	4.1%	0.4%	0.6%	0.0%	0.0%	0.0%
Homosassa Springs, FL	20,619	95.2%	4.8%	989	2.8%	0.7%	1.4%	0.0%	0.0%	0.0%
Hot Springs, AR	21,426	96.4%	3.6%	775	0.7%	1.2%	0.7%	1.0%	0.0%	0.0%
Houma-Thibodaux, LA	54,143	96.0%	4.0%	2,170	3.0%	0.9%	0.0%	0.1%	0.0%	0.0%
Houston-The Woodlands-Sugar Land, TX	1,795,490	75.8%	24.2%	434,824	15.4%	5.9%	1.1%	1.5%	0.2%	0.1%
Huntington-Ashland, WV-KY-OH	84,689	98.8%	1.2%	1,021	0.3%	0.4%	0.2%	0.0%	0.0%	0.2%
Huntsville, AL	116,099	92.3%	7.7%	8,970	3.4%	1.9%	1.4%	0.7%	0.4%	0.0%
Idaho Falls, ID	34,928	94.2%	5.8%	2,033	4.9%	0.0%	0.5%	0.4%	0.0%	0.0%
Indianapolis-Carmel-Anderson, IN	506,665	91.6%	8.4%	42,551	3.8%	2.4%	0.7%	0.9%	0.4%	0.2%
Iowa City, IA	60,642	88.4%	11.6%	7,041	2.2%	6.9%	1.9%	0.5%	0.0%	0.0%
Ithaca, NY	45,449	80.4%	19.6%	8,929	2.0%	14.5%	3.1%	0.0%	0.0%	0.0%
Jackson, MI	38,466	96.1%	3.9%	1,493	0.8%	2.3%	0.8%	0.0%	0.0%	0.0%
Jackson, MS	150,950	96.8%	3.2%	4,830	1.1%	1.0%	0.4%	0.5%	0.2%	0.0%
Jackson, TN	33,924	95.8%	4.2%	1,418	1.9%	2.1%	0.2%	0.0%	0.0%	0.0%
Jacksonville, FL	373,861	89.6%	10.4%	38,900	3.7%	3.4%	2.8%	0.1%	0.3%	0.1%
Jacksonville, NC	75,308	93.8%	6.2%	4,702	3.6%	1.3%	1.4%	0.0%	0.0%	0.0%
Jamestown-Dunkirk-Fredonia, NY	31,756	96.3%	3.7%	1,176	1.8%	0.8%	1.1%	0.1%	0.0%	0.0%
Janesville-Beloit, WI	36,704	98.5%	1.5%	568	0.6%	0.4%	0.0%	0.5%	0.0%	0.0%
Jefferson City, MO	38,312	95.3%	4.7%	1,793	0.8%	2.0%	0.2%	1.7%	0.0%	0.0%
Johnson City, TN	48,247	93.5%	6.5%	3,152	2.7%	2.0%	1.7%	0.0%	0.1%	0.0%
Johnstown, PA	30,779	97.5%	2.5%	767	0.2%	2.1%	0.2%	0.0%	0.0%	0.0%
Jonesboro, AR	36,893	97.3%	2.7%	1,009	0.2%	1.1%	0.0%	0.7%	0.7%	0.0%
Joplin, MO	43,861	95.6%	4.4%	1,920	2.8%	0.2%	1.0%	0.0%	0.0%	0.4%
Kahului-Wailuku-Lahaina, HI	39,215	82.2%	17.8%	6,990	3.8%	12.0%	0.6%	0.0%	0.0%	1.4%
Kalamazoo-Portage, MI	97,259	93.8%	6.2%	6,072	2.2%	2.1%	1.3%	0.3%	0.3%	0.0%
Kalispell, MT	20,702	93.2%	6.8%	1,403	0.0%	0.1%	5.8%	0.0%	0.9%	0.0%
Kankakee, IL	28,451	93.4%	6.6%	1,888	3.9%	1.0%	1.8%	0.0%	0.0%	0.0%
Kansas City, MO-KS	523,563	91.5%	8.5%	44,457	3.5%	3.2%	0.9%	0.7%	0.1%	0.1%
Kennewick-Richland, WA	75,872	85.3%	14.7%	11,154	10.2%	3.2%	1.3%	0.0%	0.1%	0.0%
Killeen-Temple, TX	139,806	87.5%	12.5%	17,485	6.3%	2.3%	3.2%	0.1%	0.1%	0.6%
Kingsport-Bristol-Bristol, TN-VA	66,770	97.9%	2.1%	1,405	0.7%	0.3%	0.8%	0.3%	0.0%	0.0%
Kingston, NY	41,944	92.9%	7.1%	2,982	3.1%	3.3%	0.5%	0.2%	0.0%	0.2%
Knoxville, TN	212,739	95.2%	4.8%	10,209	2.4%	1.2%	0.7%	0.1%	0.1%	0.2%
Kokomo, IN	17,889	86.3%	13.7%	2,447	10.0%	2.0%	1.4%	0.3%	0.0%	0.0%
La Crosse-Onalaska, WI-MN	40,654	95.8%	4.2%	1,707	0.8%	2.2%	1.2%	0.0%	0.0%	0.0%
Lafayette, LA	134,345	96.6%	3.4%	4,600	1.0%	1.5%	0.9%	0.0%	0.0%	0.0%
Lafayette-West Lafayette, IN	80,391	83.0%	17.0%	13,635	4.9%	10.8%	0.8%	0.3%	0.2%	0.0%
Lake Charles, LA	54,900	93.9%	6.1%	3,359	2.3%	2.9%	0.8%	0.0%	0.0%	0.0%
Lake Havasu City-Kingman, AZ	38,567	93.0%	7.0%	2,685	3.9%	2.0%	1.0%	0.0%	0.1%	0.0%
Lakeland-Winter Haven, FL	157,735	88.5%	11.5%	18,210	9.9%	0.9%	0.5%	0.1%	0.1%	0.0%
Lancaster, PA	133,315	94.3%	5.7%	7,576	2.5%	1.6%	1.5%	0.0%	0.1%	0.0%
Lansing-East Lansing, MI	145,575	91.1%	8.9%	12,949	0.7%	7.1%	0.5%	0.3%	0.3%	0.1%
Laredo, TX	76,206	74.0%	26.0%	19,826	25.7%	0.1%	0.0%	0.0%	0.2%	0.0%
Las Cruces, NM	64,094	88.8%	11.2%	7,164	8.8%	1.8%	0.0%	0.6%	0.0%	0.0%
Las Vegas-Henderson-Paradise, NV	551,377	78.0%	22.0%	121,534	12.6%	6.5%	1.5%	1.2%	0.2%	0.1%
Lawrence, KS	46,763	87.0%	13.0%	6,071	5.3%	5.3%	1.4%	0.4%	0.7%	0.0%
Lawton, OK	40,304	94.8%	5.2%	2,077	2.2%	1.6%	1.4%	0.0%	0.0%	0.0%
Lebanon, PA	29,746	97.3%	2.7%	797	1.1%	0.0%	0.6%	0.9%	0.0%	0.0%
Lewiston, ID-WA	14,434	91.3%	8.7%	1,258	3.9%	1.8%	2.9%	0.0%	0.1%	0.0%
Lewiston-Auburn, ME	24,352	92.8%	7.2%	1,754	3.3%	2.1%	0.6%	0.8%	0.3%	0.0%
Lexington-Fayette, KY	144,801	91.0%	9.0%	12,997	3.8%	3.8%	0.8%	0.1%	0.4%	0.0%
Lima, OH	25,254	99.6%	0.4%	99	0.0%	0.0%	0.4%	0.0%	0.0%	0.0%
Lincoln, NE	99,230	88.2%	11.8%	11,682	2.4%	7.2%	0.2%	1.8%	0.1%	0.1%
Little Rock-North Little Rock-Conway, AR	197,454	93.0%	7.0%	13,861	3.6%	2.6%	0.7%	0.1%	0.0%	0.0%
Logan, UT-ID	48,158	92.1%	7.9%	3,808	4.4%	2.4%	0.3%	0.8%	0.0%	0.0%
Longview, TX	52,337	91.9%	8.1%	4,214	6.6%	0.1%	0.3%	1.0%	0.0%	0.0%
Longview, WA	22,743	87.8%	12.2%	2,784	10.9%	0.0%	1.0%	0.3%	0.0%	0.0%
Los Angeles-Long Beach-Anaheim, CA	3,649,069	75.1%	24.9%	909,480	13.9%	8.9%	1.3%	0.5%	0.3%	0.1%
Louisville/Jefferson County, KY-IN	310,933	92.0%	8.0%	24,942	3.1%	2.4%	1.5%	0.7%	0.1%	0.2%
Lubbock, TX	108,228	91.5%	8.5%	9,213	3.1%	2.5%	2.0%	1.0%	0.0%	0.0%
Lumberton, NC	32,547	94.8%	5.2%	1,678	4.4%	0.2%	0.0%	0.5%	0.0%	0.0%
Lynchburg, VA	71,290	95.2%	4.8%	3,443	1.3%	2.1%	0.3%	0.8%	0.2%	0.0%
Macon, GA	57,298	95.2%	4.8%	2,759	1.8%	1.2%	1.2%	0.6%	0.0%	0.0%
Madera, CA	41,540	77.9%	22.1%	9,174	18.6%	3.2%	0.2%	0.0%	0.0%	0.0%
Madison, WI	192,036	88.8%	11.2%	21,551	2.4%	5.9%	1.9%	0.5%	0.4%	0.1%

Table C-4: Metropolitan/Micropolitan Statistical Areas—Nativity and World Region of Birth—*Continued*

	Total Millennial	Percent		Total Foreign Born	Percent of All Millennials by Region of Birth					
		Native	Foreign Born		Latin America	Asia	Europe	Africa	North America	Oceania
Manchester-Nashua, NH	98,967	89.6%	10.4%	10,294	4.0%	3.0%	1.7%	1.1%	0.5%	0.0%
Manhattan, KS	44,533	89.8%	10.2%	4,536	2.9%	3.8%	2.5%	0.9%	0.0%	0.0%
Mankato-North Mankato, MN	34,477	94.1%	5.9%	2,050	0.5%	1.0%	0.8%	3.7%	0.0%	0.0%
Mansfield, OH	27,953	99.4%	0.6%	166	0.0%	0.5%	0.1%	0.0%	0.0%	0.0%
McAllen-Edinburg-Mission, TX	231,675	76.4%	23.6%	54,691	22.9%	0.4%	0.2%	0.0%	0.0%	0.1%
Medford, OR	48,007	93.6%	6.4%	3,084	4.3%	0.6%	0.2%	0.0%	1.2%	0.3%
Memphis, TN-MS-AR	357,724	92.6%	7.4%	26,371	3.8%	1.8%	0.8%	0.8%	0.1%	0.0%
Merced, CA	78,357	74.6%	25.4%	19,899	19.2%	4.1%	2.0%	0.0%	0.1%	0.0%
Meridian, MS	27,324	97.6%	2.4%	657	0.9%	1.3%	0.2%	0.0%	0.0%	0.0%
Miami-Fort Lauderdale-West Palm Beach, FL	1,441,011	65.2%	34.8%	501,997	30.6%	2.1%	1.6%	0.3%	0.2%	0.0%
Michigan City-La Porte, IN	25,919	99.4%	0.6%	161	0.5%	0.1%	0.0%	0.0%	0.0%	0.0%
Midland, MI	20,208	97.0%	3.0%	604	2.4%	0.0%	0.6%	0.0%	0.0%	0.0%
Midland, TX	50,504	85.1%	14.9%	7,529	11.1%	3.1%	0.4%	0.0%	0.3%	0.0%
Milwaukee-Waukesha-West Allis, WI	397,142	91.7%	8.3%	32,976	4.1%	2.4%	1.2%	0.6%	0.1%	0.0%
Minneapolis-St. Paul-Bloomington, MN-WI	893,153	86.5%	13.5%	120,623	3.1%	5.6%	1.3%	3.2%	0.3%	0.0%
Missoula, MT	36,592	100.0%	0.0%	13	0.0%	0.0%	0.0%	0.0%	0.0%	0.0%
Mobile, AL	108,104	95.0%	5.0%	5,446	1.3%	1.7%	0.6%	1.4%	0.0%	0.0%
Modesto, CA	113,568	85.5%	14.5%	16,420	9.0%	3.7%	0.8%	0.4%	0.0%	0.5%
Monroe, LA	48,731	96.9%	3.1%	1,521	1.2%	1.9%	0.0%	0.0%	0.0%	0.0%
Monroe, MI	33,502	97.6%	2.4%	807	1.1%	0.9%	0.5%	0.0%	0.0%	0.0%
Montgomery, AL	98,811	97.2%	2.8%	2,755	1.1%	0.6%	0.7%	0.1%	0.2%	0.1%
Morgantown, WV	51,218	91.1%	8.9%	4,573	0.6%	8.0%	0.4%	0.0%	0.0%	0.0%
Morristown, TN	26,778	88.5%	11.5%	3,087	9.3%	0.4%	1.4%	0.0%	0.3%	0.0%
Mount Vernon-Anacortes, WA	27,287	91.6%	8.4%	2,301	4.9%	2.2%	0.9%	0.0%	0.3%	0.1%
Muncie, IN	37,184	99.6%	0.4%	167	0.0%	0.2%	0.0%	0.0%	0.3%	0.0%
Muskegon, MI	41,707	97.2%	2.8%	1,182	1.3%	0.6%	0.0%	0.6%	0.3%	0.0%
Myrtle Beach-Conway-North Myrtle Beach, SC-NC	90,587	91.2%	8.8%	7,954	3.6%	2.6%	2.3%	0.1%	0.2%	0.0%
Napa, CA	33,408	81.1%	18.9%	6,311	14.0%	3.6%	0.8%	0.0%	0.5%	0.0%
Naples-Immokalee-Marco Island, FL	67,976	69.3%	30.7%	20,882	27.3%	1.6%	1.2%	0.0%	0.7%	0.0%
Nashville-Davidson—Murfreesboro—Franklin, TN	487,986	89.3%	10.7%	52,364	4.8%	2.6%	1.2%	1.9%	0.2%	0.0%
New Bern, NC	34,596	94.8%	5.2%	1,797	1.1%	3.0%	1.0%	0.1%	0.0%	0.0%
New Castle, PA	18,906	98.2%	1.8%	345	0.9%	0.0%	0.0%	0.9%	0.0%	0.0%
New Haven-Milford, CT	220,739	84.6%	15.4%	34,037	7.6%	4.1%	2.0%	1.4%	0.3%	0.1%
New Orleans-Metairie, LA	328,881	92.8%	7.2%	23,795	4.0%	2.0%	0.6%	0.4%	0.2%	0.0%
New Philadelphia-Dover, OH	20,822	97.0%	3.0%	622	0.0%	2.8%	0.1%	0.0%	0.0%	0.0%
New York-Newark-Jersey City, NY-NJ-PA	5,196,245	73.4%	26.6%	1,382,583	13.9%	8.1%	2.8%	1.3%	0.4%	0.1%
Niles-Benton Harbor, MI	34,168	90.1%	9.9%	3,380	2.7%	3.8%	0.8%	2.2%	0.1%	0.2%
North Port-Sarasota-Bradenton, FL	138,244	86.6%	13.4%	18,581	9.4%	1.3%	2.5%	0.0%	0.1%	0.0%
Norwich-New London, CT	71,058	90.6%	9.4%	6,709	3.7%	3.9%	1.2%	0.5%	0.1%	0.1%
Ocala, FL	70,359	92.2%	7.8%	5,473	6.8%	0.5%	0.5%	0.0%	0.0%	0.0%
Ocean City, NJ	18,811	90.7%	9.3%	1,744	7.7%	1.0%	0.0%	0.6%	0.0%	0.0%
Odessa, TX	49,508	87.2%	12.8%	6,317	8.8%	1.7%	1.1%	1.2%	0.0%	0.0%
Ogden-Clearfield, UT	175,789	91.9%	8.1%	14,230	5.9%	1.2%	0.6%	0.3%	0.1%	0.1%
Ogdensburg-Massena, NY	32,089	93.9%	6.1%	1,942	0.5%	2.2%	2.7%	0.1%	0.6%	0.0%
Oklahoma City, OK	375,784	89.4%	10.6%	39,919	6.4%	3.2%	0.4%	0.6%	0.0%	0.0%
Olympia-Tumwater, WA	67,330	89.6%	10.4%	6,974	3.6%	3.8%	2.8%	0.0%	0.2%	0.0%
Omaha-Council Bluffs, NE-IA	238,509	89.2%	10.8%	25,698	5.1%	3.7%	0.7%	1.3%	0.0%	0.0%
Orangeburg, SC	22,898	97.3%	2.7%	614	1.2%	0.4%	0.4%	0.7%	0.0%	0.0%
Orlando-Kissimmee-Sanford, FL	647,918	83.5%	16.5%	107,116	11.6%	3.0%	1.0%	0.5%	0.4%	0.0%
Oshkosh-Neenah, WI	46,787	96.1%	3.9%	1,824	0.3%	2.0%	1.6%	0.0%	0.0%	0.0%
Ottawa-Peru, IL	25,216	98.4%	1.6%	399	1.2%	0.4%	0.0%	0.0%	0.0%	0.0%
Owensboro, KY	27,255	97.1%	2.9%	796	0.6%	1.8%	0.4%	0.0%	0.0%	0.0%
Oxnard-Thousand Oaks-Ventura, CA	217,504	80.1%	19.9%	43,352	14.8%	4.2%	0.6%	0.2%	0.1%	0.1%
Palm Bay-Melbourne-Titusville, FL	120,364	89.2%	10.8%	13,008	5.4%	2.9%	1.9%	0.1%	0.3%	0.2%
Panama City, FL	48,956	91.9%	8.1%	3,966	2.6%	2.5%	2.4%	0.5%	0.1%	0.0%
Parkersburg-Vienna, WV	20,168	97.9%	2.1%	415	0.0%	0.0%	1.2%	0.0%	0.9%	0.0%
Pensacola-Ferry Pass-Brent, FL	132,104	93.0%	7.0%	9,183	1.8%	3.0%	1.7%	0.1%	0.1%	0.2%
Peoria, IL	90,607	96.2%	3.8%	3,488	0.8%	2.0%	0.9%	0.2%	0.0%	0.0%
Philadelphia-Camden-Wilmington, PA-NJ-DE-MD	1,554,689	88.4%	11.6%	180,775	4.2%	4.5%	1.4%	1.3%	0.2%	0.0%
Phoenix-Mesa-Scottsdale, AZ	1,190,960	84.8%	15.2%	181,229	9.5%	3.6%	1.1%	0.8%	0.2%	0.1%
Pine Bluff, AR	22,491	98.7%	1.3%	292	0.2%	0.5%	0.3%	0.3%	0.0%	0.0%
Pittsburgh, PA	559,661	94.3%	5.7%	31,937	0.8%	2.7%	1.0%	1.1%	0.2%	0.0%
Pittsfield, MA	28,289	92.6%	7.4%	2,086	1.6%	2.8%	2.9%	0.0%	0.0%	0.0%
Pocatello, ID	24,466	93.4%	6.6%	1,625	1.7%	4.1%	0.1%	0.7%	0.0%	0.0%
Port St. Lucie, FL	121,993	94.4%	5.6%	6,777	0.7%	1.6%	1.8%	0.7%	0.7%	0.0%
Portland-South Portland, ME	614,186	85.2%	14.8%	90,740	5.9%	4.9%	2.7%	0.6%	0.3%	0.4%
Portland-Vancouver-Hillsboro, OR-WA	91,998	86.3%	13.7%	12,626	11.3%	1.4%	0.3%	0.7%	0.0%	0.0%
Pottsville, PA	30,373	98.7%	1.3%	408	1.3%	0.0%	0.1%	0.0%	0.0%	0.0%
Prescott, AZ	39,793	94.6%	5.4%	2,150	3.8%	1.3%	0.0%	0.2%	0.0%	0.0%
Providence-Warwick, RI-MA	414,862	87.7%	12.3%	50,825	5.5%	3.3%	1.6%	1.4%	0.4%	0.1%
Provo-Orem, UT	198,288	91.6%	8.4%	16,637	5.0%	2.1%	0.8%	0.2%	0.1%	0.2%
Pueblo, CO	40,672	96.4%	3.6%	1,453	2.5%	0.2%	0.9%	0.0%	0.0%	0.0%
Punta Gorda, FL	23,149	92.2%	7.8%	1,803	0.3%	6.4%	0.0%	0.0%	1.2%	0.0%
Racine, WI	45,504	97.7%	2.3%	1,054	1.4%	0.4%	0.0%	0.0%	0.5%	0.0%
Raleigh, NC	328,403	86.3%	13.7%	45,009	6.5%	4.4%	1.7%	0.7%	0.3%	0.1%

Table C-4: Metropolitan/Micropolitan Statistical Areas—Nativity and World Region of Birth—*Continued*

	Total Millennial	Percent		Total Foreign Born	Percent of All Millennials by Region of Birth					
		Native	Foreign Born		Latin America	Asia	Europe	Africa	North America	Oceania
Rapid City, SD	36,640	97.5%	2.5%	928	0.5%	0.0%	2.0%	0.0%	0.0%	0.0%
Reading, PA	103,746	91.4%	8.6%	8,898	6.2%	1.5%	0.5%	0.4%	0.0%	0.0%
Redding, CA	40,454	92.9%	7.1%	2,869	0.4%	1.8%	4.0%	0.0%	0.0%	0.9%
Reno, NV	115,549	87.7%	12.3%	14,199	7.1%	4.3%	0.4%	0.4%	0.0%	0.0%
Richmond, VA	331,236	90.7%	9.3%	30,970	3.2%	3.5%	1.4%	1.0%	0.3%	0.0%
Riverside-San Bernardino-Ontario, CA	1,242,971	84.7%	15.3%	189,812	10.8%	3.5%	0.5%	0.3%	0.1%	0.1%
Roanoke, VA	72,916	91.8%	8.2%	5,973	3.2%	2.5%	1.1%	0.9%	0.4%	0.0%
Rochester, MN	51,703	87.2%	12.8%	6,616	2.1%	5.5%	1.5%	2.8%	0.7%	0.3%
Rochester, NY	279,031	92.1%	7.9%	21,955	1.3%	3.9%	1.8%	0.7%	0.1%	0.0%
Rockford, IL	80,061	87.9%	12.1%	9,727	9.0%	1.9%	0.7%	0.5%	0.0%	0.0%
Rocky Mount, NC	33,841	97.5%	2.5%	852	1.4%	0.4%	0.8%	0.0%	0.0%	0.0%
Rome, GA	24,685	92.4%	7.6%	1,873	6.1%	0.5%	1.0%	0.0%	0.0%	0.0%
Roseburg, OR	21,577	95.8%	4.2%	896	2.5%	0.0%	1.6%	0.0%	0.0%	0.0%
Sacramento–Roseville–Arden-Arcade, CA	592,077	81.4%	18.6%	110,410	6.4%	8.3%	2.7%	0.7%	0.1%	0.4%
Saginaw, MI	48,370	92.5%	7.5%	3,612	1.0%	5.7%	0.4%	0.0%	0.3%	0.0%
Salem, OH	58,133	93.0%	7.0%	4,088	1.9%	2.5%	0.1%	2.3%	0.3%	0.0%
Salem, OR	39,437	94.3%	5.7%	2,262	2.4%	0.1%	0.7%	2.2%	0.4%	0.0%
Salinas, CA	33,339	90.6%	9.4%	3,129	4.6%	2.9%	0.3%	1.6%	0.0%	0.0%
Salisbury, MD-DE	695,032	93.3%	6.7%	46,556	1.7%	2.9%	1.2%	0.7%	0.2%	0.0%
Salt Lake City, UT	21,390	97.1%	2.9%	623	1.5%	0.0%	1.0%	0.4%	0.0%	0.0%
San Angelo, TX	106,365	84.6%	15.4%	16,387	10.4%	1.5%	0.5%	0.6%	0.4%	2.1%
San Antonio-New Braunfels, TX	118,338	71.6%	28.4%	33,600	24.0%	2.7%	0.8%	0.5%	0.3%	0.1%
San Diego-Carlsbad, CA	89,917	92.9%	7.1%	6,408	5.0%	0.9%	0.7%	0.5%	0.0%	0.0%
San Francisco-Oakland-Hayward, CA	338,055	87.0%	13.0%	43,844	6.4%	3.6%	1.0%	1.1%	0.6%	0.3%
San Jose-Sunnyvale-Santa Clara, CA	36,639	93.3%	6.7%	2,458	3.8%	1.8%	0.5%	0.3%	0.0%	0.3%
San Luis Obispo-Paso Robles-Arroyo Grande, CA	674,563	86.8%	13.2%	88,959	8.4%	2.5%	1.8%	0.3%	0.1%	0.0%
Santa Cruz-Watsonville, CA	944,397	79.9%	20.1%	189,686	9.7%	7.4%	1.8%	0.7%	0.3%	0.2%
Santa Fe, NM	1,181,069	72.7%	27.3%	321,844	9.4%	13.8%	2.4%	0.7%	0.6%	0.4%
Santa Maria-Santa Barbara, CA	508,745	66.0%	34.0%	172,999	10.3%	20.2%	2.1%	0.6%	0.6%	0.2%
Santa Rosa, CA	81,571	89.9%	10.1%	8,234	6.3%	2.7%	0.9%	0.0%	0.2%	0.0%
Savannah, GA	81,439	82.9%	17.1%	13,889	11.0%	4.1%	1.0%	0.3%	0.4%	0.2%
Scranton–Wilkes-Barre–Hazleton, PA	30,994	86.1%	13.9%	4,295	8.8%	0.7%	4.2%	0.0%	0.0%	0.1%
Seattle-Tacoma-Bellevue, WA	136,421	78.6%	21.4%	29,166	14.4%	4.5%	2.0%	0.3%	0.2%	0.0%
Sebastian-Vero Beach, FL	118,618	81.9%	18.1%	21,454	12.7%	3.1%	1.8%	0.3%	0.2%	0.0%
Sebring, FL	110,241	92.0%	8.0%	8,871	3.1%	2.4%	1.6%	0.9%	0.0%	0.0%
Sheboygan, WI	130,840	95.2%	4.8%	6,225	2.3%	2.0%	0.2%	0.2%	0.0%	0.0%
Sherman-Denison, TX	993,581	79.2%	20.8%	207,125	5.1%	9.9%	3.5%	1.3%	0.6%	0.4%
Show Low, AZ	26,890	92.1%	7.9%	2,120	3.8%	0.3%	2.7%	0.6%	0.4%	0.0%
Shreveport-Bossier City, LA	17,160	90.5%	9.5%	1,638	7.1%	0.0%	1.9%	0.6%	0.0%	0.0%
Sierra Vista-Douglas, AZ	24,958	86.0%	14.0%	3,491	7.7%	3.9%	2.4%	0.0%	0.0%	0.0%
Sioux City, IA-NE-SD	29,792	89.7%	10.3%	3,083	7.8%	1.0%	1.5%	0.0%	0.0%	0.0%
Sioux Falls, SD	26,103	99.2%	0.8%	218	0.5%	0.4%	0.0%	0.0%	0.0%	0.0%
South Bend-Mishawaka, IN-MI	115,714	95.2%	4.8%	5,503	2.4%	1.6%	0.8%	0.0%	0.0%	0.0%
Spartanburg, SC	29,422	85.9%	14.1%	4,146	12.0%	1.4%	0.6%	0.0%	0.0%	0.1%
Spokane-Spokane Valley, WA	40,932	90.1%	9.9%	4,048	7.9%	0.2%	0.1%	1.7%	0.0%	0.0%
Springfield, IL	66,928	90.5%	9.5%	6,377	1.7%	3.6%	1.8%	2.3%	0.2%	0.0%
Springfield, MA	84,142	91.2%	8.8%	7,419	3.3%	2.6%	0.6%	2.4%	0.0%	0.0%
Springfield, MO	79,956	93.2%	6.8%	5,424	3.0%	0.7%	3.0%	0.1%	0.0%	0.0%
Springfield, OH	144,143	91.4%	8.6%	12,426	1.0%	2.3%	3.2%	0.8%	0.7%	0.7%
St. Cloud, MN	51,217	94.0%	6.0%	3,090	1.3%	3.8%	0.6%	0.1%	0.2%	0.0%
St. George, UT	179,075	90.5%	9.5%	16,973	2.7%	3.1%	2.7%	0.7%	0.2%	0.1%
St. Joseph, MO-KS	127,743	95.3%	4.7%	6,066	1.4%	1.5%	1.1%	0.5%	0.2%	0.1%
St. Louis, MO-IL	31,343	98.6%	1.4%	438	0.8%	0.0%	0.0%	0.6%	0.0%	0.0%
State College, PA	67,059	87.9%	12.1%	8,108	1.3%	8.6%	1.5%	0.0%	0.7%	0.0%
Staunton-Waynesboro, VA	28,708	97.3%	2.7%	783	1.0%	1.7%	0.0%	0.0%	0.0%	0.0%
Stockton-Lodi, CA	194,976	78.0%	22.0%	42,955	13.2%	8.0%	0.3%	0.6%	0.0%	0.0%
Sumter, SC	29,989	97.5%	2.5%	741	0.8%	1.0%	0.4%	0.0%	0.3%	0.0%
Sunbury, PA	20,330	99.0%	1.0%	213	0.0%	0.0%	1.0%	0.0%	0.0%	0.0%
Syracuse, NY	172,604	92.0%	8.0%	13,752	1.6%	4.0%	1.2%	0.7%	0.5%	0.0%
Tallahassee, FL	131,206	90.8%	9.2%	12,046	3.9%	2.6%	1.4%	0.7%	0.4%	0.2%
Tampa-St. Petersburg-Clearwater, FL	687,275	85.4%	14.6%	100,028	8.9%	2.8%	1.9%	0.7%	0.3%	0.0%
Terre Haute, IN	47,389	98.9%	1.1%	517	0.9%	0.0%	0.0%	0.2%	0.0%	0.0%
Texarkana, TX-AR	36,299	98.8%	1.2%	443	1.1%	0.1%	0.0%	0.0%	0.0%	0.0%
The Villages, FL	11,009	98.0%	2.0%	218	0.0%	0.0%	0.0%	0.5%	1.5%	0.0%
Toledo, OH	163,570	96.3%	3.7%	6,005	0.6%	1.9%	0.3%	0.7%	0.2%	0.0%
Topeka, KS	54,373	97.5%	2.5%	1,337	0.5%	1.1%	0.4%	0.3%	0.0%	0.2%
Torrington, CT	36,755	90.9%	9.1%	3,328	4.1%	1.7%	2.5%	0.8%	0.0%	0.0%
Traverse City, MI	31,729	95.9%	4.1%	1,305	1.0%	1.6%	1.1%	0.0%	0.4%	0.0%
Trenton, NJ	96,611	75.4%	24.6%	23,785	11.3%	7.6%	4.1%	1.6%	0.0%	0.1%
Truckee-Grass Valley, CA	18,893	92.3%	7.7%	1,446	1.7%	0.7%	4.0%	0.6%	0.6%	0.0%
Tucson, AZ	265,127	85.2%	14.8%	39,254	9.1%	3.4%	1.2%	0.9%	0.1%	0.2%
Tullahoma-Manchester, TN	23,694	95.4%	4.6%	1,091	1.5%	3.1%	0.0%	0.0%	0.0%	0.0%
Tulsa, OK	248,733	89.5%	10.5%	26,086	6.9%	2.4%	0.7%	0.3%	0.1%	0.0%
Tupelo, MS	33,847	97.4%	2.6%	880	2.4%	0.0%	0.0%	0.0%	0.2%	0.0%
Tuscaloosa, AL	80,383	95.1%	4.9%	3,929	1.6%	2.2%	0.8%	0.1%	0.2%	0.0%
Tyler, TX	59,464	94.8%	5.2%	3,109	4.3%	0.8%	0.1%	0.0%	0.0%	0.0%

Table C-4: Metropolitan/Micropolitan Statistical Areas—Nativity and World Region of Birth—*Continued*

| | Total Millennial | Percent | | Total Foreign Born | Percent of All Millennials by Region of Birth | | | | | |
		Native	Foreign Born		Latin America	Asia	Europe	Africa	North America	Oceania
Urban Honolulu, HI	273,410	84.8%	15.2%	41,598	1.0%	10.3%	1.3%	0.1%	0.1%	2.4%
Utica-Rome, NY	69,188	89.9%	10.1%	6,964	1.9%	4.6%	2.4%	1.1%	0.0%	0.0%
Valdosta, GA	46,199	95.8%	4.2%	1,932	1.1%	2.1%	0.9%	0.0%	0.0%	0.0%
Vallejo-Fairfield, CA	112,131	82.0%	18.0%	20,163	9.7%	7.1%	0.6%	0.0%	0.3%	0.3%
Victoria, TX	25,601	93.9%	6.1%	1,554	2.9%	1.7%	0.0%	1.4%	0.0%	0.0%
Vineland-Bridgeton, NJ	40,801	88.5%	11.5%	4,708	9.8%	0.8%	0.5%	0.3%	0.0%	0.0%
Virginia Beach-Norfolk-Newport News, VA-NC	507,885	92.8%	7.2%	36,715	2.3%	2.7%	1.7%	0.3%	0.2%	0.0%
Visalia-Porterville, CA	131,238	78.8%	21.2%	27,819	18.7%	1.9%	0.1%	0.1%	0.2%	0.2%
Waco, TX	78,233	89.6%	10.4%	8,104	7.6%	1.3%	0.4%	0.4%	0.6%	0.1%
Walla Walla, WA	17,618	90.0%	10.0%	1,768	4.8%	2.0%	3.2%	0.0%	0.0%	0.0%
Warner Robins, GA	49,429	96.4%	3.6%	1,773	1.3%	1.8%	0.2%	0.0%	0.0%	0.2%
Washington-Arlington-Alexandria, DC-VA-MD-WV	1,605,799	76.9%	23.1%	370,352	9.4%	7.7%	2.2%	3.5%	0.2%	0.1%
Waterloo-Cedar Falls, IA	50,906	93.5%	6.5%	3,312	4.8%	0.7%	0.8%	0.1%	0.0%	0.2%
Watertown-Fort Drum, NY	35,878	96.0%	4.0%	1,425	1.6%	0.8%	0.8%	0.0%	0.1%	0.5%
Wausau, WI	29,492	92.5%	7.5%	2,213	2.2%	4.4%	0.9%	0.0%	0.0%	0.0%
Weirton-Steubenville, WV-OH	27,390	99.0%	1.0%	276	0.8%	0.3%	0.0%	0.0%	0.0%	0.0%
Wenatchee, WA	25,938	89.5%	10.5%	2,714	10.1%	0.0%	0.4%	0.0%	0.0%	0.0%
Wheeling, WV-OH	31,989	99.1%	0.9%	303	0.6%	0.3%	0.0%	0.0%	0.0%	0.0%
Whitewater-Elkhorn, WI	27,201	90.5%	9.5%	2,589	8.7%	0.0%	0.3%	0.1%	0.4%	0.0%
Wichita Falls, TX	169,912	90.0%	10.0%	17,007	4.5%	3.8%	0.8%	0.7%	0.2%	0.0%
Wichita, KS	44,916	88.8%	11.2%	5,017	8.1%	1.4%	0.8%	0.7%	0.2%	0.0%
Williamsport, PA	28,105	97.2%	2.8%	790	0.0%	1.7%	0.4%	0.0%	0.7%	0.0%
Wilmington, NC	75,894	93.5%	6.5%	4,925	3.6%	0.7%	1.4%	0.6%	0.2%	0.0%
Winchester, VA-WV	29,424	92.8%	7.2%	2,111	5.7%	1.3%	0.1%	0.1%	0.0%	0.0%
Winston-Salem, NC	159,220	88.9%	11.1%	17,725	7.4%	2.3%	0.7%	0.6%	0.1%	0.0%
Wooster, OH	28,015	98.9%	1.1%	312	0.2%	0.1%	0.0%	0.4%	0.0%	0.3%
Worcester, MA-CT	232,320	90.0%	10.0%	23,154	3.1%	3.7%	1.4%	1.7%	0.1%	0.0%
Yakima, WA	64,342	80.1%	19.9%	12,780	18.9%	0.0%	0.2%	0.3%	0.4%	0.0%
York-Hanover, PA	102,477	96.5%	3.5%	3,623	1.3%	1.0%	0.7%	0.5%	0.0%	0.0%
Youngstown-Warren-Boardman, OH-PA	120,714	98.4%	1.6%	1,973	0.9%	0.6%	0.1%	0.0%	0.0%	0.0%
Yuba City, CA	45,459	80.7%	19.3%	8,754	9.9%	7.5%	1.5%	0.1%	0.0%	0.2%
Yuma, AZ	57,750	79.3%	20.7%	11,945	18.6%	0.6%	0.5%	0.2%	0.8%	0.0%

PART D
HOUSEHOLD RELATIONSHIP

People live in a multitude of different living arrangements, but they are all classified by the Census Bureau as living in either households or group quarters facilities. Those living in households live in either family or non-family households. A family household is comprised of two or more individuals related to the householder by blood, marriage, or adoption. Non-family households are ones where all of the individuals are unrelated or it is occupied by a single person living alone. There are no other household types. All households have a single householder which is generally the person who owns or rents the unit and is "Person 1" on the questionnaire. The relationship of other individuals in the household are all defined in relation to person 1 — the householder.

Group quarters facilities can be either institutional or non-institutional. Examples of institutional facilities include correctional facilities, nursing homes, and other institutional health facilities. Non-institutional group quarters include college student housing, military, and other group home situations. For the Millennial population described here, those living in group quarters will be predominantly college housing, and it is often easy to identify those counties and cities with a large college or university presence.

The Millennials are notable as a generation for delayed marriage and childbearing, which dramatically alters their household composition. Whereas Baby Boomers formed family households early in life, Millennials are delaying, or not forming, family households as early in their life. Today, Millennials are also faced with the unique situation of increased return to their parental home. The tables in this section focus on Millennial householders age 18 to 33 and the type of household: married couples with and without children, single male householders with and without children, single female householders with and without children, and non-family households with individuals living alone or with other non-relatives. Also included is a measure of the sons and daughters (both biological and legal) living with their parents.

More than 59 percent of Millennial householders age 18 to 24 are in non-family living situations compared to 34.5 percent of those age 25 to 33. One in four

Percent Age 25 to 33 Living With Their Parents

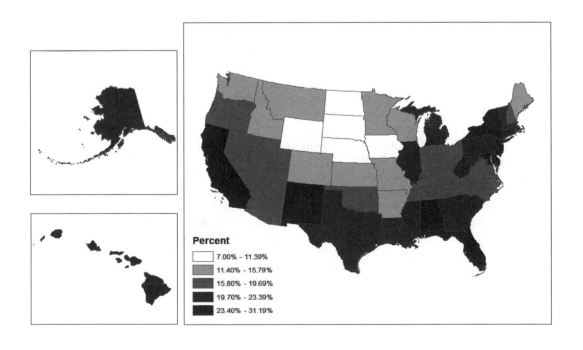

Percent
	7.00% - 11.39%
	11.40% - 15.79%
	15.80% - 19.69%
	19.70% - 23.39%
	23.40% - 31.19%

(26.9 percent) householders 18 to 24 is living alone, which is somewhat higher than those age 25 to 33 (22.6 percent). While 32.3 percent of the 18 to 24 Millennials are living with other non-relatives, that figure drops to only 13.9 percent for those age 25 to 33. More than half (51.4 percent) of Millennials age 18 to 24 are living in their parents' households, but that figure drops to only 21.4 percent of 25 to 33 year olds.

Among family households, only 16.1 percent of the 18 to 24 year olds are in married couple families (7.9 percent are with children), compared to 30.3 percent of the 25 to 33 year olds. Though there are many more 25 to 33 year olds who are married, one out of three still do not have children. Single male and female households make up the smallest share in both age categories. Single male households make up 8.1 percent of the 18 to 24 age group and only 6.8 percent of the 25 to 33 year olds. Single females account for 16.4 percent of the 18 to 24 householders and also 16.4 percent of the 25 to 33 year olds. The big difference here is single females with children, which make up 12.9 percent of 18 to 24 year old householders and 14.8 percent of the 25 to 33 age group.

Utah has by far the highest percentage of married couple households among the 18 to 24 year olds at 41.2 percent and has the highest proportion of married couples with children at 31.0 percent. Hawaii is second at 37.3 percent and Idaho is close at 30.4 percent. The District of Columbia has the lowest percentage at only 3.8 percent and all of them are without children. Nationwide, 16.1 percent of Millennial households age 18 to 24 are married couples. Marriage increases significantly for the 25 to 33 age group where 40.3 percent of Millennials are now married. Utah again has the highest percentage at 60.2 percent and the District of Columbia is still lowest at 17.9 percent.

New Jersey has the highest percentage of 18 to 24 year old single male householders with no children at 12.0 percent, and four states (the District of Columbia, Iowa, Vermont, and Wyoming) are below two percent. Among the 18 to 24 year olds, New Jersey also has the highest percentage of single females with no children at 7.8 percent, but Ohio has the highest percentage (19.5 percent) of those with children. In South Dakota, 37.0 percent of 18 to 24 year old householders are living alone but only 15.7 percent live alone in Utah. New Hampshire has the highest percentage living with other non-relatives at 53.8 percent. More than two-thirds (69.5 percent) of New Jersey Millennials age 18 to 24 are living with their parents, and in 18 states that figure is over 50 percent. In North Dakota, only 22.2 percent are living with their parents.

The percentage of Millennial householders age 25 to 33 who are married has risen from the 18 to 24 age group

mainly because the percentage of them living in non-family situations, or with their parents, has declined. Single male and female householders, with and without children, maintain similar percentages but only 36.5 percent of 25 to 33 year olds are in non-family arrangements compared to 59.2 percent of the 18 to 24 year olds. The District of Columbia has the highest percentage of non-family households at 66.5 percent and is also highest for those living alone (36.8 percent) and living with other non-relatives (29.6 percent). DC has the lowest share of married couples age 25 to 33. The percentage of 25 to 33 year old Millennials living with their parents drops by more than half from the 18 to 24 age group to 21.4 percent, with New Jersey still having the highest rate at 31.1 percent.

Among the 18 to 24 year old Millennial householders, Wilson County, TN has the highest percentage of married couples at 83.3 percent. More than 50 percent of Millennial householders are in married couple relationships in 20 of the 633 counties. There are 428 counties where the percent of single male householders is less than 10 percent but among single females householders, only 204 counties are below 10 percent. In seven counties more than 50 percent of households are single females with children. The percentage of sons and daughters living with their parents ranges from a low of 7.9 percent in Monroe County, IN to a high of 89.5 percent in Putnam County, NY.

In 170 of the 633 counties, more than 50 percent of Millennial householders age 25 to 33 are married. Bonneville County, OH is highest at 77.1 percent, and 65.4 percent are married couples with children and 11.7 percent have no children. At 65.4 percent, Bonneville County has the highest percentage of married householders with children. In Sumter County, FL, 66.9 percent of Millennial householders age 25 to 33 are single females with children while Wicomico County, MD has the highest percentage of single male householders with children at 28.9 percent. In Washington County, TN, 48.7 percent of householders are single individuals living alone. It's one of only eight counties over 40 percent. At 55.7 percent, Putnam County, NY also has the highest percentage of 25 to 33 year old Millennials living with their parents.

Rialto, CA is not a large city but all of its 18 to 24 year old Millennial households are married couples! Rialto also has the highest percentage of married couple households with children at 71.4 percent. In 172 of the 344 cities the percentage of 18 to 24 year old householders who are married couples is less than 10 percent, but 10 cities are over 50 percent married couples. Antioch, CA has the highest percentage of single female households with children at 83.9 percent. Centennial, CO and Meridian, ID are anomalies in that all of their 18 to 24 Millennial

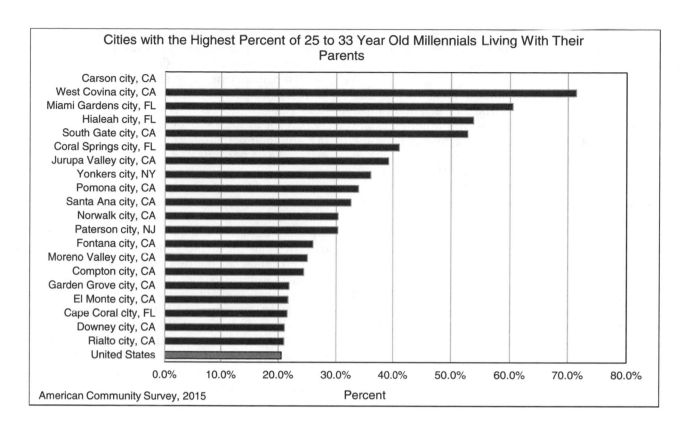

Cities with the Highest Percent of 25 to 33 Year Old Millennials Living With Their Parents

American Community Survey, 2015

Percent

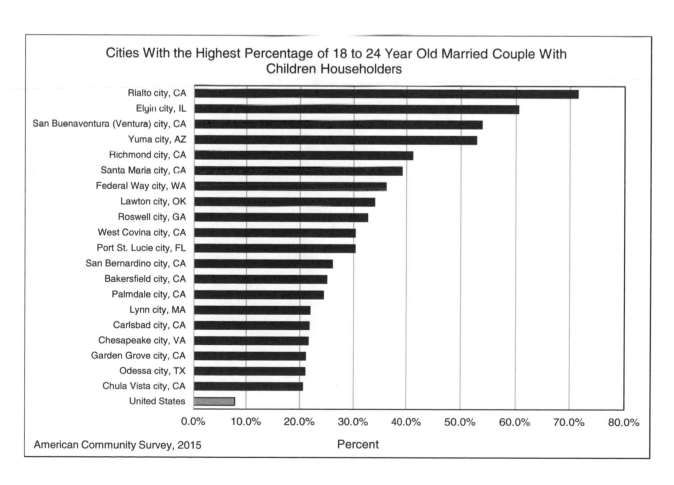

Cities With the Highest Percentage of 18 to 24 Year Old Married Couple With Children Householders

American Community Survey, 2015

Percent

householders are living alone as non-family households. In Livonia, MI 91 percent of 18 to 24 year olds are sons or daughters living with their parents.

Among the 25 to 33 year old householders, West Jordan City, UT has the highest percentage of married couple households at 75.4 percent. Fifty-seven other cities are above 50 percent married couples. Surprise, AZ has the highest percentage of married couples with children at 61.7 percent. Coral Springs, FL has the highest percentage of single male householders with children at 25.2 percent while Springfield, MA is highest for single female householders with children at 41.7 percent. Even in the older ages sons and daughters are still living with their parents, with Carson, CA having the highest percentage at 57.3 percent.

In 15 metropolitan/micropolitan areas, the percentage of 18 to 24 year old householders that are married couples is greater than 50 percent. It is highest in the Brunswick, GA metro at 70.1 percent. The Roseburg, OR micro has the highest proportion of householders who are married couples with children at 55.8 percent. Almost two-thirds (62.3 percent) of 18- to 24-year-old householders are single females with children in the Pottsville, PA micropolitan area. The percentage of younger Millennials living alone is greatest in the Ocean City, NJ metro where all (100 percent) are living alone while all (100 percent) of Hot Springs, AR metro are those living with other non-relatives. In 191 metro/micro areas, more than 50 percent of the 18 to 24 year old Millennials are living with their parents. It's highest in the The Villages, FL metro at 83.1 percent.

The Provo-Orem, OR metro has the highest percentage of 25- to 33-year-old householders who are married couples (74.3 percent). Eighty-eight metropolitan/micropolitan areas are above the 50 percent level. At 61.6 percent, the Idaho Falls, ID metro has the highest percentage of married couples with children. The Elkhart-Goshen, IN metro has the highest percentage of single male householders with children (17.5 percent), while at 66.9 percent, The Villages, FL metro is highest for single female householders. Forty-three percent of 25- to 33-year-old householders are living alone in the Orangeburg, SC micro and the Ocala, FL metro, has the highest percentage of sons and daughters living with their parents (45.5 percent).

This page is intentionally left blank.

Table D-1: States—Household Relationship

		18 to 24								
		Married Couple Households		Male, No Spouse Present		Female, No Spouse Present		Non-Family Householders		
	Total Householders	With Children	No Children	With Children	No Children	With Children	No Children	Living Alone	Not Alone	Living With Parents
United States	4,393,907	7.9%	8.2%	3.2%	4.9%	12.9%	3.5%	26.9%	32.3%	51.4%
Alabama	76,068	9.5%	8.0%	4.3%	3.7%	15.0%	3.3%	30.0%	26.2%	47.3%
Alaska	15,267	10.6%	18.7%	6.2%	7.8%	7.5%	0.2%	31.9%	17.1%	43.0%
Arizona	108,597	8.6%	7.3%	3.5%	6.5%	12.8%	4.1%	26.4%	30.7%	48.1%
Arkansas	53,654	10.6%	9.0%	4.7%	5.3%	18.6%	1.8%	25.7%	24.2%	44.2%
California	395,895	7.6%	7.4%	3.5%	8.5%	9.7%	6.6%	21.3%	35.5%	58.0%
Colorado	99,360	7.2%	8.8%	0.7%	4.7%	8.1%	3.4%	23.8%	43.2%	41.8%
Connecticut	30,370	3.2%	5.8%	7.7%	4.5%	13.7%	5.4%	28.9%	31.0%	57.6%
Delaware	8,927	4.9%	22.0%	0.7%	4.8%	9.4%	2.7%	21.5%	34.1%	52.7%
District of Columbia	11,997	0.0%	3.8%	0.0%	1.4%	7.5%	2.1%	35.2%	50.0%	25.6%
Florida	208,461	6.0%	7.0%	3.6%	6.5%	12.7%	5.5%	27.6%	31.2%	56.2%
Georgia	138,180	10.5%	8.7%	4.3%	3.8%	13.7%	3.0%	27.9%	28.0%	52.1%
Hawaii	16,358	16.9%	20.4%	0.6%	6.5%	0.9%	6.7%	19.6%	28.4%	46.1%
Idaho	27,594	11.5%	18.9%	1.0%	2.1%	10.0%	2.0%	29.0%	25.4%	40.7%
Illinois	159,687	6.8%	5.0%	2.6%	5.4%	14.6%	2.3%	32.2%	30.9%	56.6%
Indiana	119,026	8.8%	8.2%	2.7%	3.3%	14.9%	2.8%	28.6%	30.6%	46.5%
Iowa	69,471	8.2%	7.6%	2.3%	1.5%	9.1%	1.0%	27.7%	42.5%	34.3%
Kansas	58,427	6.9%	10.6%	3.0%	2.7%	10.2%	2.9%	32.1%	31.6%	39.1%
Kentucky	76,133	12.4%	12.7%	2.6%	3.9%	15.8%	1.7%	23.3%	27.7%	44.2%
Louisiana	72,681	8.5%	6.4%	3.9%	4.9%	17.4%	2.4%	32.1%	24.4%	51.1%
Maine	16,105	7.5%	8.9%	4.0%	4.7%	8.9%	1.0%	19.2%	45.8%	42.9%
Maryland	54,361	5.8%	6.8%	3.0%	5.3%	14.6%	3.3%	23.6%	37.6%	57.8%
Massachusetts	66,159	2.8%	3.4%	1.4%	7.1%	12.2%	3.7%	23.4%	46.1%	50.6%
Michigan	148,660	4.9%	6.0%	4.2%	5.8%	13.0%	2.3%	30.5%	33.2%	52.2%
Minnesota	90,968	8.4%	5.8%	2.5%	2.3%	16.5%	2.7%	25.1%	36.6%	47.3%
Mississippi	43,350	10.1%	7.6%	1.7%	4.8%	18.8%	2.2%	28.1%	26.8%	50.9%
Missouri	113,642	8.2%	7.3%	3.5%	2.9%	12.3%	1.9%	31.1%	32.9%	44.5%
Montana	22,220	8.9%	6.1%	0.0%	2.1%	17.8%	2.5%	25.5%	37.2%	35.8%
Nebraska	48,841	8.8%	6.0%	4.2%	2.5%	8.9%	3.2%	33.6%	32.8%	34.2%
Nevada	34,822	7.8%	4.9%	4.0%	6.9%	14.2%	6.3%	27.2%	28.7%	56.1%
New Hampshire	15,507	8.9%	0.4%	0.4%	3.1%	9.2%	5.0%	19.3%	53.8%	53.0%
New Jersey	52,734	7.1%	4.9%	2.3%	12.0%	13.7%	7.8%	30.6%	21.6%	69.5%
New Mexico	31,700	10.8%	6.8%	2.7%	7.8%	18.7%	3.4%	24.7%	25.2%	54.1%
New York	185,070	6.0%	4.8%	2.1%	7.2%	12.7%	5.8%	27.3%	34.1%	58.5%
North Carolina	161,504	8.5%	11.3%	3.8%	4.2%	10.9%	2.4%	25.7%	33.2%	45.8%
North Dakota	29,496	7.8%	14.4%	5.2%	2.4%	11.6%	1.2%	24.4%	33.1%	22.2%
Ohio	192,205	6.5%	7.1%	3.5%	3.4%	19.5%	2.4%	28.6%	29.0%	47.7%
Oklahoma	74,373	13.1%	11.1%	3.7%	3.8%	13.7%	1.5%	24.9%	28.2%	42.7%
Oregon	60,890	8.4%	8.0%	1.6%	3.5%	8.9%	2.8%	22.5%	44.3%	44.1%
Pennsylvania	139,406	5.4%	6.2%	2.4%	4.8%	16.8%	2.1%	28.2%	34.1%	52.5%
Rhode Island	12,049	6.6%	0.7%	5.4%	3.7%	13.3%	5.9%	23.1%	41.3%	46.7%
South Carolina	69,142	6.3%	10.0%	3.6%	3.7%	17.5%	3.8%	25.8%	29.3%	48.0%
South Dakota	21,083	4.6%	12.2%	3.2%	2.1%	7.9%	1.0%	37.0%	32.0%	37.0%
Tennessee	109,481	7.4%	11.7%	2.5%	6.0%	16.5%	2.2%	26.1%	27.6%	47.5%
Texas	421,935	11.2%	7.8%	4.3%	4.8%	13.6%	4.4%	28.1%	25.8%	53.1%
Utah	59,994	10.2%	31.0%	1.2%	3.2%	6.3%	3.8%	15.7%	28.7%	44.6%
Vermont	10,674	12.8%	8.5%	1.1%	0.0%	5.5%	0.3%	28.5%	43.4%	40.3%
Virginia	108,342	7.5%	10.1%	2.4%	3.2%	10.4%	3.9%	23.3%	39.2%	48.6%
Washington	113,025	7.2%	11.5%	3.4%	3.4%	9.6%	2.9%	23.7%	38.5%	45.7%
West Virginia	26,664	5.0%	12.1%	3.8%	2.0%	11.8%	3.1%	36.4%	25.9%	47.8%
Wisconsin	101,101	3.8%	4.4%	2.6%	3.3%	9.7%	1.9%	32.2%	42.1%	44.8%
Wyoming	12,251	10.9%	5.2%	2.8%	1.2%	5.7%	1.6%	35.4%	37.1%	34.8%

Table D-1: States—Household Relationship—*Continued*

| | | 25 to 33 | | | | | | | | |
| | | Married Couple Households | | Male, No Spouse Present | | Female, No Spouse Present | | Non-Family Householders | | |
	Total Householders	With Children	No Children	With Children	No Children	With Children	No Children	Living Alone	Not Alone	Living With Parents
United States..........................	15,842,697	27.5%	12.8%	4.4%	2.4%	14.8%	1.6%	22.6%	13.9%	21.4%
Alabama................................	231,873	29.4%	11.7%	4.7%	1.0%	20.9%	1.4%	22.8%	7.9%	25.0%
Alaska..................................	44,874	33.1%	14.7%	3.6%	1.0%	16.6%	1.0%	21.8%	8.1%	16.0%
Arizona.................................	336,057	29.2%	9.9%	6.4%	3.2%	16.0%	1.6%	21.1%	12.7%	19.6%
Arkansas...............................	155,107	35.4%	11.6%	5.3%	1.2%	15.8%	1.5%	19.7%	9.4%	15.8%
California..............................	1,752,696	26.2%	13.2%	4.8%	4.2%	12.0%	2.7%	20.0%	16.9%	26.3%
Colorado...............................	328,558	27.7%	14.5%	2.9%	2.3%	9.9%	1.1%	22.6%	19.1%	13.8%
Connecticut...........................	153,336	20.9%	14.5%	3.0%	2.8%	16.4%	1.4%	24.2%	16.9%	24.1%
Delaware...............................	43,221	29.1%	12.8%	1.8%	1.2%	19.7%	2.4%	17.3%	15.5%	24.8%
District of Columbia	63,496	5.4%	12.4%	1.6%	1.6%	10.9%	1.5%	36.8%	29.6%	9.8%
Florida..................................	843,555	23.7%	12.2%	4.7%	2.7%	17.2%	2.3%	23.2%	14.0%	26.3%
Georgia.................................	501,977	28.0%	11.8%	4.1%	2.1%	17.2%	1.7%	23.9%	11.3%	21.0%
Hawaii..................................	57,271	32.8%	18.0%	3.7%	2.3%	9.5%	3.2%	15.5%	15.0%	24.9%
Idaho....................................	85,253	37.5%	12.0%	5.4%	1.6%	12.9%	0.7%	17.4%	12.5%	15.7%
Illinois.................................	660,021	25.6%	13.5%	3.9%	1.9%	13.6%	1.7%	25.9%	14.0%	21.9%
Indiana.................................	331,955	33.2%	11.1%	5.5%	1.4%	15.8%	0.6%	22.0%	10.4%	18.2%
Iowa.....................................	180,235	30.5%	14.8%	4.3%	1.0%	13.3%	0.9%	22.4%	12.9%	11.1%
Kansas..................................	161,162	36.0%	12.1%	4.7%	1.7%	13.1%	0.9%	23.9%	7.7%	15.0%
Kentucky...............................	220,892	32.2%	12.5%	5.2%	2.4%	17.0%	0.3%	20.7%	9.8%	18.0%
Louisiana	255,366	29.6%	9.2%	3.9%	1.6%	21.2%	0.9%	22.3%	11.3%	20.9%
Maine	58,515	29.3%	14.7%	5.9%	0.6%	13.2%	1.5%	22.1%	12.8%	15.8%
Maryland...............................	268,778	24.8%	13.8%	5.8%	2.6%	13.9%	1.9%	22.7%	14.5%	25.0%
Massachusetts........................	332,132	18.1%	15.0%	2.9%	2.3%	12.9%	2.2%	23.8%	22.9%	22.2%
Michigan...............................	469,060	25.6%	12.2%	5.1%	1.7%	15.7%	1.1%	23.7%	14.9%	20.6%
Minnesota..............................	313,520	27.1%	15.0%	4.1%	1.5%	12.0%	1.0%	24.7%	14.5%	13.6%
Mississippi............................	138,084	30.5%	9.2%	4.9%	3.1%	26.4%	1.5%	17.6%	6.8%	23.4%
Missouri................................	327,983	32.2%	12.3%	5.4%	1.1%	14.6%	1.0%	22.6%	10.9%	14.8%
Montana................................	46,916	31.2%	11.1%	4.6%	0.2%	11.1%	0.2%	27.6%	14.0%	12.9%
Nebraska...............................	117,940	32.3%	10.3%	2.8%	1.4%	15.6%	1.5%	23.7%	12.4%	9.9%
Nevada..................................	154,748	23.0%	10.2%	5.6%	3.8%	16.4%	2.3%	24.4%	14.2%	19.7%
New Hampshire.......................	57,957	22.7%	18.5%	1.8%	1.2%	13.0%	0.9%	23.9%	17.9%	18.5%
New Jersey	352,703	25.5%	15.0%	3.5%	3.8%	15.0%	1.9%	21.2%	14.0%	31.1%
New Mexico	99,061	28.0%	11.2%	9.8%	3.4%	16.1%	2.5%	18.4%	10.6%	24.5%
New York	925,969	20.7%	12.1%	3.4%	3.2%	13.6%	2.4%	26.8%	17.9%	27.8%
North Carolina........................	508,647	28.0%	12.7%	4.5%	2.3%	15.9%	1.0%	23.4%	12.1%	18.4%
North Dakota..........................	53,794	32.7%	10.8%	6.2%	1.5%	6.3%	0.3%	24.9%	17.3%	7.5%
Ohio.....................................	607,199	26.8%	12.2%	3.8%	1.7%	17.6%	1.1%	24.3%	12.5%	17.5%
Oklahoma..............................	207,552	33.6%	12.3%	5.9%	2.2%	16.5%	1.0%	19.7%	8.8%	17.1%
Oregon..................................	200,773	23.4%	14.4%	5.1%	1.9%	13.5%	1.4%	21.4%	19.0%	17.0%
Pennsylvania..........................	600,475	25.2%	14.3%	4.5%	1.8%	15.3%	1.4%	23.2%	14.3%	22.2%
Rhode Island..........................	51,385	21.2%	10.1%	2.5%	2.8%	21.4%	1.1%	21.1%	19.7%	24.5%
South Carolina........................	242,174	28.8%	12.2%	3.1%	2.1%	17.3%	1.6%	23.4%	11.3%	20.4%
South Dakota..........................	51,967	31.5%	12.1%	6.3%	1.6%	11.9%	2.2%	25.5%	9.0%	9.0%
Tennessee.............................	338,215	31.1%	12.8%	4.0%	1.8%	17.2%	1.1%	20.5%	11.4%	19.0%
Texas....................................	1,473,329	31.5%	12.0%	4.2%	2.7%	15.5%	1.6%	22.3%	10.1%	20.5%
Utah.....................................	157,633	44.6%	15.6%	3.2%	1.4%	10.3%	0.8%	13.9%	10.2%	17.3%
Vermont................................	26,664	19.8%	13.0%	3.5%	0.2%	6.6%	1.2%	28.3%	27.4%	21.4%
Virginia.................................	418,209	27.3%	15.4%	3.5%	1.9%	12.6%	1.5%	22.1%	15.6%	19.5%
Washington............................	407,626	28.9%	14.8%	4.0%	1.8%	10.6%	1.1%	21.2%	17.7%	14.6%
West Virginia..........................	80,561	27.2%	12.3%	4.6%	1.1%	21.9%	1.5%	20.2%	11.1%	23.0%
Wisconsin..............................	312,797	27.6%	13.7%	4.2%	1.5%	13.2%	1.0%	24.0%	14.9%	13.6%
Wyoming...............................	33,426	39.8%	10.0%	6.3%	0.6%	10.1%	0.0%	21.1%	12.0%	11.4%

Table D-2: Counties—Household Relationship

		18 to 24								
		Married Couple Households		Male, No Spouse Present		Female, No Spouse Present		Non-Family Householders		
	Total Householders	With Children	No Children	With Children	No Children	With Children	No Children	Living Alone	Not Alone	Living With Parents
Alabama										
Baldwin County	1,708	8.2%	9.0%	8.0%	0.0%	0.0%	8.5%	8.3%	58.0%	55.0%
Calhoun County	2,219	0.0%	7.3%	0.0%	0.0%	28.0%	9.2%	27.9%	27.5%	43.3%
Etowah County	1,202	0.0%	15.9%	0.0%	5.2%	38.5%	0.0%	22.5%	17.9%	57.3%
Houston County	1,731	0.6%	0.9%	5.2%	0.9%	29.5%	4.9%	36.1%	22.0%	52.3%
Jefferson County	10,613	3.3%	8.9%	4.8%	3.8%	17.2%	1.9%	44.6%	15.5%	49.5%
Lauderdale County	2,118	17.5%	17.8%	0.0%	0.0%	18.8%	0.0%	14.8%	31.2%	20.5%
Lee County	7,586	2.3%	3.3%	10.1%	2.5%	9.5%	1.0%	42.8%	28.5%	24.8%
Madison County	4,731	10.7%	0.0%	1.0%	9.2%	19.0%	4.4%	41.8%	13.9%	46.7%
Marshall County	1,595	34.7%	2.1%	2.8%	0.0%	14.7%	0.0%	0.0%	45.7%	56.6%
Mobile County	5,550	9.1%	4.1%	5.7%	2.6%	23.8%	8.4%	25.5%	20.8%	51.3%
Montgomery County	5,559	5.3%	2.8%	13.1%	0.0%	9.7%	0.0%	38.1%	30.9%	33.9%
Morgan County	940	6.4%	44.3%	0.0%	10.1%	8.4%	0.0%	14.1%	16.7%	66.6%
Shelby County	2,054	8.2%	3.7%	0.0%	11.7%	0.0%	0.0%	20.1%	56.4%	53.4%
Tuscaloosa County	6,791	1.0%	2.0%	2.1%	11.1%	15.4%	6.7%	32.2%	29.5%	29.6%
Alaska										
Anchorage Municipality	7,804	2.3%	11.6%	5.2%	10.9%	8.1%	0.0%	39.2%	22.8%	42.5%
Fairbanks North Star Borough	2,675	26.2%	24.2%	0.0%	11.7%	11.6%	0.0%	26.2%	0.0%	32.7%
Matanuska-Susitna Borough	1,097	8.2%	25.9%	0.0%	2.7%	2.2%	0.0%	29.5%	31.4%	60.0%
Arizona										
Cochise County	2,274	15.7%	26.6%	0.0%	20.1%	11.3%	4.0%	18.8%	3.5%	44.0%
Coconino County	4,479	0.0%	5.8%	0.0%	0.0%	0.8%	0.0%	29.3%	64.1%	18.1%
Maricopa County	61,211	8.3%	5.6%	4.9%	7.1%	12.5%	5.5%	26.8%	29.3%	51.4%
Mohave County	1,898	6.7%	6.4%	9.6%	0.0%	0.0%	1.9%	37.5%	37.8%	54.3%
Navajo County	557	2.9%	65.2%	0.0%	0.0%	1.8%	12.6%	17.6%	0.0%	66.3%
Pima County	23,552	5.4%	6.9%	2.1%	6.5%	10.7%	3.2%	28.4%	36.8%	42.3%
Pinal County	2,081	14.3%	17.1%	0.0%	2.9%	18.3%	2.1%	31.5%	13.8%	59.8%
Yavapai County	3,108	1.5%	0.0%	0.0%	2.2%	26.8%	1.7%	27.0%	40.8%	41.0%
Yuma County	4,536	33.4%	24.4%	1.1%	8.9%	15.3%	1.9%	10.3%	4.8%	50.1%
Arkansas										
Benton County	2,962	12.8%	22.4%	7.5%	2.9%	10.6%	5.3%	19.8%	18.7%	56.4%
Craighead County	3,648	7.3%	10.0%	6.9%	8.5%	13.6%	0.0%	43.3%	10.4%	34.4%
Faulkner County	2,709	5.1%	10.1%	0.0%	7.6%	16.1%	0.0%	36.4%	24.7%	49.1%
Garland County	184	0.0%	0.0%	0.0%	0.0%	0.0%	0.0%	0.0%	100.0%	44.6%
Pulaski County	8,868	7.6%	5.0%	4.8%	4.2%	20.0%	0.9%	39.2%	18.3%	39.9%
Saline County	1,425	33.8%	5.4%	0.0%	0.0%	7.9%	0.0%	19.0%	33.9%	44.1%
Sebastian County	1,702	13.5%	0.0%	0.0%	0.0%	31.6%	22.6%	23.7%	8.8%	61.5%
Washington County	8,999	7.9%	12.0%	0.0%	6.7%	6.2%	0.9%	23.2%	43.1%	26.9%
California										
Alameda County	15,423	3.1%	3.1%	2.9%	13.1%	7.6%	4.8%	22.9%	42.5%	52.1%
Butte County	6,807	12.9%	3.7%	0.0%	4.2%	3.4%	5.4%	17.8%	52.6%	35.8%
Contra Costa County	6,966	11.1%	4.3%	4.7%	2.4%	18.9%	7.1%	9.1%	42.4%	69.3%
El Dorado County	711	6.8%	0.0%	0.0%	0.0%	6.8%	0.0%	47.3%	39.2%	65.8%
Fresno County	12,625	11.7%	7.7%	1.4%	10.9%	17.1%	4.9%	10.9%	35.3%	57.9%
Humboldt County	4,146	3.7%	1.8%	3.7%	0.8%	1.1%	0.0%	30.7%	58.2%	28.0%
Imperial County	423	29.1%	15.1%	0.0%	0.0%	46.1%	0.0%	0.0%	9.7%	72.4%
Kern County	9,590	13.1%	1.8%	2.4%	5.4%	22.4%	8.7%	30.8%	15.4%	64.6%
Kings County	1,847	19.2%	20.0%	10.9%	0.0%	21.3%	14.7%	0.7%	13.2%	48.9%
Los Angeles County	88,217	4.4%	4.4%	1.9%	12.2%	8.7%	9.1%	25.2%	34.1%	62.1%
Madera County	2,236	11.9%	11.5%	4.4%	17.8%	26.2%	4.6%	10.7%	13.1%	49.6%
Marin County	1,543	8.6%	6.9%	0.0%	0.0%	9.7%	16.3%	15.4%	43.0%	58.7%
Merced County	4,384	5.3%	2.5%	21.7%	20.9%	10.2%	6.3%	21.8%	11.4%	50.2%
Monterey County	3,145	1.0%	7.0%	22.1%	6.0%	5.5%	4.5%	29.0%	25.0%	57.3%
Napa County	771	17.4%	0.0%	0.0%	0.0%	0.0%	0.0%	18.8%	63.8%	65.8%
Nevada County	430	0.0%	0.0%	0.0%	0.0%	55.6%	33.0%	0.0%	11.4%	58.7%
Orange County	25,264	5.6%	9.0%	2.0%	9.7%	3.2%	6.4%	19.4%	44.6%	64.1%
Placer County	1,794	0.0%	20.8%	0.0%	0.0%	18.0%	0.0%	18.7%	42.4%	74.1%
Riverside County	17,513	11.7%	8.7%	4.6%	7.2%	13.5%	10.5%	21.7%	22.0%	68.0%
Sacramento County	17,450	6.2%	9.6%	4.3%	9.3%	9.5%	6.8%	27.1%	27.2%	59.5%
San Bernardino County	22,319	12.8%	12.5%	5.2%	6.2%	20.7%	8.8%	11.0%	22.8%	61.2%
San Diego County	38,901	7.7%	14.4%	5.3%	7.3%	6.6%	3.7%	18.9%	36.0%	50.1%
San Francisco County	9,443	0.0%	0.0%	0.3%	6.9%	5.1%	5.5%	36.2%	46.1%	35.8%
San Joaquin County	6,940	6.7%	4.4%	8.8%	3.9%	22.4%	8.9%	19.0%	25.8%	63.3%
San Luis Obispo County	6,236	5.0%	9.7%	0.0%	0.0%	0.0%	0.0%	30.9%	54.4%	27.9%
San Mateo County	3,843	9.0%	7.5%	0.0%	5.0%	6.0%	17.5%	20.8%	34.2%	64.7%
Santa Barbara County	11,045	7.1%	3.0%	2.6%	4.4%	7.1%	0.7%	16.4%	58.7%	34.9%
Santa Clara County	15,680	3.7%	7.4%	1.2%	7.7%	5.3%	5.9%	19.2%	49.7%	54.2%
Santa Cruz County	3,364	1.4%	5.5%	0.0%	0.0%	0.0%	0.0%	10.1%	83.0%	38.4%
Shasta County	3,628	10.7%	10.0%	4.5%	13.0%	9.2%	3.8%	27.4%	21.6%	35.5%
Solano County	4,199	11.2%	16.0%	6.4%	2.9%	5.6%	18.7%	22.0%	17.3%	57.8%
Sonoma County	5,719	5.8%	10.2%	3.0%	12.9%	7.7%	8.7%	17.0%	34.8%	59.8%
Stanislaus County	4,978	18.3%	4.8%	11.8%	13.7%	12.5%	5.5%	18.8%	14.6%	70.8%
Sutter County	930	0.0%	49.4%	0.0%	0.0%	0.0%	0.0%	24.7%	25.9%	65.3%
Tulare County	4,831	14.5%	1.5%	8.0%	3.0%	30.6%	2.3%	19.6%	20.5%	66.6%

Table D-2: Counties—Household Relationship—*Continued*

| | | 25 to 33 | | | | | | | | |
| | | Married Couple Households | | Male, No Spouse Present | | Female, No Spouse Present | | Non-Family Householders | | |
	Total Householders	With Children	No Children	With Children	No Children	With Children	No Children	Living Alone	Not Alone	Living With Parents
Alabama										
Baldwin County	6,287	38.0%	6.7%	8.5%	2.6%	3.4%	1.2%	36.1%	3.5%	55.0%
Calhoun County	4,788	31.7%	5.7%	14.6%	1.4%	22.3%	0.0%	21.0%	3.4%	43.3%
Etowah County	3,813	30.8%	13.6%	10.1%	1.2%	24.2%	4.1%	13.7%	2.3%	57.3%
Houston County	3,920	38.4%	7.6%	5.0%	2.6%	29.2%	0.3%	14.6%	2.2%	52.3%
Jefferson County	38,005	20.2%	13.0%	2.7%	1.3%	24.7%	2.0%	26.1%	10.0%	49.5%
Lauderdale County	3,891	20.9%	19.1%	0.0%	0.0%	30.5%	0.0%	25.5%	4.0%	20.5%
Lee County	7,574	33.2%	15.8%	1.8%	1.4%	18.3%	0.3%	25.4%	3.8%	24.8%
Madison County	23,035	32.3%	9.5%	3.0%	0.0%	10.5%	2.9%	28.7%	13.2%	46.7%
Marshall County	3,476	32.7%	18.3%	7.5%	0.5%	23.9%	0.0%	14.3%	2.8%	56.6%
Mobile County	20,594	31.4%	8.8%	3.2%	0.2%	21.3%	0.5%	26.4%	8.1%	51.3%
Montgomery County	14,411	18.9%	7.2%	4.8%	1.8%	31.1%	5.1%	24.3%	6.9%	33.9%
Morgan County	6,210	30.5%	11.6%	10.4%	2.4%	25.6%	1.2%	13.8%	4.6%	66.6%
Shelby County	9,344	35.7%	18.4%	2.0%	3.9%	9.8%	0.0%	19.0%	11.2%	53.4%
Tuscaloosa County	10,258	24.9%	9.5%	3.9%	0.0%	23.0%	0.0%	30.3%	8.3%	29.6%
Alaska										
Anchorage Municipality	20,574	33.5%	12.2%	0.7%	0.0%	23.5%	0.0%	22.5%	7.7%	42.5%
Fairbanks North Star Borough	8,638	25.9%	9.2%	10.5%	0.0%	15.5%	2.6%	30.2%	6.2%	32.7%
Matanuska-Susitna Borough	4,186	31.4%	17.4%	4.3%	0.8%	8.1%	4.7%	24.3%	8.9%	60.0%
Arizona										
Cochise County	6,414	36.3%	2.8%	0.8%	0.0%	22.1%	3.2%	30.9%	3.9%	44.0%
Coconino County	6,242	29.5%	6.6%	1.7%	3.3%	14.8%	5.2%	12.9%	26.0%	18.1%
Maricopa County	219,102	28.1%	10.8%	6.4%	3.0%	13.7%	1.3%	23.0%	13.6%	51.4%
Mohave County	7,792	21.1%	0.0%	13.8%	1.3%	36.3%	2.2%	16.3%	9.0%	54.3%
Navajo County	2,784	33.3%	7.5%	13.1%	3.0%	29.8%	0.0%	12.7%	0.6%	66.3%
Pima County	51,059	25.3%	9.7%	4.4%	4.2%	19.0%	2.1%	20.8%	14.4%	42.3%
Pinal County	12,987	36.0%	7.7%	6.0%	4.4%	24.6%	1.4%	14.1%	5.8%	59.8%
Yavapai County	7,955	47.0%	11.7%	16.6%	0.0%	10.5%	2.0%	9.2%	3.0%	41.0%
Yuma County	9,978	39.4%	13.1%	7.4%	4.6%	13.7%	0.0%	13.6%	8.2%	50.1%
Arkansas										
Benton County	14,756	37.7%	23.3%	4.4%	0.0%	11.5%	1.2%	13.5%	8.4%	56.4%
Craighead County	4,873	37.3%	8.9%	2.8%	0.0%	26.2%	0.0%	11.0%	13.6%	34.4%
Faulkner County	7,397	34.6%	5.7%	4.8%	0.8%	8.8%	12.3%	21.3%	11.7%	49.1%
Garland County	3,994	28.4%	2.4%	14.6%	6.4%	20.1%	3.1%	18.6%	6.5%	44.6%
Pulaski County	26,090	20.3%	9.4%	5.3%	1.2%	21.4%	1.6%	30.9%	9.9%	39.9%
Saline County	4,744	53.8%	4.8%	11.6%	0.0%	3.6%	0.0%	23.5%	2.7%	44.1%
Sebastian County	6,223	27.2%	8.6%	3.4%	1.1%	9.7%	0.0%	21.4%	28.6%	61.5%
Washington County	15,023	34.9%	15.2%	4.3%	0.0%	11.6%	2.5%	20.4%	11.2%	26.9%
California										
Alameda County	79,618	22.5%	20.0%	4.0%	3.9%	9.1%	2.1%	18.3%	20.2%	52.1%
Butte County	11,274	28.4%	8.0%	4.3%	0.2%	6.2%	0.5%	25.8%	26.6%	35.8%
Contra Costa County	40,794	30.5%	13.9%	3.7%	7.2%	12.0%	2.7%	12.3%	17.8%	69.3%
El Dorado County	4,920	41.2%	21.8%	0.8%	2.1%	5.0%	0.0%	25.5%	3.6%	65.8%
Fresno County	42,747	30.4%	7.2%	11.1%	2.9%	21.8%	3.8%	15.1%	7.7%	57.9%
Humboldt County	6,639	26.6%	5.3%	0.6%	2.1%	8.7%	1.5%	22.2%	33.0%	28.0%
Imperial County	5,571	49.3%	11.8%	8.7%	0.5%	12.3%	1.2%	11.8%	4.3%	72.4%
Kern County	45,724	32.2%	9.8%	8.6%	3.2%	22.1%	2.4%	14.0%	7.6%	64.6%
Kings County	9,542	35.7%	14.1%	6.9%	0.0%	15.0%	2.7%	9.3%	16.2%	48.9%
Los Angeles County	446,069	20.3%	11.6%	4.2%	5.4%	11.1%	4.0%	25.4%	18.0%	62.1%
Madera County	5,019	39.8%	11.7%	1.6%	6.7%	16.3%	1.6%	17.1%	5.2%	49.6%
Marin County	8,073	24.1%	17.8%	1.9%	1.3%	0.0%	0.0%	40.1%	14.7%	58.7%
Merced County	13,238	38.3%	5.6%	8.9%	4.6%	23.3%	0.8%	8.5%	10.0%	50.2%
Monterey County	17,427	34.9%	9.4%	9.3%	3.9%	17.3%	1.3%	13.2%	10.7%	57.3%
Napa County	5,176	32.8%	7.6%	5.8%	4.7%	13.3%	3.8%	10.8%	21.1%	65.8%
Nevada County	3,951	48.7%	8.6%	6.4%	0.0%	13.1%	2.8%	8.6%	11.8%	58.7%
Orange County	118,940	24.1%	18.5%	2.7%	4.8%	8.6%	3.8%	18.9%	18.6%	64.1%
Placer County	13,442	37.1%	9.8%	7.6%	0.6%	6.2%	1.4%	18.7%	18.5%	74.1%
Riverside County	84,566	38.7%	8.6%	7.1%	3.0%	12.3%	2.3%	17.7%	10.1%	68.0%
Sacramento County	83,094	27.5%	11.2%	4.6%	4.2%	14.8%	2.2%	21.2%	14.2%	59.5%
San Bernardino County	90,091	32.7%	10.7%	6.7%	6.2%	19.6%	3.4%	12.8%	7.8%	61.2%
San Diego County	167,698	25.6%	15.4%	4.7%	2.1%	9.5%	1.9%	21.3%	19.6%	50.1%
San Francisco County	70,630	5.4%	15.6%	0.2%	4.2%	1.0%	2.5%	31.4%	39.8%	35.8%
San Joaquin County	30,320	39.4%	6.9%	8.5%	6.6%	18.5%	1.0%	13.0%	6.0%	63.3%
San Luis Obispo County	12,218	29.5%	17.4%	5.7%	1.9%	11.4%	1.1%	9.0%	24.1%	27.9%
San Mateo County	32,845	19.1%	23.7%	3.9%	7.4%	7.3%	2.3%	17.1%	19.2%	64.7%
Santa Barbara County	14,623	24.1%	13.7%	4.4%	2.1%	19.8%	1.2%	15.8%	18.8%	34.9%
Santa Clara County	83,318	26.1%	21.5%	2.6%	4.2%	5.9%	2.5%	17.7%	19.5%	54.2%
Santa Cruz County	10,111	20.4%	11.7%	1.2%	7.8%	10.4%	0.9%	24.7%	23.0%	38.4%
Shasta County	9,137	32.3%	6.8%	0.0%	1.4%	22.3%	0.6%	15.4%	21.2%	35.5%
Solano County	18,155	34.8%	10.0%	3.3%	3.4%	22.1%	1.5%	12.9%	12.0%	57.8%
Sonoma County	18,678	23.3%	15.7%	5.2%	3.2%	13.7%	1.4%	15.6%	22.0%	59.8%
Stanislaus County	27,626	32.5%	12.4%	10.0%	2.6%	20.8%	1.2%	10.2%	10.3%	70.8%
Sutter County	4,857	41.6%	23.7%	7.1%	1.0%	15.0%	0.0%	6.7%	4.9%	65.3%
Tulare County	22,144	48.6%	4.6%	8.0%	3.9%	22.9%	0.8%	7.4%	3.7%	66.6%

Table D-2: Counties—Household Relationship—*Continued*

		18 to 24								
		Married Couple Households		Male, No Spouse Present		Female, No Spouse Present		Non-Family Householders		
	Total Householders	With Children	No Children	With Children	No Children	With Children	No Children	Living Alone	Not Alone	Living With Parents
California—Cont.										
Ventura County	5,501	21.4%	12.2%	6.0%	12.5%	3.1%	4.0%	21.8%	19.1%	67.0%
Yolo County	8,367	3.5%	2.1%	0.0%	1.0%	3.0%	5.0%	23.1%	62.3%	21.7%
Colorado										
Adams County	7,190	14.3%	8.5%	2.6%	9.5%	9.0%	0.6%	23.9%	31.6%	52.7%
Arapahoe County	8,274	4.7%	20.1%	1.2%	6.8%	9.0%	3.9%	21.4%	32.8%	63.1%
Boulder County	10,681	0.0%	2.8%	0.0%	3.0%	2.0%	2.7%	24.5%	65.1%	22.1%
Denver County	11,557	7.1%	5.3%	0.0%	7.7%	10.6%	2.2%	24.5%	42.6%	35.6%
Douglas County	4,330	13.6%	3.6%	0.0%	5.8%	3.3%	22.5%	24.0%	27.2%	60.6%
El Paso County	13,715	14.3%	14.4%	0.0%	2.3%	11.8%	1.7%	21.2%	34.3%	42.5%
Jefferson County	11,042	1.6%	6.3%	0.0%	2.3%	10.1%	8.6%	21.4%	49.6%	42.0%
Larimer County	10,544	0.0%	7.8%	1.4%	4.5%	3.2%	1.1%	11.3%	70.8%	24.7%
Mesa County	2,403	0.0%	8.2%	0.0%	12.4%	6.9%	3.3%	22.9%	46.4%	37.8%
Pueblo County	2,330	3.3%	0.0%	7.5%	1.0%	11.2%	15.0%	25.6%	36.3%	51.7%
Weld County	4,877	11.7%	8.0%	4.7%	4.8%	13.3%	0.0%	22.7%	34.9%	40.5%
Connecticut										
Fairfield County	5,592	1.1%	5.6%	6.8%	0.7%	13.4%	11.1%	34.2%	27.1%	69.2%
Hartford County	8,163	5.5%	5.2%	11.1%	9.3%	15.4%	4.9%	25.6%	23.0%	60.6%
Litchfield County	991	5.2%	0.0%	0.0%	0.0%	32.5%	0.0%	11.8%	50.5%	75.0%
Middlesex County	1,187	0.0%	9.4%	4.2%	0.0%	0.0%	0.0%	34.4%	52.0%	46.9%
New Haven County	6,246	2.2%	0.8%	7.9%	6.1%	17.4%	8.9%	30.0%	26.8%	56.5%
New London County	3,409	5.0%	21.8%	10.2%	0.0%	16.0%	0.0%	24.3%	22.7%	50.3%
Tolland County	3,225	2.9%	3.3%	0.0%	0.0%	0.0%	2.0%	39.8%	51.9%	27.6%
Windham County	1,340	0.0%	0.0%	11.7%	14.4%	13.9%	0.0%	16.5%	43.5%	41.8%
Delaware										
Kent County	2,729	1.7%	13.7%	0.0%	10.9%	13.0%	8.7%	20.7%	31.3%	39.4%
New Castle County	4,433	3.7%	14.8%	1.3%	2.9%	8.9%	0.0%	27.0%	41.3%	54.1%
Sussex County	1,765	12.6%	53.3%	0.0%	0.0%	5.0%	0.0%	8.8%	20.4%	62.5%
Florida										
Alachua County	10,078	3.3%	1.6%	0.0%	0.5%	0.3%	4.8%	36.6%	52.7%	24.4%
Bay County	1,064	5.9%	9.9%	2.3%	0.0%	19.2%	0.0%	29.6%	33.1%	66.2%
Brevard County	5,028	1.3%	9.7%	9.3%	6.5%	17.9%	0.0%	32.5%	22.7%	60.0%
Broward County	13,197	6.2%	11.4%	4.9%	5.2%	19.9%	8.0%	26.3%	18.2%	68.8%
Charlotte County	822	6.6%	0.0%	0.0%	0.0%	24.2%	69.2%	0.0%	0.0%	76.9%
Citrus County	978	0.0%	2.6%	0.0%	8.7%	19.6%	0.0%	37.2%	31.9%	44.5%
Clay County	2,034	0.0%	6.5%	0.0%	0.0%	11.9%	28.7%	43.7%	9.2%	62.4%
Collier County	1,215	11.0%	5.8%	8.6%	5.2%	14.0%	0.0%	33.3%	22.1%	69.8%
Duval County	16,314	6.4%	14.6%	3.2%	2.2%	22.3%	1.8%	16.5%	33.0%	45.9%
Escambia County	4,598	0.0%	7.2%	1.8%	12.6%	8.1%	1.2%	39.8%	29.2%	32.8%
Flagler County	914	0.0%	0.0%	0.0%	43.5%	11.7%	10.5%	5.7%	28.6%	61.7%
Hernando County	289	10.7%	12.8%	0.0%	0.0%	63.7%	0.0%	0.0%	12.8%	81.2%
Highlands County	860	0.0%	0.0%	20.7%	0.0%	4.8%	0.0%	51.4%	23.1%	49.5%
Hillsborough County	18,463	4.1%	6.5%	5.5%	3.9%	11.2%	6.3%	33.2%	29.3%	51.5%
Indian River County	566	18.2%	6.0%	32.9%	0.0%	32.0%	0.0%	4.4%	6.5%	54.1%
Lake County	3,313	11.6%	10.9%	17.2%	6.2%	4.4%	0.0%	17.4%	32.3%	64.3%
Lee County	4,037	1.8%	6.5%	3.6%	6.6%	17.8%	0.0%	32.1%	31.6%	51.3%
Leon County	17,338	1.4%	0.6%	0.0%	3.5%	4.7%	2.5%	37.2%	50.1%	19.8%
Manatee County	1,426	21.8%	5.8%	12.8%	2.0%	20.2%	2.0%	10.1%	25.3%	67.3%
Marion County	1,170	5.6%	19.9%	0.0%	0.0%	16.1%	6.0%	31.7%	20.7%	72.1%
Martin County	402	0.0%	0.0%	0.0%	0.0%	5.0%	0.0%	30.1%	64.9%	70.9%
Miami-Dade County	14,954	2.9%	5.3%	2.8%	12.4%	13.3%	8.9%	35.5%	19.0%	68.6%
Okaloosa County	4,683	18.9%	13.4%	1.3%	3.0%	9.1%	0.0%	24.9%	29.3%	38.5%
Orange County	22,092	7.5%	2.8%	1.3%	12.0%	11.6%	6.9%	23.4%	34.6%	48.4%
Osceola County	2,849	12.2%	21.2%	9.7%	0.0%	15.9%	8.4%	17.6%	15.0%	68.3%
Palm Beach County	11,207	6.4%	4.3%	4.1%	12.5%	9.1%	5.3%	27.9%	30.5%	60.6%
Pasco County	5,088	6.9%	5.2%	7.1%	7.2%	19.6%	2.1%	15.5%	36.4%	58.1%
Pinellas County	6,275	8.1%	16.8%	1.6%	5.2%	9.9%	8.4%	32.0%	18.0%	63.4%
Polk County	4,290	8.5%	5.4%	6.0%	7.3%	16.2%	3.8%	19.7%	33.0%	62.1%
Santa Rosa County	2,245	15.6%	10.0%	0.0%	0.0%	3.7%	14.0%	23.3%	33.5%	51.5%
Sarasota County	2,007	9.3%	7.3%	0.0%	5.9%	18.7%	15.7%	7.3%	35.7%	66.1%
Seminole County	1,713	30.6%	0.0%	0.0%	0.0%	23.5%	0.0%	0.0%	45.8%	55.2%
St. Johns County	2,926	5.8%	9.5%	8.5%	2.9%	3.7%	18.5%	24.4%	26.8%	62.9%
St. Lucie County	4,640	4.6%	3.7%	1.3%	5.8%	6.1%	8.4%	30.2%	40.0%	55.4%
Sumter County	326	0.0%	0.0%	89.9%	0.0%	10.1%	0.0%	0.0%	0.0%	82.9%
Volusia County	5,922	2.0%	9.7%	1.0%	16.1%	8.0%	6.3%	27.7%	29.2%	51.2%
Georgia										
Bartow County	1,499	33.3%	7.8%	38.0%	0.0%	10.5%	0.0%	3.7%	6.7%	46.5%
Bibb County	2,664	1.2%	0.0%	0.0%	0.0%	33.8%	0.0%	31.4%	33.6%	47.8%
Carroll County	3,513	5.2%	0.0%	7.5%	1.4%	19.2%	0.0%	35.1%	31.6%	41.7%
Chatham County	5,487	0.7%	9.7%	0.0%	0.8%	14.2%	0.0%	45.8%	28.7%	37.4%
Cherokee County	1,756	26.3%	14.1%	0.0%	0.0%	0.0%	1.3%	6.3%	52.1%	60.7%
Clarke County	9,038	0.0%	6.5%	0.0%	1.0%	1.3%	1.4%	32.6%	57.3%	11.4%
Clayton County	3,661	6.9%	12.6%	5.3%	5.7%	13.4%	10.3%	19.6%	26.1%	52.0%
Cobb County	9,195	10.1%	7.4%	5.1%	3.3%	7.3%	1.3%	26.3%	39.2%	55.2%
Columbia County	547	0.0%	47.2%	0.0%	0.0%	24.1%	11.5%	0.0%	17.2%	79.8%
Coweta County	2,615	25.4%	13.8%	0.0%	6.6%	0.0%	16.1%	27.4%	10.6%	56.9%

Table D-2: Counties—Household Relationship—Continued

	Total Householders	25 to 33								
		Married Couple Households		Male, No Spouse Present		Female, No Spouse Present		Non-Family Householders		
		With Children	No Children	With Children	No Children	With Children	No Children	Living Alone	Not Alone	Living With Parents
California—Cont.										
Ventura County	27,244	33.3%	14.4%	3.3%	2.8%	13.7%	5.1%	13.9%	13.6%	67.0%
Yolo County	9,604	24.2%	16.5%	0.0%	4.2%	7.7%	4.6%	21.4%	21.4%	21.7%
Colorado										
Adams County	27,333	37.5%	12.2%	5.5%	3.0%	10.6%	2.0%	14.3%	14.9%	52.7%
Arapahoe County	35,588	31.8%	15.5%	2.4%	2.4%	11.6%	0.9%	21.1%	14.1%	63.1%
Boulder County	17,315	21.0%	17.2%	0.5%	1.0%	6.1%	3.5%	23.0%	27.8%	22.1%
Denver County	68,328	12.9%	13.9%	2.2%	2.8%	7.0%	1.1%	34.0%	26.1%	35.6%
Douglas County	12,788	42.7%	20.2%	2.2%	0.0%	6.4%	0.8%	4.3%	23.5%	60.6%
El Paso County	45,329	32.6%	13.1%	3.9%	2.2%	13.9%	1.2%	21.7%	11.5%	42.5%
Jefferson County	30,311	22.2%	19.5%	4.9%	2.3%	5.3%	1.2%	22.0%	22.7%	42.0%
Larimer County	18,911	18.6%	14.6%	2.0%	1.5%	11.3%	2.6%	18.2%	31.1%	24.7%
Mesa County	8,526	34.5%	20.3%	1.1%	0.0%	11.8%	0.0%	22.4%	9.9%	37.8%
Pueblo County	8,447	38.7%	7.6%	8.6%	0.0%	19.9%	0.0%	18.2%	7.0%	51.7%
Weld County	16,519	47.0%	10.5%	1.7%	1.8%	11.4%	1.4%	17.0%	9.2%	40.5%
Connecticut										
Fairfield County	32,926	23.9%	16.6%	3.4%	2.6%	14.7%	2.4%	17.8%	18.6%	69.2%
Hartford County	41,226	21.3%	15.8%	1.6%	2.6%	20.7%	1.2%	21.5%	15.4%	60.6%
Litchfield County	6,098	27.3%	15.0%	0.6%	10.4%	6.1%	0.7%	29.1%	10.8%	75.0%
Middlesex County	6,679	11.8%	20.0%	0.8%	0.0%	12.4%	1.6%	34.9%	18.6%	46.9%
New Haven County	39,355	13.1%	10.1%	5.4%	2.4%	17.0%	1.0%	32.0%	18.9%	56.5%
New London County	14,756	30.0%	13.0%	0.8%	2.8%	15.5%	0.7%	28.0%	9.2%	50.3%
Tolland County	6,148	26.8%	25.6%	2.9%	2.6%	7.7%	0.0%	9.0%	25.4%	27.6%
Windham County	5,247	32.2%	3.1%	4.3%	4.5%	20.5%	2.6%	11.7%	21.1%	41.8%
Delaware										
Kent County	8,713	29.3%	6.3%	0.6%	1.5%	31.5%	3.0%	14.8%	12.9%	39.4%
New Castle County	26,843	25.6%	15.7%	2.1%	1.2%	16.0%	2.8%	17.5%	19.2%	54.1%
Sussex County	7,665	41.2%	10.1%	2.3%	1.2%	19.6%	0.0%	19.8%	5.8%	62.5%
Florida										
Alachua County	16,534	22.0%	16.5%	0.9%	3.9%	11.6%	1.6%	23.3%	20.2%	24.4%
Bay County	10,036	35.5%	8.5%	3.9%	1.0%	14.6%	0.5%	27.1%	8.8%	66.2%
Brevard County	20,536	28.1%	11.9%	7.7%	0.0%	17.2%	1.5%	18.6%	15.0%	60.0%
Broward County	75,321	19.1%	11.4%	6.7%	3.5%	17.1%	4.1%	24.0%	14.2%	68.8%
Charlotte County	2,166	48.3%	11.3%	7.8%	2.4%	11.6%	0.0%	7.2%	11.2%	76.9%
Citrus County	2,850	47.3%	4.8%	0.0%	2.1%	30.1%	0.0%	12.4%	3.2%	44.5%
Clay County	7,812	43.4%	6.7%	8.4%	0.6%	12.3%	0.0%	11.6%	17.1%	62.4%
Collier County	9,157	28.2%	4.6%	6.7%	3.4%	17.5%	9.8%	16.3%	13.6%	69.8%
Duval County	51,435	21.7%	14.2%	3.5%	1.0%	16.6%	2.1%	24.6%	16.4%	45.9%
Escambia County	17,149	17.3%	14.8%	3.4%	3.0%	14.8%	1.3%	30.7%	14.8%	32.8%
Flagler County	2,611	44.9%	11.4%	0.0%	6.7%	4.6%	0.0%	7.6%	24.8%	61.7%
Hernando County	5,258	26.4%	23.9%	6.4%	0.0%	28.8%	0.0%	14.5%	0.9%	01.2%
Highlands County	2,521	41.5%	7.9%	8.3%	0.0%	19.2%	0.0%	16.7%	6.4%	49.5%
Hillsborough County	80,044	18.3%	12.3%	4.9%	2.9%	19.0%	1.7%	26.4%	14.6%	51.5%
Indian River County	3,190	57.8%	14.2%	5.2%	0.0%	10.5%	0.0%	8.7%	3.6%	54.1%
Lake County	10,499	18.0%	16.8%	3.7%	2.4%	25.8%	3.6%	18.6%	11.2%	64.3%
Lee County	20,219	25.7%	6.1%	7.9%	2.4%	23.0%	2.9%	21.0%	11.0%	51.3%
Leon County	17,296	18.8%	11.8%	1.8%	0.0%	17.2%	0.9%	29.9%	19.7%	19.8%
Manatee County	9,013	25.1%	5.3%	5.7%	0.6%	30.4%	0.0%	19.2%	13.9%	67.3%
Marion County	8,464	38.3%	7.0%	1.5%	0.9%	28.4%	0.0%	16.9%	7.0%	72.1%
Martin County	4,350	24.5%	24.3%	5.2%	0.0%	2.3%	0.0%	29.7%	14.1%	70.9%
Miami-Dade County	104,958	19.4%	11.6%	4.2%	4.5%	19.1%	3.1%	26.8%	11.3%	68.6%
Okaloosa County	12,811	29.2%	20.8%	7.5%	2.6%	9.1%	0.0%	23.0%	7.7%	38.5%
Orange County	78,710	21.5%	12.2%	3.2%	3.0%	14.7%	2.7%	23.5%	19.3%	48.4%
Osceola County	11,900	29.8%	12.7%	4.3%	5.0%	17.4%	1.1%	11.5%	18.3%	68.3%
Palm Beach County	49,601	22.6%	13.0%	6.1%	5.3%	15.1%	2.8%	23.3%	11.7%	60.6%
Pasco County	16,661	34.1%	10.7%	8.2%	2.7%	14.0%	1.9%	15.0%	13.3%	58.1%
Pinellas County	37,849	17.6%	12.2%	2.9%	2.0%	13.6%	1.9%	32.5%	17.4%	63.4%
Polk County	26,572	32.1%	13.2%	7.6%	1.0%	21.0%	4.8%	12.0%	8.3%	62.1%
Santa Rosa County	7,242	36.7%	20.8%	4.9%	0.7%	5.5%	4.7%	18.5%	8.1%	51.5%
Sarasota County	12,389	13.0%	15.7%	5.0%	6.9%	23.7%	0.0%	15.0%	20.8%	66.1%
Seminole County	10,082	48.0%	8.0%	1.1%	0.0%	12.9%	0.0%	17.9%	12.1%	55.2%
St. Johns County	12,056	31.3%	11.2%	3.2%	1.9%	13.6%	2.0%	27.5%	9.2%	62.9%
St. Lucie County	22,038	25.5%	16.1%	3.8%	1.5%	11.9%	3.4%	23.9%	13.9%	55.4%
Sumter County	1,387	9.2%	2.7%	0.0%	0.0%	66.9%	0.0%	11.8%	9.3%	82.9%
Volusia County	19,985	23.2%	11.8%	0.7%	1.8%	15.0%	1.3%	24.4%	21.7%	51.2%
Georgia										
Bartow County	4,084	31.0%	10.9%	3.6%	3.4%	11.7%	0.0%	22.3%	17.0%	46.5%
Bibb County	8,305	14.7%	28.4%	2.6%	0.0%	22.5%	0.6%	23.4%	7.8%	47.8%
Carroll County	5,934	44.1%	3.3%	0.0%	0.0%	26.4%	2.3%	10.4%	13.5%	41.7%
Chatham County	19,021	24.7%	14.6%	2.0%	3.3%	17.2%	1.8%	25.5%	10.9%	37.4%
Cherokee County	10,554	43.5%	18.9%	2.8%	0.0%	6.4%	2.4%	9.6%	16.4%	60.7%
Clarke County	7,483	7.8%	13.3%	2.3%	0.0%	12.8%	1.1%	35.3%	27.3%	11.4%
Clayton County	12,070	17.0%	3.3%	9.9%	7.0%	25.7%	1.6%	27.3%	8.3%	52.0%
Cobb County	39,927	24.6%	20.8%	3.1%	2.9%	11.7%	2.8%	21.5%	12.6%	55.2%
Columbia County	7,069	51.7%	8.3%	1.7%	2.7%	11.6%	0.7%	14.0%	9.4%	79.8%
Coweta County	5,680	47.3%	12.8%	3.9%	0.0%	4.5%	0.0%	20.3%	11.2%	56.9%

Table D-2: Counties—Household Relationship—*Continued*

		18 to 24								
		Married Couple Households		Male, No Spouse Present		Female, No Spouse Present		Non-Family Householders		
	Total Householders	With Children	No Children	With Children	No Children	With Children	No Children	Living Alone	Not Alone	Living With Parents
Georgia—Cont.										
DeKalb County	8,531	3.2%	0.6%	1.6%	3.4%	11.8%	6.2%	36.4%	36.9%	45.4%
Dougherty County	1,514	8.9%	0.0%	0.0%	0.0%	17.3%	0.0%	66.7%	7.1%	52.6%
Douglas County	905	13.0%	39.7%	0.0%	0.0%	0.0%	0.0%	0.0%	47.3%	74.1%
Fayette County	448	15.6%	27.7%	0.0%	0.0%	0.0%	0.0%	36.8%	19.9%	88.9%
Floyd County	993	0.0%	11.4%	2.9%	21.5%	42.6%	0.0%	11.7%	10.0%	58.4%
Forsyth County	751	5.3%	0.0%	7.2%	0.0%	3.5%	8.9%	65.2%	9.9%	85.8%
Fulton County	16,405	2.9%	3.7%	1.5%	3.3%	14.4%	1.5%	47.0%	25.6%	42.4%
Gwinnett County	7,971	13.7%	7.1%	10.5%	8.1%	15.6%	7.8%	25.2%	12.0%	69.2%
Hall County	2,436	20.6%	12.8%	0.0%	1.5%	9.0%	0.0%	21.2%	34.9%	58.7%
Henry County	1,404	0.0%	19.2%	5.8%	32.5%	0.0%	0.0%	33.5%	9.0%	74.8%
Houston County	2,552	17.2%	16.8%	0.0%	0.0%	16.6%	0.0%	30.6%	18.8%	59.1%
Lowndes County	3,377	6.8%	5.5%	0.0%	0.0%	0.0%	2.0%	31.8%	53.9%	35.1%
Muscogee County	3,483	15.2%	13.2%	1.9%	1.3%	14.1%	2.4%	20.5%	31.4%	39.1%
Newton County	1,404	31.5%	0.0%	34.5%	1.6%	10.3%	0.0%	0.0%	22.2%	54.1%
Paulding County	431	0.0%	0.0%	0.0%	0.0%	0.0%	0.0%	70.1%	29.9%	80.9%
Richmond County	3,230	6.4%	7.8%	0.0%	0.0%	4.7%	7.7%	45.2%	28.2%	39.8%
Whitfield County	2,895	12.0%	8.2%	8.9%	14.6%	34.0%	0.0%	16.6%	5.7%	50.8%
Hawaii										
Hawaii County	1,958	1.1%	0.0%	5.4%	7.2%	4.0%	0.0%	11.3%	71.1%	49.2%
Honolulu County	13,504	20.3%	24.4%	0.0%	6.4%	0.5%	4.6%	21.7%	22.1%	43.9%
Maui County	833	0.0%	3.6%	0.0%	6.7%	0.0%	57.3%	0.0%	32.4%	58.5%
Idaho										
Ada County	6,291	8.7%	11.0%	0.0%	0.6%	6.1%	0.7%	31.6%	41.3%	38.3%
Bonneville County	1,212	24.8%	9.6%	0.0%	0.0%	22.9%	0.0%	24.6%	18.2%	36.7%
Canyon County	1,800	8.5%	12.6%	0.0%	0.0%	6.4%	17.7%	43.1%	11.8%	47.2%
Kootenai County	1,646	9.0%	0.0%	0.0%	0.0%	23.0%	0.0%	64.4%	3.6%	60.0%
Illinois										
Champaign County	10,622	2.9%	1.3%	0.0%	7.3%	1.2%	1.1%	37.3%	48.8%	21.0%
Cook County	53,671	5.4%	3.9%	2.5%	7.4%	11.4%	2.9%	32.2%	34.4%	59.1%
DeKalb County	5,467	7.2%	0.0%	0.0%	3.6%	8.4%	0.0%	36.6%	44.1%	28.1%
DuPage County	8,289	12.1%	3.5%	1.3%	6.6%	11.0%	2.4%	40.3%	22.9%	67.2%
Kane County	4,272	18.3%	6.0%	1.7%	18.3%	23.6%	7.0%	6.2%	18.9%	76.8%
Kankakee County	1,173	3.7%	15.3%	6.8%	0.0%	32.8%	0.0%	34.4%	7.0%	53.7%
Kendall County	542	0.0%	0.0%	62.9%	0.0%	0.0%	0.0%	0.0%	37.1%	82.5%
Lake County	5,364	9.7%	7.6%	0.0%	1.2%	26.1%	4.2%	32.4%	18.9%	69.8%
LaSalle County	1,440	37.2%	4.7%	0.0%	0.0%	0.0%	0.0%	58.1%	0.0%	65.2%
Macon County	2,579	11.7%	20.0%	0.0%	0.0%	11.6%	0.0%	17.6%	39.1%	73.5%
Madison County	7,070	2.4%	4.6%	1.4%	0.0%	0.0%	0.0%	36.8%	54.9%	25.5%
McHenry County	1,979	0.0%	0.0%	0.0%	0.0%	31.7%	0.0%	53.0%	15.3%	45.9%
McLean County	3,451	0.5%	0.6%	0.0%	9.4%	8.0%	14.8%	21.3%	45.5%	48.8%
Peoria County	2,634	0.8%	0.0%	0.0%	3.7%	15.2%	0.0%	41.2%	39.1%	45.9%
Rock Island County	1,531	3.3%	2.2%	0.0%	0.0%	21.2%	0.0%	41.0%	32.3%	51.8%
Sangamon County	3,749	0.0%	16.7%	0.0%	5.4%	21.9%	1.0%	39.8%	15.2%	55.3%
St. Clair County	2,382	2.9%	7.3%	0.0%	0.0%	30.4%	0.0%	28.7%	30.7%	53.9%
Tazewell County	1,758	1.0%	3.4%	0.0%	0.0%	27.7%	0.0%	53.5%	14.3%	61.4%
Will County	4,138	8.9%	4.6%	2.7%	28.0%	23.0%	4.8%	19.6%	8.5%	72.3%
Winnebago County	4,258	15.2%	5.1%	12.8%	1.6%	36.4%	0.0%	22.2%	6.6%	60.7%
Indiana										
Allen County	7,303	4.6%	10.1%	2.4%	1.4%	17.1%	5.6%	21.8%	37.0%	48.2%
Clark County	880	7.0%	8.9%	0.0%	11.3%	2.4%	14.7%	42.2%	13.6%	63.8%
Delaware County	5,871	5.7%	0.7%	0.0%	1.3%	18.0%	0.0%	26.9%	47.3%	21.7%
Elkhart County	4,845	6.1%	20.8%	0.9%	19.8%	26.8%	0.0%	8.6%	17.1%	55.5%
Hamilton County	4,086	6.8%	7.3%	0.0%	0.0%	17.2%	0.0%	35.9%	32.8%	70.9%
Hendricks County	884	10.1%	35.6%	7.4%	6.0%	0.0%	0.0%	38.7%	2.3%	73.4%
Johnson County	2,173	0.0%	12.8%	0.0%	23.1%	0.0%	0.0%	19.1%	45.0%	46.1%
Lake County	4,473	14.4%	3.3%	2.1%	0.0%	24.6%	4.3%	26.8%	24.6%	66.6%
LaPorte County	1,842	14.5%	0.0%	0.0%	0.0%	14.3%	0.0%	33.3%	37.8%	47.7%
Madison County	1,940	10.8%	19.7%	6.9%	2.5%	20.8%	4.5%	16.1%	18.8%	49.3%
Marion County	17,590	6.4%	3.5%	1.7%	5.3%	17.5%	4.6%	32.5%	28.6%	47.9%
Monroe County	8,920	0.5%	2.6%	0.0%	1.7%	3.7%	3.5%	40.6%	47.4%	7.9%
Porter County	1,769	7.5%	6.3%	0.0%	0.0%	20.5%	0.0%	13.5%	52.2%	51.4%
St. Joseph County	2,958	4.3%	6.3%	5.2%	1.6%	11.4%	8.2%	34.9%	28.1%	43.7%
Tippecanoe County	10,887	3.1%	1.6%	0.0%	0.0%	5.3%	7.1%	33.4%	49.6%	15.8%
Vanderburgh County	4,387	3.9%	5.7%	0.0%	0.0%	29.0%	0.0%	47.1%	14.4%	39.8%
Vigo County	3,530	0.0%	2.1%	1.9%	0.0%	20.6%	1.1%	42.0%	32.3%	21.8%
Iowa										
Black Hawk County	5,089	2.4%	2.3%	0.0%	2.2%	25.7%	2.0%	38.1%	27.3%	23.9%
Dubuque County	1,588	26.6%	5.2%	6.7%	0.0%	7.0%	0.0%	36.4%	18.1%	42.2%
Johnson County	8,454	0.0%	8.4%	1.7%	0.0%	0.0%	0.0%	27.1%	62.8%	11.4%
Linn County	4,713	0.9%	4.7%	0.0%	0.0%	16.1%	0.0%	43.3%	35.1%	41.9%
Polk County	8,754	8.9%	9.3%	0.0%	0.0%	15.9%	1.9%	21.6%	42.5%	40.7%
Pottawattamie County	1,644	1.3%	1.6%	0.0%	0.0%	14.2%	0.0%	31.6%	51.2%	51.7%
Scott County	1,961	9.6%	0.0%	4.2%	0.0%	13.9%	2.7%	8.0%	61.6%	46.8%
Story County	6,915	2.6%	0.0%	0.0%	1.7%	0.0%	0.0%	9.6%	86.0%	11.6%
Woodbury County	1,678	9.1%	10.5%	0.0%	0.0%	8.2%	0.0%	47.4%	24.9%	49.7%

Table D-2: Counties—Household Relationship—*Continued*

| | | 25 to 33 | | | | | | | | |
| | | Married Couple Households | | Male, No Spouse Present | | Female, No Spouse Present | | Non-Family Householders | | |
	Total Householders	With Children	No Children	With Children	No Children	With Children	No Children	Living Alone	Not Alone	Living With Parents
Georgia—Cont.										
DeKalb County	45,183	14.7%	11.6%	3.3%	2.9%	16.5%	3.3%	32.2%	15.5%	45.4%
Dougherty County	5,619	17.9%	1.0%	2.5%	0.0%	46.7%	0.0%	24.8%	7.1%	52.6%
Douglas County	6,279	24.2%	12.0%	7.1%	6.3%	16.8%	4.7%	25.3%	3.7%	74.1%
Fayette County	2,411	35.6%	8.3%	2.9%	0.0%	11.7%	0.0%	39.0%	2.4%	88.9%
Floyd County	3,852	35.5%	15.3%	5.1%	0.3%	24.0%	0.0%	18.8%	1.0%	58.4%
Forsyth County	6,869	61.0%	14.1%	2.2%	2.4%	6.9%	2.6%	3.9%	6.8%	85.8%
Fulton County	69,943	10.3%	11.8%	2.8%	1.8%	9.6%	1.7%	45.5%	16.5%	42.4%
Gwinnett County	36,832	35.1%	8.5%	5.6%	1.5%	13.1%	3.0%	18.8%	14.4%	69.2%
Hall County	7,815	41.0%	18.2%	1.3%	2.7%	14.3%	0.8%	14.5%	7.1%	58.7%
Henry County	8,146	60.2%	9.7%	3.3%	0.0%	8.1%	4.5%	10.4%	4.0%	74.8%
Houston County	8,001	24.3%	18.3%	3.4%	0.0%	28.5%	0.6%	15.2%	9.6%	59.1%
Lowndes County	5,530	45.4%	6.9%	0.5%	0.0%	13.0%	0.6%	21.3%	12.3%	35.1%
Muscogee County	12,973	30.3%	12.4%	5.2%	1.7%	14.3%	0.0%	30.3%	5.8%	39.1%
Newton County	4,125	19.0%	9.4%	3.5%	11.9%	11.9%	0.0%	31.7%	12.7%	54.1%
Paulding County	6,510	52.7%	8.4%	6.5%	0.0%	21.2%	0.0%	6.8%	4.5%	80.9%
Richmond County	12,097	25.4%	11.0%	1.5%	1.2%	26.5%	0.0%	25.3%	9.0%	39.8%
Whitfield County	4,967	35.9%	12.3%	8.3%	0.8%	19.2%	1.5%	8.3%	13.6%	50.8%
Hawaii										
Hawaii County	5,408	39.5%	12.5%	0.0%	0.0%	21.0%	5.5%	11.0%	9.9%	49.2%
Honolulu County	42,808	32.7%	17.5%	4.0%	2.5%	6.4%	3.6%	16.9%	16.4%	43.9%
Maui County	6,949	32.7%	24.7%	4.6%	0.0%	21.1%	0.1%	5.0%	11.8%	58.5%
Idaho										
Ada County	25,661	25.0%	9.1%	5.7%	2.7%	12.8%	1.5%	27.2%	15.9%	38.3%
Bonneville County	6,012	65.4%	11.7%	6.6%	0.0%	2.9%	0.0%	10.6%	2.8%	36.7%
Canyon County	8,839	29.7%	6.1%	7.5%	0.0%	26.0%	0.0%	23.6%	7.0%	47.2%
Kootenai County	7,747	30.5%	11.3%	6.6%	0.0%	20.0%	0.0%	6.3%	25.3%	60.0%
Illinois										
Champaign County	12,931	26.0%	10.2%	2.0%	0.4%	6.0%	0.0%	38.5%	16.9%	21.0%
Cook County	311,937	18.3%	14.2%	2.8%	2.7%	11.4%	2.6%	31.5%	16.5%	59.1%
DeKalb County	5,349	17.5%	12.8%	5.3%	1.1%	23.4%	0.0%	20.3%	19.7%	28.1%
DuPage County	37,727	29.3%	19.5%	2.3%	0.9%	8.1%	1.1%	22.5%	16.2%	67.2%
Kane County	19,606	45.3%	10.6%	2.3%	0.7%	17.0%	0.7%	12.6%	10.7%	76.8%
Kankakee County	5,148	28.1%	11.3%	7.8%	4.2%	30.7%	0.0%	11.7%	6.2%	53.7%
Kendall County	7,941	35.6%	28.7%	12.1%	0.0%	4.8%	2.9%	8.8%	7.1%	82.5%
Lake County	25,548	36.0%	16.3%	2.8%	3.7%	13.6%	1.6%	17.5%	8.5%	69.8%
LaSalle County	5,846	25.4%	8.3%	4.9%	5.7%	19.9%	0.0%	20.4%	15.4%	65.2%
Macon County	11,049	37.9%	10.7%	0.0%	0.7%	17.3%	0.0%	12.1%	21.4%	73.5%
Madison County	11,159	20.7%	22.3%	5.5%	1.9%	7.1%	0.8%	29.9%	11.8%	25.5%
McHenry County	4,874	25.3%	3.6%	13.3%	1.7%	22.2%	1.0%	27.4%	5.5%	45.9%
McLean County	12,644	39.0%	16.3%	3.4%	1.6%	17.9%	0.0%	9.3%	12.6%	48.8%
Peoria County	11,900	17.7%	12.2%	9.0%	0.3%	25.8%	0.0%	26.9%	8.1%	45.9%
Rock Island County	7,845	28.9%	16.0%	3.6%	0.0%	17.8%	0.0%	30.6%	3.0%	51.8%
Sangamon County	13,197	22.6%	7.1%	10.1%	1.0%	19.6%	0.6%	24.6%	14.4%	55.3%
St. Clair County	10,372	22.1%	9.8%	4.6%	1.0%	17.5%	0.0%	25.7%	19.4%	53.9%
Tazewell County	6,703	44.8%	18.1%	10.5%	1.0%	3.1%	1.9%	20.8%	0.0%	61.4%
Will County	23,530	38.5%	14.3%	2.7%	1.7%	15.0%	0.0%	17.5%	10.2%	72.3%
Winnebago County	12,627	21.9%	11.0%	3.8%	0.5%	28.0%	0.6%	19.2%	15.1%	60.7%
Indiana										
Allen County	22,252	25.0%	14.2%	9.4%	3.2%	18.8%	0.5%	19.2%	9.6%	48.2%
Clark County	5,519	45.7%	11.6%	9.8%	2.2%	12.8%	0.0%	10.4%	7.4%	63.8%
Delaware County	5,116	22.8%	11.6%	3.7%	4.0%	24.7%	5.4%	14.6%	13.2%	21.7%
Elkhart County	7,882	44.1%	5.9%	17.5%	0.0%	9.2%	0.0%	12.4%	10.9%	55.5%
Hamilton County	14,763	41.2%	20.5%	3.2%	0.9%	7.5%	0.0%	19.0%	7.8%	70.9%
Hendricks County	6,686	59.7%	8.2%	4.9%	0.0%	3.6%	2.0%	14.7%	6.8%	73.4%
Johnson County	7,510	41.6%	9.6%	3.8%	0.0%	17.6%	0.0%	12.4%	15.0%	46.1%
Lake County	19,318	30.6%	7.9%	3.0%	1.8%	22.4%	1.8%	22.1%	10.3%	66.6%
LaPorte County	5,028	21.1%	4.2%	8.5%	0.0%	38.3%	0.0%	18.4%	9.5%	47.7%
Madison County	6,082	30.8%	7.9%	10.1%	2.5%	24.4%	0.0%	20.2%	4.1%	49.3%
Marion County	69,130	17.3%	10.5%	3.7%	1.4%	19.0%	1.4%	34.6%	12.1%	47.9%
Monroe County	9,977	17.6%	20.1%	1.2%	0.0%	4.5%	0.0%	39.5%	17.1%	7.9%
Porter County	6,399	38.1%	20.3%	8.7%	0.0%	12.5%	0.0%	15.4%	5.1%	51.4%
St. Joseph County	13,368	27.6%	17.0%	3.0%	0.7%	16.5%	0.0%	22.7%	12.4%	43.7%
Tippecanoe County	10,641	30.8%	10.4%	2.1%	3.7%	9.2%	0.5%	22.3%	20.9%	15.8%
Vanderburgh County	11,270	34.0%	8.6%	8.4%	0.5%	12.5%	0.0%	28.0%	8.0%	39.8%
Vigo County	4,242	24.3%	6.6%	0.6%	0.0%	12.8%	0.0%	30.9%	24.7%	21.8%
Iowa										
Black Hawk County	8,469	32.8%	13.2%	3.6%	0.0%	11.0%	3.3%	31.7%	4.5%	23.9%
Dubuque County	5,517	41.5%	5.5%	3.0%	0.0%	15.4%	0.0%	27.0%	7.5%	42.2%
Johnson County	10,740	8.3%	27.2%	0.0%	1.7%	11.6%	5.1%	23.5%	22.7%	11.4%
Linn County	12,238	21.4%	25.3%	3.1%	0.3%	15.5%	0.0%	19.8%	14.6%	41.9%
Polk County	30,420	24.6%	14.8%	1.1%	2.2%	11.6%	0.6%	31.4%	13.8%	40.7%
Pottawattamie County	5,638	34.4%	13.9%	0.3%	0.0%	18.4%	0.0%	19.9%	13.1%	51.7%
Scott County	10,764	24.7%	13.2%	12.5%	0.0%	11.1%	0.0%	25.0%	13.5%	46.8%
Story County	6,514	27.7%	32.7%	0.0%	0.0%	1.9%	0.0%	23.2%	14.5%	11.6%
Woodbury County	7,274	33.3%	6.0%	7.1%	0.0%	26.4%	0.0%	20.0%	7.2%	49.7%

Table D-2: Counties—Household Relationship—*Continued*

		Married Couple Households		Male, No Spouse Present		Female, No Spouse Present		Non-Family Householders		
		18 to 24								
	Total Householders	With Children	No Children	With Children	No Children	With Children	No Children	Living Alone	Not Alone	Living With Parents
Kansas										
Douglas County	5,747	0.0%	0.0%	0.0%	0.0%	0.0%	7.8%	30.4%	61.8%	11.1%
Johnson County	7,032	1.8%	17.8%	1.5%	0.9%	7.2%	2.3%	30.4%	38.1%	61.3%
Sedgwick County	9,466	2.4%	8.0%	0.0%	1.2%	15.8%	3.6%	49.4%	19.7%	43.4%
Shawnee County	3,882	6.0%	5.4%	2.2%	8.5%	19.7%	2.8%	26.6%	28.8%	41.4%
Wyandotte County	3,569	2.1%	5.0%	4.5%	10.6%	16.1%	9.9%	24.9%	26.8%	52.5%
Kentucky										
Boone County	2,007	2.2%	21.9%	0.0%	0.0%	0.0%	19.7%	19.7%	36.5%	57.8%
Campbell County	1,132	7.7%	10.1%	25.9%	8.7%	4.4%	0.0%	20.6%	22.6%	46.4%
Daviess County	1,229	5.5%	0.0%	6.4%	0.0%	59.2%	0.0%	14.1%	14.8%	53.9%
Fayette County	11,295	3.7%	7.6%	0.6%	2.7%	6.6%	2.3%	29.0%	47.4%	28.7%
Hardin County	1,734	30.8%	25.6%	15.4%	0.0%	0.0%	0.0%	11.6%	16.6%	54.9%
Jefferson County	12,479	4.9%	5.3%	0.7%	6.1%	18.1%	1.6%	32.0%	31.2%	47.0%
Kenton County	2,485	5.6%	9.7%	0.0%	4.9%	22.8%	0.0%	23.9%	33.2%	54.2%
Warren County	4,866	8.4%	12.8%	0.0%	4.9%	11.9%	0.0%	39.9%	22.1%	21.2%
Louisiana										
Ascension Parish	941	21.1%	30.1%	0.0%	0.0%	0.0%	0.0%	0.0%	48.8%	80.9%
Bossier Parish	2,229	9.2%	39.7%	0.0%	0.0%	3.2%	0.0%	37.9%	10.0%	41.6%
Caddo Parish	3,597	10.6%	17.5%	2.2%	0.0%	29.3%	13.1%	18.8%	8.5%	50.9%
Calcasieu Parish	3,552	17.2%	2.1%	5.5%	9.5%	20.3%	8.1%	16.2%	21.1%	41.9%
East Baton Rouge Parish	14,606	3.2%	2.8%	3.7%	4.1%	13.4%	0.0%	39.5%	33.3%	35.5%
Jefferson Parish	5,034	9.4%	3.1%	18.7%	2.6%	14.7%	2.0%	22.7%	26.9%	69.1%
Lafayette Parish	4,702	6.3%	0.7%	0.0%	0.0%	16.1%	0.0%	38.6%	38.3%	40.8%
Lafourche Parish	1,492	3.8%	8.0%	0.0%	0.0%	7.5%	0.0%	48.8%	31.8%	51.2%
Livingston Parish	889	12.6%	0.0%	5.3%	53.9%	0.0%	2.7%	14.5%	11.0%	67.7%
Orleans Parish	4,934	3.6%	5.4%	0.0%	6.3%	14.6%	2.2%	48.5%	19.3%	48.5%
Ouachita Parish	3,044	8.3%	2.7%	0.0%	5.5%	14.9%	11.9%	32.5%	24.2%	39.2%
Rapides Parish	2,172	24.5%	8.4%	0.0%	1.0%	27.5%	0.0%	34.3%	4.4%	49.3%
St. Tammany Parish	1,907	20.1%	2.1%	11.6%	3.1%	8.1%	0.0%	27.4%	27.5%	75.1%
Tangipahoa Parish	2,747	0.0%	2.8%	0.0%	0.0%	17.2%	9.5%	42.9%	27.7%	41.1%
Terrebonne Parish	2,464	11.8%	0.0%	0.0%	25.7%	9.0%	0.0%	25.2%	28.3%	47.7%
Maine										
Androscoggin County	1,754	13.4%	8.4%	4.4%	0.0%	11.0%	0.0%	26.3%	36.4%	21.8%
Cumberland County	5,361	7.0%	0.0%	10.6%	10.0%	2.8%	0.0%	4.1%	65.5%	37.2%
Kennebec County	2,327	0.0%	0.0%	0.0%	0.0%	16.4%	0.0%	29.1%	54.4%	38.9%
Penobscot County	1,973	0.0%	0.0%	0.0%	0.0%	18.6%	6.8%	29.2%	45.4%	36.4%
York County	1,933	0.0%	0.0%	29.4%	27.7%	6.8%	0.0%	12.7%	23.4%	58.7%
Maryland										
Anne Arundel County	4,415	3.9%	25.7%	5.0%	5.3%	12.8%	0.0%	3.9%	43.4%	55.5%
Baltimore County	8,248	9.1%	1.1%	5.4%	3.9%	21.4%	3.1%	12.4%	43.7%	51.5%
Carroll County	681	0.0%	5.1%	0.0%	0.0%	10.3%	0.0%	53.5%	31.1%	77.7%
Cecil County	1,149	0.0%	6.4%	0.0%	13.4%	9.1%	0.0%	58.7%	12.5%	75.5%
Charles County	1,096	0.0%	18.1%	0.0%	0.0%	62.2%	0.0%	0.0%	19.7%	72.8%
Frederick County	2,827	6.5%	17.1%	0.0%	0.0%	5.6%	0.0%	38.7%	32.2%	59.9%
Harford County	1,734	50.8%	0.0%	0.0%	0.0%	19.6%	0.0%	18.1%	11.5%	74.3%
Howard County	2,116	0.0%	18.3%	0.0%	14.0%	0.0%	0.0%	45.4%	22.4%	75.7%
Montgomery County	7,357	0.0%	3.6%	3.5%	16.6%	1.7%	6.7%	32.3%	35.7%	70.0%
Prince George's County	6,052	8.6%	1.4%	0.0%	6.5%	14.3%	9.1%	30.0%	30.1%	57.9%
St. Mary's County	735	0.0%	0.0%	0.0%	0.0%	0.0%	0.0%	44.4%	55.6%	60.8%
Washington County	2,434	8.1%	7.4%	0.0%	0.0%	16.9%	0.0%	25.9%	41.7%	47.7%
Wicomico County	2,401	4.6%	0.0%	0.0%	0.0%	25.3%	6.0%	21.9%	42.1%	34.0%
Massachusetts										
Barnstable County	571	0.0%	28.5%	0.0%	0.0%	29.6%	0.0%	11.9%	29.9%	77.2%
Berkshire County	1,857	0.0%	8.8%	0.0%	12.5%	21.6%	9.1%	15.0%	32.9%	41.9%
Bristol County	5,870	9.8%	0.0%	0.9%	3.8%	23.5%	4.1%	31.0%	27.0%	60.6%
Essex County	5,777	3.7%	9.3%	0.0%	4.1%	15.1%	7.0%	22.6%	38.2%	63.9%
Hampden County	5,484	6.9%	4.4%	5.2%	4.8%	29.6%	0.9%	5.7%	42.5%	58.3%
Hampshire County	2,541	4.3%	2.7%	0.0%	0.0%	5.4%	0.0%	10.5%	77.1%	35.4%
Middlesex County	13,073	0.0%	1.4%	0.2%	11.2%	16.1%	0.0%	20.4%	50.6%	50.5%
Norfolk County	3,908	0.0%	0.0%	1.5%	3.7%	0.0%	2.4%	35.7%	56.6%	54.2%
Plymouth County	2,038	7.9%	0.0%	8.9%	0.0%	6.7%	4.7%	30.7%	41.2%	73.2%
Suffolk County	16,246	1.7%	1.2%	0.2%	11.1%	2.0%	7.6%	26.9%	49.3%	26.5%
Worcester County	5,862	0.0%	4.3%	6.5%	5.6%	15.4%	1.1%	17.1%	49.9%	60.4%
Michigan										
Allegan County	1,367	10.5%	6.9%	1.6%	0.0%	24.6%	0.0%	10.8%	45.6%	52.7%
Bay County	1,967	20.9%	0.0%	0.0%	3.3%	0.0%	0.0%	22.6%	53.1%	53.6%
Berrien County	2,091	2.2%	1.4%	0.0%	7.1%	18.1%	9.1%	18.8%	43.3%	45.6%
Calhoun County	1,811	2.6%	5.1%	29.1%	5.9%	0.0%	0.0%	36.7%	20.6%	55.3%
Eaton County	1,749	6.5%	9.8%	0.0%	0.0%	7.1%	4.2%	31.1%	41.2%	49.2%
Genesee County	5,806	23.1%	7.7%	9.9%	0.0%	15.6%	13.4%	19.9%	10.3%	63.5%
Ingham County	10,648	0.0%	4.2%	0.0%	5.7%	3.5%	1.8%	38.6%	46.2%	22.3%
Jackson County	1,770	3.7%	10.2%	0.0%	0.0%	37.7%	0.0%	2.0%	46.4%	48.8%
Kalamazoo County	8,134	4.1%	6.2%	0.0%	4.6%	4.5%	6.3%	35.4%	39.0%	34.5%
Kent County	9,813	6.6%	6.8%	0.0%	2.3%	19.1%	2.2%	18.5%	44.7%	49.7%

Table D-2: Counties—Household Relationship—*Continued*

		25 to 33								
		Married Couple Households		Male, No Spouse Present		Female, No Spouse Present		Non-Family Householders		Living With Parents
	Total Householders	With Children	No Children	With Children	No Children	With Children	No Children	Living Alone	Not Alone	
Kansas										
Douglas County	6,892	40.0%	13.2%	0.0%	0.0%	2.9%	0.0%	29.8%	14.0%	11.1%
Johnson County	34,620	32.9%	20.1%	3.5%	2.1%	10.1%	0.2%	21.2%	9.8%	61.3%
Sedgwick County	31,837	23.8%	9.7%	5.9%	2.9%	16.2%	0.4%	34.9%	6.2%	43.4%
Shawnee County	10,339	41.9%	5.1%	5.4%	0.0%	11.4%	0.0%	25.5%	10.7%	41.4%
Wyandotte County	9,526	34.5%	7.7%	3.6%	0.4%	18.2%	4.0%	25.6%	6.1%	52.5%
Kentucky										
Boone County	6,040	31.4%	16.9%	11.3%	2.5%	14.3%	0.0%	23.6%	0.0%	57.8%
Campbell County	4,904	26.9%	13.5%	11.1%	0.0%	12.7%	1.3%	32.1%	2.4%	46.4%
Daviess County	5,376	37.5%	11.0%	4.6%	7.0%	9.4%	0.0%	17.7%	12.8%	53.9%
Fayette County	22,228	20.7%	13.6%	4.0%	0.3%	12.4%	0.2%	34.4%	14.3%	28.7%
Hardin County	5,693	38.8%	20.7%	3.8%	0.0%	19.7%	0.0%	8.2%	9.0%	54.9%
Jefferson County	44,918	21.5%	13.8%	3.6%	3.3%	14.9%	0.3%	28.8%	13.8%	47.0%
Kenton County	10,443	26.3%	11.2%	1.1%	4.8%	12.1%	0.0%	29.9%	14.7%	54.2%
Warren County	6,410	28.1%	21.5%	6.6%	0.0%	28.0%	0.0%	7.9%	8.0%	21.2%
Louisiana										
Ascension Parish	6,896	42.3%	11.8%	1.1%	0.0%	22.0%	0.0%	15.7%	7.0%	80.9%
Bossier Parish	9,016	38.2%	9.5%	1.3%	0.5%	17.2%	0.0%	15.6%	17.7%	41.6%
Caddo Parish	13,628	26.8%	9.9%	1.3%	0.6%	26.5%	0.0%	30.3%	4.7%	50.9%
Calcasieu Parish	13,046	27.3%	5.7%	5.2%	0.0%	24.8%	0.0%	29.6%	7.4%	41.9%
East Baton Rouge Parish	27,637	19.6%	10.6%	3.6%	1.5%	20.0%	1.9%	27.8%	14.9%	35.5%
Jefferson Parish	25,553	18.2%	10.4%	7.2%	1.9%	27.3%	1.3%	23.2%	10.5%	69.1%
Lafayette Parish	16,282	25.8%	9.4%	7.0%	2.6%	14.9%	0.0%	19.7%	20.5%	40.8%
Lafourche Parish	5,078	27.4%	18.3%	2.0%	0.0%	8.5%	6.0%	22.4%	15.3%	51.2%
Livingston Parish	6,087	41.6%	18.4%	0.8%	0.0%	13.6%	0.0%	16.0%	9.5%	67.7%
Orleans Parish	27,218	9.6%	7.2%	1.9%	0.8%	15.4%	1.6%	43.3%	20.2%	48.5%
Ouachita Parish	8,007	39.3%	3.5%	5.8%	1.1%	30.2%	0.0%	14.9%	5.1%	39.2%
Rapides Parish	7,435	34.9%	9.3%	4.2%	2.4%	28.2%	0.0%	8.9%	12.2%	49.3%
St. Tammany Parish	9,294	51.2%	9.0%	0.0%	6.6%	20.3%	0.0%	6.1%	6.8%	75.1%
Tangipahoa Parish	6,576	33.3%	13.2%	0.8%	0.0%	18.3%	0.0%	30.5%	3.9%	41.1%
Terrebonne Parish	5,584	60.0%	0.0%	6.6%	0.0%	11.6%	0.0%	3.4%	18.4%	47.7%
Maine										
Androscoggin County	6,313	38.7%	10.3%	13.1%	0.0%	11.5%	0.0%	18.6%	7.9%	21.8%
Cumberland County	15,220	17.7%	16.4%	3.2%	0.5%	13.7%	3.6%	21.4%	23.5%	37.2%
Kennebec County	4,758	38.9%	23.8%	7.2%	0.0%	5.6%	0.0%	17.8%	6.7%	38.9%
Penobscot County	8,211	17.0%	13.1%	7.9%	0.0%	15.7%	0.0%	33.0%	13.3%	36.4%
York County	7,387	27.5%	30.2%	0.0%	0.0%	8.4%	0.0%	18.1%	15.9%	58.7%
Maryland										
Anne Arundel County	26,363	38.9%	10.7%	1.8%	0.6%	11.8%	0.5%	21.4%	14.3%	55.5%
Baltimore County	37,119	25.5%	13.6%	5.2%	2.3%	14.1%	2.4%	24.8%	12.0%	51.5%
Carroll County	5,949	29.3%	27.5%	2.5%	1.1%	17.4%	0.0%	10.2%	12.0%	77.7%
Cecil County	5,134	30.1%	14.5%	2.5%	3.7%	8.6%	0.0%	24.0%	16.8%	75.5%
Charles County	6,367	46.8%	12.1%	4.2%	6.8%	0.9%	1.1%	24.0%	4.2%	72.8%
Frederick County	10,100	33.5%	15.3%	7.0%	1.7%	4.7%	0.0%	21.8%	16.0%	59.9%
Harford County	10,407	38.0%	12.0%	2.8%	1.9%	21.0%	2.0%	17.5%	4.9%	74.3%
Howard County	11,705	34.8%	17.8%	4.5%	0.0%	5.8%	0.6%	23.5%	13.0%	75.7%
Montgomery County	43,495	20.9%	20.2%	3.6%	2.7%	10.0%	2.2%	24.5%	15.8%	70.0%
Prince George's County	35,580	20.5%	9.9%	11.2%	4.1%	17.7%	2.2%	21.3%	13.1%	57.9%
St. Mary's County	5,145	19.3%	10.4%	7.4%	0.0%	14.8%	13.3%	14.8%	20.0%	60.8%
Washington County	5,012	36.0%	11.4%	7.1%	5.6%	12.7%	0.0%	16.1%	11.0%	47.7%
Wicomico County	3,593	8.6%	6.1%	28.9%	0.0%	30.3%	0.0%	15.9%	10.1%	34.0%
Massachusetts										
Barnstable County	6,304	31.7%	6.6%	0.0%	0.0%	11.9%	0.0%	18.6%	31.2%	77.2%
Berkshire County	4,745	6.9%	10.8%	6.5%	0.0%	32.4%	0.0%	35.4%	8.1%	41.9%
Bristol County	25,921	17.4%	10.5%	8.4%	0.4%	28.1%	0.8%	15.1%	19.2%	60.6%
Essex County	31,976	21.5%	15.5%	4.0%	2.3%	17.4%	2.1%	24.2%	13.0%	63.9%
Hampden County	20,238	24.0%	14.4%	3.3%	1.6%	20.6%	1.6%	19.9%	14.7%	58.3%
Hampshire County	7,088	22.5%	9.5%	4.2%	0.3%	11.9%	0.0%	19.9%	31.7%	35.4%
Middlesex County	78,465	18.6%	20.9%	1.5%	2.0%	6.9%	1.9%	20.4%	27.7%	50.5%
Norfolk County	27,597	19.5%	19.3%	0.9%	3.5%	8.9%	2.0%	22.0%	23.8%	54.2%
Plymouth County	14,508	32.8%	11.1%	3.6%	0.7%	16.4%	1.3%	24.1%	9.9%	73.2%
Suffolk County	70,099	8.8%	12.9%	2.4%	2.9%	8.3%	3.9%	32.4%	28.4%	26.5%
Worcester County	33,486	24.9%	13.3%	2.7%	3.6%	15.0%	1.3%	24.7%	14.6%	60.4%
Michigan										
Allegan County	4,970	36.8%	10.9%	3.4%	0.0%	12.9%	0.0%	17.6%	18.3%	52.7%
Bay County	5,422	31.2%	14.1%	0.0%	3.5%	13.2%	0.0%	20.5%	17.5%	53.6%
Berrien County	8,181	27.0%	9.1%	7.1%	0.0%	27.0%	0.0%	22.0%	7.8%	45.6%
Calhoun County	6,719	44.9%	4.5%	6.5%	4.5%	17.7%	12.4%	7.0%	2.5%	55.3%
Eaton County	6,269	27.0%	9.3%	4.5%	1.2%	21.6%	0.0%	23.5%	12.9%	49.2%
Genesee County	17,245	25.1%	8.5%	8.4%	5.7%	17.5%	1.7%	18.0%	15.1%	63.5%
Ingham County	17,957	15.3%	17.9%	2.6%	0.0%	14.9%	1.1%	27.3%	20.9%	22.3%
Jackson County	6,955	39.1%	9.3%	11.6%	0.0%	15.6%	1.6%	18.1%	4.8%	48.8%
Kalamazoo County	13,621	16.3%	16.4%	7.8%	2.5%	11.8%	2.4%	24.9%	17.9%	34.5%
Kent County	39,055	24.5%	16.9%	3.5%	0.5%	11.2%	2.0%	23.1%	18.3%	49.7%

Table D-2: Counties—Household Relationship—*Continued*

		18 to 24								
	Total Householders	Married Couple Households		Male, No Spouse Present		Female, No Spouse Present		Non-Family Householders		Living With Parents
		With Children	No Children	With Children	No Children	With Children	No Children	Living Alone	Not Alone	
Michigan—Cont.										
Lenawee County	1,667	0.0%	0.0%	11.0%	0.0%	35.8%	0.0%	27.0%	26.3%	47.5%
Livingston County	1,571	0.0%	0.0%	0.0%	21.1%	23.3%	4.1%	32.7%	18.8%	74.7%
Macomb County	9,223	3.2%	4.9%	15.7%	8.9%	13.3%	0.0%	35.7%	18.3%	69.1%
Monroe County	1,612	0.0%	14.2%	16.1%	0.0%	3.2%	0.0%	57.4%	9.1%	78.7%
Muskegon County	1,954	7.5%	0.0%	12.4%	0.0%	19.6%	0.0%	51.3%	9.1%	59.7%
Oakland County	14,089	9.1%	12.2%	1.9%	6.5%	6.4%	0.9%	39.0%	24.0%	62.8%
Ottawa County	5,279	2.2%	6.9%	0.0%	12.8%	3.4%	3.0%	19.0%	52.7%	38.6%
Saginaw County	2,710	5.4%	18.3%	0.7%	0.0%	31.7%	0.0%	25.9%	18.1%	54.4%
St. Clair County	2,572	6.9%	1.4%	6.8%	26.5%	13.6%	0.0%	21.2%	23.6%	55.6%
Washtenaw County	14,848	0.2%	3.7%	0.0%	5.4%	4.7%	0.0%	33.4%	52.7%	22.7%
Wayne County	17,781	1.0%	1.3%	6.9%	9.6%	25.2%	5.6%	30.2%	20.1%	65.7%
Minnesota										
Anoka County	3,791	32.9%	6.3%	10.3%	8.4%	22.1%	0.0%	17.1%	3.0%	63.4%
Carver County	588	0.0%	48.8%	0.0%	0.0%	29.1%	0.0%	14.6%	7.5%	66.6%
Dakota County	4,639	14.0%	0.0%	9.4%	0.0%	12.5%	0.0%	28.5%	35.7%	67.3%
Hennepin County	20,342	9.1%	3.7%	0.0%	1.5%	4.9%	6.3%	34.0%	40.4%	45.1%
Olmsted County	2,893	0.0%	7.0%	0.0%	0.0%	23.1%	0.0%	26.0%	43.9%	48.5%
Ramsey County	7,629	3.1%	11.4%	2.0%	5.6%	6.7%	7.2%	14.8%	49.2%	45.1%
Scott County	4,087	9.1%	7.4%	0.0%	0.0%	9.1%	0.0%	15.7%	58.7%	33.7%
St. Louis County	1,151	0.0%	0.0%	0.0%	0.0%	60.0%	0.0%	40.0%	0.0%	73.5%
Stearns County	5,787	6.3%	0.0%	2.0%	2.4%	11.4%	0.0%	33.2%	44.8%	28.6%
Washington County	1,107	0.0%	0.0%	0.0%	0.0%	46.7%	0.0%	18.8%	34.5%	83.7%
Wright County	1,556	0.0%	4.2%	0.0%	0.0%	13.5%	0.0%	26.9%	55.4%	71.8%
Mississippi										
DeSoto County	2,632	3.2%	2.0%	0.0%	9.4%	12.8%	12.5%	39.6%	20.5%	60.7%
Harrison County	3,887	11.7%	17.8%	2.5%	9.7%	11.9%	0.0%	26.8%	19.7%	42.2%
Hinds County	4,139	2.8%	2.7%	4.8%	4.4%	27.1%	3.5%	36.7%	18.1%	43.4%
Jackson County	942	0.0%	5.5%	0.0%	31.4%	23.4%	0.0%	20.9%	18.8%	73.3%
Madison County	1,238	31.5%	0.0%	0.0%	0.0%	47.2%	0.0%	12.6%	8.7%	76.9%
Rankin County	1,067	15.3%	13.0%	0.0%	0.0%	0.0%	0.0%	40.5%	31.2%	70.0%
Missouri										
Boone County	9,430	5.3%	5.2%	0.2%	0.0%	0.0%	0.4%	41.2%	47.8%	18.3%
Cass County	1,198	30.4%	3.8%	0.0%	0.0%	3.6%	0.0%	27.5%	34.8%	70.3%
Clay County	2,345	6.3%	14.6%	4.4%	0.0%	2.8%	0.0%	31.5%	40.4%	56.3%
Franklin County	1,183	15.4%	0.0%	0.0%	3.0%	27.4%	0.0%	18.0%	36.2%	54.3%
Greene County	11,687	5.4%	7.3%	0.7%	1.4%	4.0%	2.5%	24.7%	54.1%	22.6%
Jackson County	13,646	6.0%	6.2%	1.7%	4.2%	18.7%	1.8%	42.5%	18.8%	49.2%
Jasper County	2,186	15.0%	0.0%	13.1%	0.0%	28.9%	0.0%	25.8%	17.3%	47.3%
Jefferson County	1,666	0.0%	0.0%	14.3%	3.1%	29.4%	0.0%	11.1%	42.0%	63.1%
Platte County	1,928	1.8%	0.0%	0.0%	0.0%	0.0%	0.0%	23.1%	75.2%	51.1%
St. Charles County	2,460	5.8%	6.6%	4.3%	0.0%	2.6%	2.2%	29.3%	49.3%	64.0%
St. Louis County	12,260	2.4%	4.6%	1.2%	7.2%	11.2%	4.0%	36.4%	33.0%	55.1%
Montana										
Flathead County	504	0.0%	31.9%	0.0%	0.0%	44.2%	0.0%	23.8%	0.0%	59.4%
Gallatin County	4,361	3.3%	0.0%	0.0%	4.6%	0.0%	2.9%	41.2%	48.0%	20.2%
Missoula County	3,557	8.2%	3.3%	0.0%	0.0%	26.4%	6.4%	19.4%	36.4%	42.7%
Yellowstone County	3,535	9.1%	4.5%	0.0%	0.0%	16.7%	1.2%	32.3%	36.2%	40.4%
Nebraska										
Douglas County	12,040	3.3%	8.9%	4.0%	1.1%	11.0%	2.3%	43.8%	25.5%	37.1%
Lancaster County	12,613	5.0%	0.0%	5.3%	4.9%	8.4%	1.1%	35.1%	40.1%	24.7%
Sarpy County	2,505	15.0%	4.6%	0.0%	0.0%	3.9%	5.6%	25.4%	45.5%	58.0%
Nevada										
Clark County	23,007	4.6%	5.3%	4.1%	8.1%	14.2%	8.6%	29.5%	25.6%	59.2%
Washoe County	7,193	4.6%	3.2%	4.8%	5.9%	16.5%	2.6%	23.9%	38.6%	43.3%
New Hampshire										
Hillsborough County	4,506	11.2%	0.6%	0.0%	2.2%	6.8%	0.0%	24.7%	54.5%	60.5%
Merrimack County	1,814	0.0%	0.0%	0.0%	0.0%	26.7%	34.0%	10.5%	28.8%	56.6%
Rockingham County	1,826	0.0%	0.0%	0.0%	6.2%	0.0%	0.0%	11.5%	82.3%	71.3%
Strafford County	3,170	0.0%	0.0%	0.0%	8.5%	0.0%	4.8%	18.5%	68.2%	31.9%
New Jersey										
Atlantic County	2,387	7.4%	2.5%	0.0%	24.8%	3.8%	0.0%	18.9%	42.6%	65.0%
Bergen County	4,684	5.7%	1.2%	0.0%	23.1%	6.5%	34.3%	17.7%	11.5%	79.1%
Burlington County	2,485	5.2%	15.0%	5.9%	1.4%	2.9%	10.1%	48.4%	11.2%	68.3%
Camden County	3,646	2.6%	0.5%	0.0%	9.4%	33.3%	14.0%	18.5%	21.8%	74.5%
Cape May County	59	0.0%	0.0%	0.0%	0.0%	0.0%	0.0%	100.0%	0.0%	76.0%
Cumberland County	1,078	9.3%	0.0%	21.8%	21.3%	17.3%	0.0%	30.2%	0.0%	69.9%
Essex County	5,546	4.2%	0.8%	4.5%	4.4%	15.3%	7.3%	52.0%	11.6%	61.8%
Gloucester County	1,763	0.0%	12.2%	0.0%	8.0%	26.1%	2.4%	15.1%	36.1%	71.8%
Hudson County	7,216	7.6%	0.7%	3.9%	18.0%	7.4%	5.1%	26.4%	30.8%	59.2%
Hunterdon County	1,018	12.0%	11.0%	0.0%	0.0%	23.5%	0.0%	53.5%	0.0%	67.9%
Mercer County	1,492	3.6%	7.4%	3.6%	15.8%	16.9%	7.8%	18.0%	27.0%	56.6%
Middlesex County	3,657	6.5%	0.0%	0.0%	15.9%	6.3%	9.7%	21.6%	40.1%	57.0%
Monmouth County	2,440	0.0%	3.0%	0.0%	2.4%	17.6%	10.8%	30.7%	35.5%	80.0%

Table D-2: Counties—Household Relationship—*Continued*

| | | 25 to 33 | | | | | | | | |
| | | Married Couple Households | | Male, No Spouse Present | | Female, No Spouse Present | | Non-Family Householders | | |
	Total Householders	With Children	No Children	With Children	No Children	With Children	No Children	Living Alone	Not Alone	Living With Parents
Michigan—Cont.										
Lenawee County	3,764	33.6%	8.5%	3.7%	0.0%	22.2%	0.7%	25.7%	5.7%	47.5%
Livingston County	5,831	25.9%	22.8%	17.5%	0.0%	3.7%	0.0%	16.8%	13.3%	74.7%
Macomb County	40,477	25.0%	13.5%	5.2%	3.2%	14.7%	0.6%	24.0%	13.9%	69.1%
Monroe County	5,097	35.9%	11.0%	3.7%	0.0%	24.6%	0.0%	16.0%	8.9%	78.7%
Muskegon County	7,832	33.4%	7.5%	6.6%	0.0%	32.7%	0.0%	9.0%	11.0%	59.7%
Oakland County	60,512	27.0%	14.8%	2.4%	1.6%	8.7%	0.3%	27.2%	17.9%	62.8%
Ottawa County	11,489	46.2%	17.4%	0.9%	1.4%	14.3%	0.0%	6.4%	13.3%	38.6%
Saginaw County	10,364	16.2%	7.6%	4.9%	4.4%	22.5%	0.0%	25.9%	18.4%	54.4%
St. Clair County	6,383	23.5%	8.7%	3.5%	0.0%	15.5%	0.0%	29.8%	18.9%	55.6%
Washtenaw County	22,754	16.9%	14.6%	4.6%	0.5%	6.6%	0.0%	33.5%	23.3%	22.7%
Wayne County	84,168	18.9%	8.9%	4.8%	2.2%	23.1%	1.7%	29.1%	11.3%	65.7%
Minnesota										
Anoka County	15,242	34.9%	16.5%	6.3%	2.2%	9.2%	0.0%	22.6%	8.3%	63.4%
Carver County	4,382	53.7%	22.4%	2.4%	0.0%	8.7%	0.0%	12.9%	0.0%	66.6%
Dakota County	20,723	30.1%	20.0%	3.8%	4.4%	12.8%	0.0%	16.6%	12.2%	67.3%
Hennepin County	91,384	16.1%	18.0%	1.1%	0.8%	9.6%	1.1%	33.5%	19.8%	45.1%
Olmsted County	8,194	48.1%	19.6%	0.0%	0.0%	3.9%	0.0%	20.6%	7.8%	48.5%
Ramsey County	37,485	24.6%	11.2%	3.1%	2.8%	13.7%	1.1%	23.6%	19.9%	45.1%
Scott County	11,356	24.2%	20.2%	4.3%	0.9%	14.5%	2.0%	16.9%	16.9%	33.7%
St. Louis County	6,727	40.9%	17.9%	2.6%	0.0%	15.7%	4.6%	10.8%	7.7%	73.5%
Stearns County	10,378	17.0%	17.1%	15.0%	0.7%	14.6%	0.0%	29.8%	5.8%	28.6%
Washington County	9,934	44.5%	4.6%	10.2%	0.0%	20.1%	0.0%	13.8%	6.9%	83.7%
Wright County	6,470	38.1%	4.5%	7.8%	10.4%	6.6%	0.0%	20.3%	12.3%	71.8%
Mississippi										
DeSoto County	6,744	44.2%	10.7%	2.3%	5.4%	7.5%	1.2%	20.6%	8.3%	60.7%
Harrison County	12,898	28.1%	9.3%	2.4%	2.2%	27.5%	1.2%	12.3%	16.9%	42.2%
Hinds County	16,508	16.0%	8.3%	3.7%	3.2%	31.3%	1.3%	28.1%	8.2%	43.4%
Jackson County	5,974	28.8%	21.0%	5.0%	0.0%	24.8%	0.4%	8.5%	11.5%	73.3%
Madison County	3,943	34.6%	10.1%	4.3%	0.0%	29.4%	2.1%	19.4%	0.0%	76.9%
Rankin County	7,886	37.2%	13.6%	0.0%	12.7%	7.8%	0.0%	23.1%	5.7%	70.0%
Missouri										
Boone County	13,066	31.4%	14.9%	1.0%	0.0%	5.1%	0.0%	33.2%	14.4%	18.3%
Cass County	5,119	56.5%	12.9%	7.7%	0.0%	5.9%	2.5%	13.9%	0.6%	70.3%
Clay County	12,002	34.6%	16.3%	4.5%	2.1%	15.2%	1.2%	16.2%	10.1%	56.3%
Franklin County	4,919	45.5%	16.4%	8.2%	5.3%	17.9%	0.0%	2.4%	4.2%	54.3%
Greene County	18,401	26.3%	11.7%	3.2%	1.7%	13.0%	0.0%	30.6%	13.5%	22.6%
Jackson County	44,782	22.7%	13.7%	6.2%	1.3%	17.1%	1.2%	26.2%	11.6%	49.2%
Jasper County	5,737	51.9%	6.1%	0.8%	0.0%	14.3%	0.0%	14.7%	12.3%	47.3%
Jefferson County	11,451	40.9%	9.6%	15.4%	0.0%	11.2%	2.8%	10.9%	9.1%	63.1%
Platte County	5,465	27.5%	13.7%	7.4%	6.6%	20.3%	0.0%	17.8%	6.7%	51.1%
St. Charles County	19,559	38.6%	11.3%	5.1%	1.0%	8.3%	2.5%	20.1%	12.9%	64.0%
St. Louis County	50,122	27.4%	12.0%	5.8%	0.8%	16.2%	0.4%	24.7%	12.6%	55.1%
Montana										
Flathead County	3,390	46.0%	26.6%	5.6%	0.0%	2.8%	0.0%	6.1%	12.9%	59.4%
Gallatin County	6,655	29.9%	20.3%	4.0%	0.0%	8.1%	0.0%	24.2%	13.6%	20.2%
Missoula County	8,129	31.6%	4.4%	8.9%	0.0%	2.4%	0.0%	37.9%	14.8%	42.7%
Yellowstone County	6,717	26.4%	2.2%	6.0%	0.2%	13.7%	0.0%	34.7%	16.7%	40.4%
Nebraska										
Douglas County	41,128	26.0%	12.7%	1.3%	3.0%	15.2%	0.3%	25.6%	15.9%	37.1%
Lancaster County	20,610	27.0%	9.6%	2.8%	0.7%	11.8%	1.6%	30.0%	16.5%	24.7%
Sarpy County	11,572	36.5%	12.7%	2.5%	0.0%	21.7%	3.7%	15.5%	7.4%	58.0%
Nevada										
Clark County	114,439	19.8%	10.7%	5.3%	4.9%	16.5%	2.2%	26.2%	14.3%	59.2%
Washoe County	26,011	29.3%	9.5%	4.1%	0.9%	17.6%	3.4%	19.5%	15.9%	43.3%
New Hampshire										
Hillsborough County	19,952	21.8%	13.8%	1.9%	1.3%	17.9%	1.1%	22.0%	20.2%	60.5%
Merrimack County	5,168	32.8%	4.7%	5.3%	0.0%	8.9%	1.9%	24.0%	22.5%	56.6%
Rockingham County	12,942	20.0%	27.4%	2.5%	0.0%	6.0%	0.0%	28.1%	16.0%	71.3%
Strafford County	5,835	27.4%	19.8%	4.0%	0.0%	8.7%	0.0%	17.5%	22.7%	31.9%
New Jersey										
Atlantic County	12,124	21.3%	6.5%	12.1%	6.0%	23.4%	0.1%	15.5%	15.0%	65.0%
Bergen County	29,721	32.7%	17.6%	0.7%	2.8%	8.9%	2.5%	22.5%	12.2%	79.1%
Burlington County	16,550	24.5%	14.7%	3.0%	3.0%	13.0%	0.9%	28.4%	12.5%	68.3%
Camden County	22,092	18.7%	18.3%	3.8%	3.2%	21.2%	1.3%	22.2%	11.3%	74.5%
Cape May County	3,746	42.7%	17.6%	4.6%	5.8%	8.9%	0.0%	15.5%	5.0%	76.0%
Cumberland County	6,175	32.6%	4.8%	7.7%	3.0%	32.2%	0.8%	8.1%	10.7%	69.9%
Essex County	33,706	13.9%	13.2%	3.9%	4.3%	24.6%	2.0%	28.7%	9.4%	61.8%
Gloucester County	11,145	30.9%	13.9%	3.0%	6.5%	15.2%	2.4%	14.5%	13.7%	71.8%
Hudson County	53,789	13.8%	18.8%	3.0%	2.6%	14.7%	1.4%	21.7%	24.0%	59.2%
Hunterdon County	2,235	15.6%	18.1%	0.0%	0.0%	7.2%	0.0%	25.0%	34.0%	67.9%
Mercer County	14,148	26.9%	13.2%	0.8%	3.5%	13.2%	5.9%	21.1%	15.4%	56.6%
Middlesex County	30,677	30.5%	15.0%	2.4%	5.8%	9.5%	3.5%	18.8%	14.5%	57.0%
Monmouth County	21,844	30.5%	15.7%	3.1%	5.4%	8.2%	1.2%	22.0%	13.7%	80.0%

Table D-2: Counties—Household Relationship—*Continued*

| | | 18 to 24 | | | | | | | | |
| | | Married Couple Households | | Male, No Spouse Present | | Female, No Spouse Present | | Non-Family Householders | | |
	Total Householders	With Children	No Children	With Children	No Children	With Children	No Children	Living Alone	Not Alone	Living With Parents
New Jersey—Cont.										
Morris County	2,240	10.8%	0.0%	0.0%	4.6%	18.1%	5.3%	34.6%	26.6%	76.3%
Ocean County	2,920	21.8%	9.4%	0.0%	1.5%	12.4%	2.0%	39.5%	13.5%	75.6%
Passaic County	1,980	20.8%	5.3%	4.5%	12.2%	35.8%	0.0%	18.0%	3.5%	73.9%
Somerset County	1,869	0.0%	14.4%	0.0%	0.0%	0.0%	0.0%	74.2%	11.4%	84.5%
Sussex County	939	27.9%	0.0%	3.2%	0.0%	20.9%	0.0%	25.2%	22.8%	84.2%
Union County	3,671	5.0%	18.9%	3.7%	30.1%	6.9%	0.0%	12.0%	23.4%	67.6%
Warren County	836	0.0%	0.0%	0.0%	0.0%	0.0%	0.0%	100.0%	0.0%	75.3%
New Mexico										
Bernalillo County	9,700	3.3%	7.1%	1.6%	10.9%	6.4%	0.8%	25.4%	44.6%	54.7%
Doña Ana County	5,541	8.4%	0.0%	0.0%	14.8%	31.2%	4.8%	17.3%	23.5%	45.4%
San Juan County	238	10.5%	0.0%	0.0%	0.0%	5.9%	0.0%	0.0%	83.6%	68.2%
Sandoval County	2,077	34.0%	6.6%	1.2%	0.0%	16.8%	16.8%	4.0%	20.6%	54.4%
Santa Fe County	1,435	0.0%	1.0%	6.0%	19.2%	0.9%	0.7%	49.1%	23.1%	55.5%
New York										
Albany County	6,645	0.0%	0.0%	0.6%	0.0%	14.6%	0.0%	41.1%	43.7%	41.6%
Bronx County	12,619	9.7%	6.7%	2.1%	13.6%	22.7%	16.6%	19.0%	9.7%	68.7%
Broome County	3,687	4.6%	2.1%	6.0%	0.0%	15.1%	9.0%	21.9%	41.2%	47.1%
Chautauqua County	1,972	0.0%	0.0%	0.0%	6.9%	14.5%	0.0%	51.3%	27.4%	47.7%
Dutchess County	1,657	4.6%	0.0%	0.0%	7.6%	0.0%	0.0%	57.2%	30.6%	57.2%
Erie County	12,432	1.6%	1.7%	0.6%	3.8%	18.2%	2.4%	30.9%	40.8%	54.3%
Jefferson County	3,047	30.1%	15.0%	0.7%	0.0%	4.6%	0.0%	30.6%	19.1%	39.8%
Kings County	26,060	8.8%	7.5%	2.8%	15.4%	9.6%	6.6%	18.3%	31.2%	63.0%
Monroe County	12,080	0.6%	4.2%	0.4%	5.1%	20.3%	2.2%	23.0%	44.3%	45.3%
Nassau County	2,853	2.0%	13.1%	0.0%	24.2%	0.0%	15.8%	6.2%	38.7%	77.2%
New York County	22,375	1.1%	0.4%	0.0%	1.3%	0.6%	2.3%	44.8%	49.5%	33.4%
Niagara County	1,578	0.0%	15.0%	4.7%	0.0%	18.1%	0.0%	36.5%	25.7%	72.2%
Oneida County	2,685	0.0%	20.7%	0.0%	8.7%	29.8%	0.0%	33.7%	7.1%	53.8%
Onondaga County	5,941	3.2%	1.8%	4.0%	1.1%	14.7%	0.7%	40.0%	34.5%	42.1%
Ontario County	1,349	10.5%	0.0%	5.7%	5.6%	18.2%	0.0%	26.2%	33.8%	47.0%
Orange County	3,657	16.8%	4.5%	11.6%	2.1%	4.1%	10.4%	28.8%	21.7%	67.1%
Oswego County	1,871	8.3%	6.1%	16.7%	0.0%	7.9%	0.0%	7.8%	53.1%	28.4%
Putnam County	133	0.0%	0.0%	0.0%	37.6%	0.0%	62.4%	0.0%	0.0%	89.5%
Queens County	15,494	7.0%	2.8%	3.1%	12.2%	12.0%	15.1%	22.5%	25.3%	68.0%
Rensselaer County	1,582	6.6%	2.1%	0.0%	9.9%	13.4%	4.6%	35.1%	28.3%	53.5%
Richmond County	2,311	10.4%	23.6%	0.0%	0.0%	25.4%	17.1%	0.0%	23.5%	76.6%
Rockland County	1,200	63.1%	12.9%	0.0%	0.0%	0.0%	0.0%	0.0%	24.0%	76.9%
Saratoga County	1,799	0.0%	0.0%	0.0%	3.0%	24.3%	0.0%	28.8%	43.9%	24.4%
Schenectady County	1,896	16.1%	0.0%	0.0%	0.0%	0.0%	0.0%	30.9%	53.1%	63.6%
St. Lawrence County	523	24.1%	5.4%	24.7%	10.3%	0.0%	0.0%	24.1%	11.5%	69.7%
Steuben County	732	12.0%	3.3%	0.0%	0.0%	12.0%	0.0%	35.4%	37.3%	69.5%
Suffolk County	3,889	4.9%	6.0%	0.0%	20.3%	11.8%	10.2%	21.4%	25.5%	73.6%
Tompkins County	4,999	0.0%	0.0%	2.0%	0.0%	1.7%	0.0%	37.6%	58.7%	9.2%
Ulster County	1,880	0.0%	17.1%	0.0%	0.0%	4.9%	0.0%	36.0%	41.9%	55.8%
Wayne County	1,353	0.0%	0.0%	0.0%	4.1%	35.5%	0.0%	24.2%	36.2%	54.4%
Westchester County	4,903	2.6%	3.5%	0.0%	23.2%	21.9%	13.3%	24.3%	11.2%	68.1%
North Carolina										
Alamance County	2,497	7.5%	3.0%	2.8%	0.0%	11.8%	0.8%	36.9%	37.1%	37.0%
Brunswick County	801	7.0%	26.7%	0.0%	0.0%	0.0%	5.0%	61.3%	0.0%	77.8%
Buncombe County	4,078	5.3%	6.5%	0.0%	3.3%	16.2%	4.7%	47.5%	16.5%	50.0%
Cabarrus County	2,152	13.7%	6.3%	3.2%	13.3%	15.1%	0.0%	26.5%	21.9%	60.0%
Catawba County	1,580	0.0%	12.4%	2.0%	11.1%	21.7%	0.0%	34.5%	18.3%	53.2%
Cleveland County	1,665	29.1%	0.0%	21.3%	3.9%	35.9%	0.0%	0.5%	9.4%	52.9%
Craven County	3,067	20.3%	35.7%	0.0%	0.0%	2.2%	0.0%	33.1%	8.6%	25.5%
Cumberland County	7,679	19.6%	26.5%	0.9%	3.2%	13.8%	3.7%	23.6%	8.7%	38.7%
Davidson County	1,183	16.0%	11.4%	0.0%	0.0%	8.3%	46.0%	7.4%	11.0%	65.2%
Durham County	7,817	0.0%	4.3%	0.0%	2.7%	13.5%	2.1%	30.5%	46.8%	29.9%
Forsyth County	5,716	0.0%	7.7%	0.0%	10.7%	21.0%	0.0%	19.6%	41.0%	39.9%
Gaston County	2,828	9.1%	9.6%	14.4%	1.9%	14.8%	3.1%	18.0%	29.2%	51.7%
Guilford County	5,991	3.8%	1.7%	2.4%	0.0%	14.7%	3.5%	23.4%	50.4%	50.5%
Harnett County	2,158	26.8%	9.7%	4.1%	3.7%	8.6%	0.0%	35.5%	11.6%	47.5%
Henderson County	1,733	19.9%	2.7%	17.3%	0.0%	0.0%	5.6%	21.0%	33.5%	39.7%
Iredell County	1,657	6.5%	4.5%	5.6%	0.0%	4.6%	5.6%	56.2%	17.0%	61.8%
Johnston County	1,121	9.7%	8.8%	7.8%	0.0%	19.6%	0.0%	11.2%	42.9%	70.6%
Mecklenburg County	17,746	3.7%	6.6%	1.7%	5.6%	5.8%	3.5%	38.3%	34.8%	45.0%
Moore County	405	4.4%	22.7%	0.0%	0.0%	0.0%	0.0%	47.4%	25.4%	69.5%
Nash County	240	0.0%	0.0%	20.0%	0.0%	0.0%	80.0%	0.0%	0.0%	53.6%
New Hanover County	6,270	10.5%	14.2%	0.0%	7.1%	1.9%	1.6%	9.1%	55.6%	30.1%
Onslow County	8,912	21.7%	35.2%	0.0%	1.7%	11.1%	0.0%	13.8%	16.5%	23.7%
Orange County	4,762	0.0%	0.9%	0.8%	0.0%	0.0%	5.9%	36.0%	56.5%	18.0%
Pitt County	7,747	0.0%	0.0%	0.0%	4.4%	1.3%	0.0%	34.3%	60.0%	17.8%
Randolph County	1,968	10.5%	32.5%	0.0%	0.0%	0.0%	0.0%	39.0%	18.0%	56.5%
Robeson County	1,221	6.4%	2.9%	3.4%	6.5%	12.0%	4.0%	24.3%	40.6%	55.7%
Rockingham County	586	26.5%	25.1%	15.9%	0.0%	6.5%	0.0%	8.2%	17.9%	53.4%
Rowan County	1,727	22.7%	10.5%	4.3%	7.6%	17.5%	0.0%	13.9%	23.5%	44.5%
Union County	2,464	16.6%	10.8%	0.0%	0.0%	12.0%	9.3%	18.9%	32.5%	63.1%

Table D-2: Counties—Household Relationship—*Continued*

		25 to 33								
		Married Couple Households		Male, No Spouse Present		Female, No Spouse Present		Non-Family Householders		
	Total Householders	With Children	No Children	With Children	No Children	With Children	No Children	Living Alone	Not Alone	Living With Parents
New Jersey—Cont.										
Morris County	15,851	25.5%	17.0%	0.5%	8.0%	11.7%	0.3%	23.7%	13.4%	76.3%
Ocean County	19,189	45.9%	12.1%	6.6%	0.0%	7.8%	1.2%	13.9%	12.6%	75.6%
Passaic County	17,230	34.0%	8.1%	4.4%	2.2%	22.2%	1.8%	21.1%	6.3%	73.9%
Somerset County	9,430	24.0%	29.1%	1.8%	0.9%	8.4%	0.7%	20.6%	14.5%	84.5%
Sussex County	4,097	42.8%	5.2%	2.1%	6.5%	1.0%	0.0%	30.1%	12.5%	84.2%
Union County	20,682	27.1%	12.0%	6.9%	4.1%	18.6%	3.8%	18.0%	9.5%	67.6%
Warren County	3,474	22.8%	19.1%	12.0%	0.0%	15.0%	0.0%	25.6%	5.5%	75.3%
New Mexico										
Bernalillo County	40,534	23.6%	11.0%	7.9%	4.3%	14.6%	3.9%	21.3%	13.4%	54.7%
Doña Ana County	9,595	30.3%	20.4%	6.3%	3.7%	17.8%	2.3%	10.1%	9.2%	45.4%
San Juan County	5,161	48.8%	12.3%	5.2%	0.8%	7.3%	0.4%	11.4%	13.8%	68.2%
Sandoval County	5,393	40.3%	12.1%	12.9%	0.0%	9.2%	3.5%	13.9%	8.1%	54.4%
Santa Fe County	5,528	19.4%	18.4%	2.2%	4.2%	19.2%	0.0%	22.2%	14.4%	55.5%
New York										
Albany County	15,176	10.0%	10.6%	6.4%	3.7%	10.0%	3.2%	30.8%	25.4%	41.6%
Bronx County	67,346	19.4%	9.4%	5.3%	5.4%	31.5%	2.6%	19.8%	6.6%	68.7%
Broome County	7,959	18.3%	15.6%	3.5%	0.8%	11.5%	0.9%	29.9%	19.7%	47.1%
Chautauqua County	4,787	15.8%	19.1%	5.0%	1.1%	15.4%	0.0%	29.7%	13.9%	47.7%
Dutchess County	10,460	22.3%	22.8%	1.8%	0.3%	15.3%	0.7%	27.8%	8.9%	57.2%
Erie County	50,700	24.3%	12.2%	2.1%	2.1%	18.8%	1.7%	22.3%	16.5%	54.3%
Jefferson County	7,384	33.5%	9.3%	0.9%	1.6%	17.1%	0.0%	29.3%	8.3%	39.8%
Kings County	157,947	18.4%	9.9%	2.7%	4.5%	11.9%	3.3%	24.7%	24.7%	63.0%
Monroe County	41,991	24.1%	12.2%	4.5%	0.6%	18.4%	1.1%	23.1%	15.9%	45.3%
Nassau County	28,466	34.0%	14.8%	3.0%	7.3%	8.3%	2.8%	19.9%	9.8%	77.2%
New York County	156,058	4.1%	11.7%	0.7%	1.9%	5.0%	1.8%	47.5%	27.3%	33.4%
Niagara County	7,980	24.1%	9.2%	4.4%	0.0%	27.2%	0.0%	19.9%	15.2%	72.2%
Oneida County	10,415	21.6%	7.4%	9.6%	1.1%	30.7%	1.3%	19.4%	8.9%	53.8%
Onondaga County	23,858	17.9%	11.1%	5.4%	0.0%	23.8%	0.6%	26.6%	14.6%	42.1%
Ontario County	5,003	44.0%	17.6%	2.5%	0.0%	5.4%	2.0%	21.6%	6.9%	47.0%
Orange County	12,866	39.0%	13.2%	0.0%	1.7%	11.4%	0.0%	23.9%	10.8%	67.1%
Oswego County	5,182	42.0%	8.3%	3.4%	1.0%	14.1%	0.0%	26.7%	4.4%	28.4%
Putnam County	1,526	38.3%	15.6%	0.0%	0.0%	13.0%	3.0%	24.4%	5.6%	89.5%
Queens County	98,696	22.5%	15.4%	3.1%	5.5%	9.8%	5.1%	21.7%	17.0%	68.0%
Rensselaer County	8,368	23.5%	4.6%	3.4%	1.2%	15.3%	0.0%	28.7%	23.3%	53.5%
Richmond County	16,214	31.0%	16.2%	1.2%	4.5%	20.9%	0.8%	17.9%	7.6%	76.6%
Rockland County	10,254	54.6%	11.5%	7.9%	0.9%	7.6%	1.3%	5.9%	10.2%	76.9%
Saratoga County	5,339	31.8%	15.1%	10.5%	0.0%	16.7%	0.0%	11.0%	14.8%	24.4%
Schenectady County	11,149	26.7%	11.3%	3.8%	1.0%	9.3%	1.5%	27.4%	19.0%	63.6%
St. Lawrence County	5,671	17.9%	6.2%	5.3%	1.9%	17.2%	1.5%	30.9%	19.1%	69.7%
Steuben County	3,623	28.6%	17.7%	6.2%	0.6%	27.1%	1.7%	10.6%	7.5%	69.5%
Suffolk County	31,263	35.6%	14.3%	4.0%	3.2%	8.5%	4.9%	22.2%	7.3%	73.6%
Tompkins County	5,142	11.5%	12.5%	5.5%	0.0%	9.8%	1.0%	43.4%	16.3%	9.2%
Ulster County	5,621	21.4%	18.6%	2.6%	5.4%	5.6%	0.0%	26.7%	19.8%	55.8%
Wayne County	3,530	47.6%	4.3%	11.8%	1.6%	18.6%	0.0%	5.2%	11.1%	54.4%
Westchester County	28,100	21.9%	14.2%	6.8%	3.2%	11.8%	3.9%	21.1%	17.3%	68.1%
North Carolina										
Alamance County	6,626	26.2%	24.5%	1.9%	0.0%	34.2%	0.0%	7.1%	6.1%	37.0%
Brunswick County	3,030	25.0%	18.4%	7.3%	2.6%	16.3%	4.1%	12.7%	13.6%	77.8%
Buncombe County	13,683	36.5%	12.6%	3.0%	0.8%	6.5%	1.0%	24.0%	15.5%	50.0%
Cabarrus County	8,327	43.7%	11.1%	8.6%	4.8%	9.2%	0.0%	13.2%	9.3%	60.0%
Catawba County	6,788	46.6%	7.0%	1.8%	0.0%	7.0%	0.0%	33.0%	4.7%	53.2%
Cleveland County	3,816	37.2%	2.4%	2.6%	0.6%	18.4%	1.4%	26.9%	10.4%	52.9%
Craven County	5,664	47.5%	8.5%	3.1%	0.0%	11.1%	0.5%	24.7%	4.6%	25.5%
Cumberland County	22,961	25.2%	12.6%	6.1%	0.4%	21.2%	2.4%	25.0%	7.1%	38.7%
Davidson County	6,928	34.1%	8.9%	6.2%	0.0%	12.1%	0.0%	30.9%	7.8%	65.2%
Durham County	22,645	16.8%	17.7%	2.7%	0.7%	14.6%	0.4%	30.0%	17.2%	29.9%
Forsyth County	20,336	32.3%	13.5%	6.7%	3.0%	8.1%	1.6%	26.6%	8.2%	39.9%
Gaston County	10,319	31.6%	14.0%	5.0%	4.1%	20.9%	0.0%	11.3%	13.1%	51.7%
Guilford County	27,875	21.9%	12.8%	4.4%	1.6%	20.8%	0.3%	24.4%	13.8%	50.5%
Harnett County	7,327	38.6%	18.0%	1.3%	1.3%	20.4%	0.8%	17.2%	2.4%	47.5%
Henderson County	4,310	20.3%	21.8%	1.7%	0.0%	28.1%	0.0%	23.2%	4.8%	39.7%
Iredell County	6,846	28.7%	17.9%	4.9%	6.7%	8.4%	1.2%	28.5%	3.7%	61.8%
Johnston County	6,783	47.1%	9.8%	6.5%	2.8%	13.5%	0.0%	12.5%	7.9%	70.6%
Mecklenburg County	71,275	16.5%	14.1%	4.0%	2.9%	11.2%	1.3%	31.5%	18.6%	45.0%
Moore County	4,057	23.4%	3.2%	2.7%	4.0%	26.3%	0.0%	21.4%	19.0%	69.5%
Nash County	4,099	17.1%	5.4%	2.6%	0.0%	41.7%	1.9%	31.1%	0.0%	53.6%
New Hanover County	12,032	16.9%	11.6%	6.3%	1.0%	23.0%	3.6%	20.3%	17.3%	30.1%
Onslow County	16,096	40.4%	9.1%	7.2%	0.7%	10.2%	0.0%	25.0%	7.4%	23.7%
Orange County	7,489	19.3%	20.1%	0.0%	3.0%	6.8%	0.0%	29.9%	20.9%	18.0%
Pitt County	12,353	20.9%	11.2%	4.7%	0.0%	22.6%	2.5%	23.7%	14.3%	17.8%
Randolph County	5,762	39.9%	13.4%	11.0%	0.0%	18.3%	0.0%	10.1%	7.3%	56.5%
Robeson County	4,868	35.6%	4.9%	8.2%	0.0%	32.1%	2.8%	13.0%	3.3%	55.7%
Rockingham County	3,291	29.5%	6.7%	7.2%	1.8%	39.0%	0.0%	9.5%	6.3%	53.4%
Rowan County	4,569	50.0%	9.8%	3.2%	6.5%	16.3%	0.0%	5.1%	9.0%	44.5%
Union County	7,014	52.4%	8.9%	1.5%	4.6%	15.9%	0.0%	10.7%	6.0%	63.1%

Table D-2: Counties—Household Relationship—*Continued*

		18 to 24								
		Married Couple Households		Male, No Spouse Present		Female, No Spouse Present		Non-Family Householders		
	Total Householders	With Children	No Children	With Children	No Children	With Children	No Children	Living Alone	Not Alone	Living With Parents
North Carolina—Cont.										
Wake County	17,427	2.1%	6.5%	11.8%	5.2%	5.5%	1.4%	25.7%	41.9%	44.1%
Wayne County	1,760	6.3%	18.8%	0.0%	0.0%	2.6%	0.0%	37.8%	34.5%	47.9%
North Dakota										
Cass County	9,999	5.1%	5.6%	11.6%	3.0%	14.0%	0.0%	23.5%	37.2%	16.7%
Ohio										
Allen County	1,970	3.8%	8.4%	0.0%	0.0%	27.3%	0.0%	43.4%	17.2%	43.2%
Ashtabula County	1,154	17.7%	14.0%	3.6%	5.2%	0.0%	4.2%	23.1%	32.4%	68.3%
Butler County	5,990	5.7%	3.7%	4.5%	5.2%	15.6%	1.3%	25.4%	38.8%	46.4%
Clark County	2,323	5.5%	24.8%	21.3%	0.0%	10.8%	4.1%	5.9%	27.6%	44.7%
Clermont County	1,773	16.5%	10.2%	2.8%	0.0%	24.0%	0.0%	5.0%	41.6%	56.6%
Columbiana County	1,699	5.5%	2.8%	0.0%	6.4%	40.2%	0.0%	15.8%	29.4%	50.4%
Cuyahoga County	19,439	4.2%	4.5%	3.1%	5.0%	18.3%	3.3%	35.0%	26.6%	54.6%
Delaware County	1,552	0.0%	17.7%	0.0%	13.3%	18.6%	5.3%	41.3%	3.8%	59.6%
Fairfield County	1,404	7.4%	46.3%	10.9%	0.0%	29.9%	0.0%	0.0%	5.5%	66.2%
Franklin County	26,513	3.1%	5.5%	3.0%	4.1%	15.6%	1.7%	34.4%	32.6%	31.3%
Geauga County	814	43.7%	0.0%	0.0%	0.0%	39.4%	0.0%	0.0%	16.8%	78.4%
Greene County	4,375	0.0%	8.1%	0.0%	5.1%	16.2%	1.6%	37.1%	31.8%	25.1%
Hamilton County	13,846	5.7%	5.7%	0.4%	1.6%	23.9%	1.0%	27.8%	33.8%	47.7%
Lake County	2,758	15.5%	0.0%	14.9%	0.0%	0.0%	5.3%	32.5%	31.8%	68.7%
Licking County	1,941	4.6%	0.0%	9.5%	0.0%	30.3%	5.0%	28.6%	21.8%	54.8%
Lorain County	2,966	2.4%	4.2%	9.6%	0.9%	36.2%	0.0%	22.0%	24.7%	60.4%
Lucas County	10,506	3.9%	2.6%	9.9%	2.7%	20.7%	5.9%	31.8%	22.5%	38.2%
Mahoning County	3,660	6.6%	8.3%	0.0%	2.3%	41.2%	6.7%	18.5%	16.4%	56.5%
Medina County	2,178	6.2%	7.5%	3.0%	0.0%	38.4%	3.8%	27.8%	13.5%	72.5%
Miami County	1,793	0.0%	0.0%	9.3%	6.3%	10.3%	0.0%	34.0%	40.0%	51.9%
Montgomery County	10,476	6.0%	6.6%	1.1%	6.3%	19.6%	2.6%	27.6%	30.2%	36.0%
Portage County	5,280	11.8%	7.1%	0.0%	0.0%	20.7%	0.0%	27.0%	33.5%	38.9%
Richland County	1,381	1.7%	17.7%	0.0%	0.0%	11.9%	11.0%	31.1%	26.4%	49.4%
Stark County	4,616	10.0%	6.2%	3.2%	3.1%	21.8%	0.0%	21.3%	34.4%	52.2%
Summit County	8,725	2.1%	3.9%	2.3%	9.2%	18.8%	4.0%	37.4%	22.4%	62.2%
Trumbull County	4,358	3.3%	16.5%	2.6%	8.7%	20.1%	1.5%	24.1%	23.2%	51.5%
Tuscarawas County	961	15.8%	16.4%	0.0%	3.0%	3.9%	8.6%	29.2%	23.0%	76.2%
Warren County	2,053	13.7%	44.5%	0.0%	1.0%	6.7%	0.0%	17.4%	16.7%	66.5%
Wayne County	1,093	18.6%	16.0%	0.0%	0.0%	17.0%	0.0%	27.0%	21.4%	54.5%
Wood County	3,770	0.4%	6.5%	9.7%	0.0%	0.0%	15.0%	38.4%	30.0%	31.2%
Oklahoma										
Canadian County	879	15.4%	0.0%	32.9%	13.7%	0.0%	0.0%	30.5%	7.6%	69.5%
Cleveland County	7,244	8.0%	13.5%	0.0%	0.0%	0.0%	0.0%	27.1%	51.4%	26.4%
Comanche County	2,178	38.0%	27.7%	0.0%	0.0%	5.9%	0.0%	20.8%	7.7%	33.1%
Oklahoma County	13,873	11.7%	6.0%	4.0%	6.1%	14.0%	1.8%	16.7%	39.7%	40.6%
Tulsa County	14,251	13.0%	7.9%	2.3%	8.1%	18.8%	2.0%	25.2%	22.6%	44.3%
Oregon										
Clackamas County	2,795	15.2%	13.8%	0.0%	0.0%	8.7%	0.0%	26.7%	35.5%	67.6%
Deschutes County	2,095	3.9%	9.5%	2.8%	1.8%	6.3%	10.7%	13.0%	52.0%	46.0%
Douglas County	510	58.6%	0.0%	10.2%	0.0%	0.0%	2.2%	12.9%	16.1%	43.1%
Jackson County	2,222	15.7%	5.7%	0.0%	0.0%	12.0%	0.0%	6.8%	59.8%	44.7%
Lane County	10,481	2.5%	4.8%	1.7%	0.6%	1.7%	4.8%	31.6%	52.3%	28.9%
Linn County	3,764	3.8%	3.7%	0.0%	6.7%	8.8%	0.0%	21.4%	55.7%	20.0%
Marion County	3,924	6.9%	12.7%	3.3%	1.4%	28.5%	4.3%	16.0%	26.8%	53.4%
Multnomah County	10,891	5.3%	4.8%	3.8%	1.0%	6.4%	1.0%	23.9%	53.8%	37.0%
Washington County	6,775	3.6%	3.9%	0.0%	9.1%	8.8%	0.0%	37.2%	37.5%	59.7%
Yamhill County	2,050	15.8%	0.0%	0.0%	16.2%	0.0%	0.0%	15.1%	52.9%	40.8%
Pennsylvania										
Adams County	752	20.3%	0.0%	22.5%	0.0%	0.0%	0.0%	23.7%	33.5%	54.1%
Allegheny County	20,694	1.7%	3.6%	0.6%	3.7%	12.0%	0.1%	42.0%	36.3%	43.4%
Beaver County	1,158	0.0%	10.6%	7.8%	12.5%	5.4%	0.0%	14.2%	49.4%	69.1%
Berks County	2,689	5.2%	2.4%	4.9%	15.9%	8.0%	0.0%	22.8%	40.9%	55.6%
Blair County	1,092	0.0%	7.6%	13.6%	0.0%	3.1%	0.0%	22.0%	53.8%	57.8%
Bucks County	2,301	0.0%	3.7%	0.0%	7.2%	19.3%	0.0%	38.6%	31.2%	78.3%
Butler County	2,593	0.0%	4.9%	4.3%	11.9%	0.0%	7.1%	38.6%	33.2%	52.7%
Cambria County	826	26.2%	16.5%	0.0%	6.8%	11.0%	0.0%	30.3%	9.3%	46.7%
Centre County	6,946	0.0%	0.3%	0.0%	1.0%	1.9%	0.0%	40.6%	56.2%	14.5%
Chester County	5,245	5.2%	7.2%	0.8%	8.6%	2.9%	0.0%	17.8%	57.5%	58.8%
Cumberland County	956	4.4%	13.4%	0.0%	0.0%	0.0%	0.0%	20.5%	61.7%	53.1%
Dauphin County	5,652	13.1%	3.8%	4.8%	9.5%	22.7%	0.0%	23.5%	22.7%	54.5%
Delaware County	2,334	4.1%	2.3%	4.4%	0.0%	42.1%	0.0%	22.9%	24.3%	59.6%
Erie County	4,519	8.7%	2.5%	0.0%	0.0%	34.1%	4.4%	15.4%	34.8%	42.7%
Fayette County	1,439	0.0%	6.3%	5.4%	4.8%	20.7%	0.0%	34.1%	28.8%	69.9%
Franklin County	1,654	17.8%	0.0%	10.2%	19.3%	18.2%	0.0%	17.2%	17.2%	68.4%
Lackawanna County	2,086	3.7%	0.0%	17.9%	3.3%	20.0%	0.0%	25.8%	29.2%	59.5%
Lancaster County	5,424	7.3%	24.4%	0.0%	1.2%	10.6%	4.5%	21.3%	30.8%	53.0%
Lebanon County	2,350	12.6%	8.4%	3.2%	17.3%	10.2%	0.0%	0.0%	48.3%	46.2%
Lehigh County	3,076	2.6%	15.1%	0.0%	7.2%	26.6%	6.6%	21.1%	20.9%	63.7%

Table D-2: Counties—Household Relationship—Continued

| | | 25 to 33 | | | | | | | | |
| | Total Householders | Married Couple Households | | Male, No Spouse Present | | Female, No Spouse Present | | Non-Family Householders | | Living With Parents |
		With Children	No Children	With Children	No Children	With Children	No Children	Living Alone	Not Alone	
North Carolina—Cont.										
Wake County	61,954	25.6%	15.9%	3.8%	1.9%	9.7%	1.3%	23.8%	18.0%	44.1%
Wayne County	6,350	35.4%	10.4%	4.5%	0.0%	13.0%	0.0%	22.8%	13.7%	47.9%
North Dakota										
Cass County	13,452	28.2%	12.6%	3.8%	1.3%	4.2%	0.0%	30.4%	19.6%	16.7%
Ohio										
Allen County	4,362	42.6%	3.0%	8.1%	2.2%	18.9%	0.0%	17.8%	7.4%	43.2%
Ashtabula County	3,047	33.0%	7.6%	1.6%	1.0%	23.3%	0.0%	7.7%	25.9%	68.3%
Butler County	16,086	31.3%	14.6%	0.8%	0.3%	16.3%	0.8%	21.8%	14.0%	46.4%
Clark County	6,116	25.6%	12.1%	6.5%	6.1%	28.4%	1.6%	15.0%	4.7%	44.7%
Clermont County	9,931	31.0%	15.3%	5.6%	2.6%	9.2%	0.3%	23.9%	12.1%	56.6%
Columbiana County	3,251	39.5%	7.3%	1.5%	6.1%	16.4%	0.0%	20.9%	8.4%	50.4%
Cuyahoga County	68,522	18.5%	13.1%	2.0%	3.1%	20.1%	1.7%	29.1%	12.3%	54.6%
Delaware County	6,492	52.0%	23.1%	0.0%	0.0%	3.0%	0.0%	10.6%	11.3%	59.6%
Fairfield County	6,655	45.7%	13.7%	5.5%	1.5%	21.3%	0.0%	9.5%	2.9%	66.2%
Franklin County	96,946	19.2%	14.8%	1.4%	1.9%	12.2%	2.8%	29.2%	18.5%	31.3%
Geauga County	3,409	32.9%	36.1%	0.0%	0.0%	4.5%	7.8%	14.8%	3.8%	78.4%
Greene County	9,905	27.1%	9.0%	4.8%	2.4%	19.7%	0.0%	21.6%	15.4%	25.1%
Hamilton County	54,286	19.0%	9.4%	2.9%	0.4%	22.1%	0.2%	30.5%	15.7%	47.7%
Lake County	10,676	23.4%	21.5%	1.9%	1.2%	9.7%	1.3%	32.5%	8.4%	68.7%
Licking County	8,064	42.0%	13.3%	3.9%	0.0%	21.7%	1.0%	10.7%	7.4%	54.8%
Lorain County	12,749	27.3%	12.4%	4.9%	0.8%	23.6%	1.8%	20.6%	8.5%	60.4%
Lucas County	24,661	21.2%	9.2%	5.1%	2.4%	22.4%	1.5%	24.0%	14.2%	38.2%
Mahoning County	11,840	17.4%	10.4%	3.9%	3.1%	21.0%	2.4%	29.6%	12.3%	56.5%
Medina County	6,606	46.4%	21.2%	1.3%	6.0%	10.0%	1.9%	9.2%	4.0%	72.5%
Miami County	4,715	52.5%	5.7%	5.9%	5.2%	7.5%	0.0%	8.3%	15.0%	51.9%
Montgomery County	30,553	22.3%	11.0%	6.0%	2.3%	21.4%	0.2%	22.9%	13.8%	36.0%
Portage County	6,897	15.0%	14.6%	12.4%	0.0%	23.0%	0.4%	18.1%	16.4%	38.9%
Richland County	4,223	32.7%	12.8%	6.7%	0.0%	18.5%	0.0%	27.5%	1.8%	49.4%
Stark County	19,037	28.6%	8.7%	4.7%	1.4%	17.1%	0.0%	28.5%	10.9%	52.2%
Summit County	31,003	22.0%	12.0%	1.7%	1.8%	16.9%	1.3%	29.7%	14.6%	62.2%
Trumbull County	8,547	27.0%	20.2%	8.2%	6.0%	14.7%	0.0%	21.7%	2.2%	51.5%
Tuscarawas County	3,268	40.9%	14.4%	15.6%	0.0%	6.2%	0.4%	10.0%	12.5%	76.2%
Warren County	8,609	47.4%	12.1%	4.5%	0.0%	6.4%	1.5%	24.0%	4.0%	66.5%
Wayne County	4,467	44.8%	13.3%	0.9%	0.8%	11.6%	0.0%	19.9%	8.8%	54.5%
Wood County	7,919	34.6%	11.0%	8.1%	6.5%	5.5%	0.0%	25.3%	9.0%	31.2%
Oklahoma										
Canadian County	5,656	46.4%	3.9%	8.4%	0.0%	8.9%	0.0%	28.6%	3.9%	69.5%
Cleveland County	16,375	25.3%	21.5%	0.0%	2.8%	7.0%	3.3%	29.4%	10.7%	26.4%
Comanche County	6,937	39.9%	0.0%	0.3%	0.7%	16.7%	0.0%	24.1%	18.2%	33.1%
Oklahoma County	51,978	23.9%	11.1%	7.0%	2.8%	17.9%	1.8%	26.6%	8.9%	40.6%
Tulsa County	40,770	26.9%	14.9%	6.6%	2.7%	17.5%	0.0%	21.5%	9.9%	44.3%
Oregon										
Clackamas County	15,572	31.1%	20.7%	6.2%	0.3%	10.1%	0.0%	10.1%	21.4%	67.6%
Deschutes County	9,484	27.5%	14.8%	0.0%	0.5%	13.7%	0.0%	21.1%	22.5%	46.0%
Douglas County	5,659	8.2%	20.7%	8.5%	1.1%	21.8%	0.0%	29.9%	9.9%	43.1%
Jackson County	8,084	35.6%	10.2%	11.4%	0.0%	13.8%	6.7%	12.4%	10.0%	44.7%
Lane County	18,216	22.9%	11.2%	6.4%	3.7%	9.6%	1.4%	26.2%	18.6%	28.9%
Linn County	5,759	33.3%	9.6%	2.8%	3.1%	18.9%	0.2%	22.2%	9.9%	20.0%
Marion County	14,649	39.6%	11.4%	7.8%	0.7%	15.0%	0.6%	11.4%	13.5%	53.4%
Multnomah County	52,589	13.0%	13.0%	3.8%	1.1%	12.3%	1.5%	28.7%	26.5%	37.0%
Washington County	31,099	21.3%	17.6%	1.2%	4.5%	10.6%	1.1%	24.7%	19.0%	59.7%
Yamhill County	3,759	32.0%	21.5%	13.2%	6.4%	9.5%	0.0%	13.5%	3.9%	40.8%
Pennsylvania										
Adams County	4,266	42.0%	11.5%	4.9%	0.0%	11.0%	0.0%	27.6%	3.0%	54.1%
Allegheny County	78,101	16.8%	16.7%	3.2%	2.2%	10.4%	1.4%	34.5%	14.8%	43.4%
Beaver County	6,706	31.9%	10.3%	1.1%	2.2%	22.6%	0.0%	19.0%	12.9%	69.1%
Berks County	17,794	32.1%	8.0%	6.6%	3.7%	21.8%	1.5%	13.2%	13.1%	55.6%
Blair County	5,059	29.8%	11.9%	6.9%	0.0%	30.3%	1.1%	7.5%	12.5%	57.8%
Bucks County	21,012	28.7%	19.6%	4.9%	2.7%	13.7%	0.3%	19.2%	10.9%	78.3%
Butler County	7,986	22.0%	23.3%	4.1%	0.3%	21.9%	1.9%	18.3%	8.2%	52.7%
Cambria County	6,234	42.2%	6.3%	2.2%	0.0%	12.4%	0.0%	20.9%	16.0%	46.7%
Centre County	9,926	20.3%	12.7%	0.0%	6.8%	9.9%	1.0%	38.8%	10.5%	14.5%
Chester County	18,598	31.9%	21.2%	4.6%	1.3%	11.1%	1.4%	17.3%	11.2%	58.8%
Cumberland County	11,448	24.0%	18.5%	1.2%	2.0%	17.3%	0.0%	24.1%	12.9%	53.1%
Dauphin County	13,139	30.0%	9.8%	8.2%	0.0%	12.7%	2.1%	19.1%	18.1%	54.5%
Delaware County	21,792	25.0%	20.4%	4.6%	3.2%	15.7%	1.2%	15.1%	14.7%	59.6%
Erie County	12,900	19.4%	5.1%	2.9%	2.3%	25.5%	0.0%	25.5%	19.3%	42.7%
Fayette County	5,609	45.4%	5.9%	0.0%	1.7%	15.4%	0.0%	27.3%	4.3%	69.9%
Franklin County	6,147	49.4%	9.4%	5.6%	0.0%	10.4%	0.0%	17.7%	7.4%	68.4%
Lackawanna County	7,949	20.3%	15.7%	11.1%	2.7%	14.9%	3.7%	12.2%	19.6%	59.5%
Lancaster County	25,003	36.5%	14.7%	3.4%	2.0%	15.4%	0.3%	12.0%	15.6%	53.0%
Lebanon County	5,536	26.2%	31.4%	4.7%	3.5%	15.7%	1.8%	13.5%	3.3%	46.2%
Lehigh County	17,027	30.2%	12.7%	4.0%	1.5%	16.8%	3.6%	19.6%	11.6%	63.7%

Table D-2: Counties—Household Relationship—*Continued*

| | | Married Couple Households | | Male, No Spouse Present | | Female, No Spouse Present | | Non-Family Householders | | |
| | | | | | 18 to 24 | | | | | | |
	Total Householders	With Children	No Children	With Children	No Children	With Children	No Children	Living Alone	Not Alone	Living With Parents
Pennsylvania—Cont.										
Luzerne County	3,136	8.8%	6.0%	2.3%	2.3%	16.6%	3.9%	30.2%	29.9%	49.9%
Lycoming County	1,219	27.9%	9.3%	0.0%	0.0%	12.2%	0.0%	45.9%	4.8%	55.4%
Mercer County	503	18.1%	32.8%	0.0%	0.0%	25.6%	0.0%	15.3%	8.2%	46.7%
Monroe County	603	0.0%	22.9%	0.0%	0.0%	0.0%	0.0%	37.6%	39.5%	71.4%
Montgomery County	4,160	0.0%	4.6%	0.0%	12.7%	20.9%	7.0%	33.4%	21.4%	69.2%
Northampton County	3,278	12.8%	0.0%	0.0%	4.2%	33.9%	0.0%	9.9%	39.3%	49.3%
Northumberland County	1,119	4.9%	2.2%	3.1%	0.0%	0.0%	37.1%	43.9%	8.8%	59.3%
Philadelphia County	20,822	0.5%	1.5%	1.6%	6.1%	21.0%	3.7%	36.4%	29.1%	45.1%
Schuylkill County	1,207	3.5%	2.9%	0.0%	0.0%	62.3%	0.0%	11.9%	19.4%	65.9%
Washington County	1,815	10.3%	0.0%	5.6%	2.4%	48.0%	7.9%	8.5%	17.4%	48.8%
Westmoreland County	3,523	11.0%	24.7%	4.3%	0.0%	12.3%	0.0%	29.2%	18.5%	60.2%
York County	2,098	10.7%	9.7%	9.5%	1.1%	0.8%	0.0%	17.3%	51.0%	61.4%
Rhode Island										
Kent County	844	0.0%	0.0%	0.0%	0.0%	8.8%	24.2%	20.1%	46.9%	75.7%
Providence County	7,871	7.0%	0.0%	8.3%	4.5%	19.4%	6.4%	21.6%	32.8%	43.6%
Washington County	1,075	22.5%	0.0%	0.0%	0.0%	0.0%	0.0%	14.8%	62.7%	50.3%
South Carolina										
Aiken County	1,749	4.3%	0.5%	22.7%	0.0%	15.6%	0.0%	48.8%	8.1%	58.6%
Anderson County	2,771	13.9%	12.7%	1.6%	7.3%	28.5%	0.3%	28.4%	7.4%	57.0%
Beaufort County	1,769	14.5%	14.7%	0.0%	3.1%	7.3%	12.1%	10.7%	37.6%	41.7%
Berkeley County	1,987	13.2%	33.4%	2.5%	1.0%	21.0%	7.5%	17.4%	4.0%	49.4%
Charleston County	5,200	5.0%	9.5%	1.0%	0.7%	10.9%	5.2%	15.1%	52.6%	33.8%
Dorchester County	1,314	1.1%	34.1%	3.8%	0.0%	17.2%	9.1%	12.9%	21.8%	57.3%
Florence County	1,729	5.0%	4.3%	12.1%	0.0%	36.3%	3.3%	27.6%	11.3%	51.6%
Greenville County	7,194	10.8%	14.5%	0.4%	3.7%	24.5%	2.0%	24.0%	20.0%	50.7%
Horry County	3,656	4.7%	6.3%	1.0%	7.9%	18.3%	1.2%	26.5%	34.2%	44.8%
Lexington County	3,181	13.0%	10.8%	4.8%	10.6%	8.4%	0.0%	15.6%	36.9%	55.9%
Pickens County	3,799	7.4%	2.4%	6.8%	0.0%	8.3%	0.0%	16.1%	59.0%	20.2%
Richland County	8,216	8.1%	0.0%	0.9%	3.0%	10.9%	7.2%	32.1%	37.7%	38.9%
Spartanburg County	4,278	7.3%	3.5%	13.3%	5.4%	17.5%	5.1%	31.3%	16.5%	52.1%
Sumter County	1,268	5.3%	6.9%	11.7%	0.0%	18.7%	0.0%	32.4%	25.1%	59.3%
York County	3,767	2.3%	13.2%	0.0%	5.0%	9.7%	12.9%	29.5%	27.3%	49.6%
South Dakota										
Minnehaha County	3,747	1.6%	0.0%	0.0%	0.0%	5.0%	4.8%	51.6%	36.9%	40.0%
Pennington County	2,267	9.1%	0.0%	18.0%	3.8%	5.4%	0.0%	46.1%	17.6%	28.6%
Tennessee										
Blount County	1,249	13.7%	5.4%	0.0%	0.0%	20.5%	0.0%	22.6%	37.9%	65.3%
Bradley County	2,432	5.0%	19.0%	0.0%	8.2%	16.7%	15.6%	17.4%	18.1%	48.0%
Davidson County	16,960	2.1%	4.3%	2.5%	5.1%	19.5%	2.3%	35.5%	28.7%	32.4%
Hamilton County	4,111	5.6%	9.3%	0.0%	8.1%	12.3%	0.6%	35.4%	28.6%	43.4%
Knox County	11,209	1.6%	15.5%	0.0%	2.5%	16.7%	2.2%	27.3%	34.2%	34.4%
Madison County	2,451	9.8%	3.9%	0.0%	18.9%	8.7%	0.0%	29.5%	29.3%	40.0%
Montgomery County	6,840	13.3%	28.1%	0.0%	4.9%	13.1%	0.0%	19.1%	21.5%	31.7%
Rutherford County	7,069	1.9%	12.6%	2.6%	14.2%	3.0%	0.0%	21.2%	44.4%	39.5%
Sevier County	2,235	5.3%	7.2%	0.0%	10.6%	0.0%	0.0%	34.6%	42.2%	41.4%
Shelby County	14,351	4.3%	7.6%	0.0%	5.3%	27.3%	3.9%	25.0%	26.7%	53.9%
Sullivan County	1,136	31.6%	6.5%	4.9%	0.0%	22.9%	0.0%	11.4%	22.6%	67.9%
Sumner County	2,118	0.0%	7.3%	0.0%	0.0%	29.2%	0.0%	26.3%	37.3%	60.7%
Washington County	3,609	0.0%	4.1%	0.0%	2.9%	27.0%	0.0%	26.2%	39.8%	39.4%
Williamson County	2,179	0.0%	19.0%	0.0%	12.6%	9.6%	0.0%	54.9%	3.9%	72.3%
Wilson County	1,164	35.3%	48.0%	0.0%	0.0%	16.7%	0.0%	0.0%	0.0%	73.1%
Texas										
Bell County	10,259	19.9%	21.9%	6.1%	2.0%	8.5%	1.4%	18.4%	21.9%	32.5%
Bexar County	26,427	8.5%	9.6%	3.9%	5.1%	15.2%	4.6%	28.0%	25.1%	53.4%
Bowie County	775	5.5%	36.9%	0.0%	0.0%	23.0%	12.3%	13.4%	8.9%	51.3%
Brazoria County	2,199	25.1%	9.0%	0.0%	6.5%	14.1%	0.0%	25.5%	19.9%	60.3%
Brazos County	15,428	2.8%	4.6%	0.0%	4.5%	2.7%	1.1%	34.4%	50.0%	12.2%
Cameron County	3,040	31.1%	8.1%	12.7%	1.3%	17.1%	10.5%	14.0%	5.2%	69.9%
Collin County	11,072	1.0%	5.5%	0.8%	14.1%	10.9%	14.9%	32.1%	20.7%	62.9%
Comal County	956	4.1%	0.0%	0.0%	27.4%	39.6%	0.0%	0.0%	28.9%	76.6%
Dallas County	40,806	9.5%	6.6%	6.1%	5.7%	16.1%	5.4%	26.4%	24.2%	57.6%
Denton County	13,947	1.3%	8.1%	0.3%	6.4%	9.0%	5.2%	32.4%	37.1%	45.8%
Ector County	3,798	18.7%	5.5%	0.0%	0.0%	19.7%	6.0%	18.0%	32.1%	52.7%
El Paso County	1,981	25.4%	9.9%	7.6%	0.0%	7.8%	0.0%	30.7%	18.5%	71.5%
Ellis County	11,284	24.4%	20.5%	3.7%	7.7%	7.9%	2.2%	26.7%	7.0%	63.6%
Fort Bend County	2,650	21.8%	10.9%	1.6%	16.0%	13.4%	0.0%	32.1%	4.3%	79.4%
Galveston County	3,771	11.0%	5.4%	6.5%	1.5%	11.3%	1.1%	39.5%	23.7%	56.5%
Grayson County	1,233	30.7%	0.0%	0.0%	0.0%	7.8%	0.0%	29.3%	32.3%	60.7%
Gregg County	2,841	24.5%	0.0%	0.0%	0.0%	10.1%	0.0%	35.1%	30.3%	26.0%
Guadalupe County	1,018	0.0%	28.6%	0.0%	17.8%	0.0%	9.7%	18.3%	25.6%	67.5%
Harris County	66,472	10.1%	5.0%	5.1%	7.0%	14.5%	6.1%	32.0%	20.3%	59.3%
Hays County	7,630	7.9%	0.0%	1.0%	1.3%	0.0%	2.4%	27.5%	59.8%	22.8%

Table D-2: Counties—Household Relationship—*Continued*

| | | 25 to 33 | | | | | | | | |
| | | Married Couple Households | | Male, No Spouse Present | | Female, No Spouse Present | | Non-Family Householders | | |
	Total Householders	With Children	No Children	With Children	No Children	With Children	No Children	Living Alone	Not Alone	Living With Parents
Pennsylvania—Cont.										
Luzerne County	13,961	18.0%	7.4%	8.9%	2.7%	28.8%	3.8%	17.5%	12.9%	49.9%
Lycoming County	5,169	37.4%	17.7%	5.1%	0.0%	17.5%	0.0%	10.3%	12.0%	55.4%
Mercer County	3,688	22.3%	17.6%	0.0%	1.3%	17.1%	0.0%	25.6%	16.2%	46.7%
Monroe County	4,582	51.0%	17.2%	0.0%	0.0%	6.8%	0.0%	11.1%	13.9%	71.4%
Montgomery County	33,901	27.7%	22.7%	2.0%	0.2%	7.9%	0.9%	17.7%	20.9%	69.2%
Northampton County	11,340	26.9%	10.1%	12.0%	3.6%	10.7%	0.0%	21.4%	15.3%	49.3%
Northumberland County	4,551	28.6%	7.1%	10.5%	0.0%	8.5%	3.7%	11.4%	30.2%	59.3%
Philadelphia County	104,959	12.3%	10.6%	3.8%	2.8%	18.0%	2.1%	32.4%	18.0%	45.1%
Schuylkill County	6,234	27.7%	8.9%	7.9%	0.0%	25.2%	0.0%	20.8%	9.4%	65.9%
Washington County	6,571	27.2%	31.0%	0.0%	0.0%	9.7%	1.5%	19.2%	11.4%	48.8%
Westmoreland County	14,105	21.9%	17.0%	7.8%	0.0%	10.2%	0.5%	32.5%	10.1%	60.2%
York County	21,313	30.6%	16.8%	5.8%	1.6%	15.5%	0.5%	18.2%	10.9%	61.4%
Rhode Island										
Kent County	7,680	30.5%	16.2%	5.0%	0.0%	3.1%	1.3%	27.6%	16.2%	75.7%
Providence County	33,793	17.7%	8.9%	2.5%	3.8%	26.6%	0.8%	19.9%	19.8%	43.6%
Washington County	4,414	26.5%	12.8%	0.0%	0.0%	22.9%	0.0%	11.0%	26.8%	50.3%
South Carolina										
Aiken County	8,180	36.7%	2.3%	8.7%	2.2%	22.9%	2.1%	18.1%	7.0%	58.6%
Anderson County	8,221	38.8%	8.2%	2.7%	0.8%	20.1%	0.0%	24.4%	4.9%	57.0%
Beaufort County	7,767	31.4%	13.3%	5.4%	2.3%	14.0%	2.2%	15.8%	15.5%	41.7%
Berkeley County	11,719	35.7%	11.6%	4.1%	2.2%	4.8%	5.4%	21.0%	15.0%	49.4%
Charleston County	25,894	21.5%	14.2%	2.1%	3.5%	8.8%	0.5%	31.3%	18.0%	33.8%
Dorchester County	8,412	31.4%	7.4%	4.1%	4.5%	11.0%	7.6%	21.4%	12.6%	57.3%
Florence County	5,828	37.0%	7.7%	0.7%	0.5%	24.2%	0.0%	18.8%	11.1%	51.6%
Greenville County	26,375	30.6%	16.7%	3.3%	2.5%	12.4%	0.2%	23.4%	11.0%	50.7%
Horry County	15,738	31.9%	11.5%	1.7%	0.8%	10.2%	1.4%	24.0%	18.5%	44.8%
Lexington County	14,659	28.5%	19.1%	2.6%	0.6%	16.2%	0.3%	19.1%	13.6%	55.9%
Pickens County	7,138	28.3%	11.9%	5.7%	5.4%	18.0%	1.6%	11.7%	17.5%	20.2%
Richland County	23,695	21.8%	13.0%	1.8%	2.8%	19.4%	3.4%	27.4%	10.5%	38.9%
Spartanburg County	13,654	40.3%	13.2%	1.3%	1.9%	16.6%	1.1%	17.6%	7.9%	52.1%
Sumter County	4,552	12.8%	16.0%	2.9%	3.9%	35.8%	0.0%	15.1%	13.5%	59.3%
York County	13,175	25.0%	16.2%	3.4%	3.3%	14.7%	0.0%	31.4%	6.0%	49.6%
South Dakota										
Minnehaha County	14,928	28.6%	18.9%	4.4%	1.2%	11.3%	1.3%	19.9%	14.4%	40.0%
Pennington County	6,978	25.0%	11.5%	14.6%	4.3%	23.6%	2.6%	12.9%	5.5%	28.6%
Tennessee										
Blount County	4,678	38.9%	10.2%	0.0%	0.0%	22.9%	0.0%	13.4%	14.5%	65.3%
Bradley County	3,494	44.2%	17.5%	2.3%	0.0%	16.9%	0.0%	11.0%	8.0%	48.0%
Davidson County	57,180	20.1%	14.8%	3.2%	2.3%	14.1%	1.1%	25.3%	19.0%	32.4%
Hamilton County	18,352	33.4%	14.8%	1.8%	1.7%	15.1%	2.2%	18.3%	12.7%	43.4%
Knox County	26,549	25.9%	13.5%	2.6%	1.9%	12.8%	1.3%	30.7%	11.3%	34.4%
Madison County	6,207	37.3%	20.3%	0.3%	0.7%	21.4%	0.0%	14.0%	6.0%	40.0%
Montgomery County	18,269	36.2%	13.0%	3.2%	2.1%	9.4%	0.0%	29.6%	6.4%	31.7%
Rutherford County	17,084	36.9%	13.4%	1.7%	2.1%	9.5%	0.8%	15.6%	20.0%	39.5%
Sevier County	4,241	33.9%	5.5%	6.6%	0.0%	33.5%	3.4%	17.0%	0.0%	41.4%
Shelby County	51,588	21.5%	7.8%	6.1%	2.9%	26.9%	0.6%	25.5%	8.8%	53.9%
Sullivan County	5,168	48.8%	18.5%	15.3%	0.0%	3.2%	0.0%	9.9%	4.4%	67.9%
Sumner County	7,107	46.7%	15.4%	5.3%	1.0%	7.0%	0.7%	16.8%	7.1%	60.7%
Washington County	6,688	21.9%	7.7%	1.9%	3.7%	15.0%	0.0%	48.7%	1.0%	39.4%
Williamson County	5,777	59.5%	15.5%	0.0%	0.0%	5.1%	0.0%	7.2%	12.7%	72.3%
Wilson County	5,459	48.1%	21.8%	0.0%	0.0%	18.8%	0.6%	7.5%	3.2%	73.1%
Texas										
Bell County	21,687	41.3%	13.3%	3.1%	1.4%	17.4%	0.0%	16.8%	6.7%	32.5%
Bexar County	96,949	27.4%	12.0%	3.5%	3.0%	17.6%	1.4%	24.8%	10.2%	53.4%
Bowie County	3,757	28.5%	7.8%	8.6%	0.0%	35.9%	2.9%	13.4%	2.8%	51.3%
Brazoria County	16,183	37.0%	9.6%	9.2%	1.1%	5.8%	2.3%	21.3%	13.7%	60.3%
Brazos County	16,356	11.2%	17.9%	1.0%	1.7%	12.2%	1.1%	30.5%	24.3%	12.2%
Cameron County	16,776	41.0%	7.2%	4.5%	2.0%	24.2%	0.5%	16.3%	4.4%	69.9%
Collin County	48,231	34.6%	17.6%	2.7%	3.0%	7.6%	1.4%	24.6%	8.6%	62.9%
Comal County	5,633	54.3%	8.0%	2.9%	0.9%	13.6%	0.0%	15.3%	5.1%	76.6%
Dallas County	157,859	22.6%	12.7%	4.1%	3.9%	17.0%	2.1%	25.8%	11.8%	57.6%
Denton County	45,432	33.9%	15.1%	2.5%	1.6%	9.1%	1.6%	24.9%	11.1%	45.8%
Ector County	10,127	48.1%	9.8%	0.0%	1.3%	19.4%	0.0%	17.4%	4.0%	52.7%
El Paso County	5,326	48.7%	18.4%	2.0%	1.5%	12.9%	0.0%	13.6%	2.8%	71.5%
Ellis County	41,178	33.9%	10.9%	9.5%	4.5%	15.3%	3.2%	18.3%	4.3%	63.6%
Fort Bend County	28,913	43.3%	15.3%	4.6%	5.4%	11.3%	0.9%	11.7%	7.5%	79.4%
Galveston County	14,882	38.7%	12.1%	2.7%	4.0%	11.2%	3.5%	11.9%	15.9%	56.5%
Grayson County	5,545	40.6%	9.5%	6.1%	0.0%	19.4%	0.0%	8.5%	15.9%	60.7%
Gregg County	5,986	29.1%	14.1%	0.0%	4.2%	14.5%	3.8%	23.3%	11.1%	26.0%
Guadalupe County	6,515	41.0%	18.9%	17.3%	1.0%	17.2%	0.0%	0.7%	4.1%	67.5%
Harris County	284,025	26.6%	12.3%	4.6%	3.6%	16.9%	1.6%	25.6%	8.8%	59.3%
Hays County	10,524	29.9%	6.6%	0.2%	0.2%	7.8%	0.6%	29.3%	25.4%	22.8%

Table D-2: Counties—Household Relationship—*Continued*

		Married Couple Households		Male, No Spouse Present		Female, No Spouse Present		Non-Family Householders		
	Total Householders	With Children	No Children	With Children	No Children	With Children	No Children	Living Alone	Not Alone	Living With Parents
Texas—Cont.										
Hidalgo County	5,689	13.9%	10.6%	2.8%	5.2%	21.8%	23.8%	21.1%	0.9%	76.4%
Jefferson County	4,631	18.6%	4.2%	3.9%	0.0%	15.0%	1.5%	20.0%	36.8%	42.2%
Johnson County	1,960	39.6%	0.0%	15.3%	0.0%	12.9%	2.1%	25.5%	4.6%	58.3%
Kaufman County	593	26.6%	0.0%	0.0%	28.0%	21.6%	0.0%	23.8%	0.0%	60.4%
Lubbock County	11,785	7.8%	7.2%	4.0%	2.1%	12.0%	2.6%	25.1%	39.1%	24.7%
McLennan County	8,616	10.7%	8.5%	2.7%	2.1%	15.0%	3.2%	40.6%	17.4%	29.8%
Midland County	3,447	10.1%	27.4%	3.5%	0.0%	16.9%	0.0%	21.1%	20.9%	53.2%
Montgomery County	4,001	17.6%	17.4%	8.4%	1.8%	5.8%	0.0%	35.7%	13.3%	76.9%
Nueces County	6,649	12.4%	10.8%	7.2%	5.0%	16.8%	2.3%	26.0%	19.5%	48.2%
Parker County	1,077	1.8%	20.4%	0.0%	0.0%	43.1%	0.0%	28.0%	6.7%	67.5%
Potter County	2,092	6.2%	1.6%	18.5%	13.5%	17.6%	0.0%	37.4%	5.2%	54.2%
Randall County	1,890	0.0%	12.0%	0.0%	4.7%	19.1%	0.0%	37.8%	26.4%	57.9%
Smith County	5,180	12.3%	4.9%	0.0%	1.4%	5.2%	0.0%	39.2%	37.0%	37.0%
Tarrant County	27,463	9.7%	8.6%	5.4%	4.3%	18.3%	4.1%	27.3%	22.3%	56.2%
Taylor County	5,103	9.4%	8.2%	1.7%	0.5%	22.0%	0.0%	13.9%	44.4%	27.4%
Tom Green County	2,523	6.1%	2.7%	0.0%	1.8%	7.0%	0.0%	50.0%	32.4%	30.6%
Travis County	21,417	4.6%	3.1%	0.9%	3.2%	4.5%	1.1%	34.7%	47.9%	33.3%
Webb County	2,288	17.0%	2.8%	11.8%	0.0%	28.7%	1.6%	20.7%	17.4%	70.8%
Wichita County	4,164	1.4%	4.6%	7.3%	3.8%	9.7%	4.7%	35.8%	32.6%	20.7%
Williamson County	5,921	1.5%	12.0%	1.7%	0.0%	10.0%	3.9%	23.8%	47.0%	58.5%
Utah										
Cache County	5,063	13.4%	28.3%	0.0%	0.0%	3.3%	0.0%	18.9%	36.1%	34.6%
Davis County	3,530	12.8%	29.2%	0.0%	2.2%	24.6%	1.0%	22.7%	7.6%	73.1%
Salt Lake County	15,055	6.0%	17.7%	1.6%	6.8%	7.8%	4.8%	19.3%	36.0%	49.7%
Utah County	17,597	13.5%	47.5%	0.9%	3.3%	0.0%	4.8%	5.9%	23.9%	34.2%
Washington County	2,705	1.4%	21.2%	3.4%	0.0%	0.0%	6.1%	1.6%	66.2%	36.1%
Weber County	5,529	2.9%	21.9%	0.0%	0.0%	23.2%	4.7%	29.7%	17.6%	47.7%
Vermont										
Chittenden County	3,229	0.0%	0.0%	0.0%	0.0%	4.9%	0.0%	29.9%	65.2%	36.4%
Virginia										
Albemarle County	1,035	0.0%	7.4%	0.0%	0.0%	0.0%	0.0%	18.7%	73.8%	42.8%
Arlington County	4,210	0.0%	0.8%	0.0%	6.8%	0.0%	0.0%	25.4%	67.0%	21.6%
Chesterfield County	2,979	0.4%	12.1%	0.0%	0.0%	13.6%	33.1%	28.2%	12.6%	67.5%
Fairfax County	7,783	0.0%	10.3%	0.0%	7.2%	10.3%	2.9%	23.9%	45.3%	67.1%
Hanover County	661	0.0%	9.8%	0.0%	0.0%	0.0%	43.9%	46.3%	0.0%	67.8%
Henrico County	4,641	4.0%	2.0%	13.0%	9.7%	17.9%	4.7%	18.7%	30.0%	59.1%
Loudoun County	2,331	0.0%	4.0%	0.0%	3.9%	3.7%	6.7%	40.2%	41.6%	70.0%
Montgomery County	4,793	0.0%	5.9%	5.9%	2.9%	5.2%	3.2%	21.7%	55.2%	12.6%
Prince William County	1,523	24.5%	1.1%	0.0%	8.3%	10.6%	22.1%	1.0%	32.5%	75.0%
Roanoke County	539	0.0%	29.3%	0.0%	0.0%	36.4%	0.0%	34.3%	0.0%	62.5%
Spotsylvania County	397	1.3%	23.7%	13.1%	0.0%	20.4%	38.3%	3.3%	0.0%	71.3%
Stafford County	1,653	24.9%	21.7%	0.0%	9.7%	0.0%	0.0%	24.0%	19.7%	54.6%
Washington										
Benton County	2,862	10.9%	17.4%	33.5%	5.2%	9.1%	0.0%	0.0%	23.9%	48.0%
Clark County	6,213	13.3%	10.0%	0.0%	8.4%	21.7%	5.7%	14.6%	26.3%	60.3%
Cowlitz County	1,765	18.3%	4.1%	0.0%	21.4%	3.0%	0.0%	0.0%	53.2%	33.2%
Grant County	3,262	4.6%	1.5%	0.0%	1.8%	2.9%	0.0%	43.9%	45.3%	32.8%
King County	28,526	5.3%	6.9%	1.3%	3.5%	2.2%	3.8%	26.8%	50.2%	44.2%
Kitsap County	3,696	11.9%	15.3%	9.0%	0.4%	6.8%	2.9%	18.4%	35.5%	42.7%
Pierce County	12,229	10.3%	27.3%	3.7%	0.4%	9.6%	2.4%	21.7%	24.6%	49.9%
Skagit County	1,856	13.5%	15.6%	6.4%	0.0%	8.6%	8.0%	15.4%	32.4%	41.9%
Snohomish County	9,809	4.9%	18.0%	0.3%	1.2%	19.2%	3.4%	14.1%	38.9%	57.2%
Spokane County	10,267	8.6%	6.3%	1.0%	1.1%	17.2%	1.1%	30.0%	34.8%	33.9%
Thurston County	4,829	4.1%	13.4%	6.0%	0.0%	0.0%	9.2%	21.3%	46.0%	51.8%
Whatcom County	5,286	0.0%	4.9%	3.0%	5.2%	0.0%	2.1%	27.2%	57.5%	26.7%
Yakima County	3,287	3.2%	8.1%	11.3%	1.5%	47.4%	0.0%	3.0%	25.5%	64.2%
West Virginia										
Berkeley County	1,499	1.9%	16.5%	0.0%	0.0%	53.0%	0.0%	23.7%	4.8%	55.5%
Cabell County	1,928	12.9%	0.0%	0.0%	0.0%	8.5%	0.0%	42.7%	35.9%	43.4%
Kanawha County	3,069	1.0%	7.2%	0.0%	2.8%	20.3%	4.7%	44.2%	19.8%	45.9%
Monongalia County	4,638	3.2%	6.9%	0.0%	0.0%	1.4%	2.2%	62.4%	23.8%	27.8%
Wisconsin										
Brown County	3,727	18.5%	0.0%	8.2%	0.9%	0.0%	8.4%	12.9%	51.0%	46.1%
Dane County	16,970	0.0%	1.6%	0.0%	2.7%	3.9%	0.9%	33.7%	57.2%	21.2%
Eau Claire County	3,329	0.0%	14.4%	4.3%	0.0%	14.7%	0.0%	37.7%	28.9%	39.6%
Fond du Lac County	701	0.0%	31.1%	20.0%	0.0%	11.1%	0.0%	6.7%	31.1%	71.0%
Kenosha County	2,480	0.0%	0.0%	0.0%	16.5%	19.2%	0.0%	21.6%	42.6%	50.7%
La Crosse County	4,139	0.5%	1.0%	0.0%	4.3%	0.0%	0.0%	16.5%	77.8%	14.8%
Marathon County	1,677	12.7%	1.4%	0.0%	8.2%	0.0%	0.0%	54.5%	23.1%	53.5%
Milwaukee County	18,465	2.1%	1.8%	2.5%	5.9%	13.3%	2.3%	40.9%	31.1%	40.9%
Outagamie County	2,130	0.0%	16.9%	0.0%	2.6%	20.8%	0.0%	33.6%	26.2%	64.3%
Racine County	1,718	34.6%	1.2%	0.0%	0.0%	0.0%	0.0%	31.2%	32.9%	73.1%

Table D-2: Counties—Household Relationship—*Continued*

| | | 25 to 33 | | | | | | | | |
| | | Married Couple Households | | Male, No Spouse Present | | Female, No Spouse Present | | Non-Family Householders | | |
	Total Householders	With Children	No Children	With Children	No Children	With Children	No Children	Living Alone	Not Alone	Living With Parents
Texas—Cont.										
Hidalgo County	30,495	46.3%	5.4%	2.6%	0.3%	25.4%	2.2%	14.4%	3.3%	76.4%
Jefferson County	13,874	40.7%	5.0%	5.2%	1.9%	17.9%	1.9%	19.6%	7.8%	42.2%
Johnson County	6,066	58.4%	7.8%	0.8%	1.0%	19.5%	1.0%	9.3%	2.2%	58.3%
Kaufman County	3,637	57.6%	7.8%	1.2%	4.4%	9.9%	1.0%	11.8%	6.2%	60.4%
Lubbock County	18,511	21.7%	8.3%	7.2%	2.0%	12.5%	1.7%	30.4%	16.3%	24.7%
McLennan County	12,072	23.6%	16.1%	3.5%	1.6%	20.1%	1.6%	19.9%	13.6%	29.8%
Midland County	11,363	44.9%	21.7%	0.7%	4.8%	7.2%	0.0%	10.3%	10.4%	53.2%
Montgomery County	23,929	36.5%	12.1%	5.0%	1.1%	14.5%	0.0%	23.5%	7.4%	76.9%
Nueces County	21,555	25.2%	7.6%	5.5%	4.5%	23.0%	1.2%	23.7%	9.3%	48.2%
Parker County	4,389	42.4%	30.9%	6.9%	0.0%	2.3%	0.0%	12.9%	4.5%	67.5%
Potter County	9,292	30.3%	10.9%	3.7%	1.0%	16.5%	0.0%	34.4%	3.2%	54.2%
Randall County	8,610	34.3%	14.0%	0.0%	0.0%	17.3%	1.2%	26.1%	7.0%	57.9%
Smith County	10,233	44.1%	4.8%	10.9%	0.3%	16.1%	0.3%	16.2%	7.4%	37.0%
Tarrant County	107,307	34.1%	11.2%	4.4%	3.0%	16.2%	1.1%	19.6%	10.4%	56.2%
Taylor County	7,348	33.2%	11.3%	3.7%	0.0%	11.9%	0.0%	26.9%	13.2%	27.4%
Tom Green County	7,533	47.8%	4.6%	3.4%	0.0%	13.9%	0.9%	13.7%	15.7%	30.6%
Travis County	100,168	16.0%	12.5%	1.3%	2.1%	9.8%	2.2%	32.4%	23.7%	33.3%
Webb County	9,457	31.5%	22.1%	6.1%	1.6%	16.2%	6.1%	14.5%	1.9%	70.8%
Wichita County	6,598	34.5%	9.8%	7.5%	0.0%	8.9%	7.7%	11.5%	20.0%	20.7%
Williamson County	22,143	31.1%	16.8%	4.7%	1.9%	11.8%	1.0%	23.8%	8.9%	58.5%
Utah										
Cache County	8,091	44.2%	20.4%	0.0%	2.9%	6.2%	0.0%	9.7%	16.7%	34.6%
Davis County	16,079	56.0%	18.6%	2.2%	0.0%	6.7%	0.0%	8.6%	7.8%	73.1%
Salt Lake County	61,718	33.1%	18.0%	3.6%	1.2%	11.0%	1.3%	20.1%	11.6%	49.7%
Utah County	28,999	53.8%	20.5%	0.6%	1.1%	8.4%	0.6%	4.4%	10.5%	34.2%
Washington County	5,629	45.8%	6.8%	0.0%	3.8%	20.6%	0.0%	11.5%	11.5%	36.1%
Weber County	14,352	53.8%	4.5%	7.1%	2.1%	13.6%	0.0%	12.6%	6.3%	47.7%
Vermont										
Chittenden County	7,901	17.3%	15.8%	0.0%	0.0%	2.8%	0.9%	27.3%	35.9%	36.4%
Virginia										
Albemarle County	6,711	24.4%	17.7%	0.0%	0.0%	9.2%	4.2%	17.2%	27.3%	42.8%
Arlington County	27,806	7.5%	20.6%	0.6%	1.2%	1.8%	0.5%	40.8%	27.2%	21.6%
Chesterfield County	12,701	35.1%	17.4%	2.7%	2.9%	13.0%	0.4%	11.4%	17.0%	67.5%
Fairfax County	46,295	23.7%	24.5%	1.9%	1.4%	7.1%	1.9%	20.0%	19.4%	67.1%
Hanover County	2,851	35.8%	36.2%	4.8%	0.0%	13.3%	0.0%	7.2%	2.7%	67.8%
Henrico County	15,214	26.3%	16.2%	5.5%	3.6%	8.7%	0.6%	26.4%	12.8%	59.1%
Loudoun County	15,763	42.0%	13.0%	0.6%	4.0%	3.7%	1.4%	17.1%	18.3%	70.0%
Montgomery County	6,790	38.2%	15.7%	1.0%	0.0%	11.7%	3.0%	7.8%	22.6%	12.6%
Prince William County	17,450	42.2%	15.2%	3.0%	1.5%	4.7%	2.0%	21.7%	9.7%	75.0%
Roanoke County	3,558	43.5%	14.4%	5.4%	0.0%	19.3%	0.0%	17.4%	0.0%	62.5%
Spotsylvania County	4,358	32.1%	7.8%	1.7%	16.3%	12.4%	0.0%	12.2%	17.6%	71.3%
Stafford County	7,129	24.9%	17.8%	8.5%	0.0%	9.8%	9.3%	19.0%	10.8%	54.6%
Washington										
Benton County	10,644	36.5%	7.9%	3.6%	0.4%	22.5%	3.0%	13.3%	12.7%	48.0%
Clark County	20,020	38.5%	12.9%	4.4%	0.4%	15.3%	0.0%	18.1%	10.3%	60.3%
Cowlitz County	5,121	46.7%	6.4%	5.8%	0.0%	17.0%	2.8%	16.9%	4.5%	33.2%
Grant County	3,724	53.7%	10.6%	5.5%	7.0%	11.5%	0.0%	0.0%	11.7%	32.8%
King County	150,927	17.3%	18.3%	2.7%	2.4%	5.5%	1.1%	26.7%	26.0%	44.2%
Kitsap County	13,808	33.5%	18.5%	4.8%	3.4%	12.4%	0.0%	17.8%	9.0%	42.7%
Pierce County	47,715	36.3%	12.9%	4.5%	1.0%	13.2%	1.0%	19.5%	11.6%	49.9%
Skagit County	6,288	28.7%	21.4%	4.4%	3.6%	6.6%	0.0%	22.6%	12.8%	41.9%
Snohomish County	38,117	34.5%	15.6%	2.6%	1.5%	11.8%	0.9%	16.3%	16.7%	57.2%
Spokane County	29,589	33.4%	12.6%	7.4%	0.0%	8.7%	3.6%	23.4%	10.8%	33.9%
Thurston County	13,798	38.8%	10.9%	5.1%	0.0%	14.9%	0.0%	15.5%	14.9%	51.8%
Whatcom County	11,235	22.7%	12.7%	3.5%	0.6%	11.5%	0.0%	25.9%	23.0%	26.7%
Yakima County	10,650	45.8%	10.1%	5.9%	1.6%	20.4%	0.0%	12.8%	3.4%	64.2%
West Virginia										
Berkeley County	5,132	17.2%	7.2%	9.1%	0.7%	27.1%	0.0%	29.2%	9.5%	55.5%
Cabell County	5,026	22.7%	14.7%	4.9%	0.0%	20.5%	8.1%	22.8%	6.3%	43.4%
Kanawha County	9,758	14.5%	7.6%	4.1%	1.7%	37.7%	0.8%	24.7%	8.9%	45.9%
Monongalia County	6,728	19.3%	16.6%	2.3%	0.0%	8.7%	3.2%	30.0%	19.9%	27.8%
Wisconsin										
Brown County	17,423	32.7%	9.9%	0.0%	0.6%	20.7%	1.5%	23.0%	11.6%	46.1%
Dane County	38,619	20.2%	18.8%	1.9%	0.9%	5.9%	0.0%	31.5%	20.8%	21.2%
Eau Claire County	6,128	29.8%	12.8%	5.0%	3.1%	1.4%	0.0%	33.9%	14.0%	39.6%
Fond du Lac County	4,435	26.4%	16.7%	0.8%	0.0%	26.2%	0.0%	21.1%	8.7%	71.0%
Kenosha County	8,029	21.0%	11.6%	6.5%	0.0%	11.9%	0.0%	34.8%	14.2%	50.7%
La Crosse County	6,110	26.6%	7.8%	4.1%	0.0%	0.3%	3.4%	33.7%	24.1%	14.8%
Marathon County	6,682	26.3%	14.2%	9.7%	5.2%	10.6%	0.0%	15.4%	18.6%	53.5%
Milwaukee County	68,332	16.3%	13.1%	2.8%	2.1%	19.1%	1.3%	30.7%	14.8%	40.9%
Outagamie County	10,917	28.8%	19.6%	6.1%	0.0%	13.4%	1.4%	17.7%	13.0%	64.3%
Racine County	9,867	26.5%	14.1%	5.6%	6.2%	21.8%	0.0%	18.5%	7.3%	73.1%

Table D-2: Counties—Household Relationship—*Continued*

| | | 18 to 24 | | | | | | | | |
| | Total Householders | Married Couple Households | | Male, No Spouse Present | | Female, No Spouse Present | | Non-Family Householders | | Living With Parents |
		With Children	No Children	With Children	No Children	With Children	No Children	Living Alone	Not Alone	
Wisconsin—Cont.										
Rock County	2,463	0.0%	1.8%	12.1%	0.0%	34.3%	0.0%	35.4%	16.4%	48.6%
Sheboygan County	1,865	35.5%	0.0%	0.0%	0.0%	0.0%	0.0%	47.5%	17.1%	56.2%
Walworth County	1,971	0.0%	0.0%	3.7%	11.0%	7.1%	0.0%	42.5%	35.8%	43.5%
Washington County	475	0.0%	22.9%	0.0%	0.0%	0.0%	0.0%	77.1%	0.0%	64.7%
Waukesha County	2,797	0.0%	2.6%	0.0%	0.0%	5.5%	1.1%	28.9%	61.9%	70.8%
Winnebago County	4,463	2.0%	0.0%	2.4%	0.0%	12.6%	0.0%	36.5%	46.5%	36.1%
Wyoming										
Laramie County	3,022	2.6%	4.3%	0.0%	0.4%	0.0%	0.0%	36.2%	56.5%	22.1%

Table D-2: Counties—Household Relationship—*Continued*

| | | 25 to 33 | | | | | | | | |
| | | Married Couple Households | | Male, No Spouse Present | | Female, No Spouse Present | | Non-Family Householders | | |
	Total Householders	With Children	No Children	With Children	No Children	With Children	No Children	Living Alone	Not Alone	Living With Parents
Wisconsin—Cont.										
Rock County	7,613	41.3%	6.9%	16.2%	0.0%	11.9%	0.0%	6.8%	16.9%	48.6%
Sheboygan County...................	5,120	32.1%	11.5%	4.7%	0.0%	17.3%	0.0%	19.6%	14.7%	56.2%
Walworth County	4,459	26.2%	15.3%	1.7%	0.0%	21.1%	1.9%	32.9%	0.8%	43.5%
Washington County...................	5,468	41.1%	14.4%	0.0%	0.0%	6.9%	0.0%	4.7%	32.9%	64.7%
Waukesha County	15,258	31.9%	19.0%	3.2%	0.8%	9.5%	3.0%	21.2%	11.4%	70.8%
Winnebago County....................	10,456	28.3%	12.8%	5.3%	2.8%	9.5%	0.0%	25.1%	16.2%	36.1%
Wyoming										
Laramie County.......................	4,172	41.6%	10.5%	5.5%	0.0%	17.4%	0.0%	9.7%	15.3%	22.1%

Table D-3: Places—Household Relationship

		Married Couple Households		Male, No Spouse Present		Female, No Spouse Present		Non-Family Householders		
	Total Householders	With Children	No Children	With Children	No Children	With Children	No Children	Living Alone	Not Alone	Living With Parents
Alabama										
Birmingham city	5,900	4.8%	1.8%	0.0%	6.1%	27.0%	0.0%	38.8%	21.5%	41.3%
Huntsville city	3,169	13.4%	0.0%	0.0%	8.4%	22.2%	0.0%	42.6%	13.5%	41.1%
Mobile city	3,610	0.0%	1.7%	3.3%	4.0%	26.7%	4.9%	35.5%	24.0%	44.0%
Montgomery city	4,552	1.4%	3.4%	16.0%	0.0%	11.9%	0.0%	37.5%	29.7%	34.8%
Tuscaloosa city	5,680	0.0%	0.0%	2.5%	11.3%	13.5%	4.3%	34.9%	33.6%	19.8%
Alaska										
Anchorage municipality	8,289	2.2%	11.0%	10.7%	10.2%	7.6%	0.0%	36.9%	21.4%	41.0%
Arizona										
Chandler city	2,322	1.5%	3.4%	0.0%	0.0%	17.6%	6.1%	27.9%	43.5%	58.2%
Glendale city	3,957	16.0%	3.7%	6.4%	2.5%	7.7%	1.4%	31.4%	30.9%	47.7%
Mesa city	8,079	13.6%	7.8%	2.8%	5.6%	7.9%	7.7%	26.6%	28.0%	53.7%
Peoria city	900	9.2%	10.2%	8.7%	0.0%	34.8%	0.0%	20.0%	17.1%	67.2%
Phoenix city	27,066	5.4%	5.7%	6.3%	10.6%	17.7%	8.5%	25.3%	20.4%	49.4%
Scottsdale city	2,667	0.0%	4.4%	11.8%	1.9%	0.0%	0.0%	45.5%	36.3%	49.4%
Surprise city	670	8.4%	6.1%	0.0%	6.7%	29.4%	0.0%	16.6%	32.8%	72.2%
Tempe city	10,429	0.9%	0.0%	0.9%	4.0%	3.2%	0.0%	27.4%	63.6%	15.1%
Tucson city	16,457	4.2%	1.9%	1.1%	8.2%	11.4%	3.4%	29.7%	40.0%	37.1%
Yuma city	2,603	52.8%	26.4%	2.0%	0.0%	0.0%	0.0%	16.4%	2.4%	49.9%
Arkansas										
Little Rock city	6,204	6.6%	6.0%	6.9%	5.3%	18.5%	1.3%	45.2%	10.3%	37.6%
California										
Anaheim city	3,156	16.0%	10.5%	1.4%	23.1%	8.4%	5.2%	11.6%	23.8%	68.5%
Antioch city	844	0.0%	0.0%	0.0%	0.0%	83.9%	0.0%	0.0%	16.1%	81.0%
Bakersfield city	4,472	25.0%	2.5%	0.0%	1.8%	12.0%	3.2%	31.9%	23.5%	62.4%
Berkeley city	5,320	0.0%	0.8%	0.0%	0.0%	1.4%	3.1%	41.0%	53.7%	6.3%
Burbank city	1,525	0.0%	0.0%	0.0%	7.9%	0.0%	0.0%	72.1%	20.1%	66.0%
Carlsbad city	991	21.7%	0.0%	0.0%	41.1%	0.0%	0.0%	3.8%	33.4%	57.1%
Chico city	4,901	10.4%	5.1%	0.0%	5.8%	0.0%	4.1%	16.2%	58.3%	24.7%
Carson city	238	0.0%	0.0%	0.0%	0.0%	60.9%	0.0%	0.0%	39.1%	78.2%
Chula Vista city	1,660	20.5%	10.1%	3.5%	9.9%	11.3%	5.6%	37.2%	1.9%	78.8%
Clovis city	397	0.0%	0.0%	0.0%	58.7%	0.0%	0.0%	18.4%	22.9%	82.2%
Compton city	653	18.8%	0.0%	0.0%	20.7%	7.7%	10.9%	0.0%	42.0%	78.8%
Concord city	773	11.5%	0.0%	0.0%	0.0%	21.7%	22.0%	7.9%	36.9%	68.2%
Corona city	1,562	10.3%	17.0%	0.0%	12.8%	0.0%	17.9%	24.3%	17.8%	66.8%
Costa Mesa city	779	0.0%	32.2%	0.0%	13.2%	0.0%	0.0%	11.4%	43.1%	61.7%
Daly City city	197	0.0%	37.1%	0.0%	0.0%	0.0%	0.0%	21.3%	41.6%	62.1%
Downey city	469	0.0%	27.1%	0.0%	25.4%	0.0%	29.6%	8.3%	9.6%	84.1%
El Cajon city	1,884	9.7%	14.5%	0.0%	10.8%	2.0%	0.0%	26.9%	36.1%	53.5%
Elk Grove city	287	0.0%	0.0%	0.0%	0.0%	0.0%	15.0%	53.3%	31.7%	80.6%
El Monte city	966	0.0%	0.0%	0.0%	20.0%	37.2%	8.4%	19.5%	15.0%	59.6%
Escondido city	1,079	3.7%	10.1%	3.6%	6.3%	19.4%	20.9%	17.6%	18.4%	68.7%
Fairfield city	1,022	0.0%	34.9%	20.3%	0.0%	11.5%	20.2%	13.1%	0.0%	61.9%
Fontana city	1,145	0.0%	20.6%	6.3%	23.6%	14.6%	20.9%	14.1%	0.0%	83.8%
Fremont city	415	17.3%	0.0%	14.2%	0.0%	0.0%	0.0%	0.0%	68.4%	69.8%
Fresno city	8,069	7.1%	9.0%	2.3%	9.8%	8.4%	5.3%	15.3%	42.9%	49.6%
Fullerton city	2,404	0.0%	2.5%	0.0%	0.0%	0.0%	8.9%	24.6%	64.0%	58.5%
Garden Grove city	717	21.1%	0.0%	0.0%	24.3%	16.5%	12.1%	0.0%	26.1%	76.3%
Glendale city	1,747	8.1%	0.0%	0.0%	21.2%	0.0%	31.7%	16.6%	22.5%	69.8%
Hayward city	1,392	4.0%	0.0%	0.0%	14.7%	0.0%	9.1%	15.2%	57.0%	58.4%
Hesperia city	1,305	14.3%	4.1%	26.1%	0.0%	10.9%	30.8%	0.0%	13.7%	64.0%
Huntington Beach city	1,570	0.0%	2.8%	0.0%	30.9%	0.0%	0.0%	14.8%	51.5%	65.9%
Inglewood city	286	9.4%	0.0%	18.9%	17.8%	0.0%	0.0%	53.8%	0.0%	77.0%
Irvine city	5,862	0.0%	1.8%	0.8%	6.7%	0.0%	2.5%	27.5%	60.7%	35.3%
Jurupa Valley city	1,161	0.0%	3.8%	7.7%	2.4%	5.9%	16.7%	45.5%	18.1%	65.7%
Lancaster city	1,406	6.0%	3.2%	4.1%	0.0%	27.7%	12.0%	30.2%	16.8%	61.2%
Long Beach city	4,773	2.1%	12.1%	2.2%	7.6%	18.7%	1.9%	22.4%	33.0%	61.9%
Los Angeles city	53,101	3.6%	4.4%	2.0%	8.5%	6.7%	8.2%	26.6%	40.1%	51.6%
Mission Viejo city	125	0.0%	0.0%	0.0%	0.0%	0.0%	0.0%	100.0%	0.0%	83.3%
Modesto city	3,171	17.7%	3.2%	15.3%	21.5%	6.5%	8.7%	17.9%	9.2%	68.5%
Moreno Valley city	1,283	5.1%	0.0%	15.5%	6.7%	21.0%	0.0%	14.7%	37.0%	67.6%
Murrieta city	1,004	8.8%	11.3%	0.0%	0.0%	29.8%	0.0%	35.3%	14.9%	71.5%
Norwalk city	45	0.0%	0.0%	0.0%	0.0%	0.0%	0.0%	100.0%	0.0%	87.7%
Oakland city	5,402	0.0%	0.0%	2.9%	21.1%	19.9%	5.6%	15.8%	34.9%	46.2%
Oceanside city	2,198	5.6%	38.9%	46.8%	0.0%	0.0%	5.2%	0.0%	3.5%	26.7%
Ontario city	1,044	3.4%	4.4%	0.0%	0.0%	27.2%	0.0%	14.8%	50.3%	79.0%
Orange city	990	10.5%	19.9%	0.0%	0.0%	0.0%	0.0%	0.0%	69.6%	60.0%
Oxnard city	1,194	7.0%	5.9%	9.2%	16.0%	14.2%	13.2%	6.7%	27.8%	65.1%
Palmdale city	1,248	24.4%	4.6%	0.0%	2.4%	53.7%	3.5%	11.5%	0.0%	69.6%
Pasadena city	1,766	0.0%	0.0%	0.0%	16.6%	8.0%	20.2%	16.3%	38.9%	55.7%
Pomona city	1,394	13.8%	4.1%	5.3%	0.0%	16.4%	0.0%	6.8%	53.6%	61.2%
Rancho Cucamonga city	1,824	12.0%	4.6%	0.0%	7.7%	23.6%	0.0%	9.5%	42.6%	62.9%
Redding city	1,678	7.2%	8.8%	9.7%	0.0%	0.0%	8.2%	31.3%	34.9%	32.9%
Rialto city	367	71.4%	28.6%	0.0%	0.0%	0.0%	0.0%	0.0%	0.0%	82.8%

Table D-3: Places—Household Relationship—*Continued*

		25 to 33								
		Married Couple Households		Male, No Spouse Present		Female, No Spouse Present		Non-Family Householders		
	Total Householders	With Children	No Children	With Children	No Children	With Children	No Children	Living Alone	Not Alone	Living With Parents
Alabama										
Birmingham city	14,159	12.6%	11.6%	2.1%	1.8%	30.0%	1.4%	27.7%	12.9%	27.3%
Huntsville city	13,079	22.5%	10.8%	3.0%	0.0%	11.8%	5.0%	32.0%	14.8%	13.4%
Mobile city	10,366	23.4%	12.8%	3.1%	0.0%	22.9%	0.9%	25.0%	11.7%	25.0%
Montgomery city	12,792	20.1%	5.3%	3.4%	2.0%	29.9%	5.8%	25.8%	7.7%	23.2%
Tuscaloosa city	5,664	8.0%	8.9%	4.0%	0.0%	26.6%	0.0%	38.8%	13.7%	21.5%
Alaska										
Anchorage municipality	19,976	34.4%	10.4%	0.7%	0.0%	24.2%	0.0%	22.5%	7.9%	17.2%
Arizona										
Chandler city	15,971	28.5%	18.2%	2.7%	5.0%	10.5%	1.2%	20.2%	13.6%	17.2%
Glendale city	12,297	29.0%	9.5%	9.8%	0.5%	16.9%	2.7%	20.4%	11.2%	25.2%
Mesa city	27,985	24.1%	8.4%	5.3%	4.2%	17.3%	0.5%	27.0%	13.2%	21.3%
Peoria city	8,382	35.2%	6.4%	20.5%	1.2%	14.7%	1.4%	16.3%	4.3%	22.4%
Phoenix city	89,133	25.6%	10.2%	5.8%	3.1%	16.8%	1.4%	23.0%	14.1%	17.8%
Scottsdale city	13,335	8.4%	8.5%	3.3%	1.3%	3.3%	0.3%	41.8%	33.2%	18.4%
Surprise city	5,180	61.7%	7.0%	8.8%	0.0%	12.5%	1.1%	6.9%	2.0%	21.9%
Tempe city	12,734	23.9%	9.2%	1.2%	5.4%	5.0%	2.8%	30.4%	22.1%	12.7%
Tucson city	31,751	22.7%	8.9%	5.0%	2.8%	20.3%	3.1%	25.7%	11.4%	17.4%
Yuma city	4,121	30.0%	18.0%	15.2%	3.1%	15.4%	0.0%	13.7%	4.8%	18.0%
Arkansas										
Little Rock city	12,585	16.4%	9.7%	2.0%	2.6%	22.3%	2.5%	27.7%	16.8%	15.5%
California										
Anaheim city	13,421	29.0%	6.9%	6.3%	6.0%	12.1%	6.4%	15.8%	17.6%	32.1%
Antioch city	4,745	30.5%	6.9%	9.0%	11.0%	19.9%	0.0%	6.6%	16.2%	25.5%
Bakersfield city	23,551	33.8%	7.1%	8.2%	4.3%	21.4%	2.9%	14.9%	7.4%	18.7%
Berkeley city	8,098	10.7%	23.8%	0.0%	6.7%	3.2%	1.6%	30.6%	23.5%	4.9%
Burbank city	6,584	14.4%	28.7%	0.0%	2.7%	5.9%	1.3%	30.6%	16.4%	21.7%
Carlsbad city	3,627	32.8%	11.2%	0.0%	3.6%	13.2%	2.9%	4.5%	31.7%	28.2%
Chico city	4,738	22.1%	10.1%	0.8%	0.0%	5.0%	0.0%	30.9%	31.1%	19.1%
Carson city	1,619	50.5%	9.9%	0.0%	7.2%	5.1%	10.1%	17.2%	0.0%	57.3%
Chula Vista city	8,860	36.9%	2.1%	10.7%	2.6%	15.8%	4.9%	10.8%	16.3%	37.9%
Clovis city	5,029	26.7%	16.0%	7.0%	1.6%	12.1%	3.8%	19.2%	13.6%	22.2%
Compton city	3,418	36.8%	3.1%	4.9%	13.4%	30.7%	8.0%	5.0%	0.0%	41.5%
Concord city	6,602	38.1%	16.1%	1.4%	1.5%	2.6%	2.3%	10.5%	27.5%	18.2%
Corona city	7,530	33.7%	9.2%	5.4%	1.8%	1.4%	2.9%	39.4%	6.1%	26.8%
Costa Mesa city	7,756	10.1%	14.6%	3.5%	7.8%	3.2%	3.6%	23.7%	33.4%	14.9%
Daly City city	6,088	17.9%	15.5%	0.0%	16.2%	6.5%	7.8%	10.5%	25.6%	26.4%
Downey city	4,168	6.5%	12.0%	0.0%	7.1%	27.5%	17.9%	20.6%	8.5%	38.6%
El Cajon city	5,821	34.3%	6.5%	12.7%	0.0%	13.3%	2.1%	10.5%	20.5%	19.0%
Elk Grove city	5,205	45.9%	17.0%	4.7%	0.0%	12.3%	0.0%	8.3%	11.3%	31.5%
El Monte city	3,575	26.2%	4.9%	16.1%	6.8%	10.6%	3.7%	20.7%	11.1%	40.7%
Escondido city	7,172	37.3%	19.8%	9.1%	0.0%	10.1%	0.9%	8.0%	14.0%	32.4%
Fairfield city	5,348	42.5%	4.7%	4.3%	4.7%	23.9%	0.0%	13.4%	6.5%	29.4%
Fontana city	7,668	39.1%	11.9%	10.7%	3.2%	20.1%	11.0%	1.2%	2.8%	42.4%
Fremont city	8,610	34.3%	36.4%	0.0%	4.6%	3.5%	0.0%	9.5%	11.5%	26.4%
Fresno city	24,606	29.1%	7.2%	11.4%	2.9%	24.0%	3.1%	16.5%	5.8%	23.4%
Fullerton city	5,627	21.1%	16.0%	2.0%	6.6%	6.2%	2.2%	20.7%	25.2%	30.8%
Garden Grove city	5,834	26.1%	12.2%	2.1%	3.1%	14.6%	6.6%	8.6%	26.8%	40.9%
Glendale city	8,910	17.4%	28.5%	0.0%	5.2%	8.2%	4.2%	26.7%	9.8%	35.7%
Hayward city	8,782	17.4%	14.7%	14.0%	5.4%	23.4%	4.3%	10.1%	10.8%	20.7%
Hesperia city	5,077	29.9%	3.8%	10.8%	0.0%	23.8%	8.1%	10.3%	13.4%	25.1%
Huntington Beach city	8,809	15.9%	13.3%	3.2%	1.1%	5.7%	4.0%	28.2%	28.6%	23.6%
Inglewood city	4,918	24.8%	8.4%	11.6%	6.6%	15.6%	1.1%	18.7%	13.2%	36.1%
Irvine city	13,906	21.4%	32.1%	0.0%	1.4%	4.2%	0.6%	21.6%	18.6%	17.4%
Jurupa Valley city	3,244	58.4%	3.4%	0.0%	2.7%	13.3%	1.6%	15.8%	4.8%	45.7%
Lancaster city	7,692	19.5%	7.6%	3.7%	1.6%	26.8%	6.0%	22.7%	12.2%	31.9%
Long Beach city	29,543	19.1%	12.3%	4.3%	5.5%	14.4%	0.4%	29.2%	14.7%	23.6%
Los Angeles city	228,748	16.2%	10.9%	3.9%	4.4%	9.5%	3.4%	30.6%	21.2%	23.1%
Mission Viejo city	2,861	20.4%	36.0%	0.0%	3.1%	4.9%	2.0%	14.8%	18.7%	35.6%
Modesto city	10,166	20.6%	11.6%	11.4%	0.0%	32.0%	0.5%	14.5%	9.4%	26.2%
Moreno Valley city	7,154	37.6%	8.7%	7.1%	7.5%	17.4%	3.4%	10.9%	7.4%	41.5%
Murrieta city	4,649	25.6%	10.8%	20.0%	11.8%	4.9%	8.4%	9.9%	8.6%	30.9%
Norwalk city	2,932	21.1%	1.3%	0.0%	10.0%	18.0%	12.1%	19.2%	18.3%	43.5%
Oakland city	27,696	16.5%	13.9%	5.2%	1.5%	9.4%	2.1%	23.8%	27.5%	15.9%
Oceanside city	5,934	26.1%	14.0%	5.4%	5.1%	9.2%	3.9%	23.4%	12.9%	18.2%
Ontario city	6,924	34.9%	7.0%	7.7%	2.2%	21.5%	7.1%	9.6%	9.8%	34.7%
Orange city	5,198	12.2%	28.1%	1.0%	11.2%	1.9%	8.5%	8.5%	28.6%	36.2%
Oxnard city	8,230	37.0%	10.9%	1.3%	3.3%	19.0%	5.1%	12.0%	11.6%	32.4%
Palmdale city	5,449	48.2%	4.6%	10.7%	0.0%	25.5%	0.0%	10.1%	1.0%	35.6%
Pasadena city	9,025	13.5%	19.9%	0.0%	4.0%	6.8%	6.9%	22.8%	26.1%	16.8%
Pomona city	4,664	34.4%	5.4%	9.0%	10.4%	15.0%	1.3%	15.3%	9.2%	44.8%
Rancho Cucamonga city	7,217	30.8%	11.5%	5.4%	18.1%	3.5%	0.0%	24.0%	6.7%	29.6%
Redding city	5,935	31.9%	6.2%	0.0%	1.5%	17.6%	0.0%	18.8%	24.0%	11.6%
Rialto city	3,072	43.2%	5.0%	7.4%	14.8%	4.7%	8.4%	9.8%	6.8%	38.4%

Table D-3: Places—Household Relationship—Continued

| | | 18 to 24 | | | | | | | | |
| | | Married Couple Households | | Male, No Spouse Present | | Female, No Spouse Present | | Non-Family Householders | | |
	Total Householders	With Children	No Children	With Children	No Children	With Children	No Children	Living Alone	Not Alone	Living With Parents
California—Cont.										
Richmond city	1,148	41.1%	0.0%	28.6%	0.0%	7.8%	4.8%	0.0%	17.8%	64.7%
Riverside city	4,583	5.0%	10.2%	8.1%	12.5%	7.2%	10.3%	19.4%	27.4%	48.7%
Roseville city	905	0.0%	32.9%	0.0%	0.0%	0.0%	0.0%	0.0%	67.1%	72.6%
Sacramento city	6,256	1.3%	14.3%	2.2%	11.0%	13.6%	5.3%	23.5%	28.7%	54.9%
Salinas city	1,378	2.2%	13.1%	14.5%	12.3%	12.5%	8.4%	33.9%	3.1%	64.5%
San Bernardino city	2,744	26.0%	0.0%	5.6%	0.0%	21.4%	6.5%	3.4%	37.2%	55.9%
San Buenaventura (Ventura) city	550	53.8%	0.0%	0.0%	0.0%	0.0%	0.0%	0.0%	46.2%	57.3%
San Diego city	23,724	4.3%	7.6%	1.5%	4.1%	6.3%	2.7%	20.9%	52.6%	40.0%
San Francisco city	9,642	0.0%	0.0%	0.3%	6.7%	5.0%	5.3%	35.4%	47.2%	35.8%
San Jose city	7,759	6.8%	8.0%	3.3%	11.2%	10.7%	6.9%	19.0%	34.2%	56.7%
San Leandro city	970	13.2%	0.0%	6.5%	25.7%	0.0%	0.0%	5.1%	49.6%	54.6%
San Marcos city	696	0.0%	68.1%	0.0%	0.0%	0.0%	23.6%	8.3%	0.0%	45.9%
San Mateo city	683	0.0%	17.6%	0.0%	0.0%	10.7%	0.0%	14.2%	57.5%	66.2%
Santa Ana city	1,845	16.9%	13.3%	10.8%	7.2%	6.8%	24.1%	1.9%	19.0%	68.7%
Santa Clara city	1,096	0.0%	0.0%	0.0%	0.0%	0.0%	0.0%	11.9%	88.1%	38.0%
Santa Clarita city	1,433	5.2%	21.6%	0.0%	16.3%	3.5%	29.6%	7.4%	16.4%	57.7%
Santa Maria city	1,667	39.2%	0.0%	9.7%	3.4%	25.6%	0.0%	0.0%	22.1%	58.1%
Santa Monica city	1,127	0.0%	0.0%	0.0%	0.0%	0.0%	0.0%	49.0%	51.0%	42.7%
Santa Rosa city	2,047	5.6%	12.0%	0.0%	15.7%	21.5%	3.2%	15.2%	26.8%	59.6%
Simi Valley city	998	4.9%	12.5%	14.4%	31.7%	0.0%	0.0%	15.9%	20.5%	69.7%
South Gate city	513	0.0%	0.0%	13.3%	32.2%	44.6%	0.0%	0.0%	9.9%	79.4%
Stockton city	4,490	3.1%	4.3%	5.5%	4.5%	25.5%	3.4%	21.7%	32.0%	54.0%
Sunnyvale city	1,684	0.0%	0.0%	0.0%	0.0%	0.0%	2.9%	33.5%	63.7%	38.7%
Temecula city	634	17.5%	19.9%	0.0%	0.0%	0.0%	0.0%	55.0%	7.6%	81.7%
Thousand Oaks city	373	0.0%	0.0%	0.0%	0.0%	0.0%	0.0%	76.1%	23.9%	79.6%
Torrance city	680	13.2%	0.0%	0.0%	19.1%	0.0%	0.0%	35.9%	31.8%	78.0%
Vacaville city	1,436	12.6%	7.9%	4.2%	8.5%	0.0%	37.3%	17.0%	12.5%	52.7%
Vallejo city	1,018	9.1%	0.0%	0.0%	0.0%	11.6%	4.1%	35.1%	40.1%	54.2%
Victorville city	1,284	5.2%	0.0%	0.0%	10.0%	64.2%	20.6%	0.0%	0.0%	56.5%
Visalia city	1,404	2.5%	3.2%	11.2%	0.0%	21.2%	0.0%	29.3%	32.6%	66.6%
Vista city	693	0.0%	16.3%	11.3%	0.0%	0.0%	11.1%	18.0%	43.3%	64.9%
West Covina city	218	30.3%	0.0%	0.0%	23.4%	0.0%	0.0%	46.3%	0.0%	76.4%
Westminster city	439	0.0%	0.0%	0.0%	0.0%	28.5%	71.5%	0.0%	0.0%	62.4%
Colorado										
Arvada city	1,083	0.0%	17.5%	0.0%	0.0%	0.0%	7.4%	42.5%	32.6%	64.3%
Aurora city	5,159	10.8%	20.4%	1.9%	9.9%	9.9%	3.4%	14.6%	29.2%	60.7%
Boulder city	8,468	0.0%	1.9%	0.0%	2.0%	1.7%	0.6%	22.6%	71.2%	6.5%
Centennial city	681	0.0%	0.0%	0.0%	0.0%	0.0%	0.0%	0.0%	100.0%	77.7%
Colorado Springs city	10,204	7.6%	14.4%	0.0%	0.8%	13.2%	2.3%	26.0%	35.7%	41.2%
Denver city	11,929	6.9%	5.1%	0.0%	8.7%	11.7%	1.0%	24.6%	42.0%	35.9%
Fort Collins city	8,679	0.0%	8.0%	0.0%	5.4%	1.3%	1.3%	12.5%	71.4%	15.0%
Greeley city	2,097	10.2%	9.1%	6.2%	3.6%	15.1%	0.0%	13.8%	42.0%	33.7%
Lakewood city	3,922	0.0%	9.0%	0.0%	5.3%	4.2%	2.3%	31.5%	47.7%	31.1%
Longmont city	500	0.0%	0.0%	0.0%	31.2%	13.4%	0.0%	36.8%	18.6%	65.1%
Pueblo city	1,732	4.4%	0.0%	6.7%	1.4%	15.1%	14.2%	30.5%	27.7%	60.0%
Thornton city	2,523	15.5%	2.9%	0.0%	3.8%	10.2%	0.0%	34.0%	33.6%	47.9%
Westminster city	2,238	5.8%	7.4%	0.0%	2.6%	0.0%	10.5%	12.6%	61.1%	41.7%
Connecticut										
Bridgeport city	2,104	0.0%	14.9%	0.0%	0.0%	18.7%	0.0%	46.1%	20.3%	50.9%
Hartford city	3,080	9.3%	0.0%	11.7%	6.3%	17.1%	4.9%	20.1%	30.7%	40.0%
New Haven city	2,839	0.0%	0.6%	12.9%	0.0%	27.7%	5.4%	43.7%	9.7%	30.1%
Stamford city	977	0.0%	0.0%	0.0%	4.1%	16.7%	25.0%	4.7%	49.5%	70.4%
Waterbury city	969	14.0%	0.0%	12.8%	0.0%	17.5%	41.4%	7.3%	6.9%	62.6%
District of Columbia										
Washington city	11,997	0.0%	3.8%	0.0%	1.4%	7.5%	2.1%	35.2%	50.0%	25.6%
Florida										
Boca Raton city	2,019	0.0%	7.1%	0.0%	4.3%	0.0%	0.0%	37.1%	51.6%	24.1%
Cape Coral city	347	6.9%	0.0%	41.8%	29.4%	0.0%	0.0%	0.0%	21.9%	69.8%
Clearwater city	502	7.8%	12.0%	8.6%	12.2%	6.8%	34.9%	17.9%	0.0%	65.7%
Coral Springs city	414	0.0%	0.0%	0.0%	0.0%	24.6%	0.0%	75.4%	0.0%	85.0%
Fort Lauderdale city	1,573	2.3%	18.3%	0.0%	0.0%	44.8%	6.7%	16.9%	11.1%	55.9%
Gainesville city	7,784	0.0%	1.6%	0.0%	0.7%	0.4%	6.2%	37.2%	53.8%	17.3%
Hialeah city	957	7.2%	0.0%	0.0%	35.3%	29.5%	28.0%	0.0%	0.0%	76.2%
Hollywood city	1,117	5.6%	4.3%	23.4%	0.0%	27.6%	0.0%	15.2%	24.0%	62.6%
Jacksonville city	15,876	6.3%	14.8%	3.3%	1.8%	22.9%	1.9%	16.7%	32.3%	45.4%
Lakeland city	1,162	4.1%	1.5%	13.3%	0.0%	16.2%	0.0%	20.3%	44.6%	50.6%
Miami city	4,867	6.0%	5.8%	0.0%	16.0%	11.5%	4.0%	40.0%	16.7%	56.2%
Miami Beach city	632	0.0%	0.0%	0.0%	44.9%	0.0%	0.0%	48.7%	6.3%	57.1%
Miami Gardens city	185	0.0%	0.0%	0.0%	0.0%	17.3%	0.0%	82.7%	0.0%	72.2%
Miramar city	748	0.0%	24.6%	0.0%	0.0%	27.1%	13.5%	34.8%	0.0%	80.5%
Orlando city	6,573	1.1%	2.5%	4.5%	9.6%	17.8%	12.0%	22.6%	29.8%	46.4%
Palm Bay city	912	0.0%	24.8%	28.8%	0.0%	28.1%	0.0%	10.1%	8.2%	72.8%
Pembroke Pines city	408	0.0%	8.3%	13.5%	0.0%	20.3%	24.8%	20.6%	12.5%	88.7%

Table D-3: Places—Household Relationship—*Continued*

	Total Householders	Married Couple Households		Male, No Spouse Present		Female, No Spouse Present		Non-Family Householders		Living With Parents
		With Children	No Children	With Children	No Children	With Children	No Children	Living Alone	Not Alone	
California—Cont.										
Richmond city	4,683	36.4%	10.8%	6.1%	16.3%	14.5%	1.6%	11.4%	2.8%	29.4%
Riverside city	14,589	32.2%	10.8%	4.8%	2.8%	13.2%	1.7%	18.6%	16.0%	34.5%
Roseville city	5,697	36.8%	4.9%	8.7%	0.0%	2.2%	0.6%	16.9%	29.8%	12.1%
Sacramento city	33,278	26.5%	10.5%	5.4%	3.2%	12.8%	1.6%	25.6%	14.5%	17.4%
Salinas city	6,983	45.7%	4.3%	7.9%	3.1%	19.3%	0.9%	10.1%	8.7%	31.0%
San Bernardino city	10,027	30.9%	4.5%	2.6%	6.0%	31.1%	3.5%	12.6%	8.8%	27.0%
San Buenaventura (Ventura) city	5,819	29.0%	10.1%	9.4%	1.9%	3.8%	12.4%	20.5%	13.0%	19.1%
San Diego city	93,487	17.5%	15.9%	2.7%	2.1%	7.7%	1.8%	27.4%	24.9%	17.6%
San Francisco city	71,292	5.4%	15.6%	0.2%	4.1%	1.0%	2.5%	31.6%	39.7%	13.6%
San Jose city	40,344	25.9%	17.2%	3.9%	5.8%	8.9%	2.3%	15.8%	20.2%	27.1%
San Leandro city	4,000	12.8%	29.3%	0.0%	9.6%	6.6%	5.0%	21.3%	15.5%	29.6%
San Marcos city	4,077	26.2%	24.2%	0.0%	0.0%	13.1%	5.7%	10.3%	20.5%	21.0%
San Mateo city	4,616	21.8%	34.8%	0.0%	0.0%	0.0%	3.6%	27.6%	12.1%	23.5%
Santa Ana city	9,789	39.7%	4.7%	4.8%	7.2%	15.8%	5.5%	9.7%	12.6%	44.7%
Santa Clara city	8,819	27.8%	33.5%	0.0%	3.0%	1.1%	0.0%	10.2%	24.4%	8.9%
Santa Clarita city	7,518	36.5%	10.0%	4.3%	6.3%	11.1%	6.2%	8.0%	17.6%	21.6%
Santa Maria city	3,689	35.6%	7.9%	5.8%	0.0%	32.6%	0.0%	6.3%	11.8%	27.3%
Santa Monica city	8,154	6.4%	11.3%	0.0%	3.5%	3.4%	0.7%	49.4%	25.2%	9.4%
Santa Rosa city	7,382	15.5%	17.7%	6.9%	1.3%	22.1%	0.0%	15.9%	20.7%	22.0%
Simi Valley city	4,018	37.4%	27.8%	2.2%	4.0%	11.6%	0.0%	5.0%	11.9%	32.3%
South Gate city	2,269	29.1%	6.5%	6.2%	0.0%	31.5%	3.6%	13.5%	9.6%	46.8%
Stockton city	14,719	31.1%	3.9%	11.2%	7.7%	23.6%	0.8%	14.2%	7.3%	27.3%
Sunnyvale city	10,636	36.5%	23.8%	2.0%	0.6%	2.9%	4.9%	16.1%	13.0%	14.9%
Temecula city	5,420	38.3%	6.0%	0.0%	11.2%	15.4%	0.0%	10.6%	18.5%	36.8%
Thousand Oaks city	2,532	33.7%	22.4%	0.0%	0.0%	12.9%	1.3%	19.2%	10.5%	37.2%
Torrance city	4,868	35.0%	23.7%	1.4%	3.3%	6.1%	1.6%	19.9%	8.9%	28.9%
Vacaville city	4,032	32.9%	20.4%	3.7%	2.5%	14.6%	1.0%	16.0%	8.9%	30.5%
Vallejo city	6,279	28.7%	4.7%	3.0%	3.4%	23.3%	3.7%	15.5%	17.7%	34.9%
Victorville city	5,311	31.5%	0.0%	8.6%	2.1%	34.7%	0.0%	19.6%	3.4%	21.7%
Visalia city	7,049	53.5%	8.4%	7.9%	1.3%	12.0%	2.5%	9.7%	4.7%	15.1%
Vista city	6,384	38.6%	13.5%	0.0%	4.6%	8.1%	0.0%	23.5%	11.7%	22.6%
West Covina city	2,740	32.9%	19.1%	2.7%	3.2%	24.4%	2.3%	6.5%	8.9%	56.4%
Westminster city	2,695	32.6%	8.3%	7.9%	18.6%	7.9%	2.7%	10.0%	12.0%	33.9%
Colorado										
Arvada city	6,272	28.5%	19.0%	7.6%	3.8%	1.0%	0.0%	17.5%	22.5%	16.7%
Aurora city	21,931	33.3%	16.6%	2.7%	4.4%	13.7%	1.2%	18.3%	9.7%	17.7%
Boulder city	7,540	3.6%	16.4%	0.0%	0.8%	4.1%	0.0%	29.5%	45.7%	1.9%
Centennial city	3,228	43.2%	18.8%	2.0%	1.9%	0.0%	0.0%	10.7%	23.4%	19.2%
Colorado Springs city	33,861	28.9%	14.3%	3.6%	3.0%	13.4%	1.4%	23.9%	11.4%	11.5%
Denver city	70,055	12.9%	14.3%	2.2%	2.7%	6.6%	0.9%	33.4%	26.9%	9.6%
Fort Collins city	11,792	17.3%	15.1%	0.7%	1.3%	12.1%	2.8%	15.6%	35.3%	7.1%
Greeley city	7,819	52.4%	8.9%	1.7%	0.9%	10.0%	0.7%	14.3%	11.2%	9.3%
Lakewood city	9,671	19.0%	22.1%	2.9%	4.6%	6.4%	0.0%	14.3%	30.8%	16.2%
Longmont city	4,121	45.0%	14.8%	0.0%	1.8%	15.4%	7.4%	7.1%	8.5%	21.7%
Pueblo city	6,146	40.5%	3.2%	8.0%	0.0%	15.4%	0.0%	23.3%	9.6%	21.2%
Thornton city	7,941	32.2%	13.8%	2.9%	2.8%	10.2%	1.8%	12.8%	23.6%	10.2%
Westminster city	6,285	39.8%	16.9%	4.3%	0.0%	8.8%	4.6%	14.1%	11.4%	14.6%
Connecticut										
Bridgeport city	7,316	16.9%	6.9%	1.7%	8.9%	35.4%	2.7%	15.3%	12.2%	28.0%
Hartford city	8,095	8.1%	14.4%	2.6%	0.8%	40.5%	3.9%	23.8%	6.0%	18.5%
New Haven city	11,630	8.3%	11.5%	0.0%	4.8%	19.4%	0.7%	39.2%	16.1%	9.6%
Stamford city	6,967	12.7%	22.0%	9.7%	0.7%	0.0%	1.7%	21.4%	31.8%	23.8%
Waterbury city	6,005	10.9%	9.4%	17.4%	0.0%	33.3%	0.0%	13.6%	15.5%	17.5%
District of Columbia										
Washington city	63,496	5.4%	12.4%	1.6%	1.6%	10.9%	1.5%	36.8%	29.6%	9.8%
Florida										
Boca Raton city	4,168	8.8%	18.0%	0.0%	3.5%	11.3%	0.0%	49.5%	8.9%	19.2%
Cape Coral city	4,934	26.1%	9.9%	7.4%	2.3%	28.9%	0.0%	18.3%	7.1%	39.7%
Clearwater city	5,196	20.9%	18.6%	0.0%	9.7%	17.2%	2.9%	19.4%	11.4%	30.1%
Coral Springs city	3,865	28.3%	0.0%	25.2%	4.0%	14.6%	0.0%	13.3%	14.5%	46.0%
Fort Lauderdale city	10,393	8.7%	8.9%	7.2%	3.4%	18.9%	0.3%	41.3%	11.3%	10.5%
Gainesville city	10,282	11.0%	18.7%	1.2%	3.7%	11.3%	2.6%	27.7%	23.8%	7.1%
Hialeah city	6,659	22.8%	5.9%	1.2%	6.3%	20.4%	10.1%	17.1%	16.0%	49.9%
Hollywood city	6,458	10.8%	13.7%	9.6%	2.3%	7.8%	4.3%	38.6%	13.0%	34.0%
Jacksonville city	49,788	20.9%	14.2%	3.6%	1.0%	17.5%	2.2%	23.9%	16.6%	18.8%
Lakeland city	4,808	20.5%	14.1%	3.8%	0.6%	31.4%	1.0%	20.9%	7.7%	25.9%
Miami city	26,181	11.0%	10.0%	5.5%	2.8%	14.4%	2.0%	40.7%	13.5%	21.9%
Miami Beach city	5,244	14.0%	20.3%	1.4%	1.0%	5.9%	0.6%	45.5%	11.3%	23.8%
Miami Gardens city	2,048	0.0%	6.1%	7.8%	5.0%	38.4%	0.0%	27.3%	15.4%	56.2%
Miramar city	5,133	19.1%	19.2%	5.9%	2.4%	24.7%	2.1%	14.9%	11.7%	32.2%
Orlando city	23,435	14.8%	8.1%	4.7%	1.7%	16.2%	1.6%	29.2%	23.6%	14.0%
Palm Bay city	4,394	27.0%	14.8%	4.2%	0.0%	34.0%	3.7%	13.1%	3.2%	27.5%
Pembroke Pines city	5,549	19.1%	29.3%	11.6%	0.9%	6.5%	0.0%	31.1%	1.5%	37.2%

Table D-3: Places—Household Relationship—*Continued*

		18 to 24								
		Married Couple Households		Male, No Spouse Present		Female, No Spouse Present		Non-Family Householders		
	Total Householders	With Children	No Children	With Children	No Children	With Children	No Children	Living Alone	Not Alone	Living With Parents
Florida—Cont.										
Plantation city	552	0.0%	17.9%	0.0%	16.5%	13.9%	26.6%	0.0%	25.0%	65.9%
Pompano Beach city	1,791	18.7%	4.6%	0.0%	0.0%	25.6%	5.6%	35.2%	10.3%	42.9%
Port St. Lucie city	618	30.3%	0.0%	0.0%	0.0%	8.1%	0.0%	0.0%	61.7%	72.0%
St. Petersburg city	2,232	0.0%	4.6%	2.5%	0.0%	22.0%	1.7%	41.1%	28.1%	55.6%
Sunrise city	552	0.0%	17.9%	0.0%	16.5%	13.9%	26.6%	0.0%	25.0%	70.0%
Tallahassee city	16,267	1.1%	0.7%	0.0%	3.7%	3.5%	2.7%	38.5%	49.9%	13.9%
Tampa city	7,492	2.7%	4.4%	4.8%	3.7%	14.1%	1.5%	38.7%	30.0%	40.9%
West Palm Beach city	985	13.1%	6.2%	0.0%	24.1%	0.0%	0.0%	35.2%	21.4%	54.7%
Georgia										
Athens-Clarke County unified govt (balance)	9,038	0.0%	6.5%	0.0%	1.0%	1.3%	1.4%	32.6%	57.3%	11.5%
Atlanta city	13,258	0.0%	3.0%	1.9%	2.9%	10.2%	2.0%	50.7%	29.2%	19.7%
Augusta-Richmond County consolidated govt (balance)	3,059	1.1%	8.2%	0.0%	0.0%	4.9%	8.2%	47.8%	29.8%	40.5%
Columbus city	3,483	15.2%	13.2%	1.9%	1.3%	14.1%	2.4%	20.5%	31.4%	38.9%
Macon-Bibb county	2,664	1.2%	0.0%	0.0%	0.0%	33.8%	0.0%	31.4%	33.6%	47.8%
Roswell city	310	32.6%	0.0%	0.0%	7.7%	0.0%	0.0%	0.0%	59.7%	60.5%
Sandy Springs city	2,063	8.2%	8.3%	0.0%	0.0%	0.0%	0.0%	65.8%	17.6%	46.8%
Savannah city	4,232	0.9%	5.4%	0.0%	1.1%	11.5%	0.0%	45.8%	35.3%	32.9%
Hawaii										
Urban Honolulu CDP	3,850	0.0%	1.0%	0.0%	8.5%	0.0%	8.5%	42.1%	39.9%	42.6%
Idaho										
Boise City city	4,928	9.5%	10.5%	0.0%	0.7%	6.6%	0.9%	32.9%	38.8%	32.1%
Meridian city	79	0.0%	0.0%	0.0%	0.0%	0.0%	0.0%	0.0%	100.0%	41.6%
Illinois										
Aurora city	2,103	16.0%	0.0%	3.5%	33.7%	14.9%	0.0%	2.3%	29.5%	67.3%
Chicago city	43,812	3.6%	3.4%	1.3%	6.7%	11.1%	1.4%	35.4%	37.1%	47.4%
Elgin city	1,484	60.4%	3.6%	0.0%	0.0%	26.5%	0.0%	4.7%	4.7%	62.2%
Joliet city	1,334	6.3%	4.4%	0.0%	25.1%	35.9%	0.0%	23.0%	5.2%	63.0%
Naperville city	2,290	12.1%	0.0%	0.0%	12.6%	11.4%	8.7%	28.9%	26.2%	53.4%
Peoria city	1,960	1.1%	0.0%	0.0%	0.0%	20.4%	0.0%	49.7%	28.8%	44.8%
Rockford city	2,635	8.6%	0.0%	20.6%	2.5%	29.6%	0.0%	34.0%	4.6%	61.7%
Springfield city	1,857	0.0%	4.7%	0.0%	0.0%	29.2%	0.0%	31.5%	34.6%	55.0%
Indiana										
Evansville city	3,196	5.3%	7.8%	0.0%	0.0%	32.9%	0.0%	45.9%	8.2%	40.4%
Fort Wayne city	5,600	6.0%	9.2%	3.2%	1.8%	16.3%	3.9%	24.3%	35.3%	46.8%
Indianapolis city (balance)	16,380	5.6%	3.8%	1.8%	5.7%	16.8%	4.9%	32.4%	29.1%	48.1%
South Bend city	904	0.0%	1.4%	0.0%	5.1%	29.4%	9.2%	30.3%	24.6%	37.3%
Iowa										
Cedar Rapids city	1,596	2.6%	6.7%	0.0%	0.0%	13.8%	0.0%	6.6%	70.3%	50.6%
Davenport city	1,360	13.9%	0.0%	6.1%	0.0%	0.0%	0.0%	0.0%	80.0%	43.4%
Des Moines city	5,187	14.5%	3.4%	0.0%	0.0%	17.0%	3.1%	28.6%	33.3%	33.3%
Kansas										
Kansas City city	2,969	2.5%	0.0%	5.4%	12.8%	19.4%	7.6%	29.9%	22.5%	52.2%
Olathe city	1,774	4.5%	4.9%	0.0%	0.0%	3.9%	0.0%	60.7%	26.0%	66.8%
Overland Park city	1,930	2.6%	32.0%	0.0%	0.0%	0.0%	8.2%	0.0%	57.2%	67.2%
Topeka city	3,572	1.8%	0.0%	2.4%	7.0%	30.0%	3.0%	26.1%	29.7%	35.5%
Wichita city	8,331	2.7%	8.1%	0.0%	0.0%	11.9%	4.1%	53.0%	20.3%	41.9%
Kentucky										
Lexington-Fayette urban county	11,445	3.6%	7.5%	0.6%	2.7%	6.5%	2.2%	29.9%	46.8%	28.2%
Louisville/Jefferson County metro govt (balance)	10,479	5.8%	6.3%	0.8%	5.2%	21.6%	1.9%	34.7%	23.6%	49.6%
Louisiana										
Baton Rouge city	8,523	5.5%	3.0%	4.2%	3.8%	11.4%	0.0%	49.3%	22.8%	37.2%
Lafayette city	1,933	0.0%	1.7%	0.0%	0.0%	24.5%	0.0%	27.3%	46.5%	42.6%
New Orleans city	5,017	3.6%	5.3%	0.0%	6.2%	14.4%	2.2%	49.4%	19.0%	48.6%
Shreveport city	3,478	8.8%	18.1%	2.2%	0.0%	30.3%	13.6%	18.3%	8.8%	50.2%
Maryland										
Baltimore city	8,477	1.3%	3.6%	7.4%	3.1%	14.6%	4.0%	22.5%	43.5%	41.2%
Massachusetts										
Boston city	15,490	1.8%	0.3%	0.2%	10.9%	2.1%	7.4%	27.7%	49.6%	23.3%
Brockton city	1,047	15.4%	0.0%	17.3%	0.0%	0.0%	9.1%	22.6%	35.6%	71.5%
Cambridge city	2,270	0.0%	4.6%	1.4%	4.4%	0.0%	0.0%	21.9%	67.6%	7.1%
Lowell city	1,442	0.0%	0.0%	0.0%	27.3%	20.0%	0.0%	21.0%	31.6%	41.0%
Lynn city	984	21.8%	0.0%	0.0%	9.0%	14.5%	10.4%	37.2%	7.0%	58.4%
New Bedford city	1,928	0.0%	0.0%	2.6%	1.5%	19.3%	3.6%	47.6%	25.4%	66.2%
Quincy city	638	0.0%	0.0%	0.0%	0.0%	0.0%	0.0%	47.5%	52.5%	54.8%
Springfield city	2,789	2.9%	0.0%	10.2%	4.7%	39.8%	0.0%	4.1%	38.3%	53.2%
Worcester city	3,266	0.0%	0.0%	3.1%	5.6%	11.9%	5.7%	25.5%	48.2%	34.1%

Table D-3: Places—Household Relationship—*Continued*

| | | 25 to 33 | | | | | | | | |
| | | Married Couple Households | | Male, No Spouse Present | | Female, No Spouse Present | | Non-Family Householders | | |
	Total Householders	With Children	No Children	With Children	No Children	With Children	No Children	Living Alone	Not Alone	Living With Parents
Florida—Cont.										
Plantation city	3,978	49.3%	15.0%	0.0%	0.9%	3.7%	2.3%	6.3%	22.6%	34.3%
Pompano Beach city	4,284	25.2%	6.6%	1.8%	4.6%	13.2%	3.6%	31.2%	13.8%	21.8%
Port St. Lucie city	6,698	21.7%	18.0%	5.2%	2.5%	11.2%	0.0%	15.1%	26.1%	18.5%
St. Petersburg city	12,176	10.3%	14.1%	2.8%	1.1%	13.9%	1.7%	37.3%	18.8%	23.2%
Sunrise city	4,096	48.3%	17.0%	0.0%	0.9%	3.6%	2.2%	6.1%	21.9%	36.7%
Tallahassee city	12,531	13.2%	9.0%	1.7%	0.0%	18.7%	1.3%	32.9%	23.2%	12.4%
Tampa city	27,441	12.3%	12.2%	2.3%	4.5%	18.1%	3.6%	34.3%	12.7%	15.9%
West Palm Beach city	6,188	26.2%	8.6%	9.3%	3.8%	19.2%	5.8%	19.5%	7.7%	18.1%
Georgia										
Athens-Clarke County unified govt (balance)	7,437	7.8%	13.4%	2.4%	0.0%	12.9%	1.1%	35.5%	26.9%	8.3%
Atlanta city	48,165	2.5%	11.0%	1.6%	1.2%	8.7%	1.7%	52.4%	20.8%	9.4%
Augusta-Richmond County consolidated govt (balance)	11,201	23.7%	11.9%	1.7%	1.3%	26.6%	0.0%	25.1%	9.8%	25.4%
Columbus city	12,973	30.3%	12.4%	5.2%	1.7%	14.3%	0.0%	30.3%	5.8%	17.5%
Macon-Bibb county	8,246	14.8%	28.6%	2.6%	0.0%	21.9%	0.6%	23.6%	7.9%	14.5%
Roswell city	3,256	31.9%	21.5%	0.0%	12.9%	1.7%	0.0%	12.2%	19.9%	12.0%
Sandy Springs city	8,517	11.1%	21.2%	2.0%	1.5%	2.8%	1.8%	37.5%	22.0%	11.0%
Savannah city	10,356	22.0%	9.1%	0.0%	5.2%	25.9%	1.2%	19.9%	16.6%	18.8%
Hawaii										
Urban Honolulu CDP	12,727	7.2%	13.6%	1.7%	2.8%	9.8%	7.9%	26.3%	30.7%	25.5%
Idaho										
Boise City city	14,296	20.5%	7.5%	8.5%	4.9%	13.2%	2.7%	24.6%	18.2%	8.7%
Meridian city	4,221	32.5%	1.8%	0.0%	0.0%	20.1%	0.0%	34.8%	10.8%	15.4%
Illinois										
Aurora city	8,856	36.0%	9.7%	6.5%	1.6%	13.6%	1.3%	12.9%	18.4%	20.4%
Chicago city	218,647	12.5%	13.9%	2.0%	2.4%	10.9%	2.3%	35.7%	20.4%	18.1%
Elgin city	3,159	32.5%	4.3%	0.0%	2.8%	34.7%	0.0%	21.7%	4.1%	32.1%
Joliet city	7,442	28.6%	13.9%	2.4%	1.6%	20.7%	0.0%	20.4%	12.5%	18.3%
Naperville city	5,266	28.1%	16.8%	2.3%	0.0%	9.8%	1.0%	27.2%	14.7%	32.3%
Peoria city	8,424	19.2%	12.4%	11.2%	0.5%	21.7%	0.0%	27.9%	7.1%	15.3%
Rockford city	8,684	25.9%	6.9%	2.3%	0.7%	32.4%	0.9%	14.0%	16.9%	23.8%
Springfield city	7,718	24.1%	13.1%	6.2%	0.0%	16.0%	0.0%	24.6%	16.0%	13.9%
Indiana										
Evansville city	7,778	32.9%	10.0%	6.1%	0.7%	10.2%	0.0%	29.9%	10.3%	12.8%
Fort Wayne city	18,374	21.1%	14.0%	10.2%	3.9%	20.6%	0.6%	18.4%	11.2%	13.3%
Indianapolis city (balance)	63,673	17.2%	9.7%	4.0%	1.0%	18.8%	1.5%	35.6%	12.1%	17.8%
South Bend city	5,420	24.8%	18.6%	3.5%	1.3%	23.5%	0.0%	18.5%	9.8%	16.0%
Iowa										
Cedar Rapids city	7,298	16.0%	30.1%	5.2%	0.4%	8.7%	0.0%	26.9%	12.7%	7.7%
Davenport city	6,670	27.8%	13.9%	10.7%	0.0%	13.5%	0.0%	18.9%	15.2%	20.3%
Des Moines city	16,589	20.0%	10.9%	1.2%	1.1%	16.7%	1.0%	34.8%	14.3%	16.2%
Kansas										
Kansas City city	8,832	35.4%	8.3%	3.9%	0.5%	15.5%	4.3%	25.6%	6.5%	13.2%
Olathe city	6,887	50.9%	9.7%	0.0%	3.0%	15.1%	0.0%	16.6%	4.5%	14.0%
Overland Park city	10,376	35.6%	23.7%	0.0%	0.0%	1.3%	0.0%	30.1%	9.3%	13.5%
Topeka city	7,603	29.3%	6.4%	7.2%	0.0%	19.1%	0.0%	23.5%	14.6%	16.4%
Wichita city	25,322	21.6%	10.7%	5.9%	2.7%	17.8%	0.5%	34.7%	6.2%	19.2%
Kentucky										
Lexington-Fayette urban county	22,541	20.8%	13.8%	3.9%	0.3%	12.5%	0.2%	34.4%	14.1%	11.1%
Louisville/Jefferson County metro govt (balance)	34,701	20.5%	15.7%	3.4%	3.6%	15.8%	0.2%	28.1%	12.8%	20.2%
Louisiana										
Baton Rouge city	16,336	19.9%	10.0%	4.7%	1.6%	14.5%	1.8%	32.4%	15.1%	18.8%
Lafayette city	11,327	26.5%	11.7%	6.1%	3.7%	10.4%	0.0%	18.9%	22.7%	13.0%
New Orleans city	27,963	9.7%	7.3%	1.9%	0.8%	15.0%	1.5%	43.4%	20.5%	20.8%
Shreveport city	11,427	26.6%	11.8%	1.5%	0.7%	23.1%	0.0%	30.7%	5.7%	22.1%
Maryland										
Baltimore city	42,657	8.8%	12.3%	6.0%	2.6%	16.6%	2.8%	28.9%	22.1%	21.5%
Massachusetts										
Boston city	65,228	8.3%	13.4%	1.5%	2.3%	7.1%	4.1%	33.5%	29.9%	12.7%
Brockton city	3,738	42.8%	7.0%	0.0%	2.8%	20.9%	0.0%	17.8%	8.7%	23.5%
Cambridge city	12,189	7.2%	21.7%	0.0%	0.5%	1.3%	3.0%	28.4%	37.8%	4.9%
Lowell city	5,889	39.1%	10.9%	1.1%	2.6%	17.9%	0.0%	10.3%	18.1%	24.0%
Lynn city	5,613	18.6%	6.6%	9.7%	6.6%	23.3%	5.0%	17.4%	12.9%	22.3%
New Bedford city	4,602	14.6%	8.8%	5.1%	1.2%	40.2%	0.0%	19.2%	10.8%	21.1%
Quincy city	5,793	11.5%	21.1%	0.0%	5.9%	6.3%	5.9%	24.6%	24.9%	28.3%
Springfield city	7,471	18.9%	5.9%	8.9%	2.5%	41.7%	1.1%	17.3%	3.8%	22.6%
Worcester city	13,872	8.6%	13.8%	3.8%	2.9%	14.0%	1.3%	39.5%	16.1%	12.5%

Table D-3: Places—Household Relationship—*Continued*

| | | 18 to 24 | | | | | | | | |
| | Total Householders | Married Couple Households | | Male, No Spouse Present | | Female, No Spouse Present | | Non-Family Householders | | Living With Parents |
		With Children	No Children	With Children	No Children	With Children	No Children	Living Alone	Not Alone	
Michigan										
Ann Arbor city	9,550	0.0%	0.0%	0.0%	4.1%	1.0%	0.0%	39.1%	55.8%	7.0%
Dearborn city	862	0.0%	8.6%	0.0%	46.6%	11.1%	0.0%	20.4%	13.2%	76.7%
Detroit city	9,614	0.0%	0.0%	12.8%	7.1%	30.2%	4.4%	32.9%	12.6%	56.2%
Flint city	2,042	17.6%	0.0%	17.5%	0.0%	40.7%	3.3%	14.1%	6.8%	39.7%
Grand Rapids city	5,949	0.0%	6.8%	0.0%	2.5%	11.5%	0.7%	23.7%	54.8%	25.9%
Lansing city	2,676	0.0%	17.7%	0.0%	8.9%	13.8%	0.0%	35.1%	24.4%	43.4%
Livonia city	166	0.0%	0.0%	0.0%	53.6%	0.0%	0.0%	0.0%	46.4%	91.4%
Sterling Heights city	1,826	0.0%	0.0%	12.7%	0.0%	0.0%	0.0%	44.9%	42.4%	72.5%
Warren city	1,126	0.0%	0.0%	30.8%	8.1%	7.7%	0.0%	22.9%	30.5%	70.3%
Minnesota										
Minneapolis city	12,676	0.7%	0.4%	0.0%	0.9%	9.6%	6.3%	38.0%	44.0%	22.6%
Rochester city	2,222	0.0%	9.1%	0.0%	0.0%	30.1%	0.0%	33.8%	27.0%	47.0%
St. Paul city	5,477	4.4%	2.6%	0.0%	7.9%	9.3%	7.2%	5.7%	62.8%	41.0%
Mississippi										
Jackson city	3,198	2.0%	0.0%	0.0%	5.7%	22.4%	4.5%	47.5%	18.0%	40.4%
Missouri										
Columbia city	6,995	7.1%	1.6%	0.2%	0.0%	0.0%	0.0%	44.1%	47.0%	19.3%
Independence city	2,470	18.6%	13.4%	2.9%	0.0%	13.6%	0.0%	38.0%	13.5%	52.9%
Kansas City city	11,354	3.4%	2.7%	1.5%	5.0%	20.9%	1.4%	31.9%	33.2%	37.6%
Lee's Summit city	814	19.7%	37.2%	0.0%	0.0%	22.1%	0.0%	9.7%	11.3%	78.0%
St. Louis city	7,458	0.0%	3.2%	0.0%	1.9%	15.3%	3.2%	52.9%	23.5%	35.9%
Springfield city	8,699	2.7%	7.1%	0.9%	1.2%	5.0%	2.2%	29.0%	51.9%	16.7%
Montana										
Billings city	2,993	4.2%	5.3%	0.0%	0.0%	16.6%	1.5%	29.7%	42.8%	33.7%
Nebraska										
Lincoln city	12,613	5.0%	0.0%	5.3%	4.9%	8.4%	1.1%	35.1%	40.1%	23.2%
Omaha city	11,241	3.5%	8.5%	4.3%	1.1%	11.7%	2.5%	45.5%	22.8%	35.5%
Nevada										
Henderson city	1,267	0.0%	7.1%	0.0%	0.0%	22.1%	3.6%	21.2%	46.0%	75.4%
Las Vegas city	6,192	4.7%	1.6%	0.0%	8.2%	22.8%	11.7%	31.3%	19.7%	55.6%
North Las Vegas city	2,231	6.4%	14.4%	20.2%	9.9%	13.2%	4.9%	22.1%	8.9%	62.0%
Reno city	5,698	7.2%	0.8%	1.4%	2.7%	14.8%	3.2%	26.5%	43.5%	29.7%
Sparks city	1,021	0.0%	9.5%	26.2%	18.4%	0.0%	0.0%	24.9%	21.1%	66.4%
New Hampshire										
Manchester city	2,929	13.7%	0.0%	0.0%	3.4%	16.4%	0.0%	21.8%	44.8%	42.6%
New Jersey										
Elizabeth city	1,725	10.7%	23.2%	7.9%	15.8%	22.6%	0.0%	6.9%	12.9%	55.8%
Jersey City city	3,417	11.4%	1.6%	2.3%	15.3%	5.4%	0.0%	33.8%	30.2%	53.1%
Newark city	2,389	9.7%	5.8%	10.3%	0.0%	13.4%	2.8%	39.6%	18.4%	58.1%
Paterson city	649	0.0%	0.0%	13.7%	0.0%	76.9%	0.0%	9.4%	0.0%	75.2%
New Mexico										
Albuquerque city	9,196	1.7%	7.5%	1.7%	11.5%	6.7%	0.9%	24.9%	45.1%	51.2%
Las Cruces city	4,317	3.1%	0.0%	0.0%	10.5%	34.8%	6.2%	15.3%	30.2%	29.9%
Rio Rancho city	185	13.5%	0.0%	0.0%	0.0%	7.6%	0.0%	0.0%	78.9%	65.2%
New York										
Albany city	4,264	0.0%	0.0%	0.0%	0.0%	22.8%	0.0%	31.5%	45.7%	23.4%
Buffalo city	5,465	1.0%	0.0%	0.0%	4.1%	26.3%	1.0%	28.1%	39.5%	41.4%
New York city	81,883	6.4%	4.7%	1.8%	9.9%	10.3%	9.0%	25.7%	32.1%	60.3%
Rochester city	6,443	1.2%	1.9%	0.0%	5.8%	29.0%	2.3%	22.0%	37.9%	36.6%
Syracuse city	4,072	2.7%	0.0%	0.0%	1.6%	20.4%	0.0%	37.3%	38.1%	18.2%
Yonkers city	1,980	0.0%	0.0%	0.0%	37.0%	20.9%	4.3%	32.0%	5.8%	76.0%
North Carolina										
Charlotte city	16,188	2.2%	3.3%	1.9%	6.8%	7.8%	3.0%	38.5%	36.5%	41.7%
Durham city	7,490	0.0%	4.5%	0.0%	2.9%	14.0%	2.2%	28.9%	47.5%	27.5%
Fayetteville city	5,760	18.9%	22.5%	1.2%	4.2%	11.2%	3.8%	26.6%	11.6%	41.3%
Greensboro city	4,627	4.9%	0.7%	0.0%	0.0%	12.6%	4.5%	29.4%	47.8%	43.4%
High Point city	1,069	0.0%	6.3%	13.7%	0.0%	17.7%	0.0%	3.8%	58.6%	59.7%
Raleigh city	12,414	2.6%	4.8%	11.3%	3.2%	5.6%	1.9%	26.6%	43.9%	29.8%
Wilmington city	3,999	9.8%	14.9%	0.0%	5.7%	3.0%	0.0%	7.3%	59.4%	23.9%
Winston-Salem city	5,161	0.0%	6.5%	3.5%	6.1%	15.5%	0.0%	22.4%	46.0%	34.1%
North Dakota										
Fargo city	7,680	6.6%	2.5%	15.2%	3.9%	5.1%	0.0%	25.5%	41.2%	19.4%
Ohio										
Akron city	5,043	0.0%	0.9%	2.6%	9.3%	20.1%	6.9%	30.1%	30.2%	47.7%
Cincinnati city	10,692	2.4%	3.8%	0.0%	0.7%	28.4%	0.7%	26.7%	37.4%	25.1%
Cleveland city	7,551	1.9%	1.5%	0.0%	3.5%	29.5%	4.5%	26.3%	32.7%	45.6%
Columbus city	22,928	2.9%	5.7%	2.1%	2.3%	19.1%	2.0%	31.6%	34.3%	26.8%
Dayton city	3,237	6.3%	3.8%	3.6%	16.8%	28.8%	0.0%	27.2%	13.4%	27.1%
Toledo city	8,207	4.5%	2.1%	8.2%	3.5%	25.8%	2.1%	31.2%	22.6%	35.7%

Table D-3: Places—Household Relationship—*Continued*

| | | 25 to 33 | | | | | | | | |
| | | Married Couple Households | | Male, No Spouse Present | | Female, No Spouse Present | | Non-Family Householders | | |
	Total Householders	With Children	No Children	With Children	No Children	With Children	No Children	Living Alone	Not Alone	Living With Parents
Michigan										
Ann Arbor city	8,896	14.0%	13.8%	1.8%	0.0%	2.1%	0.0%	41.1%	27.3%	4.9%
Dearborn city	3,751	44.2%	8.6%	0.0%	4.1%	9.3%	0.0%	17.7%	16.1%	36.6%
Detroit city	36,235	7.9%	4.8%	6.6%	3.4%	34.8%	2.7%	33.8%	6.0%	30.0%
Flint city	5,094	23.0%	0.0%	10.1%	9.9%	20.9%	3.4%	24.3%	8.3%	19.9%
Grand Rapids city	16,359	19.8%	16.4%	2.0%	0.0%	15.9%	0.8%	21.3%	23.8%	12.5%
Lansing city	9,339	14.6%	12.7%	4.1%	0.0%	18.5%	0.0%	27.8%	22.3%	12.3%
Livonia city	3,518	25.5%	19.0%	0.0%	0.0%	2.4%	3.1%	33.7%	16.3%	26.8%
Sterling Heights city	5,923	38.5%	23.7%	3.2%	12.8%	1.4%	0.9%	10.7%	8.8%	30.9%
Warren city	6,215	22.4%	9.1%	5.5%	0.0%	16.8%	1.6%	24.8%	19.7%	27.4%
Minnesota										
Minneapolis city	43,653	5.8%	18.9%	0.8%	0.7%	11.1%	1.2%	41.0%	20.5%	6.7%
Rochester city	6,869	54.6%	14.2%	0.0%	0.0%	4.6%	0.0%	17.3%	9.3%	6.9%
St. Paul city	24,127	18.0%	11.8%	1.6%	2.8%	12.7%	1.7%	30.2%	21.2%	11.0%
Mississippi										
Jackson city	12,123	14.0%	8.4%	3.2%	4.3%	27.0%	1.8%	31.0%	10.3%	26.7%
Missouri										
Columbia city	10,797	30.1%	15.4%	1.2%	0.0%	2.5%	0.0%	38.8%	12.0%	10.2%
Independence city	4,724	50.0%	12.4%	9.3%	0.0%	9.4%	0.0%	19.0%	0.0%	20.2%
Kansas City city	33,152	16.2%	14.4%	5.6%	2.1%	14.9%	1.7%	29.9%	15.1%	10.5%
Lee's Summit city	4,877	35.1%	19.6%	1.0%	3.3%	15.6%	0.0%	16.5%	8.9%	15.8%
St. Louis city	31,911	4.0%	13.1%	2.4%	1.3%	16.6%	0.8%	41.1%	20.8%	12.7%
Springfield city	13,030	18.4%	8.1%	4.1%	1.1%	17.0%	0.0%	34.2%	17.1%	6.8%
Montana										
Billings city	5,017	27.0%	2.7%	4.8%	0.0%	11.3%	0.0%	33.4%	20.7%	18.5%
Nebraska										
Lincoln city	18,990	27.1%	8.6%	3.1%	0.8%	12.8%	1.7%	29.4%	16.6%	6.7%
Omaha city	34,964	28.0%	12.6%	1.2%	3.0%	16.3%	1.9%	22.7%	14.3%	12.1%
Nevada										
Henderson city	13,032	28.1%	8.3%	2.0%	2.4%	12.5%	0.8%	31.4%	14.5%	24.5%
Las Vegas city	33,431	18.2%	11.7%	5.4%	4.2%	21.9%	2.1%	26.8%	9.8%	21.4%
North Las Vegas city	9,580	27.3%	6.4%	6.5%	7.6%	26.0%	1.6%	14.7%	10.0%	27.9%
Reno city	15,200	21.7%	11.7%	5.2%	0.8%	16.8%	3.4%	21.4%	19.0%	10.6%
Sparks city	5,636	36.4%	3.7%	1.6%	2.1%	18.8%	2.3%	25.2%	9.9%	9.6%
New Hampshire										
Manchester city	7,051	20.1%	6.0%	2.8%	2.5%	16.9%	3.1%	25.2%	23.4%	13.4%
New Jersey										
Elizabeth city	6,334	16.9%	8.8%	0.8%	9.0%	32.7%	4.1%	17.6%	10.0%	23.3%
Jersey City city	23,107	12.9%	21.2%	3.5%	2.0%	18.9%	1.4%	20.8%	19.3%	15.1%
Newark city	13,826	10.5%	6.7%	4.4%	6.4%	39.5%	2.6%	21.1%	8.8%	31.1%
Paterson city	7,470	16.9%	5.1%	10.0%	4.3%	32.0%	2.5%	24.4%	4.7%	42.5%
New Mexico										
Albuquerque city	35,647	24.4%	11.1%	6.4%	4.5%	13.0%	3.6%	22.2%	14.9%	16.1%
Las Cruces city	5,474	23.0%	16.7%	3.6%	3.9%	15.6%	4.0%	17.2%	16.1%	31.8%
Rio Rancho city	3,763	48.8%	16.8%	7.1%	0.3%	5.8%	0.0%	11.7%	9.5%	37.8%
New York										
Albany city	7,385	5.0%	7.9%	2.7%	2.5%	7.4%	0.0%	38.5%	36.1%	10.1%
Buffalo city	21,426	12.0%	11.6%	2.4%	0.0%	31.3%	0.8%	27.0%	14.9%	16.7%
New York city	509,098	15.2%	11.8%	2.4%	4.0%	12.1%	3.0%	30.3%	21.2%	26.3%
Rochester city	16,895	11.5%	7.4%	2.5%	1.6%	31.2%	2.2%	27.1%	16.4%	10.4%
Syracuse city	9,696	8.9%	7.3%	3.1%	0.0%	34.5%	1.6%	35.2%	9.4%	20.2%
Yonkers city	6,243	28.0%	2.5%	0.0%	1.8%	22.4%	7.9%	24.1%	13.3%	45.0%
North Carolina										
Charlotte city	61,624	16.7%	12.9%	4.3%	3.4%	11.0%	1.4%	32.1%	18.2%	14.5%
Durham city	21,235	16.3%	18.1%	2.2%	0.7%	14.8%	0.4%	30.0%	17.5%	12.7%
Fayetteville city	16,779	16.7%	13.1%	8.4%	0.6%	23.1%	1.8%	29.2%	7.1%	17.8%
Greensboro city	18,963	17.5%	9.6%	4.7%	2.3%	19.9%	0.4%	26.7%	18.9%	15.8%
High Point city	5,294	18.6%	21.7%	1.5%	0.0%	26.0%	0.0%	21.9%	10.4%	21.2%
Raleigh city	32,660	18.1%	14.3%	3.3%	0.8%	7.4%	2.0%	29.0%	25.2%	12.2%
Wilmington city	7,671	15.9%	8.4%	8.6%	1.5%	27.0%	0.0%	23.2%	15.5%	10.4%
Winston-Salem city	15,355	33.3%	11.0%	5.9%	1.6%	8.1%	2.1%	28.4%	9.6%	10.1%
North Dakota										
Fargo city	9,500	23.0%	15.2%	5.3%	1.8%	5.9%	0.0%	35.2%	13.7%	2.9%
Ohio										
Akron city	14,344	9.2%	12.3%	2.0%	0.0%	25.2%	0.4%	30.0%	21.0%	13.4%
Cincinnati city	30,855	9.5%	6.4%	4.1%	0.7%	24.4%	0.3%	37.6%	17.0%	8.8%
Cleveland city	27,460	8.7%	6.0%	3.4%	3.5%	32.1%	2.5%	32.7%	11.1%	13.8%
Columbus city	70,475	17.5%	12.4%	1.6%	2.1%	12.4%	2.9%	29.4%	21.6%	13.0%
Dayton city	10,024	20.4%	3.8%	8.8%	1.7%	27.1%	0.7%	25.8%	11.7%	18.2%
Toledo city	18,763	15.6%	6.4%	6.7%	3.2%	26.2%	1.9%	24.6%	15.4%	16.4%

Table D-3: Places—Household Relationship—*Continued*

| | | 18 to 24 | | | | | | | | |
| | | Married Couple Households | | Male, No Spouse Present | | Female, No Spouse Present | | Non-Family Householders | | Living With Parents |
	Total Householders	With Children	No Children	With Children	No Children	With Children	No Children	Living Alone	Not Alone	
Oklahoma										
Broken Arrow city	2,382	4.2%	0.0%	0.0%	22.0%	32.6%	12.1%	25.9%	3.2%	51.8%
Edmond city	3,095	15.1%	4.7%	12.4%	9.6%	0.0%	0.0%	18.2%	40.0%	30.6%
Lawton city	1,944	33.9%	31.0%	0.0%	0.0%	4.5%	0.0%	23.3%	7.4%	20.5%
Norman city	3,850	0.0%	18.4%	0.0%	0.0%	0.0%	0.0%	23.3%	58.3%	25.9%
Oklahoma City city	12,092	8.0%	9.7%	4.6%	5.6%	12.2%	2.0%	15.4%	42.4%	38.5%
Tulsa city	10,193	11.5%	7.3%	0.0%	8.3%	15.9%	2.8%	31.2%	22.9%	41.0%
Oregon										
Beaverton city	1,853	3.3%	5.6%	0.0%	26.0%	3.9%	0.0%	24.3%	36.9%	57.8%
Eugene city	6,320	0.9%	4.3%	2.7%	1.0%	2.8%	1.4%	43.4%	43.4%	18.5%
Gresham city	1,153	19.9%	8.2%	0.0%	0.0%	33.5%	0.0%	20.2%	18.2%	54.9%
Hillsboro city	1,060	9.9%	4.3%	0.0%	0.0%	16.8%	0.0%	12.3%	56.7%	60.6%
Portland city	9,556	1.2%	4.4%	4.4%	1.2%	4.6%	1.1%	24.1%	58.9%	32.9%
Salem city	3,468	2.5%	5.0%	0.0%	9.9%	31.7%	4.9%	11.3%	34.7%	45.7%
Pennsylvania										
Allentown city	1,365	0.0%	12.3%	0.0%	6.7%	40.4%	14.9%	14.9%	10.8%	45.0%
Erie city	1,992	5.7%	5.6%	0.0%	0.0%	43.6%	0.0%	22.4%	22.7%	45.2%
Philadelphia city	20,822	0.5%	1.5%	1.6%	6.1%	21.0%	3.7%	36.4%	29.1%	45.1%
Pittsburgh city	12,419	1.3%	3.8%	1.0%	4.7%	3.8%	0.0%	38.4%	47.0%	17.7%
Rhode Island										
Providence city	3,839	8.2%	0.0%	9.8%	3.0%	21.1%	2.7%	18.5%	36.6%	24.7%
South Carolina										
Charleston city	2,944	0.0%	1.6%	0.0%	0.0%	15.8%	5.1%	19.0%	58.6%	26.3%
Columbia city	4,462	6.4%	0.0%	1.6%	0.0%	10.6%	9.1%	29.9%	42.4%	19.5%
North Charleston city	1,648	15.9%	21.5%	0.0%	0.0%	6.1%	13.0%	6.6%	36.8%	40.5%
South Dakota										
Sioux Falls city	4,175	5.2%	8.7%	0.0%	0.0%	7.4%	0.0%	48.7%	30.1%	36.3%
Tennessee										
Chattanooga city	3,043	3.7%	6.4%	0.0%	10.9%	16.7%	0.0%	44.9%	17.3%	36.7%
Clarksville city	5,844	15.5%	29.3%	0.0%	3.4%	9.5%	0.0%	21.4%	20.9%	33.1%
Knoxville city	7,627	0.8%	13.8%	0.0%	3.7%	13.0%	3.3%	30.1%	35.2%	22.9%
Memphis city	12,344	4.7%	4.2%	0.0%	6.2%	26.2%	4.5%	26.3%	27.9%	47.9%
Murfreesboro city	4,071	1.3%	8.3%	0.8%	5.6%	1.8%	0.0%	29.8%	52.5%	29.2%
Nashville-Davidson metropolitan govt (balance)	16,627	2.1%	4.4%	2.5%	5.2%	17.3%	3.2%	36.2%	29.0%	32.4%
Texas										
Abilene city	5,111	9.4%	8.1%	1.7%	0.5%	22.1%	0.0%	13.9%	44.3%	28.2%
Allen city	680	0.0%	0.0%	0.0%	0.0%	43.8%	23.4%	32.8%	0.0%	69.8%
Amarillo city	2,979	4.4%	8.8%	7.3%	4.5%	22.8%	0.0%	36.3%	16.0%	56.4%
Arlington city	6,027	11.3%	15.2%	1.9%	3.5%	18.0%	1.9%	23.8%	24.4%	57.9%
Austin city	21,292	4.6%	3.0%	0.9%	3.2%	3.6%	1.1%	34.6%	49.0%	26.6%
Beaumont city	3,280	19.1%	0.0%	0.0%	0.0%	21.2%	2.1%	19.5%	38.1%	28.3%
Brownsville city	1,328	10.5%	0.0%	29.1%	0.0%	25.5%	7.8%	20.9%	6.3%	73.7%
Carrollton city	2,389	0.0%	1.5%	1.9%	4.7%	22.6%	2.0%	55.2%	12.1%	58.5%
College Station city	9,929	1.4%	5.0%	0.0%	7.1%	1.1%	0.5%	36.7%	48.2%	13.0%
Corpus Christi city	6,617	12.0%	10.8%	7.3%	5.0%	16.9%	2.4%	26.1%	19.6%	48.7%
Dallas city	28,882	8.2%	6.9%	7.3%	4.7%	16.5%	4.3%	25.4%	26.8%	47.7%
Denton city	6,696	0.0%	0.0%	0.0%	9.8%	7.4%	0.9%	23.2%	58.7%	16.9%
El Paso city	8,989	17.4%	25.4%	4.6%	9.6%	4.2%	2.8%	31.2%	4.8%	65.3%
Fort Worth city	12,951	12.2%	5.9%	5.8%	0.5%	21.7%	3.0%	24.7%	26.1%	51.4%
Frisco city	385	0.0%	0.0%	22.1%	0.0%	0.0%	31.4%	17.4%	29.1%	74.6%
Garland city	2,030	0.0%	8.0%	6.6%	5.7%	3.2%	16.4%	26.4%	33.8%	76.3%
Grand Prairie city	1,976	15.9%	12.2%	5.7%	2.7%	4.7%	0.0%	40.3%	18.5%	62.2%
Houston city	40,138	10.0%	4.8%	5.0%	6.8%	13.4%	5.3%	34.0%	20.8%	54.3%
Irving city	4,184	14.0%	1.5%	2.4%	8.8%	3.0%	5.7%	29.8%	34.8%	59.9%
Killeen city	4,499	12.3%	33.8%	9.6%	0.0%	10.5%	0.0%	20.6%	13.3%	44.1%
Laredo city	2,204	17.6%	2.9%	8.4%	0.0%	29.8%	1.6%	21.5%	18.1%	70.7%
Lewisville city	1,619	0.0%	12.2%	0.0%	7.8%	16.4%	3.7%	54.7%	5.2%	65.4%
Lubbock city	11,323	9.1%	6.4%	4.2%	2.2%	12.5%	2.8%	21.3%	41.6%	22.9%
McAllen city	1,294	0.0%	3.8%	0.0%	12.8%	33.9%	17.1%	28.4%	4.0%	69.3%
McKinney city	2,094	5.3%	2.8%	0.0%	0.0%	7.3%	31.1%	24.6%	28.9%	59.1%
Mesquite city	1,774	10.0%	0.0%	38.0%	15.9%	26.2%	0.0%	3.1%	6.7%	64.2%
Midland city	2,934	11.9%	32.2%	1.7%	0.0%	19.9%	0.0%	19.9%	14.4%	53.7%
Odessa city	3,386	21.0%	6.1%	0.0%	0.0%	15.7%	6.7%	19.1%	31.4%	47.7%
Pasadena city	1,971	11.1%	0.0%	6.6%	13.5%	5.6%	4.1%	23.2%	36.0%	64.6%
Pearland city	182	0.0%	0.0%	0.0%	0.0%	0.0%	0.0%	100.0%	0.0%	63.7%
Plano city	3,628	0.0%	2.9%	0.0%	25.5%	13.6%	12.6%	21.9%	23.5%	61.4%
Richardson city	1,680	0.0%	0.0%	0.0%	5.6%	13.8%	6.3%	30.1%	44.3%	61.0%
Round Rock City	2,729	0.0%	4.3%	0.0%	0.0%	10.7%	0.0%	30.8%	54.3%	54.7%
San Angelo city	2,366	6.5%	2.8%	0.0%	1.9%	6.3%	0.0%	50.2%	32.3%	30.3%
San Antonio city	23,227	9.2%	8.1%	3.2%	3.4%	15.6%	3.8%	29.7%	26.9%	51.2%
Tyler city	3,894	5.3%	2.7%	0.0%	1.4%	4.1%	0.0%	46.7%	39.8%	25.2%
Waco city	6,726	9.8%	7.0%	1.7%	0.0%	16.4%	4.1%	42.6%	18.5%	18.9%
Wichita Falls city	3,457	1.7%	5.5%	8.8%	0.0%	11.7%	5.7%	31.0%	35.6%	18.7%

Table D-3: Places—Household Relationship—*Continued*

		25 to 33								
		Married Couple Households		Male, No Spouse Present		Female, No Spouse Present		Non-Family Householders		
	Total Householders	With Children	No Children	With Children	No Children	With Children	No Children	Living Alone	Not Alone	Living With Parents
Oklahoma										
Broken Arrow city	6,191	33.1%	21.3%	5.6%	4.9%	18.9%	0.0%	10.6%	5.6%	12.1%
Edmond city	4,614	32.3%	11.1%	10.2%	0.0%	2.0%	0.0%	33.7%	10.6%	11.0%
Lawton city	5,553	38.3%	0.0%	0.0%	0.9%	17.4%	0.0%	29.2%	14.1%	28.0%
Norman city	8,537	29.1%	13.7%	0.0%	5.3%	8.4%	2.2%	36.4%	4.9%	14.0%
Oklahoma City city	40,682	23.8%	10.6%	5.9%	3.3%	17.7%	1.7%	29.4%	7.6%	17.7%
Tulsa city	27,764	23.7%	14.7%	6.0%	3.5%	18.1%	0.5%	25.5%	8.0%	12.4%
Oregon										
Beaverton city	7,108	14.8%	17.2%	1.4%	5.5%	9.6%	3.7%	27.9%	19.9%	9.8%
Eugene city	10,650	17.3%	11.1%	6.2%	1.2%	8.0%	1.8%	31.8%	22.6%	13.9%
Gresham city	5,788	30.0%	3.0%	13.8%	0.0%	24.9%	2.5%	17.1%	8.7%	17.2%
Hillsboro city	6,637	22.4%	22.1%	2.4%	5.8%	6.8%	0.0%	25.1%	15.5%	10.6%
Portland city	45,109	10.9%	14.0%	2.4%	1.3%	11.3%	1.3%	29.9%	29.0%	12.3%
Salem city	7,089	35.3%	13.6%	4.8%	1.4%	18.0%	1.2%	11.3%	14.3%	17.2%
Pennsylvania										
Allentown city	7,259	32.2%	6.5%	8.3%	2.0%	25.3%	2.7%	14.5%	8.5%	19.6%
Erie city	5,637	19.8%	6.9%	1.5%	5.2%	28.1%	0.0%	25.2%	13.4%	16.4%
Philadelphia city	105,171	12.2%	10.6%	3.8%	2.8%	18.0%	2.1%	32.5%	18.0%	21.9%
Pittsburgh city	28,825	9.6%	14.8%	0.5%	2.1%	10.6%	0.9%	40.9%	20.6%	10.5%
Rhode Island										
Providence city	12,360	13.3%	8.9%	3.0%	1.8%	31.2%	1.0%	12.7%	28.1%	13.9%
South Carolina										
Charleston city	9,837	10.1%	20.8%	2.2%	2.9%	9.0%	0.0%	29.0%	26.0%	10.2%
Columbia city	12,682	16.4%	11.7%	0.7%	0.7%	23.7%	5.8%	26.8%	14.2%	9.9%
North Charleston city	8,118	22.8%	7.8%	2.3%	6.3%	6.3%	6.1%	37.2%	11.1%	17.4%
South Dakota										
Sioux Falls city	14,736	30.7%	14.8%	2.9%	1.2%	12.1%	1.3%	22.2%	14.8%	7.7%
Tennessee										
Chattanooga city	10,948	24.8%	14.0%	1.1%	2.9%	20.2%	1.1%	18.5%	17.4%	16.9%
Clarksville city	16,145	37.8%	13.2%	2.9%	2.4%	10.2%	0.0%	26.2%	7.2%	12.9%
Knoxville city	13,991	17.9%	11.6%	3.4%	1.0%	16.5%	1.8%	34.1%	14.8%	9.5%
Memphis city	39,983	18.3%	6.7%	5.8%	1.0%	29.4%	0.8%	27.9%	9.6%	24.4%
Murfreesboro city	9,011	31.5%	14.5%	0.0%	0.4%	9.9%	0.0%	16.6%	27.1%	7.0%
Nashville-Davidson metropolitan govt (balance)	56,161	19.6%	14.8%	3.3%	2.3%	13.7%	1.0%	25.9%	19.5%	9.6%
Texas										
Abilene city	7,266	33.9%	11.4%	2.2%	0.0%	12.0%	0.0%	27.2%	13.3%	14.3%
Allen city	4,808	26.1%	17.0%	11.3%	2.1%	11.2%	0.0%	8.5%	23.0%	14.3%
Amarillo city	13,596	31.3%	12.8%	2.2%	0.7%	17.5%	0.7%	30.7%	4.0%	7.7%
Arlington city	23,481	29.1%	10.3%	4.4%	5.5%	14.2%	3.4%	23.4%	9.7%	23.8%
Austin city	86,943	13.8%	12.5%	1.5%	1.9%	9.6%	2.4%	34.3%	24.1%	9.6%
Beaumont city	8,017	34.9%	5.4%	5.5%	2.0%	17.1%	0.6%	25.7%	8.8%	12.6%
Brownsville city	7,194	47.0%	7.3%	3.1%	3.9%	23.1%	1.2%	13.1%	1.3%	33.7%
Carrollton city	9,639	17.1%	13.4%	4.5%	3.4%	4.6%	3.0%	40.6%	13.5%	11.9%
College Station city	9,671	11.7%	16.6%	1.7%	2.3%	9.2%	1.8%	31.4%	25.2%	8.1%
Corpus Christi city	19,188	24.5%	8.1%	4.2%	5.0%	23.8%	1.4%	23.4%	9.6%	19.7%
Dallas city	95,938	20.2%	13.6%	3.4%	3.8%	13.3%	1.8%	30.3%	13.6%	16.0%
Denton city	8,811	29.4%	24.3%	3.6%	0.0%	4.4%	0.6%	21.3%	16.4%	10.6%
El Paso city	33,720	32.8%	10.9%	8.9%	4.6%	14.7%	3.8%	19.0%	5.2%	30.6%
Fort Worth city	49,772	33.3%	13.1%	3.0%	3.0%	14.6%	0.4%	21.6%	10.8%	21.0%
Frisco city	5,781	44.3%	15.0%	1.3%	1.7%	8.1%	0.0%	25.0%	4.8%	22.5%
Garland city	10,869	38.4%	7.0%	3.8%	2.0%	19.3%	5.0%	15.1%	9.4%	26.1%
Grand Prairie city	9,185	35.2%	8.4%	4.0%	8.7%	17.8%	0.0%	23.5%	2.5%	27.7%
Houston city	165,609	21.4%	12.6%	4.1%	3.7%	14.9%	1.7%	30.8%	10.9%	17.6%
Irving city	17,623	23.4%	16.0%	3.3%	3.5%	12.8%	3.4%	27.1%	10.5%	13.8%
Killeen city	11,390	44.3%	11.9%	1.9%	0.0%	20.2%	0.0%	16.7%	4.9%	15.6%
Laredo city	9,403	31.7%	22.2%	6.1%	1.6%	16.3%	5.6%	14.6%	1.9%	35.4%
Lewisville city	9,643	28.9%	16.9%	2.5%	3.2%	14.9%	0.0%	25.3%	8.2%	15.1%
Lubbock city	16,945	23.6%	6.8%	5.6%	2.2%	14.1%	1.9%	30.2%	15.7%	13.6%
McAllen city	5,787	45.3%	3.4%	3.0%	0.0%	12.9%	5.4%	19.8%	10.1%	32.7%
McKinney city	6,736	43.9%	12.4%	2.2%	1.9%	6.3%	1.8%	23.1%	8.4%	19.0%
Mesquite city	6,838	21.8%	11.9%	4.1%	8.1%	27.6%	2.6%	11.5%	12.3%	25.5%
Midland city	9,465	45.6%	26.1%	0.9%	3.4%	7.5%	0.0%	8.5%	8.1%	14.0%
Odessa city	8,518	48.7%	11.7%	0.0%	1.5%	16.2%	0.0%	18.2%	3.6%	15.9%
Pasadena city	10,702	44.9%	7.2%	4.6%	4.9%	19.7%	1.9%	10.5%	6.3%	17.8%
Pearland city	5,855	36.8%	11.9%	0.0%	0.0%	4.7%	0.0%	25.2%	21.3%	19.0%
Plano city	18,099	21.5%	20.7%	1.3%	4.4%	11.3%	2.9%	30.0%	8.0%	16.0%
Richardson city	8,846	19.5%	24.0%	4.1%	7.4%	7.4%	2.7%	23.6%	11.2%	23.2%
Round Rock City	5,233	21.2%	13.4%	0.0%	3.7%	23.7%	0.0%	33.1%	4.9%	32.8%
San Angelo city	7,023	46.3%	4.3%	3.6%	0.0%	14.9%	1.0%	13.1%	16.8%	13.7%
San Antonio city	82,179	24.5%	12.7%	3.4%	3.4%	17.4%	1.3%	26.7%	10.5%	24.1%
Tyler city	5,496	39.0%	5.7%	4.5%	0.5%	15.7%	0.6%	28.4%	5.5%	18.2%
Waco city	7,345	18.1%	14.9%	3.2%	2.7%	19.3%	1.2%	23.4%	17.2%	17.2%
Wichita Falls city	5,495	40.4%	3.9%	8.5%	0.0%	10.7%	9.2%	11.2%	16.1%	12.2%

Table D-3: Places—Household Relationship—*Continued*

		Married Couple Households		Male, No Spouse Present		Female, No Spouse Present		Non-Family Householders		
										18 to 24
	Total Householders	With Children	No Children	With Children	No Children	With Children	No Children	Living Alone	Not Alone	Living With Parents
Utah										
Orem city	2,975	13.7%	46.4%	0.0%	2.9%	0.0%	14.0%	8.2%	14.7%	37.6%
Provo city	9,100	12.1%	43.0%	0.8%	4.4%	0.0%	0.0%	6.8%	32.8%	11.1%
Salt Lake City city	5,564	2.6%	18.2%	0.0%	6.6%	0.0%	3.7%	25.8%	43.2%	21.2%
Sandy city	682	0.0%	69.8%	0.0%	0.0%	0.0%	0.0%	7.9%	22.3%	57.0%
West Jordan city	1,075	5.4%	0.0%	0.0%	14.3%	0.0%	0.0%	63.5%	16.7%	53.3%
West Valley City city	1,994	6.2%	14.1%	3.5%	10.3%	21.9%	2.6%	11.0%	30.4%	50.7%
Virginia										
Alexandria city	1,711	8.9%	1.5%	0.0%	12.6%	0.0%	0.0%	42.0%	34.9%	50.5%
Chesapeake city	2,846	21.5%	18.0%	0.0%	0.0%	3.1%	15.6%	3.3%	38.4%	56.2%
Hampton city	2,832	7.3%	13.7%	0.0%	0.0%	12.9%	0.0%	19.1%	47.0%	36.3%
Newport News city	5,591	5.2%	8.1%	2.8%	0.0%	27.5%	1.4%	36.1%	18.9%	31.1%
Norfolk city	6,896	7.9%	18.8%	1.0%	2.7%	11.5%	4.3%	21.4%	32.3%	21.5%
Portsmouth city	2,209	6.7%	4.1%	0.0%	0.0%	23.4%	0.0%	49.2%	16.6%	37.0%
Richmond city	6,050	0.0%	1.9%	1.8%	4.1%	9.3%	1.3%	36.2%	45.5%	25.2%
Roanoke city	2,818	11.0%	0.0%	0.0%	0.0%	16.7%	0.0%	21.7%	50.5%	31.6%
Virginia Beach city	7,428	18.1%	12.3%	2.9%	0.0%	9.9%	2.0%	18.7%	36.0%	47.6%
Washington										
Bellevue city	1,833	0.0%	0.0%	0.0%	6.7%	0.0%	13.6%	47.4%	32.3%	53.6%
Everett city	1,785	0.0%	30.9%	0.0%	0.0%	18.6%	10.9%	22.5%	17.1%	50.8%
Federal Way city	736	36.0%	8.3%	0.0%	0.0%	0.0%	0.0%	14.4%	41.3%	52.3%
Kent city	1,363	0.0%	21.5%	0.0%	20.1%	0.0%	0.0%	20.3%	38.1%	57.1%
Renton city	595	12.9%	0.0%	17.6%	0.0%	0.0%	0.0%	0.0%	69.4%	58.9%
Seattle city	17,483	0.4%	2.3%	0.0%	3.7%	0.9%	3.4%	32.0%	57.2%	17.8%
Spokane city	4,420	2.7%	6.8%	2.4%	0.0%	19.0%	1.1%	31.3%	36.6%	28.1%
Spokane Valley city	1,948	18.8%	8.0%	0.0%	0.0%	37.9%	0.0%	23.6%	11.8%	44.4%
Tacoma city	3,400	1.6%	25.9%	0.0%	1.6%	0.0%	7.2%	29.4%	34.2%	42.9%
Vancouver city	2,186	6.4%	14.0%	0.0%	0.0%	24.7%	7.8%	19.0%	28.1%	62.6%
Yakima city	2,316	3.0%	6.1%	16.0%	0.0%	56.7%	0.0%	0.0%	18.2%	57.7%
Wisconsin										
Green Bay city	3,170	17.8%	0.0%	9.7%	1.1%	0.0%	9.9%	15.2%	46.4%	38.4%
Kenosha city	1,152	0.0%	0.0%	0.0%	35.6%	0.0%	0.0%	4.8%	59.6%	55.6%
Madison city	12,966	0.0%	1.8%	0.0%	3.5%	2.5%	1.2%	32.1%	58.9%	13.9%
Milwaukee city	12,404	3.2%	1.4%	2.9%	2.5%	19.0%	3.4%	36.0%	31.6%	40.9%

Table D-3: Places—Household Relationship—*Continued*

| | | 25 to 33 | | | | | | | | |
| | Total Householders | Married Couple Households | | Male, No Spouse Present | | Female, No Spouse Present | | Non-Family Householders | | Living With Parents |
		With Children	No Children	With Children	No Children	With Children	No Children	Living Alone	Not Alone	
Utah										
Orem city	5,106	54.2%	18.8%	1.2%	0.0%	10.0%	1.8%	2.7%	11.3%	17.6%
Provo city	7,727	39.3%	21.0%	0.0%	3.5%	6.0%	1.3%	7.6%	21.3%	4.9%
Salt Lake City city	18,780	13.8%	20.6%	3.8%	1.2%	8.9%	1.6%	32.5%	17.5%	9.7%
Sandy city	4,964	46.6%	16.2%	0.0%	0.0%	18.0%	0.0%	11.3%	7.9%	15.8%
West Jordan city	6,603	57.2%	18.1%	7.2%	0.0%	7.5%	0.0%	7.6%	2.2%	22.9%
West Valley City city	6,881	38.5%	8.5%	1.1%	0.0%	25.2%	4.2%	17.2%	5.4%	28.7%
Virginia										
Alexandria city	14,443	11.4%	19.3%	3.3%	2.2%	6.2%	2.5%	32.2%	22.8%	7.2%
Chesapeake city	12,536	38.5%	15.4%	11.1%	5.8%	13.3%	3.8%	8.0%	4.2%	18.8%
Hampton city	8,182	30.6%	7.9%	6.6%	0.0%	10.1%	0.9%	30.5%	13.5%	24.5%
Newport News city	13,169	30.1%	8.2%	4.0%	4.1%	18.5%	0.4%	30.9%	3.9%	11.2%
Norfolk city	17,084	22.4%	9.5%	0.5%	1.7%	22.2%	2.7%	24.9%	16.1%	17.8%
Portsmouth city	5,917	17.7%	7.1%	2.3%	1.1%	21.8%	0.0%	23.2%	26.7%	26.0%
Richmond city	19,508	8.3%	11.1%	4.9%	1.4%	10.1%	0.9%	39.2%	24.1%	15.2%
Roanoke city	7,636	10.8%	11.8%	1.7%	2.0%	37.6%	0.0%	27.4%	8.6%	12.8%
Virginia Beach city	29,701	29.9%	14.2%	6.3%	1.3%	12.6%	1.9%	17.3%	16.6%	15.8%
Washington										
Bellevue city	9,380	16.4%	23.1%	2.0%	0.0%	2.4%	0.0%	32.2%	23.8%	16.0%
Everett city	6,386	25.7%	22.1%	2.1%	3.2%	12.6%	0.0%	24.1%	10.2%	15.6%
Federal Way city	6,358	27.0%	16.6%	13.4%	0.0%	16.5%	4.3%	16.1%	6.1%	14.8%
Kent city	7,457	27.8%	13.6%	13.7%	1.9%	9.7%	4.3%	15.0%	13.9%	24.5%
Renton city	6,322	10.1%	12.0%	8.1%	8.7%	8.1%	4.0%	25.3%	23.6%	21.5%
Seattle city	74,990	9.4%	17.3%	0.3%	1.3%	2.1%	0.4%	34.4%	34.8%	5.0%
Spokane city	14,736	26.7%	13.6%	8.5%	0.0%	8.7%	6.3%	26.4%	9.8%	9.1%
Spokane Valley city	6,765	49.7%	12.3%	3.6%	0.0%	5.8%	0.0%	15.7%	13.0%	4.6%
Tacoma city	13,092	23.0%	13.8%	5.5%	0.9%	9.0%	2.5%	32.8%	12.5%	14.9%
Vancouver city	9,884	27.9%	10.9%	5.0%	0.8%	15.2%	0.0%	25.0%	15.2%	9.4%
Yakima city	4,207	50.3%	12.1%	1.3%	2.9%	12.9%	0.0%	20.5%	0.0%	13.9%
Wisconsin										
Green Bay city	8,240	17.8%	10.2%	0.0%	1.3%	30.7%	3.3%	28.8%	7.9%	6.2%
Kenosha city	4,077	18.1%	13.3%	12.8%	0.0%	14.9%	0.0%	28.6%	12.3%	10.3%
Madison city	20,183	12.2%	20.3%	2.0%	0.8%	4.9%	0.0%	30.8%	28.9%	6.6%
Milwaukee city	44,379	14.8%	10.4%	4.0%	0.9%	24.6%	0.9%	29.6%	14.9%	17.9%

Table D-4: Metropolitan/Micropolitan Statistical Areas—Household Relationship

| | | 18 to 24 | | | | | | | | |
| | | Married Couple Households | | Male, No Spouse Present | | Female, No Spouse Present | | Non-Family Householders | | |
	Total Householders	With Children	No Children	With Children	No Children	With Children	No Children	Living Alone	Not Alone	Living With Parents
Abilene, TX	5,272	9.1%	7.9%	2.3%	0.4%	21.5%	0.0%	15.8%	43.0%	29.2%
Adrian, MI	1,667	0.0%	0.0%	11.0%	0.0%	35.8%	0.0%	27.0%	26.3%	48.5%
Akron, OH	14,005	5.7%	5.1%	1.4%	5.7%	19.5%	2.5%	33.5%	26.6%	53.8%
Albany, GA	1,931	8.6%	0.0%	0.0%	0.0%	21.7%	3.6%	60.4%	5.6%	55.6%
Albany, OR	3,764	3.8%	3.7%	0.0%	6.7%	8.8%	0.0%	21.4%	55.7%	20.0%
Albany-Schenectady-Troy, NY	10,770	5.4%	0.6%	1.6%	1.9%	11.0%	0.7%	40.2%	38.6%	52.3%
Albertville, AL	1,595	34.7%	2.1%	2.8%	0.0%	14.7%	0.0%	0.0%	45.7%	56.6%
Albuquerque, NM	11,276	8.4%	6.1%	1.4%	9.5%	8.3%	2.1%	23.0%	41.2%	56.8%
Alexandria, LA	2,421	25.1%	7.5%	0.0%	13.1%	21.5%	0.0%	26.6%	6.2%	50.8%
Allentown-Bethlehem-Easton, PA-NJ	7,238	6.9%	6.4%	0.0%	5.0%	22.9%	2.8%	24.1%	31.9%	59.4%
Altoona, PA	1,092	0.0%	7.6%	13.6%	0.0%	3.1%	0.0%	22.0%	53.8%	59.4%
Amarillo, TX	4,041	3.2%	6.5%	9.6%	9.2%	18.1%	0.0%	37.0%	16.5%	57.4%
Ames, IA	7,059	2.5%	0.0%	0.0%	1.7%	0.0%	0.0%	9.4%	86.3%	11.5%
Anchorage, AK	8,610	5.3%	13.8%	4.7%	10.2%	7.6%	0.0%	33.8%	24.6%	46.7%
Ann Arbor, MI	14,848	0.2%	3.7%	0.0%	5.4%	4.7%	0.0%	33.4%	52.7%	22.7%
Anniston-Oxford-Jacksonville, AL	2,219	0.0%	7.3%	0.0%	0.0%	28.0%	9.2%	27.9%	27.5%	43.3%
Appleton, WI	2,706	0.0%	21.4%	5.2%	2.0%	16.4%	0.0%	26.4%	28.6%	63.9%
Asheville, NC	6,685	8.4%	12.5%	4.5%	4.3%	10.6%	4.3%	29.8%	25.6%	46.0%
Ashtabula, OH	1,154	17.7%	14.0%	3.6%	5.2%	0.0%	4.2%	23.1%	32.4%	68.3%
Athens-Clarke County, GA	9,508	1.3%	7.2%	1.3%	0.9%	1.5%	1.0%	33.2%	53.6%	22.4%
Atlanta-Sandy Springs-Roswell, GA	61,680	10.0%	6.6%	6.3%	4.4%	11.0%	4.3%	31.3%	26.1%	58.3%
Atlantic City-Hammonton, NJ	2,387	7.4%	2.5%	0.0%	24.8%	3.8%	0.0%	18.9%	42.6%	64.8%
Auburn-Opelika, AL	7,586	2.3%	3.3%	10.1%	2.5%	9.5%	1.0%	42.8%	28.5%	24.8%
Augusta-Richmond County, GA-SC	5,617	2.0%	9.8%	7.1%	0.0%	10.5%	5.6%	42.2%	22.9%	57.0%
Augusta-Waterville, ME	2,327	0.0%	0.0%	0.0%	0.0%	16.4%	0.0%	29.1%	54.4%	38.9%
Austin-Round Rock, TX	37,039	4.9%	3.9%	1.2%	3.1%	5.3%	3.0%	29.9%	48.7%	38.3%
Bakersfield, CA	9,590	13.1%	1.8%	2.4%	5.4%	22.4%	8.7%	30.8%	15.4%	64.6%
Baltimore-Columbia-Towson, MD	25,610	7.5%	7.6%	5.4%	4.3%	16.8%	2.3%	17.2%	38.9%	56.0%
Bangor, ME	1,973	0.0%	0.0%	0.0%	0.0%	18.6%	6.8%	29.2%	45.4%	36.4%
Barnstable Town, MA	571	0.0%	28.5%	0.0%	0.0%	29.6%	0.0%	11.9%	29.9%	76.7%
Baton Rouge, LA	18,087	4.3%	6.2%	4.1%	6.2%	13.3%	0.1%	35.8%	29.9%	46.3%
Battle Creek, MI	1,811	2.6%	5.1%	29.1%	5.9%	0.0%	0.0%	36.7%	20.6%	55.3%
Bay City, MI	1,967	20.9%	0.0%	0.0%	3.3%	0.0%	0.0%	22.6%	53.1%	53.6%
Beaumont-Port Arthur, TX	6,782	16.1%	3.8%	5.4%	1.8%	14.4%	2.5%	21.8%	34.3%	46.5%
Beckley, WV	1,566	6.5%	39.0%	5.6%	3.0%	1.6%	13.8%	24.3%	6.3%	48.2%
Bellingham, WA	5,286	0.0%	4.9%	3.0%	5.2%	0.0%	2.1%	27.2%	57.5%	26.7%
Bend-Redmond, OR	2,095	3.9%	9.5%	2.8%	1.8%	6.3%	10.7%	13.0%	52.0%	46.0%
Billings, MT	3,655	8.8%	4.3%	0.0%	0.0%	16.1%	1.2%	31.2%	38.3%	37.6%
Binghamton, NY	4,373	3.9%	1.7%	5.1%	0.0%	16.3%	7.6%	28.8%	36.6%	48.1%
Birmingham-Hoover, AL	13,772	5.9%	9.5%	3.7%	5.1%	12.7%	1.5%	40.2%	21.5%	53.0%
Bismarck, ND	2,336	21.1%	9.7%	0.0%	0.0%	0.0%	5.7%	8.7%	54.7%	36.2%
Blacksburg-Christiansburg-Radford, VA	8,739	1.9%	6.6%	3.2%	1.6%	3.1%	1.7%	19.3%	62.5%	11.5%
Bloomington, IL	7,124	2.4%	4.5%	1.4%	0.0%	0.0%	0.0%	37.3%	54.4%	28.8%
Bloomington, IN	9,201	1.1%	2.6%	0.0%	1.7%	3.6%	3.3%	41.8%	45.9%	8.2%
Bloomsburg-Berwick, PA	1,197	1.3%	0.0%	8.5%	0.0%	3.5%	0.0%	65.1%	21.6%	45.3%
Boise City, ID	8,436	8.3%	11.6%	0.0%	1.0%	7.9%	5.0%	33.7%	32.6%	43.8%
Boston-Cambridge-Newton, MA-NH	46,908	2.8%	2.9%	0.5%	7.8%	7.1%	3.8%	24.6%	50.5%	50.1%
Boulder, CO	10,782	0.0%	2.7%	0.0%	3.0%	2.0%	2.6%	25.2%	64.5%	21.4%
Bowling Green, KY	5,518	7.4%	12.0%	0.0%	10.2%	14.3%	0.0%	36.6%	19.5%	26.2%
Bremerton-Silverdale, WA	3,696	11.9%	15.3%	9.0%	0.4%	6.8%	2.9%	18.4%	35.5%	42.7%
Bridgeport-Stamford-Norwalk, CT	5,592	1.1%	5.6%	6.8%	0.7%	13.4%	11.1%	34.2%	27.1%	69.2%
Brownsville-Harlingen, TX	3,040	31.1%	8.1%	12.7%	1.3%	17.1%	10.5%	14.0%	5.2%	69.8%
Brunswick, GA	1,640	48.6%	21.5%	0.0%	17.0%	0.0%	0.0%	2.7%	10.2%	41.8%
Buffalo-Cheektowaga-Niagara Falls, NY	14,010	1.4%	3.2%	1.0%	3.3%	18.2%	2.1%	31.5%	39.1%	57.6%
Burlington, NC	2,497	7.5%	3.0%	2.8%	0.0%	11.8%	0.8%	36.9%	37.1%	37.0%
Burlington-South Burlington, VT	4,628	0.0%	0.0%	0.0%	0.0%	3.4%	0.0%	24.7%	72.0%	37.0%
California-Lexington Park, MD	735	0.0%	0.0%	0.0%	0.0%	0.0%	0.0%	44.4%	55.6%	60.8%
Canton-Massillon, OH	4,818	10.9%	5.9%	3.1%	3.0%	18.2%	0.0%	21.1%	37.9%	52.9%
Cape Coral-Fort Myers, FL	4,187	1.7%	6.2%	3.5%	6.4%	17.2%	0.0%	34.5%	30.5%	51.5%
Cape Girardeau, MO-IL	2,069	1.7%	5.1%	0.0%	5.1%	20.6%	2.9%	27.1%	37.5%	33.5%
Carbondale-Marion, IL	3,826	2.4%	7.9%	0.0%	2.1%	9.2%	0.0%	38.0%	40.5%	28.6%
Carson City, NV	809	29.0%	0.0%	0.0%	0.0%	0.0%	4.6%	30.9%	35.5%	37.8%
Casper, WY	1,951	9.3%	3.3%	12.7%	0.0%	3.8%	0.0%	43.3%	27.6%	38.3%
Cedar Rapids, IA	5,903	5.4%	3.7%	0.0%	0.0%	12.9%	0.0%	39.4%	38.6%	40.4%
Chambersburg-Waynesboro, PA	1,673	17.6%	0.0%	10.1%	19.1%	18.0%	0.0%	17.0%	18.2%	66.9%
Champaign-Urbana, IL	10,799	2.8%	1.5%	0.8%	7.2%	1.2%	1.1%	37.4%	48.0%	22.8%
Charleston, WV	3,069	1.0%	7.2%	0.0%	2.8%	20.3%	4.7%	44.2%	19.8%	49.3%
Charleston-North Charleston, SC	8,896	5.2%	13.0%	0.6%	2.6%	14.1%	6.6%	13.3%	44.5%	41.9%
Charlotte-Concord-Gastonia, NC-SC	35,337	7.6%	8.3%	4.0%	4.7%	12.5%	4.3%	30.7%	27.9%	52.3%
Charlottesville, VA	3,692	12.8%	3.3%	0.0%	6.0%	2.6%	0.0%	14.3%	61.1%	32.0%
Chattanooga, TN-GA	7,839	11.9%	16.8%	3.8%	9.7%	16.0%	0.6%	18.6%	22.6%	43.1%
Cheyenne, WY	3,393	2.4%	3.8%	0.0%	0.4%	0.0%	0.0%	43.1%	50.3%	22.5%
Chicago-Naperville-Elgin, IL-IN-WI	95,061	7.5%	4.2%	2.2%	7.5%	13.8%	3.0%	30.5%	31.3%	62.4%
Chico, CA	6,807	12.9%	3.7%	0.0%	4.2%	3.4%	5.4%	17.8%	52.6%	35.8%
Cincinnati, OH-KY-IN	32,070	7.5%	10.5%	2.5%	3.3%	18.5%	2.1%	23.5%	32.1%	51.6%

Table D-4: Metropolitan/Micropolitan Statistical Areas—Household Relationship—*Continued*

| | | 25 to 33 | | | | | | | | |
| | | Married Couple Households | | Male, No Spouse Present | | Female, No Spouse Present | | Non-Family Householders | | |
	Total Householders	With Children	No Children	With Children	No Children	With Children	No Children	Living Alone	Not Alone	Living With Parents
Abilene, TX	8,439	34.4%	12.1%	3.3%	0.0%	14.8%	0.0%	23.9%	11.5%	29.2%
Adrian, MI	3,764	33.6%	8.5%	3.7%	0.0%	22.2%	0.7%	25.7%	5.7%	48.5%
Akron, OH	37,900	20.7%	12.4%	3.6%	1.5%	18.0%	1.1%	27.6%	14.9%	53.8%
Albany, GA	7,921	21.0%	1.6%	4.2%	0.0%	38.4%	0.0%	23.2%	11.6%	55.6%
Albany, OR	5,759	33.3%	9.6%	2.8%	3.1%	18.9%	0.2%	22.2%	9.9%	20.0%
Albany-Schenectady-Troy, NY	42,118	18.8%	9.0%	4.9%	2.2%	12.3%	1.8%	29.6%	21.4%	52.3%
Albertville, AL	3,476	32.7%	18.3%	7.5%	0.5%	23.9%	0.0%	14.3%	2.8%	56.6%
Albuquerque, NM	49,021	26.4%	11.0%	10.3%	3.6%	13.1%	3.3%	19.3%	12.9%	56.8%
Alexandria, LA	8,022	35.1%	8.6%	4.0%	2.2%	23.8%	0.0%	15.1%	11.3%	50.8%
Allentown-Bethlehem-Easton, PA-NJ	33,932	30.0%	11.6%	8.3%	1.9%	14.0%	1.8%	20.3%	12.0%	59.4%
Altoona, PA	5,193	29.0%	11.6%	6.7%	0.0%	29.5%	1.1%	9.8%	12.1%	59.4%
Amarillo, TX	18,399	32.8%	12.1%	2.8%	0.5%	16.7%	0.5%	29.7%	4.9%	57.4%
Ames, IA	6,514	27.7%	32.7%	0.0%	0.0%	1.9%	0.0%	23.2%	14.5%	11.5%
Anchorage, AK	25,752	34.5%	13.1%	1.4%	0.1%	20.3%	0.8%	21.6%	8.2%	46.7%
Ann Arbor, MI	22,754	16.9%	14.6%	4.6%	0.5%	6.6%	0.0%	33.5%	23.3%	22.7%
Anniston-Oxford-Jacksonville, AL	4,788	31.7%	5.7%	14.6%	1.4%	22.3%	0.0%	21.0%	3.4%	43.3%
Appleton, WI	12,994	26.9%	17.5%	5.4%	0.0%	19.6%	1.2%	17.3%	12.1%	63.9%
Asheville, NC	19,080	33.8%	15.0%	2.5%	0.6%	13.3%	1.0%	22.5%	11.3%	46.0%
Ashtabula, OH	3,047	33.0%	7.6%	1.6%	1.0%	23.3%	0.0%	7.7%	25.9%	68.3%
Athens-Clarke County, GA	11,328	19.1%	9.9%	4.4%	0.9%	21.3%	1.0%	24.3%	19.1%	22.4%
Atlanta-Sandy Springs-Roswell, GA	281,135	25.7%	12.0%	4.2%	2.2%	13.9%	2.3%	26.9%	12.8%	58.3%
Atlantic City-Hammonton, NJ	11,955	22.6%	6.8%	11.9%	6.1%	23.3%	0.1%	15.3%	13.9%	64.8%
Auburn-Opelika, AL	7,574	33.2%	15.8%	1.8%	1.4%	18.3%	0.3%	25.4%	3.8%	24.8%
Augusta-Richmond County, GA-SC	29,191	34.0%	9.2%	4.5%	1.9%	22.3%	0.8%	19.2%	8.2%	57.0%
Augusta-Waterville, ME	4,758	38.9%	23.8%	7.2%	0.0%	5.6%	0.0%	17.8%	6.7%	38.9%
Austin-Round Rock, TX	135,871	20.6%	13.0%	1.9%	1.8%	10.4%	1.9%	29.5%	20.9%	38.3%
Bakersfield, CA	45,724	32.2%	9.8%	8.6%	3.2%	22.1%	2.4%	14.0%	7.6%	64.6%
Baltimore-Columbia-Towson, MD	133,758	25.2%	13.4%	4.4%	1.7%	15.0%	1.5%	24.2%	14.6%	56.0%
Bangor, ME	8,211	17.0%	13.1%	7.9%	0.0%	15.7%	0.0%	33.0%	13.3%	36.4%
Barnstable Town, MA	5,683	29.8%	7.4%	0.0%	0.0%	13.2%	0.0%	18.4%	31.3%	76.7%
Baton Rouge, LA	44,736	28.8%	11.2%	3.3%	1.0%	19.3%	1.2%	23.0%	12.4%	46.3%
Battle Creek, MI	6,719	44.9%	4.5%	6.5%	4.5%	17.7%	12.4%	7.0%	2.5%	55.3%
Bay City, MI	5,422	31.2%	14.1%	0.0%	3.5%	13.2%	0.0%	20.5%	17.5%	53.6%
Beaumont-Port Arthur, TX	22,447	43.0%	6.8%	4.2%	1.6%	13.6%	1.2%	21.2%	8.4%	46.5%
Beckley, WV	4,369	37.3%	5.4%	7.1%	0.0%	21.1%	0.0%	10.2%	18.9%	48.2%
Bellingham, WA	11,235	22.7%	12.7%	3.5%	0.6%	11.5%	0.0%	25.9%	23.0%	26.7%
Bend-Redmond, OR	9,484	27.5%	14.8%	0.0%	0.5%	13.7%	0.0%	21.1%	22.5%	46.0%
Billings, MT	6,704	27.3%	2.3%	3.6%	0.2%	13.8%	0.0%	36.2%	16.7%	37.6%
Binghamton, NY	10,628	20.7%	14.6%	4.0%	1.1%	16.5%	0.7%	24.5%	17.9%	48.1%
Birmingham-Hoover, AL	58,348	26.7%	14.6%	4.3%	1.5%	21.1%	1.3%	21.4%	9.2%	53.0%
Bismarck, ND	10,984	31.4%	16.1%	6.8%	1.5%	1.6%	0.0%	22.4%	20.2%	36.2%
Blacksburg-Christiansburg-Radford, VA	10,110	29.5%	14.4%	0.7%	0.0%	14.5%	2.0%	20.0%	19.0%	11.5%
Bloomington, IL	12,035	22.2%	19.7%	5.2%	1.8%	11.5%	0.7%	27.4%	11.6%	28.8%
Bloomington, IN	10,373	17.3%	19.4%	1.1%	0.3%	6.0%	0.0%	39.4%	16.5%	8.2%
Bloomsburg-Berwick, PA	4,475	33.8%	4.3%	9.0%	5.9%	20.8%	4.5%	8.3%	13.3%	45.3%
Boise City, ID	38,466	27.3%	10.5%	6.6%	1.8%	15.0%	1.0%	25.4%	12.4%	43.8%
Boston-Cambridge-Newton, MA-NH	237,991	17.5%	17.2%	2.4%	2.6%	9.5%	2.5%	24.4%	23.8%	50.1%
Boulder, CO	16,787	20.7%	16.7%	0.2%	1.0%	5.6%	3.6%	23.6%	28.7%	21.4%
Bowling Green, KY	9,153	37.1%	15.6%	7.6%	1.6%	22.0%	0.0%	10.5%	5.6%	26.2%
Bremerton-Silverdale, WA	13,808	33.5%	18.5%	4.8%	3.4%	12.4%	0.0%	17.8%	9.6%	42.7%
Bridgeport-Stamford-Norwalk, CT	32,926	23.9%	16.6%	3.4%	2.6%	14.7%	2.4%	17.8%	18.6%	69.2%
Brownsville-Harlingen, TX	16,727	41.1%	7.2%	4.5%	1.7%	24.3%	0.5%	16.3%	4.4%	69.8%
Brunswick, GA	5,981	38.2%	13.3%	7.6%	0.0%	17.8%	2.4%	6.5%	14.1%	41.8%
Buffalo-Cheektowaga-Niagara Falls, NY	58,099	24.4%	11.8%	2.4%	1.7%	20.1%	1.5%	21.7%	16.4%	57.6%
Burlington, NC	6,626	26.2%	24.5%	1.9%	0.0%	34.2%	0.0%	7.1%	6.1%	37.0%
Burlington-South Burlington, VT	11,560	15.5%	18.9%	0.0%	0.0%	5.3%	2.1%	27.9%	30.3%	37.0%
California-Lexington Park, MD	5,482	18.1%	9.8%	7.0%	0.0%	18.9%	12.5%	15.1%	18.7%	60.8%
Canton-Massillon, OH	19,971	28.8%	8.3%	4.5%	1.4%	17.1%	0.0%	29.4%	10.4%	52.9%
Cape Coral-Fort Myers, FL	21,327	27.0%	6.4%	7.5%	2.3%	21.8%	2.8%	21.1%	11.2%	51.5%
Cape Girardeau, MO-IL	4,864	29.9%	5.0%	0.0%	0.0%	32.4%	1.6%	26.2%	4.9%	33.5%
Carbondale-Marion, IL	7,446	28.6%	13.4%	8.7%	0.3%	18.5%	2.3%	21.9%	6.3%	28.6%
Carson City, NV	1,828	49.3%	3.7%	0.0%	0.0%	16.9%	1.0%	17.3%	11.7%	37.8%
Casper, WY	4,492	26.2%	16.8%	3.9%	1.4%	14.4%	0.0%	25.0%	12.2%	38.3%
Cedar Rapids, IA	13,929	22.3%	23.6%	3.9%	0.2%	14.3%	1.8%	18.4%	15.5%	40.4%
Chambersburg-Waynesboro, PA	6,309	48.2%	9.1%	6.9%	0.0%	10.2%	0.0%	17.2%	8.4%	66.9%
Champaign-Urbana, IL	15,234	24.6%	11.4%	2.3%	0.4%	10.7%	0.0%	33.9%	16.7%	22.8%
Charleston, WV	10,615	17.4%	9.6%	3.8%	1.5%	34.6%	0.7%	23.5%	8.8%	49.3%
Charleston-North Charleston, SC	45,552	25.4%	11.3%	3.0%	3.0%	11.4%	3.4%	27.0%	15.6%	41.9%
Charlotte-Concord-Gastonia, NC-SC	124,112	26.6%	13.9%	4.1%	3.6%	12.7%	1.1%	24.5%	13.5%	52.3%
Charlottesville, VA	12,958	21.8%	16.5%	1.7%	0.4%	9.3%	4.7%	23.1%	22.5%	32.0%
Chattanooga, TN-GA	25,536	36.0%	14.3%	1.0%	3.4%	16.6%	1.6%	15.7%	11.3%	43.1%
Cheyenne, WY	4,172	41.6%	10.5%	5.5%	0.0%	17.4%	0.0%	9.7%	15.3%	22.5%
Chicago-Naperville-Elgin, IL-IN-WI	488,363	23.8%	14.4%	3.1%	2.2%	12.2%	2.0%	27.1%	15.2%	62.4%
Chico, CA	11,274	28.4%	8.0%	4.3%	0.2%	6.2%	0.5%	25.8%	26.6%	35.8%
Cincinnati, OH-KY-IN	117,038	26.6%	11.3%	3.9%	1.2%	17.3%	0.4%	27.2%	12.3%	51.6%

Table D-4: Metropolitan/Micropolitan Statistical Areas—Household Relationship—*Continued*

		18 to 24								
		Married Couple Households		Male, No Spouse Present		Female, No Spouse Present		Non-Family Householders		
	Total Householders	With Children	No Children	With Children	No Children	With Children	No Children	Living Alone	Not Alone	Living With Parents
Clarksburg, WV	1,249	8.7%	3.0%	0.0%	0.0%	0.0%	19.3%	40.0%	29.0%	48.6%
Clarksville, TN-KY	10,022	20.1%	32.7%	0.0%	2.0%	11.6%	0.0%	13.0%	20.5%	26.6%
Cleveland, TN	2,527	4.8%	19.3%	0.0%	10.7%	16.0%	15.0%	16.8%	17.4%	50.1%
Cleveland-Elyria, OH	28,083	5.1%	4.1%	4.9%	3.6%	20.9%	3.1%	31.6%	26.7%	59.3%
Coeur d'Alene, ID	1,646	9.0%	0.0%	0.0%	0.0%	23.0%	0.0%	64.4%	3.6%	60.0%
College Station-Bryan, TX	14,593	2.9%	4.4%	0.0%	4.9%	4.1%	0.6%	34.7%	48.3%	15.4%
Colorado Springs, CO	13,715	14.3%	14.4%	0.0%	2.3%	11.8%	1.7%	21.2%	34.3%	42.5%
Columbia, MO	9,430	5.3%	5.2%	0.2%	0.0%	0.0%	0.4%	41.2%	47.8%	18.3%
Columbia, SC	12,883	8.4%	4.8%	1.7%	4.6%	9.5%	6.1%	26.4%	38.5%	44.4%
Columbus, GA-AL	4,764	13.3%	10.4%	4.5%	3.9%	15.6%	3.0%	18.3%	31.0%	42.1%
Columbus, IN	1,468	26.8%	13.6%	0.0%	27.2%	0.0%	0.0%	19.1%	13.3%	59.1%
Columbus, OH	34,698	5.9%	8.6%	3.4%	3.7%	18.0%	1.9%	30.9%	27.5%	41.6%
Concord, NH	1,115	0.0%	0.0%	0.0%	0.0%	43.5%	0.0%	17.0%	39.5%	52.3%
Cookeville, TN	3,459	11.1%	14.3%	0.0%	8.2%	3.2%	11.2%	22.0%	30.1%	20.1%
Corpus Christi, TX	7,591	8.9%	8.7%	13.1%	4.4%	15.5%	3.4%	28.9%	17.1%	49.1%
Corvallis, OR	4,731	9.0%	3.0%	0.0%	5.3%	7.0%	0.0%	24.4%	51.4%	20.2%
Crestview-Fort Walton Beach-Destin, FL	5,239	16.9%	13.7%	1.2%	2.7%	12.0%	0.0%	28.3%	25.2%	43.9%
Cumberland, MD-WV	1,132	17.6%	0.0%	1.0%	0.0%	8.4%	0.0%	18.4%	54.7%	48.2%
Dallas-Fort Worth-Arlington, TX	102,445	9.0%	7.1%	4.4%	6.2%	15.3%	5.8%	28.1%	24.1%	57.0%
Dalton, GA	3,026	14.9%	7.8%	8.6%	14.0%	32.6%	0.0%	15.9%	6.4%	47.9%
Danville, IL	1,192	3.9%	8.5%	7.0%	0.0%	54.4%	0.0%	13.7%	12.4%	50.4%
Danville, VA	1,585	8.1%	12.9%	4.1%	11.8%	22.0%	0.0%	24.6%	16.5%	49.1%
Daphne-Fairhope-Foley, AL	1,708	8.2%	9.0%	8.0%	0.0%	0.0%	8.5%	8.3%	58.0%	55.0%
Davenport-Moline-Rock Island, IA-IL	4,313	6.3%	0.8%	9.7%	0.9%	13.8%	2.8%	22.3%	43.5%	49.5%
Dayton, OH	16,382	3.9%	6.2%	1.7%	6.1%	18.0%	2.1%	29.8%	32.2%	35.0%
Decatur, AL	1,321	15.1%	39.7%	0.0%	17.3%	6.0%	0.0%	10.1%	11.9%	69.4%
Decatur, IL	1,979	0.0%	0.0%	0.0%	0.0%	31.7%	0.0%	53.0%	15.3%	45.9%
Deltona-Daytona Beach-Ormond Beach, FL	6,934	1.7%	8.2%	0.9%	19.5%	8.3%	9.0%	23.6%	28.7%	53.5%
Denver-Aurora-Lakewood, CO	40,513	6.7%	9.5%	0.5%	5.8%	10.0%	5.4%	23.7%	38.6%	50.6%
Des Moines-West Des Moines, IA	10,822	10.0%	12.6%	2.7%	0.0%	14.3%	1.5%	19.0%	40.0%	41.9%
Detroit-Warren-Dearborn, MI	46,357	4.2%	5.2%	6.8%	9.7%	15.8%	3.9%	33.3%	21.2%	65.9%
Dothan, AL	2,450	0.4%	4.4%	3.7%	0.6%	25.6%	4.2%	27.9%	33.2%	46.8%
Dover, DE	2,729	1.7%	13.7%	0.0%	10.9%	13.0%	8.7%	20.7%	31.3%	39.4%
Dubuque, IA	1,703	24.8%	4.9%	6.2%	0.0%	6.5%	0.0%	33.9%	23.6%	41.9%
Duluth, MN-WI	5,964	6.2%	2.4%	0.0%	0.0%	9.9%	0.0%	23.1%	58.4%	31.0%
Dunn, NC	2,047	22.8%	10.2%	4.3%	3.9%	9.0%	0.0%	37.5%	12.3%	47.0%
Durham-Chapel Hill, NC	13,208	0.8%	2.9%	0.3%	3.2%	8.1%	3.4%	31.3%	50.1%	28.6%
East Stroudsburg, PA	603	0.0%	22.9%	0.0%	0.0%	0.0%	0.0%	37.6%	39.5%	71.4%
Eau Claire, WI	4,981	0.0%	15.8%	2.9%	0.0%	13.2%	0.0%	38.5%	29.7%	39.7%
El Centro, CA	423	29.1%	15.1%	0.0%	0.0%	46.1%	0.0%	0.0%	9.7%	72.6%
El Paso, TX	2,886	18.5%	18.6%	9.3%	15.8%	4.9%	0.0%	21.2%	11.7%	44.4%
Elizabethtown-Fort Knox, KY	4,845	6.1%	20.8%	0.9%	19.8%	26.8%	0.0%	8.6%	17.1%	55.5%
Elkhart-Goshen, IN	1,259	8.3%	31.7%	0.0%	0.0%	22.8%	4.4%	20.9%	11.9%	53.6%
Elmira, NY	11,284	24.4%	20.5%	3.7%	7.7%	7.9%	2.2%	26.7%	7.0%	63.5%
Erie, PA	4,519	8.7%	2.5%	0.0%	0.0%	34.1%	4.4%	15.4%	34.8%	42.7%
Eugene, OR	10,481	2.5%	4.8%	1.7%	0.6%	1.7%	4.8%	31.6%	52.3%	29.0%
Eureka-Arcata-Fortuna, CA	4,146	3.7%	1.8%	3.7%	0.8%	1.1%	0.0%	30.7%	58.2%	28.0%
Evansville, IN-KY	5,920	11.7%	5.9%	3.4%	0.0%	22.8%	0.0%	42.6%	13.5%	43.0%
Fairbanks, AK	2,675	26.2%	24.2%	0.0%	11.7%	11.6%	0.0%	26.2%	0.0%	32.7%
Fargo, ND-MN	11,405	5.1%	5.4%	13.1%	2.8%	12.5%	1.7%	22.0%	37.4%	21.9%
Farmington, NM	2,077	34.0%	6.6%	1.2%	0.0%	16.8%	16.8%	4.0%	20.6%	54.4%
Fayetteville, NC	8,445	20.3%	25.2%	3.5%	2.9%	13.4%	5.2%	21.5%	8.0%	40.6%
Fayetteville-Springdale-Rogers, AR-MO.	14,078	8.2%	11.4%	4.9%	4.9%	6.2%	1.7%	25.6%	37.1%	38.3%
Flagstaff, AZ	4,479	0.0%	5.8%	0.0%	0.0%	0.8%	0.0%	29.3%	64.1%	18.1%
Flint, MI	5,806	23.1%	7.7%	9.9%	0.0%	15.6%	13.4%	19.9%	10.3%	63.8%
Florence, SC	2,447	3.6%	3.0%	8.5%	0.0%	30.3%	2.3%	32.2%	20.0%	54.7%
Florence-Muscle Shoals, AL	2,907	12.7%	17.8%	1.4%	0.0%	17.3%	0.0%	12.7%	37.9%	30.8%
Fond du Lac, WI	701	0.0%	31.1%	20.0%	0.0%	11.1%	0.0%	6.7%	31.1%	71.0%
Fort Collins, CO	10,859	0.0%	7.5%	1.4%	4.3%	3.1%	1.1%	13.8%	68.7%	24.2%
Fort Smith, AR-OK	3,569	13.1%	3.2%	0.0%	11.6%	28.5%	11.9%	18.4%	13.4%	52.8%
Fort Wayne, IN	7,718	6.9%	10.2%	3.6%	1.3%	16.5%	5.3%	21.4%	35.0%	50.6%
Fresno, CA	12,625	11.7%	7.7%	1.4%	10.9%	17.1%	4.9%	10.9%	35.3%	57.9%
Gadsden, AL	1,202	0.0%	15.9%	0.0%	5.2%	38.5%	0.0%	22.5%	17.9%	57.3%
Gainesville, FL	10,148	3.3%	1.9%	0.0%	0.5%	0.3%	4.8%	36.8%	52.4%	24.9%
Gainesville, GA	2,436	20.6%	12.8%	0.0%	1.5%	9.0%	0.0%	21.2%	34.9%	58.7%
Gettysburg, PA	752	20.3%	0.0%	22.5%	0.0%	0.0%	0.0%	23.7%	33.5%	54.1%
Glens Falls, NY	892	4.4%	4.7%	0.0%	6.8%	56.1%	0.0%	3.6%	24.4%	63.2%
Goldsboro, NC	1,760	6.3%	18.8%	0.0%	0.0%	2.6%	0.0%	37.8%	34.5%	47.9%
Grand Forks, ND-MN	5,625	4.2%	19.5%	1.6%	5.2%	2.5%	2.9%	16.9%	47.3%	22.5%
Grand Island, NE	2,256	41.4%	10.8%	0.0%	1.8%	16.5%	0.0%	10.7%	18.8%	39.8%
Grand Junction, CO	2,521	0.0%	7.8%	0.0%	11.8%	6.5%	3.1%	26.5%	44.2%	37.5%
Grand Rapids-Wyoming, MI	16,160	5.3%	7.2%	0.0%	6.4%	13.4%	2.3%	18.1%	47.4%	45.5%
Grants Pass, OR	1,167	50.5%	0.0%	0.0%	0.0%	5.3%	0.0%	9.9%	34.4%	49.1%
Great Falls, MT	1,363	10.8%	0.0%	0.0%	0.0%	14.6%	11.4%	19.7%	43.4%	38.0%
Greeley, CO	4,877	11.7%	8.0%	4.7%	4.8%	13.3%	0.0%	22.7%	34.9%	40.6%

Table D-4: Metropolitan/Micropolitan Statistical Areas—Household Relationship—*Continued*

	Total Householders	Married Couple Households		Male, No Spouse Present		Female, No Spouse Present		Non-Family Householders		Living With Parents
		With Children	No Children	With Children	No Children	With Children	No Children	Living Alone	Not Alone	
Clarksburg, WV	4,056	42.6%	13.0%	0.7%	0.0%	19.7%	0.0%	3.9%	20.2%	48.6%
Clarksville, TN-KY	24,118	37.9%	12.7%	3.0%	3.3%	10.2%	0.1%	27.6%	5.2%	26.6%
Cleveland, TN	3,917	39.4%	18.0%	2.0%	0.0%	17.6%	0.0%	9.8%	13.1%	50.1%
Cleveland-Elyria, OH	102,274	22.5%	14.6%	2.3%	2.7%	18.5%	1.8%	26.9%	10.7%	59.3%
Coeur d'Alene, ID	7,747	30.5%	11.3%	6.6%	0.0%	20.0%	0.0%	6.3%	25.3%	60.0%
College Station-Bryan, TX	16,508	13.8%	17.0%	2.2%	2.1%	12.3%	1.9%	26.9%	23.7%	15.4%
Colorado Springs, CO	46,148	33.3%	12.9%	3.8%	2.2%	13.6%	1.3%	21.6%	11.3%	42.5%
Columbia, MO	13,066	31.4%	14.9%	1.0%	0.0%	5.1%	0.0%	33.2%	14.4%	18.3%
Columbia, SC	42,488	23.2%	14.9%	2.9%	1.8%	18.7%	2.0%	25.2%	11.4%	44.4%
Columbus, GA-AL	19,038	26.1%	9.3%	4.2%	1.2%	20.5%	0.7%	31.2%	6.9%	42.1%
Columbus, IN	4,503	24.9%	21.1%	1.6%	0.9%	16.8%	0.3%	13.7%	20.7%	59.1%
Columbus, OH	129,733	26.0%	15.0%	1.7%	1.5%	13.3%	2.2%	24.5%	15.8%	41.6%
Concord, NH	4,027	31.8%	3.9%	2.4%	0.0%	11.5%	2.4%	30.8%	17.3%	52.3%
Cookeville, TN	5,412	24.3%	14.8%	1.6%	0.0%	15.4%	4.3%	19.5%	20.1%	20.1%
Corpus Christi, TX	24,047	27.6%	6.8%	5.9%	4.0%	23.1%	1.1%	22.2%	9.2%	49.1%
Corvallis, OR	6,481	29.9%	9.7%	2.5%	2.8%	17.9%	0.2%	20.8%	16.2%	20.2%
Crestview-Fort Walton Beach-Destin, FL	16,360	28.5%	16.6%	7.6%	2.1%	11.3%	0.0%	24.1%	10.0%	43.9%
Cumberland, MD-WV	4,337	21.1%	18.1%	14.3%	0.9%	21.1%	0.0%	14.3%	10.3%	48.2%
Dallas-Fort Worth-Arlington, TX	384,660	31.2%	13.2%	3.9%	3.0%	14.4%	1.6%	22.7%	10.0%	57.0%
Dalton, GA	6,227	36.8%	14.1%	7.8%	0.6%	17.8%	1.2%	10.8%	10.9%	47.9%
Danville, IL	4,510	26.1%	10.8%	7.7%	1.7%	29.0%	0.0%	8.8%	15.8%	50.4%
Danville, VA	4,932	34.8%	4.0%	0.0%	0.0%	32.0%	0.0%	12.9%	16.3%	49.1%
Daphne-Fairhope-Foley, AL	6,287	38.0%	6.7%	8.5%	2.6%	3.4%	1.2%	36.1%	3.5%	55.0%
Davenport-Moline-Rock Island, IA-IL	22,180	26.7%	13.4%	10.0%	0.2%	15.1%	0.0%	25.2%	9.4%	49.5%
Dayton, OH	45,091	26.4%	10.1%	5.8%	2.6%	19.6%	0.2%	21.1%	14.2%	35.0%
Decatur, AL	8,681	32.8%	9.8%	10.2%	1.8%	27.8%	3.6%	10.8%	3.3%	69.4%
Decatur, IL	4,874	25.3%	3.6%	13.3%	1.7%	22.2%	1.0%	27.4%	5.5%	45.9%
Deltona-Daytona Beach-Ormond Beach, FL	22,502	25.1%	11.5%	1.2%	2.4%	13.3%	1.2%	23.1%	22.2%	53.5%
Denver-Aurora-Lakewood, CO	175,016	25.3%	15.8%	3.0%	2.7%	7.7%	1.1%	24.2%	20.4%	50.6%
Des Moines-West Des Moines, IA	40,325	28.1%	16.7%	2.2%	2.2%	10.8%	0.4%	28.0%	11.6%	41.9%
Detroit-Warren-Dearborn, MI	197,645	22.9%	12.0%	4.6%	2.1%	16.1%	0.9%	26.8%	14.6%	65.9%
Dothan, AL	5,462	36.4%	9.0%	3.9%	1.9%	29.0%	0.2%	14.8%	4.8%	46.8%
Dover, DE	8,713	29.3%	6.3%	0.6%	1.5%	31.5%	3.0%	14.8%	12.9%	39.4%
Dubuque, IA	5,577	41.1%	5.4%	2.9%	1.1%	15.3%	0.0%	26.7%	7.5%	41.9%
Duluth, MN-WI	15,224	29.7%	15.5%	3.4%	1.3%	15.0%	2.3%	16.7%	16.1%	31.0%
Dunn, NC	7,168	38.2%	17.5%	1.4%	1.3%	20.9%	0.8%	17.5%	2.5%	47.0%
Durham-Chapel Hill, NC	33,310	19.7%	17.5%	1.8%	1.1%	12.5%	0.3%	28.6%	18.5%	28.6%
East Stroudsburg, PA	4,582	51.0%	17.2%	0.0%	0.0%	6.8%	0.0%	11.1%	13.9%	71.4%
Eau Claire, WI	8,074	27.8%	10.6%	6.7%	2.4%	2.2%	0.0%	35.5%	14.7%	39.7%
El Centro, CA	5,571	49.3%	11.8%	8.7%	0.5%	12.3%	1.2%	11.8%	4.3%	72.6%
El Paso, TX	7,711	40.1%	16.4%	2.0%	3.3%	19.3%	0.0%	8.8%	9.3%	44.4%
Elizabethtown-Fort Knox, KY	7,882	44.1%	5.9%	17.5%	0.0%	9.2%	0.0%	12.4%	10.9%	55.5%
Elkhart-Goshen, IN	4,043	28.6%	12.4%	9.1%	0.0%	11.3%	1.5%	25.1%	12.2%	53.6%
Elmira, NY	41,288	33.8%	11.0%	9.5%	4.5%	15.4%	3.2%	18.3%	4.3%	63.5%
Erie, PA	12,900	19.4%	5.1%	2.9%	2.3%	25.5%	0.0%	25.5%	19.3%	42.7%
Eugene, OR	18,216	22.9%	11.2%	6.4%	3.7%	9.6%	1.4%	26.2%	18.6%	29.0%
Eureka-Arcata-Fortuna, CA	6,639	26.6%	5.3%	0.6%	2.1%	8.7%	1.5%	22.2%	33.0%	28.0%
Evansville, IN-KY	17,600	37.2%	13.3%	6.7%	0.3%	12.0%	0.0%	24.0%	6.5%	43.0%
Fairbanks, AK	8,638	25.9%	9.2%	10.5%	0.0%	15.5%	2.6%	30.2%	6.2%	32.7%
Fargo, ND-MN	17,581	31.1%	11.5%	3.4%	2.0%	4.1%	0.0%	30.4%	17.5%	21.9%
Farmington, NM	5,393	40.3%	12.1%	12.9%	0.0%	9.2%	3.5%	13.9%	8.1%	54.4%
Fayetteville, NC	26,065	24.0%	11.6%	5.4%	0.4%	23.1%	2.1%	24.6%	8.8%	40.6%
Fayetteville-Springdale-Rogers, AR-MO	31,638	36.1%	18.4%	4.1%	0.0%	13.3%	1.7%	16.9%	9.6%	38.3%
Flagstaff, AZ	6,242	29.5%	6.6%	1.7%	3.3%	14.8%	5.2%	12.9%	26.0%	18.1%
Flint, MI	16,826	25.1%	8.1%	8.6%	5.8%	17.9%	1.8%	17.2%	15.5%	63.8%
Florence, SC	8,964	39.5%	5.0%	0.4%	0.3%	23.7%	0.5%	19.2%	11.2%	54.7%
Florence-Muscle Shoals, AL	5,690	23.8%	16.7%	0.0%	0.0%	23.4%	0.0%	31.7%	4.4%	30.8%
Fond du Lac, WI	4,512	26.0%	18.1%	0.8%	0.0%	25.8%	0.0%	20.7%	8.6%	71.0%
Fort Collins, CO	19,256	18.4%	14.7%	2.0%	1.5%	11.4%	2.6%	18.2%	31.2%	24.2%
Fort Smith, AR-OK	15,134	39.7%	10.2%	3.2%	3.5%	15.3%	0.2%	14.3%	13.6%	52.8%
Fort Wayne, IN	25,155	30.4%	13.1%	9.3%	2.8%	17.4%	0.4%	17.8%	8.8%	50.6%
Fresno, CA	42,747	30.4%	7.2%	11.1%	2.9%	21.8%	3.8%	15.1%	7.7%	57.9%
Gadsden, AL	3,813	30.8%	13.6%	10.1%	1.2%	24.2%	4.1%	13.7%	2.3%	57.3%
Gainesville, FL	16,685	21.8%	17.1%	0.9%	3.8%	11.9%	1.6%	22.6%	20.4%	24.9%
Gainesville, GA	7,815	41.0%	18.2%	1.3%	2.7%	14.3%	0.8%	14.5%	7.1%	58.7%
Gettysburg, PA	4,266	42.0%	11.5%	4.9%	0.0%	11.0%	0.0%	27.6%	3.0%	54.1%
Glens Falls, NY	4,271	33.4%	14.9%	7.2%	0.0%	18.1%	0.0%	7.1%	19.3%	63.2%
Goldsboro, NC	6,350	35.4%	10.4%	4.5%	0.0%	13.0%	0.0%	22.8%	13.7%	47.9%
Grand Forks, ND-MN	7,802	40.9%	5.3%	10.7%	4.7%	10.3%	2.0%	16.9%	9.3%	22.5%
Grand Island, NE	4,923	31.6%	13.3%	3.5%	0.0%	23.9%	0.0%	14.1%	13.6%	39.8%
Grand Junction, CO	8,468	34.7%	20.4%	1.1%	0.0%	11.9%	0.0%	21.9%	10.0%	37.5%
Grand Rapids-Wyoming, MI	57,072	30.6%	15.5%	3.7%	0.8%	13.2%	2.3%	17.8%	16.1%	45.5%
Grants Pass, OR	2,691	44.2%	16.3%	0.3%	0.0%	25.3%	0.0%	0.0%	14.0%	49.1%
Great Falls, MT	4,303	36.6%	9.0%	0.6%	0.8%	14.5%	0.0%	27.7%	10.8%	38.0%
Greeley, CO	16,564	47.7%	10.0%	1.7%	1.8%	11.3%	1.4%	16.9%	9.2%	40.6%

Table D-4: Metropolitan/Micropolitan Statistical Areas—Household Relationship—*Continued*

	Total Householders	Married Couple Households		Male, No Spouse Present		Female, No Spouse Present		Non-Family Householders		Living With Parents
		With Children	No Children	With Children	No Children	With Children	No Children	Living Alone	Not Alone	
					18 to 24					
Green Bay, WI	4,365	13.9%	3.3%	9.0%	1.3%	2.0%	7.2%	23.2%	40.2%	47.4%
Greensboro-High Point, NC	7,896	7.5%	13.1%	3.0%	0.0%	8.0%	2.6%	27.6%	38.2%	53.1%
Greenville, NC	7,747	0.0%	0.0%	0.0%	4.4%	1.3%	0.0%	34.3%	60.0%	17.9%
Greenville-Anderson-Mauldin, SC	13,834	9.9%	10.7%	2.4%	3.4%	20.7%	1.1%	23.3%	28.4%	46.6%
Greenwood, SC	1,552	0.0%	13.8%	18.6%	0.0%	22.2%	0.0%	19.4%	26.0%	52.1%
Gulfport-Biloxi-Pascagoula, MS	5,009	9.0%	17.2%	2.0%	13.5%	13.6%	0.0%	25.9%	18.8%	54.3%
Hagerstown-Martinsburg, MD-WV	3,933	5.8%	10.9%	0.0%	0.0%	30.7%	0.0%	25.0%	27.7%	51.1%
Hammond, LA	2,747	0.0%	2.8%	0.0%	0.0%	17.2%	9.5%	42.9%	27.7%	38.5%
Hanford-Corcoran, CA	1,847	19.2%	20.0%	10.9%	0.0%	21.3%	14.7%	0.7%	13.2%	48.9%
Harrisburg-Carlisle, PA	7,325	11.8%	4.7%	3.7%	7.4%	22.2%	0.0%	22.2%	28.1%	51.8%
Harrisonburg, VA	5,016	1.9%	4.1%	4.4%	3.5%	9.9%	0.0%	17.7%	58.5%	15.9%
Hartford-West Hartford-East Hartford, CT	11,822	4.6%	5.4%	8.1%	6.4%	9.9%	2.1%	30.1%	33.4%	53.2%
Hattiesburg, MS	2,284	3.0%	4.5%	0.0%	0.0%	14.5%	1.4%	47.3%	29.3%	43.5%
Hickory-Lenoir-Morganton, NC	2,794	5.4%	7.0%	3.5%	6.3%	14.3%	0.0%	33.7%	29.7%	59.3%
Hilo, HI	1,958	1.1%	0.0%	5.4%	7.2%	4.0%	0.0%	11.3%	71.1%	49.2%
Hilton Head Island-Bluffton-Beaufort, SC	2,040	12.5%	23.6%	0.0%	2.6%	6.3%	10.5%	11.7%	32.6%	40.8%
Hinesville, GA	2,984	34.9%	22.4%	0.0%	3.7%	8.5%	0.0%	21.4%	9.2%	46.5%
Holland, MI	1,367	10.5%	6.9%	1.6%	0.0%	24.6%	0.0%	10.8%	45.6%	52.7%
Homosassa Springs, FL	978	0.0%	2.6%	0.0%	8.7%	19.6%	0.0%	37.2%	31.9%	44.5%
Hot Springs, AR	184	0.0%	0.0%	0.0%	0.0%	0.0%	0.0%	0.0%	100.0%	44.5%
Houma-Thibodaux, LA	4,075	8.5%	2.9%	0.0%	15.5%	8.2%	0.0%	36.0%	28.8%	49.3%
Houston-The Woodlands-Sugar Land, TX	82,279	11.8%	6.4%	4.8%	6.6%	14.3%	5.0%	32.0%	19.0%	62.1%
Huntington-Ashland, WV-KY-OH	4,073	7.0%	8.7%	0.0%	0.0%	19.8%	0.0%	31.4%	33.1%	54.8%
Huntsville, AL	5,578	9.1%	0.2%	0.8%	8.0%	16.2%	3.7%	36.6%	25.4%	47.4%
Idaho Falls, ID	1,845	16.3%	20.8%	0.0%	0.0%	15.0%	0.0%	32.7%	15.1%	39.9%
Indianapolis-Carmel-Anderson, IN	30,670	7.2%	6.4%	1.9%	5.1%	17.1%	3.1%	31.3%	27.9%	55.0%
Iowa City, IA	9,037	1.3%	7.9%	1.6%	0.0%	1.2%	0.0%	29.3%	58.8%	11.4%
Ithaca, NY	4,999	0.0%	0.0%	2.0%	0.0%	1.7%	0.0%	37.6%	58.7%	10.0%
Jackson, MI	1,770	3.7%	10.2%	0.0%	0.0%	37.7%	0.0%	2.0%	46.4%	49.0%
Jackson, MS	7,113	12.9%	3.5%	2.8%	2.5%	24.9%	2.0%	28.7%	22.6%	55.9%
Jackson, TN	2,917	8.2%	6.7%	0.0%	15.9%	18.2%	0.0%	26.5%	24.6%	40.6%
Jacksonville, FL	21,321	7.5%	12.8%	2.6%	1.7%	19.2%	5.6%	19.6%	31.0%	50.2%
Jacksonville, NC	8,892	21.8%	35.3%	0.0%	1.7%	10.9%	0.0%	13.8%	16.5%	24.3%
Jamestown-Dunkirk-Fredonia, NY	1,972	0.0%	0.0%	0.0%	6.9%	14.5%	0.0%	51.3%	27.4%	47.7%
Janesville-Beloit, WI	2,463	0.0%	1.8%	12.1%	0.0%	34.3%	0.0%	35.4%	16.4%	48.6%
Jefferson City, MO	1,617	10.3%	15.2%	0.0%	24.4%	9.4%	0.0%	1.4%	39.3%	53.3%
Johnson City, TN	4,564	3.9%	4.3%	0.0%	2.3%	26.1%	0.0%	23.6%	39.9%	39.2%
Johnstown, PA	826	26.2%	16.5%	0.0%	6.8%	11.0%	0.0%	30.3%	9.3%	46.7%
Jonesboro, AR	3,777	8.2%	9.7%	6.6%	8.2%	13.2%	0.0%	44.1%	10.0%	37.0%
Joplin, MO	3,592	20.4%	6.3%	14.0%	0.0%	18.0%	0.0%	26.2%	15.1%	46.6%
Kahului-Wailuku-Lahaina, HI	833	0.0%	3.6%	0.0%	6.7%	0.0%	57.3%	0.0%	32.4%	58.5%
Kalamazoo-Portage, MI	9,379	3.9%	5.3%	4.3%	4.4%	6.7%	5.5%	33.6%	36.3%	37.2%
Kalispell, MT	504	0.0%	31.9%	0.0%	0.0%	44.2%	0.0%	23.8%	0.0%	59.4%
Kankakee, IL	1,173	3.7%	15.3%	6.8%	0.0%	32.8%	0.0%	34.4%	7.0%	53.7%
Kansas City, MO-KS	34,238	5.7%	10.4%	3.0%	3.1%	11.0%	2.2%	37.3%	27.2%	52.8%
Kennewick-Richland, WA	4,152	12.6%	12.0%	28.8%	3.6%	8.5%	0.0%	5.8%	28.6%	50.5%
Killeen-Temple, TX	12,982	21.1%	17.9%	4.8%	2.6%	12.4%	4.8%	16.0%	20.4%	32.5%
Kingsport-Bristol-Bristol, TN-VA	2,560	14.0%	12.1%	19.8%	0.0%	12.7%	0.0%	25.4%	15.9%	58.9%
Kingston, NY	1,880	0.0%	17.1%	0.0%	0.0%	4.9%	0.0%	36.0%	41.9%	56.0%
Knoxville, TN	15,531	9.0%	17.9%	0.7%	3.4%	17.8%	1.7%	22.0%	27.5%	45.2%
Kokomo, IN	905	13.6%	29.9%	0.0%	0.0%	46.0%	0.0%	10.5%	0.0%	51.1%
La Crosse-Onalaska, WI-MN	4,422	0.5%	4.6%	0.0%	4.7%	0.0%	0.0%	15.4%	74.7%	16.8%
Lafayette, LA	6,633	9.1%	3.5%	0.8%	0.0%	20.4%	0.0%	29.7%	36.5%	52.6%
Lafayette-West Lafayette, IN	11,596	2.9%	1.7%	4.1%	0.0%	5.0%	6.7%	31.5%	48.1%	18.4%
Lake Charles, LA	3,612	16.9%	1.5%	5.4%	9.3%	22.3%	8.0%	15.9%	20.8%	39.8%
Lake Havasu City-Kingman, AZ	1,898	6.7%	6.4%	9.6%	0.0%	0.0%	1.9%	37.5%	37.8%	54.1%
Lakeland-Winter Haven, FL	4,290	8.5%	5.4%	6.0%	7.3%	16.2%	3.8%	19.7%	33.0%	62.1%
Lancaster, PA	6,255	6.3%	31.6%	0.0%	1.0%	9.2%	3.9%	21.2%	26.7%	51.9%
Lansing-East Lansing, MI	12,921	0.9%	5.1%	0.0%	5.0%	3.8%	2.1%	37.0%	46.1%	29.4%
Laredo, TX	2,288	17.0%	2.8%	11.8%	0.0%	28.7%	1.6%	20.7%	17.4%	70.8%
Las Cruces, NM	5,541	8.4%	0.0%	0.0%	14.8%	31.2%	4.8%	17.3%	23.5%	45.4%
Las Vegas-Henderson-Paradise, NV	23,057	4.6%	5.3%	4.1%	8.1%	14.2%	8.5%	29.4%	25.8%	59.2%
Lawrence, KS	5,747	0.0%	0.0%	0.0%	0.0%	0.0%	7.8%	30.4%	61.8%	11.1%
Lawton, OK	2,178	38.0%	27.7%	0.0%	0.0%	5.9%	0.0%	20.8%	7.7%	32.8%
Lebanon, PA	2,350	12.6%	8.4%	3.2%	17.3%	10.2%	0.0%	0.0%	48.3%	46.2%
Lewiston, ID-WA	1,498	3.8%	0.3%	4.0%	0.0%	1.5%	0.0%	53.9%	36.5%	29.8%
Lewiston-Auburn, ME	1,754	13.4%	8.4%	4.4%	0.0%	11.0%	0.0%	26.3%	36.4%	21.8%
Lexington-Fayette, KY	11,315	4.6%	16.7%	2.3%	2.7%	7.1%	0.6%	25.4%	40.5%	40.1%
Lima, OH	1,970	3.8%	8.4%	0.0%	0.0%	27.3%	0.0%	43.4%	17.2%	43.2%
Lincoln, NE	13,343	4.7%	0.0%	5.0%	4.7%	8.0%	2.0%	37.7%	37.9%	23.9%
Little Rock-North Little Rock-Conway, AR	14,348	9.3%	7.2%	3.9%	4.0%	18.8%	0.6%	33.0%	23.2%	42.7%

Table D-4: Metropolitan/Micropolitan Statistical Areas—Household Relationship—*Continued*

	Total Householders	25 to 33									
		Married Couple Households		Male, No Spouse Present		Female, No Spouse Present		Non-Family Householders		Living With Parents
		With Children	No Children	With Children	No Children	With Children	No Children	Living Alone	Not Alone	
Green Bay, WI	20,346	32.9%	7.1%	4.4%	0.6%	20.8%	1.3%	20.1%	12.7%	47.4%
Greensboro-High Point, NC	36,257	26.3%	12.4%	6.5%	1.8%	21.2%	0.2%	20.0%	11.4%	53.1%
Greenville, NC	12,207	21.1%	11.4%	4.8%	0.0%	21.7%	2.5%	24.0%	14.5%	17.9%
Greenville-Anderson-Mauldin, SC	43,744	31.6%	14.1%	2.9%	2.5%	15.3%	0.7%	21.8%	11.0%	46.6%
Greenwood, SC	2,560	25.6%	4.6%	0.0%	4.9%	38.5%	0.0%	16.5%	9.8%	52.1%
Gulfport-Biloxi-Pascagoula, MS	20,852	31.1%	12.1%	4.3%	2.1%	22.9%	0.9%	11.7%	15.0%	54.3%
Hagerstown-Martinsburg, MD-WV	9,757	27.5%	9.6%	8.5%	3.3%	19.6%	0.0%	20.9%	10.7%	51.1%
Hammond, LA	6,576	33.3%	13.2%	0.8%	0.0%	18.3%	0.0%	30.5%	3.9%	38.5%
Hanford-Corcoran, CA	9,542	35.7%	14.1%	6.9%	0.0%	15.0%	2.7%	9.3%	16.2%	48.9%
Harrisburg-Carlisle, PA	26,980	27.9%	15.2%	4.5%	0.8%	13.7%	1.0%	21.1%	15.7%	51.8%
Harrisonburg, VA	6,088	37.2%	19.8%	3.4%	1.3%	0.6%	4.0%	21.8%	11.9%	15.9%
Hartford-West Hartford-East Hartford, CT	51,587	20.8%	16.9%	1.5%	2.3%	18.1%	1.2%	22.4%	16.9%	53.2%
Hattiesburg, MS	7,472	23.6%	10.6%	16.1%	1.2%	29.3%	1.1%	11.3%	6.9%	43.5%
Hickory-Lenoir-Morganton, NC	14,468	43.9%	8.2%	3.6%	0.0%	11.0%	0.0%	24.7%	8.7%	59.3%
Hilo, HI	5,408	39.5%	12.5%	0.0%	0.0%	21.0%	5.5%	11.6%	9.9%	49.2%
Hilton Head Island-Bluffton-Beaufort, SC	8,432	31.5%	13.3%	5.0%	3.0%	14.3%	2.7%	15.8%	14.3%	40.8%
Hinesville, GA	5,341	44.3%	7.6%	9.0%	0.0%	13.7%	3.1%	18.5%	3.9%	46.5%
Holland, MI	4,970	36.8%	10.9%	3.4%	0.0%	12.9%	0.0%	17.6%	18.3%	52.7%
Homosassa Springs, FL	2,850	47.3%	4.8%	0.0%	2.1%	30.1%	0.0%	12.4%	3.2%	44.5%
Hot Springs, AR	4,168	31.4%	2.3%	14.0%	6.1%	19.2%	3.0%	17.8%	6.2%	44.5%
Houma-Thibodaux, LA	10,933	44.2%	8.5%	5.2%	0.0%	10.6%	2.8%	12.2%	16.5%	49.3%
Houston-The Woodlands-Sugar Land, TX	377,408	30.0%	12.3%	4.8%	3.3%	15.5%	1.6%	23.6%	9.0%	62.1%
Huntington-Ashland, WV-KY-OH	13,834	29.0%	13.0%	5.9%	1.6%	21.2%	4.1%	14.2%	11.0%	54.8%
Huntsville, AL	28,199	31.8%	10.8%	2.4%	0.0%	11.7%	2.3%	26.5%	14.4%	47.4%
Idaho Falls, ID	7,029	61.6%	11.2%	5.6%	0.0%	5.0%	0.0%	9.0%	7.6%	39.9%
Indianapolis-Carmel-Anderson, IN	115,633	28.5%	11.7%	4.2%	1.0%	15.6%	1.0%	27.2%	10.9%	55.0%
Iowa City, IA	12,361	12.5%	25.8%	0.4%	1.4%	14.9%	4.4%	20.8%	19.8%	11.4%
Ithaca, NY	5,471	10.8%	17.8%	5.2%	0.0%	9.2%	1.0%	40.8%	15.3%	10.0%
Jackson, MI	7,207	37.7%	9.0%	11.2%	0.0%	18.5%	1.5%	17.4%	4.7%	49.0%
Jackson, MS	31,082	25.1%	9.4%	2.6%	4.9%	25.1%	1.0%	26.1%	5.8%	55.9%
Jackson, TN	7,411	42.9%	18.9%	0.2%	0.6%	19.8%	0.0%	11.7%	5.9%	40.6%
Jacksonville, FL	70,162	26.2%	14.3%	4.9%	0.8%	15.4%	2.0%	21.7%	14.5%	50.2%
Jacksonville, NC	16,018	40.6%	9.2%	7.2%	0.7%	9.7%	0.0%	25.1%	7.5%	24.3%
Jamestown-Dunkirk-Fredonia, NY	4,787	15.8%	19.1%	5.0%	1.1%	15.4%	0.0%	29.7%	13.9%	47.7%
Janesville-Beloit, WI	7,613	41.3%	6.9%	16.2%	0.0%	11.9%	0.0%	6.8%	16.9%	48.6%
Jefferson City, MO	7,422	35.1%	9.3%	8.5%	0.0%	10.7%	0.0%	30.7%	5.7%	53.3%
Johnson City, TN	9,472	26.6%	10.5%	1.3%	2.6%	19.6%	0.0%	36.9%	2.3%	39.2%
Johnstown, PA	6,234	42.2%	6.3%	2.2%	0.0%	12.4%	0.0%	20.9%	16.0%	46.7%
Jonesboro, AR	5,996	42.3%	8.1%	2.3%	0.0%	27.3%	0.0%	9.0%	11.1%	37.0%
Joplin, MO	8,000	55.8%	8.7%	0.6%	0.0%	14.0%	0.0%	11.8%	9.2%	46.6%
Kahului-Wailuku-Lahaina, HI	6,949	32.7%	24.7%	4.6%	0.0%	21.1%	0.1%	5.0%	11.8%	58.5%
Kalamazoo-Portage, MI	16,125	20.2%	15.5%	7.8%	2.4%	10.2%	2.0%	22.9%	19.0%	37.2%
Kalispell, MT	3,390	46.0%	26.6%	5.6%	0.0%	2.8%	0.0%	6.1%	12.9%	59.4%
Kankakee, IL	5,148	28.1%	11.3%	7.8%	4.2%	30.7%	0.0%	11.7%	6.2%	53.7%
Kansas City, MO-KS	122,337	31.2%	14.0%	5.5%	1.6%	14.1%	1.5%	22.0%	9.4%	52.8%
Kennewick-Richland, WA	18,566	41.8%	9.0%	6.9%	1.8%	16.0%	1.7%	13.5%	9.2%	50.5%
Killeen-Temple, TX	27,258	39.3%	14.1%	4.3%	3.5%	15.7%	0.1%	14.7%	8.3%	32.5%
Kingsport-Bristol-Bristol, TN-VA	12,525	49.1%	9.3%	7.2%	3.5%	16.2%	0.0%	6.2%	8.5%	58.9%
Kingston, NY	5,408	22.2%	19.4%	2.7%	4.2%	5.9%	0.0%	25.6%	20.1%	56.0%
Knoxville, TN	40,259	30.5%	11.9%	2.8%	2.1%	16.9%	1.0%	23.6%	11.2%	45.2%
Kokomo, IN	4,330	45.2%	5.9%	3.3%	1.8%	12.5%	0.0%	25.5%	5.7%	51.1%
La Crosse-Onalaska, WI-MN	6,842	25.5%	8.9%	3.6%	0.5%	0.3%	3.0%	34.8%	23.3%	16.8%
Lafayette, LA	29,601	27.9%	12.6%	5.2%	3.9%	19.7%	0.4%	18.1%	12.2%	52.6%
Lafayette-West Lafayette, IN	11,377	33.2%	9.7%	3.1%	3.4%	8.6%	0.5%	21.9%	19.6%	18.4%
Lake Charles, LA	13,312	24.4%	6.6%	5.1%	0.0%	27.7%	0.0%	29.0%	7.2%	39.8%
Lake Havasu City-Kingman, AZ	7,424	18.4%	0.0%	14.5%	1.4%	36.9%	2.3%	17.1%	9.4%	54.1%
Lakeland-Winter Haven, FL	26,572	32.1%	13.2%	7.6%	1.0%	21.0%	4.8%	12.0%	8.3%	62.1%
Lancaster, PA	25,874	36.4%	14.2%	3.3%	2.0%	15.6%	0.5%	11.6%	16.4%	51.9%
Lansing-East Lansing, MI	27,503	23.2%	14.4%	3.5%	0.3%	13.6%	0.7%	25.7%	18.6%	29.4%
Laredo, TX	9,457	31.5%	22.1%	6.1%	1.6%	16.2%	6.1%	14.5%	1.9%	70.8%
Las Cruces, NM	9,595	30.3%	20.4%	6.3%	3.7%	17.8%	2.3%	10.1%	9.2%	45.4%
Las Vegas-Henderson-Paradise, NV	115,585	19.9%	10.7%	5.3%	4.8%	16.5%	2.2%	26.4%	14.2%	59.2%
Lawrence, KS	6,892	40.0%	13.2%	0.0%	0.0%	2.9%	0.0%	29.8%	14.0%	11.1%
Lawton, OK	7,189	42.0%	0.0%	0.3%	0.7%	16.1%	0.0%	23.2%	17.6%	32.8%
Lebanon, PA	5,536	26.2%	31.4%	4.7%	3.5%	15.7%	1.8%	13.5%	3.3%	46.2%
Lewiston, ID-WA	2,179	44.7%	8.4%	1.1%	0.0%	33.4%	0.4%	3.1%	8.9%	29.8%
Lewiston-Auburn, ME	6,313	38.7%	10.3%	13.1%	0.0%	11.5%	0.0%	18.6%	7.9%	21.8%
Lexington-Fayette, KY	31,033	23.8%	12.3%	4.9%	0.8%	16.4%	0.2%	26.5%	15.1%	40.1%
Lima, OH	4,362	42.6%	3.0%	8.1%	2.2%	18.9%	0.0%	17.8%	7.4%	43.2%
Lincoln, NE	21,420	27.7%	9.7%	2.7%	0.7%	11.5%	1.5%	29.6%	16.6%	23.9%
Little Rock-North Little Rock-Conway, AR	43,219	28.0%	10.2%	5.7%	0.9%	16.3%	3.2%	26.6%	9.1%	42.7%

Table D-4: Metropolitan/Micropolitan Statistical Areas—Household Relationship—*Continued*

		18 to 24								
		Married Couple Households		Male, No Spouse Present		Female, No Spouse Present		Non-Family Householders		
	Total Householders	With Children	No Children	With Children	No Children	With Children	No Children	Living Alone	Not Alone	Living With Parents
Logan, UT-ID	5,456	12.4%	26.6%	0.0%	0.0%	8.8%	0.0%	19.3%	32.9%	34.7%
Longview, TX	3,562	25.7%	0.6%	0.0%	0.0%	12.2%	0.0%	28.0%	33.6%	38.1%
Longview, WA	1,765	18.3%	4.1%	0.0%	21.4%	3.0%	0.0%	0.0%	53.2%	32.8%
Los Angeles-Long Beach-Anaheim, CA..	113,755	4.7%	5.4%	1.9%	11.8%	7.5%	8.5%	24.0%	36.3%	62.5%
Louisville/Jefferson County, KY-IN	15,829	7.1%	7.2%	0.8%	6.7%	16.1%	2.1%	31.3%	28.6%	54.5%
Lubbock, TX	12,225	8.4%	7.0%	3.9%	2.0%	11.6%	2.6%	25.5%	39.2%	25.3%
Lumberton, NC	964	8.1%	3.6%	4.3%	8.2%	15.1%	5.1%	28.2%	27.4%	58.2%
Lynchburg, VA	4,906	3.9%	22.0%	0.0%	0.0%	1.7%	6.3%	25.0%	41.1%	33.2%
Macon, GA	4,069	0.8%	4.7%	0.0%	0.0%	29.7%	0.0%	26.9%	37.9%	46.5%
Madera, CA	2,236	11.9%	11.5%	4.4%	17.8%	26.2%	4.6%	10.7%	13.1%	49.6%
Madison, WI	18,116	0.0%	1.6%	0.0%	2.9%	4.6%	0.8%	32.6%	57.4%	26.0%
Manchester-Nashua, NH	4,680	10.8%	0.6%	0.0%	2.1%	10.3%	0.0%	23.8%	52.4%	60.7%
Manhattan, KS	5,670	17.8%	11.0%	0.0%	0.0%	0.0%	1.4%	24.0%	45.8%	10.6%
Mankato-North Mankato, MN	4,720	0.0%	0.0%	0.0%	0.0%	17.8%	0.7%	21.4%	60.2%	10.6%
Mansfield, OH	1,381	1.7%	17.7%	0.0%	0.0%	11.9%	11.0%	31.1%	26.4%	49.4%
McAllen-Edinburg-Mission, TX	5,513	14.3%	7.7%	2.9%	5.4%	22.5%	24.5%	21.8%	0.9%	76.1%
Medford, OR	2,222	15.7%	5.7%	0.0%	0.0%	12.0%	0.0%	6.8%	59.8%	44.7%
Memphis, TN-MS-AR	19,583	3.7%	7.0%	0.4%	6.4%	25.8%	4.7%	27.2%	24.9%	55.6%
Merced, CA	4,384	5.3%	2.5%	21.7%	20.9%	10.2%	6.3%	21.8%	11.4%	50.2%
Meridian, MS	1,062	0.0%	36.6%	3.6%	0.0%	0.0%	0.0%	59.8%	0.0%	58.0%
Miami-Fort Lauderdale-West Palm Beach, FL	39,333	5.0%	7.1%	3.8%	10.0%	14.3%	7.6%	30.3%	22.0%	66.9%
Michigan City-La Porte, IN	1,842	14.5%	0.0%	0.0%	0.0%	14.3%	0.0%	33.3%	37.8%	47.7%
Midland, MI	872	0.0%	0.0%	0.0%	0.0%	0.0%	0.0%	30.8%	69.2%	58.5%
Midland, TX	3,565	9.8%	26.5%	3.4%	0.0%	16.4%	0.0%	20.4%	23.6%	52.5%
Milwaukee-Waukesha-West Allis, WI	22,223	1.8%	2.3%	2.1%	4.9%	11.8%	2.0%	39.8%	35.2%	51.0%
Minneapolis-St. Paul-Bloomington, MN-WI	46,031	11.2%	6.3%	2.2%	1.5%	11.2%	4.0%	28.8%	34.9%	55.9%
Missoula, MT	3,583	8.9%	3.3%	0.0%	0.0%	26.2%	6.3%	19.3%	36.1%	42.6%
Mobile, AL	5,550	9.1%	4.1%	5.7%	2.6%	23.8%	8.4%	25.5%	20.8%	51.3%
Modesto, CA	4,274	18.3%	5.6%	13.7%	16.0%	4.8%	6.4%	18.2%	17.0%	69.9%
Monroe, LA	3,355	7.6%	1.3%	0.0%	5.0%	13.5%	10.8%	44.3%	17.6%	39.9%
Monroe, MI	1,612	0.0%	14.2%	16.1%	0.0%	3.2%	0.0%	57.4%	9.1%	78.7%
Montgomery, AL	7,003	8.2%	5.1%	10.4%	0.0%	7.7%	0.0%	38.0%	30.6%	41.4%
Morgantown, WV	5,139	2.9%	6.3%	0.0%	0.0%	1.2%	2.0%	59.5%	28.1%	25.6%
Morristown, TN	1,078	25.0%	39.1%	0.0%	22.1%	0.0%	0.0%	0.0%	13.8%	56.3%
Mount Vernon-Anacortes, WA	1,856	13.5%	15.6%	6.4%	0.0%	8.6%	8.0%	15.4%	32.4%	41.9%
Muncie, IN	5,871	5.7%	0.7%	0.0%	1.3%	18.0%	0.0%	26.9%	47.3%	21.7%
Muskegon, MI	1,954	7.5%	0.0%	12.4%	0.0%	19.6%	0.0%	51.3%	9.1%	59.7%
Myrtle Beach-Conway-North Myrtle Beach, SC-NC	4,457	5.1%	9.9%	0.8%	6.5%	15.0%	1.9%	32.7%	28.0%	53.1%
Napa, CA	771	17.4%	0.0%	0.0%	0.0%	0.0%	0.0%	18.8%	63.8%	65.8%
Naples-Immokalee-Marco Island, FL	1,215	11.0%	5.8%	8.6%	5.2%	14.0%	0.0%	33.3%	22.1%	69.8%
Nashville-Davidson–Murfreesboro–Franklin, TN	30,810	4.2%	10.0%	2.4%	6.1%	15.3%	1.3%	33.4%	27.3%	48.6%
New Bern, NC	3,735	16.7%	40.0%	0.0%	0.0%	8.6%	0.0%	27.7%	7.0%	29.6%
New Castle, PA	840	0.0%	0.0%	20.1%	0.0%	0.0%	0.0%	14.2%	65.7%	45.2%
New Haven-Milford, CT	6,275	2.2%	0.8%	7.8%	6.0%	17.3%	8.8%	30.3%	26.7%	56.5%
New Orleans-Metairie, LA	13,385	10.3%	3.8%	8.7%	5.6%	14.0%	2.0%	30.8%	24.9%	62.5%
New Philadelphia-Dover, OH	961	15.8%	16.4%	0.0%	3.0%	3.9%	8.6%	29.2%	23.0%	76.2%
New York-Newark-Jersey City, NY-NJ-PA	136,400	7.5%	5.0%	2.0%	11.4%	10.8%	9.2%	26.7%	27.5%	66.4%
Niles-Benton Harbor, MI	2,091	2.2%	1.4%	0.0%	7.1%	18.1%	9.1%	18.8%	43.3%	45.6%
North Port-Sarasota-Bradenton, FL	4,352	11.0%	8.2%	9.9%	2.6%	9.1%	13.1%	19.7%	26.3%	65.1%
Norwich-New London, CT	3,409	5.0%	21.8%	10.2%	0.0%	16.0%	0.0%	24.3%	22.7%	50.3%
Ocala, FL	1,170	5.6%	19.9%	0.0%	0.0%	16.1%	6.0%	31.7%	20.7%	72.1%
Ocean City, NJ	59	0.0%	0.0%	0.0%	0.0%	0.0%	0.0%	100.0%	0.0%	75.3%
Odessa, TX	3,798	18.7%	5.5%	0.0%	0.0%	19.7%	6.0%	18.0%	32.1%	52.7%
Ogden-Clearfield, UT	9,841	9.8%	24.0%	0.9%	0.8%	21.9%	3.6%	26.4%	12.6%	60.3%
Ogdensburg-Massena, NY	1,799	0.0%	0.0%	0.0%	3.0%	24.3%	0.0%	28.8%	43.9%	24.4%
Oklahoma City, OK	23,885	11.1%	8.4%	3.8%	4.2%	10.1%	1.0%	19.9%	41.4%	42.2%
Olympia-Tumwater, WA	4,829	4.1%	13.4%	6.0%	0.0%	0.0%	9.2%	21.3%	46.0%	51.8%
Omaha-Council Bluffs, NE-IA	17,214	4.6%	8.7%	4.2%	0.7%	9.6%	2.5%	37.4%	32.3%	43.7%
Orangeburg, SC	1,389	0.0%	6.6%	0.0%	18.1%	42.4%	0.0%	32.9%	0.0%	48.6%
Orlando-Kissimmee-Sanford, FL	32,577	7.7%	5.7%	4.2%	9.6%	10.7%	6.6%	22.4%	33.2%	54.5%
Oshkosh-Neenah, WI	4,463	2.0%	0.0%	2.4%	0.0%	12.6%	0.0%	36.5%	46.5%	36.1%
Ottawa-Peru, IL	1,440	37.2%	4.7%	0.0%	0.0%	0.0%	0.0%	58.1%	0.0%	65.2%
Owensboro, KY	1,395	6.6%	7.2%	5.7%	0.0%	52.2%	0.0%	12.4%	15.9%	50.7%
Oxnard-Thousand Oaks-Ventura, CA	5,240	17.5%	12.8%	6.3%	13.1%	3.2%	4.2%	22.9%	20.1%	67.9%
Palm Bay-Melbourne-Titusville, FL	5,028	1.3%	9.7%	9.3%	6.5%	17.9%	0.0%	32.5%	22.7%	60.0%
Panama City, FL	1,135	5.6%	15.5%	2.2%	0.0%	18.0%	0.0%	27.8%	31.0%	65.4%
Parkersburg-Vienna, WV	1,286	0.0%	6.4%	19.4%	0.0%	14.8%	0.0%	12.5%	46.9%	47.2%
Pensacola-Ferry Pass-Brent, FL	6,311	8.3%	5.2%	1.3%	9.2%	12.3%	0.9%	29.0%	33.7%	38.2%
Peoria, IL	5,402	0.7%	2.4%	2.7%	1.8%	22.6%	0.0%	42.4%	27.5%	49.6%
Philadelphia-Camden-Wilmington, PA-NJ-DE-MD	48,442	1.8%	4.9%	1.4%	7.1%	19.1%	3.8%	31.5%	30.3%	60.7%

Table D-4: Metropolitan/Micropolitan Statistical Areas—Household Relationship—Continued

		Married Couple Households		Male, No Spouse Present		Female, No Spouse Present		Non-Family Householders		
	Total Householders	With Children	No Children	With Children	No Children	With Children	No Children	Living Alone	Not Alone	Living With Parents
Logan, UT-ID	9,230	45.4%	17.8%	0.5%	2.5%	6.5%	0.0%	12.0%	15.2%	34.7%
Longview, TX	10,040	31.6%	13.1%	4.1%	2.5%	19.1%	2.3%	19.3%	8.0%	38.1%
Longview, WA	4,968	48.2%	6.6%	6.0%	0.0%	14.4%	2.8%	17.4%	4.6%	32.8%
Los Angeles-Long Beach-Anaheim, CA..	567,413	21.2%	13.0%	3.9%	5.2%	10.5%	4.0%	24.1%	18.1%	62.5%
Louisville/Jefferson County, KY-IN	64,472	27.9%	12.7%	4.4%	2.7%	15.2%	0.2%	26.0%	11.0%	54.5%
Lubbock, TX	19,679	24.5%	8.0%	6.7%	1.9%	13.1%	1.6%	28.8%	15.3%	25.3%
Lumberton, NC	4,624	37.5%	4.9%	8.6%	0.0%	28.9%	2.9%	13.7%	3.5%	58.2%
Lynchburg, VA	12,249	28.0%	18.5%	1.4%	3.9%	15.4%	2.0%	22.7%	8.0%	33.2%
Macon, GA	9,848	19.2%	25.5%	2.2%	0.5%	19.6%	0.5%	22.2%	10.2%	46.5%
Madera, CA	5,019	39.8%	11.7%	1.6%	6.7%	16.3%	1.6%	17.1%	5.2%	49.6%
Madison, WI	46,136	23.2%	17.0%	2.4%	1.4%	6.7%	0.3%	29.9%	19.1%	26.0%
Manchester-Nashua, NH	20,340	21.4%	13.5%	1.8%	1.3%	18.8%	1.1%	22.2%	19.8%	60.7%
Manhattan, KS	7,580	39.8%	16.5%	2.6%	0.0%	10.1%	0.0%	17.1%	13.9%	10.6%
Mankato-North Mankato, MN	6,350	14.6%	7.2%	2.1%	0.0%	13.3%	7.2%	39.7%	15.9%	10.6%
Mansfield, OH	4,223	32.7%	12.8%	6.7%	0.0%	18.5%	0.0%	27.5%	1.8%	49.4%
McAllen-Edinburg-Mission, TX	30,495	46.3%	5.4%	2.6%	0.3%	25.4%	2.2%	14.4%	3.3%	76.1%
Medford, OR	8,084	35.6%	10.2%	11.4%	0.0%	13.8%	6.7%	12.4%	10.0%	44.7%
Memphis, TN-MS-AR	67,659	24.9%	8.3%	5.5%	2.8%	25.8%	0.6%	24.0%	8.1%	55.6%
Merced, CA	13,238	38.3%	5.6%	8.9%	4.6%	23.3%	0.8%	8.5%	10.0%	50.2%
Meridian, MS	6,265	36.0%	8.7%	0.0%	0.0%	33.2%	1.4%	17.4%	3.4%	58.0%
Miami-Fort Lauderdale-West Palm Beach, FL	230,788	20.2%	11.9%	5.4%	4.3%	17.5%	3.3%	25.1%	12.3%	66.9%
Michigan City-La Porte, IN	5,028	21.1%	4.2%	8.5%	0.0%	38.3%	0.0%	18.4%	9.5%	47.7%
Midland, MI	4,880	31.6%	15.0%	0.0%	3.9%	14.7%	0.0%	15.5%	19.4%	58.5%
Midland, TX	11,641	44.2%	21.4%	0.7%	4.7%	7.3%	0.0%	11.5%	10.2%	52.5%
Milwaukee-Waukesha-West Allis, WI	92,496	21.6%	14.2%	2.6%	1.7%	17.1%	1.5%	26.7%	14.7%	51.0%
Minneapolis-St. Paul-Bloomington, MN-WI	208,396	26.4%	15.3%	3.4%	1.8%	12.1%	1.1%	24.1%	15.8%	55.9%
Missoula, MT	8,405	30.6%	4.2%	8.6%	0.3%	2.3%	0.0%	36.7%	17.3%	42.6%
Mobile, AL	20,594	31.4%	8.8%	3.2%	0.2%	21.3%	0.5%	26.4%	8.1%	51.3%
Modesto, CA	22,026	31.0%	12.4%	10.0%	2.5%	20.0%	0.7%	11.8%	11.5%	69.9%
Monroe, LA	8,494	42.1%	3.3%	5.9%	1.6%	28.1%	0.0%	14.1%	4.8%	39.9%
Monroe, MI	5,097	35.9%	11.0%	3.7%	0.0%	24.6%	0.0%	16.0%	8.9%	78.7%
Montgomery, AL	19,405	21.4%	10.5%	4.0%	2.2%	29.0%	3.8%	23.1%	5.9%	41.4%
Morgantown, WV	8,736	22.3%	14.0%	1.7%	0.0%	11.4%	2.5%	32.7%	15.4%	25.6%
Morristown, TN	4,454	30.5%	2.4%	13.5%	3.9%	24.7%	0.0%	17.0%	0.0%	56.3%
Mount Vernon-Anacortes, WA	6,288	28.7%	21.4%	4.4%	3.6%	6.6%	0.0%	22.6%	12.8%	41.9%
Muncie, IN	5,116	22.8%	11.6%	3.7%	4.0%	24.7%	5.4%	14.6%	13.2%	21.7%
Muskegon, MI	7,832	33.4%	7.5%	6.6%	0.0%	32.7%	0.0%	9.0%	11.0%	59.7%
Myrtle Beach-Conway-North Myrtle Beach, SC-NC	18,768	30.8%	12.6%	2.6%	1.1%	11.2%	1.8%	22.2%	17.7%	53.1%
Napa, CA	5,176	32.8%	7.6%	5.8%	4.7%	13.3%	3.8%	10.8%	21.1%	65.8%
Naples-Immokalee-Marco Island, FL	9,157	28.2%	4.6%	6.7%	3.4%	17.5%	9.8%	16.3%	13.6%	69.8%
Nashville-Davidson–Murfreesboro–Franklin, TN	107,897	29.3%	16.3%	3.2%	1.7%	12.9%	0.6%	20.0%	16.0%	48.6%
New Bern, NC	7,237	47.1%	12.4%	3.9%	0.0%	10.6%	0.4%	21.5%	4.1%	29.6%
New Castle, PA	3,488	28.0%	26.2%	6.2%	0.0%	16.1%	5.8%	4.7%	13.0%	45.2%
New Haven-Milford, CT	39,535	13.1%	10.4%	5.4%	2.4%	17.0%	1.0%	31.9%	18.9%	56.5%
New Orleans-Metairie, LA	69,664	21.4%	8.2%	4.8%	2.2%	22.1%	1.3%	26.8%	13.2%	62.5%
New Philadelphia-Dover, OH	3,268	40.9%	14.4%	15.6%	0.0%	6.2%	0.4%	10.0%	12.5%	76.2%
New York-Newark-Jersey City, NY-NJ-PA	880,680	21.0%	13.3%	2.9%	3.8%	12.3%	2.7%	26.4%	17.5%	66.4%
Niles-Benton Harbor, MI	8,181	27.0%	9.1%	7.1%	0.0%	27.0%	0.0%	22.0%	7.8%	45.6%
North Port-Sarasota-Bradenton, FL	21,069	28.6%	8.7%	4.3%	1.3%	20.8%	1.1%	24.0%	11.2%	65.1%
Norwich-New London, CT	14,756	30.0%	13.0%	0.8%	2.8%	15.5%	0.7%	28.0%	9.2%	50.3%
Ocala, FL	8,464	38.3%	7.0%	1.5%	0.9%	28.4%	0.0%	16.9%	7.0%	72.1%
Ocean City, NJ	3,746	42.7%	17.6%	4.6%	5.8%	8.9%	0.0%	15.5%	5.0%	75.3%
Odessa, TX	10,127	48.1%	9.8%	0.0%	1.3%	19.4%	0.0%	17.4%	4.0%	52.7%
Ogden-Clearfield, UT	32,882	56.4%	11.7%	4.4%	1.1%	9.8%	0.0%	9.8%	6.7%	60.3%
Ogdensburg-Massena, NY	5,339	31.8%	15.1%	10.5%	0.0%	16.7%	0.0%	11.0%	14.8%	24.4%
Oklahoma City, OK	81,938	27.9%	13.2%	6.2%	2.5%	14.6%	1.8%	25.4%	8.3%	42.2%
Olympia-Tumwater, WA	13,798	38.8%	10.9%	5.1%	0.0%	14.9%	0.0%	15.5%	14.9%	51.8%
Omaha-Council Bluffs, NE-IA	62,624	30.4%	12.5%	1.4%	2.2%	15.8%	0.9%	22.9%	14.0%	43.7%
Orangeburg, SC	4,741	13.5%	9.1%	1.9%	0.0%	24.9%	0.0%	43.2%	7.3%	48.6%
Orlando-Kissimmee-Sanford, FL	124,583	23.0%	13.1%	3.5%	2.9%	15.8%	2.6%	21.9%	17.3%	54.5%
Oshkosh-Neenah, WI	10,456	28.3%	12.8%	5.3%	2.8%	9.5%	0.0%	25.1%	16.2%	36.1%
Ottawa-Peru, IL	5,846	25.4%	8.3%	4.9%	5.7%	19.9%	0.0%	20.4%	15.4%	65.2%
Owensboro, KY	6,597	41.2%	9.0%	3.8%	5.7%	14.3%	0.0%	15.8%	10.4%	50.7%
Oxnard-Thousand Oaks-Ventura, CA	26,969	33.4%	14.6%	3.3%	2.8%	13.5%	5.1%	13.8%	13.5%	67.9%
Palm Bay-Melbourne-Titusville, FL	20,536	28.1%	11.9%	7.7%	0.0%	17.2%	1.5%	18.6%	15.0%	60.0%
Panama City, FL	10,524	33.9%	8.8%	3.8%	1.0%	17.2%	0.5%	26.1%	8.8%	65.4%
Parkersburg-Vienna, WV	4,094	36.3%	29.4%	0.0%	0.0%	14.4%	0.0%	18.4%	1.6%	47.2%
Pensacola-Ferry Pass-Brent, FL	27,016	28.9%	12.3%	2.5%	1.9%	14.2%	0.8%	25.4%	13.9%	38.2%
Peoria, IL	20,837	27.6%	14.1%	8.7%	0.5%	19.1%	0.6%	23.6%	5.9%	49.6%
Philadelphia-Camden-Wilmington, PA-NJ-DE-MD	282,728	21.3%	15.8%	3.6%	2.6%	15.3%	1.6%	23.8%	16.0%	60.7%

Table D-4: Metropolitan/Micropolitan Statistical Areas—Household Relationship—*Continued*

		Married Couple Households		Male, No Spouse Present		Female, No Spouse Present		Non-Family Householders		
	Total Householders	With Children	No Children	With Children	No Children	With Children	No Children	Living Alone	Not Alone	Living With Parents
Phoenix-Mesa-Scottsdale, AZ	64,468	8.4%	5.9%	4.7%	7.2%	12.6%	5.3%	26.7%	29.3%	51.3%
Pine Bluff, AR	1,084	4.8%	0.0%	26.0%	7.0%	32.7%	0.0%	29.4%	0.0%	51.8%
Pittsburgh, PA	31,579	3.0%	6.4%	2.1%	4.0%	12.5%	1.1%	36.5%	34.5%	49.8%
Pittsfield, MA	1,857	0.0%	8.8%	0.0%	12.5%	21.6%	9.1%	15.0%	32.9%	42.2%
Pocatello, ID	2,260	6.0%	12.8%	5.4%	0.0%	13.7%	0.0%	21.5%	40.5%	29.8%
Port St. Lucie, FL	6,451	5.8%	9.1%	8.8%	8.3%	4.3%	0.0%	5.5%	58.1%	41.3%
Portland-South Portland, ME	29,672	8.2%	6.8%	1.4%	5.3%	10.5%	1.8%	24.1%	41.9%	52.5%
Portland-Vancouver-Hillsboro, OR-WA	2,409	7.8%	6.1%	0.0%	4.9%	16.4%	13.1%	11.1%	40.6%	67.7%
Pottsville, PA	1,207	3.5%	2.9%	0.0%	0.0%	62.3%	0.0%	11.9%	19.4%	65.9%
Prescott, AZ	3,108	1.5%	0.0%	0.0%	2.2%	26.8%	1.7%	27.0%	40.8%	41.0%
Providence-Warwick, RI-MA	17,989	7.6%	0.5%	3.9%	3.7%	16.6%	4.7%	25.8%	37.2%	51.2%
Provo-Orem, UT	18,247	15.1%	45.2%	0.9%	3.2%	0.0%	4.7%	8.1%	22.7%	34.5%
Pueblo, CO	2,330	3.3%	0.0%	7.5%	1.0%	11.2%	15.0%	25.6%	36.3%	53.9%
Punta Gorda, FL	822	6.6%	0.0%	0.0%	0.0%	24.2%	69.2%	0.0%	0.0%	76.9%
Racine, WI	1,718	34.6%	1.2%	0.0%	0.0%	0.0%	0.0%	31.2%	32.9%	73.1%
Raleigh, NC	19,098	2.8%	6.5%	11.2%	4.7%	6.4%	1.2%	25.7%	41.5%	48.3%
Rapid City, SD	2,789	7.4%	1.9%	14.6%	9.0%	11.2%	0.0%	41.7%	14.3%	34.5%
Reading, PA	2,689	5.2%	2.4%	4.9%	15.9%	8.0%	0.0%	22.8%	40.9%	55.7%
Redding, CA	3,343	11.6%	10.8%	4.8%	14.1%	9.9%	4.1%	21.2%	23.5%	34.2%
Reno, NV	6,783	4.9%	3.3%	5.1%	6.2%	17.5%	2.7%	25.3%	34.9%	44.2%
Richmond, VA	16,185	2.5%	5.2%	6.1%	4.3%	12.6%	9.7%	28.8%	30.8%	54.3%
Riverside-San Bernardino-Ontario, CA	39,200	12.5%	10.7%	4.4%	6.8%	17.6%	9.7%	15.9%	22.4%	64.6%
Roanoke, VA	4,172	7.5%	5.2%	0.0%	5.2%	21.6%	0.0%	18.9%	41.6%	50.6%
Rochester, MN	4,445	0.6%	13.4%	0.0%	0.8%	19.4%	0.0%	27.7%	38.2%	47.9%
Rochester, NY	15,645	2.5%	3.6%	1.1%	4.3%	22.3%	1.7%	22.8%	41.8%	46.4%
Rockford, IL	4,841	13.4%	8.9%	11.2%	1.4%	32.1%	0.0%	27.2%	5.8%	62.2%
Rocky Mount, NC	1,404	0.0%	6.1%	19.4%	0.0%	58.5%	13.7%	2.4%	0.0%	50.7%
Rome, GA	993	0.0%	11.4%	2.9%	21.5%	42.6%	0.0%	11.7%	10.0%	58.4%
Roseburg, OR	477	55.8%	0.0%	10.9%	0.0%	0.0%	2.3%	13.8%	17.2%	42.7%
Sacramento–Roseville–Arden-Arcade, CA	28,270	5.0%	7.9%	2.3%	6.1%	8.1%	5.6%	26.1%	38.9%	55.2%
Saginaw, MI	2,710	5.4%	18.3%	0.7%	0.0%	31.7%	0.0%	25.9%	18.1%	54.4%
Salem, OH	5,818	6.2%	0.0%	2.0%	2.4%	11.3%	0.0%	33.5%	44.6%	36.0%
Salem, OR	2,705	1.4%	21.2%	3.4%	0.0%	0.0%	6.1%	1.6%	66.2%	36.1%
Salinas, CA	1,855	6.8%	17.8%	0.0%	0.0%	17.6%	3.4%	12.7%	41.7%	38.2%
Salisbury, MD-DE	34,153	3.6%	5.0%	1.9%	4.7%	14.5%	3.9%	35.7%	30.7%	54.1%
Salt Lake City, UT	1,699	5.5%	2.8%	0.0%	6.4%	40.2%	0.0%	15.8%	29.4%	50.4%
San Angelo, TX	5,437	10.9%	7.6%	2.4%	6.3%	20.6%	3.1%	9.8%	39.3%	50.0%
San Antonio-New Braunfels, TX	3,145	1.0%	7.0%	22.1%	6.0%	5.5%	4.5%	29.0%	25.0%	57.0%
San Diego-Carlsbad, CA	5,207	6.4%	19.9%	0.0%	0.0%	13.4%	2.8%	14.1%	43.4%	44.4%
San Francisco-Oakland-Hayward, CA	15,967	7.2%	17.9%	2.1%	6.4%	7.3%	5.0%	19.4%	34.7%	49.4%
San Jose-Sunnyvale-Santa Clara, CA	2,641	5.8%	2.5%	0.0%	1.7%	6.7%	0.0%	47.8%	35.4%	30.8%
San Luis Obispo-Paso Robles-Arroyo Grande, CA	30,834	8.8%	9.5%	3.7%	5.8%	14.6%	4.6%	28.2%	25.0%	55.6%
Santa Cruz-Watsonville, CA	39,688	7.5%	14.1%	5.2%	7.2%	6.5%	3.7%	18.7%	37.1%	50.2%
Santa Fe, NM	37,443	4.6%	2.8%	2.1%	8.1%	8.9%	6.8%	23.2%	43.4%	55.8%
Santa Maria-Santa Barbara, CA	15,888	3.7%	7.3%	1.2%	8.9%	5.2%	5.8%	18.9%	49.0%	55.1%
Santa Rosa, CA	6,236	5.0%	9.7%	0.0%	0.0%	0.0%	0.0%	30.9%	54.4%	27.9%
Savannah, GA	3,364	1.4%	5.5%	0.0%	0.0%	0.0%	0.0%	10.1%	83.0%	38.4%
Scranton–Wilkes-Barre–Hazleton, PA	1,435	0.0%	1.0%	6.0%	19.2%	0.9%	0.7%	49.1%	23.1%	55.5%
Seattle-Tacoma-Bellevue, WA	11,045	7.1%	3.0%	2.6%	4.4%	7.1%	0.7%	16.4%	58.7%	34.9%
Sebastian-Vero Beach, FL	5,719	5.8%	10.2%	3.0%	12.9%	7.7%	8.7%	17.0%	34.8%	59.8%
Sebring, FL	8,941	6.0%	10.6%	0.0%	1.7%	13.3%	0.0%	35.5%	32.9%	36.1%
Sheboygan, WI	5,316	6.4%	3.6%	7.0%	2.6%	19.7%	2.3%	27.9%	30.4%	53.2%
Sherman-Denison, TX	50,715	6.4%	14.1%	1.7%	2.4%	7.3%	3.4%	23.7%	41.0%	47.9%
Show Low, AZ	566	18.2%	6.0%	32.9%	0.0%	32.0%	0.0%	4.4%	6.5%	54.1%
Shreveport-Bossier City, LA	860	0.0%	0.0%	20.7%	0.0%	4.8%	0.0%	51.4%	23.1%	49.6%
Sierra Vista-Douglas, AZ	1,865	35.5%	0.0%	0.0%	0.0%	0.0%	0.0%	47.5%	17.1%	56.2%
Sioux City, IA-NE-SD	1,233	30.7%	0.0%	0.0%	0.0%	7.8%	0.0%	29.3%	32.3%	60.5%
Sioux Falls, SD	557	2.9%	65.2%	0.0%	0.0%	1.8%	12.6%	17.6%	0.0%	66.3%
South Bend-Mishawaka, IN-MI	6,569	11.5%	23.3%	1.2%	0.6%	17.3%	7.2%	23.2%	15.8%	45.8%
Spartanburg, SC	2,274	15.7%	26.6%	0.0%	20.1%	11.3%	4.0%	18.8%	3.5%	44.0%
Spokane-Spokane Valley, WA	2,091	10.2%	11.1%	0.0%	0.0%	6.6%	0.0%	40.5%	31.7%	54.6%
Springfield, IL	6,736	4.1%	5.4%	0.0%	0.0%	5.0%	2.7%	56.6%	26.2%	36.3%
Springfield, MA	4,000	4.0%	4.7%	13.8%	2.0%	13.6%	6.1%	29.2%	26.7%	46.4%
Springfield, MO	4,395	7.1%	4.2%	13.0%	5.3%	17.4%	5.0%	30.5%	17.6%	54.9%
Springfield, OH	10,494	9.3%	6.1%	1.0%	1.5%	16.8%	1.4%	29.3%	34.5%	35.2%
St. Cloud, MN	2,436	2.8%	7.2%	0.0%	0.0%	29.7%	0.0%	30.3%	30.0%	55.4%
St. George, UT	7,750	6.2%	4.0%	3.7%	3.4%	22.7%	0.6%	10.8%	48.5%	47.3%
St. Joseph, MO-KS	13,526	5.2%	7.7%	0.6%	1.4%	7.6%	3.2%	26.1%	48.2%	30.1%
St. Louis, MO-IL	2,323	5.5%	24.8%	21.3%	0.0%	10.8%	4.1%	5.9%	27.6%	44.7%
State College, PA	6,946	0.0%	0.3%	0.0%	1.0%	1.9%	0.0%	40.6%	56.2%	14.5%
Staunton-Waynesboro, VA	1,436	9.4%	18.1%	17.2%	0.0%	0.0%	0.0%	17.2%	38.1%	36.7%
Stockton-Lodi, CA	6,940	6.7%	4.4%	8.8%	3.9%	22.4%	8.9%	19.0%	25.8%	63.3%
Sumter, SC	1,268	5.3%	6.9%	11.7%	0.0%	18.7%	0.0%	32.4%	25.1%	59.3%
Sunbury, PA	1,119	4.9%	2.2%	3.1%	0.0%	0.0%	37.1%	43.9%	8.8%	59.3%

Table D-4: Metropolitan/Micropolitan Statistical Areas—Household Relationship—*Continued*

		Married Couple Households		Male, No Spouse Present		Female, No Spouse Present		Non-Family Householders		
	Total Householders	With Children	No Children	With Children	No Children	With Children	No Children	Living Alone	Not Alone	Living With Parents
					25 to 33					
Phoenix-Mesa-Scottsdale, AZ	233,775	28.5%	10.7%	6.2%	3.1%	14.3%	1.4%	22.5%	13.2%	51.3%
Pine Bluff, AR	5,103	19.6%	7.0%	6.3%	0.4%	32.2%	0.0%	33.0%	1.6%	51.8%
Pittsburgh, PA	120,696	21.3%	17.3%	3.4%	1.6%	11.6%	1.2%	30.4%	13.2%	49.8%
Pittsfield, MA	4,643	7.1%	11.0%	6.6%	0.0%	33.1%	0.0%	34.0%	8.3%	42.2%
Pocatello, ID	4,998	49.9%	2.3%	9.5%	0.0%	9.7%	2.2%	17.8%	8.7%	29.8%
Port St. Lucie, FL	24,318	23.5%	20.0%	2.2%	1.3%	11.5%	3.0%	21.0%	17.6%	41.3%
Portland-South Portland, ME	126,522	22.9%	15.0%	4.1%	1.9%	12.2%	0.9%	22.7%	20.3%	52.5%
Portland-Vancouver-Hillsboro, OR-WA	16,739	16.0%	17.9%	5.1%	5.1%	18.1%	0.0%	18.8%	19.1%	67.7%
Pottsville, PA	6,234	27.7%	8.9%	7.9%	0.0%	25.2%	0.0%	20.8%	9.4%	65.9%
Prescott, AZ	7,955	47.0%	11.7%	16.6%	0.0%	10.5%	2.0%	9.2%	3.0%	41.0%
Providence-Warwick, RI-MA	76,967	19.9%	10.2%	4.5%	2.0%	23.4%	1.0%	19.2%	19.7%	51.2%
Provo-Orem, UT	28,804	53.5%	20.9%	0.6%	1.1%	8.4%	0.7%	4.4%	10.3%	34.5%
Pueblo, CO	8,386	40.9%	7.7%	8.6%	0.0%	14.4%	0.0%	20.8%	7.6%	53.9%
Punta Gorda, FL	2,166	48.3%	11.3%	7.8%	2.4%	11.6%	0.0%	7.2%	11.2%	76.9%
Racine, WI	9,867	26.5%	14.1%	5.6%	6.2%	21.8%	0.0%	18.5%	7.3%	73.1%
Raleigh, NC	71,571	27.3%	14.9%	4.1%	1.9%	11.0%	1.1%	22.4%	17.1%	48.3%
Rapid City, SD	9,302	19.4%	12.3%	12.0%	3.2%	18.9%	9.1%	14.6%	10.5%	34.5%
Reading, PA	17,967	32.4%	7.9%	6.5%	3.6%	21.6%	1.5%	13.5%	13.0%	55.7%
Redding, CA	8,934	33.1%	7.0%	0.0%	1.4%	21.4%	0.6%	14.9%	21.7%	34.2%
Reno, NV	25,674	29.6%	9.8%	3.8%	0.9%	16.9%	2.9%	19.9%	16.1%	44.2%
Richmond, VA	61,588	22.5%	14.3%	5.4%	2.0%	12.0%	0.6%	27.1%	16.1%	54.3%
Riverside-San Bernardino-Ontario, CA	174,393	35.5%	9.7%	7.1%	4.6%	15.9%	2.9%	15.3%	9.0%	64.6%
Roanoke, VA	16,876	23.5%	12.0%	1.7%	0.9%	26.0%	0.0%	23.6%	12.2%	50.6%
Rochester, MN	10,458	45.2%	17.8%	0.0%	0.3%	5.1%	0.0%	23.5%	8.1%	47.9%
Rochester, NY	54,868	29.5%	12.1%	4.8%	0.8%	16.2%	1.1%	21.8%	13.7%	46.4%
Rockford, IL	14,871	23.9%	9.9%	6.7%	0.4%	25.7%	1.9%	17.4%	14.1%	62.2%
Rocky Mount, NC	6,164	14.9%	8.3%	1.8%	3.5%	44.7%	1.3%	23.8%	1.8%	50.7%
Rome, GA	4,085	33.5%	14.4%	10.5%	0.3%	22.6%	0.0%	17.7%	0.9%	58.4%
Roseburg, OR	5,659	8.2%	20.7%	8.5%	1.1%	21.8%	0.0%	29.9%	9.9%	42.7%
Sacramento–Roseville–Arden-Arcade, CA	110,897	29.0%	12.0%	4.4%	3.7%	12.7%	2.2%	21.0%	15.1%	55.2%
Saginaw, MI	10,364	16.2%	7.6%	4.9%	4.4%	22.5%	0.0%	25.9%	18.4%	54.4%
Salem, OH	12,652	18.3%	18.5%	12.3%	0.6%	19.1%	0.0%	22.1%	9.1%	36.0%
Salem, OR	5,629	45.8%	6.8%	0.0%	3.8%	20.6%	0.0%	11.5%	11.5%	36.1%
Salinas, CA	6,672	33.3%	9.3%	1.5%	0.9%	27.4%	1.9%	13.0%	12.7%	38.2%
Salisbury, MD-DE	152,966	28.0%	11.9%	6.3%	1.1%	15.4%	0.9%	23.2%	13.1%	54.1%
Salt Lake City, UT	3,251	39.5%	7.3%	1.5%	6.1%	16.4%	0.0%	20.9%	8.4%	50.4%
San Angelo, TX	17,802	38.7%	12.1%	9.2%	1.9%	13.8%	0.5%	12.2%	11.6%	50.0%
San Antonio-New Braunfels, TX	17,097	35.0%	9.6%	8.1%	4.0%	17.7%	1.3%	13.4%	10.9%	57.0%
San Diego-Carlsbad, CA	14,584	33.0%	8.1%	9.3%	2.2%	21.2%	0.0%	16.3%	9.9%	44.4%
San Francisco-Oakland-Hayward, CA	65,854	34.6%	17.2%	3.8%	1.2%	11.4%	1.3%	19.0%	11.5%	49.4%
San Jose-Sunnyvale-Santa Clara, CA	7,753	47.0%	4.4%	3.3%	0.0%	13.5%	0.9%	15.6%	15.3%	30.8%
San Luis Obispo-Paso Robles-Arroyo Grande, CA	117,297	30.1%	12.3%	4.0%	2.8%	17.5%	1.3%	22.7%	9.3%	55.6%
Santa Cruz-Watsonville, CA	168,207	25.6%	15.0%	4.6%	2.1%	9.4%	1.9%	21.2%	20.1%	50.2%
Santa Fe, NM	232,596	18.2%	18.1%	2.7%	4.9%	6.5%	2.3%	22.0%	25.4%	55.8%
Santa Maria-Santa Barbara, CA	84,717	26.5%	21.1%	2.5%	4.4%	6.2%	2.5%	17.6%	19.2%	55.1%
Santa Rosa, CA	12,218	29.5%	17.4%	5.7%	1.9%	11.4%	1.1%	9.0%	24.1%	27.9%
Savannah, GA	10,111	20.4%	11.7%	1.2%	7.8%	10.4%	0.9%	24.7%	23.0%	38.4%
Scranton–Wilkes-Barre–Hazleton, PA	5,528	19.4%	18.4%	2.2%	4.2%	19.2%	0.0%	22.2%	14.4%	55.5%
Seattle-Tacoma-Bellevue, WA	14,623	24.1%	13.7%	4.4%	2.1%	19.8%	1.2%	15.8%	18.8%	34.9%
Sebastian-Vero Beach, FL	18,678	23.3%	15.7%	5.2%	3.2%	13.7%	1.4%	15.6%	22.0%	59.8%
Sebring, FL	23,308	26.8%	13.1%	2.4%	2.7%	15.8%	3.0%	24.8%	11.4%	36.1%
Sheboygan, WI	22,639	19.0%	10.3%	9.0%	2.6%	23.5%	3.6%	17.2%	14.8%	53.2%
Sherman-Denison, TX	238,816	23.7%	16.6%	3.1%	2.0%	8.0%	1.1%	23.9%	21.7%	47.9%
Show Low, AZ	3,190	57.8%	14.2%	5.2%	0.0%	10.5%	0.0%	8.7%	3.6%	54.1%
Shreveport-Bossier City, LA	2,521	41.5%	7.9%	8.3%	0.0%	19.2%	0.0%	16.7%	6.4%	49.6%
Sierra Vista-Douglas, AZ	5,120	32.1%	11.5%	4.7%	0.0%	17.3%	0.0%	19.6%	14.7%	56.2%
Sioux City, IA-NE-SD	5,545	40.6%	9.5%	6.1%	0.0%	19.4%	0.0%	8.5%	15.9%	60.5%
Sioux Falls, SD	2,784	33.3%	7.5%	13.1%	3.0%	29.8%	0.0%	12.7%	0.6%	66.3%
South Bend-Mishawaka, IN-MI	25,341	31.9%	9.2%	1.4%	0.7%	22.0%	0.0%	24.3%	10.4%	45.8%
Spartanburg, SC	6,414	36.3%	2.8%	0.8%	0.0%	22.1%	3.2%	30.9%	3.9%	44.0%
Spokane-Spokane Valley, WA	9,783	33.7%	11.3%	7.1%	0.0%	22.7%	0.0%	15.8%	9.4%	54.6%
Springfield, IL	18,427	32.4%	16.5%	3.8%	0.9%	10.8%	1.1%	20.8%	13.7%	36.3%
Springfield, MA	15,142	30.3%	16.4%	2.6%	1.0%	14.8%	0.0%	20.0%	14.8%	46.4%
Springfield, MO	14,455	43.3%	12.5%	1.9%	1.8%	15.7%	1.0%	16.3%	7.5%	54.9%
Springfield, OH	30,810	31.9%	12.1%	7.6%	0.0%	11.2%	3.5%	23.2%	10.6%	35.2%
St. Cloud, MN	11,038	22.6%	9.2%	4.3%	0.9%	19.2%	0.0%	24.9%	18.9%	55.4%
St. George, UT	27,407	23.3%	13.1%	3.5%	1.3%	19.9%	1.2%	19.9%	17.8%	47.3%
St. Joseph, MO-KS	26,066	33.9%	12.5%	3.4%	1.2%	13.0%	0.3%	25.9%	9.9%	30.1%
St. Louis, MO-IL	6,116	25.6%	12.1%	6.5%	6.1%	28.4%	1.6%	15.0%	4.7%	44.7%
State College, PA	9,926	20.3%	12.7%	0.0%	6.8%	9.9%	1.0%	38.8%	10.5%	14.5%
Staunton-Waynesboro, VA	6,081	39.6%	7.0%	0.0%	0.0%	24.4%	0.8%	16.8%	11.4%	36.7%
Stockton-Lodi, CA	30,320	39.4%	6.9%	8.5%	6.6%	18.5%	1.0%	13.0%	6.0%	63.3%
Sumter, SC	4,552	12.8%	16.0%	2.9%	3.9%	35.8%	0.0%	15.1%	13.5%	59.3%
Sunbury, PA	4,551	28.6%	7.1%	10.5%	0.0%	8.5%	3.7%	11.4%	30.2%	59.3%

Table D-4: Metropolitan/Micropolitan Statistical Areas—Household Relationship—*Continued*

| | | 18 to 24 | | | | | | | | |
| | | Married Couple Households | | Male, No Spouse Present | | Female, No Spouse Present | | Non-Family Householders | | |
	Total Householders	With Children	No Children	With Children	No Children	With Children	No Children	Living Alone	Not Alone	Living With Parents
Syracuse, NY	8,133	4.6%	2.7%	7.1%	0.0%	14.1%	0.5%	30.6%	40.4%	38.6%
Tallahassee, FL	18,163	1.3%	2.0%	0.4%	3.5%	5.8%	2.4%	35.8%	48.9%	21.3%
Tampa-St. Petersburg-Clearwater, FL	30,989	5.3%	8.2%	4.7%	4.6%	12.0%	6.0%	29.3%	29.9%	57.0%
Terre Haute, IN	4,102	11.7%	1.0%	2.1%	0.0%	18.3%	1.0%	39.0%	26.9%	32.6%
Texarkana, TX-AR	1,858	5.5%	17.5%	14.3%	6.1%	27.8%	9.5%	11.2%	8.1%	52.0%
The Villages, FL	326	0.0%	0.0%	89.9%	0.0%	10.1%	0.0%	0.0%	0.0%	83.7%
Toledo, OH	15,968	3.2%	2.6%	6.5%	1.8%	14.3%	5.1%	33.3%	33.2%	34.2%
Topeka, KS	4,106	5.7%	5.1%	2.0%	8.0%	21.6%	2.6%	27.7%	27.2%	44.1%
Torrington, CT	991	5.2%	0.0%	0.0%	0.0%	32.5%	0.0%	11.8%	50.5%	75.0%
Traverse City, MI	882	0.0%	0.0%	0.0%	3.5%	0.0%	0.0%	47.7%	48.8%	59.4%
Trenton, NJ	1,492	3.6%	7.4%	3.6%	15.8%	16.9%	7.8%	18.0%	27.0%	56.6%
Truckee-Grass Valley, CA	430	0.0%	0.0%	0.0%	0.0%	55.6%	33.0%	0.0%	11.4%	58.7%
Tucson, AZ	23,373	5.5%	7.0%	2.1%	6.5%	10.8%	3.2%	28.6%	36.4%	42.3%
Tullahoma-Manchester, TN	1,644	8.2%	0.0%	0.0%	0.0%	6.2%	0.0%	56.0%	29.6%	51.2%
Tulsa, OK	19,226	15.0%	12.4%	2.4%	6.6%	18.4%	1.5%	22.7%	20.9%	47.9%
Tupelo, MS	3,339	7.0%	11.4%	1.5%	15.1%	6.4%	0.0%	26.4%	32.2%	42.9%
Tuscaloosa, AL	6,791	1.0%	2.0%	2.1%	11.1%	15.4%	6.7%	32.2%	29.5%	33.0%
Tyler, TX	5,180	12.3%	4.9%	0.0%	1.4%	5.2%	0.0%	39.2%	37.0%	37.3%
Urban Honolulu, HI	13,504	20.3%	24.4%	0.0%	6.4%	0.5%	4.6%	21.7%	22.1%	43.9%
Utica-Rome, NY	2,845	0.0%	19.6%	0.0%	8.2%	28.1%	0.0%	37.4%	6.7%	57.8%
Valdosta, GA	3,829	6.0%	6.3%	0.0%	7.3%	0.0%	1.7%	28.1%	50.7%	37.9%
Vallejo-Fairfield, CA	4,199	11.2%	16.0%	6.4%	2.9%	5.6%	18.7%	22.0%	17.3%	57.8%
Victoria, TX	1,752	25.5%	0.0%	19.7%	11.4%	9.2%	0.0%	25.6%	8.7%	69.1%
Vineland-Bridgeton, NJ	1,078	9.3%	0.0%	21.8%	21.3%	17.3%	0.0%	30.2%	0.0%	70.4%
Virginia Beach-Norfolk-Newport News, VA-NC	29,758	10.8%	13.7%	1.4%	0.5%	15.1%	3.0%	23.8%	31.8%	42.8%
Visalia-Porterville, CA	4,831	14.5%	1.5%	8.0%	3.0%	30.6%	2.3%	19.6%	20.5%	66.6%
Waco, TX	8,742	10.8%	8.3%	2.6%	2.0%	15.9%	3.1%	40.0%	17.1%	31.0%
Walla Walla, WA	616	0.0%	14.1%	0.0%	14.9%	5.7%	0.0%	65.3%	0.0%	49.9%
Warner Robins, GA	3,831	11.5%	14.2%	0.0%	0.0%	19.0%	0.0%	27.1%	28.2%	52.1%
Washington-Arlington-Alexandria, DC-VA-MD-WV	52,804	4.8%	7.3%	0.7%	6.1%	9.0%	4.1%	28.8%	39.2%	58.6%
Waterloo-Cedar Falls, IA	5,579	2.2%	6.6%	0.0%	2.0%	23.5%	1.9%	36.5%	27.4%	26.4%
Watertown-Fort Drum, NY	3,047	30.1%	15.0%	0.7%	0.0%	4.6%	0.0%	30.6%	19.1%	39.9%
Wausau, WI	1,677	12.7%	1.4%	0.0%	8.2%	0.0%	0.0%	54.5%	23.1%	53.5%
Weirton-Steubenville, WV-OH	905	0.0%	0.0%	0.0%	57.9%	6.7%	0.0%	6.7%	28.6%	53.2%
Wenatchee, WA	1,009	1.4%	2.4%	0.0%	1.6%	7.9%	0.0%	32.8%	53.9%	76.1%
Wheeling, WV-OH	1,615	0.0%	0.0%	8.6%	32.4%	9.7%	0.0%	4.2%	45.0%	49.3%
Whitewater-Elkhorn, WI	1,971	0.0%	0.0%	3.7%	11.0%	7.1%	0.0%	42.5%	35.8%	43.5%
Wichita Falls, TX	12,305	5.7%	10.8%	0.3%	0.9%	16.8%	2.8%	41.5%	21.2%	45.0%
Wichita, KS	4,336	1.4%	6.3%	7.0%	3.7%	9.3%	4.5%	36.5%	31.3%	24.5%
Williamsport, PA	1,219	27.9%	9.3%	0.0%	0.0%	12.2%	0.0%	45.9%	4.8%	55.4%
Wilmington, NC	6,865	9.6%	13.4%	0.0%	14.7%	1.7%	1.5%	8.3%	50.8%	32.7%
Winchester, VA-WV	457	6.3%	11.2%	0.0%	0.0%	0.0%	0.0%	0.0%	82.5%	60.6%
Winston-Salem, NC	8,640	4.0%	17.8%	1.1%	12.2%	15.5%	6.3%	17.0%	26.1%	49.4%
Wooster, OH	1,093	18.6%	16.0%	0.0%	0.0%	17.0%	0.0%	27.0%	21.4%	54.5%
Worcester, MA-CT	7,324	0.0%	3.5%	7.3%	7.1%	14.9%	2.5%	16.7%	47.9%	57.7%
Yakima, WA	3,287	3.2%	8.1%	11.3%	1.5%	47.4%	0.0%	3.0%	25.5%	64.2%
York-Hanover, PA	2,098	10.7%	9.7%	9.5%	1.1%	0.8%	0.0%	17.3%	51.0%	61.5%
Youngstown-Warren-Boardman, OH-PA	8,013	4.3%	14.3%	1.4%	5.8%	31.4%	3.1%	19.9%	19.8%	52.2%
Yuba City, CA	2,135	8.6%	22.6%	3.4%	0.0%	0.0%	0.0%	29.7%	35.7%	57.4%
Yuma, AZ	4,536	33.4%	24.4%	1.1%	8.9%	15.3%	1.9%	10.3%	4.8%	50.1%

Table D-4: Metropolitan/Micropolitan Statistical Areas—Household Relationship—*Continued*

| | | 25 to 33 | | | | | | | | |
| | | Married Couple Households | | Male, No Spouse Present | | Female, No Spouse Present | | Non-Family Householders | | |
	Total Householders	With Children	No Children	With Children	No Children	With Children	No Children	Living Alone	Not Alone	Living With Parents
Syracuse, NY	31,546	23.0%	10.0%	5.8%	0.2%	21.5%	0.5%	25.5%	13.5%	38.6%
Tallahassee, FL	20,485	21.7%	11.6%	1.8%	0.0%	18.2%	0.8%	27.9%	18.0%	21.3%
Tampa-St. Petersburg-Clearwater, FL	139,671	20.4%	12.2%	4.8%	2.5%	17.2%	1.7%	26.3%	14.8%	57.0%
Terre Haute, IN	7,169	40.3%	6.2%	2.6%	0.0%	8.3%	0.5%	22.9%	19.3%	32.6%
Texarkana, TX-AR	7,143	32.3%	8.0%	4.5%	0.0%	27.0%	1.5%	15.2%	11.4%	52.0%
The Villages, FL	1,387	9.2%	2.7%	0.0%	0.0%	66.9%	0.0%	11.8%	9.3%	83.7%
Toledo, OH	33,533	23.2%	10.3%	6.8%	1.9%	18.7%	1.1%	24.9%	13.2%	34.2%
Topeka, KS	12,578	43.6%	4.8%	5.0%	0.0%	14.5%	0.0%	22.0%	10.1%	44.1%
Torrington, CT	6,098	27.3%	15.0%	0.6%	10.4%	6.1%	0.7%	29.1%	10.8%	75.0%
Traverse City, MI	5,682	31.2%	10.7%	0.0%	0.0%	3.8%	0.0%	27.5%	26.8%	59.4%
Trenton, NJ	14,263	26.7%	13.1%	0.8%	3.5%	13.9%	5.8%	20.9%	15.3%	56.6%
Truckee-Grass Valley, CA	3,951	48.7%	8.6%	6.4%	0.0%	13.1%	2.8%	8.6%	11.8%	58.7%
Tucson, AZ	50,667	25.0%	9.7%	4.4%	4.2%	19.1%	2.2%	21.0%	14.3%	42.3%
Tullahoma-Manchester, TN	4,148	44.7%	9.9%	4.2%	1.6%	8.3%	16.2%	15.1%	0.0%	51.2%
Tulsa, OK	57,030	32.5%	12.3%	7.1%	2.4%	16.4%	0.1%	19.8%	9.4%	47.9%
Tupelo, MS	6,175	38.6%	9.1%	12.0%	7.1%	13.8%	3.7%	10.9%	4.8%	42.9%
Tuscaloosa, AL	11,436	22.8%	11.6%	6.6%	0.0%	23.7%	0.0%	27.2%	8.0%	33.0%
Tyler, TX	10,164	44.4%	4.2%	11.0%	0.3%	16.2%	0.3%	16.3%	7.4%	37.3%
Urban Honolulu, HI	42,808	32.7%	17.5%	4.0%	2.5%	6.4%	3.6%	16.9%	16.4%	43.9%
Utica-Rome, NY	11,744	24.8%	6.8%	11.3%	1.0%	28.3%	1.2%	18.4%	8.3%	57.8%
Valdosta, GA	7,101	47.3%	5.3%	0.4%	0.0%	15.7%	2.5%	16.6%	12.1%	37.9%
Vallejo-Fairfield, CA	18,155	34.8%	10.0%	3.3%	3.4%	22.1%	1.5%	12.9%	12.0%	57.8%
Victoria, TX	4,603	61.2%	8.4%	0.0%	2.9%	4.5%	0.0%	17.3%	5.6%	69.1%
Vineland-Bridgeton, NJ	6,306	31.9%	5.6%	7.6%	2.9%	31.6%	0.8%	9.2%	10.5%	70.4%
Virginia Beach-Norfolk-Newport News, VA-NC	103,582	31.2%	11.6%	4.6%	2.3%	16.6%	1.6%	19.2%	13.0%	42.8%
Visalia-Porterville, CA	22,144	48.6%	4.6%	8.0%	3.9%	22.9%	0.8%	7.4%	3.7%	66.6%
Waco, TX	12,230	24.4%	15.9%	3.4%	1.6%	19.9%	1.6%	19.6%	13.5%	31.0%
Walla Walla, WA	4,044	38.9%	15.2%	5.3%	0.0%	18.0%	0.2%	15.1%	7.3%	49.9%
Warner Robins, GA	9,770	28.6%	16.1%	2.8%	0.0%	26.6%	0.5%	14.3%	11.1%	52.1%
Washington-Arlington-Alexandria, DC-VA-MD-WV	308,547	21.1%	16.8%	4.0%	2.4%	9.4%	2.0%	25.7%	18.8%	58.6%
Waterloo-Cedar Falls, IA	11,157	31.5%	15.0%	3.7%	0.0%	12.5%	2.5%	30.2%	4.7%	26.4%
Watertown-Fort Drum, NY	7,519	32.9%	9.2%	0.9%	1.6%	17.8%	0.0%	29.3%	8.4%	39.9%
Wausau, WI	6,682	26.3%	14.2%	9.7%	5.2%	10.6%	0.0%	15.4%	18.6%	53.5%
Weirton-Steubonville, WV OH	5,137	25.5%	4.5%	8.2%	0.0%	29.1%	1.4%	24.6%	6.7%	53.2%
Wenatchee, WA	3,563	34.2%	7.2%	3.2%	2.2%	24.1%	7.2%	11.1%	10.9%	76.1%
Wheeling, WV-OH	5,357	25.7%	4.3%	7.9%	1.5%	27.9%	1.3%	24.7%	6.7%	49.3%
Whitewater-Elkhorn, WI	4,459	26.2%	15.3%	1.7%	0.0%	21.1%	1.9%	32.9%	0.8%	43.5%
Wichita Falls, TX	39,173	27.7%	10.8%	5.4%	3.2%	14.9%	0.3%	31.8%	5.9%	45.0%
Wichita, KS	6,801	36.1%	10.0%	7.1%	0.0%	8.8%	7.5%	11.1%	19.4%	24.5%
Williamsport, PA	5,169	37.4%	17.7%	5.1%	0.0%	17.5%	0.0%	10.3%	12.0%	55.4%
Wilmington, NC	14,625	21.2%	10.5%	7.0%	1.5%	19.9%	3.0%	21.2%	15.7%	32.7%
Winchester, VA-WV	4,035	23.8%	23.4%	11.0%	0.0%	20.2%	1.0%	7.5%	13.0%	60.6%
Winston-Salem, NC	31,494	33.8%	11.9%	6.5%	2.4%	11.3%	1.0%	25.4%	7.7%	49.4%
Wooster, OH	4,467	44.8%	13.3%	0.9%	0.8%	11.6%	0.0%	19.9%	8.8%	54.5%
Worcester, MA-CT	39,353	25.6%	11.9%	2.9%	3.6%	16.0%	1.4%	23.1%	15.5%	57.7%
Yakima, WA	10,650	45.8%	10.1%	5.9%	1.6%	20.4%	0.0%	12.8%	3.4%	64.2%
York-Hanover, PA	21,677	30.1%	16.6%	5.7%	1.6%	15.3%	0.5%	19.2%	11.1%	61.5%
Youngstown-Warren-Boardman, OH-PA	22,734	19.6%	15.1%	4.8%	4.1%	18.9%	1.3%	26.3%	9.8%	52.2%
Yuba City, CA	8,372	46.7%	15.8%	10.1%	0.6%	14.1%	0.0%	7.7%	5.1%	57.4%
Yuma, AZ	9,978	39.4%	13.1%	7.4%	4.6%	13.7%	0.0%	13.6%	8.2%	50.1%

PART E
EDUCATIONAL ATTAINMENT

Unlike the Baby Boom generation, completion of a bachelor's degree is more universally expected of the Millennials. Today's economy is more knowledge based, and Millennials find that in many fields even a bachelor's degree isn't sufficient for advancement. Millennials are also facing a very different economic climate having weathered the Great Recession and a slow recovery of the labor market. Yet, as the largest generation in the United States, they will be an important driver of the economy in the future. As noted by the President's Council of Economic Advisors, "this is the first generation to have had access to the Internet during their formative years."[1]

The Millennial age categories defined here span the ages where they are entering or completing their education (18 to 24) or are at the beginning of their careers (25 to 33). As expected, these two age groups vary in levels of educational accomplishment, though the 18 to 24 year olds likely aren't finished with formal schooling. In comparison to older Americans, less than one in four (22.2 percent) of those age 65 and over have a bachelor's degree or higher, but among the 25 to 33 age group, 34.1 percent have already attained that level of education.

The Millennial generation is also highly diverse, and many Millennials are immigrants having entered this country on student visas. In 1983 there were 339,000 foreign students being educated in the U.S., but by 2015 that number swelled to more than 1 million.[2] This is a generation facing a very different economic climate, labor force competition, and continued advancement of educational attainment for women.

Education

Nationally, 30.5 percent of Millennials age 18 to 24 have only a high school education, and that percentage falls to 23.9 percent for the 25 to 33 year olds. For the population age 65 and over, 33.9 percent have only a high school or equivalent education. Younger Millennials continue their education as 40.6 percent have had some college experience and 5.2 percent have attained an associate's

degree. Nearly 10 percent have gone on and hold a bachelor's degree or higher. Among the 25 to 33 year olds, fewer have some college (23.0 percent), but 34.1 percent have completed a bachelor's or advanced degree.

By state, Montana has the highest percentage of 18 to 24 year olds with only a high school education (37.7 percent) while North Dakota is lowest at 22.1 percent. In 30 states more than 30 percent of the younger Millennials stopped their educations after high school. In Wyoming, 9.9 percent have an associate's degree but only 1.2 percent in the District of Columbia. DC also has the highest percentage in this age group with a bachelor's or advanced degree (20.2 percent), while Idaho has the lowest percentage at 4.2 percent. West Virginia has the highest percentage of 25 to 33 year olds who have only a high school education (34.2 percent). The District of Columbia is lowest at 11.9 percent. Associates degrees are held by 14.0 percent of North Dakota's older Millennials. The District of Columbia has the highest percentage with bachelor's degrees (35.4 percent) and advanced degrees (35.7 percent). In total, nearly three-quarters (72.6 percent) of DC's older Millennials have a bachelor's degree or higher. New Mexico has the lowest percentage with a bachelor's degree (14.7 percent), and Nevada is lowest for advanced degrees at 5.2 percent followed closely by Alaska at 5.3 percent. Virtually all 13- to 17-year-old Millennials are still enrolled in school (96.8 percent). Wyoming is lowest at 92.0 percent.

Parker County, TX has the highest percentage of 18 to 24 year olds who have only a high school education (60.3 percent), but in 87 additional counties, high school is the highest level of accomplishment for 40 or more percent of this younger group. Tompkins County, NY (home of Cornell University) has the lowest percentage at 9.0 percent. In Arlington County, VA more than half (58.2 percent) of the 18 to 24 year olds have attained a bachelor's degree or higher. In 377 counties, less than 10 percent have completed that level of education. Among the older 25 to 33 age group, Highlands County, FL has the highest percentage who have only completed high school (53.1 percent). Many in this age group have at least experienced college, with some attaining an associate's degree. In 121 counties, more than 40 percent have an associate's degree or some college experience. A bachelor's degree is held by 56.0 percent in Delaware County, OH (home of Ohio Wesleyan University), where an additional 14 percent hold an advanced degree. Indian River County, FL has the lowest percentage holding a

---

1 Council of Economic Advisors, Executive Office of the President, "15 Economic Facts About Millennials," October 2014.
2 Institute of International Education, Open Doors Data, International Students, http://www.iie.org/Research-and-Publications/Open-Doors/Data/International-Students.

Percent Age 25 to 33 Holding an Advanced Degree

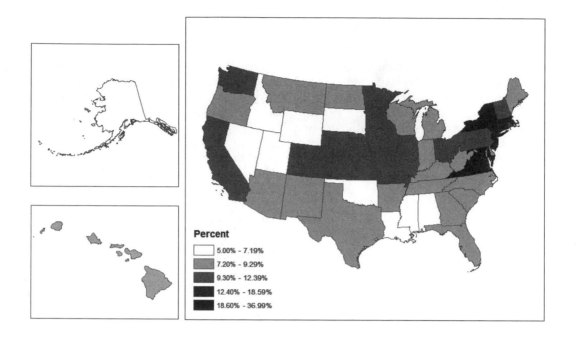

Percent
- 5.00% - 7.19%
- 7.20% - 9.29%
- 9.30% - 12.39%
- 12.40% - 18.59%
- 18.60% - 36.99%

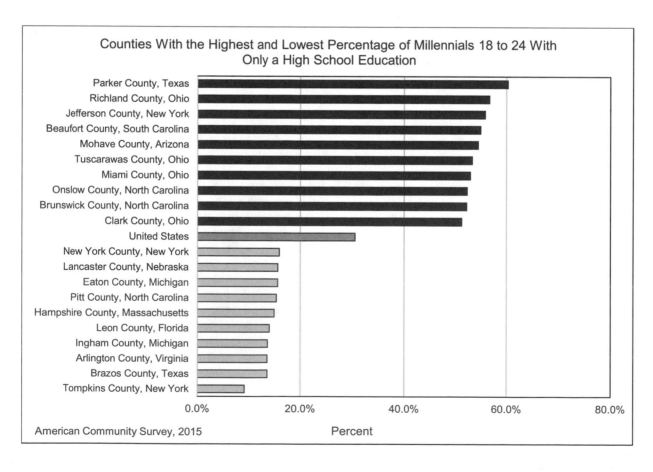

Counties With the Highest and Lowest Percentage of Millennials 18 to 24 With Only a High School Education

American Community Survey, 2015

bachelor's degree at 5.1 percent. Most 13 to 17 year olds are enrolled in school, but in Geauga County, OH only 69 percent are enrolled. In 21 counties the percentage is less than 90 percent.

Santa Monica, CA has the lowest percentage of 18 to 24 year olds with only a high school education, at 12.8 percent while Oceanside, CA is highest at 55.1 percent. Sixty-nine percent College Station, TX have already experienced some college time, and in Gresham, OR 18.7 percent have attained an associate's degree. Bachelor's degrees are held by 42.4 percent of younger Millennials in Sandy Springs, GA. Among the older Millennial age group, 47.6 percent in Paterson City, NJ still have only completed high school. Cambridge City, MA has the lowest percentage at 2.2 percent. In 20 cities less than 10 percent of older Millennials have only completed High School. In 65 cities more than one-third hold a bachelor's degree, and Santa Monica, CA is highest at 56.2 percent. In Cambridge, MA more than half of older Millennials hold an advanced degree (53.9 percent). In 75 cities, less than five percent of the 25 to 33 year olds hold an advanced degree. Richmond, VA has the lowest percentage of the 13 to 17 population enrolled in school (78.4 percent), but 150 cities are above 98 percent.

The Mansfield, OH metropolitan area has the highest percentage of 18 to 24 year olds with only a high school education (56.7 percent), while the Ithaca, NY metro is lowest at 9.3 percent. In 215 metros more than 40 percent of younger Millennials have experienced some college. The Mankato-North Mankato, MN metro is highest at 81.4 percent. The Madison, WI metro has the highest percentage with a bachelor's degree or higher (25.7 percent). Among the older Millennials, the Morristown, TN metro has the highest percentage (53.9 percent) with only a high school education. The Ithaca, NY metro is lowest at 7.4 percent. The Mankato-North Mankato metro has the highest percentage with an associate's degree at 30.6 percent, but an associate's degree is held by less than 10 percent in 241 metros. The Ithaca, NY metro (home to Cornell University and Ithaca College) has the highest percentage with a bachelor's or advanced degree (71.9 percent). The Burlington-South Burlington, VT metro is highest for just a bachelor's degree (University of Vermont) but the Ithaca, NY metro is again highest for advanced degrees (31.3 percent). At the metro/micro level the percentage of 13 to 17 year olds enrolled in school is below 90 percent in 17 areas. The Sunbury, PA micropolitan area is lowest at 76.2 percent.

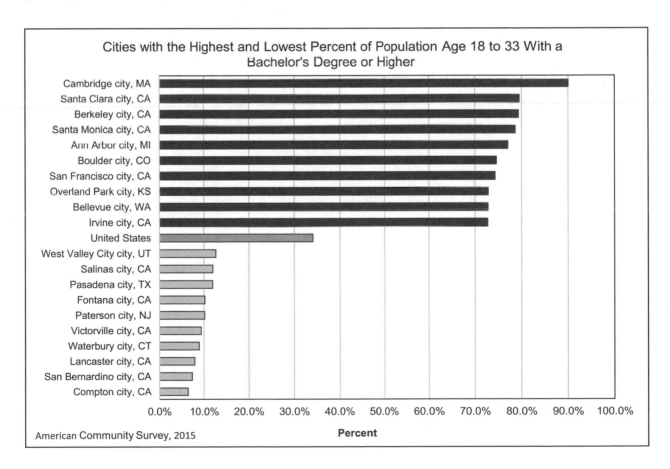

American Community Survey, 2015

Table E-1: States—Educational Attainment

	15 to 17		18 to 24					25 to 33					
				Percent					Percent				
	Total Population	Percent Enrolled in School	Total Population	High School	Some College	Associates Degree	Bachelors Degree	Total Population	High School	Some College	Associates Degree	Bachelors Degree	Advanced Degree
United States...............	12,560,034	96.8%	31,345,795	30.5%	40.6%	5.2%	9.5%	39,598,655	23.9%	23.0%	8.7%	24.1%	10.0%
Alabama........................	195,035	96.8%	469,138	31.8%	41.1%	4.5%	6.2%	564,102	26.2%	27.3%	8.3%	18.4%	6.8%
Alaska..........................	29,767	94.7%	84,225	35.1%	38.5%	3.7%	5.5%	107,424	30.0%	29.2%	8.0%	21.1%	5.3%
Arizona.........................	275,814	95.5%	672,348	30.3%	38.9%	5.4%	6.9%	820,094	24.2%	27.4%	8.8%	19.4%	7.5%
Arkansas.......................	118,111	94.6%	282,731	32.7%	42.2%	4.9%	6.5%	350,285	30.5%	27.5%	7.7%	16.6%	7.3%
California......................	1,535,966	97.8%	3,948,553	29.7%	43.6%	4.8%	8.9%	5,254,544	21.8%	23.9%	7.7%	24.4%	9.6%
Colorado.......................	205,790	95.4%	524,617	30.2%	41.0%	4.7%	10.5%	750,842	21.2%	23.2%	8.7%	29.4%	10.6%
Connecticut..................	142,674	96.6%	355,738	28.3%	42.6%	4.3%	13.0%	394,429	22.4%	19.7%	7.0%	28.2%	15.6%
Delaware.......................	34,981	95.9%	87,509	30.7%	38.3%	6.3%	8.6%	114,870	25.3%	24.3%	7.3%	22.6%	8.9%
District of Columbia........	15,198	98.1%	81,910	25.2%	45.8%	1.2%	20.2%	139,024	11.9%	8.3%	2.1%	35.7%	36.9%
Florida.........................	718,068	96.4%	1,779,978	29.4%	36.0%	9.4%	8.1%	2,343,934	27.2%	21.9%	11.6%	21.5%	7.7%
Georgia........................	425,869	96.0%	1,029,333	32.4%	38.7%	4.1%	7.5%	1,239,622	24.3%	24.5%	8.0%	21.4%	9.1%
Hawaii..........................	45,680	96.3%	136,529	36.6%	39.7%	8.5%	9.2%	189,145	27.5%	27.0%	10.1%	23.6%	7.3%
Idaho...........................	71,752	95.7%	157,480	33.5%	41.8%	5.8%	4.2%	197,546	26.8%	28.2%	11.3%	18.2%	5.7%
Illinois........................	509,080	96.9%	1,238,041	29.1%	40.3%	5.7%	12.1%	1,587,753	21.3%	21.3%	8.2%	28.3%	12.4%
Indiana.........................	273,193	95.3%	676,810	31.7%	40.0%	3.2%	9.2%	756,911	26.4%	24.2%	9.0%	21.3%	7.6%
Iowa............................	123,805	97.3%	321,381	25.1%	47.0%	7.8%	9.4%	359,741	21.7%	23.8%	13.1%	25.0%	9.7%
Kansas.........................	119,415	95.2%	296,205	27.2%	43.3%	7.1%	8.8%	348,071	21.5%	23.5%	10.4%	24.8%	10.1%
Kentucky......................	173,949	97.0%	424,621	34.9%	40.2%	4.1%	6.5%	503,547	28.2%	26.4%	9.1%	18.3%	8.1%
Louisiana.....................	187,168	95.7%	459,157	30.9%	41.3%	3.0%	7.0%	607,358	28.0%	23.9%	7.6%	20.0%	7.1%
Maine..........................	48,223	96.6%	115,050	31.0%	43.6%	3.4%	9.4%	135,710	28.9%	22.7%	9.6%	24.8%	8.2%
Maryland.......................	227,569	96.2%	558,491	28.6%	42.5%	5.0%	12.6%	746,445	22.1%	20.8%	6.7%	26.0%	15.1%
Massachusetts...............	250,516	97.7%	698,392	27.9%	41.2%	3.4%	16.0%	858,018	19.2%	16.8%	6.6%	32.7%	18.6%
Michigan.......................	400,539	96.3%	986,321	29.2%	43.6%	4.9%	9.2%	1,107,296	23.0%	26.4%	10.1%	23.3%	9.0%
Minnesota.....................	215,951	97.9%	504,157	29.3%	39.0%	5.6%	13.2%	670,737	19.4%	19.9%	13.4%	30.8%	10.6%
Mississippi...................	123,742	97.0%	312,903	28.6%	40.9%	7.6%	6.5%	332,474	27.6%	25.9%	12.2%	16.6%	6.0%
Missouri.......................	240,779	96.5%	598,165	30.3%	41.3%	5.5%	8.5%	722,354	24.6%	25.4%	9.4%	21.9%	9.7%
Montana.......................	37,052	95.1%	101,521	37.7%	38.5%	3.8%	4.7%	113,247	29.7%	22.5%	11.1%	20.3%	8.6%
Nebraska......................	75,068	96.9%	194,933	24.7%	45.0%	5.5%	12.9%	226,504	18.5%	27.0%	10.8%	26.0%	9.6%
Nevada.........................	108,914	97.5%	254,487	34.7%	37.8%	4.3%	4.6%	374,679	28.4%	28.6%	8.0%	17.0%	5.2%
New Hampshire..............	50,867	97.5%	129,612	30.9%	40.7%	4.1%	12.1%	136,348	22.5%	20.5%	9.6%	30.4%	11.3%
New Jersey...................	351,098	97.3%	792,038	27.6%	40.3%	5.6%	14.0%	1,039,533	23.6%	18.0%	7.2%	30.3%	13.2%
New Mexico...................	81,517	96.1%	208,652	28.0%	43.4%	6.1%	4.5%	243,894	26.1%	28.1%	8.8%	14.7%	7.3%
New York......................	720,612	97.3%	1,939,899	26.1%	40.1%	6.5%	14.1%	2,606,528	20.1%	17.2%	8.2%	29.6%	14.8%
North Carolina...............	389,275	96.0%	991,444	31.0%	40.3%	4.6%	9.1%	1,180,843	22.3%	24.4%	9.5%	22.7%	8.9%
North Dakota.................	26,021	98.4%	93,505	22.1%	47.4%	6.4%	12.6%	102,820	22.2%	22.5%	14.0%	27.3%	9.2%
Ohio............................	467,654	96.7%	1,090,850	33.8%	39.1%	3.6%	9.4%	1,339,989	26.3%	23.7%	9.7%	22.6%	9.6%
Oklahoma.....................	154,069	96.4%	391,812	31.9%	38.2%	4.1%	6.4%	480,214	30.4%	25.0%	7.8%	19.2%	5.9%
Oregon.........................	148,764	97.1%	365,845	29.2%	41.0%	5.1%	9.2%	493,914	22.7%	26.3%	8.3%	24.4%	9.2%
Pennsylvania.................	475,280	96.2%	1,210,947	33.1%	39.0%	4.2%	10.8%	1,486,228	26.3%	18.0%	9.8%	25.6%	12.1%
Rhode Island.................	37,117	97.2%	114,262	27.4%	43.9%	5.1%	12.4%	129,246	22.3%	23.9%	7.8%	26.6%	11.2%
South Carolina...............	189,881	97.7%	487,869	33.1%	41.9%	3.7%	7.7%	570,627	26.1%	24.5%	8.2%	21.2%	8.7%
South Dakota.................	34,011	93.6%	84,382	28.4%	38.5%	5.3%	11.4%	103,467	26.3%	23.1%	12.6%	23.2%	5.4%
Tennessee....................	258,293	97.1%	633,501	35.2%	40.9%	3.8%	8.4%	784,794	29.2%	23.5%	6.9%	21.8%	9.0%
Texas..........................	1,186,275	96.6%	2,780,856	32.7%	39.4%	4.1%	7.2%	3,594,612	25.5%	24.9%	7.1%	21.6%	7.7%
Utah............................	145,531	97.5%	345,362	29.3%	41.3%	9.0%	6.7%	394,649	23.8%	26.9%	11.2%	24.5%	6.5%
Vermont.......................	22,925	98.6%	67,578	29.2%	47.9%	3.0%	10.6%	65,969	27.7%	16.5%	5.1%	32.1%	9.8%
Virginia........................	312,713	96.9%	826,162	30.3%	42.8%	4.5%	11.3%	1,054,594	22.4%	22.7%	8.1%	26.5%	12.9%
Washington...................	268,408	97.2%	662,648	32.3%	36.6%	7.5%	9.6%	954,135	23.2%	23.6%	9.4%	24.7%	10.4%
West Virginia.................	66,815	97.7%	163,675	35.8%	41.9%	3.8%	7.6%	195,789	34.2%	23.5%	8.2%	16.8%	9.0%
Wisconsin.....................	222,282	97.6%	555,679	31.7%	40.1%	5.6%	10.9%	648,840	21.4%	23.9%	13.4%	25.9%	8.3%
Wyoming	20,958	92.0%	58,493	35.2%	32.4%	9.9%	4.2%	74,916	25.1%	28.0%	13.2%	19.4%	6.4%

Table E-2: Counties—Educational Attainment

	15 to 17		18 to 24					25 to 33					
				Percent					Percent				
	Total Population	Percent Enrolled in School	Total Population	High School	Some College	Associates Degree	Bachelors Degree	Total Population	High School	Some College	Associates Degree	Bachelors Degree	Advanced Degree
Alabama													
Baldwin County	7,453	100.0%	14,381	35.6%	27.1%	5.1%	14.1%	20,047	29.4%	28.8%	7.8%	21.7%	3.3%
Calhoun County	4,735	95.4%	12,942	27.6%	46.8%	3.5%	5.0%	12,913	33.7%	27.1%	7.8%	13.3%	7.5%
Etowah County	3,849	93.8%	9,075	28.9%	31.6%	10.4%	10.3%	9,578	26.2%	26.2%	5.9%	14.9%	7.2%
Houston County	4,558	95.7%	8,753	30.7%	39.1%	5.2%	8.2%	11,594	29.7%	25.8%	10.9%	11.6%	7.0%
Jefferson County	24,976	95.0%	58,661	33.8%	42.8%	4.3%	10.6%	84,794	23.2%	25.2%	5.2%	24.4%	13.9%
Lauderdale County	5,116	97.5%	8,925	28.1%	42.9%	2.7%	11.6%	9,028	36.0%	19.7%	10.1%	10.9%	7.1%
Lee County	5,316	92.3%	30,660	20.4%	60.5%	5.0%	6.6%	18,813	21.1%	35.7%	2.6%	22.9%	12.3%
Madison County	13,998	99.1%	32,804	36.2%	35.8%	4.9%	9.6%	44,089	19.4%	21.4%	12.1%	27.2%	11.2%
Marshall County	3,863	100.0%	8,881	27.2%	42.9%	6.2%	7.3%	9,155	26.2%	25.2%	7.1%	14.0%	4.3%
Mobile County	17,044	97.1%	37,483	34.9%	34.7%	2.3%	10.0%	53,577	23.3%	32.6%	7.2%	22.3%	4.2%
Montgomery County	9,013	94.9%	24,526	30.1%	41.7%	4.0%	9.5%	29,847	24.4%	30.1%	6.4%	18.8%	2.5%
Morgan County	5,755	93.8%	9,544	48.6%	22.5%	5.2%	6.5%	13,728	24.7%	30.3%	11.1%	13.6%	2.7%
Shelby County	8,768	97.4%	17,928	21.5%	59.6%	2.4%	3.3%	22,775	21.0%	22.5%	7.2%	37.3%	5.6%
Tuscaloosa County	7,734	98.8%	36,240	26.6%	53.9%	4.3%	4.6%	28,303	22.1%	23.7%	9.0%	21.2%	5.5%
Alaska													
Anchorage Municipality	11,687	93.5%	34,631	29.1%	38.9%	4.2%	9.9%	46,476	23.1%	30.9%	9.7%	23.3%	7.1%
Fairbanks North Star Borough	4,177	100.0%	15,158	35.6%	49.4%	7.9%	2.9%	15,499	24.9%	29.7%	10.8%	21.8%	5.4%
Matanuska-Susitna Borough	4,476	88.1%	10,694	48.8%	25.0%	1.8%	3.9%	12,719	44.5%	30.6%	4.8%	14.9%	0.3%
Arizona													
Cochise County	5,031	99.5%	9,550	42.2%	26.6%	6.8%	9.4%	14,841	34.6%	27.3%	9.5%	12.2%	5.4%
Coconino County	4,964	94.8%	29,687	29.2%	51.6%	4.1%	8.1%	17,120	27.0%	22.5%	16.9%	18.5%	10.5%
Maricopa County	172,695	96.0%	388,313	29.7%	37.8%	6.3%	8.6%	522,456	21.8%	26.6%	8.9%	22.4%	8.3%
Mohave County	6,887	90.6%	12,747	54.5%	18.2%	3.5%	4.0%	19,918	43.9%	25.9%	3.5%	7.2%	4.0%
Navajo County	4,733	94.3%	9,752	42.5%	24.0%	3.3%	1.7%	11,618	45.8%	28.6%	5.8%	8.0%	1.3%
Pima County	37,301	95.6%	119,343	26.8%	45.7%	4.6%	7.4%	110,798	20.9%	30.0%	9.8%	19.2%	8.6%
Pinal County	16,531	98.1%	30,975	27.6%	25.8%	4.7%	1.2%	45,270	28.9%	32.2%	7.2%	8.8%	3.1%
Yavapai County	6,488	84.4%	15,292	45.6%	40.9%	1.4%	5.0%	18,013	39.8%	26.9%	8.0%	12.9%	3.5%
Yuma County	9,130	93.2%	23,041	31.9%	41.1%	3.2%	3.3%	25,579	27.2%	27.3%	8.5%	13.2%	3.8%
Arkansas													
Benton County	10,696	96.6%	20,016	40.8%	25.7%	4.8%	11.6%	32,298	28.8%	21.5%	3.5%	21.4%	11.5%
Craighead County	5,131	99.0%	13,278	28.9%	50.0%	5.1%	5.6%	13,143	38.7%	20.4%	7.4%	21.5%	1.0%
Faulkner County	6,455	96.6%	17,473	30.5%	50.4%	4.9%	7.8%	16,220	27.2%	25.3%	11.2%	21.0%	5.3%
Garland County	3,373	88.4%	7,994	42.3%	40.5%	11.2%	0.7%	9,677	33.0%	35.4%	6.6%	13.6%	3.4%
Pulaski County	14,105	91.7%	35,650	31.3%	40.4%	2.4%	12.0%	53,734	19.9%	28.5%	7.2%	23.1%	12.6%
Saline County	4,687	84.2%	8,571	31.8%	52.2%	4.6%	5.2%	13,673	28.4%	26.8%	13.8%	9.5%	11.5%
Sebastian County	6,264	99.1%	11,525	34.8%	41.2%	7.9%	0.9%	14,618	28.4%	28.4%	10.9%	14.5%	2.3%
Washington County	8,062	95.3%	33,225	25.1%	50.7%	3.0%	12.5%	31,607	24.5%	29.3%	2.4%	19.2%	13.4%
California													
Alameda County	53,319	97.6%	140,673	27.2%	42.2%	3.3%	17.6%	239,328	17.4%	18.9%	5.5%	33.3%	16.6%
Butte County	7,589	99.1%	33,576	25.5%	48.2%	9.2%	7.6%	25,179	16.0%	37.5%	10.7%	19.0%	6.7%
Contra Costa County	45,591	98.6%	96,186	31.8%	37.9%	5.9%	12.9%	122,501	18.7%	24.1%	8.3%	28.6%	9.1%
El Dorado County	7,758	98.2%	13,743	21.0%	34.2%	8.3%	20.0%	16,584	24.5%	23.2%	18.7%	21.0%	7.5%
Fresno County	44,793	97.3%	106,206	28.1%	48.8%	5.9%	4.2%	129,871	26.8%	27.6%	8.1%	13.5%	4.6%
Humboldt County	3,629	100.0%	18,225	20.8%	58.8%	6.3%	6.9%	16,198	17.9%	38.5%	9.2%	18.9%	3.2%
Imperial County	8,239	96.1%	19,969	32.0%	37.0%	5.7%	4.0%	21,437	20.6%	23.2%	13.2%	16.3%	3.4%
Kern County	39,801	98.5%	96,404	41.2%	34.7%	2.7%	3.9%	119,068	32.7%	26.1%	5.8%	10.8%	4.2%
Kings County	6,293	99.1%	16,771	26.1%	38.4%	7.3%	3.9%	23,428	27.5%	26.5%	7.7%	10.1%	4.0%
Los Angeles County	386,428	97.4%	1,014,132	27.7%	45.2%	4.2%	10.1%	1,415,100	21.4%	23.1%	7.1%	26.4%	8.4%
Madera County	6,628	98.2%	15,683	31.2%	35.6%	4.9%	5.4%	19,229	28.8%	24.8%	4.7%	10.8%	2.1%
Marin County	8,607	100.0%	16,482	38.2%	27.8%	4.7%	10.1%	22,077	11.6%	19.6%	3.1%	37.2%	13.3%
Merced County	12,527	97.3%	32,689	28.1%	44.1%	5.7%	7.3%	33,141	28.6%	28.1%	6.9%	8.5%	4.7%
Monterey County	17,627	95.5%	46,279	29.2%	44.2%	5.7%	4.4%	56,147	21.2%	21.2%	9.7%	16.7%	3.5%
Napa County	5,350	98.4%	13,069	38.9%	38.3%	2.8%	7.9%	14,989	12.2%	32.0%	7.4%	33.7%	5.7%
Nevada County	3,189	79.8%	6,149	24.9%	59.2%	1.3%	4.3%	9,555	28.7%	31.6%	11.4%	20.8%	3.3%
Orange County	123,617	98.9%	301,487	28.2%	44.8%	5.5%	11.2%	398,540	16.5%	22.6%	7.6%	31.0%	11.1%
Placer County	15,343	95.1%	28,790	32.8%	43.8%	6.5%	8.5%	37,376	20.9%	27.2%	12.8%	26.2%	6.1%
Riverside County	107,174	97.3%	238,122	37.5%	38.9%	5.1%	4.7%	278,626	33.8%	28.0%	7.1%	12.4%	4.4%
Sacramento County	58,746	98.3%	136,870	27.9%	44.3%	5.9%	7.3%	204,701	22.3%	30.1%	10.4%	21.0%	6.7%
San Bernardino County	99,038	97.5%	235,348	35.1%	40.1%	4.7%	5.9%	287,689	30.5%	29.0%	9.1%	12.6%	4.5%
San Diego County	118,337	97.8%	352,621	33.1%	44.5%	4.3%	9.2%	473,319	20.3%	25.3%	7.9%	26.6%	11.2%
San Francisco County	17,062	97.0%	62,672	17.8%	37.7%	5.2%	34.8%	177,181	6.5%	10.6%	4.6%	51.6%	22.7%
San Joaquin County	33,581	98.1%	72,442	30.4%	45.2%	4.4%	4.3%	88,953	27.9%	29.9%	8.8%	11.6%	4.5%
San Luis Obispo County	8,526	98.7%	42,216	29.6%	52.1%	8.5%	3.8%	30,829	19.7%	29.9%	11.5%	20.0%	8.0%
San Mateo County	25,268	98.7%	57,300	24.9%	40.9%	7.0%	16.9%	95,118	14.0%	16.3%	8.3%	34.8%	18.3%
Santa Barbara County	16,101	99.2%	71,192	17.8%	60.2%	5.1%	7.9%	49,128	19.1%	22.1%	5.9%	24.5%	9.0%
Santa Clara County	67,386	97.7%	163,775	27.8%	41.8%	4.1%	17.0%	260,069	14.0%	16.8%	6.6%	30.1%	24.0%
Santa Cruz County	8,920	95.9%	42,214	20.9%	56.8%	2.8%	9.1%	30,305	21.1%	15.5%	8.6%	25.5%	9.9%
Shasta County	6,856	100.0%	13,747	28.7%	40.4%	4.6%	9.2%	21,145	23.4%	27.7%	10.3%	18.8%	8.7%
Solano County	16,430	95.8%	40,269	32.5%	38.9%	4.5%	9.2%	55,432	23.2%	29.1%	10.4%	18.4%	6.6%
Sonoma County	17,598	97.7%	43,756	29.9%	40.9%	6.5%	11.2%	57,264	20.4%	32.7%	9.8%	20.5%	6.8%
Stanislaus County	25,520	97.1%	54,104	38.3%	38.8%	3.8%	4.2%	70,720	30.1%	30.3%	7.5%	12.9%	2.9%
Sutter County	3,016	100.0%	8,221	21.7%	54.4%	5.7%	7.2%	13,924	35.7%	32.6%	11.0%	7.4%	2.9%
Tulare County	23,180	98.5%	48,480	32.6%	42.9%	5.0%	4.1%	59,578	33.7%	25.6%	7.1%	13.4%	3.1%

Table E-2: Counties—Educational Attainment—*Continued*

	15 to 17		18 to 24					25 to 33					
	Total Population	Percent Enrolled in School	Total Population	High School	Some College	Associates Degree	Bachelors Degree	Total Population	High School	Some College	Associates Degree	Bachelors Degree	Advanced Degree
California—Cont.													
Ventura County	35,077	98.3%	83,642	25.3%	44.6%	7.6%	7.0%	101,797	21.7%	23.1%	9.5%	21.5%	9.0%
Yolo County	7,308	100.0%	40,315	28.7%	50.9%	3.1%	12.6%	26,201	15.0%	22.3%	6.7%	35.4%	13.8%
Colorado													
Adams County	23,017	97.3%	42,953	42.0%	28.5%	5.8%	8.4%	71,561	26.7%	25.1%	9.6%	23.5%	5.0%
Arapahoe County	25,766	97.1%	54,292	32.9%	35.5%	6.5%	10.7%	86,269	19.0%	26.5%	10.0%	29.2%	8.0%
Boulder County	11,992	97.4%	50,331	18.9%	55.5%	3.7%	17.2%	37,559	14.9%	17.5%	6.4%	39.0%	21.4%
Denver County	16,454	89.3%	57,164	26.4%	36.7%	5.6%	15.4%	139,346	16.2%	16.8%	4.8%	37.4%	17.8%
Douglas County	15,941	99.5%	24,273	33.9%	43.4%	2.3%	8.9%	27,302	11.3%	19.1%	8.0%	42.9%	17.3%
El Paso County	26,582	95.9%	72,805	29.0%	47.8%	3.4%	8.8%	97,677	23.5%	28.7%	12.9%	22.8%	5.9%
Jefferson County	20,072	95.4%	49,253	31.8%	36.9%	6.1%	12.5%	70,252	19.8%	19.7%	6.5%	34.9%	14.3%
Larimer County	11,319	96.8%	45,152	22.9%	49.5%	3.9%	16.2%	45,352	16.6%	25.3%	11.6%	32.5%	11.2%
Mesa County	5,555	98.4%	15,236	18.3%	55.2%	5.0%	1.7%	17,924	29.4%	23.9%	10.6%	20.3%	2.6%
Pueblo County	6,500	87.8%	15,312	37.1%	35.8%	4.6%	8.0%	18,784	28.7%	36.7%	10.7%	15.7%	1.6%
Weld County	13,752	97.5%	28,999	31.7%	45.9%	5.8%	4.3%	35,019	24.9%	29.0%	9.6%	17.2%	7.3%
Connecticut													
Fairfield County	40,383	95.3%	85,139	25.3%	37.6%	4.5%	19.0%	97,867	20.7%	18.0%	6.8%	29.9%	16.2%
Hartford County	34,275	98.1%	82,956	27.8%	41.7%	4.5%	13.8%	102,090	20.1%	18.2%	7.1%	30.6%	17.8%
Litchfield County	6,694	99.0%	13,568	35.9%	31.4%	3.2%	24.6%	16,493	27.0%	23.5%	7.2%	27.2%	8.3%
Middlesex County	6,930	95.1%	15,193	21.9%	51.4%	4.8%	11.4%	15,292	18.4%	22.3%	8.1%	31.2%	16.3%
New Haven County	33,371	97.4%	87,071	31.6%	42.2%	3.1%	13.2%	99,378	25.4%	20.0%	6.1%	24.6%	15.4%
New London County	10,589	92.9%	28,636	40.2%	36.4%	5.7%	8.4%	31,833	30.4%	22.2%	6.2%	25.8%	11.0%
Tolland County	5,274	97.6%	28,023	17.2%	64.2%	5.5%	8.7%	15,393	10.6%	19.6%	7.2%	41.0%	19.5%
Windham County	4,391	97.7%	11,899	26.5%	53.3%	6.0%	8.9%	13,501	25.0%	27.5%	15.4%	10.6%	12.6%
Delaware													
Kent County	6,870	99.1%	18,762	25.6%	47.3%	4.0%	4.5%	20,537	31.3%	30.6%	8.4%	13.9%	3.7%
New Castle County	21,630	96.4%	52,593	30.7%	36.6%	6.6%	13.1%	74,577	22.7%	22.9%	5.5%	28.0%	11.5%
Sussex County	6,481	90.8%	15,661	36.2%	33.0%	8.2%	7.0%	19,639	29.3%	23.1%	12.8%	11.4%	3.9%
Florida													
Alachua County	7,575	100.0%	56,248	18.3%	50.8%	11.2%	14.4%	35,666	20.3%	13.4%	15.9%	26.8%	18.5%
Bay County	6,058	97.9%	14,840	34.6%	29.3%	5.6%	2.5%	23,476	31.2%	31.4%	11.1%	14.0%	4.4%
Brevard County	20,157	97.4%	45,039	30.1%	37.2%	8.5%	6.2%	55,168	25.2%	28.0%	12.8%	20.0%	7.7%
Broward County	69,903	96.5%	155,585	28.3%	36.0%	9.6%	9.4%	229,354	25.0%	20.5%	12.0%	23.9%	8.8%
Charlotte County	4,383	100.0%	9,538	38.7%	28.5%	13.8%	1.1%	9,228	46.1%	17.3%	11.3%	9.5%	2.9%
Citrus County	3,920	96.6%	7,713	43.5%	17.6%	5.5%	2.7%	8,986	44.4%	9.9%	20.1%	12.4%	0.4%
Clay County	9,230	100.0%	17,559	31.4%	42.0%	2.2%	8.1%	21,120	24.4%	26.4%	16.8%	16.3%	6.1%
Collier County	11,293	96.9%	25,881	40.6%	28.5%	2.6%	10.0%	30,802	27.6%	15.6%	10.7%	22.2%	6.3%
Duval County	33,512	97.8%	86,478	34.9%	32.3%	6.9%	10.1%	129,731	27.3%	25.2%	8.6%	22.9%	9.1%
Escambia County	10,853	95.7%	40,469	30.3%	44.4%	6.2%	9.1%	40,786	28.1%	18.4%	19.8%	19.0%	6.6%
Flagler County	3,714	100.0%	7,889	20.0%	35.4%	9.3%	1.1%	7,123	37.9%	26.6%	1.1%	31.6%	2.8%
Hernando County	6,734	98.6%	11,462	39.6%	34.8%	11.3%	4.2%	15,819	36.4%	30.8%	9.6%	10.3%	1.0%
Highlands County	3,780	96.0%	6,061	38.8%	26.1%	6.5%	0.0%	7,645	53.1%	16.8%	6.1%	6.0%	4.5%
Hillsborough County	52,057	98.4%	123,236	27.5%	33.9%	9.2%	12.6%	182,022	25.1%	20.7%	10.4%	24.4%	9.6%
Indian River County	4,007	92.7%	11,503	38.6%	17.4%	22.8%	5.3%	11,380	43.6%	29.5%	8.7%	5.1%	4.7%
Lake County	12,165	96.2%	21,516	37.1%	24.1%	7.3%	4.6%	29,837	26.6%	25.9%	14.2%	19.7%	5.6%
Lee County	21,786	94.1%	49,430	28.3%	29.8%	12.1%	5.1%	68,198	33.6%	21.4%	8.7%	14.2%	5.6%
Leon County	8,756	96.8%	65,175	14.0%	50.5%	16.1%	14.7%	35,299	21.4%	18.9%	12.3%	28.7%	13.8%
Manatee County	12,403	98.1%	26,302	37.1%	25.8%	11.3%	4.8%	33,040	34.8%	23.4%	6.8%	10.7%	6.3%
Marion County	11,395	94.1%	25,183	30.4%	33.3%	6.2%	10.0%	33,781	38.7%	28.2%	8.6%	11.4%	3.4%
Martin County	4,770	100.0%	11,404	34.3%	22.5%	9.0%	3.8%	11,689	23.9%	19.6%	15.6%	24.2%	10.1%
Miami-Dade County	95,700	95.2%	236,693	29.8%	35.5%	11.9%	8.7%	346,035	27.7%	19.2%	11.7%	21.5%	10.0%
Okaloosa County	6,455	96.8%	18,979	32.2%	33.3%	9.5%	6.3%	29,242	20.8%	35.0%	10.2%	22.0%	4.8%
Orange County	49,222	95.7%	144,127	26.8%	40.5%	10.9%	10.4%	188,528	20.6%	22.3%	12.0%	29.3%	9.1%
Osceola County	14,495	97.2%	31,196	41.6%	31.7%	7.5%	5.0%	40,058	32.6%	28.2%	14.7%	15.2%	5.1%
Palm Beach County	49,340	97.5%	109,088	25.3%	39.5%	7.7%	10.0%	146,764	20.5%	22.6%	10.2%	26.3%	7.0%
Pasco County	18,634	92.5%	36,830	31.2%	33.9%	7.4%	10.2%	46,830	28.0%	22.3%	13.7%	18.1%	7.7%
Pinellas County	27,753	96.5%	65,800	30.0%	34.6%	6.7%	10.7%	98,785	28.3%	21.2%	12.3%	23.7%	7.0%
Polk County	25,335	95.3%	56,070	34.4%	35.8%	4.2%	5.2%	76,330	34.5%	20.2%	8.9%	15.0%	4.2%
Santa Rosa County	10,149	99.2%	17,562	31.2%	40.5%	7.2%	10.1%	21,335	18.4%	16.3%	8.7%	40.8%	10.8%
Sarasota County	10,234	97.8%	22,151	27.2%	35.2%	5.1%	5.6%	31,750	31.7%	26.1%	13.9%	8.8%	3.2%
Seminole County	6,524	93.5%	13,125	39.2%	24.5%	10.9%	6.0%	21,224	18.6%	20.3%	19.4%	23.0%	7.0%
St. Johns County	10,927	96.5%	23,480	36.5%	35.1%	6.0%	6.8%	31,760	30.2%	23.9%	9.2%	25.1%	4.3%
St. Lucie County	18,121	98.2%	39,304	25.2%	38.6%	17.5%	7.2%	55,902	18.3%	18.4%	24.1%	26.3%	5.9%
Sumter County	2,181	100.0%	4,730	24.4%	18.1%	6.2%	2.6%	3,888	29.3%	25.2%	13.3%	12.9%	2.7%
Volusia County	16,444	98.2%	42,400	28.1%	41.2%	10.2%	7.0%	53,825	34.9%	25.1%	12.6%	17.9%	5.2%
Georgia													
Bartow County	4,382	92.9%	9,293	30.9%	39.4%	3.6%	4.1%	10,921	25.6%	20.7%	11.2%	21.6%	2.7%
Bibb County	6,082	94.4%	16,246	32.0%	45.1%	3.0%	5.1%	18,545	25.0%	23.8%	7.8%	25.1%	9.5%
Carroll County	5,101	94.9%	15,447	23.2%	53.6%	2.8%	4.3%	13,544	32.1%	30.9%	2.2%	18.0%	6.9%
Chatham County	9,149	92.0%	33,626	30.5%	46.6%	1.8%	9.6%	42,779	18.1%	37.8%	5.2%	18.1%	10.0%
Cherokee County	10,961	100.0%	19,073	31.9%	34.4%	3.3%	4.9%	25,158	19.7%	23.4%	6.7%	32.3%	10.1%
Clarke County	2,635	100.0%	36,550	19.0%	58.2%	3.2%	13.3%	16,374	14.6%	16.2%	6.6%	33.2%	18.4%
Clayton County	11,973	95.6%	27,620	41.3%	33.7%	2.0%	6.5%	36,094	34.0%	29.8%	6.0%	14.3%	2.4%
Cobb County	29,813	97.3%	66,221	24.8%	39.9%	3.8%	15.5%	94,327	15.5%	21.6%	8.5%	31.5%	11.8%
Columbia County	6,372	97.6%	12,592	33.5%	36.0%	11.7%	7.4%	19,341	16.8%	30.0%	10.8%	26.2%	5.9%

Table E-2: Counties—Educational Attainment—*Continued*

	15 to 17		18 to 24					25 to 33					
				Percent						Percent			
	Total Population	Percent Enrolled in School	Total Population	High School	Some College	Associates Degree	Bachelors Degree	Total Population	High School	Some College	Associates Degree	Bachelors Degree	Advanced Degree
Georgia—Cont.													
Coweta County	6,566	97.0%	11,521	24.2%	42.3%	5.8%	11.6%	15,096	37.4%	28.0%	6.2%	21.4%	4.5%
DeKalb County	24,716	96.2%	65,575	29.1%	35.6%	3.3%	13.9%	110,091	16.3%	23.8%	5.6%	26.9%	14.9%
Dougherty County	3,869	93.5%	11,312	35.7%	27.2%	7.9%	1.2%	9,967	34.0%	22.3%	14.1%	16.0%	2.3%
Douglas County	6,733	98.2%	13,139	30.4%	40.4%	4.5%	4.4%	15,463	29.6%	19.6%	6.5%	25.9%	11.3%
Fayette County	6,314	98.2%	10,448	23.2%	39.9%	3.2%	12.7%	6,653	33.2%	13.2%	6.9%	24.6%	10.4%
Floyd County	3,826	99.5%	9,179	34.9%	36.8%	0.0%	1.8%	11,390	34.8%	24.2%	5.4%	12.7%	10.3%
Forsyth County	10,460	100.0%	15,074	38.4%	26.1%	2.8%	14.2%	18,563	14.0%	22.3%	8.9%	26.6%	20.2%
Fulton County	38,991	98.5%	99,071	21.0%	46.1%	3.4%	16.4%	148,188	14.8%	16.9%	5.0%	37.2%	17.6%
Gwinnett County	43,096	95.6%	82,834	32.7%	35.3%	6.5%	9.0%	102,945	21.5%	17.2%	10.1%	26.6%	10.4%
Hall County	8,761	99.9%	18,304	36.3%	35.8%	2.5%	2.5%	21,584	21.9%	29.2%	10.2%	12.4%	4.5%
Henry County	12,656	94.3%	23,115	50.3%	20.5%	7.4%	6.4%	21,023	22.8%	28.5%	5.0%	28.3%	3.7%
Houston County	6,296	99.8%	14,662	35.3%	35.6%	5.7%	5.4%	17,833	21.4%	33.1%	15.0%	13.6%	9.7%
Lowndes County	4,318	96.9%	18,196	24.4%	44.0%	14.2%	6.2%	16,568	14.9%	28.2%	17.3%	15.9%	7.0%
Muscogee County	6,809	99.2%	24,221	36.5%	37.3%	6.4%	5.7%	29,648	24.5%	33.1%	6.1%	18.3%	10.6%
Newton County	6,061	96.9%	8,171	23.0%	54.1%	4.1%	9.9%	12,360	32.6%	33.8%	9.2%	13.8%	0.8%
Paulding County	7,701	96.2%	14,317	45.8%	34.8%	0.0%	6.7%	16,727	41.8%	24.0%	7.2%	10.8%	7.6%
Richmond County	7,388	92.2%	23,706	39.8%	32.2%	1.6%	5.2%	30,218	24.5%	28.6%	14.0%	15.1%	8.4%
Whitfield County	4,558	93.0%	10,390	33.2%	33.7%	3.9%	2.6%	13,342	27.1%	23.1%	5.5%	16.6%	1.1%
Hawaii													
Hawaii County	6,367	94.5%	16,321	36.2%	32.4%	16.6%	5.5%	21,668	32.1%	27.6%	6.1%	19.9%	7.0%
Honolulu County	30,847	97.5%	104,107	36.8%	40.3%	7.5%	10.3%	138,456	25.9%	26.5%	10.7%	25.1%	7.6%
Maui County	5,710	91.0%	12,607	33.2%	42.9%	7.2%	11.8%	20,898	29.4%	30.6%	11.2%	19.4%	4.2%
Idaho													
Ada County	18,067	98.1%	37,337	40.3%	37.3%	4.6%	6.0%	57,353	24.2%	28.2%	9.5%	23.7%	7.7%
Bonneville County	4,160	96.7%	8,924	47.2%	24.0%	8.1%	4.3%	14,384	23.7%	26.1%	13.1%	18.4%	6.6%
Canyon County	10,595	96.4%	19,059	33.6%	44.1%	3.5%	1.7%	23,454	40.2%	24.1%	7.8%	10.3%	1.8%
Kootenai County	5,612	97.3%	11,742	39.0%	34.2%	3.8%	7.8%	17,751	23.8%	30.7%	10.7%	11.9%	9.6%
Illinois													
Champaign County	5,420	98.0%	50,803	16.8%	63.7%	4.7%	8.7%	24,074	10.3%	17.4%	4.6%	36.2%	29.0%
Cook County	192,674	96.4%	478,190	27.0%	39.8%	4.7%	15.7%	749,255	19.5%	17.9%	6.4%	33.0%	15.3%
DeKalb County	3,392	96.1%	21,847	29.6%	45.0%	7.0%	15.8%	12,654	17.2%	27.8%	11.1%	23.9%	12.5%
DuPage County	37,895	98.4%	84,758	28.9%	38.4%	5.7%	19.4%	103,130	16.6%	22.2%	8.2%	35.0%	12.1%
Kane County	24,307	99.4%	48,293	29.1%	38.9%	5.5%	11.8%	55,269	22.5%	26.3%	5.8%	21.3%	7.2%
Kankakee County	4,612	99.4%	11,549	32.5%	44.4%	3.4%	8.5%	12,290	38.2%	18.8%	9.6%	23.4%	3.9%
Kendall County	6,586	96.8%	11,323	47.7%	26.5%	7.9%	2.3%	14,670	18.3%	30.3%	9.9%	28.6%	6.3%
Lake County	34,382	99.6%	71,265	32.0%	36.0%	6.6%	15.2%	68,950	21.6%	23.3%	3.6%	25.7%	12.5%
LaSalle County	4,432	95.8%	8,885	27.6%	36.0%	11.6%	12.0%	11,899	27.7%	42.2%	6.1%	10.7%	1.9%
Macon County	14,878	98.3%	26,318	37.4%	30.7%	5.4%	14.4%	27,547	24.4%	22.2%	12.6%	23.3%	11.4%
Madison County	6,408	92.0%	30,701	19.6%	60.8%	7.5%	6.5%	19,902	17.4%	22.1%	10.2%	37.2%	9.5%
McHenry County	3,953	99.5%	10,188	39.8%	34.3%	5.1%	7.3%	10,459	31.2%	31.2%	11.9%	16.2%	3.1%
McLean County	10,067	95.4%	22,983	25.9%	48.7%	7.9%	6.3%	31,871	24.7%	25.5%	15.6%	19.5%	7.6%
Peoria County	7,213	90.2%	17,561	26.8%	46.8%	5.5%	9.3%	24,949	18.0%	21.4%	8.3%	24.4%	17.1%
Rock Island County	5,147	98.9%	12,821	31.1%	46.4%	2.0%	8.0%	14,721	19.5%	30.6%	11.4%	23.0%	5.6%
Sangamon County	10,070	95.2%	22,071	32.6%	38.4%	5.1%	8.9%	30,890	22.1%	27.7%	15.1%	19.0%	5.2%
St. Clair County	8,412	91.6%	17,501	21.9%	33.9%	3.7%	16.8%	22,066	17.7%	31.8%	5.1%	23.3%	12.3%
Tazewell County	5,099	100.0%	9,581	32.6%	39.8%	10.7%	6.9%	15,526	24.0%	20.7%	14.9%	23.0%	10.8%
Will County	32,614	97.3%	61,876	33.1%	35.5%	5.4%	14.9%	70,359	24.4%	24.8%	9.0%	21.4%	11.5%
Winnebago County	11,431	95.8%	24,727	35.2%	37.0%	4.5%	7.3%	32,181	24.7%	18.7%	11.2%	24.7%	5.9%
Indiana													
Allen County	15,457	94.3%	35,877	30.0%	41.0%	2.1%	11.2%	43,159	20.5%	28.1%	9.9%	23.8%	6.9%
Clark County	4,287	86.3%	8,677	40.7%	43.1%	6.5%	0.9%	13,802	26.5%	28.9%	12.2%	19.9%	4.6%
Delaware County	3,898	93.9%	22,931	25.2%	61.0%	3.9%	4.8%	10,355	28.3%	29.3%	6.3%	13.6%	7.3%
Elkhart County	9,847	91.9%	18,907	40.3%	30.1%	2.3%	5.7%	22,639	35.0%	23.5%	5.9%	14.0%	4.7%
Hamilton County	15,860	96.2%	22,137	34.0%	29.2%	4.0%	19.7%	32,351	10.4%	23.2%	6.4%	43.7%	11.7%
Hendricks County	6,868	93.1%	12,782	37.1%	28.8%	10.5%	15.8%	19,120	22.5%	27.5%	5.3%	34.0%	7.3%
Johnson County	6,498	96.7%	12,661	28.6%	37.1%	5.7%	14.3%	16,374	16.0%	27.1%	9.1%	29.7%	8.7%
Lake County	22,134	95.5%	42,669	33.1%	38.5%	3.4%	5.5%	50,962	27.7%	25.9%	10.2%	19.5%	6.7%
LaPorte County	4,374	96.8%	8,713	43.5%	32.0%	2.1%	6.1%	12,832	34.2%	24.9%	5.2%	10.1%	2.7%
Madison County	5,357	100.0%	11,939	34.8%	46.3%	1.8%	4.5%	14,351	28.7%	31.6%	11.3%	14.6%	3.1%
Marion County	33,953	96.6%	87,972	32.0%	34.7%	2.4%	13.7%	143,605	22.3%	20.5%	8.0%	25.6%	9.4%
Monroe County	4,057	95.0%	40,498	16.6%	64.6%	2.0%	14.1%	19,522	15.9%	27.0%	4.2%	30.7%	15.4%
Porter County	7,257	99.4%	16,289	46.4%	30.1%	1.5%	6.1%	16,606	24.3%	21.5%	12.0%	18.4%	13.7%
St. Joseph County	11,323	91.8%	30,022	31.2%	41.2%	0.8%	9.9%	30,257	20.9%	28.1%	7.9%	25.9%	9.7%
Tippecanoe County	5,390	99.8%	45,635	23.4%	53.5%	0.4%	14.3%	23,119	15.1%	25.2%	6.2%	26.5%	22.9%
Vanderburgh County	5,989	93.0%	18,215	30.6%	39.9%	2.4%	9.1%	23,223	22.4%	23.5%	7.1%	25.1%	10.8%
Vigo County	3,899	97.6%	17,396	19.0%	52.3%	3.3%	11.9%	11,877	23.6%	27.7%	4.2%	19.9%	4.9%
Iowa													
Black Hawk County	4,554	99.3%	20,218	17.6%	59.3%	3.5%	7.9%	16,522	19.7%	31.5%	9.9%	26.7%	6.7%
Dubuque County	4,498	100.0%	10,631	24.3%	47.2%	13.7%	7.5%	10,173	30.1%	14.3%	8.2%	19.6%	19.5%
Johnson County	4,586	100.0%	30,445	26.5%	52.5%	3.6%	15.5%	20,149	20.0%	14.0%	9.8%	30.2%	22.5%
Linn County	8,896	98.3%	20,556	26.9%	45.2%	6.4%	10.9%	26,946	15.3%	28.5%	14.1%	30.8%	9.5%
Polk County	17,901	97.0%	42,356	25.7%	46.8%	5.2%	13.0%	63,811	18.7%	18.3%	9.1%	34.8%	11.5%
Pottawattamie County	3,531	99.6%	7,635	32.1%	40.1%	11.9%	5.9%	10,697	26.2%	20.4%	16.4%	19.3%	7.8%

Table E-2: Counties—Educational Attainment—*Continued*

| | 15 to 17 | | 18 to 24 | | | | | 25 to 33 | | | | | |
| | Total Population | Percent Enrolled in School | Total Population | Percent | | | | Total Population | Percent | | | | |
				High School	Some College	Associates Degree	Bachelors Degree		High School	Some College	Associates Degree	Bachelors Degree	Advanced Degree
Iowa—Cont.													
Scott County	6,340	97.6%	14,919	30.8%	41.2%	9.1%	9.0%	21,279	27.4%	20.2%	12.1%	26.1%	7.4%
Story County	2,650	100.0%	30,499	16.5%	65.9%	5.8%	9.0%	12,160	17.5%	19.6%	9.7%	27.1%	24.0%
Woodbury County	5,066	99.2%	10,216	36.0%	36.7%	3.9%	2.8%	13,035	22.6%	29.2%	8.4%	17.2%	7.6%
Kansas													
Douglas County	2,982	95.1%	27,314	21.4%	62.3%	7.9%	8.1%	16,467	18.2%	17.8%	6.6%	25.6%	23.0%
Johnson County	25,281	97.5%	45,453	21.1%	39.5%	7.5%	17.9%	72,191	11.5%	15.5%	7.9%	42.4%	19.6%
Sedgwick County	21,925	92.4%	42,104	26.9%	41.7%	4.9%	8.1%	69,848	20.9%	24.5%	10.4%	22.7%	8.0%
Shawnee County	7,605	96.8%	15,601	31.8%	39.6%	2.5%	10.1%	20,868	23.7%	27.4%	14.6%	18.1%	11.6%
Wyandotte County	6,907	91.3%	15,957	37.2%	34.0%	4.8%	7.9%	20,784	25.2%	22.2%	10.1%	15.1%	6.8%
Kentucky													
Boone County	5,241	100.0%	10,603	40.4%	42.2%	4.6%	5.6%	14,062	34.3%	33.8%	4.3%	13.5%	4.7%
Campbell County	2,719	99.2%	10,150	46.0%	27.8%	1.0%	13.5%	12,171	22.3%	24.9%	5.1%	22.7%	12.3%
Daviess County	4,096	98.6%	8,278	42.0%	30.0%	7.0%	7.7%	10,870	20.5%	46.2%	10.8%	16.3%	2.8%
Fayette County	9,984	98.5%	43,094	20.7%	55.7%	2.8%	13.4%	44,691	19.2%	24.8%	6.3%	30.3%	15.3%
Hardin County	5,842	100.0%	8,702	45.7%	29.9%	4.8%	5.2%	13,182	27.6%	30.5%	7.8%	12.4%	7.7%
Jefferson County	28,047	98.4%	67,483	29.8%	43.3%	4.6%	8.6%	97,019	21.8%	21.5%	7.7%	26.7%	14.9%
Kenton County	6,292	98.0%	13,201	34.8%	33.9%	3.6%	13.1%	21,440	22.8%	22.9%	11.1%	25.8%	6.3%
Warren County	5,132	100.0%	20,247	28.6%	52.4%	1.5%	12.7%	13,584	10.7%	28.8%	10.8%	31.1%	9.3%
Louisiana													
Ascension Parish	5,994	100.0%	9,930	37.8%	42.0%	1.1%	4.0%	15,246	23.2%	21.4%	8.0%	25.2%	9.0%
Bossier Parish	5,398	100.0%	10,378	41.1%	30.2%	1.3%	8.7%	18,823	28.0%	24.4%	11.0%	15.4%	9.3%
Caddo Parish	9,885	98.0%	22,950	28.6%	44.6%	3.8%	4.1%	31,201	23.9%	37.1%	5.8%	13.6%	5.6%
Calcasieu Parish	8,228	97.4%	19,191	41.5%	29.3%	2.8%	8.1%	25,818	36.0%	26.2%	7.0%	12.1%	6.5%
East Baton Rouge Parish	16,677	97.5%	64,836	22.7%	51.2%	3.3%	13.2%	60,253	25.0%	24.3%	6.0%	28.4%	8.1%
Jefferson Parish	14,162	97.6%	35,832	38.5%	35.5%	2.0%	7.7%	59,422	26.2%	23.6%	7.1%	21.7%	7.1%
Lafayette Parish	9,654	96.1%	25,132	29.1%	49.1%	3.0%	7.9%	35,178	20.8%	24.6%	8.5%	32.1%	7.2%
Lafourche Parish	3,944	94.6%	9,010	29.3%	43.3%	6.7%	4.1%	12,284	38.1%	16.7%	10.4%	12.8%	3.6%
Livingston Parish	4,931	90.9%	12,429	25.8%	36.7%	1.0%	11.2%	18,143	23.2%	27.0%	6.9%	23.4%	10.6%
Orleans Parish	11,869	97.1%	36,913	23.6%	48.2%	1.5%	13.0%	64,511	19.0%	23.3%	3.6%	29.4%	16.0%
Ouachita Parish	6,570	94.0%	16,254	20.9%	53.3%	3.7%	6.0%	21,022	26.5%	24.3%	5.2%	23.0%	9.2%
Rapides Parish	5,581	99.7%	12,171	34.2%	36.9%	5.0%	8.6%	15,027	29.1%	24.1%	12.0%	9.8%	6.0%
St. Tammany Parish	10,828	92.9%	17,848	25.2%	35.9%	5.7%	3.2%	27,347	20.9%	24.1%	6.8%	26.2%	8.8%
Tangipahoa Parish	5,276	92.1%	15,212	33.3%	49.0%	0.0%	1.3%	16,082	34.1%	24.4%	8.6%	14.6%	2.1%
Terrebonne Parish	3,910	92.8%	9,054	43.2%	32.2%	3.8%	6.2%	14,608	33.7%	21.1%	9.8%	22.6%	0.0%
Maine													
Androscoggin County	4,002	96.7%	9,422	31.3%	47.9%	0.0%	7.1%	10,928	33.1%	32.9%	8.8%	12.7%	10.1%
Cumberland County	11,424	96.8%	27,405	26.7%	44.6%	5.7%	14.6%	32,599	26.4%	18.8%	7.5%	32.7%	10.5%
Kennebec County	4,104	100.0%	10,420	39.4%	36.2%	1.2%	6.9%	11,402	32.8%	22.7%	9.9%	24.2%	5.3%
Penobscot County	5,200	97.9%	17,405	16.3%	56.2%	3.7%	8.0%	18,251	24.4%	23.1%	14.3%	19.0%	9.1%
York County	8,207	100.0%	14,898	40.8%	40.0%	6.1%	5.2%	21,412	25.8%	22.0%	8.9%	30.5%	9.1%
Maryland													
Anne Arundel County	20,440	99.3%	49,519	27.9%	42.8%	6.9%	9.7%	72,114	20.1%	22.1%	9.1%	24.0%	16.9%
Baltimore County	29,283	96.4%	75,812	30.1%	42.1%	5.1%	14.5%	102,913	23.1%	20.3%	8.4%	28.5%	14.8%
Carroll County	7,587	98.8%	15,086	32.8%	40.5%	7.1%	12.5%	15,451	22.5%	19.2%	11.9%	24.6%	14.7%
Cecil County	4,087	71.5%	10,116	40.9%	33.7%	7.9%	7.9%	10,550	45.4%	23.3%	2.5%	21.0%	4.0%
Charles County	7,369	98.9%	14,616	31.5%	43.6%	6.0%	13.0%	17,558	35.4%	20.1%	7.2%	18.4%	12.9%
Frederick County	10,064	100.0%	23,610	20.9%	44.0%	4.7%	23.7%	25,527	21.9%	21.9%	7.0%	31.9%	14.0%
Harford County	10,052	99.4%	21,193	37.4%	37.1%	5.4%	12.6%	27,303	24.3%	26.1%	10.0%	24.9%	9.2%
Howard County	14,442	100.0%	24,724	23.3%	39.9%	6.9%	21.9%	35,451	14.2%	20.6%	6.9%	31.4%	22.4%
Montgomery County	39,976	95.1%	80,631	23.8%	42.8%	6.2%	20.0%	121,975	15.2%	15.5%	6.2%	32.0%	21.5%
Prince George's County	32,415	96.0%	92,320	28.1%	45.5%	3.8%	9.6%	119,847	22.2%	22.7%	4.5%	23.5%	12.4%
St. Mary's County	4,664	98.1%	11,172	36.0%	35.8%	3.4%	14.3%	12,744	21.6%	32.6%	7.3%	21.7%	10.5%
Washington County	6,110	95.5%	12,974	35.5%	36.8%	3.7%	7.5%	17,314	33.4%	22.5%	7.8%	16.4%	7.0%
Wicomico County	3,726	92.5%	15,548	25.8%	52.2%	7.1%	4.9%	10,832	28.0%	29.9%	4.9%	17.9%	12.4%
Massachusetts													
Barnstable County	7,085	98.3%	14,470	28.6%	47.5%	7.5%	4.5%	16,446	23.8%	29.1%	12.5%	26.2%	5.1%
Berkshire County	4,505	99.3%	13,356	22.2%	51.8%	3.7%	7.6%	10,784	31.0%	24.7%	10.7%	20.2%	6.4%
Bristol County	20,144	96.9%	53,784	33.5%	35.0%	6.0%	10.9%	64,980	27.6%	23.8%	8.1%	20.9%	8.0%
Essex County	31,668	97.4%	70,510	31.6%	33.3%	5.2%	14.4%	86,690	23.0%	19.9%	8.6%	26.1%	12.7%
Hampden County	18,698	94.6%	51,064	30.2%	46.0%	1.9%	7.2%	52,638	25.9%	16.7%	8.0%	22.8%	11.3%
Hampshire County	7,555	99.2%	30,446	15.0%	64.2%	2.0%	10.6%	19,802	21.2%	20.8%	12.1%	26.7%	14.3%
Middlesex County	56,272	97.1%	151,267	26.4%	36.9%	3.4%	24.2%	217,135	14.6%	11.4%	4.5%	37.9%	27.9%
Norfolk County	31,491	99.5%	56,434	28.4%	34.6%	2.0%	27.0%	74,387	15.3%	18.5%	5.5%	38.0%	20.2%
Plymouth County	20,867	99.2%	47,932	30.8%	39.2%	4.7%	15.2%	45,305	27.9%	18.8%	7.3%	29.6%	11.2%
Suffolk County	20,344	97.4%	109,239	23.5%	46.7%	1.8%	20.0%	164,411	13.5%	13.1%	4.2%	41.4%	22.7%
Worcester County	34,713	99.9%	79,420	36.6%	34.7%	4.0%	14.7%	86,588	23.3%	21.5%	8.4%	27.7%	11.7%
Michigan													
Allegan County	5,166	93.7%	9,792	48.6%	33.7%	6.4%	3.8%	11,964	38.9%	31.0%	6.1%	15.9%	4.5%
Bay County	4,086	97.7%	8,750	38.1%	34.5%	5.5%	3.5%	11,393	21.6%	37.3%	9.2%	24.1%	3.2%
Berrien County	5,752	97.5%	12,450	32.8%	34.9%	6.6%	8.6%	15,966	29.8%	20.8%	14.9%	22.4%	7.4%
Calhoun County	5,674	97.0%	10,750	37.8%	32.8%	5.1%	6.0%	15,498	41.5%	20.2%	10.9%	16.5%	3.3%
Eaton County	4,272	98.5%	10,308	15.7%	55.0%	8.1%	6.9%	11,088	25.8%	37.5%	7.5%	23.5%	4.9%
Genesee County	16,854	96.0%	37,578	33.0%	37.5%	3.3%	4.8%	44,026	23.8%	34.8%	10.8%	14.9%	6.1%

Table E-2: Counties—Educational Attainment—Continued

| | 15 to 17 | | 18 to 24 | | | | | 25 to 33 | | | | | |
	Total Population	Percent Enrolled in School	Total Population	High School	Some College	Associates Degree	Bachelors Degree	Total Population	High School	Some College	Associates Degree	Bachelors Degree	Advanced Degree
Michigan—Cont.													
Ingham County	10,505	94.7%	55,890	13.6%	66.3%	2.1%	12.2%	36,809	15.1%	21.5%	8.5%	28.8%	18.8%
Jackson County	5,866	95.0%	13,858	30.1%	46.5%	3.7%	4.2%	18,291	29.4%	25.7%	14.5%	16.5%	4.5%
Kalamazoo County	9,165	99.0%	40,695	20.3%	49.4%	8.6%	11.1%	30,665	12.2%	23.8%	10.5%	39.5%	10.2%
Kent County	27,026	95.3%	59,053	28.1%	44.5%	3.3%	7.5%	86,654	18.3%	24.3%	9.2%	32.5%	8.4%
Lenawee County	3,813	95.2%	10,515	41.7%	35.8%	8.0%	3.8%	8,941	26.5%	25.5%	12.2%	17.6%	7.1%
Livingston County	8,688	96.5%	16,204	31.4%	42.4%	6.5%	6.1%	16,311	18.0%	24.6%	11.6%	32.5%	9.4%
Macomb County	35,897	96.8%	72,892	32.7%	34.9%	7.6%	11.6%	96,953	25.1%	29.2%	12.8%	19.9%	6.0%
Monroe County	6,328	99.2%	11,950	36.4%	35.6%	9.0%	12.7%	15,224	23.1%	24.9%	12.6%	18.9%	7.9%
Muskegon County	6,611	99.4%	14,864	32.9%	46.5%	5.2%	2.8%	20,232	29.7%	27.7%	10.0%	13.8%	4.8%
Oakland County	50,089	98.0%	99,353	25.6%	39.7%	4.5%	18.5%	138,448	12.4%	22.2%	7.8%	34.5%	17.6%
Ottawa County	12,481	100.0%	37,740	24.9%	50.6%	2.8%	11.9%	29,180	24.0%	25.4%	9.1%	26.9%	8.1%
Saginaw County	6,999	97.1%	20,018	38.0%	40.9%	4.4%	5.5%	21,353	19.5%	32.7%	13.2%	23.7%	2.3%
St. Clair County	6,981	90.7%	12,939	35.0%	38.6%	8.1%	3.9%	15,197	24.7%	29.3%	19.3%	18.2%	2.2%
Washtenaw County	11,948	99.4%	65,988	19.3%	49.0%	3.6%	23.1%	45,342	10.3%	19.0%	6.3%	38.3%	23.3%
Wayne County	73,059	94.4%	161,271	32.8%	42.4%	3.8%	5.9%	209,958	26.9%	28.0%	8.8%	17.3%	7.8%
Minnesota													
Anoka County	15,096	96.3%	28,545	35.8%	32.4%	5.9%	9.3%	37,263	21.5%	17.8%	16.2%	29.7%	11.1%
Carver County	3,719	100.0%	8,836	27.6%	23.5%	9.0%	24.4%	9,344	27.9%	11.9%	21.7%	23.0%	12.8%
Dakota County	17,986	99.0%	32.562	33.8%	28.8%	3.6%	20.6%	48,217	17.9%	17.8%	12.7%	40.9%	4.4%
Hennepin County	43,301	98.3%	102,085	26.1%	36.0%	3.6%	23.1%	187,052	13.5%	15.9%	9.0%	39.6%	17.3%
Olmsted County	5,235	100.0%	13,039	28.0%	25.3%	4.8%	13.7%	18,471	11.3%	15.3%	14.1%	28.3%	26.2%
Ramsey County	18,827	98.0%	53,476	21.8%	41.6%	4.5%	16.8%	80,179	21.1%	18.5%	8.0%	33.9%	11.4%
Scott County	6,719	97.3%	23,823	24.5%	57.1%	2.6%	5.2%	24,077	19.3%	31.2%	20.3%	18.8%	6.9%
St. Louis County	6,813	100.0%	10,039	24.3%	35.6%	8.9%	16.2%	15,996	16.6%	20.9%	15.2%	34.7%	10.4%
Stearns County	5,859	96.7%	23,336	25.9%	46.6%	10.0%	13.4%	18,068	15.6%	25.8%	9.8%	27.2%	4.7%
Washington County	11,153	99.2%	18,451	40.7%	33.7%	3.2%	13.6%	27,927	14.5%	28.2%	15.7%	27.3%	9.2%
Wright County	5,782	98.8%	9,108	29.9%	36.0%	14.9%	14.5%	12,796	30.4%	20.7%	20.3%	25.7%	2.5%
Mississippi													
DeSoto County	8,936	96.6%	15,974	25.0%	45.8%	3.0%	6.8%	18,056	22.1%	26.3%	10.8%	21.0%	7.2%
Harrison County	8,197	98.5%	20,500	27.7%	45.3%	4.9%	5.5%	26,456	28.4%	25.8%	13.0%	20.5%	3.1%
Hinds County	9,867	93.9%	27,627	24.5%	43.0%	4.5%	9.0%	33,590	24.9%	27.7%	7.4%	23.7%	9.9%
Jackson County	5,936	100.0%	11,665	35.1%	32.8%	15.1%	2.6%	15,749	16.1%	48.2%	14.6%	13.7%	5.5%
Madison County	4,534	98.7%	9,529	20.2%	54.9%	9.7%	1.6%	11,625	29.5%	27.3%	9.4%	19.9%	6.4%
Rankin County	7,049	100.0%	11,450	27.4%	28.9%	7.9%	24.9%	18,537	22.9%	22.6%	15.9%	20.4%	13.3%
Missouri													
Boone County	5,971	100.0%	35,010	19.7%	53.8%	3.2%	15.3%	24,966	13.9%	20.3%	8.3%	36.9%	19.2%
Cass County	4,002	91.6%	7,815	34.4%	32.5%	14.0%	3.6%	10,753	37.7%	30.5%	6.4%	10.7%	5.1%
Clay County	9,693	98.2%	19,014	36.5%	32.3%	3.3%	11.0%	29,294	32.6%	16.1%	12.1%	24.6%	8.6%
Franklin County	4,357	94.7%	7,688	39.8%	27.9%	1.1%	0.0%	10,968	38.3%	21.9%	12.8%	12.5%	6.3%
Greene County	10,087	100.0%	39,311	18.9%	56.8%	7.7%	9.1%	38,002	19.7%	29.1%	12.3%	21.4%	9.4%
Jackson County	25,581	97.0%	58,643	30.6%	37.0%	4.5%	12.1%	92,397	19.8%	26.1%	8.1%	24.8%	10.6%
Jasper County	5,894	100.0%	12,573	44.5%	39.8%	5.4%	2.9%	13,205	26.1%	34.2%	11.4%	19.4%	2.3%
Jefferson County	9,707	98.6%	17,003	29.9%	40.0%	9.0%	3.2%	26,185	30.5%	33.3%	10.3%	13.9%	4.3%
Platte County	3,846	100.0%	8,083	31.2%	33.0%	7.2%	11.5%	12,428	12.2%	34.6%	11.7%	31.0%	6.7%
St. Charles County	15,995	99.8%	34,021	23.0%	52.2%	5.9%	10.5%	43,865	19.4%	23.9%	14.5%	23.4%	12.3%
St. Louis County	40,499	97.8%	91,525	25.5%	44.3%	3.6%	14.2%	110,930	16.5%	26.9%	9.6%	26.6%	15.0%
Montana													
Flathead County	3,906	93.1%	7,110	49.1%	22.2%	1.3%	2.3%	8,899	40.5%	13.5%	18.0%	16.8%	8.2%
Gallatin County	3,825	98.6%	17,676	35.0%	49.7%	2.9%	6.1%	13,205	19.4%	19.5%	9.0%	34.4%	15.0%
Missoula County	4,387	100.0%	14,743	28.4%	37.4%	6.6%	7.7%	16,851	16.1%	23.6%	15.9%	21.4%	10.3%
Yellowstone County	4,798	94.0%	15,272	43.2%	33.5%	2.3%	6.1%	18,802	30.3%	21.0%	11.8%	21.0%	10.0%
Nebraska													
Douglas County	21,857	98.9%	48,111	24.6%	35.9%	4.1%	21.0%	79,252	15.3%	25.7%	7.5%	29.0%	11.5%
Lancaster County	9,211	92.9%	44,746	15.7%	59.4%	3.3%	17.0%	40,689	18.6%	26.4%	11.0%	22.6%	13.9%
Sarpy County	7,461	97.3%	15,963	27.1%	48.1%	6.3%	8.7%	21,981	11.7%	35.9%	9.3%	33.4%	8.1%
Nevada													
Clark County	80,669	97.3%	185,462	34.7%	37.2%	4.1%	5.3%	282,745	28.7%	29.1%	8.1%	16.6%	4.8%
Washoe County	16,519	97.7%	40,531	33.7%	42.2%	4.7%	4.3%	58,769	23.9%	27.4%	7.1%	20.5%	9.2%
New Hampshire													
Hillsborough County	16,014	99.5%	36,372	28.6%	30.1%	6.8%	17.4%	44,349	24.2%	18.0%	10.3%	29.7%	7.8%
Merrimack County	6,225	97.7%	15,345	31.8%	48.0%	2.8%	9.8%	14,153	16.4%	27.0%	15.4%	30.8%	8.2%
Rockingham County	11,728	95.1%	24,833	32.6%	36.4%	2.1%	13.4%	29,641	13.5%	17.4%	8.7%	42.6%	15.5%
Strafford County	4,611	95.7%	20,330	23.0%	57.1%	1.4%	8.9%	14,256	16.6%	24.5%	4.5%	31.3%	18.7%
New Jersey													
Atlantic County	10,031	97.4%	26,461	37.0%	39.1%	2.0%	9.0%	30,078	33.4%	26.2%	6.7%	15.8%	7.9%
Bergen County	37,455	98.8%	76,394	24.9%	44.3%	4.7%	18.0%	94,035	18.4%	16.8%	4.7%	41.9%	13.6%
Burlington County	18,067	99.4%	40,215	32.3%	32.8%	7.7%	15.4%	49,139	20.4%	23.5%	11.0%	31.2%	7.5%
Camden County	19,864	96.7%	45,187	30.0%	34.4%	4.7%	17.3%	63,339	26.0%	20.9%	7.0%	27.1%	11.4%
Cape May County	3,824	99.5%	6,462	30.7%	55.2%	3.6%	7.2%	8,863	28.5%	20.6%	6.3%	29.0%	11.9%
Cumberland County	5,907	99.6%	12,525	48.2%	26.9%	3.8%	4.7%	21,371	50.4%	8.4%	9.7%	13.7%	2.1%
Essex County	31,320	95.8%	73,719	26.8%	41.7%	5.5%	14.7%	94,290	28.6%	17.8%	6.7%	25.5%	9.9%
Gloucester County	11,825	94.9%	25,009	26.7%	37.1%	11.9%	11.5%	32,711	27.9%	20.2%	10.6%	27.8%	9.3%
Hudson County	20,002	98.6%	57,454	21.5%	43.0%	4.3%	17.8%	126,934	16.6%	11.5%	5.3%	39.8%	21.0%

Table E-2: Counties—Educational Attainment—*Continued*

	15 to 17		18 to 24					25 to 33					
				Percent						Percent			
	Total Population	Percent Enrolled in School	Total Population	High School	Some College	Associates Degree	Bachelors Degree	Total Population	High School	Some College	Associates Degree	Bachelors Degree	Advanced Degree
New Jersey—Cont.													
Hunterdon County	6,353	98.0%	11,277	28.2%	27.1%	8.2%	21.4%	9,540	19.2%	27.8%	4.7%	38.2%	9.3%
Mercer County	14,182	96.2%	42,896	28.6%	47.2%	1.4%	13.0%	39,044	27.8%	22.6%	3.1%	17.9%	19.1%
Middlesex County	31,955	97.6%	80,167	16.2%	54.4%	5.0%	14.8%	102,594	17.8%	14.9%	6.4%	34.1%	18.6%
Monmouth County	26,652	97.9%	52,405	25.7%	42.8%	6.3%	15.3%	61,769	21.7%	17.3%	9.0%	35.7%	10.0%
Morris County	21,633	97.6%	42,026	25.0%	35.5%	4.6%	20.4%	50,784	15.1%	17.8%	7.0%	36.7%	20.4%
Ocean County	20,954	96.7%	42,927	31.3%	34.5%	9.8%	13.5%	58,565	24.0%	21.7%	11.7%	28.9%	8.3%
Passaic County	20,397	95.2%	50,193	36.3%	38.4%	5.8%	9.5%	61,390	32.9%	19.6%	8.4%	21.5%	7.3%
Somerset County	13,336	99.6%	26,813	25.6%	28.7%	5.6%	30.2%	32,010	16.1%	19.3%	4.5%	33.2%	24.1%
Sussex County	6,130	100.0%	12,181	29.3%	35.3%	8.6%	13.3%	12,390	22.7%	20.7%	12.4%	34.9%	4.5%
Union County	22,014	93.6%	49,137	33.1%	36.4%	6.3%	11.0%	61,904	27.9%	20.5%	7.6%	21.2%	9.8%
Warren County	4,483	97.2%	8,731	24.3%	40.8%	7.2%	16.9%	9,650	24.6%	15.8%	12.8%	21.6%	5.8%
New Mexico													
Bernalillo County	27,407	97.7%	65,746	24.4%	45.3%	5.8%	6.6%	89,698	19.4%	28.7%	9.4%	16.5%	9.7%
Doña Ana County	8,988	100.0%	30,410	23.0%	54.6%	8.9%	0.4%	24,696	22.0%	42.0%	7.1%	11.2%	6.4%
San Juan County	6,020	93.0%	10,605	34.7%	45.3%	3.0%	2.6%	16,172	30.1%	33.8%	8.4%	16.4%	2.6%
Sandoval County	4,993	97.8%	11,608	25.1%	42.0%	5.9%	7.0%	14,031	27.6%	26.1%	6.3%	13.2%	3.6%
Santa Fe County	4,909	99.6%	11,025	31.1%	44.0%	2.7%	7.9%	15,060	15.8%	24.0%	7.9%	22.1%	12.6%
New York													
Albany County	10,630	95.2%	44,077	24.8%	36.6%	9.7%	20.8%	35,898	19.8%	20.5%	10.6%	25.7%	18.2%
Bronx County	58,939	98.3%	158,547	25.3%	37.7%	7.7%	7.5%	203,054	24.1%	21.7%	7.4%	18.1%	5.9%
Broome County	7,744	99.1%	28,337	26.1%	40.0%	9.0%	13.8%	18,852	20.8%	22.8%	13.7%	22.0%	16.6%
Chautauqua County	5,229	99.0%	13,664	28.4%	44.7%	10.8%	6.5%	12,863	30.4%	20.0%	14.9%	15.9%	7.4%
Dutchess County	11,448	96.7%	33,766	28.3%	45.5%	6.1%	9.0%	30,439	27.2%	16.7%	12.6%	26.2%	12.2%
Erie County	33,991	99.0%	89,778	27.4%	40.4%	8.3%	15.0%	116,105	21.9%	18.4%	11.5%	26.4%	14.1%
Jefferson County	4,181	94.5%	15,128	55.9%	24.5%	9.7%	3.9%	16,116	25.8%	33.2%	11.2%	14.1%	5.3%
Kings County	90,537	97.4%	234,279	25.6%	37.6%	6.2%	17.9%	428,199	19.7%	16.7%	5.5%	33.8%	14.4%
Monroe County	27,880	96.7%	79,736	23.1%	45.5%	6.3%	13.8%	94,106	19.4%	19.2%	10.8%	26.1%	15.9%
Nassau County	55,111	97.5%	121,410	25.1%	39.0%	6.9%	21.6%	138,159	14.2%	14.8%	9.0%	34.4%	18.7%
New York County	32,021	97.4%	148,981	16.0%	39.3%	2.5%	33.5%	339,281	7.6%	7.3%	3.5%	46.6%	28.4%
Niagara County	7,822	98.2%	19,504	34.4%	32.5%	6.9%	11.8%	22,101	30.5%	22.3%	9.4%	12.5%	12.0%
Oneida County	7,889	93.6%	22,344	24.5%	41.9%	9.7%	11.3%	27,104	30.9%	20.4%	9.1%	19.4%	7.2%
Onondaga County	19,605	95.2%	48,374	25.9%	45.4%	6.1%	11.5%	55,218	16.0%	23.7%	11.2%	26.0%	12.7%
Ontario County	4,273	85.4%	11,498	32.9%	37.4%	4.6%	8.8%	10,546	23.7%	16.4%	10.4%	30.5%	8.5%
Orange County	17,935	88.2%	41,203	29.8%	41.9%	8.6%	13.1%	37,039	26.0%	20.0%	13.2%	17.9%	11.0%
Oswego County	5,206	99.5%	13,878	28.2%	49.2%	11.3%	5.3%	13,002	27.6%	21.4%	18.3%	10.1%	7.7%
Putnam County	4,496	100.0%	9,244	35.8%	32.8%	4.4%	20.9%	7,803	23.6%	18.5%	17.9%	25.6%	10.9%
Queens County	73,248	98.7%	196,744	24.6%	41.9%	5.1%	16.5%	338,427	20.4%	18.0%	8.6%	31.1%	12.0%
Rensselaer County	5,272	98.3%	17,497	30.0%	41.5%	8.9%	11.5%	19,891	19.1%	22.1%	11.8%	27.9%	12.6%
Richmond County	19,035	96.9%	42,440	26.7%	36.1%	4.8%	20.6%	57,132	29.4%	16.5%	7.7%	22.0%	15.6%
Rockland County	14,714	97.6%	31,709	26.9%	32.0%	10.7%	16.3%	32,409	27.0%	17.2%	9.8%	23.7%	10.8%
Saratoga County	3,881	96.3%	15,881	26.4%	55.5%	4.1%	4.1%	12,327	37.9%	14.8%	8.9%	14.7%	12.1%
Schenectady County	8,697	93.7%	17,709	22.9%	47.8%	5.6%	8.7%	23,614	22.0%	17.1%	16.2%	26.3%	17.3%
St. Lawrence County	6,230	96.8%	13,854	27.8%	33.9%	10.0%	11.1%	18,362	20.9%	16.5%	16.0%	28.7%	11.4%
Steuben County	4,443	92.8%	8,644	35.7%	26.0%	11.3%	4.5%	9,588	30.4%	19.6%	9.4%	19.4%	9.1%
Suffolk County	60,924	99.4%	135,673	29.3%	37.6%	6.3%	18.4%	154,323	23.5%	19.3%	7.0%	26.3%	13.2%
Tompkins County	2,564	100.0%	30,661	9.0%	69.9%	7.2%	13.9%	11,325	7.7%	6.8%	12.6%	42.1%	28.7%
Ulster County	5,593	100.0%	19,614	32.5%	41.8%	10.2%	8.9%	18,145	26.1%	26.9%	10.4%	20.9%	10.4%
Wayne County	3,794	100.0%	7,192	32.7%	23.2%	6.7%	11.2%	9,606	36.9%	18.8%	14.2%	14.9%	3.5%
Westchester County	41,838	98.7%	88,759	26.6%	38.9%	3.5%	19.3%	96,832	17.7%	16.5%	6.4%	29.3%	17.3%
North Carolina													
Alamance County	6,420	99.1%	14,754	34.2%	38.7%	2.9%	5.1%	16,654	26.1%	21.9%	8.9%	17.0%	4.9%
Brunswick County	3,773	99.6%	8,370	52.2%	16.1%	6.2%	13.8%	9,184	27.2%	24.8%	15.5%	14.6%	2.0%
Buncombe County	8,783	91.5%	21,142	30.8%	42.5%	9.8%	5.6%	32,129	21.8%	18.7%	7.4%	26.2%	11.9%
Cabarrus County	8,592	94.2%	15,855	32.2%	33.6%	4.7%	9.7%	20,760	16.4%	32.1%	12.2%	23.3%	4.8%
Catawba County	6,952	100.0%	13,521	36.1%	27.9%	5.4%	11.4%	15,886	24.4%	28.6%	11.5%	17.8%	5.5%
Cleveland County	3,536	93.0%	9,470	39.9%	38.3%	5.6%	2.5%	9,222	34.0%	25.9%	13.8%	10.8%	1.1%
Craven County	2,915	100.0%	12,867	41.2%	45.5%	3.4%	1.0%	12,859	19.6%	35.9%	12.8%	23.5%	1.6%
Cumberland County	12,421	97.7%	40,795	40.8%	41.8%	2.3%	5.9%	48,094	23.3%	37.7%	8.4%	19.1%	6.1%
Davidson County	7,031	95.6%	12,567	36.5%	31.4%	6.7%	6.3%	16,728	25.3%	27.6%	8.1%	19.9%	4.1%
Durham County	9,831	96.6%	29,901	22.8%	42.2%	1.2%	21.1%	50,048	13.2%	18.2%	4.7%	31.7%	19.7%
Forsyth County	14,264	96.6%	34,812	30.9%	38.4%	3.1%	11.6%	43,345	15.4%	22.3%	10.7%	28.0%	13.1%
Gaston County	8,147	91.8%	17,543	40.6%	31.5%	8.2%	4.1%	25,240	29.0%	22.3%	9.2%	19.8%	6.9%
Guilford County	20,720	93.2%	53,978	29.0%	46.2%	3.9%	9.7%	62,889	23.5%	23.5%	5.8%	23.2%	9.3%
Harnett County	5,419	99.6%	13,395	27.8%	49.0%	4.8%	5.7%	17,089	30.3%	30.3%	9.8%	14.5%	4.1%
Henderson County	2,993	97.9%	7,290	37.2%	36.3%	8.7%	8.4%	10,238	29.1%	39.9%	5.3%	11.9%	5.3%
Iredell County	8,299	99.5%	14,699	41.5%	28.6%	7.4%	9.0%	16,137	24.9%	21.4%	14.6%	19.4%	7.6%
Johnston County	8,185	92.8%	14,762	20.0%	48.7%	4.7%	6.3%	18,964	21.3%	34.8%	9.6%	13.7%	2.4%
Mecklenburg County	37,568	97.4%	95,025	25.4%	41.7%	6.1%	14.6%	153,249	15.8%	19.7%	6.4%	33.8%	14.1%
Moore County	3,880	99.1%	6,442	43.4%	29.9%	0.8%	10.8%	9,173	23.6%	27.3%	10.4%	20.2%	9.6%
Nash County	3,826	100.0%	7,992	33.8%	29.0%	0.9%	7.1%	9,719	36.2%	25.3%	15.0%	5.9%	
New Hanover County	7,739	94.8%	28,270	26.5%	42.6%	7.8%	17.7%	26,458	15.9%	25.8%	17.6%	26.4%	6.3%
Onslow County	5,861	99.0%	37,365	52.3%	34.0%	5.9%	4.9%	33,337	24.9%	33.6%	16.0%	13.7%	2.1%
Orange County	4,940	94.7%	27,135	26.9%	45.5%	2.3%	19.5%	17,241	14.1%	9.4%	5.2%	36.2%	29.4%
Pitt County	6,349	100.0%	32,609	15.4%	67.6%	2.4%	7.5%	22,584	20.5%	25.3%	13.9%	19.8%	10.3%

Table E-2: Counties—Educational Attainment—*Continued*

| | 15 to 17 | | 18 to 24 | | | | | 25 to 33 | | | | | |
| | Total Population | Percent Enrolled in School | Total Population | Percent | | | | Total Population | Percent | | | | |
				High School	Some College	Associates Degree	Bachelors Degree		High School	Some College	Associates Degree	Bachelors Degree	Advanced Degree
North Carolina—Cont.													
Randolph County	5,468	97.3%	12,051	33.7%	32.9%	11.3%	1.5%	14,689	30.6%	30.9%	13.2%	12.9%	2.1%
Robeson County	5,668	94.9%	15,277	34.2%	39.6%	1.0%	3.4%	13,861	31.3%	22.4%	9.6%	12.5%	3.1%
Rockingham County	3,614	99.4%	6,545	34.2%	43.9%	2.3%	2.3%	8,972	25.4%	36.0%	5.5%	19.1%	1.9%
Rowan County	5,287	86.9%	12,526	39.9%	35.1%	4.9%	4.0%	14,692	27.0%	21.2%	11.5%	14.2%	3.3%
Union County	11,693	99.5%	20,842	26.1%	32.4%	5.4%	15.6%	18,713	27.8%	26.4%	4.6%	25.4%	1.4%
Wake County	40,874	97.5%	92,700	20.5%	44.5%	3.3%	15.9%	135,921	14.2%	17.5%	7.3%	36.3%	16.6%
Wayne County	4,258	100.0%	12,124	31.8%	44.6%	2.7%	10.7%	16,422	18.7%	31.1%	7.3%	20.3%	6.0%
North Dakota													
Cass County	4,825	99.5%	28,541	17.7%	59.8%	1.5%	9.8%	24,162	18.8%	26.7%	9.9%	27.9%	12.9%
Ohio													
Allen County	4,020	99.1%	9,702	47.9%	28.3%	2.7%	4.9%	11,532	29.6%	30.2%	11.0%	17.4%	8.6%
Ashtabula County	4,992	93.3%	7,835	49.2%	16.6%	3.9%	3.4%	9,787	49.1%	18.0%	11.3%	9.8%	3.7%
Butler County	15,977	98.3%	45,123	33.7%	44.9%	2.5%	9.7%	39,877	33.5%	19.9%	10.5%	20.1%	6.3%
Clark County	5,603	98.7%	11,991	51.2%	35.7%	0.1%	2.9%	13,749	23.8%	38.2%	7.7%	14.0%	6.1%
Clermont County	9,004	96.9%	15,117	41.4%	30.9%	3.7%	12.2%	23,530	24.6%	26.1%	20.8%	18.9%	3.4%
Columbiana County	4,005	94.4%	7,504	42.7%	30.8%	1.9%	3.2%	9,881	43.0%	21.5%	10.9%	12.3%	2.7%
Cuyahoga County	46,290	98.3%	113,117	33.9%	37.0%	3.1%	13.6%	147,659	21.8%	23.3%	7.0%	25.2%	13.7%
Delaware County	9,153	100.0%	14,652	25.7%	42.0%	5.5%	10.8%	16,882	13.8%	10.9%	2.4%	56.0%	14.4%
Fairfield County	6,608	100.0%	12,209	30.1%	29.9%	8.7%	3.2%	14,860	21.5%	35.6%	19.3%	17.6%	3.4%
Franklin County	45,137	98.2%	120,906	27.2%	44.7%	2.3%	15.8%	202,024	19.7%	21.4%	6.9%	33.2%	11.8%
Geauga County	4,337	68.9%	7,905	20.7%	27.4%	7.1%	16.9%	6,927	28.4%	27.8%	8.1%	21.7%	7.6%
Greene County	5,937	95.4%	20,661	24.4%	54.4%	0.3%	13.6%	19,019	19.0%	22.4%	4.6%	27.3%	17.0%
Hamilton County	30,906	98.3%	72,838	34.2%	36.2%	2.6%	13.3%	107,089	23.4%	20.9%	9.3%	28.6%	13.1%
Lake County	9,398	93.1%	18,278	37.0%	33.2%	6.7%	14.3%	21,640	27.1%	21.1%	10.7%	23.5%	10.9%
Licking County	7,293	98.4%	15,948	29.7%	35.4%	3.7%	5.4%	17,374	25.9%	31.6%	17.1%	10.4%	7.7%
Lorain County	13,388	96.2%	26,120	27.3%	45.4%	4.2%	7.5%	30,309	24.5%	30.9%	12.3%	13.5%	9.5%
Lucas County	16,806	96.9%	41,038	29.6%	44.3%	1.7%	10.5%	54,283	23.9%	29.2%	13.6%	18.7%	7.1%
Mahoning County	8,365	93.5%	20,268	38.7%	36.1%	4.0%	4.9%	25,603	32.3%	26.1%	8.0%	20.3%	8.4%
Medina County	7,493	99.9%	13,547	40.1%	32.4%	1.0%	11.2%	17,648	27.4%	19.9%	6.6%	27.4%	11.2%
Miami County	4,948	97.4%	7,784	53.0%	31.3%	2.7%	7.8%	10,561	22.0%	30.1%	9.3%	26.8%	8.7%
Montgomery County	19,440	98.2%	47,493	32.8%	38.4%	4.2%	8.4%	64,115	24.3%	27.1%	7.9%	22.0%	9.6%
Portage County	6,294	99.5%	27,140	25.2%	48.3%	0.7%	13.5%	16,223	26.3%	27.2%	5.4%	22.1%	13.2%
Richland County	4,664	96.8%	10,805	56.7%	17.6%	2.7%	8.0%	12,484	36.9%	23.6%	9.5%	10.8%	2.9%
Stark County	14,912	95.2%	32,535	32.9%	43.6%	2.5%	7.9%	40,681	28.3%	29.7%	10.5%	15.3%	8.0%
Summit County	19,791	98.5%	47,666	29.2%	38.0%	9.1%	10.6%	61,441	25.0%	19.2%	10.2%	25.4%	11.3%
Trumbull County	8,438	95.6%	17,104	41.8%	28.2%	4.4%	7.8%	18,634	45.6%	23.4%	5.8%	13.3%	3.1%
Tuscarawas County	4,220	91.8%	7,080	53.3%	22.5%	4.9%	10.9%	9,522	43.1%	16.9%	4.7%	20.8%	11.5%
Warren County	11,507	100.0%	17,277	33.2%	37.8%	5.9%	13.9%	21,167	21.0%	20.5%	14.6%	26.6%	8.8%
Wayne County	5,538	77.8%	11,242	33.2%	36.6%	0.1%	3.6%	11,235	27.7%	15.8%	12.6%	14.4%	11.2%
Wood County	6,803	100.0%	17,983	30.8%	47.0%	5.0%	7.6%	18,327	24.0%	25.7%	18.4%	20.0%	9.8%
Oklahoma													
Canadian County	4,902	98.9%	10,745	21.9%	54.3%	0.5%	10.7%	16,997	28.2%	33.2%	11.1%	15.7%	4.4%
Cleveland County	10,792	100.0%	39,790	23.3%	46.8%	4.6%	13.2%	37,668	19.8%	24.1%	10.4%	28.6%	11.7%
Comanche County	4,742	99.9%	14,998	33.1%	37.6%	8.9%	3.2%	19,817	28.2%	36.6%	6.5%	13.6%	0.9%
Oklahoma County	26,652	92.3%	70,303	24.7%	45.4%	2.3%	11.0%	111,707	29.9%	23.3%	5.0%	20.2%	7.4%
Tulsa County	26,366	96.7%	58,292	34.5%	34.5%	4.3%	7.3%	81,376	25.5%	20.0%	8.5%	26.4%	7.3%
Oregon													
Clackamas County	17,870	99.6%	32,507	31.8%	36.6%	9.3%	11.6%	41,000	19.4%	27.3%	9.0%	23.8%	10.2%
Deschutes County	5,366	100.0%	12,522	23.4%	38.9%	6.0%	11.1%	19,618	16.7%	26.9%	10.3%	30.9%	9.7%
Douglas County	3,303	93.1%	7,578	41.1%	31.8%	1.6%	5.7%	10,988	37.8%	26.0%	5.6%	10.2%	14.1%
Jackson County	7,333	97.1%	16,260	29.9%	24.4%	3.3%	6.5%	24,414	34.0%	25.2%	10.9%	11.9%	3.3%
Lane County	12,849	94.4%	46,498	28.0%	47.9%	2.8%	12.0%	42,066	19.7%	31.9%	7.7%	23.0%	8.8%
Linn County	4,217	97.3%	12,827	22.4%	58.3%	4.0%	5.6%	11,296	21.7%	22.5%	10.9%	17.3%	14.4%
Marion County	14,733	99.6%	32,049	31.0%	39.6%	4.3%	5.7%	38,868	37.5%	22.6%	8.8%	14.7%	4.9%
Multnomah County	22,350	97.5%	64,956	25.7%	43.2%	6.2%	14.1%	130,045	16.9%	23.5%	7.2%	35.1%	11.2%
Washington County	23,839	97.4%	46,192	30.9%	33.8%	6.3%	10.7%	78,390	16.9%	24.4%	8.1%	27.9%	14.6%
Yamhill County	4,387	99.7%	11,578	27.3%	51.7%	0.5%	12.4%	10,384	21.5%	32.5%	6.1%	25.9%	2.8%
Pennsylvania													
Adams County	4,180	100.0%	8,558	47.3%	30.2%	3.8%	4.8%	10,662	33.1%	24.6%	10.3%	22.7%	4.7%
Allegheny County	41,256	96.6%	110,343	26.1%	41.9%	4.4%	17.5%	166,066	19.1%	14.9%	10.7%	30.0%	19.9%
Beaver County	6,300	100.0%	12,689	49.8%	30.5%	4.1%	6.4%	18,443	27.5%	25.5%	12.0%	19.4%	11.1%
Berks County	16,614	97.8%	41,286	32.3%	38.7%	2.6%	10.2%	44,483	27.3%	24.7%	14.3%	16.4%	8.2%
Blair County	5,226	96.8%	9,841	36.0%	38.7%	3.2%	15.7%	13,578	43.5%	18.3%	8.0%	22.4%	1.6%
Bucks County	25,062	99.5%	49,616	36.3%	36.4%	4.0%	11.6%	59,844	20.6%	21.3%	13.0%	27.4%	13.0%
Butler County	7,222	99.8%	16,278	34.1%	45.1%	5.7%	7.7%	19,823	20.9%	19.9%	12.7%	28.7%	14.9%
Cambria County	5,489	99.6%	12,403	34.4%	46.0%	5.0%	5.0%	12,887	33.7%	24.8%	12.5%	15.6%	8.7%
Centre County	3,835	98.0%	41,020	29.3%	48.8%	2.6%	12.2%	22,204	23.3%	16.8%	5.9%	33.7%	15.7%
Chester County	20,281	96.8%	46,694	28.9%	37.9%	2.1%	19.1%	51,777	18.5%	15.4%	5.0%	40.3%	14.8%
Cumberland County	9,199	98.1%	24,633	27.3%	51.6%	0.8%	5.9%	26,980	34.0%	14.4%	12.0%	24.8%	11.8%
Dauphin County	10,319	91.5%	26,451	27.1%	36.6%	3.6%	9.8%	29,124	27.3%	15.1%	12.6%	27.3%	10.6%
Delaware County	22,183	95.2%	57,565	29.5%	43.9%	5.9%	10.9%	63,379	23.9%	18.7%	9.0%	28.5%	14.0%
Erie County	11,465	96.8%	28,432	24.0%	46.8%	3.8%	12.0%	31,135	31.1%	17.1%	14.2%	20.2%	8.3%
Fayette County	4,931	98.2%	9,656	47.5%	21.1%	3.5%	7.4%	13,469	51.2%	17.6%	11.5%	7.9%	4.5%
Franklin County	5,437	96.0%	14,051	49.3%	20.3%	1.4%	1.4%	15,211	45.2%	18.0%	7.2%	18.1%	3.5%

Table E-2: Counties—Educational Attainment—*Continued*

| | 15 to 17 | | 18 to 24 | | | | | 25 to 33 | | | | | |
	Total Population	Percent Enrolled in School	Total Population	High School	Some College	Associates Degree	Bachelors Degree	Total Population	High School	Some College	Associates Degree	Bachelors Degree	Advanced Degree
Pennsylvania—Cont.													
Lackawanna County	8,194	96.7%	19,620	33.1%	42.8%	1.3%	14.1%	22,958	23.6%	22.0%	9.1%	22.8%	10.3%
Lancaster County	22,070	90.2%	49,519	41.1%	26.1%	4.0%	9.2%	58,006	26.3%	17.6%	9.8%	21.6%	9.5%
Lebanon County	4,416	96.3%	12,415	35.0%	30.7%	9.6%	14.8%	12,915	31.1%	22.4%	12.3%	16.6%	4.0%
Lehigh County	16,197	96.1%	33,016	39.6%	35.1%	6.0%	8.6%	41,803	21.4%	23.1%	12.1%	23.5%	9.7%
Luzerne County	11,546	96.4%	31,241	32.5%	43.3%	2.0%	13.9%	32,819	25.9%	22.2%	12.6%	19.4%	10.4%
Lycoming County	3,675	92.7%	12,018	37.7%	41.8%	1.5%	8.6%	12,412	31.1%	9.0%	8.3%	28.1%	8.6%
Mercer County	5,096	98.1%	10,204	39.7%	36.1%	6.0%	6.0%	10,723	31.4%	9.6%	11.3%	31.8%	4.0%
Monroe County	7,360	99.5%	18,241	29.1%	48.4%	0.0%	4.0%	16,475	23.2%	14.5%	7.7%	40.1%	2.0%
Montgomery County	29,425	99.4%	65,670	29.7%	36.2%	5.9%	17.4%	91,032	22.9%	12.7%	7.3%	36.2%	16.9%
Northampton County	11,123	100.0%	31,759	30.5%	50.2%	4.3%	7.7%	29,745	25.2%	18.9%	13.4%	28.6%	12.0%
Northumberland County	3,106	76.2%	6,642	49.0%	23.4%	5.4%	7.5%	10,582	33.4%	14.6%	15.0%	16.9%	6.7%
Philadelphia County	53,344	95.1%	165,336	30.1%	40.6%	3.8%	13.5%	266,596	22.4%	19.5%	4.9%	27.6%	15.3%
Schuylkill County	5,347	100.0%	10,180	49.1%	21.6%	8.2%	8.3%	14,846	35.9%	13.9%	18.9%	17.5%	6.8%
Washington County	6,857	100.0%	18,388	44.6%	30.7%	6.2%	8.9%	20,742	35.0%	16.5%	10.7%	26.0%	7.3%
Westmoreland County	13,511	98.7%	28,973	27.3%	36.2%	5.1%	19.9%	31,727	23.8%	20.2%	19.3%	26.8%	5.9%
York County	16,615	95.8%	34,225	41.6%	31.6%	4.9%	8.8%	50,402	38.4%	16.5%	11.6%	19.3%	5.3%
Rhode Island													
Kent County	5,736	97.0%	11,627	30.6%	43.8%	4.1%	10.9%	20,408	24.6%	18.2%	11.8%	29.9%	9.1%
Providence County	22,065	97.9%	70,500	26.4%	43.7%	4.9%	13.5%	84,965	22.8%	24.1%	6.9%	24.9%	11.9%
Washington County	4,344	98.8%	17,643	29.9%	44.7%	7.6%	12.7%	10,535	15.2%	29.1%	10.9%	30.7%	10.2%
South Carolina													
Aiken County	6,478	100.0%	14,965	28.8%	43.9%	2.8%	7.2%	18,220	24.7%	29.5%	4.8%	17.8%	4.2%
Anderson County	8,898	96.8%	17,655	34.5%	37.8%	5.4%	9.7%	17,931	28.7%	27.0%	13.3%	11.1%	5.2%
Beaufort County	4,910	100.0%	16,479	55.0%	26.2%	2.3%	1.5%	20,810	33.6%	27.2%	5.3%	20.7%	3.3%
Berkeley County	8,654	98.6%	17,806	34.1%	40.3%	1.0%	6.6%	28,825	25.0%	25.2%	8.6%	26.5%	7.4%
Charleston County	14,511	99.1%	38,878	23.8%	50.1%	3.7%	12.6%	56,973	19.4%	18.8%	6.0%	38.1%	11.1%
Dorchester County	5,235	100.0%	12,198	37.6%	37.4%	0.8%	3.9%	22,400	29.4%	30.7%	10.5%	14.7%	6.2%
Florence County	5,538	100.0%	13,112	32.2%	45.9%	5.0%	4.4%	15,454	35.5%	27.8%	9.9%	13.5%	4.6%
Greenville County	19,624	96.7%	47,357	29.4%	38.3%	4.4%	11.4%	60,082	22.9%	19.3%	8.2%	22.0%	15.4%
Horry County	10,824	95.6%	24,882	42.1%	35.9%	5.2%	6.8%	33,554	26.5%	22.6%	8.5%	24.0%	8.0%
Lexington County	11,295	98.0%	23,719	31.1%	43.1%	3.2%	8.2%	34,276	21.3%	25.0%	8.3%	25.3%	11.8%
Pickens County	4,994	96.4%	18,664	28.8%	48.8%	3.2%	10.7%	15,557	28.4%	26.7%	8.1%	13.0%	8.0%
Richland County	16,757	97.6%	64,258	31.3%	46.2%	2.3%	11.0%	52,538	20.6%	27.0%	3.7%	26.5%	15.2%
Spartanburg County	11,773	100.0%	28,689	28.9%	43.5%	6.0%	7.1%	33,740	25.3%	27.4%	10.7%	15.2%	5.9%
Sumter County	4,406	91.1%	13,392	38.7%	36.7%	3.7%	0.9%	12,191	25.9%	31.8%	7.7%	6.4%	6.9%
York County	10,926	99.6%	22,732	31.1%	44.5%	2.9%	9.3%	27,355	28.2%	16.3%	12.1%	28.4%	8.2%
South Dakota													
Minnehaha County	6,496	84.4%	15,505	27.6%	32.7%	4.8%	20.9%	29,060	22.3%	21.2%	13.9%	28.8%	6.4%
Pennington County	4,331	94.0%	8,522	29.9%	51.0%	1.8%	7.5%	14,959	22.8%	34.1%	12.2%	20.5%	4.6%
Tennessee													
Blount County	4,936	99.6%	10,726	39.0%	41.4%	3.6%	3.5%	12,700	38.2%	27.6%	5.5%	14.3%	9.8%
Bradley County	4,930	99.0%	10,032	29.5%	49.7%	3.6%	8.9%	12,385	37.4%	18.7%	5.5%	21.5%	2.0%
Davidson County	20,832	98.8%	69,835	30.8%	37.8%	1.8%	18.9%	116,613	19.2%	18.4%	6.7%	32.9%	16.6%
Hamilton County	12,276	96.3%	32,702	25.1%	51.8%	3.9%	9.2%	44,034	21.2%	25.2%	6.4%	24.1%	11.4%
Knox County	17,800	96.3%	56,420	26.6%	46.5%	4.4%	13.8%	52,327	21.5%	19.4%	8.2%	26.7%	13.7%
Madison County	3,796	100.0%	10,544	31.0%	52.0%	0.8%	7.2%	10,779	28.5%	26.6%	12.2%	22.2%	2.4%
Montgomery County	7,374	95.9%	22,027	40.8%	40.9%	6.9%	8.7%	35,085	23.0%	33.8%	9.3%	23.9%	7.3%
Rutherford County	12,608	94.9%	39,666	33.2%	45.1%	3.0%	9.2%	37,880	24.3%	27.6%	6.6%	27.4%	8.8%
Sevier County	4,319	100.0%	8,480	28.5%	46.6%	9.4%	6.5%	8,556	51.2%	20.7%	2.5%	14.7%	3.5%
Shelby County	40,130	97.2%	91,576	33.1%	43.3%	4.2%	8.4%	123,261	27.0%	27.0%	5.8%	21.5%	9.1%
Sullivan County	7,445	90.9%	12,331	40.7%	44.8%	4.5%	3.9%	14,272	31.1%	21.5%	11.3%	16.0%	8.3%
Sumner County	6,878	99.4%	14,595	28.4%	46.9%	1.5%	14.2%	19,768	31.2%	23.7%	6.9%	22.8%	8.6%
Washington County	4,303	97.9%	15,505	33.5%	50.4%	7.4%	3.9%	13,799	28.9%	18.1%	4.6%	26.3%	12.8%
Williamson County	11,788	97.6%	15,560	21.9%	38.3%	1.5%	22.9%	14,755	12.7%	7.5%	10.1%	45.7%	22.3%
Wilson County	5,150	98.0%	10,983	35.6%	44.5%	8.2%	6.2%	12,081	17.6%	23.1%	9.1%	34.5%	8.0%
Texas													
Bell County	13,872	96.0%	40,033	35.5%	44.6%	2.5%	4.4%	51,420	24.6%	37.6%	8.3%	16.5%	5.8%
Bexar County	81,443	96.8%	195,287	33.1%	41.8%	4.1%	6.0%	265,647	26.3%	29.3%	8.8%	18.9%	5.8%
Bowie County	3,541	93.6%	8,627	46.5%	16.8%	9.4%	0.0%	10,857	39.2%	33.9%	10.3%	8.6%	0.0%
Brazoria County	17,237	100.0%	29,299	32.8%	40.0%	6.3%	7.3%	42,280	24.0%	26.2%	6.8%	27.7%	5.4%
Brazos County	6,520	97.5%	58,803	13.6%	69.0%	2.3%	10.0%	31,962	16.3%	19.4%	5.9%	31.5%	16.5%
Cameron County	23,240	96.5%	44,967	45.6%	30.0%	4.7%	2.3%	46,269	26.8%	27.1%	7.4%	13.5%	4.0%
Collin County	43,267	97.3%	71,235	30.2%	40.0%	4.5%	14.3%	102,770	17.2%	18.1%	8.7%	34.1%	15.4%
Comal County	5,581	96.5%	10,469	37.2%	31.9%	2.7%	3.9%	12,595	31.9%	22.8%	8.8%	24.3%	4.9%
Dallas County	103,457	95.0%	247,751	33.1%	35.6%	3.5%	9.2%	361,996	22.6%	21.5%	5.5%	23.0%	10.3%
Denton County	33,504	97.0%	72,368	25.6%	48.0%	6.1%	9.9%	104,559	19.8%	25.0%	8.2%	32.5%	8.6%
Ector County	7,443	94.4%	18,034	39.9%	40.7%	3.2%	4.2%	24,031	36.1%	31.1%	6.5%	13.0%	1.6%
El Paso County	8,424	98.0%	14,510	27.8%	40.5%	8.3%	6.7%	17,753	37.9%	30.0%	5.1%	11.3%	2.5%
Ellis County	38,124	96.4%	94,081	29.0%	47.1%	5.2%	5.4%	110,389	24.7%	30.6%	8.1%	21.4%	4.7%
Fort Bend County	34,703	96.7%	60,267	31.2%	43.1%	3.1%	8.2%	79,344	21.1%	27.0%	5.5%	25.9%	12.5%
Galveston County	13,541	90.8%	28,761	30.1%	34.2%	4.7%	8.9%	36,906	17.2%	28.9%	5.5%	23.4%	12.0%
Grayson County	4,923	96.3%	12,296	40.7%	29.2%	5.7%	1.4%	12,857	39.1%	24.3%	9.8%	16.7%	0.6%

Table E-2: Counties—Educational Attainment—*Continued*

	15 to 17		18 to 24					25 to 33					
				Percent					Percent				
	Total Population	Percent Enrolled in School	Total Population	High School	Some College	Associates Degree	Bachelors Degree	Total Population	High School	Some College	Associates Degree	Bachelors Degree	Advanced Degree
Texas—Cont.													
Gregg County	4,911	100.0%	12,091	25.2%	33.1%	4.7%	14.7%	14,705	46.4%	21.0%	5.0%	16.9%	3.5%
Guadalupe County	7,395	98.1%	12,985	44.8%	28.0%	7.1%	4.2%	17,571	30.1%	26.6%	15.2%	13.6%	6.1%
Harris County	191,385	96.6%	431,721	32.7%	35.1%	4.0%	10.1%	649,252	23.0%	22.5%	6.4%	23.4%	9.3%
Hays County	7,234	97.7%	34,323	18.3%	61.2%	5.9%	7.4%	25,058	22.3%	26.6%	4.2%	35.4%	6.1%
Hidalgo County	44,577	97.7%	93,515	32.4%	38.4%	4.4%	5.2%	98,073	24.3%	24.8%	7.6%	15.5%	4.6%
Jefferson County	10,267	95.6%	23,959	26.6%	48.9%	1.5%	8.9%	33,763	27.2%	27.9%	6.2%	16.1%	5.6%
Johnson County	7,363	89.1%	14,217	37.6%	39.1%	4.4%	2.6%	17,692	35.9%	27.2%	5.8%	14.5%	3.8%
Kaufman County	4,752	95.4%	9,480	35.2%	34.2%	1.2%	6.5%	13,508	31.6%	21.8%	9.0%	21.8%	4.2%
Lubbock County	11,457	96.8%	50,728	19.7%	56.9%	3.1%	10.7%	40,214	21.3%	31.2%	8.2%	20.4%	10.0%
McLennan County	10,718	100.0%	35,986	32.1%	38.4%	5.3%	12.6%	28,137	23.9%	25.6%	12.5%	17.1%	8.1%
Midland County	7,423	97.2%	16,182	43.9%	25.2%	5.7%	4.7%	25,270	37.6%	25.0%	6.9%	16.9%	3.5%
Montgomery County	23,918	99.1%	46,093	36.6%	35.0%	2.7%	8.2%	58,593	29.2%	22.9%	3.7%	22.9%	8.9%
Nueces County	15,956	95.8%	36,530	41.3%	33.2%	2.5%	5.2%	48,054	28.8%	28.4%	9.6%	17.4%	3.3%
Parker County	5,976	100.0%	10,442	60.3%	21.8%	3.4%	6.8%	11,100	29.8%	29.0%	3.8%	22.8%	5.5%
Potter County	4,489	98.9%	11,257	29.1%	50.0%	4.2%	1.9%	16,547	25.8%	31.3%	5.9%	12.8%	4.3%
Randall County	5,217	100.0%	13,490	31.3%	40.7%	7.3%	8.7%	17,543	19.3%	36.4%	13.6%	16.6%	6.3%
Smith County	8,942	93.6%	23,359	26.3%	46.1%	3.3%	11.0%	28,402	27.5%	29.7%	5.3%	16.1%	4.9%
Tarrant County	87,586	96.4%	183,333	34.4%	37.6%	6.1%	8.9%	260,714	23.5%	25.2%	7.7%	22.6%	8.1%
Taylor County	5,383	98.9%	20,854	39.2%	45.9%	0.8%	4.8%	17,073	28.4%	35.9%	8.3%	17.5%	5.3%
Tom Green County	4,482	98.0%	14,946	30.0%	44.7%	4.5%	15.9%	16,337	30.6%	23.9%	10.3%	21.0%	3.3%
Travis County	39,547	94.9%	112,029	23.7%	47.5%	3.7%	13.3%	212,482	17.5%	18.7%	5.4%	37.0%	12.1%
Webb County	14,816	95.7%	30,472	42.5%	28.7%	4.7%	4.7%	30,918	33.9%	23.5%	5.1%	14.8%	3.8%
Wichita County	4,865	88.5%	19,000	50.0%	34.0%	3.4%	5.6%	17,480	35.5%	19.5%	10.3%	16.3%	6.9%
Williamson County	23,089	97.3%	39,815	31.7%	45.7%	2.3%	12.3%	59,894	21.1%	25.7%	12.4%	23.9%	10.4%
Utah													
Cache County	6,289	99.9%	21,031	23.1%	45.3%	8.2%	13.9%	17,230	21.8%	32.4%	14.9%	21.8%	5.9%
Davis County	17,354	99.3%	32,376	30.3%	40.8%	8.1%	7.1%	42,554	20.0%	30.3%	15.8%	24.3%	5.8%
Salt Lake County	49,421	96.7%	107,190	30.6%	37.2%	7.6%	7.8%	159,139	23.4%	24.4%	9.2%	25.5%	8.5%
Utah County	30,240	96.8%	94,406	23.5%	47.5%	11.3%	7.5%	72,255	16.4%	27.6%	13.4%	32.4%	6.3%
Washington County	7,485	99.4%	16,709	30.2%	46.6%	10.6%	4.1%	15,243	33.6%	28.3%	12.6%	15.8%	4.1%
Weber County	11,020	93.3%	23,746	36.6%	35.5%	7.5%	2.1%	33,518	31.8%	26.8%	10.5%	18.4%	2.7%
Vermont													
Chittenden County	6,437	99.5%	25,155	30.2%	48.2%	0.5%	15.5%	19,823	18.2%	10.3%	6.1%	51.5%	10.5%
Virginia													
Albemarle County	2,381	100.0%	13,562	31.4%	41.2%	3.5%	13.8%	13,254	25.4%	21.8%	7.7%	21.3%	20.4%
Arlington County	4,667	88.6%	17,377	13.6%	19.2%	0.7%	58.2%	55,450	3.3%	8.3%	3.5%	44.2%	35.8%
Chesterfield County	15,836	96.6%	31,432	32.1%	40.9%	3.5%	12.6%	33,832	26.1%	31.2%	8.0%	20.4%	10.8%
Fairfax County	44,237	97.6%	95,712	25.5%	38.7%	2.2%	22.3%	142,057	12.4%	17.4%	5.8%	37.1%	21.2%
Hanover County	4,844	99.1%	9,818	19.6%	34.9%	2.5%	12.6%	8,198	37.4%	23.2%	9.3%	17.8%	5.1%
Henrico County	12,260	99.4%	26,484	26.3%	35.5%	3.4%	15.7%	40,556	19.7%	24.5%	6.2%	33.4%	11.4%
Loudoun County	16,911	99.4%	24,373	25.6%	37.8%	3.8%	19.1%	43,326	13.8%	19.1%	3.9%	42.0%	16.5%
Montgomery County	2,557	98.2%	27,532	17.9%	60.9%	9.6%	9.7%	12,992	15.2%	16.0%	3.7%	46.0%	15.4%
Prince William County	20,839	97.2%	40,126	37.3%	36.8%	5.6%	11.5%	55,830	21.4%	22.4%	7.3%	26.4%	12.1%
Roanoke County	4,231	100.0%	7,175	37.0%	36.8%	3.2%	15.7%	10,124	15.3%	32.8%	14.7%	25.2%	11.6%
Spotsylvania County	6,337	95.9%	12,088	38.5%	38.0%	3.8%	6.4%	13,377	36.5%	29.3%	4.7%	18.6%	6.4%
Stafford County	6,019	98.3%	15,338	39.8%	30.8%	5.7%	13.1%	16,712	25.8%	28.8%	7.8%	25.8%	9.2%
Washington													
Benton County	9,462	96.8%	17,372	34.7%	30.5%	7.4%	3.9%	21,311	21.4%	26.9%	12.9%	15.5%	7.6%
Clark County	20,695	99.0%	39,349	39.9%	31.2%	9.1%	5.7%	54,151	26.9%	28.0%	8.2%	20.6%	6.4%
Cowlitz County	3,440	92.7%	6,662	38.8%	39.6%	7.4%	2.1%	12,951	30.6%	25.1%	10.3%	8.2%	10.1%
Grant County	3,102	89.1%	11,592	20.2%	51.9%	9.5%	5.3%	10,034	30.5%	28.4%	3.7%	14.3%	3.6%
King County	68,176	98.4%	171,924	24.7%	36.2%	6.4%	20.9%	327,984	14.6%	15.9%	7.5%	37.4%	18.4%
Kitsap County	9,762	95.2%	27,430	49.4%	27.5%	4.2%	6.4%	32,727	26.2%	35.4%	10.0%	17.5%	5.4%
Pierce County	32,839	95.6%	78,851	37.0%	34.0%	9.0%	6.8%	113,567	27.7%	29.8%	13.5%	18.0%	4.2%
Skagit County	4,657	98.3%	8,948	32.6%	42.1%	3.4%	4.2%	13,682	27.2%	36.3%	9.5%	15.8%	2.3%
Snohomish County	30,570	95.9%	64,465	39.1%	33.7%	9.2%	7.1%	97,289	24.6%	25.6%	10.4%	23.8%	8.3%
Spokane County	19,071	96.4%	48,491	29.4%	45.3%	5.1%	9.6%	68,066	32.9%	25.4%	9.8%	16.0%	8.4%
Thurston County	9,282	100.0%	24,902	37.4%	39.3%	7.0%	6.5%	33,146	27.6%	24.1%	8.1%	21.1%	3.7%
Whatcom County	7,277	100.0%	30,613	27.7%	37.6%	17.5%	6.9%	26,325	19.0%	31.3%	16.2%	22.0%	6.0%
Yakima County	11,331	95.7%	25,431	39.5%	29.6%	5.5%	3.1%	27,580	36.9%	18.0%	7.9%	7.2%	4.1%
West Virginia													
Berkeley County	4,078	98.2%	9,972	29.5%	45.3%	3.3%	4.6%	12,772	41.6%	23.0%	9.2%	13.6%	4.8%
Cabell County	4,250	95.9%	11,420	34.8%	40.8%	0.4%	14.3%	10,967	30.3%	16.4%	18.4%	15.5%	14.4%
Kanawha County	6,215	99.4%	14,130	41.7%	33.8%	4.3%	9.8%	20,325	35.1%	17.7%	10.3%	16.1%	11.0%
Monongalia County	3,293	100.0%	21,629	19.8%	63.5%	0.9%	14.7%	18,112	17.3%	25.0%	6.3%	24.7%	23.9%
Wisconsin													
Brown County	9,272	100.0%	23,305	28.2%	43.6%	5.3%	7.1%	32,699	18.0%	24.4%	22.2%	19.3%	2.4%
Dane County	17,602	98.9%	67,409	25.3%	36.7%	3.8%	31.8%	73,996	10.4%	18.7%	8.5%	40.7%	18.9%
Eau Claire County	4,486	99.2%	15,224	27.5%	46.2%	8.1%	8.8%	12,710	10.5%	20.6%	16.9%	37.8%	2.5%
Fond du Lac County	5,121	99.6%	8,500	31.9%	45.0%	1.0%	6.2%	10,541	30.8%	17.1%	20.0%	13.8%	5.1%
Kenosha County	7,132	97.4%	17,148	42.5%	37.1%	2.7%	6.2%	17,742	26.6%	26.4%	15.0%	20.8%	5.6%
La Crosse County	4,026	98.4%	19,238	25.7%	58.2%	4.7%	8.0%	12,539	19.1%	27.1%	14.0%	23.1%	12.5%

Table E-2: Counties—Educational Attainment—*Continued*

	15 to 17		18 to 24					25 to 33					
				Percent						Percent			
	Total Population	Percent Enrolled in School	Total Population	High School	Some College	Associates Degree	Bachelors Degree	Total Population	High School	Some College	Associates Degree	Bachelors Degree	Advanced Degree
Wisconsin—Cont.													
Marathon County	5,541	93.1%	9,696	41.3%	24.9%	12.5%	11.2%	14,255	18.4%	20.3%	17.8%	28.8%	7.9%
Milwaukee County.....................	35,510	98.7%	95,959	27.4%	47.2%	3.4%	7.2%	136,081	18.2%	24.8%	7.8%	29.5%	10.9%
Outagamie County.....................	7,237	100.0%	15,392	28.5%	42.4%	8.1%	10.4%	23,277	20.6%	26.0%	16.1%	22.7%	8.5%
Racine County...........................	8,017	100.0%	17,832	46.5%	35.0%	7.5%	3.6%	19,655	29.5%	25.4%	10.9%	21.9%	3.5%
Rock County	6,618	100.0%	14,815	39.1%	37.1%	0.8%	8.5%	15,271	21.6%	25.7%	20.9%	21.1%	4.4%
Sheboygan County.....................	4,661	98.3%	8,517	35.6%	25.9%	3.9%	22.7%	11,780	35.9%	19.7%	6.1%	22.1%	4.8%
Walworth County	3,868	100.0%	13,278	25.7%	42.1%	10.0%	8.3%	10,055	22.3%	28.2%	9.4%	20.3%	3.7%
Washington County....................	4,784	100.0%	10,356	35.5%	26.7%	6.8%	24.6%	12,465	22.1%	21.4%	20.1%	30.7%	5.7%
Waukesha County	17,531	98.8%	29,887	26.3%	42.1%	7.3%	13.0%	35,375	17.5%	23.0%	16.4%	29.3%	12.2%
Winnebago County.....................	6,316	97.3%	19,273	19.1%	53.8%	10.0%	6.2%	21,198	12.3%	32.7%	21.4%	22.4%	6.2%
Wyoming													
Laramie County..........................	3,281	100.0%	13,912	34.3%	33.6%	12.7%	6.0%	9,429	24.1%	26.5%	15.7%	22.9%	7.9%

Table E-3: Places—Educational Attainment

	15 to 17		18 to 24					25 to 33					
				Percent					Percent				
	Total Population	Percent Enrolled in School	Total Population	High School	Some College	Associates Degree	Bachelors Degree	Total Population	High School	Some College	Associates Degree	Bachelors Degree	Advanced Degree
Alabama													
Birmingham city	7,925	90.2%	24,765	33.2%	43.4%	2.0%	10.3%	32,586	28.4%	30.3%	4.8%	18.7%	9.4%
Huntsville city	6,976	98.2%	19,309	40.5%	35.5%	4.8%	8.8%	24,297	19.5%	24.7%	8.4%	31.5%	7.0%
Mobile city	7,829	95.6%	20,136	25.3%	40.1%	3.1%	12.8%	26,961	23.8%	31.9%	6.5%	20.4%	6.1%
Montgomery city	8,010	94.3%	21,793	29.1%	42.0%	4.2%	6.1%	26,837	23.8%	30.4%	6.8%	19.6%	1.7%
Tuscaloosa city	3,709	97.5%	25,864	24.5%	60.1%	4.1%	4.3%	13,727	13.2%	15.1%	13.5%	32.9%	6.1%
Alaska													
Anchorage municipality	11,771	93.5%	34,552	29.6%	37.4%	4.3%	8.9%	46,126	23.6%	32.4%	9.2%	23.2%	5.8%
Arizona													
Chandler city	11,641	97.7%	21,152	24.8%	40.9%	8.2%	9.0%	36,119	13.0%	25.3%	8.6%	26.3%	18.1%
Glendale city	11,712	98.4%	24,197	38.1%	29.9%	5.2%	5.7%	31,617	28.7%	26.7%	8.6%	15.6%	2.9%
Mesa city	19,020	94.6%	45,282	35.9%	36.4%	6.3%	5.7%	63,020	24.7%	29.1%	8.5%	18.2%	5.5%
Peoria city	7,196	95.1%	13,727	29.7%	48.1%	7.2%	5.8%	21,111	27.4%	31.2%	9.4%	16.1%	5.9%
Phoenix city	65,047	96.7%	156,250	31.2%	30.8%	6.9%	7.8%	211,638	24.1%	24.5%	8.5%	20.2%	6.8%
Scottsdale city	6,947	98.5%	15,416	14.6%	37.5%	7.7%	27.1%	30,246	6.3%	28.7%	6.4%	48.7%	6.8%
Surprise city	5,937	99.0%	7,602	39.4%	44.9%	5.6%	6.3%	13,542	29.3%	21.7%	12.5%	17.1%	4.8%
Tempe city	5,572	100.0%	44,340	17.7%	54.5%	4.3%	12.7%	28,260	17.8%	25.6%	4.7%	20.4%	23.7%
Tucson city	20,366	92.8%	83,057	25.1%	48.2%	3.3%	6.6%	66,272	22.2%	29.2%	9.5%	18.1%	8.4%
Yuma city	5,336	98.1%	11,281	37.5%	41.9%	4.1%	0.9%	10,968	28.7%	26.3%	6.7%	13.1%	5.7%
Arkansas													
Little Rock city	6,883	84.9%	17,815	33.2%	42.8%	0.7%	13.8%	28,900	16.7%	26.7%	6.1%	23.8%	17.7%
California													
Anaheim city	14,855	98.5%	38,451	31.6%	45.3%	5.1%	6.3%	51,581	18.7%	29.4%	8.0%	19.9%	4.0%
Antioch city	5,261	100.0%	13,849	24.0%	37.2%	11.0%	6.4%	12,047	30.0%	32.8%	5.4%	17.9%	5.8%
Bakersfield city	16,886	98.6%	45,417	41.6%	33.0%	4.6%	5.6%	53,945	33.4%	24.3%	5.7%	14.4%	4.4%
Berkeley city	3,615	100.0%	25,791	27.6%	46.6%	3.0%	19.5%	20,092	5.0%	10.7%	4.5%	48.6%	30.7%
Burbank city	3,997	89.1%	7,065	20.2%	41.8%	6.2%	17.4%	16,868	9.4%	28.2%	6.5%	38.8%	16.0%
Carlsbad city	4,657	100.0%	8,757	22.1%	50.1%	5.7%	18.1%	12,465	10.3%	27.5%	6.0%	40.3%	13.0%
Chico city	3,606	100.0%	20,214	25.8%	48.7%	10.6%	5.9%	11,738	8.6%	38.7%	14.3%	20.6%	7.5%
Carson city	4,723	100.0%	9,998	20.2%	48.6%	12.8%	8.3%	11,282	17.6%	28.4%	6.8%	33.7%	3.9%
Chula Vista city	11,333	100.0%	29,347	43.2%	43.4%	6.5%	3.2%	32,687	24.9%	29.9%	8.4%	21.3%	1.7%
Clovis city	4,019	100.0%	8,292	32.5%	47.3%	4.6%	5.9%	13,995	16.0%	30.2%	4.6%	26.4%	11.3%
Compton city	4,704	94.7%	13,133	32.8%	40.3%	2.0%	1.2%	12,685	32.8%	27.7%	4.2%	6.3%	0.0%
Concord city	4,254	100.0%	10,042	25.0%	48.1%	10.7%	10.6%	16,439	20.7%	18.9%	8.1%	29.5%	14.4%
Corona city	6,654	97.6%	14,784	36.3%	38.0%	8.3%	2.8%	20,907	33.8%	25.4%	8.5%	18.3%	4.1%
Costa Mesa city	5,843	99.0%	10,854	28.9%	42.4%	9.7%	11.9%	19,681	10.2%	23.7%	9.2%	34.2%	16.1%
Daly City city	2,037	100.0%	10,375	23.0%	44.9%	10.9%	13.7%	17,192	17.3%	22.7%	8.6%	36.2%	9.5%
Downey city	4,610	97.0%	13,983	22.5%	43.4%	8.2%	7.6%	15,220	20.3%	31.1%	16.3%	20.3%	2.9%
El Cajon city	3,902	100.0%	11,079	41.0%	39.2%	2.0%	2.2%	15,091	35.3%	35.4%	7.5%	10.4%	4.3%
Elk Grove city	7,032	100.0%	17,398	22.7%	43.2%	8.7%	6.4%	17,220	17.5%	29.6%	8.8%	24.3%	9.3%
El Monte city	5,200	97.7%	12,404	35.3%	34.4%	5.5%	6.3%	15,964	35.2%	17.1%	7.2%	15.3%	5.0%
Escondido city	5,350	93.9%	17,660	28.5%	49.2%	3.7%	3.2%	24,192	23.6%	26.1%	10.9%	15.3%	6.8%
Fairfield city	4,659	100.0%	10,589	36.8%	37.8%	2.6%	6.3%	15,995	19.3%	21.5%	10.9%	18.0%	7.2%
Fontana city	8,977	97.6%	23,408	40.4%	39.7%	6.2%	1.7%	31,601	34.5%	30.7%	4.4%	8.7%	1.5%
Fremont city	8,496	98.3%	19,330	35.2%	40.2%	2.5%	12.4%	31,000	15.2%	13.8%	3.3%	35.1%	30.8%
Fresno city	24,032	97.0%	61,204	27.7%	50.6%	6.1%	4.2%	75,584	27.2%	30.2%	7.7%	13.4%	4.0%
Fullerton city	6,182	100.0%	18,398	23.6%	46.0%	6.9%	11.8%	19,400	17.1%	21.2%	4.4%	30.0%	9.8%
Garden Grove city	6,763	98.7%	17,516	29.9%	37.6%	6.2%	11.4%	22,763	24.5%	25.9%	7.2%	22.3%	4.6%
Glendale city	5,276	96.8%	15,025	15.4%	56.1%	7.8%	15.4%	28,888	17.8%	24.9%	6.6%	33.1%	12.3%
Hayward city	5,564	93.4%	15,039	27.8%	47.9%	6.3%	9.6%	27,067	34.2%	20.0%	5.1%	26.7%	7.2%
Hesperia city	5,305	96.6%	8,864	37.0%	32.6%	4.1%	8.6%	12,931	37.2%	20.1%	6.8%	14.0%	3.8%
Huntington Beach city	4,928	97.9%	14,445	31.4%	43.1%	5.2%	14.1%	25,026	11.4%	23.9%	7.5%	38.4%	11.2%
Inglewood city	4,406	97.7%	11,548	29.8%	53.6%	2.3%	1.0%	15,749	19.5%	31.0%	9.3%	17.1%	3.3%
Irvine city	10,459	99.6%	36,009	27.5%	43.6%	3.7%	16.3%	36,640	4.8%	13.3%	5.8%	46.3%	26.4%
Jurupa Valley city	4,584	100.0%	12,342	43.6%	35.4%	7.5%	1.9%	13,050	32.0%	29.6%	4.6%	13.0%	7.1%
Lancaster city	8,963	98.6%	14,851	40.2%	36.0%	5.0%	0.5%	25,394	33.4%	30.4%	18.6%	6.1%	1.8%
Long Beach city	19,352	97.8%	47,955	28.1%	45.2%	5.2%	7.4%	70,119	21.6%	25.3%	7.8%	23.9%	6.9%
Los Angeles city	143,058	97.6%	429,036	26.7%	44.5%	3.8%	11.3%	636,484	20.7%	20.6%	5.9%	28.7%	9.3%
Mission Viejo city	3,523	100.0%	9,478	19.4%	42.9%	12.4%	18.5%	9,308	10.6%	22.8%	14.4%	33.0%	11.8%
Modesto city	8,314	96.4%	23,005	43.0%	32.7%	2.1%	7.5%	25,866	28.0%	33.9%	6.3%	12.8%	4.0%
Moreno Valley city	11,841	97.6%	27,021	42.5%	37.0%	2.0%	5.0%	27,577	33.9%	27.9%	6.3%	14.7%	3.1%
Murrieta city	6,786	100.0%	9,635	34.9%	40.8%	6.8%	5.1%	14,030	25.5%	36.7%	9.6%	11.6%	6.0%
Norwalk city	3,355	92.0%	13,714	23.6%	56.9%	1.5%	6.3%	13,620	20.1%	35.9%	11.2%	18.1%	3.6%
Oakland city	13,374	96.9%	34,194	22.4%	38.8%	4.3%	19.7%	74,769	17.3%	18.0%	5.5%	29.4%	14.5%
Oceanside city	4,874	95.5%	23,119	55.1%	26.7%	6.2%	2.9%	17,362	16.4%	40.1%	5.2%	20.1%	6.4%
Ontario city	8,214	99.3%	18,889	32.8%	45.7%	4.8%	5.8%	24,428	29.3%	28.3%	7.3%	13.7%	3.4%
Orange city	5,015	98.9%	17,383	25.0%	59.3%	3.2%	5.3%	21,674	14.3%	21.7%	14.1%	31.3%	9.7%
Oxnard city	8,739	99.9%	21,543	29.0%	46.9%	8.9%	1.9%	32,007	19.6%	24.3%	9.9%	12.3%	5.5%
Palmdale city	7,740	100.0%	16,298	25.8%	48.2%	5.5%	1.6%	18,322	32.0%	22.9%	11.1%	12.6%	2.2%
Pasadena city	2,678	94.0%	11,802	25.3%	44.7%	3.7%	15.9%	22,282	13.0%	19.8%	6.2%	34.9%	19.2%
Pomona city	6,661	100.0%	20,281	31.3%	43.9%	3.1%	8.6%	21,771	23.0%	20.1%	8.8%	23.5%	6.5%
Rancho Cucamonga city	6,933	99.0%	21,193	28.0%	48.5%	4.0%	11.1%	21,999	20.7%	35.1%	8.8%	20.2%	11.4%
Redding city	4,610	100.0%	7,140	35.9%	38.8%	2.3%	2.0%	13,090	23.4%	31.9%	9.0%	17.5%	9.9%
Rialto city	5,279	98.4%	12,693	34.2%	48.3%	3.3%	1.7%	14,882	40.2%	20.0%	4.6%	13.3%	1.7%

Table E-3: Places—Educational Attainment—Continued

| | 15 to 17 | | 18 to 24 | | | | | 25 to 33 | | | | | |
| | | | | Percent | | | | | Percent | | | | |
	Total Population	Percent Enrolled in School	Total Population	High School	Some College	Associates Degree	Bachelors Degree	Total Population	High School	Some College	Associates Degree	Bachelors Degree	Advanced Degree
California—Cont.													
Richmond city	2,574	100.0%	13,367	35.6%	35.1%	3.3%	6.0%	16,605	23.6%	24.9%	4.6%	20.2%	4.6%
Riverside city	12,088	99.0%	47,199	31.0%	49.2%	5.4%	6.0%	49,657	31.2%	25.2%	8.4%	14.5%	8.1%
Roseville city	5,797	94.7%	12,503	36.6%	42.2%	3.5%	11.0%	14,296	15.1%	26.2%	17.8%	32.7%	4.3%
Sacramento city	19,543	98.7%	44,442	28.7%	47.3%	3.5%	7.5%	78,271	22.0%	25.9%	9.1%	22.2%	8.0%
Salinas city	7,118	89.0%	16,341	25.6%	41.0%	5.5%	2.8%	21,776	23.9%	17.7%	6.6%	10.4%	1.6%
San Bernardino city	10,249	96.7%	27,676	36.9%	37.2%	5.5%	4.7%	30,586	36.6%	24.9%	7.8%	5.3%	2.0%
San Buenaventura (Ventura) city.	3,800	91.0%	8,974	20.9%	41.6%	3.1%	10.5%	14,855	30.6%	29.5%	5.9%	23.3%	5.3%
San Diego city	48,032	97.5%	163,607	25.6%	50.4%	4.3%	11.9%	233,373	16.0%	21.9%	6.2%	32.0%	17.1%
San Francisco city	17,062	97.0%	63,520	18.1%	37.4%	5.1%	33.4%	178,135	6.5%	10.6%	4.7%	51.5%	22.8%
San Jose city	37,124	96.6%	93,229	30.1%	43.0%	4.0%	11.2%	139,521	19.4%	20.4%	7.6%	26.4%	16.1%
San Leandro city	3,246	98.3%	6,738	26.6%	34.6%	2.3%	25.7%	12,776	15.7%	24.9%	6.6%	42.4%	5.0%
San Marcos city	3,908	100.0%	9,325	23.6%	55.5%	1.6%	7.3%	11,169	18.5%	24.1%	8.0%	28.2%	12.4%
San Mateo city	4,395	97.4%	7,418	35.0%	26.0%	3.8%	23.6%	12,624	9.2%	6.2%	10.7%	38.8%	30.4%
Santa Ana city	15,351	98.4%	34,544	30.8%	41.1%	5.2%	4.9%	51,773	32.2%	23.1%	4.4%	12.9%	2.5%
Santa Clara city	2,783	100.0%	13,344	29.3%	38.6%	4.8%	17.8%	23,466	4.6%	9.8%	2.3%	38.1%	41.4%
Santa Clarita city	6,978	97.5%	18,469	33.3%	41.3%	4.1%	11.1%	22,326	20.7%	25.8%	10.0%	28.1%	6.1%
Santa Maria city	6,003	100.0%	12,496	31.2%	36.6%	5.7%	1.2%	12,057	13.3%	33.3%	5.0%	12.6%	1.0%
Santa Monica city	2,793	100.0%	5,866	12.8%	52.8%	0.8%	24.8%	16,013	6.8%	10.6%	1.9%	56.2%	22.4%
Santa Rosa city	5,788	94.0%	15,634	23.2%	45.9%	5.0%	14.2%	23,024	20.8%	33.0%	9.5%	19.4%	6.7%
Simi Valley city	6,362	98.6%	12,530	24.3%	40.1%	8.0%	12.2%	13,848	20.0%	18.6%	14.2%	32.7%	10.7%
South Gate city	4,348	96.0%	11,254	35.7%	40.0%	1.8%	3.3%	12,675	28.8%	21.6%	9.1%	8.9%	4.0%
Stockton city	15,603	97.6%	34,010	31.2%	44.4%	3.6%	4.0%	42,335	25.1%	31.3%	7.3%	12.5%	2.3%
Sunnyvale city	4,139	97.9%	8,863	19.0%	31.2%	3.1%	27.3%	28,799	5.1%	12.8%	6.2%	30.6%	37.9%
Temecula city	6,828	100.0%	10,102	30.3%	47.6%	11.1%	3.3%	13,346	20.9%	42.1%	7.3%	23.0%	3.1%
Thousand Oaks city	5,906	98.9%	10,437	24.6%	52.5%	5.2%	8.5%	9,958	26.7%	11.2%	6.3%	24.6%	25.7%
Torrance city	4,539	97.5%	15,100	22.5%	48.4%	6.2%	11.0%	15,611	13.6%	26.5%	12.6%	33.0%	11.4%
Vacaville city	4,170	100.0%	9,533	23.2%	52.9%	7.6%	5.0%	12,759	27.5%	22.6%	16.1%	19.4%	5.7%
Vallejo city	4,350	90.2%	11,449	33.1%	27.1%	5.0%	16.8%	17,933	21.1%	37.6%	7.9%	20.3%	6.9%
Victorville city	8,236	100.0%	11,547	30.3%	39.1%	5.9%	0.6%	16,953	35.3%	36.2%	7.2%	4.8%	4.6%
Visalia city	4,868	98.4%	12,737	26.5%	54.6%	6.0%	4.6%	16,358	32.3%	20.5%	10.4%	17.4%	7.4%
Vista city	3,531	98.0%	11,904	32.0%	44.3%	6.0%	9.5%	16,140	30.9%	20.0%	16.8%	12.2%	7.1%
West Covina city	4,608	97.5%	9,485	48.0%	37.6%	4.8%	3.3%	15,248	21.8%	31.8%	5.0%	27.0%	5.7%
Westminster city	2,846	97.3%	6,615	13.6%	51.5%	15.1%	8.2%	12,305	19.0%	29.1%	8.3%	27.8%	5.2%
Colorado													
Arvada city	4,928	99.3%	7,135	28.0%	35.9%	9.3%	12.7%	13,764	19.3%	21.5%	8.7%	32.6%	14.6%
Aurora city	16,434	96.8%	33,948	36.2%	32.0%	8.8%	5.9%	51,712	23.5%	27.0%	10.4%	24.6%	5.7%
Boulder city	2,515	100.0%	32,366	18.9%	58.2%	4.3%	17.4%	15,823	4.1%	15.8%	5.5%	45.7%	28.9%
Centennial city	5,451	98.8%	7,611	37.4%	33.5%	1.2%	14.8%	11,724	12.5%	36.8%	13.9%	23.6%	10.3%
Colorado Springs city	17,229	98.6%	45,198	30.6%	43.6%	4.1%	10.4%	69,650	26.2%	25.6%	12.3%	23.0%	6.1%
Denver city	16,768	89.5%	58,231	25.8%	36.8%	5.4%	13.1%	142,282	16.1%	16.3%	4.8%	37.3%	18.5%
Fort Collins city	5,342	100.0%	32,030	18.7%	53.8%	2.8%	19.4%	27,412	12.0%	24.2%	9.5%	40.6%	11.1%
Greeley city	5,241	100.0%	12,337	41.8%	39.8%	4.7%	3.4%	14,747	24.7%	35.2%	6.8%	17.1%	7.9%
Lakewood city	6,096	94.5%	16,380	35.7%	34.3%	5.3%	12.1%	21,541	16.0%	26.9%	5.4%	30.0%	15.5%
Longmont city	4,481	97.2%	7,630	20.8%	54.9%	2.7%	5.1%	9,521	25.3%	21.2%	5.6%	31.2%	14.3%
Pueblo city	5,026	88.4%	10,047	42.5%	22.5%	4.5%	9.5%	13,992	28.0%	37.3%	10.2%	13.9%	2.2%
Thornton city	6,397	98.7%	11,352	46.4%	22.8%	6.0%	10.2%	17,167	24.9%	22.8%	12.3%	27.8%	2.5%
Westminster city	4,832	98.0%	9,356	30.7%	43.0%	4.0%	14.5%	15,866	21.7%	17.1%	6.2%	40.1%	11.4%
Connecticut													
Bridgeport city	5,260	90.1%	17,826	29.7%	39.9%	5.4%	6.2%	20,882	24.7%	32.6%	5.9%	17.7%	7.1%
Hartford city	5,079	100.0%	21,070	24.0%	53.8%	1.9%	6.0%	17,959	27.4%	26.9%	2.7%	17.0%	11.4%
New Haven city	5,062	99.8%	21,920	32.2%	39.4%	1.3%	6.5%	25,481	24.9%	15.3%	2.2%	25.0%	20.5%
Stamford city	5,078	94.0%	12,444	31.5%	28.5%	3.0%	20.4%	20,672	12.7%	15.6%	5.2%	34.2%	25.0%
Waterbury city	4,419	97.2%	10,362	35.8%	36.5%	2.4%	6.6%	13,325	42.3%	21.4%	8.2%	5.6%	3.3%
District of Columbia													
Washington city	15,198	98.1%	81,910	25.2%	45.8%	1.2%	20.2%	139,024	11.9%	8.3%	2.1%	35.7%	36.9%
Florida													
Boca Raton city	3,722	100.0%	9,141	21.3%	43.3%	12.7%	15.6%	8,790	15.7%	18.9%	3.8%	42.3%	13.8%
Cape Coral city	7,548	92.0%	10,150	39.1%	24.6%	14.7%	0.7%	19,627	44.1%	16.6%	9.4%	8.4%	10.7%
Clearwater city	2,921	88.5%	7,867	33.9%	26.8%	7.7%	9.1%	14,213	23.2%	31.4%	14.9%	19.1%	4.5%
Coral Springs city	8,390	98.7%	11,711	22.2%	46.5%	5.7%	10.8%	12,738	26.1%	24.7%	11.1%	25.2%	7.2%
Fort Lauderdale city	5,657	90.7%	10,504	42.5%	20.8%	4.6%	7.6%	24,714	21.1%	15.8%	8.3%	24.3%	10.8%
Gainesville city	3,533	100.0%	41,812	12.3%	57.1%	11.9%	12.1%	20,893	18.7%	13.1%	13.2%	25.3%	21.8%
Hialeah city	7,047	92.0%	18,916	36.8%	34.1%	8.1%	2.5%	28,617	39.7%	17.6%	11.4%	16.5%	4.7%
Hollywood city	2,825	98.6%	11,392	38.8%	29.3%	5.2%	6.7%	18,482	31.9%	16.0%	10.2%	24.5%	9.7%
Jacksonville city	30,124	97.5%	82,935	34.0%	33.0%	7.2%	9.9%	123,515	27.1%	25.3%	8.0%	23.2%	9.2%
Lakeland city	3,907	95.6%	10,492	24.2%	42.2%	8.7%	3.6%	13,360	37.1%	19.3%	7.0%	14.9%	3.3%
Miami city	11,941	99.6%	33,513	30.7%	34.1%	10.5%	8.5%	64,897	25.9%	18.0%	9.1%	21.0%	13.8%
Miami Beach city	2,617	94.5%	5,622	16.5%	41.9%	14.8%	11.2%	13,576	14.9%	20.6%	9.7%	31.9%	19.9%
Miami Gardens city	4,341	90.5%	11,382	39.5%	43.3%	2.7%	3.7%	15,208	25.8%	41.6%	9.4%	12.4%	2.4%
Miramar city	4,891	100.0%	12,731	18.1%	41.1%	13.9%	13.8%	17,018	10.5%	24.9%	19.1%	23.1%	12.2%
Orlando city	9,660	97.2%	28,207	34.6%	31.5%	9.6%	9.3%	54,102	21.6%	25.5%	10.3%	25.7%	8.6%
Palm Bay city	4,245	93.4%	9,453	26.0%	45.1%	8.2%	7.4%	10,233	15.1%	33.5%	10.3%	21.0%	8.7%
Pembroke Pines city	6,575	100.0%	16,234	26.0%	32.8%	15.3%	13.5%	18,884	10.2%	22.3%	14.1%	31.2%	13.8%

Table E-3: Places—Educational Attainment—Continued

| | 15 to 17 | | 18 to 24 | | | | | 25 to 33 | | | | | |
| | Total Population | Percent Enrolled in School | Total Population | Percent | | | | Total Population | Percent | | | | |
				High School	Some College	Associates Degree	Bachelors Degree		High School	Some College	Associates Degree	Bachelors Degree	Advanced Degree
Florida—Cont.													
Plantation city	2,831	79.3%	6,199	30.4%	35.1%	5.7%	9.1%	12,841	25.5%	26.8%	10.7%	20.5%	10.2%
Pompano Beach city	3,744	95.2%	8,856	36.5%	20.4%	14.8%	7.2%	12,129	26.1%	24.9%	5.7%	16.7%	8.5%
Port St. Lucie city	6,234	96.3%	14,357	17.5%	32.7%	6.2%	5.9%	18,502	36.5%	27.1%	16.4%	10.4%	3.4%
St. Petersburg city	9,050	98.3%	20,729	23.6%	42.0%	7.0%	9.7%	32,599	30.9%	16.6%	9.8%	24.7%	9.3%
Sunrise city	3,246	81.9%	6,979	25.5%	40.7%	6.0%	8.1%	14,792	25.3%	29.7%	9.3%	21.3%	8.5%
Tallahassee city	5,791	95.2%	57,815	12.0%	51.3%	17.5%	13.5%	26,618	21.0%	18.6%	13.9%	27.4%	14.8%
Tampa city	13,115	97.5%	39,114	24.7%	38.1%	7.5%	12.3%	57,156	28.6%	17.5%	7.0%	27.7%	12.3%
West Palm Beach city	4,037	100.0%	9,024	22.7%	43.2%	8.3%	8.8%	14,859	30.5%	18.5%	6.6%	20.4%	5.6%
Georgia													
Athens-Clarke County unified govt (balance)	2,635	100.0%	36,399	18.9%	58.2%	3.2%	11.2%	15,629	14.3%	16.9%	6.9%	34.7%	19.3%
Atlanta city	10,765	98.2%	59,522	12.2%	56.6%	2.1%	18.5%	89,857	14.2%	18.8%	2.8%	36.0%	20.9%
Augusta-Richmond County consolidated govt (balance)	7,388	92.2%	23,296	40.2%	31.4%	1.7%	5.1%	28,678	25.8%	25.5%	14.2%	15.7%	8.8%
Columbus city	6,999	99.2%	24,389	36.5%	37.3%	6.4%	5.7%	29,720	24.7%	33.0%	6.1%	18.2%	10.5%
Macon-Bibb county	6,082	94.4%	16,246	32.0%	45.1%	3.0%	4.2%	18,486	24.8%	23.9%	7.8%	25.2%	9.6%
Roswell city	4,937	100.0%	7,219	23.8%	29.0%	9.0%	9.5%	8,771	15.8%	22.5%	3.2%	39.0%	11.4%
Sandy Springs city	4,514	95.4%	7,991	14.8%	24.0%	1.1%	42.4%	17,561	12.3%	11.3%	6.6%	39.0%	25.0%
Savannah city	5,973	91.7%	24,692	27.9%	53.5%	1.6%	8.1%	24,507	15.3%	38.7%	6.5%	20.0%	6.9%
Hawaii													
Urban Honolulu CDP	9,278	95.1%	30,770	31.1%	43.6%	8.3%	9.4%	44,550	25.1%	18.9%	8.9%	30.2%	10.7%
Idaho													
Boise City city	9,105	96.2%	20,288	28.5%	40.4%	7.9%	9.0%	32,766	21.8%	28.3%	6.8%	26.4%	9.1%
Meridian city	2,627	100.0%	5,891	39.4%	38.4%	3.8%	1.0%	9,187	24.0%	38.0%	1.4%	30.1%	5.9%
Illinois													
Aurora city	8,412	100.0%	20,391	37.6%	35.5%	9.1%	5.7%	26,219	18.2%	23.3%	7.0%	20.8%	5.8%
Chicago city	93,491	95.7%	284,971	25.6%	40.2%	3.7%	16.1%	482,562	17.6%	15.9%	5.1%	35.6%	17.9%
Elgin city	3,346	95.3%	11,159	21.7%	47.0%	7.3%	9.3%	11,983	18.3%	31.8%	8.6%	23.2%	7.1%
Joliet city	7,526	97.7%	16,026	40.1%	37.0%	5.3%	7.0%	16,306	24.6%	30.9%	9.9%	16.5%	5.3%
Naperville city	6,360	100.0%	12,952	29.9%	38.0%	7.0%	19.7%	14,606	15.9%	19.9%	3.1%	42.4%	13.3%
Peoria city	4,986	96.5%	11,731	23.7%	46.2%	5.1%	10.9%	18,154	15.7%	25.4%	4.3%	23.4%	18.3%
Rockford city	6,451	95.0%	14,392	31.2%	32.1%	6.2%	8.3%	19,160	28.8%	20.1%	10.5%	26.7%	5.0%
Springfield city	5,399	96.4%	11,083	17.1%	37.9%	3.2%	12.1%	15,469	14.3%	33.8%	4.2%	20.8%	13.4%
Indiana													
Evansville city	4,094	89.7%	12,756	29.8%	36.5%	1.4%	9.8%	15,885	22.9%	19.4%	4.8%	29.4%	14.1%
Fort Wayne city	9,722	93.9%	27,427	27.9%	43.0%	2.7%	9.2%	33,623	20.7%	28.7%	10.0%	23.1%	5.3%
Indianapolis city (balance)	31,292	96.3%	80,525	30.1%	35.6%	2.5%	13.7%	132,231	22.3%	20.0%	8.1%	25.2%	9.5%
South Bend city	3,566	91.7%	13,865	28.0%	46.4%	1.0%	5.3%	12,052	26.1%	30.3%	7.4%	19.7%	7.1%
Iowa													
Cedar Rapids city	5,952	97.5%	12,970	18.5%	49.7%	6.3%	14.1%	16,437	12.5%	30.0%	12.7%	30.4%	12.2%
Davenport city	4,284	96.4%	9,454	28.8%	47.5%	7.6%	8.9%	14,051	25.7%	23.8%	10.8%	22.6%	7.8%
Des Moines city	7,504	94.5%	22,640	24.6%	51.7%	2.9%	9.0%	32,683	22.3%	22.2%	9.8%	24.3%	9.1%
Kansas													
Kansas City city	6,296	90.4%	14,303	37.7%	33.1%	5.4%	6.0%	19,764	25.4%	21.3%	10.1%	15.7%	6.5%
Olathe city	8,205	98.6%	11,229	24.4%	40.7%	4.9%	13.2%	14,204	14.0%	22.9%	14.0%	33.5%	10.4%
Overland Park city	8,063	93.7%	12,995	16.1%	37.2%	8.0%	19.8%	24,843	6.7%	12.1%	6.6%	42.2%	30.7%
Topeka city	5,658	95.8%	13,134	33.2%	39.0%	1.7%	8.6%	14,998	27.2%	23.5%	14.7%	12.4%	13.0%
Wichita city	16,955	94.6%	32,837	27.1%	39.9%	5.3%	5.9%	55,499	22.4%	25.2%	9.6%	21.2%	7.8%
Kentucky													
Lexington-Fayette urban county	9,984	98.5%	43,864	20.8%	55.7%	2.8%	11.7%	45,356	19.2%	24.9%	6.2%	30.4%	15.3%
Louisville/Jefferson County metro govt (balance)	24,339	98.2%	56,727	31.0%	41.6%	5.0%	7.0%	77,705	23.1%	21.7%	8.6%	25.5%	13.7%
Louisiana													
Baton Rouge city	8,509	97.1%	37,552	25.8%	46.4%	1.6%	8.8%	35,081	25.5%	22.4%	6.5%	30.3%	8.6%
Lafayette city	6,834	95.6%	14,704	25.6%	53.1%	5.1%	5.5%	22,933	17.1%	25.2%	9.8%	33.9%	8.6%
New Orleans city	12,156	96.7%	37,387	23.5%	48.1%	1.5%	13.0%	66,489	18.9%	23.4%	3.6%	29.5%	16.0%
Shreveport city	9,120	97.9%	18,974	31.5%	39.7%	3.8%	4.7%	26,743	21.7%	39.0%	5.5%	14.5%	5.6%
Maryland													
Baltimore city	19,693	94.0%	64,583	30.3%	38.1%	1.7%	13.1%	107,588	24.8%	17.5%	4.7%	25.7%	16.1%
Massachusetts													
Boston city	17,511	96.9%	100,784	22.3%	47.4%	1.9%	18.9%	148,487	11.1%	12.7%	4.2%	43.0%	24.6%
Brockton city	4,506	100.0%	11,101	42.0%	32.7%	5.4%	5.2%	11,438	33.6%	24.4%	10.6%	19.1%	7.4%
Cambridge city	2,146	100.0%	20,489	16.1%	49.9%	0.0%	30.2%	29,303	2.2%	5.5%	1.9%	36.1%	53.9%
Lowell city	2,964	97.9%	15,564	30.4%	38.4%	6.4%	11.3%	16,486	27.5%	21.8%	9.7%	19.0%	9.5%
Lynn city	3,391	100.0%	8,414	30.0%	30.2%	8.5%	10.8%	13,547	20.5%	19.9%	12.5%	15.8%	7.1%
New Bedford city	3,127	91.5%	11,109	36.9%	37.9%	3.3%	5.7%	11,068	25.7%	25.0%	6.1%	20.6%	3.6%
Quincy city	3,017	97.6%	7,210	34.1%	34.2%	0.0%	22.9%	14,553	8.4%	20.9%	4.3%	43.7%	17.5%
Springfield city	6,944	94.5%	20,703	23.0%	52.4%	2.5%	4.3%	19,325	29.0%	17.3%	7.9%	18.9%	3.7%
Worcester city	6,744	99.5%	27,597	33.5%	47.3%	3.6%	8.6%	27,695	20.6%	20.7%	9.2%	27.4%	10.7%

Table E-3: Places—Educational Attainment—*Continued*

| | 15 to 17 | | 18 to 24 | | | | | 25 to 33 | | | | | |
| | Total Population | Percent Enrolled in School | Total Population | Percent | | | | Total Population | Percent | | | | |
				High School	Some College	Associates Degree	Bachelors Degree		High School	Some College	Associates Degree	Bachelors Degree	Advanced Degree
Michigan													
Ann Arbor city	2,655	100.0%	36,381	19.8%	47.8%	2.2%	28.1%	18,044	4.4%	9.9%	6.0%	43.9%	33.1%
Dearborn city	3,770	100.0%	10,993	30.7%	45.1%	5.2%	7.0%	10,651	18.0%	31.5%	4.4%	23.8%	13.6%
Detroit city	29,159	93.1%	72,501	35.6%	38.6%	2.0%	4.9%	87,500	31.9%	28.6%	6.3%	13.0%	4.6%
Flint city	3,995	95.7%	10,233	27.8%	33.0%	5.1%	1.4%	11,405	19.5%	39.4%	2.8%	18.0%	0.7%
Grand Rapids city	5,500	95.2%	23,662	19.3%	53.8%	4.5%	9.2%	34,970	13.7%	17.1%	9.5%	36.2%	12.3%
Lansing city	4,753	91.8%	14,440	14.6%	51.0%	5.0%	17.7%	19,226	16.9%	27.3%	11.1%	24.3%	13.8%
Livonia city	3,284	97.1%	7,617	30.9%	45.5%	6.4%	13.0%	9,580	14.5%	34.4%	5.1%	28.8%	15.9%
Sterling Heights city	2,768	100.0%	12,536	19.9%	44.9%	7.4%	19.0%	17,324	29.6%	26.0%	12.9%	18.1%	7.9%
Warren city	6,260	97.7%	11,076	36.9%	31.2%	9.6%	8.2%	14,106	26.8%	31.9%	11.9%	16.9%	0.9%
Minnesota													
Minneapolis city	12,450	98.2%	51,927	20.7%	41.2%	3.7%	23.3%	83,500	12.6%	13.6%	6.9%	38.1%	21.3%
Rochester city	4,658	100.0%	10,947	24.8%	25.2%	4.9%	16.3%	15,378	11.9%	15.2%	14.1%	26.6%	28.9%
St. Paul city	10,755	96.8%	36,831	24.8%	39.9%	2.7%	14.5%	51,958	21.8%	16.4%	7.2%	31.4%	14.0%
Mississippi													
Jackson city	6,436	91.5%	20,753	20.4%	48.1%	5.0%	10.6%	25,800	25.7%	24.8%	7.2%	25.3%	10.2%
Missouri													
Columbia city	5,270	100.0%	28,768	20.8%	55.0%	2.5%	14.3%	21,450	14.3%	20.2%	7.3%	40.5%	16.1%
Independence city	3,777	96.3%	10,903	35.3%	29.7%	3.5%	8.7%	13,982	29.9%	36.3%	3.7%	16.3%	4.9%
Kansas City city	17,336	97.6%	43,621	27.6%	35.1%	3.3%	13.4%	67,268	21.4%	23.9%	8.3%	24.4%	11.6%
Lee's Summit city	4,379	100.0%	6,966	20.7%	54.4%	3.1%	13.7%	10,667	6.3%	25.9%	9.8%	38.3%	17.2%
St. Louis city	9,510	95.7%	32,067	23.4%	39.9%	2.1%	16.4%	56,718	15.0%	22.5%	5.2%	33.7%	18.5%
Springfield city	5,320	100.0%	29,221	18.2%	56.1%	7.5%	11.4%	25,949	20.5%	26.1%	13.7%	25.0%	8.8%
Montana													
Billings city	3,531	98.6%	11,573	40.2%	36.4%	2.0%	7.8%	14,982	30.4%	19.5%	14.3%	17.7%	11.9%
Nebraska													
Lincoln city	8,961	92.7%	43,889	16.0%	58.6%	3.3%	17.2%	37,574	19.2%	27.7%	10.7%	22.6%	13.2%
Omaha city	18,185	99.3%	43,003	24.3%	37.8%	4.5%	17.9%	68,472	16.7%	25.3%	6.8%	28.3%	10.7%
Nevada													
Henderson city	9,529	95.4%	19,103	35.4%	36.4%	5.6%	10.2%	32,425	22.4%	30.0%	7.4%	23.7%	7.0%
Las Vegas city	23,875	97.7%	51,195	34.0%	34.6%	2.9%	6.8%	83,225	25.4%	29.6%	8.3%	14.0%	4.8%
North Las Vegas city	12,834	95.9%	24,584	32.8%	41.2%	2.5%	4.1%	29,623	32.9%	26.3%	9.1%	15.1%	2.6%
Reno city	8,710	97.2%	26,890	26.6%	53.0%	4.0%	5.2%	33,201	20.9%	26.0%	6.5%	25.4%	10.0%
Sparks city	3,973	97.5%	8,371	48.1%	23.0%	7.3%	1.2%	12,093	26.2%	28.8%	9.5%	13.5%	6.9%
New Hampshire													
Manchester city	2,790	100.0%	12,737	28.8%	25.0%	11.2%	18.9%	14,766	40.5%	17.6%	8.7%	19.3%	4.7%
New Jersey													
Elizabeth city	4,828	84.9%	12,521	42.7%	25.2%	4.5%	4.6%	17,452	36.5%	17.3%	4.6%	7.1%	6.9%
Jersey City city	8,066	98.3%	22,866	17.4%	39.4%	3.5%	20.3%	52,020	17.6%	12.3%	4.8%	35.7%	25.8%
Newark city	9,931	95.7%	30,454	32.7%	39.6%	5.1%	8.0%	39,268	36.4%	17.6%	8.1%	14.1%	5.9%
Paterson city	6,290	98.2%	15,741	39.1%	39.6%	4.4%	1.5%	19,161	47.6%	20.1%	6.8%	9.4%	0.7%
New Mexico													
Albuquerque city	21,907	97.7%	52,676	27.1%	44.1%	6.3%	7.4%	76,537	16.0%	30.4%	9.5%	17.0%	10.4%
Las Cruces city	2,309	100.0%	16,110	27.5%	55.9%	10.5%	0.0%	12,066	17.3%	54.5%	5.6%	5.3%	12.2%
Rio Rancho city	4,635	99.8%	7,176	41.1%	39.0%	4.5%	2.3%	11,744	23.8%	35.2%	8.3%	19.5%	3.0%
New York													
Albany city	2,732	100.0%	20,054	22.2%	40.6%	8.0%	13.2%	14,733	18.1%	21.2%	5.4%	26.3%	23.9%
Buffalo city	9,138	97.0%	30,353	28.9%	35.8%	6.3%	13.0%	41,937	26.3%	19.1%	7.7%	22.7%	10.6%
New York city	278,549	97.9%	794,431	23.5%	38.9%	5.5%	16.1%	1,396,089	17.8%	15.3%	6.2%	33.7%	16.1%
Rochester city	7,207	89.0%	31,126	23.4%	37.7%	5.2%	14.4%	33,485	20.3%	23.4%	11.3%	17.0%	10.0%
Syracuse city	5,491	91.3%	26,102	21.0%	57.7%	2.2%	8.5%	21,880	18.5%	19.9%	4.9%	27.8%	11.7%
Yonkers city	8,135	95.8%	17,714	30.3%	35.1%	6.6%	12.7%	25,135	18.6%	26.1%	8.3%	24.8%	9.7%
North Carolina													
Charlotte city	28,275	96.5%	80,539	24.4%	42.9%	5.7%	14.4%	130,930	16.8%	19.2%	5.8%	33.4%	13.7%
Durham city	9,001	96.2%	26,426	23.3%	40.6%	1.4%	22.4%	46,023	12.1%	19.6%	4.1%	31.9%	20.6%
Fayetteville city	9,411	96.9%	26,213	33.1%	47.4%	2.7%	4.8%	33,692	22.5%	38.5%	8.6%	17.7%	6.7%
Greensboro city	11,226	96.8%	34,822	27.2%	48.4%	3.8%	7.8%	37,660	23.9%	23.9%	5.4%	24.8%	8.9%
High Point city	5,491	97.6%	11,419	33.8%	41.9%	8.0%	6.6%	12,920	17.0%	21.0%	8.4%	18.7%	10.1%
Raleigh city	16,199	95.8%	60,811	16.1%	50.4%	2.9%	14.4%	72,032	13.7%	17.6%	5.7%	38.0%	15.5%
Wilmington city	4,024	90.8%	18,340	29.6%	40.0%	8.0%	17.3%	15,528	14.5%	22.7%	20.8%	27.2%	7.4%
Winston-Salem city	9,000	99.5%	27,896	32.8%	39.1%	2.0%	10.5%	32,107	15.9%	23.9%	6.9%	27.5%	15.6%
North Dakota													
Fargo city	3,266	99.3%	23,310	19.5%	55.5%	1.8%	9.7%	18,285	18.2%	30.5%	7.2%	31.7%	9.7%
Ohio													
Akron city	6,706	98.5%	21,704	31.6%	48.5%	5.5%	3.5%	25,847	27.2%	21.0%	9.8%	19.6%	10.1%
Cincinnati city	11,568	97.8%	39,313	31.8%	42.9%	1.4%	12.5%	51,501	23.7%	21.9%	7.9%	28.0%	14.5%
Cleveland city	16,100	96.4%	42,414	32.4%	34.6%	1.7%	11.2%	52,322	23.7%	27.5%	7.4%	17.5%	7.5%
Columbus city	30,465	97.8%	102,832	24.9%	48.3%	2.3%	13.5%	148,625	19.8%	20.6%	6.5%	32.2%	12.4%
Dayton city	5,329	100.0%	18,882	29.8%	48.3%	2.0%	2.2%	21,241	28.6%	27.7%	5.9%	11.7%	9.9%
Toledo city	9,679	94.7%	31,522	30.2%	43.8%	1.2%	8.8%	39,064	27.9%	32.0%	11.7%	13.4%	5.1%

Table E-3: Places—Educational Attainment—Continued

	15 to 17		18 to 24					25 to 33					
				Percent						Percent			
	Total Population	Percent Enrolled in School	Total Population	High School	Some College	Associates Degree	Bachelors Degree	Total Population	High School	Some College	Associates Degree	Bachelors Degree	Advanced Degree
Oklahoma													
Broken Arrow city	4,714	93.8%	8,531	43.8%	25.8%	8.3%	7.4%	12,389	27.9%	22.8%	4.9%	29.8%	7.5%
Edmond city	3,774	100.0%	10,918	18.0%	52.4%	0.0%	20.5%	12,496	23.0%	17.8%	1.5%	33.7%	14.9%
Lawton city	3,148	99.8%	11,092	35.0%	34.8%	10.7%	4.3%	16,128	23.7%	39.1%	8.0%	14.5%	0.9%
Norman city	5,369	100.0%	20,878	22.1%	49.9%	3.0%	10.7%	20,146	26.5%	28.4%	10.0%	19.7%	8.0%
Oklahoma City city	21,088	97.2%	58,633	23.0%	46.5%	2.3%	9.3%	91,854	27.4%	24.8%	6.5%	18.2%	8.6%
Tulsa city	16,858	96.4%	39,469	34.2%	35.7%	4.8%	6.3%	56,285	24.5%	21.5%	9.2%	26.4%	8.7%
Oregon													
Beaverton city	3,900	100.0%	8,713	28.2%	26.6%	14.8%	9.1%	15,605	13.1%	28.5%	7.6%	33.7%	12.2%
Eugene city	6,130	91.4%	28,228	25.0%	52.6%	2.5%	13.0%	23,017	18.5%	29.6%	6.1%	24.9%	12.3%
Gresham city	4,869	97.8%	8,610	28.9%	25.8%	18.7%	6.2%	14,493	25.0%	25.8%	14.5%	16.2%	1.3%
Hillsboro city	4,363	95.5%	7,420	24.4%	29.8%	1.1%	14.7%	15,643	11.5%	19.4%	10.9%	22.0%	23.0%
Portland city	16,496	97.9%	53,244	24.0%	46.9%	4.0%	14.9%	110,931	14.7%	22.6%	6.8%	38.9%	12.5%
Salem city	6,919	98.9%	20,256	23.8%	51.7%	2.8%	6.3%	18,923	31.2%	26.6%	5.3%	19.2%	6.6%
Pennsylvania													
Allentown city	5,383	97.2%	12,462	41.2%	37.5%	2.7%	2.2%	17,006	18.9%	29.3%	13.7%	8.1%	6.6%
Erie city	4,110	100.0%	11,232	23.9%	43.2%	2.4%	13.3%	13,416	36.1%	21.5%	9.7%	13.4%	8.0%
Philadelphia city	53,368	95.1%	165,390	30.1%	40.7%	3.8%	13.0%	267,013	22.4%	19.4%	4.8%	27.6%	15.4%
Pittsburgh city	6,884	98.4%	54,164	21.2%	51.1%	1.9%	14.9%	56,978	18.0%	15.5%	5.6%	30.9%	25.5%
Rhode Island													
Providence city	6,580	91.9%	30,753	27.1%	47.4%	3.9%	11.0%	28,981	18.6%	23.2%	2.1%	28.4%	14.8%
South Carolina													
Charleston city	4,583	100.0%	17,312	16.5%	58.0%	5.9%	13.1%	24,013	16.5%	16.3%	4.3%	46.3%	12.7%
Columbia city	4,730	95.8%	31,398	29.7%	47.3%	2.8%	11.9%	23,959	20.8%	21.5%	5.8%	26.2%	19.1%
North Charleston city	4,033	99.8%	15,502	42.3%	34.9%	5.3%	3.4%	16,951	20.1%	27.6%	12.3%	20.6%	5.6%
South Dakota													
Sioux Falls city	5,773	87.6%	15,217	22.7%	35.2%	4.0%	21.5%	27,656	21.4%	20.7%	12.4%	30.1%	3.9%
Tennessee													
Chattanooga city	5,427	93.7%	20,231	22.8%	52.9%	3.8%	9.0%	25,035	24.0%	23.2%	6.3%	23.2%	12.4%
Clarksville city	5,737	94.7%	18,369	40.5%	40.4%	8.3%	7.4%	29,491	21.5%	32.1%	10.5%	24.7%	8.2%
Knoxville city	4,887	99.1%	35,254	26.3%	48.6%	4.8%	12.5%	25,085	17.6%	23.5%	8.4%	27.0%	12.6%
Memphis city	25,478	97.7%	69,993	34.0%	42.9%	4.4%	5.7%	92,279	27.5%	27.3%	5.4%	20.2%	8.1%
Murfreesboro city	4,888	92.3%	23,078	27.8%	49.7%	3.0%	10.1%	17,931	22.8%	27.5%	5.6%	28.0%	10.4%
Nashville-Davidson metropolitan govt (balance)	20,461	98.7%	69,435	30.4%	38.4%	1.8%	17.7%	114,997	18.8%	18.5%	6.8%	33.1%	16.7%
Texas													
Abilene city	5,597	99.0%	21,140	39.8%	45.2%	0.8%	4.0%	16,864	28.5%	34.9%	8.6%	17.7%	5.4%
Allen city	5,367	87.0%	6,626	30.6%	32.3%	10.0%	13.4%	10,327	25.0%	14.7%	11.9%	19.7%	15.0%
Amarillo city	8,179	99.4%	18,732	27.0%	44.8%	7.8%	4.0%	26,111	23.2%	32.2%	8.4%	16.1%	6.5%
Arlington city	18,096	97.2%	43,654	33.0%	44.0%	6.0%	6.4%	55,832	18.3%	25.7%	7.2%	23.0%	9.3%
Austin city	28,970	95.9%	104,338	22.8%	49.7%	3.6%	12.8%	185,237	17.0%	18.1%	5.0%	37.0%	13.3%
Beaumont city	5,380	95.7%	13,486	27.2%	50.2%	0.9%	9.6%	15,950	24.5%	34.4%	4.8%	18.0%	6.3%
Brownsville city	11,231	96.4%	21,099	50.2%	24.4%	4.1%	2.9%	20,990	23.4%	32.3%	6.3%	14.1%	4.6%
Carrollton city	4,881	99.0%	11,583	17.0%	51.0%	7.3%	13.5%	17,833	13.6%	17.7%	6.2%	39.0%	13.7%
College Station city	3,634	95.5%	37,239	14.7%	69.0%	1.7%	9.2%	18,592	16.8%	15.4%	6.2%	31.8%	18.8%
Corpus Christi city	13,601	95.0%	34,598	41.3%	33.5%	2.7%	3.9%	43,340	30.8%	27.8%	8.8%	18.0%	3.4%
Dallas city	48,617	94.6%	129,994	30.3%	34.6%	2.9%	10.9%	205,380	20.9%	18.0%	3.6%	27.8%	11.0%
Denton city	4,468	98.2%	27,287	17.4%	64.2%	7.0%	5.1%	21,384	18.9%	28.4%	12.7%	24.3%	8.3%
El Paso city	28,494	95.5%	76,155	28.8%	45.7%	5.5%	5.0%	86,901	25.9%	29.6%	8.6%	21.7%	5.0%
Fort Worth city	33,297	93.4%	79,020	37.6%	35.8%	5.2%	8.0%	121,870	26.3%	24.5%	6.4%	19.7%	7.3%
Frisco city	7,287	96.0%	7,961	21.6%	43.3%	7.0%	7.6%	14,063	13.7%	20.4%	13.7%	39.0%	8.8%
Garland city	10,634	100.0%	21,680	28.5%	37.8%	5.8%	4.6%	30,466	25.9%	31.2%	8.5%	16.7%	4.8%
Grand Prairie city	10,716	94.1%	20,178	37.4%	33.0%	2.8%	5.2%	22,919	25.4%	24.9%	6.9%	19.3%	5.8%
Houston city	93,941	96.0%	240,690	33.0%	35.4%	2.8%	10.1%	360,129	23.1%	19.9%	5.5%	23.2%	12.1%
Irving city	9,469	93.2%	25,563	30.0%	36.2%	5.0%	8.7%	36,665	18.5%	17.2%	3.7%	26.0%	16.3%
Killeen city	6,374	100.0%	15,698	28.2%	46.5%	4.0%	3.0%	25,678	24.1%	43.1%	6.6%	17.3%	2.2%
Laredo city	14,630	95.7%	29,370	43.5%	27.3%	4.7%	4.9%	29,722	34.8%	22.1%	5.2%	15.4%	4.0%
Lewisville city	4,534	100.0%	8,657	49.2%	25.5%	4.4%	9.4%	19,980	21.6%	20.4%	8.1%	37.2%	6.4%
Lubbock city	9,455	97.3%	46,318	18.8%	58.3%	3.1%	8.8%	34,892	20.5%	32.4%	7.5%	21.0%	9.7%
McAllen city	6,846	98.5%	16,256	29.7%	41.0%	3.5%	7.6%	16,372	21.6%	23.3%	11.9%	22.4%	4.4%
McKinney city	9,271	98.3%	12,154	43.0%	35.2%	1.8%	8.5%	17,200	23.4%	14.6%	13.1%	28.7%	10.0%
Mesquite city	5,771	100.0%	13,465	45.2%	41.3%	2.7%	1.0%	19,751	30.2%	28.3%	5.1%	10.9%	4.0%
Midland city	6,210	98.5%	13,875	42.8%	24.9%	4.6%	5.5%	20,114	37.8%	18.8%	8.4%	19.2%	3.6%
Odessa city	5,341	92.2%	13,032	40.2%	38.6%	3.4%	4.1%	18,578	33.6%	30.7%	7.6%	13.5%	1.1%
Pasadena city	6,315	100.0%	12,998	41.2%	26.3%	10.3%	1.1%	22,286	34.4%	21.2%	8.3%	9.5%	2.4%
Pearland city	4,899	100.0%	8,269	25.9%	52.8%	5.8%	2.2%	15,825	24.7%	24.0%	7.2%	36.8%	6.6%
Plano city	11,238	98.5%	22,643	27.8%	47.7%	1.9%	13.1%	36,726	11.3%	19.2%	6.0%	37.4%	20.3%
Richardson city	2,899	100.0%	11,884	31.6%	45.8%	1.3%	7.2%	17,044	10.5%	14.6%	7.7%	40.4%	15.3%
Round Rock City	6,601	98.8%	11,091	23.3%	53.4%	4.0%	12.7%	13,486	20.2%	26.0%	17.0%	18.1%	9.0%
San Angelo city	4,068	97.8%	13,635	31.4%	42.7%	3.4%	16.9%	14,415	32.1%	22.7%	6.5%	23.0%	3.7%
San Antonio city	61,440	96.6%	156,359	33.6%	42.3%	3.2%	5.0%	217,816	27.0%	28.8%	8.2%	18.7%	5.2%
Tyler city	3,782	97.8%	13,986	23.2%	49.2%	4.4%	13.5%	13,900	20.3%	26.9%	6.5%	21.5%	7.9%
Waco city	3,985	100.0%	24,361	27.1%	44.3%	3.3%	14.7%	17,077	24.6%	25.3%	12.1%	19.1%	8.3%
Wichita Falls city	4,169	86.6%	14,773	52.3%	30.5%	4.4%	3.9%	14,603	37.1%	16.8%	9.6%	17.2%	8.2%

Table E-3: Places—Educational Attainment—*Continued*

| | 15 to 17 | | 18 to 24 | | | | | 25 to 33 | | | | | |
| | Total Population | Percent Enrolled in School | Total Population | Percent | | | | Total Population | Percent | | | | |
				High School	Some College	Associates Degree	Bachelors Degree		High School	Some College	Associates Degree	Bachelors Degree	Advanced Degree
Utah													
Orem city	5,042	98.1%	15,666	30.0%	39.2%	14.9%	4.4%	14,174	17.5%	34.1%	13.0%	24.9%	6.6%
Provo city	3,590	95.7%	40,901	13.7%	60.3%	11.2%	10.2%	18,730	8.9%	26.7%	8.7%	43.7%	9.5%
Salt Lake City city	6,540	92.7%	26,245	19.8%	47.2%	9.6%	13.6%	38,151	18.0%	21.6%	9.3%	29.5%	15.7%
Sandy city	4,736	98.6%	7,641	39.9%	34.3%	2.8%	11.5%	10,924	20.6%	24.1%	9.6%	32.6%	7.1%
West Jordan city	8,374	96.7%	8,837	41.0%	34.1%	3.4%	3.6%	15,277	25.8%	31.3%	8.2%	23.7%	4.8%
West Valley City city	6,673	95.4%	15,698	35.2%	35.1%	7.6%	0.0%	19,357	36.8%	26.8%	7.4%	7.7%	5.0%
Virginia													
Alexandria city	2,989	100.0%	7,083	32.6%	31.6%	1.3%	23.8%	33,380	14.0%	14.6%	4.3%	30.1%	28.6%
Chesapeake city	9,636	96.1%	21,785	37.2%	33.4%	3.3%	10.0%	31,728	24.9%	28.1%	8.2%	24.2%	5.6%
Hampton city	4,331	92.3%	16,083	18.7%	55.5%	8.3%	9.7%	19,819	19.6%	31.8%	14.5%	22.3%	6.4%
Newport News city	6,474	97.7%	23,978	30.4%	51.1%	3.8%	6.1%	28,073	25.5%	36.4%	10.0%	15.6%	4.7%
Norfolk city	6,550	100.0%	46,891	31.0%	53.1%	4.6%	4.5%	42,408	31.3%	25.7%	10.1%	17.0%	7.9%
Portsmouth city	3,820	95.2%	10,240	39.6%	39.1%	0.0%	10.6%	15,009	20.9%	22.4%	8.5%	21.0%	10.6%
Richmond city	5,033	78.4%	29,893	23.8%	49.6%	4.7%	13.0%	41,924	22.1%	19.5%	4.8%	32.0%	12.8%
Roanoke city	2,205	100.0%	10,176	27.3%	35.3%	5.6%	9.8%	13,759	31.3%	29.0%	6.9%	19.5%	4.1%
Virginia Beach city	17,334	98.3%	46,490	31.9%	47.3%	6.4%	8.1%	69,123	23.1%	28.8%	13.1%	21.2%	8.4%
Washington													
Bellevue city	5,358	100.0%	10,338	24.7%	31.3%	6.8%	21.9%	22,217	8.6%	13.5%	1.7%	44.1%	28.7%
Everett city	4,917	92.7%	10,760	46.5%	28.0%	13.6%	3.0%	14,826	19.9%	25.2%	6.3%	27.8%	7.3%
Federal Way city	4,438	88.6%	6,788	36.5%	35.5%	6.7%	7.0%	15,447	27.4%	27.7%	10.3%	17.4%	2.8%
Kent city	6,346	98.7%	12,389	32.1%	30.0%	9.4%	3.4%	21,384	29.9%	21.8%	11.6%	13.3%	4.3%
Renton city	4,197	100.0%	5,919	35.7%	26.8%	8.4%	13.2%	14,615	18.7%	10.4%	17.4%	39.0%	4.4%
Seattle city	13,730	99.5%	75,581	14.4%	43.5%	5.3%	30.9%	147,020	9.4%	14.5%	4.4%	44.7%	24.5%
Spokane city	7,010	95.0%	21,782	29.6%	47.2%	5.7%	7.6%	33,095	31.0%	26.4%	9.7%	19.7%	7.5%
Spokane Valley city	3,944	100.0%	7,006	27.4%	38.7%	6.8%	12.6%	13,846	33.2%	30.0%	8.1%	13.2%	10.2%
Tacoma city	8,090	96.3%	19,387	30.9%	46.5%	8.8%	2.0%	31,332	22.6%	26.0%	13.1%	21.9%	4.8%
Vancouver city	7,309	100.0%	15,490	38.2%	24.0%	11.7%	5.9%	22,130	22.3%	27.0%	7.6%	20.0%	11.1%
Yakima city	3,524	100.0%	11,512	33.3%	33.6%	7.5%	2.5%	10,350	33.7%	23.2%	7.2%	9.7%	8.5%
Wisconsin													
Green Bay city	2,817	100.0%	13,082	28.2%	44.3%	5.0%	7.0%	14,708	21.3%	33.4%	18.1%	19.2%	2.9%
Kenosha city	3,809	95.1%	10,817	41.2%	33.5%	3.6%	7.0%	10,402	24.3%	35.1%	8.9%	17.2%	9.2%
Madison city	9,540	99.7%	51,806	22.0%	40.0%	1.4%	31.3%	39,715	8.6%	20.2%	7.7%	38.1%	23.8%
Milwaukee city	27,315	99.6%	69,180	27.3%	45.7%	1.6%	6.8%	89,811	21.5%	25.0%	7.9%	25.7%	9.6%

Table E-4: Metropolitan/Micropolitan Statistical Areas—Educational Attainment

	15 to 17		18 to 24					25 to 33					
				Percent					Percent				
	Total Population	Percent Enrolled in School	Total Population	High School	Some College	Associates Degree	Bachelors Degree	Total Population	High School	Some College	Associates Degree	Bachelors Degree	Advanced Degree
Abilene, TX	6,929	98.2%	23,544	40.3%	43.7%	1.3%	5.1%	19,761	29.2%	34.2%	8.0%	17.1%	5.4%
Adrian, MI	3,649	95.0%	10,309	41.6%	35.4%	8.1%	3.9%	8,941	26.5%	25.5%	12.2%	17.6%	7.1%
Akron, OH	26,085	98.8%	74,806	27.8%	41.7%	6.1%	11.7%	77,664	25.3%	20.8%	9.2%	24.7%	11.7%
Albany, GA	6,505	95.4%	16,195	31.5%	26.9%	10.4%	1.1%	16,784	31.2%	23.7%	13.9%	13.5%	3.2%
Albany, OR	4,217	97.3%	12,827	22.4%	58.3%	4.0%	5.6%	11,441	22.7%	22.2%	10.8%	17.0%	14.2%
Albany-Schenectady-Troy, NY	32,357	95.8%	98,107	25.7%	39.5%	8.7%	15.2%	102,488	21.5%	19.7%	12.9%	26.2%	14.9%
Albertville, AL	3,863	100.0%	8,881	27.2%	42.9%	6.2%	7.3%	9,155	26.2%	25.2%	7.1%	14.0%	4.3%
Albuquerque, NM	35,349	95.7%	84,613	26.2%	44.2%	5.2%	6.1%	113,245	21.7%	28.9%	10.0%	16.4%	8.2%
Alexandria, LA	6,747	99.7%	14,235	33.9%	38.7%	4.0%	7.2%	17,893	29.3%	27.0%	11.5%	9.5%	2.5%
Allentown-Bethlehem-Easton, PA-NJ	33,424	97.7%	76,390	33.8%	41.0%	6.2%	9.7%	84,989	22.8%	21.1%	13.3%	24.6%	9.5%
Altoona, PA	5,226	96.8%	10,242	35.3%	37.2%	6.3%	15.1%	13,712	43.0%	18.2%	7.9%	23.1%	1.6%
Amarillo, TX	10,506	99.5%	25,578	29.7%	43.8%	6.2%	5.4%	35,841	22.6%	34.0%	9.8%	14.7%	5.1%
Ames, IA	2,650	100.0%	30,643	16.9%	65.6%	5.8%	9.0%	12,175	17.6%	19.6%	9.7%	27.1%	24.0%
Anchorage, AK	16,511	91.8%	45,782	34.2%	36.2%	3.6%	7.6%	60,722	28.6%	31.3%	7.8%	21.3%	5.5%
Ann Arbor, MI	11,948	99.4%	65,988	19.3%	49.0%	3.6%	23.1%	45,342	10.3%	19.0%	6.3%	38.3%	23.3%
Anniston-Oxford-Jacksonville, AL	4,735	95.4%	12,942	27.6%	46.8%	3.5%	5.0%	12,913	33.7%	27.1%	7.8%	13.3%	7.5%
Appleton, WI	10,185	100.0%	19,110	30.5%	42.1%	6.5%	10.2%	29,121	23.3%	23.8%	16.6%	20.8%	8.2%
Asheville, NC	14,327	93.8%	33,465	29.9%	45.5%	6.9%	5.2%	44,992	23.3%	24.0%	8.0%	22.7%	9.5%
Ashtabula, OH	4,992	93.3%	7,835	49.2%	16.6%	3.9%	3.4%	9,787	49.1%	18.0%	11.3%	9.8%	3.7%
Athens-Clarke County, GA	6,948	98.3%	40,739	22.2%	51.8%	6.0%	11.4%	24,866	25.0%	20.3%	5.8%	26.3%	13.3%
Atlanta-Sandy Springs-Roswell, GA	248,760	96.2%	524,244	31.0%	37.8%	4.0%	10.5%	691,741	21.4%	21.9%	7.3%	27.0%	11.2%
Atlantic City-Hammonton, NJ	9,931	97.4%	27,015	36.3%	40.4%	2.0%	8.8%	29,552	32.7%	25.6%	6.8%	16.9%	8.1%
Auburn-Opelika, AL	5,316	92.3%	30,660	20.4%	60.5%	5.0%	6.6%	18,813	21.1%	35.7%	2.6%	22.9%	12.3%
Augusta-Richmond County, GA-SC	24,023	96.4%	57,885	35.7%	34.9%	4.1%	5.9%	77,257	25.9%	27.0%	9.5%	17.9%	6.1%
Augusta-Waterville, ME	4,104	100.0%	10,420	39.4%	36.2%	1.2%	6.9%	11,402	32.8%	22.7%	9.9%	24.2%	5.3%
Austin-Round Rock, TX	77,358	96.3%	201,829	26.1%	47.6%	3.6%	11.2%	307,346	19.5%	20.9%	6.7%	33.0%	10.9%
Bakersfield, CA	39,801	98.5%	96,404	41.2%	34.7%	2.7%	3.9%	119,068	32.7%	26.1%	5.8%	10.8%	4.2%
Baltimore-Columbia-Towson, MD	101,865	97.8%	251,659	30.1%	40.7%	5.1%	13.4%	360,376	22.3%	20.6%	7.7%	26.3%	15.7%
Bangor, ME	5,200	97.9%	17,405	16.3%	56.2%	3.7%	8.0%	18,251	24.4%	23.1%	14.3%	19.0%	9.1%
Barnstable Town, MA	6,996	98.4%	14,201	29.2%	46.5%	7.6%	4.6%	15,825	23.3%	29.1%	13.0%	26.0%	5.3%
Baton Rouge, LA	33,148	95.8%	98,596	25.1%	47.8%	3.0%	11.0%	107,608	25.4%	23.9%	6.7%	25.0%	8.6%
Battle Creek, MI	5,674	97.0%	10,750	37.8%	32.8%	5.1%	6.0%	15,498	41.5%	20.2%	10.9%	16.5%	3.3%
Bay City, MI	4,086	97.7%	8,750	38.1%	34.5%	5.5%	3.5%	11,393	21.6%	37.3%	9.2%	24.1%	3.2%
Beaumont-Port Arthur, TX	17,406	95.4%	37,714	31.4%	43.1%	3.7%	6.2%	52,493	30.4%	28.6%	8.1%	14.8%	5.5%
Beckley, WV	3,897	100.0%	9,532	45.2%	41.8%	1.8%	2.4%	12,971	36.9%	33.7%	6.0%	5.8%	7.5%
Bellingham, WA	7,277	100.0%	30,613	27.7%	37.6%	17.5%	6.9%	26,325	19.0%	31.3%	16.2%	22.0%	6.0%
Bend-Redmond, OR	5,366	100.0%	12,522	23.4%	38.9%	6.0%	11.1%	19,618	16.7%	26.9%	10.3%	30.9%	9.7%
Billings, MT	4,423	93.4%	16,307	42.5%	35.6%	2.0%	5.9%	19,898	29.8%	21.2%	11.3%	21.8%	10.5%
Binghamton, NY	9,502	99.3%	32,990	29.8%	37.9%	7.9%	13.5%	24,016	23.2%	20.5%	12.7%	22.5%	15.4%
Birmingham-Hoover, AL	47,453	96.3%	99,509	30.9%	44.2%	4.4%	6.8%	138,701	25.0%	25.1%	7.6%	22.9%	10.3%
Bismarck, ND	4,432	98.6%	10,971	23.3%	36.3%	8.8%	16.1%	18,784	17.5%	13.3%	18.9%	35.6%	11.3%
Blacksburg-Christiansburg-Radford, VA	4,812	99.0%	40,796	16.5%	61.4%	7.9%	12.0%	20,223	18.3%	14.9%	6.5%	36.7%	19.7%
Bloomington, IL	7,181	88.7%	32,433	21.8%	57.9%	7.2%	6.3%	22,102	19.0%	25.7%	9.5%	34.7%	7.2%
Bloomington, IN	4,840	95.8%	41,299	16.4%	64.7%	2.0%	13.8%	20,887	17.3%	26.7%	4.4%	29.6%	14.9%
Bloomsburg-Berwick, PA	2,251	78.3%	10,392	32.6%	41.1%	1.6%	16.0%	10,893	23.2%	15.6%	17.5%	20.5%	10.2%
Boise City, ID	30,255	96.4%	58,208	35.0%	41.7%	4.6%	4.3%	85,278	27.6%	27.3%	10.6%	19.9%	5.7%
Boston-Cambridge-Newton, MA-NH	172,606	97.7%	476,078	27.2%	39.4%	3.2%	20.1%	621,558	17.0%	15.1%	5.8%	36.2%	21.2%
Boulder, CO	11,543	97.3%	49,567	18.1%	56.2%	3.8%	17.4%	37,556	14.6%	16.8%	5.6%	38.9%	22.1%
Bowling Green, KY	6,726	100.0%	22,855	28.2%	49.4%	2.2%	12.0%	18,892	17.9%	30.3%	10.4%	24.8%	8.7%
Bremerton-Silverdale, WA	9,762	95.2%	27,430	49.4%	27.5%	4.2%	6.4%	32,727	26.2%	35.4%	10.0%	17.5%	5.4%
Bridgeport-Stamford-Norwalk, CT	40,383	95.3%	85,139	25.3%	37.6%	4.5%	19.0%	97,867	20.7%	18.0%	6.8%	29.9%	16.2%
Brownsville-Harlingen, TX	23,240	96.5%	44,883	45.7%	29.9%	4.7%	2.3%	45,622	27.2%	26.2%	7.5%	13.6%	4.1%
Brunswick, GA	4,512	100.0%	9,393	36.9%	34.2%	0.3%	5.5%	12,722	30.6%	34.1%	8.1%	11.4%	2.6%
Buffalo-Cheektowaga-Niagara Falls, NY	41,259	98.8%	108,353	28.7%	38.9%	7.9%	14.5%	137,249	23.4%	19.2%	11.2%	23.8%	13.8%
Burlington, NC	6,420	99.1%	14,754	34.2%	38.7%	2.9%	5.1%	16,654	26.1%	21.9%	8.9%	17.0%	4.9%
Burlington-South Burlington, VT	7,394	98.8%	30,542	27.3%	51.5%	0.4%	16.0%	26,095	18.8%	12.8%	6.6%	45.1%	12.7%
California-Lexington Park, MD	4,721	98.1%	11,172	36.0%	35.8%	3.4%	14.3%	13,081	23.2%	31.7%	7.1%	21.6%	10.2%
Canton-Massillon, OH	16,276	95.6%	34,570	33.7%	42.3%	2.3%	8.3%	42,794	27.4%	30.4%	11.9%	14.6%	8.0%
Cape Coral-Fort Myers, FL	22,116	94.2%	50,309	28.1%	30.2%	11.9%	5.3%	69,819	33.0%	21.5%	9.2%	14.4%	5.6%
Cape Girardeau, MO-IL	3,293	96.8%	10,731	21.3%	59.9%	4.7%	1.8%	11,904	23.4%	24.6%	16.5%	14.0%	4.9%
Carbondale-Marion, IL	5,731	97.6%	18,633	37.0%	37.3%	6.6%	8.5%	14,854	23.7%	31.3%	4.7%	18.9%	11.9%
Carson City, NV	2,019	100.0%	5,225	31.1%	49.8%	0.0%	0.0%	4,314	28.5%	32.8%	7.6%	1.0%	0.0%
Casper, WY	2,779	81.5%	7,113	36.8%	22.0%	10.4%	4.4%	10,786	26.6%	19.8%	22.5%	11.2%	6.1%
Cedar Rapids, IA	10,560	98.6%	24,636	27.9%	44.4%	7.7%	9.5%	30,774	16.5%	28.0%	12.5%	29.8%	9.5%
Chambersburg-Waynesboro, PA	5,730	96.9%	13,646	48.4%	21.5%	1.5%	2.9%	15,478	44.5%	18.4%	7.5%	18.2%	3.4%
Champaign-Urbana, IL	7,284	93.5%	52,890	18.2%	61.9%	4.5%	8.4%	28,892	14.1%	20.3%	6.0%	31.7%	24.5%
Charleston, WV	7,510	99.5%	15,789	44.7%	31.5%	3.9%	9.6%	23,511	33.5%	16.9%	11.8%	15.6%	11.0%
Charleston-North Charleston, SC	26,310	98.4%	69,521	30.4%	44.8%	3.7%	10.0%	108,893	21.4%	22.6%	6.9%	30.3%	10.0%
Charlotte-Concord-Gastonia, NC-SC	101,553	96.5%	213,700	31.1%	36.5%	5.7%	11.2%	288,787	21.8%	21.7%	8.6%	27.7%	9.3%
Charlottesville, VA	7,040	97.0%	29,757	32.1%	42.2%	2.2%	13.9%	30,260	26.4%	24.9%	7.3%	19.4%	18.0%
Chattanooga, TN-GA	20,908	97.1%	51,185	30.5%	47.6%	4.2%	6.6%	65,730	21.3%	27.7%	9.2%	19.3%	9.0%
Cheyenne, WY	3,412	100.0%	14,476	33.0%	34.9%	12.3%	6.9%	9,573	25.3%	26.1%	15.4%	22.6%	7.8%
Chicago-Naperville-Elgin, IL-IN-WI	389,155	97.3%	895,906	29.8%	38.5%	5.0%	14.7%	1,219,063	20.4%	20.3%	7.2%	30.1%	13.6%
Chico, CA	7,589	99.1%	33,684	25.7%	48.0%	9.2%	7.5%	25,312	15.9%	37.7%	10.7%	19.0%	6.7%

Table E-4: Metropolitan/Micropolitan Statistical Areas—Educational Attainment—*Continued*

| | 15 to 17 | | 18 to 24 | | | | | 25 to 33 | | | | | |
| | | | | Percent | | | | | Percent | | | | |
	Total Population	Percent Enrolled in School	Total Population	High School	Some College	Associates Degree	Bachelors Degree	Total Population	High School	Some College	Associates Degree	Bachelors Degree	Advanced Degree
Cincinnati, OH-KY-IN	89,722	97.4%	198,140	35.9%	37.6%	3.2%	11.5%	254,917	25.8%	22.3%	10.8%	24.4%	9.1%
Clarksburg, WV	3,332	99.2%	7,633	37.3%	31.8%	5.3%	13.1%	8,720	28.7%	32.5%	4.9%	23.4%	7.7%
Clarksville, TN-KY	10,047	96.0%	32,686	48.2%	33.4%	4.8%	6.1%	48,376	26.3%	32.7%	10.8%	19.2%	5.8%
Cleveland, TN	5,473	99.1%	12,021	28.1%	49.7%	3.6%	7.6%	13,353	36.8%	20.7%	6.0%	19.9%	2.4%
Cleveland-Elyria, OH	80,973	96.1%	178,155	32.8%	37.2%	3.5%	12.6%	225,453	23.2%	23.6%	8.0%	23.8%	12.4%
Coeur d'Alene, ID	5,612	97.3%	11,742	39.0%	34.2%	3.8%	7.8%	17,751	23.8%	30.7%	10.7%	11.9%	9.6%
College Station-Bryan, TX	7,537	97.8%	59,179	16.1%	65.6%	2.2%	9.6%	33,688	19.1%	19.3%	5.7%	31.0%	14.1%
Colorado Springs, CO	27,550	96.1%	75,550	29.7%	47.6%	3.2%	8.5%	98,970	23.5%	28.9%	12.8%	22.5%	6.1%
Columbia, MO	5,971	100.0%	35,010	19.7%	53.8%	3.2%	15.3%	24,966	13.9%	20.3%	8.3%	36.9%	19.2%
Columbia, SC	32,495	97.9%	99,606	31.4%	45.7%	2.4%	10.1%	96,626	22.2%	26.4%	6.0%	24.5%	13.2%
Columbus, GA-AL	12,697	97.3%	36,082	37.4%	36.4%	4.6%	7.0%	44,311	28.8%	29.2%	6.7%	16.9%	8.8%
Columbus, IN	3,580	93.3%	7,290	27.2%	37.2%	1.2%	16.3%	9,971	22.7%	24.2%	8.9%	22.7%	16.9%
Columbus, OH	80,315	98.6%	185,106	29.8%	41.2%	3.5%	12.3%	280,282	21.6%	22.7%	8.1%	30.2%	10.5%
Concord, NH	4,264	98.2%	10,518	22.7%	57.2%	4.1%	6.7%	11,368	15.6%	30.3%	12.5%	30.2%	9.7%
Cookeville, TN	4,586	93.9%	14,332	40.3%	37.2%	5.1%	9.2%	11,763	36.9%	18.2%	3.2%	24.7%	8.3%
Corpus Christi, TX	18,927	96.4%	44,738	41.2%	33.1%	3.4%	4.3%	55,956	30.0%	27.3%	8.8%	16.0%	2.8%
Corvallis, OR	4,969	97.7%	15,283	23.1%	54.4%	6.1%	7.2%	12,337	23.2%	23.7%	10.0%	17.7%	13.2%
Crestview-Fort Walton Beach-Destin, FL	7,454	97.9%	23,985	33.7%	31.2%	8.4%	5.0%	37,896	24.5%	35.2%	10.5%	18.2%	4.1%
Cumberland, MD-WV	3,828	97.5%	11,906	31.9%	48.3%	4.9%	6.6%	10,515	36.8%	26.5%	7.6%	13.3%	4.4%
Dallas-Fort Worth-Arlington, TX	308,719	96.0%	651,831	33.0%	38.2%	4.6%	9.2%	913,935	23.1%	23.3%	6.9%	24.4%	9.3%
Dalton, GA	5,983	88.4%	13,690	37.5%	29.3%	2.9%	2.2%	17,664	26.4%	21.9%	6.3%	16.5%	3.5%
Danville, IL	3,371	92.2%	5,300	46.2%	23.7%	6.1%	3.7%	9,809	37.9%	19.6%	19.1%	10.7%	2.2%
Danville, VA	4,169	100.0%	7,826	37.8%	40.6%	7.4%	3.4%	10,281	33.7%	27.8%	4.8%	13.2%	6.5%
Daphne-Fairhope-Foley, AL	7,453	100.0%	14,381	35.6%	27.1%	5.1%	14.1%	20,047	29.4%	28.8%	7.8%	21.7%	3.3%
Davenport-Moline-Rock Island, IA-IL	13,302	98.0%	34,932	31.1%	42.9%	6.3%	8.4%	42,931	24.8%	26.2%	11.8%	23.0%	6.7%
Dayton, OH	30,117	97.5%	74,740	33.1%	41.1%	3.0%	9.9%	93,470	23.0%	26.4%	7.4%	23.6%	11.0%
Decatur, AL	6,237	94.3%	12,140	54.3%	18.8%	4.1%	6.0%	17,056	25.4%	29.4%	10.9%	15.0%	3.5%
Decatur, IL	3,953	99.5%	10,188	39.8%	34.3%	5.1%	7.3%	10,459	31.2%	31.2%	11.9%	16.2%	3.1%
Deltona-Daytona Beach-Ormond Beach, FL	20,948	98.6%	51,286	27.7%	40.1%	10.0%	6.0%	60,527	34.4%	24.9%	12.0%	19.8%	4.7%
Denver-Aurora-Lakewood, CO	108,723	96.0%	234,203	33.3%	34.9%	5.3%	12.0%	402,449	19.0%	20.8%	7.6%	32.8%	12.9%
Des Moines-West Des Moines, IA	26,423	97.0%	53,771	24.1%	46.3%	6.2%	12.4%	84,680	20.3%	19.3%	9.3%	32.6%	11.6%
Detroit-Warren-Dearborn, MI	177,606	96.0%	368,804	30.8%	40.3%	5.1%	10.2%	481,372	21.9%	26.6%	9.9%	23.2%	10.1%
Dothan, AL	6,001	96.8%	12,120	29.9%	40.7%	4.5%	7.9%	16,153	30.2%	27.9%	10.7%	10.8%	6.4%
Dover, DE	6,870	99.1%	18,762	25.6%	47.3%	4.0%	4.5%	20,537	31.3%	30.6%	8.4%	13.9%	3.7%
Dubuque, IA	4,498	100.0%	10,770	24.2%	47.7%	13.5%	7.4%	10,320	29.7%	14.9%	8.1%	19.3%	19.2%
Duluth, MN-WI	9,153	99.1%	31,513	23.7%	53.1%	5.7%	8.0%	32,043	22.4%	29.5%	21.5%	16.7%	5.7%
Dunn, NC	5,255	99.5%	13,083	27.9%	49.4%	3.9%	5.9%	16,703	30.4%	30.7%	9.0%	14.4%	4.2%
Durham-Chapel Hill, NC	18,854	96.8%	65,360	25.3%	44.1%	1.5%	18.3%	77,519	15.1%	17.4%	5.3%	31.5%	19.7%
East Stroudsburg, PA	7,360	99.5%	18,241	29.1%	48.4%	0.0%	4.0%	16,475	23.2%	14.5%	7.7%	40.1%	2.0%
Eau Claire, WI	5,827	98.9%	22,132	31.6%	41.8%	10.0%	7.0%	19,765	15.9%	21.7%	16.3%	29.6%	4.1%
El Centro, CA	8,239	96.1%	20,115	31.7%	37.4%	5.6%	3.9%	21,437	20.6%	23.2%	13.2%	16.3%	3.4%
El Paso, TX	6,816	97.8%	13,120	48.2%	31.3%	3.5%	3.4%	17,336	31.3%	27.2%	9.1%	11.5%	6.5%
Elizabethtown-Fort Knox, KY	9,847	91.9%	18,907	40.3%	30.1%	2.3%	5.7%	22,639	35.0%	23.5%	5.9%	14.0%	4.7%
Elkhart-Goshen, IN	2,587	97.1%	7,341	24.7%	33.4%	8.8%	7.5%	11,023	25.7%	30.7%	7.6%	19.9%	6.7%
Elmira, NY	38,189	96.4%	94,502	29.2%	46.9%	5.2%	5.4%	110,937	24.7%	30.8%	8.1%	21.3%	4.7%
Erie, PA	11,465	96.8%	28,432	24.0%	46.8%	3.8%	12.0%	31,135	31.1%	17.1%	14.2%	20.2%	8.3%
Eugene, OR	12,770	94.4%	46,350	27.8%	48.0%	2.8%	12.0%	41,900	19.8%	31.6%	7.7%	23.1%	8.9%
Eureka-Arcata-Fortuna, CA	3,629	100.0%	18,225	20.8%	58.8%	6.3%	6.9%	16,198	17.9%	38.5%	9.2%	18.9%	3.2%
Evansville, IN-KY	11,986	92.0%	28,292	34.7%	38.6%	3.4%	7.2%	37,384	25.4%	26.4%	6.2%	23.2%	10.5%
Fairbanks, AK	4,177	100.0%	15,158	35.6%	49.4%	7.9%	2.9%	15,499	24.9%	29.7%	10.8%	21.8%	5.4%
Fargo, ND-MN	7,350	98.7%	36,712	21.2%	55.6%	1.9%	9.7%	32,049	20.5%	25.1%	10.4%	27.7%	12.1%
Farmington, NM	4,993	97.8%	11,608	25.1%	42.0%	5.9%	7.0%	14,031	27.6%	26.1%	6.3%	13.2%	3.6%
Fayetteville, NC	14,516	97.8%	45,468	38.0%	41.0%	2.2%	4.8%	54,810	24.6%	36.8%	7.8%	17.9%	6.3%
Fayetteville-Springdale-Rogers, AR-MO	20,389	96.3%	56,968	30.6%	41.3%	4.4%	11.1%	67,776	27.7%	25.7%	3.4%	18.9%	11.7%
Flagstaff, AZ	4,964	94.8%	29,687	29.2%	51.6%	4.1%	8.1%	17,120	27.0%	22.5%	16.9%	18.5%	10.5%
Flint, MI	16,466	95.9%	36,729	32.7%	37.9%	3.5%	4.5%	43,078	23.5%	35.7%	10.8%	14.1%	6.3%
Florence, SC	8,423	100.0%	19,018	34.3%	43.4%	3.8%	5.4%	21,857	33.4%	29.7%	10.5%	11.8%	5.0%
Florence-Muscle Shoals, AL	6,982	97.0%	13,870	23.9%	49.3%	4.4%	8.2%	13,856	35.2%	19.3%	9.6%	9.8%	4.6%
Fond du Lac, WI	5,336	99.6%	8,500	31.9%	45.0%	1.0%	6.2%	10,842	29.9%	16.6%	21.6%	14.1%	5.0%
Fort Collins, CO	11,319	96.8%	46,073	22.9%	49.3%	3.8%	16.5%	46,242	17.0%	24.8%	11.4%	32.9%	11.1%
Fort Smith, AR-OK	10,280	98.5%	24,092	34.2%	39.0%	6.1%	1.4%	34,033	31.7%	24.8%	9.0%	17.0%	2.0%
Fort Wayne, IN	18,479	95.2%	42,894	32.1%	39.6%	2.5%	10.5%	49,413	22.4%	27.0%	10.2%	23.4%	6.7%
Fresno, CA	44,793	97.3%	106,206	28.1%	48.8%	5.9%	4.2%	129,871	26.8%	27.6%	8.1%	13.5%	4.6%
Gadsden, AL	3,849	93.8%	9,075	28.9%	31.6%	10.4%	10.3%	9,578	26.2%	26.2%	5.9%	14.9%	7.2%
Gainesville, FL	8,410	97.1%	56,926	18.9%	50.3%	11.1%	14.1%	37,325	21.4%	13.1%	15.8%	26.2%	17.7%
Gainesville, GA	8,761	99.9%	18,304	36.3%	35.8%	2.5%	2.5%	21,584	21.9%	29.2%	10.2%	12.4%	4.5%
Gettysburg, PA	4,180	100.0%	8,558	47.3%	30.2%	3.8%	4.8%	10,662	33.1%	24.6%	10.3%	22.7%	4.7%
Glens Falls, NY	4,808	100.0%	9,770	32.1%	35.7%	4.9%	10.9%	12,268	33.5%	18.9%	7.8%	23.8%	8.2%
Goldsboro, NC	4,258	100.0%	12,124	31.8%	44.6%	2.7%	10.7%	16,422	18.7%	31.1%	7.3%	20.3%	6.0%
Grand Forks, ND-MN	3,660	94.9%	19,039	17.8%	51.0%	5.8%	17.0%	13,706	23.9%	20.3%	17.1%	25.8%	9.1%
Grand Island, NE	3,594	100.0%	7,909	41.1%	35.2%	3.5%	1.9%	9,116	27.5%	28.4%	4.4%	20.2%	7.1%
Grand Junction, CO	5,453	98.3%	15,516	18.8%	54.4%	5.0%	2.4%	17,801	29.6%	24.0%	10.7%	20.1%	2.6%
Grand Rapids-Wyoming, MI	44,884	96.0%	108,123	28.0%	46.2%	3.0%	8.8%	129,931	21.4%	25.0%	9.3%	28.9%	7.9%
Grants Pass, OR	3,979	89.3%	6,319	48.2%	36.3%	2.8%	4.8%	6,561	31.3%	40.1%	15.1%	7.0%	5.6%
Great Falls, MT	2,295	91.1%	8,457	34.4%	39.4%	2.9%	2.2%	9,734	29.0%	24.8%	10.0%	14.5%	5.4%
Greeley, CO	13,960	97.5%	29,769	32.8%	44.6%	5.9%	4.2%	35,416	25.6%	28.4%	9.6%	17.2%	7.2%

Table E-4: Metropolitan/Micropolitan Statistical Areas—Educational Attainment—*Continued*

| | 15 to 17 | | 18 to 24 | | | | | 25 to 33 | | | | | |
	Total Population	Percent Enrolled in School	Total Population	High School	Some College	Associates Degree	Bachelors Degree	Total Population	High School	Some College	Associates Degree	Bachelors Degree	Advanced Degree
Green Bay, WI	12,115	99.9%	27,413	31.7%	38.9%	5.4%	7.0%	38,825	19.5%	27.0%	19.9%	20.2%	2.0%
Greensboro-High Point, NC	30,214	94.3%	71,418	31.0%	43.5%	5.2%	7.4%	85,526	25.4%	25.3%	7.4%	20.3%	7.1%
Greenville, NC	6,240	100.0%	31,790	15.6%	67.3%	2.5%	7.7%	22,438	20.6%	24.9%	14.0%	19.9%	10.4%
Greenville-Anderson-Mauldin, SC	34,925	96.6%	85,925	30.2%	40.2%	4.8%	10.4%	99,564	25.2%	23.2%	8.5%	17.9%	12.1%
Greenwood, SC	3,615	100.0%	10,427	37.2%	38.8%	1.8%	5.0%	8,790	33.0%	26.0%	15.8%	14.0%	5.0%
Gulfport-Biloxi-Pascagoula, MS	16,274	99.3%	36,927	30.8%	40.9%	8.0%	4.5%	46,488	23.1%	32.6%	14.0%	18.1%	4.4%
Hagerstown-Martinsburg, MD-WV	9,406	96.5%	22,794	33.1%	40.4%	3.2%	6.3%	29,667	36.4%	22.7%	8.5%	15.4%	6.1%
Hammond, LA	4,906	91.5%	14,495	34.9%	46.5%	0.0%	1.4%	16,082	34.1%	24.4%	8.6%	14.6%	2.1%
Hanford-Corcoran, CA	6,293	99.1%	16,771	26.1%	38.4%	7.3%	3.9%	23,428	27.5%	26.5%	7.7%	10.1%	4.0%
Harrisburg-Carlisle, PA	21,005	93.6%	54,749	26.9%	45.0%	2.4%	7.7%	60,293	31.4%	14.6%	11.9%	25.7%	11.3%
Harrisonburg, VA	4,355	92.7%	25,737	25.8%	59.9%	2.6%	8.4%	14,315	19.8%	12.5%	14.6%	28.1%	15.3%
Hartford-West Hartford-East Hartford, CT...	44,663	97.5%	115,378	25.3%	46.9%	4.8%	12.6%	127,732	18.8%	18.5%	7.2%	32.2%	18.1%
Hattiesburg, MS	5,118	98.5%	20,046	23.9%	43.8%	10.4%	12.0%	16,974	32.1%	19.4%	12.2%	16.4%	4.3%
Hickory-Lenoir-Morganton, NC	14,991	94.8%	31,801	38.6%	27.8%	6.0%	7.3%	35,052	23.5%	29.4%	13.3%	13.7%	5.1%
Hilo, HI	6,367	94.5%	16,321	36.2%	32.4%	16.6%	5.5%	21,668	32.1%	27.6%	6.1%	19.9%	7.0%
Hilton Head Island-Bluffton-Beaufort, SC...	5,903	98.7%	18,348	52.5%	26.6%	2.1%	4.7%	24,204	31.0%	27.4%	5.1%	23.1%	4.4%
Hinesville, GA	2,966	85.7%	13,060	52.3%	30.9%	3.9%	0.3%	11,083	25.4%	44.0%	8.0%	12.3%	2.7%
Holland, MI	5,166	93.7%	9,792	48.6%	33.7%	6.4%	3.8%	11,964	38.9%	31.0%	6.1%	15.9%	4.5%
Homosassa Springs, FL	3,920	96.6%	7,713	43.5%	17.6%	5.5%	2.7%	8,986	44.4%	9.9%	20.1%	12.4%	0.4%
Hot Springs, AR	3,413	86.5%	8,016	42.2%	40.6%	11.2%	0.7%	9,997	32.6%	35.3%	6.4%	13.2%	3.3%
Houma-Thibodaux, LA	8,204	94.0%	18,255	35.9%	38.0%	5.2%	5.1%	27,684	36.1%	18.9%	9.8%	18.3%	1.6%
Houston-The Woodlands-Sugar Land, TX...	291,005	96.8%	615,008	32.6%	36.6%	4.1%	9.1%	889,477	23.3%	23.3%	6.2%	23.5%	9.4%
Huntington-Ashland, WV-KY-OH	14,789	98.0%	33,330	40.6%	33.0%	4.8%	7.2%	36,570	35.4%	19.3%	12.4%	14.6%	9.2%
Huntsville, AL	18,099	99.3%	40,619	34.4%	36.7%	4.5%	10.4%	57,381	20.7%	21.9%	10.9%	24.0%	12.0%
Idaho Falls, ID	6,345	89.2%	11,332	47.5%	28.9%	7.1%	3.4%	17,251	21.1%	25.8%	11.5%	23.1%	7.0%
Indianapolis-Carmel-Anderson, IN	79,646	96.3%	174,852	33.1%	34.7%	4.1%	13.4%	252,167	22.1%	22.6%	8.2%	27.4%	8.7%
Iowa City, IA	5,895	100.0%	31,586	26.3%	52.9%	3.5%	15.4%	23,161	18.5%	19.4%	11.1%	28.0%	20.0%
Ithaca, NY	2,679	100.0%	30,987	9.3%	69.4%	7.1%	13.7%	11,783	7.4%	6.6%	12.1%	40.7%	31.3%
Jackson, MI	5,934	95.0%	13,908	30.3%	46.4%	3.7%	4.2%	18,624	30.7%	25.2%	14.2%	16.2%	4.4%
Jackson, MS	25,345	94.8%	54,327	24.5%	43.5%	6.2%	11.1%	71,278	23.1%	27.1%	10.8%	22.6%	9.9%
Jackson, TN	4,733	100.0%	13,904	34.4%	50.6%	0.6%	6.2%	15,287	33.5%	23.1%	11.0%	19.5%	4.7%
Jacksonville, FL	57,918	97.9%	130,435	33.7%	34.7%	6.4%	10.0%	185,508	26.3%	25.1%	9.4%	23.6%	8.5%
Jacksonville, NC	5,861	99.0%	36,464	52.1%	34.1%	5.8%	5.0%	32,983	24.4%	33.8%	15.9%	13.8%	2.1%
Jamestown-Dunkirk-Fredonia, NY	5,229	99.0%	13,664	28.4%	44.7%	10.8%	6.5%	12,863	30.4%	20.0%	14.9%	15.9%	7.4%
Janesville-Beloit, WI	6,618	100.0%	14,815	39.1%	37.1%	0.8%	8.5%	15,271	21.6%	25.7%	20.9%	21.1%	4.4%
Jefferson City, MO	6,315	97.4%	14,684	24.4%	51.7%	1.8%	9.0%	17,313	33.7%	17.6%	3.5%	20.9%	9.7%
Johnson City, TN	6,659	98.5%	20,537	34.0%	48.0%	6.2%	5.1%	21,051	35.4%	18.8%	3.9%	22.9%	10.6%
Johnstown, PA	5,489	99.6%	12,403	34.4%	46.0%	5.0%	5.0%	12,887	33.7%	24.8%	12.5%	15.6%	8.7%
Jonesboro, AR	5,913	99.1%	15,635	27.5%	48.2%	4.7%	5.3%	15,345	37.3%	21.8%	7.5%	18.7%	1.2%
Joplin, MO	7,806	100.0%	17,379	38.5%	41.0%	6.3%	5.7%	18,676	33.2%	29.8%	10.8%	17.0%	2.3%
Kahului-Wailuku-Lahaina, HI	5,710	91.0%	12,607	33.2%	42.9%	7.2%	11.8%	20,898	29.4%	30.6%	11.2%	19.4%	4.2%
Kalamazoo-Portage, MI	12,475	99.3%	48,185	21.2%	45.7%	9.4%	11.3%	36,599	13.9%	23.2%	11.6%	36.0%	10.7%
Kalispell, MT	3,906	93.1%	7,110	49.1%	22.2%	1.3%	2.3%	9,686	45.3%	12.4%	16.5%	15.4%	7.5%
Kankakee, IL	4,612	99.4%	11,549	32.5%	44.4%	3.4%	8.5%	12,290	38.2%	18.8%	9.6%	23.4%	3.9%
Kansas City, MO-KS	84,123	96.7%	180,675	29.5%	37.6%	6.7%	12.0%	258,765	20.7%	22.4%	8.9%	27.7%	11.5%
Kennewick-Richland, WA	13,135	97.3%	27,475	30.7%	28.5%	11.2%	3.6%	35,262	26.9%	22.2%	12.4%	15.0%	8.3%
Killeen-Temple, TX	18,742	96.1%	53,911	38.1%	40.0%	3.5%	5.0%	67,153	27.3%	36.7%	7.9%	15.4%	5.3%
Kingsport-Bristol-Bristol, TN-VA	12,611	94.6%	23,375	37.8%	41.7%	5.6%	5.0%	30,784	35.3%	24.3%	10.9%	14.4%	5.6%
Kingston, NY	5,489	100.0%	19,374	32.1%	42.0%	10.3%	9.0%	17,081	25.0%	26.6%	10.4%	21.8%	11.1%
Knoxville, TN	32,103	96.2%	88,102	34.6%	41.0%	3.5%	10.4%	92,534	29.9%	22.2%	7.0%	18.1%	10.6%
Kokomo, IN	3,329	100.0%	6,039	28.1%	22.7%	6.3%	11.2%	8,521	21.2%	29.7%	11.1%	17.1%	3.9%
La Crosse-Onalaska, WI-MN	4,668	97.4%	21,809	26.9%	54.5%	5.4%	8.8%	14,177	20.3%	26.2%	13.0%	25.0%	11.4%
Lafayette, LA	21,756	96.9%	47,710	36.1%	41.9%	3.0%	7.6%	64,879	26.8%	25.8%	8.6%	21.3%	5.3%
Lafayette-West Lafayette, IN	6,539	99.4%	48,319	25.2%	51.1%	0.4%	13.8%	25,533	18.3%	24.8%	6.9%	25.3%	20.4%
Lake Charles, LA	8,364	97.4%	19,506	39.5%	29.2%	2.7%	8.2%	27,030	37.3%	24.4%	7.5%	12.0%	6.2%
Lake Havasu City-Kingman, AZ	6,427	94.5%	12,700	54.3%	18.3%	3.5%	4.0%	19,440	43.3%	26.0%	3.5%	7.2%	4.1%
Lakeland-Winter Haven, FL	25,335	95.3%	56,070	34.4%	35.8%	4.2%	5.2%	76,330	34.5%	20.2%	8.9%	15.0%	4.2%
Lancaster, PA	22,072	90.2%	51,481	40.5%	27.0%	4.7%	8.8%	59,762	25.8%	17.9%	9.8%	21.5%	9.7%
Lansing-East Lansing, MI	18,026	96.4%	71,250	16.2%	62.7%	2.8%	10.8%	56,299	18.7%	24.9%	9.2%	28.3%	14.0%
Laredo, TX	14,816	95.7%	30,472	42.5%	28.7%	4.7%	4.7%	30,918	33.9%	23.5%	5.1%	14.8%	3.8%
Las Cruces, NM	8,988	100.0%	30,410	23.0%	54.6%	8.9%	0.4%	24,696	22.0%	42.0%	7.1%	11.2%	6.4%
Las Vegas-Henderson-Paradise, NV	80,966	97.3%	186,180	34.7%	37.1%	4.0%	5.3%	284,231	28.7%	29.0%	8.2%	16.6%	4.8%
Lawrence, KS	2,982	95.1%	27,314	21.4%	62.3%	7.9%	8.1%	16,467	18.2%	17.8%	6.6%	25.6%	23.0%
Lawton, OK	4,823	99.9%	15,217	33.6%	37.1%	8.8%	3.1%	20,264	27.8%	36.5%	6.7%	13.3%	0.9%
Lebanon, PA	4,416	96.3%	12,415	35.0%	30.7%	9.6%	14.8%	12,915	31.1%	22.4%	12.3%	16.6%	4.0%
Lewiston, ID-WA	1,867	100.0%	6,370	18.8%	55.8%	7.9%	4.1%	6,197	38.0%	12.7%	14.6%	20.1%	7.7%
Lewiston-Auburn, ME	4,002	96.7%	9,422	31.3%	47.9%	0.0%	7.1%	10,928	33.1%	32.9%	8.8%	12.7%	10.1%
Lexington-Fayette, KY	18,842	95.8%	58,755	28.0%	46.7%	3.4%	10.1%	67,204	24.5%	24.1%	7.7%	25.2%	11.7%
Lima, OH	4,020	99.1%	9,702	47.9%	28.3%	2.7%	4.9%	11,532	29.6%	30.2%	11.0%	17.4%	8.6%
Lincoln, NE	9,830	93.2%	46,333	15.2%	58.3%	3.3%	18.7%	43,067	18.5%	25.7%	11.3%	22.4%	14.0%
Little Rock-North Little Rock-Conway, AR...	28,782	92.6%	71,322	32.8%	45.4%	3.1%	8.8%	97,350	23.9%	27.3%	9.4%	20.8%	10.4%
Logan, UT-ID	6,533	99.9%	22,240	24.4%	45.1%	7.6%	13.0%	19,385	20.8%	33.5%	13.8%	21.1%	7.6%
Longview, TX	8,120	98.9%	19,837	30.8%	33.9%	3.5%	10.4%	24,380	43.0%	22.0%	7.0%	15.6%	3.2%
Longview, WA	3,413	92.6%	6,540	39.5%	39.3%	7.6%	2.1%	12,790	29.7%	25.4%	10.4%	8.3%	10.3%
Los Angeles-Long Beach-Anaheim, CA...	510,482	97.8%	1,319,589	27.7%	45.2%	4.5%	10.3%	1,818,998	20.3%	22.9%	7.2%	27.5%	9.0%

Table E-4: Metropolitan/Micropolitan Statistical Areas—Educational Attainment—*Continued*

	15 to 17		18 to 24					25 to 33					
				Percent					Percent				
	Total Population	Percent Enrolled in School	Total Population	High School	Some College	Associates Degree	Bachelors Degree	Total Population	High School	Some College	Associates Degree	Bachelors Degree	Advanced Degree
Louisville/Jefferson County, KY-IN	51,081	97.1%	108,623	34.6%	39.8%	4.7%	7.1%	151,229	22.8%	24.0%	9.2%	23.2%	11.9%
Lubbock, TX	12,342	97.0%	53,067	20.6%	55.9%	3.0%	10.5%	42,819	22.6%	30.7%	7.7%	19.7%	9.9%
Lumberton, NC	5,362	95.6%	13,854	37.3%	39.4%	1.1%	3.7%	13,331	31.7%	21.5%	10.0%	11.6%	3.2%
Lynchburg, VA	10,793	92.0%	32,903	31.7%	45.1%	6.9%	9.7%	27,594	23.9%	26.8%	10.0%	21.9%	7.6%
Macon, GA	8,744	93.3%	25,465	30.2%	41.6%	4.3%	5.2%	23,089	22.8%	24.4%	9.0%	23.0%	8.3%
Madera, CA	6,628	98.2%	15,683	31.2%	35.6%	4.9%	5.4%	19,229	28.8%	24.8%	4.7%	10.8%	2.1%
Madison, WI	23,576	99.0%	79,957	26.9%	36.8%	3.8%	27.5%	88,503	14.0%	21.1%	9.3%	36.7%	15.1%
Manchester-Nashua, NH	16,014	99.5%	37,376	28.1%	31.7%	6.7%	16.9%	45,577	25.0%	18.2%	10.0%	29.5%	7.6%
Manhattan, KS	3,864	100.0%	23,702	25.6%	61.0%	3.9%	5.9%	16,967	18.0%	46.4%	8.3%	21.2%	3.1%
Mankato-North Mankato, MN	3,863	99.4%	18,713	10.3%	81.4%	1.5%	3.1%	11,901	16.8%	24.4%	30.6%	23.2%	5.0%
Mansfield, OH	4,664	96.8%	10,805	56.7%	17.6%	2.7%	8.0%	12,484	36.9%	23.6%	9.5%	10.8%	2.9%
McAllen-Edinburg-Mission, TX	43,446	97.6%	91,885	31.9%	38.8%	4.5%	5.3%	96,344	24.2%	24.7%	7.6%	15.3%	4.7%
Medford, OR	7,333	97.1%	16,260	29.9%	24.4%	3.3%	6.5%	24,414	34.0%	25.2%	10.9%	11.9%	3.3%
Memphis, TN-MS-AR	60,612	97.2%	128,977	33.6%	41.2%	4.6%	8.0%	168,135	27.5%	25.9%	6.9%	19.8%	8.5%
Merced, CA	12,527	97.3%	32,689	28.1%	44.1%	5.7%	7.3%	33,141	28.6%	28.1%	6.9%	8.5%	4.7%
Meridian, MS	4,691	98.4%	10,313	32.9%	38.7%	7.3%	9.5%	12,320	18.7%	36.8%	17.8%	7.2%	3.4%
Miami-Fort Lauderdale-West Palm Beach, FL	215,129	96.2%	501,872	28.3%	36.6%	10.2%	9.2%	724,010	25.4%	20.3%	11.5%	23.3%	9.0%
Michigan City-La Porte, IN	4,374	96.8%	8,713	43.5%	32.0%	2.1%	6.1%	12,832	34.2%	24.9%	5.2%	10.1%	2.7%
Midland, MI	3,948	97.6%	6,706	42.6%	32.6%	4.4%	3.4%	9,554	23.0%	39.0%	6.4%	22.7%	3.8%
Midland, TX	7,619	97.3%	17,003	43.6%	25.2%	5.4%	5.0%	25,882	37.7%	24.5%	6.7%	16.5%	4.1%
Milwaukee-Waukesha-West Allis, WI	62,538	98.6%	143,449	28.4%	43.4%	4.8%	10.2%	191,155	18.1%	24.3%	10.1%	29.8%	11.0%
Minneapolis-St. Paul-Bloomington, MN-WI	141,393	98.3%	291,586	30.5%	34.8%	5.2%	17.3%	460,174	18.6%	18.4%	11.9%	34.3%	11.5%
Missoula, MT	4,696	100.0%	14,769	28.3%	37.4%	6.6%	7.7%	17,127	15.8%	24.1%	15.7%	21.7%	10.2%
Mobile, AL	17,044	97.1%	37,483	34.9%	34.7%	2.3%	10.0%	53,577	23.3%	32.6%	7.2%	22.3%	4.2%
Modesto, CA	20,440	97.4%	41,049	39.2%	37.3%	5.0%	5.6%	52,079	30.0%	30.9%	7.1%	14.5%	3.1%
Monroe, LA	7,508	91.4%	17,986	21.6%	51.4%	4.1%	5.4%	23,237	26.5%	26.0%	4.7%	22.3%	8.3%
Monroe, MI	6,328	99.2%	11,950	36.4%	35.6%	9.0%	12.7%	15,224	23.1%	24.9%	12.6%	18.9%	7.9%
Montgomery, AL	15,184	94.7%	36,863	31.6%	37.9%	3.2%	8.2%	46,764	24.2%	30.3%	7.5%	18.2%	2.9%
Morgantown, WV	3,909	100.0%	25,885	20.0%	63.6%	0.7%	14.2%	21,424	18.3%	24.0%	5.4%	25.9%	23.6%
Morristown, TN	6,348	98.0%	9,800	39.4%	41.6%	6.7%	3.9%	10,630	53.9%	18.7%	4.5%	8.4%	1.9%
Mount Vernon-Anacortes, WA	4,657	98.3%	8,948	32.6%	42.1%	3.4%	4.2%	13,682	27.2%	36.3%	9.5%	15.8%	2.3%
Muncie, IN	3,898	93.9%	22,931	25.2%	61.0%	3.9%	4.8%	10,355	28.3%	29.3%	6.3%	13.6%	7.3%
Muskegon, MI	6,611	99.4%	14,864	32.9%	46.5%	5.2%	2.8%	20,232	29.7%	27.7%	10.0%	13.8%	4.8%
Myrtle Beach-Conway-North Myrtle Beach, SC-NC	14,597	96.6%	33,252	44.7%	30.9%	5.5%	8.5%	42,738	26.6%	23.1%	10.0%	21.9%	6.7%
Napa, CA	5,350	98.4%	13,069	38.9%	38.3%	2.8%	7.9%	14,989	12.2%	32.0%	7.4%	33.7%	5.7%
Naples-Immokalee-Marco Island, FL	11,293	96.9%	25,881	40.6%	28.5%	2.6%	10.0%	30,802	27.6%	15.6%	10.7%	22.2%	6.3%
Nashville-Davidson–Murfreesboro–Franklin, TN	73,518	97.8%	175,465	33.1%	39.9%	2.8%	13.5%	239,003	25.1%	20.2%	7.3%	28.0%	12.4%
New Bern, NC	4,030	90.8%	15,041	40.1%	43.4%	5.2%	1.7%	15,525	20.0%	38.6%	12.7%	20.0%	1.3%
New Castle, PA	3,319	99.2%	6,676	43.7%	42.7%	2.1%	2.5%	8,911	31.4%	14.9%	19.4%	10.1%	12.0%
New Haven-Milford, CT	33,493	97.5%	87,288	31.6%	42.1%	3.1%	13.2%	99,958	25.3%	20.1%	6.1%	24.7%	15.3%
New Orleans-Metairie, LA	47,760	96.7%	107,258	30.9%	40.2%	3.0%	9.0%	173,863	24.5%	23.5%	6.6%	24.2%	10.1%
New Philadelphia-Dover, OH	4,220	91.8%	7,080	53.3%	22.5%	4.9%	10.9%	9,522	43.1%	16.9%	4.7%	20.8%	11.5%
New York-Newark-Jersey City, NY-NJ-PA	739,304	97.6%	1,823,529	25.3%	39.6%	5.8%	17.5%	2,633,412	19.5%	16.3%	6.9%	32.2%	15.3%
Niles-Benton Harbor, MI	5,752	97.5%	12,450	32.8%	34.9%	6.6%	8.6%	15,966	29.8%	20.8%	14.9%	22.4%	7.4%
North Port-Sarasota-Bradenton, FL	23,491	97.4%	49,953	36.7%	30.2%	8.8%	6.0%	64,800	32.5%	23.6%	8.0%	17.7%	5.3%
Norwich-New London, CT	10,589	92.9%	28,636	40.2%	36.4%	5.7%	8.4%	31,833	30.4%	22.2%	6.2%	25.8%	11.0%
Ocala, FL	11,395	94.1%	25,183	30.4%	33.3%	6.2%	10.0%	33,781	38.7%	28.2%	8.6%	11.4%	3.4%
Ocean City, NJ	3,824	99.5%	6,265	31.7%	54.8%	2.6%	7.4%	8,722	28.9%	20.3%	5.8%	29.1%	12.1%
Odessa, TX	7,443	94.4%	18,034	39.9%	40.7%	3.2%	4.2%	24,031	36.1%	31.1%	6.5%	13.0%	1.6%
Ogden-Clearfield, UT	30,773	97.2%	61,568	34.3%	37.6%	7.5%	4.8%	83,448	25.6%	28.5%	12.9%	22.1%	4.5%
Ogdensburg-Massena, NY	3,881	96.3%	15,881	26.4%	55.5%	4.1%	4.1%	12,327	37.9%	14.8%	8.9%	14.7%	12.1%
Oklahoma City, OK	51,434	95.5%	139,317	26.2%	45.0%	2.7%	10.0%	185,033	27.5%	25.2%	7.3%	21.1%	7.7%
Olympia-Tumwater, WA	9,282	100.0%	24,902	37.4%	39.3%	7.0%	6.5%	33,146	27.6%	24.1%	8.1%	21.1%	3.7%
Omaha-Council Bluffs, NE-IA	37,769	98.8%	80,083	26.5%	38.4%	5.5%	17.1%	120,657	16.8%	26.8%	9.0%	28.5%	10.0%
Orangeburg, SC	3,765	100.0%	7,609	33.2%	38.5%	7.1%	3.6%	11,524	36.9%	27.4%	13.0%	8.4%	3.4%
Orlando-Kissimmee-Sanford, FL	95,185	96.5%	235,677	29.8%	36.9%	11.0%	8.6%	317,056	22.6%	22.7%	14.6%	25.6%	7.6%
Oshkosh-Neenah, WI	6,316	97.3%	19,273	19.1%	53.8%	10.0%	6.2%	21,198	12.3%	32.7%	21.4%	22.4%	6.2%
Ottawa-Peru, IL	4,432	95.8%	8,885	27.6%	36.0%	11.6%	12.0%	11,899	27.7%	42.2%	6.1%	10.7%	1.9%
Owensboro, KY	4,641	98.8%	9,474	41.8%	31.9%	7.2%	6.9%	13,140	21.1%	46.9%	10.2%	14.6%	4.0%
Oxnard-Thousand Oaks-Ventura, CA	34,640	98.3%	82,021	25.4%	44.9%	7.4%	6.9%	100,843	21.6%	23.2%	9.3%	21.5%	9.1%
Palm Bay-Melbourne-Titusville, FL	20,157	97.4%	45,039	30.1%	37.2%	8.5%	6.2%	55,168	25.2%	28.0%	12.8%	20.0%	7.7%
Panama City, FL	7,111	93.6%	16,270	34.2%	30.1%	5.6%	2.7%	25,575	31.4%	31.0%	11.3%	13.1%	4.5%
Parkersburg-Vienna, WV	3,452	100.0%	7,321	26.0%	46.5%	6.7%	2.6%	9,395	32.8%	29.1%	6.3%	19.7%	5.5%
Pensacola-Ferry Pass-Brent, FL	17,090	94.8%	53,366	32.4%	39.6%	7.4%	8.4%	61,648	25.0%	19.1%	19.6%	20.2%	6.7%
Peoria, IL	14,472	96.1%	31,355	30.5%	43.5%	7.3%	7.8%	44,780	22.6%	21.4%	11.4%	21.6%	13.2%
Philadelphia-Camden-Wilmington, PA-NJ-DE-MD	228,602	96.5%	558,640	30.7%	38.1%	5.1%	14.2%	767,447	23.3%	19.1%	7.0%	29.6%	13.3%
Phoenix-Mesa-Scottsdale, AZ	190,301	96.2%	427,612	29.4%	37.2%	6.1%	8.1%	573,047	22.3%	27.0%	8.6%	21.2%	8.0%
Pine Bluff, AR	3,536	98.2%	9,044	42.7%	27.4%	6.9%	5.9%	9,911	35.8%	31.3%	4.9%	17.1%	7.4%
Pittsburgh, PA	82,813	97.8%	202,145	30.9%	39.0%	4.8%	14.4%	274,703	23.6%	16.8%	12.0%	27.0%	15.1%
Pittsfield, MA	4,397	99.3%	13,210	22.4%	51.3%	3.7%	7.7%	10,682	31.3%	24.9%	10.8%	19.4%	6.5%
Pocatello, ID	3,418	100.0%	9,910	31.3%	43.9%	2.7%	2.5%	11,138	26.7%	28.7%	10.4%	19.2%	8.0%
Port St. Lucie, FL	19,311	94.7%	46,415	32.5%	42.3%	4.9%	12.7%	56,267	24.4%	20.2%	8.1%	32.5%	10.5%
Portland-South Portland, ME	92,345	98.0%	201,224	30.9%	38.2%	6.9%	10.8%	320,617	19.6%	25.7%	7.7%	28.4%	10.7%

Table E-4: Metropolitan/Micropolitan Statistical Areas—Educational Attainment—*Continued*

| | 15 to 17 | | 18 to 24 | | | | | 25 to 33 | | | | | |
| | | | | Percent | | | | | Percent | | | | |
	Total Population	Percent Enrolled in School	Total Population	High School	Some College	Associates Degree	Bachelors Degree	Total Population	High School	Some College	Associates Degree	Bachelors Degree	Advanced Degree
Portland-Vancouver-Hillsboro, OR-WA	15,004	98.5%	33,555	29.6%	30.9%	6.4%	4.9%	43,439	29.6%	24.4%	14.4%	12.9%	5.0%
Pottsville, PA	5,347	100.0%	10,180	49.1%	21.6%	8.2%	8.3%	14,846	35.9%	13.9%	18.9%	17.5%	6.8%
Prescott, AZ	6,488	84.4%	15,292	45.6%	40.9%	1.4%	5.0%	18,013	39.8%	26.9%	8.0%	12.9%	3.5%
Providence-Warwick, RI-MA	56,940	97.6%	165,357	29.1%	41.4%	5.4%	12.8%	192,565	24.1%	24.0%	7.9%	24.7%	10.0%
Provo-Orem, UT	30,616	96.9%	94,597	23.5%	46.9%	11.2%	7.1%	73,075	16.6%	27.9%	13.1%	32.1%	6.2%
Pueblo, CO	6,532	87.8%	15,000	37.3%	34.2%	4.7%	8.2%	19,140	29.5%	34.5%	9.9%	17.0%	1.6%
Punta Gorda, FL	4,383	100.0%	9,538	38.7%	28.5%	13.8%	1.1%	9,228	46.1%	17.3%	11.3%	9.5%	2.9%
Racine, WI	8,017	100.0%	17,832	46.5%	35.0%	7.5%	3.6%	19,655	29.5%	25.4%	10.9%	21.9%	3.5%
Raleigh, NC	51,758	96.8%	113,029	20.7%	44.0%	3.4%	14.2%	163,616	15.9%	19.6%	7.7%	32.6%	14.1%
Rapid City, SD	6,086	95.8%	11,262	29.7%	54.1%	1.4%	6.7%	19,292	29.3%	31.6%	12.6%	18.0%	3.9%
Reading, PA	17,087	96.5%	41,421	32.5%	38.6%	2.5%	10.2%	45,238	27.0%	25.0%	14.3%	16.1%	8.2%
Redding, CA	6,824	100.0%	12,988	27.0%	42.8%	2.6%	9.5%	20,642	23.5%	27.5%	10.0%	18.8%	8.9%
Reno, NV	16,893	97.8%	40,446	34.0%	41.9%	4.6%	4.1%	58,210	23.7%	27.5%	7.2%	20.4%	9.3%
Richmond, VA	49,670	96.2%	122,167	29.4%	39.3%	4.6%	12.6%	159,399	26.8%	23.7%	6.7%	25.3%	10.8%
Riverside-San Bernardino-Ontario, CA	204,993	97.4%	473,053	36.4%	39.6%	4.8%	5.3%	564,925	32.2%	28.5%	8.1%	12.6%	4.5%
Roanoke, VA	10,656	100.0%	27,298	37.2%	36.1%	4.1%	8.8%	34,962	26.4%	26.1%	11.5%	23.0%	7.7%
Rochester, MN	7,236	98.4%	20,720	29.5%	32.2%	6.7%	12.0%	23,747	16.4%	15.4%	13.0%	28.3%	21.2%
Rochester, NY	40,645	95.7%	110,492	25.3%	42.3%	6.9%	12.9%	127,894	22.8%	20.6%	11.3%	23.7%	13.2%
Rockford, IL	14,502	96.7%	28,540	33.9%	36.8%	3.9%	9.6%	37,019	26.3%	20.3%	11.1%	23.1%	6.3%
Rocky Mount, NC	6,288	98.0%	13,362	40.7%	28.7%	1.5%	4.8%	14,191	35.8%	24.4%	14.8%	7.0%	1.7%
Rome, GA	3,826	99.5%	9,179	34.9%	36.8%	0.0%	1.8%	11,680	36.0%	23.6%	5.3%	12.4%	10.0%
Roseburg, OR	3,303	93.1%	7,366	41.8%	32.7%	1.7%	5.9%	10,908	38.0%	25.6%	5.6%	10.2%	14.2%
Sacramento-Roseville-Arden-Arcade, CA	88,953	97.9%	218,161	28.2%	44.7%	5.7%	9.2%	284,963	21.5%	28.8%	10.8%	22.9%	7.3%
Saginaw, MI	6,999	97.1%	20,018	38.0%	40.9%	4.4%	5.5%	21,353	19.5%	32.7%	13.2%	23.7%	2.3%
Salem, OH	8,303	97.7%	25,879	24.9%	44.6%	9.4%	12.8%	23,951	16.5%	23.6%	11.1%	32.8%	4.5%
Salem, OR	7,485	99.4%	16,709	30.2%	46.6%	10.6%	4.1%	15,243	33.6%	28.3%	12.6%	15.8%	4.1%
Salinas, CA	5,145	99.0%	11,288	44.4%	26.0%	0.4%	7.6%	16,906	37.2%	24.0%	6.5%	15.5%	2.7%
Salisbury, MD-DE	110,903	97.3%	248,328	27.4%	42.8%	5.0%	10.6%	335,801	21.1%	25.8%	11.2%	23.6%	11.4%
Salt Lake City, UT	4,005	94.4%	7,504	42.7%	30.8%	1.9%	3.2%	9,881	43.0%	21.5%	10.9%	12.3%	2.7%
San Angelo, TX	18,605	99.6%	40,898	30.2%	43.0%	3.5%	6.4%	46,862	34.1%	25.4%	8.4%	16.3%	4.1%
San Antonio-New Braunfels, TX	16,757	95.3%	45,593	28.8%	44.3%	5.6%	4.2%	55,988	20.9%	21.4%	9.7%	16.8%	3.5%
San Diego-Carlsbad, CA	13,202	91.9%	39,103	30.4%	46.7%	6.4%	5.2%	37,612	26.5%	28.0%	10.1%	15.1%	6.7%
San Francisco-Oakland-Hayward, CA	53,238	96.9%	114,848	31.6%	36.8%	7.5%	7.6%	169,969	24.0%	24.7%	9.1%	25.0%	8.5%
San Jose-Sunnyvale-Santa Clara, CA	4,513	98.0%	15,384	30.2%	44.2%	4.4%	16.1%	16,742	30.5%	23.3%	10.1%	20.4%	4.2%
San Luis Obispo-Paso Robles Arroyo Grande, CA	104,960	97.2%	246,793	35.1%	39.0%	4.1%	5.6%	322,810	27.3%	28.8%	9.1%	18.1%	6.1%
Santa Cruz-Watsonville, CA	117,600	97.8%	352,905	32.6%	44.8%	4.3%	9.3%	473,892	20.3%	25.2%	7.8%	26.4%	11.5%
Santa Fe, NM	149,580	98.2%	375,073	27.1%	39.5%	4.9%	18.9%	656,416	13.9%	17.1%	6.1%	37.9%	17.1%
Santa Maria-Santa Barbara, CA	69,917	97.8%	171,407	27.6%	42.1%	4.2%	16.4%	267,421	14.2%	16.8%	7.0%	29.6%	23.3%
Santa Rosa, CA	8,526	98.7%	42,216	29.6%	52.1%	8.5%	3.8%	30,829	19.7%	29.9%	11.5%	20.0%	8.0%
Savannah, GA	8,920	95.9%	42,214	20.9%	56.8%	2.8%	9.1%	30,305	21.1%	15.5%	8.6%	25.5%	9.9%
Scranton-Wilkes-Barre-Hazleton, PA	4,909	99.6%	11,025	31.1%	44.0%	2.7%	7.9%	15,060	15.8%	24.0%	7.9%	22.1%	12.6%
Seattle-Tacoma-Bellevue, WA	16,101	99.2%	71,192	17.8%	60.2%	5.1%	7.9%	49,128	19.1%	22.1%	5.9%	24.5%	9.0%
Sebastian-Vero Beach, FL	17,598	97.7%	43,756	29.9%	40.9%	6.5%	11.2%	57,264	20.4%	32.7%	9.8%	20.5%	6.8%
Sebring, FL	11,545	91.6%	47,166	28.3%	50.4%	1.7%	7.5%	51,530	21.3%	36.8%	5.6%	17.4%	9.4%
Sheboygan, WI	20,854	96.7%	51,810	31.3%	43.6%	2.4%	13.6%	58,176	24.1%	22.2%	11.8%	21.3%	10.2%
Sherman-Denison, TX	132,418	97.1%	317,404	30.6%	35.1%	7.6%	14.7%	543,759	19.1%	20.8%	9.2%	30.9%	13.5%
Show Low, AZ	4,007	92.7%	11,503	38.6%	17.4%	22.8%	5.3%	11,380	43.6%	29.5%	8.7%	5.1%	4.7%
Shreveport-Bossier City, LA	3,191	95.2%	6,255	38.1%	25.1%	6.3%	0.0%	7,714	52.6%	18.1%	6.0%	6.0%	4.5%
Sierra Vista-Douglas, AZ	4,661	98.3%	8,517	35.6%	25.9%	3.9%	22.7%	11,780	35.9%	19.7%	6.1%	22.1%	4.8%
Sioux City, IA-NE-SD	4,855	96.2%	12,228	40.3%	29.3%	5.7%	1.4%	12,709	39.0%	24.0%	9.9%	16.8%	0.6%
Sioux Falls, SD	4,733	94.3%	9,752	42.5%	24.0%	3.3%	1.7%	11,618	45.8%	28.6%	5.8%	8.0%	1.3%
South Bend-Mishawaka, IN-MI	17,025	98.6%	40,935	30.3%	42.3%	2.8%	5.4%	57,754	24.6%	31.5%	9.4%	14.7%	6.8%
Spartanburg, SC	5,031	99.5%	9,550	42.2%	26.6%	6.8%	9.4%	14,841	34.6%	27.3%	9.5%	12.2%	5.4%
Spokane-Spokane Valley, WA	7,620	98.4%	14,972	32.9%	37.4%	6.9%	3.5%	18,340	24.0%	30.4%	10.1%	17.1%	6.6%
Springfield, IL	8,740	88.4%	22,812	25.2%	38.1%	5.2%	18.1%	35,376	20.9%	21.5%	12.9%	29.3%	6.1%
Springfield, MA	14,300	93.5%	35,054	29.8%	39.3%	2.5%	10.5%	34,788	21.3%	27.0%	9.9%	24.5%	9.4%
Springfield, MO	13,581	100.0%	31,299	27.8%	44.1%	5.5%	6.7%	35,076	25.6%	27.6%	11.1%	16.4%	5.6%
Springfield, OH	20,669	96.5%	51,658	30.6%	44.6%	4.7%	9.0%	71,816	32.6%	26.7%	9.6%	15.7%	8.2%
St. Cloud, MN	9,140	89.4%	18,486	23.0%	32.8%	3.5%	16.2%	23,591	18.5%	33.1%	5.0%	22.4%	11.8%
St. George, UT	25,492	95.5%	81,426	23.7%	54.4%	1.9%	8.4%	72,157	24.8%	18.6%	9.0%	23.3%	12.5%
St. Joseph, MO-KS	16,991	98.0%	54,905	23.8%	50.8%	7.5%	9.0%	55,847	22.8%	29.3%	11.2%	19.3%	8.4%
St. Louis, MO-IL	5,603	98.7%	11,991	51.2%	35.7%	0.1%	2.9%	13,749	23.8%	38.2%	7.7%	14.0%	6.1%
State College, PA	3,835	96.0%	41,020	29.3%	48.8%	2.6%	12.2%	22,204	23.3%	16.8%	5.9%	33.7%	15.7%
Staunton-Waynesboro, VA	3,536	95.7%	13,370	33.4%	46.5%	2.7%	4.6%	11,802	44.0%	19.4%	9.5%	17.6%	2.3%
Stockton-Lodi, CA	33,581	98.1%	72,442	30.4%	45.2%	4.4%	4.3%	88,953	27.9%	29.9%	8.8%	11.6%	4.5%
Sumter, SC	4,406	91.1%	13,392	38.7%	36.7%	3.7%	0.9%	12,191	25.9%	31.8%	7.7%	6.4%	6.9%
Sunbury, PA	3,106	76.2%	6,642	49.0%	23.4%	5.4%	7.5%	10,582	33.4%	14.6%	15.0%	16.9%	6.7%
Syracuse, NY	27,214	95.6%	71,499	27.1%	49.1%	6.3%	8.9%	73,891	19.9%	23.7%	12.5%	21.9%	11.0%
Tallahassee, FL	12,444	93.8%	70,917	14.8%	48.8%	16.2%	14.1%	47,845	25.0%	20.9%	10.1%	23.7%	11.0%
Tampa-St. Petersburg-Clearwater, FL	104,762	96.9%	239,308	29.2%	34.2%	8.4%	11.5%	343,205	26.8%	21.6%	11.4%	22.9%	8.1%
Terre Haute, IN	7,338	97.6%	21,742	26.1%	45.9%	5.1%	9.5%	18,309	28.9%	24.9%	9.3%	15.0%	4.5%
Texarkana, TX-AR	5,896	95.6%	13,517	40.6%	28.7%	7.8%	1.6%	16,886	31.9%	42.7%	8.1%	8.5%	0.9%
The Villages, FL	2,181	100.0%	4,981	28.2%	17.2%	5.8%	2.4%	3,847	29.6%	25.5%	13.4%	13.0%	2.7%
Toledo, OH	24,573	97.9%	67,145	27.2%	48.6%	2.6%	9.9%	71,852	24.5%	27.5%	12.8%	20.0%	8.8%

Table E-4: Metropolitan/Micropolitan Statistical Areas—Educational Attainment—*Continued*

| | 15 to 17 | | 18 to 24 | | | | | 25 to 33 | | | | | |
	Total Population	Percent Enrolled in School	Total Population	High School	Some College	Associates Degree	Bachelors Degree	Total Population	High School	Some College	Associates Degree	Bachelors Degree	Advanced Degree
Topeka, KS	9,187	97.4%	19,269	29.0%	42.3%	3.4%	8.6%	25,917	23.0%	26.3%	13.0%	20.3%	12.2%
Torrington, CT	6,694	99.0%	13,568	35.9%	31.4%	3.2%	24.6%	16,493	27.0%	23.5%	7.2%	27.2%	8.3%
Traverse City, MI	5,897	96.9%	11,620	30.5%	30.8%	10.7%	15.0%	14,212	16.9%	30.5%	16.6%	18.4%	10.9%
Trenton, NJ	14,301	96.2%	42,985	28.5%	47.2%	1.4%	13.0%	39,325	27.6%	22.4%	3.1%	17.8%	19.0%
Truckee-Grass Valley, CA	3,189	79.8%	6,149	24.9%	59.2%	1.3%	4.3%	9,555	28.7%	31.6%	11.4%	20.8%	3.3%
Tucson, AZ	37,110	95.6%	118,139	26.9%	45.7%	4.7%	7.5%	109,878	21.0%	30.3%	9.9%	19.1%	8.2%
Tullahoma-Manchester, TN	4,072	100.0%	9,870	46.2%	39.5%	1.0%	0.8%	9,752	35.2%	15.9%	8.4%	13.1%	2.1%
Tulsa, OK	39,744	95.9%	90,037	36.3%	32.8%	4.2%	6.2%	118,952	27.6%	23.6%	9.0%	22.5%	6.5%
Tupelo, MS	5,865	91.8%	13,296	34.6%	25.9%	9.8%	10.2%	14,686	30.8%	16.9%	21.4%	14.6%	6.2%
Tuscaloosa, AL	8,900	98.9%	40,320	25.4%	53.6%	3.8%	4.1%	31,163	24.5%	24.5%	9.3%	19.7%	5.0%
Tyler, TX	8,737	93.4%	22,578	24.8%	47.1%	3.5%	11.4%	28,149	27.8%	30.0%	5.4%	15.8%	4.7%
Urban Honolulu, HI	30,847	97.5%	104,107	36.8%	40.3%	7.5%	10.3%	138,456	25.9%	26.5%	10.7%	25.1%	7.6%
Utica-Rome, NY	10,563	95.2%	27,051	26.0%	43.6%	8.2%	11.6%	31,574	30.0%	21.4%	9.7%	19.5%	8.0%
Valdosta, GA	5,450	97.5%	21,265	25.2%	45.7%	12.1%	5.6%	19,484	18.4%	27.1%	15.2%	14.3%	6.6%
Vallejo-Fairfield, CA	16,430	95.8%	40,269	32.5%	38.9%	4.5%	9.2%	55,432	23.2%	29.1%	10.4%	18.4%	6.6%
Victoria, TX	4,352	100.0%	9,641	44.0%	17.5%	1.0%	0.6%	11,608	26.2%	34.5%	2.0%	19.3%	6.2%
Vineland-Bridgeton, NJ	6,209	99.6%	12,703	48.2%	27.3%	3.8%	4.7%	21,889	50.6%	8.3%	9.6%	13.5%	2.7%
Virginia Beach-Norfolk-Newport News, VA-NC	65,605	97.5%	196,229	30.3%	47.7%	5.1%	8.5%	246,051	24.6%	28.5%	11.5%	20.6%	7.3%
Visalia-Porterville, CA	23,180	98.5%	48,480	32.6%	42.9%	5.0%	4.1%	59,578	33.7%	25.6%	7.1%	13.4%	3.1%
Waco, TX	11,522	100.0%	37,304	32.5%	38.2%	5.6%	12.2%	29,407	23.6%	25.7%	13.6%	16.5%	7.8%
Walla Walla, WA	2,280	89.6%	6,587	26.2%	47.4%	12.1%	3.1%	8,751	24.6%	14.9%	17.7%	14.3%	18.2%
Warner Robins, GA	7,432	96.5%	20,524	35.3%	37.4%	5.4%	4.4%	21,473	20.7%	33.7%	13.8%	12.0%	9.5%
Washington-Arlington-Alexandria, DC-VA-MD-WV	226,857	96.8%	547,140	27.7%	40.3%	3.9%	18.2%	831,802	17.0%	17.4%	5.1%	31.8%	20.7%
Waterloo-Cedar Falls, IA	5,818	99.4%	23,786	17.7%	56.9%	6.4%	8.0%	21,302	20.3%	30.1%	11.1%	25.5%	7.1%
Watertown-Fort Drum, NY	4,197	94.5%	15,185	55.7%	24.7%	9.7%	3.9%	16,496	26.6%	32.6%	10.9%	13.8%	5.2%
Wausau, WI	5,541	93.1%	9,696	41.3%	24.9%	12.5%	11.2%	14,255	18.4%	20.3%	17.8%	28.8%	7.9%
Weirton-Steubenville, WV-OH	4,018	95.1%	11,083	35.4%	51.4%	3.2%	1.5%	12,289	28.5%	26.9%	15.9%	14.8%	6.4%
Wenatchee, WA	4,331	96.6%	9,272	37.3%	33.9%	3.6%	6.6%	12,335	39.3%	20.8%	8.1%	11.7%	1.6%
Wheeling, WV-OH	4,754	95.9%	13,727	36.6%	48.3%	5.1%	2.1%	13,508	26.9%	27.2%	16.3%	17.3%	5.4%
Whitewater-Elkhorn, WI	3,868	100.0%	13,278	25.7%	42.1%	10.0%	8.3%	10,055	22.3%	28.2%	9.4%	20.3%	3.7%
Wichita Falls, TX	29,379	94.2%	55,459	27.8%	41.2%	5.5%	8.3%	85,074	22.1%	23.9%	10.0%	22.4%	8.7%
Wichita, KS	5,511	89.8%	20,494	49.1%	34.9%	3.2%	5.2%	18,911	35.5%	19.9%	10.0%	16.1%	6.5%
Williamsport, PA	3,675	92.7%	12,018	37.7%	41.8%	1.5%	8.6%	12,412	31.1%	9.0%	8.3%	28.1%	8.6%
Wilmington, NC	10,816	96.3%	32,247	25.8%	42.7%	6.8%	15.8%	32,831	18.2%	24.5%	16.1%	25.2%	7.8%
Winchester, VA-WV	4,392	97.2%	12,202	25.0%	61.4%	1.7%	5.2%	12,830	33.9%	19.8%	10.2%	16.7%	8.4%
Winston-Salem, NC	26,937	96.3%	59,671	33.3%	36.4%	4.4%	9.0%	72,612	21.2%	24.9%	9.3%	22.5%	9.0%
Wooster, OH	5,538	77.8%	11,242	33.2%	36.6%	0.1%	3.6%	11,235	27.7%	15.8%	12.6%	14.4%	11.2%
Worcester, MA-CT	39,211	99.6%	92,272	35.1%	37.2%	4.2%	14.0%	100,837	23.4%	22.5%	9.3%	25.5%	11.7%
Yakima, WA	11,331	95.7%	25,431	39.5%	29.6%	5.5%	3.1%	27,580	36.9%	18.0%	7.9%	7.2%	4.1%
York-Hanover, PA	16,774	95.8%	34,937	41.4%	31.6%	5.6%	8.6%	50,766	38.1%	16.4%	11.8%	19.2%	5.6%
Youngstown-Warren-Boardman, OH-PA	21,208	95.4%	46,437	38.8%	34.8%	4.5%	6.4%	53,069	37.3%	20.6%	8.3%	19.6%	5.6%
Yuba City, CA	6,570	99.9%	15,545	27.7%	39.4%	6.3%	12.0%	23,344	32.7%	32.2%	10.7%	7.6%	3.0%
Yuma, AZ	9,130	93.2%	23,041	31.9%	41.1%	3.2%	3.3%	25,579	27.2%	27.3%	8.5%	13.2%	3.8%

PART F
FIELD OF DEGREE

PART F. FIELD OF DEGREE

The Millennial generation and the technological world they are growing into is far different from the decades when the Baby Boomers were this age. The President's Council of Economic Advisors notes that they are "the first generation to have had access to the Internet during their formative years."[1] Yet that technological advantage may not be required in the industry sectors where employment is increasing most rapidly. One of their challenges will be obtaining an education in the appropriate fields for future employment and growth. The American Community Survey questions respondents on their bachelor's degree field of study. The data are used primarily by the National Science Foundation to study the characteristics of the population in science and engineering fields, but they are more generally applicable to understanding the educational focus of the Millennials. The question is asked only of persons with a bachelor's degree or higher. Tables presented here follow the Census Bureau's category scheme for field of degree classification.

Nationwide, Millennials age 18 to 33 with a bachelor's degree or higher favor Business as their primary field of study. At 20.7 percent, Business is chosen at a rate more than twice that of the Science and Engineering Related (9.8 percent). While Business stands out for almost one in five degree holders, other disciplines are pretty evenly distributed, as seen in Table 1.

Business is the field of choice for more than 20 percent of Millennials in 28 states. Florida is highest at 26.0 percent, but Arkansas is a close second at 24.9 percent. Vermont has the lowest percentage of Business degree holders at 12.9 percent. The Millennials are thought of as the "tech" generation, but 31.1 percent in the District of Columbia hold degrees in the Social Sciences. Virginia is a distant second at 12.4 percent, and North Dakota has the lowest percentage at 2.1 percent. Engineering is most prevalent in Texas (10.7 percent), but five other states are also above 10 percent: Arizona, California, Delaware, Michigan and Wyoming. Fields related to Science and Engineering are most important in Mississippi (17.1 percent). Degrees in Computers and Mathematics are held by 9.5 percent of Millennials in Delaware. In the Biological Sciences, Vermont is highest at 15.4 percent

followed closely by Maine at 15.0 percent. Twenty-two states have more than 10 percent in the Biological Sciences. The Education fields also have large percentages with 24 states having more than 10 percent degree holders. South Dakota is the highest at 18.8 percent while the District of Columbia is lowest at 2.8 percent.

Table 1: Percent of Population 18 to 31 with a Bachelor's Degree or Higher

Field of Study	Percent
Business	20.7%
Social Science	9.8%
Science and Engineering Related	8.8%
Education	8.6%
Biological Sciences	8.1%
Engineering	7.8%
Psychology	6.4%
Communications	6.1%
Visual and Performing Arts	6.0%
Liberal Arts	5.6%
Literature	4.8%
Computers and Mathematical	4.3%
Physical Sciences	3.0%

Science and Engineering Related, Business, the Biological Sciences, Psychology, and Education are the field of degree categories with the highest percentages at the county level. Rankin County, MS (43.7 percent) has the highest percentage in the Science and Engineering Related category. In Business, Bay County, MI is at the top with 46.5 percent of Millennials holding business degrees. Biological Science degrees are held by 40.6 percent in Highlands County, FL, and in Psychology, Nash County, NC is highest at 56.9 percent. Kendall County, IL tops the list for Education degrees at 54.0 percent. Greg County, TX (27.2 percent) has the highest percentage of Engineering degree holders. In 322 counties, one out of every five degree holder Millennials holds a degree in Business.

Among cities, Business ranks highest in Rialto, CA at 60.4 percent. Only three other cities have more than

---

1 The Council of Economic Advisors, "15 Economic Facts About Millennials," Executive Office of the President, October 2014.

Percent of Millennials Age 18 to 33 with Business Field of Degree

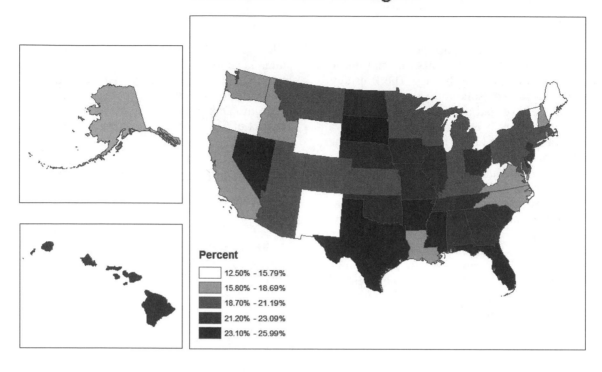

Percent
	12.50% - 15.79%
	15.80% - 18.69%
	18.70% - 21.19%
	21.20% - 23.09%
	23.10% - 25.99%

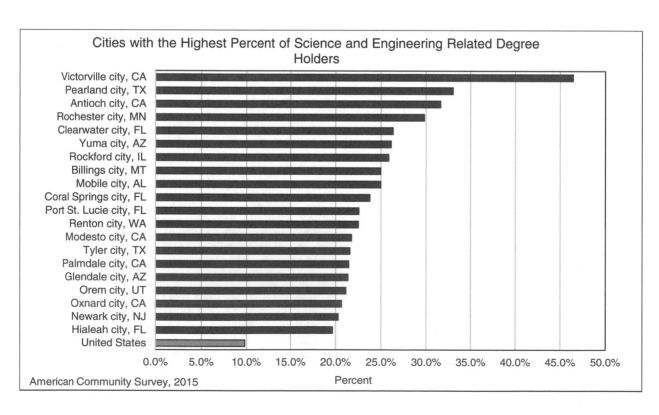

Cities with the Highest Percent of Science and Engineering Related Degree Holders

American Community Survey, 2015

50 percent business degree holders: Boca Raton, FL, Palm Bay, FL and Garland, TX. Engineering degree holders are highest in Sunnyvale City, CA (33.5 percent), and Science and Engineering Related fields are tops in another California city—Victorville at 46.4 percent. San Bernardino, CA and Bellevue, WA are nearly tied for the top concentration of degree holders in Computers and Mathematics with 27.3 percent and 27.4 percent, respectively. Business is important in 95 cities where the percentage of degree holders exceeds 25 percent. Flint City, MI is highest in the Biological Sciences at 34.5 percent. The proportion of Education degree holders is highest in Surprise, AZ (32.8 percent), and Yuma, AZ (32.6 percent).

The Wheeling, WV-OH metropolitan area has the largest percentage of its Millennials in the Education field at 41.0 percent. It's one of 28 metro/micro areas with more than 25 percent of its degree holders in Education. In Science and Engineering Related fields, Kalispell, MT ranks highest at 36.1 percent, with The Villages, FL close behind at 34.3 percent. Five other metros are over 30 percent. Business degree holders are most prevalent in Hinesville, GA, where more than half (54.8 percent) of Millennials are business minded. The Biological Sciences are strong in Sebring, FL (40.6 percent) while Rocky Mount, NC has the highest percentage of Psychology degree holders (35.8 percent).

Table F-1: States—Educational Field of Study

	Total Millennial Population with Bachelor's or Higher	Percent of the Population 18 to 33 with a Bachelor's Degree or Higher by Field of Study												
		Engineering	Computers and Math	Science and Engineering Related	Business	Physical Science	Social Science	Communications	Biological Sciences	Literature	Liberal Arts	Psychology	Education	Visual and Performing Arts
United States	15,349,537	8.1%	5.6%	9.8%	20.7%	3.0%	8.6%	6.1%	8.8%	4.3%	4.8%	6.4%	7.8%	6.0%
Alabama	155,509	7.7%	4.8%	13.0%	21.3%	2.3%	4.2%	5.5%	9.3%	3.8%	4.7%	5.1%	12.1%	6.1%
Alaska	30,508	9.1%	1.7%	11.4%	22.2%	3.1%	5.2%	3.0%	15.4%	4.8%	5.7%	5.1%	6.5%	6.7%
Arizona	246,430	10.3%	6.1%	10.0%	20.0%	3.3%	8.3%	7.4%	7.3%	3.2%	3.1%	5.6%	10.5%	4.9%
Arkansas	94,918	6.5%	5.7%	11.6%	24.9%	2.1%	3.6%	4.1%	12.6%	3.1%	5.5%	4.6%	12.6%	3.1%
California	2,006,773	10.0%	7.0%	7.6%	18.6%	2.8%	11.4%	6.3%	8.6%	4.8%	5.4%	6.4%	3.0%	8.1%
Colorado	328,526	8.4%	4.9%	9.1%	19.3%	4.2%	9.7%	5.6%	9.8%	4.2%	4.2%	7.3%	6.6%	6.7%
Connecticut	205,300	9.3%	5.0%	8.8%	19.6%	2.5%	8.6%	7.0%	7.0%	5.3%	6.0%	7.5%	7.1%	6.2%
Delaware	41,304	10.2%	9.5%	10.0%	22.4%	5.1%	6.5%	3.7%	7.7%	3.5%	2.4%	6.2%	10.2%	2.5%
District of Columbia	111,788	4.3%	3.6%	4.7%	14.5%	1.5%	31.1%	7.3%	5.4%	6.5%	9.5%	4.5%	2.8%	4.2%
Florida	768,590	6.7%	4.6%	12.2%	26.0%	2.4%	7.7%	5.8%	8.4%	2.7%	3.9%	7.2%	7.5%	4.8%
Georgia	427,906	8.4%	5.9%	10.2%	22.4%	3.1%	7.0%	6.4%	7.0%	3.4%	3.8%	5.4%	10.5%	6.5%
Hawaii	64,084	6.6%	5.5%	10.6%	21.5%	1.3%	10.5%	4.0%	8.4%	4.8%	5.1%	8.9%	7.9%	4.8%
Idaho	48,697	7.0%	3.0%	12.6%	16.5%	2.0%	3.8%	6.3%	12.2%	5.3%	7.4%	5.5%	12.3%	6.0%
Illinois	747,763	7.4%	6.0%	9.9%	22.0%	2.7%	7.8%	7.3%	8.1%	4.1%	3.5%	6.8%	8.1%	6.3%
Indiana	256,484	7.6%	4.8%	12.8%	20.0%	3.5%	6.4%	5.7%	6.6%	3.6%	7.0%	4.2%	12.8%	5.1%
Iowa	141,902	7.8%	4.0%	7.6%	22.2%	2.6%	6.2%	4.3%	14.5%	2.7%	5.8%	6.2%	12.6%	3.6%
Kansas	136,473	9.6%	5.3%	12.2%	19.8%	2.2%	5.4%	3.9%	12.0%	3.2%	4.2%	5.3%	11.4%	5.4%
Kentucky	151,794	5.9%	3.8%	12.9%	21.1%	2.9%	6.5%	7.1%	9.7%	4.4%	5.5%	6.7%	10.2%	3.1%
Louisiana	184,286	8.7%	2.5%	12.5%	17.3%	2.7%	5.2%	4.9%	11.1%	3.9%	9.0%	5.9%	10.1%	6.3%
Maine	48,860	8.3%	2.8%	9.7%	15.1%	2.6%	11.4%	6.4%	15.0%	4.2%	1.8%	8.6%	9.2%	4.9%
Maryland	350,270	9.5%	7.9%	7.6%	19.9%	2.0%	11.9%	6.1%	8.8%	3.8%	4.4%	6.1%	6.5%	5.3%
Massachusetts	518,155	9.2%	5.0%	7.6%	20.9%	3.4%	10.5%	5.3%	9.1%	5.4%	5.3%	8.5%	4.0%	5.7%
Michigan	406,515	10.4%	4.6%	11.9%	20.7%	3.2%	5.3%	5.8%	10.4%	4.4%	4.2%	6.1%	8.8%	4.4%
Minnesota	314,932	8.3%	5.2%	10.2%	20.4%	2.7%	7.7%	6.4%	10.4%	3.9%	3.2%	6.2%	8.4%	7.1%
Mississippi	83,724	4.9%	2.1%	17.1%	23.9%	3.2%	3.8%	3.5%	11.1%	2.3%	4.5%	5.9%	14.2%	3.3%
Missouri	253,458	6.5%	4.5%	9.8%	22.2%	2.5%	5.4%	6.9%	9.7%	4.0%	4.7%	7.1%	11.1%	5.5%
Montana	34,447	5.8%	2.0%	13.7%	20.4%	2.0%	7.1%	2.7%	10.2%	3.8%	10.0%	6.9%	12.0%	3.5%
Nebraska	95,859	4.6%	5.1%	12.5%	22.7%	4.2%	3.6%	6.5%	11.0%	3.4%	4.7%	5.1%	12.4%	4.1%
Nevada	84,943	6.9%	4.8%	9.2%	23.9%	3.5%	6.8%	7.5%	8.8%	5.0%	4.2%	6.2%	7.4%	5.9%
New Hampshire	67,754	9.2%	6.9%	12.6%	18.1%	1.5%	7.0%	5.7%	7.5%	5.5%	6.0%	7.2%	8.3%	4.6%
New Jersey	527,861	7.7%	8.3%	8.1%	23.0%	2.7%	7.9%	6.1%	7.0%	3.9%	4.5%	6.9%	9.1%	4.8%
New Mexico	56,423	9.3%	3.8%	8.7%	15.1%	4.8%	10.1%	4.1%	9.8%	5.8%	4.7%	6.2%	12.5%	5.1%
New York	1,367,856	5.0%	5.7%	7.9%	20.8%	2.8%	10.9%	6.8%	6.2%	5.5%	4.7%	7.1%	7.2%	9.4%
North Carolina	419,717	7.0%	6.4%	9.2%	18.5%	3.4%	8.0%	6.6%	10.3%	4.2%	5.5%	7.5%	9.7%	3.8%
North Dakota	43,980	6.9%	5.3%	15.7%	22.3%	4.0%	2.1%	3.8%	14.0%	2.2%	4.0%	7.2%	9.8%	2.7%
Ohio	497,942	7.9%	4.6%	12.7%	21.7%	3.0%	6.7%	5.5%	8.8%	3.5%	4.4%	5.6%	10.4%	5.2%
Oklahoma	134,727	9.0%	3.3%	11.3%	22.1%	4.7%	5.8%	6.2%	10.9%	2.6%	4.7%	5.2%	10.6%	3.7%
Oregon	184,852	6.3%	5.0%	10.3%	15.7%	3.3%	11.8%	5.4%	10.6%	6.7%	5.8%	5.8%	4.6%	8.6%
Pennsylvania	645,461	7.1%	4.6%	12.6%	19.9%	3.7%	6.5%	6.2%	9.3%	4.0%	3.9%	7.0%	10.8%	4.3%
Rhode Island	59,069	6.5%	6.4%	11.6%	18.2%	4.7%	9.3%	5.4%	10.7%	3.0%	3.6%	4.9%	9.5%	6.2%
South Carolina	190,459	7.8%	4.0%	10.1%	21.7%	3.8%	6.6%	4.9%	8.5%	4.0%	5.9%	6.4%	9.8%	6.5%
South Dakota	35,888	3.6%	3.1%	15.5%	23.4%	1.8%	5.8%	4.6%	10.1%	2.2%	2.4%	6.8%	18.8%	1.9%
Tennessee	269,257	6.1%	4.2%	11.3%	21.3%	3.1%	6.5%	6.2%	9.9%	4.4%	5.9%	5.5%	9.6%	6.0%
Texas	1,156,670	10.7%	5.6%	9.9%	23.5%	3.5%	6.9%	5.9%	8.9%	3.7%	4.2%	5.2%	7.7%	4.2%
Utah	128,552	6.7%	5.2%	13.1%	19.9%	2.3%	6.3%	7.3%	7.0%	6.4%	2.7%	5.6%	10.4%	7.0%
Vermont	34,265	4.9%	6.2%	4.1%	12.9%	1.6%	8.8%	5.9%	15.4%	7.7%	7.8%	7.1%	10.1%	7.5%
Virginia	472,628	9.0%	7.2%	8.8%	17.6%	3.0%	12.4%	4.9%	8.0%	4.7%	5.9%	7.2%	6.1%	5.1%
Washington	376,989	9.5%	9.5%	9.0%	17.1%	3.0%	10.9%	5.1%	9.4%	4.7%	5.5%	5.8%	4.9%	5.6%
West Virginia	56,214	7.9%	3.5%	14.9%	13.5%	3.9%	7.9%	6.2%	14.3%	3.6%	2.4%	6.1%	10.8%	5.1%
Wisconsin	264,286	8.1%	4.2%	10.6%	20.6%	3.1%	7.2%	7.2%	11.4%	4.6%	3.5%	5.0%	8.7%	5.7%
Wyoming	18,489	10.2%	1.5%	12.7%	13.0%	4.5%	10.5%	3.7%	14.7%	3.1%	7.8%	4.8%	11.7%	1.6%

Table F-2: Counties—Educational Field of Study

	Total Millennial Population with Bachelor's or Higher	Percent of the Population 18 to 33 by Field of Study												
		Engineering	Computers and Math	Science and Engineering Related	Business	Physical Science	Social Science	Communications	Biological Sciences	Literature	Liberal Arts	Psychology	Education	Visual and Performing Arts
Alabama														
Baldwin County	6,283	7.7%	0.3%	26.4%	12.9%	0.0%	1.1%	1.6%	16.5%	0.0%	10.4%	0.0%	14.8%	8.3%
Calhoun County	2,353	14.7%	6.7%	9.8%	17.2%	0.0%	0.0%	8.8%	8.1%	4.5%	2.5%	3.7%	14.4%	9.6%
Etowah County	3,051	3.6%	4.4%	11.6%	11.8%	6.6%	0.0%	14.1%	14.9%	2.9%	7.1%	0.4%	22.6%	0.0%
Houston County	2,756	9.9%	1.2%	18.7%	16.8%	9.3%	0.0%	1.4%	5.7%	0.8%	1.8%	11.0%	20.2%	3.2%
Jefferson County	35,862	3.9%	2.0%	10.9%	25.9%	3.1%	6.9%	6.1%	8.1%	4.9%	4.4%	4.4%	12.7%	6.8%
Lauderdale County	2,558	6.6%	2.3%	0.0%	28.8%	6.3%	9.6%	19.5%	4.5%	2.2%	6.8%	0.6%	10.8%	1.9%
Lee County	7,273	5.1%	0.8%	3.6%	16.1%	0.0%	4.0%	1.7%	30.6%	6.8%	4.3%	8.3%	11.2%	7.5%
Madison County	18,235	19.0%	9.4%	6.4%	24.1%	2.3%	3.1%	3.1%	5.6%	6.3%	3.5%	7.0%	3.0%	7.0%
Marshall County	1,705	1.9%	12.2%	19.8%	20.9%	0.0%	0.0%	9.0%	18.5%	0.0%	0.0%	0.0%	17.8%	0.0%
Mobile County	16,033	7.5%	6.3%	24.8%	11.2%	5.4%	0.8%	12.0%	6.6%	3.0%	4.6%	2.6%	13.8%	1.4%
Montgomery County	7,425	4.9%	6.4%	7.5%	23.0%	1.3%	4.5%	9.3%	3.3%	3.6%	2.5%	17.2%	5.8%	10.8%
Morgan County	2,769	25.4%	3.3%	14.2%	14.3%	0.0%	0.0%	0.0%	7.9%	0.0%	0.0%	0.0%	22.1%	12.7%
Shelby County	9,866	3.5%	4.3%	15.3%	30.9%	0.0%	0.0%	8.5%	5.7%	6.3%	9.0%	4.4%	6.3%	5.8%
Tuscaloosa County	6,691	9.5%	2.9%	4.2%	27.2%	0.0%	20.8%	6.5%	5.2%	5.0%	0.7%	4.2%	9.4%	4.3%
Alaska														
Anchorage Municipality	16,025	14.9%	2.3%	14.1%	11.4%	3.0%	7.7%	5.0%	21.4%	4.0%	3.7%	3.5%	6.0%	3.1%
Fairbanks North Star Borough	4,281	2.1%	0.0%	9.7%	31.1%	9.7%	4.3%	0.0%	6.6%	11.1%	6.5%	15.0%	3.8%	0.0%
Matanuska-Susitna Borough	2,222	0.0%	2.2%	2.1%	21.9%	1.7%	0.0%	5.6%	8.9%	6.0%	7.4%	0.0%	6.2%	38.1%
Arizona														
Cochise County	3,421	3.9%	22.8%	9.7%	13.1%	5.1%	20.4%	5.0%	5.6%	0.0%	1.7%	7.7%	0.5%	4.5%
Coconino County	6,415	4.2%	0.0%	1.9%	16.7%	12.0%	11.1%	1.8%	13.5%	7.5%	0.5%	2.3%	22.5%	5.9%
Maricopa County	177,731	10.2%	6.4%	10.4%	21.4%	2.7%	7.3%	8.6%	6.4%	2.5%	3.1%	5.5%	10.3%	5.2%
Mohave County	2,650	0.0%	9.1%	11.4%	31.8%	6.0%	6.1%	0.0%	5.8%	2.0%	0.0%	0.0%	27.8%	0.0%
Navajo County	1,059	2.2%	5.9%	21.2%	4.6%	0.0%	2.5%	0.0%	14.4%	10.2%	0.0%	13.0%	20.6%	5.4%
Pima County	36,673	13.7%	4.3%	6.2%	14.7%	4.2%	14.2%	5.3%	10.6%	5.2%	3.9%	6.1%	6.8%	4.9%
Pinal County	4,938	6.6%	7.8%	14.9%	26.4%	1.7%	2.1%	6.9%	5.4%	2.8%	0.5%	6.8%	12.1%	6.0%
Yavapai County	2,922	14.9%	7.1%	0.0%	26.2%	0.0%	0.0%	0.0%	12.7%	9.7%	14.9%	6.5%	3.6%	4.6%
Yuma County	3,776	6.4%	0.0%	23.0%	22.4%	0.0%	1.7%	0.9%	1.0%	0.0%	2.6%	6.7%	34.1%	1.4%
Arkansas														
Benton County	12,346	7.2%	3.5%	11.6%	35.6%	0.0%	6.4%	3.5%	5.3%	3.4%	3.2%	4.7%	11.7%	4.0%
Craighead County	3,073	3.9%	1.8%	16.9%	22.8%	0.0%	2.6%	3.4%	9.5%	0.0%	15.5%	4.5%	16.4%	2.7%
Faulkner County	5,510	1.7%	10.3%	24.3%	19.4%	2.6%	0.0%	6.2%	8.5%	1.4%	1.4%	1.6%	16.5%	6.2%
Garland County	1,349	0.0%	11.5%	3.9%	7.9%	9.6%	2.8%	3.6%	0.0%	4.5%	20.6%	0.0%	33.1%	2.5%
Pulaski County	20,926	6.7%	7.3%	12.3%	20.6%	3.0%	5.5%	7.1%	18.9%	2.9%	4.8%	3.1%	5.2%	2.5%
Saline County	2,970	5.2%	6.6%	17.2%	6.0%	4.3%	0.0%	0.0%	23.9%	2.7%	10.7%	4.4%	19.0%	0.0%
Sebastian County	1,944	7.6%	0.0%	8.7%	8.7%	5.3%	5.9%	0.0%	20.8%	0.0%	10.5%	0.0%	32.4%	0.0%
Washington County	13,055	13.7%	2.0%	4.6%	37.5%	1.9%	5.5%	5.6%	11.0%	4.7%	2.9%	2.0%	3.0%	4.1%
California														
Alameda County	136,767	13.3%	11.8%	6.8%	16.9%	4.7%	12.4%	3.5%	6.9%	5.8%	3.8%	5.4%	2.2%	6.5%
Butte County	7,376	5.7%	3.2%	12.3%	12.3%	1.3%	10.0%	11.0%	11.3%	7.2%	2.9%	6.7%	5.8%	10.4%
Contra Costa County	53,125	7.3%	3.8%	9.5%	18.8%	1.7%	12.9%	4.1%	10.0%	5.9%	8.0%	7.3%	2.1%	8.5%
El Dorado County	6,503	14.4%	9.1%	4.6%	7.2%	3.3%	14.6%	3.8%	7.8%	8.9%	7.6%	5.5%	2.1%	11.0%
Fresno County	25,835	6.2%	4.1%	12.5%	12.5%	0.0%	12.6%	6.8%	9.8%	7.7%	10.0%	8.5%	4.5%	4.8%
Humboldt County	4,115	4.8%	3.5%	8.8%	10.5%	2.8%	10.8%	0.5%	30.0%	2.8%	3.9%	3.5%	8.5%	9.6%
Imperial County	4,339	4.4%	12.8%	2.1%	22.3%	4.1%	3.7%	0.0%	1.7%	0.6%	9.5%	21.9%	10.3%	6.6%
Kern County	18,881	14.8%	6.1%	3.2%	12.3%	5.4%	3.9%	5.6%	8.0%	3.5%	12.3%	5.6%	14.0%	5.1%
Kings County	3,776	7.8%	6.0%	10.0%	25.2%	4.4%	12.4%	0.0%	11.3%	0.0%	5.7%	1.9%	15.3%	0.0%
Los Angeles County	556,456	6.9%	4.6%	7.2%	18.4%	2.0%	12.7%	9.0%	6.5%	5.0%	4.9%	6.9%	2.9%	13.2%
Madera County	3,325	18.0%	7.2%	11.4%	19.7%	0.0%	14.1%	3.6%	4.8%	0.0%	6.1%	15.1%	0.0%	0.0%
Marin County	10,678	1.6%	4.0%	10.9%	19.7%	2.7%	10.7%	2.7%	9.8%	7.3%	4.0%	3.6%	6.2%	16.6%
Merced County	5,039	0.0%	0.0%	10.1%	29.4%	3.1%	5.0%	5.2%	12.3%	1.4%	19.0%	9.2%	5.3%	0.0%
Monterey County	12,249	7.8%	2.9%	9.2%	18.8%	0.8%	16.4%	4.2%	5.1%	3.0%	13.3%	6.3%	2.1%	10.0%
Napa County	6,323	12.1%	2.7%	6.0%	29.6%	0.0%	10.1%	1.3%	12.4%	4.8%	6.7%	2.3%	1.7%	10.2%
Nevada County	2,063	6.0%	9.2%	10.7%	2.2%	0.0%	11.2%	0.0%	11.6%	5.0%	14.6%	10.7%	8.2%	10.5%
Orange County	187,642	10.3%	5.5%	7.8%	22.0%	3.1%	10.2%	5.5%	9.4%	4.7%	5.3%	5.7%	3.2%	7.1%
Placer County	13,457	5.2%	1.0%	8.8%	25.2%	2.0%	10.5%	4.0%	10.9%	10.0%	8.6%	3.1%	3.1%	7.6%
Riverside County	52,515	7.5%	4.1%	9.5%	24.7%	4.5%	10.4%	4.3%	6.5%	4.9%	8.9%	4.9%	5.3%	4.5%
Sacramento County	58,651	9.9%	3.1%	8.0%	16.0%	2.0%	12.5%	6.5%	13.0%	4.5%	7.1%	9.6%	3.4%	4.4%
San Bernardino County	57,889	4.5%	6.4%	14.8%	24.8%	4.3%	8.8%	3.3%	8.3%	3.5%	4.2%	9.0%	2.7%	5.3%
San Diego County	193,987	11.0%	6.5%	8.0%	17.6%	3.8%	11.0%	7.3%	9.8%	3.8%	6.9%	6.3%	3.1%	4.9%
San Francisco County	147,173	10.4%	9.5%	4.8%	21.4%	2.0%	13.9%	6.0%	9.2%	5.1%	3.5%	4.6%	0.9%	8.8%
San Joaquin County	15,091	5.9%	5.7%	10.9%	20.6%	2.4%	10.0%	5.2%	19.2%	2.8%	6.8%	2.5%	4.7%	3.3%
San Luis Obispo County	9,348	13.5%	4.8%	2.0%	9.6%	7.3%	6.2%	2.8%	12.2%	7.7%	13.8%	10.5%	3.9%	5.7%
San Mateo County	57,195	11.2%	11.5%	7.1%	20.1%	2.2%	10.7%	5.3%	9.4%	2.9%	5.3%	4.6%	2.6%	7.0%
Santa Barbara County	20,100	11.9%	7.2%	4.6%	13.6%	7.0%	12.9%	5.2%	9.4%	5.6%	7.9%	6.3%	1.2%	7.1%
Santa Clara County	161,144	23.0%	16.8%	5.7%	16.2%	2.6%	8.3%	4.6%	7.1%	4.1%	1.9%	5.2%	1.6%	3.0%
Santa Cruz County	13,437	12.1%	1.1%	7.6%	9.0%	3.4%	14.9%	2.8%	16.4%	6.5%	5.5%	8.5%	4.5%	7.7%
Shasta County	6,504	0.0%	3.3%	3.4%	16.6%	0.0%	4.5%	11.3%	15.9%	3.5%	25.9%	6.0%	4.3%	5.3%
Solano County	14,249	10.9%	1.1%	10.9%	17.7%	1.1%	13.2%	5.3%	9.8%	5.6%	8.3%	8.8%	2.6%	4.5%
Sonoma County	17,746	10.9%	8.6%	5.9%	19.3%	2.6%	12.5%	3.9%	9.6%	3.1%	7.0%	10.2%	1.0%	5.3%
Stanislaus County	11,849	5.5%	7.2%	16.0%	15.3%	0.7%	9.6%	4.2%	12.8%	5.8%	5.1%	9.3%	2.7%	5.9%
Sutter County	1,933	0.0%	10.8%	17.3%	15.2%	0.0%	5.2%	0.0%	19.2%	15.5%	9.6%	2.3%	5.0%	0.0%
Tulare County	10,722	2.1%	6.1%	13.5%	25.1%	4.9%	6.2%	6.0%	10.2%	0.0%	5.5%	8.0%	9.9%	2.3%

Table F-2: Counties—Educational Field of Study—*Continued*

	Total Millennial Population with Bachelor's or Higher	Percent of the Population 18 to 33 by Field of Study												
		Engineering	Computers and Math	Science and Engineering Related	Business	Physical Science	Social Science	Communications	Biological Sciences	Literature	Liberal Arts	Psychology	Education	Visual and Performing Arts
California—Cont.														
Ventura County	34,708	5.0%	7.8%	11.3%	18.4%	1.5%	8.4%	7.0%	11.5%	5.2%	5.4%	8.2%	6.1%	4.1%
Yolo County	16,821	5.3%	5.7%	8.0%	12.6%	8.8%	14.0%	0.7%	26.3%	4.8%	2.9%	6.0%	2.8%	2.1%
Colorado														
Adams County	21,929	8.5%	3.9%	13.1%	19.6%	1.8%	14.0%	4.4%	7.0%	1.9%	6.6%	5.8%	4.6%	8.9%
Arapahoe County	35,222	8.1%	5.0%	10.5%	23.4%	4.9%	8.3%	4.1%	10.9%	3.1%	3.2%	7.1%	7.1%	4.5%
Boulder County	30,162	9.0%	7.7%	7.7%	15.4%	5.9%	4.3%	3.6%	10.4%	8.0%	4.0%	12.2%	5.5%	6.5%
Denver County	79,952	7.7%	3.4%	8.2%	20.9%	2.0%	11.7%	9.1%	8.0%	4.0%	5.3%	6.9%	3.6%	9.1%
Douglas County	16,496	10.6%	4.4%	7.3%	26.4%	2.2%	7.7%	2.6%	7.1%	2.6%	2.8%	5.2%	14.9%	6.2%
El Paso County	31,416	12.1%	4.8%	11.6%	13.5%	6.3%	10.7%	4.9%	8.0%	4.1%	4.3%	10.3%	7.5%	1.8%
Jefferson County	36,278	14.2%	6.5%	8.7%	18.7%	4.7%	9.0%	3.9%	9.0%	2.5%	3.3%	8.4%	4.5%	6.6%
Larimer County	24,167	8.1%	4.7%	8.3%	12.7%	9.7%	10.1%	3.0%	14.9%	6.0%	2.9%	6.1%	7.1%	6.4%
Mesa County	3,767	0.0%	4.1%	11.4%	15.9%	2.4%	12.0%	4.6%	7.4%	2.4%	0.0%	22.0%	6.9%	10.7%
Pueblo County	3,853	3.8%	11.1%	12.5%	32.9%	0.0%	8.1%	3.3%	3.9%	8.1%	4.7%	1.5%	5.1%	5.1%
Weld County	8,409	3.3%	4.1%	8.7%	22.7%	1.3%	5.9%	7.6%	10.7%	7.2%	1.9%	11.8%	11.7%	3.1%
Connecticut														
Fairfield County	57,369	6.4%	3.5%	8.1%	25.6%	3.0%	8.7%	8.8%	5.0%	6.3%	5.4%	8.0%	6.4%	4.9%
Hartford County	55,253	9.9%	4.3%	10.3%	19.9%	1.0%	8.1%	8.2%	7.1%	3.3%	5.8%	8.4%	7.4%	6.0%
Litchfield County	7,727	7.6%	5.7%	12.1%	20.4%	0.0%	4.2%	2.9%	4.4%	8.0%	8.7%	5.5%	7.5%	12.7%
Middlesex County	8,463	4.3%	4.5%	14.4%	21.3%	10.9%	5.5%	3.4%	11.5%	6.0%	1.6%	4.8%	7.5%	4.2%
New Haven County	47,245	9.7%	7.4%	7.9%	17.7%	2.0%	10.7%	4.9%	8.3%	5.0%	9.3%	5.1%	4.3%	7.7%
New London County	13,089	15.6%	5.3%	6.0%	11.0%	1.6%	10.7%	2.1%	10.7%	5.0%	4.2%	12.1%	10.7%	4.8%
Tolland County	11,195	17.6%	6.5%	6.0%	9.9%	2.0%	5.2%	7.4%	3.1%	9.9%	0.0%	10.0%	14.1%	8.2%
Windham County	3,657	10.9%	2.9%	6.9%	2.7%	5.4%	5.5%	21.7%	12.9%	3.6%	2.1%	7.2%	18.0%	0.0%
Delaware														
Kent County	4,262	0.0%	5.2%	7.6%	19.4%	7.2%	7.5%	0.0%	6.8%	0.0%	2.6%	8.9%	33.7%	1.0%
New Castle County	33,541	12.6%	11.0%	10.5%	23.3%	4.1%	7.1%	4.3%	6.5%	4.3%	2.1%	4.7%	6.8%	2.5%
Sussex County	3,384	0.0%	0.0%	7.3%	18.5%	12.5%	0.0%	0.0%	20.7%	0.0%	5.2%	17.9%	14.2%	3.8%
Florida														
Alachua County	23,134	13.6%	6.4%	12.1%	10.1%	3.1%	9.3%	2.7%	24.3%	2.9%	2.3%	3.9%	3.8%	5.4%
Bay County	4,582	17.5%	5.1%	10.6%	21.3%	1.7%	1.8%	2.9%	10.1%	0.0%	3.6%	13.5%	7.6%	4.3%
Brevard County	16,921	12.5%	7.0%	11.2%	27.5%	5.3%	2.5%	2.7%	5.2%	2.8%	1.1%	9.7%	11.1%	1.3%
Broward County	82,441	5.7%	5.7%	11.6%	30.8%	2.4%	5.4%	6.3%	6.9%	2.7%	1.3%	10.6%	6.3%	4.3%
Charlotte County	1,126	0.0%	0.0%	32.4%	6.9%	0.0%	9.0%	0.0%	7.4%	7.6%	0.0%	5.2%	31.5%	0.0%
Citrus County	1,359	0.0%	4.6%	18.4%	18.0%	0.0%	6.5%	9.4%	34.4%	0.0%	0.0%	8.7%	0.0%	0.0%
Clay County	5,291	15.0%	2.0%	5.1%	14.2%	2.9%	2.4%	0.0%	13.5%	4.4%	10.9%	24.8%	0.0%	5.0%
Collier County	10,972	6.0%	0.9%	7.1%	25.7%	8.0%	12.4%	8.4%	10.4%	0.0%	5.0%	0.5%	7.4%	8.2%
Duval County	44,851	9.2%	4.5%	12.9%	25.4%	1.9%	7.8%	8.4%	5.4%	1.6%	3.9%	4.9%	9.2%	4.9%
Escambia County	12,485	1.7%	8.6%	12.3%	23.4%	2.5%	6.1%	9.5%	11.1%	1.6%	5.2%	3.9%	12.1%	1.9%
Flagler County	2,454	0.0%	11.7%	19.4%	18.5%	0.0%	5.8%	0.0%	21.8%	5.5%	0.0%	10.0%	0.0%	7.3%
Hernando County	2,008	0.0%	5.1%	37.9%	29.7%	0.0%	0.0%	0.0%	7.0%	0.0%	4.3%	0.0%	2.7%	13.3%
Highlands County	711	0.0%	0.0%	0.0%	6.6%	0.0%	9.1%	0.0%	40.6%	0.0%	0.0%	7.7%	35.9%	0.0%
Hillsborough County	72,022	3.5%	4.5%	11.6%	24.2%	3.3%	10.2%	7.5%	6.6%	3.1%	5.3%	10.1%	6.9%	3.2%
Indian River County	1,664	20.3%	0.0%	10.3%	21.5%	3.1%	8.9%	1.7%	4.9%	0.0%	8.3%	10.5%	7.5%	3.0%
Lake County	8,136	6.1%	5.3%	9.6%	19.1%	0.0%	2.9%	8.4%	7.5%	0.0%	0.8%	12.1%	15.7%	12.4%
Lee County	13,704	2.6%	1.6%	13.2%	25.4%	2.6%	6.3%	5.6%	10.3%	0.0%	7.1%	6.7%	10.5%	8.1%
Leon County	22,402	4.8%	4.0%	8.4%	18.3%	4.6%	15.3%	2.7%	8.0%	8.5%	4.2%	7.1%	5.8%	8.3%
Manatee County	6,216	3.0%	1.6%	13.3%	18.8%	1.8%	17.4%	2.1%	8.9%	7.8%	2.8%	3.2%	8.6%	10.6%
Marion County	7,022	12.7%	0.6%	3.8%	41.5%	1.2%	0.7%	1.9%	26.0%	0.0%	0.0%	1.5%	10.1%	0.0%
Martin County	3,248	5.7%	0.0%	6.7%	26.5%	0.0%	0.0%	8.2%	3.8%	6.7%	3.7%	20.6%	5.7%	12.5%
Miami-Dade County	119,181	8.1%	3.6%	11.6%	26.1%	2.0%	7.4%	5.9%	7.9%	3.6%	4.0%	7.5%	7.5%	4.8%
Okaloosa County	8,197	22.4%	3.5%	14.5%	24.7%	3.2%	9.2%	4.6%	5.3%	1.6%	2.1%	0.3%	5.6%	3.1%
Orange County	80,917	5.7%	5.5%	13.3%	34.3%	1.7%	6.9%	7.0%	5.0%	2.2%	2.1%	4.8%	5.3%	6.1%
Osceola County	7,960	13.1%	7.3%	17.9%	20.0%	0.0%	2.9%	6.4%	16.1%	9.6%	0.0%	1.1%	4.0%	1.5%
Palm Beach County	54,052	5.4%	4.4%	10.9%	33.6%	1.4%	8.2%	5.7%	10.6%	2.5%	4.3%	7.0%	3.9%	2.4%
Pasco County	14,741	3.0%	9.2%	16.6%	20.1%	2.3%	10.4%	3.2%	5.6%	0.8%	6.9%	6.9%	10.7%	4.3%
Pinellas County	34,827	4.9%	6.2%	12.3%	21.9%	2.0%	9.2%	5.5%	9.7%	3.0%	3.9%	7.9%	7.0%	6.4%
Polk County	15,224	6.9%	2.6%	7.3%	23.6%	2.0%	5.7%	1.4%	7.6%	0.5%	6.1%	9.9%	18.2%	8.3%
Santa Rosa County	11,536	9.3%	3.3%	26.4%	14.4%	5.3%	3.0%	7.3%	11.4%	0.9%	6.1%	4.3%	5.4%	3.0%
Sarasota County	3,904	0.0%	1.0%	14.5%	12.6%	0.0%	13.9%	0.0%	6.5%	2.7%	21.8%	7.2%	14.9%	4.8%
Seminole County	6,991	9.5%	1.1%	9.4%	20.4%	1.7%	15.1%	9.8%	6.5%	0.0%	5.2%	1.2%	20.1%	0.0%
St. Johns County	10,439	3.9%	6.4%	12.2%	22.3%	7.6%	8.8%	5.2%	4.2%	4.5%	4.0%	4.0%	13.0%	3.9%
St. Lucie County	18,262	4.9%	5.7%	12.6%	27.7%	0.6%	5.8%	8.6%	6.0%	3.9%	6.7%	5.0%	7.3%	5.2%
Sumter County	728	0.0%	0.0%	34.3%	26.8%	0.0%	6.5%	16.8%	15.7%	0.0%	0.0%	0.0%	0.0%	0.0%
Volusia County	12,882	7.2%	2.5%	11.0%	27.7%	4.4%	5.3%	5.6%	8.5%	2.7%	5.0%	9.1%	6.5%	4.5%
Georgia														
Bartow County	2,594	6.3%	0.0%	13.1%	20.4%	9.5%	15.4%	3.9%	0.0%	0.0%	5.3%	0.0%	16.4%	9.8%
Bibb County	6,984	4.8%	2.8%	14.8%	25.7%	9.1%	5.3%	8.0%	11.2%	5.3%	9.9%	5.4%	3.6%	2.8%
Carroll County	3,964	5.2%	0.0%	4.2%	15.3%	0.3%	15.1%	9.3%	2.8%	0.0%	8.6%	0.0%	31.5%	7.7%
Chatham County	14,432	10.3%	4.6%	9.6%	22.5%	2.8%	4.9%	9.1%	6.7%	1.6%	3.8%	2.3%	10.9%	11.0%
Cherokee County	10,667	2.2%	4.2%	13.6%	15.1%	1.4%	6.1%	7.0%	8.0%	3.3%	6.9%	4.8%	12.1%	15.3%
Clarke County	12,114	4.5%	6.0%	7.5%	10.3%	6.1%	8.8%	6.0%	16.5%	9.1%	2.6%	8.7%	8.6%	5.4%
Clayton County	7,183	4.6%	12.6%	10.5%	17.0%	0.0%	12.2%	4.0%	8.4%	7.4%	0.9%	8.3%	9.9%	4.2%
Cobb County	47,230	11.0%	7.5%	6.4%	25.7%	5.0%	10.5%	7.1%	6.5%	2.2%	2.1%	2.5%	6.8%	6.7%
Columbia County	7,008	1.8%	1.6%	13.9%	19.5%	11.7%	5.7%	3.6%	6.4%	1.2%	4.4%	8.4%	20.2%	1.6%
Coweta County	4,653	6.6%	5.3%	6.8%	31.3%	2.7%	2.1%	2.8%	0.0%	1.0%	5.9%	8.9%	3.5%	23.2%

Table F-2: Counties—Educational Field of Study—*Continued*

	Total Millennial Population with Bachelor's or Higher	Percent of the Population 18 to 33 by Field of Study												
		Engineering	Computers and Math	Science and Engineering Related	Business	Physical Science	Social Science	Communications	Biological Sciences	Literature	Liberal Arts	Psychology	Education	Visual and Performing Arts
Georgia—Cont.														
DeKalb County	51,923	8.3%	8.6%	8.5%	24.0%	1.9%	6.8%	8.2%	6.3%	5.2%	3.5%	5.0%	7.1%	6.7%
Dougherty County	1,927	0.0%	0.0%	6.0%	0.0%	0.0%	7.3%	6.2%	10.3%	0.0%	5.9%	12.1%	16.3%	35.8%
Douglas County	6,217	0.0%	0.0%	19.6%	28.6%	1.0%	10.2%	9.5%	6.5%	5.9%	5.4%	3.9%	0.9%	8.5%
Fayette County	3,341	9.1%	4.0%	14.4%	30.9%	1.9%	2.6%	0.0%	4.9%	3.1%	4.7%	9.5%	7.6%	7.1%
Floyd County	2,701	1.3%	10.3%	14.1%	24.4%	0.0%	4.7%	3.7%	3.3%	0.0%	6.0%	0.0%	28.4%	3.9%
Forsyth County	10,679	15.0%	6.1%	6.4%	23.5%	4.2%	5.5%	7.5%	2.8%	2.8%	1.6%	8.4%	11.9%	4.3%
Fulton County	90,197	11.7%	7.2%	9.0%	24.9%	3.1%	7.3%	6.1%	6.0%	2.8%	2.6%	7.1%	6.1%	6.2%
Gwinnett County	41,712	9.1%	4.3%	10.8%	26.5%	2.2%	6.2%	7.5%	7.0%	4.8%	5.0%	4.8%	7.2%	4.7%
Hall County	3,459	6.2%	1.4%	7.3%	11.1%	0.0%	3.1%	10.4%	3.3%	0.0%	4.6%	8.5%	39.8%	4.2%
Henry County	7,781	0.0%	6.2%	19.6%	20.5%	0.0%	1.6%	0.0%	7.2%	1.7%	5.1%	5.4%	21.4%	11.3%
Houston County	4,504	3.6%	3.8%	13.2%	17.9%	0.0%	2.5%	3.8%	12.2%	4.5%	2.8%	0.0%	29.6%	6.0%
Lowndes County	4,786	5.4%	8.0%	5.3%	21.2%	2.8%	10.9%	3.4%	11.0%	0.0%	2.3%	4.5%	25.3%	0.0%
Muscogee County	9,301	17.1%	3.5%	18.5%	19.6%	1.2%	14.4%	4.2%	4.2%	1.7%	2.9%	5.5%	3.4%	3.8%
Newton County	2,426	0.0%	0.0%	10.6%	22.9%	0.0%	2.3%	14.6%	0.0%	0.0%	0.0%	4.7%	32.3%	12.8%
Paulding County	3,447	0.3%	7.2%	29.4%	7.1%	0.0%	5.6%	12.4%	9.4%	2.4%	5.2%	1.9%	13.7%	5.3%
Richmond County	7,763	13.3%	3.2%	11.2%	17.6%	0.7%	3.9%	10.9%	12.0%	5.6%	2.2%	5.6%	5.8%	8.1%
Whitfield County	2,469	0.0%	9.5%	9.2%	20.4%	8.3%	3.3%	19.6%	2.3%	9.4%	0.0%	0.0%	18.0%	0.0%
Hawaii														
Hawaii County	6,720	4.8%	8.5%	10.3%	18.5%	0.4%	12.7%	6.8%	2.1%	1.9%	5.6%	12.7%	12.4%	3.3%
Honolulu County	49,408	7.8%	4.7%	7.0%	22.1%	1.0%	11.4%	3.7%	8.4%	5.6%	5.3%	8.9%	7.6%	5.7%
Maui County	6,006	0.8%	10.9%	28.5%	19.6%	2.3%	4.1%	2.1%	15.6%	2.8%	3.3%	3.8%	6.1%	0.0%
Idaho														
Ada County	18,963	7.9%	4.9%	11.8%	19.1%	0.4%	4.8%	9.3%	6.8%	4.1%	10.0%	6.3%	8.8%	5.7%
Bonneville County	3,422	7.0%	0.0%	25.1%	14.2%	2.3%	0.0%	0.8%	13.5%	2.2%	2.4%	0.0%	29.4%	3.3%
Canyon County	3,160	10.6%	0.0%	22.5%	26.0%	0.0%	0.0%	4.2%	1.1%	11.2%	1.3%	9.9%	10.4%	2.8%
Kootenai County	3,675	7.0%	0.0%	8.5%	12.2%	0.0%	0.0%	4.0%	21.4%	0.0%	14.7%	17.3%	4.4%	10.4%
Illinois														
Champaign County	18,535	17.8%	6.0%	5.0%	16.0%	5.5%	7.7%	5.5%	17.2%	6.9%	1.2%	4.5%	3.3%	3.2%
Cook County	409,498	7.5%	6.0%	7.8%	24.2%	2.5%	9.7%	7.6%	7.7%	4.3%	3.5%	6.8%	5.3%	7.1%
DeKalb County	7,727	2.3%	3.7%	12.5%	17.6%	1.6%	12.6%	1.7%	2.7%	8.0%	0.0%	23.0%	8.8%	4.9%
DuPage County	59,374	8.2%	5.9%	11.0%	23.6%	2.3%	5.1%	8.7%	7.6%	3.6%	3.9%	8.1%	7.1%	4.9%
Kane County	19,762	3.5%	4.5%	18.3%	21.3%	4.5%	5.6%	9.5%	3.9%	3.3%	1.9%	3.1%	12.3%	8.4%
Kankakee County	3,430	3.1%	20.8%	19.1%	11.4%	0.0%	0.0%	17.1%	0.7%	3.6%	0.0%	9.6%	14.3%	0.1%
Kendall County	5,246	3.2%	0.0%	7.0%	1.0%	1.6%	3.8%	0.0%	1.2%	1.4%	0.0%	19.1%	54.0%	7.6%
Lake County	33,774	7.7%	6.8%	9.9%	19.2%	2.9%	6.6%	7.2%	12.4%	5.6%	6.4%	3.7%	7.0%	4.5%
LaSalle County	2,192	18.6%	5.7%	5.5%	17.0%	9.5%	14.7%	2.3%	9.2%	1.7%	0.0%	0.8%	10.2%	4.7%
Macon County	11,746	6.4%	3.9%	13.6%	18.4%	2.6%	10.5%	9.0%	3.3%	5.2%	4.3%	7.7%	10.7%	4.4%
Madison County	10,916	4.9%	13.8%	9.1%	23.2%	1.7%	8.8%	7.3%	2.9%	4.2%	3.8%	6.5%	5.4%	8.4%
McHenry County	2,191	12.4%	4.8%	0.0%	22.1%	0.0%	9.8%	12.9%	2.9%	4.5%	0.0%	0.0%	24.0%	6.6%
McLean County	9,244	11.7%	9.2%	14.0%	19.0%	5.1%	4.2%	4.8%	8.9%	0.0%	3.9%	5.7%	12.8%	0.6%
Peoria County	11,620	10.4%	7.7%	19.5%	16.3%	4.7%	0.7%	5.0%	8.3%	2.8%	3.0%	6.9%	8.5%	6.3%
Rock Island County	4,550	10.5%	2.5%	4.1%	42.4%	6.1%	1.6%	3.9%	8.6%	3.1%	0.0%	7.1%	10.2%	0.0%
Sangamon County	8,350	0.6%	20.2%	8.9%	17.9%	3.3%	1.9%	14.4%	4.0%	2.7%	1.6%	10.1%	10.9%	3.5%
St. Clair County	10,365	14.6%	5.3%	12.1%	15.6%	0.8%	2.2%	3.8%	11.6%	4.7%	8.4%	7.9%	11.2%	1.8%
Tazewell County	5,691	2.7%	1.3%	20.6%	24.2%	0.0%	3.9%	3.2%	8.9%	2.1%	3.6%	5.5%	7.3%	16.6%
Will County	29,323	4.3%	8.0%	16.9%	18.4%	3.2%	4.8%	5.4%	7.5%	1.6%	2.7%	7.3%	14.6%	5.1%
Winnebago County	10,048	11.0%	0.4%	27.7%	9.8%	1.3%	4.1%	3.3%	11.7%	3.2%	0.4%	2.3%	15.6%	9.2%
Indiana														
Allen County	15,247	9.3%	0.3%	13.8%	26.6%	2.6%	7.8%	5.5%	6.2%	1.6%	3.9%	4.5%	13.9%	4.0%
Clark County	3,250	7.2%	3.0%	20.2%	26.2%	5.0%	3.9%	0.0%	9.6%	5.3%	5.9%	2.6%	5.1%	6.0%
Delaware County	2,713	0.0%	5.1%	21.6%	2.7%	4.7%	8.4%	6.2%	21.4%	4.7%	5.8%	2.5%	14.7%	2.2%
Elkhart County	4,836	7.5%	9.2%	1.9%	26.0%	0.9%	4.6%	0.0%	0.0%	2.6%	16.6%	7.8%	20.5%	2.3%
Hamilton County	19,510	4.9%	4.5%	10.0%	29.0%	2.0%	2.6%	6.8%	7.9%	4.7%	3.0%	4.2%	12.8%	7.5%
Hendricks County	8,325	4.4%	9.4%	27.7%	14.7%	0.0%	3.2%	3.9%	4.4%	3.9%	5.4%	4.8%	17.9%	0.5%
Johnson County	7,346	13.3%	7.8%	21.3%	12.9%	0.0%	13.5%	2.7%	0.0%	0.0%	7.1%	4.1%	8.8%	8.5%
Lake County	14,452	5.4%	1.8%	16.9%	24.8%	3.8%	6.2%	7.9%	7.3%	4.8%	4.7%	4.2%	10.9%	1.4%
LaPorte County	1,591	0.0%	4.7%	14.5%	26.8%	0.0%	8.8%	9.7%	13.1%	0.0%	4.8%	0.0%	17.7%	0.0%
Madison County	2,334	4.8%	3.9%	15.6%	19.5%	0.0%	3.0%	0.0%	11.7%	0.0%	5.9%	5.6%	28.1%	1.9%
Marion County	56,022	5.4%	6.3%	10.9%	19.5%	3.1%	8.4%	7.2%	6.9%	3.8%	9.7%	4.6%	10.9%	3.4%
Monroe County	13,703	3.6%	5.2%	2.8%	22.4%	5.9%	7.1%	3.2%	6.6%	3.3%	8.3%	1.5%	11.7%	18.2%
Porter County	5,872	6.8%	0.0%	23.3%	11.0%	1.1%	6.0%	2.6%	2.3%	5.6%	8.6%	11.1%	11.9%	9.7%
St. Joseph County	12,411	7.7%	4.8%	9.7%	23.4%	2.4%	9.7%	5.8%	3.9%	2.4%	10.5%	3.5%	9.1%	7.2%
Tippecanoe County	16,874	17.8%	2.8%	7.7%	18.6%	11.3%	5.2%	1.1%	13.9%	5.9%	2.5%	1.6%	7.1%	4.6%
Vanderburgh County	9,222	4.0%	2.6%	16.3%	13.8%	11.0%	1.3%	22.9%	5.2%	1.4%	4.2%	0.0%	11.5%	5.8%
Vigo County	4,723	22.5%	10.1%	12.4%	7.7%	3.7%	3.4%	0.0%	4.6%	0.8%	3.6%	10.3%	19.1%	1.7%
Iowa														
Black Hawk County	6,500	12.3%	0.0%	13.3%	20.6%	0.0%	1.3%	5.1%	13.9%	1.9%	14.8%	5.9%	9.8%	1.1%
Dubuque County	4,218	10.1%	2.1%	6.1%	10.5%	0.0%	2.8%	4.6%	4.3%	0.0%	6.6%	15.8%	33.5%	3.4%
Johnson County	14,764	0.8%	4.9%	6.9%	11.8%	6.3%	8.3%	2.3%	21.2%	8.9%	5.2%	10.5%	5.7%	7.1%
Linn County	12,613	4.9%	12.2%	9.1%	28.7%	0.0%	1.7%	3.3%	14.4%	2.6%	5.1%	9.2%	8.4%	0.4%
Polk County	31,909	6.9%	3.6%	4.3%	27.6%	1.2%	8.3%	5.6%	14.7%	2.0%	6.9%	4.9%	9.0%	5.2%
Pottawattamie County	2,924	5.6%	0.0%	28.4%	42.6%	0.0%	0.0%	2.5%	2.2%	0.0%	0.0%	0.0%	15.4%	3.3%
Scott County	7,718	8.4%	4.2%	7.0%	29.3%	2.5%	7.9%	0.0%	13.1%	0.0%	6.8%	4.7%	13.5%	2.5%
Story County	7,585	25.2%	1.2%	4.7%	13.2%	8.9%	7.4%	4.8%	16.8%	7.0%	1.9%	4.5%	2.9%	1.5%
Woodbury County	2,562	0.0%	0.0%	1.4%	9.9%	1.6%	2.0%	0.0%	11.0%	6.5%	14.7%	0.0%	37.9%	15.1%

Table F-2: Counties—Educational Field of Study—*Continued*

	Total Millennial Population with Bachelor's or Higher	Percent of the Population 18 to 33 by Field of Study												
		Engineering	Computers and Math	Science and Engineering Related	Business	Physical Science	Social Science	Communications	Biological Sciences	Literature	Liberal Arts	Psychology	Education	Visual and Performing Arts
Kansas														
Douglas County	9,458	19.4%	4.1%	3.4%	11.4%	7.0%	2.4%	1.9%	10.1%	9.9%	5.9%	13.8%	6.3%	4.5%
Johnson County	47,279	9.8%	8.2%	11.1%	21.3%	1.5%	6.1%	4.6%	10.0%	4.1%	2.8%	4.9%	9.6%	5.9%
Sedgwick County	23,831	9.4%	5.4%	15.3%	20.7%	1.0%	6.2%	3.8%	12.7%	0.2%	4.4%	5.4%	8.5%	7.1%
Shawnee County	6,825	1.6%	7.0%	10.8%	21.0%	1.9%	13.3%	6.0%	1.7%	1.8%	6.0%	9.2%	14.4%	5.3%
Wyandotte County	5,463	3.4%	10.0%	5.8%	20.4%	0.0%	3.5%	7.3%	12.1%	2.7%	4.8%	4.5%	14.4%	11.1%
Kentucky														
Boone County	2,735	10.0%	0.0%	13.1%	41.2%	0.0%	0.0%	0.0%	0.0%	14.1%	0.0%	0.0%	19.0%	2.5%
Campbell County	5,465	14.9%	5.7%	19.1%	26.5%	0.0%	8.7%	1.9%	1.7%	6.2%	1.0%	2.4%	10.7%	1.4%
Daviess County	2,650	4.6%	2.2%	12.9%	15.9%	0.0%	0.0%	7.1%	15.3%	0.0%	6.6%	11.9%	18.5%	5.0%
Fayette County	24,789	7.4%	6.4%	10.9%	15.1%	4.0%	10.9%	8.2%	14.8%	5.5%	3.6%	4.9%	5.6%	2.7%
Hardin County	2,820	12.3%	0.0%	24.5%	18.5%	0.0%	2.6%	0.0%	0.0%	2.6%	0.0%	22.8%	16.8%	0.0%
Jefferson County	42,675	6.5%	4.5%	9.8%	22.2%	2.5%	6.8%	8.6%	9.5%	4.4%	8.5%	6.2%	8.1%	2.3%
Kenton County	8,338	1.8%	4.3%	5.3%	30.5%	4.4%	10.5%	4.6%	5.5%	3.7%	6.4%	1.7%	11.9%	9.5%
Warren County	8,059	3.8%	0.0%	6.8%	19.9%	1.1%	3.4%	11.8%	17.1%	7.2%	5.0%	10.3%	11.5%	2.1%
Louisiana														
Ascension Parish	5,187	18.5%	1.7%	3.1%	29.7%	5.8%	9.7%	0.0%	9.8%	1.8%	10.3%	2.0%	7.7%	0.0%
Bossier Parish	5,361	10.2%	11.4%	21.8%	11.1%	3.0%	2.2%	13.1%	4.7%	1.4%	4.0%	3.6%	10.2%	3.3%
Caddo Parish	6,685	5.0%	4.7%	5.9%	24.0%	1.6%	4.6%	0.0%	15.0%	1.3%	11.1%	13.3%	2.5%	11.0%
Calcasieu Parish	5,631	8.4%	1.8%	12.1%	6.9%	4.6%	5.3%	3.0%	18.1%	2.2%	19.2%	0.0%	18.6%	0.0%
East Baton Rouge Parish	28,540	17.1%	2.4%	11.3%	11.8%	1.9%	5.1%	5.2%	13.2%	3.6%	5.5%	6.2%	9.5%	7.2%
Jefferson Parish	18,017	4.9%	1.1%	12.9%	27.3%	3.7%	5.6%	4.4%	13.9%	1.6%	5.4%	5.8%	8.4%	5.0%
Lafayette Parish	14,718	7.6%	2.7%	14.6%	15.8%	7.0%	0.8%	3.5%	14.1%	2.8%	13.7%	1.5%	13.2%	2.8%
Lafourche Parish	2,199	0.0%	4.7%	20.1%	8.4%	0.0%	0.0%	5.2%	8.2%	0.0%	25.7%	0.0%	13.4%	14.3%
Livingston Parish	7,373	1.6%	0.0%	5.1%	13.7%	0.0%	3.4%	1.8%	9.8%	19.2%	8.8%	2.5%	33.2%	0.9%
Orleans Parish	31,904	7.4%	2.4%	8.5%	15.7%	4.8%	11.3%	7.9%	9.7%	5.7%	7.6%	8.1%	3.0%	7.7%
Ouachita Parish	6,772	13.0%	3.6%	9.0%	21.6%	0.0%	8.1%	1.6%	12.1%	4.6%	7.6%	4.4%	8.1%	6.3%
Rapides Parish	3,231	9.9%	0.0%	6.8%	25.6%	2.7%	15.7%	0.0%	5.8%	1.6%	7.2%	4.1%	1.2%	19.3%
St. Tammany Parish	9,001	6.7%	2.1%	18.6%	20.2%	1.7%	1.2%	8.0%	4.0%	2.4%	11.5%	4.8%	7.6%	11.4%
Tangipahoa Parish	1,991	0.0%	0.0%	26.1%	18.3%	0.0%	5.6%	6.3%	0.0%	3.1%	18.3%	1.4%	14.7%	6.2%
Terrebonne Parish	3,510	10.4%	8.3%	23.2%	14.7%	0.0%	0.0%	0.0%	0.0%	0.0%	14.2%	5.8%	2.4%	21.1%
Maine														
Androscoggin County	2,447	7.7%	5.6%	10.8%	8.2%	0.0%	10.7%	0.0%	32.0%	0.0%	0.0%	11.9%	13.0%	0.0%
Cumberland County	16,793	6.0%	2.7%	10.2%	16.8%	2.7%	9.6%	13.3%	8.4%	2.5%	1.1%	10.3%	6.7%	9.6%
Kennebec County	3,435	7.9%	12.8%	8.4%	13.9%	0.0%	15.6%	0.0%	17.6%	3.3%	2.4%	8.7%	7.9%	1.5%
Penobscot County	5,202	14.5%	4.2%	8.6%	15.8%	5.2%	4.8%	1.8%	15.9%	2.9%	0.0%	9.7%	9.3%	7.3%
York County	7,488	13.1%	0.0%	6.1%	5.4%	8.5%	11.5%	6.0%	12.6%	0.0%	0.0%	16.3%	18.7%	1.8%
Maryland														
Anne Arundel County	31,997	12.9%	10.5%	4.8%	19.6%	2.5%	13.7%	7.2%	4.5%	3.6%	7.0%	7.5%	1.8%	4.4%
Baltimore County	51,813	10.7%	8.2%	10.7%	20.9%	2.5%	7.5%	6.5%	6.0%	1.8%	5.7%	4.4%	9.9%	5.1%
Carroll County	7,019	10.8%	6.7%	14.4%	15.6%	2.9%	3.9%	6.2%	17.5%	3.0%	1.8%	0.0%	13.0%	4.3%
Cecil County	3,319	12.4%	6.8%	0.0%	31.4%	0.0%	8.6%	0.0%	8.3%	0.0%	6.8%	3.3%	16.9%	5.5%
Charles County	6,821	12.9%	17.9%	4.2%	15.5%	0.0%	7.8%	6.5%	1.4%	11.5%	3.2%	2.5%	8.4%	8.2%
Frederick County	15,158	5.1%	8.9%	5.4%	23.9%	0.6%	8.8%	8.2%	9.3%	3.0%	3.7%	8.5%	10.7%	3.8%
Harford County	11,207	7.7%	6.3%	9.9%	19.0%	3.4%	10.1%	4.5%	8.6%	5.5%	5.4%	4.2%	12.5%	2.8%
Howard County	22,639	17.2%	12.6%	8.2%	15.5%	0.4%	5.9%	6.0%	11.2%	3.0%	1.3%	9.0%	4.8%	5.0%
Montgomery County	75,713	5.6%	6.0%	7.2%	23.7%	1.5%	16.3%	5.4%	8.8%	5.2%	4.7%	6.9%	4.7%	3.9%
Prince George's County	45,533	8.8%	8.4%	8.1%	18.8%	2.5%	17.1%	5.6%	10.0%	2.1%	2.3%	6.0%	5.7%	4.5%
St. Mary's County	4,977	26.0%	10.6%	1.8%	15.2%	3.3%	13.6%	2.1%	6.7%	1.4%	4.9%	3.7%	5.3%	5.4%
Washington County	4,431	1.9%	8.7%	8.5%	19.7%	2.9%	4.4%	11.4%	3.7%	3.5%	7.4%	8.4%	13.5%	6.1%
Wicomico County	3,197	0.0%	8.0%	7.3%	13.2%	6.9%	1.1%	2.2%	32.6%	3.9%	1.7%	0.0%	17.0%	6.3%
Massachusetts														
Barnstable County	5,479	4.8%	3.3%	12.1%	31.2%	1.2%	7.2%	2.6%	9.3%	3.6%	7.5%	7.9%	4.7%	4.5%
Berkshire County	3,198	10.3%	1.7%	13.5%	14.5%	0.8%	4.9%	7.8%	5.5%	3.2%	18.6%	12.3%	0.8%	6.2%
Bristol County	21,885	9.3%	5.0%	6.3%	29.4%	2.2%	8.4%	4.7%	6.4%	1.3%	3.5%	10.0%	8.5%	5.1%
Essex County	40,863	5.0%	5.3%	8.0%	22.6%	2.0%	6.8%	6.0%	9.6%	6.2%	6.2%	10.0%	5.1%	7.2%
Hampden County	19,499	6.1%	3.5%	10.0%	14.0%	2.7%	7.5%	7.4%	7.9%	3.0%	6.3%	16.9%	4.9%	9.7%
Hampshire County	10,443	4.3%	0.5%	6.8%	12.4%	3.9%	12.1%	3.5%	9.4%	9.6%	8.0%	13.4%	5.0%	11.1%
Middlesex County	167,765	12.9%	6.1%	8.3%	19.1%	4.1%	9.4%	4.9%	8.3%	5.8%	4.3%	7.3%	3.8%	5.8%
Norfolk County	54,364	10.2%	5.8%	8.0%	23.4%	1.6%	10.2%	6.9%	8.1%	3.7%	6.6%	8.2%	4.2%	3.1%
Plymouth County	23,073	9.0%	4.5%	7.9%	21.7%	1.0%	7.7%	5.4%	7.9%	1.9%	9.3%	9.6%	9.3%	4.9%
Suffolk County	117,456	7.1%	3.3%	6.5%	25.5%	2.4%	14.7%	5.6%	9.9%	5.6%	4.5%	7.5%	1.7%	5.6%
Worcester County	42,202	6.6%	6.2%	6.8%	17.9%	5.2%	8.4%	4.9%	13.3%	7.7%	5.8%	8.0%	5.0%	4.1%
Michigan														
Allegan County	2,426	0.5%	2.8%	9.2%	21.1%	13.8%	0.0%	11.1%	9.4%	0.0%	0.0%	2.5%	12.0%	17.6%
Bay County	3,233	6.2%	0.0%	6.1%	46.5%	0.0%	9.8%	3.8%	14.3%	3.5%	1.9%	0.8%	3.4%	3.8%
Berrien County	5,192	17.7%	0.0%	20.2%	15.9%	0.0%	3.7%	1.8%	6.5%	0.8%	10.7%	11.8%	8.3%	2.6%
Calhoun County	3,530	3.8%	0.0%	8.1%	32.1%	0.0%	0.0%	1.3%	2.5%	0.0%	5.9%	2.8%	28.2%	15.2%
Eaton County	3,507	6.3%	6.6%	18.5%	24.2%	0.0%	4.0%	4.3%	15.8%	0.0%	0.7%	5.7%	13.9%	0.0%
Genesee County	9,886	4.8%	1.6%	14.4%	25.9%	2.7%	2.9%	2.4%	12.8%	4.8%	4.8%	8.1%	12.0%	2.9%
Ingham County	22,265	6.3%	4.8%	7.7%	9.3%	5.1%	3.4%	4.1%	23.1%	5.3%	5.9%	7.8%	10.1%	7.0%
Jackson County	3,882	7.7%	4.4%	13.3%	26.3%	2.6%	3.3%	0.0%	6.5%	6.0%	2.2%	15.0%	10.5%	2.2%
Kalamazoo County	17,697	4.7%	6.4%	7.6%	24.8%	3.5%	4.2%	8.5%	9.8%	10.0%	4.8%	5.5%	10.2%	0.0%
Kent County	35,196	3.0%	3.9%	13.8%	29.3%	3.5%	3.8%	8.0%	8.3%	3.6%	4.8%	4.5%	8.1%	5.3%
Lenawee County	1,625	10.5%	6.7%	6.3%	12.8%	0.0%	6.0%	16.9%	7.0%	4.7%	0.0%	6.3%	19.3%	3.4%
Livingston County	6,144	17.0%	8.1%	17.6%	16.6%	0.0%	1.7%	2.3%	5.7%	2.7%	2.1%	6.9%	11.8%	7.6%

Table F-2: Counties—Educational Field of Study—*Continued*

	Total Millennial Population with Bachelor's or Higher	Percent of the Population 18 to 33 by Field of Study												
		Engineering	Computers and Math	Science and Engineering Related	Business	Physical Science	Social Science	Communications	Biological Sciences	Literature	Liberal Arts	Psychology	Education	Visual and Performing Arts
Michigan—Cont.														
Macomb County	30,033	12.5%	4.2%	20.5%	23.9%	0.8%	2.6%	8.7%	9.9%	1.1%	2.9%	4.9%	4.2%	3.8%
Monroe County	4,492	4.2%	2.3%	20.1%	24.3%	4.6%	2.7%	3.7%	5.2%	3.7%	3.9%	4.5%	14.1%	6.6%
Muskegon County	3,050	8.6%	3.4%	17.5%	28.5%	0.0%	0.0%	0.0%	0.0%	0.0%	8.5%	4.3%	29.3%	0.0%
Oakland County	84,157	16.9%	3.8%	9.6%	20.6%	1.8%	5.2%	8.8%	8.8%	4.9%	2.0%	4.6%	8.6%	4.5%
Ottawa County	11,910	10.8%	1.1%	13.2%	28.4%	0.0%	3.4%	1.9%	7.6%	4.1%	9.1%	7.2%	10.4%	2.8%
Saginaw County	6,206	7.3%	9.6%	15.5%	24.7%	6.0%	4.6%	4.3%	6.6%	4.3%	1.4%	6.2%	9.3%	0.0%
St. Clair County	3,130	8.5%	0.0%	8.9%	20.0%	4.5%	3.1%	7.2%	13.7%	0.0%	8.9%	7.1%	16.2%	1.9%
Washtenaw County	39,240	14.1%	5.7%	10.8%	7.8%	6.5%	12.8%	2.8%	11.6%	5.6%	5.7%	7.7%	4.0%	5.0%
Wayne County	57,851	9.1%	7.1%	11.3%	20.8%	3.9%	6.1%	5.7%	9.9%	4.5%	4.5%	6.2%	6.9%	4.0%
Minnesota														
Anoka County	16,376	5.8%	2.7%	18.9%	24.4%	0.0%	6.5%	3.7%	10.4%	0.7%	3.4%	5.7%	8.7%	8.9%
Carver County	4,558	6.1%	11.1%	16.5%	12.4%	0.0%	5.4%	1.9%	9.3%	14.2%	0.0%	6.4%	12.1%	4.6%
Dakota County	25,934	5.8%	5.2%	8.3%	22.0%	4.2%	6.1%	8.8%	9.9%	0.9%	2.9%	8.6%	8.6%	8.7%
Hennepin County	120,604	13.0%	7.0%	6.7%	21.8%	2.3%	9.4%	7.9%	9.1%	2.8%	1.9%	7.0%	4.7%	6.3%
Olmsted County	10,887	0.0%	5.6%	27.0%	9.6%	5.2%	10.2%	2.7%	28.0%	2.9%	4.6%	2.7%	1.6%	0.0%
Ramsey County	41,839	4.2%	5.4%	6.6%	14.4%	4.4%	8.1%	5.9%	11.0%	7.2%	4.2%	5.1%	9.9%	13.7%
Scott County	6,620	1.7%	6.3%	9.5%	25.4%	8.5%	4.1%	1.8%	18.5%	3.3%	2.5%	3.5%	11.5%	3.2%
St. Louis County	7,281	6.4%	0.0%	24.8%	26.2%	0.0%	9.0%	0.4%	5.4%	6.3%	3.2%	1.0%	15.7%	1.6%
Stearns County	8,389	1.2%	1.7%	3.3%	23.9%	3.0%	7.0%	16.8%	7.0%	14.2%	4.2%	4.9%	12.7%	0.0%
Washington County	10,573	7.6%	2.9%	11.2%	28.5%	1.6%	6.4%	4.3%	7.9%	6.3%	5.6%	3.0%	1.8%	13.0%
Wright County	4,722	15.2%	1.1%	4.7%	20.6%	0.0%	0.0%	29.3%	1.0%	0.0%	4.6%	7.9%	11.0%	4.7%
Mississippi														
DeSoto County	5,659	5.5%	0.0%	26.5%	27.1%	2.6%	5.5%	5.1%	7.0%	4.6%	2.1%	1.9%	11.5%	0.7%
Harrison County	6,950	1.9%	1.2%	16.1%	14.2%	7.9%	6.1%	4.6%	17.4%	5.7%	2.0%	5.1%	9.5%	8.2%
Hinds County	13,164	7.2%	3.9%	10.0%	24.2%	8.8%	2.1%	5.3%	12.4%	0.8%	2.1%	6.0%	11.8%	5.5%
Jackson County	2,427	5.3%	0.0%	14.3%	32.2%	0.0%	0.0%	0.0%	0.0%	0.0%	4.0%	4.6%	39.6%	0.0%
Madison County	2,536	0.0%	0.0%	10.5%	26.5%	0.0%	12.4%	5.2%	10.8%	2.0%	5.5%	14.6%	9.0%	3.4%
Rankin County	8,692	2.3%	2.0%	43.7%	15.7%	1.5%	1.9%	0.0%	4.6%	1.0%	11.8%	3.7%	9.7%	2.3%
Missouri														
Boone County	18,111	17.0%	10.1%	9.1%	6.9%	4.0%	5.3%	5.1%	17.3%	7.3%	1.8%	4.3%	8.0%	3.7%
Cass County	1,689	11.2%	0.0%	12.4%	4.1%	6.5%	0.0%	0.0%	12.1%	0.0%	2.0%	14.6%	31.3%	5.9%
Clay County	10,750	1.8%	3.9%	14.5%	21.9%	3.7%	2.0%	4.9%	2.9%	1.3%	1.8%	16.1%	21.0%	4.1%
Franklin County	1,872	1.1%	0.0%	5.6%	24.6%	0.0%	3.6%	15.9%	17.5%	0.0%	0.0%	14.1%	12.6%	5.1%
Greene County	13,154	1.1%	0.7%	11.4%	22.3%	2.3%	7.2%	4.7%	5.3%	3.2%	10.4%	11.5%	15.1%	4.9%
Jackson County	36,132	5.0%	5.2%	13.0%	21.9%	3.0%	4.9%	7.0%	6.4%	5.8%	5.9%	6.7%	6.6%	8.7%
Jasper County	3,144	0.5%	2.6%	8.7%	26.2%	0.0%	10.8%	1.4%	13.2%	3.5%	19.6%	0.0%	13.5%	0.0%
Jefferson County	4,820	6.5%	3.1%	11.2%	24.2%	3.3%	2.1%	19.1%	1.9%	0.0%	9.5%	0.0%	17.3%	1.7%
Platte County	4,995	0.3%	3.6%	8.8%	39.9%	2.1%	1.2%	7.3%	16.4%	0.2%	2.4%	3.0%	11.7%	3.1%
St. Charles County	17,398	7.8%	5.2%	8.7%	30.1%	0.0%	7.9%	6.0%	3.6%	2.5%	1.8%	9.8%	11.8%	4.8%
St. Louis County	53,016	7.1%	3.9%	7.7%	28.6%	1.7%	6.5%	8.9%	6.3%	3.8%	3.2%	6.4%	7.7%	8.2%
Montana														
Flathead County	2,102	0.0%	5.1%	36.1%	9.9%	0.0%	0.0%	0.0%	0.0%	3.9%	14.6%	0.0%	19.5%	10.9%
Gallatin County	7,044	4.7%	4.2%	13.8%	23.8%	0.7%	6.8%	3.7%	5.5%	4.4%	9.0%	11.9%	7.6%	3.9%
Missoula County	5,703	0.0%	0.0%	0.0%	25.5%	0.0%	9.7%	5.2%	17.2%	3.1%	18.8%	7.2%	4.9%	8.3%
Yellowstone County	6,002	12.4%	0.0%	19.3%	19.6%	1.4%	2.1%	0.0%	9.5%	5.8%	14.1%	3.7%	10.5%	1.5%
Nebraska														
Douglas County	38,240	3.7%	5.4%	12.5%	24.5%	3.1%	0.8%	8.9%	11.6%	4.6%	6.1%	4.0%	11.5%	3.4%
Lancaster County	20,662	8.7%	2.2%	12.4%	14.5%	9.0%	9.0%	8.9%	8.3%	3.8%	2.8%	4.7%	10.6%	5.2%
Sarpy County	9,591	7.8%	10.0%	9.3%	27.8%	0.0%	1.2%	3.5%	8.4%	1.1%	9.2%	4.3%	14.9%	2.6%
Nevada														
Clark County	61,784	6.8%	4.2%	10.2%	21.8%	3.2%	7.7%	7.6%	9.6%	4.5%	3.6%	7.0%	6.2%	7.5%
Washoe County	17,427	5.9%	4.2%	6.9%	33.0%	3.2%	3.1%	8.3%	8.5%	5.3%	5.3%	5.3%	8.9%	2.1%
New Hampshire														
Hillsborough County	21,304	9.2%	6.7%	9.6%	23.6%	1.7%	7.0%	6.2%	10.5%	3.3%	3.3%	6.8%	7.4%	4.7%
Merrimack County	6,501	10.2%	8.2%	6.2%	9.6%	0.0%	15.8%	3.3%	3.1%	5.5%	7.9%	5.3%	20.3%	4.5%
Rockingham County	18,282	8.8%	5.6%	11.5%	21.5%	0.7%	7.5%	7.1%	5.0%	4.5%	3.9%	10.2%	9.0%	4.8%
Strafford County	8,373	6.9%	12.8%	16.0%	13.4%	0.9%	1.0%	4.0%	9.7%	9.6%	2.7%	3.3%	10.6%	9.1%
New Jersey														
Atlantic County	8,620	3.4%	3.1%	18.1%	12.0%	2.7%	9.5%	4.7%	11.6%	4.0%	6.8%	2.7%	15.1%	6.2%
Bergen County	61,034	7.1%	6.8%	7.2%	30.0%	2.2%	6.1%	7.5%	6.9%	4.4%	2.6%	6.6%	8.8%	3.7%
Burlington County	23,100	7.7%	6.3%	7.3%	23.1%	0.7%	6.9%	9.3%	6.5%	4.8%	6.3%	5.4%	12.8%	2.8%
Camden County	27,988	2.4%	3.8%	6.9%	18.7%	0.5%	12.4%	6.2%	11.3%	4.5%	5.7%	8.3%	14.3%	5.0%
Cape May County	3,561	0.0%	0.0%	15.8%	11.3%	0.0%	9.4%	5.6%	8.9%	8.8%	9.7%	3.1%	19.7%	7.7%
Cumberland County	3,686	16.4%	0.0%	11.3%	29.7%	0.0%	5.0%	0.0%	7.8%	0.0%	5.5%	9.7%	14.7%	0.0%
Essex County	40,213	6.3%	6.2%	9.8%	21.4%	1.9%	6.1%	6.6%	8.6%	3.6%	2.3%	11.3%	7.7%	8.1%
Gloucester County	13,661	6.3%	5.7%	11.6%	18.8%	0.7%	5.5%	7.9%	5.0%	6.3%	2.9%	11.3%	13.1%	5.0%
Hudson County	82,943	13.7%	13.7%	4.8%	27.0%	3.6%	8.6%	4.4%	4.0%	3.5%	3.7%	4.6%	3.7%	4.7%
Hunterdon County	6,580	1.9%	2.7%	4.7%	33.3%	4.4%	8.1%	5.9%	8.2%	7.8%	10.0%	5.6%	6.1%	1.4%
Mercer County	18,873	9.3%	5.7%	5.2%	16.3%	5.1%	19.6%	4.6%	7.0%	3.3%	4.1%	13.3%	1.4%	5.1%
Middlesex County	62,793	9.5%	12.1%	8.8%	19.9%	3.6%	8.4%	4.0%	8.2%	2.4%	3.6%	5.9%	8.9%	4.7%
Monmouth County	32,315	5.3%	7.0%	8.8%	25.8%	1.4%	5.7%	9.9%	5.5%	2.1%	6.9%	7.3%	11.8%	2.3%
Morris County	34,386	7.5%	9.1%	10.2%	22.1%	2.1%	6.2%	8.4%	8.3%	3.6%	4.3%	8.0%	5.1%	5.3%
Ocean County	25,362	5.2%	2.8%	11.4%	19.1%	4.3%	4.5%	2.8%	7.6%	2.2%	11.4%	6.8%	18.8%	3.1%
Passaic County	20,295	3.3%	7.6%	4.2%	26.3%	1.2%	10.9%	6.5%	6.1%	6.2%	9.3%	5.9%	7.9%	4.5%

Table F-2: Counties—Educational Field of Study—*Continued*

	Total Millennial Population with Bachelor's or Higher	Percent of the Population 18 to 33 by Field of Study												
		Engineering	Computers and Math	Science and Engineering Related	Business	Physical Science	Social Science	Communications	Biological Sciences	Literature	Liberal Arts	Psychology	Education	Visual and Performing Arts
New Jersey—Cont.														
Somerset County	24,511	7.2%	12.4%	9.0%	18.3%	3.5%	5.9%	6.4%	10.0%	5.5%	0.1%	6.5%	8.4%	6.9%
Sussex County	5,628	1.3%	4.7%	6.5%	12.9%	4.1%	8.4%	12.3%	3.5%	2.6%	8.9%	16.5%	11.5%	6.8%
Union County	22,891	6.5%	6.1%	11.6%	25.9%	5.9%	5.7%	5.7%	5.9%	6.7%	1.7%	1.9%	10.0%	6.4%
Warren County	3,752	8.2%	7.6%	2.2%	19.0%	1.8%	3.4%	3.7%	3.9%	4.8%	9.2%	4.4%	28.5%	3.3%
New Mexico														
Bernalillo County	24,946	9.7%	4.4%	8.7%	14.0%	6.1%	10.8%	4.6%	9.1%	7.5%	8.6%	5.9%	6.4%	4.3%
Doña Ana County	3,341	0.0%	4.2%	7.3%	25.5%	3.2%	15.9%	2.8%	23.9%	9.5%	0.6%	0.0%	6.9%	0.0%
San Juan County	2,806	4.4%	0.0%	8.8%	25.2%	16.9%	7.8%	0.0%	4.5%	5.0%	0.0%	17.0%	10.4%	0.0%
Sandoval County	2,995	26.5%	0.0%	9.7%	8.7%	0.0%	6.6%	0.0%	2.2%	5.6%	0.0%	6.4%	28.4%	5.8%
Santa Fe County	5,395	8.9%	5.1%	7.4%	12.7%	1.1%	8.1%	7.8%	8.7%	7.1%	2.8%	9.0%	5.7%	15.5%
New York														
Albany County	23,531	3.8%	7.7%	8.9%	17.1%	2.9%	13.3%	10.5%	8.4%	5.5%	3.4%	8.5%	7.7%	2.4%
Bronx County	53,765	3.7%	7.6%	8.0%	27.5%	1.9%	9.3%	4.7%	5.8%	3.4%	4.4%	12.2%	7.0%	4.4%
Broome County	10,167	4.0%	12.8%	7.2%	7.9%	12.0%	14.8%	3.5%	11.1%	4.3%	0.4%	5.0%	14.2%	2.7%
Chautauqua County	3,119	1.5%	2.1%	8.4%	14.1%	0.0%	4.2%	4.0%	14.9%	5.5%	6.0%	6.0%	19.4%	13.8%
Dutchess County	12,853	5.7%	9.8%	2.4%	16.7%	4.0%	7.5%	4.9%	6.2%	7.5%	4.2%	8.6%	15.3%	7.3%
Erie County	54,648	7.1%	3.6%	11.4%	19.5%	3.4%	9.7%	6.6%	9.1%	5.8%	2.5%	6.2%	10.4%	4.6%
Jefferson County	3,206	5.9%	4.1%	2.8%	16.8%	5.0%	11.1%	8.7%	9.5%	5.9%	8.7%	6.3%	12.1%	3.2%
Kings County	234,808	4.2%	4.9%	7.3%	17.0%	2.0%	12.7%	7.2%	4.5%	6.4%	6.9%	7.5%	4.6%	14.9%
Monroe County	47,406	7.6%	6.9%	11.7%	20.2%	3.8%	7.7%	6.1%	6.1%	5.1%	3.1%	4.9%	10.0%	6.7%
Nassau County	92,121	4.2%	3.7%	12.6%	23.4%	2.6%	7.3%	6.5%	8.5%	4.7%	3.0%	7.4%	11.1%	4.8%
New York County	291,633	5.0%	6.3%	3.4%	21.6%	2.0%	15.4%	7.9%	5.0%	6.1%	5.1%	6.1%	1.2%	14.8%
Niagara County	6,706	8.8%	8.8%	8.7%	17.8%	1.2%	5.6%	2.2%	9.0%	10.8%	1.5%	3.0%	18.7%	3.8%
Oneida County	9,215	3.4%	7.2%	12.2%	19.6%	1.7%	7.5%	4.7%	1.8%	2.5%	1.7%	18.2%	10.8%	8.6%
Onondaga County	25,233	9.6%	4.4%	10.9%	18.0%	2.1%	9.9%	6.5%	9.2%	5.1%	4.0%	4.6%	11.8%	3.7%
Ontario County	4,571	2.6%	11.0%	13.3%	28.0%	1.0%	7.8%	4.8%	2.9%	5.0%	1.0%	5.1%	16.6%	0.8%
Orange County	14,399	2.2%	7.5%	13.7%	21.6%	1.9%	5.6%	4.3%	4.3%	6.1%	4.4%	10.3%	14.2%	4.0%
Oswego County	2,343	1.1%	0.0%	1.8%	34.9%	0.0%	15.7%	3.6%	3.3%	3.2%	12.1%	4.1%	15.2%	4.9%
Putnam County	4,379	3.6%	4.6%	6.8%	14.2%	2.1%	10.0%	2.4%	15.8%	0.0%	6.0%	4.1%	26.0%	4.4%
Queens County	167,553	4.9%	6.7%	9.6%	23.4%	2.3%	9.7%	6.8%	6.0%	5.2%	4.8%	5.3%	5.4%	9.7%
Rensselaer County	8,925	10.9%	5.9%	9.2%	24.6%	5.7%	4.4%	1.8%	6.5%	12.7%	4.9%	6.6%	3.7%	2.9%
Richmond County	28,956	3.2%	2.8%	7.9%	28.5%	6.1%	5.8%	5.0%	4.7%	2.0%	3.0%	11.5%	15.3%	4.1%
Rockland County	15,480	1.8%	3.9%	10.5%	27.5%	2.5%	7.5%	5.5%	9.2%	3.6%	4.5%	6.1%	12.8%	4.7%
Saratoga County	3,322	8.2%	3.9%	14.1%	12.6%	8.1%	3.0%	3.2%	10.7%	0.0%	14.2%	13.2%	8.7%	0.0%
Schenectady County	10,744	9.3%	2.8%	3.5%	23.9%	2.0%	7.5%	7.3%	13.5%	2.3%	6.2%	1.7%	15.7%	4.3%
St. Lawrence County	8,355	12.1%	3.7%	4.4%	16.6%	10.8%	9.7%	7.0%	6.2%	7.6%	4.3%	9.2%	8.5%	0.0%
Steuben County	2,832	0.7%	1.4%	6.3%	14.3%	3.4%	0.0%	22.7%	5.3%	1.4%	1.9%	16.9%	22.0%	3.7%
Suffolk County	79,905	4.6%	5.2%	11.3%	21.9%	3.9%	7.1%	5.8%	6.6%	4.8%	2.6%	7.5%	12.9%	5.8%
Tompkins County	12,018	12.0%	11.5%	4.7%	4.5%	20.4%	9.5%	0.0%	12.4%	1.9%	3.0%	10.5%	5.8%	3.9%
Ulster County	7,319	6.6%	1.6%	6.0%	13.3%	1.3%	9.8%	2.9%	6.1%	7.6%	3.9%	8.6%	28.2%	4.0%
Wayne County	2,028	2.6%	2.6%	3.0%	9.0%	2.8%	22.6%	3.7%	7.1%	9.8%	0.0%	9.0%	13.3%	14.5%
Westchester County	57,302	6.6%	5.2%	8.9%	25.0%	1.9%	10.7%	6.5%	4.4%	4.5%	4.3%	7.8%	8.7%	5.6%
North Carolina														
Alamance County	4,001	1.7%	0.0%	5.7%	29.9%	2.9%	9.1%	10.4%	14.5%	4.1%	2.1%	3.8%	12.8%	2.9%
Brunswick County	2,194	9.2%	2.8%	8.0%	17.4%	11.8%	15.1%	9.3%	2.0%	0.0%	1.1%	1.2%	14.7%	7.4%
Buncombe County	11,184	7.5%	5.1%	4.9%	17.0%	4.1%	6.3%	5.6%	10.2%	6.5%	4.5%	12.9%	10.9%	4.6%
Cabarrus County	6,178	11.0%	5.3%	12.4%	31.3%	0.0%	6.7%	2.0%	4.7%	0.0%	3.6%	3.0%	10.5%	9.6%
Catawba County	4,765	8.9%	0.0%	2.3%	15.7%	0.0%	3.1%	6.4%	25.1%	2.7%	8.9%	0.0%	25.4%	1.4%
Cleveland County	1,047	5.9%	19.5%	16.5%	0.0%	0.0%	0.0%	8.1%	6.3%	9.8%	5.9%	0.0%	27.9%	0.0%
Craven County	2,758	3.3%	17.2%	11.4%	10.6%	7.1%	3.4%	2.8%	2.7%	1.1%	14.3%	7.2%	19.1%	0.0%
Cumberland County	12,289	3.2%	4.8%	12.6%	21.7%	0.4%	7.2%	4.1%	6.4%	6.5%	8.9%	5.1%	10.8%	8.2%
Davidson County	3,977	0.0%	0.0%	21.2%	36.4%	0.0%	4.0%	3.4%	10.5%	3.2%	2.9%	8.9%	5.3%	4.0%
Durham County	30,556	6.8%	6.4%	6.8%	11.2%	3.4%	11.1%	3.9%	18.9%	8.3%	7.2%	5.5%	3.4%	7.0%
Forsyth County	18,966	12.0%	6.0%	10.5%	14.6%	4.3%	5.1%	7.2%	13.2%	1.7%	5.3%	7.1%	10.7%	2.3%
Gaston County	6,988	4.0%	12.8%	15.8%	22.5%	2.8%	17.7%	0.8%	2.8%	2.9%	0.0%	6.1%	11.6%	0.0%
Guilford County	22,042	5.2%	4.6%	10.9%	15.5%	2.8%	8.2%	6.1%	10.2%	7.1%	6.7%	7.0%	10.4%	5.3%
Harnett County	3,320	11.1%	2.3%	17.3%	15.5%	2.7%	1.2%	5.7%	12.3%	3.0%	5.3%	11.4%	8.5%	3.6%
Henderson County	1,777	12.7%	7.5%	25.3%	7.6%	0.0%	0.0%	0.0%	7.9%	0.0%	0.0%	15.5%	23.5%	0.0%
Iredell County	5,395	10.9%	4.9%	14.9%	24.7%	0.0%	7.4%	9.6%	6.0%	1.2%	0.0%	7.7%	8.4%	4.2%
Johnston County	3,335	3.7%	0.0%	16.3%	17.2%	0.0%	4.4%	13.2%	6.8%	0.0%	16.5%	2.5%	13.4%	6.0%
Mecklenburg County	79,053	9.0%	7.6%	6.7%	27.7%	1.9%	7.5%	9.9%	5.5%	2.9%	4.1%	7.5%	6.0%	3.6%
Moore County	3,147	1.3%	7.2%	0.0%	12.8%	11.2%	15.7%	5.3%	1.3%	5.2%	17.5%	6.0%	16.5%	0.0%
Nash County	1,142	0.0%	0.0%	0.0%	8.0%	0.0%	0.0%	0.0%	13.0%	0.0%	0.0%	56.9%	13.7%	8.4%
New Hanover County	12,275	1.7%	2.9%	10.7%	18.4%	2.0%	9.0%	5.0%	12.1%	4.9%	7.2%	8.7%	13.4%	3.9%
Onslow County	6,608	4.1%	11.1%	8.2%	15.8%	5.0%	9.6%	6.5%	14.6%	0.0%	4.9%	8.0%	9.1%	3.0%
Orange County	15,678	3.1%	11.4%	6.4%	3.3%	4.5%	21.5%	3.9%	11.6%	13.2%	4.6%	11.4%	3.6%	1.4%
Pitt County	7,489	0.0%	0.0%	10.5%	8.1%	13.1%	0.0%	11.7%	18.9%	2.5%	5.0%	13.6%	15.2%	1.4%
Randolph County	1,956	0.0%	3.5%	23.8%	5.0%	0.0%	5.4%	5.4%	6.8%	7.4%	4.3%	12.7%	25.8%	0.0%
Robeson County	1,694	4.2%	0.0%	18.9%	12.7%	12.7%	0.0%	10.5%	13.5%	1.8%	4.1%	0.0%	21.7%	0.0%
Rockingham County	1,764	3.4%	0.0%	31.6%	6.4%	0.0%	6.1%	0.0%	15.6%	5.7%	2.1%	0.0%	23.8%	5.2%
Rowan County	2,773	0.0%	2.8%	4.7%	31.3%	6.2%	10.1%	2.6%	19.8%	6.6%	0.0%	3.5%	8.4%	3.9%
Union County	7,294	1.7%	3.3%	2.6%	20.9%	8.2%	3.6%	7.8%	8.2%	1.5%	8.8%	10.2%	21.9%	1.4%
Wake County	79,990	10.6%	9.5%	7.7%	17.9%	3.6%	8.7%	7.0%	10.8%	2.6%	5.5%	5.3%	7.1%	3.7%
Wayne County	4,570	0.0%	2.4%	1.0%	24.8%	17.7%	6.1%	7.1%	0.0%	8.4%	8.8%	6.0%	13.6%	4.1%
North Dakota														
Cass County	10,458	4.5%	11.0%	14.5%	30.9%	5.8%	3.3%	10.0%	6.2%	4.9%	1.3%	1.4%	4.5%	1.6%

Table F-2: Counties—Educational Field of Study—*Continued*

	Total Millennial Population with Bachelor's or Higher	Percent of the Population 18 to 33 by Field of Study												
		Engineering	Computers and Math	Science and Engineering Related	Business	Physical Science	Social Science	Communications	Biological Sciences	Literature	Liberal Arts	Psychology	Education	Visual and Performing Arts
Ohio														
Allen County	3,231	8.1%	0.6%	30.6%	19.3%	5.2%	11.0%	0.0%	3.4%	2.9%	3.3%	2.7%	12.8%	0.0%
Ashtabula County	1,548	0.0%	11.0%	11.0%	25.6%	11.1%	0.0%	3.9%	14.9%	11.2%	0.0%	3.3%	2.6%	5.4%
Butler County	14,122	8.8%	2.5%	16.0%	27.7%	1.5%	7.7%	1.8%	5.9%	2.7%	5.9%	2.9%	12.3%	4.3%
Clark County	2,542	4.8%	9.5%	16.1%	29.6%	0.0%	10.0%	6.2%	0.0%	6.6%	1.8%	6.3%	5.5%	3.6%
Clermont County	6,189	4.4%	6.4%	8.1%	39.3%	2.2%	2.6%	1.6%	5.2%	6.3%	7.5%	7.1%	6.8%	2.5%
Columbiana County	1,600	3.9%	4.3%	5.7%	9.9%	6.9%	3.6%	0.0%	13.4%	0.0%	0.0%	5.8%	26.8%	26.5%
Cuyahoga County	67,673	9.8%	4.5%	12.8%	18.9%	2.2%	7.8%	5.9%	9.8%	3.7%	6.1%	6.9%	6.9%	4.6%
Delaware County	12,667	4.9%	4.9%	13.3%	24.8%	0.4%	10.1%	10.0%	8.8%	3.1%	3.8%	2.2%	6.7%	6.9%
Fairfield County	2,679	3.8%	8.7%	11.5%	11.9%	2.7%	12.8%	6.6%	6.6%	0.0%	8.1%	4.9%	3.8%	18.7%
Franklin County	100,933	7.5%	3.7%	9.6%	23.8%	2.8%	8.3%	6.0%	10.1%	4.6%	3.3%	7.0%	8.3%	5.0%
Geauga County	2,813	2.3%	21.8%	28.3%	15.1%	0.3%	0.0%	3.3%	8.6%	2.3%	0.0%	4.6%	12.9%	0.5%
Greene County	10,418	12.4%	5.5%	14.3%	24.3%	4.7%	5.1%	3.3%	6.5%	3.8%	5.9%	7.8%	5.3%	1.2%
Hamilton County	50,972	8.2%	4.8%	10.7%	19.8%	4.1%	6.7%	8.5%	8.6%	2.9%	4.4%	5.7%	7.8%	7.9%
Lake County	9,214	8.7%	10.5%	15.4%	17.9%	2.9%	3.0%	11.4%	5.1%	3.0%	0.5%	4.8%	15.0%	1.9%
Licking County	4,007	4.2%	2.2%	6.5%	28.2%	5.7%	4.0%	2.5%	10.6%	0.0%	5.4%	7.1%	17.9%	5.6%
Lorain County	8,224	9.1%	2.3%	13.2%	30.5%	4.0%	3.1%	3.9%	4.2%	3.2%	1.6%	5.9%	19.1%	0.0%
Lucas County	16,276	10.2%	4.9%	13.0%	21.9%	1.8%	4.2%	7.0%	12.6%	0.9%	5.7%	2.3%	10.2%	5.1%
Mahoning County	6,979	1.5%	11.0%	19.3%	23.7%	4.4%	4.3%	2.7%	1.6%	7.0%	4.1%	3.2%	13.1%	3.9%
Medina County	6,687	11.1%	3.7%	21.7%	22.5%	1.7%	6.4%	0.0%	4.7%	0.0%	4.6%	2.2%	19.1%	2.2%
Miami County	4,357	8.3%	0.5%	7.8%	13.4%	2.9%	8.6%	9.3%	15.5%	2.2%	2.8%	7.2%	11.5%	10.1%
Montgomery County	22,531	12.6%	3.6%	13.3%	20.2%	2.3%	8.2%	4.5%	9.9%	1.9%	3.4%	5.3%	9.1%	5.7%
Portage County	9,051	4.7%	4.1%	7.6%	30.3%	8.6%	8.0%	0.0%	7.1%	4.9%	3.0%	3.9%	13.0%	4.8%
Richland County	2,069	0.0%	7.7%	9.5%	10.9%	0.0%	0.0%	0.0%	1.6%	0.0%	7.4%	21.4%	38.1%	3.2%
Stark County	11,450	3.0%	4.2%	12.5%	26.5%	3.0%	3.5%	4.6%	16.1%	3.1%	0.9%	2.2%	15.8%	4.7%
Summit County	25,300	10.3%	5.1%	13.3%	22.9%	4.0%	4.9%	3.3%	6.8%	5.4%	5.0%	5.6%	7.4%	6.1%
Trumbull County	3,845	3.0%	13.9%	13.5%	15.5%	4.3%	10.1%	10.8%	3.8%	3.8%	2.2%	3.0%	14.3%	1.7%
Tuscarawas County	3,661	7.5%	1.8%	10.2%	12.5%	0.2%	8.3%	0.0%	20.9%	3.2%	14.3%	0.0%	16.7%	4.3%
Warren County	8,940	8.6%	15.3%	7.8%	30.1%	0.9%	4.3%	7.1%	4.3%	4.7%	0.0%	2.8%	10.1%	4.0%
Wayne County	3,145	3.2%	0.0%	10.2%	7.6%	5.5%	10.1%	16.2%	4.4%	6.7%	0.0%	5.1%	30.9%	0.0%
Wood County	6,034	11.0%	6.1%	16.8%	22.0%	4.7%	5.9%	4.4%	8.0%	5.2%	2.2%	0.5%	11.7%	1.3%
Oklahoma														
Canadian County	4,021	11.3%	0.0%	3.3%	23.5%	13.8%	8.3%	3.2%	25.6%	0.0%	0.0%	0.0%	9.2%	1.9%
Cleveland County	19,156	14.5%	2.3%	4.5%	20.4%	12.3%	6.2%	8.5%	10.3%	3.2%	9.1%	0.9%	4.9%	2.9%
Comanche County	2,827	0.0%	0.0%	18.7%	23.9%	4.2%	8.8%	0.0%	8.8%	3.5%	0.0%	12.1%	13.8%	6.0%
Oklahoma County	35,615	8.0%	3.5%	11.5%	32.9%	0.9%	7.5%	3.3%	8.0%	3.5%	3.9%	4.2%	9.3%	3.6%
Tulsa County	28,188	10.0%	5.9%	8.6%	21.9%	4.3%	3.7%	4.7%	8.9%	3.1%	4.1%	6.5%	13.6%	4.7%
Oregon														
Clackamas County	15,169	5.2%	4.5%	19.8%	21.7%	3.6%	6.0%	4.6%	5.3%	4.8%	6.2%	8.8%	5.8%	3.8%
Deschutes County	8,147	10.9%	0.7%	4.9%	15.1%	4.1%	5.6%	4.5%	17.5%	3.0%	5.2%	6.9%	8.0%	13.7%
Douglas County	2,772	8.6%	0.0%	16.2%	4.1%	4.4%	19.1%	14.6%	18.0%	3.6%	0.0%	1.8%	4.9%	4.7%
Jackson County	3,790	2.7%	4.0%	10.1%	15.0%	0.0%	12.6%	8.7%	10.3%	3.8%	20.6%	5.6%	3.5%	3.2%
Lane County	17,767	1.3%	2.8%	10.6%	8.9%	1.2%	22.8%	4.9%	0.1%	8.7%	7.7%	3.8%	4.3%	14.9%
Linn County	3,861	10.3%	6.4%	19.5%	4.7%	4.3%	3.6%	0.0%	16.3%	1.9%	7.3%	2.9%	16.2%	6.6%
Marion County	9,074	4.8%	4.8%	9.0%	19.2%	3.3%	11.8%	1.5%	2.6%	3.0%	17.0%	5.2%	14.1%	3.6%
Multnomah County	65,317	4.6%	3.6%	8.1%	16.6%	3.2%	13.1%	6.4%	10.5%	8.9%	4.6%	5.4%	2.8%	12.1%
Washington County	35,681	12.9%	10.9%	9.9%	16.1%	3.4%	10.6%	5.7%	8.6%	5.3%	3.1%	7.4%	2.5%	3.7%
Yamhill County	3,219	1.4%	0.0%	0.0%	19.9%	5.4%	18.8%	0.0%	16.0%	4.7%	15.6%	8.7%	0.0%	9.7%
Pennsylvania														
Adams County	2,986	0.0%	2.1%	6.6%	30.9%	0.0%	3.5%	3.0%	5.7%	4.7%	8.9%	5.9%	11.9%	16.7%
Allegheny County	97,804	8.8%	6.5%	11.2%	21.3%	4.0%	7.8%	6.7%	7.2%	4.2%	3.8%	8.0%	6.6%	4.0%
Beaver County	5,822	5.0%	1.4%	4.7%	22.6%	0.0%	1.6%	12.2%	13.4%	2.0%	2.2%	16.7%	18.2%	0.0%
Berks County	13,861	2.8%	3.7%	14.6%	16.8%	0.0%	7.5%	1.2%	13.1%	5.7%	3.9%	7.2%	19.1%	4.4%
Blair County	4,355	0.0%	0.0%	14.1%	23.7%	3.4%	1.6%	3.8%	0.8%	3.5%	5.9%	14.7%	24.4%	4.2%
Bucks County	27,333	6.7%	3.3%	11.2%	21.3%	2.2%	5.4%	7.2%	8.6%	2.6%	5.2%	6.4%	14.8%	5.1%
Butler County	8,970	12.6%	1.4%	14.7%	24.1%	5.8%	4.9%	8.8%	7.0%	0.4%	2.6%	2.3%	10.6%	4.7%
Cambria County	3,617	6.5%	0.6%	34.5%	23.2%	0.0%	3.0%	1.9%	0.0%	0.3%	0.0%	16.5%	13.5%	0.0%
Centre County	15,128	9.1%	13.2%	4.9%	5.3%	17.0%	7.2%	6.3%	11.4%	6.5%	3.0%	5.9%	9.3%	0.7%
Chester County	33,384	10.2%	6.7%	12.9%	24.4%	1.5%	6.1%	4.3%	8.5%	6.0%	1.9%	4.6%	8.9%	4.0%
Cumberland County	9,587	10.9%	2.1%	12.9%	25.7%	2.3%	6.4%	5.5%	5.0%	3.7%	4.8%	8.5%	11.3%	0.9%
Dauphin County	11,573	4.5%	8.1%	12.4%	20.2%	1.0%	6.8%	5.5%	4.3%	3.9%	3.1%	11.6%	15.8%	2.9%
Delaware County	31,336	4.3%	3.5%	14.5%	27.8%	3.7%	6.9%	8.5%	3.2%	5.3%	4.2%	6.4%	8.7%	3.0%
Erie County	11,541	6.7%	6.1%	6.3%	24.1%	2.8%	5.9%	13.3%	5.7%	4.5%	0.8%	9.7%	11.6%	2.4%
Fayette County	2,317	9.1%	0.0%	24.5%	11.5%	0.0%	11.2%	3.6%	4.0%	11.0%	0.0%	2.9%	14.6%	7.7%
Franklin County	3,161	0.0%	2.5%	23.2%	28.8%	0.0%	9.9%	6.9%	3.4%	0.0%	0.0%	7.7%	4.3%	13.4%
Lackawanna County	8,614	2.3%	4.0%	16.7%	21.2%	11.4%	2.2%	6.5%	7.2%	3.2%	4.8%	4.7%	14.4%	1.5%
Lancaster County	20,603	7.9%	3.6%	11.6%	17.2%	6.2%	2.8%	4.3%	12.2%	5.7%	1.7%	7.0%	13.9%	5.9%
Lebanon County	4,339	2.9%	5.1%	7.3%	29.5%	3.0%	14.0%	5.5%	13.0%	1.5%	0.0%	1.8%	13.9%	2.4%
Lehigh County	15,245	9.9%	4.7%	7.8%	19.2%	4.3%	1.9%	4.8%	14.6%	0.9%	5.0%	7.9%	14.9%	4.1%
Luzerne County	11,157	0.9%	1.3%	17.2%	19.3%	1.9%	9.8%	9.4%	3.6%	3.9%	6.4%	8.4%	17.5%	0.4%
Lycoming County	4,596	4.7%	0.6%	12.0%	7.9%	5.6%	1.2%	0.9%	17.6%	9.6%	14.6%	17.2%	7.7%	0.5%
Mercer County	4,027	1.9%	0.0%	14.5%	25.8%	0.0%	6.3%	0.0%	8.1%	5.2%	8.7%	0.0%	26.7%	2.8%
Monroe County	6,042	0.0%	0.0%	13.0%	31.3%	3.7%	7.7%	0.0%	10.3%	1.3%	0.0%	7.8%	7.7%	17.1%
Montgomery County	56,108	9.1%	5.0%	12.7%	20.8%	5.5%	5.6%	5.6%	11.1%	4.4%	3.8%	3.5%	8.4%	4.6%
Northampton County	13,979	4.4%	1.5%	20.7%	17.5%	4.2%	3.0%	5.0%	13.7%	3.7%	2.7%	9.1%	12.1%	2.2%
Northumberland County	2,785	1.0%	0.0%	7.6%	18.0%	1.3%	21.2%	1.0%	11.5%	0.0%	0.0%	9.3%	21.0%	8.0%
Philadelphia County	130,086	7.2%	4.2%	12.6%	17.7%	2.5%	8.6%	6.8%	12.2%	3.8%	5.0%	6.8%	6.4%	6.0%

Table F-2: Counties—Educational Field of Study—*Continued*

	Total Millennial Population with Bachelor's or Higher	Percent of the Population 18 to 33 by Field of Study												
		Engineering	Computers and Math	Science and Engineering Related	Business	Physical Science	Social Science	Communications	Biological Sciences	Literature	Liberal Arts	Psychology	Education	Visual and Performing Arts
Pennsylvania—Cont.														
Schuylkill County	3,699	11.9%	1.5%	29.8%	8.1%	0.0%	3.1%	0.0%	7.4%	0.0%	0.0%	15.7%	22.5%	0.0%
Washington County	7,922	7.4%	4.7%	10.6%	18.6%	6.3%	2.4%	9.2%	7.5%	3.2%	4.4%	10.6%	8.4%	6.8%
Westmoreland County	14,560	3.6%	4.8%	10.3%	25.0%	7.2%	3.2%	6.7%	7.0%	3.3%	2.4%	6.9%	19.1%	0.5%
York County	13,411	3.9%	3.2%	11.0%	17.8%	1.8%	3.9%	9.3%	10.5%	6.5%	6.0%	5.9%	16.9%	3.4%
Rhode Island														
Kent County	8,182	3.4%	4.7%	7.7%	20.2%	3.8%	5.9%	7.2%	18.7%	0.0%	11.1%	4.7%	9.4%	3.2%
Providence County	37,095	7.0%	8.6%	9.7%	15.8%	5.2%	11.5%	3.8%	8.3%	4.6%	2.0%	5.3%	10.7%	7.5%
Washington County	6,013	5.2%	0.0%	15.4%	24.1%	6.9%	7.2%	10.4%	14.1%	0.0%	0.0%	0.8%	5.5%	10.3%
South Carolina														
Aiken County	4,951	0.0%	1.2%	4.2%	29.4%	2.2%	7.6%	12.4%	9.4%	1.9%	2.1%	12.6%	7.0%	10.1%
Anderson County	4,506	8.1%	3.2%	8.5%	20.8%	2.6%	4.3%	5.5%	10.6%	0.0%	8.9%	4.7%	16.6%	6.2%
Beaufort County	4,869	3.0%	11.6%	4.2%	19.4%	2.3%	10.1%	10.5%	15.9%	0.6%	6.0%	6.4%	7.7%	2.3%
Berkeley County	9,467	14.5%	2.6%	14.8%	19.1%	3.3%	7.6%	4.0%	4.2%	8.2%	6.2%	2.9%	4.9%	7.8%
Charleston County	29,470	9.4%	3.6%	12.1%	19.7%	6.5%	4.3%	4.5%	8.2%	6.0%	5.4%	6.3%	6.2%	7.9%
Dorchester County	4,480	1.8%	4.6%	22.6%	20.3%	1.0%	3.7%	2.1%	13.5%	4.4%	4.4%	9.2%	9.0%	3.3%
Florence County	3,150	11.6%	0.0%	2.5%	8.2%	3.2%	15.5%	11.6%	5.3%	12.2%	2.2%	2.2%	19.9%	5.6%
Greenville County	25,578	12.5%	2.1%	10.2%	23.1%	3.1%	5.9%	4.0%	7.0%	3.9%	8.8%	4.0%	11.5%	3.9%
Horry County	10,915	3.0%	4.6%	17.9%	20.9%	4.6%	9.1%	7.4%	5.9%	6.5%	2.2%	9.4%	7.2%	1.3%
Lexington County	12,966	8.9%	2.4%	12.8%	22.5%	0.7%	6.0%	4.8%	11.3%	2.7%	6.7%	9.0%	8.7%	3.3%
Pickens County	4,893	2.3%	1.3%	9.1%	26.9%	5.3%	7.0%	0.0%	22.7%	0.0%	8.1%	5.7%	5.5%	6.1%
Richland County	26,299	7.0%	3.7%	6.5%	25.2%	3.6%	9.9%	5.5%	6.5%	4.1%	7.7%	7.2%	8.1%	4.8%
Spartanburg County	7,956	2.7%	4.1%	4.0%	22.1%	4.4%	7.3%	3.1%	11.9%	2.9%	3.2%	8.8%	14.6%	10.8%
Sumter County	1,742	0.0%	0.0%	8.0%	38.3%	0.0%	0.0%	0.0%	15.7%	2.9%	2.0%	2.6%	20.5%	10.0%
York County	11,255	7.3%	10.6%	6.7%	22.2%	5.8%	6.2%	5.3%	3.5%	4.1%	5.9%	5.8%	9.2%	7.3%
South Dakota														
Minnehaha County	11,624	0.0%	3.8%	16.7%	20.0%	2.5%	2.8%	3.1%	6.2%	2.3%	1.4%	13.7%	22.8%	4.7%
Pennington County	3,862	6.3%	0.0%	12.2%	25.0%	6.1%	5.0%	7.6%	20.7%	0.0%	0.8%	0.0%	16.3%	0.0%
Tennessee														
Blount County	3,179	0.0%	0.0%	13.0%	21.1%	0.0%	20.2%	9.3%	4.3%	1.5%	4.7%	10.5%	4.8%	10.5%
Bradley County	3,530	3.9%	0.0%	4.3%	32.2%	0.0%	10.2%	7.7%	6.3%	3.7%	8.8%	6.2%	4.2%	12.3%
Davidson County	65,534	4.4%	4.6%	8.5%	20.0%	3.8%	8.8%	9.1%	8.8%	4.4%	9.4%	3.8%	5.4%	9.0%
Hamilton County	16,977	8.9%	9.3%	6.9%	20.8%	2.0%	7.7%	4.2%	11.4%	7.0%	4.6%	2.4%	9.3%	5.5%
Knox County	24,853	7.2%	1.3%	11.3%	19.6%	3.3%	7.2%	6.0%	12.1%	6.5%	3.4%	4.9%	8.4%	8.7%
Madison County	2,973	0.0%	2.0%	16.0%	38.7%	0.8%	10.0%	4.2%	18.5%	0.8%	0.0%	0.0%	5.9%	3.1%
Montgomery County	10,571	10.4%	1.1%	15.8%	11.5%	3.2%	3.2%	5.3%	3.5%	3.2%	9.4%	9.5%	17.4%	6.6%
Rutherford County	14,777	4.2%	8.6%	9.8%	13.7%	4.8%	7.5%	7.8%	7.7%	6.9%	1.0%	10.0%	14.3%	3.7%
Sevier County	1,972	0.0%	3.1%	7.4%	36.1%	0.0%	0.0%	1.6%	9.9%	5.9%	0.0%	18.1%	18.0%	0.0%
Shelby County	42,353	9.4%	5.4%	10.9%	24.6%	2.5%	5.2%	4.6%	10.4%	4.6%	4.8%	4.2%	8.4%	5.0%
Sullivan County	3,445	11.1%	0.0%	19.6%	27.2%	0.0%	1.7%	5.5%	8.2%	6.4%	3.1%	3.9%	13.4%	0.0%
Sumner County	7,666	0.7%	0.0%	15.6%	20.2%	2.8%	5.5%	1.1%	22.6%	8.5%	2.5%	2.2%	13.5%	4.8%
Washington County	5,057	2.0%	1.9%	14.9%	7.9%	1.9%	12.2%	7.1%	18.5%	6.8%	1.0%	3.5%	14.6%	7.8%
Williamson County	12,505	5.3%	8.8%	12.7%	30.5%	2.2%	2.3%	5.7%	11.0%	2.8%	4.6%	5.0%	7.0%	2.1%
Wilson County	4,925	3.2%	0.0%	15.6%	19.6%	10.9%	2.2%	4.0%	3.2%	3.8%	15.6%	1.4%	13.8%	6.8%
Texas														
Bell County	11,325	8.9%	1.5%	12.4%	16.2%	6.2%	7.8%	2.6%	12.8%	6.7%	7.1%	5.1%	9.0%	3.7%
Bexar County	70,838	6.4%	7.3%	11.3%	22.6%	2.3%	7.2%	6.7%	10.9%	5.5%	2.7%	5.0%	7.9%	4.2%
Bowie County	668	0.0%	0.0%	21.6%	43.9%	0.0%	2.8%	7.3%	24.4%	0.0%	0.0%	0.0%	0.0%	0.0%
Brazoria County	13,710	13.9%	0.9%	24.5%	22.2%	2.5%	3.1%	6.2%	10.3%	1.9%	3.1%	1.2%	7.6%	2.4%
Brazos County	18,616	18.4%	5.9%	4.9%	13.1%	5.1%	8.5%	2.9%	19.1%	4.4%	5.9%	7.9%	3.3%	0.6%
Cameron County	7,809	4.4%	0.2%	11.2%	11.1%	5.4%	5.1%	7.3%	8.6%	7.8%	2.9%	7.4%	25.1%	3.6%
Collin County	55,254	11.8%	12.2%	10.8%	22.9%	1.1%	6.8%	3.4%	8.5%	2.5%	2.6%	3.9%	8.5%	5.2%
Comal County	3,677	9.2%	2.0%	8.6%	17.3%	8.8%	10.2%	12.9%	6.3%	10.4%	3.7%	0.0%	8.7%	2.0%
Dallas County	131,083	9.1%	5.0%	8.8%	31.1%	1.6%	6.1%	7.7%	7.2%	4.3%	3.9%	5.8%	4.5%	4.9%
Denton County	46,352	4.4%	4.9%	9.2%	27.2%	2.6%	9.5%	5.6%	7.1%	3.2%	5.1%	8.5%	5.3%	7.4%
Ector County	4,179	18.8%	0.0%	2.2%	31.8%	0.0%	6.8%	2.5%	14.8%	3.9%	2.0%	1.4%	14.0%	1.7%
El Paso County	3,168	0.0%	7.4%	20.7%	7.5%	0.0%	8.9%	0.6%	17.8%	0.0%	3.6%	10.2%	21.0%	2.3%
Ellis County	29,369	12.3%	2.1%	12.4%	24.4%	3.9%	7.8%	4.6%	11.9%	1.8%	3.2%	5.9%	8.7%	1.2%
Fort Bend County	31,637	15.0%	7.7%	7.7%	31.6%	1.2%	5.0%	4.6%	11.2%	2.7%	1.9%	3.5%	5.0%	2.9%
Galveston County	14,710	16.9%	2.5%	14.9%	16.9%	4.8%	8.1%	2.4%	14.8%	0.3%	3.2%	4.0%	7.4%	3.7%
Grayson County	1,982	2.4%	0.0%	7.5%	16.6%	10.2%	9.7%	0.0%	1.0%	0.0%	2.1%	11.2%	30.1%	9.1%
Gregg County	4,423	27.2%	0.0%	19.4%	18.1%	0.0%	0.0%	0.0%	5.7%	0.0%	0.0%	0.0%	29.6%	0.0%
Guadalupe County	3,633	4.5%	6.2%	27.2%	18.3%	3.3%	10.7%	3.9%	1.9%	0.0%	4.2%	7.5%	8.1%	4.2%
Harris County	236,871	14.9%	5.9%	9.4%	25.1%	4.4%	6.1%	5.3%	8.2%	3.2%	3.6%	4.4%	5.6%	3.9%
Hays County	11,311	3.9%	13.0%	0.5%	22.9%	4.0%	19.1%	8.4%	2.7%	2.1%	4.2%	7.3%	10.1%	1.9%
Hidalgo County	21,307	7.7%	2.7%	12.2%	21.5%	8.4%	5.5%	3.8%	5.8%	5.4%	5.5%	6.4%	12.5%	2.7%
Jefferson County	8,846	18.4%	4.7%	17.7%	11.2%	9.3%	1.8%	5.1%	6.9%	1.8%	6.5%	3.5%	12.3%	1.0%
Johnson County	3,183	8.8%	2.1%	12.9%	15.6%	0.0%	1.5%	0.8%	6.1%	2.9%	26.3%	4.1%	19.0%	0.0%
Kaufman County	3,980	0.0%	1.3%	10.9%	6.4%	2.5%	12.8%	2.8%	13.7%	0.0%	6.9%	11.8%	24.2%	6.6%
Lubbock County	15,539	9.8%	4.4%	8.5%	19.7%	5.0%	5.3%	8.1%	13.5%	0.9%	4.1%	9.1%	6.9%	4.5%
McLennan County	10,773	2.7%	6.5%	8.4%	28.0%	1.3%	4.5%	5.7%	10.7%	5.0%	7.9%	5.5%	6.3%	7.4%
Midland County	5,299	25.3%	0.0%	16.5%	11.2%	14.2%	1.2%	1.8%	9.9%	5.5%	0.0%	6.1%	7.1%	1.1%
Montgomery County	20,934	9.9%	8.5%	4.8%	25.2%	4.7%	5.3%	13.6%	5.5%	1.8%	6.3%	1.1%	11.0%	2.5%
Nueces County	10,811	7.4%	1.1%	9.4%	26.0%	4.4%	11.2%	8.2%	6.7%	2.0%	1.0%	8.0%	12.8%	1.8%
Parker County	3,791	8.5%	0.0%	5.9%	38.1%	5.3%	6.2%	3.4%	15.4%	0.0%	7.9%	0.0%	6.6%	2.5%

Table F-2: Counties—Educational Field of Study—*Continued*

	Total Millennial Population with Bachelor's or Higher	Percent of the Population 18 to 33 by Field of Study												
		Engineering	Computers and Math	Science and Engineering Related	Business	Physical Science	Social Science	Communications	Biological Sciences	Literature	Liberal Arts	Psychology	Education	Visual and Performing Arts
Texas—Cont.														
Potter County	2,328	0.0%	0.0%	14.0%	21.3%	0.0%	22.9%	2.4%	3.9%	5.1%	6.4%	9.6%	11.0%	2.5%
Randall County	4,347	12.7%	6.3%	6.5%	10.6%	0.0%	0.0%	9.5%	15.0%	2.0%	14.4%	0.0%	19.8%	3.2%
Smith County	7,950	8.5%	3.7%	18.4%	26.9%	1.2%	3.5%	1.9%	8.8%	4.3%	3.8%	0.8%	14.9%	3.3%
Tarrant County	85,541	7.7%	5.0%	11.5%	24.9%	3.0%	7.1%	5.4%	7.9%	3.3%	6.0%	4.9%	9.7%	3.5%
Taylor County	4,593	8.8%	0.0%	15.1%	24.1%	0.0%	4.1%	6.5%	6.2%	9.2%	7.7%	5.9%	6.4%	5.9%
Tom Green County	5,148	0.0%	6.7%	14.6%	27.8%	7.0%	4.1%	6.5%	10.0%	1.0%	0.6%	4.2%	10.7%	6.9%
Travis County	113,691	12.0%	6.5%	5.1%	19.6%	4.1%	9.9%	9.8%	6.0%	6.0%	4.2%	5.5%	4.4%	7.0%
Webb County	6,387	0.8%	0.8%	11.8%	30.9%	2.1%	7.0%	6.4%	7.2%	1.3%	4.0%	17.1%	10.9%	0.0%
Wichita County	4,745	14.8%	0.0%	12.1%	24.6%	3.2%	3.0%	1.5%	3.7%	0.0%	2.4%	9.8%	22.2%	2.6%
Williamson County	23,250	12.0%	11.1%	10.7%	20.1%	2.0%	5.3%	2.5%	8.4%	7.6%	3.2%	4.7%	7.2%	5.3%
Utah														
Cache County	6,439	7.3%	5.4%	20.2%	19.5%	1.9%	4.0%	0.9%	12.8%	4.2%	4.4%	2.8%	6.2%	10.2%
Davis County	12,788	8.3%	3.2%	8.1%	24.1%	1.0%	9.1%	7.7%	2.8%	3.2%	2.0%	8.6%	15.5%	6.5%
Salt Lake County	55,530	6.6%	5.9%	10.5%	22.0%	2.5%	8.1%	8.6%	7.6%	6.5%	2.8%	5.2%	7.9%	5.7%
Utah County	29,406	4.0%	6.2%	16.2%	16.1%	3.5%	3.6%	6.6%	5.0%	10.1%	3.7%	5.4%	12.0%	7.6%
Washington County	3,559	13.4%	14.6%	15.4%	8.5%	0.0%	0.0%	14.2%	11.9%	0.0%	0.0%	5.7%	1.6%	14.7%
Weber County	6,947	5.6%	2.2%	19.0%	23.8%	2.1%	2.1%	1.7%	7.0%	4.9%	2.1%	4.4%	15.1%	9.9%
Vermont														
Chittenden County	14,695	6.2%	11.3%	3.0%	12.4%	1.2%	4.4%	2.9%	13.6%	11.1%	12.2%	7.6%	6.9%	7.1%
Virginia														
Albemarle County	6,720	8.9%	11.5%	16.0%	17.1%	3.0%	11.4%	1.0%	11.3%	3.9%	3.6%	2.8%	8.0%	1.4%
Arlington County	52,025	8.0%	7.7%	7.4%	19.8%	4.1%	25.3%	5.1%	5.5%	2.9%	5.1%	3.9%	2.1%	3.0%
Chesterfield County	12,405	8.3%	4.7%	9.2%	20.0%	1.8%	6.4%	7.1%	13.2%	3.6%	6.7%	5.9%	6.9%	6.2%
Fairfax County	98,651	13.0%	11.0%	5.5%	17.4%	3.0%	12.6%	5.3%	6.6%	5.6%	4.2%	6.2%	5.7%	3.9%
Hanover County	2,869	1.7%	0.0%	12.6%	15.7%	1.0%	19.8%	3.1%	2.1%	6.9%	7.0%	14.2%	5.5%	10.5%
Henrico County	19,976	8.2%	7.1%	10.4%	19.2%	2.1%	8.7%	4.6%	7.7%	3.5%	9.8%	9.6%	7.0%	2.0%
Loudoun County	27,993	5.8%	8.4%	8.3%	22.2%	1.5%	14.8%	6.6%	5.3%	1.9%	6.6%	7.1%	6.6%	4.8%
Montgomery County	9,831	19.7%	8.7%	12.0%	10.4%	6.5%	2.8%	0.6%	22.7%	1.6%	2.9%	4.5%	4.1%	3.4%
Prince William County	22,864	8.3%	6.6%	5.9%	21.9%	2.2%	11.5%	7.7%	5.6%	3.3%	5.7%	7.7%	5.2%	8.4%
Roanoke County	4,505	26.1%	4.3%	5.0%	11.6%	8.2%	18.4%	4.6%	4.6%	0.0%	0.0%	13.6%	3.2%	0.3%
Spotsylvania County	3,722	6.4%	11.1%	5.3%	18.1%	0.9%	15.8%	2.9%	0.0%	3.8%	11.7%	11.9%	9.6%	2.4%
Stafford County	6,577	9.6%	3.3%	6.8%	12.1%	0.0%	26.5%	11.9%	5.4%	1.1%	7.0%	4.1%	5.3%	6.7%
Washington														
Benton County	5,354	5.1%	3.0%	8.1%	17.9%	6.9%	11.8%	4.0%	6.8%	5.6%	8.4%	4.5%	17.9%	0.0%
Clark County	15,272	6.6%	5.6%	10.0%	21.3%	0.0%	7.0%	6.7%	6.4%	4.5%	5.8%	8.2%	11.1%	6.9%
Cowlitz County	2,161	1.4%	0.0%	27.6%	19.4%	0.0%	3.8%	0.0%	18.2%	0.0%	0.0%	5.1%	24.3%	0.0%
Grant County	2,018	0.0%	11.4%	21.2%	20.4%	0.0%	14.2%	0.0%	29.0%	3.8%	0.0%	0.0%	0.0%	0.0%
King County	208,442	11.4%	12.3%	8.4%	17.3%	3.1%	10.8%	4.9%	9.1%	4.7%	4.5%	4.7%	2.5%	6.3%
Kitsap County	8,518	15.4%	2.5%	7.3%	13.9%	0.0%	11.5%	9.8%	8.0%	0.8%	11.7%	5.3%	7.6%	6.2%
Pierce County	26,795	2.5%	6.3%	9.7%	18.5%	1.6%	14.8%	7.0%	7.0%	4.7%	7.6%	9.1%	7.3%	3.8%
Skagit County	2,548	7.6%	0.0%	2.9%	15.8%	5.0%	11.6%	0.4%	23.2%	7.3%	4.7%	12.7%	8.5%	0.4%
Snohomish County	34,304	13.7%	8.1%	10.0%	19.6%	1.4%	10.9%	5.4%	4.1%	4.7%	5.7%	5.6%	4.7%	6.0%
Spokane County	18,469	3.5%	2.7%	11.0%	21.0%	0.9%	10.6%	6.5%	11.6%	5.6%	6.5%	5.4%	12.2%	2.5%
Thurston County	9,249	7.2%	6.6%	12.2%	5.5%	0.7%	16.9%	3.4%	17.5%	5.6%	3.4%	11.8%	5.6%	3.6%
Whatcom County	8,693	2.3%	3.8%	4.2%	20.5%	9.2%	7.2%	7.4%	6.9%	9.1%	9.7%	6.9%	2.4%	10.6%
Yakima County	3,764	0.0%	2.2%	17.0%	3.3%	6.1%	15.1%	1.0%	11.9%	3.4%	18.9%	6.8%	6.1%	8.3%
West Virginia														
Berkeley County	2,165	3.2%	0.0%	11.5%	30.4%	0.5%	5.2%	9.1%	0.0%	12.7%	10.9%	8.5%	5.4%	2.7%
Cabell County	4,530	2.2%	5.1%	17.9%	13.0%	7.3%	5.1%	3.9%	14.6%	3.0%	4.3%	12.5%	5.7%	5.4%
Kanawha County	5,733	7.6%	0.0%	33.2%	13.8%	8.8%	4.4%	10.4%	10.7%	0.0%	0.0%	7.0%	2.5%	1.5%
Monongalia County	9,720	16.2%	0.6%	14.2%	16.1%	3.7%	9.1%	6.1%	24.8%	1.9%	0.6%	1.3%	3.4%	2.0%
Wisconsin														
Brown County	8,568	14.5%	5.3%	8.4%	23.8%	0.0%	6.0%	12.5%	4.3%	10.2%	0.7%	1.2%	12.0%	1.2%
Dane County	61,509	15.0%	5.7%	6.7%	13.7%	3.9%	9.2%	6.9%	15.3%	6.8%	4.0%	4.2%	2.3%	6.3%
Eau Claire County	5,863	0.0%	0.0%	12.5%	41.6%	0.0%	0.2%	16.9%	1.1%	1.7%	10.1%	0.8%	15.1%	0.0%
Fond du Lac County	2,316	1.9%	3.6%	6.2%	36.8%	6.1%	0.0%	15.4%	0.0%	3.7%	0.0%	9.2%	13.2%	3.9%
Kenosha County	4,090	2.6%	3.3%	15.2%	28.0%	5.0%	15.7%	9.0%	4.9%	0.0%	5.6%	0.0%	5.6%	5.1%
La Crosse County	5,438	3.5%	2.7%	21.1%	23.7%	1.2%	6.1%	5.6%	16.5%	0.0%	0.0%	13.3%	6.3%	0.0%
Marathon County	6,067	8.1%	5.3%	13.6%	16.3%	3.5%	8.4%	18.4%	9.8%	0.0%	0.5%	8.3%	6.9%	0.8%
Milwaukee County	57,814	7.7%	4.2%	12.4%	19.7%	4.7%	7.8%	9.4%	9.3%	4.1%	2.8%	4.8%	5.2%	7.9%
Outagamie County	8,536	2.9%	8.8%	9.6%	23.5%	0.0%	5.2%	0.0%	15.1%	9.7%	1.2%	2.0%	6.5%	15.5%
Racine County	5,520	10.7%	0.0%	12.5%	33.3%	3.5%	5.1%	1.6%	1.5%	15.1%	2.9%	1.2%	9.5%	3.2%
Rock County	5,106	4.0%	7.4%	5.3%	17.7%	4.2%	4.3%	4.5%	2.5%	7.1%	6.6%	20.1%	5.4%	10.9%
Sheboygan County	3,951	7.6%	8.6%	17.2%	5.9%	0.0%	0.0%	10.3%	5.6%	0.9%	15.1%	0.0%	23.4%	5.4%
Walworth County	3,067	10.5%	1.7%	5.3%	15.9%	0.0%	9.9%	8.3%	24.2%	1.8%	3.9%	1.6%	17.0%	0.0%
Washington County	6,797	0.0%	0.0%	3.8%	28.6%	3.0%	2.9%	6.1%	19.7%	5.5%	4.2%	0.0%	21.3%	4.9%
Waukesha County	16,893	8.3%	6.6%	11.3%	27.9%	0.7%	6.2%	7.0%	3.3%	5.3%	2.2%	6.8%	12.5%	2.1%
Winnebago County	6,696	0.0%	1.8%	7.5%	40.8%	1.8%	1.7%	1.9%	3.0%	0.0%	3.7%	0.0%	28.6%	9.3%
Wyoming														
Laramie County	3,402	9.4%	0.0%	7.7%	13.3%	3.8%	16.1%	1.1%	22.9%	2.0%	8.5%	5.8%	7.0%	2.4%

Table F-3: Places—Educational Field of Study

	Total Millennial Population with Bachelor's or Higher	Percent of the Population 18 to 33 by Field of Study												
		Engineering	Computers and Math	Science and Engineering Related	Business	Physical Science	Social Science	Communications	Biological Sciences	Literature	Liberal Arts	Psychology	Education	Visual and Performing Arts
Alabama														
Birmingham city	10,847	2.2%	2.8%	7.4%	22.1%	4.8%	6.7%	7.6%	8.3%	3.7%	4.0%	8.7%	13.1%	8.5%
Huntsville city	10,678	18.3%	8.7%	7.7%	21.3%	2.2%	2.8%	1.5%	4.3%	9.2%	0.6%	10.0%	2.3%	11.1%
Mobile city	9,074	10.6%	5.5%	25.0%	8.9%	6.1%	0.7%	10.6%	10.8%	2.5%	4.3%	1.9%	10.5%	2.5%
Montgomery city	6,651	5.4%	7.1%	8.4%	25.7%	1.4%	5.0%	9.5%	3.0%	4.0%	1.0%	16.1%	4.0%	9.2%
Tuscaloosa city	4,536	12.7%	3.2%	0.0%	29.2%	0.0%	18.8%	4.3%	7.6%	2.3%	0.0%	6.1%	9.4%	6.4%
Alaska														
Anchorage municipality	15,090	14.9%	2.5%	13.9%	12.1%	3.2%	8.2%	5.3%	18.4%	4.3%	3.9%	3.7%	6.4%	3.3%
Arizona														
Chandler city	16,450	9.1%	11.9%	11.7%	18.1%	4.5%	7.7%	6.9%	5.6%	2.3%	1.5%	6.0%	13.0%	1.6%
Glendale city	6,958	5.6%	5.9%	21.4%	17.9%	5.2%	1.4%	1.6%	14.9%	1.4%	5.0%	4.3%	4.1%	11.4%
Mesa city	16,753	10.1%	2.3%	7.7%	17.0%	3.8%	12.2%	8.1%	16.2%	1.8%	0.8%	2.5%	15.4%	2.2%
Peoria city	4,989	7.4%	1.4%	15.0%	18.2%	1.5%	1.8%	14.2%	11.7%	3.9%	2.8%	5.9%	9.7%	6.5%
Phoenix city	63,876	10.6%	6.4%	10.1%	20.5%	1.8%	7.4%	7.2%	5.2%	3.3%	4.1%	6.4%	9.6%	7.4%
Scottsdale city	20,138	4.5%	5.0%	3.8%	37.2%	1.8%	8.5%	13.9%	4.2%	1.3%	6.3%	3.4%	5.7%	4.4%
Surprise city	3,194	1.8%	0.0%	17.5%	20.2%	6.4%	3.7%	6.8%	2.8%	3.0%	0.0%	2.2%	32.8%	2.9%
Tempe city	16,877	28.2%	13.6%	6.0%	7.4%	4.4%	4.4%	6.6%	5.2%	2.0%	3.4%	7.6%	7.9%	3.5%
Tucson city	21,843	15.0%	4.5%	2.2%	12.3%	4.9%	17.5%	4.2%	11.8%	6.2%	3.3%	6.6%	6.4%	4.9%
Yuma city	1,880	10.8%	0.0%	26.1%	16.9%	0.0%	3.4%	1.9%	0.0%	0.0%	5.2%	3.2%	32.6%	0.0%
Arkansas														
Little Rock city	12,455	6.6%	6.8%	10.8%	17.8%	3.7%	6.8%	6.0%	23.3%	1.9%	6.1%	0.8%	5.8%	3.7%
California														
Anaheim city	14,091	11.7%	10.7%	2.3%	17.5%	3.4%	8.9%	4.0%	11.4%	10.0%	3.7%	4.5%	4.5%	7.6%
Antioch city	3,242	5.6%	7.8%	31.6%	8.3%	0.0%	8.9%	0.0%	6.4%	3.5%	24.2%	1.9%	0.0%	1.6%
Bakersfield city	11,297	12.8%	7.1%	3.4%	12.9%	6.1%	5.2%	3.1%	7.6%	3.9%	9.3%	5.5%	16.6%	6.6%
Berkeley city	20,462	16.1%	6.1%	4.9%	9.4%	9.6%	17.4%	1.5%	7.9%	8.4%	4.2%	7.3%	0.7%	6.5%
Burbank city	9,745	1.9%	9.8%	6.4%	13.6%	0.0%	8.8%	18.6%	3.5%	2.8%	3.1%	3.9%	2.0%	25.5%
Carlsbad city	8,008	8.7%	1.0%	12.1%	17.8%	6.8%	9.3%	7.9%	13.4%	6.8%	3.6%	8.7%	0.0%	3.9%
Chico city	4,404	9.6%	2.2%	3.0%	10.9%	2.2%	13.6%	18.4%	13.8%	9.3%	0.0%	1.7%	7.8%	7.4%
Carson city	4,946	1.4%	10.2%	17.6%	18.3%	1.5%	13.9%	14.6%	5.7%	0.0%	0.0%	10.9%	0.0%	5.8%
Chula Vista city	6,875	22.1%	0.0%	5.9%	15.7%	1.2%	6.7%	1.6%	15.0%	3.4%	13.4%	6.6%	2.9%	5.5%
Clovis city	5,523	15.2%	4.4%	6.4%	14.4%	0.0%	19.9%	10.1%	6.5%	9.2%	4.6%	4.8%	0.9%	3.6%
Compton city	928	17.5%	0.0%	13.6%	33.7%	0.0%	0.0%	0.0%	0.0%	0.0%	0.0%	23.1%	0.0%	12.2%
Concord city	7,347	11.0%	2.2%	14.0%	17.4%	2.2%	14.5%	2.8%	12.5%	3.5%	9.9%	4.0%	1.3%	4.6%
Corona city	4,128	10.0%	5.1%	13.4%	11.7%	2.4%	5.6%	5.0%	7.4%	1.3%	19.9%	7.0%	3.6%	7.7%
Costa Mesa city	10,406	14.9%	3.2%	10.5%	25.0%	3.9%	2.1%	5.4%	2.3%	6.3%	12.0%	2.6%	7.8%	4.2%
Daly City city	8,660	6.7%	5.7%	10.2%	26.3%	1.5%	5.0%	5.1%	7.0%	0.0%	10.2%	5.3%	5.8%	11.1%
Downey city	3,467	0.0%	6.2%	7.4%	22.4%	8.6%	6.0%	3.2%	18.5%	7.8%	0.0%	14.9%	4.9%	0.0%
El Cajon city	2,194	12.2%	16.6%	10.4%	18.8%	0.0%	3.3%	2.9%	26.4%	2.9%	3.8%	2.6%	0.0%	0.0%
Elk Grove city	6,195	8.3%	5.6%	13.2%	21.3%	0.0%	10.8%	14.1%	13.9%	2.8%	1.5%	3.5%	4.9%	0.0%
El Monte city	3,677	20.7%	1.8%	6.9%	23.8%	0.0%	8.5%	0.0%	9.2%	7.8%	1.2%	11.4%	8.6%	0.0%
Escondido city	5,020	2.4%	1.8%	16.0%	16.0%	2.9%	0.0%	4.7%	21.6%	10.0%	7.1%	1.9%	1.6%	14.0%
Fairfield city	3,153	13.4%	4.8%	12.3%	14.9%	2.6%	5.7%	14.8%	6.3%	5.0%	13.2%	7.0%	0.0%	0.0%
Fontana city	3,439	6.5%	2.8%	12.2%	36.6%	0.0%	5.1%	0.0%	0.0%	0.0%	15.0%	21.8%	0.0%	0.0%
Fremont city	22,697	22.2%	24.2%	6.2%	16.4%	4.1%	7.0%	2.4%	4.9%	1.3%	2.6%	2.4%	2.6%	3.8%
Fresno city	14,538	4.1%	5.1%	14.5%	10.2%	0.0%	11.7%	7.3%	8.3%	6.4%	9.5%	12.6%	3.7%	6.5%
Fullerton city	8,826	8.6%	1.9%	9.6%	22.4%	2.2%	6.8%	5.9%	5.0%	11.1%	8.3%	1.5%	2.1%	14.6%
Garden Grove city	7,924	5.8%	3.2%	15.5%	20.9%	3.4%	8.1%	2.1%	12.0%	6.5%	3.2%	5.1%	8.1%	6.0%
Glendale city	14,700	7.4%	7.8%	12.4%	14.6%	1.0%	12.6%	8.9%	4.5%	3.3%	4.7%	5.8%	0.5%	16.5%
Hayward city	10,254	11.4%	7.3%	15.7%	27.8%	7.4%	8.0%	1.5%	7.2%	0.0%	1.0%	5.6%	5.4%	1.6%
Hesperia city	2,999	0.0%	6.3%	12.8%	0.0%	15.3%	7.2%	2.8%	0.0%	27.4%	4.2%	15.0%	9.1%	0.0%
Huntington Beach city	13,598	16.8%	3.7%	6.9%	16.6%	1.7%	10.8%	6.9%	12.8%	3.9%	4.9%	6.3%	2.5%	6.2%
Inglewood city	2,860	0.0%	0.0%	17.1%	22.8%	0.0%	19.4%	9.9%	1.5%	0.0%	10.2%	3.2%	3.0%	12.8%
Irvine city	32,178	16.0%	13.5%	4.6%	18.7%	6.6%	13.3%	2.2%	8.6%	3.9%	2.1%	3.7%	1.0%	5.6%
Jurupa Valley city	2,796	6.2%	12.9%	14.9%	28.6%	0.0%	14.7%	0.0%	5.1%	4.7%	0.0%	2.2%	2.3%	8.3%
Lancaster city	2,042	2.3%	3.0%	13.0%	37.5%	1.6%	8.6%	2.5%	5.5%	0.0%	6.5%	16.6%	0.0%	3.0%
Long Beach city	23,771	6.1%	5.3%	12.6%	21.3%	0.8%	13.5%	5.0%	6.2%	5.2%	8.4%	6.4%	2.1%	7.2%
Los Angeles city	276,750	7.2%	3.8%	5.8%	16.7%	2.1%	13.1%	10.3%	5.3%	5.2%	4.7%	6.3%	2.1%	17.4%
Mission Viejo city	5,473	1.2%	8.7%	4.7%	28.9%	1.8%	6.7%	5.2%	8.2%	1.2%	8.9%	8.5%	2.9%	13.1%
Modesto city	5,559	2.5%	4.9%	21.7%	7.4%	0.0%	11.9%	9.0%	16.3%	10.8%	1.4%	8.0%	0.0%	6.1%
Moreno Valley city	6,054	8.9%	2.5%	15.7%	14.2%	1.5%	7.8%	1.0%	9.6%	13.4%	5.7%	5.5%	10.5%	3.7%
Murrieta city	2,287	9.6%	4.8%	16.2%	16.4%	0.0%	5.1%	21.0%	1.4%	3.7%	12.8%	0.0%	0.0%	9.1%
Norwalk city	3,539	6.6%	5.6%	4.4%	9.9%	4.2%	20.2%	5.1%	15.9%	8.5%	6.0%	11.1%	1.9%	0.7%
Oakland city	36,360	7.8%	6.1%	5.5%	8.4%	5.3%	14.6%	5.5%	9.0%	10.3%	7.1%	8.8%	1.2%	10.4%
Oceanside city	5,046	6.6%	4.6%	14.2%	14.9%	4.1%	8.2%	9.6%	12.5%	6.5%	3.7%	5.0%	1.2%	8.8%
Ontario city	4,807	8.2%	4.2%	19.5%	23.0%	3.0%	12.6%	2.1%	7.3%	2.8%	4.2%	8.3%	0.0%	4.8%
Orange city	9,267	9.1%	0.0%	5.8%	30.2%	0.6%	11.4%	5.7%	6.6%	3.1%	3.1%	7.8%	6.1%	10.6%
Oxnard city	5,882	2.4%	0.0%	20.6%	15.5%	1.2%	6.2%	6.2%	7.2%	0.7%	11.3%	10.4%	13.8%	4.5%
Palmdale city	2,430	19.0%	0.0%	21.4%	5.9%	4.4%	8.9%	7.7%	8.7%	11.1%	0.0%	5.6%	3.8%	3.4%
Pasadena city	13,636	9.8%	3.7%	12.1%	15.1%	5.5%	12.8%	6.2%	6.9%	7.9%	1.7%	4.0%	1.0%	13.4%
Pomona city	7,445	13.6%	3.3%	4.9%	12.2%	7.1%	11.2%	2.7%	12.7%	1.3%	3.9%	14.5%	1.6%	11.1%
Rancho Cucamonga city	8,080	4.9%	8.5%	7.6%	30.0%	5.7%	9.1%	3.2%	2.1%	3.5%	6.2%	11.8%	4.2%	3.3%
Redding city	3,439	0.0%	0.9%	1.8%	19.7%	0.0%	6.5%	8.2%	17.0%	2.9%	28.1%	11.3%	3.4%	0.0%
Rialto city	2,308	0.0%	6.1%	2.6%	60.4%	0.0%	5.5%	15.3%	2.9%	0.0%	4.0%	0.0%	1.6%	1.7%

Table F-3: Places—Educational Field of Study—*Continued*

	Total Millennial Population with Bachelor's or Higher	Percent of the Population 18 to 33 by Field of Study												
		Engineering	Computers and Math	Science and Engineering Related	Business	Physical Science	Social Science	Communications	Biological Sciences	Literature	Liberal Arts	Psychology	Education	Visual and Performing Arts
California—Cont.														
Richmond city..................	4,915	5.4%	7.1%	8.0%	13.9%	0.0%	20.6%	2.1%	11.6%	4.1%	2.4%	6.6%	3.7%	14.5%
Riverside city.....................	13,104	9.5%	5.4%	5.2%	23.5%	10.7%	13.2%	3.2%	5.2%	3.0%	4.3%	10.7%	3.8%	2.3%
Roseville city....................	6,148	7.9%	0.0%	15.3%	37.9%	2.6%	1.6%	4.6%	6.6%	5.1%	7.3%	2.7%	4.5%	3.9%
Sacramento city..................	24,257	9.0%	2.0%	5.2%	15.9%	1.6%	15.7%	6.3%	13.1%	5.8%	6.9%	10.5%	3.4%	4.5%
Salinas city........................	2,625	0.0%	3.2%	0.0%	20.9%	0.0%	20.8%	14.5%	7.8%	0.0%	4.6%	0.0%	0.0%	28.3%
San Bernardino city............	3,228	3.8%	27.3%	11.6%	12.4%	1.8%	11.3%	2.9%	9.0%	0.0%	10.9%	1.8%	2.5%	4.6%
San Buenaventura (Ventura) city..................................	4,431	7.0%	7.6%	4.5%	10.9%	0.0%	18.1%	4.9%	11.6%	22.5%	6.2%	4.7%	2.2%	0.0%
San Diego city....................	125,552	13.2%	7.6%	6.7%	17.0%	3.9%	13.1%	6.3%	9.1%	2.7%	7.4%	5.8%	2.5%	4.8%
San Francisco city..............	148,317	10.4%	9.5%	4.7%	21.3%	2.1%	14.0%	6.0%	9.2%	5.2%	3.6%	4.6%	0.9%	8.7%
San Jose city.....................	67,236	18.4%	13.1%	5.6%	20.5%	2.4%	9.0%	6.8%	6.5%	3.6%	2.5%	4.8%	2.0%	4.8%
San Leandro city................	6,910	4.2%	8.3%	14.0%	28.8%	4.3%	12.5%	7.2%	8.5%	2.3%	5.4%	1.6%	1.6%	1.2%
San Marcos city..................	4,383	3.7%	4.8%	16.7%	17.2%	0.0%	11.2%	6.8%	10.0%	11.2%	0.0%	0.0%	5.8%	12.5%
San Mateo city...................	10,088	21.1%	19.8%	3.9%	14.8%	2.9%	12.9%	4.3%	5.8%	1.9%	0.0%	3.6%	4.6%	4.4%
Santa Ana city....................	9,027	3.1%	4.6%	6.8%	28.2%	1.1%	16.0%	8.1%	8.5%	4.6%	2.2%	9.9%	2.0%	4.9%
Santa Clara city.................	20,967	25.0%	25.3%	3.6%	17.1%	2.1%	5.3%	4.3%	4.9%	1.5%	1.7%	7.3%	2.0%	0.0%
Santa Clarita city...............	8,921	2.3%	1.4%	6.2%	16.3%	2.5%	14.8%	16.9%	0.9%	9.9%	7.0%	9.3%	4.0%	8.4%
Santa Maria city.................	1,468	4.2%	3.7%	4.8%	13.4%	8.0%	0.0%	3.7%	4.0%	0.0%	12.5%	12.3%	5.6%	27.9%
Santa Monica city...............	13,308	6.7%	2.8%	5.6%	25.7%	1.9%	10.9%	18.5%	5.9%	5.9%	1.7%	6.8%	1.4%	6.2%
Santa Rosa city..................	7,149	12.8%	6.2%	13.2%	8.1%	2.6%	11.6%	0.0%	11.6%	3.7%	8.6%	17.5%	0.0%	4.0%
Simi Valley city..................	6,895	9.3%	10.8%	13.8%	14.4%	1.9%	7.3%	11.3%	5.0%	2.5%	1.2%	11.4%	3.9%	7.1%
South Gate city..................	1,790	11.1%	0.0%	8.8%	8.9%	2.1%	25.9%	0.0%	15.7%	0.0%	0.0%	7.8%	15.1%	4.6%
Stockton city......................	6,896	6.3%	6.4%	6.0%	27.2%	2.4%	12.2%	5.9%	7.9%	3.8%	7.6%	5.5%	7.4%	1.4%
Sunnyvale city....................	22,400	33.5%	25.3%	4.7%	10.4%	1.0%	6.7%	3.3%	5.3%	2.5%	1.6%	2.6%	1.3%	1.9%
Temecula city.....................	3,813	12.9%	9.0%	0.0%	38.0%	0.0%	17.1%	3.7%	1.4%	2.0%	6.4%	0.0%	2.3%	7.2%
Thousand Oaks city............	5,917	4.1%	16.8%	7.5%	12.7%	3.8%	7.8%	12.5%	9.6%	1.5%	4.2%	5.0%	10.3%	4.2%
Torrance city......................	8,128	11.1%	10.1%	12.6%	18.7%	2.8%	12.4%	3.1%	5.2%	5.2%	5.9%	4.9%	4.4%	3.6%
Vacaville city......................	3,085	13.5%	0.0%	9.6%	4.2%	2.5%	15.4%	0.0%	7.7%	8.1%	20.8%	9.3%	1.5%	7.5%
Vallejo city.........................	6,151	5.4%	0.0%	12.7%	21.4%	0.0%	16.5%	1.7%	12.6%	6.4%	0.8%	11.0%	4.8%	6.8%
Victorville city....................	1,656	0.0%	0.0%	46.4%	16.4%	21.8%	0.0%	0.0%	0.0%	4.2%	11.2%	0.0%	0.0%	0.0%
Visalia city.........................	3,971	1.7%	0.0%	16.2%	27.6%	2.8%	1.7%	14.0%	20.6%	0.0%	1.3%	7.8%	0.0%	6.3%
Vista city............................	3,920	2.2%	8.4%	13.4%	16.3%	7.8%	8.7%	5.9%	12.0%	3.0%	10.4%	7.7%	1.5%	2.8%
West Covina city................	4,792	1.0%	0.0%	10.0%	39.1%	2.4%	13.4%	0.0%	6.8%	5.2%	5.5%	7.1%	5.6%	3.9%
Westminster city................	4,268	20.6%	4.4%	14.4%	15.8%	1.9%	5.6%	13.1%	10.2%	1.4%	6.7%	4.2%	1.6%	0.0%
Colorado														
Arvada city........................	6,220	25.9%	5.9%	9.3%	18.1%	4.1%	7.4%	4.1%	7.4%	3.0%	0.0%	7.4%	3.1%	4.3%
Aurora city.........................	16,464	4.9%	3.1%	12.7%	21.9%	4.8%	6.2%	3.3%	14.1%	3.0%	2.2%	8.0%	10.6%	5.1%
Boulder city.......................	17,221	8.0%	8.4%	3.3%	10.4%	8.9%	4.9%	5.2%	10.2%	9.5%	5.1%	14.8%	2.8%	8.6%
Centennial city...................	4,968	17.3%	6.6%	7.1%	26.5%	4.0%	9.4%	3.4%	8.5%	0.0%	6.5%	6.8%	0.0%	3.8%
Colorado Springs city...........	22,549	12.5%	4.6%	12.8%	14.2%	5.9%	9.4%	6.2%	7.9%	4.8%	4.2%	10.0%	6.7%	0.9%
Denver city........................	82,270	7.7%	3.4%	8.3%	20.0%	2.2%	11.4%	9.3%	7.8%	3.8%	5.4%	6.9%	4.0%	9.7%
Fort Collins city..................	18,480	9.0%	5.8%	8.7%	14.2%	8.8%	8.7%	3.3%	15.2%	6.4%	2.2%	6.3%	4.5%	6.9%
Greeley city.......................	3,049	2.6%	0.0%	10.1%	28.9%	0.0%	9.2%	10.0%	17.2%	3.0%	0.0%	11.6%	4.4%	3.1%
Lakewood city....................	11,333	6.5%	8.5%	8.8%	19.1%	4.6%	5.9%	4.4%	12.0%	1.0%	7.1%	9.0%	5.2%	8.0%
Longmont city....................	4,631	6.0%	6.5%	1.5%	34.0%	2.1%	7.0%	2.5%	9.3%	4.6%	1.2%	8.3%	17.0%	0.0%
Pueblo city........................	2,663	5.6%	11.5%	18.1%	25.8%	0.0%	3.9%	3.2%	3.1%	11.7%	2.9%	2.1%	4.9%	7.3%
Thornton city......................	6,070	13.0%	0.0%	14.3%	18.6%	0.0%	16.9%	1.4%	12.2%	2.4%	7.1%	2.4%	6.3%	5.4%
Westminster city................	8,865	11.9%	4.5%	13.4%	28.6%	2.7%	11.5%	5.8%	3.8%	1.4%	2.5%	5.4%	4.0%	4.6%
Connecticut														
Bridgeport city...................	5,893	18.0%	4.2%	7.0%	22.8%	1.5%	4.3%	7.8%	2.5%	10.7%	4.7%	5.1%	8.1%	3.2%
Hartford city......................	5,637	10.1%	2.5%	6.3%	16.6%	5.8%	14.3%	6.2%	10.1%	0.0%	7.1%	7.3%	7.3%	6.4%
New Haven city...................	12,562	4.6%	2.5%	7.2%	12.4%	3.8%	21.8%	3.4%	12.6%	9.8%	6.9%	8.1%	0.9%	5.9%
Stamford city.....................	14,560	6.7%	3.8%	2.7%	25.6%	3.0%	13.9%	7.7%	4.7%	5.9%	8.9%	10.7%	3.4%	3.0%
Waterbury city....................	1,992	8.9%	7.1%	0.0%	11.2%	0.0%	3.5%	5.4%	11.7%	6.1%	11.5%	23.4%	6.1%	5.1%
District of Columbia														
Washington city..................	111,788	4.3%	3.6%	4.7%	14.5%	1.5%	31.1%	7.3%	5.4%	6.5%	9.5%	4.5%	2.8%	4.2%
Florida														
Boca Raton city..................	5,063	3.4%	4.8%	2.0%	51.3%	0.0%	2.6%	7.7%	13.0%	0.0%	3.6%	5.5%	6.1%	0.0%
Cape Coral city...................	3,653	0.0%	0.0%	6.1%	35.0%	0.0%	6.5%	2.5%	1.5%	0.0%	2.6%	6.2%	22.9%	16.7%
Clearwater city...................	3,560	6.2%	17.2%	26.3%	17.8%	0.0%	8.9%	4.9%	5.7%	3.7%	1.2%	1.8%	4.8%	1.5%
Coral Springs city................	5,261	2.4%	7.2%	23.8%	21.4%	1.5%	2.2%	29.6%	4.6%	0.0%	1.6%	1.2%	4.7%	0.0%
Fort Lauderdale city............	8,620	5.6%	6.2%	9.7%	36.1%	0.0%	5.0%	2.0%	5.9%	1.3%	2.5%	12.5%	6.0%	7.1%
Gainesville city...................	15,048	14.5%	9.8%	10.7%	8.7%	4.6%	8.1%	3.0%	22.4%	3.4%	3.6%	3.1%	3.2%	4.9%
Hialeah city........................	5,494	9.0%	2.0%	19.7%	23.9%	4.1%	3.1%	0.0%	3.4%	2.5%	1.6%	1.5%	14.5%	14.8%
Hollywood city....................	6,804	3.3%	0.0%	3.7%	39.4%	0.0%	16.1%	2.2%	7.7%	3.2%	2.2%	9.2%	9.3%	3.5%
Jacksonville city.................	42,946	8.1%	4.7%	13.5%	26.1%	1.3%	7.9%	8.5%	5.3%	1.6%	3.8%	5.1%	9.2%	4.9%
Lakeland city.....................	2,233	0.0%	0.0%	1.4%	27.5%	0.0%	6.4%	0.0%	1.4%	2.0%	13.8%	9.6%	21.7%	16.1%
Miami city..........................	24,540	3.0%	0.9%	12.6%	24.5%	1.5%	11.5%	11.6%	9.1%	6.6%	3.3%	5.2%	4.1%	6.1%
Miami Beach city.................	7,202	7.2%	3.6%	4.9%	32.7%	1.2%	6.6%	5.1%	5.4%	7.2%	10.1%	10.5%	4.0%	1.4%
Miami Gardens city.............	2,373	2.9%	0.0%	11.1%	24.6%	0.0%	20.1%	0.0%	3.1%	1.9%	0.0%	21.8%	14.5%	0.0%
Miramar city.......................	6,085	10.1%	11.4%	14.5%	14.1%	4.7%	3.0%	3.7%	8.7%	2.9%	0.7%	9.8%	16.4%	0.0%
Orlando city.......................	18,709	5.5%	4.2%	10.1%	40.3%	1.7%	7.9%	5.9%	3.3%	3.0%	1.4%	5.5%	3.7%	7.5%
Palm Bay city.....................	3,368	2.2%	7.4%	13.7%	50.7%	0.0%	0.0%	2.3%	0.0%	3.1%	0.0%	13.0%	4.2%	3.4%
Pembroke Pines city............	9,476	8.4%	7.1%	14.9%	29.6%	1.8%	5.4%	1.7%	6.5%	3.0%	1.2%	7.5%	8.8%	4.0%

Table F-3: Places—Educational Field of Study—*Continued*

	Total Millennial Population with Bachelor's or Higher	Percent of the Population 18 to 33 by Field of Study												
		Engineering	Computers and Math	Science and Engineering Related	Business	Physical Science	Social Science	Communications	Biological Sciences	Literature	Liberal Arts	Psychology	Education	Visual and Performing Arts
Florida—Cont.														
Plantation city	4,526	5.2%	8.0%	11.9%	22.3%	0.0%	5.8%	5.5%	9.5%	15.7%	0.0%	10.4%	4.4%	1.3%
Pompano Beach city	3,504	9.3%	10.7%	6.9%	14.6%	5.3%	6.1%	1.4%	6.4%	4.4%	0.0%	21.0%	5.9%	7.8%
Port St. Lucie city	2,520	0.0%	1.6%	22.5%	16.0%	0.0%	5.7%	0.0%	10.1%	0.0%	19.3%	2.4%	15.0%	7.4%
St. Petersburg city	12,565	6.6%	6.8%	12.8%	15.0%	1.7%	11.0%	4.5%	9.9%	2.2%	4.0%	13.3%	3.7%	8.5%
Sunrise city	4,982	4.8%	9.3%	10.8%	23.9%	0.0%	4.0%	5.0%	9.6%	16.5%	0.0%	9.5%	4.0%	2.7%
Tallahassee city	18,339	3.3%	4.6%	8.0%	18.5%	5.6%	14.6%	2.4%	6.9%	9.7%	3.5%	7.8%	6.1%	8.9%
Tampa city	26,352	2.7%	3.7%	10.4%	24.7%	5.0%	10.4%	7.8%	8.2%	3.9%	8.9%	9.7%	2.8%	1.9%
West Palm Beach city	4,715	4.1%	5.5%	9.2%	39.0%	0.0%	9.7%	3.1%	7.2%	0.0%	13.3%	3.5%	4.4%	1.0%
Georgia														
Athens-Clarke County unified govt (balance)	12,114	4.5%	6.0%	7.5%	10.3%	6.1%	8.8%	6.0%	16.5%	9.1%	2.6%	8.7%	8.6%	5.4%
Atlanta city	59,305	13.7%	5.7%	8.3%	23.0%	3.2%	6.6%	7.9%	7.7%	3.1%	3.4%	5.4%	4.8%	7.2%
Augusta-Richmond County consolidated govt (balance)	7,704	13.4%	3.2%	10.6%	17.8%	0.7%	3.9%	11.0%	12.1%	5.6%	2.2%	5.6%	5.9%	8.1%
Columbus city	9,301	17.1%	3.5%	18.5%	19.6%	1.2%	14.4%	4.2%	4.2%	1.7%	2.9%	5.5%	3.4%	3.8%
Macon-Bibb county	6,984	4.8%	2.8%	14.8%	17.0%	9.1%	5.3%	8.0%	11.2%	5.3%	9.9%	5.4%	3.6%	2.8%
Roswell city	4,808	21.8%	7.6%	1.4%	23.7%	0.0%	7.9%	10.1%	0.0%	0.9%	0.0%	14.3%	7.9%	4.4%
Sandy Springs city	14,014	9.9%	8.7%	4.9%	38.3%	4.6%	4.6%	4.1%	2.0%	5.0%	2.3%	6.0%	4.5%	5.0%
Savannah city	7,985	13.6%	3.6%	15.2%	16.5%	2.8%	5.3%	9.8%	6.9%	2.8%	6.0%	2.9%	5.1%	9.4%
Hawaii														
Urban Honolulu CDP	20,010	10.0%	5.0%	6.4%	26.3%	1.3%	10.7%	5.0%	12.8%	6.2%	2.7%	8.0%	1.3%	4.4%
Idaho														
Boise City city	12,645	7.7%	5.0%	7.1%	16.7%	0.7%	5.5%	9.4%	8.3%	6.1%	12.1%	4.5%	8.5%	8.6%
Meridian city	3,024	0.0%	4.6%	18.2%	43.9%	0.0%	0.0%	14.7%	0.0%	0.0%	16.6%	2.0%	0.0%	0.0%
Illinois														
Aurora city	7,119	5.2%	2.6%	16.2%	27.8%	5.5%	1.5%	8.3%	4.0%	2.4%	3.2%	3.4%	10.1%	9.7%
Chicago city	293,161	6.4%	5.9%	6.7%	23.9%	2.5%	10.7%	8.7%	7.3%	4.9%	3.7%	6.6%	4.7%	8.0%
Elgin city	4,211	18.6%	3.3%	16.0%	22.5%	2.6%	2.8%	5.8%	8.2%	0.0%	0.0%	6.2%	6.2%	7.9%
Joliet city	4,358	12.6%	17.1%	4.2%	4.7%	2.1%	1.8%	10.2%	9.1%	3.1%	4.6%	7.0%	11.2%	12.2%
Naperville city	9,586	5.6%	4.5%	13.9%	25.5%	7.7%	5.4%	5.8%	8.9%	3.8%	0.0%	4.1%	8.4%	6.5%
Peoria city	8,838	9.7%	10.1%	18.8%	16.3%	4.7%	0.9%	4.7%	8.2%	1.2%	2.9%	8.4%	6.9%	7.0%
Rockford city	5,914	13.7%	0.8%	25.9%	7.2%	2.2%	6.9%	3.2%	14.1%	3.5%	0.7%	1.8%	10.3%	9.8%
Springfield city	7,004	14.5%	5.2%	13.2%	17.3%	1.1%	3.2%	3.2%	14.2%	3.3%	7.2%	5.9%	10.5%	1.3%
Indiana														
Evansville city	7,384	4.1%	3.3%	15.8%	12.6%	13.7%	1.6%	23.5%	6.5%	0.0%	5.2%	0.0%	8.6%	5.1%
Fort Wayne city	10,768	9.6%	0.0%	17.1%	27.2%	1.4%	4.7%	6.8%	4.5%	2.3%	2.6%	5.0%	13.9%	4.9%
Indianapolis city (balance)	51,239	5.4%	4.6%	11.4%	19.3%	3.4%	7.7%	7.4%	6.7%	3.8%	10.6%	4.8%	11.6%	3.3%
South Bend city	3,932	6.8%	6.2%	3.9%	19.5%	4.9%	17.6%	10.6%	8.0%	0.9%	6.5%	3.4%	7.4%	4.5%
Iowa														
Cedar Rapids city	8,534	3.3%	18.1%	9.1%	25.1%	0.0%	0.4%	3.2%	15.0%	3.8%	7.5%	10.0%	4.0%	0.6%
Davenport city	4,355	8.4%	4.2%	2.8%	38.0%	4.5%	11.2%	0.0%	10.7%	0.0%	4.1%	5.7%	10.3%	0.0%
Des Moines city	11,681	4.3%	3.1%	2.1%	22.3%	2.3%	9.6%	5.3%	23.0%	4.4%	4.9%	6.9%	3.3%	8.5%
Kansas														
Kansas City city	5,093	2.1%	10.7%	6.2%	21.0%	0.0%	3.7%	7.9%	13.0%	1.9%	5.1%	2.7%	13.7%	11.9%
Olathe city	6,399	16.4%	7.2%	12.9%	18.5%	1.7%	3.7%	6.5%	13.3%	2.4%	2.8%	8.9%	1.5%	4.3%
Overland Park city	19,238	8.6%	12.8%	6.5%	20.3%	0.8%	4.6%	6.3%	8.7%	6.0%	3.1%	4.1%	9.6%	8.7%
Topeka city	4,424	1.8%	8.3%	11.7%	22.2%	0.0%	16.3%	0.0%	2.7%	2.7%	1.6%	13.7%	15.3%	3.8%
Wichita city	17,420	7.9%	6.2%	15.2%	20.3%	1.9%	4.5%	5.4%	13.4%	0.3%	6.5%	6.7%	7.0%	4.7%
Kentucky														
Lexington-Fayette urban county	25,152	7.3%	6.3%	10.8%	15.7%	3.9%	10.7%	8.4%	15.0%	5.4%	3.5%	4.8%	5.5%	2.6%
Louisville/Jefferson County metro govt (balance)	31,995	6.8%	4.6%	11.1%	22.8%	3.4%	6.8%	8.7%	8.6%	3.2%	6.7%	5.6%	10.4%	1.3%
Louisiana														
Baton Rouge city	18,146	20.2%	2.9%	8.9%	11.1%	2.9%	4.0%	5.0%	13.9%	3.3%	5.4%	7.7%	7.1%	7.6%
Lafayette city	9,668	5.6%	4.1%	9.2%	16.8%	10.7%	1.2%	0.9%	17.2%	2.6%	18.4%	1.1%	9.9%	2.3%
New Orleans city	33,044	7.2%	2.4%	8.4%	15.8%	4.8%	11.0%	8.6%	9.4%	5.9%	7.5%	8.5%	2.9%	7.6%
Shreveport city	6,020	5.5%	5.2%	6.6%	25.4%	1.1%	0.0%	0.0%	14.4%	0.0%	12.4%	14.8%	2.5%	12.2%
Maryland														
Baltimore city	50,033	9.0%	5.3%	7.9%	17.7%	2.0%	12.4%	6.2%	11.0%	4.0%	5.0%	5.9%	3.5%	10.0%
Massachusetts														
Boston city	112,773	7.0%	3.4%	6.3%	25.9%	2.4%	14.2%	5.6%	10.0%	5.6%	4.7%	7.4%	1.7%	5.7%
Brockton city	3,384	5.6%	6.4%	1.3%	17.6%	0.0%	14.6%	1.6%	13.8%	3.5%	5.7%	15.0%	6.1%	8.7%
Cambridge city	32,371	18.9%	10.2%	6.0%	9.0%	10.5%	15.4%	2.2%	8.6%	5.1%	3.0%	7.2%	0.8%	3.2%
Lowell city	6,051	7.6%	14.5%	12.6%	28.2%	7.8%	5.1%	0.0%	3.0%	5.5%	3.2%	6.6%	3.0%	2.8%
Lynn city	3,808	1.9%	6.8%	5.4%	25.4%	11.0%	3.7%	10.0%	9.4%	2.8%	1.6%	11.4%	4.3%	6.4%
New Bedford city	3,403	0.0%	15.8%	9.3%	9.6%	0.0%	0.0%	8.1%	7.7%	4.6%	5.4%	16.9%	14.0%	8.4%
Quincy city	10,086	7.7%	18.7%	2.7%	21.8%	2.0%	16.0%	9.6%	5.4%	2.2%	3.1%	5.8%	3.0%	2.0%
Springfield city	4,484	3.4%	3.2%	3.7%	10.1%	0.5%	3.8%	9.6%	6.7%	5.1%	1.0%	25.0%	8.2%	19.6%
Worcester city	12,021	5.8%	10.9%	6.8%	12.1%	4.2%	18.3%	4.7%	18.6%	3.7%	3.4%	5.9%	2.8%	2.9%

Table F-3: Places—Educational Field of Study—*Continued*

	Total Millennial Population with Bachelor's or Higher	Percent of the Population 18 to 33 by Field of Study												
		Engineering	Computers and Math	Science and Engineering Related	Business	Physical Science	Social Science	Communications	Biological Sciences	Literature	Liberal Arts	Psychology	Education	Visual and Performing Arts
Michigan														
Ann Arbor city	23,052	15.8%	5.5%	8.7%	5.7%	8.4%	13.2%	1.1%	12.4%	4.8%	6.8%	8.7%	3.5%	5.5%
Dearborn city	4,652	15.3%	8.8%	19.2%	8.9%	0.0%	6.1%	3.7%	12.5%	2.6%	5.1%	11.8%	3.2%	2.7%
Detroit city	17,108	7.2%	8.2%	7.5%	17.9%	4.1%	10.4%	5.3%	9.9%	4.7%	9.5%	7.2%	1.9%	6.2%
Flint city	2,132	0.0%	0.0%	2.7%	19.8%	0.0%	0.0%	0.0%	34.5%	0.0%	0.0%	23.7%	19.4%	0.0%
Grand Rapids city	17,906	3.1%	4.7%	12.3%	21.3%	2.8%	5.7%	9.6%	12.6%	4.2%	2.3%	4.8%	9.2%	7.2%
Lansing city	8,815	5.0%	5.5%	10.4%	10.6%	4.0%	3.0%	5.1%	16.8%	5.5%	7.5%	8.6%	8.3%	9.6%
Livonia city	4,697	4.5%	16.1%	4.4%	19.5%	1.7%	7.2%	14.8%	10.4%	1.8%	7.4%	7.0%	2.7%	2.5%
Sterling Heights city	6,665	14.7%	6.3%	13.5%	18.2%	0.0%	0.0%	21.7%	15.7%	0.0%	0.0%	7.2%	2.7%	0.0%
Warren city	2,802	30.8%	10.9%	4.1%	24.7%	4.2%	0.0%	7.9%	0.0%	3.1%	0.0%	3.0%	7.4%	4.0%
Minnesota														
Minneapolis city	55,972	11.5%	6.9%	6.5%	13.5%	3.5%	11.1%	7.7%	8.4%	5.8%	3.0%	8.8%	2.4%	11.0%
Rochester city	9,457	0.0%	5.4%	29.8%	7.6%	5.9%	11.7%	3.1%	26.2%	3.3%	5.3%	1.7%	0.0%	0.0%
St. Paul city	26,803	3.0%	2.7%	7.4%	14.2%	6.3%	8.8%	2.8%	10.8%	7.9%	4.9%	5.6%	12.0%	13.7%
Mississippi														
Jackson city	11,188	6.5%	3.1%	11.2%	20.2%	10.3%	2.4%	4.1%	14.6%	1.0%	2.2%	7.1%	11.8%	5.6%
Missouri														
Columbia city	15,089	18.8%	11.0%	7.4%	5.1%	4.1%	5.0%	6.1%	15.6%	7.4%	2.2%	5.1%	7.8%	4.5%
Independence city	3,463	1.3%	8.9%	3.8%	32.4%	3.2%	15.9%	0.0%	2.5%	7.4%	6.0%	4.3%	11.7%	1.8%
Kansas City city	28,327	4.5%	3.5%	13.8%	19.2%	2.3%	5.3%	8.4%	7.9%	4.3%	5.7%	10.4%	8.1%	6.7%
Lee's Summit city	6,301	2.9%	6.7%	18.3%	22.6%	0.8%	2.3%	4.1%	7.2%	8.5%	5.8%	3.4%	17.3%	0.0%
St. Louis city	32,206	7.8%	4.9%	4.8%	20.5%	4.7%	8.4%	8.5%	14.7%	5.5%	4.9%	8.2%	2.8%	4.5%
Springfield city	10,302	1.3%	0.9%	11.6%	26.5%	2.9%	5.0%	4.3%	4.4%	2.4%	8.3%	8.9%	17.2%	6.2%
Montana														
Billings city	4,651	10.9%	0.0%	25.0%	7.5%	0.0%	2.7%	0.0%	9.8%	7.5%	16.3%	4.8%	13.6%	1.9%
Nebraska														
Lincoln city	19,692	9.1%	2.3%	11.3%	14.1%	9.4%	9.5%	9.4%	8.1%	4.0%	2.9%	4.4%	10.6%	5.0%
Omaha city	32,190	3.9%	2.8%	13.9%	24.7%	3.6%	1.3%	9.4%	11.5%	5.4%	4.5%	3.5%	12.7%	2.7%
Nevada														
Henderson city	10,154	2.6%	4.1%	6.3%	24.2%	4.2%	10.5%	7.8%	12.3%	3.2%	3.9%	11.3%	3.8%	5.9%
Las Vegas city	17,360	7.5%	2.9%	11.5%	18.5%	1.8%	7.2%	10.0%	7.3%	5.3%	4.3%	8.9%	6.5%	8.4%
North Las Vegas city	5,642	10.7%	2.9%	9.7%	19.1%	1.4%	16.9%	3.5%	11.9%	6.8%	2.6%	5.5%	9.1%	0.0%
Reno city	12,023	4.6%	3.5%	7.3%	35.0%	2.4%	3.9%	7.3%	6.9%	6.5%	7.1%	5.9%	7.1%	2.5%
Sparks city	2,320	12.3%	0.0%	3.6%	42.9%	5.3%	0.0%	13.8%	10.8%	0.0%	0.0%	7.5%	3.6%	0.0%
New Hampshire														
Manchester city	5,852	3.5%	3.5%	11.9%	44.1%	1.5%	7.5%	1.7%	5.8%	1.6%	5.2%	4.5%	5.3%	4.0%
New Jersey														
Elizabeth city	2,739	10.5%	1.9%	6.9%	24.6%	0.0%	0.0%	2.4%	7.1%	21.9%	2.2%	0.0%	8.3%	14.3%
Jersey City city	36,952	18.6%	18.3%	5.8%	26.1%	1.9%	7.3%	2.3%	4.8%	2.4%	2.6%	2.9%	1.8%	5.2%
Newark city	9,342	5.2%	3.0%	20.3%	27.3%	0.8%	5.9%	1.7%	11.9%	0.7%	3.9%	12.6%	4.7%	2.0%
Paterson city	1,814	0.0%	0.0%	0.0%	44.7%	0.0%	5.5%	8.2%	8.7%	7.4%	6.3%	0.0%	17.4%	1.8%
New Mexico														
Albuquerque city	22,851	9.2%	4.2%	8.9%	14.1%	6.1%	10.2%	5.0%	9.0%	7.4%	8.6%	5.9%	6.8%	4.7%
Las Cruces city	1,507	0.0%	0.0%	9.2%	21.8%	0.0%	28.5%	6.2%	25.3%	9.0%	0.0%	0.0%	0.0%	0.0%
Rio Rancho city	2,413	5.1%	0.0%	10.3%	28.4%	19.6%	9.0%	0.0%	5.2%	0.0%	0.0%	10.2%	12.1%	0.0%
New York														
Albany city	10,279	2.1%	8.1%	11.9%	11.5%	2.9%	19.0%	8.2%	12.4%	4.8%	5.4%	6.2%	4.2%	3.2%
Buffalo city	17,152	6.0%	3.6%	9.6%	19.6%	4.1%	10.2%	8.2%	8.8%	8.4%	3.3%	6.1%	6.9%	5.2%
New York city	796,971	4.5%	6.0%	6.3%	21.2%	2.1%	12.6%	7.3%	5.1%	5.7%	5.4%	7.0%	4.0%	12.6%
Rochester city	13,175	2.2%	8.4%	8.3%	17.4%	4.5%	11.2%	5.5%	8.8%	8.0%	4.4%	5.9%	4.4%	11.0%
Syracuse city	10,886	12.2%	3.1%	11.2%	12.1%	2.1%	10.0%	4.6%	12.5%	9.5%	2.8%	4.7%	7.9%	7.2%
Yonkers city	10,561	11.8%	3.7%	11.1%	33.4%	0.0%	10.6%	4.2%	2.2%	6.8%	4.6%	5.4%	4.8%	1.6%
North Carolina														
Charlotte city	66,383	8.4%	6.8%	6.4%	28.8%	2.2%	6.9%	10.2%	5.2%	3.2%	4.5%	7.2%	6.4%	3.8%
Durham city	28,971	6.8%	6.8%	6.9%	11.3%	3.6%	10.5%	4.2%	18.5%	8.0%	7.1%	5.5%	3.4%	7.3%
Fayetteville city	7,870	4.9%	2.6%	11.9%	19.5%	0.7%	8.7%	4.1%	6.8%	8.5%	10.3%	4.8%	5.4%	12.0%
Greensboro city	13,889	5.4%	3.2%	11.0%	13.9%	3.9%	9.6%	8.2%	9.6%	6.6%	7.5%	5.5%	10.0%	5.4%
High Point city	3,648	8.4%	7.5%	12.6%	9.3%	2.0%	11.0%	9.3%	1.7%	8.3%	0.9%	10.7%	8.3%	10.0%
Raleigh city	44,368	6.9%	7.5%	7.8%	18.9%	5.0%	11.6%	7.9%	10.4%	2.3%	5.7%	6.7%	6.3%	3.1%
Wilmington city	7,584	1.7%	4.7%	9.0%	10.3%	0.8%	14.5%	8.1%	5.8%	8.0%	11.7%	5.6%	15.1%	4.7%
Winston-Salem city	14,834	13.6%	7.7%	8.9%	13.4%	3.9%	3.7%	6.0%	14.4%	2.2%	4.0%	8.7%	10.2%	3.3%
North Dakota														
Fargo city	7,912	6.0%	7.4%	16.9%	27.5%	5.7%	2.3%	9.6%	6.5%	6.5%	1.7%	1.8%	5.9%	2.1%
Ohio														
Akron city	7,681	10.5%	1.6%	9.1%	25.7%	8.4%	4.5%	0.8%	7.1%	7.4%	8.2%	9.4%	4.7%	2.6%
Cincinnati city	26,183	9.4%	2.9%	9.5%	19.3%	5.2%	7.6%	9.0%	9.0%	2.9%	5.5%	5.7%	5.3%	8.7%
Cleveland city	16,864	11.6%	5.6%	10.9%	15.1%	2.7%	10.9%	7.9%	11.0%	2.1%	6.3%	8.5%	2.4%	5.1%
Columbus city	74,806	6.9%	4.0%	9.8%	22.6%	3.0%	8.2%	5.5%	10.6%	5.5%	3.8%	5.5%	8.2%	6.4%
Dayton city	4,689	10.3%	4.2%	7.0%	21.3%	4.1%	4.6%	4.8%	8.6%	6.0%	2.0%	1.1%	13.1%	12.8%
Toledo city	8,447	13.9%	4.7%	14.7%	15.7%	2.9%	4.1%	3.6%	14.7%	0.0%	6.4%	3.0%	10.0%	6.2%

Table F-3: Places—Educational Field of Study—*Continued*

	Total Millennial Population with Bachelor's or Higher	Percent of the Population 18 to 33 by Field of Study												
		Engineering	Computers and Math	Science and Engineering Related	Business	Physical Science	Social Science	Communications	Biological Sciences	Literature	Liberal Arts	Psychology	Education	Visual and Performing Arts
Oklahoma														
Broken Arrow city	4,538	4.8%	17.2%	6.9%	26.8%	7.3%	2.4%	0.0%	8.6%	1.9%	0.0%	6.6%	10.1%	7.4%
Edmond city	8,038	0.0%	7.9%	19.1%	26.8%	0.0%	2.4%	4.6%	7.4%	2.6%	8.0%	3.9%	13.1%	4.2%
Lawton city	2,431	0.0%	0.0%	19.0%	27.8%	4.9%	0.0%	0.0%	10.3%	4.1%	0.0%	14.1%	12.8%	7.0%
Norman city	8,207	25.1%	2.3%	9.5%	18.6%	7.3%	7.2%	7.5%	3.1%	2.1%	8.8%	1.0%	2.1%	5.5%
Oklahoma City city	29,304	11.8%	0.7%	11.7%	29.3%	3.2%	5.5%	4.4%	8.7%	3.7%	5.4%	3.8%	8.1%	3.9%
Tulsa city	20,179	10.2%	6.7%	7.0%	25.4%	5.0%	2.8%	5.4%	7.7%	3.4%	4.1%	5.3%	10.8%	6.3%
Oregon														
Beaverton city	8,134	16.1%	5.2%	9.3%	17.7%	1.2%	22.2%	6.8%	3.2%	4.9%	1.0%	5.8%	2.6%	4.0%
Eugene city	11,785	0.5%	3.1%	12.2%	8.4%	1.3%	20.3%	5.7%	12.3%	9.0%	5.2%	4.9%	3.5%	13.6%
Gresham city	2,750	5.6%	5.3%	12.0%	4.3%	15.2%	12.5%	5.8%	9.0%	3.4%	0.0%	4.7%	7.1%	15.2%
Hillsboro city	7,471	22.1%	19.4%	10.1%	8.2%	1.1%	6.6%	2.4%	10.9%	2.4%	2.8%	6.1%	1.3%	6.7%
Portland city	61,417	4.8%	3.6%	8.4%	17.2%	2.7%	12.8%	6.6%	10.2%	9.5%	4.5%	5.6%	2.3%	11.9%
Salem city	5,975	3.7%	4.9%	11.7%	22.9%	4.3%	8.1%	1.0%	1.2%	2.9%	12.2%	10.3%	12.0%	4.7%
Pennsylvania														
Allentown city	2,381	0.0%	6.7%	17.3%	12.3%	5.2%	8.7%	0.0%	26.5%	0.0%	2.1%	3.4%	17.8%	0.0%
Erie city	3,983	8.6%	12.7%	14.4%	18.4%	3.1%	5.3%	17.9%	2.4%	2.9%	1.0%	5.0%	4.9%	3.4%
Philadelphia city	130,503	7.2%	4.2%	12.6%	17.7%	2.5%	8.6%	6.8%	12.2%	3.9%	5.0%	6.8%	6.4%	6.1%
Pittsburgh city	40,423	10.7%	10.5%	7.9%	16.8%	2.4%	11.3%	3.8%	11.0%	3.8%	4.9%	7.2%	5.3%	4.3%
Rhode Island														
Providence city	15,905	6.8%	11.0%	5.6%	11.9%	6.6%	14.3%	3.2%	11.9%	4.8%	1.7%	5.7%	6.6%	9.9%
South Carolina														
Charleston city	15,487	7.4%	3.1%	9.1%	22.6%	8.4%	2.2%	5.7%	9.4%	2.9%	4.1%	5.6%	9.3%	10.3%
Columbia city	14,088	9.3%	4.9%	4.9%	18.4%	2.8%	9.1%	6.3%	7.5%	5.1%	5.3%	11.3%	7.6%	7.6%
North Charleston city	4,938	9.3%	8.5%	6.8%	22.6%	2.2%	5.0%	4.7%	1.0%	3.9%	18.2%	1.1%	2.6%	14.0%
South Dakota														
Sioux Falls city	11,219	0.0%	8.0%	13.1%	21.5%	2.4%	2.9%	4.4%	1.8%	2.4%	3.0%	13.1%	25.5%	2.1%
Tennessee														
Chattanooga city	9,766	6.9%	11.6%	4.8%	19.3%	3.5%	7.8%	3.6%	7.8%	9.2%	2.7%	3.1%	10.1%	9.6%
Clarksville city	9,547	8.8%	1.2%	15.6%	11.2%	3.5%	2.7%	5.8%	3.9%	2.3%	7.9%	10.5%	19.3%	7.3%
Knoxville city	12,642	8.9%	1.1%	12.7%	17.9%	6.2%	8.6%	5.3%	11.1%	6.3%	3.4%	6.9%	5.7%	6.0%
Memphis city	29,126	7.2%	6.8%	9.6%	26.7%	1.2%	5.9%	6.0%	9.5%	4.7%	4.5%	5.1%	6.6%	6.1%
Murfreesboro city	8,209	4.2%	10.0%	7.6%	7.8%	3.4%	6.9%	10.6%	9.5%	5.5%	0.0%	12.3%	18.9%	3.3%
Nashville-Davidson metropolitan govt (balance)	65,419	4.4%	4.6%	8.4%	20.1%	3.8%	8.9%	9.4%	8.8%	4.3%	9.5%	3.8%	5.0%	9.0%
Texas														
Abilene city	4,593	8.8%	0.0%	15.1%	24.1%	0.0%	4.1%	6.5%	6.2%	9.2%	7.7%	5.9%	6.4%	5.9%
Allen city	4,141	11.2%	6.7%	18.2%	21.1%	5.7%	11.4%	4.5%	15.7%	0.0%	0.0%	0.0%	5.4%	0.0%
Amarillo city	5,489	9.9%	3.9%	8.1%	16.2%	0.0%	9.7%	7.0%	10.8%	3.1%	10.1%	4.1%	15.5%	1.6%
Arlington city	18,563	8.9%	3.2%	10.2%	22.7%	1.5%	8.5%	6.6%	7.0%	4.1%	7.9%	5.1%	10.4%	3.9%
Austin city	102,633	11.8%	6.8%	5.2%	19.4%	4.3%	10.9%	8.4%	6.1%	6.0%	4.1%	5.9%	4.0%	7.2%
Beaumont city	5,320	25.5%	2.4%	8.8%	8.3%	13.5%	0.0%	6.4%	11.5%	2.9%	1.7%	4.7%	13.3%	1.1%
Brownsville city	4,380	3.0%	0.3%	5.3%	12.9%	0.0%	0.0%	13.0%	13.3%	6.3%	5.2%	7.9%	32.8%	0.0%
Carrollton city	10,516	7.8%	6.3%	8.6%	34.0%	3.5%	2.5%	6.9%	6.7%	0.8%	5.1%	7.5%	4.4%	5.8%
College Station city	11,154	17.7%	2.0%	2.1%	15.4%	4.1%	10.1%	3.4%	20.2%	4.4%	5.8%	12.2%	2.6%	0.0%
Corpus Christi city	9,899	6.2%	1.2%	9.5%	26.0%	4.8%	11.0%	8.9%	5.0%	2.2%	0.5%	8.8%	13.9%	2.0%
Dallas city	87,850	6.5%	4.1%	8.9%	31.2%	2.2%	6.4%	9.2%	7.4%	4.9%	4.4%	5.4%	4.2%	5.3%
Denton city	7,072	8.8%	5.7%	5.1%	16.8%	1.7%	16.2%	3.7%	5.1%	4.2%	9.4%	8.4%	2.1%	12.9%
El Paso city	23,404	14.8%	1.6%	11.2%	22.9%	3.9%	8.1%	4.8%	12.7%	2.0%	3.6%	5.7%	7.4%	1.1%
Fort Worth city	36,179	4.2%	4.7%	10.3%	27.2%	4.8%	8.8%	5.5%	7.2%	2.9%	6.5%	5.1%	8.8%	3.8%
Frisco city	7,217	7.4%	10.7%	12.6%	31.3%	0.0%	8.3%	0.0%	9.9%	3.8%	3.4%	1.7%	4.4%	6.5%
Garland city	7,061	2.6%	3.5%	8.6%	52.5%	1.8%	4.0%	5.2%	2.8%	4.0%	1.2%	8.4%	1.3%	4.1%
Grand Prairie city	6,117	7.5%	5.6%	4.4%	27.5%	0.0%	4.2%	7.6%	13.1%	6.1%	1.7%	4.1%	7.9%	10.1%
Houston city	144,091	15.6%	5.1%	9.9%	24.6%	4.4%	5.9%	5.0%	9.4%	3.1%	3.1%	4.6%	4.6%	4.7%
Irving city	17,384	21.8%	12.8%	7.4%	25.3%	0.0%	4.2%	4.7%	8.4%	2.1%	1.5%	4.7%	5.2%	2.0%
Killeen city	4,557	11.0%	0.8%	10.7%	21.7%	0.0%	16.0%	2.1%	11.5%	3.7%	5.0%	6.8%	10.8%	0.0%
Laredo city	6,387	0.8%	0.8%	11.8%	30.9%	2.1%	7.0%	6.4%	7.2%	1.3%	4.0%	17.1%	10.9%	0.0%
Lewisville city	9,082	2.1%	6.2%	8.3%	31.3%	5.5%	6.5%	2.8%	9.9%	0.0%	12.0%	6.7%	4.4%	4.3%
Lubbock city	13,256	9.8%	4.7%	10.0%	20.9%	5.0%	4.6%	8.6%	13.9%	0.0%	4.2%	7.6%	6.6%	4.2%
McAllen city	5,278	4.1%	0.9%	11.4%	34.7%	5.3%	9.8%	6.4%	1.8%	3.8%	5.2%	12.0%	4.6%	0.0%
McKinney city	7,292	8.6%	6.2%	11.3%	24.1%	0.0%	9.4%	3.6%	13.5%	5.0%	0.9%	2.2%	12.2%	3.1%
Mesquite city	2,717	7.0%	0.0%	5.6%	32.4%	0.0%	0.0%	11.4%	2.0%	0.0%	4.0%	2.3%	20.6%	14.6%
Midland city	4,883	26.4%	0.0%	16.7%	10.6%	15.4%	1.3%	1.9%	7.1%	5.0%	0.0%	6.6%	7.7%	1.2%
Odessa city	3,250	21.8%	0.0%	2.9%	31.7%	0.0%	5.0%	3.3%	15.6%	0.0%	2.6%	1.8%	15.3%	0.0%
Pasadena city	2,744	16.8%	4.8%	4.3%	29.1%	11.8%	2.9%	2.6%	2.8%	0.0%	4.6%	0.0%	16.6%	3.8%
Pearland city	5,950	4.4%	2.2%	33.0%	24.2%	0.0%	0.0%	13.2%	11.1%	4.4%	0.0%	4.6%	1.3%	1.6%
Plano city	22,344	12.0%	18.3%	7.9%	22.1%	1.5%	5.8%	3.0%	8.9%	1.1%	2.6%	3.4%	7.0%	6.4%
Richardson city	9,694	13.4%	11.4%	11.9%	25.3%	0.8%	5.0%	6.7%	5.2%	3.9%	1.7%	9.6%	1.9%	3.2%
Round Rock City	4,844	8.9%	11.1%	11.5%	29.3%	3.6%	9.5%	0.0%	9.3%	1.4%	4.9%	8.2%	0.0%	2.4%
San Angelo city	5,013	0.0%	6.9%	15.0%	28.6%	7.1%	4.2%	5.8%	10.3%	1.0%	0.0%	4.3%	9.8%	7.0%
San Antonio city	55,616	6.1%	7.6%	10.5%	22.6%	2.9%	7.4%	6.5%	11.8%	5.5%	2.2%	5.3%	7.6%	4.1%
Tyler city	5,868	3.8%	2.9%	21.6%	28.3%	1.6%	3.6%	2.6%	6.4%	0.0%	3.9%	1.1%	20.0%	4.4%
Waco city	7,864	3.7%	5.4%	9.1%	25.8%	1.8%	5.5%	5.2%	9.0%	6.8%	9.1%	6.0%	5.9%	6.7%
Wichita Falls city	4,004	5.5%	0.0%	14.4%	22.7%	3.8%	3.5%	1.7%	4.4%	0.0%	2.9%	11.6%	26.3%	3.1%

Table F-3: Places—Educational Field of Study—*Continued*

	Total Millennial Population with Bachelor's or Higher	Percent of the Population 18 to 33 by Field of Study												
		Engineering	Computers and Math	Science and Engineering Related	Business	Physical Science	Social Science	Communications	Biological Sciences	Literature	Liberal Arts	Psychology	Education	Visual and Performing Arts
Utah														
Orem city	4,344	6.9%	2.2%	21.1%	14.0%	6.9%	5.6%	9.8%	4.4%	5.0%	0.0%	4.1%	14.6%	5.2%
Provo city	11,052	3.3%	5.9%	11.2%	12.3%	2.5%	5.0%	7.6%	7.5%	18.8%	2.7%	4.2%	10.0%	9.1%
Salt Lake City city	19,338	5.2%	5.2%	12.0%	20.4%	1.6%	11.8%	4.6%	11.7%	5.7%	3.7%	4.1%	8.2%	5.8%
Sandy city	3,952	0.0%	12.5%	2.3%	28.2%	3.3%	2.3%	7.9%	10.2%	8.0%	5.4%	8.8%	8.4%	2.7%
West Jordan city	4,413	11.1%	0.0%	11.4%	30.0%	6.9%	0.0%	0.0%	4.8%	3.1%	0.0%	8.3%	20.0%	4.4%
West Valley City city	2,466	9.9%	17.3%	3.2%	22.0%	0.0%	0.0%	8.6%	10.8%	6.0%	0.0%	17.8%	4.4%	0.0%
Virginia														
Alexandria city	20,022	8.3%	5.4%	5.8%	17.4%	1.1%	19.6%	6.9%	8.9%	5.4%	8.5%	4.0%	3.3%	5.6%
Chesapeake city	10,472	8.9%	5.9%	12.0%	23.6%	2.4%	7.4%	8.2%	6.9%	3.2%	2.8%	3.4%	11.8%	3.6%
Hampton city	6,319	2.7%	8.3%	9.2%	19.0%	7.4%	4.3%	2.6%	1.4%	13.1%	8.8%	11.2%	6.8%	5.1%
Newport News city	7,132	10.1%	11.7%	6.4%	24.2%	2.3%	0.9%	6.1%	5.2%	4.0%	0.0%	11.5%	11.7%	5.9%
Norfolk city	11,158	10.6%	9.6%	13.2%	13.6%	3.6%	3.9%	5.4%	12.1%	6.1%	2.1%	3.9%	3.7%	12.1%
Portsmouth city	5,558	8.5%	4.3%	15.8%	4.4%	3.9%	4.1%	4.5%	17.6%	9.0%	6.6%	4.1%	2.0%	15.3%
Richmond city	20,912	2.9%	4.2%	9.9%	15.8%	4.8%	13.6%	2.0%	14.9%	6.9%	7.7%	4.8%	4.3%	8.2%
Roanoke city	3,884	2.9%	0.0%	10.9%	23.0%	0.0%	4.5%	6.9%	11.9%	8.7%	5.6%	10.7%	10.8%	4.0%
Virginia Beach city	21,615	9.3%	8.2%	12.2%	13.6%	3.6%	8.5%	6.0%	5.8%	6.4%	6.7%	7.2%	7.3%	5.2%
Washington														
Bellevue city	19,006	15.0%	27.4%	7.5%	15.7%	1.2%	8.2%	5.3%	2.6%	2.9%	3.3%	4.3%	1.9%	4.7%
Everett city	5,372	11.6%	3.3%	11.8%	31.5%	6.8%	8.8%	2.2%	2.9%	4.1%	6.4%	6.9%	1.7%	1.9%
Federal Way city	3,113	8.4%	0.0%	16.3%	15.2%	2.8%	4.5%	3.8%	0.0%	11.4%	0.0%	22.8%	9.4%	5.4%
Kent city	3,623	0.0%	6.5%	18.6%	4.3%	0.0%	33.0%	4.3%	15.8%	0.0%	8.2%	0.0%	3.9%	5.5%
Renton city	6,671	11.5%	13.8%	22.5%	9.5%	1.9%	15.9%	2.2%	10.2%	4.9%	2.2%	0.0%	0.0%	5.3%
Seattle city	119,925	10.6%	9.9%	7.3%	16.2%	3.4%	11.9%	5.1%	10.9%	6.1%	4.6%	4.6%	2.3%	7.2%
Spokane city	9,290	3.0%	2.1%	10.1%	19.3%	1.1%	13.6%	5.3%	7.5%	6.3%	7.0%	5.4%	16.8%	2.5%
Spokane Valley city	3,790	5.1%	3.7%	12.3%	31.0%	0.0%	9.4%	15.4%	5.4%	1.6%	3.8%	4.5%	7.7%	0.0%
Tacoma city	7,955	1.6%	6.6%	10.2%	17.4%	1.9%	8.1%	17.5%	6.7%	4.9%	4.8%	10.7%	6.4%	3.3%
Vancouver city	6,680	10.0%	4.6%	4.1%	12.4%	0.0%	9.1%	10.3%	7.4%	2.7%	6.8%	12.1%	8.8%	11.7%
Yakima city	2,244	0.0%	3.6%	15.9%	5.6%	7.8%	10.6%	0.0%	8.4%	0.0%	31.8%	4.1%	8.2%	4.1%
Wisconsin														
Green Bay city	4,075	25.7%	0.0%	8.7%	29.9%	0.0%	4.5%	0.0%	7.3%	14.4%	0.0%	2.4%	4.4%	2.6%
Kenosha city	2,018	5.3%	6.7%	14.4%	36.5%	0.0%	10.3%	11.4%	0.0%	0.0%	0.0%	0.0%	9.6%	5.8%
Madison city	39,669	16.1%	5.9%	5.4%	11.6%	3.9%	11.9%	6.9%	18.3%	7.8%	3.8%	2.3%	1.9%	4.2%
Milwaukee city	33,988	7.2%	5.2%	12.5%	20.9%	0.8%	9.7%	8.4%	11.5%	4.6%	3.9%	3.2%	4.5%	7.7%

Table F-4: Metropolitan/Micropolitan Statistical Areas—Educational Field of Study

	Total Millennial Population with Bachelor's or Higher	Percent of the Population 18 to 33 by Field of Study Degree												
		Engineering	Computers and Math	Science and Engineering Related	Business	Physical Science	Social Science	Communications	Biological Sciences	Literature	Liberal Arts	Psychology	Education	Visual and Performing Arts
Abilene, TX	5,132	7.9%	2.9%	13.5%	23.1%	0.0%	3.7%	5.8%	7.7%	10.4%	6.9%	5.3%	7.5%	5.3%
Adrian, MI	1,625	10.5%	6.7%	6.3%	12.8%	0.0%	6.0%	16.9%	7.0%	4.7%	0.0%	6.3%	19.3%	3.4%
Akron, OH	34,351	8.8%	4.8%	11.8%	24.8%	5.2%	5.7%	2.4%	6.8%	5.3%	4.5%	5.1%	8.9%	5.8%
Albany, GA	2,842	0.0%	4.5%	7.3%	8.5%	0.0%	6.2%	4.2%	16.0%	0.0%	5.5%	8.2%	15.4%	24.2%
Albany, OR	3,861	10.3%	6.4%	19.5%	4.7%	4.3%	3.6%	0.0%	16.3%	1.9%	7.3%	2.9%	16.2%	6.6%
Albany-Schenectady-Troy, NY	52,427	7.4%	5.9%	7.2%	19.4%	4.4%	9.7%	7.6%	8.9%	6.2%	4.3%	6.8%	9.5%	2.7%
Albertville, AL	1,705	1.9%	12.2%	19.8%	20.9%	0.0%	0.0%	9.0%	18.5%	0.0%	0.0%	0.0%	17.8%	0.0%
Albuquerque, NM	29,657	9.5%	3.7%	11.3%	14.4%	6.8%	10.7%	3.9%	8.2%	6.8%	7.3%	6.1%	6.4%	5.0%
Alexandria, LA	2,930	10.9%	0.0%	8.7%	28.3%	3.0%	14.7%	0.0%	6.5%	1.7%	14.6%	4.5%	1.3%	5.8%
Allentown-Bethlehem-Easton, PA-NJ	33,943	7.9%	3.7%	11.9%	18.7%	3.9%	3.2%	5.5%	11.7%	2.1%	4.1%	7.9%	16.3%	3.1%
Altoona, PA	4,489	0.0%	0.0%	13.6%	23.0%	3.3%	1.6%	6.6%	0.8%	3.4%	5.7%	14.3%	23.7%	4.1%
Amarillo, TX	6,903	8.0%	4.0%	8.8%	16.1%	0.0%	7.7%	7.6%	10.8%	3.0%	11.2%	3.2%	16.7%	2.9%
Ames, IA	7,585	25.2%	1.2%	4.7%	13.2%	8.9%	7.4%	4.8%	16.8%	7.0%	1.9%	4.5%	2.9%	1.5%
Anchorage, AK	17,952	12.6%	2.3%	13.0%	14.4%	2.9%	5.6%	5.1%	18.5%	4.3%	4.2%	4.4%	6.1%	6.5%
Ann Arbor, MI	39,240	14.1%	5.7%	10.8%	7.8%	6.5%	12.8%	2.8%	11.6%	5.6%	5.7%	7.7%	4.0%	5.0%
Anniston-Oxford-Jacksonville, AL	2,353	14.7%	6.7%	9.8%	17.2%	0.0%	0.0%	8.8%	8.1%	4.5%	2.5%	3.7%	14.4%	9.6%
Appleton, WI	9,994	2.9%	8.3%	9.2%	22.4%	1.4%	4.4%	3.6%	12.9%	8.3%	1.0%	3.9%	7.4%	14.1%
Asheville, NC	13,212	8.1%	5.5%	5.0%	17.7%	4.4%	5.6%	4.7%	10.0%	5.7%	3.9%	13.5%	11.6%	4.3%
Ashtabula, OH	1,548	0.0%	11.0%	11.0%	25.6%	11.1%	0.0%	3.9%	14.9%	11.2%	0.0%	3.3%	2.6%	5.4%
Athens-Clarke County, GA	13,410	2.2%	5.2%	10.7%	12.7%	5.8%	7.2%	5.3%	16.4%	9.1%	2.3%	7.7%	11.5%	3.9%
Atlanta-Sandy Springs-Roswell, GA	296,335	9.2%	6.7%	9.7%	24.1%	2.7%	7.5%	6.8%	6.0%	3.4%	3.4%	5.3%	8.6%	6.7%
Atlantic City-Hammonton, NJ	8,853	3.3%	3.0%	17.6%	12.1%	2.6%	9.3%	4.6%	11.3%	3.9%	6.6%	3.9%	15.7%	6.1%
Auburn-Opelika, AL	7,273	5.1%	0.8%	3.6%	16.1%	0.0%	4.0%	1.7%	30.6%	6.8%	4.3%	8.3%	11.2%	7.5%
Augusta-Richmond County, GA-SC	20,852	5.5%	2.0%	9.7%	21.1%	4.7%	6.3%	8.7%	8.8%	2.9%	3.0%	7.9%	12.3%	7.0%
Augusta-Waterville, ME	3,435	7.9%	12.8%	8.4%	13.9%	0.0%	15.6%	0.0%	17.6%	3.3%	2.4%	8.7%	7.9%	1.5%
Austin-Round Rock, TX	148,094	11.2%	7.7%	5.6%	19.9%	3.8%	10.1%	8.5%	6.4%	5.9%	3.8%	5.4%	5.4%	6.3%
Bakersfield, CA	18,881	14.8%	6.1%	3.2%	12.3%	5.4%	3.9%	5.6%	8.0%	3.5%	12.3%	5.6%	14.0%	5.1%
Baltimore-Columbia-Towson, MD	171,116	11.5%	8.3%	8.5%	18.8%	2.2%	9.9%	6.1%	8.4%	3.1%	5.0%	6.0%	6.3%	6.0%
Bangor, ME	5,202	14.5%	4.2%	8.6%	15.8%	5.2%	4.8%	1.8%	15.9%	2.9%	0.0%	9.7%	9.3%	7.3%
Barnstable Town, MA	5,277	5.0%	3.4%	12.6%	30.0%	1.3%	7.4%	2.7%	8.3%	3.7%	7.8%	8.2%	4.9%	4.7%
Baton Rouge, LA	43,907	14.1%	1.5%	10.0%	16.2%	1.9%	5.0%	4.0%	12.6%	5.4%	6.4%	4.7%	13.3%	4.8%
Battle Creek, MI	3,530	3.8%	0.0%	8.1%	32.1%	0.0%	0.0%	1.3%	2.5%	0.0%	5.9%	2.8%	28.2%	15.2%
Bay City, MI	3,233	6.2%	0.0%	6.1%	46.5%	0.0%	9.8%	3.8%	14.3%	3.5%	1.9%	0.8%	3.4%	3.8%
Beaumont-Port Arthur, TX	11,829	16.2%	3.5%	13.9%	12.4%	7.9%	3.5%	3.9%	10.5%	4.2%	5.2%	3.1%	14.8%	0.7%
Beckley, WV	1,856	7.2%	7.1%	19.7%	7.6%	13.8%	2.5%	8.0%	8.4%	5.5%	2.7%	9.9%	7.7%	0.0%
Bellingham, WA	8,693	2.3%	3.8%	4.2%	20.5%	9.2%	7.2%	7.4%	6.9%	9.1%	9.7%	6.9%	2.4%	10.6%
Bend-Redmond, OR	8,147	10.9%	0.7%	4.9%	15.1%	4.1%	5.6%	4.5%	17.5%	3.0%	5.2%	6.9%	8.0%	13.7%
Billings, MT	6,612	11.2%	0.0%	17.6%	19.6%	1.3%	1.9%	0.0%	9.8%	5.3%	16.5%	6.0%	9.6%	1.3%
Binghamton, NY	12,447	5.6%	10.8%	10.7%	8.7%	9.8%	14.8%	4.2%	9.8%	4.3%	0.9%	5.4%	12.7%	2.2%
Birmingham-Hoover, AL	49,305	3.7%	2.4%	12.8%	26.2%	2.5%	4.4%	6.3%	7.8%	4.9%	6.0%	3.9%	12.6%	6.6%
Bismarck, ND	9,625	4.6%	5.2%	19.1%	35.7%	2.6%	0.8%	1.5%	13.3%	0.0%	5.2%	4.8%	7.0%	0.0%
Blacksburg-Christiansburg-Radford, VA	15,267	23.5%	6.9%	10.9%	11.6%	5.9%	3.9%	1.2%	21.6%	1.0%	2.6%	2.9%	5.9%	2.2%
Bloomington, IL	10,937	5.1%	13.0%	9.9%	24.1%	0.3%	8.3%	7.5%	3.8%	4.2%	2.6%	7.0%	5.4%	8.9%
Bloomington, IN	14,005	3.6%	5.1%	3.4%	22.2%	5.8%	6.9%	3.1%	7.0%	3.3%	8.1%	1.8%	11.8%	17.9%
Bloomsburg-Berwick, PA	4,591	0.6%	1.8%	27.1%	20.5%	1.6%	17.1%	0.6%	7.1%	0.0%	0.0%	10.2%	12.5%	0.9%
Boise City, ID	22,765	8.3%	4.1%	11.8%	17.5%	1.0%	4.0%	7.9%	7.1%	6.3%	9.7%	6.3%	9.6%	6.6%
Boston-Cambridge-Newton, MA-NH	418,697	9.7%	5.2%	7.9%	21.6%	2.9%	10.3%	5.5%	9.0%	5.5%	4.8%	8.0%	4.1%	5.4%
Boulder, CO	30,251	9.4%	9.2%	7.7%	14.4%	5.8%	4.3%	3.6%	9.6%	7.6%	3.7%	12.3%	5.8%	6.6%
Bowling Green, KY	9,057	3.4%	0.0%	8.6%	19.7%	1.0%	3.1%	11.9%	15.2%	6.4%	4.4%	11.4%	13.0%	1.9%
Bremerton-Silverdale, WA	8,518	15.4%	2.5%	7.3%	13.9%	0.0%	11.5%	9.8%	8.0%	0.8%	11.7%	5.3%	7.6%	6.2%
Bridgeport-Stamford-Norwalk, CT	57,369	6.4%	3.5%	8.1%	25.6%	3.0%	8.7%	8.8%	5.0%	6.3%	5.4%	8.0%	6.4%	4.9%
Brownsville-Harlingen, TX	7,760	4.4%	0.2%	11.2%	11.2%	5.4%	5.1%	7.3%	8.7%	7.8%	3.0%	7.4%	24.6%	3.6%
Brunswick, GA	2,252	10.6%	0.0%	12.9%	36.2%	0.0%	0.0%	2.4%	7.7%	0.0%	3.0%	17.1%	10.3%	0.0%
Buffalo-Cheektowaga-Niagara Falls, NY	60,565	7.4%	3.9%	11.2%	19.4%	3.2%	8.9%	6.2%	9.2%	6.5%	2.4%	5.9%	11.5%	4.2%
Burlington, NC	4,001	1.7%	0.0%	5.7%	29.9%	2.9%	9.1%	10.4%	14.5%	4.1%	2.1%	3.8%	12.8%	2.9%
Burlington-South Burlington, VT	18,366	5.4%	9.1%	2.4%	11.1%	1.0%	8.6%	6.3%	16.6%	9.2%	10.1%	7.3%	5.9%	7.0%
California-Lexington Park, MD	5,039	25.7%	10.4%	1.7%	15.0%	3.3%	13.4%	2.1%	7.9%	1.4%	4.8%	3.6%	5.3%	5.3%
Canton-Massillon, OH	11,909	2.9%	4.0%	13.0%	26.1%	2.8%	3.4%	4.4%	15.5%	3.0%	0.9%	4.4%	15.2%	4.5%
Cape Coral-Fort Myers, FL	14,171	2.5%	1.6%	12.8%	25.5%	2.5%	6.1%	5.4%	9.9%	0.0%	7.6%	6.5%	11.2%	8.3%
Cape Girardeau, MO-IL	2,305	2.9%	6.5%	10.8%	23.8%	0.0%	8.8%	1.7%	8.4%	0.0%	17.2%	4.9%	10.1%	4.9%
Carbondale-Marion, IL	5,604	1.5%	0.8%	17.5%	4.0%	2.3%	2.8%	10.2%	8.8%	11.5%	11.1%	13.5%	9.4%	6.6%
Carson City, NV	45	0.0%	0.0%	0.0%	0.0%	0.0%	0.0%	0.0%	0.0%	100.0%	0.0%	0.0%	0.0%	0.0%
Casper, WY	1,903	14.5%	0.0%	19.2%	21.1%	9.8%	7.1%	0.0%	10.4%	6.0%	0.0%	0.0%	8.3%	3.6%
Cedar Rapids, IA	13,883	7.4%	11.1%	10.1%	29.0%	0.0%	1.6%	3.0%	13.1%	2.3%	4.6%	8.3%	8.0%	1.5%
Chambersburg-Waynesboro, PA	3,417	0.0%	2.3%	21.4%	26.6%	0.0%	9.1%	6.4%	3.2%	1.6%	5.9%	7.1%	4.0%	12.4%
Champaign-Urbana, IL	19,041	17.4%	5.9%	5.3%	15.8%	5.5%	8.3%	5.5%	17.1%	6.7%	1.4%	4.5%	3.3%	3.4%
Charleston, WV	6,588	6.6%	0.0%	33.0%	16.3%	7.7%	3.9%	9.5%	9.3%	0.0%	0.0%	6.1%	6.4%	1.3%
Charleston-North Charleston, SC	45,870	10.4%	4.5%	12.4%	19.5%	5.0%	3.3%	5.1%	7.6%	5.0%	4.6%	6.6%	7.9%	8.0%
Charlotte-Concord-Gastonia, NC-SC	117,571	8.0%	7.8%	7.8%	26.4%	2.8%	7.4%	7.6%	5.5%	2.8%	3.8%	7.1%	8.0%	4.9%
Charlottesville, VA	14,262	7.1%	6.8%	11.7%	16.4%	4.2%	12.8%	3.1%	10.7%	3.7%	4.4%	6.3%	10.2%	2.6%
Chattanooga, TN-GA	20,074	8.1%	9.0%	8.3%	19.7%	2.0%	7.5%	3.6%	10.5%	6.5%	4.4%	5.0%	10.6%	4.7%
Cheyenne, WY	3,579	13.9%	0.0%	7.3%	12.7%	3.6%	15.3%	1.0%	21.8%	1.9%	8.1%	5.5%	6.7%	2.2%
Chicago-Naperville-Elgin, IL-IN-WI	616,412	6.9%	5.8%	9.5%	23.0%	2.7%	8.6%	7.5%	7.4%	4.2%	3.7%	7.0%	7.1%	6.6%
Chico, CA	7,400	5.7%	3.2%	12.3%	12.2%	1.3%	9.9%	11.0%	11.2%	7.1%	2.9%	6.7%	5.8%	10.7%

Table F-4: Metropolitan/Micropolitan Statistical Areas—Educational Field of Study—*Continued*

	Total Millennial Population with Bachelor's or Higher	Percent of the Population 18 to 33 by Field of Study Degree												
		Engineering	Computers and Math	Science and Engineering Related	Business	Physical Science	Social Science	Communications	Biological Sciences	Literature	Liberal Arts	Psychology	Education	Visual and Performing Arts
Cincinnati, OH-KY-IN	100,248	7.7%	5.1%	11.6%	25.3%	2.9%	6.7%	6.1%	7.0%	3.7%	4.2%	4.4%	9.4%	6.1%
Clarksburg, WV	3,430	2.1%	3.1%	29.4%	18.2%	2.1%	7.7%	0.0%	9.4%	8.6%	0.6%	10.6%	2.4%	5.6%
Clarksville, TN-KY	11,536	9.5%	1.0%	15.8%	13.0%	2.9%	2.9%	4.8%	3.4%	2.9%	9.1%	10.3%	18.2%	6.2%
Cleveland, TN	3,621	3.8%	0.0%	4.2%	31.3%	0.0%	10.0%	7.5%	6.2%	3.6%	8.6%	6.1%	6.6%	12.0%
Cleveland-Elyria, OH	95,124	9.8%	4.7%	14.6%	19.9%	2.1%	6.6%	5.9%	8.5%	3.5%	4.6%	6.6%	9.7%	3.6%
Coeur d'Alene, ID	3,675	7.0%	0.0%	8.5%	12.2%	0.0%	0.0%	4.0%	21.4%	0.0%	14.7%	17.3%	4.4%	10.4%
College Station-Bryan, TX	17,927	18.8%	6.5%	4.1%	13.6%	4.5%	7.7%	2.2%	17.7%	3.9%	7.0%	8.2%	3.4%	2.3%
Colorado Springs, CO	31,708	12.0%	4.8%	11.5%	13.4%	6.2%	10.6%	4.9%	7.9%	4.0%	4.3%	10.2%	8.4%	1.8%
Columbia, MO	18,111	17.0%	10.1%	9.1%	6.9%	4.0%	5.3%	5.1%	17.3%	7.3%	1.8%	4.3%	8.0%	3.7%
Columbia, SC	41,832	7.7%	3.1%	8.2%	23.6%	2.5%	9.8%	5.1%	7.6%	3.7%	6.9%	8.3%	9.3%	4.1%
Columbus, GA-AL	12,849	12.4%	5.1%	18.0%	17.5%	0.8%	10.7%	3.1%	6.4%	1.3%	4.7%	8.9%	8.4%	2.7%
Columbus, IN	4,709	27.0%	4.2%	18.2%	16.1%	5.3%	0.0%	7.2%	0.9%	1.6%	8.1%	3.9%	5.1%	2.5%
Columbus, OH	125,503	7.0%	3.9%	10.2%	23.8%	2.8%	8.0%	6.1%	9.6%	3.8%	3.6%	6.5%	8.8%	5.9%
Concord, NH	4,964	13.4%	10.8%	8.2%	5.7%	0.0%	17.7%	2.8%	4.1%	7.2%	9.5%	1.7%	14.2%	4.8%
Cookeville, TN	4,559	17.2%	0.7%	15.7%	30.4%	1.2%	13.3%	0.0%	3.6%	0.0%	0.0%	4.2%	13.8%	0.0%
Corpus Christi, TX	11,370	8.6%	1.0%	8.5%	27.4%	4.2%	10.7%	7.8%	6.1%	1.9%	1.0%	7.6%	13.5%	1.8%
Corvallis, OR	4,272	9.3%	5.8%	17.6%	8.9%	6.0%	4.3%	0.0%	14.7%	1.8%	6.6%	2.6%	16.4%	6.0%
Crestview-Fort Walton Beach-Destin, FL	8,791	21.1%	3.3%	16.5%	25.6%	2.7%	7.1%	4.2%	4.9%	0.8%	2.0%	1.2%	6.4%	4.2%
Cumberland, MD-WV	2,451	0.0%	9.9%	9.7%	11.3%	4.5%	1.3%	11.5%	2.1%	15.2%	9.2%	11.1%	3.9%	10.2%
Dallas-Fort Worth-Arlington, TX	334,962	8.4%	6.2%	10.1%	26.4%	2.0%	6.9%	5.9%	7.9%	3.4%	4.7%	5.8%	7.3%	4.9%
Dalton, GA	3,630	9.4%	7.7%	9.2%	21.3%	5.6%	2.2%	13.4%	1.5%	9.3%	0.0%	6.6%	13.7%	0.0%
Danville, IL	1,233	0.0%	0.0%	10.0%	23.3%	0.0%	12.2%	22.1%	1.1%	0.0%	1.5%	9.5%	17.7%	2.7%
Danville, VA	2,086	6.8%	12.9%	2.1%	37.5%	0.0%	0.0%	0.0%	23.3%	2.5%	1.9%	6.9%	2.5%	3.6%
Daphne-Fairhope-Foley, AL	6,283	7.7%	0.3%	26.4%	12.9%	0.0%	1.1%	1.6%	16.5%	0.0%	10.4%	0.0%	14.8%	8.3%
Davenport-Moline-Rock Island, IA-IL	14,229	9.3%	3.1%	5.7%	30.5%	4.3%	5.6%	1.4%	10.6%	2.1%	4.4%	5.2%	16.1%	1.7%
Dayton, OH	37,224	12.1%	3.8%	13.0%	20.6%	3.0%	7.4%	4.8%	9.6%	2.4%	4.0%	6.2%	8.2%	4.9%
Decatur, AL	3,784	21.6%	2.4%	19.6%	22.7%	0.0%	0.0%	0.0%	8.2%	0.0%	0.0%	0.0%	16.2%	9.3%
Decatur, IL	2,191	12.4%	4.8%	0.0%	22.1%	0.0%	9.8%	12.9%	2.9%	4.5%	0.0%	0.0%	24.0%	6.6%
Deltona-Daytona Beach-Ormond Beach, FL	15,349	6.0%	4.0%	13.8%	25.5%	3.7%	5.4%	4.7%	11.3%	2.3%	4.2%	9.3%	5.4%	4.5%
Denver-Aurora-Lakewood, CO	195,169	9.2%	5.0%	9.4%	21.6%	3.3%	9.7%	5.7%	8.5%	3.4%	4.1%	6.8%	5.9%	7.2%
Des Moines-West Des Moines, IA	40,496	5.9%	5.0%	4.1%	28.6%	1.2%	7.3%	5.4%	12.4%	1.8%	6.3%	5.8%	12.1%	4.1%
Detroit-Warren-Dearborn, MI	181,564	13.2%	5.0%	12.4%	21.3%	2.1%	4.8%	7.6%	9.5%	4.1%	3.1%	5.1%	7.6%	4.1%
Dothan, AL	3,569	8.5%	0.9%	19.2%	15.2%	7.2%	0.0%	2.5%	5.9%	1.1%	1.9%	10.5%	16.1%	11.1%
Dover, DE	4,262	0.0%	5.2%	7.6%	19.4%	7.2%	7.6%	0.0%	6.0%	0.0%	2.0%	8.9%	33.7%	1.0%
Dubuque, IA	4,210	10.1%	2.1%	6.1%	10.5%	0.0%	2.8%	4.6%	4.3%	0.0%	6.6%	15.8%	33.5%	3.4%
Duluth, MN-WI	8,746	1.3%	5.2%	8.3%	20.3%	7.4%	4.0%	1.4%	19.1%	2.6%	4.9%	3.3%	17.8%	4.3%
Dunn, NC	3,254	11.3%	2.4%	17.7%	13.7%	2.7%	1.3%	5.8%	12.5%	3.1%	5.4%	11.6%	8.6%	3.7%
Durham-Chapel Hill, NC	49,177	5.5%	7.6%	7.0%	8.5%	3.8%	14.1%	4.4%	16.1%	9.4%	7.0%	7.5%	4.2%	4.8%
East Stroudsburg, PA	6,042	0.0%	0.0%	13.0%	31.3%	3.7%	7.7%	0.0%	10.3%	1.3%	0.0%	7.8%	7.7%	17.1%
Eau Claire, WI	7,204	2.1%	0.0%	12.2%	33.8%	3.0%	0.9%	16.6%	4.3%	1.4%	8.2%	2.4%	15.0%	0.0%
El Centro, CA	4,339	4.4%	12.8%	2.1%	22.3%	4.1%	3.7%	0.0%	1.7%	0.6%	9.5%	21.9%	10.3%	6.6%
El Paso, TX	3,281	10.6%	0.0%	21.0%	15.9%	2.0%	10.1%	0.0%	0.0%	2.2%	0.0%	22.6%	15.5%	0.0%
Elizabethtown-Fort Knox, KY	4,836	7.5%	9.2%	1.9%	26.0%	0.9%	4.6%	0.0%	0.0%	2.6%	16.6%	7.8%	20.5%	2.3%
Elkhart-Goshen, IN	3,305	7.4%	12.8%	1.5%	22.3%	1.1%	7.1%	19.5%	1.7%	1.7%	1.7%	18.7%	10.0%	2.5%
Elmira, NY	29,369	12.3%	2.1%	12.4%	24.4%	3.9%	7.8%	4.6%	11.9%	1.8%	3.2%	5.9%	8.7%	1.2%
Erie, PA	11,541	6.7%	6.1%	6.3%	24.1%	2.8%	5.9%	13.3%	5.7%	4.5%	0.8%	9.7%	11.6%	2.4%
Eugene, OR	17,767	1.3%	2.8%	10.6%	8.9%	1.2%	22.8%	4.9%	8.1%	8.7%	7.7%	3.8%	4.3%	14.9%
Eureka-Arcata-Fortuna, CA	4,115	4.8%	3.5%	8.8%	10.5%	2.8%	10.8%	0.5%	30.0%	2.8%	3.9%	3.5%	8.5%	9.6%
Evansville, IN-KY	13,533	3.4%	8.1%	18.5%	19.7%	7.5%	2.0%	16.5%	4.8%	0.9%	3.2%	0.7%	10.6%	4.1%
Fairbanks, AK	4,281	2.1%	0.0%	9.7%	31.1%	9.7%	4.3%	0.0%	6.6%	11.1%	6.5%	15.0%	3.8%	0.0%
Fargo, ND-MN	13,866	7.6%	8.3%	13.8%	28.5%	4.4%	5.2%	8.2%	8.7%	4.4%	1.5%	1.6%	4.1%	3.6%
Farmington, NM	2,995	26.5%	0.0%	9.7%	8.7%	0.0%	6.6%	0.0%	2.2%	5.6%	0.0%	6.4%	28.4%	5.8%
Fayetteville, NC	13,266	2.9%	1.5%	16.0%	24.5%	0.4%	6.8%	3.8%	6.3%	6.7%	8.3%	4.4%	10.8%	7.6%
Fayetteville-Springdale-Rogers, AR-MO	25,033	10.6%	2.7%	8.0%	37.3%	1.0%	5.3%	4.6%	8.3%	4.1%	2.8%	3.1%	7.7%	4.3%
Flagstaff, AZ	6,415	4.2%	0.0%	1.9%	16.7%	12.0%	11.1%	1.8%	13.5%	7.5%	0.5%	2.3%	22.5%	5.9%
Flint, MI	9,252	5.1%	1.7%	15.4%	27.4%	2.9%	3.1%	0.4%	13.6%	4.4%	4.2%	7.1%	12.8%	1.9%
Florence, SC	4,201	8.7%	0.0%	7.3%	8.1%	4.9%	13.1%	8.7%	10.3%	9.1%	9.0%	1.6%	14.9%	4.2%
Florence-Muscle Shoals, AL	2,913	7.1%	2.1%	2.7%	25.3%	5.5%	8.4%	20.8%	3.9%	3.9%	7.6%	0.5%	10.6%	1.6%
Fond du Lac, WI	2,393	1.9%	3.5%	6.0%	38.9%	5.9%	0.0%	14.9%	0.0%	3.6%	0.0%	8.9%	12.7%	3.8%
Fort Collins, CO	24,971	7.8%	4.6%	8.3%	12.5%	10.1%	9.8%	2.9%	14.6%	5.8%	2.8%	6.4%	8.2%	6.2%
Fort Smith, AR-OK	5,595	5.3%	16.5%	15.3%	12.1%	8.1%	5.1%	0.0%	8.4%	1.2%	4.8%	2.5%	16.1%	4.8%
Fort Wayne, IN	17,276	9.5%	1.4%	14.7%	23.7%	2.3%	7.6%	5.9%	5.5%	1.8%	3.6%	5.4%	14.4%	4.3%
Fresno, CA	25,835	6.2%	4.1%	12.5%	12.5%	0.0%	12.6%	6.8%	9.8%	7.7%	10.0%	8.5%	4.5%	4.8%
Gadsden, AL	3,051	3.6%	4.4%	11.6%	11.8%	6.6%	0.0%	14.1%	14.9%	2.9%	7.1%	0.4%	22.6%	0.0%
Gainesville, FL	23,265	13.5%	6.3%	12.3%	10.4%	3.1%	9.8%	2.7%	24.1%	2.7%	2.3%	3.9%	3.4%	5.4%
Gainesville, GA	3,459	6.2%	1.4%	7.3%	11.1%	0.0%	3.1%	10.4%	3.3%	0.0%	4.6%	8.5%	39.8%	4.2%
Gettysburg, PA	2,986	0.0%	2.1%	6.6%	30.9%	0.0%	3.5%	3.0%	5.7%	4.7%	8.9%	5.9%	11.9%	16.7%
Glens Falls, NY	4,574	2.9%	2.9%	5.1%	15.7%	0.0%	10.5%	2.8%	12.5%	7.0%	9.2%	11.6%	19.1%	0.7%
Goldsboro, NC	4,570	0.0%	2.4%	1.0%	24.8%	17.7%	6.1%	7.1%	0.0%	8.4%	8.8%	6.0%	13.6%	4.1%
Grand Forks, ND-MN	7,469	1.6%	1.3%	17.1%	9.3%	0.0%	5.3%	2.2%	8.5%	3.2%	4.2%	17.7%	17.0%	12.5%
Grand Island, NE	2,420	1.8%	5.1%	9.7%	8.5%	12.2%	5.4%	0.0%	20.6%	10.7%	4.3%	4.1%	17.7%	0.0%
Grand Junction, CO	3,827	0.0%	4.1%	11.3%	15.7%	2.4%	11.8%	3.0%	7.2%	2.4%	0.0%	24.8%	6.8%	10.6%
Grand Rapids-Wyoming, MI	49,695	5.0%	3.2%	13.6%	27.9%	2.6%	3.8%	6.1%	7.8%	3.9%	5.9%	5.4%	9.3%	5.5%
Grants Pass, OR	830	0.0%	0.0%	5.2%	5.6%	6.4%	11.0%	8.4%	31.8%	0.0%	1.8%	28.9%	0.0%	0.0%
Great Falls, MT	1,770	12.5%	4.5%	15.9%	11.5%	0.0%	7.6%	0.0%	11.6%	1.8%	0.0%	0.0%	34.6%	0.0%
Greeley, CO	8,498	3.3%	4.0%	8.6%	22.4%	1.3%	5.9%	7.5%	12.0%	7.9%	1.9%	10.5%	11.6%	3.1%

Table F-4: Metropolitan/Micropolitan Statistical Areas—Educational Field of Study—*Continued*

	Total Millennial Population with Bachelor's or Higher	Percent of the Population 18 to 33 by Field of Study Degree												
		Engineering	Computers and Math	Science and Engineering Related	Business	Physical Science	Social Science	Communications	Biological Sciences	Literature	Liberal Arts	Psychology	Education	Visual and Performing Arts
Green Bay, WI	9,735	12.8%	4.7%	14.4%	21.3%	0.0%	5.3%	12.5%	6.5%	5.3%	3.1%	1.0%	11.6%	1.4%
Greensboro-High Point, NC	24,948	4.9%	4.4%	13.7%	13.5%	2.2%	7.1%	5.8%	9.9%	7.2%	6.4%	7.4%	12.4%	5.0%
Greenville, NC	7,489	0.0%	0.0%	10.5%	8.1%	13.1%	0.0%	11.7%	18.9%	2.5%	5.0%	13.6%	15.2%	1.4%
Greenville-Anderson-Mauldin, SC	35,977	10.3%	2.1%	11.3%	22.1%	3.2%	6.2%	3.6%	9.4%	3.7%	8.9%	3.8%	11.2%	4.4%
Greenwood, SC	1,941	5.6%	4.8%	26.4%	24.1%	0.0%	2.8%	0.0%	19.3%	0.0%	3.2%	1.6%	12.1%	0.0%
Gulfport-Biloxi-Pascagoula, MS	10,785	4.8%	0.8%	13.7%	19.0%	5.1%	4.0%	5.0%	12.4%	3.7%	3.4%	4.3%	18.6%	5.3%
Hagerstown-Martinsburg, MD-WV	6,596	2.3%	5.8%	9.4%	23.2%	2.1%	4.7%	10.6%	2.5%	6.5%	8.5%	8.4%	10.9%	5.0%
Hammond, LA	1,991	0.0%	0.0%	26.1%	18.3%	0.0%	5.6%	6.3%	0.0%	3.1%	18.3%	1.4%	14.7%	6.2%
Hanford-Corcoran, CA	3,776	7.8%	6.0%	10.0%	25.2%	4.4%	12.4%	0.0%	11.3%	0.0%	5.7%	1.9%	15.3%	0.0%
Harrisburg-Carlisle, PA	22,405	7.0%	5.1%	12.6%	22.7%	1.5%	7.2%	5.2%	6.1%	3.6%	3.0%	10.0%	14.1%	1.8%
Harrisonburg, VA	7,887	0.5%	2.0%	12.8%	15.8%	1.3%	11.0%	2.9%	6.4%	7.1%	9.8%	12.4%	8.9%	9.0%
Hartford-West Hartford-East Hartford, CT	72,417	10.6%	4.5%	9.9%	19.0%	2.2%	7.5%	7.3%	7.3%	4.6%	4.5%	8.4%	8.5%	5.6%
Hattiesburg, MS	4,950	5.5%	0.0%	5.3%	43.9%	0.0%	0.2%	14.2%	11.4%	3.7%	1.7%	3.6%	8.1%	2.3%
Hickory-Lenoir-Morganton, NC	8,122	8.6%	0.0%	15.4%	15.1%	0.0%	4.5%	3.9%	19.8%	1.6%	7.1%	5.8%	17.3%	0.8%
Hilo, HI	6,720	4.8%	8.5%	10.3%	18.5%	0.4%	12.7%	6.8%	2.1%	1.9%	5.6%	12.7%	12.4%	3.3%
Hilton Head Island-Bluffton-Beaufort, SC	6,546	3.6%	8.6%	3.1%	31.4%	1.7%	7.9%	7.8%	12.6%	0.5%	7.4%	4.8%	5.7%	4.8%
Hinesville, GA	1,366	4.5%	0.0%	0.0%	54.8%	0.0%	15.5%	0.0%	6.1%	0.0%	0.0%	0.0%	14.1%	5.1%
Holland, MI	2,426	0.5%	2.8%	9.2%	21.1%	13.8%	0.0%	11.1%	9.4%	0.0%	0.0%	2.5%	12.0%	17.6%
Homosassa Springs, FL	1,359	0.0%	4.6%	18.4%	18.0%	0.0%	6.5%	9.4%	34.4%	0.0%	0.0%	8.7%	0.0%	0.0%
Hot Springs, AR	1,349	0.0%	11.5%	3.9%	7.9%	9.6%	2.8%	3.6%	0.0%	4.5%	20.6%	0.0%	33.1%	2.5%
Houma-Thibodaux, LA	5,883	6.2%	6.7%	24.3%	11.9%	0.0%	0.0%	2.0%	3.1%	0.0%	18.1%	3.5%	6.4%	18.0%
Houston-The Woodlands-Sugar Land, TX	320,124	14.4%	5.8%	9.9%	25.1%	4.0%	5.9%	5.6%	9.0%	2.8%	3.6%	4.0%	6.3%	3.6%
Huntington-Ashland, WV-KY-OH	10,358	4.0%	2.4%	21.5%	10.0%	6.6%	5.6%	7.3%	12.4%	2.3%	3.9%	5.5%	14.4%	4.2%
Huntsville, AL	22,503	18.7%	10.5%	6.1%	24.2%	2.7%	3.1%	2.9%	6.6%	6.0%	3.1%	5.8%	3.4%	6.9%
Idaho Falls, ID	4,569	5.2%	5.0%	24.7%	20.5%	3.6%	0.0%	3.0%	10.1%	1.6%	1.8%	0.0%	22.0%	2.5%
Indianapolis-Carmel-Anderson, IN	100,587	5.8%	6.3%	13.5%	20.1%	2.4%	7.3%	6.2%	6.6%	3.4%	7.8%	4.6%	11.9%	4.1%
Iowa City, IA	15,405	1.1%	4.9%	6.6%	11.3%	7.3%	8.0%	2.9%	20.9%	8.5%	5.2%	10.0%	6.4%	6.8%
Ithaca, NY	12,476	11.5%	11.1%	4.7%	4.4%	23.1%	9.1%	0.0%	11.9%	1.8%	2.9%	10.1%	5.6%	3.8%
Jackson, MI	3,882	7.7%	4.4%	13.3%	26.3%	2.6%	3.3%	0.0%	6.5%	6.0%	2.2%	15.0%	10.5%	2.2%
Jackson, MS	27,062	4.7%	2.5%	21.5%	23.0%	6.1%	2.9%	3.3%	8.9%	1.1%	5.4%	7.1%	9.5%	4.0%
Jackson, TN	3,733	0.0%	1.6%	13.9%	41.3%	2.4%	8.0%	3.3%	14.7%	0.6%	7.0%	0.0%	4.7%	2.4%
Jacksonville, FL	65,245	9.4%	4.0%	14.7%	22.4%	2.5%	6.5%	7.3%	7.2%	1.6%	4.9%	6.5%	8.6%	4.4%
Jacksonville, NC	6,608	4.1%	11.1%	8.2%	15.8%	5.0%	9.6%	6.5%	14.6%	0.0%	4.9%	8.0%	9.1%	3.0%
Jamestown-Dunkirk-Fredonia, NY	3,119	1.5%	2.1%	8.4%	14.1%	0.0%	4.2%	4.0%	14.9%	5.5%	6.0%	6.0%	19.4%	13.8%
Janesville-Beloit, WI	5,106	4.0%	7.4%	5.3%	17.7%	4.2%	4.3%	4.5%	2.5%	7.1%	6.6%	20.1%	5.4%	10.9%
Jefferson City, MO	5,222	11.4%	2.9%	3.0%	22.3%	1.3%	5.0%	16.2%	15.5%	6.0%	2.2%	0.4%	13.7%	0.0%
Johnson City, TN	7,046	1.9%	1.4%	17.6%	7.1%	1.3%	8.7%	12.3%	17.8%	5.5%	2.0%	4.2%	13.0%	7.2%
Johnstown, PA	3,617	6.5%	0.6%	34.5%	23.2%	0.0%	3.0%	1.9%	0.0%	0.3%	0.0%	16.5%	13.5%	0.0%
Jonesboro, AR	3,209	3.7%	1.7%	19.4%	18.0%	0.0%	2.5%	3.2%	11.7%	0.0%	14.9%	4.3%	15.7%	4.9%
Joplin, MO	4,380	0.3%	1.8%	20.8%	26.0%	0.0%	7.7%	1.0%	9.5%	3.4%	14.1%	2.0%	13.3%	0.0%
Kahului-Wailuku-Lahaina, HI	6,006	0.8%	10.9%	28.5%	19.6%	2.3%	4.1%	2.1%	15.6%	2.8%	3.3%	3.8%	6.1%	0.0%
Kalamazoo-Portage, MI	20,117	5.6%	6.2%	8.0%	25.1%	3.8%	3.7%	7.7%	10.6%	10.0%	4.4%	4.9%	10.0%	0.0%
Kalispell, MT	2,102	0.0%	5.1%	36.1%	9.9%	0.0%	0.0%	0.0%	0.0%	3.9%	14.6%	0.0%	19.5%	10.9%
Kankakee, IL	3,430	3.1%	20.8%	19.1%	11.4%	0.0%	0.0%	17.1%	0.7%	3.6%	0.0%	9.6%	14.3%	0.1%
Kansas City, MO-KS	111,293	6.4%	6.3%	11.5%	21.8%	2.2%	5.1%	5.4%	9.1%	4.0%	4.9%	6.5%	10.2%	6.6%
Kennewick-Richland, WA	8,811	5.3%	4.4%	9.4%	15.2%	5.8%	14.4%	3.0%	13.9%	4.7%	6.1%	4.6%	13.3%	0.0%
Killeen-Temple, TX	13,838	9.6%	4.6%	10.4%	14.0%	5.1%	6.4%	5.1%	10.8%	5.8%	7.1%	5.3%	10.5%	5.4%
Kingsport-Bristol-Bristol, TN-VA	6,304	6.1%	5.8%	23.1%	29.2%	0.0%	0.9%	5.7%	7.0%	6.7%	1.7%	3.4%	10.4%	0.0%
Kingston, NY	7,251	6.7%	1.6%	6.1%	13.5%	1.3%	9.9%	2.9%	6.1%	7.7%	3.0%	8.7%	28.5%	4.0%
Knoxville, TN	30,993	6.8%	2.0%	12.1%	21.4%	3.4%	7.7%	6.2%	10.4%	5.3%	4.4%	5.2%	7.7%	7.5%
Kokomo, IN	2,214	0.0%	3.5%	28.6%	15.2%	1.5%	0.0%	16.9%	1.0%	0.0%	11.9%	0.0%	7.9%	13.4%
La Crosse-Onalaska, WI-MN	6,536	5.6%	6.2%	17.6%	20.2%	1.0%	5.1%	4.9%	14.7%	3.2%	0.0%	11.1%	8.0%	2.5%
Lafayette, LA	19,035	7.5%	2.9%	14.2%	13.8%	5.4%	1.9%	5.2%	17.5%	2.5%	12.4%	2.6%	11.9%	2.1%
Lafayette-West Lafayette, IN	17,245	17.4%	2.7%	7.5%	18.1%	9.7%	6.1%	1.1%	14.4%	5.7%	2.4%	2.6%	7.8%	4.5%
Lake Charles, LA	5,899	8.0%	1.7%	12.6%	6.5%	4.4%	5.0%	2.8%	17.3%	3.8%	20.1%	0.0%	17.7%	0.0%
Lake Havasu City-Kingman, AZ	2,602	0.0%	9.3%	11.6%	32.4%	6.1%	6.2%	0.0%	6.0%	0.2%	0.0%	0.0%	28.3%	0.0%
Lakeland-Winter Haven, FL	15,224	6.9%	2.6%	7.3%	23.6%	2.0%	5.7%	1.4%	7.6%	0.5%	6.1%	9.9%	18.2%	8.3%
Lancaster, PA	21,197	8.1%	3.5%	12.1%	17.0%	6.6%	2.8%	4.2%	11.8%	5.8%	2.2%	6.8%	13.5%	5.7%
Lansing-East Lansing, MI	28,294	5.9%	5.5%	9.1%	13.5%	4.2%	4.1%	4.1%	20.1%	4.5%	5.6%	7.8%	10.1%	5.5%
Laredo, TX	6,387	0.8%	0.8%	11.8%	30.9%	2.1%	7.0%	6.4%	7.2%	1.3%	4.0%	17.1%	10.9%	0.0%
Las Cruces, NM	3,341	0.0%	4.2%	7.3%	25.5%	3.2%	15.9%	2.8%	23.9%	9.5%	0.6%	0.0%	6.9%	0.0%
Las Vegas-Henderson-Paradise, NV	62,061	6.8%	4.4%	10.4%	21.7%	3.2%	7.7%	7.6%	9.6%	4.4%	3.6%	6.9%	6.2%	7.4%
Lawrence, KS	9,458	19.4%	4.1%	3.4%	11.4%	7.0%	2.4%	1.9%	10.1%	9.9%	5.9%	13.8%	6.3%	4.5%
Lawton, OK	2,827	0.0%	0.0%	18.7%	23.9%	4.2%	8.8%	0.0%	8.8%	3.5%	0.0%	12.1%	13.8%	6.0%
Lebanon, PA	4,339	2.9%	5.1%	7.3%	29.5%	3.0%	14.0%	5.5%	13.0%	1.5%	0.0%	1.8%	13.9%	2.4%
Lewiston, ID-WA	1,835	7.2%	0.0%	11.7%	23.7%	9.0%	12.9%	0.0%	17.4%	3.7%	7.7%	2.6%	3.1%	1.1%
Lewiston-Auburn, ME	2,447	7.7%	5.6%	10.8%	8.2%	0.0%	10.7%	0.0%	32.0%	0.0%	0.0%	11.9%	13.0%	0.0%
Lexington-Fayette, KY	28,860	6.8%	5.2%	12.1%	16.5%	3.7%	9.3%	8.1%	12.6%	4.8%	6.3%	5.7%	6.7%	2.3%
Lima, OH	3,231	8.1%	0.6%	30.6%	19.3%	5.2%	11.0%	0.0%	3.4%	2.9%	3.3%	2.7%	12.8%	0.0%
Lincoln, NE	22,162	8.1%	2.0%	12.1%	15.7%	8.4%	8.4%	9.1%	9.9%	3.6%	2.7%	5.1%	10.1%	4.8%
Little Rock-North Little Rock-Conway, AR	33,428	6.2%	7.1%	14.8%	19.5%	2.8%	3.8%	5.5%	17.7%	2.7%	5.5%	2.6%	9.4%	2.6%
Logan, UT-ID	7,250	12.7%	5.4%	18.6%	17.0%	1.7%	3.6%	0.8%	11.9%	3.7%	8.5%	2.5%	4.5%	9.1%

Table F-4: Metropolitan/Micropolitan Statistical Areas—Educational Field of Study—*Continued*

	Total Millennial Population with Bachelor's or Higher	Percent of the Population 18 to 33 by Field of Study Degree												
		Engineering	Computers and Math	Science and Engineering Related	Business	Physical Science	Social Science	Communications	Biological Sciences	Literature	Liberal Arts	Psychology	Education	Visual and Performing Arts
Longview, TX	6,226	22.1%	0.0%	14.8%	18.1%	3.4%	4.0%	0.0%	4.0%	0.4%	4.3%	0.0%	28.8%	0.0%
Longview, WA	2,161	1.4%	0.0%	27.6%	19.4%	0.0%	3.8%	0.0%	18.2%	0.0%	0.0%	5.1%	24.3%	0.0%
Los Angeles-Long Beach-Anaheim, CA.	746,571	7.8%	4.8%	7.3%	19.2%	2.2%	12.1%	8.1%	7.2%	4.9%	5.0%	6.6%	2.9%	11.8%
Louisville/Jefferson County, KY-IN	56,336	6.2%	4.2%	10.4%	23.4%	2.8%	6.9%	7.4%	9.8%	4.2%	7.8%	6.5%	7.7%	2.8%
Lubbock, TX	15,847	9.6%	4.5%	8.5%	19.3%	4.9%	5.7%	7.9%	13.6%	0.9%	4.5%	9.0%	6.8%	4.7%
Lumberton, NC	1,694	4.2%	0.0%	18.9%	12.7%	12.7%	0.0%	10.5%	13.5%	1.8%	4.1%	0.0%	21.7%	0.0%
Lynchburg, VA	10,119	3.1%	3.0%	14.0%	14.9%	0.5%	12.6%	1.6%	4.7%	4.9%	6.5%	17.5%	11.3%	5.5%
Macon, GA	8,277	4.0%	3.5%	12.5%	16.4%	7.7%	4.5%	7.5%	9.4%	5.6%	9.1%	5.4%	6.9%	7.6%
Madera, CA	3,325	18.0%	7.2%	11.4%	19.7%	0.0%	14.1%	3.6%	4.8%	0.0%	6.1%	15.1%	0.0%	0.0%
Madison, WI	63,764	14.1%	5.7%	7.6%	13.6%	3.9%	8.0%	6.5%	15.2%	7.1%	3.9%	4.7%	3.2%	6.4%
Manchester-Nashua, NH	21,595	9.1%	6.6%	10.5%	23.3%	1.7%	6.9%	6.1%	10.3%	3.3%	3.5%	6.7%	7.3%	4.7%
Manhattan, KS	4,576	20.0%	0.0%	7.8%	10.3%	3.9%	3.3%	6.1%	15.9%	1.2%	10.5%	1.2%	14.8%	5.0%
Mankato-North Mankato, MN	3,110	10.8%	0.7%	12.6%	26.8%	0.7%	0.3%	9.2%	13.8%	4.8%	0.0%	12.3%	8.0%	0.0%
Mansfield, OH	2,069	0.0%	7.7%	9.5%	10.9%	0.0%	0.0%	0.0%	1.6%	0.0%	7.4%	21.4%	38.1%	3.2%
McAllen-Edinburg-Mission, TX	20,851	7.8%	2.7%	12.5%	21.9%	8.6%	5.6%	3.9%	4.9%	4.8%	5.6%	6.5%	12.8%	2.4%
Medford, OR	3,790	2.7%	4.0%	10.1%	15.0%	0.0%	12.6%	8.7%	10.3%	3.8%	20.6%	5.6%	3.5%	3.2%
Memphis, TN-MS-AR	53,408	8.1%	4.6%	12.5%	24.7%	2.4%	5.0%	4.2%	10.0%	4.1%	4.8%	4.8%	10.5%	4.2%
Merced, CA	5,039	0.0%	0.0%	10.1%	29.4%	3.1%	5.0%	5.2%	12.3%	1.4%	19.0%	9.2%	5.3%	0.0%
Meridian, MS	1,513	0.0%	0.0%	21.9%	18.1%	0.0%	1.3%	0.0%	28.7%	1.2%	2.4%	0.0%	26.4%	0.0%
Miami-Fort Lauderdale-West Palm Beach, FL	256,013	6.7%	4.4%	11.4%	29.3%	2.0%	6.9%	6.0%	8.2%	3.1%	3.1%	8.3%	6.4%	4.2%
Michigan City-La Porte, IN	1,591	0.0%	4.7%	14.5%	26.8%	0.0%	8.8%	9.7%	13.1%	0.0%	4.8%	0.0%	17.7%	0.0%
Midland, MI	2,759	4.2%	0.0%	7.2%	46.5%	0.0%	7.6%	2.8%	16.7%	4.1%	2.2%	0.9%	3.3%	4.5%
Midland, TX	5,575	24.1%	0.0%	17.5%	10.7%	13.5%	4.3%	1.7%	9.4%	5.3%	0.0%	5.8%	6.7%	1.1%
Milwaukee-Waukesha-West Allis, WI	86,057	6.8%	4.2%	11.6%	23.0%	4.0%	7.5%	7.7%	9.0%	4.3%	3.0%	4.7%	8.2%	6.1%
Minneapolis-St. Paul-Bloomington, MN-WI	238,991	9.3%	5.4%	8.9%	21.4%	2.5%	7.1%	7.2%	9.5%	3.4%	2.7%	7.0%	7.8%	7.9%
Missoula, MT	5,816	0.0%	0.0%	0.0%	27.0%	0.0%	9.5%	5.1%	16.8%	3.1%	18.5%	7.1%	4.8%	8.2%
Mobile, AL	16,033	7.5%	6.3%	24.8%	11.2%	5.4%	0.8%	12.0%	6.6%	3.0%	4.6%	2.6%	13.8%	1.4%
Modesto, CA	10,369	2.3%	6.5%	17.8%	16.9%	0.8%	9.2%	4.8%	12.3%	6.6%	3.7%	9.7%	2.4%	6.8%
Monroe, LA	7,113	12.3%	3.4%	8.6%	21.2%	0.0%	7.7%	1.5%	12.1%	4.4%	7.7%	4.1%	10.9%	6.0%
Monroe, MI	4,492	4.2%	2.3%	20.1%	24.3%	4.6%	2.7%	3.7%	5.2%	3.7%	3.9%	4.5%	14.1%	6.6%
Montgomery, AL	11,408	4.7%	9.0%	12.4%	25.3%	0.8%	3.1%	6.0%	6.9%	2.3%	3.0%	12.9%	3.9%	9.5%
Morgantown, WV	11,927	15.6%	0.5%	12.5%	18.1%	3.0%	9.9%	5.0%	23.5%	1.9%	1.7%	1.0%	2.8%	4.5%
Morristown, TN	1,482	6.6%	13.0%	6.4%	27.2%	0.0%	0.0%	2.1%	0.0%	0.0%	0.0%	24.0%	20.7%	0.0%
Mount Vernon-Anacortes, WA	2,548	7.6%	0.0%	2.9%	15.8%	5.0%	11.6%	0.4%	23.2%	7.3%	4.7%	12.7%	8.5%	0.4%
Muncie, IN	2,713	0.0%	5.1%	21.6%	2.7%	4.7%	8.4%	6.2%	21.4%	4.7%	5.8%	2.5%	14.7%	2.2%
Muskegon, MI	3,050	8.6%	3.4%	17.5%	28.5%	0.0%	0.0%	0.0%	0.0%	0.0%	8.5%	4.3%	29.3%	0.0%
Myrtle Beach-Conway-North Myrtle Beach, SC-NC	13,109	4.0%	4.3%	16.3%	20.3%	5.8%	10.1%	7.7%	5.2%	5.4%	2.0%	8.0%	8.5%	2.3%
Napa, CA	6,323	12.1%	2.7%	6.0%	29.6%	0.0%	10.1%	1.3%	12.4%	4.8%	6.7%	2.3%	1.7%	10.2%
Naples-Immokalee-Marco Island, FL	10,972	6.0%	0.9%	7.1%	25.7%	8.0%	12.4%	8.4%	10.4%	0.0%	5.0%	0.5%	7.4%	8.2%
Nashville-Davidson–Murfreesboro–Franklin, TN	108,763	4.4%	4.8%	10.6%	20.9%	3.8%	6.7%	7.1%	10.7%	4.0%	7.3%	5.5%	7.9%	6.4%
New Bern, NC	2,967	3.0%	20.2%	11.1%	9.8%	6.6%	3.1%	2.6%	3.8%	1.0%	13.3%	6.7%	18.9%	0.0%
New Castle, PA	1,967	1.3%	0.0%	4.4%	13.8%	0.0%	10.1%	6.8%	4.3%	4.5%	0.0%	14.6%	38.7%	1.5%
New Haven-Milford, CT	47,519	9.7%	7.3%	8.1%	17.6%	2.0%	10.8%	4.9%	8.2%	5.2%	9.2%	5.1%	4.3%	7.6%
New Orleans-Metairie, LA	63,673	7.0%	1.8%	12.0%	20.1%	3.6%	7.5%	6.6%	9.8%	3.8%	7.4%	6.9%	6.4%	7.2%
New Philadelphia-Dover, OH	3,661	7.5%	1.8%	10.2%	12.5%	0.2%	8.3%	0.0%	20.9%	3.2%	14.3%	0.0%	16.7%	4.3%
New York-Newark-Jersey City, NY-NJ-PA	1,471,149	5.5%	6.7%	7.6%	22.4%	2.6%	10.2%	6.6%	5.9%	5.0%	4.8%	7.0%	6.7%	9.0%
Niles-Benton Harbor, MI	5,192	17.7%	0.0%	20.2%	15.9%	0.0%	3.7%	1.8%	6.5%	0.8%	10.7%	11.8%	8.3%	2.6%
North Port-Sarasota-Bradenton, FL	16,788	3.6%	4.6%	12.5%	20.8%	5.4%	12.7%	4.0%	5.9%	5.7%	3.5%	3.7%	11.3%	6.3%
Norwich-New London, CT	13,089	15.6%	5.3%	6.0%	11.0%	1.6%	10.7%	2.1%	10.7%	5.0%	4.2%	12.1%	10.7%	4.8%
Ocala, FL	7,022	12.7%	0.6%	3.8%	41.5%	1.2%	0.7%	1.9%	26.0%	0.0%	0.0%	1.5%	10.1%	0.0%
Ocean City, NJ	3,522	0.0%	0.0%	16.0%	11.4%	0.0%	9.5%	5.7%	9.0%	8.9%	9.8%	3.1%	20.0%	6.7%
Odessa, TX	4,179	18.8%	0.0%	2.2%	31.8%	0.0%	6.8%	2.5%	14.8%	3.9%	2.0%	1.4%	14.0%	1.7%
Ogden-Clearfield, UT	22,000	8.8%	2.6%	12.4%	23.6%	1.3%	6.0%	5.0%	4.6%	3.9%	1.8%	8.0%	14.8%	7.2%
Ogdensburg-Massena, NY	3,322	8.2%	3.9%	14.1%	12.6%	8.1%	3.0%	3.2%	10.7%	0.0%	14.2%	13.2%	8.7%	0.0%
Oklahoma City, OK	61,959	10.6%	2.8%	8.8%	28.1%	5.2%	7.6%	4.5%	9.9%	3.6%	5.0%	2.8%	8.0%	3.1%
Olympia-Tumwater, WA	9,249	7.2%	6.6%	12.2%	5.5%	0.7%	16.9%	3.4%	17.5%	5.6%	3.4%	11.8%	5.6%	3.6%
Omaha-Council Bluffs, NE-IA	54,408	4.2%	6.7%	12.5%	25.8%	2.2%	1.1%	7.1%	10.5%	3.7%	5.9%	3.7%	13.1%	3.6%
Orangeburg, SC	1,297	3.6%	0.0%	1.8%	20.5%	0.0%	19.1%	0.0%	39.5%	4.4%	1.9%	0.0%	0.0%	9.2%
Orlando-Kissimmee-Sanford, FL	114,408	6.0%	5.7%	13.5%	30.7%	1.2%	6.5%	7.2%	6.2%	2.9%	2.6%	5.0%	6.5%	6.1%
Oshkosh-Neenah, WI	6,696	0.0%	1.8%	7.5%	40.8%	1.8%	1.7%	1.9%	3.0%	0.0%	3.7%	0.0%	28.6%	9.3%
Ottawa-Peru, IL	2,192	18.6%	5.7%	5.5%	17.0%	9.5%	14.7%	2.3%	9.2%	1.7%	0.0%	0.8%	10.2%	4.7%
Owensboro, KY	2,975	4.1%	1.9%	18.9%	16.3%	0.0%	0.0%	6.3%	15.0%	0.0%	5.9%	10.6%	16.5%	4.5%
Oxnard-Thousand Oaks-Ventura, CA	34,454	4.5%	7.8%	11.4%	18.6%	1.5%	8.4%	7.0%	11.6%	5.3%	5.5%	8.3%	6.0%	4.2%
Palm Bay-Melbourne-Titusville, FL	16,921	12.5%	7.0%	11.2%	27.5%	5.3%	2.5%	2.7%	5.2%	2.8%	1.1%	9.7%	11.1%	1.3%
Panama City, FL	4,800	17.5%	4.8%	10.1%	21.9%	1.6%	1.7%	2.8%	9.6%	0.0%	3.7%	12.9%	9.2%	4.1%
Parkersburg-Vienna, WV	2,271	8.4%	6.1%	13.1%	20.3%	0.0%	7.8%	6.7%	8.7%	2.9%	0.0%	3.4%	18.5%	4.1%
Pensacola-Ferry Pass-Brent, FL	19,317	4.5%	5.7%	11.3%	22.5%	2.2%	9.4%	9.1%	9.6%	1.1%	5.3%	3.0%	15.1%	1.3%
Peoria, IL	17,288	8.2%	6.0%	18.9%	19.0%	3.1%	1.8%	4.9%	9.7%	2.6%	3.4%	6.4%	6.9%	9.1%
Philadelphia-Camden-Wilmington, PA-NJ-DE-MD	379,277	7.7%	5.2%	11.5%	21.0%	2.7%	7.5%	6.4%	9.5%	4.4%	4.4%	6.1%	9.2%	4.5%
Phoenix-Mesa-Scottsdale, AZ	184,928	10.3%	6.5%	10.4%	21.3%	2.9%	7.2%	8.5%	6.5%	2.6%	3.0%	5.6%	10.2%	5.1%
Pine Bluff, AR	2,795	0.0%	4.1%	6.7%	18.0%	0.0%	2.9%	0.0%	15.6%	0.0%	0.0%	13.3%	37.5%	2.1%

Table F-4: Metropolitan/Micropolitan Statistical Areas—Educational Field of Study—*Continued*

	Total Millennial Population with Bachelor's or Higher	Percent of the Population 18 to 33 by Field of Study Degree												
		Engineering	Computers and Math	Science and Engineering Related	Business	Physical Science	Social Science	Communications	Biological Sciences	Literature	Liberal Arts	Psychology	Education	Visual and Performing Arts
Pittsburgh, PA	137,014	8.1%	5.2%	11.7%	21.5%	4.3%	6.5%	7.2%	7.4%	3.7%	3.6%	8.0%	8.9%	3.7%
Pittsfield, MA	3,096	10.6%	1.8%	14.0%	15.0%	0.8%	5.1%	8.0%	5.7%	0.0%	19.2%	12.7%	0.8%	6.4%
Pocatello, ID	2,928	15.4%	4.4%	10.0%	11.9%	9.7%	9.1%	3.3%	5.1%	0.0%	11.9%	2.7%	16.7%	0.0%
Port St. Lucie, FL	27,114	8.8%	1.9%	8.3%	14.6%	3.6%	10.4%	10.4%	14.8%	2.0%	0.7%	8.8%	9.1%	6.5%
Portland–South Portland, ME	134,796	7.0%	5.8%	9.8%	17.5%	3.0%	11.1%	5.9%	9.1%	7.1%	4.7%	6.8%	4.0%	8.2%
Portland-Vancouver-Hillsboro, OR-WA	7,152	2.6%	0.6%	11.0%	18.9%	0.0%	7.6%	3.7%	5.3%	4.5%	13.6%	13.3%	10.7%	8.3%
Pottsville, PA	3,699	11.9%	1.5%	29.8%	8.1%	0.0%	3.1%	0.0%	7.4%	0.0%	0.0%	15.7%	22.5%	0.0%
Prescott, AZ	2,922	14.9%	7.1%	0.0%	26.2%	0.0%	0.0%	0.0%	12.7%	9.7%	14.9%	6.5%	3.6%	4.6%
Providence-Warwick, RI-MA	79,623	7.4%	5.7%	10.3%	21.5%	4.1%	9.4%	5.1%	8.9%	2.6%	3.6%	6.5%	9.2%	5.7%
Provo-Orem, UT	29,099	4.0%	6.2%	16.4%	16.7%	3.6%	3.7%	6.7%	4.6%	9.6%	3.5%	5.1%	12.1%	7.8%
Pueblo, CO	4,169	3.6%	14.2%	11.5%	30.4%	0.0%	7.5%	3.0%	3.6%	11.1%	4.3%	1.3%	4.7%	4.7%
Punta Gorda, FL	1,126	0.0%	0.0%	32.4%	6.9%	0.0%	9.0%	0.0%	7.4%	7.6%	0.0%	5.2%	31.5%	0.0%
Racine, WI	5,520	10.7%	0.0%	12.5%	33.3%	3.5%	5.1%	1.6%	1.5%	15.1%	2.9%	1.2%	9.5%	3.2%
Raleigh, NC	85,018	10.3%	9.1%	7.9%	18.0%	3.4%	8.4%	7.1%	10.9%	2.5%	6.0%	5.1%	7.5%	3.8%
Rapid City, SD	4,343	5.6%	0.0%	10.8%	31.9%	5.5%	4.5%	6.7%	18.4%	0.0%	2.1%	0.0%	14.5%	0.0%
Reading, PA	13,933	2.8%	3.6%	14.5%	16.7%	0.0%	7.5%	1.2%	13.0%	5.6%	3.9%	7.2%	19.5%	4.4%
Redding, CA	6,379	0.0%	3.4%	3.5%	16.4%	0.0%	4.6%	11.5%	16.3%	2.1%	26.4%	6.1%	4.4%	5.4%
Reno, NV	17,196	6.0%	4.2%	6.9%	32.1%	3.2%	3.1%	8.4%	8.7%	5.4%	5.4%	5.4%	9.0%	2.2%
Richmond, VA	64,834	6.7%	5.0%	10.1%	18.0%	2.7%	10.5%	4.1%	10.1%	4.5%	8.1%	8.8%	6.2%	5.1%
Riverside-San Bernardino-Ontario, CA	110,655	5.9%	5.3%	12.2%	24.8%	4.4%	9.5%	3.7%	7.6%	4.1%	6.4%	7.0%	4.0%	5.0%
Roanoke, VA	11,955	13.7%	2.7%	9.9%	17.0%	3.1%	10.4%	3.7%	8.6%	2.8%	5.4%	11.8%	6.5%	4.5%
Rochester, MN	13,228	3.4%	6.6%	26.8%	8.5%	4.2%	8.5%	2.3%	24.5%	4.1%	4.3%	2.7%	2.7%	1.2%
Rochester, NY	56,704	6.0%	6.9%	10.8%	19.7%	3.1%	8.6%	6.6%	7.0%	4.4%	3.0%	6.8%	11.2%	5.9%
Rockford, IL	12,033	10.9%	0.9%	23.1%	13.7%	1.1%	4.7%	4.5%	11.5%	5.2%	0.3%	2.0%	14.6%	7.6%
Rocky Mount, NC	1,880	0.0%	5.2%	11.6%	4.8%	3.9%	0.0%	4.2%	13.7%	0.0%	0.0%	35.8%	15.7%	5.1%
Rome, GA	2,701	1.3%	10.3%	14.1%	24.4%	0.0%	4.7%	3.7%	3.3%	0.0%	6.0%	0.0%	28.4%	3.9%
Roseburg, OR	2,772	8.6%	0.0%	16.2%	4.1%	4.4%	19.1%	14.6%	18.0%	3.6%	0.0%	1.8%	4.9%	4.7%
Sacramento–Roseville–Arden-Arcade, CA	95,287	8.7%	3.6%	7.6%	16.3%	3.1%	12.7%	5.1%	14.7%	5.7%	6.6%	7.9%	3.2%	4.8%
Saginaw, MI	6,206	7.3%	9.6%	15.5%	24.7%	6.0%	4.6%	4.3%	6.6%	4.3%	1.4%	6.2%	9.3%	0.0%
Salem, OH	11,056	4.7%	1.3%	4.7%	18.5%	2.6%	5.3%	12.8%	5.7%	10.8%	3.2%	12.7%	17.7%	0.0%
Salem, OR	3,559	13.4%	14.6%	15.4%	8.5%	0.0%	0.0%	14.2%	11.9%	0.0%	0.0%	5.7%	1.6%	14.7%
Salinas, CA	3,692	31.6%	16.1%	15.0%	6.7%	2.3%	1.3%	3.4%	9.1%	0.0%	2.9%	1.7%	8.3%	1.7%
Salisbury, MD-DE	130,466	6.8%	5.6%	7.9%	24.4%	2.2%	6.6%	8.9%	7.9%	3.3%	3.5%	7.2%	10.1%	5.5%
Salt Lake City, UT	1,600	3.9%	4.3%	5.7%	9.9%	0.0%	3.6%	0.0%	13.4%	0.0%	0.0%	5.8%	26.8%	26.5%
San Angelo, TX	11,355	4.2%	3.9%	7.2%	19.0%	4.1%	14.0%	1.2%	5.3%	2.8%	18.0%	6.6%	10.0%	3.5%
San Antonio-New Braunfels, TX	12,125	7.9%	3.0%	8.4%	19.0%	0.8%	16.6%	4.2%	5.2%	3.0%	13.3%	6.4%	2.1%	10.1%
San Diego-Carlsbad, CA	8,289	0.3%	5.1%	6.5%	14.3%	8.5%	3.6%	4.9%	21.7%	1.5%	3.7%	9.5%	15.3%	5.1%
San Francisco-Oakland-Hayward, CA	58,814	7.1%	5.6%	10.9%	21.2%	2.4%	7.7%	8.3%	8.0%	6.4%	2.7%	5.5%	8.4%	5.9%
San Jose-Sunnyvale-Santa Clara, CA	5,424	0.0%	6.4%	15.7%	26.4%	6.6%	7.1%	6.2%	9.5%	0.9%	0.6%	4.0%	10.1%	6.5%
San Luis Obispo-Paso Robles-Arroyo Grande, CA	83,168	6.3%	6.9%	12.7%	21.9%	3.0%	7.4%	6.4%	10.3%	5.1%	2.7%	4.7%	8.7%	3.9%
Santa Cruz-Watsonville, CA	195,101	11.4%	6.8%	7.8%	17.4%	3.8%	11.3%	6.7%	9.9%	3.8%	6.9%	6.3%	3.1%	4.8%
Santa Fe, NM	407,273	10.8%	9.6%	6.5%	19.2%	2.9%	12.8%	4.7%	8.6%	5.2%	4.5%	5.2%	1.9%	8.0%
Santa Maria-Santa Barbara, CA	162,126	22.8%	16.6%	5.8%	16.2%	2.6%	8.4%	4.6%	7.1%	4.2%	2.1%	5.2%	1.6%	3.0%
Santa Rosa, CA	9,348	13.5%	4.8%	2.0%	9.6%	7.3%	6.2%	2.8%	12.2%	7.7%	13.8%	10.5%	3.9%	5.7%
Savannah, GA	13,437	12.1%	1.1%	7.6%	9.0%	3.4%	14.9%	2.8%	16.4%	6.5%	5.5%	8.5%	4.5%	7.7%
Scranton–Wilkes-Barre–Hazleton, PA	5,395	8.9%	5.1%	7.4%	12.7%	1.1%	8.1%	7.8%	8.7%	7.1%	2.8%	9.0%	5.7%	15.5%
Seattle-Tacoma-Bellevue, WA	20,100	11.9%	7.2%	4.6%	13.6%	7.0%	12.9%	5.2%	9.4%	5.6%	7.9%	6.3%	1.2%	7.1%
Sebastian-Vero Beach, FL	17,746	10.9%	8.6%	5.9%	19.3%	2.6%	12.5%	3.9%	9.6%	3.1%	7.0%	10.2%	1.0%	5.3%
Sebring, FL	16,023	9.0%	5.0%	9.2%	21.8%	2.5%	5.8%	7.8%	6.8%	2.7%	3.4%	2.3%	13.5%	10.2%
Sheboygan, WI	20,262	1.5%	2.5%	15.8%	19.1%	6.1%	5.4%	7.9%	6.3%	3.8%	5.6%	5.9%	19.6%	0.6%
Sherman-Denison, TX	272,244	10.9%	11.2%	8.7%	17.6%	2.7%	11.3%	5.2%	8.2%	4.7%	4.7%	5.3%	3.3%	6.1%
Show Low, AZ	1,664	20.3%	10.6%	10.3%	21.5%	3.1%	8.9%	1.7%	4.9%	0.0%	8.3%	10.5%	7.5%	3.0%
Shreveport-Bossier City, LA	711	0.0%	0.0%	0.0%	6.6%	0.0%	9.1%	0.0%	40.6%	0.0%	0.0%	7.7%	35.9%	0.0%
Sierra Vista-Douglas, AZ	3,951	7.6%	8.6%	17.2%	5.9%	0.0%	0.0%	10.3%	5.6%	0.9%	15.1%	0.0%	23.4%	5.4%
Sioux City, IA-NE-SD	1,982	2.4%	0.0%	7.5%	16.6%	10.2%	9.7%	0.0%	1.0%	0.0%	2.1%	11.2%	30.1%	9.1%
Sioux Falls, SD	1,059	2.2%	5.9%	21.2%	4.6%	0.0%	2.5%	0.0%	14.4%	10.2%	0.0%	13.0%	20.6%	5.4%
South Bend-Mishawaka, IN-MI	13,984	6.8%	7.9%	11.6%	20.5%	1.9%	3.0%	5.0%	10.1%	1.2%	8.9%	8.2%	7.2%	7.7%
Spartanburg, SC	3,421	3.9%	22.8%	9.7%	13.1%	5.1%	20.4%	5.0%	5.6%	0.0%	1.7%	7.7%	0.5%	4.5%
Spokane-Spokane Valley, WA	3,520	0.0%	0.0%	1.8%	15.7%	5.5%	1.4%	0.0%	13.0%	4.7%	10.7%	0.7%	29.4%	17.1%
Springfield, IL	14,623	0.0%	6.2%	13.3%	23.2%	2.3%	2.2%	4.3%	6.0%	1.9%	2.3%	10.9%	23.8%	3.7%
Springfield, MA	13,814	7.8%	4.8%	9.5%	25.9%	3.3%	8.7%	5.3%	5.0%	2.1%	9.0%	2.6%	9.7%	6.5%
Springfield, MO	8,671	2.5%	3.8%	6.2%	21.6%	5.4%	6.7%	2.8%	12.5%	2.9%	3.0%	8.2%	13.4%	10.9%
Springfield, OH	18,928	3.7%	2.6%	10.3%	21.0%	0.8%	10.4%	6.3%	12.8%	5.5%	6.8%	5.2%	11.9%	2.5%
St. Cloud, MN	10,645	14.2%	5.2%	12.5%	15.6%	1.0%	2.1%	3.7%	11.8%	4.5%	8.4%	7.6%	10.9%	2.3%
St. George, UT	29,844	5.6%	2.4%	9.6%	13.8%	3.1%	9.5%	5.6%	8.4%	5.0%	7.0%	14.5%	5.2%	10.2%
St. Joseph, MO-KS	17,580	0.8%	0.7%	11.3%	21.1%	3.1%	6.8%	4.6%	8.0%	4.1%	8.8%	10.6%	15.3%	4.8%
St. Louis, MO-IL	2,542	4.8%	9.5%	16.1%	29.6%	0.0%	10.0%	6.2%	0.0%	6.6%	1.8%	6.3%	5.5%	3.6%
State College, PA	15,128	9.1%	13.2%	4.9%	5.3%	17.0%	7.2%	6.3%	11.4%	6.5%	3.0%	5.9%	9.3%	0.7%
Staunton-Waynesboro, VA	2,734	5.4%	7.4%	14.8%	25.2%	0.0%	6.3%	0.0%	6.1%	5.3%	2.6%	0.0%	9.0%	17.9%
Stockton-Lodi, CA	15,091	5.9%	5.7%	10.9%	20.6%	2.4%	10.0%	5.2%	19.2%	2.8%	6.8%	2.5%	4.7%	3.3%
Sumter, SC	1,742	0.0%	0.0%	8.0%	38.3%	0.0%	0.0%	0.0%	15.7%	2.9%	2.0%	2.6%	20.5%	10.0%
Sunbury, PA	2,785	1.0%	0.0%	7.6%	18.0%	1.3%	21.2%	1.0%	11.5%	0.0%	0.0%	9.3%	21.0%	8.0%
Syracuse, NY	27,852	7.9%	3.8%	9.8%	22.2%	1.9%	9.7%	6.4%	8.7%	4.6%	5.7%	3.9%	12.8%	2.5%
Tallahassee, FL	24,445	4.7%	3.6%	9.9%	18.8%	4.2%	14.6%	2.4%	7.7%	7.8%	4.2%	7.2%	6.9%	8.0%
Tampa-St. Petersburg-Clearwater, FL	124,411	3.9%	5.6%	13.1%	23.2%	2.8%	9.9%	6.3%	7.1%	2.7%	4.9%	8.7%	7.3%	4.4%

Table F-4: Metropolitan/Micropolitan Statistical Areas—Educational Field of Study—*Continued*

	Total Millennial Population with Bachelor's or Higher	Engineering	Computers and Math	Science and Engineering Related	Business	Physical Science	Social Science	Communications	Biological Sciences	Literature	Liberal Arts	Psychology	Education	Visual and Performing Arts
					Percent of the Population 18 to 33 by Field of Study Degree									
Terre Haute, IN	5,200	12.5%	6.9%	13.4%	7.9%	5.3%	3.9%	0.0%	9.6%	0.8%	2.4%	9.2%	26.6%	1.5%
Texarkana, TX-AR	1,504	0.0%	0.0%	12.7%	22.4%	0.0%	1.3%	3.3%	10.8%	8.2%	18.0%	16.4%	3.3%	3.7%
The Villages, FL	728	0.0%	0.0%	34.3%	26.8%	0.0%	6.5%	16.8%	15.7%	0.0%	0.0%	0.0%	0.0%	0.0%
Toledo, OH	25,020	10.3%	4.1%	12.1%	23.3%	2.1%	5.0%	7.5%	8.6%	1.3%	5.2%	4.6%	11.0%	5.0%
Topeka, KS	9,086	3.4%	5.9%	8.4%	19.8%	1.4%	14.0%	5.5%	2.8%	1.6%	9.5%	9.8%	12.4%	5.6%
Torrington, CT	7,727	7.6%	5.7%	12.1%	20.4%	0.0%	4.2%	2.9%	4.4%	8.0%	8.7%	5.5%	7.5%	12.7%
Traverse City, MI	5,498	1.9%	3.8%	9.8%	39.5%	3.1%	9.7%	0.0%	3.5%	5.6%	3.4%	2.4%	5.4%	11.8%
Trenton, NJ	18,873	9.3%	5.7%	5.2%	16.3%	5.1%	19.6%	4.6%	7.0%	3.3%	4.1%	13.3%	1.4%	5.1%
Truckee-Grass Valley, CA	2,063	6.0%	9.2%	10.7%	2.2%	0.0%	11.2%	0.0%	11.6%	5.0%	14.6%	10.7%	8.2%	10.5%
Tucson, AZ	35,987	13.9%	4.4%	6.3%	14.4%	4.3%	14.4%	5.4%	10.2%	5.3%	3.9%	6.2%	7.0%	4.3%
Tullahoma-Manchester, TN	1,510	21.8%	10.7%	3.6%	1.3%	5.6%	5.6%	0.0%	0.0%	5.5%	10.2%	0.0%	13.7%	22.1%
Tulsa, OK	35,073	9.5%	6.3%	8.9%	21.0%	4.2%	5.1%	4.8%	10.2%	2.6%	4.4%	5.9%	11.9%	5.1%
Tupelo, MS	3,158	9.3%	2.6%	7.1%	24.1%	0.0%	10.3%	0.0%	17.7%	1.4%	3.3%	0.0%	24.3%	0.0%
Tuscaloosa, AL	6,834	9.3%	2.9%	4.1%	27.4%	0.0%	20.4%	6.4%	5.1%	4.9%	0.7%	5.4%	9.2%	4.2%
Tyler, TX	7,886	8.6%	3.8%	18.6%	27.1%	1.2%	2.7%	1.9%	8.9%	4.4%	3.8%	0.8%	15.1%	3.3%
Urban Honolulu, HI	49,408	7.8%	4.7%	7.9%	22.1%	1.0%	11.4%	3.7%	8.4%	5.6%	5.3%	8.9%	7.6%	5.7%
Utica-Rome, NY	10,836	2.9%	7.6%	12.4%	18.8%	1.4%	7.8%	4.2%	2.3%	3.1%	3.4%	16.3%	11.5%	8.3%
Valdosta, GA	5,109	5.0%	7.5%	5.0%	21.7%	2.6%	10.2%	3.2%	11.3%	0.0%	2.2%	7.6%	23.7%	0.0%
Vallejo-Fairfield, CA	14,249	10.9%	1.1%	10.9%	17.7%	1.1%	13.2%	5.3%	9.8%	5.6%	8.3%	8.8%	2.6%	4.5%
Victoria, TX	2,657	25.7%	3.5%	0.0%	25.0%	5.5%	12.4%	0.0%	24.2%	1.4%	0.0%	0.0%	0.0%	2.3%
Vineland-Bridgeton, NJ	3,854	15.7%	0.0%	11.7%	28.4%	0.0%	4.7%	0.0%	7.5%	2.0%	5.2%	9.3%	15.4%	0.0%
Virginia Beach-Norfolk-Newport News, VA-NC	76,104	10.1%	6.8%	10.2%	15.9%	3.7%	5.9%	5.0%	8.9%	6.6%	5.2%	8.4%	7.0%	6.4%
Visalia-Porterville, CA	10,722	2.1%	6.1%	13.5%	25.1%	4.9%	6.2%	6.0%	10.2%	0.0%	5.5%	8.0%	9.9%	2.3%
Waco, TX	10,800	2.7%	6.5%	8.4%	27.9%	1.6%	4.5%	5.6%	10.7%	4.9%	7.8%	5.5%	6.3%	7.4%
Walla Walla, WA	3,056	2.9%	4.0%	11.6%	15.0%	3.9%	30.5%	8.6%	8.8%	2.4%	0.0%	0.0%	12.3%	0.0%
Warner Robins, GA	5,091	3.2%	3.3%	11.7%	20.7%	0.0%	2.2%	4.6%	10.8%	4.0%	2.5%	0.8%	27.5%	8.5%
Washington-Arlington-Alexandria, DC-VA-MD-WV	494,254	7.9%	7.2%	6.1%	18.8%	2.1%	19.1%	6.0%	6.9%	4.7%	5.8%	5.8%	4.9%	4.5%
Waterloo-Cedar Falls, IA	8,222	10.5%	0.0%	15.1%	19.7%	0.0%	1.0%	4.1%	15.0%	1.5%	13.1%	5.9%	13.1%	0.9%
Watertown-Fort Drum, NY	3,206	5.9%	4.1%	2.8%	16.8%	5.0%	11.1%	8.7%	9.5%	5.9%	8.7%	6.3%	12.1%	3.2%
Wausau, WI	6,067	8.1%	5.3%	13.6%	16.3%	3.5%	8.4%	18.4%	9.8%	0.0%	0.5%	8.3%	6.9%	0.8%
Weirton-Steubenville, WV-OH	2,744	2.0%	14.2%	0.0%	19.7%	3.0%	5.9%	0.0%	5.6%	0.9%	3.6%	10.3%	34.7%	0.0%
Wenatchee, WA	2,246	2.3%	2.1%	4.1%	14.9%	4.8%	4.6%	0.0%	10.4%	8.4%	0.0%	13.8%	18.0%	16.4%
Wheeling, WV-OH	2,826	2.0%	13.8%	0.2%	19.1%	0.0%	5.7%	0.0%	2.8%	0.8%	4.5%	10.0%	41.0%	0.0%
Whitewater-Elkhorn, WI	3,067	10.5%	1.7%	5.3%	15.9%	0.0%	9.9%	8.3%	24.2%	1.8%	3.9%	1.6%	17.0%	0.0%
Wichita Falls, TX	29,801	11.5%	4.4%	14.2%	22.0%	1.6%	4.9%	3.1%	12.6%	0.1%	3.5%	4.8%	10.9%	6.3%
Wichita, KS	4,913	14.3%	0.0%	11.7%	23.8%	3.1%	2.9%	1.4%	4.6%	0.0%	2.4%	9.7%	23.6%	2.5%
Williamsport, PA	4,596	4.7%	0.6%	12.0%	7.9%	5.6%	1.2%	0.9%	17.6%	9.6%	14.6%	17.2%	7.7%	0.5%
Wilmington, NC	14,401	1.5%	2.5%	13.8%	17.5%	2.4%	9.6%	4.8%	12.5%	5.2%	6.1%	9.5%	11.5%	3.3%
Winchester, VA-WV	3,267	0.0%	0.0%	32.9%	20.2%	9.3%	2.1%	1.6%	6.8%	4.8%	6.2%	4.2%	10.7%	1.1%
Winston-Salem, NC	24,385	10.9%	4.7%	14.7%	18.2%	3.3%	5.2%	5.6%	11.6%	1.8%	4.6%	7.5%	9.5%	2.4%
Wooster, OH	3,145	3.2%	0.0%	10.2%	7.6%	5.5%	10.1%	16.2%	4.4%	6.7%	0.0%	5.1%	30.9%	0.0%
Worcester, MA-CT	46,277	6.8%	5.9%	6.8%	16.5%	5.3%	8.6%	6.2%	13.1%	7.3%	5.7%	7.9%	6.0%	3.7%
Yakima, WA	3,764	0.0%	2.2%	17.0%	3.3%	6.1%	15.1%	1.0%	11.9%	3.4%	18.9%	6.8%	6.1%	8.3%
York-Hanover, PA	13,612	3.8%	3.2%	11.2%	17.5%	1.8%	4.9%	9.2%	10.3%	6.4%	5.9%	5.8%	16.6%	3.4%
Youngstown-Warren-Boardman, OH-PA	14,004	2.1%	9.3%	16.0%	22.3%	2.8%	5.9%	3.5%	3.8%	5.0%	5.1%	2.4%	18.4%	3.2%
Yuba City, CA	4,118	8.9%	5.1%	15.3%	11.9%	0.0%	8.3%	0.0%	23.0%	7.3%	11.3%	1.1%	7.8%	0.0%
Yuma, AZ	3,776	6.4%	0.0%	23.0%	22.4%	0.0%	1.7%	0.9%	1.0%	0.0%	2.6%	6.7%	34.1%	1.4%

PART G
LANGUAGE SPOKEN AT HOME

The nation continues to grow more racially and ethnically diverse—even in the smallest of communities. That diversity is also mirrored in the growth of foreign languages spoken at home. Today, immigration from many different origin countries, especially Latin America and Asia, has added to the mix of languages spoken. These differences are shown in the data on education and language spoken. Some estimates indicate that as many as 800 different languages are spoken in New York City.[1]

American Community Survey data on language is gathered through a question on whether each person speaks a language other than English at home and a write-in response of what that language is. The respondent is then asked a question on how well they speak English—Very

Well, Well, Not Well, or Not At All. The data presented in the following tables report on the percentage of population by major categories of Language Spoken at Home and how well the population speaks English.

There is an interesting difference between today's Millennial generation and the population 65 and over. Nationwide, more than 85 percent of the population over age 65 speaks English at home, while only 76 percent of Millennials speak only English. And while Spanish is spoken by only 7.0 percent of the older population, 15.7 percent of Millennials speak Spanish at home. Indo-European and Asian languages are spoken by 3.6 percent and 3.4 percent of Millennials, respectively. By state, Montana (95.7 percent) and West Virginia (95.6 percent) have the highest percentage of the younger generation speaking only English, while California is lowest with a little over half the population (52.8 percent) speaking English. California also has the highest percentage of

1 "Say What?" *The Economist*, September 10, 2011, http://www.economist.com/node/21528592, accessed 7/7/2015.

Percent of Millennials Who Speak Spanish at Home

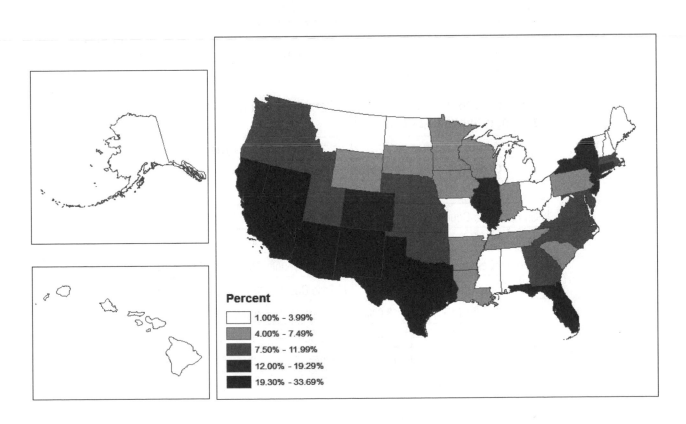

Percent
- 1.00% - 3.99%
- 4.00% - 7.49%
- 7.50% - 11.99%
- 12.00% - 19.29%
- 19.30% - 33.69%

those speaking Spanish at home at 33.6 percent. More than 90 percent of the Millennial population speaks only English in 16 states, and in five additional states Spanish is spoken by more than 20 percent of the younger population—Arizona (24.5 percent), Florida (24.1 percent), Nevada (27.1 percent), New Mexico (25.9 percent), and Texas (31.6 percent). Asian languages are spoken at home by 15.0 percent of Hawaii's Millennials and by 8.5 percent in California. Massachusetts, New Jersey and New York have the highest percentage who speak Indo-European languages at 8.7 percent, 8.0 percent and 8.2 percent, respectively.

While many languages can be spoken in the home, the ability to speak English is an important measure of assimilation. The question on ability to speak English is only asked of those who speak a language other than English at home. North Dakota has the highest percentage of Millennials who speak another language and speak English "Very Well" (84.3 percent) while Iowa is lowest at 58.5 percent. In Alabama, 23.1 percent speak another language at home and speak English "Not Well" or "Not At All."

Virtually everyone (99.2 percent) in Columbiana County, OH speaks only English at home, and 231 counties are above the 90 percent mark. Webb County, TX has the lowest percentage at 11.1 percent where it's also the highest for Spanish speaking population with 88.8 percent speaking Spanish at home. Rockland County, NY has the highest percentage of those speaking Indo-European languages (21.3 percent) while Santa Clara County, CA tops the list for Asian languages at 21.9 percent.

Of Millennials who speak another language at home, more than 90 percent indicate that they speak English "Very Well" in 36 counties. The lowest percentage who speak English "Very Well" is in Boone County, KY (11.7 percent) which also has the highest percentage of those who speak English "Not Well" or "Not At All" at 60.8 percent.

In Billings, MT, 97.2 percent of Millennials speak only English at home, but in 51 cities less than 50 percent of the generation speaks English at home. It's lowest in Hialeah City, FL at 7.5 percent where 91.8 percent speak Spanish at home. Hialeah is followed closely by South Gate, CA at 90.3 percent and Laredo, TX at 88.8 percent. Spanish is spoken at home by more than 25 percent in 104 cities. At 36.2 percent, Glendale City, CA has the highest percentage who speak Indo-European languages (45.4 percent) and Fremont, CA has the most speaking Asian languages (34.2 percent). Of those who speak a language other than English, Flint, MI and Portsmouth, VA are reported as 100 percent speaking English "Very Well." Huntsville, AL has the highest percentage who speak English "Not Well" or "Not At All" at 40.3 percent.

In 171 metropolitan/micropolitan areas English is spoken at home by more than 90 percent of Millennials over age 15. The Salem, OH micro is highest at 99.2 percent, but 26 other metro/micros are above 97 percent. Spanish is the primary language in the Laredo, TX metro with 88.8 percent, but in 24 metro/micros, less than one percent speak Spanish at home. Indo-European languages are spoken by 15.4 percent in the Wooster, OH

Table 1: Counties with the Highest Percentage of Another Language Spoken At Home

Asian Language		Spanish Language	
County	Percent	County	Percent
Santa Clara County, CA	21.9%	Webb County, TX	88.8%
San Francisco County, CA	19.6%	Hidalgo County, TX	85.2%
Alameda County, CA	16.8%	Imperial County, CA	77.1%
Honolulu County, HI	16.3%	Cameron County, TX	74.9%
San Mateo County, CA	16.0%	El Paso County, TX	67.3%
Ramsey County, MN	13.6%	Miami-Dade County, FL	62.2%
Queens County, NY	12.9%	Yuma County, AZ	54.5%
Yolo County, CA	12.5%	Monterey County, CA	51.5%
Champaign County, IL	12.5%	Bronx County, NY	51.3%
Orange County, CA	12.3%	Merced County, CA	50.9%

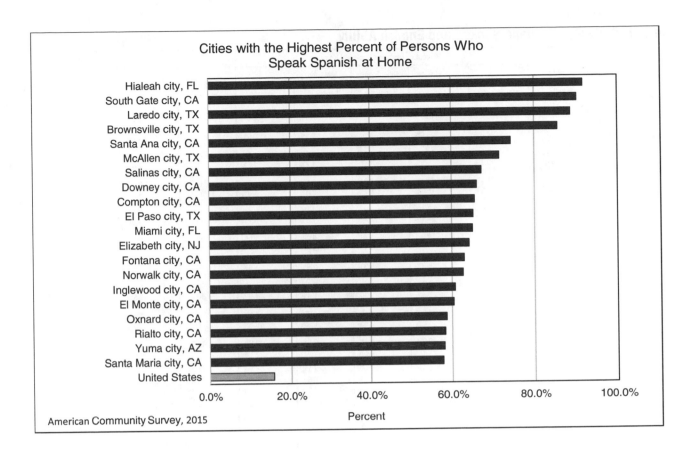

Cities with the Highest Percent of Persons Who Speak Spanish at Home

American Community Survey, 2015

micro and in the San Jose-Sunnyvale-Santa Clara, CA metro, 21.1 percent speak Asian languages at home. Among those who speak a language other than English, 100 percent in the Salem, OH micropolitan area are reported as speaking English "Not Well" or "Not At All." Five metro/micros are over 40 percent. Eleven metro/micros report that 100 percent of those who don't speak English at home speak English "Very Well."

Table G-1: States—Language Spoken and English Ability

	Millennial Population 15 to 33	Percent by Language Spoken at Home					Percent by Ability to Speak English			
		English Only	Spanish	Other Indo-European Language	Asian and Pacific Island Language	Other Language	Speak English "Very Well"	Speak English "Well"	Speak English "Not Well"	Speak English "Not at All"
United States	83,504,484	76.0%	15.7%	3.6%	3.4%	1.2%	17.4%	3.6%	2.1%	0.9%
Alabama	1,228,275	94.2%	4.0%	0.5%	0.8%	0.5%	3.5%	1.0%	1.0%	0.3%
Alaska	221,416	82.0%	4.9%	2.8%	5.0%	5.3%	13.4%	4.3%	0.3%	0.0%
Arizona	1,768,256	69.2%	24.5%	1.6%	2.2%	2.5%	24.6%	3.1%	1.8%	1.3%
Arkansas	751,127	90.3%	6.9%	1.0%	1.2%	0.6%	5.7%	2.0%	1.6%	0.5%
California	10,739,063	52.8%	33.6%	3.9%	8.5%	1.1%	35.8%	6.1%	3.6%	1.7%
Colorado	1,481,249	81.4%	13.4%	2.1%	2.1%	1.0%	14.0%	2.3%	1.8%	0.5%
Connecticut	892,841	74.3%	15.3%	6.8%	2.3%	1.3%	18.7%	4.3%	1.8%	0.9%
Delaware	237,360	82.6%	10.6%	3.0%	2.5%	1.4%	13.0%	2.2%	1.8%	0.4%
District of Columbia	236,132	83.0%	7.4%	4.8%	2.5%	2.4%	13.2%	2.4%	0.9%	0.5%
Florida	4,841,980	67.9%	24.1%	5.7%	1.6%	0.7%	23.7%	4.2%	2.6%	1.5%
Georgia	2,694,824	84.3%	9.6%	2.8%	2.3%	1.0%	10.5%	2.6%	2.0%	0.6%
Hawaii	371,354	77.0%	3.6%	1.1%	15.0%	3.4%	14.2%	7.0%	1.8%	0.0%
Idaho	426,778	86.5%	9.9%	1.4%	1.1%	1.1%	9.9%	2.4%	1.1%	0.1%
Illinois	3,334,874	74.2%	16.3%	5.3%	2.9%	1.3%	19.4%	3.6%	2.3%	0.5%
Indiana	1,706,914	89.7%	5.5%	2.4%	1.8%	0.7%	6.6%	2.2%	1.2%	0.3%
Iowa	804,927	89.4%	5.5%	1.4%	2.5%	1.1%	6.2%	2.4%	1.3%	0.6%
Kansas	763,691	85.1%	9.4%	2.1%	2.4%	1.0%	10.4%	2.5%	1.5%	0.6%
Kentucky	1,102,117	92.6%	3.9%	1.7%	0.9%	1.1%	5.0%	1.4%	0.9%	0.2%
Louisiana	1,253,683	92.1%	4.3%	1.4%	1.7%	0.5%	5.2%	1.4%	0.9%	0.4%
Maine	298,983	94.5%	1.3%	2.5%	0.9%	0.8%	4.4%	0.8%	0.4%	0.0%
Maryland	1,532,505	80.2%	9.9%	4.8%	3.0%	2.0%	13.9%	2.9%	2.2%	0.8%
Massachusetts	1,806,926	73.8%	11.1%	8.7%	4.9%	1.5%	19.7%	4.0%	1.9%	0.6%
Michigan	2,494,156	89.4%	3.5%	2.8%	1.9%	2.3%	7.5%	2.1%	0.7%	0.3%
Minnesota	1,390,845	85.0%	4.9%	2.5%	4.4%	3.1%	10.2%	3.0%	1.4%	0.3%
Mississippi	769,119	95.2%	3.3%	0.6%	0.6%	0.3%	3.0%	0.8%	0.7%	0.2%
Missouri	1,561,298	92.4%	3.6%	1.7%	1.6%	0.8%	5.3%	1.4%	0.6%	0.3%
Montana	251,820	95.7%	1.2%	1.5%	0.3%	1.3%	3.3%	0.4%	0.5%	0.1%
Nebraska	496,505	85.5%	9.2%	1.8%	1.9%	1.7%	9.4%	3.1%	1.6%	0.4%
Nevada	738,080	65.2%	27.1%	2.2%	4.4%	1.2%	26.4%	4.3%	2.7%	1.3%
New Hampshire	316,827	91.8%	3.1%	2.3%	2.1%	0.7%	5.9%	1.5%	0.8%	0.1%
New Jersey	2,182,669	66.9%	19.3%	8.0%	4.1%	1.8%	24.3%	4.6%	3.0%	1.3%
New Mexico	534,063	67.2%	25.9%	1.0%	1.1%	4.8%	26.3%	3.4%	2.1%	0.9%
New York	5,267,039	67.7%	17.0%	8.2%	5.1%	1.9%	22.7%	5.4%	3.3%	0.9%
North Carolina	2,561,562	85.7%	10.0%	1.9%	1.7%	0.7%	9.3%	2.2%	1.9%	0.9%
North Dakota	222,346	94.0%	1.3%	2.9%	0.9%	0.9%	5.1%	0.7%	0.3%	0.0%
Ohio	2,898,493	91.2%	2.9%	2.9%	1.7%	1.2%	6.0%	1.8%	0.8%	0.2%
Oklahoma	1,026,095	87.2%	9.3%	1.0%	1.9%	0.6%	8.4%	2.2%	1.5%	0.7%
Oregon	1,008,523	81.3%	12.0%	2.5%	3.4%	0.9%	13.5%	3.0%	1.6%	0.7%
Pennsylvania	3,172,455	86.9%	6.0%	3.7%	2.6%	0.8%	9.3%	2.3%	1.2%	0.3%
Rhode Island	280,625	73.4%	15.6%	6.2%	3.9%	0.8%	20.1%	4.3%	1.6%	0.6%
South Carolina	1,248,377	91.8%	5.6%	1.4%	0.9%	0.3%	5.3%	1.5%	1.2%	0.2%
South Dakota	221,860	89.6%	4.3%	2.7%	0.8%	2.5%	7.1%	1.5%	1.4%	0.3%
Tennessee	1,676,588	91.4%	5.1%	1.3%	1.1%	1.0%	5.5%	1.5%	1.2%	0.4%
Texas	7,561,743	62.5%	31.6%	2.2%	2.7%	1.0%	26.6%	5.5%	3.3%	2.1%
Utah	885,542	84.2%	10.8%	1.7%	2.1%	1.2%	12.3%	1.9%	1.3%	0.3%
Vermont	156,472	91.8%	1.8%	5.4%	0.6%	0.4%	6.3%	0.8%	1.1%	0.0%
Virginia	2,193,469	82.3%	8.4%	3.8%	3.7%	1.8%	12.8%	2.9%	1.6%	0.4%
Washington	1,885,191	77.2%	11.4%	4.6%	5.8%	1.1%	16.2%	3.7%	2.2%	0.8%
West Virginia	426,279	95.6%	2.2%	1.2%	1.0%	0.1%	3.3%	0.9%	0.2%	0.0%
Wisconsin	1,426,801	88.5%	6.2%	2.2%	2.6%	0.5%	8.0%	2.3%	1.1%	0.1%
Wyoming	154,367	90.4%	7.0%	1.3%	0.8%	0.4%	6.2%	1.5%	1.7%	0.2%

Table G-2: Counties—Language Spoken and English Ability

	Millennial Population 15 to 33	Percent by Language Spoken at Home					Percent by Ability to Speak English			
		English Only	Spanish	Other Indo-European Language	Asian and Pacific Island Language	Other Language	Speak English "Very Well"	Speak English "Well"	Speak English "Not Well"	Speak English "Not at All"
Alabama										
Baldwin County	41,881	93.5%	5.6%	0.7%	0.1%	0.0%	6.5%	0.0%	0.0%	0.0%
Calhoun County	30,590	96.6%	2.1%	1.0%	0.0%	0.4%	3.4%	0.0%	0.0%	0.0%
Etowah County	22,502	97.7%	2.2%	0.0%	0.0%	0.1%	0.9%	0.2%	1.3%	0.0%
Houston County	24,905	94.3%	4.5%	0.1%	0.8%	0.3%	3.1%	0.0%	0.2%	2.4%
Jefferson County	168,431	93.2%	3.7%	0.6%	1.0%	1.4%	3.5%	1.4%	1.8%	0.2%
Lauderdale County	23,069	88.4%	10.3%	0.2%	0.0%	1.1%	5.0%	6.1%	0.5%	0.0%
Lee County	54,789	96.6%	1.4%	1.0%	0.9%	0.1%	1.9%	0.5%	1.0%	0.0%
Madison County	90,891	92.3%	5.2%	1.0%	1.3%	0.1%	4.8%	1.1%	1.7%	0.1%
Marshall County	21,899	93.0%	4.7%	1.4%	0.9%	0.0%	3.2%	1.6%	1.8%	0.4%
Mobile County	108,104	93.1%	3.3%	0.7%	1.7%	1.1%	3.6%	0.8%	2.0%	0.5%
Montgomery County	63,386	96.6%	1.9%	0.8%	0.5%	0.1%	2.0%	0.5%	0.5%	0.4%
Morgan County	29,027	94.5%	4.6%	0.5%	0.4%	0.0%	2.8%	0.7%	2.0%	0.0%
Shelby County	49,471	88.3%	9.2%	0.4%	1.0%	1.1%	9.0%	0.5%	1.1%	1.1%
Tuscaloosa County	72,277	94.0%	2.7%	0.5%	2.5%	0.3%	3.8%	1.4%	0.2%	0.6%
Alaska										
Anchorage Municipality	92,794	79.0%	6.8%	2.2%	7.4%	4.6%	14.8%	6.2%	0.0%	0.0%
Fairbanks North Star Borough	34,834	83.9%	5.0%	5.5%	4.0%	1.6%	13.0%	3.1%	0.0%	0.0%
Matanuska-Susitna Borough	27,889	90.9%	4.8%	2.4%	1.1%	0.8%	6.9%	0.7%	1.5%	0.0%
Arizona										
Cochise County	29,422	50.8%	45.4%	1.6%	0.6%	1.6%	43.2%	2.6%	2.1%	1.4%
Coconino County	51,771	81.8%	8.0%	1.7%	2.5%	6.0%	15.7%	2.2%	0.2%	0.0%
Maricopa County	1,083,464	69.5%	24.4%	2.0%	2.6%	1.5%	24.1%	3.0%	2.0%	1.4%
Mohave County	39,552	86.4%	11.4%	0.7%	0.3%	1.3%	9.6%	3.4%	0.6%	0.0%
Navajo County	26,103	59.0%	2.0%	0.3%	0.2%	38.4%	35.2%	5.1%	0.5%	0.2%
Pima County	267,442	68.5%	26.8%	1.2%	2.2%	1.4%	25.8%	3.4%	1.7%	0.7%
Pinal County	92,776	73.6%	23.1%	0.9%	1.0%	1.4%	21.9%	2.3%	0.8%	1.4%
Yavapai County	39,793	89.5%	7.2%	1.3%	1.3%	0.7%	9.2%	0.4%	0.6%	0.2%
Yuma County	57,750	43.3%	54.5%	0.4%	0.2%	1.7%	42.6%	5.9%	4.6%	3.7%
Arkansas										
Benton County	63,010	84.2%	10.6%	1.4%	2.9%	0.9%	10.4%	2.2%	3.1%	0.2%
Craighead County	31,552	93.6%	4.2%	1.0%	1.2%	0.0%	4.9%	0.1%	1.3%	0.0%
Faulkner County	40,148	95.2%	3.5%	0.0%	1.2%	0.1%	2.6%	0.8%	1.3%	0.0%
Garland County	21,044	95.3%	3.5%	0.2%	1.0%	0.0%	3.0%	0.0%	1.7%	0.0%
Pulaski County	103,489	89.5%	6.1%	2.0%	1.7%	0.6%	5.7%	3.1%	0.6%	1.1%
Saline County	26,931	90.9%	7.6%	1.2%	0.2%	0.0%	7.9%	0.5%	0.8%	0.0%
Sebastian County	32,407	82.3%	10.8%	1.3%	4.4%	1.2%	13.0%	2.1%	1.9%	0.8%
Washington County	72,894	79.5%	13.7%	1.2%	2.5%	3.1%	9.2%	5.5%	4.1%	1.8%
California										
Alameda County	433,320	53.4%	19.8%	7.6%	16.8%	2.4%	33.4%	8.2%	3.7%	1.3%
Butte County	66,344	79.2%	13.4%	0.0%	4.7%	1.9%	18.0%	1.5%	0.7%	0.0%
Contra Costa County	264,278	59.9%	24.0%	4.5%	10.4%	1.3%	28.3%	6.7%	3.7%	1.5%
El Dorado County	38,085	87.2%	8.0%	0.9%	3.1%	0.8%	9.1%	1.9%	1.8%	0.0%
Fresno County	280,870	50.7%	37.7%	3.5%	7.2%	1.0%	36.7%	5.1%	3.4%	4.2%
Humboldt County	38,052	81.9%	11.7%	2.3%	2.6%	1.5%	14.6%	1.2%	2.3%	0.0%
Imperial County	49,645	21.8%	77.1%	0.5%	0.5%	0.0%	55.0%	13.2%	6.6%	3.3%
Kern County	255,273	50.4%	44.9%	1.9%	2.0%	0.7%	36.4%	6.3%	4.4%	2.4%
Kings County	46,492	55.8%	39.0%	1.6%	3.2%	0.4%	28.1%	7.7%	6.9%	1.4%
Los Angeles County	2,815,660	41.6%	43.9%	4.6%	8.9%	1.0%	45.6%	6.9%	4.3%	1.7%
Madera County	41,540	48.3%	47.9%	2.4%	0.8%	0.6%	39.0%	4.5%	1.9%	6.3%
Marin County	47,166	73.5%	17.1%	4.6%	4.3%	0.5%	15.7%	3.8%	4.9%	2.2%
Merced County	78,357	39.1%	50.9%	4.6%	4.7%	0.7%	42.0%	8.5%	6.3%	4.0%
Monterey County	120,053	43.6%	51.5%	1.5%	2.6%	0.9%	36.2%	6.5%	6.0%	7.8%
Napa County	33,408	59.5%	34.1%	1.3%	4.5%	0.6%	28.9%	7.2%	3.0%	1.4%
Nevada County	18,893	94.0%	3.6%	1.1%	0.7%	0.6%	1.9%	1.8%	2.3%	0.0%
Orange County	823,644	52.0%	31.3%	3.4%	12.3%	1.0%	35.8%	6.5%	4.2%	1.6%
Placer County	81,509	83.4%	9.5%	2.8%	3.7%	0.6%	12.8%	1.8%	1.8%	0.3%
Riverside County	623,922	53.9%	40.6%	1.6%	3.1%	0.7%	37.0%	4.6%	2.8%	1.7%
Sacramento County	400,317	65.1%	17.2%	7.4%	8.9%	1.3%	25.9%	5.7%	2.6%	0.7%
San Bernardino County	622,075	56.7%	36.7%	1.3%	4.3%	1.0%	34.3%	5.3%	2.6%	1.1%
San Diego County	944,277	60.0%	28.9%	2.8%	6.7%	1.7%	31.5%	5.4%	2.2%	1.0%
San Francisco County	256,915	62.2%	10.4%	6.4%	19.6%	1.3%	28.6%	7.1%	1.5%	0.5%
San Joaquin County	194,976	54.6%	31.2%	4.8%	8.8%	0.6%	33.7%	5.3%	4.9%	1.6%
San Luis Obispo County	81,571	78.3%	17.2%	1.1%	2.7%	0.7%	17.5%	3.1%	1.1%	0.0%
San Mateo County	177,686	53.3%	23.3%	6.3%	16.0%	1.1%	35.0%	7.8%	3.0%	1.0%
Santa Barbara County	136,421	55.1%	36.6%	2.5%	4.7%	1.1%	31.0%	5.5%	2.8%	5.6%
Santa Clara County	491,230	47.1%	21.6%	8.1%	21.9%	1.3%	39.9%	8.0%	4.3%	0.7%
Santa Cruz County	81,439	64.3%	26.6%	2.6%	5.2%	1.3%	25.3%	4.5%	2.7%	3.3%
Shasta County	41,748	91.7%	5.6%	1.6%	1.2%	0.0%	7.5%	0.7%	0.1%	0.0%
Solano County	112,131	69.5%	22.4%	1.2%	6.7%	0.3%	22.7%	3.9%	2.7%	1.2%
Sonoma County	118,618	70.7%	23.8%	2.0%	3.3%	0.2%	18.8%	5.4%	4.1%	1.2%
Stanislaus County	150,344	53.8%	37.3%	4.5%	2.1%	2.4%	35.7%	6.0%	3.4%	1.1%
Sutter County	25,161	64.3%	20.7%	11.1%	3.9%	0.0%	24.1%	4.0%	6.2%	1.4%
Tulare County	131,238	46.4%	50.4%	1.8%	1.1%	0.3%	37.2%	7.9%	4.0%	4.5%
Ventura County	220,516	56.0%	36.9%	2.3%	3.7%	1.2%	30.5%	3.7%	4.3%	5.5%
Yolo County	73,824	60.4%	20.6%	5.3%	12.5%	1.1%	30.3%	6.0%	2.3%	1.0%

Table G-2: Counties—Language Spoken and English Ability—*Continued*

	Millennial Population 15 to 33	Percent by Language Spoken at Home					Percent by Ability to Speak English			
		English Only	Spanish	Other Indo-European Language	Asian and Pacific Island Language	Other Language	Speak English "Very Well"	Speak English "Well"	Speak English "Not Well"	Speak English "Not at All"
Colorado										
Adams County	137,531	69.8%	24.8%	1.4%	3.5%	0.5%	24.0%	3.2%	1.9%	1.1%
Arapahoe County	166,327	74.1%	16.6%	3.8%	3.1%	2.4%	17.7%	3.3%	3.7%	1.2%
Boulder County	99,882	83.1%	9.3%	4.1%	2.5%	0.9%	13.6%	1.6%	1.5%	0.2%
Denver County	212,964	73.4%	20.7%	1.9%	2.4%	1.7%	19.3%	3.3%	3.1%	1.1%
Douglas County	67,516	91.2%	4.1%	2.8%	1.9%	0.0%	7.3%	1.1%	0.3%	0.1%
El Paso County	197,064	88.5%	7.7%	1.9%	1.4%	0.5%	9.1%	1.7%	0.4%	0.3%
Jefferson County	139,577	88.0%	8.2%	1.6%	1.7%	0.4%	10.0%	0.5%	1.4%	0.1%
Larimer County	101,823	87.8%	7.6%	2.8%	1.1%	0.7%	10.3%	1.4%	0.6%	0.0%
Mesa County	38,715	92.2%	6.3%	0.7%	0.8%	0.0%	4.9%	2.9%	0.0%	0.0%
Pueblo County	40,596	87.8%	10.4%	1.8%	0.0%	0.0%	11.6%	0.4%	0.2%	0.0%
Weld County	77,770	80.6%	17.2%	0.5%	1.1%	0.6%	13.2%	3.3%	2.0%	0.9%
Connecticut										
Fairfield County	223,389	66.8%	20.0%	9.6%	2.9%	0.8%	21.5%	6.6%	3.2%	1.9%
Hartford County	219,321	69.3%	16.9%	9.2%	2.3%	2.3%	25.0%	3.7%	1.3%	0.6%
Litchfield County	36,755	89.4%	3.9%	3.6%	2.4%	0.7%	8.5%	0.4%	1.3%	0.3%
Middlesex County	37,415	87.8%	4.6%	4.6%	1.5%	1.6%	10.3%	0.6%	1.3%	0.0%
New Haven County	219,820	75.1%	16.8%	5.1%	1.6%	1.5%	17.8%	4.9%	1.6%	0.7%
New London County	71,058	86.3%	7.8%	3.3%	2.2%	0.4%	10.1%	2.7%	1.0%	0.0%
Tolland County	48,690	86.7%	3.7%	3.9%	4.5%	1.2%	10.7%	2.3%	0.2%	0.0%
Windham County	29,791	81.6%	15.5%	1.2%	1.7%	0.0%	10.3%	3.3%	2.7%	2.1%
Delaware										
Kent County	46,169	90.1%	5.5%	2.8%	1.6%	0.0%	5.2%	1.9%	2.1%	0.6%
New Castle County	148,800	79.8%	11.2%	3.5%	3.3%	2.3%	16.6%	2.3%	0.9%	0.4%
Sussex County	41,781	84.1%	14.1%	1.2%	0.5%	0.0%	9.1%	2.4%	4.4%	0.0%
Florida										
Alachua County	99,489	84.3%	6.9%	4.1%	3.9%	0.8%	12.5%	2.0%	0.8%	0.4%
Bay County	44,374	94.7%	2.9%	1.4%	1.0%	0.0%	4.0%	0.0%	1.3%	0.0%
Brevard County	120,364	87.0%	8.7%	1.5%	0.4%	2.3%	9.6%	1.5%	1.0%	0.9%
Broward County	454,842	56.7%	27.6%	13.1%	1.5%	1.1%	32.2%	5.7%	3.2%	2.2%
Charlotte County	23,149	85.3%	8.2%	0.7%	3.2%	2.6%	9.6%	0.3%	4.8%	0.0%
Citrus County	20,619	94.4%	4.4%	0.8%	0.4%	0.0%	3.5%	0.6%	0.4%	1.2%
Clay County	47,909	87.7%	10.3%	1.7%	0.2%	0.0%	11.3%	0.2%	0.5%	0.2%
Collier County	67,976	50.9%	41.6%	7.4%	0.1%	0.0%	37.6%	3.2%	4.3%	4.1%
Duval County	249,721	86.3%	6.0%	4.0%	2.9%	0.8%	10.2%	1.6%	1.6%	0.3%
Escambia County	92,108	92.0%	4.1%	1.3%	2.5%	0.1%	5.0%	2.7%	0.1%	0.3%
Flagler County	18,726	91.6%	4.5%	2.3%	1.6%	0.0%	5.3%	3.0%	0.1%	0.0%
Hernando County	34,015	88.9%	9.7%	1.4%	0.0%	0.0%	8.8%	1.7%	0.0%	0.6%
Highlands County	17,486	76.6%	22.8%	0.0%	0.0%	0.5%	15.8%	5.0%	2.5%	0.0%
Hillsborough County	357,315	68.4%	24.9%	3.4%	2.1%	1.3%	24.4%	3.1%	2.4%	1.7%
Indian River County	26,890	78.1%	18.9%	2.7%	0.3%	0.0%	17.7%	2.4%	1.5%	0.2%
Lake County	63,518	84.2%	14.9%	1.0%	0.0%	0.0%	11.4%	3.9%	0.3%	0.3%
Lee County	139,414	72.0%	24.0%	3.0%	0.8%	0.2%	18.8%	3.7%	3.6%	1.8%
Leon County	109,230	89.6%	4.8%	2.8%	1.6%	1.3%	8.8%	1.6%	0.0%	0.0%
Manatee County	71,745	76.5%	20.1%	2.0%	1.2%	0.1%	14.3%	3.5%	4.9%	0.7%
Marion County	70,359	88.3%	8.4%	2.9%	0.5%	0.0%	10.3%	0.7%	0.6%	0.2%
Martin County	27,863	81.0%	16.5%	1.8%	0.0%	0.7%	12.6%	0.5%	3.9%	2.0%
Miami-Dade County	678,428	27.8%	62.2%	8.5%	0.9%	0.6%	53.5%	9.0%	5.6%	4.1%
Okaloosa County	54,676	89.3%	7.5%	1.2%	1.7%	0.3%	7.5%	1.3%	1.6%	0.4%
Orange County	381,877	64.1%	24.8%	7.0%	3.2%	0.9%	27.3%	5.5%	2.0%	1.1%
Osceola County	85,749	45.4%	49.3%	3.2%	1.0%	1.0%	41.1%	9.4%	2.3%	1.8%
Palm Beach County	305,192	63.2%	22.4%	11.8%	1.9%	0.6%	25.9%	5.2%	4.3%	1.4%
Pasco County	102,294	84.8%	11.7%	1.4%	1.2%	0.9%	13.2%	1.1%	0.8%	0.1%
Pinellas County	192,338	82.2%	9.7%	5.3%	2.3%	0.6%	11.8%	3.0%	2.1%	0.8%
Polk County	157,735	72.4%	22.3%	3.8%	1.4%	0.1%	19.0%	3.3%	2.6%	2.7%
Santa Rosa County	49,046	86.1%	4.6%	6.5%	2.7%	0.1%	9.2%	4.6%	0.1%	0.0%
Sarasota County	64,135	72.7%	16.8%	8.3%	2.2%	0.0%	19.6%	3.9%	2.3%	1.5%
Seminole County	40,873	93.6%	3.8%	0.4%	2.3%	0.0%	5.1%	0.0%	0.1%	1.3%
St. Johns County	66,167	81.7%	11.2%	5.8%	0.8%	0.4%	11.7%	3.6%	2.9%	0.2%
St. Lucie County	113,327	77.8%	16.7%	3.9%	0.4%	1.2%	18.7%	1.7%	1.9%	0.0%
Sumter County	10,799	88.9%	8.6%	2.6%	0.0%	0.0%	9.8%	1.4%	0.0%	0.0%
Volusia County	112,669	83.0%	12.6%	1.7%	1.2%	1.5%	12.5%	3.5%	0.7%	0.3%
Georgia										
Bartow County	24,596	90.8%	8.4%	0.0%	0.6%	0.2%	7.8%	0.9%	0.6%	0.0%
Bibb County	40,873	92.9%	3.8%	2.4%	0.8%	0.1%	5.2%	0.8%	0.4%	0.8%
Carroll County	34,092	90.0%	9.5%	0.6%	0.0%	0.0%	3.7%	2.3%	4.1%	0.0%
Chatham County	85,554	85.9%	6.9%	4.7%	2.0%	0.5%	9.6%	2.4%	0.9%	1.3%
Cherokee County	55,192	85.2%	12.9%	1.3%	0.3%	0.3%	9.2%	0.8%	3.4%	1.4%
Clarke County	55,559	85.2%	7.5%	3.7%	2.7%	0.9%	8.4%	4.3%	1.9%	0.1%
Clayton County	75,687	81.9%	11.0%	2.3%	3.4%	1.3%	12.0%	2.0%	2.7%	1.4%
Cobb County	190,361	75.2%	15.4%	5.3%	2.8%	1.3%	17.4%	2.1%	3.8%	1.6%
Columbia County	38,305	88.3%	7.2%	0.4%	1.4%	2.6%	8.4%	1.7%	1.6%	0.0%
Coweta County	33,183	93.4%	4.9%	1.5%	0.1%	0.0%	4.5%	2.0%	0.0%	0.0%
DeKalb County	200,382	78.3%	8.8%	3.5%	4.3%	5.0%	11.2%	4.6%	4.8%	1.1%
Dougherty County	25,148	94.5%	1.7%	2.8%	0.0%	1.0%	3.0%	2.5%	0.0%	0.0%
Douglas County	35,335	90.0%	8.8%	0.6%	0.3%	0.3%	8.4%	1.3%	0.0%	0.3%

Table G-2: Counties—Language Spoken and English Ability—*Continued*

	Millennial Population 15 to 33	Percent by Language Spoken at Home					Percent by Ability to Speak English			
		English Only	Spanish	Other Indo-European Language	Asian and Pacific Island Language	Other Language	Speak English "Very Well"	Speak English "Well"	Speak English "Not Well"	Speak English "Not at All"
Georgia—Cont.										
Fayette County	23,415	88.9%	4.5%	2.8%	3.9%	0.0%	7.8%	2.4%	0.0%	0.9%
Floyd County	24,395	89.9%	9.4%	0.5%	0.0%	0.2%	6.3%	2.0%	0.9%	0.9%
Forsyth County	44,097	76.0%	11.3%	7.7%	4.7%	0.3%	17.8%	4.1%	2.1%	0.0%
Fulton County	286,250	82.1%	6.4%	6.1%	3.7%	1.7%	12.7%	3.5%	1.4%	0.2%
Gwinnett County	228,875	63.4%	21.7%	6.0%	6.8%	2.1%	23.7%	6.2%	5.1%	1.5%
Hall County	48,649	68.8%	28.8%	0.9%	1.1%	0.4%	17.5%	7.2%	3.9%	2.5%
Henry County	56,794	87.0%	8.2%	2.2%	2.3%	0.3%	11.0%	1.3%	0.2%	0.4%
	38,791	90.3%	7.4%	0.8%	1.2%	0.4%	7.7%	1.0%	1.0%	0.0%
Houston County	39,082	95.0%	2.7%	2.1%	0.2%	0.0%	3.3%	1.1%	0.4%	0.2%
Lowndes County	60,678	88.2%	6.5%	1.9%	3.4%	0.1%	8.8%	1.5%	1.2%	0.3%
Muscogee County	26,592	91.1%	5.6%	3.2%	0.0%	0.0%	5.3%	2.2%	1.4%	0.0%
Newton County	38,745	90.7%	7.0%	2.3%	0.0%	0.0%	8.3%	0.4%	0.6%	0.0%
Paulding County	61,312	93.6%	3.0%	1.6%	1.5%	0.2%	6.1%	0.2%	0.0%	0.0%
Richmond County	28,290	54.7%	42.4%	1.8%	0.5%	0.6%	32.8%	6.2%	2.9%	3.4%
Whitfield County										
Hawaii										
Hawaii County	44,356	80.3%	2.8%	0.1%	10.9%	5.9%	13.5%	4.4%	1.7%	0.0%
Honolulu County	273,410	76.0%	3.6%	1.4%	16.3%	2.7%	14.4%	7.8%	1.8%	0.0%
Maui County	39,215	79.2%	5.1%	0.3%	9.9%	5.5%	15.2%	4.8%	0.9%	0.0%
Idaho										
Ada County	112,757	86.4%	8.5%	2.2%	0.4%	2.3%	8.4%	3.3%	1.9%	0.0%
Bonneville County	27,468	87.5%	11.5%	0.4%	0.6%	0.0%	8.8%	3.0%	0.4%	0.2%
Canyon County	53,108	80.1%	16.6%	2.9%	0.5%	0.0%	17.2%	1.7%	0.9%	0.1%
Kootenai County	35,105	98.6%	0.8%	0.2%	0.4%	0.0%	0.9%	0.1%	0.4%	0.0%
Illinois										
Champaign County	80,297	74.2%	6.1%	6.6%	12.5%	0.5%	17.8%	6.3%	1.7%	0.0%
Cook County	1,420,119	62.4%	23.4%	7.9%	4.0%	2.3%	28.9%	5.2%	2.8%	0.7%
DeKalb County	37,893	88.0%	9.6%	0.7%	1.7%	0.0%	8.6%	1.6%	1.0%	0.8%
DuPage County	225,783	70.6%	13.6%	11.1%	3.7%	1.0%	22.7%	4.2%	2.2%	0.3%
Kane County	127,899	63.3%	32.0%	2.1%	1.3%	1.3%	25.4%	4.7%	5.3%	1.4%
Kankakee County	28,451	89.8%	8.8%	0.4%	0.8%	0.3%	7.1%	0.9%	1.8%	0.4%
Kendall County	32,579	82.2%	11.0%	2.8%	4.1%	0.0%	13.1%	0.8%	3.9%	0.0%
Lake County	174,597	68.1%	23.3%	4.9%	3.2%	0.5%	24.2%	3.5%	2.8%	1.4%
LaSalle County	25,216	90.1%	7.2%	1.3%	1.4%	0.0%	7.3%	0.8%	1.8%	0.0%
Macon County	68,743	84.1%	12.0%	3.4%	0.4%	0.1%	12.0%	2.0%	1.8%	0.1%
Madison County	57,011	93.4%	2.5%	0.8%	3.3%	0.0%	4.5%	1.0%	1.2%	0.0%
McHenry County	24,600	93.5%	5.0%	1.5%	0.0%	0.0%	5.2%	1.0%	0.3%	0.0%
McLean County	64,921	95.4%	2.7%	0.4%	1.6%	0.0%	2.4%	1.6%	0.7%	0.0%
Peoria County	49,723	87.6%	5.0%	3.6%	3.3%	0.5%	7.3%	1.1%	4.0%	0.0%
Rock Island County	32,689	83.3%	9.1%	3.0%	2.1%	2.5%	10.7%	2.1%	3.9%	0.0%
Sangamon County	63,031	93.8%	2.0%	3.1%	0.9%	0.2%	3.8%	1.3%	0.6%	0.4%
St. Clair County	47,979	93.1%	2.3%	2.3%	2.2%	0.1%	6.2%	0.7%	0.0%	0.0%
Tazewell County	30,206	97.7%	0.7%	0.4%	1.2%	0.0%	1.5%	0.3%	0.5%	0.0%
Will County	164,849	79.6%	15.1%	3.2%	1.3%	0.8%	14.1%	4.3%	1.3%	0.7%
Winnebago County	68,339	78.8%	17.9%	1.1%	1.4%	0.9%	13.5%	3.2%	3.7%	0.8%
Indiana										
Allen County	94,493	87.9%	5.9%	2.2%	3.6%	0.4%	7.3%	2.5%	1.5%	0.7%
Clark County	26,766	93.5%	5.2%	1.3%	0.0%	0.0%	3.9%	1.8%	0.7%	0.0%
Delaware County	37,184	95.5%	2.5%	1.0%	0.9%	0.0%	4.0%	0.0%	0.5%	0.0%
Elkhart County	51,393	82.1%	11.8%	5.3%	0.3%	0.5%	11.5%	4.4%	2.0%	0.0%
Hamilton County	70,348	90.7%	3.2%	3.3%	2.3%	0.5%	8.0%	1.0%	0.3%	0.0%
Hendricks County	38,770	86.7%	4.5%	2.3%	0.3%	6.2%	7.4%	5.5%	0.3%	0.0%
Johnson County	35,533	94.7%	2.7%	0.6%	1.6%	0.4%	4.4%	0.9%	0.0%	0.0%
Lake County	115,765	86.4%	9.5%	2.4%	0.7%	0.9%	10.0%	2.7%	0.8%	0.1%
LaPorte County	25,919	96.3%	2.3%	1.4%	0.1%	0.0%	2.4%	1.3%	0.0%	0.9%
Madison County	31,647	94.5%	3.7%	1.8%	0.0%	0.0%	3.1%	0.4%	1.1%	0.9%
Marion County	265,530	85.8%	9.4%	2.1%	1.5%	1.1%	7.9%	2.5%	3.0%	0.8%
Monroe County	64,077	87.7%	2.5%	2.1%	7.0%	0.8%	6.7%	4.7%	0.9%	0.0%
Porter County	40,152	90.9%	3.2%	4.0%	1.8%	0.1%	8.3%	0.6%	0.2%	0.0%
St. Joseph County	71,602	85.8%	6.9%	1.9%	2.8%	2.6%	10.3%	2.5%	1.0%	0.4%
Tippecanoe County	74,144	79.0%	6.6%	3.2%	10.7%	0.6%	10.6%	8.8%	1.3%	0.3%
Vanderburgh County	47,427	94.8%	3.3%	0.5%	1.0%	0.5%	4.2%	0.4%	0.5%	0.1%
Vigo County	33,172	97.4%	1.4%	0.7%	0.5%	0.0%	1.3%	1.3%	0.0%	0.0%
Iowa										
Black Hawk County	41,294	89.8%	6.0%	2.3%	0.4%	1.5%	7.8%	0.0%	2.2%	0.1%
Dubuque County	25,302	97.0%	0.7%	1.4%	0.0%	0.9%	1.2%	1.7%	0.0%	0.0%
Johnson County	55,180	87.9%	3.4%	1.8%	6.4%	0.5%	9.0%	2.8%	0.3%	0.0%
Linn County	56,398	91.9%	2.2%	1.0%	4.7%	0.2%	4.8%	3.1%	0.2%	0.0%
Polk County	124,068	83.3%	7.7%	2.0%	2.9%	4.1%	11.4%	1.9%	2.6%	0.8%
Pottawattamie County	21,863	89.6%	8.9%	0.0%	1.5%	0.0%	6.6%	1.5%	2.2%	0.1%
Scott County	42,538	92.4%	4.1%	1.2%	2.1%	0.2%	6.0%	1.4%	0.3%	0.0%
Story County	45,309	89.2%	0.7%	0.4%	9.1%	0.6%	4.3%	6.3%	0.2%	0.0%
Woodbury County	28,317	74.6%	18.4%	0.6%	4.0%	2.5%	13.0%	6.5%	3.9%	2.0%
Kansas										
Douglas County	46,763	83.2%	8.0%	6.7%	0.9%	1.2%	11.6%	2.6%	2.6%	0.0%

Table G-2: Counties—Language Spoken and English Ability—*Continued*

	Millennial Population 15 to 33	Percent by Language Spoken at Home					Percent by Ability to Speak English			
		English Only	Spanish	Other Indo-European Language	Asian and Pacific Island Language	Other Language	Speak English "Very Well"	Speak English "Well"	Speak English "Not Well"	Speak English "Not at All"
Kansas—Cont.										
Johnson County	142,925	86.3%	5.7%	3.2%	4.0%	0.9%	9.6%	2.3%	1.6%	0.2%
Sedgwick County	133,877	84.5%	9.9%	1.3%	2.7%	1.5%	12.2%	2.7%	0.3%	0.2%
Shawnee County	44,074	92.8%	5.6%	0.0%	0.4%	1.1%	6.8%	0.4%	0.0%	0.0%
Wyandotte County	43,648	66.4%	25.1%	1.9%	3.7%	2.9%	18.2%	6.5%	5.8%	3.0%
Kentucky										
Boone County	29,906	92.1%	6.5%	0.0%	0.0%	1.4%	0.9%	2.2%	4.8%	0.0%
Campbell County	25,040	88.7%	6.2%	3.1%	1.7%	0.4%	7.4%	0.8%	3.1%	0.0%
Daviess County	23,244	97.2%	1.4%	0.2%	0.8%	0.4%	1.3%	0.2%	0.9%	0.3%
Fayette County	97,769	87.0%	6.9%	2.0%	2.1%	2.0%	7.4%	3.4%	1.9%	0.2%
Hardin County	27,726	90.8%	5.7%	1.6%	2.0%	0.0%	6.9%	2.4%	0.0%	0.0%
Jefferson County	192,549	88.9%	4.6%	3.1%	0.9%	2.5%	7.2%	2.3%	1.3%	0.3%
Kenton County	40,933	96.9%	2.0%	0.8%	0.3%	0.0%	2.0%	0.6%	0.2%	0.2%
Warren County	38,963	86.5%	4.8%	2.9%	1.9%	3.8%	8.0%	4.7%	0.8%	0.0%
Louisiana										
Ascension Parish	31,170	92.2%	6.2%	0.0%	1.4%	0.3%	7.2%	0.6%	0.0%	0.0%
Bossier Parish	34,599	91.6%	3.1%	0.6%	2.0%	2.6%	5.7%	2.3%	0.4%	0.0%
Caddo Parish	64,036	96.5%	2.0%	0.2%	1.3%	0.0%	2.2%	0.0%	0.6%	0.7%
Calcasieu Parish	53,237	92.1%	2.0%	4.0%	0.9%	1.0%	5.0%	2.6%	0.3%	0.0%
East Baton Rouge Parish	141,766	89.9%	4.3%	2.2%	3.3%	0.2%	4.9%	2.7%	1.4%	1.1%
Jefferson Parish	109,416	81.1%	12.5%	1.8%	2.7%	2.0%	10.3%	5.4%	2.6%	0.7%
Lafayette Parish	69,964	91.4%	4.6%	1.5%	2.0%	0.6%	6.0%	1.5%	1.1%	0.0%
Lafourche Parish	25,238	90.6%	5.4%	3.3%	0.7%	0.0%	9.2%	0.3%	0.0%	0.0%
Livingston Parish	35,503	98.8%	1.2%	0.0%	0.0%	0.0%	1.2%	0.0%	0.0%	0.0%
Orleans Parish	113,293	90.6%	4.2%	1.8%	3.4%	0.0%	5.9%	1.6%	1.2%	0.8%
Ouachita Parish	43,846	96.3%	1.7%	0.1%	1.9%	0.1%	3.5%	0.2%	0.0%	0.0%
Rapides Parish	32,779	94.1%	2.4%	1.6%	1.4%	0.6%	5.3%	0.0%	0.6%	0.0%
St. Tammany Parish	56,023	92.1%	5.9%	0.7%	1.3%	0.0%	5.3%	1.1%	1.4%	0.0%
Tangipahoa Parish	36,570	91.0%	8.0%	0.3%	0.8%	0.0%	9.0%	0.0%	0.0%	0.0%
Terrebonne Parish	27,572	87.8%	3.7%	0.5%	7.9%	0.0%	10.2%	0.4%	1.6%	0.0%
Maine										
Androscoggin County	24,352	87.1%	4.8%	5.1%	1.6%	1.3%	9.0%	3.6%	0.2%	0.0%
Cumberland County	71,428	92.7%	1.4%	3.6%	1.3%	1.0%	5.4%	1.3%	0.6%	0.0%
Kennebec County	25,926	94.3%	1.8%	0.3%	2.2%	1.4%	4.9%	0.0%	0.8%	0.0%
Penobscot County	40,856	95.8%	1.0%	2.5%	0.3%	0.4%	3.5%	0.7%	0.0%	0.0%
York County	44,517	96.3%	1.6%	0.9%	0.6%	0.6%	3.5%	0.2%	0.0%	0.0%
Maryland										
Anne Arundel County	142,073	87.5%	6.9%	3.2%	1.5%	0.9%	7.7%	2.6%	2.1%	0.1%
Baltimore County	208,008	84.2%	5.3%	5.5%	2.3%	2.6%	11.5%	2.3%	1.8%	0.2%
Carroll County	38,124	94.5%	2.5%	2.2%	0.6%	0.2%	5.2%	0.3%	0.0%	0.0%
Cecil County	24,753	96.0%	1.5%	1.6%	0.9%	0.0%	2.5%	0.0%	1.5%	0.0%
Charles County	39,543	94.4%	1.1%	0.8%	3.5%	0.1%	4.3%	0.7%	0.1%	0.4%
Frederick County	59,201	83.9%	8.6%	3.2%	3.5%	0.8%	13.2%	1.5%	0.2%	1.3%
Harford County	58,548	90.9%	5.6%	2.6%	0.7%	0.2%	6.9%	1.6%	0.6%	0.0%
Howard County	74,617	74.0%	6.8%	10.0%	7.5%	1.7%	20.9%	2.2%	2.4%	0.5%
Montgomery County	242,582	56.9%	22.4%	9.0%	7.3%	4.3%	33.6%	4.8%	3.1%	1.7%
Prince George's County	244,582	72.3%	17.7%	4.2%	2.4%	3.5%	15.6%	5.3%	4.6%	2.2%
St. Mary's County	28,580	94.9%	3.0%	1.3%	0.5%	0.2%	1.9%	2.2%	1.0%	0.0%
Washington County	36,398	91.3%	3.5%	4.2%	0.3%	0.7%	8.0%	0.6%	0.0%	0.1%
Wicomico County	30,106	88.7%	4.3%	5.4%	0.4%	1.2%	9.3%	1.2%	0.5%	0.3%
Massachusetts										
Barnstable County	38,001	85.5%	4.8%	7.2%	0.3%	2.2%	13.0%	1.2%	0.2%	0.0%
Berkshire County	28,645	90.9%	5.3%	1.8%	1.9%	0.0%	5.8%	2.4%	0.3%	0.6%
Bristol County	138,908	80.5%	7.8%	9.4%	1.6%	0.6%	15.5%	2.2%	1.8%	0.0%
Essex County	188,868	69.7%	21.0%	6.0%	2.0%	1.2%	20.3%	5.3%	3.1%	1.5%
Hampden County	122,400	69.0%	23.0%	5.4%	2.1%	0.5%	24.6%	2.8%	3.0%	0.7%
Hampshire County	57,803	89.1%	3.5%	2.7%	3.7%	1.0%	8.8%	1.3%	0.7%	0.1%
Middlesex County	424,674	72.9%	7.4%	10.1%	7.8%	1.8%	21.6%	3.6%	1.4%	0.6%
Norfolk County	162,312	75.5%	4.3%	10.7%	7.7%	1.8%	20.1%	3.2%	1.2%	0.1%
Plymouth County	114,104	83.2%	3.6%	12.3%	0.9%	0.0%	13.5%	1.8%	1.5%	0.0%
Suffolk County	293,994	61.5%	17.6%	11.2%	6.8%	2.9%	27.6%	6.6%	3.0%	1.2%
Worcester County	200,721	83.1%	8.2%	4.4%	3.1%	1.2%	11.8%	3.6%	1.2%	0.3%
Michigan										
Allegan County	26,922	94.0%	5.1%	0.9%	0.0%	0.0%	3.8%	1.3%	0.0%	0.9%
Bay County	24,229	98.6%	0.5%	0.9%	0.0%	0.0%	1.4%	0.0%	0.0%	0.0%
Berrien County	34,168	92.3%	3.1%	1.1%	1.9%	1.6%	5.1%	2.4%	0.2%	0.0%
Calhoun County	31,922	94.3%	2.0%	1.5%	2.3%	0.0%	3.4%	1.9%	0.3%	0.1%
Eaton County	25,668	93.4%	2.8%	1.5%	2.3%	0.0%	2.6%	3.5%	0.5%	0.0%
Genesee County	98,458	96.6%	1.3%	0.8%	0.2%	1.1%	2.8%	0.3%	0.2%	0.1%
Ingham County	103,204	86.6%	2.3%	3.4%	6.1%	1.6%	9.2%	4.1%	0.1%	0.0%
Jackson County	38,015	94.6%	2.3%	1.7%	1.3%	0.0%	3.6%	1.6%	0.1%	0.0%
Kalamazoo County	80,525	90.5%	3.6%	3.1%	0.9%	1.8%	6.9%	2.3%	0.3%	0.0%
Kent County	172,733	84.7%	8.0%	2.5%	3.9%	0.9%	10.6%	2.2%	1.8%	0.6%
Lenawee County	23,269	96.2%	1.7%	0.7%	0.0%	1.4%	2.5%	0.3%	0.7%	0.4%
Livingston County	41,203	96.8%	1.5%	1.0%	0.0%	0.7%	2.8%	0.0%	0.3%	0.0%

Table G-2: Counties—Language Spoken and English Ability—*Continued*

	Millennial Population 15 to 33	Percent by Language Spoken at Home					Percent by Ability to Speak English			
		English Only	Spanish	Other Indo-European Language	Asian and Pacific Island Language	Other Language	Speak English "Very Well"	Speak English "Well"	Speak English "Not Well"	Speak English "Not at All"
Michigan—Cont.										
Macomb County	205,742	86.5%	1.7%	5.2%	1.2%	5.5%	9.7%	2.8%	0.8%	0.2%
Monroe County	33,502	97.3%	1.5%	0.4%	0.8%	0.0%	0.6%	1.0%	0.5%	0.6%
Muskegon County	41,707	94.6%	4.1%	0.7%	0.0%	0.6%	4.7%	0.0%	0.8%	0.0%
Oakland County	287,890	85.5%	3.4%	4.5%	4.0%	2.5%	9.3%	3.6%	1.4%	0.2%
Ottawa County	79,401	88.4%	8.3%	2.0%	1.2%	0.1%	8.0%	1.7%	1.3%	0.6%
Saginaw County	48,370	94.0%	2.0%	0.3%	1.5%	2.1%	1.4%	3.8%	0.0%	0.8%
St. Clair County	35,117	97.5%	1.6%	0.0%	0.6%	0.3%	2.0%	0.4%	0.2%	0.0%
Washtenaw County	123,278	85.6%	2.4%	4.2%	5.7%	2.1%	11.7%	2.5%	0.3%	0.0%
Wayne County	444,288	84.9%	5.0%	3.9%	0.9%	5.3%	11.5%	2.1%	1.0%	0.5%
Minnesota										
Anoka County	80,904	86.9%	3.7%	1.8%	5.3%	2.3%	9.7%	2.9%	0.6%	0.0%
Carver County	21,899	87.6%	5.6%	1.9%	4.3%	0.6%	12.4%	0.0%	0.0%	0.0%
Dakota County	98,765	87.0%	6.0%	1.7%	5.0%	0.2%	7.2%	3.2%	2.1%	0.6%
Hennepin County	332,438	77.8%	5.5%	4.6%	5.9%	6.1%	15.6%	4.2%	2.0%	0.3%
Olmsted County	36,745	91.1%	2.8%	3.2%	1.0%	1.9%	5.4%	0.8%	2.7%	0.0%
Ramsey County	152,482	72.9%	5.3%	2.0%	13.6%	6.2%	17.3%	6.0%	2.8%	1.0%
Scott County	54,619	92.6%	3.5%	0.9%	1.9%	1.1%	7.0%	0.4%	0.0%	0.0%
St. Louis County	32,848	78.9%	8.4%	6.4%	6.2%	0.0%	14.5%	1.0%	2.9%	2.7%
Stearns County	47,263	88.8%	5.3%	2.0%	1.6%	2.3%	6.9%	3.5%	0.8%	0.0%
Washington County	57,531	86.3%	3.9%	2.2%	5.0%	2.5%	10.4%	2.5%	0.8%	0.0%
Wright County	27,686	94.1%	4.5%	1.4%	0.0%	0.0%	5.4%	0.0%	0.6%	0.0%
Mississippi										
DeSoto County	42,966	93.2%	5.3%	0.0%	1.3%	0.2%	5.1%	0.2%	1.1%	0.3%
Harrison County	55,153	89.0%	6.0%	0.8%	3.0%	1.3%	8.4%	2.0%	0.5%	0.2%
Hinds County	71,084	96.5%	1.7%	1.0%	0.3%	0.5%	1.7%	0.5%	0.5%	0.9%
Jackson County	33,350	91.5%	6.2%	0.9%	1.3%	0.2%	6.8%	0.8%	0.8%	0.0%
Madison County	25,688	94.8%	3.6%	0.8%	0.5%	0.3%	2.4%	0.5%	1.8%	0.5%
Rankin County	37,036	96.5%	1.6%	0.3%	1.5%	0.0%	1.8%	1.5%	0.2%	0.0%
Missouri										
Boone County	65,947	92.7%	1.8%	1.6%	3.1%	0.8%	4.5%	2.5%	0.4%	0.0%
Cass County	22,570	92.2%	5.0%	1.7%	0.0%	1.0%	4.0%	2.1%	0.0%	1.7%
Clay County	58,001	93.8%	3.2%	1.5%	1.0%	0.5%	4.0%	1.1%	0.5%	0.5%
Franklin County	23,013	96.9%	1.9%	0.2%	1.0%	0.0%	1.5%	1.2%	0.4%	0.0%
Greene County	87,400	92.9%	3.1%	1.2%	2.1%	0.8%	4.9%	1.7%	0.4%	0.0%
Jackson County	176,621	88.7%	8.4%	1.2%	1.3%	0.4%	8.4%	1.7%	0.8%	0.4%
Jasper County	31,672	92.1%	7.1%	0.0%	0.8%	0.0%	5.1%	1.0%	1.8%	0.0%
Jefferson County	52,895	98.0%	0.7%	0.8%	0.6%	0.0%	1.8%	0.0%	0.2%	0.0%
Platte County	24,357	92.9%	2.2%	2.4%	1.3%	1.3%	6.5%	0.6%	0.0%	0.0%
St. Charles County	93,881	91.1%	4.5%	1.7%	2.4%	0.3%	6.5%	0.9%	1.5%	0.0%
St. Louis County	242,954	90.8%	2.2%	2.7%	2.8%	1.4%	6.0%	1.6%	0.5%	0.9%
Montana										
Flathead County	19,915	96.7%	0.0%	3.1%	0.1%	0.0%	3.3%	0.0%	0.0%	0.0%
Gallatin County	34,706	98.1%	1.6%	0.3%	0.0%	0.0%	0.9%	1.0%	0.1%	0.0%
Missoula County	35,981	98.6%	0.6%	0.7%	0.0%	0.0%	0.9%	0.0%	0.5%	0.0%
Yellowstone County	38,872	95.5%	0.7%	0.1%	1.1%	2.7%	3.2%	1.3%	0.0%	0.0%
Nebraska										
Douglas County	149,220	81.1%	10.8%	3.3%	3.2%	1.5%	12.6%	2.9%	2.4%	1.0%
Lancaster County	94,646	83.1%	7.1%	2.6%	4.0%	3.1%	9.1%	5.6%	2.1%	0.1%
Sarpy County	45,405	92.2%	5.5%	1.3%	0.9%	0.0%	6.1%	0.8%	0.9%	0.0%
Nevada										
Clark County	548,876	61.9%	28.9%	2.4%	5.3%	1.5%	28.8%	4.7%	3.1%	1.5%
Washoe County	115,819	73.0%	21.9%	2.1%	2.7%	0.3%	20.3%	4.1%	2.0%	0.7%
New Hampshire										
Hillsborough County	96,735	87.0%	6.1%	2.9%	2.5%	1.5%	8.6%	2.7%	1.4%	0.3%
Merrimack County	35,723	94.7%	0.1%	3.8%	1.1%	0.4%	4.5%	0.8%	0.0%	0.0%
Rockingham County	66,202	90.8%	3.4%	3.2%	2.1%	0.4%	6.7%	1.9%	0.6%	0.0%
Strafford County	39,197	93.4%	0.1%	2.1%	3.8%	0.6%	5.6%	0.3%	0.6%	0.0%
New Jersey										
Atlantic County	66,570	68.7%	21.5%	6.9%	2.7%	0.2%	22.5%	6.9%	1.4%	0.5%
Bergen County	207,884	59.0%	18.1%	11.5%	8.9%	2.5%	33.8%	4.0%	3.0%	0.2%
Burlington County	107,421	87.9%	6.6%	3.3%	1.9%	0.3%	8.9%	1.7%	1.4%	0.1%
Camden County	128,390	76.0%	15.8%	4.9%	2.8%	0.4%	16.7%	3.1%	3.2%	0.9%
Cape May County	19,149	84.7%	14.3%	0.5%	0.0%	0.5%	11.4%	2.7%	1.2%	0.0%
Cumberland County	39,803	73.8%	20.8%	2.2%	1.2%	2.0%	17.2%	3.0%	2.3%	3.7%
Essex County	199,329	64.9%	21.4%	9.8%	1.5%	2.4%	24.4%	5.1%	3.8%	1.8%
Gloucester County	69,545	87.5%	6.3%	2.3%	1.9%	2.0%	11.0%	0.5%	0.4%	0.6%
Hudson County	204,390	42.5%	34.9%	10.5%	8.0%	4.1%	43.6%	7.9%	3.6%	2.5%
Hunterdon County	27,170	90.4%	4.9%	2.6%	1.4%	0.7%	6.0%	1.1%	2.5%	0.0%
Mercer County	96,122	68.8%	17.0%	7.7%	5.4%	1.1%	21.7%	5.0%	3.8%	0.7%
Middlesex County	214,716	60.7%	17.3%	13.2%	6.8%	2.0%	28.9%	5.7%	3.6%	1.1%
Monmouth County	140,826	77.9%	10.6%	8.0%	2.7%	0.8%	16.3%	3.7%	1.8%	0.3%
Morris County	114,443	72.9%	13.8%	6.5%	5.3%	1.4%	20.2%	4.5%	2.2%	0.1%
Ocean County	122,446	88.9%	6.4%	2.6%	0.7%	1.3%	6.9%	2.3%	1.4%	0.4%
Passaic County	131,980	49.0%	37.8%	8.0%	2.1%	3.0%	39.5%	5.0%	3.9%	2.7%

Table G-2: Counties—Language Spoken and English Ability—Continued

	Millennial Population 15 to 33	Percent by Language Spoken at Home					Percent by Ability to Speak English			
		English Only	Spanish	Other Indo-European Language	Asian and Pacific Island Language	Other Language	Speak English "Very Well"	Speak English "Well"	Speak English "Not Well"	Speak English "Not at All"
New Jersey—Cont.										
Somerset County	72,159	69.6%	14.2%	7.3%	7.6%	1.4%	24.6%	3.5%	2.3%	0.0%
Sussex County	30,701	93.5%	4.3%	1.0%	0.6%	0.6%	4.9%	1.3%	0.3%	0.0%
Union County	133,055	52.6%	33.0%	10.8%	2.0%	1.6%	29.6%	6.8%	5.9%	5.2%
Warren County	22,864	88.0%	7.6%	3.9%	0.2%	0.3%	7.6%	1.2%	1.9%	1.3%
New Mexico										
Bernalillo County	182,851	69.0%	24.7%	2.1%	1.6%	2.6%	22.2%	4.6%	3.1%	1.2%
Doña Ana County	64,094	50.9%	47.3%	0.1%	1.0%	0.7%	42.3%	4.3%	1.5%	1.0%
San Juan County	32,797	76.4%	13.3%	0.3%	0.8%	9.3%	22.9%	0.5%	0.0%	0.2%
Sandoval County	30,632	69.7%	11.9%	0.0%	0.1%	18.3%	25.8%	2.2%	2.3%	0.0%
Santa Fe County	30,994	66.4%	29.1%	1.6%	0.6%	2.2%	29.8%	0.6%	1.3%	1.9%
New York										
Albany County	90,605	85.3%	3.0%	5.1%	5.9%	0.6%	11.2%	1.5%	1.9%	0.0%
Bronx County	420,540	38.5%	51.3%	5.1%	1.3%	3.8%	43.7%	8.0%	6.3%	3.5%
Broome County	54,933	87.3%	2.3%	3.4%	6.0%	1.0%	10.2%	1.5%	0.9%	0.2%
Chautauqua County	31,756	89.7%	6.2%	1.7%	2.1%	0.4%	7.2%	2.0%	1.1%	0.0%
Dutchess County	75,653	84.6%	9.8%	2.7%	2.0%	0.9%	11.5%	2.5%	0.9%	0.5%
Erie County	239,874	86.2%	4.3%	4.3%	3.5%	1.7%	9.7%	2.4%	1.5%	0.2%
Jefferson County	35,425	95.8%	3.2%	1.1%	0.0%	0.0%	3.4%	0.2%	0.1%	0.5%
Kings County	753,015	56.7%	16.4%	15.6%	7.9%	3.3%	28.9%	8.2%	5.5%	0.8%
Monroe County	201,722	83.7%	7.1%	4.4%	3.4%	1.5%	10.5%	3.9%	1.7%	0.1%
Nassau County	314,680	70.0%	15.4%	9.5%	3.7%	1.3%	21.2%	5.0%	3.0%	0.7%
New York County	520,283	63.7%	19.8%	6.3%	8.0%	2.3%	27.9%	5.3%	2.0%	1.2%
Niagara County	49,427	97.4%	1.6%	0.8%	0.0%	0.2%	1.5%	0.7%	0.3%	0.0%
Oneida County	57,337	84.7%	4.7%	4.9%	2.1%	3.6%	9.6%	4.1%	1.1%	0.4%
Onondaga County	123,197	86.7%	4.2%	3.2%	3.0%	3.0%	10.7%	1.7%	0.8%	0.1%
Ontario County	26,317	87.4%	4.1%	5.3%	3.2%	0.0%	8.4%	3.8%	0.4%	0.0%
Orange County	96,177	72.9%	14.6%	10.3%	1.5%	0.7%	20.3%	3.9%	2.5%	0.5%
Oswego County	32,086	93.6%	2.7%	2.1%	1.3%	0.3%	4.9%	1.2%	0.3%	0.0%
Putnam County	21,543	91.0%	7.7%	0.8%	0.4%	0.0%	7.3%	1.2%	0.4%	0.0%
Queens County	608,419	43.1%	26.2%	15.4%	12.9%	2.4%	38.5%	10.9%	6.4%	1.2%
Rensselaer County	42,660	88.6%	4.4%	2.2%	4.3%	0.6%	8.2%	2.2%	0.6%	0.5%
Richmond County	118,607	68.9%	11.0%	11.4%	5.3%	3.3%	24.0%	3.5%	3.2%	0.4%
Rockland County	78,832	58.7%	16.3%	21.3%	2.4%	1.2%	24.7%	11.1%	5.0%	0.4%
Saratoga County	32,089	90.5%	1.8%	5.9%	0.3%	1.5%	7.4%	1.7%	0.5%	0.0%
Schenectady County	50,020	95.2%	1.5%	2.8%	0.6%	0.0%	3.3%	0.9%	0.7%	0.0%
St. Lawrence County	38,446	86.5%	4.2%	4.3%	2.8%	2.3%	8.3%	4.3%	0.7%	0.1%
Steuben County	22,675	96.6%	0.4%	2.9%	0.2%	0.0%	1.6%	1.1%	0.7%	0.0%
Suffolk County	350,920	73.5%	17.7%	5.2%	2.8%	0.8%	18.5%	4.4%	2.5%	1.2%
Tompkins County	44,550	80.9%	1.6%	4.4%	12.2%	0.8%	16.1%	2.9%	0.0%	0.0%
Ulster County	43,352	86.8%	6.9%	3.6%	1.6%	1.1%	11.0%	1.9%	0.3%	0.1%
Wayne County	20,592	93.7%	3.9%	2.1%	0.0%	0.2%	4.7%	0.3%	1.0%	0.2%
Westchester County	227,429	65.1%	24.4%	7.0%	2.8%	0.8%	26.2%	5.2%	3.1%	0.4%
North Carolina										
Alamance County	37,828	81.7%	16.6%	0.9%	0.8%	0.1%	9.6%	4.1%	3.6%	1.1%
Brunswick County	21,327	92.6%	4.9%	2.5%	0.0%	0.0%	3.7%	2.3%	1.4%	0.0%
Buncombe County	62,054	85.1%	9.1%	4.0%	1.8%	0.0%	8.5%	2.2%	1.6%	2.6%
Cabarrus County	45,207	89.4%	8.8%	0.4%	1.4%	0.0%	7.6%	1.0%	1.5%	0.5%
Catawba County	36,359	79.9%	12.2%	0.4%	7.5%	0.0%	9.4%	6.7%	4.0%	0.0%
Cleveland County	22,228	87.2%	11.6%	1.1%	0.0%	0.0%	8.9%	3.9%	0.0%	0.0%
Craven County	28,641	92.2%	3.2%	1.2%	2.3%	1.1%	3.7%	1.4%	2.7%	0.0%
Cumberland County	101,310	86.6%	9.6%	1.7%	0.9%	1.2%	10.0%	2.0%	1.2%	0.2%
Davidson County	36,326	89.4%	10.2%	0.0%	0.4%	0.0%	7.5%	1.0%	0.6%	1.4%
Durham County	89,780	73.8%	15.2%	4.7%	3.6%	2.6%	17.2%	3.1%	1.9%	4.0%
Forsyth County	92,421	82.3%	12.8%	2.2%	2.3%	0.5%	11.9%	2.2%	2.8%	0.8%
Gaston County	50,930	89.6%	8.1%	1.9%	0.2%	0.2%	6.2%	1.7%	1.6%	0.9%
Guilford County	137,587	85.6%	8.4%	2.8%	2.6%	0.7%	9.3%	2.6%	1.7%	0.8%
Harnett County	35,903	83.4%	13.4%	2.4%	0.8%	0.0%	13.5%	0.7%	2.4%	0.0%
Henderson County	20,521	83.6%	14.2%	0.0%	2.2%	0.0%	7.7%	3.7%	2.7%	2.3%
Iredell County	39,135	85.5%	10.2%	1.0%	3.3%	0.0%	11.6%	1.9%	0.0%	0.9%
Johnston County	41,911	85.5%	14.2%	0.1%	0.2%	0.0%	7.8%	2.6%	4.1%	0.0%
Mecklenburg County	285,842	79.2%	12.3%	3.9%	3.3%	1.3%	13.1%	3.4%	3.2%	1.2%
Moore County	19,495	91.8%	8.2%	0.0%	0.0%	0.0%	4.9%	3.1%	0.2%	0.0%
Nash County	21,537	92.0%	7.4%	0.0%	0.6%	0.0%	6.6%	0.3%	1.1%	0.0%
New Hanover County	62,467	90.9%	5.3%	0.8%	1.1%	1.9%	6.7%	1.4%	1.0%	0.0%
Onslow County	76,563	87.5%	10.8%	0.7%	0.9%	0.1%	8.7%	2.7%	0.6%	0.5%
Orange County	49,316	83.1%	7.4%	1.5%	6.0%	2.0%	13.7%	1.6%	0.8%	0.8%
Pitt County	61,542	94.5%	4.3%	0.1%	0.8%	0.3%	3.6%	1.0%	0.9%	0.0%
Randolph County	32,208	85.1%	14.3%	0.3%	0.4%	0.0%	11.4%	0.8%	1.3%	1.5%
Robeson County	34,806	91.0%	8.1%	0.0%	0.2%	0.7%	6.1%	0.9%	1.4%	0.6%
Rockingham County	19,131	92.0%	7.3%	0.0%	0.0%	0.7%	6.5%	0.3%	1.2%	0.0%
Rowan County	32,505	83.7%	14.9%	0.6%	0.8%	0.0%	11.0%	1.6%	1.7%	2.0%
Union County	51,248	86.6%	11.5%	0.8%	0.6%	0.6%	7.0%	1.9%	3.5%	1.0%
Wake County	269,495	82.3%	9.2%	4.6%	3.1%	0.9%	12.6%	2.9%	1.7%	0.5%
Wayne County	32,804	86.2%	10.4%	1.9%	0.6%	1.0%	5.3%	3.0%	3.3%	2.3%
North Dakota										
Cass County	57,528	93.6%	0.2%	3.7%	1.9%	0.6%	5.4%	0.8%	0.2%	0.0%

Table G-2: Counties—Language Spoken and English Ability—*Continued*

	Millennial Population 15 to 33	Percent by Language Spoken at Home					Percent by Ability to Speak English			
		English Only	Spanish	Other Indo-European Language	Asian and Pacific Island Language	Other Language	Speak English "Very Well"	Speak English "Well"	Speak English "Not Well"	Speak English "Not at All"
Ohio										
Allen County	25,254	97.3%	0.6%	1.0%	1.1%	0.0%	1.9%	0.8%	0.0%	0.0%
Ashtabula County	22,614	89.1%	3.7%	5.9%	1.3%	0.0%	8.6%	1.5%	0.8%	0.0%
Butler County	100,977	88.5%	4.7%	2.8%	2.7%	1.3%	7.4%	2.0%	2.0%	0.0%
Clark County	31,343	96.7%	1.1%	2.0%	0.0%	0.2%	2.4%	0.0%	0.6%	0.3%
Clermont County	47,651	97.6%	0.5%	0.8%	1.1%	0.0%	1.6%	0.8%	0.0%	0.0%
Columbiana County	21,390	99.2%	0.8%	0.0%	0.0%	0.0%	0.0%	0.0%	0.8%	0.2%
Cuyahoga County	307,066	85.5%	5.1%	4.2%	2.5%	2.6%	10.4%	1.9%	2.0%	0.2%
Delaware County	40,687	92.9%	1.5%	2.4%	3.2%	0.0%	6.7%	0.4%	0.0%	0.0%
Fairfield County	33,757	94.9%	1.0%	3.7%	0.1%	0.3%	4.2%	0.9%	0.0%	0.0%
Franklin County	368,067	85.7%	4.4%	3.2%	3.5%	3.1%	8.9%	3.3%	1.7%	0.4%
Geauga County	19,169	82.8%	0.0%	17.2%	0.0%	0.0%	13.6%	2.6%	1.0%	0.0%
Greene County	45,617	94.7%	1.3%	1.6%	1.2%	1.1%	2.7%	2.2%	0.3%	0.0%
Hamilton County	210,833	91.7%	2.5%	2.7%	1.4%	1.7%	5.4%	2.1%	0.7%	0.0%
Lake County	49,316	93.1%	2.2%	2.8%	0.4%	1.4%	3.9%	2.4%	0.0%	0.6%
Licking County	40,615	93.7%	2.5%	1.6%	1.7%	0.5%	4.7%	1.3%	0.0%	0.3%
Lorain County	69,817	89.9%	7.1%	1.5%	1.5%	0.0%	7.4%	1.9%	0.7%	0.1%
Lucas County	112,127	91.9%	2.7%	2.1%	1.5%	1.7%	5.5%	1.9%	0.7%	0.6%
Mahoning County	54,236	92.5%	4.6%	2.7%	0.2%	0.0%	5.2%	0.7%	1.0%	0.6%
Medina County	38,688	90.2%	3.7%	5.4%	0.0%	0.8%	7.5%	2.3%	0.0%	0.0%
Miami County	23,293	98.1%	0.5%	0.7%	0.7%	0.0%	1.2%	0.7%	0.0%	0.0%
Montgomery County	131,048	91.9%	2.3%	0.9%	2.7%	2.1%	6.2%	1.3%	0.5%	0.1%
Portage County	49,657	90.3%	2.9%	2.9%	2.0%	1.9%	6.3%	1.8%	1.6%	0.0%
Richland County	27,953	93.5%	2.2%	2.1%	1.5%	0.8%	5.3%	1.2%	0.0%	0.0%
Stark County	88,128	95.8%	1.9%	1.5%	0.6%	0.2%	2.4%	0.3%	0.7%	0.9%
Summit County	128,898	92.9%	1.3%	3.0%	2.3%	0.6%	5.0%	1.0%	1.1%	0.0%
Trumbull County	44,176	94.8%	1.2%	4.0%	0.0%	0.0%	4.2%	0.9%	0.1%	0.0%
Tuscarawas County	20,822	92.6%	1.3%	6.2%	0.0%	0.0%	4.0%	3.1%	0.3%	0.0%
Warren County	49,951	92.6%	2.2%	1.1%	4.2%	0.0%	5.9%	1.0%	0.5%	0.0%
Wayne County	28,015	79.5%	3.8%	15.4%	0.0%	1.3%	10.4%	9.5%	0.6%	0.0%
Wood County	43,113	94.3%	1.5%	1.3%	0.9%	2.0%	3.7%	1.4%	0.0%	0.5%
Oklahoma										
Canadian County	32,644	88.4%	5.9%	3.3%	2.2%	0.2%	10.2%	1.4%	0.0%	0.0%
Cleveland County	88,250	85.6%	4.7%	2.5%	6.3%	0.9%	11.9%	2.4%	0.1%	0.0%
Comanche County	39,557	90.0%	7.6%	0.2%	2.2%	0.0%	7.7%	2.1%	0.2%	0.0%
Oklahoma County	208,662	80.2%	16.2%	0.9%	2.3%	0.5%	12.6%	3.5%	2.4%	1.3%
Tulsa County	166,034	82.9%	12.7%	1.6%	2.4%	0.5%	9.5%	3.0%	3.1%	1.5%
Oregon										
Clackamas County	91,377	85.7%	8.4%	2.9%	2.7%	0.4%	11.4%	2.5%	0.4%	0.0%
Deschutes County	37,506	94.1%	4.8%	0.0%	0.5%	0.6%	3.4%	1.6%	0.4%	0.4%
Douglas County	21,869	95.8%	4.2%	0.0%	0.0%	0.0%	1.8%	1.0%	0.0%	1.4%
Jackson County	48,007	89.7%	9.0%	0.0%	1.2%	0.2%	7.5%	2.1%	0.6%	0.0%
Lane County	101,413	90.8%	5.4%	1.0%	2.6%	0.2%	6.1%	1.3%	1.5%	0.2%
Linn County	28,340	84.9%	8.5%	0.8%	4.6%	1.3%	9.7%	2.6%	0.0%	2.8%
Marion County	85,650	69.1%	25.3%	1.8%	2.1%	1.7%	22.9%	4.3%	2.4%	1.3%
Multnomah County	217,351	77.9%	10.0%	4.6%	6.0%	1.5%	15.8%	3.5%	2.3%	0.6%
Washington County	148,421	72.9%	15.4%	4.7%	5.9%	1.1%	18.1%	5.1%	3.0%	0.9%
Yamhill County	26,349	80.2%	17.3%	0.9%	1.2%	0.4%	15.7%	1.4%	0.1%	2.6%
Pennsylvania										
Adams County	23,400	93.2%	6.4%	0.4%	0.0%	0.0%	4.2%	0.7%	1.8%	0.0%
Allegheny County	317,665	90.3%	2.0%	3.7%	2.4%	1.6%	6.5%	2.3%	0.8%	0.1%
Beaver County	37,432	97.2%	1.3%	0.8%	0.8%	0.0%	1.7%	0.8%	0.4%	0.0%
Berks County	102,383	78.4%	18.6%	1.6%	0.9%	0.5%	16.9%	1.5%	2.0%	1.2%
Blair County	28,645	96.6%	0.4%	1.8%	0.4%	0.8%	3.2%	0.2%	0.0%	0.0%
Bucks County	134,522	89.8%	4.0%	4.3%	1.5%	0.4%	7.6%	1.9%	0.4%	0.2%
Butler County	43,323	94.9%	2.5%	1.7%	0.6%	0.3%	3.7%	1.4%	0.0%	0.0%
Cambria County	30,779	95.6%	0.5%	1.4%	2.1%	0.4%	1.8%	2.6%	0.0%	0.0%
Centre County	67,059	84.7%	2.7%	6.4%	6.1%	0.1%	12.7%	2.4%	0.2%	0.0%
Chester County	118,752	84.9%	7.1%	4.7%	3.2%	0.0%	9.2%	3.5%	1.3%	1.1%
Cumberland County	60,812	88.3%	2.4%	5.6%	3.3%	0.3%	7.5%	4.2%	0.0%	0.0%
Dauphin County	65,894	88.4%	4.3%	4.0%	2.1%	1.3%	7.5%	2.4%	1.5%	0.2%
Delaware County	143,127	88.3%	3.4%	4.9%	2.5%	0.9%	9.7%	1.1%	0.8%	0.2%
Erie County	71,032	91.5%	2.1%	2.2%	2.2%	1.9%	5.3%	2.3%	0.2%	0.6%
Fayette County	28,056	96.5%	0.9%	2.0%	0.2%	0.5%	3.4%	0.1%	0.0%	0.0%
Franklin County	34,699	91.5%	4.6%	3.9%	0.0%	0.0%	6.8%	0.3%	1.3%	0.0%
Lackawanna County	50,772	92.3%	4.2%	2.2%	1.3%	0.1%	3.4%	2.3%	1.2%	0.8%
Lancaster County	129,595	78.4%	10.6%	9.4%	1.5%	0.0%	16.3%	3.9%	1.1%	0.3%
Lebanon County	29,746	84.5%	9.7%	3.8%	1.2%	0.9%	13.0%	1.3%	1.2%	0.0%
Lehigh County	91,016	72.8%	21.9%	1.1%	2.9%	1.3%	17.3%	7.5%	1.6%	0.8%
Luzerne County	75,606	86.4%	11.7%	1.1%	0.5%	0.2%	9.7%	1.9%	1.3%	0.7%
Lycoming County	28,105	92.9%	2.9%	2.9%	1.4%	0.0%	5.8%	1.1%	0.2%	0.0%
Mercer County	26,023	95.3%	0.9%	3.8%	0.0%	0.0%	3.3%	1.0%	0.4%	0.0%
Monroe County	42,076	80.9%	9.4%	7.2%	2.1%	0.5%	16.7%	1.7%	0.2%	0.5%
Montgomery County	186,127	84.4%	4.9%	4.5%	5.5%	0.6%	11.6%	2.3%	1.6%	0.2%
Northampton County	72,627	85.3%	8.2%	3.5%	2.5%	0.5%	11.0%	2.8%	0.8%	0.0%
Northumberland County	20,330	97.7%	1.3%	1.0%	0.0%	0.0%	1.4%	0.9%	0.0%	0.0%
Philadelphia County	485,276	77.6%	9.7%	4.6%	6.4%	1.7%	15.2%	3.7%	3.2%	0.3%

Table G-2: Counties—Language Spoken and English Ability—*Continued*

	Millennial Population 15 to 33	Percent by Language Spoken at Home					Percent by Ability to Speak English			
		English Only	Spanish	Other Indo-European Language	Asian and Pacific Island Language	Other Language	Speak English "Very Well"	Speak English "Well"	Speak English "Not Well"	Speak English "Not at All"
Pennsylvania—Cont.										
Schuylkill County	30,373	93.4%	5.5%	1.1%	0.0%	0.0%	5.6%	1.1%	0.0%	0.0%
Washington County	45,987	93.6%	3.2%	1.4%	1.6%	0.3%	4.3%	1.7%	0.5%	0.0%
Westmoreland County	74,211	97.2%	1.1%	1.3%	0.3%	0.1%	1.8%	0.3%	0.7%	0.0%
York County	101,242	93.2%	4.5%	1.2%	0.6%	0.5%	5.0%	1.3%	0.4%	0.1%
Rhode Island										
Kent County	37,771	89.6%	5.1%	4.1%	1.2%	0.0%	9.4%	1.0%	0.0%	0.0%
Providence County	177,530	64.0%	21.6%	8.4%	5.2%	0.8%	27.0%	6.0%	2.2%	0.8%
Washington County	32,522	93.5%	4.2%	0.4%	1.7%	0.2%	4.0%	1.8%	0.6%	0.0%
South Carolina										
Aiken County	39,663	90.7%	8.0%	0.2%	1.1%	0.0%	4.1%	0.6%	4.6%	0.0%
Anderson County	44,484	93.8%	5.2%	1.0%	0.0%	0.0%	5.5%	0.4%	0.3%	0.0%
Beaufort County	42,199	86.9%	12.1%	0.4%	0.7%	0.0%	10.6%	1.2%	1.0%	0.3%
Berkeley County	55,285	94.4%	2.0%	2.1%	1.3%	0.2%	4.1%	0.8%	0.8%	0.0%
Charleston County	110,362	93.9%	3.3%	1.6%	0.9%	0.3%	3.9%	0.3%	1.8%	0.1%
Dorchester County	39,833	97.8%	0.8%	0.7%	0.8%	0.0%	1.5%	0.8%	0.0%	0.0%
Florence County	34,104	97.6%	1.6%	0.6%	0.3%	0.0%	1.3%	0.8%	0.3%	0.0%
Greenville County	127,063	86.5%	9.5%	1.7%	2.1%	0.3%	7.3%	3.6%	1.4%	1.2%
Horry County	69,260	91.7%	5.3%	1.1%	1.5%	0.4%	5.2%	1.8%	1.3%	0.0%
Lexington County	69,290	88.9%	7.8%	1.7%	1.4%	0.2%	5.1%	3.3%	2.2%	0.5%
Pickens County	39,215	92.7%	5.3%	0.9%	1.1%	0.0%	6.4%	0.9%	0.0%	0.0%
Richland County	133,553	91.3%	4.5%	2.0%	1.1%	1.2%	4.8%	3.1%	0.7%	0.1%
Spartanburg County	74,202	88.7%	6.4%	4.3%	0.5%	0.1%	9.7%	1.0%	0.3%	0.3%
Sumter County	29,989	93.7%	5.0%	0.7%	0.6%	0.0%	5.2%	0.9%	0.2%	0.0%
York County	61,013	90.5%	5.7%	1.4%	2.4%	0.0%	7.7%	0.7%	1.1%	0.0%
South Dakota										
Minnehaha County	51,061	86.2%	4.5%	5.6%	0.6%	3.0%	7.1%	2.7%	2.7%	1.3%
Pennington County	27,812	91.9%	2.9%	0.4%	0.0%	4.9%	7.9%	0.0%	0.2%	0.0%
Tennessee										
Blount County	28,362	94.3%	4.2%	0.7%	0.2%	0.5%	5.7%	0.0%	0.0%	0.0%
Bradley County	27,347	88.6%	9.3%	0.6%	0.9%	0.6%	7.8%	2.4%	0.7%	0.5%
Davidson County	207,280	81.5%	9.4%	3.5%	1.9%	3.8%	10.5%	3.2%	3.6%	1.3%
Hamilton County	89,012	93.5%	3.6%	0.8%	2.1%	0.0%	2.9%	1.8%	1.6%	0.2%
Knox County	126,547	93.0%	4.6%	0.8%	1.0%	0.6%	3.8%	0.9%	2.0%	0.3%
Madison County	25,119	93.9%	4.1%	0.1%	1.1%	0.8%	4.4%	0.0%	0.0%	1.7%
Montgomery County	64,486	90.3%	6.3%	1.5%	1.4%	0.4%	7.7%	1.0%	1.0%	0.0%
Rutherford County	90,154	87.2%	6.6%	1.3%	2.5%	2.4%	7.9%	2.6%	1.5%	0.8%
Sevier County	21,355	90.6%	5.6%	3.6%	0.2%	0.0%	5.2%	2.1%	0.6%	1.7%
Shelby County	254,967	89.2%	6.5%	1.4%	1.9%	0.9%	7.7%	1.9%	0.8%	0.4%
Sullivan County	34,048	98.4%	1.4%	0.3%	0.0%	0.0%	1.1%	0.0%	0.5%	0.0%
Sumner County	41,241	93.3%	4.4%	1.5%	0.8%	0.0%	3.8%	2.0%	0.8%	0.0%
Washington County	33,607	92.4%	3.3%	1.2%	1.4%	1.7%	7.6%	0.0%	0.0%	0.0%
Williamson County	42,103	93.0%	2.7%	3.0%	1.0%	0.3%	5.8%	0.5%	0.4%	0.4%
Wilson County	28,214	94.4%	3.3%	0.5%	0.5%	1.2%	3.5%	2.1%	0.0%	0.0%
Texas										
Bell County	105,325	76.8%	17.1%	3.2%	1.8%	1.2%	16.8%	3.3%	2.5%	0.6%
Bexar County	542,377	64.6%	31.9%	1.2%	1.8%	0.5%	28.5%	3.6%	2.1%	1.2%
Bowie County	23,025	97.3%	2.7%	0.0%	0.0%	0.0%	1.6%	0.0%	0.0%	1.1%
Brazoria County	88,816	72.5%	20.5%	0.8%	4.6%	1.5%	22.0%	2.3%	1.7%	1.4%
Brazos County	97,285	79.7%	12.6%	2.5%	4.2%	0.9%	12.8%	4.6%	1.4%	1.5%
Cameron County	114,476	24.7%	74.9%	0.1%	0.3%	0.0%	61.7%	6.2%	4.1%	3.4%
Collin County	217,272	72.0%	13.0%	7.3%	6.0%	1.6%	18.1%	5.8%	2.8%	1.3%
Comal County	28,645	73.9%	22.8%	1.5%	0.8%	1.0%	21.0%	0.9%	1.5%	2.8%
Dallas County	713,204	52.2%	39.1%	2.9%	3.5%	2.3%	29.1%	9.7%	6.5%	2.4%
Denton County	210,431	76.4%	15.0%	2.9%	4.7%	1.1%	18.6%	2.9%	1.5%	0.6%
Ector County	49,508	49.3%	47.7%	0.7%	0.8%	1.5%	40.0%	4.7%	3.3%	2.7%
El Paso County	40,687	75.9%	23.3%	0.0%	0.6%	0.2%	15.7%	3.5%	4.3%	0.6%
Ellis County	242,594	30.0%	67.3%	1.3%	0.7%	0.7%	53.5%	11.4%	3.1%	2.0%
Fort Bend County	174,314	61.6%	20.9%	6.8%	9.5%	1.3%	28.8%	5.1%	3.5%	1.1%
Galveston County	79,208	78.1%	16.4%	1.5%	2.5%	1.6%	16.7%	1.8%	2.3%	1.2%
Grayson County	30,076	84.3%	14.5%	0.4%	0.0%	0.9%	12.5%	1.3%	1.3%	0.7%
Gregg County	31,707	82.7%	16.0%	1.3%	0.0%	0.0%	13.0%	1.8%	0.3%	2.3%
Guadalupe County	37,951	88.6%	9.5%	0.2%	1.7%	0.0%	8.4%	2.5%	0.6%	0.0%
Harris County	1,272,358	53.9%	36.9%	3.5%	4.2%	1.5%	29.7%	7.4%	4.5%	4.5%
Hays County	66,615	73.7%	24.3%	1.8%	0.2%	0.0%	23.4%	0.9%	1.3%	0.7%
Hidalgo County	236,165	14.1%	85.2%	0.1%	0.5%	0.0%	68.0%	9.0%	5.8%	3.1%
Jefferson County	67,989	70.4%	24.4%	1.7%	3.1%	0.4%	21.4%	2.6%	4.4%	1.1%
Johnson County	39,272	79.4%	17.8%	2.6%	0.1%	0.1%	15.4%	4.3%	0.9%	0.0%
Kaufman County	27,740	81.8%	16.7%	0.0%	1.5%	0.0%	9.5%	5.5%	0.9%	2.4%
Lubbock County	102,399	75.6%	18.4%	3.9%	1.5%	0.5%	20.9%	2.8%	0.6%	0.1%
McLennan County	74,841	77.1%	19.4%	1.4%	1.8%	0.4%	9.8%	9.5%	2.4%	1.3%
Midland County	48,875	66.2%	29.2%	0.2%	3.6%	0.8%	23.3%	5.0%	5.4%	0.1%
Montgomery County	128,604	77.5%	19.6%	1.3%	1.2%	0.5%	17.3%	2.2%	2.2%	0.8%
Nueces County	100,540	70.1%	27.4%	0.1%	1.8%	0.6%	26.2%	2.3%	1.0%	0.3%
Parker County	27,518	90.7%	9.1%	0.0%	0.2%	0.0%	5.8%	2.9%	0.6%	0.0%

Table G-2: Counties—Language Spoken and English Ability—*Continued*

	Millennial Population 15 to 33	Percent by Language Spoken at Home					Percent by Ability to Speak English			
		English Only	Spanish	Other Indo-European Language	Asian and Pacific Island Language	Other Language	Speak English "Very Well"	Speak English "Well"	Speak English "Not Well"	Speak English "Not at All"
Texas—Cont.										
Potter County	32,293	61.9%	33.3%	0.7%	1.2%	2.9%	26.8%	5.0%	3.6%	2.7%
Randall County	36,250	84.6%	11.5%	1.8%	2.1%	0.0%	12.3%	2.5%	0.5%	0.0%
Smith County	60,703	82.7%	15.7%	0.8%	0.8%	0.0%	10.6%	2.6%	2.6%	1.4%
Tarrant County	531,633	68.8%	24.3%	2.3%	3.0%	1.6%	21.3%	5.5%	3.3%	1.1%
Taylor County	43,310	82.5%	13.0%	2.9%	1.3%	0.3%	14.8%	2.1%	0.6%	0.0%
Tom Green County	35,765	71.5%	24.8%	1.6%	1.5%	0.6%	21.5%	4.3%	2.0%	0.6%
Travis County	364,058	67.2%	24.7%	3.0%	3.7%	1.4%	22.6%	3.7%	3.8%	2.8%
Webb County	76,206	11.1%	88.8%	0.0%	0.0%	0.0%	65.1%	11.0%	5.2%	7.7%
Wichita County	41,345	83.8%	13.6%	1.1%	0.8%	0.7%	8.1%	7.6%	0.4%	0.1%
Williamson County	122,798	78.8%	15.5%	2.1%	3.3%	0.4%	15.2%	3.2%	2.1%	0.7%
Utah										
Cache County	44,550	88.8%	7.8%	1.0%	1.4%	1.0%	8.3%	1.3%	1.0%	0.6%
Davis County	92,284	88.2%	8.4%	2.0%	1.2%	0.3%	9.1%	1.5%	0.9%	0.3%
Salt Lake County	315,750	78.8%	14.6%	2.0%	3.1%	1.5%	16.4%	2.5%	1.8%	0.5%
Utah County	196,901	86.1%	9.2%	1.7%	2.5%	0.5%	10.8%	2.0%	1.1%	0.1%
Washington County	39,437	87.0%	7.6%	3.1%	1.8%	0.6%	11.6%	1.0%	0.4%	0.0%
Weber County	68,284	84.3%	13.6%	0.3%	1.3%	0.5%	9.8%	2.8%	2.8%	0.3%
Vermont										
Chittenden County	51,415	90.1%	2.1%	6.8%	0.8%	0.2%	8.6%	0.9%	0.4%	0.0%
Virginia										
Albemarle County	29,197	85.3%	5.7%	4.2%	4.5%	0.3%	12.2%	2.0%	0.4%	0.0%
Arlington County	77,494	71.3%	13.6%	6.4%	6.0%	2.8%	21.7%	4.2%	2.4%	0.4%
Chesterfield County	81,100	87.4%	8.3%	2.1%	1.9%	0.3%	7.7%	2.1%	2.0%	0.7%
Fairfax County	282,006	58.8%	16.8%	8.4%	11.2%	4.7%	31.0%	5.8%	3.8%	0.6%
Hanover County	22,860	96.4%	1.3%	0.8%	1.5%	0.0%	2.8%	0.2%	0.6%	0.0%
Henrico County	79,300	82.1%	3.7%	4.0%	5.7%	4.5%	11.4%	4.6%	1.6%	0.2%
Loudoun County	84,610	64.7%	13.1%	9.6%	8.2%	4.5%	25.5%	7.5%	1.9%	0.5%
Montgomery County	43,081	87.1%	4.0%	4.2%	4.4%	0.4%	9.2%	3.0%	0.7%	0.0%
Prince William County	116,795	68.2%	20.5%	7.2%	2.4%	1.8%	22.2%	5.9%	2.4%	1.3%
Roanoke County	21,530	94.5%	3.4%	2.1%	0.0%	0.0%	5.4%	0.1%	0.0%	0.0%
Spotsylvania County	31,802	93.0%	4.8%	0.4%	0.0%	1.8%	5.3%	1.7%	0.0%	0.0%
Stafford County	38,069	88.6%	6.0%	1.7%	1.9%	1.7%	9.8%	1.0%	0.5%	0.1%
Washington										
Benton County	48,145	60.5%	24.9%	4.9%	0.7%	0.0%	23.2%	5.5%	0.2%	1.5%
Clark County	114,195	81.8%	8.6%	6.7%	2.5%	0.5%	12.4%	3.8%	1.7%	0.2%
Cowlitz County	23,053	85.2%	11.6%	0.4%	1.4%	1.3%	8.6%	3.2%	1.0%	1.9%
Grant County	24,728	69.6%	25.6%	0.9%	3.5%	0.4%	13.7%	6.5%	8.1%	2.0%
King County	568,084	70.6%	8.4%	6.6%	11.9%	2.4%	20.0%	5.7%	3.0%	0.6%
Kitsap County	69,919	94.4%	3.1%	1.2%	1.4%	0.0%	4.9%	0.5%	0.3%	0.0%
Pierce County	225,257	82.2%	8.9%	4.1%	4.4%	0.4%	13.4%	2.5%	1.5%	0.4%
Skagit County	27,287	84.5%	13.6%	0.3%	1.0%	0.6%	12.0%	1.5%	1.3%	0.8%
Snohomish County	192,324	76.4%	9.0%	7.4%	6.6%	0.5%	16.8%	3.4%	2.7%	0.6%
Spokane County	135,628	89.6%	2.9%	4.4%	1.6%	1.5%	8.4%	1.6%	0.3%	0.0%
Thurston County	67,330	84.5%	6.7%	3.0%	4.7%	1.1%	10.1%	4.0%	1.1%	0.3%
Whatcom County	64,215	87.7%	7.3%	3.1%	1.8%	0.1%	7.9%	3.3%	0.3%	0.8%
Yakima County	64,342	49.2%	50.5%	0.0%	0.0%	0.3%	38.3%	2.9%	4.4%	5.3%
West Virginia										
Berkeley County	26,822	95.3%	4.1%	0.7%	0.0%	0.0%	3.8%	0.9%	0.0%	0.0%
Cabell County	26,637	98.9%	0.3%	0.0%	0.8%	0.0%	0.8%	0.3%	0.0%	0.0%
Kanawha County	40,670	95.8%	1.4%	0.6%	1.5%	0.7%	3.6%	0.4%	0.0%	0.2%
Monongalia County	43,034	84.8%	5.9%	7.1%	2.3%	0.0%	12.3%	2.4%	0.5%	0.0%
Wisconsin										
Brown County	65,276	84.4%	10.7%	0.1%	4.6%	0.2%	10.3%	2.2%	3.1%	0.0%
Dane County	159,007	82.9%	4.8%	5.3%	6.2%	0.8%	11.8%	4.6%	0.7%	0.0%
Eau Claire County	32,420	94.0%	0.3%	0.1%	5.3%	0.3%	1.9%	1.3%	2.8%	0.0%
Fond du Lac County	24,162	92.6%	4.7%	0.0%	2.7%	0.0%	6.3%	1.1%	0.0%	0.0%
Kenosha County	42,022	86.5%	10.8%	0.6%	1.6%	0.4%	9.0%	2.6%	1.8%	0.0%
La Crosse County	35,803	86.3%	5.9%	2.3%	5.5%	0.0%	6.2%	5.6%	1.0%	0.9%
Marathon County	29,492	88.0%	3.3%	1.8%	6.8%	0.0%	5.0%	6.7%	0.0%	0.3%
Milwaukee County	267,550	83.0%	11.0%	2.4%	2.5%	1.1%	12.5%	2.9%	1.5%	0.2%
Outagamie County	45,906	88.5%	3.7%	2.8%	4.5%	0.5%	7.6%	1.9%	2.1%	0.0%
Racine County	45,504	90.1%	6.5%	1.5%	1.9%	0.0%	8.2%	1.7%	0.0%	0.0%
Rock County	36,704	88.2%	9.0%	1.9%	0.4%	0.5%	11.1%	0.7%	0.0%	0.0%
Sheboygan County	24,958	80.2%	9.8%	3.3%	6.7%	0.0%	11.6%	3.1%	5.1%	0.0%
Walworth County	27,201	84.6%	14.0%	1.4%	0.0%	0.0%	9.1%	4.4%	1.8%	0.0%
Washington County	27,605	96.4%	3.1%	0.5%	0.0%	0.0%	3.6%	0.0%	0.0%	0.0%
Waukesha County	82,793	91.2%	4.3%	1.7%	2.9%	0.0%	6.3%	1.5%	1.0%	0.0%
Winnebago County	46,787	92.5%	3.4%	2.0%	2.1%	0.0%	6.1%	1.4%	0.0%	0.0%
Wyoming										
Laramie County	26,622	91.6%	3.8%	2.6%	1.7%	0.3%	4.3%	4.2%	0.0%	0.0%

Table G-3: Places—Language Spoken and English Ability

	Millennial Population 15 to 33	Percent by Language Spoken at Home					Percent by Ability to Speak English			
		English Only	Spanish	Other Indo-European Language	Asian and Pacific Island Language	Other Language	Speak English "Very Well"	Speak English "Well"	Speak English "Not Well"	Speak English "Not at All"
Alabama										
Birmingham city	65,276	94.6%	3.1%	0.4%	0.9%	1.0%	2.9%	1.5%	1.0%	0.0%
Huntsville city	50,582	92.2%	6.2%	1.2%	0.2%	0.2%	3.1%	1.6%	3.0%	0.2%
Mobile city	54,926	92.4%	3.5%	1.4%	2.4%	0.3%	3.7%	1.0%	1.9%	0.9%
Montgomery city	56,640	96.7%	2.0%	0.9%	0.3%	0.0%	1.9%	0.4%	0.5%	0.5%
Tuscaloosa city	43,300	93.6%	2.1%	0.0%	3.7%	0.6%	4.6%	0.8%	0.0%	1.0%
Alaska										
Anchorage municipality	92,449	78.9%	6.8%	2.1%	7.4%	4.7%	14.9%	6.2%	0.0%	0.0%
Arizona										
Chandler city	68,912	73.4%	14.8%	1.7%	9.3%	0.7%	20.3%	4.8%	1.1%	0.4%
Glendale city	67,526	68.4%	24.0%	2.3%	3.7%	1.6%	24.6%	2.6%	1.8%	2.6%
Mesa city	128,122	76.1%	20.0%	1.4%	1.5%	1.0%	18.4%	2.4%	2.4%	0.8%
Peoria city	42,034	82.6%	13.0%	2.1%	2.0%	0.2%	13.5%	2.4%	1.0%	0.4%
Phoenix city	432,935	58.0%	36.4%	2.2%	1.7%	1.8%	33.1%	3.5%	2.8%	2.6%
Scottsdale city	52,609	87.9%	8.7%	0.8%	2.1%	0.5%	9.4%	0.6%	0.9%	1.2%
Surprise city	27,081	79.6%	15.8%	1.4%	0.4%	2.7%	16.3%	2.0%	1.4%	0.7%
Tempe city	78,172	68.6%	18.3%	4.0%	7.5%	1.6%	25.0%	5.3%	1.0%	0.1%
Tucson city	169,695	65.8%	28.2%	1.2%	2.9%	1.8%	27.6%	3.4%	2.2%	0.9%
Yuma city	27,585	39.9%	58.1%	0.3%	0.2%	1.5%	46.4%	5.5%	3.6%	4.5%
Arkansas										
Little Rock city	53,598	85.7%	9.1%	2.6%	1.6%	1.0%	8.9%	2.9%	0.7%	1.7%
California										
Anaheim city	104,887	36.3%	51.4%	3.0%	8.1%	1.3%	45.6%	6.9%	7.2%	4.1%
Antioch city	31,157	55.2%	28.0%	3.4%	12.1%	1.3%	32.0%	5.8%	3.6%	3.4%
Bakersfield city	116,248	48.2%	44.6%	3.2%	2.5%	1.5%	39.1%	5.3%	5.5%	1.9%
Berkeley city	49,498	57.5%	9.4%	11.0%	20.8%	1.3%	33.5%	8.4%	0.6%	0.0%
Burbank city	27,930	54.0%	23.7%	15.7%	3.5%	3.1%	38.3%	7.2%	0.5%	0.0%
Carlsbad city	25,879	81.9%	11.9%	2.5%	3.7%	0.0%	17.8%	0.0%	0.3%	0.0%
Chico city	35,558	75.8%	17.8%	0.8%	2.1%	3.5%	22.1%	1.4%	0.7%	0.0%
Carson city	26,003	52.9%	27.1%	1.7%	17.7%	0.6%	40.3%	6.4%	0.4%	0.0%
Chula Vista city	73,367	42.7%	49.6%	0.4%	6.8%	0.5%	45.9%	8.6%	1.8%	1.1%
Clovis city	26,306	75.8%	13.2%	6.2%	4.7%	0.0%	20.5%	1.5%	0.8%	1.5%
Compton city	30,522	31.4%	65.5%	0.3%	0.6%	2.2%	55.0%	7.2%	4.4%	2.0%
Concord city	30,735	64.8%	21.5%	2.1%	10.6%	1.1%	24.0%	7.5%	3.7%	0.0%
Corona city	42,345	61.4%	30.4%	1.1%	4.7%	2.4%	32.6%	3.2%	1.9%	0.9%
Costa Mesa city	36,378	71.9%	17.7%	2.3%	4.1%	3.9%	24.1%	2.5%	1.5%	0.0%
Daly City city	29,604	52.7%	17.5%	3.1%	25.8%	0.9%	32.0%	11.5%	3.4%	0.5%
Downey city	33,813	27.8%	66.0%	0.7%	5.5%	0.0%	66.3%	3.9%	1.1%	0.9%
El Cajon city	30,072	61.7%	18.6%	3.8%	0.8%	15.1%	31.3%	5.1%	1.9%	0.0%
Elk Grove city	41,650	70.8%	9.9%	6.9%	11.5%	0.8%	20.2%	5.9%	3.0%	0.1%
El Monte city	33,568	19.9%	60.3%	0.4%	19.2%	0.1%	55.7%	7.7%	8.2%	8.6%
Escondido city	47,202	54.1%	37.9%	0.9%	5.0%	2.0%	30.0%	5.8%	5.7%	4.3%
Fairfield city	31,243	65.4%	26.4%	0.4%	7.8%	0.0%	23.3%	3.5%	5.4%	2.3%
Fontana city	63,986	33.8%	62.9%	0.7%	2.6%	0.0%	56.3%	6.4%	2.6%	0.9%
Fremont city	58,826	38.5%	11.5%	14.4%	34.2%	1.5%	52.6%	8.1%	0.9%	0.0%
Fresno city	160,820	53.5%	31.2%	4.1%	9.6%	1.6%	35.3%	5.5%	2.3%	3.4%
Fullerton city	43,980	52.0%	32.6%	2.4%	11.9%	1.2%	33.0%	8.5%	5.5%	1.0%
Garden Grove city	47,042	27.0%	37.0%	2.2%	32.5%	1.3%	59.2%	9.8%	3.3%	0.6%
Glendale city	49,189	28.7%	13.7%	45.4%	12.1%	0.1%	52.7%	13.0%	4.9%	0.8%
Hayward city	47,670	44.1%	37.2%	9.9%	7.9%	1.0%	38.1%	11.8%	4.0%	2.0%
Hesperia city	27,100	62.0%	36.5%	0.0%	1.6%	0.0%	30.9%	3.5%	3.6%	0.0%
Huntington Beach city	44,399	71.3%	18.4%	0.7%	8.5%	1.1%	19.9%	4.0%	1.9%	2.9%
Inglewood city	31,703	35.2%	60.7%	3.1%	0.0%	0.9%	53.8%	7.7%	2.6%	0.6%
Irvine city	83,108	54.2%	9.0%	10.0%	25.3%	1.6%	33.4%	7.8%	4.0%	0.6%
Jurupa Valley city	29,976	42.9%	47.7%	3.2%	6.0%	0.2%	45.1%	9.6%	1.9%	0.5%
Lancaster city	49,208	83.4%	15.9%	0.0%	0.3%	0.4%	13.0%	1.8%	1.0%	0.7%
Long Beach city	137,426	47.8%	41.9%	2.4%	7.6%	0.3%	43.8%	4.1%	2.9%	1.4%
Los Angeles city	1,208,578	39.2%	45.8%	5.9%	7.7%	1.4%	46.0%	7.4%	5.4%	2.1%
Mission Viejo city	22,309	76.2%	13.8%	3.7%	4.8%	1.5%	19.0%	3.2%	1.1%	0.4%
Modesto city	57,185	58.4%	31.4%	3.9%	3.1%	3.2%	32.6%	6.3%	1.6%	1.1%
Moreno Valley city	66,439	46.9%	48.8%	0.8%	1.8%	1.7%	46.1%	3.7%	2.1%	1.3%
Murrieta city	30,451	77.9%	15.6%	3.4%	3.2%	0.0%	18.5%	2.4%	0.0%	1.2%
Norwalk city	30,689	28.4%	62.6%	1.1%	7.1%	0.8%	51.5%	13.9%	5.2%	1.0%
Oakland city	122,337	59.2%	24.9%	2.6%	9.3%	4.0%	23.2%	7.2%	7.9%	2.3%
Oceanside city	45,355	76.9%	17.0%	0.5%	4.8%	0.8%	17.3%	3.6%	1.9%	0.3%
Ontario city	51,531	44.1%	48.3%	0.5%	6.9%	0.1%	44.3%	5.5%	3.6%	2.4%
Orange city	44,072	54.6%	33.8%	3.7%	7.2%	0.7%	35.4%	5.4%	3.3%	1.2%
Oxnard city	62,289	36.8%	58.6%	0.1%	3.6%	0.8%	40.4%	5.6%	7.4%	9.8%
Palmdale city	42,360	63.1%	32.6%	1.3%	2.4%	0.6%	29.5%	5.4%	2.0%	0.0%
Pasadena city	36,762	48.4%	38.0%	5.1%	8.2%	0.3%	40.5%	6.1%	3.5%	1.5%
Pomona city	48,713	32.2%	55.0%	0.5%	11.9%	0.3%	55.4%	7.2%	3.7%	1.4%
Rancho Cucamonga city	50,125	69.5%	17.7%	6.4%	4.7%	1.6%	25.9%	3.9%	0.7%	0.0%
Redding city	24,840	93.6%	4.5%	0.5%	1.4%	0.0%	6.0%	0.2%	0.2%	0.0%
Rialto city	32,854	37.1%	58.3%	0.0%	3.1%	1.5%	45.7%	11.4%	2.5%	3.4%

Table G-3: Places—Language Spoken and English Ability—*Continued*

	Millennial Population 15 to 33	Percent by Language Spoken at Home					Percent by Ability to Speak English			
		English Only	Spanish	Other Indo-European Language	Asian and Pacific Island Language	Other Language	Speak English "Very Well"	Speak English "Well"	Speak English "Not Well"	Speak English "Not at All"
California—Cont.										
Richmond city	32,546	35.4%	43.6%	2.5%	16.5%	2.0%	48.1%	7.6%	5.8%	3.1%
Riverside city	108,944	55.8%	37.4%	1.8%	4.2%	0.9%	35.2%	3.7%	4.4%	1.0%
Roseville city	32,596	82.7%	8.0%	2.7%	5.5%	1.1%	14.0%	2.7%	0.6%	0.0%
Sacramento city	142,256	56.1%	23.6%	6.4%	12.6%	1.3%	33.1%	6.2%	3.4%	1.2%
Salinas city	45,235	30.3%	67.1%	0.5%	2.1%	0.0%	43.4%	6.8%	10.4%	9.1%
San Bernardino city	68,511	39.3%	52.3%	1.2%	4.7%	2.5%	40.6%	10.8%	6.6%	2.7%
San Buenaventura (Ventura) city	27,629	66.8%	29.2%	1.3%	2.7%	0.0%	22.4%	1.8%	3.9%	5.1%
San Diego city	445,012	59.4%	26.1%	3.9%	9.6%	1.0%	32.3%	5.5%	2.1%	0.7%
San Francisco city	258,717	62.2%	10.5%	6.3%	19.7%	1.3%	28.6%	7.2%	1.6%	0.5%
San Jose city	269,874	46.4%	26.8%	5.3%	20.5%	1.0%	39.5%	7.8%	5.4%	0.9%
San Leandro city	22,760	53.5%	16.0%	5.1%	24.6%	0.8%	32.1%	10.5%	3.3%	0.5%
San Marcos city	24,402	57.9%	30.1%	1.8%	9.7%	0.5%	30.3%	5.9%	2.0%	3.9%
San Mateo city	24,437	51.1%	18.3%	12.6%	16.9%	1.1%	39.2%	7.0%	2.2%	0.5%
Santa Ana city	101,668	17.6%	74.3%	0.7%	7.4%	0.1%	61.7%	9.1%	8.3%	3.3%
Santa Clara city	39,593	42.9%	10.7%	17.8%	26.5%	2.1%	45.6%	9.2%	2.4%	0.0%
Santa Clarita city	47,773	67.3%	21.8%	3.0%	6.6%	1.4%	26.2%	4.0%	1.9%	0.7%
Santa Maria city	30,556	39.6%	57.8%	0.0%	1.6%	1.0%	35.7%	4.5%	3.0%	17.2%
Santa Monica city	24,672	72.1%	16.2%	7.5%	3.7%	0.5%	24.1%	2.3%	1.6%	0.0%
Santa Rosa city	44,446	64.0%	29.5%	2.2%	4.2%	0.1%	22.2%	9.5%	3.3%	1.0%
Simi Valley city	32,740	70.0%	20.5%	3.2%	4.9%	1.4%	27.2%	1.7%	0.6%	0.5%
South Gate city	28,277	8.9%	90.3%	0.0%	0.7%	0.0%	72.7%	7.4%	7.5%	3.4%
Stockton city	91,948	51.3%	32.9%	3.0%	11.9%	0.9%	36.4%	6.2%	4.7%	1.4%
Sunnyvale city	41,801	42.4%	14.1%	15.2%	27.4%	0.9%	42.9%	9.3%	4.8%	0.6%
Temecula city	30,276	83.5%	12.5%	1.9%	2.1%	0.0%	15.2%	1.3%	0.0%	0.0%
Thousand Oaks city	26,301	75.9%	15.2%	3.2%	5.5%	0.3%	15.3%	4.3%	2.7%	1.8%
Torrance city	35,250	60.5%	16.3%	4.7%	16.9%	1.7%	30.5%	7.5%	1.1%	0.4%
Vacaville city	26,462	79.5%	17.3%	1.4%	1.8%	0.0%	12.9%	5.0%	2.2%	0.5%
Vallejo city	33,732	65.9%	21.5%	1.0%	10.8%	0.7%	29.0%	3.2%	1.2%	0.7%
Victorville city	36,736	65.7%	32.8%	0.7%	0.4%	0.4%	29.2%	3.4%	1.7%	0.0%
Visalia city	33,963	70.7%	24.6%	0.2%	3.7%	0.8%	18.2%	5.5%	2.1%	3.5%
Vista city	31,575	59.5%	35.8%	0.3%	4.0%	0.4%	31.6%	5.0%	3.7%	0.1%
West Covina city	29,341	40.6%	47.4%	0.1%	11.9%	0.0%	52.3%	4.9%	2.0%	0.3%
Westminster city	21,766	39.8%	29.5%	1.6%	27.9%	1.2%	46.6%	7.3%	4.1%	2.2%
Colorado										
Arvada city	25,827	90.3%	8.2%	0.9%	0.0%	0.6%	5.8%	0.2%	3.6%	0.0%
Aurora city	102,094	65.1%	24.2%	3.4%	3.6%	3.7%	22.8%	5.3%	5.0%	1.9%
Boulder city	50,704	83.6%	6.0%	6.2%	3.0%	1.1%	13.9%	1.8%	0.6%	0.1%
Centennial city	24,786	79.2%	7.9%	9.2%	3.0%	0.7%	15.6%	2.1%	3.1%	0.0%
Colorado Springs city	132,077	88.1%	7.7%	2.0%	1.6%	0.6%	9.5%	1.6%	0.5%	0.4%
Denver city	217,281	73.2%	20.9%	1.9%	2.4%	1.6%	19.5%	3.1%	3.0%	1.1%
Fort Collins city	64,784	91.1%	4.3%	2.2%	1.4%	1.0%	8.0%	0.9%	0.0%	0.0%
Greeley city	32,325	82.5%	15.7%	0.7%	1.1%	0.0%	12.2%	3.7%	1.1%	0.5%
Lakewood city	44,017	87.1%	8.5%	2.0%	2.0%	0.5%	11.2%	0.4%	1.2%	0.0%
Longmont city	21,632	80.4%	17.4%	1.3%	0.8%	0.0%	16.0%	2.0%	1.2%	0.4%
Pueblo city	29,065	86.7%	12.5%	0.8%	0.0%	0.0%	12.9%	0.3%	0.0%	0.0%
Thornton city	34,916	70.9%	25.8%	0.3%	3.0%	0.0%	20.6%	2.8%	3.2%	2.5%
Westminster city	30,054	78.7%	14.0%	0.9%	6.4%	0.0%	16.4%	2.7%	2.2%	0.0%
Connecticut										
Bridgeport city	43,968	50.8%	29.6%	15.0%	2.9%	1.6%	34.6%	9.0%	3.5%	2.1%
Hartford city	44,108	52.0%	36.8%	6.2%	1.7%	3.4%	38.7%	4.6%	3.1%	1.6%
New Haven city	52,463	60.7%	30.6%	3.0%	4.8%	0.9%	25.4%	8.8%	2.8%	2.3%
Stamford city	38,194	55.0%	25.2%	12.2%	7.3%	0.3%	29.7%	9.7%	4.8%	0.8%
Waterbury city	28,106	56.1%	34.5%	9.0%	0.1%	0.3%	35.4%	3.0%	4.2%	1.3%
District of Columbia										
Washington city	236,132	83.0%	7.4%	4.8%	2.5%	2.4%	13.2%	2.4%	0.9%	0.5%
Florida										
Boca Raton city	21,653	73.3%	14.5%	9.3%	2.2%	0.7%	20.5%	3.5%	2.2%	0.5%
Cape Coral city	37,325	73.8%	24.5%	1.7%	0.0%	0.0%	19.6%	3.6%	3.0%	0.0%
Clearwater city	25,001	73.1%	21.0%	5.6%	0.3%	0.0%	19.3%	3.9%	3.0%	0.6%
Coral Springs city	32,839	61.3%	24.4%	11.5%	1.1%	1.7%	25.3%	7.7%	5.3%	0.4%
Fort Lauderdale city	40,875	63.2%	23.0%	12.1%	0.6%	1.0%	17.7%	7.2%	7.7%	4.2%
Gainesville city	66,238	82.0%	7.8%	4.9%	4.9%	0.4%	14.3%	2.3%	0.9%	0.6%
Hialeah city	54,580	7.5%	91.8%	0.6%	0.1%	0.0%	63.5%	9.7%	9.0%	10.3%
Hollywood city	32,699	51.5%	35.4%	7.4%	2.3%	3.4%	38.3%	5.4%	2.8%	2.0%
Jacksonville city	236,574	86.2%	6.1%	4.2%	2.7%	0.8%	10.4%	1.4%	1.7%	0.3%
Lakeland city	27,759	83.9%	12.3%	1.2%	2.1%	0.5%	10.7%	2.9%	2.3%	0.3%
Miami city	110,351	27.5%	64.9%	7.1%	0.4%	0.1%	48.1%	10.6%	6.4%	7.4%
Miami Beach city	21,815	35.0%	42.7%	19.0%	1.0%	2.3%	49.0%	11.4%	1.8%	2.8%
Miami Gardens city	30,931	50.1%	29.0%	20.8%	0.2%	0.0%	44.4%	3.9%	1.7%	0.0%
Miramar city	34,640	53.9%	33.3%	8.8%	3.4%	0.6%	38.3%	3.6%	2.2%	2.1%
Orlando city	91,969	63.0%	27.9%	6.6%	1.3%	1.2%	27.3%	5.7%	2.6%	1.3%
Palm Bay city	23,931	86.0%	12.4%	0.0%	0.0%	1.7%	12.8%	0.0%	1.3%	0.0%
Pembroke Pines city	41,693	52.5%	37.0%	5.6%	4.1%	0.8%	36.0%	5.7%	4.4%	1.5%
Plantation city	21,871	56.1%	23.4%	15.2%	2.2%	3.1%	27.1%	14.3%	0.9%	1.6%

Table G-3: Places—Language Spoken and English Ability—Continued

	Millennial Population 15 to 33	Percent by Language Spoken at Home					Percent by Ability to Speak English			
		English Only	Spanish	Other Indo-European Language	Asian and Pacific Island Language	Other Language	Speak English "Very Well"	Speak English "Well"	Speak English "Not Well"	Speak English "Not at All"
Florida—Cont.										
Pompano Beach city	24,729	61.0%	23.1%	14.1%	1.6%	0.2%	30.5%	2.9%	2.8%	2.9%
Port St. Lucie city	39,093	74.5%	13.7%	9.4%	2.4%	0.0%	18.1%	6.2%	0.6%	0.7%
St. Petersburg city	62,378	86.9%	4.2%	5.1%	3.2%	0.6%	9.3%	1.8%	2.1%	0.0%
Sunrise city	25,017	54.0%	27.2%	13.3%	1.9%	3.6%	30.8%	13.0%	0.8%	1.4%
Tallahassee city	90,224	89.7%	4.3%	3.1%	1.6%	1.3%	8.8%	1.5%	0.0%	0.0%
Tampa city	109,385	72.6%	20.8%	3.7%	1.7%	1.1%	21.0%	3.8%	1.4%	1.2%
West Palm Beach city	27,920	63.0%	23.9%	9.9%	2.6%	0.7%	23.3%	5.4%	6.7%	1.5%
Georgia										
Athens-Clarke County unified govt (balance)	54,663	85.0%	7.6%	3.8%	2.7%	0.9%	8.5%	4.4%	2.0%	0.1%
Atlanta city	160,144	88.8%	4.0%	2.9%	3.4%	0.9%	7.0%	2.9%	0.9%	0.4%
Augusta-Richmond County consolidated govt (balance)	59,362	93.5%	3.1%	1.7%	1.4%	0.2%	6.2%	0.3%	0.0%	0.0%
Columbus city	61,108	88.3%	6.4%	1.8%	3.4%	0.1%	8.7%	1.5%	1.2%	0.3%
Macon-Bibb county	40,814	92.8%	3.8%	2.4%	0.8%	0.1%	5.2%	0.8%	0.4%	0.8%
Roswell city	20,927	74.9%	13.7%	4.1%	3.4%	4.0%	13.7%	6.7%	4.7%	0.0%
Sandy Springs city	30,066	64.1%	12.1%	18.0%	3.1%	2.7%	24.1%	10.6%	1.3%	0.0%
Savannah city	55,172	86.5%	6.3%	5.3%	1.7%	0.1%	10.0%	2.4%	1.1%	0.0%
Hawaii										
Urban Honolulu CDP	84,598	63.9%	1.6%	2.1%	27.5%	4.9%	18.8%	13.2%	4.1%	0.0%
Idaho										
Boise City city	62,159	86.2%	8.9%	1.5%	0.7%	2.7%	8.5%	2.5%	2.7%	0.0%
Meridian city	17,705	88.0%	4.1%	3.7%	0.0%	4.2%	3.4%	6.1%	2.5%	0.0%
Illinois										
Aurora city	55,022	51.0%	41.7%	4.3%	0.3%	2.7%	33.7%	6.7%	6.8%	1.8%
Chicago city	861,024	64.3%	23.5%	6.4%	4.2%	1.6%	27.1%	5.1%	2.6%	0.9%
Elgin city	26,488	53.3%	39.5%	3.8%	1.8%	1.6%	31.0%	9.4%	5.6%	0.8%
Joliet city	39,858	72.8%	25.6%	1.3%	0.0%	0.2%	17.2%	5.3%	3.5%	1.2%
Naperville city	33,918	78.9%	8.6%	7.9%	3.0%	1.5%	17.5%	2.9%	0.0%	0.8%
Peoria city	34,871	85.2%	5.3%	4.3%	4.5%	0.7%	8.6%	1.1%	5.0%	0.0%
Rockford city	40,012	77.6%	17.7%	1.0%	2.3%	1.5%	15.5%	4.5%	2.4%	0.0%
Springfield city	31,951	93.5%	2.4%	2.4%	1.5%	0.2%	6.2%	0.3%	0.0%	0.0%
Indiana										
Evansville city	32,735	95.5%	2.5%	0.5%	1.3%	0.3%	3.6%	0.5%	0.3%	0.1%
Fort Wayne city	70,772	86.1%	6.7%	2.2%	4.4%	0.5%	8.5%	2.4%	2.0%	1.0%
Indianapolis city (balance)	244,048	85.6%	9.5%	2.3%	1.6%	1.0%	7.7%	2.6%	3.2%	0.8%
South Bend city	29,483	82.4%	11.8%	2.9%	2.1%	0.8%	13.9%	1.6%	1.5%	0.5%
Iowa										
Cedar Rapids city	35,359	88.2%	3.3%	0.7%	7.4%	0.4%	7.2%	4.3%	0.3%	0.0%
Davenport city	27,789	94.0%	3.5%	0.6%	1.6%	0.4%	4.4%	1.2%	0.4%	0.0%
Des Moines city	62,827	80.5%	8.3%	2.0%	2.8%	6.5%	12.1%	2.9%	3.8%	0.8%
Kansas										
Kansas City city	40,363	66.3%	25.1%	2.1%	4.0%	2.6%	18.8%	5.7%	6.0%	3.2%
Olathe city	33,638	85.1%	8.9%	2.7%	2.2%	1.1%	9.9%	2.0%	2.2%	0.7%
Overland Park city	45,901	85.7%	3.6%	5.1%	5.6%	0.0%	11.7%	2.2%	0.4%	0.0%
Topeka city	33,790	88.1%	10.0%	0.0%	0.6%	1.3%	9.9%	1.9%	0.0%	0.0%
Wichita city	105,291	84.7%	10.2%	1.1%	2.4%	1.7%	12.2%	2.7%	0.2%	0.3%
Kentucky										
Lexington-Fayette urban county	99,204	86.9%	6.8%	2.1%	2.1%	2.1%	7.6%	3.4%	1.9%	0.2%
Louisville/Jefferson County metro govt (balance)	158,771	88.4%	5.1%	3.0%	0.9%	2.6%	7.5%	2.5%	1.3%	0.3%
Louisiana										
Baton Rouge city	81,142	88.9%	4.8%	3.2%	2.6%	0.4%	6.4%	2.0%	1.5%	1.2%
Lafayette city	44,471	88.4%	6.7%	2.1%	2.3%	0.5%	7.5%	2.4%	1.7%	0.0%
New Orleans city	116,032	90.4%	4.4%	1.9%	3.3%	0.0%	6.1%	1.5%	1.2%	0.8%
Shreveport city	54,837	96.0%	2.2%	0.2%	1.6%	0.0%	2.4%	0.0%	0.7%	0.9%
Maryland										
Baltimore city	191,864	88.4%	4.6%	3.6%	2.1%	1.3%	8.0%	2.1%	1.0%	0.5%
Massachusetts										
Boston city	266,782	64.4%	14.6%	11.5%	6.9%	2.6%	26.5%	5.9%	2.5%	0.7%
Brockton city	27,045	51.2%	11.8%	35.4%	1.6%	0.0%	36.4%	7.7%	4.7%	0.0%
Cambridge city	51,938	63.7%	8.7%	13.8%	10.3%	3.5%	34.0%	2.1%	0.3%	0.0%
Lowell city	35,014	51.3%	14.7%	7.8%	20.6%	5.6%	35.1%	7.8%	4.6%	1.2%
Lynn city	25,352	43.6%	36.5%	11.1%	8.1%	0.7%	37.1%	6.7%	9.5%	3.1%
New Bedford city	25,304	66.1%	18.9%	11.2%	3.8%	0.0%	24.8%	4.4%	4.7%	0.0%
Quincy city	24,780	59.2%	1.8%	11.9%	26.0%	1.1%	26.3%	9.4%	4.4%	0.6%
Springfield city	46,972	58.5%	36.0%	2.3%	3.2%	0.1%	31.4%	4.0%	4.4%	1.7%
Worcester city	62,036	71.5%	13.1%	6.1%	7.4%	1.8%	17.8%	8.5%	1.7%	0.5%
Michigan										
Ann Arbor city	57,080	80.6%	2.4%	5.1%	10.5%	1.4%	15.5%	3.4%	0.5%	0.0%
Dearborn city	25,414	56.2%	0.6%	4.1%	1.4%	37.7%	38.9%	2.7%	1.4%	0.7%

Table G-3: Places—Language Spoken and English Ability—*Continued*

	Millennial Population 15 to 33	Percent by Language Spoken at Home					Percent by Ability to Speak English			
		English Only	Spanish	Other Indo-European Language	Asian and Pacific Island Language	Other Language	Speak English "Very Well"	Speak English "Well"	Speak English "Not Well"	Speak English "Not at All"
Michigan—Cont.										
Detroit city	189,160	86.3%	8.3%	3.3%	0.0%	2.1%	9.8%	2.3%	1.1%	0.6%
Flint city	25,633	93.5%	2.5%	1.7%	0.0%	2.4%	6.5%	0.0%	0.0%	0.0%
Grand Rapids city	64,132	85.1%	9.7%	0.9%	2.9%	1.3%	10.5%	1.8%	1.0%	1.6%
Lansing city	38,419	93.3%	3.0%	0.6%	3.1%	0.0%	5.6%	1.1%	0.0%	0.0%
Livonia city	20,481	95.8%	1.7%	2.1%	0.4%	0.0%	3.1%	0.6%	0.5%	0.0%
Sterling Heights city	32,628	65.4%	0.0%	9.1%	4.7%	20.8%	24.0%	6.0%	3.4%	1.3%
Warren city	31,442	87.2%	1.1%	8.9%	0.9%	1.9%	9.1%	2.9%	0.8%	0.0%
Minnesota										
Minneapolis city	147,877	75.2%	7.8%	4.7%	5.8%	6.5%	15.6%	5.4%	3.1%	0.8%
Rochester city	30,983	90.7%	3.3%	2.6%	1.2%	2.3%	5.5%	0.9%	2.9%	0.0%
St. Paul city	99,544	67.0%	6.9%	1.5%	16.4%	8.2%	20.4%	7.6%	3.9%	1.1%
Mississippi										
Jackson city	52,989	96.1%	1.9%	0.9%	0.4%	0.7%	2.0%	0.3%	0.4%	1.2%
Missouri										
Columbia city	55,488	93.6%	1.8%	0.9%	2.7%	1.0%	3.5%	2.4%	0.4%	0.0%
Independence city	28,662	90.3%	6.4%	1.0%	2.3%	0.0%	6.7%	1.6%	0.6%	0.8%
Kansas City city	128,225	88.6%	8.2%	1.2%	1.3%	0.7%	7.9%	1.8%	0.9%	0.8%
Lee's Summit city	22,012	90.5%	6.5%	1.2%	1.4%	0.5%	7.5%	0.7%	1.3%	0.0%
St. Louis city	98,295	87.8%	4.2%	2.0%	2.8%	3.2%	9.0%	2.6%	0.4%	0.1%
Springfield city	60,490	92.6%	3.1%	1.0%	2.8%	0.4%	5.0%	1.8%	0.6%	0.0%
Montana										
Billings city	30,086	97.2%	0.8%	0.1%	1.4%	0.4%	1.4%	1.4%	0.0%	0.0%
Nebraska										
Lincoln city	90,424	83.2%	7.1%	2.7%	4.1%	2.9%	9.2%	5.8%	1.7%	0.1%
Omaha city	129,660	79.3%	13.1%	3.1%	2.9%	1.7%	13.5%	3.4%	2.6%	1.2%
Nevada										
Henderson city	61,057	77.6%	12.3%	2.4%	7.0%	0.7%	17.8%	3.0%	1.5%	0.2%
Las Vegas city	158,295	60.5%	33.0%	1.6%	4.5%	0.4%	29.6%	4.4%	3.3%	2.2%
North Las Vegas city	67,041	57.2%	41.3%	0.2%	1.3%	0.0%	35.7%	3.0%	2.4%	1.6%
Reno city	68,801	73.7%	20.7%	2.5%	3.0%	0.1%	19.8%	3.5%	2.3%	0.8%
Sparks city	24,437	65.0%	31.6%	0.6%	1.5%	1.2%	26.7%	4.7%	2.7%	0.8%
New Hampshire										
Manchester city	30,293	80.5%	9.7%	4.4%	1.4%	4.0%	13.9%	2.9%	1.9%	0.8%
New Jersey										
Elizabeth city	34,801	23.4%	64.1%	10.8%	0.5%	1.2%	43.6%	6.8%	14.4%	11.9%
Jersey City city	82,952	42.3%	22.9%	14.1%	14.4%	6.3%	42.9%	10.8%	2.9%	1.1%
Newark city	79,653	56.0%	28.5%	11.2%	0.3%	3.9%	31.0%	5.7%	5.2%	2.2%
Paterson city	41,192	38.6%	48.9%	8.8%	1.0%	2.7%	43.9%	8.2%	6.6%	2.6%
New Mexico										
Albuquerque city	151,120	71.2%	21.8%	2.4%	1.9%	2.6%	21.2%	3.9%	3.2%	0.5%
Las Cruces city	30,485	64.0%	33.0%	0.0%	1.7%	1.4%	34.1%	1.3%	0.7%	0.0%
Rio Rancho city	23,555	76.2%	15.5%	0.0%	0.0%	8.4%	23.4%	0.1%	0.0%	0.3%
New York										
Albany city	37,519	83.3%	3.7%	4.4%	7.8%	0.8%	11.1%	2.1%	3.5%	0.0%
Buffalo city	81,428	80.5%	8.8%	5.0%	2.9%	2.7%	13.5%	2.6%	2.7%	0.5%
New York city	2,469,069	52.3%	25.4%	11.5%	7.9%	2.9%	33.4%	7.9%	5.0%	1.4%
Rochester city	71,818	79.0%	12.0%	2.9%	4.1%	2.1%	11.3%	6.6%	2.8%	0.4%
Syracuse city	53,473	79.0%	7.0%	3.9%	5.3%	4.8%	17.0%	2.2%	1.6%	0.3%
Yonkers city	50,984	51.3%	37.4%	8.4%	1.2%	1.6%	37.5%	7.9%	2.8%	0.6%
North Carolina										
Charlotte city	239,744	78.8%	13.1%	3.7%	3.4%	1.0%	12.6%	3.8%	3.4%	1.4%
Durham city	81,450	73.4%	14.6%	5.1%	4.0%	2.9%	18.2%	2.8%	1.3%	4.3%
Fayetteville city	69,316	88.0%	9.1%	1.0%	0.8%	1.1%	7.7%	2.4%	1.5%	0.3%
Greensboro city	83,708	85.6%	9.4%	1.6%	2.5%	0.9%	9.7%	1.9%	2.3%	0.6%
High Point city	29,830	82.2%	9.6%	5.0%	2.7%	0.5%	10.8%	3.5%	2.8%	0.8%
Raleigh city	149,042	82.8%	9.7%	4.2%	2.6%	0.6%	11.8%	2.9%	2.2%	0.3%
Wilmington city	37,892	92.5%	4.9%	1.0%	0.7%	0.9%	5.5%	0.6%	1.4%	0.0%
Winston-Salem city	69,003	81.1%	14.0%	2.6%	1.9%	0.3%	13.0%	2.1%	2.9%	0.9%
North Dakota										
Fargo city	44,861	93.5%	0.3%	3.5%	2.3%	0.5%	6.2%	0.1%	0.2%	0.0%
Ohio										
Akron city	54,257	93.8%	0.4%	2.1%	2.8%	0.9%	4.4%	0.9%	0.9%	0.0%
Cincinnati city	102,382	91.4%	2.8%	2.4%	2.1%	1.3%	5.9%	1.8%	0.8%	0.1%
Cleveland city	110,836	83.1%	9.0%	2.3%	3.2%	2.4%	11.3%	3.0%	2.2%	0.4%
Columbus city	281,922	84.9%	4.6%	3.5%	3.5%	3.5%	9.5%	3.0%	1.8%	0.5%
Dayton city	45,452	91.2%	2.6%	0.8%	5.1%	0.3%	7.0%	1.0%	0.6%	0.2%
Toledo city	80,265	90.3%	3.4%	2.3%	2.0%	1.9%	6.3%	2.6%	0.8%	0.0%
Oklahoma										
Broken Arrow city	25,634	80.4%	14.2%	2.1%	3.3%	0.0%	13.6%	2.8%	2.7%	0.5%

Table G-3: Places—Language Spoken and English Ability—*Continued*

	Millennial Population 15 to 33	Percent by Language Spoken at Home					Percent by Ability to Speak English			
		English Only	Spanish	Other Indo-European Language	Asian and Pacific Island Language	Other Language	Speak English "Very Well"	Speak English "Well"	Speak English "Not Well"	Speak English "Not at All"
Oklahoma—Cont.										
Edmond city	27,188	89.7%	4.7%	2.5%	1.9%	1.2%	5.5%	3.6%	1.2%	0.0%
Lawton city	30,368	89.7%	7.4%	0.0%	2.9%	0.0%	7.8%	2.5%	0.0%	0.0%
Norman city	46,393	86.3%	3.5%	2.2%	6.2%	1.8%	11.2%	2.4%	0.0%	0.0%
Oklahoma City city	171,575	77.7%	17.8%	1.0%	3.2%	0.3%	13.9%	4.4%	2.6%	1.4%
Tulsa city	112,612	82.5%	11.2%	2.2%	3.1%	1.0%	10.6%	3.2%	2.6%	1.1%
Oregon										
Beaverton city	28,218	71.0%	16.4%	6.4%	5.3%	0.9%	16.1%	6.6%	4.1%	2.1%
Eugene city	57,375	89.5%	5.8%	1.3%	3.4%	0.0%	6.9%	2.0%	1.2%	0.4%
Gresham city	27,972	65.2%	25.6%	6.4%	1.6%	1.3%	23.2%	6.6%	3.1%	1.9%
Hillsboro city	27,426	67.0%	17.0%	7.9%	8.0%	0.2%	20.8%	8.3%	1.3%	2.6%
Portland city	180,671	79.3%	7.7%	4.3%	7.0%	1.7%	14.6%	3.5%	1.9%	0.6%
Salem city	46,098	68.9%	26.6%	0.9%	2.3%	1.3%	22.3%	4.1%	2.3%	2.3%
Pennsylvania										
Allentown city	34,851	46.7%	50.7%	1.3%	0.3%	1.1%	33.9%	14.8%	2.5%	2.1%
Erie city	28,758	88.6%	3.0%	3.7%	2.1%	2.7%	5.8%	3.8%	0.3%	1.6%
Philadelphia city	485,771	77.6%	9.7%	4.6%	6.4%	1.7%	15.2%	3.7%	3.2%	0.3%
Pittsburgh city	118,026	85.6%	2.7%	5.4%	5.3%	1.0%	10.0%	3.5%	0.8%	0.0%
Rhode Island										
Providence city	66,314	50.0%	34.9%	5.0%	8.3%	1.8%	34.6%	8.9%	4.5%	2.0%
South Carolina										
Charleston city	45,908	96.5%	1.6%	1.5%	0.2%	0.3%	2.3%	0.2%	1.0%	0.0%
Columbia city	60,087	90.1%	4.9%	1.3%	1.5%	2.2%	3.5%	4.6%	1.6%	0.2%
North Charleston city	36,486	89.7%	7.9%	0.7%	1.6%	0.1%	5.6%	1.0%	3.5%	0.2%
South Dakota										
Sioux Falls city	48,646	83.5%	5.1%	7.3%	1.1%	3.2%	8.5%	2.9%	3.8%	1.4%
Tennessee										
Chattanooga city	50,693	91.7%	4.3%	0.9%	3.1%	0.0%	3.6%	2.3%	2.0%	0.3%
Clarksville city	53,597	89.0%	7.2%	1.6%	1.7%	0.5%	8.9%	1.1%	1.1%	0.0%
Knoxville city	65,226	92.8%	5.1%	0.6%	0.9%	0.7%	3.5%	1.2%	1.9%	0.6%
Memphis city	187,750	89.7%	6.9%	1.3%	1.2%	0.8%	7.5%	1.5%	0.9%	0.5%
Murfreesboro city	45,897	91.8%	4.7%	1.0%	1.9%	0.6%	4.7%	2.4%	1.2%	0.0%
Nashville-Davidson metropolitan govt (balance)	204,893	81.4%	9.3%	3.6%	1.9%	3.8%	10.7%	3.2%	3.4%	1.2%
Texas										
Abilene city	43,601	82.5%	13.0%	2.9%	1.3%	0.3%	14.8%	2.0%	0.6%	0.0%
Allen city	22,320	76.1%	11.5%	5.3%	3.7%	3.5%	17.8%	0.2%	4.6%	1.4%
Amarillo city	53,022	73.5%	21.6%	1.1%	2.0%	1.8%	20.4%	2.8%	1.9%	1.4%
Arlington city	117,582	66.1%	24.4%	2.7%	4.3%	2.5%	23.4%	4.9%	4.7%	0.8%
Austin city	318,545	66.0%	25.5%	3.0%	4.4%	1.1%	23.4%	3.8%	3.9%	3.0%
Beaumont city	34,816	73.2%	21.4%	1.4%	3.7%	0.3%	21.6%	1.3%	3.9%	0.0%
Brownsville city	53,320	14.2%	85.7%	0.0%	0.1%	0.0%	70.8%	7.7%	3.6%	3.7%
Carrollton city	34,297	60.7%	22.6%	5.6%	9.8%	1.4%	29.1%	6.9%	2.5%	0.7%
College Station city	59,465	76.7%	14.5%	2.7%	4.7%	1.3%	14.4%	5.1%	2.1%	1.7%
Corpus Christi city	91,539	69.5%	28.1%	0.1%	2.0%	0.4%	27.1%	2.6%	0.8%	0.1%
Dallas city	383,991	52.2%	40.4%	2.2%	3.2%	1.9%	27.4%	9.5%	7.5%	3.3%
Denton city	53,139	80.6%	12.1%	2.3%	2.7%	2.4%	15.1%	2.6%	1.0%	0.7%
El Paso city	191,550	32.0%	65.1%	1.6%	0.5%	0.8%	52.9%	10.3%	3.2%	1.6%
Fort Worth city	234,187	66.6%	28.1%	1.9%	2.5%	1.0%	23.8%	5.0%	2.9%	1.7%
Frisco city	29,311	72.3%	16.9%	3.7%	4.2%	2.9%	22.9%	1.9%	2.3%	0.6%
Garland city	62,780	53.3%	33.7%	2.2%	8.6%	2.3%	34.8%	5.6%	4.7%	1.7%
Grand Prairie city	53,813	45.7%	44.7%	1.5%	4.6%	3.5%	26.9%	15.5%	9.2%	2.7%
Houston city	694,760	47.9%	41.1%	4.4%	4.4%	2.1%	33.2%	8.4%	5.4%	5.1%
Irving city	71,697	39.3%	41.8%	10.7%	5.9%	2.2%	42.1%	8.6%	8.2%	1.8%
Killeen city	47,750	73.2%	17.1%	5.0%	2.1%	2.6%	21.8%	3.1%	1.9%	0.0%
Laredo city	73,722	11.1%	88.8%	0.0%	0.0%	0.0%	65.0%	11.1%	5.3%	7.5%
Lewisville city	33,171	64.1%	24.1%	3.5%	8.3%	0.0%	24.4%	7.9%	1.6%	2.0%
Lubbock city	90,665	74.9%	19.4%	3.4%	1.4%	0.7%	22.0%	2.5%	0.5%	0.1%
McAllen city	39,474	25.4%	71.4%	0.7%	2.4%	0.0%	59.2%	8.9%	4.7%	1.7%
McKinney city	38,625	74.4%	21.2%	2.1%	2.1%	0.1%	19.3%	1.4%	2.1%	2.7%
Mesquite city	38,987	53.6%	40.8%	1.7%	1.8%	2.1%	32.0%	5.9%	6.5%	2.0%
Midland city	40,199	66.3%	30.8%	0.0%	1.9%	0.9%	24.4%	4.3%	4.8%	0.1%
Odessa city	36,951	46.7%	50.7%	0.5%	0.4%	1.6%	44.1%	3.8%	3.1%	2.2%
Pasadena city	41,599	61.6%	36.9%	0.2%	1.3%	0.0%	25.2%	1.7%	6.0%	5.5%
Pearland city	28,993	74.5%	11.8%	2.8%	7.7%	3.3%	23.3%	0.4%	0.0%	1.9%
Plano city	70,607	66.5%	10.5%	12.1%	9.5%	1.4%	19.0%	10.0%	3.5%	1.1%
Richardson city	31,827	51.8%	23.5%	7.0%	10.6%	7.1%	33.0%	6.1%	7.2%	1.9%
Round Rock City	31,178	78.1%	16.0%	1.2%	3.3%	1.4%	17.3%	2.0%	2.1%	0.5%
San Angelo city	32,118	73.0%	23.6%	1.2%	1.6%	0.7%	19.4%	4.7%	2.2%	0.7%
San Antonio city	435,615	61.7%	34.3%	1.5%	1.9%	0.6%	30.4%	4.2%	2.3%	1.5%
Tyler city	31,668	80.8%	17.2%	0.8%	1.2%	0.0%	11.5%	3.7%	2.2%	1.8%
Waco city	45,423	72.2%	23.0%	2.3%	1.8%	0.6%	10.8%	12.7%	2.8%	1.5%
Wichita Falls city	33,545	83.2%	13.6%	1.4%	1.0%	0.8%	8.9%	7.2%	0.5%	0.2%

Table G-3: Places—Language Spoken and English Ability—*Continued*

	Millennial Population 15 to 33	Percent by Language Spoken at Home					Percent by Ability to Speak English			
		English Only	Spanish	Other Indo-European Language	Asian and Pacific Island Language	Other Language	Speak English "Very Well"	Speak English "Well"	Speak English "Not Well"	Speak English "Not at All"
Utah										
Orem city	34,882	80.7%	11.1%	0.9%	5.6%	1.7%	13.0%	3.6%	2.6%	0.0%
Provo city	63,221	83.9%	10.9%	2.9%	2.1%	0.3%	14.3%	1.5%	0.3%	0.0%
Salt Lake City city	70,936	76.5%	14.2%	3.2%	5.0%	1.1%	19.0%	1.5%	2.6%	0.3%
Sandy city	23,301	84.9%	9.5%	1.8%	3.9%	0.0%	12.9%	1.3%	1.0%	0.0%
West Jordan city	32,488	86.9%	7.4%	1.5%	3.0%	1.2%	9.5%	3.1%	0.0%	0.5%
West Valley City city	41,728	67.6%	25.5%	1.2%	5.2%	0.5%	22.5%	3.2%	5.1%	1.6%
Virginia										
Alexandria city	43,452	60.3%	17.0%	7.3%	3.3%	12.1%	29.0%	5.1%	3.9%	1.7%
Chesapeake city	63,149	90.5%	7.7%	0.2%	1.4%	0.1%	7.3%	0.1%	1.8%	0.3%
Hampton city	40,233	92.4%	3.7%	0.5%	1.6%	1.8%	6.3%	0.3%	1.1%	0.0%
Newport News city	58,525	87.2%	6.1%	4.4%	1.8%	0.5%	9.0%	3.1%	0.6%	0.1%
Norfolk city	95,849	88.0%	6.6%	3.2%	1.7%	0.5%	8.8%	1.7%	1.5%	0.0%
Portsmouth city	29,069	94.5%	2.4%	2.0%	0.8%	0.3%	5.5%	0.0%	0.0%	0.0%
Richmond city	76,850	87.2%	6.6%	2.5%	2.3%	1.5%	8.0%	2.7%	1.1%	1.1%
Roanoke city	26,140	90.0%	2.1%	6.8%	0.3%	0.8%	6.2%	3.8%	0.0%	0.0%
Virginia Beach city	132,947	88.1%	4.3%	3.1%	4.3%	0.2%	9.8%	1.6%	0.6%	0.0%
Washington										
Bellevue city	37,913	51.9%	5.8%	18.9%	23.1%	0.2%	34.8%	8.9%	3.4%	0.9%
Everett city	30,503	76.5%	8.8%	9.9%	4.6%	0.2%	15.8%	2.8%	2.7%	2.2%
Federal Way city	26,673	66.6%	18.4%	4.4%	10.0%	0.6%	21.2%	5.8%	6.1%	0.3%
Kent city	40,119	56.9%	20.4%	6.1%	11.0%	5.6%	21.7%	10.8%	7.9%	2.7%
Renton city	24,731	61.1%	12.7%	7.5%	16.0%	2.7%	25.9%	5.0%	7.4%	0.6%
Seattle city	236,331	78.7%	4.4%	4.1%	9.9%	2.8%	14.9%	4.2%	1.8%	0.4%
Spokane city	61,887	90.2%	3.2%	3.2%	1.9%	1.5%	7.2%	2.0%	0.6%	0.0%
Spokane Valley city	24,796	89.2%	0.7%	8.9%	1.1%	0.0%	9.9%	0.8%	0.0%	0.0%
Tacoma city	58,809	81.4%	11.3%	4.3%	2.3%	0.6%	12.8%	2.1%	3.1%	0.6%
Vancouver city	44,929	76.1%	14.1%	6.8%	2.1%	0.8%	14.2%	5.5%	3.7%	0.5%
Yakima city	25,386	56.2%	43.4%	0.0%	0.0%	0.4%	31.6%	3.4%	5.9%	2.8%
Wisconsin										
Green Bay city	30,607	74.9%	18.2%	0.0%	6.5%	0.4%	17.7%	3.8%	3.6%	0.0%
Kenosha city	25,028	87.2%	10.2%	0.0%	2.6%	0.0%	9.1%	3.7%	0.0%	0.0%
Madison city	101,061	83.0%	3.3%	6.6%	6.8%	0.3%	12.2%	4.1%	0.7%	0.0%
Milwaukee city	186,306	81.3%	13.6%	1.4%	2.7%	1.0%	13.0%	3.3%	2.1%	0.3%

Table G-4: Metropolitan/Micropolitan Statistical Areas—Language Spoken and English Ability

	Millennial Population 15 to 33	Percent by Language Spoken at Home					Percent by Ability to Speak English			
		English Only	Spanish	Other Indo-European Language	Asian and Pacific Island Language	Other Language	Speak English "Very Well"	Speak English "Well"	Speak English "Not Well"	Speak English "Not at All"
Abilene, TX	50,234	82.9%	13.1%	2.5%	1.1%	0.3%	14.6%	1.8%	0.5%	0.2%
Adrian, MI	22,899	96.1%	1.7%	0.7%	0.0%	1.4%	2.5%	0.3%	0.7%	0.4%
Akron, OH	178,555	92.2%	1.8%	2.9%	2.2%	0.9%	5.4%	1.2%	1.2%	0.0%
Albany, GA	39,484	96.0%	1.6%	1.8%	0.0%	0.7%	2.0%	2.0%	0.0%	0.0%
Albany, OR	28,485	84.4%	8.9%	0.8%	4.6%	1.3%	9.7%	2.6%	0.5%	2.8%
Albany-Schenectady-Troy, NY	232,952	88.7%	3.2%	3.8%	3.6%	0.7%	8.2%	1.9%	1.1%	0.1%
Albertville, AL	21,899	93.0%	4.7%	1.4%	0.9%	0.0%	3.2%	1.6%	1.8%	0.4%
Albuquerque, NM	233,207	70.6%	22.6%	1.8%	1.4%	3.7%	21.9%	3.9%	2.4%	1.2%
Alexandria, LA	38,875	94.5%	2.0%	1.9%	1.1%	0.5%	4.9%	0.0%	0.5%	0.0%
Allentown-Bethlehem-Easton, PA-NJ	194,803	79.8%	14.5%	2.6%	2.3%	0.7%	13.9%	4.5%	1.2%	0.5%
Altoona, PA	29,180	96.7%	0.4%	1.8%	0.4%	0.8%	3.1%	0.2%	0.0%	0.0%
Amarillo, TX	71,925	73.6%	22.0%	1.5%	1.6%	1.3%	19.4%	3.8%	2.0%	1.2%
Ames, IA	45,468	89.3%	0.7%	0.4%	9.0%	0.6%	4.3%	6.3%	0.2%	0.0%
Anchorage, AK	123,015	82.5%	6.0%	2.3%	5.7%	3.7%	12.4%	4.8%	0.3%	0.0%
Ann Arbor, MI	123,278	85.6%	2.4%	4.2%	5.7%	2.1%	11.7%	2.5%	0.3%	0.0%
Anniston-Oxford-Jacksonville, AL	30,590	96.6%	2.1%	1.0%	0.0%	0.4%	3.4%	0.0%	0.0%	0.0%
Appleton, WI	58,416	89.8%	4.0%	2.2%	3.6%	0.4%	6.6%	1.9%	1.6%	0.0%
Asheville, NC	92,784	86.4%	9.0%	3.3%	1.3%	0.0%	8.1%	2.3%	1.0%	2.3%
Ashtabula, OH	22,614	89.1%	3.7%	5.9%	1.3%	0.0%	8.6%	1.5%	0.8%	0.0%
Athens-Clarke County, GA	72,553	87.9%	6.7%	2.9%	1.8%	0.7%	7.5%	2.8%	1.7%	0.1%
Atlanta-Sandy Springs-Roswell, GA	1,464,745	80.2%	10.9%	4.0%	3.2%	1.6%	13.1%	3.2%	2.7%	0.8%
Atlantic City-Hammonton, NJ	66,498	68.8%	21.4%	6.9%	2.7%	0.2%	22.5%	6.9%	1.4%	0.5%
Auburn-Opelika, AL	54,789	96.6%	1.4%	1.0%	0.9%	0.1%	1.9%	0.5%	1.0%	0.0%
Augusta-Richmond County, GA-SC	159,165	91.8%	5.4%	1.0%	1.1%	0.8%	5.7%	0.7%	1.9%	0.0%
Augusta-Waterville, ME	25,926	94.3%	1.8%	0.3%	2.2%	1.4%	4.9%	0.0%	0.8%	0.0%
Austin-Round Rock, TX	586,533	70.8%	22.7%	2.5%	3.0%	1.0%	20.9%	3.1%	3.2%	2.0%
Bakersfield, CA	255,273	50.4%	44.9%	1.9%	2.0%	0.7%	36.4%	6.3%	4.4%	2.4%
Baltimore-Columbia-Towson, MD	713,900	86.2%	5.5%	4.5%	2.3%	1.5%	9.9%	2.1%	1.6%	0.2%
Bangor, ME	40,856	95.8%	1.0%	2.5%	0.3%	0.4%	3.5%	0.7%	0.0%	0.0%
Barnstable Town, MA	37,022	85.5%	4.9%	7.0%	0.3%	2.2%	13.0%	1.3%	0.2%	0.0%
Baton Rouge, LA	239,352	92.7%	3.7%	1.3%	2.1%	0.2%	4.0%	1.7%	0.9%	0.7%
Battle Creek, MI	31,922	94.3%	2.0%	1.5%	2.3%	0.0%	3.4%	1.9%	0.3%	0.1%
Bay City, MI	24,229	98.6%	0.5%	0.9%	0.0%	0.0%	1.4%	0.0%	0.0%	0.0%
Beaumont-Port Arthur, TX	107,613	78.8%	17.3%	1.1%	2.6%	0.3%	15.0%	2.4%	3.1%	0.7%
Beckley, WV	26,400	91.5%	6.3%	1.5%	0.6%	0.0%	5.4%	2.4%	0.7%	0.0%
Bellingham, WA	64,215	87.7%	7.3%	3.1%	1.8%	0.1%	7.9%	3.3%	0.3%	0.8%
Bend-Redmond, OR	37,506	94.1%	4.8%	0.0%	0.5%	0.6%	3.4%	1.6%	0.4%	0.4%
Billings, MT	40,628	95.1%	1.3%	0.1%	1.1%	2.5%	3.4%	1.5%	0.0%	0.0%
Binghamton, NY	66,508	89.0%	2.2%	2.8%	5.3%	0.8%	8.7%	1.3%	0.7%	0.3%
Birmingham-Hoover, AL	285,663	93.1%	4.3%	0.7%	0.8%	1.0%	4.2%	1.1%	1.2%	0.4%
Bismarck, ND	34,187	95.3%	0.3%	4.2%	0.0%	0.2%	4.7%	0.0%	0.0%	0.0%
Blacksburg-Christiansburg-Radford, VA	65,831	88.4%	3.0%	3.9%	4.4%	0.4%	8.7%	2.5%	0.5%	0.0%
Bloomington, IL	61,716	94.3%	2.3%	0.9%	2.5%	0.0%	3.7%	0.9%	1.1%	0.0%
Bloomington, IN	67,026	88.0%	2.5%	2.1%	6.7%	0.7%	6.6%	4.5%	0.8%	0.0%
Bloomsburg-Berwick, PA	23,536	95.7%	2.8%	1.3%	0.1%	0.0%	2.3%	1.3%	0.7%	0.0%
Boise City, ID	173,741	85.5%	10.3%	2.2%	0.5%	1.5%	10.1%	3.1%	1.3%	0.0%
Boston-Cambridge-Newton, MA-NH	1,270,242	72.7%	10.6%	9.4%	5.6%	1.7%	20.4%	4.2%	2.0%	0.7%
Boulder, CO	98,666	83.4%	8.6%	4.2%	2.9%	0.9%	13.5%	1.5%	1.5%	0.2%
Bowling Green, KY	48,473	87.0%	5.3%	3.1%	1.6%	3.1%	8.6%	3.8%	0.6%	0.0%
Bremerton-Silverdale, WA	69,919	94.4%	3.1%	1.2%	1.4%	0.0%	4.9%	0.5%	0.3%	0.0%
Bridgeport-Stamford-Norwalk, CT	223,389	66.8%	20.0%	9.6%	2.9%	0.8%	21.5%	6.6%	3.2%	1.9%
Brownsville-Harlingen, TX	113,745	24.8%	74.8%	0.1%	0.3%	0.0%	61.6%	6.1%	4.1%	3.4%
Brunswick, GA	26,627	90.8%	7.3%	1.3%	0.6%	0.0%	6.2%	1.4%	1.7%	0.0%
Buffalo-Cheektowaga-Niagara Falls, NY	286,861	88.0%	3.8%	3.7%	2.9%	1.5%	8.3%	2.2%	1.3%	0.2%
Burlington, NC	37,828	81.7%	16.6%	0.9%	0.8%	0.1%	9.6%	4.1%	3.6%	1.1%
Burlington-South Burlington, VT	64,031	87.6%	2.0%	8.9%	0.9%	0.6%	10.8%	1.1%	0.4%	0.0%
California-Lexington Park, MD	28,974	95.0%	3.0%	1.3%	0.5%	0.2%	1.9%	2.2%	1.0%	0.0%
Canton-Massillon, OH	93,640	95.9%	1.8%	1.5%	0.5%	0.2%	2.4%	0.2%	0.6%	0.8%
Cape Coral-Fort Myers, FL	142,244	71.5%	24.3%	3.2%	0.8%	0.2%	19.5%	3.7%	3.6%	1.8%
Cape Girardeau, MO-IL	25,928	97.8%	0.4%	0.6%	1.2%	0.0%	1.9%	0.2%	0.0%	0.0%
Carbondale-Marion, IL	39,218	95.3%	2.5%	1.6%	0.5%	0.1%	3.4%	1.3%	0.0%	0.0%
Carson City, NV	11,558	75.0%	24.8%	0.0%	0.0%	0.2%	17.5%	4.7%	0.0%	2.8%
Casper, WY	20,678	91.1%	7.5%	0.0%	1.4%	0.0%	8.9%	0.0%	0.0%	0.0%
Cedar Rapids, IA	65,970	91.5%	3.0%	1.0%	4.2%	0.2%	4.6%	2.6%	0.6%	0.6%
Chambersburg-Waynesboro, PA	34,854	90.8%	5.4%	3.8%	0.0%	0.0%	7.3%	0.3%	1.6%	0.0%
Champaign-Urbana, IL	89,066	76.7%	5.6%	6.0%	11.3%	0.4%	16.1%	5.6%	1.6%	0.0%
Charleston, WV	46,810	96.4%	1.2%	0.5%	1.3%	0.6%	3.1%	0.3%	0.0%	0.2%
Charleston-North Charleston, SC	204,724	93.9%	4.1%	1.3%	0.6%	0.2%	4.2%	0.3%	1.5%	0.0%
Charlotte-Concord-Gastonia, NC-SC	604,040	84.7%	10.2%	2.3%	2.1%	0.6%	10.0%	2.4%	2.1%	0.8%
Charlottesville, VA	67,057	86.3%	4.8%	3.7%	4.4%	0.9%	9.6%	3.2%	0.8%	0.1%
Chattanooga, TN-GA	137,823	93.9%	3.4%	0.8%	1.9%	0.0%	2.9%	1.5%	1.5%	0.2%
Cheyenne, WY	27,461	91.8%	3.7%	2.6%	1.6%	0.3%	4.2%	4.0%	0.0%	0.0%
Chicago-Naperville-Elgin, IL-IN-WI	2,504,124	68.4%	20.3%	6.5%	3.2%	1.6%	24.0%	4.4%	2.6%	0.7%
Chico, CA	66,585	79.2%	13.4%	0.8%	4.7%	1.9%	18.6%	1.5%	0.7%	0.0%
Cincinnati, OH-KY-IN	542,779	92.4%	3.0%	2.0%	1.6%	1.0%	4.9%	1.5%	1.1%	0.1%
Clarksburg, WV	19,685	98.7%	1.0%	0.3%	0.1%	0.0%	1.3%	0.0%	0.1%	0.0%

Table G-4: Metropolitan/Micropolitan Statistical Areas—Language Spoken and English Ability—*Continued*

	Millennial Population 15 to 33	Percent by Language Spoken at Home					Percent by Ability to Speak English			
		English Only	Spanish	Other Indo-European Language	Asian and Pacific Island Language	Other Language	Speak English "Very Well"	Speak English "Well"	Speak English "Not Well"	Speak English "Not at All"
Clarksville, TN-KY	91,109	91.7%	5.2%	1.4%	1.2%	0.4%	6.8%	0.8%	0.6%	0.0%
Cleveland, TN	30,847	89.0%	9.1%	0.5%	0.8%	0.5%	7.8%	2.1%	0.6%	0.5%
Cleveland-Elyria, OH	484,581	87.1%	4.8%	4.5%	1.9%	1.8%	9.2%	2.2%	1.3%	0.2%
Coeur d'Alene, ID	35,105	98.6%	0.8%	0.2%	0.4%	0.0%	0.9%	0.1%	0.4%	0.0%
College Station-Bryan, TX	100,404	78.5%	14.5%	2.5%	3.7%	0.8%	13.6%	5.2%	1.6%	1.1%
Colorado Springs, CO	202,070	88.8%	7.5%	1.9%	1.4%	0.5%	8.9%	1.7%	0.4%	0.3%
Columbia, MO	65,947	92.7%	1.8%	1.6%	3.1%	0.8%	4.5%	2.5%	0.4%	0.0%
Columbia, SC	228,727	90.9%	5.5%	1.7%	1.1%	0.8%	4.8%	2.9%	1.1%	0.2%
Columbus, GA-AL	93,090	89.8%	6.4%	1.4%	2.3%	0.0%	7.1%	1.2%	1.0%	0.8%
Columbus, IN	20,841	86.2%	7.1%	4.2%	2.5%	0.0%	10.2%	1.4%	1.4%	0.9%
Columbus, OH	545,703	88.5%	3.7%	2.8%	2.8%	2.2%	7.6%	2.5%	1.2%	0.3%
Concord, NH	26,150	94.1%	0.1%	3.9%	1.6%	0.4%	5.2%	0.8%	0.0%	0.0%
Cookeville, TN	30,681	89.0%	7.2%	1.3%	1.3%	1.2%	8.1%	2.8%	0.1%	0.0%
Corpus Christi, TX	119,621	69.5%	28.0%	0.2%	1.9%	0.5%	26.6%	2.1%	1.5%	0.3%
Corvallis, OR	32,589	83.4%	9.4%	1.7%	4.4%	1.1%	11.4%	2.3%	0.4%	2.5%
Crestview-Fort Walton Beach-Destin, FL	69,335	90.5%	6.4%	1.1%	1.7%	0.2%	6.7%	1.0%	1.5%	0.3%
Cumberland, MD-WV	26,249	93.9%	3.6%	1.0%	1.2%	0.2%	3.9%	1.6%	0.6%	0.0%
Dallas-Fort Worth-Arlington, TX	1,874,485	65.2%	26.7%	3.0%	3.4%	1.6%	22.6%	6.6%	4.0%	1.5%
Dalton, GA	37,337	62.8%	34.9%	1.3%	0.6%	0.5%	27.8%	4.7%	2.2%	2.6%
Danville, IL	18,480	96.2%	2.6%	0.1%	1.2%	0.0%	2.4%	0.4%	1.0%	0.0%
Danville, VA	22,276	91.6%	6.4%	1.5%	0.4%	0.0%	6.1%	0.9%	1.4%	0.0%
Daphne-Fairhope-Foley, AL	41,881	93.5%	5.6%	0.7%	0.1%	0.0%	6.5%	0.0%	0.0%	0.0%
Davenport-Moline-Rock Island, IA-IL	91,165	89.4%	5.9%	1.9%	1.8%	1.0%	7.1%	1.7%	1.9%	0.0%
Dayton, OH	198,327	93.2%	1.9%	1.0%	2.1%	1.7%	4.8%	1.5%	0.4%	0.0%
Decatur, AL	35,433	94.3%	4.9%	0.4%	0.3%	0.0%	3.0%	1.0%	1.6%	0.0%
Decatur, IL	24,600	93.5%	5.0%	1.5%	0.0%	0.0%	5.2%	1.0%	0.3%	0.0%
Deltona-Daytona Beach-Ormond Beach, FL	132,761	84.3%	11.4%	1.8%	1.3%	1.2%	11.5%	3.4%	0.6%	0.2%
Denver-Aurora-Lakewood, CO	745,375	77.9%	15.8%	2.3%	2.7%	1.3%	16.3%	2.6%	2.4%	0.9%
Des Moines-West Des Moines, IA	164,874	85.3%	7.1%	1.9%	2.7%	3.1%	9.8%	1.9%	2.0%	1.1%
Detroit-Warren-Dearborn, MI	1,027,782	86.7%	3.5%	4.0%	1.8%	4.0%	9.6%	2.5%	1.0%	0.3%
Dothan, AL	34,274	95.1%	3.9%	0.1%	0.6%	0.2%	3.0%	0.0%	0.2%	1.7%
Dover, DE	46,169	90.1%	5.5%	2.8%	1.6%	0.0%	5.2%	1.9%	2.1%	0.6%
Dubuque, IA	25,588	97.0%	0.7%	1.3%	0.0%	0.9%	1.2%	1.7%	0.0%	0.0%
Duluth, MN-WI	72,709	94.1%	2.9%	0.7%	1.7%	0.6%	5.2%	0.7%	0.0%	0.0%
Dunn, NC	35,041	83.3%	13.4%	2.5%	0.8%	0.0%	13.5%	0.7%	2.5%	0.0%
Durham-Chapel Hill, NC	161,733	78.6%	12.4%	3.1%	3.9%	2.0%	14.6%	2.5%	1.7%	2.5%
East Stroudsburg, PA	42,076	80.9%	9.4%	7.2%	2.1%	0.5%	16.7%	1.7%	0.2%	0.5%
Eau Claire, WI	47,724	94.3%	0.7%	0.9%	3.7%	0.4%	2.5%	1.0%	2.2%	0.0%
El Centro, CA	49,791	21.8%	77.2%	0.5%	0.5%	0.0%	54.9%	13.4%	6.6%	3.3%
El Paso, TX	37,272	92.3%	4.6%	1.6%	1.5%	0.0%	5.6%	2.0%	0.0%	0.0%
Elizabethtown-Fort Knox, KY	51,393	82.1%	11.8%	5.3%	0.3%	0.5%	11.5%	4.4%	2.0%	0.0%
Elkhart-Goshen, IN	20,951	97.8%	0.5%	0.7%	1.1%	0.0%	1.7%	0.3%	0.2%	0.0%
Elmira, NY	243,628	30.0%	67.3%	1.3%	0.7%	0.7%	53.5%	11.4%	3.1%	2.0%
Erie, PA	71,032	91.5%	2.1%	2.2%	2.2%	1.9%	5.3%	2.3%	0.2%	0.6%
Eugene, OR	101,020	90.9%	5.4%	0.9%	2.6%	0.2%	6.1%	1.3%	1.5%	0.2%
Eureka-Arcata-Fortuna, CA	38,052	81.9%	11.7%	2.3%	2.6%	1.5%	14.6%	1.2%	2.3%	0.0%
Evansville, IN-KY	77,662	95.7%	2.1%	0.6%	1.4%	0.3%	3.4%	0.5%	0.3%	0.1%
Fairbanks, AK	34,834	83.9%	5.0%	5.5%	4.0%	1.6%	13.0%	3.1%	0.0%	0.0%
Fargo, ND-MN	76,111	93.5%	0.9%	3.2%	1.7%	0.8%	5.2%	0.9%	0.5%	0.0%
Farmington, NM	30,632	69.7%	11.9%	0.0%	0.1%	18.3%	25.8%	2.2%	2.3%	0.0%
Fayetteville, NC	114,794	88.0%	8.6%	1.5%	0.9%	1.0%	8.9%	1.9%	1.1%	0.2%
Fayetteville-Springdale-Rogers, AR-MO	145,133	82.3%	11.8%	1.4%	2.6%	1.9%	9.4%	3.9%	3.4%	1.0%
Flagstaff, AZ	51,771	81.8%	8.0%	1.7%	2.5%	6.0%	15.7%	2.2%	0.2%	0.0%
Flint, MI	96,273	96.6%	1.3%	0.8%	0.2%	1.1%	2.9%	0.3%	0.2%	0.1%
Florence, SC	49,298	97.9%	1.5%	0.4%	0.2%	0.0%	0.9%	0.6%	0.6%	0.0%
Florence-Muscle Shoals, AL	34,708	90.0%	9.1%	0.2%	0.0%	0.7%	5.1%	4.6%	0.3%	0.0%
Fond du Lac, WI	24,678	92.7%	4.6%	0.0%	2.7%	0.0%	6.2%	1.1%	0.0%	0.0%
Fort Collins, CO	103,634	88.0%	7.5%	2.8%	1.1%	0.7%	10.1%	1.3%	0.6%	0.0%
Fort Smith, AR-OK	68,405	85.5%	10.3%	0.8%	2.8%	0.6%	10.0%	2.1%	2.1%	0.4%
Fort Wayne, IN	110,786	88.6%	5.1%	2.8%	3.1%	0.3%	7.1%	2.4%	1.3%	0.6%
Fresno, CA	280,870	50.7%	37.7%	3.5%	7.2%	1.0%	36.7%	5.1%	3.4%	4.2%
Gadsden, AL	22,502	97.7%	2.2%	0.0%	0.0%	0.1%	0.9%	0.2%	1.3%	0.0%
Gainesville, FL	102,661	84.9%	6.8%	3.9%	3.7%	0.8%	12.0%	1.9%	0.8%	0.4%
Gainesville, GA	48,649	68.8%	28.8%	0.9%	1.1%	0.4%	17.5%	7.2%	3.9%	2.5%
Gettysburg, PA	23,400	93.2%	6.4%	0.4%	0.0%	0.0%	4.2%	0.7%	1.8%	0.0%
Glens Falls, NY	26,846	94.7%	2.1%	2.3%	0.9%	0.0%	3.9%	0.6%	0.9%	0.0%
Goldsboro, NC	32,804	86.2%	10.4%	1.9%	0.6%	1.0%	5.3%	3.0%	3.3%	2.3%
Grand Forks, ND-MN	36,405	90.5%	3.4%	1.2%	1.8%	3.1%	6.8%	2.0%	0.7%	0.0%
Grand Island, NE	20,619	86.7%	11.5%	0.3%	0.2%	1.3%	6.3%	5.5%	1.4%	0.0%
Grand Junction, CO	38,770	92.2%	6.3%	0.7%	0.8%	0.0%	4.9%	2.9%	0.0%	0.0%
Grand Rapids-Wyoming, MI	282,938	86.7%	7.5%	2.4%	2.8%	0.6%	9.2%	2.0%	1.5%	0.5%
Grants Pass, OR	16,859	86.6%	9.8%	3.6%	0.0%	0.0%	9.6%	2.8%	0.0%	1.0%
Great Falls, MT	20,486	94.4%	0.0%	5.6%	0.0%	0.0%	5.5%	0.1%	0.0%	0.0%
Greeley, CO	79,145	80.0%	17.8%	0.5%	1.1%	0.5%	13.7%	3.3%	1.9%	1.1%
Green Bay, WI	78,353	86.1%	9.0%	0.3%	4.5%	0.1%	9.5%	1.9%	2.4%	0.1%
Greensboro-High Point, NC	187,158	86.5%	9.1%	2.0%	1.7%	0.6%	9.0%	2.1%	1.5%	0.8%

Table G-4: Metropolitan/Micropolitan Statistical Areas—Language Spoken and English Ability—*Continued*

	Millennial Population 15 to 33	Percent by Language Spoken at Home					Percent by Ability to Speak English			
		English Only	Spanish	Other Indo-European Language	Asian and Pacific Island Language	Other Language	Speak English "Very Well"	Speak English "Well"	Speak English "Not Well"	Speak English "Not at All"
Greenville, NC	60,468	94.5%	4.3%	0.1%	0.8%	0.3%	3.5%	1.0%	0.9%	0.0%
Greenville-Anderson-Mauldin, SC	220,414	89.2%	7.9%	1.4%	1.4%	0.2%	6.8%	2.3%	1.0%	0.7%
Greenwood, SC	22,832	93.2%	6.0%	0.4%	0.4%	0.0%	6.6%	0.2%	0.0%	0.0%
Gulfport-Biloxi-Pascagoula, MS	99,689	90.2%	6.1%	0.8%	2.1%	0.8%	7.0%	2.2%	0.5%	0.1%
Hagerstown-Martinsburg, MD-WV	61,867	93.1%	3.5%	2.8%	0.2%	0.4%	6.1%	0.8%	0.0%	0.0%
Hammond, LA	35,483	90.7%	8.2%	0.3%	0.8%	0.0%	9.3%	0.0%	0.0%	0.0%
Hanford-Corcoran, CA	46,492	55.8%	39.0%	1.6%	3.2%	0.4%	28.1%	7.7%	6.9%	1.4%
Harrisburg-Carlisle, PA	136,047	89.0%	3.3%	4.7%	2.5%	0.5%	7.1%	3.1%	0.7%	0.1%
Harrisonburg, VA	44,407	85.7%	8.3%	2.3%	2.8%	1.0%	9.6%	1.9%	2.9%	0.0%
Hartford-West Hartford-East Hartford, CT	287,773	74.3%	13.0%	8.0%	2.5%	2.1%	21.0%	3.1%	1.2%	0.4%
Hattiesburg, MS	42,138	95.5%	2.5%	1.3%	0.3%	0.4%	2.4%	1.7%	0.4%	0.0%
Hickory-Lenoir-Morganton, NC	81,844	86.9%	8.3%	0.2%	4.2%	0.4%	7.3%	3.5%	2.1%	0.1%
Hilo, HI	44,356	80.3%	2.8%	0.1%	10.9%	5.9%	13.5%	4.4%	1.7%	0.0%
Hilton Head Island-Bluffton-Beaufort, SC	48,455	86.3%	12.5%	0.7%	0.6%	0.0%	9.8%	2.5%	1.2%	0.2%
Hinesville, GA	27,109	87.1%	9.9%	0.7%	2.3%	0.0%	8.4%	2.0%	1.4%	1.1%
Holland, MI	26,922	94.0%	5.1%	0.9%	0.0%	0.0%	3.8%	1.3%	0.0%	0.9%
Homosassa Springs, FL	20,619	94.4%	4.4%	0.8%	0.4%	0.0%	3.5%	0.6%	0.4%	1.2%
Hot Springs, AR	21,426	95.4%	3.5%	0.2%	1.0%	0.0%	2.9%	0.0%	1.7%	0.0%
Houma-Thibodaux, LA	54,143	88.7%	4.8%	1.8%	4.7%	0.0%	9.8%	0.3%	0.8%	0.3%
Houston-The Woodlands-Sugar Land, TX	1,795,490	58.9%	31.9%	3.4%	4.3%	1.5%	27.4%	6.2%	3.9%	3.6%
Huntington-Ashland, WV-KY-OH	84,689	98.5%	0.5%	0.4%	0.5%	0.0%	1.1%	0.3%	0.0%	0.0%
Huntsville, AL	116,099	92.7%	5.3%	0.8%	1.1%	0.1%	4.3%	0.9%	1.8%	0.3%
Idaho Falls, ID	34,928	84.3%	15.0%	0.3%	0.4%	0.0%	11.9%	2.5%	1.1%	0.2%
Indianapolis-Carmel-Anderson, IN	506,665	89.3%	6.4%	1.9%	1.3%	1.2%	6.6%	2.0%	1.7%	0.5%
Iowa City, IA	60,642	87.9%	3.5%	2.2%	5.9%	0.5%	9.2%	2.6%	0.3%	0.0%
Ithaca, NY	45,449	81.1%	1.7%	4.3%	12.1%	0.8%	16.0%	2.8%	0.0%	0.0%
Jackson, MI	38,466	94.7%	2.3%	1.7%	1.3%	0.0%	3.6%	1.6%	0.1%	0.0%
Jackson, MS	150,950	95.4%	3.0%	0.8%	0.5%	0.2%	2.5%	0.6%	0.6%	0.8%
Jackson, TN	33,924	95.1%	3.0%	0.2%	1.0%	0.6%	3.6%	0.0%	0.0%	1.2%
Jacksonville, FL	373,861	87.2%	6.2%	3.8%	2.3%	0.5%	9.8%	1.7%	1.2%	0.2%
Jacksonville, NC	75,308	87.6%	10.6%	0.7%	1.0%	0.1%	8.5%	2.7%	0.6%	0.5%
Jamestown-Dunkirk-Fredonia, NY	31,756	89.7%	6.2%	1.7%	2.1%	0.4%	7.2%	2.0%	1.1%	0.0%
Janesville-Beloit, WI	36,704	88.2%	9.0%	1.9%	0.4%	0.5%	11.1%	0.7%	0.0%	0.0%
Jefferson City, MO	38,312	94.2%	2.0%	0.4%	1.2%	2.2%	4.7%	1.1%	0.0%	0.0%
Johnson City, TN	48,247	94.0%	2.6%	1.0%	1.2%	1.2%	5.6%	0.4%	0.0%	0.0%
Johnstown, PA	30,779	95.6%	0.5%	1.4%	2.1%	0.4%	1.8%	2.6%	0.0%	0.0%
Jonesboro, AR	36,893	94.5%	3.6%	0.9%	1.0%	0.0%	4.2%	0.1%	1.1%	0.0%
Joplin, MO	43,861	92.5%	6.9%	0.0%	0.6%	0.0%	5.4%	0.9%	1.3%	0.0%
Kahului-Wailuku-Lahaina, HI	39,215	79.2%	5.1%	0.3%	9.9%	5.5%	15.2%	4.8%	0.9%	0.0%
Kalamazoo-Portage, MI	97,259	90.5%	4.3%	2.7%	0.8%	1.7%	7.0%	2.2%	0.4%	0.0%
Kalispell, MT	20,702	96.9%	0.0%	3.0%	0.1%	0.0%	3.1%	0.0%	0.0%	0.0%
Kankakee, IL	28,451	89.8%	8.8%	0.4%	0.8%	0.3%	7.1%	0.9%	1.8%	0.4%
Kansas City, MO-KS	523,563	87.9%	7.2%	1.9%	2.1%	0.9%	8.3%	2.0%	1.3%	0.6%
Kennewick-Richland, WA	75,872	64.0%	31.3%	3.8%	0.9%	0.0%	28.7%	5.1%	1.0%	1.2%
Killeen-Temple, TX	139,806	78.0%	15.7%	3.1%	1.9%	1.4%	15.9%	3.2%	2.0%	1.0%
Kingsport-Bristol-Bristol, TN-VA	66,770	98.3%	0.9%	0.5%	0.1%	0.1%	1.1%	0.1%	0.5%	0.0%
Kingston, NY	41,944	86.9%	6.9%	3.4%	1.7%	1.2%	10.8%	1.9%	0.3%	0.1%
Knoxville, TN	212,739	93.7%	4.1%	1.0%	0.8%	0.4%	3.9%	0.5%	1.4%	0.5%
Kokomo, IN	17,889	87.5%	9.8%	1.4%	0.7%	0.5%	1.4%	9.8%	1.3%	0.0%
La Crosse-Onalaska, WI-MN	40,654	86.0%	5.4%	2.6%	6.0%	0.0%	6.7%	5.4%	1.1%	0.8%
Lafayette, LA	134,345	92.5%	3.4%	1.9%	1.7%	0.5%	5.5%	0.9%	0.9%	0.2%
Lafayette-West Lafayette, IN	80,391	79.4%	7.6%	2.6%	9.9%	0.5%	10.1%	8.1%	2.1%	0.3%
Lake Charles, LA	54,900	92.5%	1.9%	1.9%	4.2%	0.5%	5.1%	2.1%	0.3%	0.0%
Lake Havasu City-Kingman, AZ	38,567	87.1%	10.7%	0.6%	0.3%	1.3%	8.9%	3.4%	0.6%	0.0%
Lakeland-Winter Haven, FL	157,735	72.4%	22.3%	3.8%	1.4%	0.1%	19.0%	3.3%	2.6%	2.7%
Lancaster, PA	133,315	78.4%	10.6%	9.4%	1.5%	0.1%	16.3%	3.8%	1.1%	0.4%
Lansing-East Lansing, MI	145,575	88.8%	2.7%	2.7%	4.7%	1.1%	7.0%	3.9%	0.3%	0.0%
Laredo, TX	76,206	11.1%	88.8%	0.0%	0.0%	0.0%	65.1%	11.0%	5.2%	7.7%
Las Cruces, NM	64,094	50.9%	47.3%	0.1%	1.0%	0.7%	42.3%	4.3%	1.5%	1.0%
Las Vegas-Henderson-Paradise, NV	551,377	62.0%	28.9%	2.4%	5.3%	1.4%	28.7%	4.7%	3.1%	1.5%
Lawrence, KS	46,763	83.2%	8.0%	6.7%	0.9%	1.2%	11.6%	2.6%	2.6%	0.0%
Lawton, OK	40,304	89.8%	7.7%	0.2%	2.2%	0.0%	7.9%	2.1%	0.2%	0.0%
Lebanon, PA	29,746	84.5%	9.7%	3.8%	1.2%	0.9%	13.0%	1.3%	1.2%	0.0%
Lewiston, ID-WA	14,434	87.6%	9.4%	0.4%	2.7%	0.0%	7.7%	2.2%	2.5%	0.0%
Lewiston-Auburn, ME	24,352	87.1%	4.8%	5.1%	1.6%	1.3%	9.0%	3.6%	0.2%	0.0%
Lexington-Fayette, KY	144,801	89.0%	6.4%	1.5%	1.7%	1.5%	6.6%	2.6%	1.5%	0.4%
Lima, OH	25,254	97.3%	0.6%	1.0%	1.1%	0.0%	1.9%	0.8%	0.0%	0.0%
Lincoln, NE	99,230	83.7%	7.0%	2.5%	3.9%	3.0%	8.8%	5.4%	2.0%	0.1%
Little Rock-North Little Rock-Conway, AR	197,454	91.3%	5.6%	1.5%	1.2%	0.3%	5.1%	2.3%	0.7%	0.6%
Logan, UT-ID	48,158	89.4%	7.4%	0.9%	1.4%	0.9%	7.8%	1.3%	0.9%	0.6%
Longview, TX	52,337	83.7%	15.3%	1.0%	0.0%	0.0%	12.6%	1.5%	0.9%	1.4%
Longview, WA	22,743	85.0%	11.8%	0.4%	1.4%	1.3%	8.7%	3.2%	1.1%	1.9%
Los Angeles-Long Beach-Anaheim, CA	3,649,069	43.9%	41.1%	4.4%	9.6%	1.0%	43.4%	6.8%	4.3%	1.6%
Louisville/Jefferson County, KY-IN	310,933	90.7%	4.6%	2.3%	0.7%	1.6%	6.3%	1.8%	1.0%	0.2%
Lubbock, TX	108,228	75.1%	18.9%	3.9%	1.5%	0.6%	21.0%	2.9%	0.7%	0.3%
Lumberton, NC	32,547	91.3%	7.8%	0.0%	0.2%	0.7%	5.8%	0.9%	1.5%	0.5%
Lynchburg, VA	71,290	94.0%	2.6%	0.8%	2.0%	0.6%	3.0%	2.2%	0.2%	0.5%
Macon, GA	57,298	94.3%	3.1%	1.8%	0.7%	0.1%	4.0%	0.6%	0.5%	0.5%

Table G-4: Metropolitan/Micropolitan Statistical Areas—Language Spoken and English Ability—*Continued*

	Millennial Population 15 to 33	Percent by Language Spoken at Home					Percent by Ability to Speak English			
		English Only	Spanish	Other Indo-European Language	Asian and Pacific Island Language	Other Language	Speak English "Very Well"	Speak English "Well"	Speak English "Not Well"	Speak English "Not at All"
Madera, CA	41,540	48.3%	47.9%	2.4%	0.8%	0.6%	39.0%	4.5%	1.9%	6.3%
Madison, WI	192,036	85.4%	4.3%	4.7%	4.8%	0.7%	10.4%	3.6%	0.6%	0.0%
Manchester-Nashua, NH	98,967	87.0%	6.1%	2.9%	2.4%	1.6%	8.5%	2.8%	1.5%	0.3%
Manhattan, KS	44,533	89.0%	4.7%	1.8%	2.5%	2.0%	4.9%	4.7%	1.4%	0.0%
Mankato-North Mankato, MN	34,477	92.3%	1.4%	2.4%	0.7%	3.2%	3.7%	3.7%	0.4%	0.0%
Mansfield, OH	27,953	93.5%	2.2%	2.1%	1.5%	0.8%	5.3%	1.2%	0.0%	0.0%
McAllen-Edinburg-Mission, TX	231,675	14.0%	85.4%	0.1%	0.5%	0.0%	68.0%	9.0%	5.9%	3.1%
Medford, OR	48,007	89.7%	9.0%	0.0%	1.2%	0.2%	7.5%	2.1%	0.6%	0.0%
Memphis, TN-MS-AR	357,724	90.9%	5.8%	1.0%	1.5%	0.8%	6.5%	1.5%	0.8%	0.3%
Merced, CA	78,357	39.1%	50.9%	4.6%	4.7%	0.7%	42.0%	8.5%	6.3%	4.0%
Meridian, MS	27,324	97.3%	1.4%	1.3%	0.1%	0.0%	2.1%	0.1%	0.6%	0.0%
Miami-Fort Lauderdale-West Palm Beach, FL	1,441,011	44.5%	42.7%	10.7%	1.3%	0.8%	40.9%	7.2%	4.6%	2.9%
Michigan City-La Porte, IN	25,919	96.3%	2.3%	1.4%	0.1%	0.0%	2.4%	1.3%	0.0%	0.0%
Midland, MI	20,208	98.4%	0.6%	1.0%	0.0%	0.0%	1.6%	0.0%	0.0%	0.0%
Midland, TX	50,504	66.5%	29.1%	0.2%	3.5%	0.7%	22.7%	5.2%	5.4%	0.1%
Milwaukee-Waukesha-West Allis, WI	397,142	85.9%	8.9%	2.1%	2.3%	0.8%	10.3%	2.4%	1.3%	0.1%
Minneapolis-St. Paul-Bloomington, MN-WI	893,153	82.6%	5.0%	2.8%	5.9%	3.6%	11.9%	3.4%	1.7%	0.4%
Missoula, MT	36,592	98.6%	0.6%	0.7%	0.0%	0.0%	0.9%	0.0%	0.5%	0.0%
Mobile, AL	108,104	93.1%	3.3%	0.7%	1.7%	1.1%	3.6%	0.8%	2.0%	0.5%
Modesto, CA	113,568	58.4%	32.8%	4.3%	2.1%	2.5%	31.6%	5.9%	3.1%	1.0%
Monroe, LA	48,731	96.0%	2.2%	0.1%	1.7%	0.0%	3.5%	0.2%	0.3%	0.0%
Monroe, MI	33,502	97.3%	1.5%	0.4%	0.8%	0.0%	0.6%	1.0%	0.5%	0.6%
Montgomery, AL	98,811	97.0%	1.9%	0.6%	0.5%	0.1%	1.9%	0.3%	0.5%	0.3%
Morgantown, WV	51,218	85.3%	5.3%	6.2%	3.2%	0.0%	11.4%	2.7%	0.6%	0.0%
Morristown, TN	26,778	86.4%	11.1%	2.3%	0.2%	0.0%	6.6%	1.9%	3.3%	1.9%
Mount Vernon-Anacortes, WA	27,287	84.5%	13.6%	0.3%	1.0%	0.6%	12.0%	1.5%	1.3%	0.8%
Muncie, IN	37,184	95.5%	2.5%	1.0%	0.9%	0.0%	4.0%	0.0%	0.5%	0.0%
Muskegon, MI	41,707	94.6%	4.1%	0.7%	0.0%	0.6%	4.7%	0.0%	0.8%	0.0%
Myrtle Beach-Conway-North Myrtle Beach, SC-NC	90,587	91.9%	5.2%	1.4%	1.1%	0.3%	4.9%	1.9%	1.3%	0.0%
Napa, CA	33,408	59.5%	34.1%	1.3%	4.5%	0.6%	28.9%	7.2%	3.0%	1.4%
Naples-Immokalee-Marco Island, FL	67,976	50.9%	41.6%	7.4%	0.1%	0.0%	37.6%	3.2%	4.3%	4.1%
Nashville-Davidson–Murfreesboro–Franklin, TN	487,986	87.8%	6.6%	2.1%	1.4%	2.1%	7.3%	2.2%	1.9%	0.7%
New Bern, NC	34,596	93.1%	3.2%	1.0%	1.9%	0.9%	3.5%	1.1%	2.3%	0.0%
New Castle, PA	18,906	98.6%	0.2%	1.2%	0.0%	0.0%	0.4%	1.0%	0.0%	0.0%
New Haven-Milford, CT	220,739	75.1%	16.8%	5.0%	1.6%	1.5%	17.8%	4.9%	1.5%	0.7%
New Orleans-Metairie, LA	328,881	87.9%	7.5%	1.6%	2.3%	0.7%	7.5%	2.5%	1.5%	0.5%
New Philadelphia-Dover, OH	20,822	92.6%	1.3%	6.2%	0.0%	0.0%	4.0%	3.1%	0.3%	0.0%
New York-Newark-Jersey City, NY-NJ-PA	5,196,245	59.9%	22.1%	10.0%	5.8%	2.3%	28.6%	6.3%	3.9%	1.3%
Niles-Benton Harbor, MI	34,168	92.3%	3.1%	1.1%	1.9%	1.6%	5.1%	2.4%	0.2%	0.0%
North Port-Sarasota-Bradenton, FL	138,244	79.1%	15.8%	3.8%	1.0%	0.2%	13.0%	3.6%	3.9%	0.4%
Norwich-New London, CT	71,058	86.3%	7.8%	3.3%	2.2%	0.4%	10.1%	2.7%	1.0%	0.0%
Ocala, FL	70,359	88.3%	8.4%	2.9%	0.5%	0.0%	10.3%	0.7%	0.6%	0.2%
Ocean City, NJ	18,811	84.6%	14.5%	0.3%	0.0%	0.6%	11.4%	2.8%	1.3%	0.0%
Odessa, TX	49,508	49.3%	47.7%	0.7%	0.8%	1.5%	40.0%	4.7%	3.3%	2.7%
Ogden-Clearfield, UT	175,789	86.8%	10.2%	1.3%	1.3%	0.4%	9.2%	2.0%	1.6%	0.4%
Ogdensburg-Massena, NY	32,089	90.5%	1.8%	5.9%	0.3%	1.5%	7.4%	1.7%	0.5%	0.0%
Oklahoma City, OK	375,784	83.8%	11.3%	1.4%	3.0%	0.6%	11.3%	2.8%	1.4%	0.7%
Olympia-Tumwater, WA	67,330	84.5%	6.7%	3.0%	4.7%	1.1%	10.1%	4.0%	1.1%	0.3%
Omaha-Council Bluffs, NE-IA	238,509	85.2%	9.1%	2.4%	2.3%	1.0%	10.1%	2.2%	1.8%	0.6%
Orangeburg, SC	22,898	94.8%	1.8%	3.3%	0.0%	0.0%	5.2%	0.0%	0.0%	0.0%
Orlando-Kissimmee-Sanford, FL	647,918	66.4%	25.4%	5.2%	2.1%	0.8%	25.6%	5.2%	1.8%	0.9%
Oshkosh-Neenah, WI	46,787	92.5%	3.4%	2.0%	2.1%	0.0%	6.1%	1.4%	0.0%	0.0%
Ottawa-Peru, IL	25,216	90.1%	7.2%	1.3%	1.4%	0.0%	7.3%	0.8%	1.8%	0.0%
Owensboro, KY	27,255	97.7%	1.2%	0.2%	0.7%	0.3%	1.1%	0.2%	0.8%	0.3%
Oxnard-Thousand Oaks-Ventura, CA	217,504	56.3%	36.6%	2.3%	3.7%	1.1%	30.5%	3.7%	4.3%	5.2%
Palm Bay-Melbourne-Titusville, FL	120,364	87.0%	8.7%	1.5%	0.4%	2.3%	9.6%	1.5%	1.0%	0.9%
Panama City, FL	48,956	94.3%	2.9%	1.7%	0.9%	0.2%	4.2%	0.0%	1.5%	0.0%
Parkersburg-Vienna, WV	20,168	98.8%	1.0%	0.0%	0.2%	0.0%	1.2%	0.0%	0.0%	0.0%
Pensacola-Ferry Pass-Brent, FL	132,104	92.5%	4.0%	1.0%	2.4%	0.1%	5.0%	1.8%	0.1%	0.6%
Peoria, IL	90,607	91.1%	4.0%	2.2%	2.3%	0.4%	5.5%	1.0%	2.4%	0.0%
Philadelphia-Camden-Wilmington, PA-NJ-DE-MD	1,554,689	82.5%	8.2%	4.2%	4.0%	1.1%	12.5%	2.6%	2.0%	0.4%
Phoenix-Mesa-Scottsdale, AZ	1,190,960	69.6%	24.4%	1.9%	2.5%	1.5%	24.1%	3.0%	1.9%	1.4%
Pine Bluff, AR	22,491	97.1%	1.7%	0.7%	0.0%	0.4%	2.5%	0.4%	0.0%	0.0%
Pittsburgh, PA	559,661	92.8%	1.9%	2.7%	1.6%	1.0%	4.8%	1.7%	0.6%	0.1%
Pittsfield, MA	28,289	90.8%	5.4%	1.8%	2.0%	0.0%	5.9%	2.4%	0.3%	0.6%
Pocatello, ID	24,466	90.1%	4.9%	0.0%	1.5%	3.5%	5.0%	4.4%	0.2%	0.2%
Port St. Lucie, FL	121,993	93.7%	1.1%	3.2%	1.0%	1.0%	5.0%	0.9%	0.4%	0.0%
Portland-South Portland, ME	614,186	79.0%	11.0%	4.5%	4.5%	1.0%	14.8%	3.7%	1.9%	0.6%
Portland-Vancouver-Hillsboro, OR-WA	91,998	75.2%	16.7%	6.4%	1.5%	0.2%	17.5%	2.9%	2.8%	1.7%
Pottsville, PA	30,373	93.4%	5.5%	1.1%	0.0%	0.0%	5.6%	1.1%	0.0%	0.0%
Prescott, AZ	39,793	89.5%	7.2%	1.3%	1.3%	0.7%	9.2%	0.4%	0.6%	0.2%
Providence-Warwick, RI-MA	414,862	76.5%	12.5%	7.3%	3.0%	0.7%	18.0%	3.5%	1.7%	0.4%

Table G-4: Metropolitan/Micropolitan Statistical Areas—Language Spoken and English Ability—*Continued*

	Millennial Population 15 to 33	Percent by Language Spoken at Home					Percent by Ability to Speak English			
		English Only	Spanish	Other Indo-European Language	Asian and Pacific Island Language	Other Language	Speak English "Very Well"	Speak English "Well"	Speak English "Not Well"	Speak English "Not at All"
Provo-Orem, UT	198,288	86.0%	9.4%	1.6%	2.5%	0.5%	10.9%	1.9%	1.1%	0.1%
Pueblo, CO	40,672	87.1%	11.1%	1.8%	0.0%	0.0%	11.8%	0.9%	0.2%	0.0%
Punta Gorda, FL	23,149	85.3%	8.2%	0.7%	3.2%	2.6%	9.6%	0.3%	4.8%	0.0%
Racine, WI	45,504	90.1%	6.5%	1.5%	1.9%	0.0%	8.2%	1.7%	0.0%	0.0%
Raleigh, NC	328,403	83.1%	9.8%	3.8%	2.6%	0.7%	11.6%	2.8%	2.0%	0.5%
Rapid City, SD	36,640	90.2%	4.0%	2.1%	0.0%	3.7%	8.0%	1.6%	0.2%	0.0%
Reading, PA	103,746	78.2%	18.8%	1.6%	0.9%	0.5%	17.0%	1.5%	2.0%	1.3%
Redding, CA	40,454	91.6%	5.5%	1.6%	1.2%	0.0%	7.5%	0.7%	0.1%	0.0%
Reno, NV	115,549	73.1%	22.0%	2.0%	2.6%	0.3%	20.2%	4.0%	2.0%	0.7%
Richmond, VA	331,236	88.0%	5.5%	2.5%	2.6%	1.5%	7.8%	2.5%	1.2%	0.5%
Riverside-San Bernardino-Ontario, CA	1,242,971	55.4%	38.6%	1.5%	3.7%	0.8%	35.6%	4.9%	2.7%	1.4%
Roanoke, VA	72,916	90.4%	4.3%	4.1%	0.1%	1.1%	6.9%	2.5%	0.2%	0.0%
Rochester, MN	51,703	88.5%	3.7%	3.0%	1.6%	3.2%	7.8%	1.0%	2.3%	0.5%
Rochester, NY	279,031	86.3%	6.0%	4.1%	2.5%	1.1%	9.1%	3.2%	1.3%	0.2%
Rockford, IL	80,061	80.6%	16.5%	1.0%	1.2%	0.7%	12.0%	3.4%	3.4%	0.7%
Rocky Mount, NC	33,841	93.8%	5.7%	0.1%	0.4%	0.0%	5.2%	0.2%	0.8%	0.0%
Rome, GA	24,685	90.0%	9.3%	0.5%	0.0%	0.2%	6.2%	1.9%	0.9%	0.9%
Roseburg, OR	21,577	96.3%	3.7%	0.0%	0.0%	0.0%	1.3%	1.0%	0.0%	1.4%
Sacramento–Roseville-Arden-Arcade, CA	592,077	68.5%	16.0%	6.1%	8.2%	1.2%	23.5%	4.9%	2.4%	0.6%
Saginaw, MI	48,370	94.0%	2.0%	0.3%	1.5%	2.1%	1.4%	3.8%	0.0%	0.8%
Salem, OH	58,133	90.6%	4.5%	1.7%	1.3%	1.8%	5.8%	2.9%	0.7%	0.0%
Salem, OR	39,437	87.0%	7.6%	3.1%	1.8%	0.6%	11.6%	1.0%	0.4%	0.0%
Salinas, CA	33,339	92.4%	5.7%	1.8%	0.0%	0.1%	3.4%	2.1%	1.6%	0.4%
Salisbury, MD-DE	695,032	92.7%	2.6%	1.9%	2.0%	1.0%	5.1%	1.3%	0.6%	0.4%
Salt Lake City, UT	21,390	99.2%	0.8%	0.0%	0.0%	0.0%	0.0%	0.0%	0.8%	0.0%
San Angelo, TX	106,365	71.2%	23.7%	1.7%	2.0%	1.4%	21.4%	3.7%	2.0%	1.7%
San Antonio-New Braunfels, TX	118,338	43.7%	51.4%	1.5%	2.6%	0.7%	35.8%	6.4%	6.3%	7.8%
San Diego-Carlsbad, CA	89,917	88.4%	8.1%	2.6%	0.5%	0.5%	7.8%	1.5%	2.2%	0.1%
San Francisco-Oakland-Hayward, CA	338,055	79.5%	14.1%	2.0%	3.0%	1.5%	15.9%	2.4%	1.7%	0.5%
San Jose-Sunnyvale-Santa Clara, CA	36,639	71.3%	25.0%	1.6%	1.4%	0.6%	21.1%	4.7%	2.3%	0.6%
San Luis Obispo-Paso Robles-Arroyo Grande, CA	674,563	67.0%	29.8%	1.1%	1.6%	0.5%	26.4%	3.4%	1.9%	1.2%
Santa Cruz-Watsonville, CA	944,397	59.8%	28.9%	2.8%	6.8%	1.7%	31.6%	5.4%	2.2%	1.0%
Santa Fe, NM	1,181,069	57.6%	19.0%	6.3%	15.4%	1.6%	30.7%	7.4%	3.2%	1.1%
Santa Maria-Santa Barbara, CA	508,745	46.9%	22.8%	7.8%	21.2%	1.3%	39.8%	7.9%	4.3%	1.1%
Santa Rosa, CA	81,571	78.3%	17.2%	1.1%	2.7%	0.7%	17.5%	3.1%	1.1%	0.0%
Savannah, GA	81,439	64.3%	26.6%	2.6%	5.2%	1.3%	25.3%	4.5%	2.7%	3.3%
Scranton–Wilkes-Barre–Hazleton, PA	30,994	66.4%	29.1%	1.6%	0.6%	2.2%	29.8%	0.6%	1.3%	1.9%
Seattle-Tacoma-Bellevue, WA	136,421	55.1%	36.6%	2.5%	4.7%	1.1%	31.0%	5.5%	2.8%	5.6%
Sebastian-Vero Beach, FL	118,618	70.7%	23.8%	2.0%	3.3%	0.2%	18.8%	5.4%	4.1%	1.2%
Sebring, FL	110,241	88.4%	5.6%	3.8%	1.8%	0.4%	8.3%	2.0%	0.9%	0.4%
Sheboygan, WI	130,840	89.3%	8.2%	1.6%	0.8%	0.1%	6.9%	1.9%	1.2%	0.7%
Sherman-Denison, TX	993,581	74.5%	8.6%	6.2%	9.1%	1.6%	17.9%	4.5%	2.6%	0.6%
Show Low, AZ	26,890	78.1%	18.9%	2.7%	0.3%	0.0%	17.7%	2.4%	1.5%	0.2%
Shreveport-Bossier City, LA	17,160	79.3%	20.1%	0.0%	0.0%	0.6%	13.0%	5.1%	2.5%	0.0%
Sierra Vista-Douglas, AZ	24,958	80.2%	9.8%	3.3%	6.7%	0.0%	11.6%	3.1%	5.1%	0.0%
Sioux City, IA-NE-SD	29,792	84.4%	14.4%	0.4%	0.0%	0.9%	12.4%	1.3%	1.3%	0.7%
Sioux Falls, SD	26,103	59.0%	2.0%	0.3%	0.2%	38.4%	35.2%	5.1%	0.5%	0.2%
South Bend-Mishawaka, IN-MI	115,714	95.0%	2.1%	0.4%	1.4%	1.1%	3.4%	0.8%	0.5%	0.4%
Spartanburg, SC	29,422	50.8%	45.4%	1.6%	0.6%	1.6%	43.2%	2.6%	2.1%	1.4%
Spokane-Spokane Valley, WA	40,932	79.4%	15.7%	0.4%	2.8%	1.7%	11.7%	4.5%	3.0%	1.4%
Springfield, IL	66,928	85.1%	5.8%	5.7%	1.0%	2.3%	9.0%	2.1%	2.7%	1.0%
Springfield, MA	84,142	86.7%	6.9%	1.8%	2.3%	2.2%	9.8%	2.1%	1.0%	0.3%
Springfield, MO	79,956	89.5%	6.0%	3.9%	0.5%	0.1%	9.1%	0.9%	0.3%	0.2%
Springfield, OH	144,143	89.6%	3.7%	3.7%	1.5%	1.5%	8.4%	1.6%	0.3%	0.1%
St. Cloud, MN	51,217	93.4%	2.2%	2.3%	2.0%	0.1%	5.9%	0.6%	0.1%	0.0%
St. George, UT	179,075	75.1%	16.6%	4.6%	3.0%	0.7%	19.8%	2.3%	2.3%	0.5%
St. Joseph, MO-KS	127,743	93.5%	2.9%	1.5%	1.5%	0.5%	4.8%	1.3%	0.3%	0.1%
St. Louis, MO-IL	31,343	96.7%	1.1%	2.0%	0.0%	0.2%	2.4%	0.0%	0.6%	0.3%
State College, PA	67,059	84.7%	2.7%	6.4%	6.1%	0.1%	12.7%	2.4%	0.2%	0.0%
Staunton-Waynesboro, VA	28,708	97.1%	2.5%	0.4%	0.0%	0.0%	2.5%	0.3%	0.0%	0.1%
Stockton-Lodi, CA	194,976	54.6%	31.2%	4.8%	8.8%	0.6%	33.7%	5.3%	4.9%	1.6%
Sumter, SC	29,989	93.7%	5.0%	0.7%	0.6%	0.0%	5.2%	0.9%	0.2%	0.0%
Sunbury, PA	20,330	97.7%	1.3%	1.0%	0.0%	0.0%	1.4%	0.9%	0.0%	0.0%
Syracuse, NY	172,604	89.6%	3.3%	2.6%	2.4%	2.1%	8.2%	1.4%	0.6%	0.1%
Tallahassee, FL	131,206	88.9%	5.0%	3.0%	1.8%	1.3%	8.8%	2.0%	0.2%	0.0%
Tampa-St. Petersburg-Clearwater, FL	687,275	75.8%	17.8%	3.6%	1.9%	0.9%	18.3%	2.8%	1.9%	1.2%
Terre Haute, IN	47,389	97.1%	1.7%	1.1%	0.1%	0.0%	1.7%	0.6%	0.4%	0.1%
Texarkana, TX-AR	36,299	97.6%	2.3%	0.0%	0.1%	0.0%	1.4%	0.2%	0.2%	0.7%
The Villages, FL	11,009	89.1%	8.4%	2.5%	0.0%	0.0%	9.6%	1.3%	0.0%	0.0%
Toledo, OH	163,570	91.6%	3.1%	1.8%	1.8%	1.7%	5.2%	1.8%	0.7%	0.7%
Topeka, KS	54,373	94.0%	4.3%	0.5%	0.4%	0.9%	5.4%	0.3%	0.2%	0.0%
Torrington, CT	36,755	89.4%	3.9%	3.6%	2.4%	0.7%	8.5%	0.4%	1.3%	0.3%
Traverse City, MI	31,729	93.3%	2.6%	2.2%	1.9%	0.1%	4.8%	1.8%	0.1%	0.0%
Trenton, NJ	96,611	68.7%	17.2%	7.7%	5.3%	1.1%	21.5%	5.2%	4.0%	0.7%
Truckee-Grass Valley, CA	18,893	94.0%	3.6%	1.1%	0.7%	0.6%	1.9%	1.8%	2.3%	0.0%
Tucson, AZ	265,127	68.4%	26.8%	1.3%	2.1%	1.4%	25.7%	3.4%	1.7%	0.7%

Table G-4: Metropolitan/Micropolitan Statistical Areas—Language Spoken and English Ability—*Continued*

	Millennial Population 15 to 33	Percent by Language Spoken at Home					Percent by Ability to Speak English			
		English Only	Spanish	Other Indo-European Language	Asian and Pacific Island Language	Other Language	Speak English "Very Well"	Speak English "Well"	Speak English "Not Well"	Speak English "Not at All"
Tullahoma-Manchester, TN	23,694	95.0%	4.1%	0.9%	0.0%	0.0%	5.0%	0.0%	0.0%	0.0%
Tulsa, OK	248,733	86.4%	9.9%	1.1%	2.1%	0.5%	7.9%	2.5%	2.2%	1.1%
Tupelo, MS	33,847	94.4%	5.4%	0.0%	0.2%	0.0%	3.4%	0.3%	1.9%	0.0%
Tuscaloosa, AL	80,383	94.6%	2.4%	0.4%	2.2%	0.3%	3.4%	1.3%	0.2%	0.5%
Tyler, TX	59,464	82.8%	15.5%	0.8%	0.9%	0.0%	10.5%	2.6%	2.6%	1.5%
Urban Honolulu, HI	273,410	76.0%	3.6%	1.4%	16.3%	2.7%	14.4%	7.8%	1.8%	0.0%
Utica-Rome, NY	69,188	86.5%	4.1%	4.4%	2.0%	3.0%	8.6%	3.6%	0.9%	0.4%
Valdosta, GA	46,199	95.2%	2.4%	1.8%	0.6%	0.0%	2.8%	1.5%	0.3%	0.1%
Vallejo-Fairfield, CA	112,131	69.5%	22.4%	1.2%	6.7%	0.3%	22.7%	3.9%	2.7%	1.2%
Victoria, TX	25,601	83.5%	13.2%	0.6%	0.9%	1.7%	13.5%	0.8%	2.1%	0.0%
Vineland-Bridgeton, NJ	40,801	73.6%	21.1%	2.2%	1.2%	1.9%	17.3%	3.3%	2.2%	3.6%
Virginia Beach-Norfolk-Newport News, VA-NC	507,885	89.9%	5.2%	2.1%	2.4%	0.4%	7.6%	1.4%	1.0%	0.1%
Visalia-Porterville, CA	131,238	46.4%	50.4%	1.8%	1.1%	0.3%	37.2%	7.9%	4.0%	4.5%
Waco, TX	78,233	77.3%	19.2%	1.4%	1.7%	0.4%	10.0%	9.1%	2.3%	1.2%
Walla Walla, WA	17,618	76.8%	20.7%	0.9%	1.6%	0.0%	19.6%	1.7%	0.0%	1.8%
Warner Robins, GA	49,429	92.1%	5.9%	0.6%	1.1%	0.3%	6.2%	0.8%	0.9%	0.0%
Washington-Arlington-Alexandria, DC-VA-MD-WV	1,605,799	70.8%	14.8%	6.0%	5.1%	3.3%	21.2%	4.3%	2.6%	1.1%
Waterloo-Cedar Falls, IA	50,906	90.9%	5.6%	1.8%	0.4%	1.3%	6.6%	0.1%	2.3%	0.1%
Watertown-Fort Drum, NY	35,878	95.8%	3.1%	1.1%	0.0%	0.0%	3.3%	0.2%	0.1%	0.5%
Wausau, WI	29,492	88.0%	3.3%	1.8%	6.8%	0.0%	5.0%	6.7%	0.0%	0.3%
Weirton-Steubenville, WV-OH	27,390	98.2%	0.7%	0.3%	0.5%	0.2%	1.7%	0.1%	0.0%	0.0%
Wenatchee, WA	25,938	67.3%	31.4%	1.2%	0.0%	0.1%	26.4%	1.8%	1.6%	2.9%
Wheeling, WV-OH	31,989	98.4%	0.6%	0.3%	0.6%	0.2%	1.5%	0.2%	0.0%	0.0%
Whitewater-Elkhorn, WI	27,201	84.6%	14.0%	1.4%	0.0%	0.0%	9.1%	4.4%	1.8%	0.0%
Wichita Falls, TX	169,912	84.9%	9.6%	1.2%	3.0%	1.3%	12.0%	2.5%	0.3%	0.2%
Wichita, KS	44,916	83.0%	14.4%	1.2%	0.7%	0.6%	8.3%	7.7%	0.7%	0.3%
Williamsport, PA	28,105	92.9%	2.9%	2.9%	1.4%	0.0%	5.8%	1.1%	0.2%	0.0%
Wilmington, NC	75,894	90.5%	5.8%	1.2%	0.9%	1.6%	6.3%	2.4%	0.8%	0.0%
Winchester, VA-WV	29,424	84.4%	11.9%	2.9%	0.7%	0.1%	10.8%	1.3%	3.6%	0.0%
Winston-Salem, NC	159,220	85.3%	11.7%	1.3%	1.3%	0.4%	10.4%	1.7%	1.7%	0.8%
Wooster, OH	28,015	79.5%	3.8%	15.4%	0.0%	1.3%	10.4%	9.5%	0.6%	0.0%
Worcester, MA-CT	232,320	82.9%	9.2%	4.0%	2.9%	1.0%	11.6%	3.6%	1.4%	0.6%
Yakima, WA	64,342	49.2%	50.5%	0.0%	0.0%	0.3%	38.3%	2.9%	4.4%	5.3%
York-Hanover, PA	102,477	93.2%	4.5%	1.2%	0.6%	0.5%	5.1%	1.3%	0.4%	0.1%
Youngstown-Warren-Boardman, OH-PA	120,714	94.0%	2.7%	3.3%	0.1%	0.0%	4.4%	0.9%	0.6%	0.3%
Yuba City, CA	45,459	63.8%	21.9%	10.1%	4.2%	0.0%	25.5%	4.2%	4.5%	2.0%
Yuma, AZ	57,750	43.3%	54.5%	0.4%	0.2%	1.7%	42.6%	5.9%	4.6%	3.7%

PART H

EMPLOYMENT AND LABOR FORCE STATUS

Understanding the employment situation of the Millennials is complicated by changes in the economy, its impact on labor force participation, and the fact that many Millennials are still pursuing formal education. Younger Millennials who are still in school are not generally captured as part of the labor force by official U.S. Bureau of Labor Statistics (BLS) standards because they are not "looking for work." However, their response to employment questions in the American Community Survey may well have them classified as labor force participants if they are working while in school.

Official BLS employment data for 2016 show an unemployment rate for younger Millennials age 18 to 24 of 9.6 percent, down from 14.4 percent in 2013. Yet in 2008 during the depth of the recession the unemployment rate for that age group was only 11.6 percent. This apparent anomaly illustrates the importance of looking at the size of the labor force in addition to the number of unemployed. While the population base increased between 2008 and 2013, the size of the labor force declined slightly indicating that labor force participation declined during this period. The labor force for this age group continued to decline in 2016. Employment status is a dynamic process with individuals moving in and out of the labor force as education and life cycle changes take place.

About two-thirds (67.7 percent) of younger Millennials are engaged in the civilian labor force meaning they are not in the military and are either employed or unemployed and actively looking for work. More than half (58.0 percent) of all persons age 18 to 24 are employed, but more than 85 percent of those in the labor force are employed while 12.4 percent are unemployed and 1.9 percent are in the armed forces. The remaining young Millennials are classified as not in the labor force. While 11.0 percent of the population is unemployed, the overall unemployment rate for those age 18 to 24 is 12.6 percent because the unemployment rate is based on the civilian labor force not the total population.

The highest unemployment rate for younger Millennials is in Mississippi at 17.9 percent while the lowest is in North Dakota (3.8 percent). Minnesota has the highest percentage of young Millennials participating in the labor force at 79.6 percent. The Mississippi is lowest at 59.2 percent. Vermont has the highest percentage of employed (93.2 percent), and only one state is below

Percent of Millennials Age 18 to 33 Who Are Employed

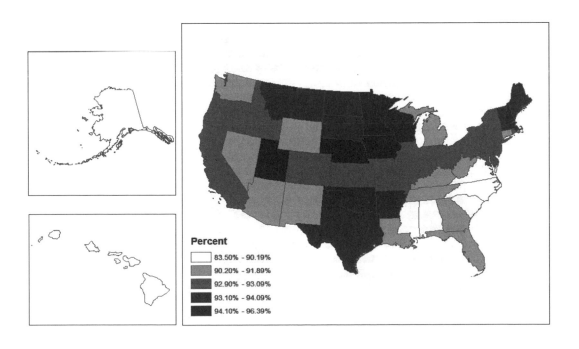

Percent	
	83.50% - 90.19%
	90.20% - 91.89%
	92.90% - 93.09%
	93.10% - 94.09%
	94.10% - 96.39%

75 percent: the Hawaii (74.9 percent). Among the older age group, the highest rate of unemployment is in Mississippi at 10.5 percent, and Iowa is lowest at 3.4 percent though four other states are below four percent: Minnesota, Nebraska, North Dakota and Utah. Labor force participation is high nationwide, at 82.2 percent and it's above 80 percent in 42 states. It's highest in the District of Columbia (90.3 percent) and lowest in New Mexico at 75.8 percent. Hawaii has the highest percentage of older Millennials in the armed forces (9.6 percent). At 96.3 percent, Iowa has the highest percentage of 25- to 33-year-olds that are employed though Minnesota and Utah are also just over 96 percent.

Participation in the civilian labor force among Millennials age 18 to 24 is highest (91.2 percent) in Wright County, MN and lowest in Tompkins County, NY at 40.8 percent. Woodbury County, IA has the highest percentage of the younger labor force who are employed, reported at 100 percent, and in 191 counties more than nine out of ten of the younger age group is employed. Local unemployment can be very high with 160 counties having unemployment rates greater than 15 percent. Dougherty County, GA has the highest rate at 39.3 percent, and 12 other counties are above 25 percent. Unemployment declines for the older Millennial age group where the highest rate is 26.6 percent in Sumter County, SC and lowest in Eau Claire County,

WI reporting no unemployment. Unemployment is less than seven percent in 369 counties. Labor force participation ranges from a low of 52.4 percent in Navajo County, AZ to Kendall County, IL where 97.5 percent of persons 25 to 33 are employed. A number of counties have a high percentage of armed forces population such as Onslow County, NC at 32.9 percent. Twenty-five counties are above 10 percent.

In Warren, MI, 89.3 percent of Millennials age 18 to 24 are participating in the labor force, and in 77 cities the rate is above 75 percent. The lowest rate (38.3 percent) is in Gainesville, FL. In Davenport, IA, 99.6 percent of the younger labor forces is employed but 37.4 percent are employed in Oceanside, CA. That is mostly because the armed forces presence is highest in Oceanside City, CA at 60.1 percent due to the nearby Camp Pendleton Marine Corps base. The city with the highest rate of unemployment is Victorville, CA at 39.7 percent. Thirty-four cities have unemployment rates above 20 percent while 56 cities are below seven percent.

Almost all 25 to 33 year olds are reported to be participating in the labor force in Fargo, ND (97.0 percent), but just over one-half (59.6 percent) are participating in Killeen, TX. However, Killeen also has the largest armed forces percentage at 26.4 percent due to nearby Ft. Hood, a U.S. Army base. The ACS reports that all

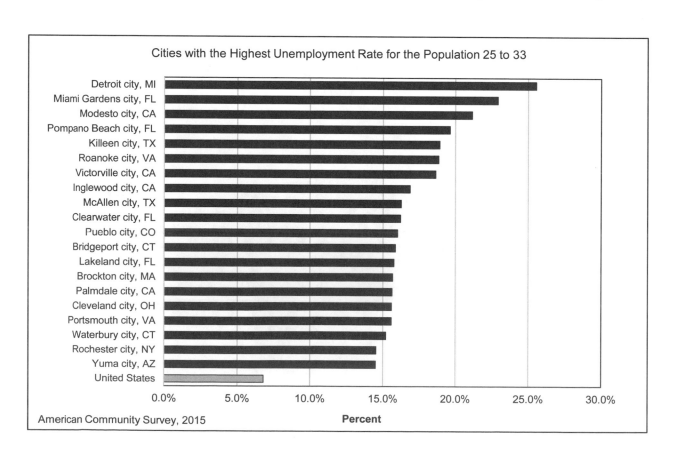

Cities with the Highest Unemployment Rate for the Population 25 to 33

American Community Survey, 2015

Percent

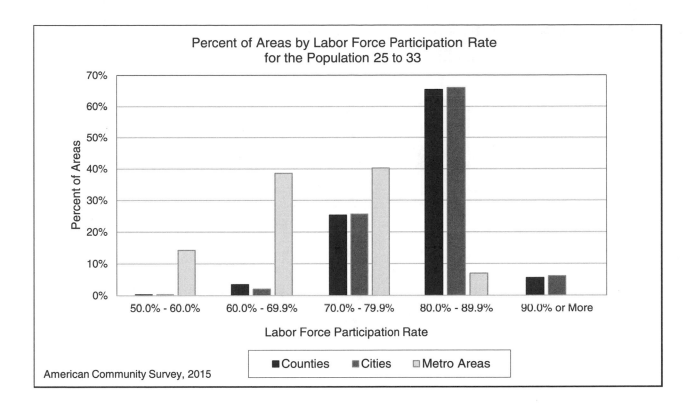

Percent of Areas by Labor Force Participation Rate
for the Population 25 to 33

American Community Survey, 2015

older Millennials are employed in Independence, MO, Edmond, OK and Pearland, TX. The percent employed is greater than 90 percent in 255 cities. Unemployment among this age group is below four percent in 83 cities, but it's also greater than 15 percent in 16 cities, with Detroit City, MI having the highest rate at 25.6 percent.

The Grand Island, NE metropolitan area reports the highest percent of young Millennials participating in the labor force at 97.4 percent while the Show Low, AZ micro area is lowest at 52.4 percent. Labor force participation is above 85 percent in 89 metro and micro areas but less than 70 percent in 19. The highest percentage of employed 18 to 24 year olds in the Holland, MI metro area is reported at 100 percent and the lowest is in the Jacksonville, NC metro (59.3 percent). The Jacksonville,

NC metro has the highest percentage (33.1 percent) of young Millennials in the armed forces and is home to the U.S. Marine Corps base Camp Lejeune. Unemployment, at 26.6 percent, is highest in the Sumter, SC metro area.

Among Millennials age 25 to 33, labor force participation ranges from a low of 41.2 percent in the Ithaca, NY metro to a high of 89.1 percent in the Holland, MI metro. Ithaca is understandably low because of the large college populations at Cornell University and Ithaca College. The Kalispell, MT micropolitan area reports the highest percentage of older Millennials who are employed at 100 percent. The unemployment rate for older Millennials is highest in the Albany, GA metro area at 38.5 percent and above 20 percent in 30 other metropolitan areas.

Table H-1: States—Labor Force Status

	18 to 24					25 to 33				
		Percent					Percent			
	In the Labor Force	Employed	Unemployed	In Armed Forces	Labor Force Participation Rate	In the Labor Force	Employed	Unemployed	In Armed Forces	Labor Force Participation Rate
United States......................	21,217,063	85.7%	12.4%	1.9%	67.7%	32,534,665	92.2%	6.7%	1.1%	82.2%
Alabama................................	300,638	84.0%	15.4%	0.6%	64.1%	447,888	89.7%	9.6%	0.6%	79.4%
Alaska..................................	67,016	78.8%	9.6%	11.7%	79.6%	87,158	83.4%	7.1%	9.5%	81.1%
Arizona.................................	458,309	85.1%	13.6%	1.3%	68.2%	643,603	91.9%	7.1%	1.0%	78.5%
Arkansas...............................	185,586	86.2%	13.2%	0.6%	65.6%	273,183	93.1%	6.4%	0.5%	78.0%
California..............................	2,541,485	83.2%	14.4%	2.4%	64.4%	4,255,953	92.0%	7.0%	1.0%	81.0%
Colorado	381,671	88.2%	8.4%	3.4%	72.8%	638,989	92.4%	6.0%	1.6%	85.1%
Connecticut...........................	245,947	87.3%	11.3%	1.4%	69.1%	335,788	91.4%	7.8%	0.7%	85.1%
Delaware	55,278	87.0%	11.8%	1.1%	63.2%	94,468	92.8%	5.7%	1.5%	82.2%
District of Columbia	50,796	82.3%	12.7%	5.0%	62.0%	125,560	93.8%	5.4%	0.8%	90.3%
Florida..................................	1,156,753	85.1%	13.4%	1.5%	65.0%	1,909,172	91.2%	7.7%	1.1%	81.5%
Georgia	657,067	82.2%	15.3%	2.5%	63.8%	1,006,835	91.0%	7.0%	2.0%	81.2%
Hawaii	103,306	74.4%	8.7%	16.8%	75.7%	159,242	85.6%	4.8%	9.6%	84.2%
Idaho....................................	113,408	87.7%	11.4%	0.9%	72.0%	155,587	93.0%	5.1%	1.9%	78.8%
Illinois..................................	855,492	85.0%	14.0%	0.9%	69.1%	1,334,792	92.4%	7.1%	0.4%	84.1%
Indiana.................................	477,826	88.0%	11.9%	0.1%	70.6%	624,224	92.5%	7.3%	0.1%	82.5%
Iowa.....................................	236,500	92.4%	7.6%	0.0%	73.6%	311,983	96.3%	3.4%	0.2%	86.7%
Kansas	215,845	88.5%	8.5%	3.0%	72.9%	295,066	92.3%	5.2%	2.4%	84.8%
Kentucky...............................	303,608	86.1%	11.8%	2.1%	71.5%	400,108	91.5%	7.7%	0.8%	79.5%
Louisiana..............................	300,777	83.9%	14.4%	1.7%	65.5%	475,211	90.6%	8.3%	1.1%	78.2%
Maine	87,917	89.2%	10.5%	0.3%	76.4%	111,907	93.3%	6.0%	0.7%	82.5%
Maryland...............................	379,162	85.0%	12.5%	2.6%	67.9%	632,315	92.9%	5.8%	1.3%	84.7%
Massachusetts.......................	481,383	88.9%	10.9%	0.2%	68.9%	734,275	93.5%	6.2%	0.2%	85.6%
Michigan	715,131	86.3%	13.6%	0.1%	72.5%	903,797	91.7%	8.2%	0.2%	81.6%
Minnesota	401,304	91.7%	8.2%	0.1%	79.6%	589,194	96.1%	3.8%	0.1%	87.8%
Mississippi............................	185,256	79.2%	17.9%	2.9%	59.2%	260,745	88.4%	10.5%	1.1%	78.4%
Missouri................................	436,574	86.9%	10.3%	2.8%	73.0%	599,875	93.0%	6.0%	1.0%	83.0%
Montana................................	67,981	90.0%	8.6%	1.4%	67.0%	93,928	94.1%	5.1%	0.9%	82.9%
Nebraska	147,429	92.7%	5.9%	1.4%	75.6%	193,996	95.4%	3.7%	1.0%	85.6%
Nevada	187,800	86.2%	12.6%	1.2%	73.8%	306,102	90.5%	8.2%	1.2%	81.7%
New Hampshire.....................	97,341	91.8%	8.0%	0.2%	75.1%	117,622	95.2%	4.3%	0.5%	86.3%
New Jersey	499,421	84.7%	14.6%	0.7%	63.1%	866,102	92.9%	6.7%	0.4%	83.3%
New Mexico	142,393	82.2%	15.0%	2.8%	68.2%	184,953	91.0%	7.7%	1.3%	75.8%
New York...............................	1,182,701	85.6%	13.5%	0.9%	61.0%	2,173,292	92.5%	7.2%	0.3%	83.4%
North Carolina.......................	666,638	81.9%	13.5%	4.6%	67.2%	963,955	90.2%	7.2%	2.7%	81.6%
North Dakota.........................	70,870	91.6%	3.8%	4.6%	75.8%	92,171	93.4%	3.8%	2.8%	89.6%
Ohio.....................................	786,194	87.2%	12.7%	0.1%	72.1%	1,124,639	92.5%	7.3%	0.2%	83.9%
Oklahoma..............................	265,490	88.7%	8.7%	2.6%	67.8%	381,814	93.2%	5.5%	1.3%	79.5%
Oregon..................................	259,077	86.9%	13.1%	0.1%	70.8%	406,211	92.6%	7.3%	0.2%	82.2%
Pennsylvania.........................	795,513	87.1%	12.9%	0.0%	65.7%	1,230,473	93.0%	6.9%	0.1%	82.8%
Rhode Island.........................	76,358	87.6%	12.0%	0.4%	66.8%	107,659	92.5%	6.1%	1.4%	83.3%
South Carolina	325,958	79.7%	15.6%	4.8%	66.8%	470,121	89.7%	8.7%	1.6%	82.4%
South Dakota	63,611	88.3%	10.5%	1.2%	75.4%	88,851	94.0%	4.5%	1.5%	85.9%
Tennessee.............................	436,884	87.9%	11.1%	1.0%	69.0%	631,842	91.2%	7.4%	1.4%	80.5%
Texas....................................	1,836,112	86.4%	11.4%	2.2%	66.0%	2,886,261	93.2%	5.7%	1.1%	80.3%
Utah	264,943	92.6%	7.1%	0.3%	76.7%	317,295	96.1%	3.5%	0.4%	80.4%
Vermont................................	46,265	93.2%	6.8%	0.0%	68.5%	55,187	93.7%	6.3%	0.1%	83.7%
Virginia.................................	567,676	80.9%	11.2%	7.9%	68.7%	884,976	89.5%	6.2%	4.3%	83.9%
Washington...........................	468,480	85.8%	10.9%	3.2%	70.7%	777,210	91.5%	6.1%	2.5%	81.5%
West Virginia.........................	97,423	84.6%	15.3%	0.1%	59.5%	150,121	90.6%	9.2%	0.2%	76.7%
Wisconsin	427,965	92.3%	7.7%	0.0%	77.0%	562,540	95.3%	4.6%	0.1%	86.7%
Wyoming	42,505	89.7%	9.1%	1.2%	72.7%	60,426	91.5%	6.3%	2.2%	80.7%

Table H-2: Counties—Labor Force Status

| | 18 to 24 | | | | | 25 to 33 | | | | |
| | | Percent | | | | | Percent | | | |
	In the Labor Force	Employed	Unemployed	In Armed Forces	Labor Force Participation Rate	In the Labor Force	Employed	Unemployed	In Armed Forces	Labor Force Participation Rate
Alabama										
Baldwin County	11,207	81.3%	18.7%	0.0%	77.9%	15,435	91.5%	8.5%	0.0%	77.0%
Calhoun County	10,143	89.1%	10.9%	0.0%	78.4%	10,420	89.0%	10.4%	0.6%	80.7%
Etowah County	6,487	93.9%	6.1%	0.0%	71.5%	7,149	94.6%	5.4%	0.0%	74.6%
Houston County	6,112	77.2%	14.5%	8.2%	69.8%	8,916	79.4%	17.4%	3.2%	76.9%
Jefferson County	42,068	86.0%	14.0%	0.0%	71.7%	74,192	91.5%	8.5%	0.0%	87.5%
Lauderdale County	6,679	88.8%	11.2%	0.0%	74.8%	6,600	95.3%	4.7%	0.0%	73.1%
Lee County	17,346	93.5%	6.5%	0.0%	56.6%	15,343	90.2%	9.3%	0.5%	81.6%
Madison County	22,073	87.2%	12.2%	0.5%	67.3%	37,283	91.9%	8.0%	0.1%	84.6%
Marshall County	5,970	90.5%	9.5%	0.0%	67.2%	7,070	88.6%	11.4%	0.0%	77.2%
Mobile County	22,442	82.0%	18.0%	0.0%	59.9%	42,507	91.0%	8.1%	0.9%	79.3%
Montgomery County	16,765	78.0%	18.9%	3.1%	68.4%	23,788	90.4%	6.9%	2.7%	79.7%
Morgan County	5,202	75.3%	24.7%	0.0%	54.5%	10,139	88.2%	11.8%	0.0%	73.9%
Shelby County	13,051	92.6%	7.4%	0.0%	72.8%	18,853	97.6%	2.4%	0.0%	82.8%
Tuscaloosa County	19,098	87.1%	12.9%	0.0%	52.7%	20,737	91.3%	8.7%	0.0%	73.3%
Alaska										
Anchorage Municipality	27,754	75.5%	11.6%	12.9%	80.1%	39,916	81.8%	7.2%	11.0%	85.9%
Fairbanks North Star Borough	12,500	83.0%	1.6%	15.4%	82.5%	12,522	77.3%	6.5%	16.2%	80.8%
Matanuska-Susitna Borough	7,883	93.7%	5.8%	0.5%	73.7%	10,108	93.7%	4.7%	1.6%	79.5%
Arizona										
Cochise County	5,113	65.0%	12.9%	22.1%	53.5%	8,700	80.3%	8.2%	11.5%	58.6%
Coconino County	16,913	82.6%	17.4%	0.1%	57.0%	14,180	92.0%	6.6%	1.4%	82.8%
Maricopa County	277,640	89.0%	10.7%	0.3%	71.5%	426,791	93.7%	5.9%	0.5%	81.7%
Mohave County	9,958	89.5%	10.5%	0.0%	78.1%	15,478	93.0%	7.0%	0.0%	77.7%
Navajo County	4,067	69.1%	30.9%	0.0%	41.7%	6,089	80.8%	19.2%	0.0%	52.4%
Pima County	80,320	79.6%	18.1%	2.3%	67.3%	88,001	89.3%	8.6%	2.1%	79.4%
Pinal County	18,756	82.7%	17.3%	0.0%	60.6%	27,928	90.4%	9.3%	0.3%	61.7%
Yavapai County	10,904	86.4%	13.6%	0.0%	71.3%	14,777	96.2%	3.8%	0.0%	82.0%
Yuma County	15,457	70.9%	18.2%	10.9%	67.1%	19,801	80.8%	13.8%	5.4%	77.4%
Arkansas										
Benton County	14,597	91.1%	7.3%	1.6%	72.9%	25,611	98.3%	1.7%	0.0%	79.3%
Craighead County	9,713	83.7%	16.3%	0.0%	73.2%	9,256	90.4%	8.2%	1.4%	70.4%
Faulkner County	10,348	88.2%	11.8%	0.0%	59.2%	12,042	96.4%	3.2%	0.4%	74.2%
Garland County	5,154	88.8%	11.2%	0.0%	64.5%	7,072	93.4%	6.6%	0.0%	73.1%
Pulaski County	24,319	87.6%	8.9%	3.5%	68.2%	44,087	92.3%	5.3%	2.4%	82.0%
Saline County	6,385	89.7%	10.3%	0.0%	74.5%	11,705	95.4%	4.6%	0.0%	85.6%
Sebastian County	7,211	82.9%	17.1%	0.0%	62.6%	11,626	98.2%	1.8%	0.0%	79.5%
Washington County	20,761	91.5%	8.5%	0.0%	62.5%	25,065	95.4%	4.6%	0.0%	79.3%
California										
Alameda County	88,389	86.7%	12.5%	0.9%	62.8%	199,199	94.8%	5.1%	0.1%	83.2%
Butte County	22,310	76.4%	23.6%	0.0%	66.4%	20,708	90.1%	9.9%	0.0%	82.2%
Contra Costa County	67,134	84.8%	15.2%	0.0%	69.8%	103,383	92.7%	7.2%	0.1%	84.4%
El Dorado County	8,296	92.4%	7.6%	0.0%	60.4%	15,065	89.1%	10.9%	0.0%	90.8%
Fresno County	65,842	81.8%	18.2%	0.0%	62.0%	99,549	88.9%	11.1%	0.0%	76.7%
Humboldt County	11,280	84.5%	15.5%	0.0%	61.9%	10,795	94.4%	5.6%	0.0%	66.6%
Imperial County	12,982	65.9%	31.5%	2.6%	65.0%	14,623	77.4%	22.4%	0.2%	68.2%
Kern County	63,415	82.8%	15.5%	1.6%	65.8%	89,602	88.0%	11.0%	1.0%	75.3%
Kings County	10,299	62.4%	16.6%	21.0%	61.4%	15,918	80.7%	8.6%	10.7%	67.9%
Los Angeles County	621,838	85.3%	14.6%	0.1%	61.3%	1,152,067	92.8%	7.1%	0.1%	81.4%
Madera County	10,441	91.2%	8.8%	0.0%	66.6%	11,768	96.4%	3.6%	0.0%	61.2%
Marin County	10,564	84.9%	15.0%	0.1%	64.1%	18,077	98.4%	1.6%	0.0%	81.9%
Merced County	21,423	76.1%	23.9%	0.0%	65.5%	23,258	91.7%	8.0%	0.3%	70.2%
Monterey County	31,259	78.3%	11.3%	10.4%	67.5%	41,994	88.7%	7.3%	4.0%	74.8%
Napa County	8,606	91.9%	8.1%	0.0%	65.9%	13,394	92.6%	7.4%	0.0%	89.4%
Nevada County	4,212	87.0%	9.9%	3.0%	68.5%	8,208	89.0%	9.7%	1.3%	85.9%
Orange County	193,551	88.3%	11.4%	0.3%	64.2%	333,675	94.8%	4.7%	0.5%	83.7%
Placer County	19,305	88.8%	11.2%	0.0%	67.1%	30,509	95.3%	3.5%	1.1%	81.6%
Riverside County	157,899	80.0%	19.7%	0.3%	66.3%	218,741	89.1%	10.3%	0.5%	78.5%
Sacramento County	87,860	84.0%	16.0%	0.0%	64.2%	167,602	90.8%	8.7%	0.5%	81.9%
San Bernardino County	156,722	78.8%	16.4%	4.7%	66.6%	220,469	88.7%	9.5%	1.9%	76.6%
San Diego County	250,084	74.5%	10.8%	14.7%	70.9%	391,326	89.3%	5.6%	5.0%	82.7%
San Francisco County	41,466	85.1%	14.9%	0.0%	66.2%	157,266	96.8%	3.2%	0.0%	88.8%
San Joaquin County	47,097	79.4%	20.6%	0.0%	65.0%	68,143	91.2%	8.7%	0.1%	76.6%
San Luis Obispo County	23,027	88.4%	5.9%	5.6%	54.5%	25,558	90.1%	7.3%	2.5%	82.9%
San Mateo County	40,960	86.8%	13.2%	0.0%	71.5%	84,015	95.6%	4.4%	0.0%	88.3%
Santa Barbara County	43,678	88.5%	10.4%	1.0%	61.4%	40,628	94.2%	4.4%	1.4%	82.7%
Santa Clara County	103,774	89.3%	10.7%	0.0%	63.4%	216,549	94.6%	5.3%	0.2%	83.3%
Santa Cruz County	24,658	89.7%	10.3%	0.0%	58.4%	23,853	94.3%	5.7%	0.1%	78.7%
Shasta County	9,601	96.3%	3.7%	0.0%	69.8%	17,339	93.0%	7.0%	0.0%	82.0%
Solano County	27,541	77.8%	17.7%	4.4%	68.4%	45,482	85.7%	9.6%	4.7%	82.1%
Sonoma County	32,994	85.8%	13.6%	0.7%	75.4%	48,546	95.5%	3.5%	1.0%	84.8%
Stanislaus County	35,634	76.7%	23.3%	0.0%	65.9%	54,249	85.9%	13.3%	0.8%	76.7%
Sutter County	5,834	70.1%	27.4%	2.5%	71.0%	10,500	92.8%	4.8%	2.4%	75.4%

Table H-2: Counties—Labor Force Status—*Continued*

	18 to 24					25 to 33				
		Percent					Percent			
	In the Labor Force	Employed	Unemployed	In Armed Forces	Labor Force Participation Rate	In the Labor Force	Employed	Unemployed	In Armed Forces	Labor Force Participation Rate
California—Cont.										
Tulare County	26,892	84.9%	15.1%	0.0%	55.5%	46,286	92.6%	7.3%	0.1%	77.7%
Ventura County	59,888	85.1%	12.5%	2.4%	71.6%	85,535	92.8%	5.8%	1.4%	84.0%
Yolo County	22,299	84.0%	15.7%	0.3%	55.3%	20,958	94.8%	4.7%	0.5%	80.0%
Colorado										
Adams County	34,636	89.1%	10.5%	0.4%	80.6%	60,550	93.0%	6.2%	0.8%	84.6%
Arapahoe County	41,762	89.8%	9.8%	0.3%	76.9%	73,432	92.5%	7.1%	0.4%	85.1%
Boulder County	31,831	89.2%	10.8%	0.0%	63.2%	33,000	96.4%	3.6%	0.0%	87.9%
Denver County	37,588	96.7%	3.3%	0.0%	65.8%	123,296	95.0%	4.9%	0.1%	88.5%
Douglas County	20,248	89.3%	8.4%	2.3%	83.4%	23,617	97.8%	2.2%	0.0%	86.5%
El Paso County	57,340	76.4%	6.8%	16.8%	78.8%	79,244	82.6%	6.4%	11.0%	81.1%
Jefferson County	36,197	91.7%	8.3%	0.0%	73.5%	62,510	94.2%	5.5%	0.3%	89.0%
Larimer County	34,709	94.1%	5.3%	0.6%	76.9%	38,922	93.7%	6.3%	0.0%	85.8%
Mesa County	9,834	85.1%	13.8%	1.1%	64.5%	14,529	80.3%	18.7%	1.0%	81.1%
Pueblo County	10,897	77.3%	21.4%	1.4%	71.2%	14,256	86.3%	12.6%	1.1%	75.9%
Weld County	20,055	94.4%	5.6%	0.0%	69.2%	27,900	95.3%	4.0%	0.7%	79.7%
Connecticut										
Fairfield County	59,233	86.0%	14.0%	0.0%	69.6%	84,592	90.7%	9.0%	0.3%	86.4%
Hartford County	55,929	87.6%	12.4%	0.0%	67.4%	87,521	92.0%	7.9%	0.1%	85.7%
Litchfield County	11,120	92.4%	7.6%	0.0%	82.0%	14,683	90.7%	9.3%	0.0%	89.0%
Middlesex County	10,283	91.4%	8.6%	0.0%	67.7%	12,761	91.4%	8.6%	0.0%	83.4%
New Haven County	55,159	88.4%	11.6%	0.0%	63.3%	83,131	92.0%	8.0%	0.1%	83.7%
New London County	23,370	75.0%	10.2%	14.9%	81.6%	26,518	86.1%	6.3%	7.7%	83.3%
Tolland County	19,963	94.4%	5.6%	0.0%	71.2%	12,508	97.3%	2.7%	0.0%	81.3%
Windham County	9,045	92.5%	7.5%	0.0%	76.0%	11,856	95.4%	3.6%	1.0%	87.8%
Delaware										
Kent County	12,181	83.5%	11.4%	5.1%	64.9%	17,576	88.2%	5.8%	6.0%	85.6%
New Castle County	32,538	89.7%	10.3%	0.0%	61.9%	60,905	93.6%	5.9%	0.4%	81.7%
Sussex County	10,251	82.5%	17.5%	0.0%	65.5%	15,870	94.4%	4.6%	1.0%	80.8%
Florida										
Alachua County	25,490	88.4%	11.6%	0.0%	45.3%	27,400	98.0%	2.0%	0.0%	76.8%
Bay County	10,643	73.6%	24.9%	1.6%	71.7%	18,470	85.2%	6.5%	8.4%	78.7%
Brevard County	27,908	84.2%	15.0%	0.8%	62.0%	45,917	92.6%	5.8%	1.5%	83.2%
Broward County	105,964	84.3%	15.6%	0.0%	68.1%	200,390	90.8%	9.2%	0.1%	87.4%
Charlotte County	6,041	86.7%	13.3%	0.0%	63.3%	7,400	94.8%	5.2%	0.0%	80.2%
Citrus County	4,537	89.9%	10.1%	0.0%	58.8%	7,752	81.7%	18.3%	0.0%	86.3%
Clay County	13,324	88.2%	11.8%	0.0%	75.9%	16,478	84.9%	11.0%	4.1%	78.0%
Collier County	18,677	91.3%	8.7%	0.0%	72.2%	25,202	96.4%	3.6%	0.0%	81.8%
Duval County	65,581	81.2%	11.4%	7.4%	75.8%	111,163	87.9%	7.5%	4.6%	85.7%
Escambia County	30,653	70.1%	8.7%	21.2%	75.7%	33,865	84.6%	9.8%	5.6%	83.0%
Flagler County	3,925	81.3%	18.7%	0.0%	49.8%	5,143	90.3%	9.7%	0.0%	72.2%
Hernando County	7,595	86.5%	13.5%	0.0%	66.3%	12,750	93.1%	6.9%	0.0%	80.6%
Highlands County	3,633	65.6%	34.4%	0.0%	59.9%	5,904	91.9%	8.1%	0.0%	77.2%
Hillsborough County	77,523	85.2%	14.1%	0.8%	62.9%	153,093	90.3%	8.2%	1.5%	84.1%
Indian River County	7,329	84.9%	15.1%	0.0%	63.7%	9,385	88.0%	12.0%	0.0%	82.5%
Lake County	13,559	82.2%	17.8%	0.0%	63.0%	22,950	94.7%	5.3%	0.0%	76.9%
Lee County	36,030	87.5%	12.4%	0.1%	72.9%	50,832	89.8%	9.3%	0.8%	74.5%
Leon County	43,664	87.7%	12.3%	0.0%	67.0%	29,642	92.8%	7.2%	0.0%	84.0%
Manatee County	19,103	90.3%	9.5%	0.2%	72.6%	25,036	89.2%	10.8%	0.0%	75.8%
Marion County	12,727	70.6%	29.4%	0.0%	50.5%	25,032	90.4%	9.6%	0.0%	74.1%
Martin County	8,794	96.2%	3.8%	0.0%	77.1%	10,203	95.2%	4.8%	0.0%	87.3%
Miami-Dade County	135,981	85.8%	13.9%	0.2%	57.5%	279,908	92.5%	7.5%	0.1%	80.9%
Okaloosa County	15,043	72.3%	7.1%	20.6%	79.3%	23,230	77.9%	6.4%	15.6%	79.4%
Orange County	94,578	89.6%	10.4%	0.0%	65.6%	159,767	93.8%	6.1%	0.0%	84.7%
Osceola County	20,054	90.8%	9.2%	0.0%	64.3%	33,670	94.2%	5.6%	0.2%	84.1%
Palm Beach County	79,700	85.3%	14.7%	0.0%	73.1%	122,748	92.9%	7.1%	0.0%	83.6%
Pasco County	26,070	88.6%	11.4%	0.0%	70.8%	38,044	91.6%	7.9%	0.5%	81.2%
Pinellas County	46,786	87.7%	11.8%	0.5%	71.1%	80,709	91.9%	7.6%	0.5%	81.7%
Polk County	34,831	81.6%	18.4%	0.0%	62.1%	59,290	93.2%	6.8%	0.0%	77.7%
Santa Rosa County	10,363	86.8%	13.2%	0.0%	59.0%	17,343	92.6%	7.0%	0.4%	81.3%
Sarasota County	17,452	77.9%	22.1%	0.0%	78.8%	23,910	94.3%	4.8%	0.9%	75.3%
Seminole County	8,857	87.4%	9.3%	3.4%	67.5%	17,010	86.8%	5.4%	7.8%	80.1%
St. Johns County	14,950	87.8%	12.2%	0.0%	63.7%	26,052	92.2%	7.8%	0.0%	82.0%
St. Lucie County	22,337	85.3%	14.1%	0.6%	56.8%	45,689	91.4%	7.1%	1.5%	81.7%
Sumter County	2,385	72.9%	27.1%	0.0%	50.4%	2,348	93.1%	6.9%	0.0%	60.4%
Volusia County	21,678	88.4%	11.3%	0.3%	51.1%	43,299	92.3%	7.5%	0.2%	80.4%
Georgia										
Bartow County	6,455	95.7%	4.3%	0.0%	69.5%	8,760	96.2%	3.8%	0.0%	80.2%
Bibb County	8,560	84.1%	15.3%	0.5%	52.7%	15,114	90.9%	9.1%	0.0%	81.5%
Carroll County	11,671	75.3%	24.7%	0.0%	75.6%	11,084	96.3%	3.7%	0.0%	81.8%
Chatham County	23,078	76.2%	18.5%	5.2%	68.6%	36,279	88.9%	8.0%	3.1%	84.8%
Cherokee County	15,832	97.5%	2.5%	0.0%	83.0%	20,329	97.0%	2.6%	0.4%	80.8%
Clarke County	19,366	91.9%	8.1%	0.0%	53.0%	13,564	94.6%	5.4%	0.0%	82.8%
Clayton County	15,416	79.1%	20.6%	0.4%	55.8%	28,369	92.3%	7.7%	0.0%	78.6%

Table H-2: Counties—Labor Force Status—*Continued*

	18 to 24					25 to 33				
		Percent					Percent			
	In the Labor Force	Employed	Unemployed	In Armed Forces	Labor Force Participation Rate	In the Labor Force	Employed	Unemployed	In Armed Forces	Labor Force Participation Rate
Georgia—Cont.										
Cobb County	47,660	88.5%	11.5%	0.0%	72.0%	81,486	92.9%	7.1%	0.0%	86.4%
Columbia County	7,814	84.6%	13.3%	2.1%	62.1%	16,547	79.8%	8.9%	11.4%	85.6%
Coweta County	8,184	90.9%	9.1%	0.0%	71.0%	13,925	92.6%	7.4%	0.0%	92.2%
DeKalb County	44,608	77.9%	22.1%	0.1%	68.0%	95,384	92.0%	7.8%	0.2%	86.6%
Dougherty County	7,399	60.7%	39.3%	0.0%	65.4%	6,866	90.9%	9.1%	0.0%	68.9%
Douglas County	8,654	87.2%	12.8%	0.0%	65.9%	14,138	86.8%	13.2%	0.0%	91.4%
Fayette County	5,838	95.9%	4.1%	0.0%	55.9%	6,053	83.3%	16.1%	0.6%	91.0%
Floyd County	6,168	82.5%	17.5%	0.0%	67.2%	9,076	98.2%	1.8%	0.0%	79.7%
Forsyth County	10,473	93.0%	7.0%	0.0%	69.5%	15,272	91.2%	8.3%	0.5%	82.3%
Fulton County	65,285	81.9%	18.0%	0.1%	65.9%	128,488	93.8%	5.9%	0.3%	86.7%
Gwinnett County	51,245	87.9%	12.1%	0.0%	61.9%	84,816	95.3%	4.7%	0.0%	82.4%
Hall County	13,039	87.8%	12.2%	0.0%	71.2%	15,635	95.0%	5.0%	0.0%	72.4%
Henry County	14,822	87.4%	12.6%	0.0%	64.1%	16,997	92.2%	7.8%	0.0%	80.8%
Houston County	9,953	81.1%	13.3%	5.6%	67.9%	15,279	87.1%	9.2%	3.6%	85.7%
Lowndes County	10,286	84.6%	11.3%	4.1%	56.5%	13,386	78.1%	14.3%	7.5%	80.8%
Muscogee County	16,058	58.7%	17.1%	24.2%	66.3%	24,185	74.6%	6.9%	18.5%	81.6%
Newton County	5,746	87.3%	12.7%	0.0%	70.3%	11,006	86.1%	10.9%	3.0%	89.0%
Paulding County	10,508	90.6%	9.4%	0.0%	73.4%	14,365	93.1%	6.9%	0.0%	85.9%
Richmond County	15,406	61.7%	12.5%	25.9%	65.0%	23,516	80.5%	6.8%	12.7%	77.8%
Whitfield County	6,999	90.6%	9.4%	0.0%	67.4%	10,596	96.8%	3.2%	0.0%	79.4%
Hawaii										
Hawaii County	12,804	92.1%	7.9%	0.0%	78.5%	16,965	90.1%	9.5%	0.4%	78.3%
Honolulu County	77,714	68.6%	9.1%	22.3%	74.6%	115,514	83.5%	4.4%	12.1%	83.4%
Maui County	9,952	90.6%	9.4%	0.0%	78.9%	19,058	92.0%	4.9%	3.1%	91.2%
Idaho										
Ada County	26,476	88.3%	11.7%	0.0%	70.9%	47,500	90.9%	7.2%	1.9%	82.8%
Bonneville County	6,178	87.5%	12.5%	0.0%	69.2%	11,320	94.4%	5.6%	0.0%	78.7%
Canyon County	13,998	83.5%	16.5%	0.0%	73.4%	16,679	92.2%	7.5%	0.4%	71.1%
Kootenai County	9,099	98.4%	1.6%	0.0%	77.5%	13,823	96.8%	3.2%	0.0%	77.9%
Illinois										
Champaign County	22,007	92.5%	7.5%	0.0%	43.3%	20,557	94.3%	5.7%	0.0%	85.4%
Cook County	312,268	81.5%	18.3%	0.2%	65.3%	630,061	92.4%	7.5%	0.1%	84.1%
DeKalb County	14,450	79.5%	20.5%	0.0%	66.1%	10,556	98.7%	1.3%	0.0%	83.4%
DuPage County	62,581	89.8%	10.2%	0.0%	73.8%	89,603	94.5%	5.5%	0.0%	86.9%
Kane County	38,175	89.4%	10.6%	0.0%	79.0%	46,235	92.6%	7.2%	0.2%	83.7%
Kankakee County	8,059	85.4%	14.6%	0.0%	69.8%	10,130	91.9%	8.1%	0.0%	82.4%
Kendall County	8,929	90.2%	9.8%	0.0%	78.9%	14,307	96.1%	3.9%	0.0%	97.5%
Lake County	54,498	78.3%	9.7%	12.0%	76.5%	56,687	87.5%	7.1%	5.4%	82.2%
LaSalle County	6,602	81.2%	18.0%	0.0%	75.3%	10,295	90.5%	9.5%	0.0%	86.5%
Macon County	21,925	92.9%	7.1%	0.0%	83.3%	24,104	99.0%	1.0%	0.0%	87.5%
Madison County	22,321	89.5%	10.5%	0.0%	72.7%	18,442	96.2%	3.8%	0.0%	92.7%
McHenry County	7,154	83.6%	16.4%	0.0%	70.2%	8,897	95.1%	4.9%	0.0%	85.1%
McLean County	16,232	85.3%	14.7%	0.0%	70.6%	26,310	94.8%	4.7%	0.4%	82.6%
Peoria County	12,115	72.6%	27.4%	0.0%	69.0%	21,108	90.9%	9.1%	0.0%	84.6%
Rock Island County	9,408	88.1%	11.9%	0.0%	73.4%	12,692	91.9%	8.1%	0.0%	86.2%
Sangamon County	17,071	83.6%	13.2%	3.2%	77.3%	26,595	85.1%	10.8%	4.1%	86.1%
St. Clair County	10,786	89.6%	10.4%	0.0%	61.6%	18,289	89.9%	8.9%	1.1%	82.9%
Tazewell County	8,155	93.7%	6.0%	0.3%	85.1%	13,294	95.5%	1.9%	2.6%	85.6%
Will County	47,617	91.6%	8.4%	0.0%	77.0%	60,064	92.8%	7.1%	0.1%	85.4%
Winnebago County	19,606	87.8%	12.2%	0.0%	79.3%	27,009	91.3%	8.7%	0.0%	83.9%
Indiana										
Allen County	25,866	88.8%	11.2%	0.0%	72.1%	36,712	93.7%	6.3%	0.0%	85.1%
Clark County	7,547	94.2%	5.8%	0.0%	87.0%	11,509	92.2%	7.8%	0.0%	83.4%
Delaware County	15,743	86.4%	13.6%	0.0%	68.7%	8,253	98.3%	1.7%	0.0%	79.7%
Elkhart County	14,186	91.7%	8.3%	0.0%	75.0%	16,230	95.1%	4.9%	0.0%	71.7%
Hamilton County	17,439	96.9%	3.1%	0.0%	78.8%	27,939	96.1%	3.1%	0.8%	86.4%
Hendricks County	11,610	97.5%	2.5%	0.0%	90.8%	16,793	97.6%	2.4%	0.0%	87.8%
Johnson County	8,715	93.7%	6.3%	0.0%	68.8%	13,982	90.1%	9.0%	0.9%	85.4%
Lake County	29,325	84.1%	15.9%	0.0%	68.7%	41,911	91.7%	8.3%	0.0%	82.2%
LaPorte County	6,169	88.4%	11.6%	0.0%	70.8%	9,507	83.6%	16.4%	0.0%	74.1%
Madison County	8,617	86.1%	13.9%	0.0%	72.2%	11,485	92.4%	7.1%	0.5%	80.0%
Marion County	66,501	85.0%	14.8%	0.2%	75.6%	120,649	90.1%	9.9%	0.0%	84.0%
Monroe County	19,433	87.2%	12.8%	0.0%	48.0%	16,215	90.8%	9.2%	0.0%	83.1%
Porter County	10,993	79.7%	20.3%	0.0%	67.5%	13,086	88.6%	11.4%	0.0%	78.8%
St. Joseph County	17,361	89.1%	10.9%	0.0%	57.8%	24,184	95.2%	4.4%	0.3%	79.9%
Tippecanoe County	26,932	93.2%	6.8%	0.0%	59.0%	19,427	95.6%	4.4%	0.0%	84.0%
Vanderburgh County	11,352	92.1%	7.9%	0.0%	62.3%	20,533	98.8%	1.2%	0.0%	88.4%
Vigo County	12,436	77.4%	22.6%	0.0%	71.5%	8,347	81.2%	18.8%	0.0%	70.3%
Iowa										
Black Hawk County	14,624	94.4%	5.6%	0.0%	72.3%	13,655	96.8%	3.2%	0.0%	82.6%
Dubuque County	7,863	94.4%	5.6%	0.0%	74.0%	9,356	93.6%	6.4%	0.0%	92.0%
Johnson County	19,115	89.8%	10.2%	0.0%	62.8%	18,316	97.4%	2.6%	0.0%	90.9%

Table H-2: Counties—Labor Force Status—*Continued*

	18 to 24					25 to 33				
	In the Labor Force	Percent				In the Labor Force	Percent			
		Employed	Unemployed	In Armed Forces	Labor Force Participation Rate		Employed	Unemployed	In Armed Forces	Labor Force Participation Rate
Iowa—Cont.										
Linn County	16,313	87.2%	12.8%	0.0%	79.4%	22,218	97.2%	2.8%	0.0%	82.5%
Polk County	34,560	87.0%	13.0%	0.0%	81.6%	54,576	96.6%	3.4%	0.0%	85.5%
Pottawattamie County	6,244	97.4%	2.6%	0.0%	81.8%	8,275	93.5%	5.0%	1.6%	77.4%
Scott County	9,984	99.7%	0.3%	0.0%	66.9%	17,659	94.7%	4.4%	0.9%	83.0%
Story County	18,839	93.5%	6.5%	0.0%	61.8%	10,075	95.6%	3.1%	1.3%	82.9%
Woodbury County	6,123	100.0%	0.0%	0.0%	59.9%	11,408	95.7%	4.3%	0.0%	87.5%
Kansas										
Douglas County	18,803	87.4%	12.6%	0.0%	68.8%	15,354	94.5%	4.8%	0.7%	93.2%
Johnson County	35,164	91.3%	8.7%	0.0%	77.4%	66,024	96.5%	3.4%	0.1%	91.5%
Sedgwick County	30,412	92.3%	5.8%	1.8%	72.2%	57,449	92.7%	5.6%	1.7%	82.2%
Shawnee County	11,644	92.9%	7.1%	0.0%	74.6%	17,967	88.1%	10.8%	1.1%	86.1%
Wyandotte County	11,888	89.0%	11.0%	0.0%	74.5%	17,900	91.5%	8.5%	0.0%	86.1%
Kentucky										
Boone County	8,511	80.5%	19.5%	0.0%	80.3%	12,165	86.0%	14.0%	0.0%	86.5%
Campbell County	6,373	87.7%	12.3%	0.0%	62.8%	9,585	99.1%	0.9%	0.0%	78.8%
Daviess County	6,689	76.4%	23.6%	0.0%	80.8%	9,039	92.7%	7.3%	0.0%	83.2%
Fayette County	29,706	93.0%	7.0%	0.0%	68.9%	39,127	95.9%	4.1%	0.0%	87.6%
Hardin County	7,121	81.2%	14.4%	4.5%	81.8%	10,582	88.4%	10.2%	1.4%	80.3%
Jefferson County	51,716	89.2%	10.6%	0.2%	76.6%	83,665	94.1%	5.7%	0.2%	86.2%
Kenton County	9,182	89.6%	10.4%	0.0%	69.6%	18,384	91.4%	8.6%	0.0%	85.7%
Warren County	14,982	88.5%	11.0%	0.5%	74.0%	10,426	93.2%	6.8%	0.0%	76.8%
Louisiana										
Ascension Parish	6,873	92.9%	7.1%	0.0%	69.2%	12,450	90.9%	9.1%	0.0%	81.7%
Bossier Parish	8,091	66.4%	11.2%	22.3%	78.0%	14,789	87.6%	3.2%	9.2%	78.6%
Caddo Parish	11,738	85.4%	14.6%	0.0%	51.1%	25,734	90.5%	8.6%	0.9%	82.5%
Calcasieu Parish	12,320	85.7%	14.3%	0.0%	64.2%	21,261	92.0%	7.8%	0.2%	82.3%
East Baton Rouge Parish	45,687	87.1%	12.9%	0.0%	70.5%	51,543	91.3%	8.2%	0.5%	85.5%
Jefferson Parish	23,888	91.0%	8.0%	1.0%	66.7%	49,139	92.4%	7.0%	0.6%	82.7%
Lafayette Parish	17,871	84.2%	15.8%	0.0%	71.1%	29,473	98.0%	2.0%	0.0%	83.8%
Lafourche Parish	7,169	83.7%	16.3%	0.0%	79.6%	9,394	98.5%	1.5%	0.0%	76.5%
Livingston Parish	8,275	89.6%	10.4%	0.0%	66.6%	12,745	93.3%	6.7%	0.0%	70.2%
Orleans Parish	22,250	80.0%	19.8%	0.2%	60.3%	53,795	89.8%	9.1%	1.1%	83.4%
Ouachita Parish	9,442	79.8%	20.2%	0.0%	58.1%	16,254	88.9%	11.1%	0.0%	77.3%
Rapides Parish	9,006	64.0%	17.6%	18.4%	74.0%	10,847	84.1%	4.1%	11.9%	72.2%
St. Tammany Parish	13,292	70.6%	29.4%	0.0%	74.5%	23,135	96.6%	3.4%	0.0%	84.6%
Tangipahoa Parish	10,802	87.7%	12.3%	0.0%	71.0%	12,233	90.5%	9.5%	0.0%	76.1%
Terrebonne Parish	6,742	99.2%	0.8%	0.0%	74.5%	9,935	95.2%	4.1%	0.7%	68.0%
Maine										
Androscoggin County	7,161	96.8%	3.2%	0.0%	76.0%	8,966	98.3%	1.7%	0.0%	82.0%
Cumberland County	22,174	89.4%	10.6%	0.0%	80.9%	28,463	94.2%	5.0%	0.8%	87.3%
Kennebec County	7,869	93.7%	6.2%	0.1%	75.5%	9,595	94.1%	5.8%	0.1%	84.2%
Penobscot County	11,390	79.1%	18.6%	2.4%	65.4%	14,195	92.7%	7.3%	0.0%	77.8%
York County	11,847	88.8%	11.2%	0.0%	79.5%	19,290	95.8%	3.9%	0.2%	90.1%
Maryland										
Anne Arundel County	38,240	74.7%	9.0%	16.3%	77.2%	61,177	89.7%	5.0%	5.4%	84.8%
Baltimore County	52,921	89.2%	9.9%	0.8%	69.8%	89,535	95.6%	4.2%	0.1%	87.0%
Carroll County	10,659	88.9%	11.1%	0.0%	70.7%	12,823	94.2%	4.7%	1.1%	83.0%
Cecil County	7,719	84.7%	15.3%	0.0%	76.3%	9,408	84.4%	15.6%	0.0%	89.2%
Charles County	9,016	91.7%	7.2%	1.1%	61.7%	14,669	94.9%	1.4%	3.7%	83.5%
Frederick County	17,621	86.4%	13.0%	0.6%	74.6%	24,156	95.8%	3.8%	0.4%	94.6%
Harford County	15,967	82.9%	14.3%	2.7%	75.3%	22,981	92.1%	5.8%	2.1%	84.2%
Howard County	18,735	93.9%	4.1%	2.0%	75.8%	29,906	94.9%	3.7%	1.4%	84.4%
Montgomery County	58,116	84.2%	14.7%	1.2%	72.1%	106,125	93.1%	5.8%	1.1%	87.0%
Prince George's County	60,550	85.1%	14.0%	0.9%	65.6%	101,725	92.7%	6.7%	0.7%	84.9%
St. Mary's County	8,132	82.2%	15.0%	2.8%	72.8%	10,683	94.6%	2.7%	2.6%	83.8%
Washington County	8,878	83.4%	15.6%	1.0%	68.4%	12,718	95.4%	4.6%	0.0%	73.5%
Wicomico County	8,359	89.1%	10.6%	0.3%	53.8%	7,380	83.8%	16.2%	0.0%	68.1%
Massachusetts										
Barnstable County	9,371	89.1%	9.0%	2.0%	64.8%	14,570	96.0%	2.8%	1.3%	88.6%
Berkshire County	9,314	90.4%	9.6%	0.0%	69.7%	9,864	92.6%	7.4%	0.0%	91.5%
Bristol County	42,274	86.8%	13.2%	0.0%	78.6%	53,259	91.4%	8.3%	0.3%	82.0%
Essex County	52,341	90.7%	9.0%	0.3%	74.2%	73,821	93.8%	6.0%	0.1%	85.2%
Hampden County	35,339	86.9%	13.1%	0.0%	69.2%	40,560	90.4%	9.6%	0.0%	77.1%
Hampshire County	20,268	86.0%	14.0%	0.0%	66.6%	17,089	93.7%	6.3%	0.0%	86.3%
Middlesex County	104,147	92.1%	7.6%	0.3%	68.8%	190,295	94.8%	4.9%	0.3%	87.6%
Norfolk County	38,555	88.3%	11.7%	0.0%	68.3%	65,238	93.0%	7.0%	0.0%	87.7%
Plymouth County	36,335	87.4%	12.6%	0.0%	75.8%	39,200	91.9%	8.1%	0.0%	86.5%
Suffolk County	69,991	87.7%	12.1%	0.2%	64.1%	143,462	96.0%	3.7%	0.3%	87.3%
Worcester County	57,274	88.3%	11.7%	0.0%	72.1%	71,354	90.4%	9.5%	0.1%	82.4%
Michigan										
Allegan County	8,727	96.7%	3.3%	0.0%	89.1%	9,487	100.0%	0.0%	0.0%	79.3%
Bay County	7,052	87.3%	11.5%	1.2%	80.6%	10,470	95.7%	4.3%	0.0%	91.9%

Table H-2: Counties—Labor Force Status—*Continued*

| | 18 to 24 | | | | | 25 to 33 | | | | |
| | | Percent | | | | | Percent | | | |
	In the Labor Force	Employed	Unemployed	In Armed Forces	Labor Force Participation Rate	In the Labor Force	Employed	Unemployed	In Armed Forces	Labor Force Participation Rate
Michigan—Cont.										
Berrien County	10,069	84.4%	15.6%	0.0%	80.9%	12,730	89.2%	10.8%	0.0%	79.7%
Calhoun County	7,931	84.6%	15.4%	0.0%	73.8%	12,041	97.9%	2.1%	0.0%	77.7%
Eaton County	7,346	92.4%	6.2%	1.4%	71.3%	9,435	93.7%	6.3%	0.0%	85.1%
Genesee County	25,793	82.9%	17.1%	0.0%	68.6%	34,217	90.1%	9.9%	0.0%	77.7%
Ingham County	33,265	84.7%	15.3%	0.0%	59.5%	30,657	96.0%	4.0%	0.0%	83.3%
Jackson County	9,999	83.7%	16.3%	0.0%	72.2%	12,799	94.5%	5.5%	0.0%	70.0%
Kalamazoo County	30,834	84.5%	15.5%	0.0%	75.8%	26,967	87.4%	11.5%	1.0%	87.9%
Kent County	47,007	91.2%	8.8%	0.0%	79.6%	76,464	93.3%	6.5%	0.2%	88.2%
Lenawee County	7,428	84.1%	15.9%	0.0%	70.6%	6,452	97.4%	2.6%	0.0%	72.2%
Livingston County	12,880	90.2%	9.8%	0.0%	79.5%	13,106	91.2%	8.8%	0.0%	80.4%
Macomb County	57,995	87.8%	11.9%	0.3%	79.6%	81,217	92.9%	6.9%	0.3%	83.8%
Monroe County	8,884	84.7%	15.3%	0.0%	74.3%	12,572	93.2%	6.8%	0.0%	82.6%
Muskegon County	10,390	87.2%	12.8%	0.0%	69.9%	14,722	90.3%	9.7%	0.0%	72.8%
Oakland County	75,406	91.3%	8.7%	0.0%	75.9%	120,319	95.4%	4.5%	0.1%	86.9%
Ottawa County	29,592	92.3%	7.7%	0.0%	78.4%	24,500	95.6%	4.1%	0.3%	84.0%
Saginaw County	15,341	76.5%	23.5%	0.0%	76.6%	17,880	94.9%	5.1%	0.0%	83.7%
St. Clair County	10,090	80.2%	19.8%	0.0%	78.0%	12,799	88.3%	11.7%	0.0%	84.2%
Washtenaw County	42,295	88.1%	11.9%	0.0%	64.1%	38,488	94.9%	4.9%	0.2%	84.9%
Wayne County	110,994	79.0%	20.9%	0.1%	68.8%	165,535	84.6%	15.4%	0.0%	78.8%
Minnesota										
Anoka County	23,169	86.1%	12.8%	1.1%	81.2%	31,824	95.3%	4.7%	0.0%	85.4%
Carver County	6,487	99.5%	0.5%	0.0%	73.4%	8,876	96.7%	3.3%	0.0%	95.0%
Dakota County	27,096	95.0%	5.0%	0.0%	83.2%	44,797	96.9%	3.1%	0.0%	92.9%
Hennepin County	78,334	92.3%	7.5%	0.2%	76.7%	167,755	98.0%	2.0%	0.0%	89.7%
Olmsted County	11,053	98.0%	2.0%	0.0%	84.8%	15,677	95.9%	4.1%	0.0%	84.9%
Ramsey County	40,313	86.0%	14.0%	0.0%	75.4%	67,342	95.3%	4.7%	0.0%	84.0%
Scott County	18,498	86.6%	13.4%	0.0%	77.6%	21,459	96.3%	3.7%	0.0%	89.1%
St. Louis County	7,020	90.7%	9.3%	0.0%	69.9%	14,342	97.0%	3.0%	0.0%	89.7%
Stearns County	20,020	95.1%	4.9%	0.0%	85.8%	14,700	98.1%	1.9%	0.0%	81.4%
Washington County	14,345	90.6%	9.4%	0.0%	77.7%	23,054	93.7%	6.3%	0.0%	82.6%
Wright County	8,308	98.9%	1.1%	0.0%	91.2%	11,655	97.3%	2.7%	0.0%	91.1%
Mississippi										
DeSoto County	12,136	81.9%	18.1%	0.0%	76.0%	14,238	89.7%	10.3%	0.0%	78.9%
Harrison County	16,801	61.9%	10.9%	27.3%	77.5%	22,149	77.3%	14.1%	8.7%	83.7%
Hinds County	13,550	88.3%	11.7%	0.0%	49.0%	26,116	92.9%	7.1%	0.0%	77.7%
Jackson County	8,040	80.0%	19.1%	0.9%	68.9%	11,893	94.5%	4.7%	0.8%	75.5%
Madison County	5,780	83.8%	14.3%	1.9%	60.7%	10,139	88.7%	11.3%	0.0%	87.2%
Rankin County	8,792	81.2%	18.8%	0.0%	76.8%	15,780	96.8%	2.6%	0.7%	85.1%
Missouri										
Boone County	17,555	87.3%	11.9%	0.8%	60.1%	19,055	96.2%	3.8%	0.0%	79.5%
Cass County	5,927	96.4%	3.6%	0.0%	75.8%	9,633	96.4%	3.6%	0.0%	89.6%
Clay County	15,674	92.0%	8.0%	0.0%	82.4%	25,266	95.6%	4.4%	0.0%	86.2%
Franklin County	6,259	89.8%	10.2%	0.0%	81.4%	9,267	96.0%	4.0%	0.0%	84.5%
Greene County	31,028	92.1%	7.9%	0.0%	78.9%	30,502	96.7%	2.9%	0.4%	80.3%
Jackson County	41,251	89.1%	10.9%	0.0%	70.3%	76,949	94.4%	5.6%	0.0%	83.3%
Jasper County	10,070	93.0%	7.0%	0.0%	80.1%	11,321	94.5%	5.5%	0.0%	85.7%
Jefferson County	15,147	81.1%	18.9%	0.0%	89.1%	20,819	97.7%	2.3%	0.0%	79.5%
Platte County	6,652	97.0%	3.0%	0.0%	82.3%	10,608	96.3%	2.9%	0.9%	85.4%
St. Charles County	27,064	93.3%	6.7%	0.0%	79.6%	39,060	96.6%	3.4%	0.0%	89.0%
St. Louis County	67,824	88.8%	11.2%	0.0%	74.1%	98,030	93.2%	6.8%	0.0%	88.4%
Montana										
Flathead County	3,612	100.0%	0.0%	0.0%	50.8%	8,291	99.7%	0.3%	0.0%	93.2%
Gallatin County	13,055	91.7%	8.3%	0.0%	73.9%	11,800	93.2%	6.8%	0.0%	89.4%
Missoula County	11,766	87.2%	12.8%	0.0%	79.8%	13,395	97.9%	2.1%	0.0%	79.5%
Yellowstone County	11,199	86.5%	12.9%	0.7%	73.3%	16,116	97.4%	1.7%	0.8%	85.7%
Nebraska										
Douglas County	38,666	92.8%	5.5%	1.7%	80.4%	68,856	96.1%	3.5%	0.5%	86.9%
Lancaster County	29,007	94.3%	5.7%	0.0%	64.8%	34,352	94.8%	4.2%	1.0%	84.4%
Sarpy County	13,642	82.8%	7.5%	9.7%	85.5%	19,038	90.9%	2.8%	6.4%	86.6%
Nevada										
Clark County	135,090	85.1%	13.4%	1.4%	72.8%	230,782	90.4%	8.3%	1.3%	81.6%
Washoe County	30,920	89.0%	11.0%	0.0%	76.3%	50,512	91.6%	7.6%	0.7%	86.0%
New Hampshire										
Hillsborough County	28,754	92.9%	7.1%	0.0%	79.1%	38,374	97.6%	2.3%	0.2%	86.5%
Merrimack County	12,734	95.5%	4.5%	0.0%	83.0%	11,853	94.2%	4.9%	0.9%	83.7%
Rockingham County	19,057	95.1%	3.9%	1.0%	76.7%	27,229	96.1%	3.3%	0.6%	91.9%
Strafford County	15,508	90.5%	9.5%	0.0%	76.3%	12,682	96.8%	1.3%	1.9%	89.0%
New Jersey										
Atlantic County	18,159	70.3%	28.6%	1.2%	68.6%	24,408	87.3%	12.7%	0.0%	81.1%
Bergen County	40,292	88.8%	11.2%	0.0%	52.7%	80,194	95.3%	4.7%	0.0%	85.3%
Burlington County	29,212	76.1%	16.7%	7.2%	72.6%	40,939	86.8%	8.7%	4.5%	83.3%
Camden County	31,042	85.3%	14.1%	0.6%	68.7%	53,769	90.6%	8.7%	0.7%	84.9%

Table H-2: Counties—Labor Force Status—*Continued*

	18 to 24					25 to 33				
	In the Labor Force	Percent				In the Labor Force	Percent			
		Employed	Unemployed	In Armed Forces	Labor Force Participation Rate		Employed	Unemployed	In Armed Forces	Labor Force Participation Rate
New Jersey—Cont.										
Cape May County	4,763	68.3%	17.3%	14.3%	73.7%	7,891	91.6%	6.5%	1.9%	89.0%
Cumberland County	9,093	85.3%	14.7%	0.0%	72.6%	12,951	94.3%	5.7%	0.0%	60.6%
Essex County	44,334	76.2%	23.8%	0.0%	60.1%	76,964	91.5%	8.5%	0.0%	81.6%
Gloucester County	17,394	86.8%	13.2%	0.0%	69.6%	27,381	91.4%	8.6%	0.0%	83.7%
Hudson County	36,598	84.3%	15.7%	0.0%	63.7%	109,370	94.9%	5.0%	0.1%	86.2%
Hunterdon County	7,389	86.9%	13.1%	0.0%	65.5%	8,144	97.1%	2.9%	0.0%	85.4%
Mercer County	25,325	81.9%	18.1%	0.0%	59.0%	30,856	90.8%	9.2%	0.0%	79.0%
Middlesex County	36,185	88.8%	11.2%	0.0%	45.1%	83,251	93.6%	5.9%	0.5%	81.1%
Monmouth County	31,977	87.9%	12.1%	0.0%	61.0%	52,907	93.9%	5.9%	0.2%	85.7%
Morris County	27,912	89.7%	10.3%	0.0%	66.4%	46,050	94.4%	5.6%	0.0%	90.7%
Ocean County	32,332	91.6%	8.4%	0.0%	75.3%	49,116	92.1%	7.3%	0.6%	83.9%
Passaic County	28,759	89.1%	10.9%	0.0%	57.3%	46,389	95.2%	4.8%	0.0%	75.6%
Somerset County	19,782	92.0%	8.0%	0.0%	73.8%	28,499	95.8%	4.2%	0.0%	89.0%
Sussex County	9,767	90.0%	10.0%	0.0%	80.2%	9,799	94.1%	5.5%	0.4%	79.1%
Union County	35,711	80.9%	19.1%	0.0%	72.7%	52,980	90.9%	9.1%	0.0%	85.6%
Warren County	7,102	87.4%	12.3%	0.4%	81.3%	7,871	91.1%	8.9%	0.0%	81.6%
New Mexico										
Bernalillo County	46,371	82.4%	14.9%	2.6%	70.5%	73,425	91.7%	7.9%	0.5%	81.9%
Doña Ana County	21,360	82.0%	17.8%	0.1%	70.2%	17,014	88.7%	6.7%	4.6%	68.9%
San Juan County	8,473	85.6%	14.4%	0.0%	79.9%	12,899	88.8%	10.8%	0.4%	79.8%
Sandoval County	7,995	92.6%	7.4%	0.0%	68.9%	9,664	92.1%	7.9%	0.0%	68.9%
Santa Fe County	6,655	91.0%	9.0%	0.0%	60.4%	11,139	98.1%	1.7%	0.2%	74.0%
New York										
Albany County	27,127	93.5%	6.5%	0.0%	61.5%	32,497	92.7%	7.0%	0.4%	90.5%
Bronx County	91,109	77.2%	22.7%	0.1%	57.5%	158,960	88.0%	12.0%	0.0%	78.3%
Broome County	16,062	83.6%	16.4%	0.0%	56.7%	15,780	95.5%	4.5%	0.0%	83.7%
Chautauqua County	8,490	79.9%	20.1%	0.0%	62.1%	10,170	86.7%	13.3%	0.0%	79.1%
Dutchess County	20,551	86.6%	13.4%	0.0%	60.9%	25,663	91.9%	8.1%	0.0%	84.3%
Erie County	61,419	92.1%	7.9%	0.0%	68.4%	95,916	93.0%	6.9%	0.1%	82.6%
Jefferson County	11,731	56.8%	7.3%	35.9%	77.5%	12,589	71.5%	4.8%	23.7%	78.1%
Kings County	131,897	84.0%	15.8%	0.2%	56.3%	354,863	92.3%	7.6%	0.0%	82.9%
Monroe County	55,850	87.0%	12.9%	0.1%	70.0%	81,001	92.7%	7.3%	0.0%	86.1%
Nassau County	74,408	86.2%	13.3%	0.5%	61.3%	119,268	94.0%	5.9%	0.1%	86.3%
New York County	81,455	84.8%	15.2%	0.0%	54.7%	298,387	94.8%	5.1%	0.0%	87.9%
Niagara County	13,207	85.8%	13.5%	0.7%	67.7%	17,943	89.9%	10.1%	0.0%	81.2%
Oneida County	15,075	89.8%	10.2%	0.0%	67.5%	22,122	89.7%	10.3%	0.0%	81.6%
Onondaga County	28,621	84.2%	15.2%	0.6%	59.2%	46,239	95.2%	4.8%	0.0%	83.7%
Ontario County	7,458	91.4%	8.6%	0.0%	64.9%	9,308	92.6%	7.4%	0.0%	88.3%
Orange County	27,730	80.3%	10.4%	9.4%	67.3%	29,272	92.9%	5.3%	1.8%	79.0%
Oswego County	9,343	85.5%	14.5%	0.0%	67.3%	9,629	90.8%	9.2%	0.0%	74.1%
Putnam County	7,165	89.5%	10.5%	0.0%	77.5%	5,929	100.0%	0.0%	0.0%	76.0%
Queens County	117,794	84.8%	15.1%	0.1%	59.9%	283,888	92.6%	7.3%	0.1%	83.9%
Rensselaer County	10,923	90.8%	9.2%	0.0%	62.4%	17,676	94.4%	5.6%	0.0%	88.9%
Richmond County	21,394	86.3%	13.7%	0.0%	50.4%	44,400	93.7%	5.9%	0.4%	77.7%
Rockland County	21,588	86.7%	13.3%	0.0%	68.1%	26,327	93.0%	6.8%	0.1%	81.2%
Saratoga County	7,143	90.0%	10.0%	0.0%	45.0%	9,111	83.4%	11.8%	4.7%	73.9%
Schenectady County	13,772	75.9%	16.0%	8.1%	77.8%	19,867	88.0%	6.3%	5.8%	84.1%
St. Lawrence County	9,031	86.7%	13.3%	0.0%	65.2%	16,059	92.8%	7.0%	0.1%	87.5%
Steuben County	6,175	86.7%	13.3%	0.0%	71.4%	7,233	89.4%	10.6%	0.0%	75.4%
Suffolk County	90,355	91.1%	8.7%	0.2%	66.6%	130,797	92.1%	7.6%	0.3%	84.8%
Tompkins County	12,503	94.1%	5.9%	0.0%	40.8%	8,427	95.0%	5.0%	0.0%	74.4%
Ulster County	11,428	91.9%	8.1%	0.0%	58.3%	14,287	94.3%	5.7%	0.0%	78.7%
Wayne County	4,593	81.5%	18.5%	0.0%	63.9%	7,473	82.6%	17.4%	0.0%	77.8%
Westchester County	53,877	86.2%	13.8%	0.0%	60.7%	83,574	93.3%	6.6%	0.1%	86.3%
North Carolina										
Alamance County	10,031	82.9%	17.1%	0.0%	68.0%	13,511	93.2%	6.8%	0.0%	81.1%
Brunswick County	6,352	92.0%	7.5%	0.5%	75.9%	7,730	94.0%	3.2%	2.8%	84.2%
Buncombe County	15,727	83.5%	16.5%	0.0%	74.4%	24,711	93.6%	5.4%	1.0%	76.9%
Cabarrus County	12,156	79.5%	20.5%	0.0%	76.7%	17,580	97.1%	2.3%	0.6%	84.7%
Catawba County	9,778	83.4%	16.6%	0.0%	72.3%	12,433	94.6%	5.4%	0.0%	78.3%
Cleveland County	6,295	85.4%	14.6%	0.0%	66.5%	7,146	94.4%	5.6%	0.0%	77.5%
Craven County	10,580	66.8%	5.9%	27.3%	82.2%	10,688	73.3%	11.1%	15.6%	83.1%
Cumberland County	30,259	57.1%	12.3%	30.6%	74.2%	39,281	69.6%	9.1%	21.3%	81.7%
Davidson County	9,482	77.8%	22.2%	0.0%	75.5%	12,996	87.4%	12.6%	0.0%	77.7%
Durham County	19,586	90.6%	9.4%	0.0%	65.5%	42,219	96.3%	3.5%	0.2%	84.4%
Forsyth County	21,125	86.5%	13.2%	0.3%	60.7%	36,436	91.4%	8.3%	0.3%	84.1%
Gaston County	11,614	87.5%	12.5%	0.0%	66.2%	19,853	90.4%	9.6%	0.0%	78.7%
Guilford County	30,450	89.0%	11.0%	0.0%	56.4%	52,699	94.0%	5.8%	0.2%	83.8%
Harnett County	7,720	79.2%	18.3%	2.4%	57.6%	12,978	79.2%	7.9%	13.0%	75.9%
Henderson County	5,416	92.7%	7.3%	0.0%	74.3%	6,968	94.8%	5.2%	0.0%	68.1%
Iredell County	11,458	88.3%	11.7%	0.0%	78.0%	13,333	89.5%	10.5%	0.0%	82.6%
Johnston County	10,091	80.3%	19.7%	0.0%	68.4%	16,953	91.7%	8.3%	0.0%	89.4%
Mecklenburg County	66,694	87.1%	12.9%	0.0%	70.2%	134,280	93.9%	6.1%	0.0%	87.6%
Moore County	3,989	74.6%	22.8%	2.6%	61.9%	7,236	77.5%	12.6%	9.9%	78.9%

Table H-2: Counties—Labor Force Status—*Continued*

	18 to 24					25 to 33				
		Percent						Percent		
	In the Labor Force	Employed	Unemployed	In Armed Forces	Labor Force Participation Rate	In the Labor Force	Employed	Unemployed	In Armed Forces	Labor Force Participation Rate
North Carolina—Cont.										
Nash County	6,010	87.5%	12.5%	0.0%	75.2%	8,286	88.9%	11.1%	0.0%	85.3%
New Hanover County	16,914	87.0%	11.5%	1.6%	59.8%	22,637	89.0%	11.0%	0.0%	85.6%
Onslow County	32,383	43.6%	9.2%	47.2%	86.7%	26,472	59.5%	7.5%	32.9%	79.4%
Orange County	18,533	97.4%	2.6%	0.0%	68.3%	13,719	95.1%	4.9%	0.0%	79.6%
Pitt County	24,262	81.3%	18.7%	0.0%	74.4%	18,510	87.4%	12.6%	0.0%	82.0%
Randolph County	8,668	82.6%	17.4%	0.0%	71.9%	12,645	95.8%	3.3%	0.8%	86.1%
Robeson County	7,817	71.5%	26.7%	1.8%	51.2%	9,584	91.4%	8.6%	0.0%	69.1%
Rockingham County	3,919	86.5%	13.5%	0.0%	59.9%	7,616	89.0%	11.0%	0.0%	84.9%
Rowan County	8,522	84.5%	15.5%	0.0%	68.0%	11,406	86.0%	14.0%	0.0%	77.6%
Union County	16,515	86.6%	13.4%	0.0%	79.2%	15,426	91.2%	8.8%	0.0%	82.4%
Wake County	56,657	92.0%	7.8%	0.2%	61.1%	113,749	94.7%	5.2%	0.1%	83.7%
Wayne County	9,014	78.2%	10.1%	11.8%	74.3%	12,000	90.7%	5.6%	3.7%	73.1%
North Dakota										
Cass County	22,161	96.1%	3.9%	0.0%	77.6%	23,415	98.8%	1.2%	0.0%	96.9%
Ohio										
Allen County	6,530	88.2%	11.8%	0.0%	67.3%	10,318	90.3%	9.7%	0.0%	89.5%
Ashtabula County	5,154	82.0%	18.0%	0.0%	65.8%	8,000	90.8%	9.2%	0.0%	81.7%
Butler County	29,018	90.2%	9.8%	0.0%	64.3%	32,146	95.2%	4.8%	0.0%	80.6%
Clark County	9,147	88.6%	11.4%	0.0%	76.3%	11,651	90.9%	9.1%	0.0%	84.7%
Clermont County	11,753	90.6%	9.4%	0.0%	77.7%	20,572	97.2%	2.8%	0.0%	87.4%
Columbiana County	6,170	86.5%	13.5%	0.0%	82.2%	6,763	84.1%	15.9%	0.0%	68.4%
Cuyahoga County	86,117	82.1%	17.9%	0.0%	76.1%	124,756	90.1%	9.8%	0.1%	84.5%
Delaware County	8,997	91.0%	9.0%	0.0%	61.4%	14,660	97.3%	2.7%	0.0%	86.8%
Fairfield County	8,959	91.1%	8.9%	0.0%	72.9%	12,419	94.7%	4.0%	1.2%	83.6%
Franklin County	89,491	90.7%	9.0%	0.2%	74.0%	177,183	95.1%	4.9%	0.1%	87.7%
Geauga County	4,968	95.7%	4.3%	0.0%	62.8%	6,041	96.4%	3.6%	0.0%	87.2%
Greene County	14,792	84.3%	12.6%	3.1%	71.6%	16,803	82.5%	13.6%	3.9%	88.3%
Hamilton County	52,590	86.2%	13.8%	0.0%	72.2%	94,478	94.2%	5.8%	0.0%	88.2%
Lake County	13,643	93.3%	6.7%	0.0%	74.6%	19,419	94.5%	5.5%	0.0%	89.7%
Licking County	10,680	79.5%	20.5%	0.0%	67.0%	15,098	92.4%	7.6%	0.0%	86.9%
Lorain County	18,414	84.7%	15.3%	0.0%	70.5%	25,193	94.5%	5.5%	0.0%	83.1%
Lucas County	29,722	87.2%	12.7%	0.1%	72.4%	47,450	89.1%	10.9%	0.0%	87.4%
Mahoning County	14,107	77.6%	22.4%	0.0%	69.6%	22,452	85.0%	15.0%	0.0%	87.7%
Medina County	9,877	85.6%	14.0%	0.4%	72.9%	15,205	99.3%	0.7%	0.0%	86.2%
Miami County	6,985	80.5%	19.5%	0.0%	89.7%	9,741	91.4%	8.6%	0.0%	92.2%
Montgomery County	34,551	82.0%	17.4%	0.6%	72.7%	50,681	91.3%	7.3%	1.4%	79.0%
Portage County	17,237	82.7%	17.3%	0.0%	63.5%	13,688	92.6%	7.4%	0.0%	84.4%
Richland County	6,941	82.9%	17.1%	0.0%	64.2%	8,109	92.7%	7.3%	0.0%	65.0%
Stark County	24,883	89.7%	10.3%	0.0%	76.5%	34,220	89.4%	10.6%	0.0%	84.1%
Summit County	34,678	88.9%	11.1%	0.0%	72.8%	51,430	92.1%	7.9%	0.0%	83.7%
Trumbull County	13,986	88.5%	11.5%	0.0%	81.8%	14,510	91.7%	8.3%	0.0%	77.9%
Tuscarawas County	5,090	93.1%	6.9%	0.0%	71.9%	7,288	98.7%	1.3%	0.0%	76.5%
Warren County	11,494	91.1%	8.9%	0.0%	66.5%	16,622	95.8%	4.2%	0.0%	78.5%
Wayne County	9,297	88.0%	12.0%	0.0%	82.7%	9,620	98.0%	2.0%	0.0%	85.6%
Wood County	14,306	92.3%	7.7%	0.0%	79.6%	16,084	88.6%	11.4%	0.0%	87.8%
Oklahoma										
Canadian County	7,699	98.2%	1.8%	0.0%	71.7%	13,789	100.0%	0.0%	0.0%	81.1%
Cleveland County	25,628	90.8%	6.0%	3.3%	64.4%	33,889	95.1%	3.6%	1.3%	90.0%
Comanche County	11,518	52.5%	9.7%	37.8%	76.8%	15,922	86.2%	2.9%	10.9%	80.3%
Oklahoma County	51,553	91.3%	6.5%	2.2%	73.3%	89,847	92.2%	6.4%	1.4%	80.4%
Tulsa County	42,782	88.6%	11.0%	0.4%	73.4%	68,123	95.1%	4.7%	0.2%	83.7%
Oregon										
Clackamas County	24,958	91.6%	8.4%	0.0%	76.8%	33,503	92.9%	6.9%	0.2%	81.7%
Deschutes County	10,144	87.8%	12.2%	0.0%	81.0%	16,028	96.4%	3.6%	0.0%	81.7%
Douglas County	5,280	76.1%	23.8%	0.1%	69.7%	9,216	93.7%	6.3%	0.0%	83.9%
Jackson County	10,118	85.7%	14.3%	0.0%	62.2%	17,911	90.6%	9.4%	0.0%	73.4%
Lane County	32,536	86.9%	13.1%	0.0%	70.0%	34,779	93.3%	6.7%	0.0%	82.7%
Linn County	7,007	95.3%	4.7%	0.0%	54.6%	9,112	89.7%	10.3%	0.0%	80.7%
Marion County	21,800	89.6%	10.4%	0.0%	68.0%	32,285	90.0%	9.6%	0.4%	83.1%
Multnomah County	47,243	85.3%	14.7%	0.0%	72.7%	113,505	92.6%	7.2%	0.2%	87.3%
Washington County	33,700	81.9%	18.1%	0.0%	73.0%	65,697	92.8%	7.2%	0.0%	83.8%
Yamhill County	9,147	92.4%	7.6%	0.0%	79.0%	8,512	90.0%	10.0%	0.0%	82.0%
Pennsylvania										
Adams County	6,072	96.7%	3.3%	0.0%	71.0%	9,679	90.3%	9.7%	0.0%	90.8%
Allegheny County	73,808	89.1%	10.9%	0.0%	66.9%	140,667	93.4%	6.6%	0.0%	84.7%
Beaver County	9,413	87.2%	12.8%	0.0%	74.2%	16,004	94.3%	5.7%	0.0%	86.8%
Berks County	29,833	85.1%	14.7%	0.2%	72.3%	39,165	93.2%	6.8%	0.0%	88.0%
Blair County	6,836	91.0%	9.0%	0.0%	69.5%	10,907	96.1%	3.9%	0.0%	80.3%
Bucks County	36,083	88.9%	11.1%	0.0%	72.7%	51,782	93.6%	6.4%	0.0%	86.5%
Butler County	11,892	90.0%	10.0%	0.0%	73.1%	17,722	96.8%	2.1%	1.1%	89.4%
Cambria County	6,758	82.6%	17.4%	0.0%	54.5%	10,634	89.1%	10.9%	0.0%	82.5%
Centre County	18,886	92.4%	7.6%	0.0%	46.0%	16,671	96.8%	3.2%	0.0%	75.1%
Chester County	31,149	88.8%	11.2%	0.0%	66.7%	45,599	93.3%	5.5%	1.2%	88.1%

Table H-2: Counties—Labor Force Status—*Continued*

	18 to 24					25 to 33				
		Percent						Percent		
	In the Labor Force	Employed	Unemployed	In Armed Forces	Labor Force Participation Rate	In the Labor Force	Employed	Unemployed	In Armed Forces	Labor Force Participation Rate
Pennsylvania—Cont.										
Cumberland County	17,377	92.6%	7.3%	0.1%	70.5%	23,470	97.8%	2.2%	0.0%	87.0%
Dauphin County	19,193	86.8%	13.2%	0.0%	72.6%	24,934	96.7%	3.3%	0.0%	85.6%
Delaware County	34,104	88.3%	11.7%	0.0%	59.2%	53,650	92.9%	7.1%	0.0%	84.6%
Erie County	19,796	92.3%	7.7%	0.0%	69.6%	26,728	88.2%	11.8%	0.0%	85.8%
Fayette County	6,914	94.0%	6.0%	0.0%	71.6%	9,072	81.9%	18.1%	0.0%	67.4%
Franklin County	9,365	84.3%	15.7%	0.0%	66.7%	14,184	95.9%	4.1%	0.0%	93.2%
Lackawanna County	12,380	90.6%	9.4%	0.0%	63.1%	19,211	90.7%	9.3%	0.0%	83.7%
Lancaster County	34,263	87.4%	12.6%	0.0%	69.2%	49,446	96.4%	3.6%	0.0%	85.2%
Lebanon County	9,808	93.3%	6.7%	0.0%	79.0%	10,778	98.8%	0.0%	1.2%	83.5%
Lehigh County	24,269	87.9%	12.1%	0.0%	73.5%	35,098	92.9%	7.1%	0.0%	84.0%
Luzerne County	18,795	87.5%	12.5%	0.0%	60.2%	27,232	92.8%	7.2%	0.0%	83.0%
Lycoming County	7,736	85.7%	14.3%	0.0%	64.4%	9,191	92.9%	7.1%	0.0%	74.0%
Mercer County	5,485	88.0%	12.0%	0.0%	53.8%	8,758	95.3%	4.7%	0.0%	81.7%
Monroe County	14,257	80.6%	19.4%	0.0%	78.2%	14,420	86.1%	12.8%	1.1%	87.5%
Montgomery County	43,750	86.6%	13.4%	0.0%	66.6%	76,939	94.1%	5.7%	0.2%	84.5%
Northampton County	20,394	87.0%	13.0%	0.0%	64.2%	25,318	96.5%	3.5%	0.0%	85.1%
Northumberland County	4,787	84.4%	15.6%	0.0%	72.1%	9,148	97.3%	2.7%	0.0%	86.4%
Philadelphia County	92,921	82.1%	17.9%	0.0%	56.2%	210,580	89.3%	10.7%	0.0%	79.0%
Schuylkill County	6,435	78.0%	22.0%	0.0%	63.2%	11,556	93.8%	6.2%	0.0%	77.8%
Washington County	13,642	82.9%	17.1%	0.0%	74.2%	17,259	92.8%	7.2%	0.0%	83.2%
Westmoreland County	20,681	88.2%	11.8%	0.0%	71.4%	26,814	94.1%	5.9%	0.0%	84.5%
York County	27,076	90.3%	9.5%	0.2%	79.1%	42,404	94.8%	5.2%	0.0%	84.1%
Rhode Island										
Kent County	9,528	84.9%	15.1%	0.0%	81.9%	18,548	91.6%	8.4%	0.0%	90.9%
Providence County	46,526	87.4%	12.6%	0.0%	66.0%	69,008	93.5%	6.2%	0.4%	81.2%
Washington County	12,429	85.9%	14.1%	0.0%	70.4%	8,856	94.7%	5.3%	0.0%	84.1%
South Carolina										
Aiken County	10,654	77.4%	22.6%	0.0%	71.2%	13,633	91.9%	8.1%	0.0%	74.8%
Anderson County	12,531	86.6%	13.4%	0.0%	71.0%	14,715	90.0%	9.3%	0.7%	82.1%
Beaufort County	12,826	65.0%	5.8%	29.2%	77.8%	18,884	81.8%	11.6%	6.6%	90.7%
Berkeley County	12,146	75.5%	9.2%	15.3%	68.2%	22,481	90.2%	8.3%	1.5%	78.0%
Charleston County	24,800	85.6%	5.2%	9.1%	63.8%	47,881	92.4%	5.6%	2.0%	84.0%
Dorchester County	7,967	84.2%	7.5%	8.2%	65.3%	17,172	91.4%	7.4%	1.2%	76.7%
Florence County	9,133	75.3%	24.7%	0.0%	69.7%	12,427	82.9%	17.1%	0.0%	80.4%
Greenville County	30,345	85.7%	14.0%	0.3%	64.1%	49,867	92.0%	8.0%	0.0%	83.0%
Horry County	17,969	87.8%	12.2%	0.0%	72.2%	28,317	89.3%	10.5%	0.2%	84.4%
Lexington County	15,829	86.4%	13.6%	0.0%	66.7%	29,391	95.4%	4.0%	0.6%	85.7%
Pickens County	10,344	90.1%	9.9%	0.0%	55.4%	13,279	93.4%	6.6%	0.0%	85.4%
Richland County	42,721	75.4%	12.3%	12.3%	66.5%	44,540	89.6%	5.9%	4.5%	84.8%
Spartanburg County	22,088	82.6%	17.4%	0.0%	77.0%	26,169	91.1%	8.3%	0.6%	77.6%
Sumter County	8,671	83.2%	16.1%	0.8%	64.7%	9,606	70.3%	26.6%	3.1%	78.8%
York County	17,161	84.0%	16.0%	0.0%	75.5%	24,006	93.9%	6.1%	0.0%	87.8%
South Dakota										
Minnehaha County	11,313	88.7%	11.3%	0.0%	73.0%	24,608	99.4%	0.0%	0.6%	84.7%
Pennington County	6,738	83.6%	4.9%	11.4%	79.1%	13,416	83.7%	8.7%	7.6%	89.7%
Tennessee										
Blount County	7,895	82.0%	18.0%	0.0%	73.6%	10,935	93.5%	6.5%	0.0%	86.1%
Bradley County	7,373	81.1%	18.9%	0.0%	73.5%	9,053	86.8%	13.2%	0.0%	73.1%
Davidson County	49,642	89.5%	10.3%	0.2%	71.1%	100,641	97.3%	2.7%	0.0%	86.3%
Hamilton County	21,942	88.8%	11.2%	0.0%	67.1%	36,896	90.0%	9.6%	0.4%	83.8%
Knox County	40,260	93.2%	6.8%	0.0%	71.4%	43,571	91.7%	8.1%	0.2%	83.3%
Madison County	6,268	92.0%	8.0%	0.0%	59.4%	8,487	93.4%	6.6%	0.0%	78.7%
Montgomery County	15,384	64.7%	9.5%	25.8%	69.8%	28,642	66.3%	8.6%	25.0%	81.6%
Rutherford County	32,261	93.8%	6.2%	0.0%	81.3%	31,580	95.4%	4.6%	0.0%	83.4%
Sevier County	6,814	100.0%	0.0%	0.0%	80.4%	5,943	99.0%	1.0%	0.0%	69.5%
Shelby County	60,501	82.7%	17.2%	0.1%	66.1%	101,465	91.9%	7.7%	0.4%	82.3%
Sullivan County	8,819	81.2%	18.8%	0.0%	71.5%	10,279	89.3%	10.7%	0.0%	72.0%
Sumner County	10,048	93.4%	6.6%	0.0%	68.8%	16,756	95.1%	4.9%	0.0%	84.8%
Washington County	9,914	84.2%	15.8%	0.0%	63.9%	10,458	95.8%	4.2%	0.0%	75.8%
Williamson County	11,877	92.1%	7.9%	0.0%	76.3%	12,460	90.4%	9.6%	0.0%	84.4%
Wilson County	8,616	91.8%	8.2%	0.0%	78.4%	10,283	88.6%	11.4%	0.0%	85.1%
Texas										
Bell County	32,027	63.8%	11.0%	25.2%	80.0%	41,578	70.1%	10.4%	19.5%	80.9%
Bexar County	136,004	84.9%	11.4%	3.7%	69.6%	214,095	91.8%	5.4%	2.8%	80.6%
Bowie County	5,206	72.0%	28.0%	0.0%	60.3%	7,515	94.0%	6.0%	0.0%	69.2%
Brazoria County	19,089	82.1%	17.9%	0.0%	65.2%	34,187	97.2%	2.8%	0.0%	80.9%
Brazos County	29,070	96.9%	3.1%	0.0%	49.4%	25,839	95.7%	4.3%	0.0%	80.8%
Cameron County	26,282	85.7%	14.3%	0.0%	58.4%	35,064	90.9%	9.1%	0.0%	75.8%
Collin County	47,825	88.6%	11.2%	0.3%	67.1%	86,696	96.8%	2.5%	0.7%	84.4%
Comal County	6,941	96.3%	3.7%	0.0%	66.3%	10,116	95.6%	4.4%	0.0%	80.3%
Dallas County	175,237	89.0%	10.9%	0.1%	70.7%	298,459	94.8%	5.1%	0.1%	82.4%
Denton County	51,981	88.8%	11.2%	0.0%	71.8%	90,131	95.2%	4.8%	0.0%	86.2%

Table H-2: Counties—Labor Force Status—*Continued*

| | 18 to 24 | | | | | 25 to 33 | | | | |
| | In the Labor Force | Percent | | | | In the Labor Force | Percent | | | |
		Employed	Unemployed	In Armed Forces	Labor Force Participation Rate		Employed	Unemployed	In Armed Forces	Labor Force Participation Rate
Texas—Cont.										
Ector County	11,796	84.1%	15.9%	0.0%	65.4%	18,501	97.2%	2.8%	0.0%	77.0%
El Paso County	10,285	95.9%	4.1%	0.0%	70.9%	13,917	91.3%	8.2%	0.5%	78.4%
Ellis County	62,339	78.5%	9.2%	12.3%	66.3%	89,637	86.4%	6.5%	7.1%	81.2%
Fort Bend County	38,768	91.8%	8.2%	0.0%	64.3%	62,221	96.0%	3.0%	1.0%	78.4%
Galveston County	20,403	81.4%	17.4%	1.1%	70.9%	29,298	93.4%	5.7%	0.9%	79.4%
Grayson County	8,602	85.6%	13.1%	1.3%	70.0%	10,741	95.5%	2.5%	2.0%	83.5%
Gregg County	8,260	94.7%	5.3%	0.0%	68.3%	12,594	89.8%	10.2%	0.0%	85.6%
Guadalupe County	8,119	92.6%	7.4%	0.0%	62.5%	13,655	94.7%	3.6%	1.7%	77.7%
Harris County	292,082	87.6%	12.2%	0.2%	67.7%	533,770	94.6%	5.4%	0.1%	82.2%
Hays County	22,789	89.7%	10.3%	0.0%	66.4%	21,194	93.2%	6.4%	0.4%	84.6%
Hidalgo County	51,006	79.4%	20.6%	0.0%	54.5%	72,239	88.1%	11.2%	0.6%	73.7%
Jefferson County	15,545	91.7%	8.1%	0.2%	64.9%	22,841	92.6%	7.4%	0.0%	67.7%
Johnson County	8,357	84.0%	16.0%	0.0%	58.8%	13,583	93.1%	6.9%	0.0%	76.8%
Kaufman County	6,926	67.7%	32.3%	0.0%	73.1%	10,986	95.1%	4.9%	0.0%	81.3%
Lubbock County	28,209	92.3%	7.7%	0.0%	55.6%	33,584	98.0%	2.0%	0.0%	83.5%
McLennan County	22,595	90.0%	9.5%	0.5%	62.8%	21,880	94.1%	5.9%	0.0%	77.8%
Midland County	12,733	92.5%	7.5%	0.0%	78.7%	20,696	97.9%	2.1%	0.0%	81.9%
Montgomery County	29,030	93.7%	6.3%	0.0%	63.0%	49,440	86.8%	13.2%	0.0%	84.4%
Nueces County	22,872	78.0%	18.9%	3.1%	62.6%	39,931	92.1%	7.4%	0.5%	83.1%
Parker County	7,315	93.7%	6.3%	0.0%	70.1%	8,756	92.6%	7.2%	0.2%	78.9%
Potter County	7,611	90.0%	10.0%	0.0%	67.6%	13,616	99.1%	0.9%	0.0%	82.3%
Randall County	9,709	95.6%	3.7%	0.7%	72.0%	14,538	96.7%	3.3%	0.0%	82.9%
Smith County	14,155	92.7%	7.3%	0.0%	60.6%	20,554	97.4%	2.6%	0.0%	72.4%
Tarrant County	130,694	92.7%	7.1%	0.2%	71.3%	216,230	94.9%	5.0%	0.1%	82.9%
Taylor County	15,491	75.0%	5.4%	19.7%	74.3%	14,399	90.8%	2.9%	6.3%	84.3%
Tom Green County	9,026	78.1%	2.2%	19.8%	60.4%	12,749	88.5%	2.9%	8.6%	78.0%
Travis County	70,081	91.2%	8.8%	0.1%	62.6%	186,080	96.3%	3.7%	0.0%	87.6%
Webb County	18,857	87.0%	13.0%	0.0%	61.9%	21,239	93.9%	6.1%	0.0%	68.7%
Wichita County	14,435	61.1%	7.2%	31.7%	76.0%	12,265	90.0%	6.5%	3.5%	70.2%
Williamson County	28,201	88.4%	11.5%	0.1%	70.8%	49,028	94.8%	4.0%	1.2%	81.9%
Utah										
Cache County	15,769	95.3%	4.7%	0.0%	75.0%	13,468	96.3%	3.7%	0.0%	78.2%
Davis County	23,663	90.6%	7.4%	2.0%	73.1%	34,358	93.8%	4.5%	1.7%	80.7%
Salt Lake County	85,998	92.6%	7.4%	0.0%	80.2%	133,814	96.3%	3.5%	0.2%	84.1%
Utah County	70,737	93.5%	6.5%	0.0%	74.9%	54,993	97.1%	2.8%	0.2%	76.1%
Washington County	12,220	93.3%	6.7%	0.0%	73.1%	12,161	98.4%	1.6%	0.0%	79.8%
Weber County	19,353	90.3%	8.7%	1.0%	81.5%	26,492	94.2%	4.4%	1.4%	79.0%
Vermont										
Chittenden County	16,578	94.9%	5.1%	0.0%	65.9%	17,196	93.9%	5.9%	0.2%	86.7%
Virginia										
Albemarle County	7,359	98.6%	1.4%	0.0%	54.3%	10,999	93.1%	6.2%	0.7%	83.0%
Arlington County	13,928	86.6%	8.5%	5.0%	80.2%	52,231	94.9%	4.2%	0.8%	94.2%
Chesterfield County	23,813	91.1%	8.9%	0.0%	75.8%	28,280	91.5%	7.8%	0.7%	83.6%
Fairfax County	69,885	85.9%	13.4%	0.7%	73.0%	125,816	94.1%	4.0%	1.9%	88.6%
Hanover County	6,661	90.8%	9.2%	0.0%	67.8%	7,110	93.4%	6.6%	0.0%	86.7%
Henrico County	20,235	83.9%	16.1%	0.0%	76.4%	36,037	94.1%	5.9%	0.0%	88.9%
Loudoun County	18,289	91.5%	4.7%	3.8%	75.0%	36,770	95.9%	3.2%	0.9%	84.9%
Montgomery County	12,027	93.2%	6.8%	0.0%	43.7%	10,306	97.9%	2.1%	0.0%	79.3%
Prince William County	28,759	80.9%	15.1%	4.0%	71.7%	48,156	91.2%	5.7%	3.1%	86.3%
Roanoke County	5,722	92.0%	8.0%	0.0%	79.7%	9,247	92.3%	7.1%	0.6%	91.3%
Spotsylvania County	9,486	76.3%	13.8%	9.9%	78.5%	11,299	87.4%	7.0%	5.7%	84.5%
Stafford County	10,265	68.5%	15.5%	16.1%	66.9%	14,272	90.7%	4.5%	4.8%	85.4%
Washington										
Benton County	12,086	85.4%	14.6%	0.0%	69.6%	16,996	95.2%	4.8%	0.0%	79.8%
Clark County	29,776	87.0%	12.9%	0.1%	75.7%	44,033	93.7%	5.0%	1.3%	81.3%
Cowlitz County	4,889	98.5%	1.3%	0.2%	73.4%	10,670	95.9%	4.1%	0.0%	82.4%
Grant County	6,255	89.2%	10.8%	0.0%	54.0%	8,302	92.1%	7.9%	0.0%	82.7%
King County	120,868	90.6%	9.1%	0.3%	70.3%	282,595	95.6%	4.3%	0.1%	86.2%
Kitsap County	21,329	61.4%	15.7%	22.9%	77.8%	26,374	73.0%	5.1%	21.9%	80.6%
Pierce County	57,368	77.9%	12.1%	10.0%	72.8%	89,535	87.7%	6.2%	6.1%	78.8%
Skagit County	7,246	69.7%	15.8%	14.5%	81.0%	11,783	78.4%	10.1%	11.5%	86.1%
Snohomish County	47,834	88.9%	10.3%	0.8%	74.2%	80,686	91.5%	6.7%	1.8%	82.9%
Spokane County	30,351	86.4%	11.8%	1.8%	62.6%	49,324	89.3%	7.5%	3.2%	72.5%
Thurston County	17,092	90.4%	8.2%	1.4%	68.6%	27,411	88.1%	8.4%	3.5%	82.7%
Whatcom County	22,833	95.1%	4.9%	0.0%	74.6%	20,429	89.6%	9.7%	0.6%	77.6%
Yakima County	19,540	80.1%	19.9%	0.1%	76.8%	20,689	88.9%	10.6%	0.5%	75.0%
West Virginia										
Berkeley County	6,067	77.5%	21.4%	1.2%	60.8%	10,415	87.4%	12.6%	0.0%	81.5%
Cabell County	6,246	89.1%	10.9%	0.0%	54.7%	8,264	100.0%	0.0%	0.0%	75.4%
Kanawha County	9,756	80.9%	19.1%	0.0%	69.0%	16,941	91.9%	8.1%	0.0%	83.4%
Monongalia County	8,975	91.9%	8.1%	0.0%	41.5%	13,066	98.0%	2.0%	0.0%	72.1%

Table H-2: Counties—Labor Force Status—*Continued*

	18 to 24					25 to 33				
	In the Labor Force	Percent				In the Labor Force	Percent			
		Employed	Unemployed	In Armed Forces	Labor Force Participation Rate		Employed	Unemployed	In Armed Forces	Labor Force Participation Rate
Wisconsin										
Brown County	18,536	91.3%	8.7%	0.0%	79.5%	28,624	97.3%	2.7%	0.0%	87.5%
Dane County	52,592	93.4%	6.6%	0.0%	78.0%	65,655	96.0%	3.9%	0.1%	88.7%
Eau Claire County	10,646	97.1%	2.9%	0.0%	69.9%	11,236	100.0%	0.0%	0.0%	88.4%
Fond du Lac County	6,639	88.3%	11.7%	0.0%	78.1%	9,728	92.4%	7.6%	0.0%	92.3%
Kenosha County	13,856	88.1%	11.9%	0.0%	80.8%	15,341	92.7%	5.4%	1.8%	86.5%
La Crosse County	12,808	94.3%	5.7%	0.0%	66.6%	10,952	92.4%	7.6%	0.0%	87.3%
Marathon County	8,396	96.7%	3.3%	0.0%	86.6%	12,377	97.9%	2.1%	0.0%	86.8%
Milwaukee County	66,508	88.2%	11.8%	0.0%	69.3%	114,346	93.8%	6.2%	0.0%	84.0%
Outagamie County	13,549	94.0%	6.0%	0.0%	88.0%	21,264	97.8%	2.2%	0.0%	91.4%
Racine County	13,887	90.8%	9.2%	0.0%	77.9%	17,369	92.0%	8.0%	0.0%	88.4%
Rock County	12,389	88.4%	11.6%	0.0%	83.6%	13,110	96.0%	4.0%	0.0%	85.8%
Sheboygan County	6,603	89.2%	10.8%	0.0%	77.5%	10,114	98.8%	1.2%	0.0%	85.9%
Walworth County	10,761	96.7%	3.3%	0.0%	81.0%	8,998	95.7%	4.3%	0.0%	89.5%
Washington County	8,953	94.4%	5.6%	0.0%	86.5%	10,438	94.8%	5.2%	0.0%	83.7%
Waukesha County	23,300	93.6%	6.4%	0.0%	78.0%	32,738	97.7%	2.3%	0.0%	92.5%
Winnebago County	15,362	94.6%	5.4%	0.0%	79.7%	17,967	97.2%	2.8%	0.0%	84.8%
Wyoming										
Laramie County	9,519	88.0%	6.6%	5.5%	68.4%	8,185	86.4%	5.9%	7.7%	86.8%

Table H-3: Places—Labor Force Status

| | 18 to 24 | | | | | 25 to 33 | | | | |
| | In the Labor Force | Percent | | | | In the Labor Force | Percent | | | |
		Employed	Unemployed	In Armed Forces	Labor Force Participation Rate		Employed	Unemployed	In Armed Forces	Labor Force Participation Rate
Alabama										
Birmingham city	16,391	79.2%	20.8%	0.0%	66.2%	27,766	88.0%	12.0%	0.0%	85.2%
Huntsville city	13,108	84.0%	16.0%	0.0%	67.9%	19,462	90.4%	9.6%	0.0%	80.1%
Mobile city	10,995	80.8%	19.2%	0.0%	54.6%	22,055	90.6%	8.2%	1.2%	81.8%
Montgomery city	14,751	77.0%	19.5%	3.5%	67.7%	21,876	90.1%	7.5%	2.4%	81.5%
Tuscaloosa city	13,928	84.5%	15.5%	0.0%	53.9%	10,528	95.0%	5.0%	0.0%	76.7%
Alaska										
Anchorage municipality	27,714	76.7%	10.3%	12.9%	80.2%	38,931	81.3%	7.4%	11.3%	84.4%
Arizona										
Chandler city	15,969	90.1%	9.9%	0.0%	75.5%	30,591	96.0%	3.2%	0.8%	84.7%
Glendale city	16,378	91.1%	7.7%	1.2%	67.7%	23,587	89.3%	9.0%	1.7%	74.6%
Mesa city	33,531	89.3%	10.7%	0.0%	74.0%	52,465	93.8%	6.0%	0.1%	82.2%
Peoria city	10,309	88.5%	11.5%	0.0%	75.1%	17,896	91.9%	8.1%	0.0%	84.8%
Phoenix city	109,583	87.4%	12.6%	0.0%	70.1%	168,841	93.1%	6.8%	0.2%	79.8%
Scottsdale city	11,310	89.0%	11.0%	0.0%	73.4%	27,298	96.4%	3.6%	0.0%	90.3%
Surprise city	6,358	92.0%	8.0%	0.0%	83.6%	11,949	89.9%	8.5%	1.6%	88.2%
Tempe city	28,630	91.5%	8.5%	0.0%	64.6%	23,965	92.8%	6.6%	0.7%	84.8%
Tucson city	53,140	76.5%	20.6%	3.0%	64.0%	53,175	89.6%	8.7%	1.7%	80.2%
Yuma city	7,807	86.0%	8.6%	5.4%	69.2%	8,510	82.0%	13.9%	4.1%	77.6%
Arkansas										
Little Rock city	12,988	92.8%	7.0%	0.2%	72.9%	23,603	94.3%	4.5%	1.2%	81.7%
California										
Anaheim city	29,081	88.0%	12.0%	0.0%	75.6%	43,287	93.8%	6.2%	0.0%	83.9%
Antioch city	8,750	84.1%	15.9%	0.0%	63.2%	10,804	92.3%	7.7%	0.0%	89.7%
Bakersfield city	32,941	82.8%	14.7%	2.4%	72.5%	45,306	87.0%	13.0%	0.0%	84.0%
Berkeley city	12,398	89.8%	10.2%	0.0%	48.1%	16,365	94.1%	5.9%	0.0%	81.5%
Burbank city	4,478	80.1%	19.9%	0.0%	63.4%	14,186	92.6%	7.4%	0.0%	84.1%
Carlsbad city	6,078	95.9%	4.1%	0.0%	69.4%	10,378	93.4%	3.8%	2.8%	83.3%
Chico city	12,715	68.0%	32.0%	0.0%	62.9%	9,815	94.9%	5.1%	0.0%	83.6%
Carson city	6,546	87.0%	13.0%	0.0%	65.5%	9,384	94.0%	6.0%	0.0%	83.2%
Chula Vista city	18,475	83.5%	7.3%	9.2%	63.0%	25,159	85.5%	8.7%	5.8%	77.0%
Clovis city	6,082	82.4%	17.6%	0.0%	73.3%	10,990	93.2%	6.8%	0.0%	78.5%
Compton city	9,472	75.8%	24.2%	0.0%	72.1%	10,806	92.3%	7.7%	0.0%	85.2%
Concord city	8,021	90.3%	9.7%	0.0%	79.9%	14,854	94.6%	5.4%	0.0%	90.4%
Corona city	10,955	76.6%	23.4%	0.0%	74.1%	15,200	93.4%	6.6%	0.0%	72.7%
Costa Mesa city	7,972	89.6%	8.5%	1.9%	73.4%	16,690	95.2%	4.8%	0.0%	84.8%
Daly City city	7,530	89.7%	10.3%	0.0%	72.6%	14,642	93.9%	6.1%	0.0%	85.2%
Downey city	7,806	91.6%	8.4%	0.0%	55.8%	12,035	94.2%	5.8%	0.0%	79.1%
El Cajon city	7,966	85.2%	10.6%	4.1%	71.9%	12,967	91.5%	5.8%	2.8%	85.9%
Elk Grove city	10,287	87.9%	12.1%	0.0%	59.1%	15,168	86.6%	13.4%	0.0%	88.1%
El Monte city	6,208	93.8%	6.2%	0.0%	50.0%	11,724	98.7%	1.3%	0.0%	73.4%
Escondido city	13,996	88.8%	10.7%	0.5%	79.3%	20,209	90.6%	8.0%	1.4%	83.5%
Fairfield city	8,193	76.2%	14.0%	9.8%	77.4%	12,667	79.4%	13.1%	7.5%	79.2%
Fontana city	15,961	84.5%	15.5%	0.0%	68.2%	25,987	89.4%	10.6%	0.0%	82.2%
Fremont city	11,417	86.7%	13.3%	0.0%	59.1%	23,465	98.2%	1.8%	0.0%	75.7%
Fresno city	39,903	83.2%	16.8%	0.0%	65.2%	58,094	88.0%	12.0%	0.0%	76.9%
Fullerton city	13,207	89.2%	10.8%	0.0%	71.8%	14,964	97.7%	2.3%	0.0%	77.1%
Garden Grove city	11,087	86.7%	13.3%	0.0%	63.3%	19,276	95.3%	4.7%	0.0%	84.7%
Glendale city	9,105	83.3%	16.7%	0.0%	60.6%	23,856	92.5%	7.5%	0.0%	82.6%
Hayward city	9,222	92.6%	7.4%	0.0%	61.3%	22,304	96.4%	3.6%	0.0%	82.4%
Hesperia city	5,588	70.2%	29.8%	0.0%	63.0%	9,852	88.8%	11.2%	0.0%	76.2%
Huntington Beach city	11,243	89.4%	10.6%	0.0%	77.8%	22,293	96.8%	2.7%	0.5%	89.1%
Inglewood city	8,499	83.7%	16.3%	0.0%	73.6%	13,682	83.1%	16.9%	0.0%	86.9%
Irvine city	15,636	87.6%	12.4%	0.0%	43.4%	28,632	98.4%	1.6%	0.0%	78.1%
Jurupa Valley city	8,606	79.7%	20.3%	0.0%	69.7%	10,405	92.6%	7.4%	0.0%	79.7%
Lancaster city	7,067	84.8%	15.2%	0.0%	47.6%	14,344	92.0%	6.4%	1.6%	56.5%
Long Beach city	30,778	87.5%	12.5%	0.0%	64.2%	57,323	93.5%	6.3%	0.2%	81.8%
Los Angeles city	263,018	85.6%	14.3%	0.1%	61.3%	522,674	93.0%	7.0%	0.1%	82.1%
Mission Viejo city	6,794	80.9%	19.1%	0.0%	71.7%	7,445	98.9%	1.1%	0.0%	80.0%
Modesto city	15,405	73.7%	26.3%	0.0%	67.0%	19,977	78.8%	21.2%	0.0%	77.2%
Moreno Valley city	17,615	80.8%	19.2%	0.0%	65.2%	22,293	90.6%	8.7%	0.7%	80.8%
Murrieta city	6,237	78.1%	20.7%	1.2%	64.7%	11,167	86.1%	13.9%	0.0%	79.6%
Norwalk city	7,368	85.0%	15.0%	0.0%	53.7%	10,516	96.8%	3.2%	0.0%	77.2%
Oakland city	23,187	84.0%	16.0%	0.0%	67.8%	63,723	93.9%	6.1%	0.0%	85.2%
Oceanside city	19,642	37.4%	2.5%	60.1%	85.0%	13,356	79.6%	3.8%	16.7%	76.9%
Ontario city	13,203	86.0%	14.0%	0.0%	69.9%	20,665	91.2%	8.8%	0.0%	84.6%
Orange city	9,717	88.5%	11.5%	0.0%	55.9%	19,343	92.6%	7.4%	0.0%	89.2%
Oxnard city	15,936	86.5%	8.1%	5.4%	74.0%	26,786	89.9%	7.4%	2.7%	83.7%
Palmdale city	8,586	70.9%	28.0%	1.1%	52.7%	13,314	84.4%	15.6%	0.0%	72.7%
Pasadena city	8,172	86.6%	13.4%	0.0%	69.2%	19,621	94.4%	5.6%	0.0%	88.1%
Pomona city	12,834	86.8%	12.6%	0.6%	63.3%	16,178	89.8%	10.2%	0.0%	74.3%
Rancho Cucamonga city	13,868	88.5%	11.5%	0.0%	65.4%	19,162	92.0%	8.0%	0.0%	87.1%

Table H-3: Places—Labor Force Status—*Continued*

	18 to 24					25 to 33				
	In the Labor Force	Percent				In the Labor Force	Percent			
		Employed	Unemployed	In Armed Forces	Labor Force Participation Rate		Employed	Unemployed	In Armed Forces	Labor Force Participation Rate
California—Cont.										
Redding city	5,106	95.6%	4.4%	0.0%	71.5%	11,261	91.4%	8.6%	0.0%	86.0%
Rialto city	8,009	81.5%	18.5%	0.0%	63.1%	11,761	86.8%	13.2%	0.0%	79.0%
Richmond city	9,272	82.2%	17.8%	0.0%	69.4%	12,000	92.4%	7.6%	0.0%	72.3%
Riverside city	29,436	86.6%	13.4%	0.0%	62.4%	40,271	90.4%	9.6%	0.0%	81.1%
Roseville city	8,375	85.9%	14.1%	0.0%	67.0%	12,177	94.2%	4.4%	1.3%	85.2%
Sacramento city	27,396	80.9%	19.1%	0.0%	61.6%	63,069	91.5%	7.5%	0.9%	80.6%
Salinas city	11,418	87.7%	12.3%	0.0%	69.9%	15,871	89.5%	10.1%	0.4%	72.9%
San Bernardino city	18,153	77.8%	22.2%	0.0%	65.6%	21,968	90.5%	9.5%	0.0%	71.8%
San Buenaventura (Ventura) city	5,929	83.5%	16.5%	0.0%	66.1%	12,164	97.4%	2.6%	0.0%	81.9%
San Diego city	113,257	77.1%	10.6%	12.3%	69.2%	196,910	89.6%	5.2%	5.1%	84.4%
San Francisco city	42,236	85.4%	14.6%	0.0%	66.5%	158,113	96.8%	3.2%	0.0%	88.8%
San Jose city	60,664	87.8%	12.2%	0.0%	65.1%	115,101	95.1%	4.6%	0.3%	82.5%
San Leandro city	5,405	86.4%	7.1%	6.5%	80.2%	11,469	98.4%	1.6%	0.0%	89.8%
San Marcos city	7,367	91.5%	7.1%	1.4%	79.0%	10,099	98.0%	2.0%	0.0%	90.4%
San Mateo city	4,693	94.0%	6.0%	0.0%	63.3%	11,464	96.1%	3.9%	0.0%	90.8%
Santa Ana city	22,373	91.2%	8.8%	0.0%	64.8%	41,780	95.3%	4.7%	0.0%	80.7%
Santa Clara city	9,126	95.6%	4.4%	0.0%	68.4%	19,823	96.9%	2.6%	0.5%	84.5%
Santa Clarita city	13,120	86.5%	13.5%	0.0%	71.0%	18,951	92.8%	6.1%	1.1%	84.9%
Santa Maria city	9,588	84.5%	15.5%	0.0%	76.7%	10,620	90.8%	6.6%	2.6%	88.1%
Santa Monica city	4,138	80.4%	19.6%	0.0%	70.5%	14,848	98.4%	1.6%	0.0%	92.7%
Santa Rosa city	12,266	92.2%	7.8%	0.0%	78.5%	19,417	97.3%	2.7%	0.0%	84.3%
Simi Valley city	9,124	84.6%	15.4%	0.0%	72.8%	11,847	94.3%	5.7%	0.0%	85.6%
South Gate city	8,048	82.8%	17.2%	0.0%	71.5%	9,388	87.4%	12.6%	0.0%	74.1%
Stockton city	22,822	72.3%	27.7%	0.0%	67.1%	31,146	90.5%	9.2%	0.3%	73.6%
Sunnyvale city	6,493	89.3%	10.7%	0.0%	73.3%	24,162	88.4%	11.6%	0.0%	83.9%
Temecula city	6,250	76.8%	19.1%	4.0%	61.9%	11,648	92.3%	5.4%	2.4%	87.3%
Thousand Oaks city	8,132	85.4%	14.6%	0.0%	77.9%	9,124	92.3%	7.7%	0.0%	91.6%
Torrance city	10,918	89.1%	10.9%	0.0%	72.3%	12,677	95.7%	4.3%	0.0%	81.2%
Vacaville city	6,884	86.0%	12.7%	1.3%	72.2%	10,756	81.2%	10.2%	8.6%	84.3%
Vallejo city	6,727	76.2%	23.8%	0.0%	58.8%	14,806	95.4%	4.6%	0.0%	82.6%
Victorville city	7,808	60.3%	39.7%	0.0%	67.6%	11,721	81.4%	18.6%	0.0%	69.1%
Visalia city	6,888	94.0%	6.0%	0.0%	54.1%	12,596	93.7%	6.3%	0.0%	77.0%
Vista city	8,930	91.3%	5.8%	2.8%	75.0%	13,347	92.8%	3.6%	3.7%	82.7%
West Covina city	6,661	79.5%	20.5%	0.0%	70.2%	12,832	90.5%	9.5%	0.0%	84.2%
Westminster city	4,027	95.5%	4.5%	0.0%	60.9%	8,889	94.5%	5.5%	0.0%	72.2%
Colorado										
Arvada city	4,826	95.6%	4.4%	0.0%	67.6%	12,475	88.7%	10.4%	0.9%	90.6%
Aurora city	24,896	88.7%	10.8%	0.5%	73.3%	44,695	93.8%	5.4%	0.8%	86.4%
Boulder city	18,241	91.6%	8.4%	0.0%	56.4%	14,004	97.5%	2.5%	0.0%	88.5%
Centennial city	5,541	94.2%	5.8%	0.0%	72.8%	9,433	96.3%	3.7%	0.0%	80.5%
Colorado Springs city	35,039	86.9%	7.7%	5.4%	77.5%	57,372	84.5%	7.0%	8.5%	82.4%
Denver city	37,347	97.3%	2.7%	0.0%	64.1%	126,455	94.9%	5.0%	0.1%	88.9%
Fort Collins city	24,771	93.8%	5.4%	0.8%	77.3%	23,552	92.9%	7.1%	0.0%	85.9%
Greeley city	8,553	94.5%	5.5%	0.0%	69.3%	11,452	95.5%	4.5%	0.0%	77.7%
Lakewood city	12,321	90.8%	9.2%	0.0%	75.2%	18,978	94.5%	5.5%	0.0%	88.1%
Longmont city	5,342	93.8%	6.2%	0.0%	70.0%	7,878	93.5%	6.5%	0.0%	82.7%
Pueblo city	6,863	79.5%	18.3%	2.2%	68.3%	11,023	82.8%	15.8%	1.4%	78.8%
Thornton city	9,588	90.1%	8.6%	1.3%	84.5%	15,296	96.2%	3.4%	0.4%	89.1%
Westminster city	7,700	88.3%	10.1%	1.7%	82.3%	13,616	94.2%	5.8%	0.0%	85.8%
Connecticut										
Bridgeport city	13,154	84.1%	15.9%	0.0%	73.8%	18,107	83.6%	15.8%	0.6%	86.7%
Hartford city	11,146	75.7%	24.3%	0.0%	52.9%	15,195	90.5%	9.5%	0.0%	84.6%
New Haven city	13,484	88.1%	11.8%	0.1%	61.5%	19,915	89.0%	10.8%	0.2%	78.2%
Stamford city	9,777	94.7%	5.3%	0.0%	78.6%	17,752	94.4%	5.0%	0.6%	85.9%
Waterbury city	7,401	85.4%	14.6%	0.0%	71.4%	9,577	84.8%	15.2%	0.0%	71.9%
District of Columbia										
Washington city	50,796	82.3%	12.7%	5.0%	62.0%	125,560	93.8%	5.4%	0.8%	90.3%
Florida										
Boca Raton city	5,580	88.5%	11.5%	0.0%	61.0%	7,038	99.8%	0.2%	0.0%	80.1%
Cape Coral city	7,740	89.0%	11.0%	0.0%	76.3%	14,225	85.3%	11.7%	3.0%	72.5%
Clearwater city	5,255	91.6%	8.4%	0.0%	66.8%	12,227	83.8%	16.2%	0.0%	86.0%
Coral Springs city	7,223	82.2%	17.8%	0.0%	61.7%	11,526	86.5%	13.5%	0.0%	90.5%
Fort Lauderdale city	7,797	79.0%	21.0%	0.0%	74.2%	21,182	87.3%	12.2%	0.6%	85.7%
Gainesville city	16,028	89.6%	10.4%	0.0%	38.3%	15,979	96.6%	3.4%	0.0%	76.5%
Hialeah city	10,317	84.9%	15.1%	0.0%	54.5%	22,738	91.8%	8.2%	0.0%	79.5%
Hollywood city	8,205	80.7%	19.3%	0.0%	72.0%	16,814	91.0%	9.0%	0.0%	91.0%
Jacksonville city	62,874	81.2%	11.9%	6.9%	75.8%	106,244	87.9%	7.8%	4.3%	86.0%
Lakeland city	6,995	71.5%	28.5%	0.0%	66.7%	9,777	84.2%	15.8%	0.0%	73.2%
Miami city	23,617	83.7%	16.3%	0.0%	70.5%	52,812	93.0%	7.0%	0.0%	81.4%
Miami Beach city	2,494	85.6%	14.4%	0.0%	44.4%	11,562	94.6%	5.4%	0.0%	85.2%
Miami Gardens city	6,496	81.7%	18.3%	0.0%	57.1%	11,154	77.1%	22.9%	0.0%	73.3%
Miramar city	7,146	83.0%	17.0%	0.0%	56.1%	13,687	95.6%	4.4%	0.0%	80.4%

Table H-3: Places—Labor Force Status—*Continued*

	18 to 24					25 to 33				
		Percent					Percent			
	In the Labor Force	Employed	Unemployed	In Armed Forces	Labor Force Participation Rate	In the Labor Force	Employed	Unemployed	In Armed Forces	Labor Force Participation Rate
Florida—Cont.										
Orlando city	19,252	91.0%	9.0%	0.0%	68.3%	46,245	91.3%	8.6%	0.1%	85.5%
Palm Bay city	5,607	74.2%	25.8%	0.0%	59.3%	8,413	95.7%	3.3%	0.9%	82.2%
Pembroke Pines city	10,558	89.7%	9.9%	0.5%	65.0%	15,723	97.6%	2.4%	0.0%	83.3%
Plantation city	4,003	90.3%	9.7%	0.0%	64.6%	9,674	97.0%	3.0%	0.0%	75.3%
Pompano Beach city	6,834	88.2%	11.8%	0.0%	77.2%	10,280	80.0%	19.5%	0.5%	84.8%
Port St. Lucie city	12,320	75.4%	24.6%	0.0%	85.8%	13,640	95.3%	3.0%	1.6%	73.7%
St. Petersburg city	14,060	81.8%	18.2%	0.0%	67.8%	24,825	91.2%	8.1%	0.7%	76.2%
Sunrise city	4,552	91.5%	8.5%	0.0%	65.2%	11,391	97.5%	2.5%	0.0%	77.0%
Tallahassee city	38,618	87.9%	12.1%	0.0%	66.8%	22,309	95.1%	4.9%	0.0%	83.8%
Tampa city	25,942	80.0%	18.6%	1.4%	66.3%	48,414	87.9%	11.0%	1.1%	84.7%
West Palm Beach city	6,378	89.6%	10.4%	0.0%	70.7%	12,097	93.3%	6.7%	0.0%	81.4%
Georgia										
Athens-Clarke County unified govt (balance)	19,215	91.8%	8.2%	0.0%	52.8%	12,831	94.3%	5.7%	0.0%	82.1%
Atlanta city	35,073	84.5%	15.0%	0.4%	58.9%	77,870	94.2%	5.6%	0.2%	86.7%
Augusta-Richmond County consolidated govt (balance)	15,104	62.6%	12.7%	24.7%	64.8%	22,041	80.2%	6.5%	13.3%	76.9%
Columbus city	16,180	58.7%	17.3%	24.0%	66.3%	24,257	74.6%	6.9%	18.4%	81.6%
Macon-Bibb county	8,560	84.1%	15.3%	0.5%	52.7%	15,055	90.8%	9.2%	0.0%	81.4%
Roswell city	4,629	91.4%	8.6%	0.0%	64.1%	7,135	98.8%	0.0%	1.2%	81.3%
Sandy Springs city	6,132	91.1%	8.9%	0.0%	76.7%	15,881	92.8%	5.3%	1.9%	90.4%
Savannah city	15,975	78.9%	15.5%	5.6%	64.7%	20,774	86.5%	9.0%	4.5%	84.8%
Hawaii										
Urban Honolulu CDP	18,528	89.6%	10.1%	0.3%	60.2%	38,540	92.0%	5.4%	2.6%	86.5%
Idaho										
Boise City city	13,766	84.5%	15.5%	0.0%	67.9%	27,004	93.2%	6.7%	0.1%	82.4%
Meridian city	3,877	88.1%	11.9%	0.0%	65.8%	6,361	88.2%	11.8%	0.0%	69.2%
Illinois										
Aurora city	15,503	88.1%	11.9%	0.0%	76.0%	22,688	91.7%	8.3%	0.0%	86.5%
Chicago city	180,618	79.8%	19.9%	0.3%	63.4%	414,421	92.6%	7.4%	0.0%	85.9%
Elgin city	8,209	93.0%	7.0%	0.0%	73.6%	9,424	96.0%	4.0%	0.0%	78.6%
Joliet city	13,603	94.9%	5.1%	0.0%	84.9%	13,932	96.4%	3.2%	0.4%	85.4%
Naperville city	9,278	92.1%	7.9%	0.0%	71.6%	12,413	91.7%	8.3%	0.0%	85.0%
Peoria city	9,047	68.8%	31.2%	0.0%	77.1%	14,864	88.6%	11.4%	0.0%	81.9%
Rockford city	11,189	80.0%	20.0%	0.0%	77.7%	16,528	91.8%	8.2%	0.0%	86.2%
Springfield city	6,776	87.1%	12.9%	0.0%	61.1%	13,137	88.0%	10.4%	1.6%	84.9%
Indiana										
Evansville city	8,576	90.6%	9.4%	0.0%	67.2%	14,642	99.2%	0.8%	0.0%	92.2%
Fort Wayne city	19,044	88.1%	11.9%	0.0%	69.4%	28,287	93.4%	6.6%	0.0%	84.1%
Indianapolis city (balance)	60,182	86.6%	13.2%	0.2%	74.7%	111,060	91.3%	8.7%	0.0%	84.0%
South Bend city	7,500	89.2%	10.8%	0.0%	54.1%	9,403	94.3%	5.7%	0.0%	78.0%
Iowa										
Cedar Rapids city	9,446	86.4%	13.6%	0.0%	72.8%	12,274	98.9%	1.1%	0.0%	74.7%
Davenport city	6,300	99.6%	0.4%	0.0%	66.6%	11,694	93.8%	4.9%	1.3%	83.2%
Des Moines city	18,820	82.7%	17.3%	0.0%	83.1%	27,465	95.0%	5.0%	0.0%	84.0%
Kansas										
Kansas City city	10,713	87.8%	12.2%	0.0%	74.9%	16,919	91.0%	9.0%	0.0%	85.6%
Olathe city	8,306	92.7%	7.3%	0.0%	74.0%	12,686	94.9%	4.4%	0.7%	89.3%
Overland Park city	8,355	91.9%	8.1%	0.0%	64.3%	22,211	95.1%	4.9%	0.0%	89.4%
Topeka city	9,952	90.9%	9.1%	0.0%	75.8%	13,440	85.2%	13.5%	1.4%	89.6%
Wichita city	23,321	93.7%	5.3%	1.0%	71.0%	45,982	93.6%	4.9%	1.5%	82.9%
Kentucky										
Lexington-Fayette urban county	29,825	93.0%	7.0%	0.0%	68.0%	39,750	95.7%	4.3%	0.0%	87.6%
Louisville/Jefferson County metro govt (balance)	44,304	91.8%	8.0%	0.2%	78.1%	66,379	93.3%	6.5%	0.3%	85.4%
Louisiana										
Baton Rouge city	27,194	87.2%	12.8%	0.0%	72.4%	30,099	94.6%	4.9%	0.6%	85.8%
Lafayette city	10,782	82.0%	18.0%	0.0%	73.3%	20,521	97.2%	2.8%	0.0%	89.5%
New Orleans city	22,511	80.2%	19.6%	0.2%	60.2%	55,383	90.1%	8.8%	1.0%	83.3%
Shreveport city	9,634	86.8%	13.2%	0.0%	50.8%	22,030	89.2%	9.8%	1.0%	82.4%
Maryland										
Baltimore city	35,956	80.8%	18.5%	0.7%	55.7%	86,887	91.4%	8.5%	0.1%	80.8%
Massachusetts										
Boston city	64,384	87.7%	12.1%	0.2%	63.9%	129,676	95.7%	4.0%	0.3%	87.3%
Brockton city	9,327	83.3%	16.7%	0.0%	64.0%	10,111	84.3%	15.7%	0.0%	88.4%
Cambridge city	12,495	95.7%	3.5%	0.8%	61.0%	26,109	97.2%	2.5%	0.3%	89.1%
Lowell city	9,758	87.7%	12.3%	0.0%	62.7%	13,332	87.1%	12.9%	0.0%	80.9%
Lynn city	6,066	85.9%	14.1%	0.0%	72.1%	11,984	90.6%	9.4%	0.0%	88.5%
New Bedford city	8,938	87.4%	12.6%	0.0%	80.5%	8,732	90.2%	9.8%	0.0%	78.9%
Quincy city	5,035	96.2%	3.8%	0.0%	69.8%	12,874	94.1%	5.9%	0.0%	88.5%

Table H-3: Places—Labor Force Status—*Continued*

	18 to 24					25 to 33				
	In the Labor Force	Percent				In the Labor Force	Percent			
		Employed	Unemployed	In Armed Forces	Labor Force Participation Rate		Employed	Unemployed	In Armed Forces	Labor Force Participation Rate
Massachusetts—Cont.										
Springfield city	13,888	89.5%	10.5%	0.0%	67.1%	12,756	89.6%	10.4%	0.0%	66.0%
Worcester city	15,594	88.4%	11.6%	0.0%	56.5%	21,043	91.5%	8.5%	0.0%	76.0%
Michigan										
Ann Arbor city	18,989	83.9%	16.1%	0.0%	52.2%	15,149	94.7%	4.8%	0.4%	84.0%
Dearborn city	6,435	85.5%	14.5%	0.0%	58.5%	7,229	95.4%	4.6%	0.0%	67.9%
Detroit city	46,790	67.8%	32.2%	0.0%	64.5%	67,467	74.4%	25.6%	0.0%	77.1%
Flint city	6,706	72.5%	27.5%	0.0%	65.5%	8,120	90.3%	9.7%	0.0%	71.2%
Grand Rapids city	18,486	90.8%	9.2%	0.0%	78.1%	30,677	90.9%	8.5%	0.5%	87.7%
Lansing city	11,066	87.9%	12.1%	0.0%	76.6%	15,741	96.6%	3.4%	0.0%	81.9%
Livonia city	6,331	85.8%	14.2%	0.0%	83.1%	8,296	95.9%	4.1%	0.0%	86.6%
Sterling Heights city	9,945	88.5%	11.5%	0.0%	79.3%	13,155	96.8%	3.2%	0.0%	75.9%
Warren city	9,886	80.6%	19.4%	0.0%	89.3%	11,603	89.6%	10.4%	0.0%	82.3%
Minnesota										
Minneapolis city	38,848	92.6%	7.4%	0.0%	74.8%	76,818	97.5%	2.5%	0.0%	92.0%
Rochester city	8,996	97.6%	2.4%	0.0%	82.2%	13,446	97.5%	2.5%	0.0%	87.4%
St. Paul city	27,908	81.9%	18.1%	0.0%	75.8%	43,771	94.3%	5.7%	0.0%	84.2%
Mississippi										
Jackson city	10,384	90.7%	9.3%	0.0%	50.0%	20,449	92.2%	7.8%	0.0%	79.3%
Missouri										
Columbia city	14,828	86.3%	12.8%	1.0%	51.5%	16,506	98.1%	1.9%	0.0%	77.0%
Independence city	6,601	93.3%	6.7%	0.0%	60.5%	10,138	100.0%	0.0%	0.0%	72.5%
Kansas City city	33,945	89.0%	11.0%	0.0%	77.8%	56,705	93.8%	6.1%	0.2%	84.3%
Lee's Summit city	4,992	81.5%	18.5%	0.0%	71.7%	9,557	98.5%	1.5%	0.0%	89.6%
St. Louis city	20,081	78.2%	21.8%	0.0%	62.6%	50,754	90.3%	9.2%	0.5%	89.5%
Springfield city	21,683	92.0%	8.0%	0.0%	74.2%	20,852	95.2%	4.3%	0.5%	80.4%
Montana										
Billings city	8,948	91.3%	7.9%	0.8%	77.3%	12,946	97.3%	1.6%	1.0%	86.4%
Nebraska										
Lincoln city	28,903	94.2%	5.8%	0.0%	65.9%	32,019	94.4%	4.5%	1.1%	85.2%
Omaha city	34,563	94.1%	4.1%	1.9%	80.4%	58,881	95.7%	4.3%	0.0%	86.0%
Nevada										
Henderson city	12,841	92.2%	7.8%	0.0%	67.2%	26,875	92.7%	5.8%	1.4%	82.9%
Las Vegas city	35,267	84.8%	14.5%	0.7%	68.9%	65,860	91.0%	7.9%	1.1%	79.1%
North Las Vegas city	17,433	82.5%	14.0%	3.6%	70.9%	23,288	87.4%	8.7%	3.9%	78.6%
Reno city	20,698	88.7%	11.3%	0.0%	77.0%	28,899	92.1%	7.9%	0.0%	87.0%
Sparks city	6,443	91.4%	8.6%	0.0%	77.0%	10,723	91.4%	8.6%	0.0%	88.7%
New Hampshire										
Manchester city	10,797	94.3%	5.7%	0.0%	84.8%	11,781	95.8%	4.2%	0.0%	79.8%
New Jersey										
Elizabeth city	8,734	79.6%	20.4%	0.0%	69.8%	14,723	94.0%	6.0%	0.0%	84.4%
Jersey City city	13,299	81.9%	18.1%	0.0%	58.2%	42,583	95.5%	4.4%	0.2%	81.9%
Newark city	19,216	70.0%	30.0%	0.0%	63.1%	28,888	89.7%	10.3%	0.0%	73.6%
Paterson city	8,230	87.4%	12.6%	0.0%	52.3%	12,550	95.0%	5.0%	0.0%	65.5%
New Mexico										
Albuquerque city	37,555	84.7%	12.1%	3.2%	71.3%	63,970	90.8%	8.7%	0.5%	83.6%
Las Cruces city	11,520	77.6%	22.4%	0.0%	71.5%	9,299	88.1%	7.2%	4.7%	77.1%
Rio Rancho city	6,024	82.7%	17.3%	0.0%	83.9%	9,409	86.5%	13.0%	0.5%	80.1%
New York										
Albany city	11,577	89.7%	10.3%	0.0%	57.7%	14,090	93.0%	7.0%	0.0%	95.6%
Buffalo city	19,325	89.5%	10.5%	0.0%	63.7%	32,269	89.8%	10.2%	0.0%	76.9%
New York city	451,758	83.1%	16.8%	0.1%	56.9%	1,165,315	92.5%	7.4%	0.1%	83.5%
Rochester city	22,191	77.2%	22.8%	0.0%	71.3%	27,285	85.5%	14.5%	0.0%	81.5%
Syracuse city	11,296	77.1%	22.9%	0.0%	43.3%	17,828	93.8%	6.2%	0.0%	81.5%
Yonkers city	9,898	84.6%	15.4%	0.0%	55.9%	20,505	94.0%	6.0%	0.0%	81.6%
North Carolina										
Charlotte city	56,867	87.4%	12.6%	0.0%	70.6%	114,693	93.5%	6.5%	0.0%	87.6%
Durham city	17,476	91.7%	8.3%	0.0%	66.1%	39,340	96.1%	3.7%	0.2%	85.5%
Fayetteville city	18,537	70.0%	12.1%	17.9%	70.7%	28,786	71.7%	10.6%	17.7%	85.4%
Greensboro city	17,209	88.4%	11.6%	0.0%	49.4%	30,695	95.9%	3.7%	0.4%	81.5%
High Point city	6,956	90.4%	9.6%	0.0%	60.9%	10,636	85.7%	14.3%	0.0%	82.3%
Raleigh city	32,887	95.8%	3.9%	0.3%	54.1%	60,714	95.2%	4.6%	0.2%	84.3%
Wilmington city	10,571	88.7%	11.3%	0.0%	57.6%	13,156	86.8%	13.2%	0.0%	84.7%
Winston-Salem city	15,188	86.0%	13.6%	0.4%	54.4%	27,280	92.1%	7.5%	0.4%	85.0%
North Dakota										
Fargo city	17,727	95.9%	4.1%	0.0%	76.0%	17,745	98.4%	1.6%	0.0%	97.0%
Ohio										
Akron city	16,176	89.7%	10.3%	0.0%	74.5%	22,034	87.6%	12.4%	0.0%	85.2%

Table H-3: Places—Labor Force Status—*Continued*

| | 18 to 24 | | | | 25 to 33 | | | |
| | | Percent | | | | Percent | | |
	In the Labor Force	Employed	Unemployed	In Armed Forces	Labor Force Participation Rate	In the Labor Force	Employed	Unemployed	In Armed Forces	Labor Force Participation Rate
Ohio—Cont.										
Cincinnati city	26,944	80.6%	19.4%	0.0%	68.5%	44,491	93.4%	6.5%	0.1%	86.4%
Cleveland city	30,516	71.0%	29.0%	0.0%	71.9%	40,131	84.1%	15.5%	0.4%	76.7%
Columbus city	74,299	91.3%	8.7%	0.0%	72.3%	130,735	94.4%	5.6%	0.0%	88.0%
Dayton city	12,822	83.0%	16.6%	0.5%	67.9%	15,531	88.0%	9.6%	2.4%	73.1%
Toledo city	22,584	84.2%	15.7%	0.1%	71.6%	34,407	89.0%	11.0%	0.0%	88.1%
Oklahoma										
Broken Arrow city	6,895	90.7%	9.3%	0.0%	80.8%	10,576	97.8%	2.2%	0.0%	85.4%
Edmond city	8,998	95.4%	4.6%	0.0%	82.4%	10,566	100.0%	0.0%	0.0%	84.6%
Lawton city	9,112	46.5%	5.7%	47.8%	82.1%	13,182	85.0%	1.9%	13.1%	81.7%
Norman city	13,617	89.8%	7.0%	3.2%	65.2%	18,278	90.9%	6.7%	2.4%	90.7%
Oklahoma City city	43,350	91.7%	5.7%	2.6%	73.9%	72,588	91.7%	6.1%	2.2%	79.0%
Tulsa city	28,418	90.6%	9.4%	0.0%	72.0%	46,584	94.8%	4.9%	0.4%	82.8%
Oregon										
Beaverton city	5,765	80.6%	19.4%	0.0%	66.2%	12,963	91.6%	8.4%	0.0%	83.1%
Eugene city	18,668	87.6%	12.4%	0.0%	66.1%	19,265	92.4%	7.6%	0.0%	83.7%
Gresham city	6,368	80.4%	19.6%	0.0%	74.0%	11,623	94.4%	5.6%	0.0%	80.2%
Hillsboro city	5,576	79.4%	20.6%	0.0%	75.1%	12,275	95.0%	5.0%	0.0%	78.5%
Portland city	38,250	85.9%	14.1%	0.0%	71.8%	98,441	92.1%	7.7%	0.2%	88.7%
Salem city	12,974	91.0%	9.0%	0.0%	64.1%	16,565	90.3%	9.7%	0.0%	87.5%
Pennsylvania										
Allentown city	9,132	85.5%	14.5%	0.0%	73.3%	13,805	87.2%	12.8%	0.0%	81.2%
Erie city	8,266	85.8%	14.2%	0.0%	73.6%	11,449	92.5%	7.5%	0.0%	85.3%
Philadelphia city	92,921	82.1%	17.9%	0.0%	56.2%	210,886	89.3%	10.7%	0.0%	79.0%
Pittsburgh city	29,868	93.0%	7.0%	0.0%	55.1%	46,297	90.2%	9.8%	0.0%	81.3%
Rhode Island										
Providence city	17,361	85.8%	14.2%	0.0%	56.5%	22,484	93.1%	6.9%	0.0%	77.6%
South Carolina										
Charleston city	9,686	94.9%	3.9%	1.2%	55.9%	21,580	95.9%	3.4%	0.8%	89.9%
Columbia city	21,797	69.0%	11.5%	19.6%	69.4%	20,585	89.5%	3.8%	6.7%	85.9%
North Charleston city	11,321	65.3%	9.5%	25.2%	73.0%	13,302	84.3%	10.8%	5.0%	78.5%
South Dakota										
Sioux Falls city	11,041	90.4%	9.6%	0.0%	72.6%	22,975	95.7%	3.6%	0.6%	83.1%
Tennessee										
Chattanooga city	12,742	87.6%	12.4%	0.0%	63.0%	20,529	94.5%	5.1%	0.4%	82.0%
Clarksville city	12,898	65.6%	7.7%	26.8%	70.2%	24,455	72.5%	5.6%	22.0%	82.9%
Knoxville city	25,576	94.0%	6.0%	0.0%	72.5%	20,873	94.5%	5.5%	0.0%	83.2%
Memphis city	46,545	80.0%	20.0%	0.0%	66.5%	75,768	91.9%	8.0%	0.2%	82.1%
Murfreesboro city	18,963	92.5%	7.5%	0.0%	82.2%	15,138	92.1%	7.9%	0.0%	84.4%
Nashville-Davidson metropolitan govt (balance)	49,316	89.3%	10.5%	0.2%	71.0%	99,102	97.5%	2.5%	0.0%	86.2%
Texas										
Abilene city	15,817	74.9%	5.8%	19.3%	74.8%	14,331	90.8%	2.9%	6.3%	85.0%
Allen city	3,944	79.6%	20.4%	0.0%	59.5%	8,163	91.6%	8.4%	0.0%	79.0%
Amarillo city	13,052	92.4%	7.1%	0.5%	69.7%	21,843	98.0%	2.0%	0.0%	83.7%
Arlington city	28,880	94.7%	4.9%	0.4%	66.2%	46,952	95.5%	4.5%	0.0%	84.1%
Austin city	64,029	90.8%	9.2%	0.1%	61.4%	162,853	96.7%	3.3%	0.0%	87.9%
Beaumont city	8,654	93.9%	6.1%	0.0%	64.2%	11,859	95.3%	4.7%	0.0%	74.4%
Brownsville city	10,708	89.1%	10.9%	0.0%	50.8%	17,264	93.3%	6.7%	0.0%	82.2%
Carrollton city	8,795	92.0%	8.0%	0.0%	75.9%	15,524	95.9%	4.1%	0.0%	87.1%
College Station city	18,993	97.0%	3.0%	0.0%	51.0%	14,714	98.3%	1.7%	0.0%	79.1%
Corpus Christi city	21,958	80.0%	18.2%	1.8%	63.5%	36,193	92.9%	6.7%	0.4%	83.5%
Dallas city	91,200	89.6%	10.2%	0.2%	70.2%	167,686	95.6%	4.3%	0.1%	81.6%
Denton city	17,441	85.2%	14.8%	0.0%	63.9%	17,814	93.8%	6.2%	0.0%	83.3%
El Paso city	50,013	80.1%	10.1%	9.8%	65.7%	70,856	86.4%	6.7%	6.9%	81.5%
Fort Worth city	57,772	91.0%	8.7%	0.3%	73.1%	100,086	93.5%	6.2%	0.3%	82.1%
Frisco city	5,132	96.9%	3.1%	0.0%	64.5%	12,160	98.7%	1.3%	0.0%	86.5%
Garland city	15,121	91.9%	8.1%	0.0%	69.7%	24,793	92.9%	6.7%	0.3%	81.4%
Grand Prairie city	13,969	84.1%	15.9%	0.0%	69.2%	19,981	92.5%	7.5%	0.0%	87.2%
Houston city	162,607	88.6%	11.2%	0.2%	67.6%	298,675	94.6%	5.1%	0.2%	82.9%
Irving city	17,030	93.3%	6.7%	0.0%	66.6%	30,853	96.8%	3.2%	0.0%	84.1%
Killeen city	11,918	63.3%	15.0%	21.7%	75.9%	20,852	59.6%	13.9%	26.4%	81.2%
Laredo city	18,195	86.6%	13.4%	0.0%	62.0%	20,326	93.6%	6.4%	0.0%	68.4%
Lewisville city	6,905	92.8%	7.2%	0.0%	79.8%	17,816	98.6%	1.4%	0.0%	89.2%
Lubbock city	26,178	92.6%	7.4%	0.0%	56.5%	28,841	98.6%	1.4%	0.0%	82.7%
McAllen city	9,229	76.4%	23.6%	0.0%	56.8%	13,176	82.7%	16.1%	1.3%	80.5%
McKinney city	8,407	95.0%	5.0%	0.0%	69.2%	14,062	96.7%	2.9%	0.4%	81.8%
Mesquite city	11,102	90.2%	9.8%	0.0%	82.5%	16,337	93.3%	6.7%	0.0%	82.7%
Midland city	10,852	93.5%	6.5%	0.0%	78.2%	16,205	99.6%	0.4%	0.0%	80.6%
Odessa city	9,289	83.0%	17.0%	0.0%	71.3%	14,049	96.5%	3.5%	0.0%	75.6%
Pasadena city	8,328	82.1%	15.1%	2.8%	64.1%	18,753	91.3%	8.3%	0.5%	84.1%
Pearland city	5,375	97.5%	1.1%	1.4%	65.0%	14,405	100.0%	0.0%	0.0%	91.0%

Table H-3: Places—Labor Force Status—*Continued*

	18 to 24					25 to 33				
	In the Labor Force	Percent				In the Labor Force	Percent			
		Employed	Unemployed	In Armed Forces	Labor Force Participation Rate		Employed	Unemployed	In Armed Forces	Labor Force Participation Rate
Texas—Cont.										
Plano city	14,274	85.3%	13.8%	0.9%	63.0%	32,140	97.8%	2.2%	0.0%	87.5%
Richardson city	7,587	84.3%	15.7%	0.0%	63.8%	14,572	93.0%	7.0%	0.0%	85.5%
Round Rock City	8,721	88.9%	10.9%	0.2%	78.6%	11,528	94.5%	4.1%	1.4%	85.5%
San Angelo city	7,978	79.1%	2.4%	18.4%	58.5%	11,337	87.9%	3.2%	8.8%	78.6%
San Antonio city	108,731	85.9%	10.4%	3.7%	69.5%	174,803	91.9%	5.9%	2.2%	80.3%
Tyler city	8,859	93.3%	6.7%	0.0%	63.3%	9,582	95.4%	4.6%	0.0%	68.9%
Waco city	14,502	89.5%	9.7%	0.8%	59.5%	13,122	99.2%	0.8%	0.0%	76.8%
Wichita Falls city	11,474	62.1%	7.0%	30.9%	77.7%	10,272	88.9%	7.1%	4.0%	70.3%
Utah										
Orem city	11,314	94.1%	5.9%	0.0%	72.2%	10,576	98.8%	1.2%	0.0%	74.6%
Provo city	30,193	93.2%	6.8%	0.0%	73.8%	14,186	99.4%	0.6%	0.0%	75.7%
Salt Lake City city	18,589	95.0%	5.0%	0.0%	70.8%	33,343	95.2%	4.5%	0.3%	87.4%
Sandy city	5,953	95.0%	5.0%	0.0%	77.9%	8,530	94.9%	5.1%	0.0%	78.1%
West Jordan city	7,812	91.1%	8.9%	0.0%	88.4%	12,921	98.6%	1.4%	0.0%	84.6%
West Valley City city	13,795	95.0%	5.0%	0.0%	87.9%	17,410	93.7%	6.3%	0.0%	89.9%
Virginia										
Alexandria city	5,586	98.3%	1.3%	0.4%	78.9%	30,808	95.3%	1.1%	3.6%	92.3%
Chesapeake city	16,499	74.0%	6.2%	19.8%	75.7%	25,117	83.3%	7.0%	9.7%	79.2%
Hampton city	12,028	77.7%	8.8%	13.5%	74.8%	17,427	84.6%	4.1%	11.2%	87.9%
Newport News city	17,512	65.5%	10.2%	24.3%	73.0%	21,801	83.6%	5.1%	11.4%	77.7%
Norfolk city	36,614	45.7%	12.6%	41.6%	78.1%	33,242	72.1%	5.1%	22.9%	78.4%
Portsmouth city	7,835	65.9%	9.9%	24.2%	76.5%	11,839	77.3%	14.3%	8.4%	78.9%
Richmond city	18,944	84.5%	14.5%	1.0%	63.4%	35,776	92.2%	6.9%	0.9%	85.3%
Roanoke city	7,359	90.7%	9.3%	0.0%	72.3%	11,610	81.2%	18.8%	0.0%	84.4%
Virginia Beach city	37,413	64.4%	9.2%	26.4%	80.5%	60,074	77.2%	5.7%	17.0%	86.9%
Washington										
Bellevue city	6,945	98.0%	2.0%	0.0%	67.2%	18,054	95.6%	4.4%	0.0%	81.3%
Everett city	8,824	88.4%	7.4%	4.1%	82.0%	12,365	88.9%	5.2%	5.9%	83.4%
Federal Way city	5,216	89.5%	8.5%	2.1%	76.8%	13,106	96.0%	3.2%	0.8%	84.8%
Kent city	8,762	88.3%	11.7%	0.0%	70.7%	16,971	93.5%	6.5%	0.0%	79.4%
Renton city	3,928	92.4%	7.6%	0.0%	66.4%	11,508	96.1%	3.9%	0.0%	78.7%
Seattle city	54,329	91.0%	8.8%	0.2%	71.9%	132,466	96.6%	3.4%	0.1%	90.1%
Spokane city	13,130	84.4%	15.6%	0.0%	60.3%	24,025	86.6%	9.7%	3.7%	72.6%
Spokane Valley city	5,138	92.2%	7.8%	0.0%	73.3%	11,229	94.7%	5.3%	0.0%	81.1%
Tacoma city	13,738	90.6%	8.2%	1.2%	70.9%	24,208	90.7%	6.1%	3.2%	77.3%
Vancouver city	11,666	95.8%	4.2%	0.0%	75.3%	17,889	96.0%	4.0%	0.0%	80.8%
Yakima city	9,024	77.3%	22.7%	0.0%	78.4%	8,131	89.8%	10.2%	0.0%	78.6%
Wisconsin										
Green Bay city	10,590	88.7%	11.3%	0.0%	81.0%	13,553	97.9%	2.1%	0.0%	92.1%
Kenosha city	8,276	95.0%	5.0%	0.0%	76.5%	9,086	97.2%	2.8%	0.0%	87.3%
Madison city	38,310	91.4%	8.6%	0.0%	73.9%	35,862	96.6%	3.2%	0.2%	90.3%
Milwaukee city	46,299	86.6%	13.4%	0.0%	66.9%	73,295	91.7%	8.3%	0.0%	81.6%

Table H-4: Metropolitan/Micropolitan Statistical Areas—Labor Force Status

| | 18 to 24 | | | | | 25 to 33 | | | | |
| | | Percent | | | | | Percent | | | |
	In the Labor Force	Employed	Unemployed	In Armed Forces	Labor Force Participation Rate	In the Labor Force	Employed	Unemployed	In Armed Forces	Labor Force Participation Rate
Abilene, TX	17,129	76.7%	5.5%	17.8%	72.8%	16,016	90.7%	3.6%	5.7%	81.0%
Adrian, MI	7,317	83.8%	16.2%	0.0%	71.0%	6,452	97.4%	2.6%	0.0%	72.2%
Akron, OH	51,915	86.9%	13.1%	0.0%	69.4%	65,118	92.2%	7.8%	0.0%	83.8%
Albany, GA	10,059	61.5%	38.5%	0.0%	62.1%	11,780	86.7%	12.2%	1.1%	70.2%
Albany, OR	7,007	95.3%	4.7%	0.0%	54.6%	9,257	89.8%	10.2%	0.0%	80.9%
Albany-Schenectady-Troy, NY	63,537	87.8%	10.5%	1.8%	64.8%	89,822	91.8%	6.7%	1.4%	87.6%
Albertville, AL	5,970	90.5%	9.5%	0.0%	67.2%	7,070	88.6%	11.4%	0.0%	77.2%
Albuquerque, NM	60,030	83.2%	14.8%	2.0%	70.9%	91,803	91.2%	8.4%	0.4%	81.1%
Alexandria, LA	10,235	68.6%	16.1%	15.3%	71.9%	12,017	84.7%	4.6%	10.7%	67.2%
Allentown-Bethlehem-Easton, PA-NJ	53,716	87.5%	12.4%	0.0%	70.3%	71,600	94.2%	5.8%	0.0%	84.2%
Altoona, PA	7,237	90.5%	9.5%	0.0%	70.7%	11,041	96.1%	3.9%	0.0%	80.5%
Amarillo, TX	17,855	93.3%	6.3%	0.4%	69.8%	29,386	98.0%	2.0%	0.0%	82.0%
Ames, IA	18,983	93.6%	6.4%	0.0%	61.9%	10,090	95.6%	3.1%	1.3%	82.9%
Anchorage, AK	35,566	79.7%	10.9%	9.4%	77.7%	50,901	84.5%	6.6%	8.9%	83.8%
Ann Arbor, MI	42,295	88.1%	11.9%	0.0%	64.1%	38,488	94.9%	4.9%	0.2%	84.9%
Anniston-Oxford-Jacksonville, AL	10,143	89.1%	10.9%	0.0%	78.4%	10,420	89.0%	10.4%	0.6%	80.7%
Appleton, WI	16,495	94.8%	5.2%	0.0%	86.3%	26,717	96.2%	3.8%	0.0%	91.7%
Asheville, NC	23,905	83.0%	17.0%	0.0%	71.4%	33,683	93.6%	5.7%	0.7%	74.9%
Ashtabula, OH	5,154	82.0%	18.0%	0.0%	66.8%	8,000	90.8%	9.2%	0.0%	01.7%
Athens-Clarke County, GA	21,691	90.1%	9.4%	0.5%	53.2%	19,668	93.6%	6.4%	0.0%	79.1%
Atlanta-Sandy Springs-Roswell, GA	350,272	85.1%	14.8%	0.0%	66.8%	583,234	93.0%	6.8%	0.2%	84.3%
Atlantic City-Hammonton, NJ	18,728	68.3%	28.5%	3.2%	69.3%	23,950	87.1%	12.9%	0.0%	01.1%
Auburn-Opelika, AL	17,346	93.5%	6.5%	0.0%	56.6%	15,343	90.2%	9.3%	0.5%	81.6%
Augusta-Richmond County, GA-SC	37,148	72.5%	17.0%	10.5%	64.2%	58,912	83.6%	8.4%	8.0%	76.3%
Augusta-Waterville, ME	7,869	93.7%	6.2%	0.1%	75.5%	9,595	94.1%	5.8%	0.1%	84.2%
Austin-Round Rock, TX	132,632	89.7%	10.2%	0.0%	65.7%	262,222	95.7%	4.0%	0.3%	85.3%
Bakersfield, CA	63,415	82.8%	15.5%	1.6%	65.8%	89,602	88.0%	11.0%	1.0%	75.3%
Baltimore-Columbia-Towson, MD	174,642	84.5%	11.0%	4.5%	69.4%	303,171	92.9%	5.7%	1.5%	84.1%
Bangor, ME	11,390	79.1%	18.6%	2.4%	65.4%	14,195	92.7%	7.3%	0.0%	77.8%
Barnstable Town, MA	9,192	88.9%	9.1%	2.0%	64.7%	14,137	95.8%	2.9%	1.3%	89.3%
Baton Rouge, LA	69,720	87.6%	12.2%	0.2%	70.7%	85,509	91.1%	8.5%	0.3%	79.5%
Battle Creek, MI	7,931	84.6%	15.4%	0.0%	73.8%	12,041	97.9%	2.1%	0.0%	77.7%
Bay City, MI	7,052	87.3%	11.5%	1.2%	80.6%	10,470	95.7%	4.3%	0.0%	91.9%
Beaumont-Port Arthur, TX	25,326	90.0%	9.8%	0.1%	67.2%	37,905	93.9%	6.1%	0.0%	72.2%
Beckley, WV	4,990	77.6%	22.4%	0.0%	52.3%	8,958	88.0%	10.3%	1.7%	69.1%
Bellingham, WA	22,833	95.1%	4.9%	0.0%	74.6%	20,429	89.6%	9.7%	0.6%	77.6%
Bend-Redmond, OR	10,144	87.8%	12.2%	0.0%	81.0%	16,028	96.4%	3.6%	0.0%	81.7%
Billings, MT	12,056	88.1%	11.3%	0.6%	73.9%	16,677	97.1%	2.1%	0.8%	83.8%
Binghamton, NY	19,919	85.8%	14.2%	0.0%	60.4%	20,237	95.4%	4.6%	0.0%	84.3%
Birmingham-Hoover, AL	68,277	84.6%	15.4%	0.0%	68.6%	115,491	92.6%	7.4%	0.0%	83.3%
Bismarck, ND	8,514	95.0%	3.9%	1.1%	77.6%	17,244	98.6%	1.4%	0.0%	91.8%
Blacksburg-Christiansburg-Radford, VA	17,238	92.8%	7.2%	0.0%	42.3%	16,172	95.8%	4.2%	0.0%	80.0%
Bloomington, IL	23,684	89.8%	10.2%	0.0%	73.0%	20,315	95.9%	4.0%	0.1%	91.9%
Bloomington, IN	20,074	87.6%	12.4%	0.0%	48.6%	17,361	90.2%	9.0%	0.8%	83.1%
Bloomsburg-Berwick, PA	5,909	90.5%	9.5%	0.0%	56.9%	8,773	90.8%	9.2%	0.0%	80.5%
Boise City, ID	41,510	87.5%	12.5%	0.0%	71.3%	69,117	92.6%	6.0%	1.4%	81.0%
Boston-Cambridge-Newton, MA-NH	331,375	90.1%	9.7%	0.2%	69.6%	544,124	94.3%	5.4%	0.3%	87.5%
Boulder, CO	30,881	90.3%	9.7%	0.0%	62.3%	33,067	96.7%	3.3%	0.0%	88.0%
Bowling Green, KY	16,891	89.8%	9.7%	0.4%	73.9%	13,653	94.2%	5.8%	0.0%	72.3%
Bremerton-Silverdale, WA	21,329	61.4%	15.7%	22.9%	77.8%	26,374	73.0%	5.1%	21.9%	80.6%
Bridgeport-Stamford-Norwalk, CT	59,233	86.0%	14.0%	0.0%	69.6%	84,592	90.7%	9.0%	0.3%	86.4%
Brownsville-Harlingen, TX	26,282	85.7%	14.3%	0.0%	58.6%	34,576	90.8%	9.2%	0.0%	75.8%
Brunswick, GA	5,757	82.1%	4.7%	13.2%	61.3%	9,579	83.5%	4.3%	12.2%	75.3%
Buffalo-Cheektowaga-Niagara Falls, NY	73,913	91.1%	8.8%	0.1%	68.2%	113,010	92.5%	7.4%	0.1%	82.3%
Burlington, NC	10,031	82.9%	17.1%	0.0%	68.0%	13,511	93.2%	6.8%	0.0%	81.1%
Burlington-South Burlington, VT	20,696	94.0%	6.0%	0.0%	67.8%	22,733	95.4%	4.4%	0.2%	87.1%
California-Lexington Park, MD	8,132	82.2%	15.0%	2.8%	72.8%	11,020	94.8%	2.6%	2.6%	84.2%
Canton-Massillon, OH	26,628	89.3%	10.7%	0.0%	77.0%	36,095	90.0%	10.0%	0.0%	84.3%
Cape Coral-Fort Myers, FL	36,653	87.7%	12.2%	0.1%	72.9%	52,317	90.1%	9.1%	0.8%	74.9%
Cape Girardeau, MO-IL	7,818	92.5%	7.5%	0.0%	72.9%	9,215	95.6%	4.4%	0.0%	77.4%
Carbondale-Marion, IL	11,026	78.7%	21.3%	0.0%	59.2%	11,962	92.3%	7.7%	0.0%	80.5%
Carson City, NV	4,075	95.9%	4.1%	0.0%	78.0%	3,385	74.2%	19.9%	5.9%	78.5%
Casper, WY	5,290	83.9%	16.1%	0.0%	74.4%	8,248	90.3%	9.7%	0.0%	76.5%
Cedar Rapids, IA	18,769	88.9%	11.1%	0.0%	76.2%	25,890	97.5%	2.5%	0.0%	84.1%
Chambersburg-Waynesboro, PA	9,490	83.9%	16.1%	0.0%	69.5%	14,289	95.3%	4.7%	0.0%	92.3%
Champaign-Urbana, IL	23,669	92.4%	7.6%	0.0%	44.8%	24,328	94.2%	5.7%	0.1%	84.2%
Charleston, WV	11,283	82.1%	17.9%	0.0%	71.5%	19,062	92.8%	7.2%	0.0%	81.1%
Charleston-North Charleston, SC	46,130	81.7%	8.6%	9.7%	66.4%	88,970	91.5%	5.6%	2.9%	81.7%
Charlotte-Concord-Gastonia, NC-SC	154,014	85.0%	15.0%	0.0%	72.1%	245,849	92.8%	7.2%	0.1%	85.1%
Charlottesville, VA	16,106	90.2%	8.3%	1.5%	54.1%	24,752	94.3%	5.1%	0.6%	81.8%
Chattanooga, TN-GA	36,373	88.8%	11.2%	0.0%	71.1%	53,944	92.6%	7.1%	0.3%	82.1%
Cheyenne, WY	9,890	88.4%	6.3%	5.3%	68.3%	8,185	86.4%	5.9%	7.7%	85.5%
Chicago-Naperville-Elgin, IL-IN-WI	626,055	84.2%	14.7%	1.1%	69.9%	1,028,645	92.5%	7.1%	0.4%	84.4%
Chico, CA	22,310	76.4%	23.6%	0.0%	66.2%	20,841	90.1%	9.9%	0.0%	82.3%

Table H-4: Metropolitan/Micropolitan Statistical Areas—Labor Force Status—*Continued*

	18 to 24					25 to 33				
	In the Labor Force	Percent				In the Labor Force	Percent			
		Employed	Unemployed	In Armed Forces	Labor Force Participation Rate		Employed	Unemployed	In Armed Forces	Labor Force Participation Rate
Cincinnati, OH-KY-IN	139,611	88.4%	11.6%	0.0%	70.5%	217,179	93.8%	6.2%	0.0%	85.2%
Clarksburg, WV	4,959	86.8%	13.2%	0.0%	65.0%	7,300	93.0%	7.0%	0.0%	83.7%
Clarksville, TN-KY	24,663	55.4%	9.8%	34.8%	75.5%	38,912	70.3%	6.6%	23.1%	80.4%
Cleveland, TN	8,881	84.1%	15.9%	0.0%	73.9%	9,523	87.4%	12.6%	0.0%	71.3%
Cleveland-Elyria, OH	133,632	84.2%	15.8%	0.0%	75.0%	191,243	92.0%	7.9%	0.1%	84.8%
Coeur d'Alene, ID	9,099	98.4%	1.6%	0.0%	77.5%	13,823	96.8%	3.2%	0.0%	77.9%
College Station-Bryan, TX	29,785	96.3%	3.7%	0.0%	50.3%	26,905	94.7%	5.3%	0.0%	79.9%
Colorado Springs, CO	59,763	73.5%	8.3%	18.2%	79.1%	80,411	82.7%	6.4%	11.0%	81.2%
Columbia, MO	17,555	87.3%	11.9%	0.8%	50.1%	19,855	96.2%	3.8%	0.0%	79.5%
Columbia, SC	66,393	77.1%	13.7%	9.2%	66.7%	81,975	92.1%	5.2%	2.7%	84.8%
Columbus, GA-AL	22,576	63.5%	18.5%	18.0%	62.6%	35,112	74.6%	11.1%	14.3%	79.2%
Columbus, IN	5,661	98.1%	1.9%	0.0%	77.7%	8,418	90.7%	9.3%	0.0%	84.4%
Columbus, OH	131,989	90.2%	9.6%	0.1%	71.3%	240,082	94.6%	5.2%	0.1%	85.7%
Concord, NH	8,116	95.0%	5.0%	0.0%	77.2%	9,155	92.5%	6.3%	1.2%	80.5%
Cookeville, TN	7,332	87.8%	12.2%	0.0%	51.2%	9,695	95.3%	4.7%	0.0%	82.4%
Corpus Christi, TX	27,628	80.1%	17.3%	2.6%	61.8%	44,326	91.7%	7.9%	0.4%	79.2%
Corvallis, OR	8,154	95.9%	4.1%	0.0%	53.4%	10,153	90.0%	10.0%	0.0%	82.3%
Crestview-Fort Walton Beach-Destin, FL	18,535	73.1%	10.2%	16.7%	77.3%	30,382	80.2%	5.9%	13.9%	80.2%
Cumberland, MD-WV	6,158	89.3%	10.7%	0.0%	51.7%	8,762	94.0%	6.0%	0.0%	83.3%
Dallas-Fort Worth-Arlington, TX	455,288	89.7%	10.2%	0.1%	69.8%	756,526	94.9%	4.9%	0.2%	82.8%
Dalton, GA	8,727	86.2%	13.8%	0.0%	63.7%	13,804	97.6%	2.4%	0.0%	78.1%
Danville, IL	3,351	84.3%	15.7%	0.0%	63.2%	7,695	88.6%	11.4%	0.0%	78.4%
Danville, VA	5,708	81.3%	18.7%	0.0%	72.9%	7,879	81.0%	19.0%	0.0%	76.6%
Daphne-Fairhope-Foley, AL	11,207	81.3%	18.7%	0.0%	77.9%	15,435	91.5%	8.5%	0.0%	77.0%
Davenport-Moline-Rock Island, IA-IL	23,522	93.2%	6.8%	0.0%	67.3%	36,056	92.9%	6.7%	0.4%	84.0%
Dayton, OH	55,339	82.2%	16.6%	1.2%	74.0%	77,000	89.4%	8.8%	1.8%	82.4%
Decatur, AL	6,715	73.7%	26.3%	0.0%	55.3%	12,709	89.4%	10.6%	0.0%	74.5%
Decatur, IL	7,154	83.6%	16.4%	0.0%	70.2%	8,897	95.1%	4.9%	0.0%	85.1%
Deltona-Daytona Beach-Ormond Beach, FL	26,540	87.1%	12.7%	0.2%	51.7%	48,260	92.0%	7.8%	0.2%	79.7%
Denver-Aurora-Lakewood, CO	174,696	91.4%	7.9%	0.7%	74.6%	350,733	94.5%	5.2%	0.3%	87.1%
Des Moines-West Des Moines, IA	43,299	88.3%	11.7%	0.0%	80.5%	73,605	96.6%	3.4%	0.0%	86.9%
Detroit-Warren-Dearborn, MI	272,294	85.1%	14.8%	0.1%	73.8%	396,545	89.9%	10.0%	0.1%	82.4%
Dothan, AL	8,896	76.7%	14.3%	9.0%	73.4%	12,894	78.0%	18.3%	3.8%	79.8%
Dover, DE	12,181	83.5%	11.4%	5.1%	64.9%	17,576	88.2%	5.8%	6.0%	85.6%
Dubuque, IA	8,002	94.5%	5.5%	0.0%	74.3%	9,503	93.1%	6.9%	0.0%	92.1%
Duluth, MN-WI	23,545	91.6%	8.4%	0.0%	74.7%	27,800	94.8%	5.2%	0.0%	86.8%
Dunn, NC	7,539	80.2%	18.8%	1.0%	57.6%	12,722	78.8%	8.0%	13.2%	76.2%
Durham-Chapel Hill, NC	45,044	92.2%	7.8%	0.0%	68.9%	63,849	95.4%	4.5%	0.1%	82.4%
East Stroudsburg, PA	14,257	80.6%	19.4%	0.0%	78.2%	14,420	86.1%	12.8%	1.1%	87.5%
Eau Claire, WI	16,102	92.6%	7.4%	0.0%	72.8%	16,944	97.0%	3.0%	0.0%	85.7%
El Centro, CA	12,982	65.9%	31.5%	2.6%	64.5%	14,623	77.4%	22.4%	0.2%	68.2%
El Paso, TX	10,490	82.2%	14.7%	3.1%	80.0%	13,774	90.4%	8.2%	1.4%	79.5%
Elizabethtown-Fort Knox, KY	14,186	91.7%	8.3%	0.0%	75.0%	16,230	95.1%	4.9%	0.0%	71.7%
Elkhart-Goshen, IN	4,972	91.4%	8.6%	0.0%	67.7%	8,552	92.5%	7.5%	0.0%	77.6%
Elmira, NY	62,694	78.6%	9.2%	12.3%	66.3%	90,129	86.5%	6.5%	7.0%	81.2%
Erie, PA	19,796	92.3%	7.7%	0.0%	69.6%	26,728	88.2%	11.8%	0.0%	85.8%
Eugene, OR	32,461	86.9%	13.1%	0.0%	70.0%	34,723	93.4%	6.6%	0.0%	82.9%
Eureka-Arcata-Fortuna, CA	11,280	84.5%	15.5%	0.0%	61.9%	10,795	94.4%	5.6%	0.0%	66.6%
Evansville, IN-KY	19,235	91.9%	8.1%	0.0%	68.0%	32,967	97.0%	2.5%	0.5%	88.2%
Fairbanks, AK	12,500	83.0%	1.6%	15.4%	82.5%	12,522	77.3%	6.5%	16.2%	80.8%
Fargo, ND-MN	28,556	95.0%	5.0%	0.0%	77.8%	30,661	97.5%	2.5%	0.0%	95.7%
Farmington, NM	7,995	92.6%	7.4%	0.0%	68.9%	9,664	92.1%	7.9%	0.0%	68.9%
Fayetteville, NC	32,171	57.5%	14.4%	28.1%	70.8%	43,707	71.3%	9.9%	18.8%	79.7%
Fayetteville-Springdale-Rogers, AR-MO	38,491	91.1%	8.3%	0.6%	67.6%	53,078	96.1%	3.9%	0.0%	78.3%
Flagstaff, AZ	16,913	82.6%	17.4%	0.1%	57.0%	14,180	92.0%	6.6%	1.4%	82.8%
Flint, MI	25,586	83.3%	16.7%	0.0%	69.7%	33,567	89.9%	10.1%	0.0%	77.9%
Florence, SC	12,681	73.0%	27.0%	0.0%	66.7%	17,685	86.0%	14.0%	0.0%	80.9%
Florence-Muscle Shoals, AL	9,903	90.1%	9.9%	0.0%	71.4%	10,319	92.0%	8.0%	0.0%	74.5%
Fond du Lac, WI	6,639	88.3%	11.7%	0.0%	78.1%	9,892	92.5%	7.5%	0.0%	91.2%
Fort Collins, CO	35,564	94.2%	5.2%	0.6%	77.2%	39,763	92.9%	6.6%	0.5%	86.0%
Fort Smith, AR-OK	16,022	87.9%	11.9%	0.2%	66.5%	25,666	96.3%	3.7%	0.0%	75.4%
Fort Wayne, IN	32,000	89.7%	10.3%	0.0%	74.6%	42,264	94.5%	5.5%	0.0%	85.5%
Fresno, CA	65,842	81.8%	18.2%	0.0%	62.0%	99,549	88.9%	11.1%	0.0%	76.7%
Gadsden, AL	6,487	93.9%	6.1%	0.0%	71.5%	7,149	94.6%	5.4%	0.0%	74.6%
Gainesville, FL	25,934	88.5%	11.5%	0.0%	45.6%	28,295	98.0%	2.0%	0.0%	75.8%
Gainesville, GA	13,039	87.8%	12.2%	0.0%	71.2%	15,635	95.0%	5.0%	0.0%	72.4%
Gettysburg, PA	6,072	96.7%	3.3%	0.0%	71.0%	9,679	90.3%	9.7%	0.0%	90.8%
Glens Falls, NY	7,413	89.1%	10.5%	0.5%	75.9%	10,456	94.1%	5.9%	0.0%	85.2%
Goldsboro, NC	9,014	78.2%	10.1%	11.8%	74.3%	12,000	90.7%	5.6%	3.7%	73.1%
Grand Forks, ND-MN	14,630	92.1%	5.8%	2.1%	76.8%	12,596	91.8%	2.0%	6.2%	91.9%
Grand Island, NE	6,731	93.1%	6.9%	0.0%	85.1%	8,877	94.5%	5.5%	0.0%	97.4%
Grand Junction, CO	10,022	85.4%	13.6%	1.0%	64.6%	14,406	81.3%	17.8%	1.0%	80.9%
Grand Rapids-Wyoming, MI	84,070	91.1%	8.9%	0.0%	77.8%	111,026	93.7%	6.1%	0.2%	85.4%
Grants Pass, OR	5,597	89.6%	10.4%	0.0%	88.6%	4,884	95.7%	4.3%	0.0%	74.4%

Table H-4: Metropolitan/Micropolitan Statistical Areas—Labor Force Status—*Continued*

	18 to 24					25 to 33				
	In the Labor Force	Percent			Labor Force Participation Rate	In the Labor Force	Percent			Labor Force Participation Rate
		Employed	Unemployed	In Armed Forces			Employed	Unemployed	In Armed Forces	
Great Falls, MT	5,280	77.4%	12.9%	9.8%	62.4%	6,859	88.7%	6.9%	4.4%	70.5%
Greeley, CO	20,781	93.1%	6.9%	0.0%	69.8%	27,988	95.3%	4.0%	0.7%	79.0%
Green Bay, WI	22,294	91.2%	8.8%	0.0%	81.3%	34,419	97.6%	2.4%	0.0%	88.7%
Greensboro-High Point, NC	42,612	87.3%	12.7%	0.0%	59.7%	71,564	93.8%	6.1%	0.1%	83.7%
Greenville, NC	24,102	81.2%	18.8%	0.0%	75.8%	18,510	87.4%	12.6%	0.0%	82.5%
Greenville-Anderson-Mauldin, SC	54,110	86.0%	13.8%	0.2%	63.0%	82,832	91.5%	8.2%	0.3%	83.2%
Greenwood, SC	7,566	72.4%	27.6%	0.0%	72.6%	6,027	90.9%	9.1%	0.0%	68.6%
Gulfport-Biloxi-Pascagoula, MS	26,349	70.0%	13.3%	16.7%	71.4%	37,315	84.0%	10.9%	5.1%	80.3%
Hagerstown-Martinsburg, MD-WV	14,865	80.9%	18.1%	1.1%	65.2%	22,714	91.8%	8.2%	0.0%	76.6%
Hammond, LA	10,126	86.8%	13.2%	0.0%	69.9%	12,233	90.5%	9.5%	0.0%	76.1%
Hanford-Corcoran, CA	10,299	62.4%	16.6%	21.0%	61.4%	15,918	80.7%	8.6%	10.7%	67.9%
Harrisburg-Carlisle, PA	39,457	90.1%	9.9%	0.0%	72.1%	52,073	97.4%	2.6%	0.0%	86.4%
Harrisonburg, VA	13,755	90.1%	9.9%	0.0%	53.4%	12,072	88.7%	11.3%	0.0%	84.3%
Hartford-West Hartford-East Hartford, CT	78,808	90.1%	9.9%	0.0%	68.3%	108,485	92.4%	7.6%	0.1%	84.9%
Hattiesburg, MS	14,103	85.8%	14.2%	0.0%	70.4%	13,287	81.5%	18.1%	0.4%	78.3%
Hickory-Lenoir-Morganton, NC	24,005	86.5%	13.5%	0.0%	75.5%	27,591	92.5%	7.5%	0.0%	78.7%
Hilo, HI	12,804	92.1%	7.9%	0.0%	78.5%	16,965	90.1%	9.5%	0.4%	78.3%
Hilton Head Island-Bluffton-Beaufort, SC	14,273	67.7%	5.2%	27.1%	77.8%	21,812	84.2%	10.1%	5.7%	90.1%
Hinesville, GA	9,666	61.3%	6.5%	32.2%	74.0%	9,090	73.7%	6.1%	20.3%	73.0%
Holland, MI	8,727	96.7%	3.3%	0.0%	89.1%	9,487	100.0%	0.0%	0.0%	79.3%
Homosassa Springs, FL	4,537	89.9%	10.1%	0.0%	58.8%	7,752	81.7%	18.3%	0.0%	86.3%
Hot Springs, AR	5,154	88.8%	11.2%	0.0%	64.3%	7,392	91.7%	8.3%	0.0%	73.9%
Houma-Thibodaux, LA	14,102	91.4%	8.6%	0.0%	77.3%	19,600	96.9%	2.8%	0.4%	70.8%
Houston-The Woodlands-Sugar Land, TX	411,550	87.8%	12.0%	0.2%	66.9%	724,094	94.2%	5.7%	0.2%	81.4%
Huntington-Ashland, WV-KY-OH	20,831	88.1%	11.9%	0.0%	62.5%	26,497	95.7%	4.3%	0.0%	72.5%
Huntsville, AL	28,418	86.0%	13.0%	1.1%	70.0%	47,431	90.7%	9.2%	0.1%	82.7%
Idaho Falls, ID	8,318	90.7%	9.3%	0.0%	73.4%	14,013	95.5%	4.5%	0.0%	81.2%
Indianapolis-Carmel-Anderson, IN	132,965	89.1%	10.8%	0.1%	76.0%	212,851	91.8%	8.0%	0.3%	84.4%
Iowa City, IA	20,011	90.0%	10.0%	0.0%	63.4%	20,678	97.7%	2.3%	0.0%	89.3%
Ithaca, NY	12,758	93.2%	6.8%	0.0%	41.2%	8,860	95.2%	4.8%	0.0%	75.2%
Jackson, MI	10,049	83.8%	16.2%	0.0%	72.3%	13,051	94.6%	5.4%	0.0%	70.1%
Jackson, MS	31,712	83.4%	15.9%	0.6%	58.4%	58,432	92.9%	6.9%	0.2%	82.0%
Jackson, TN	7,620	92.9%	6.6%	0.6%	54.8%	12,392	94.7%	5.3%	0.0%	81.1%
Jacksonville, FL	95,436	83.2%	11.7%	5.1%	73.2%	155,434	88.0%	8.0%	3.9%	83.8%
Jacksonville, NC	31,482	43.4%	9.5%	47.1%	86.3%	26,196	59.3%	7.6%	33.1%	79.4%
Jamestown-Dunkirk-Fredonia, NY	8,490	79.9%	20.1%	0.0%	62.1%	10,170	86.7%	13.3%	0.0%	79.1%
Janesville-Beloit, WI	12,389	88.4%	11.6%	0.0%	83.6%	13,110	96.0%	4.0%	0.0%	85.8%
Jefferson City, MO	10,699	88.6%	10.9%	0.6%	72.9%	13,986	98.1%	0.9%	1.0%	80.8%
Johnson City, TN	13,835	85.1%	14.9%	0.0%	67.4%	15,928	95.2%	4.8%	0.0%	75.7%
Johnstown, PA	6,758	82.6%	17.4%	0.0%	54.5%	10,634	89.1%	10.9%	0.0%	82.5%
Jonesboro, AR	11,031	82.4%	17.6%	0.0%	70.6%	10,219	91.3%	7.5%	1.3%	66.6%
Joplin, MO	14,033	92.5%	7.5%	0.0%	80.7%	15,677	96.0%	4.0%	0.0%	83.9%
Kahului-Wailuku-Lahaina, HI	9,952	90.6%	9.4%	0.0%	78.9%	19,058	92.0%	4.9%	3.1%	91.2%
Kalamazoo-Portage, MI	36,556	84.6%	15.4%	0.0%	75.9%	31,853	88.1%	11.0%	0.9%	87.0%
Kalispell, MT	3,612	100.0%	0.0%	0.0%	50.8%	8,291	99.7%	0.3%	0.0%	85.6%
Kankakee, IL	8,059	85.4%	14.6%	0.0%	69.8%	10,130	91.9%	8.1%	0.0%	82.4%
Kansas City, MO-KS	135,486	89.4%	9.0%	1.6%	75.0%	222,027	94.6%	4.7%	0.7%	85.8%
Kennewick-Richland, WA	18,968	88.0%	12.0%	0.0%	69.0%	27,802	94.4%	5.6%	0.0%	78.8%
Killeen-Temple, TX	42,051	64.1%	9.1%	26.8%	78.0%	52,176	72.1%	9.9%	18.1%	77.7%
Kingsport-Bristol-Bristol, TN-VA	15,889	85.6%	14.4%	0.0%	68.0%	23,810	91.3%	8.7%	0.0%	77.3%
Kingston, NY	11,316	91.8%	8.2%	0.0%	58.4%	13,491	95.7%	4.3%	0.0%	79.0%
Knoxville, TN	60,721	90.5%	9.5%	0.0%	68.9%	74,519	91.7%	8.2%	0.1%	80.5%
Kokomo, IN	4,581	81.7%	18.3%	0.0%	75.9%	7,549	95.2%	4.8%	0.0%	88.6%
La Crosse-Onalaska, WI-MN	15,083	92.1%	7.9%	0.0%	69.2%	12,392	93.3%	6.7%	0.0%	87.4%
Lafayette, LA	34,052	83.5%	16.5%	0.0%	71.4%	52,908	91.7%	7.9%	0.4%	81.5%
Lafayette-West Lafayette, IN	29,330	93.0%	7.0%	0.0%	60.7%	21,118	96.5%	3.5%	0.0%	82.7%
Lake Charles, LA	12,662	86.1%	13.9%	0.0%	64.9%	22,079	92.3%	7.5%	0.2%	81.7%
Lake Havasu City-Kingman, AZ	9,911	89.4%	10.6%	0.0%	78.0%	15,337	93.0%	7.0%	0.0%	78.9%
Lakeland-Winter Haven, FL	34,831	81.6%	18.4%	0.0%	62.1%	59,290	93.2%	6.8%	0.0%	77.7%
Lancaster, PA	35,793	87.9%	12.1%	0.0%	69.5%	50,396	96.5%	3.5%	0.0%	84.3%
Lansing-East Lansing, MI	44,722	86.1%	13.6%	0.2%	62.8%	47,041	95.5%	4.5%	0.0%	83.6%
Laredo, TX	18,857	87.0%	13.0%	0.0%	61.9%	21,239	93.9%	6.1%	0.0%	68.7%
Las Cruces, NM	21,360	82.0%	17.8%	0.1%	70.2%	17,014	88.7%	6.7%	4.6%	68.9%
Las Vegas-Henderson-Paradise, NV	135,471	85.2%	13.4%	1.4%	72.8%	232,057	90.5%	8.2%	1.3%	81.6%
Lawrence, KS	18,803	87.4%	12.6%	0.0%	68.8%	15,354	94.5%	4.8%	0.7%	93.2%
Lawton, OK	11,663	53.1%	9.6%	37.4%	76.6%	16,163	85.9%	3.4%	10.7%	79.8%
Lebanon, PA	9,808	93.3%	6.7%	0.0%	79.0%	10,778	98.8%	0.0%	1.2%	83.5%
Lewiston, ID-WA	3,525	93.5%	6.5%	0.0%	55.3%	4,877	91.4%	8.6%	0.0%	78.7%
Lewiston-Auburn, ME	7,161	96.8%	3.2%	0.0%	76.0%	8,966	98.3%	1.7%	0.0%	82.0%
Lexington-Fayette, KY	40,177	90.4%	9.6%	0.0%	68.4%	58,366	94.4%	5.2%	0.4%	86.8%
Lima, OH	6,530	88.2%	11.8%	0.0%	67.3%	10,318	90.3%	9.7%	0.0%	89.5%
Lincoln, NE	30,271	94.1%	5.9%	0.0%	65.3%	36,503	95.1%	3.9%	0.9%	84.8%
Little Rock-North Little Rock-Conway, AR	47,744	89.0%	9.2%	1.8%	66.9%	78,682	93.5%	5.0%	1.5%	80.8%
Logan, UT-ID	16,560	95.3%	4.7%	0.0%	74.5%	14,723	95.2%	3.4%	1.4%	76.0%

Table H-4: Metropolitan/Micropolitan Statistical Areas—Labor Force Status—*Continued*

	18 to 24					25 to 33				
	In the Labor Force	Percent				In the Labor Force	Percent			
		Employed	Unemployed	In Armed Forces	Labor Force Participation Rate		Employed	Unemployed	In Armed Forces	Labor Force Participation Rate
Longview, TX	13,494	85.0%	15.0%	0.0%	68.0%	19,651	91.9%	8.1%	0.0%	80.6%
Longview, WA	4,822	98.5%	1.3%	0.2%	73.7%	10,509	95.9%	4.1%	0.0%	82.2%
Los Angeles-Long Beach-Anaheim, CA	817,423	86.0%	13.8%	0.2%	61.9%	1,489,963	93.3%	6.6%	0.2%	81.9%
Louisville/Jefferson County, KY-IN	82,315	88.3%	11.6%	0.1%	75.8%	128,250	93.3%	6.3%	0.4%	84.8%
Lubbock, TX	29,856	92.7%	7.3%	0.0%	56.3%	35,404	97.8%	2.2%	0.0%	82.7%
Lumberton, NC	7,206	69.0%	29.0%	2.0%	52.0%	9,304	91.2%	8.8%	0.0%	69.8%
Lynchburg, VA	17,793	89.4%	10.6%	0.0%	54.1%	21,780	94.0%	6.0%	0.0%	78.9%
Macon, GA	12,551	83.6%	16.1%	0.4%	49.3%	18,882	90.3%	9.5%	0.2%	81.8%
Madera, CA	10,441	91.2%	8.8%	0.0%	66.6%	11,768	96.4%	3.6%	0.0%	61.2%
Madison, WI	60,900	93.4%	6.6%	0.0%	76.2%	77,981	96.7%	3.2%	0.1%	88.1%
Manchester-Nashua, NH	29,606	93.1%	6.9%	0.0%	79.2%	38,912	97.6%	2.2%	0.2%	85.4%
Manhattan, KS	15,874	65.9%	6.5%	27.6%	67.0%	12,946	61.8%	7.2%	30.9%	76.3%
Mankato-North Mankato, MN	14,606	94.5%	5.5%	0.0%	78.1%	11,365	93.5%	5.3%	1.2%	95.5%
Mansfield, OH	6,941	82.9%	17.1%	0.0%	64.2%	8,109	92.7%	7.3%	0.0%	65.0%
McAllen-Edinburg-Mission, TX	49,946	79.3%	20.7%	0.0%	54.4%	70,790	88.2%	11.1%	0.7%	73.5%
Medford, OR	10,118	85.7%	14.3%	0.0%	62.2%	17,911	90.6%	9.4%	0.0%	73.4%
Memphis, TN-MS-AR	86,419	83.5%	16.4%	0.1%	67.0%	135,575	90.7%	9.0%	0.3%	80.6%
Merced, CA	21,423	76.1%	23.9%	0.0%	65.5%	23,258	91.7%	8.0%	0.3%	70.2%
Meridian, MS	6,304	62.1%	27.4%	10.5%	61.1%	10,210	90.0%	8.5%	1.5%	82.9%
Miami-Fort Lauderdale-West Palm Beach, FL	321,589	85.1%	14.8%	0.1%	64.1%	604,996	92.1%	7.9%	0.0%	83.6%
Michigan City-La Porte, IN	6,169	88.4%	11.6%	0.0%	70.8%	9,507	83.6%	16.4%	0.0%	74.1%
Midland, MI	5,549	89.6%	10.4%	0.0%	82.7%	8,960	98.0%	2.0%	0.0%	93.8%
Midland, TX	13,108	91.9%	8.1%	0.0%	77.1%	21,067	97.9%	2.1%	0.0%	81.4%
Milwaukee-Waukesha-West Allis, WI	105,067	90.6%	9.4%	0.0%	73.2%	163,534	94.7%	5.2%	0.1%	85.6%
Minneapolis-St..Paul-Bloomington, MN-WI	229,764	91.8%	8.1%	0.2%	78.8%	405,320	96.5%	3.5%	0.0%	88.1%
Missoula, MT	11,766	87.2%	12.8%	0.0%	79.7%	13,643	97.9%	2.1%	0.0%	79.7%
Mobile, AL	22,442	82.0%	18.0%	0.0%	59.9%	42,507	91.0%	8.1%	0.9%	79.3%
Modesto, CA	27,024	77.6%	22.4%	0.0%	65.8%	40,349	85.2%	14.8%	0.0%	77.5%
Monroe, LA	10,394	79.6%	20.4%	0.0%	57.8%	17,846	87.5%	12.5%	0.0%	76.8%
Monroe, MI	8,884	84.7%	15.3%	0.0%	74.3%	12,572	93.2%	6.8%	0.0%	82.6%
Montgomery, AL	23,162	78.3%	19.2%	2.5%	62.8%	36,647	91.4%	6.8%	1.8%	78.4%
Morgantown, WV	11,024	90.9%	9.1%	0.0%	42.6%	15,698	97.8%	2.2%	0.0%	73.3%
Morristown, TN	6,349	96.3%	3.7%	0.0%	64.8%	7,874	99.2%	0.8%	0.0%	74.1%
Mount Vernon-Anacortes, WA	7,246	69.7%	15.8%	14.5%	81.0%	11,783	78.4%	10.1%	11.5%	86.1%
Muncie, IN	15,743	86.4%	13.6%	0.0%	68.7%	8,253	98.3%	1.7%	0.0%	79.7%
Muskegon, MI	10,390	87.2%	12.8%	0.0%	69.9%	14,722	90.3%	9.7%	0.0%	72.8%
Myrtle Beach-Conway-North Myrtle Beach, SC-NC	24,321	88.9%	11.0%	0.1%	73.1%	36,047	90.3%	8.9%	0.8%	84.3%
Napa, CA	8,606	91.9%	8.1%	0.0%	65.9%	13,394	92.6%	7.4%	0.0%	89.4%
Naples-Immokalee-Marco Island, FL	18,677	91.3%	8.7%	0.0%	72.2%	25,202	96.4%	3.6%	0.0%	81.8%
Nashville-Davidson–Murfreesboro–Franklin, TN	130,159	92.1%	7.8%	0.1%	74.2%	201,948	95.4%	4.5%	0.1%	84.5%
New Bern, NC	12,337	67.0%	9.6%	23.4%	82.0%	12,773	71.4%	11.6%	17.0%	82.3%
New Castle, PA	5,466	76.5%	23.5%	0.0%	81.9%	6,771	96.5%	3.5%	0.0%	76.0%
New Haven-Milford, CT	55,188	88.4%	11.6%	0.0%	63.2%	83,711	91.9%	8.1%	0.1%	83.7%
New Orleans-Metairie, LA	70,324	83.2%	16.3%	0.5%	65.6%	144,551	91.7%	7.7%	0.7%	83.1%
New Philadelphia-Dover, OH	5,090	93.1%	6.9%	0.0%	71.9%	7,288	98.7%	1.3%	0.0%	76.5%
New York-Newark-Jersey City, NY-NJ-PA	1,094,365	85.2%	14.4%	0.4%	60.0%	2,208,796	93.0%	6.8%	0.1%	83.9%
Niles-Benton Harbor, MI	10,069	84.4%	15.6%	0.0%	80.9%	12,730	89.2%	10.8%	0.0%	79.7%
North Port-Sarasota-Bradenton, FL	34,224	88.8%	11.0%	0.1%	68.5%	51,088	90.7%	9.3%	0.0%	78.8%
Norwich-New London, CT	23,370	75.0%	10.2%	14.9%	81.6%	26,518	86.1%	6.3%	7.7%	83.3%
Ocala, FL	12,727	70.6%	29.4%	0.0%	50.5%	25,032	90.4%	9.6%	0.0%	74.1%
Ocean City, NJ	4,566	67.0%	18.1%	14.9%	72.9%	7,750	91.4%	6.6%	2.0%	88.9%
Odessa, TX	11,796	84.1%	15.9%	0.0%	65.4%	18,501	97.2%	2.8%	0.0%	77.0%
Ogden-Clearfield, UT	47,748	91.0%	7.6%	1.4%	77.6%	66,918	94.1%	4.5%	1.4%	80.2%
Ogdensburg-Massena, NY	7,143	90.0%	10.0%	0.0%	45.0%	9,111	83.4%	11.8%	4.7%	73.9%
Oklahoma City, OK	96,724	90.7%	7.1%	2.1%	69.4%	152,113	93.6%	5.2%	1.1%	82.2%
Olympia-Tumwater, WA	17,092	90.4%	8.2%	1.4%	68.6%	27,411	88.1%	8.4%	3.5%	82.7%
Omaha-Council Bluffs, NE-IA	64,503	91.4%	5.6%	3.1%	80.5%	103,334	95.0%	3.3%	1.6%	85.6%
Orangeburg, SC	5,176	64.9%	35.1%	0.0%	68.0%	10,054	78.5%	21.5%	0.0%	87.2%
Orlando-Kissimmee-Sanford, FL	151,202	88.3%	11.6%	0.1%	64.2%	263,381	93.5%	6.2%	0.3%	83.1%
Oshkosh-Neenah, WI	15,362	94.6%	5.4%	0.0%	79.7%	17,967	97.2%	2.8%	0.0%	84.8%
Ottawa-Peru, IL	6,692	81.2%	18.8%	0.0%	75.3%	10,295	90.5%	9.5%	0.0%	86.5%
Owensboro, KY	7,486	75.6%	24.4%	0.0%	79.0%	11,066	91.5%	7.1%	1.5%	84.2%
Oxnard-Thousand Oaks-Ventura, CA	59,364	85.0%	12.6%	2.4%	72.4%	84,720	92.9%	5.7%	1.4%	84.0%
Palm Bay-Melbourne-Titusville, FL	27,908	84.2%	15.0%	0.8%	62.0%	45,917	92.6%	5.8%	1.5%	83.2%
Panama City, FL	11,556	74.0%	24.6%	1.4%	71.0%	19,566	85.4%	6.8%	7.9%	76.5%
Parkersburg-Vienna, WV	5,017	79.1%	20.9%	0.0%	68.5%	7,976	97.6%	2.4%	0.0%	84.9%
Pensacola-Ferry Pass-Brent, FL	39,399	73.9%	8.8%	17.3%	73.8%	50,558	85.4%	8.4%	6.3%	82.0%
Peoria, IL	23,365	82.7%	17.2%	0.1%	74.5%	37,716	93.0%	6.4%	0.6%	84.2%
Philadelphia-Camden-Wilmington, PA-NJ-DE-MD	358,659	85.3%	14.1%	0.6%	64.2%	633,992	91.3%	8.3%	0.5%	82.6%
Phoenix-Mesa-Scottsdale, AZ	300,438	88.5%	11.2%	0.3%	70.3%	458,343	93.5%	6.1%	0.4%	80.0%
Pine Bluff, AR	4,805	80.3%	19.7%	0.0%	53.1%	7,474	93.4%	6.6%	0.0%	75.4%

Table H-4: Metropolitan/Micropolitan Statistical Areas—Labor Force Status—*Continued*

	18 to 24				25 to 33			
		Percent				Percent		
	In the Labor Force	Employed	Unemployed	In Armed Forces	Labor Force Participation Rate	In the Labor Force	Employed	Unemployed	In Armed Forces	Labor Force Participation Rate
Pittsburgh, PA	138,492	87.9%	12.1%	0.0%	68.5%	231,246	93.2%	6.7%	0.1%	84.2%
Pittsfield, MA	9,168	90.5%	9.5%	0.0%	69.4%	9,762	92.5%	7.5%	0.0%	91.4%
Pocatello, ID	6,444	81.7%	18.3%	0.0%	65.0%	7,991	92.6%	4.8%	2.6%	71.7%
Port St. Lucie, FL	37,174	90.3%	9.7%	0.0%	80.1%	49,567	92.7%	5.8%	1.5%	88.1%
Portland-South Portland, ME	150,360	86.3%	13.6%	0.1%	74.7%	270,108	92.9%	6.8%	0.3%	84.2%
Portland-Vancouver-Hillsboro, OR-WA	26,246	84.0%	16.0%	0.0%	78.2%	34,113	94.5%	4.8%	0.7%	78.5%
Pottsville, PA	6,435	78.0%	22.0%	0.0%	63.2%	11,556	93.8%	6.2%	0.0%	77.8%
Prescott, AZ	10,904	86.4%	13.6%	0.0%	71.3%	14,777	96.2%	3.8%	0.0%	82.0%
Providence-Warwick, RI-MA	117,230	87.4%	12.3%	0.3%	70.9%	159,626	92.2%	6.8%	1.0%	82.9%
Provo-Orem, UT	70,109	93.6%	6.4%	0.0%	74.1%	55,714	97.1%	2.7%	0.2%	76.2%
Pueblo, CO	10,647	78.3%	20.3%	1.4%	71.0%	14,687	86.5%	12.4%	1.1%	76.7%
Punta Gorda, FL	6,041	86.7%	13.3%	0.0%	63.3%	7,400	94.8%	5.2%	0.0%	80.2%
Racine, WI	13,887	90.8%	9.2%	0.0%	77.9%	17,369	92.0%	8.0%	0.0%	88.4%
Raleigh, NC	70,349	89.1%	10.7%	0.1%	62.2%	138,549	93.9%	6.0%	0.1%	84.7%
Rapid City, SD	8,853	76.7%	14.7%	8.7%	78.6%	17,557	87.2%	7.0%	5.8%	91.0%
Reading, PA	29,968	85.2%	14.6%	0.2%	72.3%	39,920	93.3%	6.7%	0.0%	88.2%
Redding, CA	8,893	96.0%	4.0%	0.0%	68.5%	17,042	92.9%	7.1%	0.0%	82.6%
Reno, NV	30,790	89.0%	11.0%	0.0%	76.1%	50,006	91.7%	7.5%	0.8%	85.9%
Richmond, VA	87,268	85.9%	12.0%	1.6%	71.4%	132,982	91.8%	7.2%	1.0%	83.4%
Riverside-San Bernardino-Ontario, CA	314,765	79.4%	18.1%	2.5%	66.5%	438,393	88.9%	9.9%	1.2%	77.6%
Roanoke, VA	21,179	93.8%	6.2%	0.0%	77.6%	29,999	88.1%	11.4%	0.5%	85.8%
Rochester, MN	17,265	95.8%	4.2%	0.0%	83.3%	20,359	96.0%	4.0%	0.0%	85.7%
Rochester, NY	74,522	88.5%	11.4%	0.1%	67.4%	108,332	92.1%	7.9%	0.0%	84.7%
Rockford, IL	22,214	87.8%	12.2%	0.0%	77.8%	31,609	90.6%	9.4%	0.0%	85.4%
Rocky Mount, NC	9,546	91.9%	8.1%	0.0%	71.4%	11,904	88.5%	11.5%	0.0%	83.9%
Rome, GA	6,168	82.5%	17.5%	0.0%	67.2%	9,366	98.3%	1.7%	0.0%	80.2%
Roseburg, OR	5,123	75.4%	24.5%	0.1%	69.5%	9,136	94.3%	5.7%	0.0%	83.8%
Sacramento–Roseville–Arden-Arcade, CA	136,452	85.0%	15.0%	0.0%	62.5%	234,338	91.5%	7.9%	0.6%	82.2%
Saginaw, MI	15,341	76.5%	23.5%	0.0%	76.6%	17,880	94.9%	5.1%	0.0%	83.7%
Salem, OH	21,797	95.0%	5.0%	0.0%	84.2%	20,046	94.7%	4.5%	0.8%	83.7%
Salem, OR	12,220	93.3%	6.7%	0.0%	73.1%	12,161	98.4%	1.6%	0.0%	79.8%
Salinas, CA	9,198	93.5%	6.5%	0.0%	81.5%	12,119	91.8%	7.2%	1.0%	71.7%
Salisbury, MD-DE	186,163	87.4%	12.2%	0.4%	75.0%	291,006	93.4%	6.0%	0.5%	86.7%
Salt Lake City, UT	6,170	86.5%	13.5%	0.0%	82.2%	6,763	84.1%	15.9%	0.0%	68.4%
San Angelo, TX	28,674	89.7%	10.3%	0.0%	70.1%	38,772	89.9%	9.8%	0.3%	82.7%
San Antonio-New Braunfels, TX	30,571	77.8%	11.5%	10.7%	67.1%	41,588	89.1%	6.8%	4.1%	74.3%
San Diego-Carlsbad, CA	22,100	86.9%	13.0%	0.1%	56.5%	28,718	92.0%	7.5%	0.5%	76.4%
San Francisco-Oakland-Hayward, CA	92,302	92.7%	7.3%	0.0%	80.4%	142,734	96.0%	3.8%	0.2%	84.0%
San Jose-Sunnyvale-Santa Clara, CA	9,401	77.9%	3.1%	19.0%	61.1%	13,029	88.8%	2.8%	8.4%	77.8%
San Luis Obispo-Paso Robles-Arroyo Grande, CA	168,251	85.4%	11.6%	3.0%	68.2%	258,212	91.8%	5.7%	2.5%	80.0%
Santa Cruz-Watsonville, CA	250,602	75.0%	10.8%	14.2%	71.0%	391,721	89.4%	5.6%	5.0%	82.7%
Santa Fe, NM	249,505	86.0%	13.7%	0.3%	66.5%	562,594	95.2%	4.8%	0.1%	85.7%
Santa Maria-Santa Barbara, CA	108,780	88.9%	10.7%	0.4%	63.5%	221,177	94.4%	5.3%	0.3%	82.7%
Santa Rosa, CA	23,027	88.4%	5.9%	5.6%	54.5%	25,558	90.1%	7.3%	2.5%	82.9%
Savannah, GA	24,658	89.7%	10.3%	0.0%	58.4%	23,853	94.3%	5.7%	0.1%	78.7%
Scranton–Wilkes-Barre–Hazleton, PA	6,655	91.0%	9.0%	0.0%	60.4%	11,139	98.1%	1.7%	0.2%	74.0%
Seattle-Tacoma-Bellevue, WA	43,678	88.5%	10.4%	1.0%	61.4%	40,628	94.2%	4.4%	1.4%	82.7%
Sebastian-Vero Beach, FL	32,994	85.8%	13.6%	0.7%	75.4%	48,546	95.5%	3.5%	1.0%	84.8%
Sebring, FL	30,947	74.2%	17.7%	8.1%	65.6%	42,892	89.2%	7.0%	3.8%	83.2%
Sheboygan, WI	31,900	88.1%	11.9%	0.0%	61.6%	48,070	91.9%	8.1%	0.0%	82.6%
Sherman-Denison, TX	228,085	86.9%	10.0%	3.1%	71.9%	456,709	93.1%	5.2%	1.7%	84.0%
Show Low, AZ	7,329	84.9%	15.1%	0.0%	63.7%	9,385	88.0%	12.0%	0.0%	82.5%
Shreveport-Bossier City, LA	3,596	68.1%	31.9%	0.0%	57.5%	6,015	92.1%	7.9%	0.0%	78.0%
Sierra Vista-Douglas, AZ	6,603	89.2%	10.8%	0.0%	77.5%	10,114	98.8%	1.2%	0.0%	85.9%
Sioux City, IA-NE-SD	8,534	86.3%	12.4%	1.3%	69.8%	10,663	95.5%	2.5%	2.0%	83.9%
Sioux Falls, SD	4,067	69.1%	30.9%	0.0%	41.7%	6,089	80.8%	19.2%	0.0%	52.4%
South Bend-Mishawaka, IN-MI	24,599	80.3%	11.4%	8.2%	60.1%	45,680	89.5%	6.7%	3.8%	79.1%
Spartanburg, SC	5,113	65.0%	12.9%	22.1%	53.5%	8,700	80.3%	8.2%	11.5%	58.6%
Spokane-Spokane Valley, WA	9,550	99.7%	0.3%	0.0%	63.8%	16,061	96.0%	4.0%	0.0%	87.6%
Springfield, IL	16,920	90.0%	10.0%	0.0%	74.2%	29,588	96.7%	2.8%	0.5%	83.6%
Springfield, MA	21,187	87.9%	12.1%	0.0%	60.4%	27,966	94.8%	4.9%	0.3%	80.4%
Springfield, MO	22,598	83.0%	17.0%	0.0%	72.2%	27,483	91.6%	7.8%	0.6%	78.4%
Springfield, OH	32,367	86.7%	11.6%	1.7%	62.7%	51,183	89.1%	7.8%	3.1%	71.3%
St. Cloud, MN	11,561	89.9%	10.1%	0.0%	62.5%	19,762	90.0%	8.8%	1.1%	83.8%
St. George, UT	54,029	87.1%	12.9%	0.0%	78.0%	57,775	91.6%	8.4%	0.0%	80.1%
St. Joseph, MO-KS	42,643	91.1%	8.9%	0.0%	77.7%	44,292	94.7%	5.0%	0.2%	79.3%
St. Louis, MO-IL	9,147	88.6%	11.4%	0.0%	76.3%	11,651	90.9%	9.1%	0.0%	84.7%
State College, PA	18,886	92.4%	7.6%	0.0%	46.0%	16,671	96.8%	3.2%	0.0%	75.1%
Staunton-Waynesboro, VA	7,885	92.3%	7.7%	0.0%	59.0%	8,199	95.5%	3.6%	0.8%	69.5%
Stockton-Lodi, CA	47,097	79.4%	20.6%	0.0%	65.0%	68,143	91.2%	8.7%	0.1%	76.6%
Sumter, SC	8,671	83.2%	16.1%	0.8%	64.7%	9,606	70.3%	26.6%	3.1%	78.8%
Sunbury, PA	4,787	84.4%	15.6%	0.0%	72.1%	9,148	97.3%	2.7%	0.0%	86.4%
Syracuse, NY	42,157	85.8%	13.8%	0.4%	59.0%	59,634	93.9%	6.0%	0.1%	80.7%
Tallahassee, FL	47,293	87.4%	12.6%	0.0%	66.7%	36,202	91.8%	8.0%	0.3%	75.7%

Table H-4: Metropolitan/Micropolitan Statistical Areas—Labor Force Status—*Continued*

	18 to 24					25 to 33				
	In the Labor Force	Percent				In the Labor Force	Percent			
		Employed	Unemployed	In Armed Forces	Labor Force Participation Rate		Employed	Unemployed	In Armed Forces	Labor Force Participation Rate
Tampa-St. Petersburg-Clearwater, FL............	160,070	86.5%	13.0%	0.5%	66.9%	284,837	90.9%	8.1%	1.0%	83.0%
Terre Haute, IN..................................	15,053	81.1%	18.9%	0.0%	69.2%	13,349	85.7%	14.3%	0.0%	72.9%
Texarkana, TX-AR...............................	8,909	81.8%	18.2%	0.0%	65.9%	12,115	91.2%	8.8%	0.0%	71.7%
The Villages, FL.................................	2,495	74.1%	25.9%	0.0%	50.1%	2,348	93.1%	6.9%	0.0%	61.0%
Toledo, OH......................................	49,223	87.8%	12.2%	0.1%	73.3%	63,172	89.4%	10.6%	0.0%	87.9%
Topeka, KS......................................	13,716	93.9%	6.1%	0.0%	71.2%	22,076	87.7%	9.0%	3.3%	85.2%
Torrington, CT...................................	11,120	92.4%	7.6%	0.0%	82.0%	14,683	90.7%	9.3%	0.0%	89.0%
Traverse City, MI................................	8,416	86.6%	11.9%	1.5%	72.4%	12,140	95.2%	2.1%	2.7%	85.4%
Trenton, NJ......................................	25,325	81.9%	18.1%	0.0%	58.9%	31,022	90.9%	9.1%	0.0%	78.9%
Truckee-Grass Valley, CA........................	4,212	87.0%	9.9%	3.0%	68.5%	8,208	89.0%	9.7%	1.3%	85.9%
Tucson, AZ......................................	79,401	79.5%	18.2%	2.3%	67.2%	87,261	89.2%	8.7%	2.1%	79.4%
Tullahoma-Manchester, TN.......................	6,938	92.1%	7.7%	0.2%	70.3%	7,323	96.9%	3.1%	0.0%	75.1%
Tulsa, OK.......................................	65,730	90.3%	9.4%	0.3%	73.0%	97,680	94.7%	4.9%	0.4%	82.1%
Tupelo, MS......................................	9,731	81.7%	18.3%	0.0%	73.2%	12,001	92.5%	7.5%	0.0%	81.7%
Tuscaloosa, AL..................................	20,545	82.8%	17.2%	0.0%	51.0%	23,047	92.1%	7.9%	0.0%	74.0%
Tyler, TX..	13,407	92.9%	7.1%	0.0%	59.4%	20,301	97.4%	2.6%	0.0%	72.1%
Urban Honolulu, HI..............................	77,714	68.6%	9.1%	22.3%	74.6%	115,514	83.5%	4.4%	12.1%	83.4%
Utica-Rome, NY..................................	19,060	88.3%	11.7%	0.0%	70.5%	26,034	90.6%	9.3%	0.1%	82.5%
Valdosta, GA....................................	11,873	83.9%	12.6%	3.6%	55.8%	15,105	77.9%	15.4%	6.7%	77.5%
Vallejo-Fairfield, CA.............................	27,541	77.8%	17.7%	4.4%	68.4%	45,482	85.7%	9.6%	4.7%	82.1%
Victoria, TX.....................................	6,150	87.8%	12.2%	0.0%	63.8%	9,902	89.8%	9.7%	0.5%	85.3%
Vineland-Bridgeton, NJ...........................	9,271	85.6%	14.4%	0.0%	73.0%	13,440	94.5%	5.5%	0.0%	61.4%
Virginia Beach-Norfolk-Newport News, VA-NC.....................................	147,272	65.0%	11.4%	23.6%	75.1%	201,499	80.6%	6.4%	13.0%	81.9%
Visalia-Porterville, CA............................	26,892	84.9%	15.1%	0.0%	55.5%	46,286	92.6%	7.3%	0.1%	77.7%
Waco, TX..	23,393	89.8%	9.7%	0.5%	62.7%	22,878	93.9%	6.1%	0.0%	77.8%
Walla Walla, WA.................................	3,611	81.5%	18.5%	0.0%	54.8%	7,120	95.9%	4.1%	0.0%	81.4%
Warner Robins, GA..............................	13,124	79.0%	16.8%	4.2%	63.9%	18,283	88.2%	8.7%	3.0%	85.1%
Washington-Arlington-Alexandria, DC-VA-MD-WV....................................	381,751	84.2%	13.0%	2.8%	69.8%	730,514	93.2%	5.1%	1.6%	87.8%
Waterloo-Cedar Falls, IA..........................	17,717	94.6%	5.4%	0.0%	74.5%	18,161	96.0%	4.0%	0.0%	85.3%
Watertown-Fort Drum, NY........................	11,754	56.9%	7.3%	35.9%	77.4%	12,886	72.2%	4.6%	23.2%	78.1%
Wausau, WI.....................................	8,396	96.7%	3.3%	0.0%	86.6%	12,377	97.9%	2.1%	0.0%	86.8%
Weirton-Steubenville, WV-OH.....................	7,527	90.5%	9.5%	0.0%	67.9%	8,666	93.6%	5.3%	1.1%	70.5%
Wenatchee, WA..................................	6,668	93.6%	6.4%	0.0%	71.9%	10,246	95.8%	3.7%	0.5%	83.1%
Wheeling, WV-OH................................	9,829	90.5%	9.5%	0.0%	71.6%	9,532	94.2%	4.8%	1.0%	70.6%
Whitewater-Elkhorn, WI..........................	10,761	96.7%	3.3%	0.0%	81.0%	8,998	95.7%	4.3%	0.0%	89.5%
Wichita Falls, TX................................	41,112	91.6%	7.0%	1.3%	74.1%	69,863	93.0%	5.6%	1.4%	82.1%
Wichita, KS.....................................	15,386	62.8%	7.5%	29.7%	75.1%	13,359	90.5%	6.2%	3.2%	70.6%
Williamsport, PA................................	7,736	85.7%	14.3%	0.0%	64.4%	9,191	92.9%	7.1%	0.0%	74.0%
Wilmington, NC..................................	19,470	85.3%	12.6%	2.1%	60.4%	27,958	89.0%	10.8%	0.2%	85.2%
Winchester, VA-WV..............................	6,614	97.1%	2.9%	0.0%	54.2%	10,802	91.3%	8.7%	0.0%	84.2%
Winston-Salem, NC..............................	38,883	83.1%	16.7%	0.1%	65.2%	59,425	90.7%	9.1%	0.2%	81.8%
Wooster, OH....................................	9,297	88.0%	12.0%	0.0%	82.7%	9,620	98.0%	2.0%	0.0%	85.6%
Worcester, MA-CT...............................	66,758	88.9%	11.1%	0.0%	72.3%	83,548	91.1%	8.7%	0.2%	82.9%
Yakima, WA.....................................	19,540	80.1%	19.9%	0.1%	76.8%	20,689	88.9%	10.6%	0.5%	75.0%
York-Hanover, PA...............................	27,330	89.5%	10.3%	0.2%	78.2%	42,768	94.8%	5.2%	0.0%	84.2%
Youngstown-Warren-Boardman, OH-PA.......	33,375	85.2%	14.8%	0.0%	71.9%	43,820	88.7%	11.3%	0.0%	82.6%
Yuba City, CA...................................	10,606	75.9%	19.8%	4.3%	68.2%	17,329	90.4%	6.8%	2.9%	74.2%
Yuma, AZ.......................................	15,457	70.9%	18.2%	10.9%	67.1%	19,801	80.8%	13.8%	5.4%	77.4%

PART I

INCOME AND POVERTY

Income reported in the American Community Survey pertains only to the population age 15 and older. While some Millennials who are 15 to 17 will have income, they are not included in the following tables because of their small numbers and low income. The Census definition of income includes all sources of cash income: wages and salary, social security, retirement, interest, dividends and rent, for example. However, sources such as social security and retirement income are largely not applicable to a younger population. The Census money income definition also does not include measures of assets.

The Census Bureau reports that median household income for householders under age 25 increased from $25,391 in 2013 to $28,411 in 2015, but this masks the fact that median income in 2015 is just slightly above the $27,047 figure from 2008 as the recession took hold. This is another indication of the difficult economic climate faced by Millennials as they continue their formal education and move into the work force. The tables presented here reflect individual incomes rather than household income, which is an important difference. The median income of young Millennials age 18 to 24 was only $6,249 in 2015, but for those age 25 to 33 it was $25,315. These

incomes suggest that younger working Millennials are still struggling with job opportunities or are continuing their education while older Millennials are moving forward into their career paths and higher incomes.

INCOME

Not surprisingly, most young Millennials age 18 to 24 have low incomes. Nationwide, 61 percent have less than $10,000 in income from all sources and only 2.2 percent have incomes over $50,000. Almost one out of five (19.3 percent) have between $10,000 and $19,999 in annual income. Mississippi has the highest percentage of low income Millennials at 69.1 percent and 27 states exceed 60 percent. By this measure, Alaska is doing the best with the lowest percentage at 39.2 percent. At the higher income levels, Wyoming has the highest percentage (6.4 percent) with incomes over $50,000. Only eight states have more than three percent of this youngest age group making over $50,000. Incomes rise with age, and only one-quarter (25.4 percent) of the older Millennial age group has income below $10,000. Mississippi has the highest percentage at 32.3 percent, while North

Percent of Millennials Age 18 to 33 With Income Over $100,000

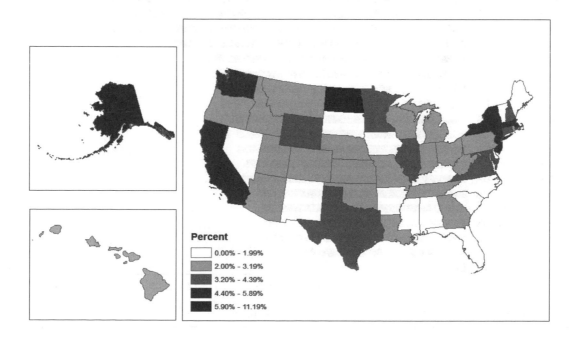

Percent
- 0.00% - 1.99%
- 2.00% - 3.19%
- 3.20% - 4.39%
- 4.40% - 5.89%
- 5.90% - 11.19%

Dakota is lowest at 14.9 percent. Some older Millennials are doing quite well, with incomes over $150,000. The District of Columbia has the highest percentage at 3.2 percent, but it's one of only three states above two percent with New York (2.4 percent) and North Dakota (2.9 percent).

Champaign County, IL has the highest percentage of younger Millennials in the under $10,000 category at 82.8 percent but is followed closely by Bibb County, GA at 82.4 percent. More than 140 counties have more than two-thirds of the 18 to 24 year olds in the lowest income category. Onslow County, NC has the lowest percentage at 32.7 percent. Arlington County, VA has the highest percentage of young, high income Millennials where 15.3 percent have incomes above $50,000, but in 366 counties less than two percent of this group is in the high income category. Among the older Millennial age category, those making under $10,000 range from a low of 5.5 percent in Kendall County, IL to a high of 59.2 percent in Navajo County, AZ. In 13 counties, more than 10 percent of those age 25 to 33 make more than $100,000 and in San Francisco, CA 22.5 percent have over $100,000. In New York County, NY (Manhattan) 10.6 percent make over $150,000.

More than 80 percent of those age 18 to 24 in Gainesville, FL have incomes below $10,000, and in 82 cities more than two-thirds of the younger population is in the low income category. Oceanside City, CA has the lowest percentage (24.1 percent) of low income persons. In San Francisco, CA, 12.4 percent of young Millennials make more than $50,000, and it is one of only six cities above 10 percent. In Fargo, ND only 8.7 percent of older Millennials are in the lowest income category. More than half (50.7 percent) in Meridian, ID make under $10,000. In the high income categories, 16 cities have greater than 15 percent of the 25 to 33 year old population making more than $75,000. The highest is Sunnyvale city, CA at 38.1 percent. In San Francisco city, CA, 5.1 percent make more than $150,000.

In 26 metropolitan/micropolitan areas more than 75 percent of Millennials in the younger age group make less than $10,000. The Albany, GA metro is the highest at 85.9 percent, while the Fairbanks, AK metro is lowest with 33.1 percent. Only 6.7 percent of older Millennials make less than $10,000 in the Torrington, CT micro, but more than half (54.6 percent) are low income earners in the Show Low, AZ micropolitan area. It's one of only three areas above 50 percent; also included are

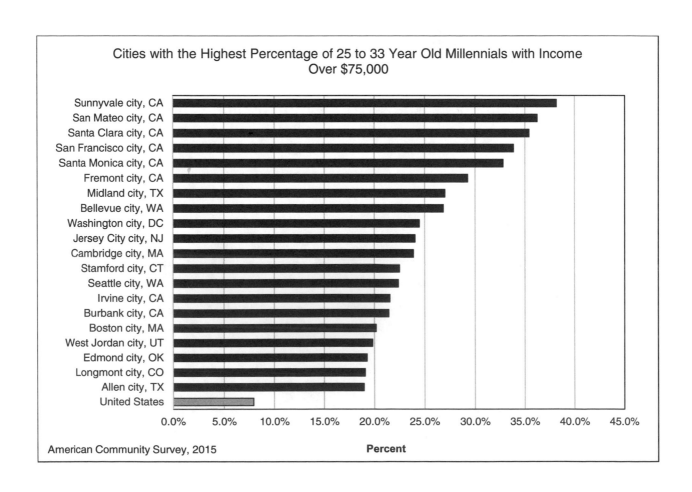

Cities with the Highest Percentage of 25 to 33 Year Old Millennials with Income Over $75,000

American Community Survey, 2015

Percent

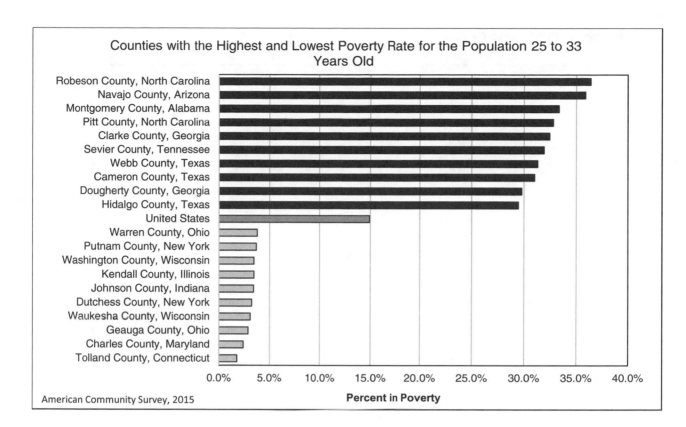

Counties with the Highest and Lowest Poverty Rate for the Population 25 to 33 Years Old

American Community Survey, 2015

the Panama City, FL and the Rocky Mount, NC metropolitan areas. High income earners are most prevalent in the San Jose-Sunnyvale, CA metro area where more than one in five (20.7 percent) make more than $75,000. Fifteen metro/micros have more than 15 percent of the older Millennials in the high income category.

POVERTY

Poverty status is determined by comparing total family or unrelated individual income to the established national poverty thresholds which vary by size and type of household and number of children. When a family or single person household is determined to be in poverty, every member of the family is so defined. College students living in group quarters (dormitories or other college housing) are not part of the poverty population universe so the poverty data presented here is only for the 25- to 33-year-old Millennials to minimize the effect of college populations.

The national poverty rate for all persons from the 2015 ACS is 14.7 percent, and the poverty rate for the older Millennials is only slightly higher with 14.9 percent

having incomes below the poverty level. Mississippi has the highest poverty rate at 23.4 percent while Maryland is lowest at 10.4 percent though seven other states are also below 11 percent. Of the 633 counties, 303 have poverty rates above the national average for Millennials. Tolland County, CT has the lowest rate of poverty at 1.8 percent. Poverty was highest in Robeson County, NC at 36.4 percent. However, Robeson County is the home of the University of North Carolina at Pembroke and while college students living in dormitories are excluded from the poverty definition, college students living in non-university, private housing off-campus are included. For this reason, most large college counties and cities will still have very high poverty rates.

Flint, MI has the highest poverty rate for older Millennials at 47.8 percent. Ten cities have poverty rates above 30 percent but 74 cities have poverty rates below 10 percent. San Mateo, CA is lowest at 0.7 percent. The impact of college populations is less important at the metropolitan level but the Lumberton, NC micropolitan area (University of North Carolina at Pembroke) still has the highest poverty rate at 36.2 percent. More than 25 percent of Millennials are in poverty in 44 metro/micro areas. The Bismarck, ND metro is lowest at 1.8 percent.

Table I-1: States—Income Class by Age

		Personal Income, Percent by Income Class, ages 18 to 24						
	Total Millennials	Under $10,000	$10,000 to $19,999	$20,000 to $29,999	$30,000 to $49,999	$50,000 to $74,999	$75,000 to $99,999	$100,000 or More
United States	31,345,795	61.0%	19.3%	10.8%	6.8%	1.7%	0.3%	0.2%
Alabama	469,138	66.1%	18.7%	9.3%	4.7%	1.0%	0.1%	0.2%
Alaska	84,225	39.2%	25.6%	21.9%	9.2%	3.8%	0.3%	0.0%
Arizona	672,348	58.8%	22.7%	10.9%	5.9%	1.6%	0.0%	0.1%
Arkansas	282,731	63.3%	19.1%	9.3%	6.5%	1.2%	0.2%	0.3%
California	3,948,553	62.7%	19.3%	10.0%	5.9%	1.5%	0.3%	0.3%
Colorado	524,617	53.0%	22.9%	13.0%	8.6%	2.1%	0.2%	0.2%
Connecticut	355,738	60.3%	18.6%	10.1%	8.2%	2.3%	0.3%	0.1%
Delaware	87,509	64.4%	18.4%	8.1%	6.4%	2.6%	0.2%	0.0%
District of Columbia	81,910	62.7%	14.2%	8.5%	8.5%	5.2%	0.2%	0.6%
Florida	1,779,978	61.7%	20.8%	11.0%	5.2%	1.1%	0.2%	0.1%
Georgia	1,029,333	65.1%	18.1%	10.6%	4.9%	1.0%	0.2%	0.1%
Hawaii	136,529	51.4%	15.1%	18.9%	11.1%	2.4%	1.0%	0.1%
Idaho	157,480	62.6%	21.1%	10.0%	5.1%	1.2%	0.0%	0.1%
Illinois	1,238,041	63.1%	18.0%	10.0%	6.6%	1.9%	0.2%	0.1%
Indiana	676,810	62.3%	19.2%	10.1%	6.9%	1.3%	0.1%	0.1%
Iowa	321,381	57.3%	21.4%	9.9%	9.1%	1.9%	0.1%	0.3%
Kansas	296,205	56.4%	21.6%	12.2%	7.8%	1.9%	0.1%	0.1%
Kentucky	424,621	57.6%	21.9%	12.2%	6.7%	1.3%	0.2%	0.1%
Louisiana	459,157	62.7%	19.5%	8.8%	6.2%	1.6%	0.5%	0.6%
Maine	115,050	57.7%	21.1%	11.2%	7.1%	2.6%	0.2%	0.0%
Maryland	558,491	61.2%	17.6%	10.6%	7.9%	2.3%	0.3%	0.1%
Massachusetts	698,392	63.4%	16.8%	9.0%	7.5%	2.5%	0.4%	0.4%
Michigan	986,321	60.0%	20.7%	10.3%	6.8%	1.9%	0.2%	0.1%
Minnesota	504,157	52.1%	22.2%	12.6%	10.5%	2.2%	0.3%	0.1%
Mississippi	312,903	69.2%	17.2%	7.9%	4.6%	0.9%	0.1%	0.1%
Missouri	598,165	59.3%	20.5%	11.8%	6.8%	1.4%	0.1%	0.0%
Montana	101,521	53.5%	25.3%	10.4%	8.3%	1.5%	0.3%	0.7%
Nebraska	194,933	53.8%	20.5%	13.8%	9.1%	1.8%	0.5%	0.5%
Nevada	254,487	53.8%	24.0%	12.3%	7.9%	1.4%	0.5%	0.2%
New Hampshire	129,612	60.8%	17.9%	11.0%	8.2%	1.7%	0.4%	0.0%
New Jersey	792,038	65.6%	16.5%	8.7%	6.5%	2.1%	0.4%	0.1%
New Mexico	208,652	62.1%	21.0%	10.7%	4.7%	1.2%	0.2%	0.0%
New York	1,939,899	66.0%	15.5%	8.8%	6.8%	2.1%	0.5%	0.4%
North Carolina	991,444	62.7%	18.7%	11.0%	6.5%	0.9%	0.1%	0.1%
North Dakota	93,505	46.8%	19.2%	14.3%	14.7%	3.1%	0.7%	1.2%
Ohio	1,090,850	58.9%	20.9%	11.1%	7.1%	1.7%	0.2%	0.1%
Oklahoma	391,812	55.2%	22.5%	12.8%	6.9%	2.1%	0.2%	0.1%
Oregon	365,845	59.9%	19.8%	12.3%	6.0%	1.8%	0.3%	0.0%
Pennsylvania	1,210,947	64.5%	16.8%	9.9%	6.8%	1.7%	0.3%	0.1%
Rhode Island	114,262	62.0%	18.5%	9.8%	8.2%	1.4%	0.0%	0.1%
South Carolina	487,869	61.5%	20.4%	10.9%	5.7%	1.1%	0.2%	0.1%
South Dakota	84,382	55.0%	18.4%	13.9%	10.7%	0.9%	0.4%	0.7%
Tennessee	633,501	61.3%	18.8%	11.3%	6.9%	1.4%	0.3%	0.2%
Texas	2,780,856	59.1%	19.1%	11.7%	7.3%	2.2%	0.5%	0.2%
Utah	345,362	54.0%	22.6%	12.8%	8.9%	1.1%	0.3%	0.3%
Vermont	67,578	60.2%	17.8%	10.7%	8.9%	2.2%	0.1%	0.0%
Virginia	826,162	59.3%	18.4%	11.5%	8.1%	2.0%	0.4%	0.2%
Washington	662,648	56.0%	18.7%	13.8%	7.7%	2.8%	0.6%	0.4%
West Virginia	163,675	67.1%	15.8%	9.7%	3.8%	2.5%	0.6%	0.5%
Wisconsin	555,679	55.2%	22.2%	12.2%	8.4%	1.8%	0.1%	0.0%
Wyoming	58,493	50.9%	23.9%	10.6%	8.2%	1.4%	1.8%	3.1%

Table I-1: States—Income Class by Age—*Continued*

	Personal Income, Percent by Income Class, ages 25 to 33									
	Total Millennials	Under $10,000	$10,000 to $19,999	$20,000 to $29,999	$30,000 to $49,999	$50,000 to $74,999	$75,000 to $99,999	$100,000 to $149,999	$150,000 or More	Poverty Rate
United States	39,598,655	25.4%	15.1%	15.8%	23.0%	12.8%	4.4%	2.5%	1.0%	14.9%
Alabama	564,102	31.4%	18.0%	15.7%	20.5%	9.7%	3.0%	1.4%*	0.4%	20.6%
Alaska	107,424	21.1%	12.9%	13.7%	23.7%	17.0%	5.2%	4.6%	1.8%	10.7%
Arizona	820,094	29.2%	14.8%	15.7%	24.3%	10.3%	3.6%	1.7%	0.5%	17.7%
Arkansas	350,285	29.9%	17.5%	17.9%	20.9%	9.4%	2.9%	1.1%	0.4%	20.1%
California	5,254,544	26.1%	16.5%	15.1%	20.1%	12.1%	5.0%	3.6%	1.5%	14.2%
Colorado	750,842	21.2%	12.1%	15.6%	27.3%	15.3%	5.3%	2.2%	0.8%	11.6%
Connecticut	394,429	22.8%	12.7%	13.4%	23.8%	17.0%	5.9%	3.4%	1.0%	12.7%
Delaware	114,870	27.4%	13.5%	14.3%	25.4%	15.5%	2.1%	1.9%	0.0%	12.7%
District of Columbia	139,024	15.8%	7.2%	9.5%	17.4%	25.6%	13.3%	8.0%	3.2%	10.5%
Florida	2,343,934	27.4%	17.5%	18.1%	23.1%	9.7%	2.6%	1.3%	0.4%	16.2%
Georgia	1,239,622	28.1%	16.0%	16.9%	23.0%	10.6%	3.2%	1.6%	0.6%	16.7%
Hawaii	189,145	21.9%	12.1%	17.7%	26.3%	15.3%	4.0%	2.3%	0.5%	10.6%
Idaho	197,546	29.5%	19.3%	18.1%	21.0%	7.8%	2.1%	1.8%	0.4%	16.0%
Illinois	1,587,753	23.7%	14.0%	15.2%	22.5%	15.1%	5.3%	2.8%	1.4%	14.1%
Indiana	756,911	27.1%	14.9%	16.4%	24.2%	12.0%	3.0%	1.6%	0.8%	15.2%
Iowa	359,741	19.5%	14.0%	15.7%	31.0%	14.4%	3.5%	1.7%	0.3%	14.0%
Kansas	348,071	21.3%	14.6%	16.7%	27.8%	13.1%	3.4%	2.0%	1.1%	12.9%
Kentucky	503,547	29.0%	17.1%	16.4%	22.9%	10.1%	2.7%	1.1%	0.6%	19.6%
Louisiana	607,358	31.0%	15.6%	14.1%	20.8%	10.9%	4.6%	2.3%	0.6%	19.6%
Maine	135,710	24.3%	16.1%	18.3%	23.4%	13.6%	2.7%	0.9%	0.6%	15.6%
Maryland	746,445	23.5%	12.7%	13.5%	23.1%	16.1%	7.2%	2.9%	1.1%	10.4%
Massachusetts	858,018	20.0%	11.4%	12.4%	24.2%	19.3%	7.3%	3.7%	1.6%	11.8%
Michigan	1,107,296	27.6%	16.4%	15.9%	22.1%	12.3%	3.5%	1.6%	0.7%	17.1%
Minnesota	670,737	17.2%	11.9%	15.5%	28.9%	17.4%	5.1%	3.2%	0.8%	10.7%
Mississippi	332,474	32.3%	17.7%	17.7%	21.4%	7.6%	2.5%	0.8%	0.1%	23.4%
Missouri	722,354	23.9%	17.0%	17.5%	24.7%	11.6%	3.0%	1.5%	0.7%	16.5%
Montana	113,247	24.9%	18.6%	15.2%	22.7%	13.4%	2.8%	1.6%	0.6%	16.9%
Nebraska	226,504	20.2%	13.3%	17.9%	27.5%	14.9%	3.8%	1.6%	0.8%	14.5%
Nevada	374,679	25.9%	14.6%	17.8%	26.4%	11.1%	2.6%	1.3%	0.3%	14.3%
New Hampshire	136,348	18.3%	12.4%	12.6%	32.3%	14.7%	5.9%	2.3%	1.6%	10.5%
New Jersey	1,039,533	24.5%	13.4%	13.9%	20.4%	15.8%	6.7%	3.7%	1.5%	11.3%
New Mexico	243,894	31.8%	15.8%	20.8%	19.9%	7.1%	3.0%	1.3%	0.4%	18.9%
New York	2,606,528	24.3%	13.5%	13.5%	21.6%	15.6%	5.8%	3.4%	2.4%	13.9%
North Carolina	1,180,843	27.1%	16.9%	17.2%	23.8%	10.1%	2.9%	1.4%	0.5%	17.7%
North Dakota	102,820	14.0%	11.4%	14.7%	25.9%	16.4%	7.6%	6.2%	2.9%	10.5%
Ohio	1,339,989	24.6%	16.4%	15.7%	24.5%	13.2%	3.5%	1.6%	0.5%	16.4%
Oklahoma	480,214	26.4%	16.2%	16.9%	23.9%	10.5%	2.9%	2.3%	0.8%	17.2%
Oregon	493,914	26.5%	16.7%	17.7%	21.3%	11.0%	3.9%	1.7%	1.2%	17.2%
Pennsylvania	1,486,228	24.3%	13.1%	15.9%	24.2%	14.8%	4.8%	2.2%	0.7%	14.0%
Rhode Island	129,246	24.5%	16.7%	13.6%	25.3%	14.1%	3.2%	2.0%	0.6%	16.0%
South Carolina	570,627	27.6%	16.2%	18.1%	23.8%	9.9%	2.5%	1.1%	0.7%	16.6%
South Dakota	103,467	20.1%	12.8%	19.6%	32.4%	11.5%	2.1%	1.3%	0.4%	15.3%
Tennessee	784,794	28.1%	16.6%	17.9%	22.3%	10.2%	2.6%	2.1%	0.3%	17.5%
Texas	3,594,612	26.4%	15.1%	15.9%	22.3%	12.5%	4.2%	2.7%	1.0%	14.8%
Utah	394,649	27.9%	13.0%	16.3%	25.2%	11.2%	3.2%	2.1%	1.0%	11.1%
Vermont	65,969	21.3%	15.0%	20.8%	26.9%	11.6%	3.4%	0.1%	0.8%	10.8%
Virginia	1,054,594	23.8%	13.9%	14.1%	23.1%	14.5%	6.5%	3.3%	0.7%	12.3%
Washington	954,135	23.5%	13.4%	15.4%	22.9%	13.7%	5.7%	4.2%	1.2%	13.3%
West Virginia	195,789	31.8%	17.0%	14.3%	23.0%	8.4%	3.3%	1.9%	0.4%	22.0%
Wisconsin	648,840	19.1%	13.8%	17.0%	30.0%	13.8%	3.6%	1.8%	0.9%	11.5%
Wyoming	74,916	23.6%	12.6%	15.8%	23.2%	12.9%	8.0%	3.1%	0.8%	11.8%

Table I-2: Counties—Income Class by Age

		Personal Income, Percent by Income Class, ages 18 to 24						
	Total Millennials	Under $10,000	$10,000 to $19,999	$20,000 to $29,999	$30,000 to $49,999	$50,000 to $74,999	$75,000 to $99,999	$100,000 or More
Alabama								
Baldwin County	14,381	54.9%	24.4%	4.8%	9.9%	6.1%	0.0%	0.0%
Calhoun County	12,942	51.8%	29.2%	15.0%	2.0%	1.4%	0.7%	0.0%
Etowah County	9,075	50.4%	24.1%	17.5%	7.6%	0.5%	0.0%	0.0%
Houston County	8,753	61.9%	22.0%	11.5%	3.8%	0.7%	0.2%	0.0%
Jefferson County	58,661	59.9%	22.5%	10.5%	5.2%	1.8%	0.0%	0.0%
Lauderdale County	8,925	43.4%	21.0%	29.1%	5.9%	0.6%	0.0%	0.0%
Lee County	30,660	72.8%	10.8%	11.8%	4.6%	0.0%	0.0%	0.0%
Madison County	32,804	67.9%	18.1%	9.4%	4.2%	0.0%	0.4%	0.0%
Marshall County	8,881	69.0%	23.9%	6.1%	0.3%	0.6%	0.0%	0.0%
Mobile County	37,483	69.2%	15.7%	7.5%	7.0%	0.6%	0.0%	0.0%
Montgomery County	24,526	63.6%	21.6%	7.6%	5.4%	0.0%	0.0%	1.7%
Morgan County	9,544	64.4%	24.6%	7.3%	2.0%	1.6%	0.0%	0.0%
Shelby County	17,928	72.6%	16.2%	6.9%	3.6%	0.7%	0.0%	0.0%
Tuscaloosa County	36,240	67.7%	17.7%	9.4%	3.5%	0.9%	0.0%	0.9%
Alaska								
Anchorage Municipality	34,631	34.1%	30.1%	18.9%	11.9%	4.3%	0.7%	0.0%
Fairbanks North Star Borough	15,158	38.8%	24.7%	28.4%	5.2%	3.0%	0.0%	0.0%
Matanuska-Susitna Borough	10,694	49.9%	27.2%	13.8%	6.8%	2.3%	0.0%	0.0%
Arizona								
Cochise County	9,550	52.0%	30.6%	8.8%	6.3%	2.3%	0.0%	0.0%
Coconino County	29,687	80.3%	14.7%	2.8%	1.7%	0.5%	0.0%	0.0%
Maricopa County	388,313	55.9%	23.9%	11.3%	6.9%	1.9%	0.0%	0.0%
Mohave County	12,747	42.2%	36.5%	8.0%	9.2%	1.8%	0.0%	2.3%
Navajo County	9,752	81.9%	13.5%	3.7%	0.9%	0.0%	0.0%	0.0%
Pima County	119,343	60.0%	21.6%	11.3%	5.5%	1.4%	0.1%	0.1%
Pinal County	30,975	61.0%	22.0%	14.9%	2.1%	0.0%	0.0%	0.0%
Yavapai County	15,292	58.9%	22.6%	13.8%	3.1%	1.6%	0.0%	0.0%
Yuma County	23,041	57.3%	19.2%	15.6%	5.6%	2.3%	0.0%	0.0%
Arkansas								
Benton County	20,016	56.4%	21.5%	13.2%	6.6%	2.2%	0.0%	0.0%
Craighead County	13,278	67.1%	14.9%	11.1%	6.5%	0.5%	0.0%	0.0%
Faulkner County	17,473	63.9%	22.1%	10.3%	3.6%	0.0%	0.0%	0.0%
Garland County	7,994	65.7%	15.0%	8.4%	10.8%	0.0%	0.0%	0.0%
Pulaski County	35,650	57.2%	18.9%	8.8%	12.7%	0.6%	1.6%	0.2%
Saline County	8,571	51.2%	33.3%	9.5%	3.0%	2.1%	0.0%	1.0%
Sebastian County	11,525	64.1%	19.8%	8.5%	3.7%	2.0%	0.0%	1.9%
Washington County	33,225	64.4%	13.3%	14.2%	7.1%	1.1%	0.0%	0.0%
California								
Alameda County	140,673	58.7%	18.3%	10.0%	9.3%	3.3%	0.2%	0.2%
Butte County	33,576	73.0%	19.2%	5.8%	1.6%	0.4%	0.0%	0.1%
Contra Costa County	96,186	61.1%	18.5%	11.7%	6.0%	2.0%	0.6%	0.1%
El Dorado County	13,743	56.4%	23.3%	14.0%	5.5%	0.7%	0.0%	0.0%
Fresno County	106,206	68.2%	20.2%	6.3%	4.2%	1.0%	0.0%	0.1%
Humboldt County	18,225	64.6%	26.3%	5.2%	3.5%	0.0%	0.0%	0.4%
Imperial County	19,969	72.9%	14.8%	6.4%	4.4%	1.3%	0.0%	0.1%
Kern County	96,404	59.6%	20.3%	10.8%	6.0%	2.6%	0.0%	0.8%
Kings County	16,771	64.3%	16.2%	13.4%	6.1%	0.1%	0.0%	0.0%
Los Angeles County	1,014,132	64.1%	18.9%	9.3%	5.6%	1.5%	0.4%	0.2%
Madera County	15,683	61.6%	19.0%	14.9%	4.5%	0.0%	0.0%	0.0%
Marin County	16,482	63.0%	20.4%	8.4%	5.9%	0.8%	0.0%	1.6%
Merced County	32,689	60.0%	20.5%	13.1%	5.7%	0.4%	0.2%	0.0%
Monterey County	46,279	55.1%	23.6%	16.8%	4.0%	0.5%	0.0%	0.0%
Napa County	13,069	65.2%	16.9%	8.4%	7.7%	1.8%	0.0%	0.0%
Nevada County	6,149	68.1%	14.6%	13.9%	3.2%	0.2%	0.0%	0.0%
Orange County	301,487	64.5%	18.4%	9.2%	5.7%	1.7%	0.3%	0.2%
Placer County	28,790	68.5%	16.0%	8.8%	3.4%	3.3%	0.0%	0.0%
Riverside County	238,122	64.5%	19.1%	11.5%	4.2%	0.6%	0.1%	0.1%
Sacramento County	136,870	66.8%	19.6%	8.2%	4.4%	0.8%	0.1%	0.0%
San Bernardino County	235,348	61.8%	20.6%	11.0%	5.7%	0.8%	0.0%	0.0%
San Diego County	352,621	55.3%	22.7%	12.6%	7.2%	2.0%	0.2%	0.1%
San Francisco County	62,672	59.8%	12.5%	8.5%	6.8%	8.0%	1.3%	3.1%
San Joaquin County	72,442	65.5%	19.5%	8.6%	5.5%	0.9%	0.0%	0.0%
San Luis Obispo County	42,216	71.1%	16.2%	4.5%	8.0%	0.0%	0.3%	0.0%
San Mateo County	57,300	57.6%	21.0%	12.6%	5.9%	1.7%	0.6%	0.5%
Santa Barbara County	71,192	59.7%	20.7%	13.6%	4.6%	0.5%	0.4%	0.6%
Santa Clara County	163,775	61.1%	16.2%	8.9%	8.9%	3.2%	0.6%	1.1%
Santa Cruz County	42,214	74.2%	17.1%	6.5%	1.6%	0.5%	0.0%	0.0%
Shasta County	13,747	61.0%	21.8%	9.2%	6.5%	0.3%	1.2%	0.0%
Solano County	40,269	59.5%	20.0%	11.5%	5.4%	2.0%	0.9%	0.8%
Sonoma County	43,756	57.3%	19.0%	9.7%	11.7%	1.6%	0.6%	0.2%
Stanislaus County	54,104	66.8%	18.1%	9.9%	4.4%	0.8%	0.0%	0.0%
Sutter County	8,221	66.7%	14.8%	6.8%	9.2%	2.5%	0.0%	0.0%
Tulare County	48,480	68.2%	19.4%	7.9%	4.2%	0.3%	0.0%	0.0%
Ventura County	83,642	58.8%	21.7%	11.0%	7.2%	1.0%	0.3%	0.0%
Yolo County	40,315	70.3%	19.1%	6.5%	3.9%	0.1%	0.0%	0.1%

Table I-2: Counties—Income Class by Age—*Continued*

	Personal Income, Percent by Income Class, ages 25 to 33								
	Total Millennials	Under $10,000	$10,000 to $19,999	$20,000 to $29,999	$30,000 to $49,999	$50,000 to $74,999	$75,000 to $99,999	$100,000 to $149,999	$150,000 or More	Poverty Rate
Alabama										
Baldwin County	20,047	29.0%	24.2%	13.5%	20.0%	6.1%	4.6%	2.3%	0.3%	19.9%
Calhoun County	12,913	31.1%	21.5%	7.7%	25.3%	10.3%	0.3%	1.8%	2.0%	22.1%
Etowah County	9,578	29.8%	19.0%	15.4%	21.0%	9.0%	0.0%	5.8%	0.0%	19.0%
Houston County	11,594	43.0%	15.6%	14.0%	20.5%	3.6%	1.7%	0.9%	0.7%	22.4%
Jefferson County	84,794	23.0%	18.9%	15.1%	23.1%	13.3%	3.3%	2.4%	0.9%	18.9%
Lauderdale County	9,028	39.6%	16.0%	16.4%	19.4%	2.9%	5.2%	0.6%	0.0%	29.4%
Lee County	18,813	35.3%	12.7%	9.7%	31.9%	8.3%	1.4%	0.6%	0.0%	26.4%
Madison County	44,089	25.2%	17.1%	20.3%	18.3%	12.3%	5.3%	1.5%	0.1%	19.1%
Marshall County	9,155	39.2%	20.1%	14.5%	15.3%	7.3%	1.8%	1.7%	0.0%	27.6%
Mobile County	53,577	31.3%	21.4%	15.8%	22.2%	7.1%	2.0%	0.2%	0.0%	19.4%
Montgomery County	29,847	38.3%	15.7%	18.6%	19.5%	4.7%	2.2%	0.3%	0.6%	33.4%
Morgan County	13,728	36.4%	11.3%	14.8%	27.6%	7.3%	2.3%	0.3%	0.0%	17.9%
Shelby County	22,775	22.6%	13.5%	9.8%	33.6%	15.3%	4.6%	0.0%	0.7%	12.1%
Tuscaloosa County	28,303	28.9%	22.1%	18.1%	14.7%	11.0%	3.8%	1.3%	0.2%	12.7%
Alaska										
Anchorage Municipality	46,476	16.7%	10.0%	15.3%	26.7%	17.6%	5.5%	4.8%	3.2%	5.9%
Fairbanks North Star Borough	15,499	23.2%	9.2%	12.8%	30.4%	13.4%	3.5%	6.7%	0.8%	16.8%
Matanuska-Susitna Borough	12,719	25.5%	21.5%	10.0%	22.8%	13.7%	2.8%	3.6%	0.2%	16.8%
Arizona										
Cochise County	14,841	45.1%	21.6%	10.0%	11.2%	7.0%	2.5%	1.4%	1.3%	29.3%
Coconino County	17,120	27.3%	17.1%	11.5%	27.2%	9.1%	6.2%	1.3%	0.3%	18.4%
Maricopa County	522,456	25.5%	13.6%	16.4%	26.3%	11.8%	3.9%	1.9%	0.6%	15.7%
Mohave County	19,918	29.6%	18.3%	19.7%	25.6%	3.0%	1.7%	2.3%	0.0%	20.7%
Navajo County	11,618	59.2%	8.8%	9.4%	17.0%	4.6%	0.6%	0.4%	0.0%	35.9%
Pima County	110,798	27.7%	18.7%	17.0%	21.6%	9.2%	3.8%	1.7%	0.3%	18.9%
Pinal County	45,270	50.7%	10.5%	12.8%	17.6%	6.2%	2.1%	0.1%	0.0%	15.2%
Yavapai County	18,013	25.6%	19.5%	16.0%	26.2%	7.1%	0.9%	3.3%	1.2%	22.7%
Yuma County	25,579	32.4%	18.5%	11.2%	28.8%	7.1%	1.6%	0.3%	0.1%	23.4%
Arkansas										
Benton County	32,298	23.4%	10.5%	23.0%	20.5%	14.7%	3.7%	2.7%	1.4%	10.9%
Craighead County	13,143	32.6%	22.6%	14.5%	22.7%	5.2%	2.4%	0.0%	0.0%	19.8%
Faulkner County	16,220	31.6%	16.4%	13.2%	26.4%	7.4%	4.6%	0.4%	0.0%	18.3%
Garland County	9,677	33.9%	17.8%	26.0%	11.8%	10.6%	0.0%	0.0%	0.0%	26.5%
Pulaski County	53,734	27.8%	16.5%	19.0%	22.9%	10.2%	2.3%	0.5%	0.7%	18.4%
Saline County	13,673	23.4%	18.2%	15.1%	31.1%	7.8%	2.8%	1.1%	0.6%	9.3%
Sebastian County	14,618	27.5%	19.6%	13.8%	25.8%	12.2%	1.0%	0.0%	0.0%	20.9%
Washington County	31,607	24.1%	13.9%	22.0%	23.3%	7.3%	6.6%	2.4%	0.4%	20.6%
California										
Alameda County	239,328	22.3%	13.8%	11.2%	21.2%	16.5%	8.3%	5.2%	1.6%	12.2%
Butte County	25,179	22.9%	25.8%	15.0%	17.5%	12.2%	4.1%	2.6%	0.0%	16.9%
Contra Costa County	122,601	22.0%	14.8%	12.9%	22.6%	14.9%	5.7%	4.8%	1.7%	10.0%
El Dorado County	16,584	24.5%	25.7%	13.1%	12.9%	10.1%	7.7%	6.0%	0.0%	6.8%
Fresno County	129,871	36.7%	19.4%	16.7%	16.2%	7.6%	2.7%	0.6%	0.2%	24.4%
Humboldt County	16,198	36.4%	13.8%	21.7%	20.4%	6.0%	0.5%	0.5%	0.6%	27.7%
Imperial County	21,437	50.3%	22.9%	5.3%	8.8%	9.1%	3.4%	0.2%	0.0%	27.8%
Kern County	119,068	34.8%	19.8%	13.2%	17.4%	8.9%	3.5%	2.1%	0.4%	23.2%
Kings County	23,428	42.2%	12.2%	10.0%	22.6%	9.7%	2.7%	0.6%	0.0%	28.8%
Los Angeles County	1,415,100	25.9%	17.4%	16.4%	20.4%	11.3%	4.6%	2.8%	1.2%	14.5%
Madera County	19,229	40.6%	22.5%	19.1%	10.0%	6.0%	0.0%	0.0%	1.7%	25.1%
Marin County	22,077	23.4%	14.7%	13.2%	18.3%	10.7%	9.1%	8.0%	2.7%	9.0%
Merced County	33,141	29.4%	21.6%	22.2%	18.3%	5.9%	1.4%	0.7%	0.5%	22.5%
Monterey County	56,147	30.1%	17.1%	21.6%	17.4%	8.3%	4.0%	0.9%	0.6%	12.8%
Napa County	14,989	19.3%	14.1%	12.9%	27.3%	15.7%	5.2%	4.8%	0.7%	6.2%
Nevada County	9,555	29.1%	7.3%	13.8%	27.9%	10.2%	8.1%	0.7%	3.1%	8.4%
Orange County	398,540	23.5%	14.8%	16.0%	20.2%	14.3%	5.7%	3.8%	1.8%	11.2%
Placer County	37,376	21.5%	15.3%	18.2%	20.4%	14.1%	4.1%	5.6%	0.7%	9.6%
Riverside County	278,626	30.6%	17.8%	15.6%	20.8%	10.0%	2.9%	1.6%	0.7%	14.9%
Sacramento County	204,701	26.4%	18.7%	14.7%	22.4%	11.0%	3.6%	2.9%	0.4%	15.0%
San Bernardino County	287,689	31.5%	18.4%	16.1%	20.0%	9.4%	2.9%	1.4%	0.2%	17.1%
San Diego County	473,319	23.5%	16.7%	14.1%	22.0%	13.5%	6.3%	3.2%	0.7%	13.1%
San Francisco County	177,181	15.7%	8.6%	7.1%	16.6%	18.1%	11.3%	13.7%	8.8%	10.2%
San Joaquin County	88,953	27.7%	20.3%	18.2%	19.8%	10.2%	2.2%	1.1%	0.3%	15.3%
San Luis Obispo County	30,829	23.4%	15.9%	19.4%	17.0%	14.8%	5.8%	2.6%	1.1%	18.2%
San Mateo County	95,118	18.9%	10.5%	13.6%	19.8%	14.7%	8.3%	9.2%	5.0%	7.3%
Santa Barbara County	49,128	20.3%	21.8%	19.0%	15.4%	13.8%	4.4%	4.5%	0.8%	13.8%
Santa Clara County	260,069	21.0%	11.3%	11.4%	18.1%	14.8%	8.2%	9.9%	5.3%	6.2%
Santa Cruz County	30,305	30.1%	20.7%	9.1%	18.6%	15.7%	2.3%	2.4%	1.2%	20.9%
Shasta County	21,145	29.0%	20.9%	15.3%	24.7%	2.8%	2.7%	4.1%	0.5%	20.7%
Solano County	55,432	25.4%	17.1%	14.5%	25.3%	11.0%	4.2%	1.8%	0.6%	9.5%
Sonoma County	57,264	20.4%	14.3%	16.9%	24.5%	18.6%	2.1%	2.4%	0.7%	8.1%
Stanislaus County	70,720	30.1%	16.3%	17.2%	21.4%	8.8%	3.3%	2.6%	0.2%	22.6%
Sutter County	13,924	26.3%	23.9%	18.9%	22.8%	6.7%	0.3%	1.0%	0.0%	15.9%
Tulare County	59,578	33.7%	20.8%	17.1%	15.3%	9.7%	1.8%	1.4%	0.2%	27.6%
Ventura County	101,797	22.4%	17.4%	18.6%	20.5%	12.6%	4.7%	2.8%	1.1%	9.3%
Yolo County	26,201	25.8%	15.4%	19.8%	21.3%	8.0%	5.1%	3.6%	1.1%	13.2%

Table I-2: Counties—Income Class by Age—*Continued*

	Total Millennials	Under $10,000	$10,000 to $19,999	$20,000 to $29,999	$30,000 to $49,999	$50,000 to $74,999	$75,000 to $99,999	$100,000 or More
				Personal Income, Percent by Income Class, ages 18 to 24				
Colorado								
Adams County	42,953	49.8%	20.7%	15.6%	11.1%	2.8%	0.0%	0.0%
Arapahoe County	54,292	46.0%	24.5%	17.1%	10.2%	2.0%	0.3%	0.0%
Boulder County	50,331	61.7%	18.9%	9.6%	8.8%	1.0%	0.0%	0.0%
Denver County	57,164	52.1%	19.9%	14.2%	9.9%	3.6%	0.1%	0.2%
Douglas County	24,273	54.6%	22.3%	10.9%	8.6%	3.1%	0.5%	0.0%
El Paso County	72,805	43.5%	28.7%	17.0%	8.7%	1.6%	0.2%	0.3%
Jefferson County	49,253	56.3%	23.1%	9.9%	9.3%	1.0%	0.4%	0.0%
Larimer County	45,152	54.4%	21.0%	11.5%	9.4%	3.5%	0.2%	0.0%
Mesa County	15,236	63.5%	17.2%	13.6%	5.0%	0.7%	0.0%	0.0%
Pueblo County	15,312	67.3%	20.4%	7.9%	3.8%	0.6%	0.0%	0.0%
Weld County	28,999	53.3%	23.5%	10.9%	9.7%	1.9%	0.4%	0.3%
Connecticut								
Fairfield County	85,139	63.7%	17.2%	8.2%	7.8%	3.0%	0.0%	0.2%
Hartford County	82,956	60.7%	16.5%	10.2%	8.8%	3.0%	0.7%	0.0%
Litchfield County	13,568	42.4%	27.3%	15.3%	13.1%	1.9%	0.0%	0.0%
Middlesex County	15,193	63.8%	21.1%	4.8%	7.8%	2.4%	0.0%	0.0%
New Haven County	87,071	58.6%	18.7%	12.8%	8.3%	1.3%	0.3%	0.1%
New London County	28,636	59.0%	17.6%	12.1%	7.5%	3.4%	0.2%	0.2%
Tolland County	28,023	62.0%	23.3%	6.9%	5.3%	1.0%	0.7%	0.7%
Windham County	11,899	63.0%	22.1%	6.4%	6.0%	2.1%	0.4%	0.0%
Delaware								
Kent County	18,762	58.0%	22.7%	8.6%	7.3%	2.4%	1.0%	0.0%
New Castle County	52,593	68.4%	17.0%	7.2%	4.8%	2.6%	0.0%	0.0%
Sussex County	15,661	59.2%	18.7%	8.6%	10.9%	2.7%	0.0%	0.0%
Florida								
Alachua County	56,248	79.1%	12.1%	4.0%	4.2%	0.6%	0.0%	0.0%
Bay County	14,840	67.1%	17.4%	10.4%	3.8%	1.3%	0.0%	0.0%
Brevard County	45,039	65.5%	18.6%	10.7%	3.8%	1.0%	0.0%	0.3%
Broward County	155,585	62.4%	19.6%	11.8%	4.7%	1.2%	0.1%	0.1%
Charlotte County	9,538	78.2%	11.7%	10.1%	0.0%	0.0%	0.0%	0.0%
Citrus County	7,713	67.4%	26.2%	4.4%	1.5%	0.0%	0.5%	0.0%
Clay County	17,559	54.0%	29.1%	9.2%	4.1%	3.6%	0.0%	0.0%
Collier County	25,881	60.0%	21.7%	14.1%	4.2%	0.0%	0.0%	0.0%
Duval County	86,478	53.0%	23.8%	13.5%	7.6%	1.8%	0.0%	0.2%
Escambia County	40,469	54.5%	24.6%	11.9%	6.6%	0.9%	0.3%	1.2%
Flagler County	7,889	77.0%	16.5%	0.0%	6.6%	0.0%	0.0%	0.0%
Hernando County	11,462	61.2%	28.6%	8.1%	2.0%	0.0%	0.0%	0.0%
Highlands County	6,061	77.7%	16.0%	2.7%	0.0%	0.0%	0.0%	3.6%
Hillsborough County	123,236	61.7%	17.7%	12.8%	5.8%	1.5%	0.3%	0.2%
Indian River County	11,503	56.7%	28.1%	13.8%	0.4%	1.0%	0.0%	0.0%
Lake County	21,516	55.0%	30.6%	11.7%	2.6%	0.0%	0.0%	0.0%
Lee County	49,430	53.6%	27.5%	12.4%	5.5%	0.9%	0.0%	0.1%
Leon County	65,175	65.8%	19.2%	10.3%	4.2%	0.6%	0.0%	0.0%
Manatee County	26,302	54.0%	26.5%	12.0%	7.1%	0.4%	0.0%	0.0%
Marion County	25,183	68.8%	16.6%	9.5%	4.4%	0.7%	0.0%	0.0%
Martin County	11,404	50.7%	25.1%	21.5%	2.6%	0.0%	0.0%	0.0%
Miami-Dade County	236,693	65.9%	19.2%	9.4%	4.3%	0.7%	0.4%	0.0%
Okaloosa County	18,979	41.2%	18.7%	23.6%	14.1%	2.0%	0.3%	0.0%
Orange County	144,127	59.4%	21.7%	12.0%	5.9%	1.0%	0.0%	0.0%
Osceola County	31,196	58.1%	26.5%	10.4%	4.3%	0.6%	0.0%	0.0%
Palm Beach County	109,088	57.2%	22.1%	11.3%	6.2%	2.6%	0.2%	0.2%
Pasco County	36,830	56.7%	24.7%	10.1%	7.6%	0.5%	0.2%	0.2%
Pinellas County	65,800	58.9%	20.1%	12.2%	7.2%	1.2%	0.4%	0.1%
Polk County	56,070	62.5%	16.7%	15.1%	4.7%	0.7%	0.0%	0.3%
Santa Rosa County	17,562	61.1%	25.4%	3.6%	9.8%	0.0%	0.0%	0.0%
Sarasota County	22,151	61.6%	20.5%	12.5%	5.0%	0.4%	0.0%	0.0%
Seminole County	13,125	61.1%	20.7%	10.5%	4.6%	0.0%	3.1%	0.0%
St. Johns County	23,480	63.0%	21.1%	8.7%	5.4%	1.8%	0.0%	0.0%
St. Lucie County	39,304	66.1%	18.7%	10.0%	3.5%	1.7%	0.0%	0.0%
Sumter County	4,730	67.1%	32.9%	0.0%	0.0%	0.0%	0.0%	0.0%
Volusia County	42,400	72.0%	17.8%	7.3%	2.2%	0.6%	0.0%	0.0%
Georgia								
Bartow County	9,293	49.2%	28.6%	17.1%	3.2%	1.8%	0.0%	0.0%
Bibb County	16,246	82.4%	7.6%	5.9%	2.2%	1.5%	0.0%	0.3%
Carroll County	15,447	67.8%	18.0%	10.6%	1.1%	2.5%	0.0%	0.0%
Chatham County	33,626	68.7%	16.3%	6.4%	7.9%	0.6%	0.0%	0.1%
Cherokee County	19,073	52.4%	27.2%	17.6%	2.9%	0.0%	0.0%	0.0%
Clarke County	36,550	76.6%	14.0%	4.7%	3.7%	1.0%	0.0%	0.0%
Clayton County	27,620	69.7%	11.0%	14.2%	3.7%	1.0%	0.0%	0.4%
Cobb County	66,221	57.0%	21.5%	12.9%	7.5%	0.6%	0.3%	0.2%
Columbia County	12,592	67.7%	8.7%	15.2%	7.1%	1.3%	0.0%	0.0%
Coweta County	11,521	58.1%	6.0%	27.3%	3.5%	3.1%	2.0%	0.0%
DeKalb County	65,575	66.3%	17.5%	9.7%	4.4%	1.9%	0.1%	0.0%
Dougherty County	11,312	76.2%	10.1%	9.2%	3.4%	1.1%	0.0%	0.0%
Douglas County	13,139	70.2%	17.7%	6.1%	3.6%	2.4%	0.0%	0.0%
Fayette County	10,448	70.2%	21.3%	6.2%	1.5%	0.8%	0.0%	0.0%

Table I-2: Counties—Income Class by Age—*Continued*

				Personal Income, Percent by Income Class, ages 25 to 33						
	Total Millennials	Under $10,000	$10,000 to $19,999	$20,000 to $29,999	$30,000 to $49,999	$50,000 to $74,999	$75,000 to $99,999	$100,000 to $149,999	$150,000 or More	Poverty Rate
Colorado										
Adams County	71,561	20.3%	15.6%	15.4%	27.7%	15.8%	3.3%	1.7%	0.3%	11.4%
Arapahoe County	86,269	21.1%	12.8%	14.6%	28.8%	15.9%	4.1%	1.6%	1.0%	12.0%
Boulder County	37,559	20.4%	11.2%	12.8%	26.2%	13.6%	10.5%	3.5%	1.8%	15.0%
Denver County	139,346	17.4%	9.2%	14.0%	27.8%	17.9%	8.1%	4.3%	1.3%	11.0%
Douglas County	27,302	17.6%	7.3%	7.2%	28.4%	22.1%	13.9%	1.5%	2.1%	4.6%
El Paso County	97,677	24.9%	14.3%	17.6%	24.9%	15.0%	2.5%	0.5%	0.3%	13.4%
Jefferson County	70,252	17.8%	11.1%	18.1%	30.6%	12.7%	6.1%	3.3%	0.3%	10.3%
Larimer County	45,352	18.0%	14.8%	18.9%	28.7%	14.2%	3.1%	1.4%	0.9%	12.8%
Mesa County	17,924	27.1%	16.3%	18.5%	19.2%	14.9%	3.5%	0.0%	0.5%	13.1%
Pueblo County	18,784	33.4%	15.4%	16.5%	23.1%	7.9%	1.5%	1.7%	0.5%	16.7%
Weld County	35,019	22.1%	9.7%	16.1%	29.2%	12.3%	5.8%	3.7%	1.2%	10.3%
Connecticut										
Fairfield County	97,867	24.1%	12.6%	12.4%	22.2%	14.6%	6.9%	5.0%	2.2%	12.0%
Hartford County	102,090	22.4%	12.1%	13.3%	21.8%	19.5%	6.7%	3.2%	1.0%	11.7%
Litchfield County	16,493	17.2%	13.6%	15.0%	32.0%	18.6%	1.7%	2.0%	0.0%	5.1%
Middlesex County	15,292	25.7%	10.8%	8.8%	19.7%	18.7%	8.6%	6.8%	0.8%	13.8%
New Haven County	99,378	24.2%	13.2%	13.9%	26.5%	15.8%	4.2%	1.9%	0.3%	17.6%
New London County	31,833	21.3%	16.2%	14.0%	20.8%	16.5%	6.5%	4.1%	0.5%	10.4%
Tolland County	15,393	18.5%	8.7%	4.5%	29.9%	24.7%	10.9%	2.8%	0.0%	1.8%
Windham County	13,501	15.7%	10.1%	28.0%	27.1%	15.7%	1.7%	1.4%	0.3%	11.7%
Delaware										
Kent County	20,537	29.2%	17.7%	14.8%	29.5%	7.9%	0.8%	0.0%	0.0%	18.2%
New Castle County	74,577	26.9%	12.8%	14.2%	23.2%	18.0%	2.3%	2.6%	0.0%	11.9%
Sussex County	19,639	27.7%	11.8%	14.2%	29.4%	13.2%	2.6%	1.0%	0.0%	10.1%
Florida										
Alachua County	35,666	32.9%	12.6%	13.6%	22.7%	13.1%	2.7%	1.2%	1.3%	23.9%
Bay County	23,476	32.7%	15.1%	19.4%	23.3%	7.3%	2.2%	0.0%	0.0%	19.7%
Brevard County	55,168	26.1%	20.0%	22.3%	20.4%	6.8%	3.2%	1.0%	0.2%	14.2%
Broward County	229,354	24.5%	17.3%	18.4%	25.4%	10.0%	2.6%	1.6%	0.3%	12.6%
Charlotte County	9,228	37.2%	16.2%	22.2%	20.2%	4.2%	0.0%	0.0%	0.0%	21.8%
Citrus County	8,986	29.2%	23.6%	26.7%	16.7%	3.7%	0.0%	0.0%	0.0%	25.5%
Clay County	21,120	30.4%	11.3%	20.5%	25.4%	12.4%	0.0%	0.0%	0.0%	22.9%
Collier County	30,802	25.2%	22.2%	15.6%	26.8%	6.6%	1.7%	1.6%	0.2%	20.0%
Duval County	129,731	25.0%	14.4%	14.7%	28.3%	12.2%	2.9%	1.9%	0.6%	14.8%
Escambia County	40,786	22.6%	18.9%	21.5%	24.9%	7.7%	2.9%	1.3%	0.2%	12.1%
Flagler County	7,123	34.2%	21.4%	17.6%	16.0%	5.3%	2.7%	0.0%	2.8%	15.0%
Hernando County	15,819	34.9%	9.6%	18.8%	30.7%	5.9%	0.0%	0.0%	0.0%	13.8%
Highlands County	7,645	36.9%	15.6%	21.1%	21.8%	2.2%	2.4%	0.0%	0.0%	28.6%
Hillsborough County	182,022	22.9%	14.7%	18.5%	24.5%	13.4%	3.4%	1.6%	1.0%	16.0%
Indian River County	11,380	30.4%	20.3%	22.3%	22.1%	4.0%	0.2%	0.0%	0.8%	14.6%
Lake County	29,837	30.6%	17.3%	17.3%	24.0%	7.6%	3.2%	0.0%	0.0%	13.3%
Lee County	68,198	35.5%	16.5%	20.0%	18.9%	6.3%	1.7%	1.1%	0.0%	21.6%
Leon County	35,299	24.5%	16.5%	18.2%	25.9%	11.3%	2.3%	0.9%	0.3%	21.1%
Manatee County	33,040	32.9%	23.0%	14.2%	22.6%	5.9%	1.0%	0.1%	0.3%	24.3%
Marion County	33,781	36.3%	14.4%	22.4%	20.3%	5.5%	0.3%	0.8%	0.0%	23.7%
Martin County	11,689	21.4%	16.2%	22.1%	19.4%	17.4%	2.9%	0.0%	0.6%	7.3%
Miami-Dade County	346,035	29.5%	18.8%	18.9%	19.6%	8.9%	2.7%	1.1%	0.5%	16.8%
Okaloosa County	29,242	21.9%	13.9%	18.4%	27.1%	12.6%	6.2%	0.1%	0.0%	9.5%
Orange County	188,528	21.6%	17.9%	18.0%	25.7%	11.7%	3.3%	1.5%	0.4%	13.9%
Osceola County	40,058	25.4%	24.9%	18.8%	20.4%	8.4%	1.1%	0.9%	0.2%	17.4%
Palm Beach County	146,764	24.0%	19.2%	18.0%	22.6%	10.3%	4.0%	1.5%	0.3%	14.9%
Pasco County	46,830	26.2%	18.0%	19.6%	24.8%	8.8%	1.7%	1.0%	0.1%	16.5%
Pinellas County	98,785	25.4%	15.6%	18.0%	24.7%	11.9%	2.8%	1.5%	0.3%	13.7%
Polk County	76,330	28.1%	19.9%	21.2%	21.3%	8.1%	1.1%	0.3%	0.0%	16.5%
Santa Rosa County	21,335	30.2%	14.1%	10.5%	21.8%	6.3%	6.2%	10.2%	0.7%	11.9%
Sarasota County	31,750	29.0%	17.6%	18.1%	22.1%	9.8%	1.4%	1.7%	0.3%	17.0%
Seminole County	21,224	30.0%	16.9%	16.5%	19.0%	8.7%	5.9%	2.2%	0.9%	17.8%
St. Johns County	31,760	23.4%	18.2%	12.5%	27.3%	14.1%	2.9%	1.3%	0.3%	11.0%
St. Lucie County	55,902	24.9%	16.2%	17.3%	26.9%	11.1%	2.2%	0.9%	0.5%	13.4%
Sumter County	3,888	45.9%	8.6%	17.6%	17.6%	10.3%	0.0%	0.0%	0.0%	23.4%
Volusia County	53,825	27.0%	20.3%	20.5%	24.1%	5.9%	1.0%	0.5%	0.7%	17.8%
Georgia										
Bartow County	10,921	23.8%	10.9%	20.5%	27.2%	12.5%	5.0%	0.0%	0.0%	6.7%
Bibb County	18,545	27.5%	16.5%	18.8%	25.9%	6.3%	2.3%	2.4%	0.2%	22.8%
Carroll County	13,544	24.0%	11.2%	19.9%	23.7%	17.0%	2.4%	0.7%	1.0%	13.4%
Chatham County	42,779	28.8%	15.7%	16.8%	24.7%	11.2%	2.1%	0.5%	0.2%	16.9%
Cherokee County	25,158	24.2%	18.6%	13.3%	26.6%	11.3%	5.0%	0.9%	0.1%	11.7%
Clarke County	16,374	30.3%	20.9%	23.6%	19.7%	3.0%	1.0%	1.3%	0.2%	32.4%
Clayton County	36,094	35.9%	21.4%	14.3%	22.2%	4.5%	1.4%	0.2%	0.0%	22.9%
Cobb County	94,327	25.5%	12.6%	15.4%	23.6%	14.1%	5.5%	2.4%	1.0%	11.6%
Columbia County	19,341	22.3%	15.1%	13.0%	30.1%	13.5%	5.7%	0.4%	0.0%	13.6%
Coweta County	15,096	17.8%	19.2%	21.7%	27.5%	7.5%	2.7%	1.5%	2.0%	5.1%
DeKalb County	110,091	23.6%	16.5%	15.7%	23.0%	14.1%	4.0%	2.0%	1.2%	15.8%
Dougherty County	9,967	36.2%	20.7%	10.8%	20.5%	10.1%	0.0%	0.0%	1.7%	29.8%
Douglas County	15,463	19.0%	15.0%	26.7%	22.0%	13.3%	4.0%	0.0%	0.0%	9.6%
Fayette County	6,653	27.0%	12.7%	11.7%	20.5%	24.2%	2.9%	1.0%	0.0%	6.6%

Table I-2: Counties—Income Class by Age—*Continued*

		Personal Income, Percent by Income Class, ages 18 to 24						
	Total Millennials	Under $10,000	$10,000 to $19,999	$20,000 to $29,999	$30,000 to $49,999	$50,000 to $74,999	$75,000 to $99,999	$100,000 or More
Georgia—Cont.								
Floyd County	9,179	72.7%	12.4%	10.3%	3.0%	1.7%	0.0%	0.0%
Forsyth County	15,074	62.5%	21.0%	5.3%	4.8%	4.7%	0.8%	0.9%
Fulton County	99,071	63.4%	19.2%	10.0%	4.5%	2.0%	0.6%	0.3%
Gwinnett County	82,834	62.9%	19.3%	12.2%	5.0%	0.3%	0.2%	0.0%
Hall County	18,304	54.3%	23.8%	12.5%	8.1%	1.2%	0.0%	0.0%
Henry County	23,115	64.8%	15.6%	16.6%	1.5%	1.0%	0.6%	0.0%
	14,662	61.8%	16.4%	14.3%	7.0%	0.2%	0.3%	0.0%
Houston County								
Lowndes County	18,196	70.9%	18.7%	7.2%	3.2%	0.0%	0.0%	0.0%
Muscogee County	24,221	64.8%	20.4%	9.4%	4.6%	0.6%	0.3%	0.0%
Newton County	8,171	63.0%	16.1%	10.1%	7.3%	0.0%	3.4%	0.0%
Paulding County	14,317	54.3%	21.0%	14.5%	10.1%	0.1%	0.0%	0.0%
Richmond County	23,706	62.1%	22.0%	10.5%	4.3%	1.0%	0.0%	0.0%
Whitfield County	10,390	50.9%	27.8%	13.5%	7.8%	0.0%	0.0%	0.0%
Hawaii								
Hawaii County	16,321	47.9%	25.4%	10.6%	13.2%	2.4%	0.5%	0.0%
Honolulu County	104,107	52.6%	13.5%	20.0%	10.0%	2.7%	1.0%	0.2%
Maui County	12,607	46.5%	12.0%	22.7%	17.7%	1.1%	0.0%	0.0%
Idaho								
Ada County	37,337	62.0%	17.1%	13.5%	5.0%	2.4%	0.0%	0.0%
Bonneville County	8,924	62.3%	29.1%	5.8%	2.8%	0.0%	0.0%	0.0%
Canyon County	19,059	70.4%	17.5%	4.8%	3.4%	3.4%	0.0%	0.5%
Kootenai County	11,742	53.4%	33.5%	12.3%	0.6%	0.0%	0.2%	0.0%
Illinois								
Champaign County	50,803	82.8%	11.4%	4.1%	1.7%	0.0%	0.0%	0.0%
Cook County	478,190	65.9%	16.8%	9.2%	5.4%	2.2%	0.3%	0.2%
DeKalb County	21,847	57.1%	23.8%	8.4%	9.7%	1.0%	0.0%	0.0%
DuPage County	84,758	58.3%	16.8%	10.7%	11.2%	2.8%	0.2%	0.0%
Kane County	48,293	53.5%	15.7%	17.2%	10.5%	2.7%	0.2%	0.2%
Kankakee County	11,549	72.0%	10.6%	5.3%	5.2%	6.8%	0.0%	0.0%
Kendall County	11,323	67.3%	14.9%	15.5%	2.3%	0.0%	0.0%	0.0%
Lake County	71,265	52.3%	23.1%	14.4%	7.6%	2.0%	0.4%	0.2%
LaSalle County	8,885	65.7%	16.1%	5.6%	8.1%	4.4%	0.0%	0.0%
Macon County	26,318	52.1%	25.1%	13.6%	7.0%	2.2%	0.0%	0.0%
Madison County	30,701	61.5%	20.9%	9.6%	7.6%	0.4%	0.0%	0.0%
McHenry County	10,188	77.0%	10.5%	3.2%	9.4%	0.0%	0.0%	0.0%
McLean County	22,983	67.4%	18.6%	7.0%	5.3%	1.8%	0.0%	0.0%
Peoria County	17,561	70.3%	19.5%	6.5%	3.1%	0.0%	0.6%	0.0%
Rock Island County	12,821	63.9%	19.3%	9.4%	6.3%	1.1%	0.0%	0.0%
Sangamon County	22,071	55.9%	21.7%	6.0%	14.0%	2.2%	0.2%	0.0%
St. Clair County	17,501	69.2%	18.5%	7.5%	3.6%	1.2%	0.0%	0.0%
Tazewell County	9,581	39.8%	34.0%	14.1%	12.2%	0.0%	0.0%	0.0%
Will County	61,876	55.5%	22.1%	14.5%	5.9%	1.8%	0.3%	0.0%
Winnebago County	24,727	64.0%	18.7%	9.2%	7.8%	0.3%	0.0%	0.0%
Indiana								
Allen County	35,877	56.4%	17.1%	14.0%	12.1%	0.4%	0.0%	0.0%
Clark County	8,677	41.7%	28.1%	13.5%	16.7%	0.0%	0.0%	0.0%
Delaware County	22,931	70.4%	18.7%	8.1%	2.8%	0.0%	0.0%	0.0%
Elkhart County	18,907	46.7%	33.9%	7.6%	8.5%	3.2%	0.0%	0.0%
Hamilton County	22,137	51.5%	26.8%	8.2%	11.1%	2.4%	0.0%	0.0%
Hendricks County	12,782	41.1%	34.6%	9.5%	10.7%	0.0%	4.0%	0.0%
Johnson County	12,661	62.1%	12.0%	5.7%	18.6%	1.6%	0.0%	0.0%
Lake County	42,669	67.4%	19.6%	8.6%	3.6%	0.3%	0.0%	0.4%
LaPorte County	8,713	68.9%	17.2%	5.5%	5.9%	2.6%	0.0%	0.0%
Madison County	11,939	67.9%	7.6%	16.1%	3.4%	4.9%	0.0%	0.0%
Marion County	87,972	59.6%	21.2%	12.6%	5.6%	0.8%	0.1%	0.1%
Monroe County	40,498	79.2%	13.9%	3.1%	2.7%	1.0%	0.0%	0.0%
Porter County	16,289	68.1%	21.9%	9.0%	1.0%	0.0%	0.0%	0.0%
St. Joseph County	30,022	70.7%	15.1%	7.6%	4.9%	0.6%	0.0%	1.1%
Tippecanoe County	45,635	69.8%	12.1%	11.5%	5.4%	1.1%	0.0%	0.2%
Vanderburgh County	18,215	67.7%	17.8%	10.8%	3.3%	0.5%	0.0%	0.0%
Vigo County	17,396	75.2%	16.4%	6.1%	2.3%	0.0%	0.0%	0.0%
Iowa								
Black Hawk County	20,218	65.1%	23.5%	4.2%	6.5%	0.8%	0.0%	0.0%
Dubuque County	10,631	57.3%	23.9%	5.6%	11.4%	1.8%	0.0%	0.0%
Johnson County	30,445	75.8%	14.5%	7.3%	1.8%	0.1%	0.0%	0.5%
Linn County	20,556	50.9%	29.7%	13.5%	4.5%	1.4%	0.0%	0.0%
Polk County	42,356	51.1%	25.7%	8.1%	13.7%	0.9%	0.5%	0.0%
Pottawattamie County	7,635	49.2%	21.6%	15.0%	10.5%	3.7%	0.0%	0.0%
Scott County	14,919	58.7%	19.5%	13.0%	5.7%	2.3%	0.8%	0.0%
Story County	30,499	64.9%	18.7%	9.0%	5.7%	1.6%	0.0%	0.0%
Woodbury County	10,216	65.7%	19.3%	9.0%	5.0%	1.0%	0.0%	0.0%
Kansas								
Douglas County	27,314	57.2%	33.9%	5.1%	2.3%	1.5%	0.0%	0.0%
Johnson County	45,453	57.9%	13.2%	13.4%	12.7%	2.3%	0.3%	0.2%
Sedgwick County	42,104	60.0%	20.6%	13.2%	4.1%	2.0%	0.0%	0.0%

Table I-2: Counties—Income Class by Age—*Continued*

	Total Millennials	Under $10,000	$10,000 to $19,999	$20,000 to $29,999	$30,000 to $49,999	$50,000 to $74,999	$75,000 to $99,999	$100,000 to $149,999	$150,000 or More	Poverty Rate
Georgia—Cont.										
Floyd County	11,390	32.6%	23.3%	22.6%	10.8%	6.7%	0.0%	0.5%	3.6%	21.5%
Forsyth County	18,563	28.8%	11.8%	12.2%	19.7%	15.4%	5.0%	5.6%	1.4%	4.3%
Fulton County	148,188	18.4%	12.5%	17.0%	26.8%	14.9%	5.0%	4.0%	1.5%	12.2%
Gwinnett County	102,945	25.9%	19.1%	15.8%	22.3%	11.6%	3.8%	1.4%	0.2%	12.4%
Hall County	21,584	30.3%	21.3%	19.6%	18.0%	6.3%	1.7%	1.1%	1.6%	19.5%
Henry County	21,023	28.6%	6.4%	13.0%	36.3%	11.6%	4.1%	0.0%	0.0%	9.4%
Houston County	17,833	25.5%	14.6%	11.3%	36.3%	10.8%	1.5%	0.0%	0.0%	14.6%
Lowndes County	16,568	38.6%	8.8%	16.6%	22.5%	8.0%	1.8%	1.1%	2.6%	24.5%
Muscogee County	29,648	25.5%	16.4%	18.3%	23.6%	10.6%	2.3%	3.2%	0.0%	14.4%
Newton County	12,360	23.9%	19.2%	21.5%	24.3%	8.5%	2.7%	0.0%	0.0%	13.0%
Paulding County	16,727	28.6%	15.0%	18.7%	25.6%	7.0%	3.9%	0.9%	0.4%	15.3%
Richmond County	30,218	34.4%	15.8%	10.9%	22.5%	12.4%	2.8%	0.8%	0.3%	23.6%
Whitfield County	13,342	27.3%	10.9%	36.5%	19.1%	5.8%	0.0%	0.3%	0.0%	20.2%
Hawaii										
Hawaii County	21,668	32.5%	10.0%	19.8%	20.7%	14.6%	1.6%	0.8%	0.0%	22.9%
Honolulu County	138,456	21.7%	11.6%	17.7%	25.9%	15.1%	4.7%	2.9%	0.4%	8.8%
Maui County	20,898	14.7%	18.3%	13.9%	32.1%	18.3%	2.0%	0.7%	0.0%	11.4%
Idaho										
Ada County	57,353	26.5%	19.1%	16.4%	22.7%	9.5%	2.8%	1.7%	1.2%	10.3%
Bonneville County	14,384	29.4%	18.7%	20.6%	19.5%	2.8%	4.0%	5.0%	0.0%	12.5%
Canyon County	23,454	40.1%	20.1%	19.3%	10.9%	6.8%	2.5%	0.4%	0.0%	16.4%
Kootenai County	17,751	29.4%	18.0%	19.3%	23.3%	3.5%	1.0%	4.4%	1.2%	23.9%
Illinois										
Champaign County	24,074	16.2%	15.2%	27.5%	26.1%	10.6%	2.8%	1.2%	0.5%	13.3%
Cook County	749,255	24.1%	13.8%	13.7%	19.8%	16.5%	6.2%	3.5%	2.3%	15.3%
DeKalb County	12,654	15.8%	15.8%	26.1%	22.7%	17.4%	0.8%	1.4%	0.0%	15.9%
DuPage County	103,130	19.7%	11.6%	15.4%	24.2%	17.3%	6.9%	3.5%	1.4%	7.2%
Kane County	55,269	19.7%	17.3%	14.1%	28.8%	12.6%	4.4%	2.8%	0.3%	11.6%
Kankakee County	12,290	27.3%	16.1%	12.2%	27.1%	13.2%	0.9%	2.4%	0.8%	18.7%
Kendall County	14,670	5.5%	21.6%	14.6%	33.8%	14.1%	3.1%	7.2%	0.0%	3.4%
Lake County	68,950	24.7%	12.5%	15.6%	21.8%	15.5%	5.3%	3.4%	1.1%	8.6%
LaSalle County	11,899	24.3%	16.5%	20.7%	20.0%	9.6%	8.1%	0.9%	0.0%	16.6%
Macon County	27,547	18.3%	12.8%	15.2%	29.8%	13.3%	7.8%	2.4%	0.3%	9.8%
Madison County	19,902	15.5%	14.2%	18.8%	26.0%	15.8%	7.2%	0.0%	1.0%	9.9%
McHenry County	10,459	25.2%	12.6%	17.8%	25.7%	15.4%	2.7%	0.6%	0.0%	22.5%
McLean County	31,871	26.8%	12.1%	13.9%	25.8%	14.3%	4.6%	2.6%	0.0%	15.6%
Peoria County	24,949	24.0%	12.9%	18.7%	21.2%	12.2%	8.9%	1.6%	0.4%	20.0%
Rock Island County	14,721	25.2%	20.2%	15.2%	20.9%	11.3%	7.2%	0.0%	0.0%	12.8%
Sangamon County	30,890	27.5%	14.3%	10.7%	24.0%	12.7%	2.5%	0.3%	0.0%	19.0%
St. Clair County	22,066	23.3%	16.5%	18.9%	23.6%	11.3%	3.3%	2.2%	1.0%	21.6%
Tazewell County	15,526	16.5%	10.0%	17.4%	32.4%	15.3%	5.1%	1.3%	2.0%	3.9%
Will County	70,359	22.6%	13.6%	16.7%	21.7%	17.6%	3.9%	2.9%	1.0%	6.0%
Winnebago County	32,181	27.3%	13.7%	20.8%	25.8%	10.2%	2.0%	0.2%	0.0%	21.8%
Indiana										
Allen County	43,159	22.1%	12.4%	17.4%	33.2%	11.5%	1.0%	1.1%	1.3%	15.3%
Clark County	13,802	30.4%	7.0%	8.2%	25.8%	20.7%	6.5%	1.4%	0.0%	13.6%
Delaware County	10,355	31.0%	16.2%	16.5%	26.4%	4.2%	2.3%	2.3%	1.1%	24.6%
Elkhart County	22,639	32.0%	17.4%	15.8%	16.1%	16.2%	1.7%	0.6%	0.3%	19.6%
Hamilton County	32,351	20.4%	9.3%	12.8%	19.1%	23.4%	6.9%	2.8%	5.2%	8.8%
Hendricks County	19,120	15.7%	6.4%	12.4%	45.6%	17.0%	1.7%	1.2%	0.0%	4.4%
Johnson County	16,374	23.0%	11.0%	14.9%	21.5%	15.6%	5.0%	6.8%	2.3%	3.4%
Lake County	50,962	29.7%	14.8%	13.2%	22.2%	13.0%	4.3%	2.3%	0.5%	17.3%
LaPorte County	12,832	36.4%	17.4%	15.8%	20.6%	5.1%	3.3%	1.4%	0.0%	27.1%
Madison County	14,351	25.9%	14.6%	18.8%	29.6%	6.5%	3.2%	0.0%	1.4%	14.4%
Marion County	143,605	27.4%	16.1%	18.2%	23.5%	9.9%	2.4%	1.8%	0.7%	17.7%
Monroe County	19,522	27.9%	20.5%	22.1%	14.8%	13.1%	1.5%	0.0%	0.0%	18.9%
Porter County	16,606	33.7%	18.2%	7.7%	18.3%	12.5%	3.2%	5.6%	0.8%	12.3%
St. Joseph County	30,257	30.7%	15.5%	18.8%	23.4%	10.6%	0.6%	0.5%	0.0%	17.4%
Tippecanoe County	23,119	21.7%	13.4%	25.7%	22.4%	12.1%	3.8%	0.9%	0.0%	16.3%
Vanderburgh County	23,223	26.1%	16.1%	21.3%	21.8%	10.8%	2.2%	1.6%	0.1%	17.2%
Vigo County	11,877	42.0%	19.7%	17.4%	13.5%	5.8%	0.5%	0.0%	1.2%	19.9%
Iowa										
Black Hawk County	16,522	25.5%	7.9%	21.2%	27.0%	9.5%	5.6%	2.0%	1.3%	16.2%
Dubuque County	10,173	15.3%	19.4%	13.6%	28.1%	18.1%	3.9%	0.0%	1.6%	11.9%
Johnson County	20,149	17.8%	19.6%	17.5%	23.3%	18.9%	2.6%	0.3%	0.0%	15.4%
Linn County	26,946	22.9%	14.5%	6.8%	38.8%	12.4%	3.7%	0.0%	0.9%	21.7%
Polk County	63,811	19.7%	11.7%	16.2%	31.0%	16.4%	2.5%	2.6%	0.0%	11.1%
Pottawattamie County	10,697	19.5%	14.5%	13.5%	33.8%	12.4%	4.8%	1.5%	0.0%	13.9%
Scott County	21,279	20.6%	11.9%	21.9%	25.6%	11.7%	5.1%	3.1%	0.0%	16.3%
Story County	12,160	20.1%	17.7%	16.7%	31.0%	14.3%	0.2%	0.0%	0.0%	11.9%
Woodbury County	13,035	25.2%	11.4%	24.9%	23.4%	11.0%	3.8%	0.3%	0.0%	25.1%
Kansas										
Douglas County	16,467	19.1%	17.6%	10.3%	34.2%	9.0%	4.6%	5.2%	0.0%	12.2%
Johnson County	72,191	12.8%	9.7%	11.7%	35.2%	19.3%	5.4%	3.4%	2.4%	7.2%
Sedgwick County	69,848	25.5%	16.1%	17.9%	23.8%	11.5%	1.8%	2.7%	0.7%	12.8%

Table I-2: Counties—Income Class by Age—*Continued*

	Total Millennials	Under $10,000	$10,000 to $19,999	$20,000 to $29,999	$30,000 to $49,999	$50,000 to $74,999	$75,000 to $99,999	$100,000 or More
				Personal Income, Percent by Income Class, ages 18 to 24				
Kansas—Cont.								
Shawnee County	15,601	51.2%	25.4%	13.9%	9.0%	0.5%	0.0%	0.0%
Wyandotte County	15,957	47.6%	18.0%	23.3%	8.4%	2.6%	0.0%	0.0%
Kentucky								
Boone County	10,603	47.5%	31.5%	13.3%	4.6%	0.0%	1.5%	1.6%
Campbell County	10,150	70.8%	10.0%	13.6%	5.0%	0.5%	0.1%	0.0%
Daviess County	8,278	62.5%	21.2%	7.5%	1.9%	6.9%	0.0%	0.0%
Fayette County	43,094	54.2%	25.6%	12.4%	6.2%	1.6%	0.0%	0.0%
Hardin County	8,702	51.0%	30.5%	12.6%	5.1%	0.8%	0.0%	0.0%
Jefferson County	67,483	57.2%	24.0%	11.3%	5.9%	1.3%	0.2%	0.2%
Kenton County	13,201	52.9%	22.3%	19.2%	4.7%	0.9%	0.0%	0.0%
Warren County	20,247	61.5%	18.4%	14.4%	5.3%	0.5%	0.0%	0.0%
Louisiana								
Ascension Parish	9,930	67.5%	9.6%	10.5%	3.3%	7.7%	0.7%	0.7%
Bossier Parish	10,378	45.3%	19.9%	22.0%	10.0%	1.8%	1.1%	0.0%
Caddo Parish	22,950	72.3%	11.7%	8.6%	4.3%	2.8%	0.3%	0.0%
Calcasieu Parish	19,191	59.6%	23.2%	7.9%	7.7%	1.7%	0.0%	0.0%
East Baton Rouge Parish	64,836	55.7%	26.7%	10.7%	4.5%	1.4%	1.0%	0.0%
Jefferson Parish	35,832	57.7%	22.9%	8.4%	8.3%	2.3%	0.3%	0.3%
Lafayette Parish	25,132	74.9%	17.9%	4.2%	1.9%	0.0%	0.0%	1.2%
Lafourche Parish	9,010	56.0%	17.4%	13.7%	5.2%	4.1%	3.6%	0.0%
Livingston Parish	12,429	55.6%	19.5%	3.1%	20.4%	0.9%	0.6%	0.0%
Orleans Parish	36,913	68.7%	17.7%	5.9%	5.3%	0.7%	1.7%	0.0%
Ouachita Parish	16,254	76.1%	15.3%	3.8%	3.6%	1.2%	0.0%	0.0%
Rapides Parish	12,171	56.4%	16.1%	17.9%	8.5%	0.2%	0.0%	0.9%
St. Tammany Parish	17,848	63.5%	19.5%	8.6%	7.6%	0.8%	0.0%	0.0%
Tangipahoa Parish	15,212	78.5%	17.9%	1.2%	2.5%	0.0%	0.0%	0.0%
Terrebonne Parish	9,054	52.4%	23.5%	14.4%	5.0%	1.9%	0.0%	2.7%
Maine								
Androscoggin County	9,422	60.2%	15.2%	9.4%	10.6%	4.6%	0.0%	0.0%
Cumberland County	27,405	47.4%	25.6%	12.2%	10.7%	3.3%	0.7%	0.0%
Kennebec County	10,420	55.4%	33.4%	4.6%	5.3%	1.3%	0.0%	0.0%
Penobscot County	17,405	74.5%	18.2%	3.9%	2.7%	0.8%	0.0%	0.0%
York County	14,898	53.9%	13.3%	16.3%	15.2%	1.3%	0.0%	0.0%
Maryland								
Anne Arundel County	49,519	52.0%	28.1%	9.6%	9.9%	0.4%	0.0%	0.0%
Baltimore County	75,812	62.4%	17.3%	12.2%	5.5%	2.7%	0.0%	0.0%
Carroll County	15,086	55.3%	22.2%	9.3%	8.4%	3.5%	1.2%	0.0%
Cecil County	10,116	42.2%	36.1%	12.4%	5.0%	4.4%	0.0%	0.0%
Charles County	14,616	59.1%	17.7%	11.2%	8.4%	3.6%	0.0%	0.0%
Frederick County	23,610	57.2%	17.4%	12.5%	8.7%	3.8%	0.3%	0.0%
Harford County	21,193	56.2%	14.6%	13.8%	12.0%	2.4%	1.0%	0.0%
Howard County	24,724	59.7%	9.0%	17.1%	7.9%	3.2%	3.0%	0.0%
Montgomery County	80,631	61.8%	15.7%	10.7%	7.9%	3.5%	0.3%	0.1%
Prince George's County	92,320	62.8%	17.7%	10.6%	7.0%	1.7%	0.1%	0.1%
St. Mary's County	11,172	55.3%	20.2%	10.7%	9.9%	3.9%	0.0%	0.0%
Washington County	12,974	62.1%	21.6%	5.7%	10.1%	0.4%	0.0%	0.0%
Wicomico County	15,548	65.9%	17.5%	5.3%	9.7%	1.6%	0.0%	0.0%
Massachusetts								
Barnstable County	14,470	69.4%	11.8%	9.4%	9.4%	0.0%	0.0%	0.0%
Berkshire County	13,356	63.5%	23.8%	7.2%	4.3%	1.2%	0.0%	0.0%
Bristol County	53,784	58.7%	17.5%	14.7%	6.3%	2.3%	0.6%	0.0%
Essex County	70,510	59.2%	19.0%	11.1%	7.4%	2.2%	0.0%	1.1%
Hampden County	51,064	63.3%	18.8%	10.0%	6.8%	0.9%	0.3%	0.0%
Hampshire County	30,446	68.5%	18.6%	7.6%	3.9%	0.9%	0.1%	0.4%
Middlesex County	151,267	61.3%	16.8%	7.6%	9.8%	3.4%	0.7%	0.4%
Norfolk County	56,434	64.0%	15.2%	8.4%	7.7%	3.1%	0.2%	1.4%
Plymouth County	47,932	59.8%	19.1%	11.2%	7.7%	2.2%	0.0%	0.0%
Suffolk County	109,239	67.9%	13.5%	8.1%	6.2%	3.4%	0.5%	0.3%
Worcester County	79,420	61.5%	17.3%	9.7%	9.5%	1.7%	0.2%	0.1%
Michigan								
Allegan County	9,792	41.9%	20.0%	15.3%	21.4%	1.4%	0.0%	0.0%
Bay County	8,750	43.1%	42.2%	9.1%	3.0%	0.0%	2.5%	0.0%
Berrien County	12,450	64.7%	17.7%	9.6%	7.6%	0.0%	0.4%	0.0%
Calhoun County	10,750	63.8%	24.3%	8.5%	3.4%	0.0%	0.0%	0.0%
Eaton County	10,308	54.6%	22.6%	15.3%	6.0%	1.6%	0.0%	0.0%
Genesee County	37,578	63.0%	24.4%	8.1%	3.0%	1.1%	0.0%	0.4%
Ingham County	55,890	66.9%	17.5%	9.0%	5.4%	1.2%	0.0%	0.0%
Jackson County	13,858	59.4%	18.1%	13.5%	7.9%	1.1%	0.0%	0.0%
Kalamazoo County	40,695	63.2%	21.3%	8.4%	4.8%	1.1%	0.5%	0.7%
Kent County	59,053	60.8%	21.6%	10.2%	5.9%	1.5%	0.0%	0.0%
Lenawee County	10,515	51.0%	28.5%	14.0%	4.3%	2.2%	0.0%	0.0%
Livingston County	16,204	52.0%	20.6%	14.6%	9.3%	1.5%	0.0%	2.0%
Macomb County	72,892	54.6%	21.6%	12.7%	8.2%	2.6%	0.3%	0.0%
Monroe County	11,950	50.2%	26.3%	12.0%	10.3%	0.4%	0.9%	0.0%
Muskegon County	14,864	59.7%	18.8%	8.9%	6.8%	5.8%	0.0%	0.0%

Table I-2: Counties—Income Class by Age—*Continued*

	Personal Income, Percent by Income Class, ages 25 to 33									
	Total Millennials	Under $10,000	$10,000 to $19,999	$20,000 to $29,999	$30,000 to $49,999	$50,000 to $74,999	$75,000 to $99,999	$100,000 to $149,999	$150,000 or More	Poverty Rate
Kansas—Cont.										
Shawnee County	20,868	28.0%	14.5%	17.0%	22.9%	13.2%	1.9%	0.0%	2.4%	18.8%
Wyandotte County	20,784	19.4%	14.6%	19.3%	32.5%	10.1%	2.7%	1.3%	0.0%	16.4%
Kentucky										
Boone County	14,062	25.3%	16.1%	18.8%	22.5%	11.9%	2.3%	1.4%	1.7%	18.8%
Campbell County	12,171	28.9%	6.1%	13.1%	29.7%	15.7%	4.1%	1.5%	0.9%	18.5%
Daviess County	10,870	22.3%	16.4%	28.8%	21.5%	9.3%	0.3%	0.0%	1.3%	13.4%
Fayette County	44,691	20.4%	15.9%	21.1%	24.5%	10.4%	2.9%	3.0%	1.8%	18.1%
Hardin County	13,182	26.4%	22.1%	16.6%	18.9%	10.2%	2.3%	2.9%	0.6%	21.2%
Jefferson County	97,019	22.6%	17.7%	14.5%	24.4%	15.4%	3.3%	1.5%	0.5%	13.5%
Kenton County	21,440	23.8%	17.0%	15.1%	28.4%	11.4%	3.1%	0.7%	0.5%	12.9%
Warren County	13,584	23.8%	16.1%	17.1%	29.3%	8.0%	2.9%	0.0%	2.7%	15.8%
Louisiana										
Ascension Parish	15,246	20.7%	11.7%	13.1%	28.4%	11.4%	9.5%	5.1%	0.0%	6.9%
Bossier Parish	18,823	27.7%	16.0%	19.5%	21.9%	7.8%	3.6%	3.3%	0.1%	18.9%
Caddo Parish	31,201	28.2%	22.8%	17.1%	19.2%	8.7%	2.4%	0.2%	1.5%	16.8%
Calcasieu Parish	25,818	30.0%	13.1%	14.7%	20.5%	12.3%	5.0%	3.4%	1.0%	16.9%
East Baton Rouge Parish	60,253	24.9%	15.8%	14.9%	24.6%	9.7%	6.1%	3.4%	0.7%	16.6%
Jefferson Parish	59,422	26.5%	14.9%	19.1%	22.4%	12.0%	2.6%	2.1%	0.4%	19.7%
Lafayette Parish	35,178	21.9%	10.7%	13.1%	25.8%	16.8%	6.0%	3.3%	2.3%	12.5%
Lafourche Parish	12,284	20.9%	20.7%	13.3%	22.7%	10.4%	7.5%	4.4%	0.0%	16.8%
Livingston Parish	18,143	37.5%	11.9%	7.1%	16.9%	15.8%	8.8%	1.0%	1.0%	13.7%
Orleans Parish	64,511	27.5%	19.3%	17.0%	19.3%	10.3%	3.1%	2.7%	0.8%	22.7%
Ouachita Parish	21,022	34.2%	19.2%	11.5%	18.8%	11.9%	2.9%	1.6%	0.0%	20.7%
Rapides Parish	15,027	31.2%	14.6%	17.3%	19.4%	6.9%	7.8%	2.6%	0.2%	22.0%
St. Tammany Parish	27,347	21.0%	11.5%	14.1%	22.4%	23.1%	2.4%	5.0%	0.5%	13.7%
Tangipahoa Parish	16,082	38.0%	12.1%	11.5%	18.7%	12.7%	7.0%	0.0%	0.0%	26.1%
Terrebonne Parish	14,608	37.9%	12.8%	8.3%	23.6%	7.0%	6.8%	3.7%	0.0%	17.8%
Maine										
Androscoggin County	10,928	14.1%	10.4%	27.3%	30.2%	11.6%	6.4%	0.0%	0.0%	12.0%
Cumberland County	32,599	20.2%	13.2%	18.6%	24.2%	16.0%	5.6%	1.6%	0.5%	16.5%
Kennebec County	11,402	19.2%	13.2%	24.9%	29.0%	13.2%	0.0%	0.5%	0.0%	3.9%
Penobscot County	18,251	34.1%	19.0%	14.0%	19.3%	10.2%	2.4%	0.0%	1.1%	29.2%
York County	21,412	16.7%	10.9%	22.2%	23.2%	16.5%	6.6%	1.0%	3.0%	5.7%
Maryland										
Anne Arundel County	72,114	22.0%	9.2%	11.4%	27.2%	15.2%	9.3%	4.7%	0.9%	7.1%
Baltimore County	102,913	20.4%	12.8%	13.9%	25.0%	18.2%	6.9%	2.0%	0.7%	7.9%
Carroll County	15,451	23.3%	15.4%	8.7%	20.9%	21.3%	7.4%	1.3%	1.6%	11.5%
Cecil County	10,550	26.1%	7.2%	14.3%	24.2%	22.6%	5.6%	0.0%	0.0%	8.7%
Charles County	17,558	22.6%	9.1%	9.8%	31.2%	13.9%	11.8%	1.5%	0.0%	2.4%
Frederick County	25,527	12.9%	12.6%	16.7%	27.6%	18.4%	7.9%	2.7%	1.0%	6.4%
Harford County	27,303	25.9%	12.9%	8.5%	25.6%	16.4%	6.9%	2.3%	1.5%	10.6%
Howard County	35,451	18.8%	7.0%	12.4%	21.2%	22.8%	11.0%	5.3%	1.6%	6.4%
Montgomery County	121,975	20.3%	13.0%	14.1%	20.0%	17.4%	8.7%	4.9%	1.5%	8.1%
Prince George's County	119,847	25.8%	13.3%	14.5%	22.7%	14.8%	6.6%	1.3%	1.1%	8.8%
St. Mary's County	12,744	21.0%	13.5%	9.5%	23.3%	22.3%	6.7%	3.1%	0.7%	11.1%
Washington County	17,314	32.5%	9.2%	15.4%	23.1%	14.3%	4.0%	0.7%	0.9%	12.7%
Wicomico County	10,832	33.5%	16.7%	19.5%	17.8%	9.7%	2.1%	0.7%	0.0%	18.7%
Massachusetts										
Barnstable County	16,446	20.7%	8.6%	15.1%	26.7%	18.7%	4.5%	3.6%	2.0%	7.9%
Berkshire County	10,784	17.2%	22.4%	24.5%	19.6%	14.4%	1.1%	0.8%	0.0%	20.6%
Bristol County	64,980	24.4%	12.8%	15.7%	24.6%	18.2%	2.3%	1.4%	0.4%	16.3%
Essex County	86,690	21.9%	14.8%	11.8%	23.3%	18.4%	5.8%	2.8%	1.1%	12.9%
Hampden County	52,638	28.2%	13.9%	12.9%	21.4%	18.1%	3.8%	1.7%	0.0%	14.6%
Hampshire County	19,802	28.6%	13.0%	15.9%	25.6%	14.1%	2.2%	0.1%	0.3%	16.4%
Middlesex County	217,135	16.9%	8.9%	10.5%	25.2%	21.9%	10.2%	4.9%	1.5%	8.7%
Norfolk County	74,387	18.4%	9.1%	11.9%	26.2%	18.0%	9.4%	4.9%	2.2%	6.9%
Plymouth County	45,305	19.8%	13.8%	13.0%	28.8%	18.2%	4.0%	1.7%	0.7%	9.1%
Suffolk County	164,411	16.8%	9.5%	10.5%	23.4%	21.4%	9.3%	5.6%	3.6%	12.5%
Worcester County	86,588	22.5%	13.3%	15.0%	23.4%	17.2%	4.7%	3.2%	0.8%	13.0%
Michigan										
Allegan County	11,964	20.0%	13.5%	23.1%	23.6%	15.4%	0.0%	4.4%	0.0%	12.5%
Bay County	11,393	7.5%	29.6%	18.8%	28.5%	7.9%	6.2%	1.2%	0.2%	12.3%
Berrien County	15,966	33.7%	14.4%	14.6%	19.7%	12.4%	2.4%	2.1%	0.7%	20.0%
Calhoun County	15,498	20.2%	13.6%	33.9%	19.4%	8.8%	3.2%	0.5%	0.4%	14.6%
Eaton County	11,088	31.1%	15.5%	20.9%	17.7%	9.0%	3.6%	1.3%	1.0%	25.4%
Genesee County	44,026	34.7%	17.6%	19.8%	17.2%	6.1%	3.6%	0.2%	0.8%	27.3%
Ingham County	36,809	24.4%	10.7%	23.4%	29.2%	9.5%	2.2%	0.6%	0.0%	15.2%
Jackson County	18,291	37.8%	8.4%	12.7%	23.7%	15.3%	2.2%	0.0%	0.0%	21.4%
Kalamazoo County	30,665	28.4%	10.2%	10.1%	31.8%	11.8%	3.2%	4.3%	0.3%	17.4%
Kent County	86,654	18.9%	19.4%	15.6%	26.9%	14.2%	3.3%	0.9%	0.9%	12.2%
Lenawee County	8,941	35.7%	9.1%	12.0%	32.0%	5.4%	2.0%	3.1%	0.7%	19.8%
Livingston County	16,311	23.2%	10.6%	18.0%	20.2%	23.2%	3.6%	1.3%	0.0%	11.8%
Macomb County	96,953	27.1%	13.8%	15.6%	23.6%	12.5%	5.3%	1.6%	0.5%	13.5%
Monroe County	15,224	27.9%	17.6%	9.2%	21.7%	16.1%	2.9%	3.7%	0.9%	15.4%
Muskegon County	20,232	33.0%	24.8%	12.8%	14.6%	13.5%	0.0%	0.0%	1.3%	20.9%

Table I-2: Counties—Income Class by Age—*Continued*

					Personal Income, Percent by Income Class, ages 18 to 24			
	Total Millennials	Under $10,000	$10,000 to $19,999	$20,000 to $29,999	$30,000 to $49,999	$50,000 to $74,999	$75,000 to $99,999	$100,000 or More
Michigan—Cont.								
Oakland County	99,353	58.4%	18.3%	10.8%	8.8%	3.2%	0.5%	0.0%
Ottawa County	37,740	57.2%	15.6%	14.6%	10.5%	1.2%	0.9%	0.0%
Saginaw County	20,018	70.5%	16.5%	7.5%	5.4%	0.1%	0.0%	0.0%
St. Clair County	12,939	46.6%	41.5%	5.7%	5.3%	0.9%	0.0%	0.0%
Washtenaw County	65,988	48.5%	23.0%	10.9%	11.3%	6.0%	0.0%	0.2%
Wayne County	161,271	65.1%	18.3%	9.4%	6.0%	1.1%	0.1%	0.0%
Minnesota								
Anoka County	28,545	50.6%	23.2%	11.4%	12.9%	1.8%	0.0%	0.0%
Carver County	8,836	49.7%	25.5%	12.1%	8.4%	4.0%	0.3%	0.0%
Dakota County	32,562	46.8%	19.8%	17.3%	11.4%	4.8%	0.0%	0.0%
Hennepin County	102,085	54.2%	20.1%	9.4%	12.9%	3.3%	0.1%	0.0%
Olmsted County	13,039	55.5%	12.2%	16.2%	7.2%	8.9%	0.0%	0.0%
Ramsey County	53,476	60.7%	20.8%	10.8%	7.0%	0.3%	0.0%	0.3%
Scott County	23,823	60.1%	23.7%	11.8%	3.5%	0.9%	0.0%	0.0%
St. Louis County	10,039	56.3%	24.4%	6.7%	12.6%	0.0%	0.0%	0.0%
Stearns County	23,336	38.7%	29.9%	13.7%	16.8%	0.8%	0.0%	0.0%
Washington County	18,451	47.5%	25.3%	19.2%	4.8%	3.2%	0.0%	0.0%
Wright County	9,108	35.9%	29.9%	13.2%	15.3%	1.9%	3.8%	0.0%
Mississippi								
DeSoto County	15,974	60.4%	24.7%	8.0%	6.1%	0.9%	0.0%	0.0%
Harrison County	20,500	53.2%	21.8%	14.2%	9.5%	0.6%	0.5%	0.2%
Hinds County	27,627	76.2%	13.8%	4.2%	5.3%	0.4%	0.0%	0.0%
Jackson County	11,665	62.6%	24.3%	8.0%	5.1%	0.0%	0.0%	0.0%
Madison County	9,529	61.7%	25.2%	6.3%	6.3%	0.5%	0.0%	0.0%
Rankin County	11,450	57.4%	22.9%	13.5%	6.1%	0.0%	0.0%	0.0%
Missouri								
Boone County	35,010	80.7%	10.6%	3.6%	2.7%	2.3%	0.0%	0.0%
Cass County	7,815	48.1%	23.3%	22.2%	4.1%	2.3%	0.0%	0.0%
Clay County	19,014	49.2%	28.9%	19.9%	2.0%	0.0%	0.0%	0.0%
Franklin County	7,688	60.0%	14.9%	22.3%	0.7%	2.1%	0.0%	0.0%
Greene County	39,311	53.6%	25.1%	12.5%	7.1%	1.7%	0.0%	0.0%
Jackson County	58,643	59.0%	15.1%	15.0%	8.4%	2.3%	0.0%	0.1%
Jasper County	12,573	56.5%	24.7%	6.8%	11.4%	0.5%	0.0%	0.0%
Jefferson County	17,003	63.5%	26.9%	4.6%	4.7%	0.3%	0.0%	0.0%
Platte County	8,083	49.6%	17.9%	28.5%	4.0%	0.0%	0.0%	0.0%
St. Charles County	34,021	57.3%	20.0%	15.3%	6.0%	1.3%	0.0%	0.0%
St. Louis County	91,525	60.8%	19.6%	10.5%	8.2%	0.8%	0.2%	0.0%
Montana								
Flathead County	7,110	73.5%	17.7%	0.0%	8.8%	0.0%	0.0%	0.0%
Gallatin County	17,676	44.8%	32.4%	14.7%	4.6%	3.0%	0.5%	0.0%
Missoula County	14,743	60.2%	22.8%	10.8%	6.2%	0.0%	0.0%	0.0%
Yellowstone County	15,272	41.3%	17.8%	15.4%	19.3%	2.1%	1.2%	2.9%
Nebraska								
Douglas County	48,111	46.9%	22.4%	14.3%	10.5%	3.9%	0.3%	1.7%
Lancaster County	44,746	68.6%	18.7%	7.1%	2.5%	1.5%	1.6%	0.0%
Sarpy County	15,963	43.0%	19.7%	19.7%	15.5%	2.1%	0.0%	0.0%
Nevada								
Clark County	185,462	56.0%	22.9%	11.9%	7.5%	1.3%	0.4%	0.0%
Washoe County	40,531	50.8%	29.7%	11.4%	6.8%	0.6%	0.1%	0.7%
New Hampshire								
Hillsborough County	36,372	53.5%	15.9%	18.7%	9.3%	2.6%	0.0%	0.0%
Merrimack County	15,345	65.2%	14.9%	12.9%	4.7%	2.3%	0.0%	0.0%
Rockingham County	24,833	58.1%	17.7%	7.9%	12.2%	2.0%	2.1%	0.0%
Strafford County	20,330	67.4%	20.1%	2.9%	6.9%	2.7%	0.0%	0.0%
New Jersey								
Atlantic County	26,461	65.6%	15.6%	6.4%	8.7%	2.0%	0.0%	1.7%
Bergen County	76,394	68.5%	14.3%	7.2%	7.6%	2.3%	0.1%	0.0%
Burlington County	40,215	61.7%	15.7%	14.4%	6.7%	1.2%	0.1%	0.2%
Camden County	45,187	58.1%	22.7%	10.7%	6.3%	2.2%	0.0%	0.0%
Cape May County	6,462	68.2%	20.7%	5.5%	5.6%	0.0%	0.0%	0.0%
Cumberland County	12,525	52.8%	22.8%	12.9%	10.1%	0.4%	0.3%	0.6%
Essex County	73,719	73.3%	11.9%	8.0%	4.6%	1.6%	0.4%	0.2%
Gloucester County	25,009	56.5%	26.9%	8.0%	4.8%	3.2%	0.6%	0.0%
Hudson County	57,454	61.3%	20.8%	7.7%	6.8%	2.6%	0.2%	0.6%
Hunterdon County	11,277	68.0%	14.4%	9.8%	3.6%	4.2%	0.0%	0.0%
Mercer County	42,896	74.3%	12.6%	9.1%	2.4%	1.4%	0.2%	0.0%
Middlesex County	80,167	72.9%	12.1%	6.7%	5.3%	2.5%	0.4%	0.0%
Monmouth County	52,405	68.6%	15.5%	6.4%	6.0%	2.8%	0.6%	0.1%
Morris County	42,026	66.6%	14.7%	6.4%	8.8%	3.0%	0.5%	0.0%
Ocean County	42,927	57.6%	22.6%	9.8%	7.9%	0.6%	1.6%	0.0%
Passaic County	50,193	67.7%	17.9%	7.2%	5.2%	1.4%	0.6%	0.0%
Somerset County	26,813	57.6%	12.4%	14.8%	11.8%	3.4%	0.0%	0.0%
Sussex County	12,181	45.9%	22.7%	20.2%	9.7%	1.0%	0.4%	0.0%
Union County	49,137	61.3%	17.6%	9.8%	8.4%	2.7%	0.1%	0.0%
Warren County	8,731	60.8%	19.7%	8.2%	7.5%	3.8%	0.0%	0.0%

Table I-2: Counties—Income Class by Age—*Continued*

	Total Millennials	Under $10,000	$10,000 to $19,999	$20,000 to $29,999	$30,000 to $49,999	$50,000 to $74,999	$75,000 to $99,999	$100,000 to $149,999	$150,000 or More	Poverty Rate
	Personal Income, Percent by Income Class, ages 25 to 33									
Michigan—Cont.										
Oakland County	138,448	20.3%	13.5%	13.6%	20.1%	19.3%	8.7%	3.0%	1.4%	9.4%
Ottawa County	29,180	20.4%	16.5%	11.9%	33.0%	15.0%	0.7%	1.2%	1.4%	9.8%
Saginaw County	21,353	23.9%	23.8%	20.5%	17.9%	9.2%	2.1%	2.1%	0.6%	20.4%
St. Clair County	15,197	20.4%	27.3%	17.7%	17.5%	14.9%	1.8%	0.3%	0.0%	16.5%
Washtenaw County	45,342	21.0%	16.9%	12.4%	24.1%	16.7%	3.6%	3.5%	1.8%	14.7%
Wayne County	209,958	36.7%	17.2%	14.1%	18.7%	9.3%	2.1%	1.3%	0.6%	24.7%
Minnesota										
Anoka County	37,263	23.4%	10.4%	11.1%	27.3%	16.4%	9.5%	1.1%	0.8%	4.3%
Carver County	9,344	12.6%	8.1%	9.0%	36.7%	22.6%	9.9%	0.6%	0.6%	9.4%
Dakota County	48,217	13.8%	12.2%	15.7%	30.9%	19.5%	4.8%	2.9%	0.0%	10.2%
Hennepin County	187,052	13.2%	11.5%	15.7%	26.5%	19.1%	7.0%	5.7%	1.4%	9.3%
Olmsted County	18,471	18.1%	8.9%	11.4%	27.2%	24.5%	5.7%	3.3%	1.0%	5.2%
Ramsey County	80,179	22.9%	14.8%	15.6%	26.3%	14.0%	3.0%	2.8%	0.6%	15.4%
Scott County	24,077	14.3%	14.9%	20.3%	31.3%	13.7%	2.0%	3.4%	0.1%	14.1%
St. Louis County	15,996	11.6%	2.4%	14.9%	37.0%	22.3%	6.5%	4.3%	1.1%	5.9%
Stearns County	18,068	20.0%	10.5%	10.2%	32.9%	23.0%	1.2%	1.9%	0.2%	12.2%
Washington County	27,927	23.3%	12.8%	17.4%	26.3%	11.2%	4.2%	4.0%	0.9%	7.5%
Wright County	12,796	13.4%	4.8%	17.9%	40.3%	12.9%	6.7%	3.9%	0.0%	4.9%
Mississippi										
DeSoto County	18,056	27.0%	14.8%	15.5%	27.1%	10.1%	4.7%	0.9%	0.0%	11.3%
Harrison County	26,456	32.2%	11.8%	17.1%	29.5%	7.9%	1.1%	0.3%	0.0%	23.5%
Hinds County	33,590	29.8%	19.0%	18.9%	23.8%	7.0%	0.8%	0.7%	0.0%	27.4%
Jackson County	15,749	16.2%	20.4%	24.0%	30.2%	8.5%	0.8%	0.0%	0.0%	12.7%
Madison County	11,625	24.6%	15.2%	16.0%	30.6%	11.8%	1.8%	0.0%	0.0%	11.9%
Rankin County	18,537	18.6%	10.9%	21.5%	28.6%	13.7%	3.9%	2.7%	0.0%	7.8%
Missouri										
Boone County	24,966	30.6%	13.6%	17.6%	21.9%	11.4%	3.7%	0.6%	0.5%	17.5%
Cass County	10,753	16.8%	12.4%	22.8%	24.6%	15.4%	6.9%	0.7%	0.4%	8.2%
Clay County	29,294	16.8%	17.5%	17.0%	29.7%	12.2%	5.4%	1.4%	0.0%	9.4%
Franklin County	10,968	15.7%	23.6%	18.6%	24.5%	8.9%	6.7%	2.1%	0.0%	14.0%
Greene County	38,002	22.3%	18.7%	19.8%	27.3%	7.3%	2.7%	1.2%	0.6%	16.1%
Jackson County	92,397	20.9%	14.2%	17.0%	28.8%	14.3%	2.1%	1.4%	1.4%	16.8%
Jasper County	13,205	15.9%	29.5%	15.3%	28.5%	10.6%	0.1%	0.1%	0.0%	8.1%
Jefferson County	26,185	24.2%	20.2%	15.8%	27.4%	7.0%	3.6%	1.7%	0.0%	16.5%
Platte County	12,428	14.8%	19.9%	11.0%	40.0%	10.5%	3.9%	0.0%	0.0%	10.7%
St. Charles County	43,865	17.2%	13.2%	14.4%	31.6%	15.1%	5.6%	1.7%	1.1%	9.8%
St. Louis County	110,930	23.0%	16.5%	16.8%	22.3%	13.5%	4.3%	3.1%	0.5%	13.2%
Montana										
Flathead County	8,899	16.4%	9.1%	15.0%	29.1%	20.5%	7.6%	0.0%	2.3%	15.2%
Gallatin County	13,205	20.1%	14.9%	14.1%	27.4%	14.6%	4.4%	3.4%	1.2%	11.8%
Missoula County	16,851	29.7%	28.8%	19.1%	13.3%	7.2%	0.5%	0.8%	0.6%	19.1%
Yellowstone County	18,802	19.7%	15.2%	9.9%	28.1%	24.3%	1.1%	1.4%	0.3%	9.5%
Nebraska										
Douglas County	79,252	18.7%	8.9%	17.8%	28.9%	17.4%	4.8%	2.7%	0.7%	12.1%
Lancaster County	40,689	26.2%	19.2%	16.8%	23.7%	8.8%	4.0%	1.0%	0.3%	23.7%
Sarpy County	21,981	19.8%	7.8%	11.2%	30.2%	23.0%	4.8%	1.0%	2.2%	7.2%
Nevada										
Clark County	282,745	26.6%	14.2%	18.5%	25.8%	11.0%	2.4%	1.1%	0.3%	14.0%
Washoe County	58,769	19.4%	15.4%	17.7%	29.8%	12.7%	2.6%	2.3%	0.3%	13.9%
New Hampshire										
Hillsborough County	44,349	18.3%	14.0%	9.0%	32.6%	14.6%	8.1%	2.1%	1.4%	10.7%
Merrimack County	14,153	27.8%	16.1%	9.9%	32.0%	13.4%	0.8%	0.0%	0.0%	6.6%
Rockingham County	29,641	9.8%	12.2%	13.7%	31.6%	17.0%	7.8%	5.4%	2.6%	4.6%
Strafford County	14,256	14.4%	15.0%	15.1%	36.1%	15.2%	1.4%	2.0%	0.7%	8.8%
New Jersey										
Atlantic County	30,078	26.8%	16.1%	16.2%	21.8%	12.9%	3.5%	2.6%	0.0%	18.0%
Bergen County	94,035	20.2%	11.1%	11.5%	20.7%	19.8%	10.2%	4.4%	2.2%	9.4%
Burlington County	49,139	25.7%	10.6%	13.7%	25.2%	15.0%	7.1%	1.3%	1.4%	9.0%
Camden County	63,339	25.9%	12.6%	15.1%	21.0%	17.2%	4.8%	2.6%	0.8%	13.1%
Cape May County	8,863	19.8%	10.4%	24.1%	28.0%	10.3%	2.3%	5.2%	0.0%	13.9%
Cumberland County	21,371	37.2%	16.4%	14.7%	16.7%	11.7%	3.4%	0.0%	0.0%	19.2%
Essex County	94,290	29.1%	15.0%	15.8%	21.0%	11.4%	4.4%	2.4%	0.9%	15.3%
Gloucester County	32,711	22.7%	15.4%	15.5%	21.7%	15.7%	6.6%	1.9%	0.4%	8.8%
Hudson County	126,934	20.2%	11.5%	11.0%	15.8%	17.4%	10.2%	8.9%	4.9%	11.9%
Hunterdon County	9,540	20.5%	12.2%	8.3%	32.1%	21.2%	3.5%	1.3%	1.0%	5.0%
Mercer County	39,044	32.7%	14.0%	14.6%	18.9%	11.2%	5.7%	1.9%	1.0%	13.6%
Middlesex County	102,594	25.9%	11.9%	10.9%	21.4%	16.6%	7.3%	4.9%	1.1%	9.1%
Monmouth County	61,769	20.8%	13.1%	16.1%	20.7%	18.4%	6.9%	3.6%	0.5%	10.8%
Morris County	50,784	15.8%	12.9%	12.2%	18.7%	23.1%	9.9%	5.6%	1.8%	6.9%
Ocean County	58,565	25.7%	13.3%	16.9%	21.5%	15.3%	3.9%	2.3%	1.0%	12.4%
Passaic County	61,390	32.2%	19.7%	12.3%	17.9%	13.7%	2.5%	1.5%	0.2%	15.8%
Somerset County	32,010	17.0%	9.1%	15.6%	23.5%	20.7%	7.5%	5.9%	0.8%	5.0%
Sussex County	12,390	23.8%	17.4%	12.7%	19.8%	18.0%	2.5%	5.0%	0.8%	5.5%
Union County	61,904	25.9%	15.7%	17.9%	20.8%	9.7%	6.5%	1.4%	2.1%	9.3%
Warren County	9,650	30.4%	12.4%	11.3%	17.9%	13.6%	11.6%	2.9%	0.0%	8.5%

Table I-2: Counties—Income Class by Age—*Continued*

			Personal Income, Percent by Income Class, ages 18 to 24					
	Total Millennials	Under $10,000	$10,000 to $19,999	$20,000 to $29,999	$30,000 to $49,999	$50,000 to $74,999	$75,000 to $99,999	$100,000 or More
New Mexico								
Bernalillo County	65,746	58.1%	25.8%	12.5%	3.1%	0.4%	0.0%	0.0%
Doña Ana County	30,410	69.4%	19.4%	5.9%	4.8%	0.6%	0.0%	0.0%
San Juan County	10,605	55.2%	31.9%	9.0%	3.8%	0.1%	0.0%	0.0%
Sandoval County	11,608	54.4%	19.3%	14.5%	10.8%	1.0%	0.0%	0.0%
Santa Fe County	11,025	59.2%	25.2%	7.7%	5.9%	2.0%	0.0%	0.0%
New York								
Albany County	44,077	67.4%	13.7%	9.6%	8.2%	1.1%	0.0%	0.0%
Bronx County	158,547	73.3%	14.5%	5.9%	5.0%	0.8%	0.2%	0.2%
Broome County	28,337	74.3%	16.4%	7.2%	1.3%	0.3%	0.0%	0.5%
Chautauqua County	13,664	70.1%	17.1%	5.5%	7.3%	0.0%	0.0%	0.0%
Dutchess County	33,766	70.2%	14.2%	9.4%	2.6%	3.3%	0.3%	0.0%
Erie County	89,778	59.4%	20.1%	10.4%	8.3%	1.3%	0.4%	0.0%
Jefferson County	15,128	47.5%	24.4%	15.4%	12.4%	0.2%	0.0%	0.0%
Kings County	234,279	66.6%	14.9%	8.0%	7.2%	2.1%	0.7%	0.5%
Monroe County	79,736	54.1%	19.8%	13.0%	10.7%	1.9%	0.4%	0.3%
Nassau County	121,410	67.9%	14.6%	8.9%	6.5%	1.5%	0.4%	0.3%
New York County	148,981	63.8%	8.7%	8.6%	8.0%	6.8%	1.9%	2.2%
Niagara County	19,504	65.7%	18.1%	9.2%	5.1%	1.9%	0.0%	0.0%
Oneida County	22,344	61.7%	25.3%	6.1%	5.7%	1.1%	0.0%	0.0%
Onondaga County	48,374	64.4%	14.7%	10.6%	6.5%	2.8%	0.5%	0.5%
Ontario County	11,498	70.9%	12.5%	9.0%	7.5%	0.0%	0.0%	0.0%
Orange County	41,203	59.4%	18.8%	9.9%	6.6%	4.4%	0.5%	0.4%
Oswego County	13,878	55.2%	21.0%	11.7%	10.0%	1.3%	0.8%	0.0%
Putnam County	9,244	64.2%	10.6%	9.9%	13.5%	1.7%	0.1%	0.0%
Queens County	196,744	66.6%	13.6%	9.2%	7.5%	2.3%	0.4%	0.3%
Rensselaer County	17,497	64.5%	19.0%	10.8%	5.7%	0.0%	0.0%	0.0%
Richmond County	42,440	73.0%	13.6%	6.0%	6.7%	0.8%	0.0%	0.0%
Rockland County	31,709	74.0%	14.8%	4.1%	3.8%	2.5%	0.8%	0.0%
Saratoga County	15,881	81.3%	12.3%	2.9%	3.5%	0.0%	0.0%	0.0%
Schenectady County	17,709	48.5%	29.7%	9.3%	9.4%	3.0%	0.0%	0.0%
St. Lawrence County	13,854	71.7%	16.8%	6.5%	5.1%	0.0%	0.0%	0.0%
Steuben County	8,644	58.1%	27.3%	8.8%	4.3%	1.1%	0.3%	0.0%
Suffolk County	135,673	62.5%	17.1%	11.1%	6.7%	2.1%	0.5%	0.0%
Tompkins County	30,661	80.0%	7.4%	5.3%	2.0%	4.9%	0.0%	0.4%
Ulster County	19,614	67.8%	18.5%	8.7%	3.5%	1.4%	0.2%	0.0%
Wayne County	7,192	63.8%	13.2%	11.4%	11.7%	0.0%	0.0%	0.0%
Westchester County	88,759	70.5%	13.2%	8.5%	5.3%	1.9%	0.2%	0.4%
North Carolina								
Alamance County	14,754	68.0%	19.2%	9.1%	3.5%	0.2%	0.0%	0.0%
Brunswick County	8,370	56.9%	21.1%	20.1%	1.9%	0.0%	0.0%	0.0%
Buncombe County	21,142	56.7%	27.6%	9.8%	4.9%	1.0%	0.0%	0.0%
Cabarrus County	15,855	59.1%	22.3%	10.8%	6.5%	1.3%	0.0%	0.0%
Catawba County	13,521	60.5%	14.3%	13.3%	8.4%	3.0%	0.6%	0.0%
Cleveland County	9,470	61.9%	20.8%	10.8%	3.8%	2.0%	0.0%	0.6%
Craven County	12,867	47.0%	16.3%	23.7%	10.4%	2.6%	0.0%	0.0%
Cumberland County	40,795	49.0%	24.7%	16.5%	9.2%	0.7%	0.0%	0.0%
Davidson County	12,567	59.3%	20.7%	8.3%	10.4%	1.2%	0.0%	0.0%
Durham County	29,901	60.6%	23.9%	8.3%	6.3%	0.6%	0.0%	0.2%
Forsyth County	34,812	72.4%	13.1%	8.1%	6.5%	0.0%	0.0%	0.0%
Gaston County	17,543	52.7%	26.5%	13.5%	5.7%	1.2%	0.4%	0.0%
Guilford County	53,978	71.5%	17.4%	5.9%	5.1%	0.1%	0.0%	0.0%
Harnett County	13,395	74.0%	9.9%	10.0%	4.3%	1.8%	0.0%	0.0%
Henderson County	7,290	64.1%	15.6%	11.9%	8.4%	0.0%	0.0%	0.0%
Iredell County	14,699	61.4%	21.6%	9.7%	6.7%	0.6%	0.0%	0.0%
Johnston County	14,762	65.4%	13.7%	10.9%	10.0%	0.0%	0.0%	0.0%
Mecklenburg County	95,025	58.3%	20.4%	10.9%	8.2%	1.5%	0.4%	0.2%
Moore County	6,442	68.8%	20.6%	8.2%	2.4%	0.0%	0.0%	0.0%
Nash County	7,992	65.4%	22.4%	11.4%	0.9%	0.0%	0.0%	0.0%
New Hanover County	28,270	68.6%	11.8%	13.3%	4.6%	1.7%	0.0%	0.0%
Onslow County	37,365	32.7%	19.0%	29.9%	15.9%	2.5%	0.0%	0.0%
Orange County	27,135	74.0%	13.9%	7.8%	4.1%	0.0%	0.0%	0.2%
Pitt County	32,609	63.2%	22.6%	10.3%	2.7%	1.2%	0.0%	0.0%
Randolph County	12,051	54.2%	30.2%	11.8%	2.6%	1.1%	0.0%	0.0%
Robeson County	15,277	74.8%	11.0%	8.8%	4.6%	0.9%	0.0%	0.0%
Rockingham County	6,545	58.7%	20.6%	12.3%	8.5%	0.0%	0.0%	0.0%
Rowan County	12,526	49.6%	23.1%	14.2%	12.6%	0.5%	0.0%	0.0%
Union County	20,842	67.8%	14.0%	9.3%	7.0%	2.0%	0.0%	0.0%
Wake County	92,700	67.5%	16.0%	8.5%	6.8%	0.9%	0.0%	0.4%
Wayne County	12,124	57.1%	16.8%	20.7%	4.2%	0.0%	1.2%	0.0%
North Dakota								
Cass County	28,541	43.4%	14.3%	17.2%	22.6%	2.5%	0.0%	0.0%
Ohio								
Allen County	9,702	58.8%	26.6%	5.6%	4.9%	2.0%	2.1%	0.0%
Ashtabula County	7,835	58.2%	19.6%	15.1%	5.3%	0.6%	1.3%	0.0%
Butler County	45,123	65.7%	21.8%	6.7%	4.8%	0.5%	0.5%	0.0%
Clark County	11,991	53.6%	22.1%	13.1%	10.6%	0.6%	0.0%	0.0%

Table I-2: Counties—Income Class by Age—*Continued*

	Total Millennials	Under $10,000	$10,000 to $19,999	$20,000 to $29,999	$30,000 to $49,999	$50,000 to $74,999	$75,000 to $99,999	$100,000 to $149,999	$150,000 or More	Poverty Rate
New Mexico										
Bernalillo County	89,698	27.1%	14.5%	22.9%	21.4%	8.0%	3.9%	2.1%	0.2%	16.2%
Doña Ana County	24,696	35.9%	25.6%	19.3%	12.7%	3.1%	2.2%	1.0%	0.0%	24.1%
San Juan County	16,172	32.9%	24.1%	11.2%	22.4%	7.3%	0.5%	0.8%	0.8%	10.0%
Sandoval County	14,031	43.1%	11.6%	18.7%	14.4%	5.9%	3.5%	1.1%	1.8%	23.7%
Santa Fe County	15,060	27.0%	14.5%	26.2%	20.4%	8.8%	1.6%	0.3%	1.1%	18.4%
New York										
Albany County	35,898	13.3%	18.1%	17.3%	23.5%	22.6%	2.8%	2.4%	0.0%	10.6%
Bronx County	203,054	35.3%	16.9%	13.4%	20.9%	9.4%	2.6%	1.1%	0.4%	23.0%
Broome County	18,852	21.8%	14.8%	20.6%	27.9%	9.0%	4.5%	0.6%	0.7%	15.6%
Chautauqua County	12,863	31.5%	17.1%	24.6%	17.5%	6.7%	1.4%	1.2%	0.0%	15.4%
Dutchess County	30,439	19.0%	8.2%	18.1%	31.4%	13.1%	6.0%	3.5%	0.7%	3.2%
Erie County	116,105	22.9%	15.1%	13.9%	29.0%	14.6%	3.3%	0.9%	0.4%	14.9%
Jefferson County	16,116	23.4%	14.6%	21.1%	20.7%	17.0%	3.3%	0.0%	0.0%	9.4%
Kings County	428,199	25.8%	13.3%	11.9%	20.2%	16.3%	6.5%	3.9%	2.1%	16.5%
Monroe County	94,106	20.7%	13.7%	16.5%	26.8%	17.0%	3.9%	0.6%	0.8%	14.3%
Nassau County	138,159	19.8%	13.2%	10.6%	22.1%	19.0%	7.9%	4.9%	2.5%	5.7%
New York County	339,281	17.3%	8.1%	8.5%	17.2%	19.9%	9.5%	8.8%	10.6%	11.7%
Niagara County	22,101	24.3%	20.8%	21.4%	20.1%	11.5%	1.0%	0.9%	0.0%	24.0%
Oneida County	27,104	29.9%	16.2%	20.5%	19.6%	10.3%	2.1%	0.6%	0.8%	22.4%
Onondaga County	55,218	24.1%	15.7%	18.2%	21.4%	15.3%	3.5%	0.7%	1.1%	19.4%
Ontario County	10,546	18.3%	21.3%	18.4%	22.7%	10.2%	5.1%	4.0%	0.0%	13.0%
Orange County	37,039	25.2%	11.1%	15.3%	25.4%	15.7%	3.9%	2.8%	0.7%	14.4%
Oswego County	13,002	28.6%	16.6%	17.2%	24.0%	12.3%	0.8%	0.5%	0.0%	14.7%
Putnam County	7,803	20.5%	25.2%	5.9%	24.6%	14.2%	2.8%	6.7%	0.0%	3.7%
Queens County	338,427	25.3%	14.1%	15.2%	20.1%	14.5%	6.4%	3.0%	1.3%	11.3%
Rensselaer County	19,891	15.0%	18.5%	14.2%	29.2%	17.6%	2.5%	2.6%	0.4%	8.9%
Richmond County	57,132	29.0%	12.6%	11.2%	19.9%	15.2%	9.2%	2.2%	0.7%	12.9%
Rockland County	32,409	26.3%	15.5%	14.4%	20.3%	12.6%	6.6%	3.0%	1.2%	11.7%
Saratoga County	12,327	33.7%	11.6%	13.9%	27.1%	10.0%	0.8%	2.9%	0.0%	19.4%
Schenectady County	23,614	18.9%	9.7%	10.1%	23.1%	26.4%	7.3%	4.4%	0.0%	5.9%
St. Lawrence County	18,362	24.7%	15.7%	14.0%	19.1%	15.9%	5.3%	4.7%	0.5%	13.5%
Steuben County	9,588	30.7%	16.7%	14.7%	27.4%	7.0%	2.4%	0.0%	1.1%	14.5%
Suffolk County	154,323	22.8%	11.8%	15.9%	22.8%	16.4%	6.8%	2.6%	0.9%	9.4%
Tompkins County	11,325	20.9%	20.0%	15.3%	24.4%	12.5%	3.5%	3.4%	0.0%	19.4%
Ulster County	18,145	23.6%	15.0%	17.9%	24.8%	15.1%	2.3%	0.8%	0.6%	18.9%
Wayne County	9,606	30.1%	18.9%	17.7%	23.5%	8.8%	0.6%	0.0%	0.4%	15.5%
Westchester County	96,832	23.8%	12.9%	12.4%	19.8%	17.7%	6.8%	3.9%	2.7%	11.3%
North Carolina										
Alamance County	16,654	28.2%	16.3%	23.5%	21.6%	6.4%	3.5%	0.6%	0.0%	21.1%
Brunswick County	9,184	26.1%	12.1%	26.3%	22.0%	11.2%	2.2%	0.0%	0.0%	21.8%
Buncombe County	32,129	25.3%	29.5%	14.9%	19.0%	9.3%	0.8%	0.4%	0.7%	21.9%
Cabarrus County	20,760	25.0%	15.1%	17.2%	25.1%	11.6%	4.3%	1.7%	0.0%	13.2%
Catawba County	15,886	28.8%	21.3%	22.4%	20.8%	6.5%	0.3%	1.0%	0.0%	16.1%
Cleveland County	9,222	23.9%	17.3%	23.6%	29.3%	3.5%	1.1%	1.3%	0.0%	14.4%
Craven County	12,859	31.1%	15.0%	14.6%	20.9%	14.5%	3.0%	0.6%	0.3%	10.7%
Cumberland County	48,094	31.5%	16.2%	18.4%	22.0%	8.4%	3.2%	0.3%	0.0%	21.9%
Davidson County	16,728	28.5%	24.0%	21.0%	22.2%	3.8%	0.0%	0.5%	0.0%	17.8%
Durham County	50,048	21.5%	20.5%	15.5%	20.0%	17.1%	3.2%	1.4%	0.8%	13.4%
Forsyth County	43,345	23.0%	15.6%	19.8%	26.7%	9.2%	2.6%	2.3%	0.7%	12.9%
Gaston County	25,240	27.9%	17.8%	20.6%	23.0%	6.5%	1.5%	2.7%	0.0%	19.6%
Guilford County	62,889	25.6%	18.3%	21.9%	24.7%	6.9%	2.3%	0.1%	0.3%	15.6%
Harnett County	17,089	34.7%	11.0%	16.5%	22.2%	13.7%	1.6%	0.3%	0.0%	18.3%
Henderson County	10,238	30.9%	16.9%	23.7%	21.4%	3.4%	1.6%	0.0%	2.1%	12.9%
Iredell County	16,137	26.5%	17.2%	12.5%	19.9%	16.8%	5.7%	1.5%	0.0%	19.1%
Johnston County	18,964	27.4%	17.8%	14.1%	23.1%	10.4%	6.2%	0.0%	1.1%	18.6%
Mecklenburg County	153,249	20.1%	13.5%	15.7%	26.1%	14.9%	5.1%	2.7%	2.0%	14.1%
Moore County	9,173	27.7%	9.3%	16.0%	28.8%	11.1%	2.4%	2.9%	1.8%	19.2%
Nash County	9,719	41.5%	20.1%	24.4%	10.8%	0.0%	0.7%	2.5%	0.0%	20.6%
New Hanover County	26,458	30.1%	15.7%	14.4%	22.1%	12.2%	4.1%	0.5%	0.9%	20.7%
Onslow County	33,337	27.8%	16.8%	20.1%	19.9%	12.6%	2.5%	0.3%	0.0%	22.6%
Orange County	17,241	26.2%	14.5%	18.9%	31.4%	6.3%	0.5%	1.9%	0.3%	22.7%
Pitt County	22,584	28.1%	19.2%	15.0%	28.9%	7.2%	1.5%	0.0%	0.0%	32.8%
Randolph County	14,689	20.3%	18.6%	19.8%	33.6%	7.6%	0.0%	0.0%	0.0%	12.7%
Robeson County	13,861	45.3%	17.7%	7.8%	24.0%	4.1%	1.0%	0.0%	0.0%	36.4%
Rockingham County	8,972	24.7%	30.9%	15.1%	25.7%	2.6%	0.4%	0.6%	0.0%	25.8%
Rowan County	14,692	32.8%	14.1%	15.7%	28.0%	5.6%	0.0%	3.8%	0.0%	21.0%
Union County	18,713	25.2%	23.3%	11.9%	23.5%	10.8%	4.4%	0.0%	0.8%	14.7%
Wake County	135,921	20.4%	12.5%	14.7%	27.1%	15.0%	6.1%	3.8%	0.4%	11.5%
Wayne County	16,422	28.5%	17.8%	19.2%	19.8%	14.1%	0.0%	0.6%	0.0%	18.8%
North Dakota										
Cass County	24,162	8.2%	18.7%	19.1%	31.3%	12.6%	4.5%	5.6%	0.0%	10.6%
Ohio										
Allen County	11,532	24.1%	22.7%	14.8%	25.8%	10.1%	0.7%	1.0%	0.7%	19.7%
Ashtabula County	9,787	27.3%	19.9%	23.7%	15.9%	8.0%	4.4%	0.8%	0.0%	16.0%
Butler County	39,877	26.5%	19.0%	13.3%	25.6%	12.1%	2.5%	0.8%	0.3%	17.4%
Clark County	13,749	23.1%	18.5%	16.5%	24.8%	14.2%	1.8%	0.5%	0.6%	14.2%

Table I-2: Counties—Income Class by Age—*Continued*

			Personal Income, Percent by Income Class, ages 18 to 24					
	Total Millennials	Under $10,000	$10,000 to $19,999	$20,000 to $29,999	$30,000 to $49,999	$50,000 to $74,999	$75,000 to $99,999	$100,000 or More
Ohio—Cont.								
Clermont County	15,117	49.4%	25.9%	15.0%	9.7%	0.1%	0.0%	0.0%
Columbiana County	7,504	61.8%	19.8%	9.6%	7.9%	0.9%	0.0%	0.0%
Cuyahoga County	113,117	60.2%	21.1%	11.2%	5.9%	1.3%	0.1%	0.1%
Delaware County	14,652	58.1%	30.2%	7.2%	1.8%	2.7%	0.0%	0.0%
Fairfield County	12,289	50.1%	30.8%	12.5%	6.6%	0.0%	0.0%	0.0%
Franklin County	120,906	53.8%	20.1%	14.6%	8.5%	3.0%	0.0%	0.0%
Geauga County	7,905	65.9%	22.5%	6.0%	5.7%	0.0%	0.0%	0.0%
Greene County	20,661	62.8%	19.8%	7.3%	9.2%	1.0%	0.0%	0.0%
Hamilton County	72,838	57.8%	22.1%	10.2%	6.9%	2.7%	0.2%	0.0%
Lake County	18,278	42.2%	26.4%	7.6%	19.0%	4.5%	0.0%	0.4%
Licking County	15,948	67.2%	19.8%	8.7%	2.9%	1.1%	0.0%	0.3%
Lorain County	26,120	57.2%	26.9%	8.3%	7.1%	0.4%	0.0%	0.0%
Lucas County	41,038	62.1%	20.8%	9.1%	7.1%	0.7%	0.0%	0.2%
Mahoning County	20,268	62.8%	23.5%	8.0%	4.7%	0.7%	0.2%	0.0%
Medina County	13,547	66.6%	16.3%	9.0%	6.1%	2.0%	0.0%	0.0%
Miami County	7,784	40.5%	18.8%	27.5%	10.0%	3.2%	0.0%	0.0%
Montgomery County	47,493	60.6%	19.9%	11.8%	6.6%	0.6%	0.5%	0.0%
Portage County	27,140	73.9%	14.4%	6.2%	3.4%	2.1%	0.0%	0.0%
Richland County	10,805	58.5%	19.5%	14.5%	7.5%	0.0%	0.0%	0.0%
Stark County	32,535	56.0%	22.5%	15.0%	3.9%	2.2%	0.2%	0.2%
Summit County	47,666	56.5%	24.0%	9.8%	8.2%	1.0%	0.2%	0.3%
Trumbull County	17,104	51.9%	27.9%	15.2%	3.5%	0.5%	0.6%	0.5%
Tuscarawas County	7,080	51.3%	23.7%	16.9%	6.2%	1.9%	0.0%	0.0%
Warren County	17,277	56.1%	30.1%	8.6%	2.9%	2.3%	0.0%	0.0%
Wayne County	11,242	59.9%	13.5%	9.7%	15.9%	1.1%	0.0%	0.0%
Wood County	17,983	58.1%	23.4%	10.8%	5.8%	1.9%	0.0%	0.0%
Oklahoma								
Canadian County	10,745	47.5%	31.7%	7.5%	12.5%	0.8%	0.0%	0.0%
Cleveland County	39,790	60.2%	19.4%	14.2%	4.7%	1.6%	0.0%	0.0%
Comanche County	14,998	53.6%	14.8%	20.9%	10.6%	0.1%	0.0%	0.0%
Oklahoma County	70,303	48.9%	25.1%	14.6%	8.3%	3.0%	0.1%	0.0%
Tulsa County	58,292	51.0%	22.3%	14.6%	9.6%	1.9%	0.1%	0.4%
Oregon								
Clackamas County	32,507	60.0%	18.8%	11.4%	9.3%	0.5%	0.0%	0.0%
Deschutes County	12,522	52.3%	22.4%	11.0%	5.3%	4.9%	4.0%	0.0%
Douglas County	7,578	65.7%	13.9%	10.8%	9.5%	0.0%	0.0%	0.0%
Jackson County	16,260	65.9%	12.8%	11.7%	9.6%	0.0%	0.0%	0.0%
Lane County	46,498	63.8%	20.1%	11.5%	3.4%	1.3%	0.0%	0.0%
Linn County	12,827	59.1%	19.8%	12.0%	4.9%	4.1%	0.0%	0.0%
Marion County	32,049	57.2%	18.8%	16.9%	4.3%	2.6%	0.2%	0.0%
Multnomah County	64,956	58.3%	20.4%	12.6%	5.9%	2.0%	0.8%	0.0%
Washington County	46,192	61.7%	18.2%	9.8%	7.9%	2.3%	0.1%	0.0%
Yamhill County	11,578	52.9%	13.0%	21.8%	12.3%	0.0%	0.0%	0.0%
Pennsylvania								
Adams County	8,558	55.4%	30.1%	4.2%	8.2%	2.1%	0.0%	0.0%
Allegheny County	110,343	65.0%	18.2%	8.2%	6.8%	1.4%	0.2%	0.1%
Beaver County	12,689	57.9%	16.1%	17.9%	4.9%	3.3%	0.0%	0.0%
Berks County	41,286	59.9%	19.9%	12.6%	6.4%	1.2%	0.0%	0.0%
Blair County	9,841	72.1%	11.0%	5.9%	4.9%	6.1%	0.0%	0.0%
Bucks County	49,616	63.4%	14.5%	12.2%	6.4%	2.3%	0.4%	0.9%
Butler County	16,278	69.1%	13.4%	8.8%	5.6%	1.8%	1.3%	0.0%
Cambria County	12,403	75.8%	16.1%	5.1%	1.2%	1.8%	0.0%	0.0%
Centre County	41,020	70.3%	12.4%	11.7%	4.8%	0.5%	0.4%	0.0%
Chester County	46,694	61.4%	16.2%	11.8%	9.3%	0.3%	0.8%	0.2%
Cumberland County	24,633	48.5%	20.6%	13.4%	12.8%	3.5%	1.2%	0.0%
Dauphin County	26,451	57.4%	19.3%	9.3%	12.5%	1.5%	0.0%	0.0%
Delaware County	57,565	68.1%	16.5%	9.7%	5.1%	0.5%	0.0%	0.0%
Erie County	28,432	63.8%	22.1%	6.6%	6.4%	1.2%	0.0%	0.0%
Fayette County	9,656	54.8%	19.8%	11.7%	10.6%	3.1%	0.0%	0.0%
Franklin County	14,051	64.9%	19.0%	7.5%	7.6%	1.1%	0.0%	0.0%
Lackawanna County	19,620	66.0%	17.6%	9.1%	6.8%	0.5%	0.0%	0.0%
Lancaster County	49,519	57.8%	18.5%	13.1%	6.9%	3.0%	0.7%	0.0%
Lebanon County	12,415	56.6%	14.9%	9.0%	18.5%	1.1%	0.0%	0.0%
Lehigh County	33,016	64.9%	19.9%	6.8%	5.8%	1.6%	0.7%	0.3%
Luzerne County	31,241	74.6%	12.1%	7.6%	3.4%	2.3%	0.0%	0.0%
Lycoming County	12,018	67.1%	18.3%	9.5%	4.3%	0.6%	0.1%	0.0%
Mercer County	10,204	70.1%	14.6%	7.8%	7.1%	0.1%	0.3%	0.0%
Monroe County	18,241	69.7%	16.8%	8.5%	1.7%	1.6%	1.0%	0.8%
Montgomery County	65,670	69.6%	12.0%	9.4%	7.3%	1.6%	0.0%	0.0%
Northampton County	31,759	57.1%	19.1%	14.2%	8.1%	1.0%	0.5%	0.0%
Northumberland County	6,642	53.7%	24.4%	11.1%	8.4%	1.0%	1.4%	0.0%
Philadelphia County	165,336	70.2%	14.4%	7.2%	5.7%	2.4%	0.1%	0.0%
Schuylkill County	10,180	63.2%	14.4%	16.3%	4.6%	1.4%	0.0%	0.0%
Washington County	18,388	58.3%	18.8%	14.0%	6.6%	1.8%	0.4%	0.0%
Westmoreland County	28,973	60.9%	16.4%	7.9%	10.7%	3.6%	0.6%	0.0%
York County	34,225	53.7%	27.7%	9.9%	6.4%	2.4%	0.0%	0.0%

Table I-2: Counties—Income Class by Age—*Continued*

	Personal Income, Percent by Income Class, ages 25 to 33								
	Total Millennials	Under $10,000	$10,000 to $19,999	$20,000 to $29,999	$30,000 to $49,999	$50,000 to $74,999	$75,000 to $99,999	$100,000 to $149,999	$150,000 or More	Poverty Rate
Ohio—Cont.										
Clermont County	23,530	21.7%	12.1%	11.1%	29.5%	20.9%	4.2%	0.3%	0.3%	13.0%
Columbiana County	9,881	36.5%	15.4%	20.8%	14.2%	6.7%	5.7%	0.7%	0.0%	17.9%
Cuyahoga County	147,659	25.2%	16.6%	15.7%	23.8%	12.4%	3.7%	2.1%	0.5%	17.1%
Delaware County	16,882	14.7%	10.7%	12.1%	28.1%	14.8%	7.8%	11.1%	0.6%	6.4%
Fairfield County	14,860	28.2%	13.2%	16.6%	19.0%	18.8%	4.3%	0.0%	0.0%	11.9%
Franklin County	202,024	19.4%	14.6%	15.6%	26.5%	16.1%	4.9%	1.9%	1.0%	13.5%
Geauga County	6,927	16.0%	12.2%	24.3%	30.5%	13.9%	2.4%	0.6%	0.0%	2.9%
Greene County	19,019	20.8%	17.7%	10.0%	28.2%	16.0%	3.0%	4.2%	0.0%	14.6%
Hamilton County	107,089	19.6%	16.7%	17.0%	24.7%	14.4%	4.6%	2.0%	1.1%	15.2%
Lake County	21,640	20.1%	12.5%	19.8%	23.1%	16.2%	6.2%	1.1%	0.9%	11.9%
Licking County	17,374	16.6%	17.9%	22.0%	25.0%	16.5%	0.7%	1.2%	0.0%	18.6%
Lorain County	30,309	25.7%	20.5%	14.3%	24.6%	11.4%	2.6%	0.9%	0.0%	22.1%
Lucas County	54,283	23.9%	18.5%	17.2%	23.0%	13.2%	1.5%	2.0%	0.7%	18.7%
Mahoning County	25,603	22.9%	29.3%	15.9%	22.7%	6.3%	2.2%	0.4%	0.3%	18.4%
Medina County	17,648	27.8%	18.6%	14.4%	16.1%	19.2%	3.0%	0.8%	0.0%	12.9%
Miami County	10,561	21.9%	20.7%	9.0%	23.2%	22.6%	1.2%	1.0%	0.6%	12.9%
Montgomery County	64,115	29.2%	14.3%	16.2%	24.5%	11.8%	3.5%	0.4%	0.1%	20.9%
Portage County	16,223	22.4%	22.4%	16.4%	22.5%	15.2%	1.0%	0.0%	0.0%	19.1%
Richland County	12,484	42.5%	22.1%	11.9%	17.1%	2.8%	1.3%	2.4%	0.0%	26.9%
Stark County	40,681	27.1%	17.7%	10.7%	25.3%	15.4%	2.6%	0.8%	0.3%	18.4%
Summit County	61,441	23.8%	17.0%	17.2%	23.1%	14.4%	1.7%	2.4%	0.5%	15.3%
Trumbull County	18,634	27.7%	20.3%	18.0%	29.6%	3.8%	0.0%	0.6%	0.0%	23.8%
Tuscarawas County	9,522	28.5%	13.4%	12.3%	25.6%	12.6%	6.2%	1.2%	0.2%	12.8%
Warren County	21,167	23.1%	13.1%	12.5%	27.5%	11.5%	8.1%	4.1%	0.1%	3.8%
Wayne County	11,235	19.5%	19.1%	17.2%	30.3%	11.5%	0.0%	0.0%	2.3%	5.7%
Wood County	18,327	21.6%	16.2%	14.9%	22.1%	19.4%	0.6%	4.2%	1.0%	10.8%
Oklahoma										
Canadian County	16,997	24.7%	24.2%	12.0%	16.6%	19.9%	0.0%	2.0%	0.6%	15.6%
Cleveland County	37,668	19.0%	13.5%	16.8%	28.8%	18.0%	3.5%	0.3%	0.0%	9.9%
Comanche County	19,817	23.8%	20.5%	21.9%	24.2%	2.1%	1.5%	2.4%	3.7%	17.2%
Oklahoma County	111,707	23.1%	18.0%	17.9%	24.3%	9.7%	3.3%	2.6%	1.0%	17.8%
Tulsa County	81,376	23.0%	15.0%	18.2%	26.5%	11.1%	2.8%	2.8%	0.6%	19.2%
Oregon										
Clackamas County	41,000	28.1%	13.3%	13.3%	20.9%	17.3%	4.0%	1.8%	1.4%	12.9%
Deschutes County	19,618	17.5%	21.5%	15.3%	21.9%	11.6%	7.3%	0.8%	4.0%	16.3%
Douglas County	10,988	32.3%	14.5%	24.9%	16.3%	11.6%	0.0%	0.0%	0.5%	27.8%
Jackson County	24,414	37.0%	20.3%	17.1%	17.0%	7.4%	1.3%	0.0%	0.0%	27.0%
Lane County	42,066	27.8%	20.5%	17.3%	23.5%	7.1%	2.6%	1.3%	0.0%	21.7%
Linn County	11,296	25.2%	26.8%	20.4%	16.4%	6.4%	3.7%	1.0%	0.0%	20.6%
Marion County	38,868	26.0%	16.6%	19.7%	25.3%	0.1%	0.0%	0.4%	0.0%	17.0%
Multnomah County	130,045	22.0%	15.3%	17.9%	23.3%	12.4%	4.4%	2.3%	2.3%	17.8%
Washington County	78,390	24.1%	14.6%	16.8%	19.0%	14.1%	6.8%	3.5%	1.2%	10.7%
Yamhill County	10,384	31.2%	20.1%	20.4%	18.1%	7.5%	1.0%	1.7%	0.0%	19.1%
Pennsylvania										
Adams County	10,662	17.6%	21.4%	16.0%	23.6%	16.7%	2.9%	0.0%	1.7%	10.0%
Allegheny County	166,066	21.0%	13.0%	16.1%	24.6%	15.6%	6.0%	2.8%	0.9%	13.5%
Beaver County	18,443	18.9%	14.4%	20.1%	25.3%	14.2%	5.7%	1.5%	0.0%	16.6%
Berks County	44,483	24.0%	12.0%	17.8%	23.4%	17.2%	2.5%	2.3%	0.7%	13.6%
Blair County	13,578	23.8%	24.4%	14.2%	23.3%	9.6%	3.1%	0.5%	1.0%	18.3%
Bucks County	59,844	23.2%	11.5%	11.2%	25.4%	15.8%	7.8%	4.4%	0.7%	6.4%
Butler County	19,823	15.8%	13.3%	16.3%	24.4%	19.6%	8.0%	2.7%	0.0%	10.8%
Cambria County	12,887	26.9%	16.7%	13.8%	15.9%	23.3%	1.3%	1.7%	0.4%	22.5%
Centre County	22,204	24.4%	10.3%	11.9%	33.7%	16.8%	2.5%	0.2%	0.2%	5.6%
Chester County	51,777	16.9%	9.1%	18.4%	17.9%	22.6%	10.3%	3.6%	1.3%	6.0%
Cumberland County	26,980	20.4%	9.2%	20.5%	28.5%	16.7%	3.3%	1.0%	0.4%	5.8%
Dauphin County	29,124	16.6%	13.9%	18.8%	32.3%	14.9%	1.0%	2.4%	0.2%	10.2%
Delaware County	63,379	26.4%	13.8%	12.5%	22.0%	15.6%	7.4%	2.2%	0.2%	15.2%
Erie County	31,135	24.9%	15.7%	21.0%	24.9%	10.4%	2.5%	0.6%	0.0%	17.7%
Fayette County	13,469	47.0%	7.1%	12.1%	16.7%	13.4%	1.9%	1.9%	0.0%	23.4%
Franklin County	15,211	13.6%	19.6%	16.3%	33.4%	11.9%	5.3%	0.0%	0.0%	9.4%
Lackawanna County	22,958	26.4%	12.3%	13.6%	29.7%	13.0%	1.5%	3.3%	0.2%	15.7%
Lancaster County	58,006	26.0%	11.0%	16.2%	24.8%	15.0%	3.7%	2.6%	0.5%	14.9%
Lebanon County	12,915	20.9%	8.7%	26.8%	26.2%	11.0%	2.5%	2.7%	1.1%	10.3%
Lehigh County	41,803	23.9%	12.9%	19.1%	26.7%	11.1%	3.0%	2.2%	1.0%	14.3%
Luzerne County	32,819	23.7%	13.8%	17.6%	31.0%	11.9%	1.4%	0.4%	0.1%	18.2%
Lycoming County	12,412	35.5%	12.3%	14.4%	21.0%	8.4%	6.8%	1.3%	0.2%	19.2%
Mercer County	10,723	26.6%	18.8%	18.9%	29.5%	6.1%	0.0%	0.0%	0.0%	13.0%
Monroe County	16,475	31.8%	5.8%	30.8%	19.4%	8.2%	0.6%	3.4%	0.0%	13.8%
Montgomery County	91,032	22.0%	11.2%	12.5%	21.9%	18.1%	9.8%	3.2%	1.2%	8.9%
Northampton County	29,745	16.1%	16.0%	18.8%	21.9%	19.8%	5.3%	2.0%	0.0%	11.1%
Northumberland County	10,582	22.2%	17.2%	24.2%	18.4%	13.0%	4.9%	0.1%	0.0%	8.8%
Philadelphia County	266,596	27.1%	12.0%	14.8%	23.0%	14.8%	4.6%	2.4%	1.2%	20.1%
Schuylkill County	14,846	25.2%	11.9%	10.5%	29.8%	17.2%	4.6%	0.2%	0.6%	15.6%
Washington County	20,742	20.2%	12.6%	12.7%	32.3%	13.2%	5.2%	2.6%	1.2%	7.9%
Westmoreland County	31,727	25.1%	15.3%	13.6%	28.5%	10.5%	4.3%	1.9%	0.8%	15.3%
York County	50,402	22.0%	14.2%	23.2%	21.0%	16.1%	1.8%	1.6%	0.0%	7.2%

Table I-2: Counties—Income Class by Age—*Continued*

	Total Millennials	Under $10,000	$10,000 to $19,999	$20,000 to $29,999	$30,000 to $49,999	$50,000 to $74,999	$75,000 to $99,999	$100,000 or More
Rhode Island								
Kent County	11,627	52.7%	19.1%	10.5%	17.7%	0.0%	0.0%	0.0%
Providence County	70,500	62.3%	17.7%	10.1%	8.0%	1.6%	0.1%	0.2%
Washington County	17,643	60.7%	27.2%	7.0%	3.7%	1.4%	0.0%	0.0%
South Carolina								
Aiken County	14,965	61.9%	26.7%	4.6%	6.0%	0.8%	0.0%	0.0%
Anderson County	17,655	52.3%	23.4%	15.5%	5.8%	3.0%	0.0%	0.0%
Beaufort County	16,479	44.9%	29.4%	17.2%	8.5%	0.0%	0.0%	0.0%
Berkeley County	17,806	66.2%	17.8%	11.0%	3.6%	1.0%	0.2%	0.3%
Charleston County	38,878	63.5%	15.6%	13.2%	4.9%	2.1%	0.3%	0.4%
Dorchester County	12,198	62.6%	19.0%	13.4%	4.0%	1.0%	0.0%	0.0%
Florence County	13,112	61.4%	19.9%	12.4%	6.3%	0.0%	0.0%	0.0%
Greenville County	47,357	64.6%	17.0%	8.0%	7.1%	3.4%	0.0%	0.0%
Horry County	24,882	54.6%	30.2%	11.4%	3.5%	0.2%	0.0%	0.0%
Lexington County	23,719	61.4%	21.7%	8.1%	7.4%	1.4%	0.0%	0.0%
Pickens County	18,664	65.7%	20.5%	7.8%	6.0%	0.0%	0.0%	0.0%
Richland County	64,258	58.0%	23.2%	11.8%	4.9%	0.6%	1.1%	0.3%
Spartanburg County	28,689	54.8%	22.8%	12.5%	8.1%	1.8%	0.0%	0.0%
Sumter County	13,392	63.8%	14.4%	15.4%	5.8%	0.5%	0.0%	0.0%
York County	22,732	62.2%	19.4%	13.1%	3.0%	1.4%	0.0%	1.0%
South Dakota								
Minnehaha County	15,505	61.0%	18.2%	13.3%	6.4%	0.4%	0.8%	0.0%
Pennington County	8,522	52.4%	21.5%	15.0%	9.5%	1.5%	0.0%	0.0%
Tennessee								
Blount County	10,726	68.7%	15.7%	11.0%	4.3%	0.4%	0.0%	0.0%
Bradley County	10,032	54.6%	18.2%	18.4%	4.3%	4.5%	0.0%	0.0%
Davidson County	69,835	49.1%	21.2%	12.8%	12.6%	3.7%	0.6%	0.0%
Hamilton County	32,702	66.4%	16.9%	9.4%	5.9%	0.2%	1.0%	0.2%
Knox County	56,420	61.8%	16.8%	12.5%	8.3%	0.5%	0.1%	0.0%
Madison County	10,544	70.8%	8.1%	16.5%	4.6%	0.0%	0.0%	0.0%
Montgomery County	22,027	49.8%	15.8%	14.3%	18.0%	1.7%	0.0%	0.5%
Rutherford County	39,666	55.0%	22.5%	10.5%	9.9%	0.9%	1.1%	0.0%
Sevier County	8,480	45.6%	32.3%	6.5%	13.5%	2.1%	0.0%	0.0%
Shelby County	91,576	66.0%	19.7%	9.4%	3.8%	0.3%	0.1%	0.8%
Sullivan County	12,331	71.8%	17.7%	6.5%	4.0%	0.0%	0.0%	0.0%
Sumner County	14,595	56.6%	22.4%	9.7%	10.4%	0.8%	0.0%	0.0%
Washington County	15,505	73.6%	17.8%	7.1%	1.5%	0.0%	0.0%	0.0%
Williamson County	15,560	59.6%	19.5%	10.8%	3.5%	6.2%	0.4%	0.0%
Wilson County	10,983	63.9%	15.1%	11.8%	8.6%	0.0%	0.6%	0.0%
Texas								
Bell County	40,033	46.5%	22.9%	23.1%	6.6%	0.5%	0.0%	0.4%
Bexar County	195,287	54.5%	22.4%	14.6%	5.9%	2.3%	0.2%	0.0%
Bowie County	8,627	74.3%	16.9%	6.6%	1.6%	0.6%	0.0%	0.0%
Brazoria County	29,299	61.7%	17.4%	7.0%	10.4%	2.5%	0.5%	0.5%
Brazos County	58,803	71.0%	16.7%	6.2%	4.7%	1.0%	0.0%	0.3%
Cameron County	44,967	67.0%	21.0%	8.6%	2.8%	0.4%	0.1%	0.0%
Collin County	71,235	61.2%	18.4%	10.5%	7.7%	1.9%	0.3%	0.0%
Comal County	10,469	61.2%	18.6%	13.6%	5.9%	0.8%	0.0%	0.0%
Dallas County	247,751	52.3%	20.9%	14.7%	9.4%	1.7%	0.9%	0.1%
Denton County	72,368	58.5%	16.5%	15.1%	8.0%	1.8%	0.0%	0.0%
Ector County	18,034	49.4%	19.4%	10.9%	13.7%	2.5%	2.6%	1.6%
El Paso County	14,510	53.5%	17.1%	15.2%	13.1%	1.0%	0.0%	0.0%
Ellis County	94,081	61.6%	18.4%	12.3%	5.5%	1.5%	0.5%	0.0%
Fort Bend County	60,267	66.7%	20.1%	5.7%	4.1%	3.5%	0.0%	0.0%
Galveston County	28,761	62.2%	21.7%	10.1%	3.7%	1.8%	0.6%	0.0%
Grayson County	12,296	63.7%	14.3%	15.4%	5.6%	1.0%	0.0%	0.0%
Gregg County	12,091	48.2%	28.2%	11.7%	8.7%	3.2%	0.0%	0.0%
Guadalupe County	12,985	62.2%	19.6%	3.8%	9.5%	3.9%	0.0%	1.0%
Harris County	431,721	56.0%	19.1%	11.6%	8.5%	3.7%	0.8%	0.3%
Hays County	34,323	55.1%	19.3%	16.0%	8.4%	0.6%	0.0%	0.7%
Hidalgo County	93,515	74.6%	14.4%	5.7%	4.1%	1.2%	0.1%	0.0%
Jefferson County	23,959	57.9%	22.1%	8.2%	9.2%	2.4%	0.0%	0.3%
Johnson County	14,217	60.8%	14.1%	19.8%	5.2%	0.2%	0.0%	0.0%
Kaufman County	9,480	67.9%	17.9%	4.5%	6.9%	2.8%	0.0%	0.0%
Lubbock County	50,728	64.4%	19.0%	7.6%	7.2%	0.9%	1.0%	0.0%
McLennan County	35,986	68.1%	17.0%	8.9%	4.1%	1.9%	0.0%	0.0%
Midland County	16,182	46.7%	10.3%	13.2%	16.8%	8.1%	4.9%	0.0%
Montgomery County	46,093	63.1%	14.6%	11.6%	6.8%	1.7%	2.2%	0.0%
Nueces County	36,530	64.0%	15.3%	12.2%	3.6%	4.9%	0.0%	0.0%
Parker County	10,442	50.6%	21.7%	22.3%	3.8%	1.6%	0.0%	0.0%
Potter County	11,257	57.7%	18.5%	10.2%	11.5%	2.0%	0.0%	0.0%
Randall County	13,490	53.1%	26.3%	11.9%	7.0%	1.7%	0.0%	0.0%
Smith County	23,359	62.3%	20.6%	9.2%	6.0%	0.6%	1.2%	0.0%
Tarrant County	183,333	56.5%	19.3%	13.4%	8.5%	1.9%	0.1%	0.2%
Taylor County	20,854	49.2%	17.5%	18.7%	13.2%	1.4%	0.0%	0.0%
Tom Green County	14,946	59.1%	14.9%	21.6%	3.9%	0.5%	0.0%	0.0%

Table I-2: Counties—Income Class by Age—*Continued*

	Personal Income, Percent by Income Class, ages 25 to 33									
	Total Millennials	Under $10,000	$10,000 to $19,999	$20,000 to $29,999	$30,000 to $49,999	$50,000 to $74,999	$75,000 to $99,999	$100,000 to $149,999	$150,000 or More	Poverty Rate
Rhode Island										
Kent County	20,408	24.8%	9.8%	12.8%	34.6%	13.6%	2.9%	1.0%	0.4%	10.5%
Providence County	84,965	24.6%	18.2%	13.6%	24.6%	13.2%	3.1%	2.2%	0.5%	16.9%
Washington County	10,535	25.0%	13.1%	13.9%	25.0%	16.0%	3.6%	1.1%	2.5%	14.9%
South Carolina										
Aiken County	18,220	34.2%	22.8%	12.1%	21.0%	9.5%	0.5%	0.0%	0.0%	20.3%
Anderson County	17,931	33.7%	15.5%	16.4%	22.0%	8.6%	3.2%	0.0%	0.5%	28.6%
Beaufort County	20,810	20.7%	23.5%	18.4%	30.7%	4.4%	0.4%	0.4%	1.6%	16.2%
Berkeley County	28,825	28.2%	10.1%	16.8%	19.8%	13.3%	7.2%	1.7%	2.9%	11.5%
Charleston County	56,973	22.9%	9.8%	16.3%	28.0%	13.7%	4.4%	2.8%	2.3%	14.1%
Dorchester County	22,400	31.5%	13.4%	15.5%	20.0%	13.0%	4.9%	0.4%	1.2%	15.7%
Florence County	15,454	29.5%	23.2%	14.7%	24.2%	5.0%	2.3%	0.6%	0.4%	14.1%
Greenville County	60,082	27.0%	13.8%	18.6%	24.2%	11.5%	3.1%	1.6%	0.2%	14.8%
Horry County	33,554	29.3%	16.3%	19.0%	21.3%	11.5%	1.6%	1.1%	0.0%	15.7%
Lexington County	34,276	18.2%	15.4%	19.8%	29.6%	10.3%	3.3%	2.1%	1.2%	12.9%
Pickens County	15,557	25.3%	15.8%	19.2%	30.4%	8.5%	0.4%	0.0%	0.5%	16.6%
Richland County	52,538	21.4%	14.9%	24.9%	23.9%	10.9%	2.4%	0.7%	0.9%	11.7%
Spartanburg County	33,740	31.2%	15.4%	17.4%	27.9%	5.2%	1.1%	1.2%	0.6%	15.1%
Sumter County	12,191	39.9%	14.6%	23.5%	14.2%	6.7%	1.1%	0.0%	0.0%	28.4%
York County	27,355	22.3%	17.7%	11.8%	25.6%	17.1%	4.6%	0.9%	0.0%	14.8%
South Dakota										
Minnehaha County	29,060	15.5%	11.1%	22.0%	41.0%	7.4%	1.1%	2.0%	0.0%	11.9%
Pennington County	14,959	15.4%	23.4%	21.3%	26.8%	6.6%	3.5%	2.6%	0.5%	19.4%
Tennessee										
Blount County	12,700	23.8%	21.0%	15.9%	27.7%	9.0%	0.3%	2.3%	0.0%	15.7%
Bradley County	12,385	35.9%	15.1%	18.1%	22.3%	5.5%	0.9%	1.0%	1.2%	28.4%
Davidson County	116,613	19.9%	14.3%	15.6%	27.2%	15.4%	4.2%	2.9%	0.5%	14.4%
Hamilton County	44,034	25.6%	16.1%	20.6%	21.7%	8.7%	3.3%	3.7%	0.2%	10.0%
Knox County	52,327	26.7%	16.9%	15.4%	23.2%	11.8%	2.6%	2.7%	0.7%	22.4%
Madison County	10,779	35.5%	17.9%	25.6%	13.4%	5.3%	1.9%	0.0%	0.4%	25.0%
Montgomery County	35,085	25.8%	13.5%	19.5%	27.4%	8.5%	2.6%	2.7%	0.0%	9.2%
Rutherford County	37,880	22.4%	12.5%	18.6%	30.3%	12.1%	1.7%	2.5%	0.0%	8.2%
Sevier County	8,556	41.1%	15.2%	19.4%	18.1%	5.2%	0.0%	0.0%	0.9%	31.9%
Shelby County	123,261	28.2%	17.8%	19.3%	19.4%	9.8%	3.4%	1.9%	0.3%	18.6%
Sullivan County	14,272	35.9%	20.4%	15.2%	19.4%	7.4%	1.4%	0.0%	0.4%	20.4%
Sumner County	19,760	21.9%	12.8%	20.8%	22.9%	14.8%	3.5%	3.3%	0.0%	8.4%
Washington County	13,799	40.1%	14.9%	14.6%	14.7%	10.2%	5.5%	0.0%	0.0%	26.7%
Williamson County	14,755	28.3%	9.0%	9.5%	12.3%	21.9%	7.4%	7.4%	4.2%	4.3%
Wilson County	12,081	21.2%	13.5%	8.2%	32.8%	13.0%	5.5%	5.9%	0.0%	3.9%
Texas										
Bell County	51,420	28.8%	13.3%	20.8%	22.1%	11.5%	3.4%	0.0%	0.0%	18.1%
Bexar County	265,647	25.8%	16.5%	17.7%	23.5%	11.1%	3.4%	1.4%	0.5%	14.7%
Bowie County	10,857	38.9%	21.5%	12.6%	17.4%	9.5%	0.0%	0.0%	0.0%	25.1%
Brazoria County	42,280	20.2%	12.7%	7.9%	28.2%	19.1%	7.4%	4.6%	0.0%	7.3%
Brazos County	31,962	25.9%	21.5%	20.5%	18.8%	8.8%	1.1%	0.9%	2.5%	22.6%
Cameron County	46,269	36.1%	21.7%	13.2%	18.0%	7.3%	1.6%	1.8%	0.2%	31.0%
Collin County	102,770	19.0%	11.8%	12.1%	24.2%	19.3%	7.9%	4.2%	1.6%	8.3%
Comal County	12,595	21.5%	14.1%	20.1%	19.5%	17.7%	2.4%	4.1%	0.5%	7.6%
Dallas County	361,996	23.8%	14.6%	17.1%	24.1%	12.9%	3.8%	2.4%	1.2%	15.7%
Denton County	104,559	19.6%	11.8%	17.6%	25.2%	15.6%	6.0%	3.1%	1.2%	7.2%
Ector County	24,031	25.8%	11.5%	13.2%	18.7%	14.2%	7.5%	7.7%	1.3%	9.1%
El Paso County	17,753	22.4%	19.2%	18.3%	23.6%	13.1%	1.8%	1.4%	0.3%	14.9%
Ellis County	110,389	26.7%	15.4%	21.8%	22.1%	10.2%	2.2%	1.3%	0.3%	15.8%
Fort Bend County	79,344	26.2%	12.8%	14.5%	22.3%	10.1%	6.7%	5.9%	1.5%	6.7%
Galveston County	36,906	25.7%	12.1%	11.1%	20.3%	18.0%	6.9%	4.9%	1.0%	13.4%
Grayson County	12,857	20.9%	16.4%	16.5%	29.1%	15.3%	1.6%	0.1%	0.0%	15.8%
Gregg County	14,705	31.5%	21.4%	11.3%	19.8%	11.8%	3.0%	1.2%	0.0%	14.9%
Guadalupe County	17,571	26.5%	9.3%	20.4%	19.8%	17.0%	3.9%	2.2%	0.8%	13.0%
Harris County	649,252	24.7%	15.3%	14.9%	21.6%	14.2%	4.7%	3.3%	1.4%	14.9%
Hays County	25,058	21.3%	14.7%	11.2%	27.9%	20.8%	1.3%	2.8%	0.1%	12.8%
Hidalgo County	98,073	38.3%	20.9%	18.4%	14.4%	4.5%	1.5%	1.1%	0.9%	29.5%
Jefferson County	33,763	40.9%	12.2%	8.0%	24.1%	10.6%	1.8%	1.9%	0.4%	20.3%
Johnson County	17,692	28.4%	16.1%	14.4%	24.2%	9.0%	4.7%	1.5%	1.7%	12.8%
Kaufman County	13,508	34.9%	8.1%	11.0%	18.5%	19.5%	6.6%	1.3%	0.2%	9.7%
Lubbock County	40,214	23.0%	16.3%	24.1%	20.1%	11.7%	1.0%	2.4%	1.4%	16.2%
McLennan County	28,137	30.8%	15.9%	18.3%	15.3%	15.7%	2.5%	0.6%	1.0%	18.9%
Midland County	25,270	17.5%	8.7%	11.7%	27.7%	10.4%	11.8%	10.3%	1.9%	5.6%
Montgomery County	58,593	26.1%	13.1%	10.7%	21.6%	15.4%	3.9%	6.0%	3.0%	11.3%
Nueces County	48,054	24.2%	16.2%	17.7%	25.1%	10.9%	3.6%	2.2%	0.1%	18.9%
Parker County	11,100	23.1%	12.8%	15.7%	20.1%	15.4%	6.4%	3.6%	2.9%	5.3%
Potter County	16,547	28.0%	16.6%	17.9%	21.9%	9.1%	4.9%	1.5%	0.0%	18.1%
Randall County	17,543	17.6%	19.6%	18.3%	25.4%	12.7%	3.2%	3.1%	0.0%	11.1%
Smith County	28,402	40.0%	16.3%	11.7%	16.4%	9.7%	1.5%	1.6%	2.8%	20.7%
Tarrant County	260,714	23.0%	14.5%	15.9%	25.6%	14.3%	3.3%	2.2%	1.1%	14.1%
Taylor County	17,073	22.4%	15.3%	17.6%	28.5%	10.4%	4.6%	0.0%	1.2%	10.7%
Tom Green County	16,337	27.4%	19.1%	15.4%	17.6%	12.9%	4.7%	2.9%	0.0%	21.0%

Table I-2: Counties—Income Class by Age—*Continued*

	Total Millennials	Under $10,000	$10,000 to $19,999	$20,000 to $29,999	$30,000 to $49,999	$50,000 to $74,999	$75,000 to $99,999	$100,000 or More
Texas—Cont.								
Travis County	112,029	59.8%	16.9%	10.9%	9.1%	2.4%	0.6%	0.3%
Webb County	30,472	62.8%	22.2%	8.1%	4.5%	2.4%	0.0%	0.0%
Wichita County	19,000	48.1%	28.4%	17.9%	2.1%	3.5%	0.0%	0.0%
Williamson County	39,815	60.2%	16.0%	15.4%	7.7%	0.4%	0.3%	0.0%
Utah								
Cache County	21,031	57.0%	26.6%	10.1%	5.4%	0.0%	0.8%	0.0%
Davis County	32,376	56.6%	25.7%	10.5%	5.7%	1.2%	0.2%	0.3%
Salt Lake County	107,190	47.8%	24.2%	16.7%	9.9%	0.9%	0.3%	0.2%
Utah County	94,406	61.0%	19.3%	9.2%	8.7%	0.7%	0.4%	0.7%
Washington County	16,709	52.0%	16.4%	13.4%	12.3%	5.4%	0.0%	0.5%
Weber County	23,746	47.1%	28.1%	15.2%	8.5%	1.1%	0.0%	0.0%
Vermont								
Chittenden County	25,155	59.3%	18.0%	9.9%	11.2%	1.7%	0.0%	0.0%
Virginia								
Albemarle County	13,562	70.0%	12.8%	10.2%	5.9%	0.9%	0.0%	0.2%
Arlington County	17,377	39.7%	16.8%	15.3%	13.0%	10.4%	3.0%	1.9%
Chesterfield County	31,432	55.5%	23.9%	8.6%	8.5%	3.5%	0.0%	0.0%
Fairfax County	95,712	61.5%	13.5%	10.9%	9.0%	3.9%	0.8%	0.4%
Hanover County	9,818	69.1%	18.6%	6.4%	3.4%	2.5%	0.0%	0.0%
Henrico County	26,484	59.1%	22.6%	12.4%	4.5%	1.2%	0.2%	0.0%
Loudoun County	24,373	56.1%	18.6%	9.6%	14.1%	0.7%	0.6%	0.3%
Montgomery County	27,532	75.3%	14.0%	6.0%	4.3%	0.4%	0.0%	0.0%
Prince William County	40,126	53.7%	19.2%	15.3%	10.8%	0.5%	0.5%	0.0%
Roanoke County	7,175	57.0%	12.8%	4.3%	15.6%	7.3%	0.0%	3.1%
Spotsylvania County	12,088	48.8%	21.6%	24.3%	4.8%	0.5%	0.0%	0.0%
Stafford County	15,338	56.8%	17.9%	11.9%	12.2%	0.0%	0.0%	1.2%
Washington								
Benton County	17,372	60.3%	16.0%	13.7%	10.1%	0.0%	0.0%	0.0%
Clark County	39,349	49.9%	23.1%	17.1%	7.6%	2.1%	0.3%	0.0%
Cowlitz County	6,662	54.1%	11.9%	17.2%	15.7%	1.1%	0.0%	0.0%
Grant County	11,592	72.5%	7.1%	9.7%	4.8%	6.0%	0.0%	0.0%
King County	171,924	56.2%	16.3%	12.8%	7.7%	4.7%	1.3%	1.0%
Kitsap County	27,430	47.3%	15.8%	25.5%	9.0%	2.4%	0.0%	0.0%
Pierce County	78,851	53.1%	16.1%	16.4%	11.0%	3.1%	0.3%	0.0%
Skagit County	8,948	51.9%	17.3%	20.0%	8.0%	1.5%	1.4%	0.0%
Snohomish County	64,465	50.3%	26.5%	12.0%	8.1%	2.5%	0.2%	0.3%
Spokane County	48,491	62.8%	21.6%	8.4%	5.2%	1.5%	0.2%	0.3%
Thurston County	24,902	57.7%	19.0%	15.1%	5.3%	2.0%	0.3%	0.5%
Whatcom County	30,613	61.1%	17.8%	13.0%	5.5%	1.9%	0.7%	0.0%
Yakima County	25,431	55.4%	23.4%	8.0%	12.4%	0.9%	0.0%	0.0%
West Virginia								
Berkeley County	9,972	66.9%	14.9%	11.3%	1.4%	5.5%	0.0%	0.0%
Cabell County	11,420	66.5%	26.3%	2.1%	3.4%	1.6%	0.0%	0.0%
Kanawha County	14,130	60.9%	24.7%	11.4%	1.1%	0.5%	0.6%	0.9%
Monongalia County	21,629	73.9%	12.4%	10.2%	2.2%	0.6%	0.7%	0.0%
Wisconsin								
Brown County	23,305	48.6%	26.8%	14.2%	9.8%	0.6%	0.0%	0.0%
Dane County	67,409	51.2%	22.0%	14.2%	10.1%	1.8%	0.8%	0.0%
Eau Claire County	15,224	65.7%	21.6%	6.9%	5.6%	0.2%	0.0%	0.0%
Fond du Lac County	8,500	51.7%	25.0%	17.7%	4.3%	1.2%	0.0%	0.0%
Kenosha County	17,148	52.0%	19.9%	18.8%	9.3%	0.0%	0.0%	0.0%
La Crosse County	19,238	62.0%	25.0%	6.9%	6.0%	0.1%	0.1%	0.0%
Marathon County	9,696	39.1%	19.9%	21.3%	15.8%	3.6%	0.2%	0.0%
Milwaukee County	95,959	63.3%	21.2%	7.9%	6.1%	1.3%	0.1%	0.0%
Outagamie County	15,392	54.6%	22.0%	14.5%	8.2%	0.7%	0.0%	0.0%
Racine County	17,832	60.0%	15.0%	14.2%	10.7%	0.1%	0.0%	0.0%
Rock County	14,815	54.9%	21.9%	15.7%	4.2%	3.3%	0.0%	0.0%
Sheboygan County	8,517	50.1%	18.9%	15.2%	7.2%	8.5%	0.0%	0.0%
Walworth County	13,278	61.9%	26.7%	2.5%	6.2%	2.7%	0.0%	0.0%
Washington County	10,356	57.8%	23.8%	7.1%	10.2%	1.1%	0.0%	0.0%
Waukesha County	29,887	61.5%	20.6%	6.2%	7.8%	4.0%	0.0%	0.0%
Winnebago County	19,273	57.7%	22.6%	14.0%	5.0%	0.6%	0.0%	0.0%
Wyoming								
Laramie County	13,912	41.4%	35.1%	8.3%	5.6%	0.6%	0.0%	9.0%

Table I-2: Counties—Income Class by Age—*Continued*

	Personal Income, Percent by Income Class, ages 25 to 33								
	Total Millennials	Under $10,000	$10,000 to $19,999	$20,000 to $29,999	$30,000 to $49,999	$50,000 to $74,999	$75,000 to $99,999	$100,000 to $149,999	$150,000 or More	Poverty Rate
Texas—Cont.										
Travis County	212,482	16.2%	13.0%	19.6%	26.9%	13.3%	6.1%	3.3%	1.6%	10.5%
Webb County	30,918	39.5%	18.9%	15.2%	12.8%	8.2%	4.9%	0.0%	0.6%	31.3%
Wichita County	17,480	41.9%	15.3%	13.9%	18.8%	5.7%	1.9%	2.0%	0.4%	19.1%
Williamson County	59,894	22.5%	12.1%	15.0%	24.4%	16.6%	5.5%	3.6%	0.2%	6.1%
Utah										
Cache County	17,230	32.9%	18.6%	16.5%	20.6%	7.7%	0.9%	0.6%	2.3%	19.3%
Davis County	42,554	29.5%	9.9%	17.1%	20.4%	16.8%	3.8%	1.8%	0.7%	6.1%
Salt Lake County	159,139	23.5%	11.5%	16.7%	28.3%	12.7%	3.7%	2.6%	0.9%	10.5%
Utah County	72,255	32.6%	14.0%	14.8%	23.8%	9.7%	2.8%	1.8%	0.7%	11.7%
Washington County	15,243	29.8%	14.4%	17.0%	21.1%	5.3%	4.7%	0.7%	7.1%	9.0%
Weber County	33,518	27.4%	10.6%	17.7%	29.3%	10.2%	2.4%	2.4%	0.0%	10.4%
Vermont										
Chittenden County	19,823	19.7%	6.9%	12.8%	31.9%	21.0%	5.0%	0.0%	2.8%	9.9%
Virginia										
Albemarle County	13,254	22.7%	8.3%	11.2%	27.5%	15.7%	10.6%	3.5%	0.5%	14.2%
Arlington County	55,450	9.4%	9.2%	7.7%	13.0%	29.7%	20.0%	8.9%	2.2%	7.0%
Chesterfield County	33,832	21.3%	11.2%	21.7%	26.0%	13.6%	3.9%	1.6%	0.7%	5.2%
Fairfax County	142,057	18.9%	11.6%	11.2%	19.6%	18.1%	11.7%	7.8%	1.2%	5.6%
Hanover County	8,198	16.8%	15.4%	16.7%	32.3%	4.8%	10.4%	2.1%	1.6%	8.4%
Henrico County	40,556	20.8%	11.5%	14.0%	28.9%	14.4%	6.7%	3.1%	0.6%	6.5%
Loudoun County	43,326	17.0%	13.7%	10.5%	21.2%	20.1%	7.8%	8.7%	1.0%	7.0%
Montgomery County	12,992	18.5%	14.2%	13.5%	27.5%	14.0%	4.9%	4.8%	2.5%	14.4%
Prince William County	55,830	23.0%	14.0%	11.5%	22.2%	15.7%	9.2%	4.2%	0.2%	9.4%
Roanoke County	10,124	26.3%	8.7%	12.2%	34.2%	16.6%	1.9%	0.0%	0.0%	11.1%
Spotsylvania County	13,377	24.9%	18.2%	11.3%	27.4%	14.7%	1.3%	1.1%	1.1%	11.2%
Stafford County	16,712	15.6%	13.4%	9.4%	23.5%	23.0%	9.7%	4.9%	0.4%	8.8%
Washington										
Benton County	21,311	22.9%	20.5%	18.5%	18.3%	14.4%	3.1%	2.3%	0.0%	21.4%
Clark County	54,151	24.3%	11.9%	17.6%	27.1%	13.2%	4.5%	1.4%	0.0%	13.8%
Cowlitz County	12,951	20.3%	20.8%	18.9%	34.8%	5.2%	0.0%	0.0%	0.0%	20.8%
Grant County	10,034	24.7%	12.1%	19.6%	30.8%	7.4%	2.6%	2.7%	0.0%	15.0%
King County	327,984	17.6%	11.0%	12.6%	21.8%	17.2%	9.1%	8.0%	2.8%	8.9%
Kitsap County	32,727	23.7%	17.4%	15.7%	24.4%	13.6%	3.2%	1.9%	0.1%	14.0%
Pierce County	113,567	25.9%	12.1%	16.3%	24.0%	14.5%	4.7%	2.1%	0.4%	13.7%
Skagit County	13,602	22.0%	10.8%	22.0%	28.8%	6.0%	8.3%	1.4%	0.0%	12.3%
Snohomish County	97,289	22.2%	11.0%	14.1%	24.0%	16.9%	6.6%	4.9%	0.4%	9.5%
Spokane County	68,066	31.0%	19.5%	13.6%	23.1%	8.4%	2.4%	1.4%	0.5%	19.0%
Thurston County	33,146	25.1%	21.0%	18.4%	19.1%	10.2%	4.1%	2.0%	0.0%	16.7%
Whatcom County	26,325	23.4%	17.2%	26.4%	20.4%	6.3%	3.7%	0.9%	1.6%	13.5%
Yakima County	27,580	33.5%	18.0%	21.6%	19.8%	4.6%	0.3%	1.1%	1.2%	24.9%
West Virginia										
Berkeley County	12,772	33.9%	18.8%	5.5%	28.0%	3.9%	8.6%	1.3%	0.0%	15.3%
Cabell County	10,967	30.3%	6.5%	24.7%	25.5%	9.6%	1.7%	1.6%	0.0%	19.3%
Kanawha County	20,325	25.0%	13.3%	15.1%	35.1%	6.3%	1.2%	3.2%	0.8%	20.6%
Monongalia County	18,112	33.4%	12.9%	10.8%	29.6%	8.0%	3.3%	2.0%	0.0%	21.8%
Wisconsin										
Brown County	32,699	21.6%	18.7%	17.9%	28.3%	11.4%	0.8%	0.7%	0.7%	13.7%
Dane County	73,996	18.0%	9.0%	19.3%	28.4%	13.2%	5.7%	3.0%	3.4%	10.7%
Eau Claire County	12,710	11.6%	16.6%	10.2%	39.3%	12.0%	8.6%	0.0%	1.7%	4.8%
Fond du Lac County	10,541	16.7%	18.3%	12.8%	36.2%	14.4%	0.0%	1.5%	0.0%	8.7%
Kenosha County	17,742	21.4%	9.5%	12.7%	40.7%	12.5%	3.1%	0.0%	0.0%	9.9%
La Crosse County	12,539	21.4%	24.7%	18.3%	16.9%	13.6%	3.5%	0.5%	1.2%	9.0%
Marathon County	14,255	14.7%	9.0%	15.2%	35.9%	19.4%	3.6%	2.2%	0.0%	10.0%
Milwaukee County	136,081	22.8%	13.1%	17.6%	26.9%	12.7%	3.7%	2.4%	0.8%	15.6%
Outagamie County	23,277	14.5%	10.1%	18.7%	40.5%	6.9%	7.0%	1.4%	0.9%	4.6%
Racine County	19,655	14.7%	14.0%	16.5%	35.2%	17.2%	0.8%	1.1%	0.6%	9.0%
Rock County	15,271	16.3%	16.2%	16.7%	18.1%	28.1%	4.4%	0.2%	0.0%	8.3%
Sheboygan County	11,780	14.3%	21.4%	14.0%	37.3%	12.4%	0.7%	0.0%	0.0%	9.5%
Walworth County	10,055	22.4%	18.8%	24.9%	24.0%	6.6%	2.4%	1.1%	0.0%	14.7%
Washington County	12,465	11.8%	18.0%	13.2%	35.5%	17.7%	2.4%	0.0%	1.3%	3.5%
Waukesha County	35,375	11.2%	14.2%	14.2%	30.4%	20.3%	6.4%	3.0%	0.4%	3.1%
Winnebago County	21,198	21.6%	11.5%	12.9%	35.0%	18.7%	0.4%	0.0%	0.0%	14.5%
Wyoming										
Laramie County	9,429	19.3%	14.0%	21.7%	26.3%	14.4%	3.3%	0.0%	0.9%	13.7%

Table I-3: Places—Income Class by Age

			Personal Income, Percent by Income Class, ages 18 to 24					
	Total Millennials	Under $10,000	$10,000 to $19,999	$20,000 to $29,999	$30,000 to $49,999	$50,000 to $74,999	$75,000 to $99,999	$100,000 or More
Alabama								
Birmingham city	24,765	66.6%	20.7%	5.4%	4.7%	2.6%	0.0%	0.0%
Huntsville city	19,309	72.8%	16.5%	5.2%	4.8%	0.0%	0.6%	0.0%
Mobile city	20,136	73.9%	15.1%	7.2%	3.4%	0.4%	0.0%	0.0%
Montgomery city	21,793	67.5%	22.1%	7.5%	2.9%	0.0%	0.0%	0.0%
Tuscaloosa city	25,864	65.8%	21.7%	7.0%	3.8%	0.6%	0.0%	1.2%
Alaska								
Anchorage municipality	34,552	32.9%	29.8%	19.0%	11.9%	5.7%	0.7%	0.0%
Arizona								
Chandler city	21,152	55.3%	27.0%	7.3%	5.7%	4.4%	0.0%	0.2%
Glendale city	24,197	59.2%	21.6%	12.3%	5.4%	1.5%	0.0%	0.0%
Mesa city	45,282	52.9%	22.0%	17.0%	5.9%	2.3%	0.0%	0.0%
Peoria city	13,727	53.3%	30.5%	12.1%	4.1%	0.0%	0.0%	0.0%
Phoenix city	156,250	57.0%	23.1%	10.5%	8.1%	1.3%	0.1%	0.0%
Scottsdale city	15,416	51.3%	24.9%	4.8%	12.9%	6.1%	0.0%	0.0%
Surprise city	7,602	46.2%	31.2%	14.8%	6.2%	1.5%	0.0%	0.0%
Tempe city	44,340	60.7%	22.2%	11.8%	3.7%	1.2%	0.0%	0.4%
Tucson city	83,057	62.0%	21.7%	11.8%	3.8%	0.7%	0.0%	0.0%
Yuma city	11,281	49.8%	24.6%	20.5%	5.2%	0.0%	0.0%	0.0%
Arkansas								
Little Rock city	17,815	56.4%	14.8%	9.9%	17.6%	0.9%	0.0%	0.4%
California								
Anaheim city	38,451	56.1%	23.2%	10.5%	7.6%	1.4%	1.2%	0.0%
Antioch city	13,849	68.0%	15.5%	9.7%	6.8%	0.0%	0.0%	0.0%
Bakersfield city	45,417	55.5%	20.5%	11.3%	6.7%	4.9%	0.0%	1.2%
Berkeley city	25,791	76.2%	9.8%	4.5%	7.7%	1.5%	0.2%	0.0%
Burbank city	7,065	63.3%	12.3%	10.4%	14.0%	0.0%	0.0%	0.0%
Carlsbad city	8,757	45.4%	34.2%	5.6%	14.0%	0.8%	0.0%	0.0%
Chico city	20,214	81.0%	11.6%	6.2%	1.1%	0.0%	0.0%	0.1%
Carson city	9,998	70.3%	8.5%	17.9%	2.3%	0.9%	0.0%	0.0%
Chula Vista city	29,347	65.0%	21.0%	6.0%	5.6%	2.0%	0.0%	0.3%
Clovis city	8,292	76.5%	10.4%	11.0%	1.1%	1.1%	0.0%	0.0%
Compton city	13,133	60.9%	19.2%	14.9%	5.0%	0.0%	0.0%	0.0%
Concord city	10,042	40.2%	34.3%	18.2%	4.8%	2.5%	0.0%	0.0%
Corona city	14,784	69.0%	15.9%	9.4%	5.8%	0.0%	0.0%	0.0%
Costa Mesa city	10,854	51.2%	22.5%	10.0%	7.8%	5.7%	2.8%	0.0%
Daly City city	10,375	55.2%	27.5%	13.7%	3.6%	0.0%	0.0%	0.0%
Downey city	13,983	66.1%	21.1%	9.9%	2.6%	0.4%	0.0%	0.0%
El Cajon city	11,079	53.9%	16.7%	21.3%	4.8%	3.3%	0.0%	0.0%
Elk Grove city	17,398	68.6%	18.6%	8.1%	3.6%	1.1%	0.0%	0.0%
El Monte city	12,404	61.9%	20.5%	12.9%	3.2%	1.4%	0.0%	0.0%
Escondido city	17,660	52.9%	27.1%	11.0%	6.9%	2.1%	0.0%	0.0%
Fairfield city	10,589	59.5%	17.3%	12.1%	4.4%	3.4%	3.3%	0.0%
Fontana city	23,408	59.7%	25.2%	10.3%	4.8%	0.0%	0.0%	0.0%
Fremont city	19,330	64.1%	8.6%	9.5%	13.4%	4.2%	0.0%	0.3%
Fresno city	61,204	64.1%	23.3%	6.6%	4.7%	1.0%	0.1%	0.1%
Fullerton city	18,398	56.2%	22.2%	11.4%	6.4%	3.8%	0.0%	0.0%
Garden Grove city	17,516	74.6%	13.0%	7.1%	2.7%	1.8%	0.4%	0.5%
Glendale city	15,025	69.4%	14.9%	8.6%	2.8%	3.1%	1.2%	0.0%
Hayward city	15,039	51.4%	24.8%	10.6%	12.1%	1.1%	0.0%	0.0%
Hesperia city	8,864	65.4%	14.1%	12.6%	8.0%	0.0%	0.0%	0.0%
Huntington Beach city	14,445	58.9%	22.2%	11.8%	5.1%	1.9%	0.0%	0.0%
Inglewood city	11,548	63.7%	25.5%	8.5%	2.3%	0.0%	0.0%	0.0%
Irvine city	36,009	77.6%	8.7%	6.3%	5.8%	1.1%	0.3%	0.3%
Jurupa Valley city	12,342	54.6%	21.1%	15.9%	8.4%	0.0%	0.0%	0.0%
Lancaster city	14,851	65.3%	13.4%	12.9%	8.0%	0.3%	0.0%	0.0%
Long Beach city	47,955	62.7%	21.2%	9.2%	4.7%	1.9%	0.2%	0.2%
Los Angeles city	429,036	61.9%	18.9%	9.8%	6.7%	1.7%	0.5%	0.4%
Mission Viejo city	9,478	62.0%	22.7%	7.8%	6.4%	0.0%	0.0%	1.1%
Modesto city	23,005	67.3%	19.2%	6.9%	5.7%	0.9%	0.0%	0.0%
Moreno Valley city	27,021	66.1%	19.3%	10.5%	3.2%	0.8%	0.0%	0.0%
Murrieta city	9,635	66.6%	15.5%	15.5%	2.4%	0.0%	0.0%	0.0%
Norwalk city	13,714	61.3%	24.9%	7.8%	2.7%	3.2%	0.0%	0.0%
Oakland city	34,194	53.6%	23.3%	10.8%	6.5%	5.1%	0.4%	0.4%
Oceanside city	23,119	24.1%	38.2%	30.6%	6.8%	0.3%	0.0%	0.0%
Ontario city	18,889	56.9%	15.1%	18.6%	9.4%	0.0%	0.0%	0.0%
Orange city	17,383	67.2%	18.0%	7.6%	4.8%	2.4%	0.0%	0.0%
Oxnard city	21,543	55.5%	25.2%	11.8%	7.5%	0.0%	0.0%	0.0%
Palmdale city	16,298	71.4%	17.9%	6.9%	3.5%	0.0%	0.0%	0.3%
Pasadena city	11,802	61.4%	21.0%	6.3%	4.7%	6.0%	0.0%	0.6%
Pomona city	20,281	65.1%	19.8%	9.2%	4.8%	0.7%	0.4%	0.0%
Rancho Cucamonga city	21,193	58.0%	24.2%	6.3%	10.9%	0.5%	0.0%	0.0%
Redding city	7,140	54.6%	27.0%	8.7%	9.7%	0.0%	0.0%	0.0%
Rialto city	12,693	65.2%	20.8%	9.6%	3.5%	0.9%	0.0%	0.0%
Richmond city	13,367	63.0%	20.2%	11.0%	4.6%	0.7%	0.6%	0.0%

Table I-3: Places—Income Class by Age—*Continued*

	Total Millennials	Under $10,000	$10,000 to $19,999	$20,000 to $29,999	$30,000 to $49,999	$50,000 to $74,999	$75,000 to $99,999	$100,000 to $149,999	$150,000 or More	Poverty Rate
Alabama										
Birmingham city	32,586	26.2%	25.5%	12.1%	20.1%	10.5%	1.8%	3.3%	0.5%	28.2%
Huntsville city	24,297	29.6%	13.7%	22.9%	15.8%	12.4%	4.4%	1.0%	0.2%	22.7%
Mobile city	26,961	29.1%	21.5%	16.7%	25.4%	5.5%	1.5%	0.4%	0.0%	17.1%
Montgomery city	26,837	38.1%	16.2%	18.3%	20.3%	3.5%	2.5%	0.3%	0.7%	34.5%
Tuscaloosa city	13,727	21.2%	26.5%	23.2%	9.1%	13.4%	6.2%	0.5%	0.0%	13.5%
Alaska										
Anchorage municipality	46,126	18.2%	10.1%	15.4%	27.4%	18.1%	4.8%	4.6%	1.4%	5.9%
Arizona										
Chandler city	36,119	21.4%	10.4%	9.6%	34.0%	14.8%	5.6%	3.4%	0.9%	9.1%
Glendale city	31,617	37.3%	19.2%	17.6%	14.6%	8.2%	2.8%	0.4%	0.0%	24.4%
Mesa city	63,820	26.8%	12.9%	20.6%	26.9%	8.8%	2.9%	1.0%	0.1%	18.4%
Peoria city	21,111	24.3%	15.3%	15.3%	28.9%	9.8%	4.2%	1.9%	0.4%	19.5%
Phoenix city	211,638	27.1%	15.7%	17.5%	23.9%	10.1%	3.6%	1.5%	0.6%	19.9%
Scottsdale city	30,246	13.6%	10.8%	10.7%	26.9%	22.6%	8.2%	3.6%	3.6%	8.7%
Surprise city	13,542	20.0%	11.6%	22.3%	26.5%	15.4%	3.7%	0.4%	0.0%	11.4%
Tempe city	28,260	22.9%	13.3%	14.7%	29.3%	9.6%	6.1%	4.2%	0.0%	12.9%
Tucson city	66,272	27.2%	20.3%	17.6%	21.9%	8.0%	2.8%	1.9%	0.2%	21.0%
Yuma city	10,968	34.7%	24.0%	4.0%	26.5%	8.0%	2.4%	0.3%	0.0%	26.1%
Arkansas										
Little Rock city	28,900	26.5%	20.8%	20.3%	21.5%	6.9%	1.9%	1.0%	1.0%	19.9%
California										
Anaheim city	51,581	24.9%	15.9%	16.6%	23.2%	9.9%	4.6%	4.6%	0.3%	10.5%
Antioch city	12,047	14.0%	14.4%	18.1%	28.1%	15.9%	4.9%	3.8%	0.7%	5.2%
Bakersfield city	53,945	30.9%	16.3%	13.9%	21.8%	10.3%	3.5%	3.2%	0.2%	20.7%
Berkeley city	20,092	19.3%	17.3%	10.3%	25.6%	15.1%	6.1%	5.5%	0.8%	15.9%
Burbank city	16,868	21.9%	10.1%	11.7%	22.1%	12.8%	8.3%	10.1%	3.0%	9.0%
Carlsbad city	12,465	16.7%	7.3%	25.2%	23.0%	9.9%	11.7%	6.2%	0.0%	2.3%
Chico city	11,738	25.3%	20.7%	16.3%	18.8%	12.4%	4.2%	2.3%	0.0%	25.3%
Carson city	11,282	30.8%	11.5%	17.1%	14.8%	19.0%	3.5%	3.2%	0.0%	11.0%
Chula Vista city	32,687	29.8%	21.8%	13.0%	18.5%	9.9%	2.4%	1.4%	3.1%	14.7%
Clovis city	13,995	33.1%	21.2%	16.9%	9.3%	13.4%	5.4%	0.5%	0.3%	20.3%
Compton city	12,685	29.2%	19.2%	27.4%	16.1%	7.9%	0.3%	0.0%	0.0%	17.9%
Concord city	16,439	13.2%	12.8%	19.4%	21.3%	14.5%	9.3%	6.7%	2.8%	7.2%
Corona city	20,907	29.0%	17.3%	15.1%	10.9%	12.8%	2.8%	2.5%	2.9%	20.3%
Costa Mesa city	19,681	18.0%	6.1%	22.1%	28.4%	17.7%	3.6%	2.6%	1.4%	7.9%
Daly City city	17,192	28.6%	7.5%	17.3%	20.0%	10.9%	6.3%	7.1%	2.3%	12.8%
Downey city	15,220	26.3%	26.0%	19.7%	14.6%	5.6%	7.5%	0.0%	0.3%	7.6%
El Cajon city	15,091	24.9%	25.4%	10.1%	22.9%	11.2%	4.7%	0.8%	0.0%	18.2%
Elk Grove city	17,220	30.7%	16.0%	12.0%	20.5%	11.9%	4.5%	4.2%	1.1%	10.3%
El Monte city	15,964	28.8%	17.1%	33.4%	12.6%	5.0%	1.5%	1.6%	0.0%	16.5%
Escondido city	24,192	29.8%	23.8%	12.0%	21.0%	10.7%	1.8%	0.9%	0.0%	13.2%
Fairfield city	15,995	28.3%	21.2%	14.8%	21.2%	8.5%	3.2%	2.8%	0.0%	9.8%
Fontana city	31,601	31.5%	14.5%	16.5%	26.0%	8.9%	1.1%	1.2%	0.3%	18.0%
Fremont city	31,000	26.1%	3.5%	5.1%	19.7%	16.3%	15.2%	10.6%	3.5%	3.5%
Fresno city	75,584	39.2%	16.7%	17.0%	17.6%	6.7%	1.9%	0.7%	0.1%	24.4%
Fullerton city	19,400	27.0%	11.2%	25.2%	18.9%	12.4%	2.5%	0.5%	2.3%	9.8%
Garden Grove city	22,763	28.6%	19.1%	16.4%	17.2%	12.2%	4.0%	2.6%	0.0%	15.9%
Glendale city	28,888	26.7%	21.3%	10.0%	19.9%	13.4%	4.8%	2.5%	1.4%	13.5%
Hayward city	27,067	18.5%	13.4%	8.9%	28.7%	16.8%	8.0%	5.6%	0.0%	12.3%
Hesperia city	12,931	31.1%	21.4%	15.2%	7.2%	22.5%	0.8%	0.8%	1.0%	24.0%
Huntington Beach city	25,026	13.1%	19.6%	17.3%	21.7%	16.2%	5.9%	4.0%	2.4%	7.4%
Inglewood city	15,749	32.2%	21.9%	19.7%	18.9%	7.3%	0.0%	0.0%	0.0%	29.0%
Irvine city	36,640	25.1%	8.1%	7.9%	17.6%	19.8%	10.7%	7.3%	3.6%	12.0%
Jurupa Valley city	13,050	28.6%	15.6%	13.6%	25.8%	10.8%	2.7%	2.7%	0.0%	11.0%
Lancaster city	25,394	49.0%	7.6%	9.5%	23.8%	6.2%	3.2%	0.0%	0.7%	24.4%
Long Beach city	70,119	24.7%	15.9%	15.7%	21.6%	14.4%	5.0%	1.9%	0.8%	15.2%
Los Angeles city	636,484	24.3%	18.2%	16.4%	20.1%	12.0%	4.4%	3.3%	1.3%	16.8%
Mission Viejo city	9,308	24.1%	12.1%	11.6%	15.9%	21.5%	7.0%	3.8%	4.0%	1.0%
Modesto city	25,866	31.2%	18.1%	17.9%	19.0%	8.8%	3.3%	0.0%	0.0%	25.2%
Moreno Valley city	27,577	24.6%	20.1%	19.6%	25.5%	8.2%	1.7%	0.3%	0.0%	8.7%
Murrieta city	14,030	33.7%	24.2%	8.7%	8.9%	15.5%	6.3%	1.8%	1.1%	13.8%
Norwalk city	13,620	30.6%	16.3%	14.5%	20.8%	8.7%	7.0%	2.1%	0.0%	11.8%
Oakland city	74,769	23.6%	20.0%	14.7%	17.3%	14.7%	5.2%	3.5%	1.0%	18.6%
Oceanside city	17,362	27.6%	13.4%	20.0%	19.5%	15.6%	2.7%	0.9%	0.4%	16.1%
Ontario city	24,428	25.3%	23.5%	14.3%	24.4%	6.7%	1.7%	4.1%	0.0%	12.7%
Orange city	21,674	16.8%	19.4%	15.0%	24.7%	13.6%	6.9%	3.3%	0.4%	7.5%
Oxnard city	32,007	24.1%	21.0%	18.9%	22.2%	8.4%	2.1%	1.9%	1.5%	13.2%
Palmdale city	18,322	37.0%	15.9%	15.2%	20.8%	7.1%	3.0%	0.9%	0.0%	15.9%
Pasadena city	22,282	21.5%	10.7%	13.1%	25.4%	17.3%	7.2%	3.4%	1.5%	14.2%
Pomona city	21,771	30.2%	22.1%	16.2%	19.7%	7.5%	2.8%	1.4%	0.0%	14.6%
Rancho Cucamonga city	21,999	23.8%	19.6%	17.2%	19.0%	14.2%	4.5%	1.1%	0.6%	8.3%
Redding city	13,090	29.3%	20.2%	15.5%	26.1%	2.5%	1.1%	4.5%	0.8%	18.3%
Rialto city	14,882	31.9%	17.2%	19.3%	22.8%	5.7%	0.0%	1.6%	1.4%	13.0%
Richmond city	16,605	32.1%	22.3%	16.6%	15.5%	8.7%	1.5%	1.9%	1.5%	22.1%

Table I-3: Places—Income Class by Age—*Continued*

			Personal Income, Percent by Income Class, ages 18 to 24					
	Total Millennials	Under $10,000	$10,000 to $19,999	$20,000 to $29,999	$30,000 to $49,999	$50,000 to $74,999	$75,000 to $99,999	$100,000 or More
California—Cont.								
Riverside city	47,199	63.8%	17.6%	12.1%	5.5%	0.9%	0.2%	0.0%
Roseville city	12,503	68.2%	15.3%	6.1%	5.0%	5.3%	0.0%	0.0%
Sacramento city	44,442	65.4%	20.1%	8.9%	4.4%	1.3%	0.0%	0.0%
Salinas city	16,341	58.2%	27.9%	8.5%	4.6%	0.8%	0.0%	0.0%
San Bernardino city	27,676	64.7%	18.7%	11.7%	5.0%	0.0%	0.0%	0.0%
San Buenaventura (Ventura) city	8,974	52.9%	24.3%	14.8%	7.4%	0.6%	0.0%	0.0%
San Diego city	163,607	59.4%	20.0%	11.1%	6.9%	2.1%	0.5%	0.0%
San Francisco city	63,520	59.2%	12.8%	8.4%	7.2%	7.9%	1.3%	3.2%
San Jose city	93,229	63.4%	16.6%	10.0%	6.8%	2.4%	0.5%	0.4%
San Leandro city	6,738	38.6%	31.0%	14.5%	15.2%	0.0%	0.0%	0.7%
San Marcos city	9,325	54.8%	26.8%	8.5%	7.1%	2.8%	0.0%	0.0%
San Mateo city	7,418	56.6%	21.3%	12.8%	1.6%	6.8%	0.0%	0.9%
Santa Ana city	34,544	54.8%	25.5%	10.7%	8.1%	0.6%	0.1%	0.3%
Santa Clara city	13,344	58.9%	9.0%	5.9%	15.7%	8.6%	0.0%	2.0%
Santa Clarita city	18,469	59.2%	21.1%	8.8%	8.3%	2.1%	0.5%	0.0%
Santa Maria city	12,496	48.9%	24.0%	23.8%	1.6%	0.9%	0.7%	0.0%
Santa Monica city	5,866	38.6%	25.0%	20.3%	13.7%	2.5%	0.0%	0.0%
Santa Rosa city	15,634	50.5%	25.4%	9.1%	14.6%	0.5%	0.0%	0.0%
Simi Valley city	12,530	55.9%	22.3%	9.6%	8.7%	3.4%	0.0%	0.0%
South Gate city	11,254	53.6%	28.3%	10.4%	7.6%	0.0%	0.0%	0.0%
Stockton city	34,010	65.6%	17.7%	9.5%	5.2%	2.0%	0.0%	0.0%
Sunnyvale city	8,863	48.6%	21.0%	6.7%	14.9%	2.7%	0.3%	5.7%
Temecula city	10,102	79.7%	9.2%	9.4%	0.5%	1.2%	0.0%	0.0%
Thousand Oaks city	10,437	67.3%	9.9%	6.7%	13.5%	2.6%	0.0%	0.0%
Torrance city	15,100	66.6%	18.7%	8.2%	2.4%	3.2%	0.9%	0.0%
Vacaville city	9,533	58.6%	16.5%	10.0%	9.3%	3.5%	0.0%	2.1%
Vallejo city	11,449	61.4%	24.0%	9.9%	3.7%	0.9%	0.0%	0.0%
Victorville city	11,547	76.1%	11.2%	5.6%	7.1%	0.0%	0.0%	0.0%
Visalia city	12,737	68.8%	12.9%	10.4%	7.5%	0.4%	0.0%	0.0%
Vista city	11,904	48.1%	35.7%	8.5%	7.7%	0.0%	0.0%	0.0%
West Covina city	9,485	69.9%	21.0%	4.5%	4.6%	0.0%	0.0%	0.0%
Westminster city	6,615	68.6%	13.4%	8.2%	9.8%	0.0%	0.0%	0.0%
Colorado								
Arvada city	7,135	64.6%	15.2%	11.4%	8.9%	0.0%	0.0%	0.0%
Aurora city	33,948	52.0%	18.9%	15.8%	12.0%	1.3%	0.0%	0.0%
Boulder city	32,366	63.6%	16.9%	9.6%	8.9%	1.0%	0.0%	0.0%
Centennial city	7,611	55.4%	19.4%	13.0%	9.8%	2.5%	0.0%	0.0%
Colorado Springs city	45,198	48.4%	24.0%	16.4%	9.5%	1.0%	0.2%	0.5%
Denver city	58,231	54.1%	18.4%	13.9%	9.5%	3.7%	0.1%	0.2%
Fort Collins city	32,030	55.8%	19.8%	9.5%	10.5%	4.2%	0.3%	0.0%
Greeley city	12,337	49.5%	27.9%	9.6%	10.4%	1.5%	0.2%	0.8%
Lakewood city	16,380	53.6%	26.6%	10.0%	7.4%	2.5%	0.0%	0.0%
Longmont city	7,630	56.6%	23.8%	12.9%	6.7%	0.0%	0.0%	0.0%
Pueblo city	10,047	62.8%	21.4%	9.7%	5.2%	0.9%	0.0%	0.0%
Thornton city	11,352	45.7%	24.3%	18.7%	8.1%	3.2%	0.0%	0.0%
Westminster city	9,356	36.7%	23.7%	20.1%	15.5%	4.1%	0.0%	0.0%
Connecticut								
Bridgeport city	17,826	58.6%	26.6%	9.5%	5.0%	0.0%	0.0%	0.2%
Hartford city	21,070	69.6%	10.7%	9.8%	9.5%	0.4%	0.0%	0.0%
New Haven city	21,920	60.0%	24.8%	9.4%	5.7%	0.0%	0.0%	0.0%
Stamford city	12,444	53.4%	20.8%	10.3%	14.9%	0.6%	0.0%	0.0%
Waterbury city	10,362	61.6%	14.4%	16.3%	6.2%	1.5%	0.0%	0.0%
District of Columbia								
Washington city	81,910	62.7%	14.2%	8.5%	8.5%	5.2%	0.2%	0.6%
Florida								
Boca Raton city	9,141	56.5%	26.6%	4.0%	6.5%	6.5%	0.0%	0.0%
Cape Coral city	10,150	45.8%	30.4%	15.0%	8.0%	0.7%	0.0%	0.0%
Clearwater city	7,867	62.1%	17.2%	12.1%	7.2%	0.9%	0.5%	0.0%
Coral Springs city	11,711	73.0%	8.1%	7.7%	5.5%	5.5%	0.3%	0.0%
Fort Lauderdale city	10,504	43.9%	35.7%	8.4%	9.3%	2.1%	0.0%	0.6%
Gainesville city	41,812	84.5%	9.9%	3.3%	1.5%	0.8%	0.0%	0.0%
Hialeah city	18,916	68.8%	15.7%	8.1%	3.4%	4.0%	0.0%	0.0%
Hollywood city	11,392	70.0%	14.9%	10.1%	4.5%	0.0%	0.4%	0.0%
Jacksonville city	82,935	53.3%	23.8%	13.9%	7.0%	1.8%	0.0%	0.2%
Lakeland city	10,492	53.6%	21.1%	20.1%	3.4%	0.0%	0.0%	1.8%
Miami city	33,513	57.0%	25.4%	8.6%	8.2%	0.9%	0.0%	0.0%
Miami Beach city	5,622	67.1%	18.6%	11.5%	2.8%	0.0%	0.0%	0.0%
Miami Gardens city	11,382	74.1%	15.8%	6.3%	3.8%	0.0%	0.0%	0.0%
Miramar city	12,731	73.2%	17.6%	7.6%	1.6%	0.0%	0.0%	0.0%
Orlando city	28,207	53.1%	21.9%	17.3%	6.3%	1.4%	0.0%	0.0%
Palm Bay city	9,453	75.1%	19.3%	5.1%	0.6%	0.0%	0.0%	0.0%
Pembroke Pines city	16,234	69.5%	17.1%	11.2%	1.4%	0.6%	0.3%	0.0%
Plantation city	6,199	57.3%	28.8%	10.4%	3.5%	0.0%	0.0%	0.0%
Pompano Beach city	8,856	44.2%	18.8%	11.4%	20.5%	4.5%	0.0%	0.6%
Port St. Lucie city	14,357	56.9%	24.9%	12.8%	5.3%	0.0%	0.0%	0.0%

Table I-3: Places—Income Class by Age—*Continued*

	Personal Income, Percent by Income Class, ages 25 to 33								
	Total Millennials	Under $10,000	$10,000 to $19,999	$20,000 to $29,999	$30,000 to $49,999	$50,000 to $74,999	$75,000 to $99,999	$100,000 to $149,999	$150,000 or More	Poverty Rate
California—Cont.										
Riverside city	49,657	27.6%	17.7%	15.9%	26.0%	10.9%	1.0%	0.5%	0.3%	13.1%
Roseville city	14,296	21.8%	10.1%	14.2%	26.9%	14.1%	4.3%	8.2%	0.4%	8.5%
Sacramento city	78,271	26.2%	16.9%	16.5%	23.2%	11.2%	4.0%	2.1%	0.0%	16.2%
Salinas city	21,776	33.0%	16.1%	25.4%	14.1%	5.5%	4.2%	0.9%	0.8%	15.1%
San Bernardino city	30,586	36.1%	21.7%	18.2%	16.5%	5.9%	1.6%	0.0%	0.0%	27.5%
San Buenaventura (Ventura) city	14,855	16.9%	16.7%	22.5%	20.0%	12.3%	8.0%	2.3%	1.3%	11.3%
San Diego city	233,373	22.2%	14.2%	12.9%	20.5%	15.7%	9.1%	4.3%	1.0%	13.0%
San Francisco city	178,135	15.6%	8.7%	7.1%	16.6%	18.1%	11.2%	13.9%	8.8%	10.3%
San Jose city	139,521	21.7%	13.7%	13.0%	19.8%	15.4%	6.5%	6.8%	3.0%	6.6%
San Leandro city	12,776	17.2%	13.9%	17.8%	19.2%	22.0%	4.6%	4.0%	1.3%	6.1%
San Marcos city	11,169	21.8%	12.0%	12.5%	25.5%	16.5%	5.6%	6.1%	0.0%	16.0%
San Mateo city	12,624	12.2%	5.7%	9.8%	15.2%	20.9%	5.9%	17.0%	13.3%	0.7%
Santa Ana city	51,773	24.1%	20.5%	25.8%	19.0%	7.4%	1.5%	1.2%	0.4%	16.7%
Santa Clara city	23,466	16.1%	4.9%	9.0%	20.8%	13.8%	12.7%	16.0%	6.7%	4.6%
Santa Clarita city	22,326	19.0%	14.0%	10.2%	25.8%	16.6%	7.8%	3.5%	3.1%	7.3%
Santa Maria city	12,057	20.3%	36.5%	21.5%	11.2%	6.0%	2.7%	1.9%	0.0%	16.8%
Santa Monica city	16,013	10.3%	10.8%	6.9%	16.6%	22.6%	18.7%	8.1%	5.9%	6.7%
Santa Rosa city	23,024	22.9%	12.0%	18.8%	26.0%	16.2%	2.3%	1.3%	0.5%	9.4%
Simi Valley city	13,848	22.8%	10.1%	15.1%	19.4%	19.3%	6.4%	4.6%	2.3%	6.5%
South Gate city	12,675	35.9%	18.7%	21.7%	16.2%	6.4%	1.2%	0.0%	0.0%	24.6%
Stockton city	42,335	24.1%	23.2%	22.0%	19.3%	7.8%	2.5%	0.7%	0.4%	16.0%
Sunnyvale city	28,799	24.2%	8.4%	7.7%	10.8%	10.7%	14.1%	16.2%	8.0%	7.0%
Temecula city	13,346	20.5%	15.5%	11.4%	25.4%	14.2%	8.0%	4.0%	1.0%	5.4%
Thousand Oaks city	9,958	23.5%	9.5%	11.6%	27.2%	12.9%	11.3%	2.7%	1.3%	5.9%
Torrance city	15,611	24.2%	14.9%	16.6%	17.4%	16.5%	5.4%	4.4%	0.6%	4.4%
Vacaville city	12,759	24.2%	20.1%	11.5%	25.7%	14.5%	1.8%	1.2%	0.9%	5.7%
Vallejo city	17,933	20.9%	13.0%	14.4%	33.5%	9.8%	5.8%	1.6%	1.1%	12.1%
Victorville city	16,953	43.6%	21.7%	15.0%	7.3%	5.4%	6.4%	0.6%	0.0%	28.8%
Visalia city	16,358	34.4%	11.3%	16.2%	23.3%	8.3%	1.0%	4.6%	0.9%	19.1%
Vista city	16,140	16.8%	21.4%	22.6%	17.4%	14.2%	4.1%	3.5%	0.0%	10.6%
West Covina city	15,248	30.4%	19.4%	19.6%	15.3%	10.1%	4.1%	0.6%	0.6%	10.3%
Westminster city	12,305	32.7%	19.6%	10.2%	19.8%	10.5%	6.0%	1.2%	0.0%	20.5%
Colorado										
Arvada city	13,764	20.8%	10.9%	17.8%	17.7%	21.4%	6.1%	5.3%	0.0%	11.2%
Aurora city	51,712	21.9%	13.9%	16.1%	32.3%	12.2%	2.7%	0.6%	0.3%	12.9%
Boulder city	15,823	20.0%	11.1%	11.9%	22.7%	19.0%	7.3%	3.8%	3.6%	18.1%
Centennial city	11,724	22.0%	16.9%	8.2%	24.1%	20.3%	4.9%	1.2%	2.5%	5.6%
Colorado Springs city	69,650	24.5%	14.6%	17.7%	25.0%	15.0%	2.5%	0.4%	0.3%	12.5%
Denver city	142,282	16.9%	9.6%	13.9%	27.1%	19.0%	8.1%	4.1%	1.3%	11.0%
Fort Collins city	27,412	15.4%	16.9%	19.2%	29.4%	12.7%	2.8%	2.1%	1.5%	15.3%
Greeley city	14,747	22.7%	8.4%	17.9%	24.4%	13.5%	7.4%	4.0%	1.7%	8.1%
Lakewood city	21,541	18.9%	11.9%	21.2%	30.3%	9.2%	4.9%	3.2%	0.3%	10.7%
Longmont city	9,521	21.4%	11.2%	12.2%	29.0%	7.0%	14.2%	4.2%	0.0%	12.1%
Pueblo city	13,992	33.0%	15.5%	16.0%	21.3%	9.3%	2.1%	2.3%	0.6%	17.2%
Thornton city	17,167	16.2%	22.5%	10.5%	32.3%	13.6%	3.3%	1.3%	0.3%	14.1%
Westminster city	15,866	18.6%	8.2%	10.1%	31.3%	21.3%	8.6%	1.9%	0.0%	11.6%
Connecticut										
Bridgeport city	20,882	32.4%	19.5%	12.8%	18.6%	11.5%	3.7%	1.1%	0.4%	21.7%
Hartford city	17,959	28.3%	13.6%	19.9%	23.5%	9.6%	4.8%	0.2%	0.0%	21.2%
New Haven city	25,481	31.4%	14.4%	13.0%	21.7%	11.7%	6.2%	1.6%	0.0%	25.8%
Stamford city	20,672	18.3%	14.9%	7.2%	19.7%	17.4%	9.6%	10.8%	2.1%	9.5%
Waterbury city	13,325	39.8%	16.5%	15.6%	18.6%	8.6%	0.5%	0.3%	0.0%	39.7%
District of Columbia										
Washington city	139,024	15.8%	7.2%	9.5%	17.4%	25.6%	13.3%	8.0%	3.2%	10.5%
Florida										
Boca Raton city	8,790	13.7%	25.9%	17.5%	13.9%	12.4%	10.9%	5.7%	0.0%	15.7%
Cape Coral city	19,627	41.0%	15.9%	16.7%	17.1%	7.5%	1.4%	0.5%	0.0%	25.2%
Clearwater city	14,213	19.6%	21.1%	24.2%	24.0%	9.1%	2.1%	0.0%	0.0%	7.9%
Coral Springs city	12,738	21.6%	25.8%	21.1%	17.0%	8.5%	0.0%	5.3%	0.6%	7.9%
Fort Lauderdale city	24,714	24.2%	14.0%	24.4%	21.5%	12.0%	1.5%	1.5%	0.8%	17.3%
Gainesville city	20,893	32.9%	14.4%	15.5%	20.8%	11.6%	2.8%	1.7%	0.3%	28.9%
Hialeah city	28,617	34.7%	24.4%	16.3%	17.6%	6.4%	0.5%	0.0%	0.0%	22.9%
Hollywood city	18,482	29.4%	7.5%	21.5%	25.5%	10.8%	4.6%	0.5%	0.2%	15.8%
Jacksonville city	123,515	25.7%	14.1%	14.6%	28.1%	12.2%	2.6%	1.8%	0.7%	16.0%
Lakeland city	13,360	38.9%	14.3%	16.8%	21.0%	7.6%	1.1%	0.4%	0.0%	22.2%
Miami city	64,897	28.2%	18.1%	22.8%	15.9%	9.7%	3.0%	1.9%	0.3%	18.7%
Miami Beach city	13,576	22.2%	15.9%	16.6%	19.3%	14.4%	4.6%	4.1%	3.0%	8.2%
Miami Gardens city	15,208	49.2%	11.0%	20.9%	17.2%	0.7%	1.1%	0.0%	0.0%	17.7%
Miramar city	17,018	24.6%	19.0%	10.7%	28.9%	13.4%	0.7%	2.7%	0.0%	11.6%
Orlando city	54,102	23.2%	19.7%	19.7%	22.8%	9.5%	3.3%	1.8%	0.1%	17.9%
Palm Bay city	10,233	22.3%	16.8%	31.1%	19.1%	6.8%	3.2%	0.0%	0.7%	15.0%
Pembroke Pines city	18,884	24.0%	13.8%	15.6%	24.4%	14.5%	4.4%	3.4%	0.0%	7.2%
Plantation city	12,841	32.1%	17.0%	9.4%	21.8%	10.7%	7.6%	0.5%	0.7%	6.3%
Pompano Beach city	12,129	33.6%	20.1%	13.2%	22.7%	3.9%	3.6%	2.8%	0.0%	17.8%
Port St. Lucie city	18,502	25.5%	12.8%	16.7%	28.3%	13.0%	0.6%	2.8%	0.5%	12.3%

Table I-3: Places—Income Class by Age—*Continued*

	Total Millennials	Under $10,000	$10,000 to $19,999	$20,000 to $29,999	$30,000 to $49,999	$50,000 to $74,999	$75,000 to $99,999	$100,000 or More
					Personal Income, Percent by Income Class, ages 18 to 24			
Florida—Cont.								
St. Petersburg city	20,729	65.2%	13.4%	12.7%	6.4%	1.2%	1.1%	0.0%
Sunrise city	6,979	55.2%	30.5%	11.2%	3.2%	0.0%	0.0%	0.0%
Tallahassee city	57,815	66.4%	19.3%	9.4%	4.1%	0.7%	0.0%	0.0%
Tampa city	39,114	59.7%	20.9%	12.2%	4.7%	1.9%	0.3%	0.3%
West Palm Beach city	9,024	60.3%	23.2%	10.5%	3.5%	2.5%	0.0%	0.0%
Georgia								
Athens-Clarke County unified govt (balance)	36,399	76.5%	14.0%	4.7%	3.7%	1.0%	0.0%	0.0%
Atlanta city	59,522	67.4%	17.5%	7.4%	3.8%	3.0%	0.5%	0.5%
Augusta-Richmond County consolidated govt (balance)	23,296	62.8%	21.9%	10.7%	3.6%	1.0%	0.0%	0.0%
Columbus city	24,389	65.0%	20.2%	9.3%	4.5%	0.6%	0.3%	0.0%
Macon-Bibb county	16,246	82.4%	7.6%	5.9%	2.2%	1.5%	0.0%	0.3%
Roswell city	7,219	59.6%	28.5%	7.2%	4.7%	0.0%	0.0%	0.0%
Sandy Springs city	7,991	33.8%	31.8%	13.1%	11.0%	5.0%	5.3%	0.0%
Savannah city	24,692	67.2%	17.5%	8.1%	6.7%	0.4%	0.0%	0.1%
Hawaii								
Urban Honolulu CDP	30,770	66.4%	14.6%	6.2%	9.0%	3.6%	0.0%	0.1%
Idaho								
Boise City city	20,288	58.7%	23.3%	11.2%	5.5%	1.4%	0.0%	0.0%
Meridian city	5,891	74.6%	5.7%	9.2%	0.0%	10.5%	0.0%	0.0%
Illinois								
Aurora city	20,391	53.4%	18.2%	17.6%	8.1%	1.8%	0.8%	0.0%
Chicago city	284,971	65.3%	16.2%	9.1%	5.8%	2.9%	0.3%	0.3%
Elgin city	11,159	61.9%	14.5%	10.2%	11.5%	1.3%	0.0%	0.7%
Joliet city	16,026	54.8%	24.1%	15.0%	5.7%	0.0%	0.4%	0.0%
Naperville city	12,952	66.2%	13.5%	13.6%	2.7%	3.0%	1.0%	0.0%
Peoria city	11,731	75.7%	15.5%	6.6%	1.4%	0.0%	0.9%	0.0%
Rockford city	14,392	66.0%	17.1%	8.4%	8.6%	0.0%	0.0%	0.0%
Springfield city	11,083	72.1%	13.8%	7.7%	5.4%	0.9%	0.0%	0.0%
Indiana								
Evansville city	12,756	69.0%	16.9%	9.4%	4.0%	0.7%	0.0%	0.0%
Fort Wayne city	27,427	55.3%	18.4%	14.1%	12.1%	0.1%	0.0%	0.0%
Indianapolis city (balance)	80,525	59.3%	20.8%	12.9%	5.8%	0.9%	0.1%	0.1%
South Bend city	13,865	73.3%	15.7%	6.6%	3.0%	0.4%	0.0%	1.0%
Iowa								
Cedar Rapids city	12,970	57.5%	24.4%	9.6%	7.2%	1.3%	0.0%	0.0%
Davenport city	9,454	56.3%	16.5%	18.8%	3.6%	3.7%	1.2%	0.0%
Des Moines city	22,640	52.2%	27.4%	6.7%	12.8%	0.4%	0.5%	0.0%
Kansas								
Kansas City city	14,303	47.2%	19.9%	22.1%	7.9%	2.9%	0.0%	0.0%
Olathe city	11,229	65.2%	14.4%	8.1%	10.1%	1.2%	1.0%	0.0%
Overland Park city	12,995	55.4%	12.5%	8.9%	17.3%	5.3%	0.0%	0.7%
Topeka city	13,134	56.5%	24.8%	13.6%	5.1%	0.0%	0.0%	0.0%
Wichita city	32,837	58.7%	22.6%	12.8%	3.0%	2.9%	0.0%	0.0%
Kentucky								
Lexington-Fayette urban county	43,864	55.0%	25.1%	12.2%	6.1%	1.5%	0.0%	0.0%
Louisville/Jefferson County metro govt (balance)	56,727	55.4%	25.1%	12.3%	5.3%	1.4%	0.2%	0.3%
Louisiana								
Baton Rouge city	37,552	60.8%	23.0%	7.9%	5.5%	1.7%	1.1%	0.0%
Lafayette city	14,704	74.9%	20.4%	3.0%	1.7%	0.0%	0.0%	0.0%
New Orleans city	37,387	69.0%	17.6%	5.8%	5.3%	0.7%	1.6%	0.0%
Shreveport city	18,974	70.2%	11.4%	9.9%	4.8%	3.4%	0.4%	0.0%
Maryland								
Baltimore city	64,583	69.2%	11.7%	8.7%	8.7%	1.0%	0.4%	0.2%
Massachusetts								
Boston city	100,784	68.1%	13.4%	7.8%	6.2%	3.6%	0.5%	0.4%
Brockton city	11,101	53.1%	30.0%	11.9%	5.0%	0.0%	0.0%	0.0%
Cambridge city	20,489	65.6%	8.9%	5.4%	11.9%	7.2%	0.8%	0.3%
Lowell city	15,564	59.4%	20.6%	8.9%	10.7%	0.1%	0.2%	0.0%
Lynn city	8,414	59.9%	9.7%	17.3%	8.3%	4.8%	0.0%	0.0%
New Bedford city	11,109	61.1%	20.4%	10.6%	5.8%	2.1%	0.0%	0.0%
Quincy city	7,210	75.5%	13.4%	2.1%	9.0%	0.0%	0.0%	0.0%
Springfield city	20,703	66.7%	14.8%	9.5%	8.6%	0.4%	0.0%	0.0%
Worcester city	27,597	76.0%	12.5%	5.5%	3.9%	1.4%	0.3%	0.4%
Michigan								
Ann Arbor city	36,381	48.0%	16.0%	13.7%	12.5%	9.5%	0.1%	0.4%
Dearborn city	10,993	68.9%	11.2%	3.2%	13.0%	3.6%	0.0%	0.0%
Detroit city	72,501	73.2%	16.2%	6.5%	3.2%	0.7%	0.3%	0.0%
Flint city	10,233	65.1%	21.0%	11.2%	2.7%	0.0%	0.0%	0.0%
Grand Rapids city	23,662	59.4%	24.4%	8.0%	5.5%	2.7%	0.0%	0.0%
Lansing city	14,440	43.4%	22.6%	22.7%	10.7%	0.6%	0.0%	0.0%

Table I-3: Places—Income Class by Age—*Continued*

	Personal Income, Percent by Income Class, ages 25 to 33								
	Total Millennials	Under $10,000	$10,000 to $19,999	$20,000 to $29,999	$30,000 to $49,999	$50,000 to $74,999	$75,000 to $99,999	$100,000 to $149,999	$150,000 or More	Poverty Rate
Florida—Cont.										
St. Petersburg city	32,599	31.4%	11.1%	17.1%	25.7%	9.8%	3.3%	1.6%	0.0%	19.6%
Sunrise city	14,792	29.5%	17.5%	10.3%	26.1%	8.8%	6.6%	0.5%	0.6%	6.9%
Tallahassee city	26,618	23.5%	17.2%	18.9%	26.2%	10.9%	2.4%	0.5%	0.5%	22.4%
Tampa city	57,156	26.3%	13.9%	20.4%	17.9%	12.8%	4.3%	2.5%	1.9%	19.7%
West Palm Beach city	14,859	29.2%	15.1%	24.8%	20.1%	6.3%	4.0%	0.5%	0.0%	26.3%
Georgia										
Athens-Clarke County unified govt (balance)	15,629	31.7%	21.3%	20.6%	20.6%	3.1%	1.1%	1.3%	0.2%	33.9%
Atlanta city	89,857	15.6%	11.0%	17.6%	26.2%	16.0%	7.3%	4.7%	1.7%	13.0%
Augusta-Richmond County consolidated govt (balance)	28,678	36.0%	16.1%	10.4%	21.5%	13.1%	1.7%	0.9%	0.3%	24.1%
Columbus city	29,720	25.7%	16.3%	18.3%	23.6%	10.6%	2.3%	3.2%	0.0%	14.3%
Macon-Bibb county	18,486	27.3%	16.6%	18.9%	26.0%	6.3%	2.3%	2.5%	0.2%	22.6%
Roswell city	8,771	22.7%	15.1%	9.8%	31.1%	11.1%	3.0%	5.3%	1.9%	4.3%
Sandy Springs city	17,561	11.2%	13.1%	14.7%	28.2%	24.6%	4.3%	2.3%	1.5%	5.8%
Savannah city	24,507	33.7%	17.9%	21.1%	14.6%	10.0%	1.7%	0.7%	0.4%	22.1%
Hawaii										
Urban Honolulu CDP	44,550	19.6%	14.8%	20.4%	23.1%	12.9%	6.3%	3.0%	0.0%	11.3%
Idaho										
Boise City city	32,766	26.4%	19.3%	14.6%	26.6%	7.7%	2.8%	0.8%	1.7%	13.6%
Meridian city	9,187	50.7%	7.0%	7.1%	19.3%	10.2%	0.8%	0.0%	4.8%	11.3%
Illinois										
Aurora city	26,219	18.1%	20.5%	18.9%	28.7%	9.2%	3.2%	1.5%	0.0%	12.9%
Chicago city	482,562	23.1%	12.9%	12.7%	18.9%	17.6%	7.1%	4.3%	3.3%	16.2%
Elgin city	11,983	23.2%	11.1%	15.0%	35.5%	9.4%	4.5%	1.4%	0.0%	11.6%
Joliet city	16,306	19.3%	16.7%	18.6%	26.3%	15.0%	2.6%	1.4%	0.0%	11.2%
Naperville city	14,606	22.5%	9.8%	13.7%	26.7%	18.3%	5.3%	3.7%	0.0%	4.9%
Peoria city	18,154	28.4%	9.0%	18.3%	19.1%	13.7%	10.5%	0.7%	0.3%	18.8%
Rockford city	19,169	26.5%	13.5%	22.7%	21.9%	13.4%	1.6%	0.3%	0.0%	20.7%
Springfield city	15,469	23.6%	17.4%	17.8%	20.7%	13.5%	3.6%	2.2%	1.2%	23.1%
Indiana										
Evansville city	15,885	25.8%	12.3%	20.5%	25.4%	11.8%	2.5%	1.8%	0.0%	17.2%
Fort Wayne city	33,623	23.1%	13.3%	16.2%	35.6%	9.1%	0.5%	1.2%	0.9%	15.9%
Indianapolis city (balance)	132,231	27.0%	16.5%	18.5%	23.6%	9.8%	2.3%	1.9%	0.4%	16.9%
South Bend city	12,062	20.0%	21.3%	21.3%	20.3%	7.2%	0.0%	1.2%	0.0%	20.3%
Iowa										
Cedar Rapids city	16,437	30.0%	12.5%	5.1%	34.8%	13.6%	2.5%	0.0%	1.4%	24.2%
Davenport city	14,051	21.4%	10.0%	26.9%	24.0%	9.8%	4.4%	3.5%	0.0%	12.3%
Des Moines city	32,683	21.0%	17.1%	18.4%	26.6%	15.5%	1.5%	0.0%	0.0%	15.9%
Kansas										
Kansas City city	19,764	20.2%	15.4%	18.3%	32.7%	9.2%	2.9%	1.4%	0.0%	17.2%
Olathe city	14,204	20.1%	10.1%	11.7%	32.2%	20.2%	4.3%	1.4%	0.0%	10.4%
Overland Park city	24,843	16.3%	10.8%	8.5%	31.7%	16.0%	6.2%	4.8%	5.6%	8.3%
Topeka city	14,998	25.5%	17.2%	17.6%	19.9%	14.0%	2.5%	0.0%	3.3%	25.9%
Wichita city	55,499	24.3%	16.9%	17.6%	24.9%	10.8%	1.8%	2.9%	0.8%	13.6%
Kentucky										
Lexington-Fayette urban county	45,356	20.5%	16.0%	20.9%	24.8%	10.2%	2.9%	2.9%	1.8%	18.0%
Louisville/Jefferson County metro govt (balance)	77,705	24.0%	17.8%	13.4%	24.6%	15.1%	3.2%	1.5%	0.4%	13.2%
Louisiana										
Baton Rouge city	35,081	24.3%	16.1%	17.1%	23.6%	10.7%	4.2%	3.9%	0.2%	15.7%
Lafayette city	22,933	19.1%	9.9%	12.6%	25.0%	19.0%	8.3%	3.0%	3.1%	8.6%
New Orleans city	66,489	27.5%	19.2%	17.0%	19.0%	10.4%	3.2%	2.8%	0.8%	22.6%
Shreveport city	26,743	28.1%	22.3%	18.2%	18.5%	8.6%	2.6%	0.0%	1.7%	15.8%
Maryland										
Baltimore city	107,588	29.9%	13.7%	13.1%	21.4%	12.1%	5.4%	3.2%	1.2%	20.6%
Massachusetts										
Boston city	148,487	17.0%	8.7%	9.8%	22.5%	21.9%	9.9%	6.3%	4.0%	12.5%
Brockton city	11,438	26.1%	16.6%	6.9%	35.5%	10.3%	3.9%	0.6%	0.0%	11.3%
Cambridge city	29,303	10.8%	6.7%	8.4%	26.2%	23.9%	12.7%	7.8%	3.3%	8.4%
Lowell city	16,486	32.4%	8.4%	11.3%	30.9%	6.6%	8.5%	1.3%	0.5%	24.2%
Lynn city	13,547	15.7%	19.0%	12.2%	31.9%	19.3%	1.1%	0.8%	0.0%	16.3%
New Bedford city	11,068	30.8%	23.3%	17.4%	15.9%	10.7%	1.9%	0.0%	0.0%	33.3%
Quincy city	14,553	22.7%	5.9%	13.8%	26.1%	19.6%	6.5%	4.8%	0.6%	9.1%
Springfield city	19,325	35.3%	16.4%	15.9%	23.1%	7.3%	1.3%	0.7%	0.0%	24.6%
Worcester city	27,695	26.3%	15.3%	13.8%	21.5%	18.0%	3.1%	0.8%	1.1%	25.0%
Michigan										
Ann Arbor city	18,044	19.3%	10.9%	17.1%	28.0%	13.7%	3.2%	6.8%	0.9%	12.3%
Dearborn city	10,651	38.0%	12.3%	16.5%	18.0%	7.0%	3.3%	4.8%	0.0%	19.5%
Detroit city	87,500	45.4%	21.9%	15.4%	12.9%	2.8%	0.4%	0.8%	0.5%	35.6%
Flint city	11,405	49.3%	22.1%	20.6%	4.5%	2.2%	0.7%	0.0%	0.5%	47.8%
Grand Rapids city	34,970	21.7%	21.0%	17.3%	23.2%	13.3%	2.1%	0.8%	0.7%	15.4%
Lansing city	19,226	25.3%	12.2%	23.5%	27.8%	7.6%	3.0%	0.6%	0.0%	19.5%

Table I-3: Places—Income Class by Age—*Continued*

	Total Millennials	Personal Income, Percent by Income Class, ages 18 to 24						
		Under $10,000	$10,000 to $19,999	$20,000 to $29,999	$30,000 to $49,999	$50,000 to $74,999	$75,000 to $99,999	$100,000 or More
Michigan—Cont.								
Livonia city	7,617	58.3%	28.9%	2.0%	8.9%	1.9%	0.0%	0.0%
Sterling Heights city	12,536	51.4%	21.2%	10.1%	15.1%	1.3%	0.9%	0.0%
Warren city	11,076	48.8%	34.4%	7.7%	4.8%	4.3%	0.0%	0.0%
Minnesota								
Minneapolis city	51,927	54.6%	22.6%	9.3%	9.9%	3.6%	0.0%	0.0%
Rochester city	10,947	55.9%	9.8%	17.5%	6.3%	10.5%	0.0%	0.0%
St. Paul city	36,831	59.5%	20.8%	11.1%	8.1%	0.4%	0.0%	0.0%
Mississippi								
Jackson city	20,753	75.1%	16.0%	2.9%	5.4%	0.6%	0.0%	0.0%
Missouri								
Columbia city	28,768	79.8%	11.2%	3.4%	2.8%	2.8%	0.0%	0.0%
Independence city	10,903	72.4%	11.4%	7.0%	8.3%	0.9%	0.0%	0.0%
Kansas City city	43,621	51.5%	22.5%	17.3%	5.7%	2.9%	0.0%	0.2%
Lee's Summit city	6,966	61.5%	9.7%	21.4%	5.0%	2.5%	0.0%	0.0%
St. Louis city	32,067	66.6%	17.0%	7.0%	6.6%	2.0%	0.2%	0.6%
Springfield city	29,221	60.5%	23.9%	9.5%	4.5%	1.7%	0.0%	0.0%
Montana								
Billings city	11,573	36.7%	16.1%	16.9%	23.1%	1.8%	1.5%	3.8%
Nebraska								
Lincoln city	43,889	68.0%	19.0%	7.2%	2.5%	1.5%	1.6%	0.0%
Omaha city	43,003	47.3%	22.7%	14.2%	9.5%	4.1%	0.3%	2.0%
Nevada								
Henderson city	19,103	58.5%	22.0%	12.7%	5.2%	1.2%	0.3%	0.0%
Las Vegas city	51,195	57.4%	24.6%	10.8%	5.7%	1.2%	0.2%	0.0%
North Las Vegas city	24,584	62.7%	15.1%	13.6%	8.6%	0.0%	0.0%	0.0%
Reno city	26,890	49.1%	33.9%	8.7%	7.7%	0.5%	0.0%	0.0%
Sparks city	8,371	49.2%	28.5%	12.9%	4.7%	1.1%	0.3%	3.2%
New Hampshire								
Manchester city	12,737	46.9%	15.1%	21.6%	15.8%	0.6%	0.0%	0.0%
New Jersey								
Elizabeth city	12,521	59.9%	21.3%	6.8%	11.2%	0.9%	0.0%	0.0%
Jersey City city	22,866	65.1%	14.5%	8.3%	7.4%	4.3%	0.4%	0.0%
Newark city	30,454	80.1%	9.3%	5.8%	3.7%	1.2%	0.0%	0.0%
Paterson city	15,741	70.8%	17.2%	9.1%	3.0%	0.0%	0.0%	0.0%
New Mexico								
Albuquerque city	52,676	54.1%	27.0%	14.7%	3.7%	0.5%	0.0%	0.0%
Las Cruces city	16,110	69.0%	18.7%	3.6%	8.1%	0.5%	0.0%	0.0%
Rio Rancho city	7,176	56.2%	31.9%	11.5%	0.5%	0.0%	0.0%	0.0%
New York								
Albany city	20,054	70.3%	14.2%	10.8%	3.8%	0.8%	0.0%	0.0%
Buffalo city	30,353	63.6%	23.2%	9.2%	2.4%	1.6%	0.0%	0.0%
New York city	794,431	67.7%	13.2%	7.9%	7.0%	2.7%	0.7%	0.7%
Rochester city	31,126	56.4%	18.4%	10.8%	12.0%	1.5%	0.8%	0.0%
Syracuse city	26,102	67.4%	14.1%	7.9%	7.8%	1.0%	1.0%	0.9%
Yonkers city	17,714	72.1%	11.5%	10.1%	5.4%	0.8%	0.0%	0.0%
North Carolina								
Charlotte city	80,539	58.2%	20.0%	11.9%	7.6%	1.7%	0.5%	0.1%
Durham city	26,426	58.0%	25.4%	8.7%	7.0%	0.7%	0.0%	0.3%
Fayetteville city	26,213	54.2%	21.1%	15.4%	8.3%	1.0%	0.0%	0.0%
Greensboro city	34,822	74.9%	15.2%	5.9%	3.8%	0.2%	0.0%	0.0%
High Point city	11,419	61.1%	21.0%	9.3%	8.6%	0.0%	0.0%	0.0%
Raleigh city	60,811	65.9%	17.1%	7.5%	8.7%	0.9%	0.0%	0.0%
Wilmington city	18,340	70.3%	11.2%	12.7%	5.3%	0.6%	0.0%	0.0%
Winston-Salem city	27,896	73.5%	13.3%	5.7%	7.5%	0.0%	0.0%	0.0%
North Dakota								
Fargo city	23,310	45.4%	15.9%	15.3%	20.4%	3.0%	0.0%	0.0%
Ohio								
Akron city	21,704	56.8%	22.9%	12.9%	5.5%	0.8%	0.4%	0.7%
Cincinnati city	39,313	58.3%	23.9%	7.9%	7.8%	1.9%	0.3%	0.0%
Cleveland city	42,414	66.9%	18.7%	9.1%	3.5%	1.3%	0.3%	0.3%
Columbus city	102,832	56.0%	19.3%	14.4%	7.5%	2.8%	0.1%	0.0%
Dayton city	18,882	68.4%	22.6%	7.1%	0.4%	0.3%	1.3%	0.0%
Toledo city	31,522	63.4%	20.6%	9.8%	5.9%	0.0%	0.0%	0.3%
Oklahoma								
Broken Arrow city	8,531	38.1%	35.4%	13.8%	10.4%	1.1%	0.0%	1.2%
Edmond city	10,918	46.7%	21.3%	12.0%	11.8%	8.2%	0.0%	0.0%
Lawton city	11,092	50.4%	12.2%	22.9%	14.4%	0.1%	0.0%	0.0%
Norman city	20,878	58.8%	21.8%	15.1%	1.2%	3.0%	0.0%	0.0%
Oklahoma City city	58,633	45.6%	27.5%	15.8%	7.9%	3.2%	0.0%	0.0%
Tulsa city	39,469	50.5%	23.9%	15.3%	9.0%	1.0%	0.0%	0.4%

Table I-3: Places—Income Class by Age—Continued

		Personal Income, Percent by Income Class, ages 25 to 33								
	Total Millennials	Under $10,000	$10,000 to $19,999	$20,000 to $29,999	$30,000 to $49,999	$50,000 to $74,999	$75,000 to $99,999	$100,000 to $149,999	$150,000 or More	Poverty Rate
Michigan—Cont.										
Livonia city	9,580	24.9%	9.8%	12.4%	24.1%	16.9%	10.7%	0.0%	1.2%	5.5%
Sterling Heights city	17,324	32.8%	6.9%	17.9%	17.9%	19.2%	3.4%	2.0%	0.0%	13.7%
Warren city	14,106	28.4%	12.6%	23.0%	23.6%	6.6%	3.4%	2.4%	0.0%	17.9%
Minnesota										
Minneapolis city	83,500	13.1%	14.8%	18.5%	27.4%	14.5%	5.8%	3.7%	2.2%	14.6%
Rochester city	15,378	13.4%	10.3%	13.4%	28.4%	22.8%	6.6%	3.9%	1.2%	4.1%
St. Paul city	51,958	23.9%	16.1%	16.5%	25.3%	13.4%	2.5%	2.3%	0.0%	19.1%
Mississippi										
Jackson city	25,800	29.1%	19.8%	17.5%	25.6%	7.1%	0.2%	0.6%	0.0%	27.6%
Missouri										
Columbia city	21,450	31.8%	12.4%	17.9%	22.8%	11.1%	3.9%	0.0%	0.0%	16.1%
Independence city	13,982	28.4%	10.1%	10.6%	31.0%	16.9%	0.8%	0.6%	1.7%	9.6%
Kansas City city	67,268	18.1%	21.9%	16.1%	26.1%	13.6%	2.8%	1.2%	0.3%	17.2%
Lee's Summit city	10,667	24.0%	7.1%	8.3%	36.5%	18.8%	3.6%	1.7%	0.0%	9.6%
St. Louis city	56,718	22.8%	10.3%	20.9%	24.1%	15.4%	3.4%	1.8%	1.3%	20.0%
Springfield city	25,949	25.4%	19.8%	18.0%	25.3%	7.5%	1.4%	1.8%	0.8%	19.6%
Montana										
Billings city	14,982	20.7%	15.8%	9.5%	24.3%	29.1%	0.7%	0.0%	0.0%	8.6%
Nebraska										
Lincoln city	37,574	24.8%	20.5%	17.3%	23.8%	8.4%	4.1%	0.9%	0.3%	23.5%
Omaha city	68,472	20.1%	9.7%	18.6%	26.1%	17.7%	4.4%	2.7%	0.8%	13.6%
Nevada										
Henderson city	32,425	22.2%	14.3%	16.4%	23.8%	17.6%	3.3%	2.1%	0.2%	10.5%
Las Vegas city	83,225	27.4%	15.9%	18.8%	24.8%	9.0%	2.3%	1.6%	0.2%	18.1%
North Las Vegas city	29,623	30.7%	12.6%	17.2%	21.9%	13.3%	3.2%	0.7%	0.3%	11.1%
Reno city	33,201	20.5%	15.1%	17.5%	29.0%	12.1%	2.5%	2.7%	0.5%	18.5%
Sparks city	12,093	18.1%	9.9%	16.4%	29.3%	22.7%	3.5%	0.0%	0.0%	7.6%
New Hampshire										
Manchester city	14,766	23.0%	14.6%	17.0%	27.1%	10.8%	7.0%	0.6%	0.0%	20.7%
New Jersey										
Elizabeth city	17,452	29.5%	20.1%	23.9%	18.8%	5.5%	1.6%	0.6%	0.0%	14.5%
Jersey City city	52,020	22.6%	11.6%	12.5%	14.0%	15.3%	11.5%	9.3%	3.3%	13.4%
Newark city	39,268	41.2%	16.9%	16.2%	16.5%	5.4%	1.3%	1.7%	0.8%	24.5%
Paterson city	19,161	37.3%	27.8%	11.4%	13.2%	8.2%	2.1%	0.0%	0.0%	30.2%
New Mexico										
Albuquerque city	76,537	25.7%	15.1%	23.2%	21.7%	8.3%	3.6%	2.2%	0.1%	16.0%
Las Cruces city	12,066	27.9%	30.3%	22.1%	12.0%	3.5%	3.6%	0.0%	0.0%	16.2%
Rio Rancho city	11,744	31.7%	23.9%	11.6%	21.7%	8.5%	0.7%	1.0%	0.8%	8.0%
New York										
Albany city	14,733	12.5%	22.7%	22.0%	18.8%	18.2%	3.5%	2.3%	0.0%	16.6%
Buffalo city	41,937	28.3%	17.6%	13.9%	25.9%	10.8%	2.1%	0.8%	0.7%	24.4%
New York city	1,396,089	25.2%	12.7%	12.0%	19.4%	15.8%	6.9%	4.4%	3.7%	14.9%
Rochester city	33,485	30.5%	13.0%	20.5%	19.2%	13.3%	2.8%	0.5%	0.2%	28.0%
Syracuse city	21,880	26.1%	21.7%	18.5%	19.1%	12.7%	1.2%	0.6%	0.0%	27.3%
Yonkers city	25,135	28.7%	11.4%	11.5%	20.5%	21.6%	4.7%	0.9%	0.8%	18.2%
North Carolina										
Charlotte city	130,930	19.5%	14.2%	15.4%	26.2%	15.3%	4.7%	2.5%	2.2%	14.7%
Durham city	46,023	20.6%	20.7%	14.9%	20.6%	17.6%	3.4%	1.5%	0.6%	13.7%
Fayetteville city	33,692	30.2%	18.7%	18.4%	18.2%	10.1%	3.9%	0.5%	0.0%	21.2%
Greensboro city	37,660	24.7%	19.0%	22.5%	28.2%	5.1%	0.3%	0.1%	0.0%	17.3%
High Point city	12,920	33.5%	16.5%	16.3%	20.8%	8.1%	3.5%	0.0%	1.2%	19.6%
Raleigh city	72,032	19.7%	12.7%	17.9%	27.6%	13.3%	5.4%	3.0%	0.3%	12.9%
Wilmington city	15,528	24.9%	21.0%	17.9%	18.7%	12.3%	2.7%	0.8%	1.5%	26.9%
Winston-Salem city	32,107	20.8%	17.6%	21.6%	25.7%	10.0%	1.5%	2.4%	0.3%	13.2%
North Dakota										
Fargo city	18,285	8.7%	20.8%	17.3%	29.1%	12.6%	5.0%	6.5%	0.0%	10.8%
Ohio										
Akron city	25,847	23.7%	20.5%	20.1%	22.9%	10.1%	0.7%	1.7%	0.3%	22.7%
Cincinnati city	51,501	18.7%	17.6%	19.4%	22.7%	13.3%	3.9%	2.6%	1.7%	20.2%
Cleveland city	52,322	35.3%	18.9%	15.0%	18.2%	9.2%	2.0%	0.9%	0.7%	31.5%
Columbus city	148,625	20.1%	16.7%	15.5%	24.7%	15.6%	4.6%	2.2%	0.7%	15.5%
Dayton city	21,241	37.0%	20.8%	15.1%	17.9%	7.0%	2.0%	0.0%	0.3%	32.1%
Toledo city	39,064	24.0%	19.2%	19.1%	24.5%	11.1%	1.5%	0.2%	0.5%	22.3%
Oklahoma										
Broken Arrow city	12,389	22.9%	10.2%	13.7%	25.8%	21.8%	1.4%	3.3%	0.9%	13.5%
Edmond city	12,496	12.2%	23.0%	18.2%	16.2%	11.1%	11.7%	5.0%	2.6%	8.9%
Lawton city	16,128	21.2%	22.3%	24.4%	24.6%	1.0%	0.6%	1.9%	4.1%	16.9%
Norman city	20,146	20.6%	13.4%	15.1%	27.5%	21.0%	1.8%	0.6%	0.0%	7.0%
Oklahoma City city	91,854	22.8%	17.9%	18.4%	22.3%	12.2%	3.3%	2.6%	0.5%	17.6%
Tulsa city	56,285	23.4%	14.7%	19.5%	25.1%	11.8%	2.8%	2.2%	0.4%	18.8%

Table I-3: Places—Income Class by Age—*Continued*

			Personal Income, Percent by Income Class, ages 18 to 24					
	Total Millennials	Under $10,000	$10,000 to $19,999	$20,000 to $29,999	$30,000 to $49,999	$50,000 to $74,999	$75,000 to $99,999	$100,000 or More
Oregon								
Beaverton city	8,713	56.7%	18.2%	10.6%	9.4%	5.1%	0.0%	0.0%
Eugene city	28,228	66.3%	15.3%	14.7%	3.1%	0.6%	0.0%	0.0%
Gresham city	8,610	52.6%	22.1%	17.7%	5.8%	0.0%	1.8%	0.0%
Hillsboro city	7,420	58.2%	20.1%	10.8%	6.7%	3.8%	0.4%	0.0%
Portland city	53,244	59.1%	20.0%	11.4%	6.3%	2.4%	0.7%	0.0%
Salem city	20,256	56.2%	18.8%	16.5%	5.8%	2.7%	0.0%	0.0%
Pennsylvania								
Allentown city	12,462	68.2%	16.9%	9.2%	5.7%	0.0%	0.0%	0.0%
Erie city	11,232	63.4%	23.5%	5.9%	6.1%	1.1%	0.0%	0.0%
Philadelphia city	165,390	70.2%	14.4%	7.2%	5.7%	2.4%	0.1%	0.0%
Pittsburgh city	54,164	70.9%	15.2%	7.3%	4.4%	1.6%	0.3%	0.2%
Rhode Island								
Providence city	30,753	72.7%	13.2%	5.9%	6.4%	1.5%	0.2%	0.1%
South Carolina								
Charleston city	17,312	65.7%	16.0%	11.2%	4.0%	3.0%	0.2%	0.0%
Columbia city	31,398	49.6%	27.5%	15.2%	7.0%	0.1%	0.0%	0.7%
North Charleston city	15,502	54.9%	15.6%	20.5%	6.7%	2.0%	0.2%	0.0%
South Dakota								
Sioux Falls city	15,217	51.1%	20.0%	19.5%	9.4%	0.0%	0.0%	0.0%
Tennessee								
Chattanooga city	20,231	65.8%	15.2%	12.8%	5.2%	0.3%	0.3%	0.3%
Clarksville city	18,369	49.4%	13.0%	14.8%	21.1%	1.6%	0.0%	0.0%
Knoxville city	35,254	60.0%	18.4%	12.7%	8.2%	0.7%	0.0%	0.0%
Memphis city	69,993	66.8%	19.3%	10.0%	3.4%	0.4%	0.1%	0.0%
Murfreesboro city	23,078	56.9%	24.7%	8.0%	8.4%	0.1%	1.9%	0.0%
Nashville-Davidson metropolitan govt (balance)	69,435	49.4%	20.5%	13.0%	12.8%	3.7%	0.6%	0.0%
Texas								
Abilene city	21,140	49.1%	17.9%	18.6%	13.0%	1.4%	0.0%	0.0%
Allen city	6,626	60.9%	11.5%	18.5%	9.1%	0.0%	0.0%	0.0%
Amarillo city	18,732	58.1%	20.1%	12.1%	7.3%	2.3%	0.0%	0.0%
Arlington city	43,654	59.3%	20.8%	10.6%	8.5%	0.7%	0.0%	0.2%
Austin city	104,338	60.5%	16.2%	11.1%	9.0%	2.4%	0.6%	0.3%
Beaumont city	13,486	54.0%	25.1%	7.8%	11.1%	1.6%	0.0%	0.4%
Brownsville city	21,099	71.8%	18.5%	7.9%	1.0%	0.8%	0.0%	0.0%
Carrollton city	11,583	55.4%	7.6%	14.4%	19.2%	3.3%	0.0%	0.0%
College Station city	37,239	70.6%	17.0%	6.0%	5.2%	0.7%	0.0%	0.5%
Corpus Christi city	34,598	63.4%	16.2%	12.3%	3.5%	4.6%	0.0%	0.0%
Dallas city	129,994	50.1%	21.6%	14.2%	11.1%	1.7%	1.1%	0.1%
Denton city	27,287	65.5%	17.9%	11.2%	5.4%	0.0%	0.0%	0.0%
El Paso city	76,155	62.1%	18.9%	11.6%	6.3%	1.2%	0.3%	0.0%
Fort Worth city	79,020	57.1%	17.4%	15.5%	7.4%	2.1%	0.3%	0.2%
Frisco city	7,961	70.3%	14.5%	9.4%	4.3%	1.6%	0.0%	0.0%
Garland city	21,680	67.9%	16.6%	10.0%	4.0%	0.8%	0.7%	0.0%
Grand Prairie city	20,178	63.0%	21.5%	6.6%	5.8%	2.9%	0.0%	0.3%
Houston city	240,690	54.2%	20.4%	12.1%	8.2%	3.8%	1.0%	0.3%
Irving city	25,563	53.3%	17.3%	15.5%	10.4%	1.6%	1.9%	0.0%
Killeen city	15,698	53.4%	15.6%	18.1%	12.0%	1.0%	0.0%	0.0%
Laredo city	29,370	62.0%	23.1%	7.9%	4.6%	2.5%	0.0%	0.0%
Lewisville city	8,657	39.5%	11.6%	26.5%	18.0%	4.4%	0.0%	0.0%
Lubbock city	46,318	64.2%	19.8%	6.8%	6.8%	1.0%	1.1%	0.2%
McAllen city	16,256	77.1%	14.1%	7.7%	0.9%	0.0%	0.3%	0.0%
McKinney city	12,154	59.5%	26.4%	7.4%	4.4%	2.2%	0.0%	0.0%
Mesquite city	13,465	50.4%	22.6%	17.0%	9.3%	0.7%	0.0%	0.0%
Midland city	13,875	47.5%	11.5%	11.2%	18.3%	8.3%	3.2%	0.0%
Odessa city	13,032	45.4%	19.1%	11.8%	15.1%	3.4%	3.0%	2.2%
Pasadena city	12,998	64.8%	11.0%	9.0%	8.3%	6.9%	0.0%	0.0%
Pearland city	8,269	56.5%	18.3%	6.8%	17.1%	1.3%	0.0%	0.0%
Plano city	22,643	65.9%	14.1%	12.7%	6.5%	0.4%	0.4%	0.0%
Richardson city	11,884	62.2%	16.2%	13.2%	3.2%	0.0%	5.3%	0.0%
Round Rock City	11,091	52.0%	12.0%	18.6%	16.2%	0.9%	0.4%	0.0%
San Angelo city	13,635	58.7%	14.1%	22.4%	4.3%	0.6%	0.0%	0.0%
San Antonio city	156,359	54.3%	23.2%	14.2%	6.4%	1.5%	0.4%	0.0%
Tyler city	13,986	58.4%	20.8%	10.8%	8.4%	0.2%	1.4%	0.0%
Waco city	24,361	70.9%	14.6%	8.5%	6.0%	0.0%	0.0%	0.0%
Wichita Falls city	14,773	48.1%	27.3%	20.7%	2.1%	1.7%	0.0%	0.0%
Utah								
Orem city	15,666	60.4%	23.4%	5.5%	8.6%	2.2%	0.0%	0.0%
Provo city	40,901	67.6%	20.1%	7.8%	4.5%	0.0%	0.0%	0.0%
Salt Lake City city	26,245	53.5%	19.0%	15.3%	9.8%	2.1%	0.2%	0.0%
Sandy city	7,641	39.9%	27.9%	24.4%	6.7%	1.0%	0.0%	0.0%
West Jordan city	8,837	45.2%	25.9%	10.3%	18.6%	0.0%	0.0%	0.0%
West Valley City city	15,698	39.2%	22.9%	26.2%	9.4%	2.2%	0.0%	0.0%

Table I-3: Places—Income Class by Age—*Continued*

| | Personal Income, Percent by Income Class, ages 25 to 33 | | | | | | | | | |
	Total Millennials	Under $10,000	$10,000 to $19,999	$20,000 to $29,999	$30,000 to $49,999	$50,000 to $74,999	$75,000 to $99,999	$100,000 to $149,999	$150,000 or More	Poverty Rate
Oregon										
Beaverton city	15,605	25.4%	20.9%	13.2%	13.3%	15.7%	5.0%	5.2%	1.2%	12.2%
Eugene city	23,017	24.9%	21.7%	21.1%	22.2%	6.8%	1.4%	1.9%	0.0%	20.9%
Gresham city	14,493	26.2%	12.4%	26.8%	23.8%	7.6%	2.6%	0.0%	0.6%	22.7%
Hillsboro city	15,643	28.2%	8.2%	16.9%	16.4%	14.9%	6.6%	6.2%	2.6%	10.2%
Portland city	110,931	21.5%	14.9%	16.2%	23.7%	13.4%	4.9%	2.8%	2.6%	17.2%
Salem city	18,923	23.2%	23.1%	15.1%	26.6%	7.8%	3.6%	0.6%	0.0%	12.5%
Pennsylvania										
Allentown city	17,006	30.8%	18.0%	16.6%	26.2%	5.5%	0.7%	2.2%	0.0%	26.0%
Erie city	13,416	23.1%	19.8%	25.0%	17.3%	9.7%	5.1%	0.0%	0.0%	25.0%
Philadelphia city	267,013	27.1%	12.0%	14.8%	23.1%	14.9%	4.6%	2.4%	1.2%	20.1%
Pittsburgh city	56,978	24.2%	12.3%	18.4%	21.9%	14.7%	4.6%	2.7%	1.3%	21.0%
Rhode Island										
Providence city	28,981	26.1%	26.8%	8.8%	21.1%	13.9%	1.4%	1.4%	0.5%	26.4%
South Carolina										
Charleston city	24,013	18.8%	8.8%	16.9%	32.2%	15.1%	2.9%	3.9%	1.5%	15.0%
Columbia city	23,959	18.9%	13.3%	22.9%	26.3%	12.9%	3.5%	1.6%	0.5%	11.9%
North Charleston city	16,951	32.9%	11.2%	14.5%	25.8%	13.7%	0.7%	1.2%	0.0%	18.9%
South Dakota										
Sioux Falls city	27,656	18.3%	8.2%	22.5%	40.2%	10.2%	0.5%	0.0%	0.0%	14.9%
Tennessee										
Chattanooga city	25,035	23.8%	16.3%	22.8%	24.4%	8.0%	1.4%	3.3%	0.0%	12.9%
Clarksville city	29,491	23.3%	14.2%	21.4%	29.4%	8.5%	1.7%	1.4%	0.0%	6.4%
Knoxville city	25,085	24.0%	19.0%	18.8%	26.5%	9.2%	1.8%	0.3%	0.4%	25.9%
Memphis city	92,279	29.0%	19.6%	20.7%	16.4%	9.4%	3.1%	1.6%	0.2%	21.8%
Murfreesboro city	17,931	23.8%	8.4%	17.8%	31.4%	15.1%	3.0%	0.4%	0.0%	8.9%
Nashville-Davidson metropolitan govt (balance)	114,997	19.5%	14.5%	16.0%	26.9%	15.3%	4.2%	3.0%	0.4%	14.0%
Texas										
Abilene city	16,864	21.8%	15.5%	17.9%	29.1%	9.9%	4.7%	0.0%	1.2%	11.2%
Allen city	10,327	12.8%	18.4%	15.4%	26.9%	7.6%	10.3%	5.8%	2.9%	5.6%
Amarillo city	26,111	20.7%	18.7%	17.4%	25.9%	10.2%	4.6%	2.5%	0.0%	15.3%
Arlington city	55,832	25.5%	16.0%	15.1%	22.3%	16.9%	2.0%	1.6%	0.7%	11.5%
Austin city	185,237	14.7%	13.3%	20.7%	27.1%	12.5%	6.6%	3.4%	1.7%	10.1%
Beaumont city	15,950	39.5%	13.4%	5.8%	25.0%	11.4%	1.3%	2.9%	0.8%	23.4%
Brownsville city	20,990	32.5%	24.0%	16.8%	18.9%	6.6%	0.0%	1.2%	0.0%	29.3%
Carrollton city	17,833	16.4%	10.0%	12.2%	30.4%	16.4%	8.7%	4.0%	1.8%	8.5%
College Station city	18,592	29.1%	18.4%	22.8%	18.2%	6.5%	1.8%	0.0%	3.1%	23.9%
Corpus Christi city	43,340	23.0%	15.8%	17.9%	26.1%	11.0%	4.0%	2.2%	0.0%	18.4%
Dallas city	205,380	23.5%	14.4%	16.6%	22.5%	14.1%	4.4%	3.1%	1.5%	18.1%
Denton city	21,384	25.9%	12.5%	20.2%	19.1%	14.3%	6.7%	1.3%	0.0%	6.6%
El Paso city	86,901	27.0%	16.1%	22.3%	23.0%	8.0%	1.8%	1.4%	0.3%	15.5%
Fort Worth city	121,870	24.3%	14.2%	16.9%	25.2%	13.2%	3.4%	1.8%	1.1%	16.4%
Frisco city	14,063	20.5%	7.2%	18.2%	25.1%	16.4%	10.0%	2.7%	0.0%	9.5%
Garland city	30,466	27.4%	12.7%	20.6%	25.7%	9.9%	1.3%	1.9%	0.5%	10.1%
Grand Prairie city	22,919	21.0%	20.0%	15.9%	29.8%	10.0%	2.8%	0.3%	0.0%	14.1%
Houston city	360,129	23.2%	16.5%	15.6%	20.7%	13.2%	4.7%	4.2%	1.9%	16.5%
Irving city	36,665	23.5%	10.7%	17.9%	24.0%	16.2%	4.5%	2.0%	1.2%	10.1%
Killeen city	25,678	30.2%	14.1%	10.4%	26.7%	15.2%	3.4%	0.0%	0.0%	19.7%
Laredo city	29,722	40.1%	18.6%	14.3%	13.3%	8.0%	5.1%	0.0%	0.6%	31.6%
Lewisville city	19,980	15.6%	11.0%	17.3%	30.1%	16.7%	4.5%	3.5%	1.4%	3.7%
Lubbock city	34,892	23.7%	17.5%	24.7%	19.7%	9.5%	0.9%	2.4%	1.6%	16.8%
McAllen city	16,372	36.8%	14.7%	12.5%	21.4%	9.2%	2.7%	0.0%	2.7%	19.2%
McKinney city	17,200	25.3%	12.5%	8.3%	22.0%	16.5%	10.7%	3.7%	0.9%	9.5%
Mesquite city	19,751	25.6%	24.4%	9.9%	26.9%	10.2%	1.8%	1.2%	0.0%	18.5%
Midland city	20,114	17.3%	8.6%	10.3%	27.5%	9.3%	13.9%	11.3%	1.8%	5.4%
Odessa city	18,578	29.3%	11.7%	9.4%	17.1%	14.1%	8.7%	8.0%	1.7%	10.6%
Pasadena city	22,286	23.2%	14.8%	22.3%	26.9%	9.9%	1.4%	1.6%	0.0%	14.9%
Pearland city	15,825	10.7%	6.8%	7.9%	38.8%	27.7%	6.7%	1.4%	0.0%	0.9%
Plano city	36,726	17.1%	16.5%	10.5%	23.1%	23.0%	5.4%	3.2%	1.3%	7.7%
Richardson city	17,044	20.9%	13.7%	15.9%	18.8%	22.5%	4.3%	3.4%	0.6%	14.1%
Round Rock City	13,486	16.4%	14.3%	20.2%	19.4%	23.3%	4.2%	2.2%	0.0%	5.7%
San Angelo city	14,415	26.9%	20.6%	15.3%	16.4%	13.9%	3.6%	3.3%	0.0%	22.7%
San Antonio city	217,816	26.3%	16.7%	17.9%	23.6%	11.0%	3.0%	1.1%	0.4%	16.0%
Tyler city	13,900	42.2%	15.2%	14.7%	13.1%	9.7%	1.2%	2.5%	1.3%	24.5%
Waco city	17,077	31.3%	14.9%	21.6%	11.8%	17.6%	1.6%	0.9%	0.3%	21.8%
Wichita Falls city	14,603	41.9%	17.5%	13.5%	16.7%	5.8%	1.7%	2.4%	0.5%	22.5%
Utah										
Orem city	14,174	28.8%	11.0%	22.3%	25.5%	9.9%	0.6%	1.9%	0.0%	10.2%
Provo city	18,730	35.4%	19.1%	18.9%	18.0%	6.6%	1.5%	0.5%	0.0%	24.7%
Salt Lake City city	38,151	18.5%	13.0%	20.6%	29.9%	11.8%	2.5%	2.6%	1.2%	12.6%
Sandy city	10,924	25.9%	18.2%	8.2%	27.4%	9.7%	7.3%	3.4%	0.0%	13.5%
West Jordan city	15,277	23.5%	10.7%	14.8%	19.4%	11.9%	9.8%	6.9%	3.2%	9.1%
West Valley City city	19,357	22.7%	12.5%	21.3%	29.5%	14.0%	0.0%	0.0%	0.0%	12.1%

Table I-3: Places—Income Class by Age—*Continued*

			Personal Income, Percent by Income Class, ages 18 to 24					
	Total Millennials	Under $10,000	$10,000 to $19,999	$20,000 to $29,999	$30,000 to $49,999	$50,000 to $74,999	$75,000 to $99,999	$100,000 or More
Virginia								
Alexandria city	7,083	35.1%	25.1%	14.5%	18.9%	6.5%	0.0%	0.0%
Chesapeake city	21,785	48.7%	21.1%	10.3%	14.6%	4.1%	1.3%	0.0%
Hampton city	16,083	49.8%	19.7%	10.4%	16.7%	2.9%	0.6%	0.0%
Newport News city	23,978	50.3%	22.0%	15.5%	10.7%	1.2%	0.3%	0.0%
Norfolk city	46,891	46.3%	20.0%	23.3%	8.9%	0.8%	0.6%	0.0%
Portsmouth city	10,240	54.5%	17.2%	10.1%	12.0%	6.2%	0.0%	0.0%
Richmond city	29,893	66.8%	16.8%	5.9%	7.9%	2.1%	0.4%	0.0%
Roanoke city	10,176	65.6%	11.8%	7.0%	15.6%	0.0%	0.0%	0.0%
Virginia Beach city	46,490	44.0%	23.7%	16.3%	12.5%	2.9%	0.7%	0.0%
Washington								
Bellevue city	10,338	53.7%	24.2%	11.0%	7.0%	1.7%	2.4%	0.0%
Everett city	10,760	47.0%	23.4%	14.0%	12.2%	1.8%	0.5%	1.2%
Federal Way city	6,788	58.2%	7.9%	16.4%	11.7%	5.7%	0.0%	0.0%
Kent city	12,389	55.9%	12.7%	12.0%	12.1%	7.3%	0.0%	0.0%
Renton city	5,919	54.1%	22.2%	14.3%	9.5%	0.0%	0.0%	0.0%
Seattle city	75,581	55.6%	15.2%	12.5%	7.5%	5.2%	2.3%	1.6%
Spokane city	21,782	64.8%	21.3%	8.5%	2.3%	2.4%	0.0%	0.7%
Spokane Valley city	7,006	48.6%	24.9%	12.8%	12.5%	0.0%	1.2%	0.0%
Tacoma city	19,387	56.6%	15.7%	11.0%	11.9%	4.8%	0.0%	0.0%
Vancouver city	15,490	49.2%	23.1%	14.2%	9.7%	3.8%	0.0%	0.0%
Yakima city	11,512	55.4%	30.5%	6.3%	5.8%	2.1%	0.0%	0.0%
Wisconsin								
Green Bay city	13,082	46.5%	24.7%	14.3%	13.5%	1.0%	0.0%	0.0%
Kenosha city	10,817	54.2%	23.5%	18.1%	4.1%	0.0%	0.0%	0.0%
Madison city	51,806	58.7%	20.6%	10.1%	7.7%	1.9%	1.0%	0.0%
Milwaukee city	69,180	67.2%	19.6%	8.3%	3.8%	1.0%	0.2%	0.0%

Table I-3: Places—Income Class by Age—*Continued*

| | Personal Income, Percent by Income Class, ages 25 to 33 | | | | | | | | | |
	Total Millennials	Under $10,000	$10,000 to $19,999	$20,000 to $29,999	$30,000 to $49,999	$50,000 to $74,999	$75,000 to $99,999	$100,000 to $149,999	$150,000 or More	Poverty Rate
Virginia										
Alexandria city	33,380	16.2%	10.9%	15.7%	17.0%	22.2%	9.2%	7.0%	1.8%	8.2%
Chesapeake city	31,728	29.9%	13.0%	18.0%	18.8%	14.3%	4.5%	1.0%	0.5%	13.2%
Hampton city	19,819	20.8%	16.3%	12.5%	26.9%	22.2%	0.9%	0.4%	0.0%	14.4%
Newport News city	28,073	30.4%	15.3%	12.7%	26.7%	8.7%	4.1%	2.0%	0.2%	19.9%
Norfolk city	42,408	31.5%	15.3%	14.9%	22.0%	12.4%	3.5%	0.5%	0.0%	17.5%
Portsmouth city	15,009	32.5%	12.3%	17.1%	22.3%	12.6%	2.2%	1.0%	0.0%	21.6%
Richmond city	41,924	22.8%	14.4%	19.5%	22.0%	13.0%	4.0%	3.5%	0.7%	17.4%
Roanoke city	13,759	26.1%	21.8%	21.5%	23.0%	6.4%	0.6%	0.4%	0.4%	20.5%
Virginia Beach city	69,123	20.5%	14.1%	16.4%	28.8%	14.3%	4.9%	0.5%	0.6%	10.0%
Washington										
Bellevue city	22,217	23.0%	12.0%	10.9%	10.2%	17.1%	13.2%	9.4%	4.3%	7.5%
Everett city	14,826	21.8%	11.0%	15.7%	27.9%	18.9%	2.4%	1.6%	0.6%	10.0%
Federal Way city	15,447	24.3%	13.4%	11.7%	32.6%	13.9%	3.1%	0.6%	0.4%	7.6%
Kent city	21,384	29.9%	13.4%	18.6%	20.5%	10.6%	4.6%	1.6%	0.7%	16.9%
Renton city	14,615	22.6%	10.0%	17.1%	23.9%	18.7%	2.1%	5.6%	0.0%	3.3%
Seattle city	147,020	12.7%	9.5%	12.0%	23.6%	19.9%	10.4%	9.8%	2.3%	9.1%
Spokane city	33,095	30.9%	19.0%	12.2%	24.2%	8.9%	1.7%	3.0%	0.2%	20.6%
Spokane Valley city	13,846	27.9%	13.1%	16.5%	25.7%	10.4%	4.5%	0.0%	1.9%	10.8%
Tacoma city	31,332	25.2%	9.8%	18.4%	22.4%	15.4%	6.0%	2.8%	0.0%	18.0%
Vancouver city	22,130	20.5%	13.5%	19.2%	28.8%	13.8%	3.9%	0.3%	0.0%	14.6%
Yakima city	10,350	28.6%	25.4%	15.0%	25.5%	3.7%	0.6%	1.2%	0.0%	22.3%
Wisconsin										
Green Bay city	14,708	19.9%	17.1%	23.1%	29.5%	8.7%	1.7%	0.0%	0.0%	14.9%
Kenosha city	10,402	23.0%	11.8%	13.8%	34.4%	14.4%	2.6%	0.0%	0.0%	13.6%
Madison city	39,715	14.5%	11.0%	19.8%	29.3%	12.1%	6.5%	3.4%	3.4%	13.1%
Milwaukee city	89,811	25.7%	11.8%	19.5%	26.4%	11.2%	2.5%	2.0%	1.0%	20.4%

Table I-4: Metropolitan/Micropolitan Statistical Areas—Income Class by Age

	Total Millennials	Under $10,000	$10,000 to $19,999	$20,000 to $29,999	$30,000 to $49,999	$50,000 to $74,999	$75,000 to $99,999	$100,000 or More
				Persons Income, Percent by Income Class 18 to 24				
Abilene, TX	23,544	50.7%	16.9%	19.0%	11.9%	1.4%	0.0%	0.2%
Adrian, MI	10,309	50.9%	29.0%	13.3%	4.4%	2.3%	0.0%	0.0%
Akron, OH	74,806	62.8%	20.5%	8.5%	6.4%	1.4%	0.1%	0.2%
Albany, GA	16,195	74.6%	13.5%	8.3%	2.6%	1.0%	0.0%	0.0%
Albany, OR	12,827	59.1%	19.8%	12.0%	4.9%	4.1%	0.0%	0.0%
Albany-Schenectady-Troy, NY	98,107	64.0%	18.3%	9.5%	7.2%	1.0%	0.0%	0.0%
Albertville, AL	8,881	69.0%	23.9%	6.1%	0.3%	0.6%	0.0%	0.0%
Albuquerque, NM	84,613	58.8%	25.3%	12.4%	3.1%	0.4%	0.0%	0.0%
Alexandria, LA	14,235	59.3%	16.4%	15.3%	7.2%	1.0%	0.0%	0.8%
Allentown-Bethlehem-Easton, PA-NJ	76,390	60.9%	19.3%	10.7%	6.8%	1.5%	0.5%	0.1%
Altoona, PA	10,242	73.2%	10.6%	5.6%	4.7%	5.9%	0.0%	0.0%
Amarillo, TX	25,578	55.7%	22.6%	11.1%	8.8%	1.8%	0.0%	0.0%
Ames, IA	30,643	65.1%	18.6%	9.0%	5.7%	1.6%	0.0%	0.0%
Anchorage, AK	45,782	39.4%	29.0%	16.5%	10.9%	3.8%	0.5%	0.0%
Ann Arbor, MI	65,988	48.5%	23.0%	10.9%	11.3%	6.0%	0.0%	0.2%
Anniston-Oxford-Jacksonville, AL	12,942	51.8%	29.2%	15.0%	2.0%	1.4%	0.7%	0.0%
Appleton, WI	19,110	53.8%	20.1%	17.8%	7.8%	0.6%	0.0%	0.0%
Asheville, NC	33,465	59.4%	24.9%	9.0%	5.6%	0.7%	0.3%	0.0%
Ashtabula, OH	7,835	58.2%	19.6%	15.1%	5.3%	0.6%	1.3%	0.0%
Athens-Clarke County, GA	40,739	76.2%	14.8%	6.1%	2.6%	0.3%	0.0%	0.0%
Atlanta-Sandy Springs-Roswell, GA	524,244	63.0%	18.8%	11.8%	4.7%	1.3%	0.3%	0.1%
Atlantic City-Hammonton, NJ	27,015	66.2%	15.9%	5.8%	8.5%	1.9%	0.0%	1.6%
Auburn-Opelika, AL	30,660	72.8%	10.8%	11.8%	4.6%	0.0%	0.0%	0.0%
Augusta-Richmond County, GA-SC	57,885	66.7%	18.4%	9.2%	4.7%	0.9%	0.0%	0.0%
Augusta-Waterville, ME	10,420	55.4%	33.4%	4.6%	5.3%	1.3%	0.0%	0.0%
Austin-Round Rock, TX	201,829	58.9%	17.5%	12.7%	8.4%	1.8%	0.4%	0.3%
Bakersfield, CA	96,404	59.6%	20.3%	10.8%	6.0%	2.6%	0.0%	0.8%
Baltimore-Columbia-Towson, MD	251,659	60.1%	17.7%	11.5%	8.1%	2.0%	0.6%	0.0%
Bangor, ME	17,405	74.5%	18.2%	3.9%	2.7%	0.8%	0.0%	0.0%
Barnstable Town, MA	14,201	69.3%	11.6%	9.6%	9.5%	0.0%	0.0%	0.0%
Baton Rouge, LA	98,596	57.5%	22.3%	10.2%	6.8%	2.0%	0.8%	0.4%
Battle Creek, MI	10,750	63.8%	24.3%	8.5%	3.4%	0.0%	0.0%	0.0%
Bay City, MI	8,750	43.1%	42.2%	9.1%	3.0%	0.0%	2.5%	0.0%
Beaumont-Port Arthur, TX	37,714	55.8%	20.6%	8.2%	10.2%	3.7%	0.8%	0.8%
Beckley, WV	9,532	79.2%	13.5%	4.1%	2.8%	0.3%	0.0%	0.0%
Bellingham, WA	30,613	61.1%	17.8%	13.0%	5.5%	1.9%	0.7%	0.0%
Bend-Redmond, OR	12,522	52.3%	22.4%	11.0%	5.3%	4.9%	4.0%	0.0%
Billings, MT	16,307	40.5%	21.1%	14.3%	19.1%	1.3%	1.1%	2.7%
Binghamton, NY	32,990	70.1%	18.6%	7.0%	3.6%	0.3%	0.0%	0.4%
Birmingham-Hoover, AL	99,509	65.4%	19.0%	10.2%	4.0%	1.4%	0.0%	0.0%
Bismarck, ND	10,971	47.7%	16.9%	16.7%	11.6%	4.8%	0.1%	2.2%
Blacksburg-Christiansburg-Radford, VA	40,796	74.9%	15.3%	5.9%	3.3%	0.6%	0.0%	0.0%
Bloomington, IL	32,433	60.7%	20.4%	9.3%	7.7%	1.9%	0.0%	0.0%
Bloomington, IN	41,299	78.2%	14.1%	3.8%	2.9%	1.0%	0.0%	0.0%
Bloomsburg-Berwick, PA	10,392	66.7%	13.0%	8.9%	6.0%	5.5%	0.0%	0.0%
Boise City, ID	58,208	64.5%	19.7%	9.1%	4.6%	1.9%	0.0%	0.2%
Boston-Cambridge-Newton, MA-NH	476,078	62.7%	16.8%	8.6%	8.0%	2.9%	0.5%	0.5%
Boulder, CO	49,567	62.3%	18.4%	9.1%	9.2%	1.0%	0.0%	0.0%
Bowling Green, KY	22,855	59.2%	21.5%	14.3%	4.7%	0.4%	0.0%	0.0%
Bremerton-Silverdale, WA	27,430	47.3%	15.8%	25.5%	9.0%	2.4%	0.0%	0.0%
Bridgeport-Stamford-Norwalk, CT	85,139	63.7%	17.2%	8.2%	7.8%	3.0%	0.0%	0.2%
Brownsville-Harlingen, TX	44,883	67.0%	21.1%	8.7%	2.8%	0.4%	0.1%	0.0%
Brunswick, GA	9,393	55.0%	29.1%	5.5%	8.5%	1.9%	0.0%	0.0%
Buffalo-Cheektowaga-Niagara Falls, NY	108,353	60.3%	19.8%	10.3%	7.8%	1.4%	0.4%	0.0%
Burlington, NC	14,754	68.0%	19.2%	9.1%	3.5%	0.2%	0.0%	0.0%
Burlington-South Burlington, VT	30,542	61.7%	15.9%	10.5%	10.5%	1.4%	0.0%	0.0%
California-Lexington Park, MD	11,172	55.3%	20.2%	10.7%	9.9%	3.9%	0.0%	0.0%
Canton-Massillon, OH	34,570	55.9%	22.6%	14.6%	4.4%	2.3%	0.2%	0.2%
Cape Coral-Fort Myers, FL	50,309	53.2%	27.9%	12.1%	5.7%	0.9%	0.0%	0.1%
Cape Girardeau, MO-IL	10,731	62.7%	26.5%	5.8%	5.0%	0.0%	0.0%	0.0%
Carbondale-Marion, IL	18,633	71.1%	17.0%	9.1%	1.0%	1.8%	0.0%	0.0%
Carson City, NV	5,225	40.1%	32.0%	5.7%	22.1%	0.0%	0.0%	0.0%
Casper, WY	7,113	52.5%	22.7%	8.8%	10.1%	1.2%	4.8%	0.0%
Cedar Rapids, IA	24,636	51.6%	29.4%	12.2%	5.2%	1.2%	0.3%	0.0%
Chambersburg-Waynesboro, PA	13,646	63.7%	20.5%	6.0%	8.7%	1.1%	0.0%	0.0%
Champaign-Urbana, IL	52,890	81.7%	11.8%	4.2%	2.1%	0.2%	0.0%	0.0%
Charleston, WV	15,789	57.0%	24.2%	16.1%	0.9%	0.4%	0.5%	0.8%
Charleston-North Charleston, SC	69,521	62.6%	17.2%	12.5%	5.4%	1.8%	0.2%	0.2%
Charlotte-Concord-Gastonia, NC-SC	213,700	59.1%	20.6%	11.4%	7.2%	1.3%	0.2%	0.2%
Charlottesville, VA	29,757	68.9%	14.3%	9.2%	4.6%	2.2%	0.8%	0.1%
Chattanooga, TN-GA	51,185	61.9%	18.7%	14.3%	4.8%	0.1%	0.1%	0.1%
Cheyenne, WY	14,476	41.1%	36.3%	8.0%	5.4%	0.5%	0.0%	8.7%
Chicago-Naperville-Elgin, IL-IN-WI	895,906	61.9%	18.4%	10.8%	6.5%	2.0%	0.2%	0.2%
Chico, CA	33,684	73.0%	19.2%	5.8%	1.6%	0.4%	0.0%	0.1%
Cincinnati, OH-KY-IN	198,140	58.3%	23.2%	10.4%	6.1%	1.6%	0.3%	0.1%
Clarksburg, WV	7,633	51.2%	20.2%	6.7%	17.3%	1.1%	3.5%	0.0%

Table I-4: Metropolitan/Micropolitan Statistical Areas—Income Class by Age—*Continued*

	Total Millennials	Under $10,000	$10,000 to $19,999	$20,000 to $29,999	$30,000 to $49,999	$50,000 to $74,999	$75,000 to $99,999	$100,000 to $149,999	$150,000 or More	Poverty Rate
				Persons Income, Percent by Income Class 25 to 33						
Abilene, TX	19,761	26.0%	14.5%	16.9%	28.3%	9.2%	4.1%	0.0%	1.0%	11.7%
Adrian, MI	8,941	35.7%	9.1%	12.0%	32.0%	5.4%	2.0%	3.1%	0.7%	19.8%
Akron, OH	77,664	23.5%	18.1%	17.0%	22.9%	14.5%	1.6%	1.9%	0.4%	16.1%
Albany, GA	16,784	37.7%	18.9%	14.3%	19.8%	7.3%	0.6%	0.3%	1.0%	30.9%
Albany, OR	11,441	24.9%	27.8%	20.2%	16.2%	6.4%	3.7%	1.0%	0.0%	20.3%
Albany-Schenectady-Troy, NY	102,488	17.8%	15.4%	14.7%	23.9%	20.5%	4.2%	3.2%	0.2%	9.9%
Albertville, AL	9,155	39.2%	20.1%	14.5%	15.3%	7.3%	1.8%	1.7%	0.0%	27.6%
Albuquerque, NM	113,245	28.1%	16.2%	21.1%	21.7%	7.6%	3.2%	1.8%	0.3%	16.3%
Alexandria, LA	17,893	34.0%	17.2%	16.6%	18.2%	6.6%	5.0%	2.2%	0.1%	20.8%
Allentown-Bethlehem-Easton, PA-NJ	84,989	21.5%	14.5%	18.3%	24.2%	13.7%	5.0%	2.3%	0.5%	12.3%
Altoona, PA	13,712	23.6%	24.2%	14.1%	24.1%	9.5%	3.0%	0.5%	1.0%	18.1%
Amarillo, TX	35,841	23.6%	18.7%	17.4%	23.0%	11.2%	3.8%	2.2%	0.0%	14.6%
Ames, IA	12,175	20.1%	17.7%	16.7%	31.0%	14.2%	0.2%	0.0%	0.0%	11.9%
Anchorage, AK	60,722	19.2%	12.5%	14.2%	25.2%	17.4%	5.0%	4.2%	2.3%	8.6%
Ann Arbor, MI	45,342	21.0%	16.9%	12.4%	24.1%	16.7%	3.6%	3.5%	1.8%	14.7%
Anniston-Oxford-Jacksonville, AL	12,913	31.1%	21.5%	7.7%	25.3%	10.3%	0.3%	1.8%	2.0%	22.1%
Appleton, WI	29,121	15.6%	10.8%	17.7%	39.0%	8.9%	5.6%	1.6%	0.8%	6.1%
Asheville, NC	44,992	27.5%	26.8%	15.4%	18.5%	9.1%	1.4%	0.5%	0.9%	20.1%
Ashtabula, OH	9,787	27.3%	19.9%	23.7%	15.9%	8.0%	4.4%	0.8%	0.0%	16.0%
Athens-Clarke County, GA	24,866	33.2%	21.5%	17.0%	19.8%	3.6%	3.4%	1.2%	0.2%	28.2%
Atlanta-Sandy Springs-Roswell, GA	691,741	24.5%	15.5%	16.6%	24.1%	12.6%	3.9%	2.0%	0.7%	13.1%
Atlantic City-Hammonton, NJ	29,552	26.9%	16.4%	15.2%	22.5%	13.0%	4.0%	2.0%	0.0%	17.9%
Auburn-Opelika, AL	18,813	35.3%	12.7%	9.7%	31.9%	8.3%	1.4%	0.6%	0.0%	26.4%
Augusta-Richmond County, GA-SC	77,257	34.4%	17.1%	12.1%	22.4%	11.0%	2.5%	0.4%	0.1%	20.7%
Augusta-Waterville, ME	11,402	19.2%	13.2%	24.9%	29.0%	13.2%	0.0%	0.5%	0.0%	3.9%
Austin-Round Rock, TX	307,346	18.7%	13.0%	18.0%	26.1%	14.3%	5.4%	3.2%	1.2%	9.9%
Bakersfield, CA	119,068	34.8%	19.8%	13.2%	17.4%	8.9%	3.5%	2.1%	0.4%	23.2%
Baltimore-Columbia-Towson, MD	360,376	23.8%	12.0%	12.4%	23.9%	16.1%	7.4%	3.2%	1.1%	11.5%
Bangor, ME	18,251	34.1%	19.0%	14.0%	19.3%	10.2%	2.4%	0.0%	1.1%	29.2%
Barnstable Town, MA	15,825	21.5%	9.0%	15.2%	25.8%	18.0%	4.7%	3.7%	2.1%	8.3%
Baton Rouge, LA	107,608	29.3%	14.1%	12.9%	22.0%	11.4%	6.6%	3.1%	0.6%	15.3%
Battle Creek, MI	15,498	20.2%	13.6%	33.9%	19.4%	8.8%	3.2%	0.5%	0.4%	14.6%
Bay City, MI	11,393	7.5%	29.6%	18.8%	28.5%	7.9%	6.2%	1.2%	0.2%	12.3%
Beaumont-Port Arthur, TX	52,493	35.8%	13.0%	9.6%	23.1%	12.3%	2.5%	3.1%	0.6%	16.8%
Beckley, WV	12,971	30.3%	16.0%	10.0%	19.1%	4.0%	3.0%	1.4%	0.0%	27.9%
Bellingham, WA	26,325	23.4%	17.2%	26.4%	20.4%	6.3%	3.7%	0.9%	1.6%	13.5%
Bend-Redmond, OR	19,618	17.5%	21.5%	15.3%	21.9%	11.6%	7.3%	0.8%	4.0%	16.3%
Billings, MT	19,898	21.5%	14.4%	9.5%	29.3%	22.9%	0.9%	1.3%	0.2%	11.0%
Binghamton, NY	24,016	20.9%	14.2%	19.4%	26.4%	12.8%	4.2%	1.6%	0.6%	13.7%
Birmingham-Hoover, AL	138,701	26.0%	16.8%	14.3%	23.8%	12.7%	3.7%	2.1%	0.6%	18.3%
Bismarck, ND	18,784	9.8%	6.5%	16.0%	30.0%	21.8%	6.3%	1.8%	7.8%	1.8%
Blacksburg-Christiansburg-Radford, VA	20,223	19.4%	16.1%	14.1%	27.5%	11.6%	6.2%	3.6%	1.6%	16.5%
Bloomington, IL	22,102	16.0%	14.5%	18.0%	27.7%	16.3%	5.3%	0.7%	1.5%	10.3%
Bloomington, IN	20,887	27.2%	19.6%	22.1%	15.7%	14.0%	1.4%	0.0%	0.0%	18.2%
Bloomsburg-Berwick, PA	10,893	30.2%	12.4%	23.3%	26.2%	4.6%	3.0%	0.2%	0.0%	12.0%
Boise City, ID	85,278	28.1%	18.5%	18.9%	21.6%	8.2%	2.6%	1.3%	0.8%	11.9%
Boston-Cambridge-Newton, MA-NH	621,558	17.7%	10.5%	11.3%	25.6%	19.9%	8.5%	4.6%	2.0%	10.1%
Boulder, CO	37,556	20.3%	11.4%	13.0%	25.0%	13.0%	11.5%	3.9%	1.8%	13.6%
Bowling Green, KY	18,892	24.4%	17.2%	16.0%	27.8%	9.8%	2.8%	0.0%	1.9%	16.0%
Bremerton-Silverdale, WA	32,727	23.7%	17.4%	15.7%	24.4%	13.6%	3.2%	1.9%	0.1%	14.0%
Bridgeport-Stamford-Norwalk, CT	97,867	24.1%	12.6%	12.4%	22.2%	14.6%	6.9%	5.0%	2.2%	12.0%
Brownsville-Harlingen, TX	45,622	36.4%	21.9%	12.4%	18.3%	7.4%	1.6%	1.9%	0.2%	31.4%
Brunswick, GA	12,722	33.9%	12.9%	17.6%	23.1%	9.7%	2.8%	0.0%	0.0%	22.4%
Buffalo-Cheektowaga-Niagara Falls, NY	137,249	23.1%	16.1%	15.2%	27.5%	14.0%	2.9%	0.9%	0.2%	16.3%
Burlington, NC	16,654	28.2%	16.3%	23.5%	21.6%	6.4%	3.5%	0.6%	0.0%	21.1%
Burlington-South Burlington, VT	26,095	19.2%	7.0%	12.4%	35.3%	19.9%	4.1%	0.0%	2.1%	10.4%
California-Lexington Park, MD	13,081	20.5%	13.1%	9.2%	24.8%	22.2%	6.5%	3.0%	0.7%	10.9%
Canton-Massillon, OH	42,794	27.6%	17.7%	11.5%	24.5%	14.7%	2.9%	0.8%	0.3%	17.8%
Cape Coral-Fort Myers, FL	69,819	34.9%	16.1%	20.7%	19.0%	6.2%	1.9%	1.0%	0.0%	21.2%
Cape Girardeau, MO-IL	11,904	17.6%	35.8%	7.5%	21.0%	11.2%	2.1%	1.7%	3.1%	21.2%
Carbondale-Marion, IL	14,854	25.1%	17.4%	17.1%	28.1%	4.8%	3.4%	2.1%	2.0%	14.8%
Carson City, NV	4,314	32.2%	28.4%	18.6%	20.9%	0.0%	0.0%	0.0%	0.0%	28.4%
Casper, WY	10,786	30.9%	10.5%	11.9%	20.9%	17.3%	6.0%	2.1%	0.4%	8.7%
Cedar Rapids, IA	30,774	20.9%	15.3%	7.6%	37.3%	13.2%	3.8%	1.1%	0.8%	20.6%
Chambersburg-Waynesboro, PA	15,478	15.3%	19.8%	14.2%	33.4%	12.2%	5.2%	0.0%	0.0%	9.5%
Champaign-Urbana, IL	28,892	18.3%	15.6%	23.9%	26.8%	11.6%	2.4%	1.1%	0.4%	14.1%
Charleston, WV	23,511	24.3%	14.7%	13.9%	35.1%	6.9%	1.7%	2.7%	0.7%	22.5%
Charleston-North Charleston, SC	108,893	24.8%	12.4%	16.5%	24.6%	12.9%	4.6%	2.4%	1.7%	13.4%
Charlotte-Concord-Gastonia, NC-SC	288,787	23.5%	14.7%	15.7%	26.1%	13.0%	3.8%	2.1%	1.1%	14.9%
Charlottesville, VA	30,260	21.4%	17.5%	11.7%	24.6%	13.3%	7.9%	3.3%	0.4%	15.6%
Chattanooga, TN-GA	65,730	26.5%	16.3%	21.1%	20.7%	8.6%	2.6%	3.9%	0.3%	12.0%
Cheyenne, WY	9,573	20.6%	13.8%	21.4%	25.9%	14.2%	3.2%	0.0%	0.9%	13.5%
Chicago-Naperville-Elgin, IL-IN-WI	1,219,063	23.4%	13.8%	14.1%	21.6%	16.1%	5.8%	3.4%	1.8%	13.2%
Chico, CA	25,312	22.8%	26.1%	14.9%	17.5%	12.1%	4.1%	2.6%	0.0%	16.8%
Cincinnati, OH-KY-IN	254,917	22.9%	15.3%	15.3%	26.1%	13.7%	4.4%	1.6%	0.8%	14.6%
Clarksburg, WV	8,720	26.8%	18.2%	18.4%	17.7%	11.1%	5.6%	2.2%	0.0%	11.9%

Table I-4: Metropolitan/Micropolitan Statistical Areas—Income Class by Age—*Continued*

	Total Millennials	Under $10,000	$10,000 to $19,999	$20,000 to $29,999	$30,000 to $49,999	$50,000 to $74,999	$75,000 to $99,999	$100,000 or More
Clarksville, TN-KY	32,686	48.0%	13.8%	15.8%	20.2%	1.8%	0.0%	0.3%
Cleveland, TN	12,021	58.4%	16.5%	17.1%	3.6%	3.7%	0.0%	0.7%
Cleveland-Elyria, OH	178,155	58.6%	22.2%	10.1%	7.4%	1.6%	0.1%	0.1%
Coeur d'Alene, ID	11,742	53.4%	33.5%	12.3%	0.6%	0.0%	0.2%	0.0%
College Station-Bryan, TX	59,179	70.9%	15.7%	6.6%	5.6%	0.8%	0.0%	0.5%
Colorado Springs, CO	75,550	44.0%	28.5%	16.8%	8.6%	1.6%	0.2%	0.3%
Columbia, MO	35,010	80.7%	10.6%	3.6%	2.7%	2.3%	0.0%	0.0%
Columbia, SC	99,606	59.3%	22.0%	10.8%	6.0%	0.8%	1.0%	0.2%
Columbus, GA-AL	36,082	66.2%	18.5%	10.2%	3.7%	1.0%	0.2%	0.2%
Columbus, IN	7,290	55.4%	22.3%	10.1%	7.9%	4.2%	0.0%	0.0%
Columbus, OH	185,106	54.8%	21.5%	13.6%	7.4%	2.6%	0.2%	0.0%
Concord, NH	10,518	69.9%	17.0%	7.8%	5.2%	0.0%	0.0%	0.0%
Cookeville, TN	14,332	62.6%	17.4%	18.8%	0.2%	1.0%	0.0%	0.0%
Corpus Christi, TX	44,738	63.0%	15.6%	11.7%	5.1%	4.1%	0.0%	0.5%
Corvallis, OR	15,283	59.2%	21.0%	10.1%	4.1%	5.6%	0.0%	0.0%
Crestview-Fort Walton Beach-Destin, FL	23,985	47.2%	17.6%	21.3%	12.7%	1.0%	0.3%	0.0%
Cumberland, MD-WV	11,906	67.1%	18.1%	6.9%	6.6%	1.4%	0.0%	0.0%
Dallas-Fort Worth-Arlington, TX	651,831	56.0%	19.5%	13.7%	8.5%	1.8%	0.4%	0.1%
Dalton, GA	13,690	55.2%	23.2%	14.3%	7.1%	0.2%	0.0%	0.0%
Danville, IL	5,300	69.1%	11.5%	7.8%	11.1%	0.5%	0.0%	0.0%
Danville, VA	7,826	61.5%	17.1%	14.6%	6.4%	0.5%	0.0%	0.0%
Daphne-Fairhope-Foley, AL	14,381	54.9%	24.4%	4.8%	9.9%	6.1%	0.0%	0.0%
Davenport-Moline-Rock Island, IA-IL	34,932	65.0%	17.2%	9.5%	6.1%	1.4%	0.7%	0.0%
Dayton, OH	74,740	59.2%	20.0%	12.4%	7.1%	1.0%	0.3%	0.0%
Decatur, AL	12,140	65.5%	25.0%	5.8%	2.5%	1.3%	0.0%	0.0%
Decatur, IL	10,188	77.0%	10.5%	3.2%	9.4%	0.0%	0.0%	0.0%
Deltona-Daytona Beach-Ormond Beach, FL	51,286	72.1%	17.5%	7.1%	2.8%	0.5%	0.0%	0.0%
Denver-Aurora-Lakewood, CO	234,203	51.9%	21.9%	13.6%	9.9%	2.3%	0.2%	0.2%
Des Moines-West Des Moines, IA	53,771	50.5%	23.9%	9.5%	14.2%	1.6%	0.4%	0.0%
Detroit-Warren-Dearborn, MI	368,804	59.8%	20.3%	10.5%	7.1%	1.9%	0.3%	0.1%
Dothan, AL	12,120	59.2%	24.1%	11.5%	4.1%	1.0%	0.1%	0.0%
Dover, DE	18,762	58.0%	22.7%	8.6%	7.3%	2.4%	1.0%	0.0%
Dubuque, IA	10,770	57.8%	23.6%	5.5%	11.3%	1.8%	0.0%	0.0%
Duluth, MN-WI	31,513	59.0%	22.7%	11.7%	5.7%	0.8%	0.0%	0.0%
Dunn, NC	13,083	74.8%	9.9%	9.9%	4.4%	1.0%	0.0%	0.0%
Durham-Chapel Hill, NC	65,360	64.8%	20.4%	8.9%	5.5%	0.3%	0.0%	0.2%
East Stroudsburg, PA	18,241	69.7%	16.8%	8.5%	1.7%	1.6%	1.0%	0.8%
Eau Claire, WI	22,132	63.1%	20.0%	11.4%	5.2%	0.3%	0.0%	0.0%
El Centro, CA	20,115	73.1%	14.7%	6.4%	4.4%	1.3%	0.0%	0.1%
El Paso, TX	13,120	53.0%	32.4%	9.6%	4.5%	0.5%	0.0%	0.0%
Elizabethtown-Fort Knox, KY	18,907	46.7%	33.9%	7.6%	8.5%	3.2%	0.0%	0.0%
Elkhart-Goshen, IN	7,341	59.7%	26.3%	11.2%	2.6%	0.2%	0.0%	0.0%
Elmira, NY	94,502	61.4%	18.4%	12.3%	5.8%	1.5%	0.5%	0.0%
Erie, PA	28,432	63.8%	22.1%	6.6%	6.4%	1.2%	0.0%	0.0%
Eugene, OR	46,350	63.8%	20.0%	11.5%	3.4%	1.3%	0.0%	0.0%
Eureka-Arcata-Fortuna, CA	18,225	64.6%	26.3%	5.2%	3.5%	0.0%	0.0%	0.4%
Evansville, IN-KY	28,292	61.7%	21.5%	9.4%	6.6%	0.6%	0.2%	0.0%
Fairbanks, AK	15,158	38.8%	24.7%	28.4%	5.2%	3.0%	0.0%	0.0%
Fargo, ND-MN	36,712	47.5%	13.2%	17.9%	18.5%	2.7%	0.3%	0.0%
Farmington, NM	11,608	54.4%	19.3%	14.5%	10.8%	1.0%	0.0%	0.0%
Fayetteville, NC	45,468	53.1%	22.9%	14.5%	8.6%	0.9%	0.0%	0.0%
Fayetteville-Springdale-Rogers, AR-MO	56,968	59.7%	16.1%	13.0%	7.9%	3.2%	0.1%	0.0%
Flagstaff, AZ	29,687	80.3%	14.7%	2.8%	1.7%	0.5%	0.0%	0.0%
Flint, MI	36,029	62.9%	24.2%	8.3%	3.1%	1.1%	0.0%	0.4%
Florence, SC	19,018	62.1%	20.7%	12.1%	5.0%	0.0%	0.0%	0.0%
Florence-Muscle Shoals, AL	13,870	52.9%	23.4%	18.9%	4.2%	0.4%	0.3%	0.0%
Fond du Lac, WI	8,500	51.7%	25.0%	17.7%	4.3%	1.2%	0.0%	0.0%
Fort Collins, CO	46,073	54.3%	21.6%	11.3%	9.2%	3.4%	0.2%	0.0%
Fort Smith, AR-OK	24,092	61.5%	21.4%	8.7%	5.1%	2.2%	0.0%	1.1%
Fort Wayne, IN	42,894	54.0%	20.7%	13.5%	11.1%	0.8%	0.0%	0.0%
Fresno, CA	106,206	68.2%	20.2%	6.3%	4.2%	1.0%	0.0%	0.1%
Gadsden, AL	9,075	50.4%	24.1%	17.5%	7.6%	0.5%	0.0%	0.0%
Gainesville, FL	56,926	78.8%	12.1%	4.4%	4.2%	0.6%	0.0%	0.0%
Gainesville, GA	18,304	54.3%	23.8%	12.5%	8.1%	1.2%	0.0%	0.0%
Gettysburg, PA	8,558	55.4%	30.1%	4.2%	8.2%	2.1%	0.0%	0.0%
Glens Falls, NY	9,770	58.3%	20.3%	15.8%	5.6%	0.0%	0.0%	0.0%
Goldsboro, NC	12,124	57.1%	16.8%	20.7%	4.2%	0.0%	1.2%	0.0%
Grand Forks, ND-MN	19,039	56.6%	18.8%	10.8%	10.5%	3.0%	0.0%	0.4%
Grand Island, NE	7,909	43.7%	24.9%	20.7%	10.2%	0.6%	0.0%	0.0%
Grand Junction, CO	15,516	62.9%	17.6%	13.9%	4.9%	0.7%	0.0%	0.0%
Grand Rapids-Wyoming, MI	108,123	60.2%	19.7%	11.1%	7.4%	1.2%	0.3%	0.0%
Grants Pass, OR	6,319	50.6%	17.2%	12.9%	16.6%	2.6%	0.0%	0.0%
Great Falls, MT	8,457	64.0%	21.0%	7.2%	7.8%	0.0%	0.0%	0.0%
Greeley, CO	29,769	53.4%	23.1%	11.2%	9.8%	1.9%	0.4%	0.3%
Green Bay, WI	27,413	47.7%	27.8%	13.6%	9.4%	1.6%	0.0%	0.0%
Greensboro-High Point, NC	71,418	66.6%	21.1%	6.9%	5.1%	0.3%	0.0%	0.0%
Greenville, NC	31,790	63.2%	23.1%	10.5%	1.9%	1.2%	0.0%	0.0%

Table I-4: Metropolitan/Micropolitan Statistical Areas—Income Class by Age—*Continued*

	Total Millennials	Under $10,000	$10,000 to $19,999	$20,000 to $29,999	$30,000 to $49,999	$50,000 to $74,999	$75,000 to $99,999	$100,000 to $149,999	$150,000 or More	Poverty Rate
					Persons Income, Percent by Income Class 25 to 33					
Clarksville, TN-KY	48,376	25.4%	14.3%	20.8%	26.1%	8.9%	2.6%	1.9%	0.0%	10.4%
Cleveland, TN	13,353	35.6%	17.2%	16.8%	21.3%	6.2%	0.8%	0.9%	1.1%	29.9%
Cleveland-Elyria, OH	225,453	24.9%	16.9%	15.9%	23.3%	13.2%	3.6%	1.7%	0.5%	16.5%
Coeur d'Alene, ID	17,751	29.4%	18.0%	19.3%	23.3%	3.5%	1.0%	4.4%	1.2%	23.9%
College Station-Bryan, TX	33,688	27.8%	20.8%	18.8%	19.7%	8.9%	1.2%	0.3%	2.6%	21.1%
Colorado Springs, CO	98,970	24.7%	14.2%	17.5%	24.9%	15.4%	2.4%	0.5%	0.3%	13.2%
Columbia, MO	24,966	30.6%	13.6%	17.6%	21.9%	11.4%	3.7%	0.6%	0.5%	17.5%
Columbia, SC	96,626	20.4%	15.7%	24.0%	24.8%	10.2%	2.7%	1.2%	0.9%	12.2%
Columbus, GA-AL	44,311	32.6%	15.4%	17.3%	20.3%	10.0%	1.6%	2.8%	0.0%	17.9%
Columbus, IN	9,971	19.0%	16.3%	12.9%	14.4%	19.4%	18.0%	0.0%	0.0%	14.0%
Columbus, OH	280,282	20.7%	14.2%	15.9%	25.9%	15.8%	4.5%	2.3%	0.7%	13.6%
Concord, NH	11,368	32.0%	13.5%	8.5%	28.4%	16.7%	1.0%	0.0%	0.0%	8.0%
Cookeville, TN	11,763	27.3%	15.2%	21.8%	26.3%	7.7%	0.8%	0.0%	0.9%	19.5%
Corpus Christi, TX	55,956	26.2%	15.6%	17.3%	23.2%	11.5%	3.3%	2.8%	0.1%	18.5%
Corvallis, OR	12,337	25.0%	27.2%	19.3%	15.0%	9.3%	3.4%	0.9%	0.0%	20.2%
Crestview-Fort Walton Beach-Destin, FL	37,896	22.9%	16.1%	19.6%	24.5%	12.3%	4.6%	0.0%	0.0%	13.1%
Cumberland, MD-WV	10,515	24.6%	25.3%	17.6%	20.7%	8.6%	2.7%	0.5%	0.0%	14.8%
Dallas-Fort Worth-Arlington, TX	913,935	23.2%	14.0%	16.1%	24.4%	14.2%	4.5%	2.5%	1.2%	13.1%
Dalton, GA	17,664	27.4%	11.4%	33.3%	21.3%	6.0%	0.3%	0.2%	0.0%	18.0%
Danville, IL	9,809	27.1%	21.8%	19.8%	18.7%	11.1%	0.7%	0.5%	0.3%	17.8%
Danville, VA	10,281	43.9%	18.4%	13.4%	15.6%	8.1%	0.6%	0.0%	0.0%	34.6%
Daphne-Fairhope-Foley, AL	20,047	29.0%	24.2%	13.5%	20.0%	6.1%	4.6%	2.3%	0.3%	19.9%
Davenport-Moline-Rock Island, IA-IL	42,931	23.8%	15.8%	18.1%	23.9%	11.4%	5.2%	1.8%	0.0%	17.2%
Dayton, OH	93,470	26.8%	15.7%	14.1%	25.0%	13.9%	3.2%	1.2%	0.1%	18.8%
Decatur, AL	17,056	34.3%	9.6%	13.6%	29.5%	6.6%	4.2%	2.2%	0.0%	16.6%
Decatur, IL	10,459	25.2%	12.6%	17.8%	25.7%	15.4%	2.7%	0.6%	0.0%	22.5%
Deltona-Daytona Beach-Ormond Beach, FL	60,527	27.6%	20.4%	20.0%	23.8%	5.7%	1.2%	0.4%	0.8%	16.8%
Denver-Aurora-Lakewood, CO	402,449	18.8%	11.3%	14.5%	28.3%	16.6%	6.6%	2.9%	0.9%	10.1%
Des Moines-West Des Moines, IA	84,680	19.2%	12.4%	14.7%	30.2%	17.0%	3.6%	2.9%	0.2%	10.1%
Detroit-Warren-Dearborn, MI	481,372	29.0%	15.4%	14.7%	20.3%	13.3%	4.7%	1.8%	0.7%	17.0%
Dothan, AL	16,153	43.1%	15.2%	12.8%	20.5%	5.1%	1.7%	0.8%	0.7%	21.3%
Dover, DE	20,537	29.2%	17.7%	14.8%	29.5%	7.9%	0.8%	0.0%	0.0%	18.2%
Dubuque, IA	10,320	15.1%	19.1%	14.0%	28.6%	17.8%	3.9%	0.0%	1.6%	11.8%
Duluth, MN-WI	32,043	18.6%	14.9%	21.3%	26.1%	12.3%	3.6%	3.1%	0.1%	14.9%
Dunn, NC	16,703	34.8%	11.2%	16.9%	22.2%	13.0%	1.7%	0.3%	0.0%	18.7%
Durham-Chapel Hill, NC	77,519	24.6%	17.4%	17.1%	23.3%	13.3%	2.4%	1.3%	0.6%	16.2%
East Stroudsburg, PA	16,475	31.8%	5.8%	30.0%	19.4%	8.2%	0.6%	3.4%	0.0%	13.8%
Eau Claire, WI	19,765	15.3%	20.3%	13.9%	33.8%	8.1%	6.2%	1.2%	1.2%	6.3%
El Centro, CA	21,437	50.3%	22.9%	5.3%	8.8%	9.1%	3.4%	0.2%	0.0%	27.8%
El Paso, TX	17,336	31.2%	20.9%	16.4%	17.5%	9.5%	1.7%	2.2%	0.5%	25.4%
Elizabethtown-Fort Knox, KY	22,639	32.0%	17.1%	15.8%	16.1%	16.2%	1.7%	0.6%	0.3%	19.6%
Elkhart-Goshen, IN	11,023	35.2%	16.5%	10.5%	20.6%	10.4%	4.0%	2.9%	1.0%	17.5%
Elmira, NY	110,937	26.6%	15.3%	21.8%	22.1%	10.3%	2.3%	1.3%	0.3%	15.8%
Erie, PA	31,135	24.9%	15.7%	21.0%	24.9%	10.4%	2.5%	0.0%	0.0%	17.7%
Eugene, OR	41,900	27.6%	20.5%	17.4%	23.5%	7.1%	2.6%	1.3%	0.0%	21.7%
Eureka-Arcata-Fortuna, CA	16,198	36.4%	13.8%	21.7%	20.4%	6.0%	0.5%	0.5%	0.6%	27.7%
Evansville, IN-KY	37,384	24.0%	14.5%	22.8%	21.4%	13.3%	2.3%	1.3%	0.5%	14.3%
Fairbanks, AK	15,499	23.2%	9.2%	12.8%	30.4%	13.4%	3.5%	6.7%	0.8%	16.8%
Fargo, ND-MN	32,049	9.6%	15.8%	16.6%	33.1%	15.8%	3.4%	5.8%	0.0%	10.3%
Farmington, NM	14,031	43.1%	11.6%	18.7%	14.4%	5.9%	3.5%	1.1%	1.8%	23.7%
Fayetteville, NC	54,810	32.7%	15.5%	17.1%	21.9%	9.6%	2.8%	0.3%	0.0%	22.7%
Fayetteville-Springdale-Rogers, AR-MO	67,776	24.9%	12.1%	22.7%	21.5%	10.9%	4.7%	2.4%	0.9%	16.7%
Flagstaff, AZ	17,120	27.3%	17.1%	11.5%	27.2%	9.1%	6.2%	1.3%	0.3%	18.4%
Flint, MI	43,078	34.8%	17.9%	19.7%	17.1%	6.3%	3.5%	0.0%	0.8%	27.6%
Florence, SC	21,857	30.7%	20.2%	16.1%	23.6%	6.0%	2.7%	0.4%	0.3%	17.7%
Florence-Muscle Shoals, AL	13,856	36.7%	12.0%	23.8%	19.3%	4.5%	3.4%	0.4%	0.0%	23.1%
Fond du Lac, WI	10,842	17.5%	17.8%	13.3%	35.2%	14.0%	0.7%	1.5%	0.0%	8.5%
Fort Collins, CO	46,242	18.2%	14.6%	18.6%	28.7%	14.5%	3.0%	1.5%	0.9%	13.2%
Fort Smith, AR-OK	34,033	27.0%	21.7%	17.0%	24.2%	7.6%	1.7%	0.4%	0.0%	25.6%
Fort Wayne, IN	49,413	23.0%	12.1%	17.3%	32.6%	11.4%	0.9%	1.3%	1.4%	14.1%
Fresno, CA	129,871	36.7%	19.4%	16.7%	16.2%	7.6%	2.7%	0.6%	0.2%	24.4%
Gadsden, AL	9,578	29.8%	19.0%	15.4%	21.0%	9.0%	0.0%	5.8%	0.0%	19.0%
Gainesville, FL	37,325	34.0%	12.1%	14.0%	21.9%	13.0%	2.6%	1.1%	1.3%	23.5%
Gainesville, GA	21,584	30.3%	21.3%	19.6%	18.0%	6.3%	1.7%	1.1%	1.6%	19.5%
Gettysburg, PA	10,662	17.6%	21.4%	16.0%	23.6%	16.7%	2.9%	0.0%	1.7%	10.0%
Glens Falls, NY	12,268	31.4%	14.9%	13.7%	27.7%	10.2%	1.9%	0.3%	0.0%	20.6%
Goldsboro, NC	16,422	28.5%	17.8%	19.2%	19.8%	14.1%	0.0%	0.6%	0.0%	18.8%
Grand Forks, ND-MN	13,706	12.4%	14.4%	22.8%	18.3%	18.7%	7.8%	5.6%	0.0%	15.9%
Grand Island, NE	9,116	10.1%	20.3%	30.7%	21.9%	8.5%	4.2%	4.3%	0.0%	23.6%
Grand Junction, CO	17,801	27.3%	16.0%	18.7%	19.0%	15.0%	3.5%	0.0%	0.5%	13.2%
Grand Rapids-Wyoming, MI	129,931	20.5%	18.1%	15.3%	27.9%	13.6%	2.8%	0.9%	0.9%	12.9%
Grants Pass, OR	6,561	27.5%	14.8%	34.9%	14.4%	4.7%	3.7%	0.0%	0.0%	18.0%
Great Falls, MT	9,734	36.1%	19.6%	17.2%	13.1%	12.3%	0.9%	0.0%	0.7%	28.2%
Greeley, CO	35,416	22.7%	10.0%	16.0%	28.6%	12.2%	5.7%	3.6%	1.2%	10.7%
Green Bay, WI	38,825	20.1%	18.1%	17.6%	29.9%	12.7%	0.0%	1.0%	0.6%	13.5%
Greensboro-High Point, NC	85,526	25.2%	19.4%	20.4%	26.1%	6.6%	1.8%	0.2%	0.2%	16.9%
Greenville, NC	22,438	27.7%	19.3%	15.1%	29.1%	7.3%	1.5%	0.0%	0.0%	32.4%

Table I-4: Metropolitan/Micropolitan Statistical Areas—Income Class by Age—*Continued*

	Total Millennials	Under $10,000	$10,000 to $19,999	$20,000 to $29,999	$30,000 to $49,999	$50,000 to $74,999	$75,000 to $99,999	$100,000 or More
Greenville-Anderson-Mauldin, SC	85,925	62.6%	18.6%	9.8%	6.4%	2.5%	0.0%	0.1%
Greenwood, SC	10,427	61.2%	21.3%	11.4%	6.0%	0.0%	0.0%	0.0%
Gulfport-Biloxi-Pascagoula, MS	36,927	59.1%	21.7%	11.3%	7.2%	0.3%	0.3%	0.1%
Hagerstown-Martinsburg, MD-WV	22,794	64.3%	18.9%	7.8%	6.4%	2.6%	0.0%	0.0%
Hammond, LA	14,495	77.4%	18.8%	1.2%	2.6%	0.0%	0.0%	0.0%
Hanford-Corcoran, CA	16,771	64.3%	16.2%	13.4%	6.1%	0.1%	0.0%	0.0%
Harrisburg-Carlisle, PA	54,749	51.1%	20.6%	12.5%	12.5%	2.8%	0.5%	0.0%
Harrisonburg, VA	25,737	77.3%	13.3%	4.3%	4.0%	1.3%	0.0%	0.0%
Hartford-West Hartford-East Hartford, CT	115,378	60.6%	19.0%	9.3%	7.7%	2.5%	0.7%	0.2%
Hattiesburg, MS	20,046	68.1%	18.2%	8.2%	4.7%	0.5%	0.0%	0.3%
Hickory-Lenoir-Morganton, NC	31,801	59.9%	19.0%	11.1%	8.5%	1.3%	0.3%	0.0%
Hilo, HI	16,321	47.9%	25.4%	10.6%	13.2%	2.4%	0.5%	0.0%
Hilton Head Island-Bluffton-Beaufort, SC	18,348	43.6%	27.5%	16.3%	12.6%	0.0%	0.0%	0.0%
Hinesville, GA	13,060	46.6%	17.0%	22.0%	14.4%	0.0%	0.0%	0.0%
Holland, MI	9,792	41.9%	20.0%	15.3%	21.4%	1.4%	0.0%	0.0%
Homosassa Springs, FL	7,713	67.4%	26.2%	4.4%	1.5%	0.0%	0.5%	0.0%
Hot Springs, AR	8,016	65.8%	15.0%	8.4%	10.8%	0.0%	0.0%	0.0%
Houma-Thibodaux, LA	18,255	54.0%	20.9%	13.9%	5.1%	3.0%	1.8%	1.3%
Houston-The Woodlands-Sugar Land, TX	615,008	58.3%	19.2%	10.6%	7.7%	3.2%	0.8%	0.2%
Huntington-Ashland, WV-KY-OH	33,330	62.4%	20.1%	11.9%	4.1%	1.5%	0.0%	0.0%
Huntsville, AL	40,619	66.4%	17.9%	10.6%	3.7%	1.2%	0.3%	0.0%
Idaho Falls, ID	11,332	58.8%	23.3%	15.8%	2.2%	0.0%	0.0%	0.0%
Indianapolis-Carmel-Anderson, IN	174,852	58.5%	20.4%	10.9%	7.9%	1.8%	0.4%	0.1%
Iowa City, IA	31,586	74.5%	15.8%	7.1%	2.0%	0.1%	0.0%	0.5%
Ithaca, NY	30,987	79.8%	7.7%	5.3%	2.0%	4.9%	0.0%	0.4%
Jackson, MI	13,908	59.2%	18.1%	13.4%	8.2%	1.1%	0.0%	0.0%
Jackson, MS	54,327	67.6%	18.4%	8.1%	5.5%	0.4%	0.0%	0.0%
Jackson, TN	13,904	72.0%	11.0%	13.3%	3.7%	0.0%	0.0%	0.0%
Jacksonville, FL	130,435	54.4%	24.7%	11.2%	7.7%	1.8%	0.0%	0.2%
Jacksonville, NC	36,464	32.3%	19.0%	29.9%	16.3%	2.5%	0.0%	0.0%
Jamestown-Dunkirk-Fredonia, NY	13,664	70.1%	17.1%	5.5%	7.3%	0.0%	0.0%	0.0%
Janesville-Beloit, WI	14,815	54.9%	21.9%	15.7%	4.2%	3.3%	0.0%	0.0%
Jefferson City, MO	14,684	63.0%	19.6%	11.3%	4.5%	1.7%	0.0%	0.0%
Johnson City, TN	20,537	70.0%	19.1%	8.7%	2.2%	0.0%	0.0%	0.0%
Johnstown, PA	12,403	75.8%	16.1%	5.1%	1.2%	1.8%	0.0%	0.0%
Jonesboro, AR	15,635	67.3%	12.9%	11.4%	7.9%	0.4%	0.2%	0.0%
Joplin, MO	17,379	53.8%	24.9%	7.1%	13.8%	0.3%	0.0%	0.0%
Kahului-Wailuku-Lahaina, HI	12,607	46.5%	12.0%	22.7%	17.7%	1.1%	0.0%	0.0%
Kalamazoo-Portage, MI	48,185	63.2%	21.2%	7.9%	5.8%	1.0%	0.4%	0.6%
Kalispell, MT	7,110	73.5%	17.7%	0.0%	8.8%	0.0%	0.0%	0.0%
Kankakee, IL	11,549	72.0%	10.6%	5.3%	5.2%	6.8%	0.0%	0.0%
Kansas City, MO-KS	180,675	55.6%	17.5%	15.9%	9.1%	1.7%	0.1%	0.1%
Kennewick-Richland, WA	27,475	59.0%	13.7%	15.7%	10.0%	0.0%	1.5%	0.0%
Killeen-Temple, TX	53,911	46.1%	23.0%	21.8%	8.4%	0.4%	0.0%	0.3%
Kingsport-Bristol-Bristol, TN-VA	23,375	68.9%	17.2%	8.8%	4.0%	1.0%	0.0%	0.0%
Kingston, NY	19,374	67.4%	18.7%	8.8%	3.5%	1.4%	0.2%	0.0%
Knoxville, TN	88,102	63.6%	16.7%	12.3%	6.3%	1.0%	0.0%	0.0%
Kokomo, IN	6,039	50.6%	32.5%	13.3%	3.6%	0.0%	0.0%	0.0%
La Crosse-Onalaska, WI-MN	21,809	63.2%	22.9%	7.3%	6.0%	0.2%	0.4%	0.0%
Lafayette, LA	47,710	70.7%	16.5%	7.5%	3.1%	1.5%	0.0%	0.6%
Lafayette-West Lafayette, IN	48,319	69.7%	12.1%	11.2%	5.5%	1.2%	0.0%	0.3%
Lake Charles, LA	19,506	60.4%	22.8%	8.2%	7.0%	1.5%	0.0%	0.0%
Lake Havasu City-Kingman, AZ	12,700	42.4%	36.3%	8.1%	9.3%	1.8%	0.0%	2.3%
Lakeland-Winter Haven, FL	56,070	62.5%	16.7%	15.1%	4.7%	0.7%	0.0%	0.3%
Lancaster, PA	51,481	57.6%	18.0%	12.6%	8.2%	2.9%	0.7%	0.0%
Lansing-East Lansing, MI	71,250	65.4%	18.0%	9.8%	5.6%	1.2%	0.0%	0.0%
Laredo, TX	30,472	62.8%	22.2%	8.1%	4.5%	2.4%	0.0%	0.0%
Las Cruces, NM	30,410	69.4%	19.4%	5.9%	4.8%	0.6%	0.0%	0.0%
Las Vegas-Henderson-Paradise, NV	186,180	55.9%	22.9%	11.9%	7.5%	1.3%	0.4%	0.0%
Lawrence, KS	27,314	57.2%	33.9%	5.1%	2.3%	1.5%	0.0%	0.0%
Lawton, OK	15,217	53.3%	14.7%	21.4%	10.5%	0.1%	0.0%	0.0%
Lebanon, PA	12,415	56.6%	14.9%	9.0%	18.5%	1.1%	0.0%	0.0%
Lewiston, ID-WA	6,370	84.9%	3.4%	4.5%	7.3%	0.0%	0.0%	0.0%
Lewiston-Auburn, ME	9,422	60.2%	15.2%	9.4%	10.6%	4.6%	0.0%	0.0%
Lexington-Fayette, KY	58,755	55.3%	21.3%	13.7%	6.9%	2.4%	0.3%	0.0%
Lima, OH	9,702	58.8%	26.6%	5.6%	4.9%	2.0%	2.1%	0.0%
Lincoln, NE	46,333	67.7%	18.9%	7.2%	3.2%	1.5%	1.5%	0.0%
Little Rock-North Little Rock-Conway, AR	71,322	57.3%	22.2%	10.3%	8.7%	0.6%	0.8%	0.2%
Logan, UT-ID	22,240	55.9%	27.7%	10.0%	5.6%	0.0%	0.8%	0.0%
Longview, TX	19,837	54.4%	24.8%	11.0%	6.7%	2.2%	0.9%	0.0%
Longview, WA	6,540	53.2%	12.1%	17.5%	16.0%	1.1%	0.0%	0.0%
Los Angeles-Long Beach-Anaheim, CA	1,319,589	64.1%	18.8%	9.3%	5.6%	1.5%	0.4%	0.2%
Louisville/Jefferson County, KY-IN	108,623	57.0%	24.7%	10.7%	6.1%	1.1%	0.2%	0.1%
Lubbock, TX	53,067	64.0%	19.2%	7.6%	7.1%	0.9%	1.0%	0.2%
Lumberton, NC	13,854	74.2%	10.1%	9.7%	5.1%	0.9%	0.0%	0.0%
Lynchburg, VA	32,903	74.1%	12.4%	8.8%	3.7%	0.0%	0.5%	0.5%
Macon, GA	25,465	78.0%	12.2%	5.5%	3.0%	1.1%	0.0%	0.2%

Table I-4: Metropolitan/Micropolitan Statistical Areas—Income Class by Age—*Continued*

	Total Millennials	Under $10,000	$10,000 to $19,999	$20,000 to $29,999	$30,000 to $49,999	$50,000 to $74,999	$75,000 to $99,999	$100,000 to $149,999	$150,000 or More	Poverty Rate
				Persons Income, Percent by Income Class 25 to 33						
Greenville-Anderson-Mauldin, SC	99,564	28.0%	14.4%	18.1%	24.5%	10.9%	2.7%	1.0%	0.3%	17.2%
Greenwood, SC	8,790	34.2%	28.7%	17.4%	8.9%	9.6%	1.2%	0.0%	0.0%	15.6%
Gulfport-Biloxi-Pascagoula, MS	46,488	26.9%	15.5%	19.0%	29.0%	8.1%	0.9%	0.3%	0.0%	20.9%
Hagerstown-Martinsburg, MD-WV	29,667	33.1%	13.5%	10.4%	25.5%	10.0%	6.0%	1.0%	0.5%	13.5%
Hammond, LA	16,082	38.0%	12.1%	11.5%	18.7%	12.7%	7.0%	0.0%	0.0%	26.1%
Hanford-Corcoran, CA	23,428	42.2%	12.2%	10.0%	22.6%	9.7%	2.7%	0.6%	0.0%	28.8%
Harrisburg-Carlisle, PA	60,293	18.4%	11.5%	18.7%	31.2%	16.3%	2.3%	1.4%	0.2%	8.2%
Harrisonburg, VA	14,315	25.6%	22.9%	11.6%	27.1%	8.3%	3.0%	1.5%	0.0%	15.0%
Hartford-West Hartford-East Hartford, CT	127,732	22.2%	11.7%	11.9%	22.1%	20.1%	7.5%	3.6%	0.9%	10.8%
Hattiesburg, MS	16,974	35.3%	17.5%	23.9%	12.4%	4.4%	6.1%	0.4%	0.0%	29.6%
Hickory-Lenoir-Morganton, NC	35,052	31.4%	18.8%	21.7%	21.1%	5.9%	0.2%	0.4%	0.5%	13.9%
Hilo, HI	21,668	32.5%	10.0%	19.8%	20.7%	14.6%	1.6%	0.8%	0.0%	22.9%
Hilton Head Island-Bluffton-Beaufort, SC	24,204	21.4%	23.6%	16.4%	30.5%	6.1%	0.3%	0.3%	1.3%	14.6%
Hinesville, GA	11,083	32.5%	10.9%	20.9%	24.1%	9.6%	1.9%	0.0%	0.0%	20.5%
Holland, MI	11,964	20.0%	13.5%	23.1%	23.6%	15.4%	0.0%	4.4%	0.0%	12.5%
Homosassa Springs, FL	8,986	29.2%	23.6%	26.7%	16.7%	3.7%	0.0%	0.0%	0.0%	25.5%
Hot Springs, AR	9,997	34.3%	17.2%	25.1%	13.1%	10.2%	0.0%	0.0%	0.0%	27.2%
Houma-Thibodaux, LA	27,684	31.2%	15.9%	10.6%	23.2%	8.3%	6.9%	3.9%	0.0%	17.1%
Houston-The Woodlands-Sugar Land, TX	889,477	25.2%	14.5%	14.0%	21.8%	14.1%	5.2%	3.9%	1.3%	13.6%
Huntington-Ashland, WV-KY-OH	36,570	35.9%	13.3%	15.3%	23.1%	8.9%	1.7%	1.4%	0.4%	21.6%
Huntsville, AL	57,381	27.8%	15.6%	18.7%	16.7%	13.0%	5.6%	1.2%	1.2%	19.0%
Idaho Falls, ID	17,251	26.0%	20.7%	20.0%	20.3%	3.9%	4.1%	4.2%	0.0%	11.9%
Indianapolis-Carmel-Anderson, IN	252,167	25.4%	13.2%	16.6%	25.5%	12.1%	3.6%	2.1%	1.5%	12.9%
Iowa City, IA	23,161	19.1%	18.1%	16.1%	25.4%	17.6%	3.4%	0.3%	0.0%	15.5%
Ithaca, NY	11,783	20.3%	19.2%	14.7%	27.1%	12.0%	3.4%	3.3%	0.0%	18.6%
Jackson, MI	10,624	37.1%	0.2%	12.7%	24.0%	15.0%	2.1%	0.0%	0.0%	21.0%
Jackson, MS	71,278	25.8%	15.3%	19.4%	26.1%	10.1%	2.5%	1.0%	0.0%	18.2%
Jackson, TN	15,287	32.9%	16.6%	27.5%	16.2%	4.6%	1.5%	0.5%	0.3%	24.3%
Jacksonville, FL	185,508	27.4%	13.7%	14.3%	27.2%	11.4%	2.8%	2.6%	0.5%	15.2%
Jacksonville, NC	32,983	27.2%	17.0%	20.2%	20.1%	12.8%	2.5%	0.3%	0.0%	21.9%
Jamestown-Dunkirk-Fredonia, NY	12,863	31.5%	17.1%	24.6%	17.5%	6.7%	1.4%	1.2%	0.0%	15.4%
Janesville-Beloit, WI	15,271	16.3%	16.2%	16.7%	18.1%	28.1%	4.4%	0.2%	0.0%	8.3%
Jefferson City, MO	17,313	20.1%	16.1%	16.0%	30.2%	11.8%	3.0%	1.8%	1.0%	18.3%
Johnson City, TN	21,051	37.7%	16.7%	16.1%	14.5%	9.2%	4.1%	1.5%	0.3%	26.8%
Johnstown, PA	12,887	26.9%	16.7%	13.8%	15.9%	23.3%	1.3%	1.7%	0.4%	22.5%
Jonesboro, AR	15,345	36.9%	19.8%	12.7%	23.0%	5.0%	2.6%	0.0%	0.0%	23.7%
Joplin, MO	18,676	19.3%	26.0%	18.6%	26.6%	8.8%	0.5%	0.1%	0.0%	6.8%
Kahului-Wailuku-Lahaina, HI	20,898	14.7%	18.3%	13.9%	32.1%	18.3%	2.0%	0.7%	0.0%	11.4%
Kalamazoo-Portage, MI	36,599	27.0%	11.4%	11.4%	30.0%	12.1%	4.0%	3.9%	0.3%	15.3%
Kalispell, MT	9,686	23.2%	8.3%	13.8%	26.7%	18.9%	7.0%	0.0%	2.1%	14.0%
Kankakee, IL	12,290	27.3%	16.1%	12.2%	27.1%	13.2%	0.9%	2.4%	0.8%	18.7%
Kansas City, MO-KS	258,765	18.3%	14.3%	15.8%	30.2%	14.6%	4.0%	1.7%	1.1%	13.0%
Kennewick-Richland, WA	35,262	25.7%	14.7%	20.0%	20.1%	14.6%	2.3%	2.6%	0.0%	18.7%
Killeen-Temple, TX	67,153	30.6%	13.5%	20.3%	22.3%	9.2%	3.3%	0.6%	0.1%	17.6%
Kingsport-Bristol-Bristol, TN-VA	30,784	32.3%	20.5%	19.2%	19.9%	6.1%	1.8%	0.0%	0.2%	22.6%
Kingston, NY	17,081	23.6%	13.6%	19.1%	24.3%	15.6%	2.4%	0.8%	0.6%	17.7%
Knoxville, TN	92,534	29.5%	18.7%	15.5%	21.3%	11.0%	1.7%	2.0%	0.3%	22.1%
Kokomo, IN	8,521	17.4%	11.7%	17.6%	36.0%	12.1%	0.9%	1.9%	2.4%	16.0%
La Crosse-Onalaska, WI-MN	14,177	21.4%	23.2%	17.3%	19.6%	12.9%	3.4%	0.7%	1.4%	8.2%
Lafayette, LA	64,879	25.8%	13.5%	13.6%	22.9%	14.0%	6.1%	2.5%	1.6%	15.9%
Lafayette-West Lafayette, IN	25,533	23.2%	15.4%	24.4%	20.7%	12.1%	3.5%	0.8%	0.0%	15.5%
Lake Charles, LA	27,030	30.6%	12.9%	14.9%	22.2%	10.5%	4.8%	3.2%	1.0%	18.1%
Lake Havasu City-Kingman, AZ	19,440	30.3%	17.0%	20.1%	25.5%	3.1%	1.7%	2.3%	0.0%	19.7%
Lakeland-Winter Haven, FL	76,330	28.1%	19.9%	21.2%	21.3%	8.1%	1.1%	0.3%	0.0%	16.5%
Lancaster, PA	59,762	26.6%	10.8%	16.3%	24.6%	14.9%	3.7%	2.5%	0.5%	14.7%
Lansing-East Lansing, MI	56,299	25.1%	13.0%	21.9%	26.5%	9.8%	2.5%	1.0%	0.2%	16.5%
Laredo, TX	30,918	39.5%	18.9%	15.2%	12.8%	8.2%	4.9%	0.0%	0.6%	31.3%
Las Cruces, NM	24,696	35.9%	25.6%	19.3%	12.7%	3.1%	2.2%	1.0%	0.0%	24.1%
Las Vegas-Henderson-Paradise, NV	284,231	26.6%	14.1%	18.5%	25.8%	11.1%	2.4%	1.1%	0.3%	14.0%
Lawrence, KS	16,467	19.1%	17.6%	10.3%	34.2%	9.0%	4.6%	5.2%	0.0%	12.2%
Lawton, OK	20,264	24.9%	20.4%	21.6%	23.6%	2.0%	1.5%	2.4%	3.6%	17.2%
Lebanon, PA	12,915	20.9%	8.7%	26.8%	26.2%	11.0%	2.5%	2.7%	1.1%	10.3%
Lewiston, ID-WA	6,197	30.2%	10.6%	28.2%	20.2%	5.7%	3.6%	1.6%	0.0%	19.3%
Lewiston-Auburn, ME	10,928	14.1%	10.4%	27.3%	30.2%	11.6%	6.4%	0.0%	0.0%	12.0%
Lexington-Fayette, KY	67,204	21.2%	17.7%	20.2%	24.7%	9.5%	3.4%	2.1%	1.1%	19.6%
Lima, OH	11,532	24.1%	22.7%	14.8%	25.8%	10.1%	0.7%	1.0%	0.7%	19.7%
Lincoln, NE	43,067	25.7%	18.6%	17.3%	24.0%	8.9%	3.8%	1.4%	0.2%	22.7%
Little Rock-North Little Rock-Conway, AR	97,350	29.0%	16.0%	16.3%	23.4%	10.7%	3.5%	0.5%	0.6%	16.7%
Logan, UT-ID	19,385	34.0%	17.5%	14.9%	19.4%	10.4%	0.8%	0.9%	2.0%	19.1%
Longview, TX	24,380	33.3%	18.7%	17.0%	16.6%	9.3%	3.7%	1.5%	0.0%	16.3%
Longview, WA	12,790	20.6%	19.9%	19.1%	35.2%	5.3%	0.0%	0.0%	0.0%	19.9%
Los Angeles-Long Beach-Anaheim, CA	1,818,998	25.4%	16.8%	16.4%	20.3%	12.0%	4.8%	3.0%	1.3%	13.8%
Louisville/Jefferson County, KY-IN	151,229	23.8%	16.2%	14.7%	25.5%	14.3%	3.8%	1.3%	0.4%	13.4%
Lubbock, TX	42,819	23.7%	16.5%	23.1%	20.6%	11.0%	1.5%	2.3%	1.3%	16.0%
Lumberton, NC	13,331	45.2%	17.1%	8.0%	24.4%	4.3%	1.1%	0.0%	0.0%	36.2%
Lynchburg, VA	27,594	23.5%	23.3%	14.4%	24.2%	11.2%	3.0%	0.4%	0.2%	16.3%
Macon, GA	23,089	28.4%	15.8%	19.5%	23.7%	7.5%	2.5%	2.4%	0.1%	20.2%

Table I-4: Metropolitan/Micropolitan Statistical Areas—Income Class by Age—*Continued*

			Persons Income, Percent by Income Class 18 to 24					
	Total Millennials	Under $10,000	$10,000 to $19,999	$20,000 to $29,999	$30,000 to $49,999	$50,000 to $74,999	$75,000 to $99,999	$100,000 or More
Madera, CA	15,683	61.6%	19.0%	14.9%	4.5%	0.0%	0.0%	0.0%
Madison, WI	79,957	53.1%	21.5%	14.1%	8.9%	1.8%	0.6%	0.0%
Manchester-Nashua, NH	37,376	52.8%	17.4%	18.2%	9.1%	2.5%	0.0%	0.0%
Manhattan, KS	23,702	59.1%	18.0%	15.6%	7.4%	0.0%	0.0%	0.0%
Mankato-North Mankato, MN	18,713	66.8%	21.5%	3.0%	8.7%	0.1%	0.0%	0.0%
Mansfield, OH	10,805	58.5%	19.5%	14.5%	7.5%	0.0%	0.0%	0.0%
McAllen-Edinburg-Mission, TX	91,885	74.4%	14.4%	5.8%	4.1%	1.3%	0.1%	0.0%
Medford, OR	16,260	65.9%	12.8%	11.7%	9.6%	0.0%	0.0%	0.0%
Memphis, TN-MS-AR	128,977	65.0%	19.6%	9.3%	4.9%	0.7%	0.0%	0.6%
Merced, CA	32,689	60.0%	20.5%	13.1%	5.7%	0.4%	0.2%	0.0%
Meridian, MS	10,313	62.7%	26.3%	5.1%	5.9%	0.0%	0.0%	0.0%
Miami-Fort Lauderdale-West Palm Beach, FL	501,872	63.0%	19.9%	10.6%	4.9%	1.3%	0.2%	0.1%
Michigan City-La Porte, IN	8,713	68.9%	17.2%	5.5%	5.9%	2.6%	0.0%	0.0%
Midland, MI	6,706	45.0%	45.5%	7.8%	0.0%	0.0%	1.7%	0.0%
Midland, TX	17,003	47.7%	10.7%	12.6%	16.0%	7.7%	4.7%	0.7%
Milwaukee-Waukesha-West Allis, WI	143,449	62.2%	21.1%	7.8%	6.8%	2.0%	0.1%	0.0%
Minneapolis-St. Paul-Bloomington, MN-WI	291,586	51.3%	22.4%	12.5%	11.0%	2.5%	0.2%	0.1%
Missoula, MT	14,769	60.2%	22.8%	10.8%	6.2%	0.0%	0.0%	0.0%
Mobile, AL	37,483	69.2%	15.7%	7.5%	7.0%	0.6%	0.0%	0.0%
Modesto, CA	41,049	65.3%	20.7%	8.2%	4.7%	1.1%	0.0%	0.0%
Monroe, LA	17,986	73.5%	17.3%	4.5%	3.7%	1.1%	0.0%	0.0%
Monroe, MI	11,950	50.2%	26.3%	12.0%	10.3%	0.4%	0.9%	0.0%
Montgomery, AL	36,863	65.8%	20.3%	6.9%	5.3%	0.5%	0.0%	1.1%
Morgantown, WV	25,885	75.2%	11.2%	9.9%	1.8%	1.2%	0.6%	0.0%
Morristown, TN	9,800	67.2%	21.7%	5.9%	2.8%	2.4%	0.0%	0.0%
Mount Vernon-Anacortes, WA	8,948	51.9%	17.3%	20.0%	8.0%	1.5%	1.4%	0.0%
Muncie, IN	22,931	70.4%	18.7%	8.1%	2.8%	0.0%	0.0%	0.0%
Muskegon, MI	14,864	59.7%	18.8%	8.9%	6.8%	5.8%	0.0%	0.0%
Myrtle Beach-Conway-North Myrtle Beach, SC-NC	33,252	55.2%	27.9%	13.6%	3.1%	0.2%	0.0%	0.0%
Napa, CA	13,069	65.2%	16.9%	8.4%	7.7%	1.8%	0.0%	0.0%
Naples-Immokalee-Marco Island, FL	25,881	60.0%	21.7%	14.1%	4.2%	0.0%	0.0%	0.0%
Nashville-Davidson–Murfreesboro–Franklin, TN	175,465	54.4%	19.9%	12.5%	10.2%	2.3%	0.6%	0.0%
New Bern, NC	15,041	49.4%	15.7%	23.3%	9.3%	2.2%	0.0%	0.0%
New Castle, PA	6,676	59.4%	23.4%	10.2%	5.3%	1.6%	0.0%	0.0%
New Haven-Milford, CT	87,288	58.7%	18.7%	12.8%	8.2%	1.3%	0.3%	0.1%
New Orleans-Metairie, LA	107,258	61.9%	20.7%	7.5%	7.4%	1.7%	0.7%	0.2%
New Philadelphia-Dover, OH	7,080	51.3%	23.7%	16.9%	6.2%	1.9%	0.0%	0.0%
New York-Newark-Jersey City, NY-NJ-PA	1,823,529	67.0%	14.6%	8.4%	6.6%	2.5%	0.6%	0.4%
Niles-Benton Harbor, MI	12,450	64.7%	17.7%	9.6%	7.6%	0.0%	0.4%	0.0%
North Port-Sarasota-Bradenton, FL	49,953	58.3%	23.9%	10.4%	6.3%	1.1%	0.0%	0.0%
Norwich-New London, CT	28,636	59.0%	17.6%	12.1%	7.5%	3.4%	0.2%	0.2%
Ocala, FL	25,183	68.8%	16.6%	9.5%	4.4%	0.7%	0.0%	0.0%
Ocean City, NJ	6,265	68.3%	21.4%	4.6%	5.8%	0.0%	0.0%	0.0%
Odessa, TX	18,034	49.4%	19.4%	10.9%	13.7%	2.5%	2.6%	1.6%
Ogden-Clearfield, UT	61,568	51.3%	26.0%	13.4%	7.8%	1.0%	0.2%	0.1%
Ogdensburg-Massena, NY	15,881	81.3%	12.3%	2.9%	3.5%	0.0%	0.0%	0.0%
Oklahoma City, OK	139,317	53.2%	24.8%	12.9%	6.7%	2.4%	0.1%	0.0%
Olympia-Tumwater, WA	24,902	57.7%	19.0%	15.1%	5.3%	2.0%	0.3%	0.5%
Omaha-Council Bluffs, NE-IA	80,083	45.4%	22.7%	15.5%	11.9%	3.1%	0.2%	1.0%
Orangeburg, SC	7,609	71.5%	13.3%	11.5%	3.7%	0.0%	0.0%	0.0%
Orlando-Kissimmee-Sanford, FL	235,677	60.0%	22.8%	11.5%	4.8%	1.0%	0.0%	0.0%
Oshkosh-Neenah, WI	19,273	57.7%	22.6%	14.0%	5.0%	0.6%	0.0%	0.0%
Ottawa-Peru, IL	8,885	65.7%	16.1%	5.6%	8.1%	4.4%	0.0%	0.0%
Owensboro, KY	9,474	64.0%	20.7%	6.5%	2.8%	6.1%	0.0%	0.0%
Oxnard-Thousand Oaks-Ventura, CA	82,021	58.4%	21.9%	11.0%	7.4%	1.0%	0.3%	0.0%
Palm Bay-Melbourne-Titusville, FL	45,039	65.5%	18.6%	10.7%	3.8%	1.0%	0.0%	0.3%
Panama City, FL	16,270	66.9%	18.5%	9.5%	3.9%	1.2%	0.0%	0.0%
Parkersburg-Vienna, WV	7,321	66.7%	15.2%	5.6%	7.8%	1.5%	3.3%	0.0%
Pensacola-Ferry Pass-Brent, FL	53,366	56.1%	23.5%	11.6%	6.1%	0.7%	1.0%	0.9%
Peoria, IL	31,355	59.4%	24.7%	8.3%	6.7%	0.5%	0.3%	0.0%
Philadelphia-Camden-Wilmington, PA-NJ-DE-MD	558,640	65.5%	16.6%	9.6%	6.1%	1.9%	0.2%	0.1%
Phoenix-Mesa-Scottsdale, AZ	427,612	56.8%	23.6%	11.4%	6.4%	1.7%	0.0%	0.0%
Pine Bluff, AR	9,044	70.1%	20.5%	4.1%	5.3%	0.0%	0.0%	0.0%
Pittsburgh, PA	202,145	63.4%	17.5%	9.6%	7.2%	1.9%	0.3%	0.1%
Pittsfield, MA	13,210	63.1%	24.0%	7.2%	4.4%	1.2%	0.0%	0.0%
Pocatello, ID	9,910	62.8%	22.0%	7.3%	7.8%	0.0%	0.0%	0.0%
Port St. Lucie, FL	46,415	48.9%	23.4%	15.8%	8.2%	3.2%	0.4%	0.0%
Portland-South Portland, ME	201,224	57.4%	19.8%	13.2%	7.6%	1.7%	0.3%	0.0%
Portland-Vancouver-Hillsboro, OR-WA	33,555	57.9%	22.1%	15.5%	4.2%	0.3%	0.0%	0.0%
Pottsville, PA	10,180	63.2%	14.4%	16.3%	4.6%	1.4%	0.0%	0.0%
Prescott, AZ	15,292	58.9%	22.6%	13.8%	3.1%	1.6%	0.0%	0.0%
Providence-Warwick, RI-MA	165,357	60.8%	18.5%	11.2%	7.7%	1.5%	0.2%	0.1%
Provo-Orem, UT	94,597	60.7%	19.7%	9.2%	8.7%	0.7%	0.4%	0.7%

Table I-4: Metropolitan/Micropolitan Statistical Areas—Income Class by Age—*Continued*

	Total Millennials	Under $10,000	$10,000 to $19,999	$20,000 to $29,999	$30,000 to $49,999	$50,000 to $74,999	$75,000 to $99,999	$100,000 to $149,999	$150,000 or More	Poverty Rate
				Persons Income, Percent by Income Class 25 to 33						
Madera, CA	19,229	40.6%	22.5%	19.1%	10.0%	6.0%	0.0%	0.0%	1.7%	25.1%
Madison, WI	88,503	18.8%	9.8%	19.0%	28.2%	13.4%	5.3%	2.9%	2.7%	11.8%
Manchester-Nashua, NH	45,577	19.1%	13.8%	9.0%	31.8%	14.5%	8.4%	2.0%	1.4%	11.8%
Manhattan, KS	16,967	30.9%	10.2%	20.7%	21.7%	13.3%	3.1%	0.0%	0.0%	19.2%
Mankato-North Mankato, MN	11,901	13.7%	19.6%	17.9%	30.8%	16.6%	0.0%	1.1%	0.4%	6.1%
Mansfield, OH	12,484	42.5%	22.1%	11.9%	17.1%	2.8%	1.3%	2.4%	0.0%	26.9%
McAllen-Edinburg-Mission, TX	96,344	38.2%	20.8%	18.1%	14.7%	4.6%	1.6%	1.1%	0.9%	29.1%
Medford, OR	24,414	37.0%	20.3%	17.1%	17.0%	7.4%	1.3%	0.0%	0.0%	27.0%
Memphis, TN-MS-AR	168,135	29.6%	17.1%	18.7%	20.2%	9.3%	3.2%	1.7%	0.2%	18.8%
Merced, CA	33,141	29.4%	21.6%	22.2%	18.3%	5.9%	1.4%	0.7%	0.5%	22.5%
Meridian, MS	12,320	27.7%	23.5%	19.9%	17.7%	9.8%	0.1%	1.4%	0.0%	25.5%
Miami-Fort Lauderdale-West Palm Beach, FL	724,010	26.7%	18.4%	18.6%	22.1%	9.6%	2.9%	1.3%	0.4%	15.1%
Michigan City-La Porte, IN	12,832	36.4%	17.4%	15.8%	20.6%	5.1%	3.3%	1.4%	0.0%	27.1%
Midland, MI	9,554	7.4%	30.0%	17.1%	28.6%	8.0%	7.2%	1.5%	0.2%	13.7%
Midland, TX	25,882	18.0%	8.6%	11.6%	27.9%	10.3%	11.7%	10.0%	1.9%	5.6%
Milwaukee-Waukesha-West Allis, WI	191,155	19.8%	13.2%	16.6%	27.9%	14.8%	4.0%	2.8%	0.8%	12.2%
Minneapolis-St. Paul-Bloomington, MN-WI	460,174	17.1%	11.6%	15.2%	27.7%	17.7%	5.8%	3.8%	1.0%	9.4%
Missoula, MT	17,127	29.4%	28.3%	18.8%	14.5%	7.1%	0.5%	0.7%	0.6%	18.8%
Mobile, AL	53,577	31.3%	21.4%	15.8%	22.2%	7.1%	2.0%	0.2%	0.0%	19.4%
Modesto, CA	52,079	28.7%	18.5%	16.2%	20.3%	9.8%	3.1%	3.0%	0.3%	22.4%
Monroe, LA	23,237	34.8%	19.3%	10.9%	19.8%	11.3%	3.1%	0.9%	0.0%	20.1%
Monroe, MI	15,224	27.9%	17.6%	9.2%	21.7%	16.1%	2.9%	3.7%	0.9%	15.4%
Montgomery, AL	46,764	35.7%	14.2%	17.6%	21.3%	8.7%	2.0%	0.2%	0.4%	27.0%
Morgantown, WV	21,424	32.7%	12.4%	11.8%	28.7%	9.5%	3.2%	1.7%	0.0%	19.8%
Morristown, TN	10,630	36.2%	19.5%	20.6%	15.5%	8.2%	0.0%	0.0%	0.0%	24.6%
Mount Vernon-Anacortes, WA	13,682	22.8%	10.8%	22.0%	28.8%	6.0%	8.3%	1.4%	0.0%	12.3%
Muncie, IN	10,355	31.0%	16.2%	16.5%	26.4%	4.2%	2.3%	2.3%	1.1%	24.6%
Muskegon, MI	20,232	33.0%	24.8%	12.8%	14.6%	13.5%	0.0%	0.0%	1.3%	20.9%
Myrtle Beach-Conway-North Myrtle Beach, SC-NC	42,738	28.6%	15.4%	20.6%	21.4%	11.4%	1.7%	0.8%	0.0%	17.0%
Napa, CA	14,989	19.3%	14.1%	12.9%	27.3%	15.7%	5.2%	4.8%	0.7%	6.2%
Naples-Immokalee-Marco Island, FL	30,802	25.2%	22.2%	15.6%	26.8%	6.6%	1.7%	1.6%	0.2%	20.0%
Nashville-Davidson–Murfreesboro–Franklin, TN	239,003	22.1%	14.9%	16.7%	25.7%	13.7%	3.3%	3.3%	0.4%	11.9%
New Bern, NC	15,525	31.4%	15.7%	13.9%	21.0%	14.4%	2.5%	0.5%	0.3%	14.9%
New Castle, PA	8,911	27.3%	15.4%	15.6%	23.4%	14.9%	3.1%	0.5%	0.0%	17.4%
New Haven-Milford, CT	99,958	24.3%	13.2%	13.8%	26.5%	15.7%	4.2%	1.9%	0.3%	17.7%
New Orleans-Metairie, LA	173,863	26.7%	16.2%	16.9%	21.0%	12.7%	3.3%	2.6%	0.5%	19.7%
New Philadelphia-Dover, OH	9,522	28.5%	13.4%	12.3%	25.6%	12.6%	6.2%	1.2%	0.2%	12.8%
New York-Newark-Jersey City, NY NJ PA	2,633,412	24.1%	12.9%	12.7%	20.3%	16.1%	6.9%	4.3%	2.8%	12.5%
Niles-Benton Harbor, MI	15,966	33.7%	14.4%	14.6%	19.7%	12.4%	2.4%	2.1%	0.7%	20.0%
North Port-Sarasota-Bradenton, FL	64,800	28.3%	20.7%	13.3%	24.9%	9.9%	2.0%	0.7%	0.3%	17.8%
Norwich-New London, CT	31,833	21.3%	16.2%	14.0%	20.8%	16.5%	6.5%	4.1%	0.5%	10.4%
Ocala, FL	33,781	36.3%	14.4%	22.4%	20.3%	5.5%	0.3%	0.8%	0.0%	23.7%
Ocean City, NJ	8,722	19.5%	10.6%	24.5%	27.4%	10.5%	2.3%	5.2%	0.0%	13.6%
Odessa, TX	24,031	25.8%	11.5%	13.2%	18.7%	14.2%	7.5%	7.7%	1.3%	9.1%
Ogden-Clearfield, UT	83,448	28.6%	10.7%	17.5%	23.6%	13.7%	3.2%	2.2%	0.4%	8.1%
Ogdensburg-Massena, NY	12,327	33.7%	11.6%	13.9%	27.1%	10.0%	0.8%	2.9%	0.0%	19.4%
Oklahoma City, OK	185,033	22.6%	17.2%	16.8%	24.8%	12.3%	3.2%	2.3%	0.9%	15.4%
Olympia-Tumwater, WA	33,146	25.1%	21.0%	18.4%	19.1%	10.2%	4.1%	2.0%	0.0%	16.7%
Omaha-Council Bluffs, NE-IA	120,657	19.2%	9.2%	16.2%	29.8%	17.8%	4.8%	2.1%	0.8%	10.7%
Orangeburg, SC	11,524	36.5%	21.1%	13.8%	26.5%	2.1%	0.0%	0.0%	0.0%	29.4%
Orlando-Kissimmee-Sanford, FL	317,056	24.0%	18.2%	17.7%	25.2%	10.7%	2.8%	1.2%	0.3%	14.2%
Oshkosh-Neenah, WI	21,198	21.6%	11.5%	12.9%	35.0%	18.7%	0.4%	0.0%	0.0%	14.5%
Ottawa-Peru, IL	11,899	24.3%	16.5%	20.7%	20.0%	9.6%	8.1%	0.9%	0.0%	16.6%
Owensboro, KY	13,140	19.7%	17.3%	32.0%	20.1%	9.4%	0.2%	0.2%	1.1%	11.6%
Oxnard-Thousand Oaks-Ventura, CA	100,843	22.4%	17.5%	18.4%	20.5%	12.5%	4.7%	2.8%	1.1%	9.3%
Palm Bay-Melbourne-Titusville, FL	55,168	26.1%	20.0%	22.3%	20.4%	6.8%	3.2%	1.0%	0.2%	14.2%
Panama City, FL	25,575	33.9%	15.9%	18.7%	22.7%	6.7%	2.1%	0.0%	0.0%	21.6%
Parkersburg-Vienna, WV	9,395	30.6%	20.3%	6.7%	28.8%	9.6%	3.9%	0.0%	0.0%	20.2%
Pensacola-Ferry Pass-Brent, FL	61,648	25.2%	18.3%	19.9%	22.5%	8.1%	3.9%	1.6%	0.4%	14.1%
Peoria, IL	44,780	22.7%	13.7%	18.1%	23.6%	12.8%	6.6%	1.6%	0.9%	15.5%
Philadelphia-Camden-Wilmington, PA-NJ-DE-MD	767,447	25.0%	12.0%	14.2%	22.5%	16.6%	6.2%	2.6%	0.9%	13.6%
Phoenix-Mesa-Scottsdale, AZ	573,047	27.6%	13.4%	16.0%	25.6%	11.4%	3.8%	1.8%	0.6%	15.7%
Pine Bluff, AR	9,911	35.1%	12.6%	13.4%	28.3%	8.4%	1.6%	0.0%	0.6%	22.9%
Pittsburgh, PA	274,703	22.4%	13.1%	15.7%	25.1%	15.0%	5.5%	2.6%	0.7%	13.5%
Pittsfield, MA	10,682	16.4%	22.6%	24.7%	19.8%	14.5%	1.2%	0.8%	0.0%	19.9%
Pocatello, ID	11,138	36.5%	14.7%	7.7%	22.1%	17.7%	0.3%	1.0%	0.0%	17.7%
Port St. Lucie, FL	56,267	19.4%	13.1%	17.5%	25.6%	17.8%	4.1%	1.5%	1.1%	12.1%
Portland-South Portland, ME	320,617	24.3%	14.4%	17.3%	22.1%	13.2%	4.9%	2.3%	1.5%	14.7%
Portland-Vancouver-Hillsboro, OR-WA	43,439	26.9%	17.2%	19.2%	21.4%	11.9%	1.8%	1.2%	0.4%	14.4%
Pottsville, PA	14,846	25.2%	11.9%	10.5%	29.8%	17.2%	4.6%	0.2%	0.6%	15.6%
Prescott, AZ	18,013	25.6%	19.5%	16.0%	26.2%	7.1%	0.9%	3.3%	1.2%	22.7%
Providence-Warwick, RI-MA	192,565	24.5%	15.0%	14.4%	25.3%	15.4%	2.9%	1.8%	0.6%	15.8%
Provo-Orem, UT	73,075	32.5%	13.9%	15.0%	23.8%	9.5%	2.9%	1.8%	0.7%	11.1%

Table I-4: Metropolitan/Micropolitan Statistical Areas—Income Class by Age—*Continued*

	Total Millennials	Under $10,000	$10,000 to $19,999	$20,000 to $29,999	$30,000 to $49,999	$50,000 to $74,999	$75,000 to $99,999	$100,000 or More
				Persons Income, Percent by Income Class 18 to 24				
Pueblo, CO	15,000	66.5%	20.3%	8.7%	3.9%	0.6%	0.0%	0.0%
Punta Gorda, FL	9,538	78.2%	11.7%	10.1%	0.0%	0.0%	0.0%	0.0%
Racine, WI	17,832	60.0%	15.0%	14.2%	10.7%	0.1%	0.0%	0.0%
Raleigh, NC	113,029	67.1%	15.6%	8.7%	7.5%	0.8%	0.0%	0.3%
Rapid City, SD	11,262	53.5%	19.9%	17.3%	8.2%	1.1%	0.0%	0.0%
Reading, PA	41,421	60.0%	19.9%	12.5%	6.4%	1.2%	0.0%	0.0%
Redding, CA	12,988	60.9%	20.9%	9.7%	6.9%	0.3%	1.3%	0.0%
Reno, NV	40,446	51.2%	30.0%	11.0%	6.5%	0.6%	0.1%	0.7%
Richmond, VA	122,167	61.8%	19.7%	9.9%	6.1%	2.3%	0.2%	0.0%
Riverside-San Bernardino-Ontario, CA	473,053	63.2%	19.9%	11.2%	5.0%	0.7%	0.0%	0.1%
Roanoke, VA	27,298	57.4%	15.0%	13.2%	11.7%	1.9%	0.0%	0.8%
Rochester, MN	20,720	55.9%	16.1%	15.2%	6.5%	5.9%	0.3%	0.0%
Rochester, NY	110,492	58.7%	17.6%	11.9%	9.7%	1.6%	0.3%	0.2%
Rockford, IL	28,540	63.0%	17.5%	10.7%	8.1%	0.2%	0.5%	0.0%
Rocky Mount, NC	13,362	61.4%	26.8%	8.3%	3.5%	0.0%	0.0%	0.0%
Rome, GA	9,179	72.7%	12.4%	10.3%	3.0%	1.7%	0.0%	0.0%
Roseburg, OR	7,366	66.9%	12.2%	11.1%	9.8%	0.0%	0.0%	0.0%
Sacramento–Roseville–Arden-Arcade, CA	218,161	67.3%	19.2%	8.2%	4.2%	1.0%	0.1%	0.0%
Saginaw, MI	20,018	70.5%	16.5%	7.5%	5.4%	0.1%	0.0%	0.0%
Salem, OH	25,879	41.2%	29.7%	12.8%	15.6%	0.7%	0.0%	0.0%
Salem, OR	16,709	52.0%	16.4%	13.4%	12.3%	5.4%	0.0%	0.5%
Salinas, CA	11,288	59.0%	20.9%	11.2%	3.1%	5.9%	0.0%	0.0%
Salisbury, MD-DE	248,328	61.0%	20.4%	10.2%	7.3%	1.1%	0.1%	0.0%
Salt Lake City, UT	7,504	61.8%	19.8%	9.6%	7.9%	0.9%	0.0%	0.0%
San Angelo, TX	40,898	56.5%	17.2%	17.9%	6.1%	2.0%	0.2%	0.0%
San Antonio-New Braunfels, TX	45,593	55.9%	22.8%	16.8%	4.1%	0.5%	0.0%	0.0%
San Diego-Carlsbad, CA	39,103	66.7%	16.1%	6.4%	8.9%	1.9%	0.0%	0.0%
San Francisco-Oakland-Hayward, CA	114,848	48.3%	23.5%	16.8%	9.9%	0.9%	0.4%	0.2%
San Jose-Sunnyvale-Santa Clara, CA	15,384	58.4%	15.5%	21.0%	3.8%	0.5%	0.0%	0.8%
San Luis Obispo-Paso Robles-Arroyo Grande, CA	246,793	57.0%	20.9%	13.5%	5.8%	2.3%	0.4%	0.1%
Santa Cruz-Watsonville, CA	352,905	55.5%	22.6%	12.5%	7.2%	1.9%	0.2%	0.1%
Santa Fe, NM	375,073	59.5%	17.9%	10.5%	7.4%	3.4%	0.6%	0.8%
Santa Maria-Santa Barbara, CA	171,407	60.9%	16.7%	9.2%	8.6%	3.1%	0.5%	1.1%
Santa Rosa, CA	42,216	71.1%	16.2%	4.5%	8.0%	0.0%	0.3%	0.0%
Savannah, GA	42,214	74.2%	17.1%	6.5%	1.6%	0.5%	0.0%	0.0%
Scranton–Wilkes-Barre–Hazleton, PA	11,025	59.2%	25.2%	7.7%	5.9%	2.0%	0.0%	0.0%
Seattle-Tacoma-Bellevue, WA	71,192	59.7%	20.7%	13.6%	4.6%	0.5%	0.4%	0.6%
Sebastian-Vero Beach, FL	43,756	57.3%	19.0%	9.7%	11.7%	1.6%	0.6%	0.2%
Sebring, FL	47,166	66.8%	17.6%	8.6%	6.4%	0.4%	0.0%	0.2%
Sheboygan, WI	51,810	70.8%	14.3%	8.7%	4.7%	1.5%	0.0%	0.0%
Sherman-Denison, TX	317,404	54.1%	18.5%	13.6%	8.6%	3.8%	0.8%	0.6%
Show Low, AZ	11,503	56.7%	28.1%	13.8%	0.4%	1.0%	0.0%	0.0%
Shreveport-Bossier City, LA	6,255	77.3%	16.6%	2.6%	0.0%	0.0%	0.0%	3.5%
Sierra Vista-Douglas, AZ	8,517	50.1%	18.9%	15.2%	7.2%	8.5%	0.0%	0.0%
Sioux City, IA-NE-SD	12,228	63.5%	14.4%	15.5%	5.7%	1.0%	0.0%	0.0%
Sioux Falls, SD	9,752	81.9%	13.5%	3.7%	0.9%	0.0%	0.0%	0.0%
South Bend-Mishawaka, IN-MI	40,935	62.0%	15.9%	12.4%	7.0%	2.0%	0.4%	0.2%
Spartanburg, SC	9,550	52.0%	30.6%	8.8%	6.3%	2.3%	0.0%	0.0%
Spokane-Spokane Valley, WA	14,972	65.9%	18.3%	8.1%	5.1%	1.1%	0.8%	0.8%
Springfield, IL	22,812	52.6%	23.3%	16.0%	7.2%	0.3%	0.5%	0.0%
Springfield, MA	35,054	70.3%	15.6%	6.9%	5.7%	0.5%	0.0%	1.0%
Springfield, MO	31,299	57.2%	21.7%	11.8%	7.6%	1.7%	0.0%	0.0%
Springfield, OH	51,658	63.6%	21.3%	7.8%	5.1%	1.6%	0.2%	0.3%
St. Cloud, MN	18,486	69.3%	18.2%	7.3%	3.8%	1.4%	0.0%	0.0%
St. George, UT	81,426	66.3%	18.0%	8.7%	5.8%	0.8%	0.2%	0.1%
St. Joseph, MO-KS	54,905	56.1%	24.0%	11.8%	6.5%	1.3%	0.3%	0.0%
St. Louis, MO-IL	11,991	53.6%	22.1%	13.1%	10.6%	0.6%	0.0%	0.0%
State College, PA	41,020	70.3%	12.4%	11.7%	4.8%	0.5%	0.4%	0.0%
Staunton-Waynesboro, VA	13,370	60.4%	27.6%	10.1%	1.9%	0.0%	0.0%	0.0%
Stockton-Lodi, CA	72,442	65.5%	19.5%	8.6%	5.5%	0.9%	0.0%	0.0%
Sumter, SC	13,392	63.8%	14.4%	15.4%	5.8%	0.5%	0.0%	0.0%
Sunbury, PA	6,642	53.7%	24.4%	11.1%	8.4%	1.0%	1.4%	0.0%
Syracuse, NY	71,499	64.6%	15.2%	11.5%	6.2%	2.0%	0.2%	0.3%
Tallahassee, FL	70,917	65.3%	19.5%	10.5%	4.0%	0.7%	0.0%	0.0%
Tampa-St. Petersburg-Clearwater, FL	239,308	59.9%	20.0%	12.1%	6.3%	1.2%	0.4%	0.1%
Terre Haute, IN	21,742	72.8%	15.3%	7.3%	4.3%	0.1%	0.0%	0.1%
Texarkana, TX-AR	13,517	62.7%	24.8%	6.9%	5.1%	0.4%	0.0%	0.0%
The Villages, FL	4,981	66.5%	31.3%	2.2%	0.0%	0.0%	0.0%	0.0%
Toledo, OH	67,145	63.7%	20.5%	8.5%	6.3%	0.8%	0.0%	0.1%
Topeka, KS	19,269	55.1%	20.6%	13.8%	10.1%	0.4%	0.0%	0.0%
Torrington, CT	13,568	42.4%	27.3%	15.3%	13.1%	1.9%	0.0%	0.0%
Traverse City, MI	11,620	55.2%	24.7%	6.0%	10.5%	3.5%	0.0%	0.0%
Trenton, NJ	42,985	74.4%	12.6%	9.0%	2.4%	1.4%	0.2%	0.0%
Truckee-Grass Valley, CA	6,149	68.1%	14.6%	13.9%	3.2%	0.2%	0.0%	0.0%
Tucson, AZ	118,139	59.9%	21.6%	11.5%	5.4%	1.4%	0.1%	0.1%
Tullahoma-Manchester, TN	9,870	66.4%	16.7%	13.2%	1.9%	1.9%	0.0%	0.0%
Tulsa, OK	90,037	51.3%	23.3%	13.5%	9.1%	2.5%	0.1%	0.3%

Table I-4: Metropolitan/Micropolitan Statistical Areas—Income Class by Age—*Continued*

	Total Millennials	Under $10,000	$10,000 to $19,999	$20,000 to $29,999	$30,000 to $49,999	$50,000 to $74,999	$75,000 to $99,999	$100,000 to $149,999	$150,000 or More	Poverty Rate
					Persons Income, Percent by Income Class 25 to 33					
Pueblo, CO	19,140	33.3%	15.2%	17.1%	22.8%	8.0%	1.5%	1.7%	0.5%	15.8%
Punta Gorda, FL	9,228	37.2%	16.2%	22.2%	20.2%	4.2%	0.0%	0.0%	0.0%	21.8%
Racine, WI	19,655	14.7%	14.0%	16.5%	35.2%	17.2%	0.8%	1.1%	0.6%	9.0%
Raleigh, NC	163,616	21.6%	14.4%	14.6%	26.2%	13.7%	6.0%	3.1%	0.4%	13.1%
Rapid City, SD	19,292	15.6%	20.6%	22.5%	26.9%	8.2%	3.8%	2.0%	0.4%	16.6%
Reading, PA	45,238	24.8%	11.8%	17.6%	23.3%	16.9%	2.6%	2.3%	0.7%	14.5%
Redding, CA	20,642	28.7%	21.3%	15.7%	23.9%	2.9%	2.8%	4.2%	0.5%	20.8%
Reno, NV	58,210	19.6%	15.4%	18.0%	29.3%	12.5%	2.6%	2.3%	0.3%	14.0%
Richmond, VA	159,399	24.1%	13.1%	18.1%	24.8%	12.2%	4.7%	2.3%	0.8%	10.8%
Riverside-San Bernardino-Ontario, CA	564,925	30.9%	18.2%	15.9%	20.4%	9.8%	2.9%	1.5%	0.5%	15.9%
Roanoke, VA	34,962	27.2%	14.7%	14.4%	30.6%	11.5%	1.2%	0.1%	0.1%	17.0%
Rochester, MN	23,747	17.5%	8.5%	14.3%	30.1%	20.5%	5.4%	2.7%	1.0%	5.0%
Rochester, NY	127,894	21.9%	14.2%	16.5%	27.5%	14.5%	3.6%	0.9%	0.8%	13.3%
Rockford, IL	37,019	26.6%	14.2%	18.5%	27.7%	10.4%	2.3%	0.2%	0.0%	20.1%
Rocky Mount, NC	14,191	42.2%	21.6%	21.3%	11.8%	0.9%	0.5%	1.7%	0.0%	28.6%
Rome, GA	11,680	33.8%	22.7%	22.5%	10.5%	6.6%	0.0%	0.5%	3.5%	22.9%
Roseburg, OR	10,908	31.9%	14.6%	25.1%	16.3%	11.5%	0.0%	0.0%	0.5%	27.4%
Sacramento–Roseville–Arden-Arcade, CA	284,963	25.6%	18.4%	15.5%	21.5%	11.1%	4.0%	3.5%	0.5%	13.7%
Saginaw, MI	21,353	23.9%	23.8%	20.5%	17.9%	9.2%	2.1%	2.1%	0.6%	20.4%
Salem, OH	23,951	23.8%	10.9%	11.3%	28.4%	21.2%	2.8%	1.5%	0.1%	11.2%
Salem, OR	15,243	29.8%	14.4%	17.0%	21.1%	5.3%	4.7%	0.7%	7.1%	9.0%
Salinas, CA	16,906	41.8%	19.1%	13.2%	19.6%	5.9%	0.4%	0.1%	0.0%	31.4%
Salisbury, MD-DE	335,801	22.8%	15.1%	17.0%	25.2%	13.1%	4.0%	2.1%	0.7%	14.8%
Salt Lake City, UT	9,881	36.5%	15.4%	20.8%	14.2%	6.7%	5.7%	0.7%	0.0%	17.9%
San Angelo, TX	46,862	26.9%	17.4%	18.9%	24.6%	9.2%	2.7%	0.3%	0.0%	17.7%
San Antonio-New Braunfels, TX	55,988	30.1%	17.6%	21.6%	16.8%	8.3%	4.1%	0.9%	0.6%	12.9%
San Diego-Carlsbad, CA	37,612	27.0%	17.4%	15.0%	23.8%	13.5%	2.1%	0.9%	0.2%	13.1%
San Francisco-Oakland-Hayward, CA	169,969	23.7%	12.0%	16.9%	27.6%	12.5%	3.6%	2.7%	0.9%	10.6%
San Jose-Sunnyvale-Santa Clara, CA	16,742	27.5%	18.6%	15.0%	18.5%	12.6%	4.9%	2.8%	0.0%	20.6%
San Luis Obispo-Paso Robles-Arroyo Grande, CA	322,810	26.3%	16.6%	17.4%	22.2%	12.0%	3.3%	1.6%	0.6%	14.5%
Santa Cruz-Watsonville, CA	473,892	23.5%	16.4%	14.1%	21.9%	13.6%	6.2%	3.3%	0.8%	13.1%
Santa Fe, NM	656,416	20.0%	12.1%	10.8%	20.0%	16.2%	8.6%	8.2%	4.1%	10.4%
Santa Maria-Santa Barbara, CA	267,421	21.4%	11.6%	11.7%	17.9%	14.6%	8.0%	9.6%	5.2%	6.0%
Santa Rosa, CA	30,829	23.4%	15.9%	19.4%	17.0%	14.8%	5.8%	2.6%	1.1%	18.2%
Savannah, GA	30,305	30.1%	20.7%	9.1%	18.6%	15.7%	2.3%	2.4%	1.2%	20.9%
Scranton–Wilkes-Barre–Hazleton, PA	15,060	27.0%	14.5%	26.2%	20.4%	8.8%	1.6%	0.3%	1.1%	18.4%
Seattle-Tacoma-Bellevue, WA	40,120	20.3%	21.8%	19.0%	15.4%	13.8%	4.4%	4.5%	0.8%	13.8%
Sebastian-Vero Beach, FL	57,264	20.4%	14.3%	16.9%	24.5%	18.6%	2.1%	2.4%	0.7%	8.1%
Sebring, FL	51,530	29.6%	13.2%	17.6%	26.3%	10.9%	1.8%	0.4%	0.2%	17.8%
Sheboygan, WI	58,176	24.6%	13.2%	16.2%	29.9%	12.5%	1.9%	1.5%	0.1%	16.5%
Sherman-Denison, TX	543,759	20.3%	11.2%	13.5%	22.8%	16.6%	7.6%	6.2%	1.9%	10.1%
Show Low, AZ	11,380	30.4%	20.3%	22.3%	22.1%	4.0%	0.2%	0.0%	0.8%	14.6%
Shreveport-Bossier City, LA	7,714	36.0%	15.4%	22.4%	21.6%	2.2%	2.4%	0.0%	0.0%	28.1%
Sierra Vista-Douglas, AZ	11,780	14.3%	21.4%	14.0%	37.3%	12.4%	0.7%	0.0%	0.0%	9.5%
Sioux City, IA-NE-SD	12,709	21.0%	16.1%	16.7%	29.5%	14.9%	1.6%	0.1%	0.0%	15.9%
Sioux Falls, SD	11,618	59.2%	8.8%	9.4%	17.0%	4.6%	0.6%	0.4%	0.0%	35.9%
South Bend-Mishawaka, IN-MI	57,754	31.3%	18.8%	16.2%	20.7%	8.1%	2.8%	1.3%	0.8%	19.0%
Spartanburg, SC	14,841	45.1%	21.6%	10.0%	11.2%	7.0%	2.5%	1.4%	1.3%	29.3%
Spokane-Spokane Valley, WA	18,340	24.2%	14.4%	21.8%	22.3%	12.6%	3.1%	1.7%	0.0%	20.8%
Springfield, IL	35,376	17.1%	10.5%	20.8%	37.2%	11.6%	1.1%	1.6%	0.0%	13.6%
Springfield, MA	34,788	29.2%	15.5%	19.3%	23.0%	10.8%	1.5%	0.7%	0.0%	15.6%
Springfield, MO	35,076	30.5%	14.8%	16.7%	28.2%	7.0%	1.1%	1.1%	0.6%	15.4%
Springfield, OH	71,816	33.2%	18.6%	13.6%	22.3%	8.1%	2.3%	1.4%	0.4%	21.0%
St. Cloud, MN	23,591	22.6%	16.4%	17.7%	24.1%	13.1%	3.2%	2.0%	0.9%	20.3%
St. George, UT	72,157	27.9%	12.9%	14.6%	22.7%	16.9%	3.4%	1.5%	0.1%	14.9%
St. Joseph, MO-KS	55,847	25.0%	17.6%	19.7%	26.8%	6.9%	2.4%	1.1%	0.5%	14.3%
St. Louis, MO-IL	13,749	23.1%	18.5%	16.5%	24.8%	14.2%	1.8%	0.5%	0.6%	14.2%
State College, PA	22,204	24.4%	10.3%	11.9%	33.7%	16.8%	2.5%	0.2%	0.2%	5.6%
Staunton-Waynesboro, VA	11,802	31.9%	6.9%	27.5%	24.9%	7.8%	1.0%	0.0%	0.0%	23.7%
Stockton-Lodi, CA	88,953	27.7%	20.3%	18.2%	19.8%	10.2%	2.2%	1.1%	0.3%	15.3%
Sumter, SC	12,191	39.9%	14.6%	23.5%	14.2%	6.7%	1.1%	0.0%	0.0%	28.4%
Sunbury, PA	10,582	22.2%	17.2%	24.2%	18.4%	13.0%	4.9%	0.1%	0.0%	8.8%
Syracuse, NY	73,891	25.4%	16.0%	16.6%	23.4%	14.3%	2.7%	0.7%	0.9%	18.7%
Tallahassee, FL	47,845	31.0%	17.8%	15.5%	22.6%	9.7%	1.9%	0.9%	0.5%	21.3%
Tampa-St. Petersburg-Clearwater, FL	343,205	24.6%	15.2%	18.6%	24.9%	11.9%	2.8%	1.4%	0.6%	15.5%
Terre Haute, IN	18,309	37.1%	16.3%	18.7%	17.7%	7.9%	1.5%	0.0%	0.8%	15.0%
Texarkana, TX-AR	16,886	34.8%	18.9%	19.9%	14.7%	11.6%	0.1%	0.0%	0.0%	24.7%
The Villages, FL	3,847	45.3%	8.7%	17.8%	17.8%	10.4%	0.0%	0.0%	0.0%	22.4%
Toledo, OH	71,852	23.1%	17.1%	16.6%	22.5%	15.4%	2.4%	2.0%	0.8%	16.5%
Topeka, KS	25,917	25.9%	15.1%	16.3%	25.1%	13.5%	2.2%	0.0%	1.9%	17.5%
Torrington, CT	16,493	17.2%	13.6%	15.0%	32.0%	18.6%	1.7%	2.0%	0.0%	5.1%
Traverse City, MI	14,212	18.1%	14.3%	25.6%	24.6%	10.6%	3.2%	3.6%	0.0%	8.5%
Trenton, NJ	39,325	32.8%	14.4%	14.5%	18.7%	11.1%	5.6%	1.9%	0.9%	13.8%
Truckee-Grass Valley, CA	9,555	29.1%	7.3%	13.8%	27.9%	10.2%	8.1%	0.7%	3.1%	8.4%
Tucson, AZ	109,878	27.8%	18.4%	17.1%	21.6%	9.2%	3.8%	1.7%	0.3%	18.8%
Tullahoma-Manchester, TN	9,752	27.8%	29.6%	9.7%	20.2%	7.2%	5.5%	0.0%	0.0%	16.7%
Tulsa, OK	118,952	24.4%	13.8%	18.6%	25.0%	12.3%	3.0%	2.6%	0.4%	17.7%

Table I-4: Metropolitan/Micropolitan Statistical Areas—Income Class by Age—*Continued*

	Total Millennials	Under $10,000	$10,000 to $19,999	$20,000 to $29,999	$30,000 to $49,999	$50,000 to $74,999	$75,000 to $99,999	$100,000 or More
				Persons Income, Percent by Income Class 18 to 24				
Tupelo, MS	13,296	55.2%	20.5%	15.0%	5.6%	1.8%	0.0%	1.9%
Tuscaloosa, AL	40,320	69.2%	17.4%	8.4%	3.3%	0.9%	0.0%	0.8%
Tyler, TX	22,578	63.9%	18.8%	9.5%	6.2%	0.7%	0.9%	0.0%
Urban Honolulu, HI	104,107	52.6%	13.5%	20.0%	10.0%	2.7%	1.0%	0.2%
Utica-Rome, NY	27,051	62.3%	24.6%	6.6%	5.6%	0.9%	0.0%	0.0%
Valdosta, GA	21,265	71.4%	16.9%	7.0%	4.7%	0.0%	0.0%	0.0%
Vallejo-Fairfield, CA	40,269	59.5%	20.0%	11.5%	5.4%	2.0%	0.9%	0.8%
Victoria, TX	9,641	63.1%	17.6%	17.2%	0.3%	0.8%	1.0%	0.0%
Vineland-Bridgeton, NJ	12,703	53.5%	22.5%	12.7%	10.0%	0.4%	0.3%	0.6%
Virginia Beach-Norfolk-Newport News, VA-NC	196,229	50.0%	21.2%	15.1%	11.0%	2.1%	0.5%	0.1%
Visalia-Porterville, CA	48,480	68.2%	19.4%	7.9%	4.2%	0.3%	0.0%	0.0%
Waco, TX	37,304	68.1%	17.2%	8.8%	4.0%	1.9%	0.0%	0.0%
Walla Walla, WA	6,587	78.5%	12.8%	3.8%	4.9%	0.0%	0.0%	0.0%
Warner Robins, GA	20,524	64.7%	16.6%	11.0%	7.2%	0.3%	0.2%	0.0%
Washington-Arlington-Alexandria, DC-VA-MD-WV	547,140	59.2%	17.0%	11.2%	8.7%	3.2%	0.4%	0.3%
Waterloo-Cedar Falls, IA	23,786	61.8%	23.2%	4.4%	8.4%	2.2%	0.0%	0.0%
Watertown-Fort Drum, NY	15,185	47.7%	24.4%	15.3%	12.4%	0.2%	0.0%	0.0%
Wausau, WI	9,696	39.1%	19.9%	21.3%	15.8%	3.6%	0.2%	0.0%
Weirton-Steubenville, WV-OH	11,083	65.1%	12.2%	16.5%	1.8%	4.3%	0.0%	0.0%
Wenatchee, WA	9,272	55.4%	30.5%	11.8%	2.0%	0.0%	0.2%	0.0%
Wheeling, WV-OH	13,727	61.9%	14.2%	15.8%	4.6%	3.5%	0.0%	0.0%
Whitewater-Elkhorn, WI	13,278	61.9%	26.7%	2.5%	6.2%	2.7%	0.0%	0.0%
Wichita Falls, TX	55,459	58.6%	19.1%	14.5%	5.5%	2.3%	0.0%	0.0%
Wichita, KS	20,494	48.3%	28.0%	17.7%	2.8%	3.3%	0.0%	0.0%
Williamsport, PA	12,018	67.1%	18.3%	9.5%	4.3%	0.6%	0.1%	0.0%
Wilmington, NC	32,247	65.9%	11.7%	16.3%	4.4%	1.6%	0.0%	0.0%
Winchester, VA-WV	12,202	56.4%	30.5%	11.7%	1.4%	0.0%	0.0%	0.0%
Winston-Salem, NC	59,671	67.6%	18.3%	7.4%	6.4%	0.4%	0.0%	0.0%
Wooster, OH	11,242	59.9%	13.5%	9.7%	15.9%	1.1%	0.0%	0.0%
Worcester, MA-CT	92,272	62.0%	17.8%	9.2%	8.9%	1.7%	0.2%	0.1%
Yakima, WA	25,431	55.4%	23.4%	8.0%	12.4%	0.9%	0.0%	0.0%
York-Hanover, PA	34,937	54.6%	27.1%	9.7%	6.3%	2.3%	0.0%	0.0%
Youngstown-Warren-Boardman, OH-PA	46,437	60.3%	23.2%	10.8%	4.6%	0.5%	0.4%	0.2%
Yuba City, CA	15,545	61.0%	13.8%	10.4%	12.4%	2.4%	0.0%	0.0%
Yuma, AZ	23,041	57.3%	19.2%	15.6%	5.6%	2.3%	0.0%	0.0%

Table I-4: Metropolitan/Micropolitan Statistical Areas—Income Class by Age—*Continued*

| | Persons Income, Percent by Income Class 25 to 33 | | | | | | | | | |
	Total Millennials	Under $10,000	$10,000 to $19,999	$20,000 to $29,999	$30,000 to $49,999	$50,000 to $74,999	$75,000 to $99,999	$100,000 to $149,999	$150,000 or More	Poverty Rate
Tupelo, MS	14,686	27.7%	17.6%	21.9%	22.7%	7.3%	2.9%	0.0%	0.0%	19.8%
Tuscaloosa, AL	31,163	29.3%	21.8%	19.3%	14.6%	10.2%	3.4%	1.2%	0.2%	13.8%
Tyler, TX	28,149	40.4%	16.2%	11.8%	16.3%	9.4%	1.5%	1.6%	2.8%	20.8%
Urban Honolulu, HI	138,456	21.7%	11.6%	17.7%	25.9%	15.1%	4.7%	2.9%	0.4%	8.8%
Utica-Rome, NY	31,574	28.5%	16.9%	20.1%	21.3%	9.7%	2.1%	0.7%	0.7%	18.8%
Valdosta, GA	19,484	42.8%	9.4%	16.2%	19.5%	7.4%	1.6%	0.9%	2.2%	29.5%
Vallejo-Fairfield, CA	55,432	25.4%	17.1%	14.5%	25.3%	11.0%	4.2%	1.8%	0.6%	9.5%
Victoria, TX	11,608	23.4%	28.3%	7.7%	23.8%	10.6%	3.1%	3.1%	0.0%	16.8%
Vineland-Bridgeton, NJ	21,889	36.4%	16.9%	14.4%	16.7%	12.0%	3.5%	0.0%	0.0%	18.8%
Virginia Beach-Norfolk-Newport News, VA-NC	246,051	27.0%	14.0%	15.4%	25.0%	13.5%	4.0%	1.0%	0.3%	14.5%
Visalia-Porterville, CA	59,578	33.7%	20.8%	17.1%	15.3%	9.7%	1.8%	1.4%	0.2%	27.6%
Waco, TX	29,407	30.7%	15.7%	18.8%	15.2%	15.7%	2.4%	0.6%	0.9%	18.2%
Walla Walla, WA	8,751	24.9%	10.5%	16.4%	26.3%	18.1%	0.0%	3.8%	0.0%	14.5%
Warner Robins, GA	21,473	25.3%	13.8%	12.8%	34.9%	11.0%	1.8%	0.5%	0.0%	12.8%
Washington-Arlington-Alexandria, DC-VA-MD-WV	831,802	19.5%	11.9%	12.0%	20.8%	19.0%	10.0%	5.4%	1.5%	8.4%
Waterloo-Cedar Falls, IA	21,302	21.9%	9.2%	21.2%	28.9%	10.9%	5.3%	1.6%	1.0%	13.0%
Watertown-Fort Drum, NY	16,496	23.8%	14.9%	21.1%	20.2%	16.6%	3.3%	0.0%	0.0%	9.7%
Wausau, WI	14,255	14.7%	9.0%	15.2%	35.9%	19.4%	3.6%	2.2%	0.0%	10.0%
Weirton-Steubenville, WV-OH	12,289	34.1%	22.9%	11.4%	20.4%	7.0%	2.5%	1.2%	0.5%	30.9%
Wenatchee, WA	12,335	27.1%	14.5%	10.8%	38.4%	4.9%	1.9%	2.4%	0.0%	16.2%
Wheeling, WV-OH	13,508	34.1%	22.8%	9.1%	21.7%	8.6%	2.3%	1.1%	0.4%	28.2%
Whitewater-Elkhorn, WI	10,055	22.4%	18.8%	24.9%	24.0%	6.6%	2.4%	1.1%	0.0%	14.7%
Wichita Falls, TX	85,074	25.1%	14.5%	18.2%	23.7%	13.3%	1.7%	2.7%	0.9%	11.8%
Wichita, KS	18,911	42.2%	16.0%	13.7%	18.6%	5.4%	1.8%	1.9%	0.4%	19.1%
Williamsport, PA	12,412	35.5%	12.3%	14.4%	21.0%	8.4%	6.8%	1.3%	0.2%	19.2%
Wilmington, NC	32,831	29.5%	15.0%	15.0%	22.1%	13.1%	4.2%	0.4%	0.7%	19.1%
Winchester, VA-WV	12,830	26.1%	19.0%	13.6%	25.7%	11.1%	1.7%	2.7%	0.0%	14.7%
Winston-Salem, NC	72,612	25.3%	19.0%	19.5%	25.0%	7.4%	1.6%	1.7%	0.4%	15.9%
Wooster, OH	11,235	19.5%	19.1%	17.2%	30.3%	11.5%	0.0%	0.0%	2.3%	5.7%
Worcester, MA-CT	100,837	21.7%	12.8%	16.7%	24.0%	17.0%	4.2%	2.9%	0.7%	13.1%
Yakima, WA	27,580	33.5%	18.0%	21.6%	19.8%	4.6%	0.3%	1.1%	1.2%	24.9%
York-Hanover, PA	50,766	21.8%	14.1%	23.2%	20.9%	16.4%	1.8%	1.8%	0.0%	7.1%
Youngstown-Warren-Boardman, OH-PA	53,069	26.9%	23.5%	16.6%	26.0%	5.5%	1.1%	0.2%	0.1%	20.2%
Yuba City, CA	23,344	30.2%	10.0%	19.9%	21.7%	7.5%	1.0%	0.8%	0.0%	19.0%
Yuma, AZ	25,579	32.4%	18.5%	11.2%	28.8%	7.1%	1.6%	0.3%	0.1%	23.4%

PART J
MOBILITY AND MIGRATION

While the mobility of younger Millennials may still be tied to their parents, the mobility of those in the 18 to 24 age group will often be related to college attendance, and the older Millennials may be following their first job or career move. People in their late 20s and early 30s typically have high rates of migration as this stage in the lifecycle is one of transition: finding jobs, finding partners, starting families, and finding a location to settle in. Today, metropolitan areas have become primary destinations. Millennials aren't so different from other generations in that sense, except that they are often staying in school longer and delaying marriage and career decisions. A recent Census Bureau report on young adult migration provides a useful portrait of the characteristics of Millennial migrants at the national level.[1] However, recent articles in popular periodicals point to some diverse trends for Millennial migration—remaking the inner cities, moving to smaller urban areas, moving to the suburbs. It's safe to say that the Millennials are a more

diverse group than previously thought and they are following a variety of settlement patterns.

The American Community Survey data comes from response to the question on residence one year ago. This is used to determine the extent of mobility and migration. From these data it is possible to identify specific migration flows such as retirees from northern states to southern states or even economic moves between specific Public Use Microdata Areas. The tables presented here are summarized to identify persons living in the same house as one year ago (non-migrants), those who have moved but were residing in the same state one year ago, those who lived in a different state but within the same Census region one year ago, those who lived in a different region, and those who lived outside of the United States one year ago (primarily foreign immigrants). It's important to remember that for someone who has moved, these data don't always represent migration. Someone who moves but stays in the same state would only be considered a migrant if their move was to or from a different county.

1 U.S. Census Bureau, "Young Adult Migration: 2007–2009 to 2010–2012," Report Number: ACS-31, March 2015.

Percent Age 25 to 33 Living in the Same House One Year Ago

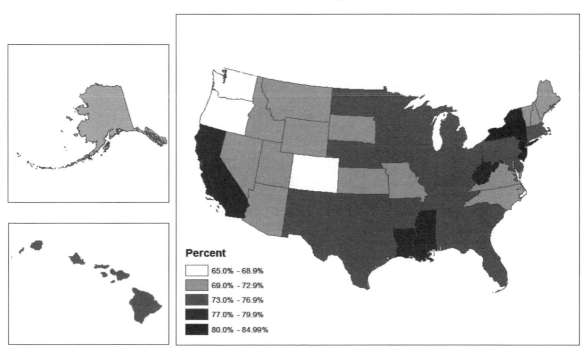

Percent
65.0% - 68.9%
69.0% - 72.9%
73.0% - 76.9%
77.0% - 79.9%
80.0% - 84.99%

Not surprisingly, 89 percent of young Millennials age 13 to 17 live in the same house as they did one year ago, but they're more mobile in Alaska where only 82.1 percent stayed in the same house. They're most stable in New York where 93.4 percent didn't move. While nearly three of every four older Millennials are still in the same house, they are much more mobile. The percentage of stable 18 to 24 and 25 to 33 year olds is 71.1 percent and 74.7 percent, respectively. When they do move, most stay within the same state—22.5 percent of the 18 to 24 age group and 19.8 percent for the 25 to 33 year olds. In both age categories, New Jersey has the lowest percent staying in the same state—10.2 percent of the younger Millennials and 14.6 percent of the older age group. Among the 18 to 24 age group, 15.7 percent of the District of Columbia residents lived in a different region one year ago. Utah has the highest percentage who lived outside the U.S. at 3.6 percent for the 18 to 24 year olds compared to 3.1 percent for those 25 to 33 in the District of Columbia.

Miami County, OH and Laramie County, WY report the highest percentage of 13 to 17 year olds who remain in the same house year to year as 100 percent. Forty-four counties have over 97 percent of this youngest age group living in the same house as one year ago. Mojave County, AZ is the most mobile with only 64.2 percent staying in the same house. Among the 18 to 24 age group, Monroe County, IN has the lowest percentage who stay home at

only 29.4 percent, compared to Richmond County, NY, where 93.8 percent are stable. In Maui County, HI only 3.0 percent live in a different house but in the same state, while Monroe County, IN has the highest percentage at 61.7 percent. Monroe County is the home of the University of Indiana Bloomington. Living in a different state from one year ago is most common in Cass County, ND, where 29.3 percent moved, but in 353 counties less than five percent of the 18 to 24 year olds lived in a different state. Martin County, FL has the highest percentage of those living abroad in the previous year at 11.3 percent. Among the older age group, 92.0 percent of residents in Robeson County, NC stayed in the same house as a year ago. The most mobile were in Mohave County, AZ, where only 51.4 percent stayed at home. Mohave County also had the highest percent of those who moved but stayed within the state at 37.9 percent. Platte County, MO has the highest percentage who changed states at 23.2 percent, and in 329 counties the percentage was below five percent. Linn County, IA has the highest percentage moving from outside the U.S. at 9.6 percent.

In Sterling Heights, MI, the ACS reports that all 13 to 17 year olds live in the same house as one year ago. It's reported as the highest, but 126 other cities are above 90 percent. Beaverton, OR has the lowest percentage (60.9 percent) of young Millennials who live in the same house. Among the 18 to 24 year olds, Patterson, NJ is the

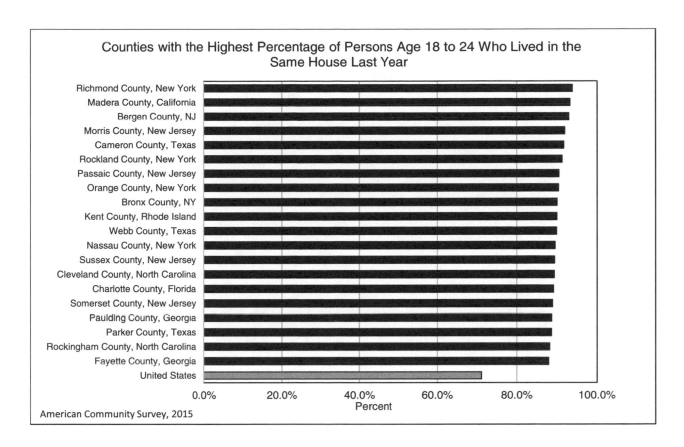

Counties with the Highest Percentage of Persons Age 18 to 24 Who Lived in the Same House Last Year

American Community Survey, 2015

most stable, with 97.5 percent not moving. In Ann Arbor, MI only 23.1 percent did not move, but 58.8 moved and stayed within Colorado—the highest for that category. In Lawton City, OK 37.1 percent previously lived in a different state, though 23.8 percent were still within the same Census region. The city with the highest percentage (12.7 percent) who lived abroad in the previous year was Arlington, VA. Patterson, NJ also had the highest percentage of 25 to 33 year olds who live in the same house as a year ago at 97.6 percent. Only eight other cities were above 90 percent. In Cambridge, MA, 21.6 percent of the older Millennials lived in a different state last year. Cambridge is home to Harvard University and MIT. Only ten other cities were above 15 percent. Foreign locations were the origin for 15.7 percent of Millennials age 25 to 33 in Cedar Rapids, IA.

More than 70 percent of the youngest Millennials live in the same house as a year ago in all by five metropolitan/ micropolitan areas. The Lake Havasu City-Kingman metro is lowest at 61.7 percent. In 163 of the 415 metro areas more than 90 percent have not moved. The Bloomington, IN metro has the lowest percentage of 18 to 24 year olds who live in the same house at 30.0 percent, while the Orangeburg, SC metro is highest (94.5 percent). The Lawton, OK metro area has the highest percentage who lived in a different state last year at 27.4 percent. Only Jacksonville, NC (26.4 percent) is also over 25 percent. In the Manhattan, KS metropolitan area, 7.6 percent of the 18 to 24 year olds lived abroad last year. Metros with less than two percent from abroad numbered 366. Among the older Millennials, the Orangeburg, SC metro also had the highest percentage (92.5) who stayed in the same house as last year, and in 183 metros more than 75 percent did not move. In the Tullahoma-Manchester, TN metro, 23.5 percent of the older Millennials lived in a different state last year while in Manhattan, KS, 10.6 percent lived abroad last year.

Table J-1: States—Mobility Status by Age

| | 15 to 17 | | 18 to 24 | | | | | | 25 to 33 | | | | | |
| | | | | | Percent Living in a Different House | | | | | | Percent Living in a Different House | | | |
	Total Population	Percent Living in Same House	Total Population	Percent Living in Same House	Same State	Different State, Same Region	Different Region	Outside US	Total Population	Percent Living in Same House	Same State	Different State, Same Region	Different Region	Outside US
United States	12,560,034	89.0%	31,345,795	71.1%	22.5%	2.6%	2.5%	1.2%	39,598,655	74.7%	19.8%	2.0%	2.2%	1.2%
Alabama	195,035	90.5%	469,138	70.1%	24.8%	3.2%	1.5%	0.3%	564,102	76.5%	19.0%	3.2%	0.9%	0.3%
Alaska	29,767	82.1%	84,225	62.0%	26.4%	3.9%	6.4%	1.3%	107,424	72.5%	17.1%	5.0%	4.7%	0.6%
Arizona	275,814	85.6%	672,348	66.2%	25.4%	4.1%	3.1%	1.3%	820,094	71.8%	21.5%	2.5%	3.2%	1.1%
Arkansas	118,111	84.5%	282,731	67.2%	27.1%	3.3%	1.8%	0.5%	350,285	73.6%	21.9%	2.5%	1.8%	0.3%
California	1,535,966	89.7%	3,948,553	76.6%	19.1%	0.9%	1.7%	1.6%	5,254,544	77.7%	18.1%	0.7%	2.0%	1.5%
Colorado	205,790	87.9%	524,617	61.2%	29.1%	3.2%	5.2%	1.4%	750,842	67.5%	23.6%	2.4%	5.4%	1.1%
Connecticut	142,674	90.3%	355,738	78.2%	15.5%	3.0%	2.1%	1.1%	394,429	75.5%	17.9%	2.9%	2.0%	1.6%
Delaware	34,981	91.0%	87,509	75.3%	15.9%	2.6%	5.8%	0.4%	114,870	75.7%	15.7%	2.7%	5.0%	1.0%
District of Columbia	15,198	89.9%	81,910	51.8%	17.3%	12.4%	15.7%	2.7%	139,024	67.4%	17.7%	8.2%	3.6%	3.1%
Florida	718,068	85.8%	1,779,978	73.6%	20.4%	1.8%	2.7%	1.6%	2,343,934	73.8%	20.3%	1.9%	2.3%	1.8%
Georgia	425,869	88.3%	1,029,333	72.4%	21.9%	2.9%	1.9%	0.9%	1,239,622	74.2%	19.8%	3.3%	1.6%	1.0%
Hawaii	45,680	92.3%	136,529	77.9%	11.6%	4.4%	4.0%	2.0%	189,145	73.6%	16.4%	3.3%	4.9%	1.7%
Idaho	71,752	85.6%	157,480	57.9%	31.8%	6.2%	2.5%	1.5%	197,546	70.2%	20.9%	5.4%	2.2%	1.2%
Illinois	509,080	91.2%	1,238,041	73.8%	20.7%	1.8%	2.4%	1.3%	1,587,753	76.5%	19.4%	1.2%	2.0%	1.0%
Indiana	273,193	89.1%	676,810	66.0%	28.3%	2.5%	2.2%	0.9%	756,911	74.7%	21.3%	1.7%	1.9%	0.4%
Iowa	123,805	86.6%	321,381	57.4%	33.8%	5.5%	2.5%	0.8%	359,741	74.8%	19.3%	1.9%	2.5%	1.6%
Kansas	119,415	89.0%	296,205	64.1%	25.5%	3.8%	4.0%	2.5%	348,071	71.4%	21.7%	2.2%	3.3%	1.3%
Kentucky	173,949	88.0%	424,621	67.9%	25.0%	2.7%	3.6%	0.8%	503,547	74.4%	19.8%	2.0%	3.0%	0.7%
Louisiana	187,168	88.5%	459,157	75.8%	19.3%	3.0%	1.5%	0.5%	607,358	77.4%	18.3%	2.4%	1.4%	0.6%
Maine	48,223	89.4%	115,050	61.7%	30.5%	5.5%	1.6%	0.6%	135,710	69.3%	26.6%	2.6%	1.4%	0.2%
Maryland	227,569	88.2%	558,491	74.9%	17.9%	2.5%	3.7%	1.1%	746,445	74.9%	17.7%	3.4%	2.6%	1.4%
Massachusetts	250,516	92.6%	698,392	72.9%	18.3%	4.0%	3.0%	1.9%	858,018	75.2%	18.5%	2.1%	2.1%	2.0%
Michigan	400,539	88.9%	986,321	67.6%	28.6%	1.1%	1.8%	0.9%	1,107,296	73.9%	22.1%	0.9%	2.1%	1.1%
Minnesota	215,951	91.8%	504,157	66.3%	27.4%	3.7%	1.8%	0.9%	670,737	74.1%	20.4%	2.0%	2.1%	1.4%
Mississippi	123,742	88.3%	312,903	72.4%	20.4%	4.3%	2.3%	0.5%	332,474	77.3%	18.2%	3.2%	0.9%	0.4%
Missouri	240,779	87.0%	598,165	65.5%	26.8%	3.0%	3.6%	1.1%	722,354	72.0%	22.0%	2.3%	2.9%	0.9%
Montana	37,052	90.0%	101,521	57.1%	33.2%	6.3%	2.9%	0.5%	113,247	72.2%	18.7%	3.0%	5.0%	1.1%
Nebraska	75,068	88.4%	194,933	59.6%	33.8%	3.0%	2.8%	0.8%	226,504	73.9%	20.8%	1.8%	2.4%	1.0%
Nevada	108,914	82.6%	254,487	68.8%	24.1%	4.2%	2.4%	0.6%	374,679	69.4%	22.2%	5.4%	2.1%	0.9%
New Hampshire	50,867	88.4%	129,612	70.3%	20.5%	6.4%	2.3%	0.5%	136,348	71.4%	17.3%	6.2%	3.4%	1.8%
New Jersey	351,098	93.3%	792,038	85.9%	10.2%	1.5%	1.2%	1.3%	1,039,533	80.7%	14.6%	2.0%	1.3%	1.4%
New Mexico	81,517	88.6%	208,652	74.9%	20.3%	0.9%	3.2%	0.7%	243,894	76.1%	17.8%	2.0%	2.8%	1.4%
New York	720,612	93.4%	1,939,899	79.4%	15.0%	1.7%	2.2%	1.8%	2,606,528	80.7%	15.1%	1.1%	1.7%	1.3%
North Carolina	389,275	87.7%	991,444	67.6%	25.1%	3.6%	2.8%	1.0%	1,180,843	72.3%	21.1%	2.8%	2.8%	1.0%
North Dakota	26,021	86.3%	93,505	47.8%	29.2%	17.4%	4.0%	1.6%	102,820	73.1%	20.2%	4.3%	2.1%	0.3%
Ohio	467,654	88.4%	1,090,850	65.9%	28.6%	1.5%	3.1%	0.9%	1,339,989	73.3%	22.6%	0.9%	2.6%	0.7%
Oklahoma	154,069	86.5%	391,812	66.4%	25.3%	3.5%	3.3%	1.5%	480,214	73.8%	21.8%	1.5%	1.9%	1.1%
Oregon	148,764	86.5%	365,845	61.7%	27.9%	7.3%	2.0%	1.1%	493,914	68.6%	24.2%	3.8%	2.3%	1.1%
Pennsylvania	475,280	89.9%	1,210,947	73.6%	20.6%	2.5%	2.2%	1.0%	1,486,228	76.3%	18.9%	1.4%	2.5%	0.9%
Rhode Island	37,117	89.4%	114,262	72.1%	18.4%	5.0%	2.5%	2.0%	129,246	75.8%	16.5%	3.1%	4.1%	0.6%
South Carolina	189,881	89.3%	487,869	70.9%	20.4%	4.0%	4.2%	0.6%	570,627	75.3%	18.6%	3.9%	1.7%	0.6%
South Dakota	34,011	90.0%	84,382	55.6%	34.6%	6.8%	2.9%	0.1%	103,467	72.8%	20.7%	3.1%	2.1%	1.3%
Tennessee	258,293	87.8%	633,501	70.0%	23.6%	3.4%	2.3%	0.6%	784,794	73.9%	20.0%	3.5%	2.0%	0.6%
Texas	1,186,275	88.9%	2,780,856	72.3%	23.4%	1.4%	1.7%	1.2%	3,594,612	73.3%	22.1%	1.2%	2.0%	1.4%
Utah	145,531	90.3%	345,362	62.5%	26.1%	4.5%	3.2%	3.6%	394,649	71.9%	23.0%	2.6%	1.7%	0.8%
Vermont	22,925	89.6%	67,578	72.8%	15.9%	6.9%	3.2%	1.3%	65,969	69.0%	24.1%	4.2%	1.4%	1.2%
Virginia	312,713	89.4%	826,162	67.0%	23.7%	3.8%	4.0%	1.4%	1,054,594	70.2%	22.2%	3.4%	2.7%	1.6%
Washington	268,408	87.1%	662,648	62.6%	29.5%	4.0%	2.7%	1.2%	954,135	68.2%	24.2%	3.0%	2.9%	1.7%
West Virginia	66,815	90.0%	163,675	74.9%	19.5%	2.9%	2.7%	0.0%	195,789	78.8%	17.3%	2.0%	1.6%	0.2%
Wisconsin	222,282	88.9%	555,679	62.8%	30.4%	4.1%	1.5%	1.1%	648,840	75.1%	20.4%	2.4%	1.5%	0.6%
Wyoming	20,958	86.9%	58,493	59.2%	24.8%	8.6%	5.9%	1.4%	74,916	71.6%	18.6%	5.6%	4.1%	0.1%

Table J-2: Counties—Mobility Status by Age

| | 15 to 17 | | 18 to 24 | | | | | | 25 to 33 | | | | | |
| | | | | | Percent Living in a Different House | | | | | | Percent Living in a Different House | | | |
	Total Population	Percent Living in Same House	Total Population	Percent Living in Same House	Same State	Different State, Same Region	Different Region	Outside US	Total Population	Percent Living in Same House	Same State	Different State, Same Region	Different Region	Outside US
Alabama														
Baldwin County	7,453	97.5%	14,381	78.4%	17.0%	0.4%	4.2%	0.0%	20,047	73.9%	20.9%	4.1%	1.1%	0.0%
Calhoun County	4,735	90.0%	12,942	60.5%	29.5%	8.3%	1.7%	0.0%	12,913	75.0%	17.5%	4.4%	3.1%	0.0%
Etowah County	3,849	79.9%	9,075	70.3%	26.0%	1.8%	1.2%	0.6%	9,578	78.5%	20.2%	0.5%	0.7%	0.0%
Houston County	4,558	93.4%	8,753	76.5%	18.0%	3.1%	2.4%	0.0%	11,594	79.0%	15.8%	4.1%	1.0%	0.0%
Jefferson County	24,976	92.2%	58,661	69.3%	24.1%	4.0%	2.1%	0.4%	84,794	74.2%	20.1%	3.7%	1.7%	0.3%
Lauderdale County	5,116	94.5%	8,925	67.2%	29.9%	1.6%	1.2%	0.0%	9,028	75.2%	20.1%	4.6%	0.0%	0.0%
Lee County	5,316	97.9%	30,660	53.6%	35.1%	9.3%	1.1%	0.8%	18,813	71.6%	17.7%	8.3%	2.2%	0.2%
Madison County	13,998	93.6%	32,804	67.5%	28.7%	2.4%	0.9%	0.5%	44,089	68.4%	22.9%	6.5%	2.0%	0.2%
Marshall County	3,863	88.1%	8,881	64.4%	35.1%	0.6%	0.0%	0.0%	9,155	80.2%	18.5%	1.2%	0.1%	0.0%
Mobile County	17,044	88.2%	37,483	75.6%	21.9%	2.0%	0.2%	0.3%	53,577	80.2%	17.4%	1.2%	0.2%	1.0%
Montgomery County	9,013	85.1%	24,526	60.5%	36.1%	2.1%	0.6%	0.8%	29,847	67.4%	30.1%	1.9%	0.5%	0.0%
Morgan County	5,755	92.9%	9,544	71.0%	26.0%	1.4%	1.3%	0.4%	13,728	82.3%	16.0%	0.9%	0.0%	0.9%
Shelby County	8,768	92.5%	17,928	68.1%	29.3%	2.0%	0.6%	0.0%	22,775	74.4%	15.6%	9.6%	0.0%	0.4%
Tuscaloosa County	7,734	87.8%	36,240	62.4%	25.6%	6.0%	5.8%	0.1%	28,303	81.2%	15.0%	2.7%	0.2%	0.9%
Alaska														
Anchorage Municipality	11,607	75.7%	34,831	42.9%	42.8%	5.4%	5.9%	3.0%	46,476	69.1%	18.6%	5.4%	6.1%	0.8%
Fairbanks North Star Borough	4,177	90.7%	15,158	69.8%	12.0%	6.5%	11.6%	0.0%	15,499	69.4%	20.8%	3.6%	4.7%	1.6%
Matanuska-Susitna Borough	4,476	83.4%	10,694	83.4%	14.5%	2.1%	0.0%	0.0%	12,719	77.9%	14.8%	5.1%	2.1%	0.0%
Arizona														
Cochise County	5,031	81.5%	9,550	60.8%	21.5%	1.3%	13.9%	2.5%	14,841	71.7%	18.7%	1.9%	6.9%	0.8%
Coconino County	4,964	85.7%	29,687	45.6%	36.7%	12.5%	3.7%	1.5%	17,120	74.1%	15.9%	5.6%	2.4%	2.0%
Maricopa County	172,695	86.8%	388,313	69.9%	23.1%	2.8%	3.0%	1.2%	522,456	72.4%	20.9%	2.4%	3.4%	0.9%
Mohave County	6,887	64.2%	12,747	56.2%	37.1%	4.2%	2.5%	0.0%	19,918	51.4%	37.9%	6.5%	2.4%	1.8%
Navajo County	4,733	97.3%	9,752	79.8%	17.4%	1.4%	1.0%	0.4%	11,618	81.3%	17.5%	0.4%	0.6%	0.1%
Pima County	37,301	84.5%	119,343	56.3%	34.3%	5.0%	2.9%	1.4%	110,798	66.8%	26.2%	2.4%	2.7%	1.9%
Pinal County	16,531	82.6%	30,975	74.9%	15.7%	7.4%	1.0%	1.1%	45,270	75.5%	17.5%	3.3%	3.0%	0.6%
Yavapai County	6,488	68.9%	15,292	59.9%	21.1%	13.3%	3.7%	2.0%	18,013	81.4%	16.6%	1.1%	0.8%	0.0%
Yuma County	9,130	95.2%	23,041	72.2%	19.4%	1.8%	5.2%	1.4%	25,579	72.3%	21.2%	0.5%	5.4%	0.6%
Arkansas														
Benton County	10,696	92.0%	20,016	83.6%	9.9%	3.2%	1.6%	1.8%	32,298	74.4%	20.9%	1.6%	1.0%	1.2%
Craighead County	5,131	77.5%	13,278	63.7%	34.2%	0.9%	1.1%	0.2%	13,143	61.9%	34.8%	2.5%	0.9%	0.0%
Faulkner County	6,455	95.7%	17,473	66.9%	28.2%	0.1%	2.8%	2.1%	16,220	81.4%	15.8%	0.5%	2.3%	0.0%
Garland County	3,373	73.1%	7,994	43.3%	51.4%	4.0%	1.2%	0.0%	9,677	61.4%	25.5%	7.0%	6.2%	0.0%
Pulaski County	14,105	85.1%	35,650	65.7%	29.6%	1.9%	2.7%	0.0%	53,734	69.6%	25.5%	2.9%	1.7%	0.3%
Saline County	4,687	70.8%	8,571	48.0%	47.6%	4.4%	0.0%	0.0%	13,673	76.7%	23.3%	0.0%	0.0%	0.0%
Sebastian County	6,264	85.1%	11,525	81.0%	13.0%	3.8%	1.0%	1.3%	14,618	73.3%	17.3%	0.0%	9.1%	0.3%
Washington County	8,062	83.8%	33,225	58.0%	31.9%	8.2%	1.1%	0.8%	31,607	79.7%	15.5%	2.0%	2.4%	0.4%
California														
Alameda County	53,319	91.8%	140,673	75.2%	19.3%	0.8%	1.6%	3.0%	239,328	78.6%	15.6%	0.8%	2.5%	2.4%
Butte County	7,589	91.1%	33,576	62.4%	36.7%	0.0%	0.1%	0.8%	25,179	69.4%	29.3%	0.0%	0.6%	0.7%
Contra Costa County	45,591	91.5%	96,186	78.7%	17.6%	1.8%	0.7%	1.1%	122,501	75.9%	19.7%	0.9%	1.8%	1.8%
El Dorado County	7,758	93.9%	13,743	86.4%	9.9%	1.2%	0.0%	2.5%	16,584	78.4%	17.7%	0.0%	2.5%	1.5%
Fresno County	44,793	89.6%	106,206	74.9%	22.4%	0.9%	0.8%	1.0%	129,871	75.1%	21.9%	0.8%	1.7%	0.4%
Humboldt County	3,629	85.6%	18,225	42.3%	57.0%	0.6%	0.0%	0.1%	16,198	70.0%	28.3%	0.4%	1.0%	0.3%
Imperial County	8,239	88.3%	19,969	81.2%	15.7%	1.4%	1.3%	0.5%	21,437	78.1%	21.7%	0.1%	0.0%	0.0%
Kern County	39,801	88.5%	96,404	79.5%	18.2%	0.5%	1.6%	0.2%	119,068	78.1%	19.0%	1.6%	0.7%	0.5%
Kings County	6,293	84.4%	16,771	65.3%	26.4%	2.3%	5.2%	0.7%	23,428	74.1%	20.2%	0.3%	5.4%	0.0%
Los Angeles County	386,428	91.0%	1,014,132	81.9%	14.1%	0.6%	1.7%	1.8%	1,415,100	81.5%	15.2%	0.4%	1.6%	1.3%
Madera County	6,628	95.2%	15,683	93.2%	6.8%	0.0%	0.0%	0.0%	19,229	87.4%	10.7%	1.9%	0.0%	0.0%
Marin County	8,607	89.4%	16,482	66.8%	29.1%	0.0%	2.9%	1.2%	22,077	73.5%	23.4%	0.0%	2.9%	0.2%
Merced County	12,527	94.4%	32,689	72.9%	22.7%	1.1%	1.4%	1.9%	33,141	81.5%	18.0%	0.0%	0.5%	0.0%
Monterey County	17,627	89.2%	46,279	75.1%	17.2%	2.5%	4.4%	0.8%	56,147	77.8%	16.5%	1.8%	1.8%	2.1%
Napa County	5,350	80.8%	13,069	84.4%	12.8%	0.1%	2.0%	0.7%	14,989	63.4%	34.1%	0.2%	1.8%	0.6%
Nevada County	3,189	97.6%	9,544	77.1%	22.9%	0.0%	0.0%	0.0%	9,555	90.9%	7.7%	1.4%	0.0%	0.0%
Orange County	123,617	88.9%	301,487	80.5%	15.6%	0.8%	1.3%	1.8%	398,540	77.1%	18.7%	0.7%	1.7%	1.8%
Placer County	15,343	90.6%	28,790	83.0%	12.2%	2.3%	1.8%	0.7%	37,376	68.7%	26.7%	2.0%	1.6%	1.0%
Riverside County	107,174	87.0%	238,122	80.2%	18.1%	0.4%	0.7%	0.5%	278,626	79.9%	17.8%	0.8%	0.8%	0.7%
Sacramento County	58,746	86.3%	136,870	74.5%	22.8%	0.6%	0.8%	1.2%	204,701	73.8%	22.8%	1.0%	1.7%	0.6%
San Bernardino County	99,038	87.6%	235,348	78.3%	17.8%	0.8%	2.2%	1.0%	287,689	80.4%	17.1%	0.5%	1.2%	0.8%
San Diego County	118,337	88.1%	352,621	73.4%	20.4%	1.0%	3.0%	2.2%	473,319	73.8%	19.8%	0.5%	3.6%	2.3%
San Francisco County	17,062	91.4%	62,672	62.5%	22.8%	2.7%	7.2%	4.9%	177,181	73.5%	17.1%	1.6%	5.4%	2.4%
San Joaquin County	33,581	90.7%	72,442	78.5%	18.4%	1.7%	0.9%	0.6%	88,953	79.1%	18.2%	1.1%	1.2%	0.5%
San Luis Obispo County	8,526	92.1%	42,216	46.9%	47.8%	1.7%	3.2%	0.5%	30,829	72.0%	24.8%	0.7%	2.3%	0.3%
San Mateo County	25,268	91.5%	57,300	79.0%	14.0%	0.0%	2.0%	4.9%	95,118	75.8%	19.0%	0.7%	2.1%	2.3%
Santa Barbara County	16,101	93.7%	71,192	51.7%	42.2%	1.3%	1.5%	3.3%	49,128	71.8%	20.9%	2.0%	4.2%	1.0%
Santa Clara County	67,386	92.2%	163,775	76.1%	17.7%	1.3%	3.0%	1.8%	260,069	73.2%	18.6%	0.8%	3.9%	3.6%
Santa Cruz County	8,920	85.8%	42,214	67.6%	28.9%	0.7%	2.0%	0.9%	30,305	76.1%	20.0%	0.0%	3.1%	0.8%
Shasta County	6,856	84.8%	13,747	77.1%	17.9%	3.1%	0.0%	1.9%	21,145	74.3%	20.6%	0.1%	2.0%	3.0%
Solano County	16,430	89.9%	40,269	72.0%	22.0%	3.1%	1.8%	1.0%	55,432	73.0%	20.8%	1.7%	2.8%	1.7%
Sonoma County	17,598	87.8%	43,756	75.6%	21.9%	1.3%	0.5%	0.7%	57,264	77.6%	17.8%	0.7%	2.5%	1.4%
Stanislaus County	25,520	89.6%	54,104	77.7%	21.4%	0.1%	0.3%	0.6%	70,720	79.4%	17.5%	0.9%	1.1%	1.0%

Table J-2: Counties—Mobility Status by Age—*Continued*

	15 to 17		18 to 24						25 to 33					
					Percent Living in a Different House						Percent Living in a Different House			
	Total Population	Percent Living in Same House	Total Population	Percent Living in Same House	Same State	Different State, Same Region	Different Region	Outside US	Total Population	Percent Living in Same House	Same State	Different State, Same Region	Different Region	Outside US
California—Cont.														
Sutter County	3,016	90.2%	8,221	75.1%	22.6%	1.6%	0.7%	0.0%	13,924	65.1%	30.4%	0.4%	4.2%	0.0%
Tulare County	23,180	91.2%	48,480	82.3%	17.0%	0.0%	0.1%	0.6%	59,578	84.8%	14.2%	0.3%	0.0%	0.7%
Ventura County	35,077	91.1%	83,642	86.7%	11.3%	0.6%	0.6%	0.7%	101,797	79.5%	18.2%	0.4%	1.3%	0.7%
Yolo County	7,308	90.1%	40,315	44.8%	49.2%	1.5%	1.0%	3.6%	26,201	64.1%	29.2%	0.6%	0.7%	5.4%
Colorado														
Adams County	23,017	87.1%	42,953	78.2%	17.0%	1.1%	2.8%	0.9%	71,561	72.3%	20.4%	2.7%	4.0%	0.7%
Arapahoe County	25,766	85.7%	54,292	70.3%	22.9%	1.9%	3.1%	1.8%	86,269	69.0%	23.6%	2.7%	3.0%	1.7%
Boulder County	11,992	91.6%	50,331	43.8%	44.1%	2.5%	7.6%	2.1%	37,559	62.9%	28.0%	1.9%	6.6%	0.7%
Denver County	16,454	91.8%	57,164	63.7%	25.1%	2.3%	7.2%	1.8%	139,346	64.7%	24.1%	2.4%	7.3%	1.6%
Douglas County	15,941	89.9%	24,273	75.4%	20.8%	3.3%	0.4%	0.0%	27,302	60.6%	26.7%	6.0%	5.9%	0.8%
El Paso County	26,582	88.7%	72,805	59.5%	26.7%	3.9%	8.6%	1.3%	97,677	63.4%	23.4%	1.4%	10.1%	1.7%
Jefferson County	20,072	86.8%	49,253	63.3%	25.8%	4.4%	6.0%	0.6%	70,252	65.4%	26.3%	1.8%	5.6%	0.9%
Larimer County	11,319	93.3%	45,152	48.9%	39.5%	5.0%	4.8%	1.8%	45,352	69.5%	25.9%	2.0%	1.9%	0.7%
Mesa County	5,555	90.3%	15,236	64.3%	30.2%	4.5%	1.1%	0.0%	17,924	75.3%	13.3%	2.6%	8.8%	0.0%
Pueblo County	6,500	83.7%	15,312	66.0%	29.7%	1.2%	3.0%	0.0%	18,784	74.1%	23.2%	1.3%	1.3%	0.0%
Weld County	13,752	84.1%	28,999	56.4%	37.7%	2.1%	2.8%	1.1%	35,019	73.0%	22.8%	1.1%	2.6%	0.5%
Connecticut														
Fairfield County	40,383	90.2%	85,139	84.4%	9.4%	2.9%	1.2%	2.0%	97,867	73.8%	17.3%	6.4%	1.1%	1.5%
Hartford County	34,275	89.6%	82,956	80.3%	13.7%	2.8%	1.7%	1.4%	102,090	74.6%	19.5%	1.7%	1.8%	2.4%
Litchfield County	6,694	96.8%	13,568	75.6%	22.2%	1.4%	0.8%	0.0%	16,493	81.1%	17.5%	0.0%	0.9%	0.5%
Middlesex County	6,930	94.4%	15,193	62.8%	28.6%	5.6%	2.9%	0.0%	15,292	70.5%	24.5%	1.5%	0.6%	2.9%
New Haven County	33,371	90.3%	87,071	82.3%	13.8%	2.0%	1.0%	0.9%	99,378	78.8%	14.8%	1.6%	3.8%	0.9%
New London County	10,589	88.7%	28,636	72.4%	14.0%	3.1%	10.5%	0.0%	31,833	74.4%	17.2%	3.5%	3.2%	1.7%
Tolland County	5,274	85.2%	28,023	58.6%	31.8%	7.0%	1.9%	0.7%	15,393	71.0%	24.4%	3.8%	0.5%	0.4%
Windham County	4,391	89.3%	11,899	69.2%	27.6%	3.2%	0.0%	0.0%	13,501	77.9%	20.3%	0.0%	0.0%	1.7%
Delaware														
Kent County	6,870	84.0%	18,762	68.2%	25.6%	0.8%	4.9%	0.5%	20,537	76.8%	17.7%	2.8%	2.5%	0.2%
New Castle County	21,630	93.9%	52,593	75.6%	14.1%	2.6%	7.7%	0.0%	74,577	75.1%	14.0%	2.5%	7.0%	1.4%
Sussex County	6,481	88.8%	15,661	81.9%	10.9%	5.1%	0.7%	1.4%	19,639	76.2%	20.2%	3.1%	0.4%	0.0%
Florida														
Alachua County	7,575	79.2%	56,248	51.0%	42.4%	2.1%	2.9%	1.7%	35,666	64.6%	31.1%	0.6%	2.3%	1.4%
Bay County	6,058	86.8%	14,840	77.7%	13.6%	3.9%	3.8%	1.0%	23,476	69.3%	23.1%	2.5%	4.8%	0.2%
Brevard County	20,157	79.5%	45,039	70.1%	19.9%	5.4%	3.9%	0.7%	55,168	72.1%	17.2%	5.2%	3.8%	1.7%
Broward County	69,903	87.0%	155,585	80.5%	14.9%	0.7%	1.5%	2.3%	229,354	72.9%	21.8%	1.0%	1.8%	2.4%
Charlotte County	4,383	77.6%	9,538	89.1%	10.3%	0.7%	0.0%	0.0%	9,228	68.3%	24.8%	0.0%	6.9%	0.0%
Citrus County	3,920	94.5%	7,713	59.7%	39.0%	0.0%	1.3%	0.0%	8,986	72.0%	24.4%	0.0%	3.0%	0.6%
Clay County	9,230	88.4%	17,559	77.3%	20.4%	0.9%	1.2%	0.3%	21,120	66.3%	28.0%	2.6%	2.4%	0.7%
Collier County	11,293	84.5%	25,881	81.9%	11.8%	1.2%	4.2%	0.8%	30,802	73.6%	16.8%	3.0%	3.5%	3.0%
Duval County	33,512	88.0%	86,478	63.6%	28.6%	2.4%	4.3%	1.1%	129,731	69.3%	25.2%	2.0%	2.0%	1.4%
Escambia County	10,853	84.2%	40,469	59.4%	19.6%	10.1%	10.5%	0.4%	40,786	70.6%	17.7%	7.6%	3.0%	1.1%
Flagler County	3,714	98.7%	7,889	85.8%	10.1%	0.0%	4.1%	0.0%	7,123	83.4%	12.7%	3.9%	0.0%	0.0%
Hernando County	6,734	89.6%	11,462	71.2%	17.2%	0.9%	8.6%	2.1%	15,819	68.3%	28.8%	2.3%	0.6%	0.0%
Highlands County	3,780	86.0%	6,061	72.8%	24.3%	1.4%	0.0%	1.6%	7,645	81.7%	14.0%	1.1%	0.6%	2.6%
Hillsborough County	52,057	83.3%	123,236	70.4%	22.4%	1.9%	3.9%	1.4%	182,022	72.7%	20.9%	1.7%	3.4%	1.3%
Indian River County	4,007	85.7%	11,503	82.8%	13.9%	2.1%	1.2%	0.0%	11,380	76.9%	15.5%	5.3%	2.0%	0.3%
Lake County	12,165	78.2%	21,516	78.8%	17.0%	2.4%	1.7%	0.0%	29,837	72.2%	19.0%	1.9%	1.8%	5.0%
Lee County	21,786	85.0%	49,430	72.4%	22.9%	1.9%	2.4%	0.4%	68,198	77.3%	16.3%	1.6%	1.9%	2.8%
Leon County	8,756	87.8%	65,175	49.7%	46.6%	2.0%	0.6%	1.1%	35,299	61.7%	31.7%	3.6%	2.0%	1.0%
Manatee County	12,403	85.9%	26,302	73.4%	20.6%	3.2%	2.6%	0.3%	33,040	74.9%	22.5%	1.5%	0.9%	0.1%
Marion County	11,395	93.5%	25,183	78.7%	15.9%	3.2%	2.2%	0.0%	33,781	71.4%	24.3%	2.1%	1.7%	0.5%
Martin County	4,770	83.9%	11,404	72.9%	10.9%	0.3%	4.5%	11.3%	11,689	71.3%	21.4%	0.0%	4.0%	3.4%
Miami-Dade County	95,700	90.3%	236,693	83.6%	12.6%	0.4%	1.0%	2.4%	346,035	82.6%	12.8%	1.0%	1.3%	2.2%
Okaloosa County	6,455	82.3%	18,979	55.2%	28.2%	8.7%	5.2%	2.7%	29,242	63.3%	22.8%	7.4%	5.3%	1.2%
Orange County	49,222	85.4%	144,127	68.5%	23.6%	1.5%	3.7%	2.6%	188,528	70.2%	23.3%	1.5%	2.7%	2.3%
Osceola County	14,495	91.8%	31,196	79.4%	16.5%	1.3%	1.1%	1.6%	40,058	70.0%	21.0%	1.9%	1.7%	5.4%
Palm Beach County	49,340	79.7%	109,088	73.6%	21.4%	1.0%	2.5%	1.6%	146,764	72.8%	21.5%	0.9%	2.7%	2.0%
Pasco County	18,634	93.2%	36,830	82.0%	15.2%	0.7%	1.0%	1.0%	46,830	78.3%	17.8%	1.5%	1.8%	0.6%
Pinellas County	27,753	79.4%	65,860	80.0%	15.0%	1.1%	2.9%	1.0%	98,785	73.8%	19.8%	1.2%	4.6%	0.7%
Polk County	25,335	87.8%	56,070	78.5%	15.8%	2.0%	2.8%	0.9%	76,330	76.5%	17.9%	2.8%	1.4%	1.3%
Santa Rosa County	10,149	79.0%	17,562	67.4%	24.5%	2.6%	5.0%	0.6%	21,335	67.7%	27.0%	1.5%	3.8%	0.0%
Sarasota County	10,234	86.3%	22,151	77.9%	17.7%	0.1%	4.3%	0.0%	31,750	70.4%	26.7%	1.9%	0.0%	1.1%
Seminole County	6,524	76.3%	13,125	69.2%	24.4%	4.2%	2.2%	0.0%	21,224	60.2%	34.7%	3.3%	1.8%	0.0%
St. Johns County	10,927	87.4%	23,480	74.6%	20.2%	0.6%	2.6%	2.0%	31,760	75.6%	16.7%	3.3%	2.8%	1.6%
St. Lucie County	18,121	91.5%	39,304	81.7%	15.0%	0.4%	2.8%	0.1%	55,902	75.0%	19.3%	1.5%	3.4%	0.9%
Sumter County	2,181	88.1%	4,730	63.7%	34.1%	2.1%	0.0%	0.0%	3,888	61.0%	36.3%	0.0%	1.5%	1.2%
Volusia County	16,444	85.8%	42,400	83.1%	10.7%	0.9%	2.1%	3.2%	53,825	80.1%	14.6%	1.5%	2.1%	1.7%
Georgia														
Bartow County	4,382	68.9%	9,293	64.5%	35.5%	0.0%	0.0%	0.0%	10,921	82.5%	12.9%	3.7%	0.0%	0.9%
Bibb County	6,082	89.6%	16,246	68.7%	29.0%	0.8%	0.4%	1.1%	18,545	78.2%	19.8%	1.3%	0.7%	0.0%
Carroll County	5,101	90.3%	15,447	65.7%	32.5%	0.0%	1.8%	0.0%	13,544	68.4%	29.0%	2.6%	0.0%	0.0%
Chatham County	9,149	87.3%	33,626	55.6%	30.5%	7.8%	3.7%	2.4%	42,779	61.6%	21.6%	7.9%	5.8%	3.0%
Cherokee County	10,961	97.8%	19,073	85.5%	11.4%	1.2%	1.9%	0.0%	25,158	81.1%	15.0%	1.9%	2.1%	0.0%

Table J-2: Counties—Mobility Status by Age—*Continued*

| | 15 to 17 | | 18 to 24 | | | | | | 25 to 33 | | | | | |
| | | | | | Percent Living in a Different House | | | | | | Percent Living in a Different House | | | |
	Total Population	Percent Living in Same House	Total Population	Percent Living in Same House	Same State	Different State, Same Region	Different Region	Outside US	Total Population	Percent Living in Same House	Same State	Different State, Same Region	Different Region	Outside US
Georgia—Cont.														
Clarke County	2,635	88.5%	36,550	44.2%	49.4%	3.3%	2.1%	1.0%	16,374	70.3%	24.4%	1.6%	1.2%	2.5%
Clayton County	11,973	85.8%	27,620	67.8%	26.6%	3.5%	1.2%	0.8%	36,094	74.1%	21.4%	3.0%	1.5%	0.0%
Cobb County	29,813	83.3%	66,221	65.8%	28.9%	2.0%	1.5%	1.8%	94,327	66.3%	27.4%	2.3%	2.2%	1.8%
Columbia County	6,372	90.7%	12,592	84.3%	10.7%	4.4%	0.7%	0.0%	19,341	85.0%	10.4%	4.2%	0.5%	0.0%
Coweta County	6,566	89.2%	11,521	74.8%	21.4%	3.0%	0.7%	0.0%	15,096	77.9%	20.5%	0.0%	1.6%	0.0%
DeKalb County	24,716	91.3%	65,575	71.2%	21.8%	2.4%	3.4%	1.3%	110,091	71.6%	21.3%	3.7%	1.6%	1.8%
Dougherty County	3,869	89.0%	11,312	68.0%	27.5%	1.7%	2.4%	0.3%	9,967	71.1%	25.6%	1.0%	2.3%	0.0%
Douglas County	6,733	97.2%	13,139	74.1%	25.9%	0.0%	0.0%	0.0%	15,463	74.3%	15.4%	6.5%	1.9%	1.9%
Fayette County	6,314	88.6%	10,448	87.9%	5.0%	7.1%	0.0%	0.0%	6,653	72.3%	23.5%	0.8%	0.0%	3.4%
Floyd County	3,826	82.5%	9,179	83.0%	15.1%	1.9%	0.0%	0.0%	11,390	69.1%	28.9%	1.9%	0.1%	0.0%
Forsyth County	10,460	91.7%	15,074	78.6%	17.7%	1.7%	1.4%	0.6%	18,563	82.0%	13.5%	1.2%	0.0%	3.3%
Fulton County	38,991	83.8%	99,071	66.5%	23.4%	5.1%	2.8%	2.2%	148,188	74.4%	19.2%	3.6%	1.8%	1.0%
Gwinnett County	43,096	89.8%	82,834	81.1%	16.2%	1.0%	1.6%	0.2%	102,945	76.4%	18.1%	2.9%	1.6%	0.9%
Hall County	8,761	84.2%	18,304	71.6%	27.2%	0.9%	0.3%	0.0%	21,584	81.8%	17.3%	0.9%	0.0%	0.0%
Henry County	12,656	90.7%	23,115	84.3%	9.3%	3.3%	3.2%	0.0%	21,023	83.1%	15.7%	0.5%	0.8%	0.0%
Houston County	6,296	81.1%	14,662	73.0%	22.4%	2.6%	2.1%	0.0%	17,833	71.4%	23.7%	2.7%	1.5%	0.8%
Lowndes County	4,318	86.9%	18,196	66.8%	28.7%	0.8%	1.5%	2.2%	16,568	65.6%	25.8%	3.2%	3.9%	1.5%
Muscogee County	6,809	85.4%	24,221	55.7%	22.9%	10.3%	10.6%	0.4%	29,648	58.6%	23.8%	9.4%	4.7%	3.6%
Newton County	6,061	95.9%	8,171	75.0%	11.8%	2.3%	9.1%	1.9%	12,360	77.2%	13.3%	4.0%	5.5%	0.0%
Paulding County	7,701	86.9%	14,317	88.6%	11.4%	0.0%	0.0%	0.0%	16,727	88.8%	11.2%	0.0%	0.0%	0.0%
Richmond County	7,388	91.1%	23,706	77.4%	9.3%	10.4%	2.6%	0.3%	30,218	70.9%	21.9%	3.4%	2.3%	1.4%
Whitfield County	4,558	94.2%	10,390	78.7%	15.8%	3.2%	1.1%	1.3%	13,342	89.0%	7.2%	1.8%	2.0%	0.0%
Hawaii														
Hawaii County	6,367	86.3%	16,321	79.5%	13.1%	6.1%	0.0%	1.3%	21,668	72.3%	22.5%	4.2%	0.0%	1.0%
Honolulu County	30,847	91.9%	104,107	76.5%	12.7%	4.0%	4.5%	2.4%	138,456	73.2%	15.8%	3.0%	6.1%	1.9%
Maui County	5,710	97.9%	12,607	84.3%	3.0%	5.9%	6.4%	0.5%	20,898	76.5%	17.2%	5.0%	0.9%	0.5%
Idaho														
Ada County	18,067	85.3%	37,337	60.2%	30.9%	5.0%	1.8%	2.1%	57,353	66.8%	24.6%	6.5%	1.1%	1.0%
Bonneville County	4,160	87.8%	8,924	46.2%	41.2%	6.0%	1.6%	4.9%	14,384	66.2%	14.5%	7.0%	8.9%	3.3%
Canyon County	10,595	82.5%	19,059	72.3%	22.1%	3.1%	2.4%	0.1%	23,454	80.2%	15.2%	3.8%	0.5%	0.3%
Kootenai County	5,612	87.3%	11,742	61.2%	34.8%	3.6%	0.2%	0.2%	17,751	69.3%	22.2%	6.7%	0.0%	1.8%
Illinois														
Champaign County	5,420	92.6%	50,803	55.8%	36.5%	0.3%	4.3%	3.1%	24,074	70.2%	21.7%	0.6%	2.8%	4.6%
Cook County	192,674	91.5%	478,190	76.2%	17.3%	2.0%	2.5%	2.0%	749,255	76.2%	18.9%	1.2%	2.2%	1.5%
DeKalb County	3,392	87.4%	21,847	52.5%	41.1%	2.8%	3.7%	0.0%	12,654	66.7%	27.4%	0.0%	4.2%	1.7%
DuPage County	37,895	93.6%	84,758	80.4%	15.8%	1.6%	1.6%	0.6%	103,130	75.1%	20.4%	1.6%	2.2%	0.6%
Kane County	24,337	88.0%	48,293	87.4%	11.0%	0.9%	0.0%	0.8%	55,269	76.6%	21.9%	0.3%	0.6%	0.6%
Kankakee County	4,612	94.0%	11,549	78.0%	16.1%	4.8%	0.0%	1.1%	12,290	85.0%	8.5%	5.1%	0.0%	1.3%
Kendall County	6,586	90.2%	11,323	70.3%	28.1%	0.0%	0.0%	1.6%	14,670	89.8%	7.2%	0.0%	3.0%	0.0%
Lake County	34,382	91.5%	71,265	74.1%	13.5%	4.2%	7.4%	0.8%	68,950	74.3%	18.6%	1.1%	5.3%	0.7%
LaSalle County	4,432	89.4%	8,885	79.0%	13.7%	0.5%	6.9%	0.0%	11,899	75.3%	24.3%	0.1%	0.3%	0.0%
Macon County	14,878	91.6%	26,318	83.1%	13.9%	0.8%	1.8%	0.3%	27,547	77.2%	21.0%	1.1%	0.4%	0.3%
Madison County	6,408	98.8%	30,701	55.5%	42.6%	0.6%	0.6%	0.7%	19,902	67.7%	28.9%	1.7%	0.8%	0.8%
McHenry County	3,953	97.5%	10,188	78.8%	16.5%	3.2%	1.5%	0.0%	10,459	82.8%	17.2%	0.0%	0.0%	0.0%
McLean County	10,067	84.4%	22,983	69.1%	27.5%	1.3%	0.9%	1.2%	31,871	77.6%	19.5%	1.8%	1.1%	0.0%
Peoria County	7,213	91.1%	17,561	56.5%	35.8%	5.3%	2.4%	0.0%	24,949	70.4%	25.4%	0.5%	2.8%	0.9%
Rock Island County	5,147	90.3%	12,821	67.7%	24.5%	1.2%	6.5%	0.0%	14,721	73.4%	16.8%	4.7%	5.0%	0.0%
Sangamon County	10,070	91.1%	22,071	77.9%	16.6%	2.0%	3.5%	0.0%	30,890	76.5%	19.3%	1.6%	2.2%	0.3%
St. Clair County	8,412	84.3%	17,501	72.8%	22.7%	0.7%	0.7%	3.1%	22,066	70.9%	24.5%	1.9%	2.7%	0.0%
Tazewell County	5,099	80.7%	9,581	69.8%	29.4%	0.0%	0.8%	0.0%	15,526	85.7%	12.9%	0.0%	0.6%	0.8%
Will County	32,614	91.9%	61,876	85.9%	12.3%	1.1%	0.2%	0.5%	70,359	84.5%	14.3%	0.2%	0.8%	0.1%
Winnebago County	11,431	91.9%	24,727	80.4%	15.9%	0.4%	3.2%	0.0%	32,181	80.5%	18.8%	0.4%	0.0%	0.3%
Indiana														
Allen County	15,457	90.2%	35,877	72.5%	21.0%	1.0%	3.9%	1.6%	43,159	69.1%	25.2%	2.6%	3.1%	0.0%
Clark County	4,287	96.2%	8,677	79.9%	15.4%	2.5%	2.3%	0.0%	13,802	79.4%	16.4%	0.0%	4.2%	0.0%
Delaware County	3,898	82.9%	22,931	48.4%	44.5%	6.5%	0.7%	0.0%	10,355	65.8%	32.1%	0.6%	1.4%	0.0%
Elkhart County	9,847	91.3%	18,907	80.4%	19.1%	0.2%	0.3%	0.0%	22,639	83.3%	13.4%	2.3%	1.0%	0.0%
Hamilton County	15,860	81.9%	22,137	74.2%	25.4%	0.4%	0.0%	0.0%	32,351	62.8%	28.6%	1.2%	7.1%	0.3%
Hendricks County	6,868	86.8%	12,782	75.3%	22.1%	0.0%	2.5%	0.0%	19,120	77.6%	17.4%	4.5%	0.5%	0.0%
Johnson County	6,498	88.1%	12,661	61.5%	31.1%	5.2%	1.8%	0.5%	16,374	72.3%	23.0%	2.1%	1.4%	1.2%
Lake County	22,134	89.5%	42,669	80.2%	13.8%	4.8%	0.6%	0.6%	50,962	76.0%	16.5%	5.9%	1.1%	0.5%
LaPorte County	4,374	88.1%	8,713	65.5%	31.6%	1.9%	1.0%	0.0%	12,832	60.1%	35.1%	2.8%	2.0%	0.0%
Madison County	5,357	75.8%	11,939	55.2%	43.8%	0.0%	0.9%	0.0%	14,351	65.3%	32.2%	1.8%	0.2%	0.5%
Marion County	33,953	90.7%	87,972	70.5%	26.0%	1.6%	1.6%	0.3%	143,605	75.3%	21.0%	0.8%	2.4%	0.5%
Monroe County	4,057	83.1%	40,498	29.4%	61.7%	2.1%	5.6%	1.2%	19,522	63.9%	24.5%	6.8%	4.4%	0.4%
Porter County	7,257	83.4%	16,289	72.5%	18.0%	0.7%	8.1%	0.7%	16,606	75.2%	21.4%	3.4%	0.0%	0.0%
St. Joseph County	11,323	90.3%	30,022	62.3%	25.6%	7.5%	2.6%	1.9%	30,257	73.1%	21.9%	2.5%	1.7%	0.8%
Tippecanoe County	5,390	90.4%	45,635	42.0%	46.0%	3.6%	2.7%	5.8%	23,119	72.6%	22.2%	0.5%	1.2%	3.5%
Vanderburgh County	5,989	78.6%	18,215	58.3%	29.7%	3.7%	7.9%	0.4%	23,223	74.8%	23.5%	0.0%	1.7%	0.0%
Vigo County	3,899	84.9%	17,396	44.8%	45.6%	3.8%	5.1%	0.8%	11,877	64.2%	34.3%	0.0%	1.5%	0.0%
Iowa														
Black Hawk County	4,554	96.4%	20,218	44.0%	46.1%	6.7%	3.0%	0.2%	16,522	76.3%	19.2%	3.4%	1.0%	0.0%

Table J-2: Counties—Mobility Status by Age—*Continued*

| | 15 to 17 | | 18 to 24 | | | | | | 25 to 33 | | | | | |
| | | | | | Percent Living in a Different House | | | | | | Percent Living in a Different House | | | |
	Total Population	Percent Living in Same House	Total Population	Percent Living in Same House	Same State	Different State, Same Region	Different Region	Outside US	Total Population	Percent Living in Same House	Same State	Different State, Same Region	Different Region	Outside US
Iowa—Cont.														
Dubuque County	4,498	79.7%	10,631	70.4%	16.2%	11.7%	1.4%	0.3%	10,173	76.6%	16.7%	4.1%	2.7%	0.0%
Johnson County	4,586	75.1%	30,445	45.7%	39.1%	8.8%	5.5%	0.9%	20,149	79.3%	13.3%	2.9%	3.5%	0.9%
Linn County	8,896	91.1%	20,556	67.5%	27.4%	1.1%	4.0%	0.0%	26,946	71.4%	14.9%	0.0%	4.1%	9.6%
Polk County	17,901	69.8%	42,356	49.3%	45.9%	4.1%	0.7%	0.1%	63,811	62.7%	31.1%	1.1%	4.8%	0.3%
Pottawattamie County	3,531	89.2%	7,635	64.0%	14.5%	16.4%	5.1%	0.0%	10,697	81.1%	13.2%	5.5%	0.0%	0.1%
Scott County	6,340	90.6%	14,919	77.0%	12.3%	7.6%	2.2%	0.8%	21,279	81.6%	11.0%	3.7%	2.7%	0.9%
Story County	2,650	89.4%	30,499	31.3%	57.1%	10.1%	1.4%	0.0%	12,160	76.1%	14.9%	1.2%	2.4%	5.4%
Woodbury County	5,066	88.6%	10,216	61.8%	28.2%	4.1%	5.9%	0.0%	13,035	87.4%	11.2%	1.4%	0.0%	0.0%
Kansas														
Douglas County	2,982	68.5%	27,314	38.8%	40.6%	5.2%	8.1%	7.3%	16,467	78.0%	12.4%	1.2%	6.8%	1.6%
Johnson County	25,281	92.3%	45,453	69.8%	19.7%	5.3%	3.2%	2.1%	72,191	67.2%	23.4%	4.7%	3.3%	1.4%
Sedgwick County	21,925	90.7%	42,104	69.8%	24.9%	1.8%	3.6%	0.0%	69,848	77.9%	19.3%	0.7%	1.3%	0.8%
Shawnee County	7,605	88.7%	15,601	48.4%	43.8%	2.8%	3.8%	1.1%	20,868	70.1%	22.5%	2.1%	4.7%	0.6%
Wyandotte County	6,907	92.2%	15,957	72.5%	20.9%	6.6%	0.0%	0.0%	20,784	70.1%	20.5%	6.7%	1.9%	0.9%
Kentucky														
Boone County	5,241	81.2%	10,603	69.0%	28.2%	0.0%	2.8%	0.0%	14,062	59.0%	30.2%	4.5%	6.3%	0.0%
Campbell County	2,719	97.2%	10,150	68.9%	11.9%	4.8%	12.9%	1.4%	12,171	81.1%	16.1%	0.0%	2.7%	0.0%
Daviess County	4,096	86.1%	8,278	78.5%	21.5%	0.0%	0.0%	0.0%	10,870	78.0%	9.2%	1.5%	4.9%	6.3%
Fayette County	9,984	84.4%	43,094	50.5%	37.8%	3.4%	7.0%	1.2%	44,691	66.2%	23.4%	4.6%	4.1%	1.8%
Hardin County	5,842	89.9%	8,702	71.2%	22.0%	2.0%	4.8%	0.0%	13,182	60.3%	24.7%	4.2%	10.8%	0.0%
Jefferson County	28,047	89.2%	67,483	70.9%	24.1%	1.1%	3.3%	0.6%	97,019	77.6%	18.3%	1.4%	2.7%	0.1%
Kenton County	6,292	92.0%	13,201	64.9%	28.6%	0.0%	6.5%	0.0%	21,440	70.4%	16.6%	2.4%	10.6%	0.0%
Warren County	5,132	84.3%	20,247	45.1%	43.6%	6.7%	3.1%	1.4%	13,584	64.2%	33.3%	0.3%	2.2%	0.0%
Louisiana														
Ascension Parish	5,994	96.6%	9,930	86.8%	12.4%	0.7%	0.0%	0.0%	15,246	86.1%	9.9%	1.6%	2.4%	0.0%
Bossier Parish	5,398	84.4%	10,378	66.8%	20.5%	6.6%	3.1%	2.9%	18,823	76.4%	18.2%	1.6%	3.3%	0.4%
Caddo Parish	9,885	84.0%	22,950	74.6%	22.8%	1.8%	0.8%	0.0%	31,201	86.6%	11.8%	1.7%	0.0%	0.0%
Calcasieu Parish	8,228	88.7%	19,191	79.1%	15.9%	3.0%	1.5%	0.4%	25,818	76.5%	17.6%	3.4%	2.6%	0.0%
East Baton Rouge Parish	16,677	89.7%	64,836	65.1%	29.4%	1.7%	2.9%	0.9%	60,253	72.4%	22.1%	3.8%	1.6%	0.0%
Jefferson Parish	14,162	93.9%	35,832	82.4%	11.2%	4.4%	1.3%	0.7%	59,422	78.4%	18.4%	1.0%	1.6%	0.7%
Lafayette Parish	9,654	75.4%	25,132	61.4%	36.6%	0.7%	1.0%	0.3%	35,178	67.5%	28.8%	2.1%	1.4%	0.2%
Lafourche Parish	3,944	91.1%	9,010	83.7%	16.3%	0.0%	0.0%	0.0%	12,284	78.0%	19.8%	2.0%	0.0%	2.2%
Livingston Parish	4,931	83.4%	12,429	83.1%	11.4%	1.5%	4.0%	0.0%	18,143	85.3%	14.7%	0.0%	0.0%	0.0%
Orleans Parish	11,869	88.8%	36,913	77.3%	15.2%	4.1%	3.2%	0.3%	64,511	75.2%	18.9%	2.1%	1.9%	1.7%
Ouachita Parish	6,570	84.1%	16,254	78.8%	17.2%	3.5%	0.4%	0.0%	21,022	74.1%	20.9%	3.4%	1.1%	0.5%
Rapides Parish	5,581	93.3%	12,171	81.2%	10.7%	5.7%	0.9%	1.6%	15,027	81.2%	11.3%	3.7%	1.4%	2.4%
St. Tammany Parish	10,828	86.5%	17,848	79.4%	15.6%	4.2%	0.7%	0.0%	27,347	77.1%	13.9%	8.6%	0.4%	0.0%
Tangipahoa Parish	5,276	81.7%	15,212	56.7%	40.0%	2.3%	1.0%	0.0%	16,082	70.1%	27.6%	2.3%	0.0%	0.0%
Terrebonne Parish	3,910	87.5%	9,054	87.3%	3.5%	6.9%	2.3%	0.0%	14,608	82.5%	12.7%	4.4%	0.5%	0.0%
Maine														
Androscoggin County	4,002	89.0%	9,422	53.2%	42.1%	2.8%	1.8%	0.0%	10,928	72.7%	27.3%	0.0%	0.0%	0.0%
Cumberland County	11,424	87.6%	27,405	57.5%	31.2%	5.2%	5.1%	1.1%	32,599	67.0%	26.0%	4.2%	2.8%	0.0%
Kennebec County	4,104	96.2%	10,420	49.5%	41.5%	7.2%	0.1%	1.8%	11,402	71.2%	28.0%	0.7%	0.1%	0.0%
Penobscot County	5,200	78.6%	17,405	58.6%	32.6%	8.8%	0.0%	0.0%	18,251	56.8%	37.9%	2.7%	2.7%	0.0%
York County	8,207	90.8%	14,898	76.1%	13.8%	9.0%	1.0%	0.0%	21,412	73.2%	16.9%	8.3%	0.7%	0.9%
Maryland														
Anne Arundel County	20,440	89.0%	49,519	81.8%	8.6%	2.6%	6.2%	0.8%	72,114	72.2%	17.2%	4.8%	4.4%	1.3%
Baltimore County	29,283	92.3%	75,812	77.7%	16.8%	0.8%	4.4%	0.3%	102,913	82.7%	13.6%	1.3%	2.1%	0.2%
Carroll County	7,587	87.6%	15,086	84.2%	13.7%	0.9%	1.2%	0.0%	15,451	83.6%	12.0%	2.6%	1.3%	0.5%
Cecil County	4,087	88.8%	10,116	68.7%	25.3%	0.0%	6.0%	0.0%	10,550	75.0%	19.2%	5.8%	0.0%	0.0%
Charles County	7,369	92.4%	14,616	78.8%	13.4%	4.4%	0.6%	2.7%	17,558	84.0%	13.4%	2.6%	0.0%	0.0%
Frederick County	10,064	94.0%	23,610	78.1%	17.3%	0.5%	4.1%	0.0%	25,527	81.0%	15.4%	1.6%	1.5%	0.4%
Harford County	10,052	92.5%	21,193	86.8%	6.5%	4.1%	1.6%	0.9%	27,303	75.7%	17.9%	3.9%	1.0%	1.5%
Howard County	14,442	92.4%	24,724	74.7%	19.0%	0.4%	3.6%	2.2%	35,451	66.1%	22.6%	3.4%	6.5%	1.4%
Montgomery County	39,976	91.3%	80,631	71.7%	19.0%	3.1%	4.3%	2.0%	121,975	74.2%	16.6%	3.5%	3.3%	2.3%
Prince George's County	32,415	81.3%	92,320	74.4%	16.7%	4.6%	2.6%	1.6%	119,847	74.8%	14.5%	6.6%	1.9%	2.3%
St. Mary's County	4,664	92.8%	11,172	84.1%	10.6%	0.5%	4.3%	0.5%	12,744	59.3%	32.8%	4.3%	2.4%	1.2%
Washington County	6,110	83.5%	12,974	69.0%	24.6%	2.4%	0.2%	3.8%	17,314	66.7%	26.9%	0.7%	5.0%	0.6%
Wicomico County	3,726	93.3%	15,548	63.0%	33.4%	1.4%	2.1%	0.0%	10,832	66.3%	32.4%	0.0%	1.2%	0.0%
Massachusetts														
Barnstable County	7,085	93.4%	14,470	81.8%	15.1%	1.8%	1.2%	0.0%	16,446	77.0%	15.2%	6.4%	1.4%	0.0%
Berkshire County	4,505	89.4%	13,356	64.7%	21.8%	9.5%	2.7%	1.3%	10,784	84.0%	8.1%	1.3%	4.9%	1.6%
Bristol County	20,144	92.3%	53,784	81.0%	15.7%	2.1%	0.5%	0.7%	64,980	77.1%	20.0%	1.3%	0.4%	1.2%
Essex County	31,668	94.5%	70,510	83.7%	12.9%	0.9%	0.9%	1.6%	86,690	79.1%	16.5%	1.0%	1.2%	2.2%
Hampden County	18,698	83.1%	51,064	80.3%	15.7%	3.5%	0.5%	0.0%	52,638	80.4%	18.3%	0.7%	0.3%	0.4%
Hampshire County	7,555	92.8%	30,446	53.0%	37.1%	5.6%	3.7%	0.6%	19,802	68.7%	26.3%	2.8%	1.8%	0.4%
Middlesex County	56,272	94.8%	151,267	76.0%	14.5%	3.7%	3.0%	2.7%	217,135	71.5%	19.1%	3.1%	3.2%	3.1%
Norfolk County	31,491	94.1%	56,434	72.7%	16.7%	5.8%	3.2%	1.6%	74,387	78.1%	14.9%	3.2%	2.3%	1.5%
Plymouth County	20,867	92.5%	47,932	83.0%	12.6%	2.3%	1.7%	0.5%	45,305	82.2%	15.0%	0.0%	1.8%	1.1%
Suffolk County	20,344	87.6%	109,239	61.3%	21.5%	6.3%	6.6%	4.2%	164,411	71.4%	21.2%	1.9%	2.8%	2.7%
Worcester County	34,713	92.3%	79,420	76.9%	16.3%	3.3%	2.2%	1.4%	86,588	80.8%	15.4%	1.2%	1.6%	1.0%

Table J-2: Counties—Mobility Status by Age—*Continued*

| | 15 to 17 | | 18 to 24 | | | | | | 25 to 33 | | | | | |
| | | | | | Percent Living in a Different House | | | | | | Percent Living in a Different House | | | |
	Total Population	Percent Living in Same House	Total Population	Percent Living in Same House	Same State	Different State, Same Region	Different Region	Outside US	Total Population	Percent Living in Same House	Same State	Different State, Same Region	Different Region	Outside US
Michigan														
Allegan County	5,166	98.8%	9,792	73.9%	23.6%	0.4%	0.4%	1.7%	11,964	83.9%	16.1%	0.0%	0.0%	0.0%
Bay County	4,086	99.7%	8,750	77.1%	20.8%	0.1%	2.0%	0.0%	11,393	82.1%	15.1%	0.0%	0.0%	2.8%
Berrien County	5,752	71.9%	12,450	63.1%	29.6%	2.5%	4.9%	0.0%	15,966	60.6%	31.1%	1.9%	5.1%	1.3%
Calhoun County	5,674	89.2%	10,750	74.5%	23.3%	1.0%	0.5%	0.8%	15,498	74.4%	24.6%	0.8%	0.2%	0.0%
Eaton County	4,272	79.4%	10,308	67.7%	30.5%	0.0%	1.8%	0.0%	11,088	59.7%	30.0%	0.0%	8.7%	1.6%
Genesee County	16,854	91.2%	37,578	77.7%	20.9%	0.0%	0.8%	0.6%	44,026	76.7%	18.0%	0.1%	5.0%	0.1%
Ingham County	10,505	84.6%	55,890	47.4%	45.8%	0.9%	3.2%	2.7%	36,809	64.8%	30.8%	1.6%	1.8%	1.0%
Jackson County	5,866	90.8%	13,858	71.3%	24.5%	0.9%	2.9%	0.4%	18,291	78.5%	19.9%	0.7%	0.9%	0.0%
Kalamazoo County	9,165	91.1%	40,695	55.3%	38.5%	3.1%	0.9%	2.1%	30,665	76.7%	21.7%	1.1%	0.4%	0.1%
Kent County	27,026	87.1%	59,053	65.9%	27.5%	1.1%	2.5%	3.0%	86,654	72.1%	24.7%	0.2%	1.0%	2.0%
Lenawee County	3,813	68.6%	10,515	69.9%	21.7%	4.2%	2.9%	1.3%	8,941	70.9%	24.9%	0.4%	2.6%	1.2%
Livingston County	8,688	87.7%	16,204	84.1%	13.5%	2.4%	0.0%	0.0%	16,311	80.4%	17.2%	0.0%	2.5%	0.0%
Macomb County	35,897	94.4%	72,892	80.3%	16.1%	1.0%	2.1%	0.5%	96,953	74.8%	21.4%	0.3%	2.3%	1.2%
Monroe County	6,328	97.0%	11,950	80.8%	18.0%	1.2%	0.0%	0.0%	15,224	78.3%	20.0%	1.6%	0.0%	0.0%
Muskegon County	6,611	80.5%	14,864	61.0%	38.0%	1.0%	0.0%	0.0%	20,232	74.2%	23.8%	0.5%	1.5%	0.0%
Oakland County	50,089	91.6%	99,353	71.9%	25.0%	0.5%	1.8%	0.8%	138,448	70.2%	23.5%	0.6%	2.6%	3.0%
Ottawa County	12,481	92.0%	37,740	58.3%	40.5%	0.8%	0.1%	0.3%	29,180	79.9%	15.0%	0.0%	1.9%	3.3%
Saginaw County	6,999	79.9%	20,018	72.6%	25.9%	0.0%	1.1%	0.5%	21,353	73.6%	24.3%	0.0%	0.8%	1.2%
St. Clair County	6,981	84.1%	12,939	75.9%	23.6%	0.0%	0.5%	0.0%	15,197	76.1%	22.4%	0.0%	1.5%	0.0%
Washtenaw County	11,948	84.7%	65,988	42.1%	45.9%	3.8%	5.2%	3.0%	45,342	59.0%	28.2%	5.0%	6.4%	1.4%
Wayne County	73,059	86.3%	161,271	77.0%	21.4%	0.4%	0.8%	0.4%	209,958	77.4%	19.7%	0.7%	1.5%	0.7%
Minnesota														
Anoka County	15,096	93.7%	28,545	72.6%	17.9%	6.0%	0.6%	2.8%	37,263	78.8%	17.0%	0.0%	4.2%	0.0%
Carver County	3,719	99.1%	8,836	77.6%	21.2%	0.0%	1.2%	0.0%	9,344	65.4%	34.2%	0.0%	0.4%	0.0%
Dakota County	17,986	93.1%	32,562	73.6%	23.4%	0.9%	1.5%	0.5%	48,217	79.4%	16.6%	1.0%	1.4%	1.7%
Hennepin County	43,301	87.7%	102,085	59.6%	33.1%	4.2%	1.9%	1.3%	187,052	70.2%	22.6%	2.0%	2.5%	2.7%
Olmsted County	5,235	94.7%	13,039	68.4%	26.6%	5.0%	0.0%	0.0%	18,471	80.9%	13.4%	0.1%	4.1%	1.5%
Ramsey County	18,827	83.9%	53,476	63.8%	25.8%	5.4%	4.4%	0.6%	80,179	66.8%	24.5%	4.6%	2.8%	1.2%
Scott County	6,719	88.1%	23,823	56.5%	35.5%	3.6%	3.7%	0.7%	24,077	80.8%	16.6%	1.0%	1.5%	0.1%
St. Louis County	6,813	95.9%	10,039	77.7%	22.3%	0.0%	0.0%	0.0%	15,996	75.2%	23.0%	0.0%	1.8%	0.0%
Stearns County	5,859	97.6%	23,336	53.2%	42.0%	3.3%	0.2%	1.4%	18,068	67.4%	31.8%	0.3%	0.4%	0.0%
Washington County	11,153	98.8%	18,451	87.2%	10.4%	0.5%	1.8%	0.0%	27,927	75.7%	16.4%	3.0%	2.2%	2.7%
Wright County	5,782	93.5%	9,108	74.7%	22.4%	0.5%	2.3%	0.0%	12,796	87.8%	9.6%	0.0%	2.6%	0.0%
Mississippi														
DeSoto County	8,936	88.9%	15,974	81.6%	13.1%	5.4%	0.0%	0.0%	18,056	79.4%	12.6%	7.1%	0.9%	0.0%
Harrison County	8,197	75.0%	20,500	53.9%	25.2%	6.2%	14.1%	0.6%	26,456	65.4%	25.2%	6.2%	0.7%	2.5%
Hinds County	9,867	87.1%	27,627	74.3%	22.8%	2.0%	0.9%	0.0%	33,590	75.9%	21.5%	2.5%	0.2%	0.0%
Jackson County	5,936	94.6%	11,665	86.6%	7.9%	5.5%	0.0%	0.0%	15,749	77.0%	18.6%	4.5%	0.0%	0.0%
Madison County	4,534	94.2%	9,529	79.8%	15.2%	3.1%	1.9%	0.0%	11,625	71.7%	23.0%	5.3%	0.0%	0.0%
Rankin County	7,049	78.4%	11,450	79.9%	18.8%	1.2%	0.0%	0.0%	18,537	78.1%	20.0%	0.0%	1.9%	0.0%
Missouri														
Boone County	5,971	77.0%	35,010	47.7%	39.3%	5.1%	5.2%	2.7%	24,966	64.6%	30.3%	0.6%	1.8%	2.7%
Cass County	4,002	90.6%	7,815	80.8%	18.9%	0.0%	0.2%	0.0%	10,753	82.1%	15.0%	1.1%	1.8%	0.0%
Clay County	9,693	91.8%	19,014	72.4%	16.4%	5.6%	2.7%	3.0%	29,294	65.1%	24.5%	6.4%	3.2%	0.7%
Franklin County	4,357	100.0%	7,688	79.2%	18.1%	0.8%	2.0%	0.0%	10,968	83.6%	15.9%	0.5%	0.0%	0.0%
Greene County	10,087	85.0%	39,311	50.5%	45.9%	0.8%	2.1%	0.7%	38,002	71.4%	26.5%	0.9%	1.0%	0.2%
Jackson County	25,581	84.8%	58,654	68.8%	25.5%	2.9%	2.6%	0.1%	92,397	75.4%	17.8%	3.2%	2.8%	0.8%
Jasper County	5,894	91.8%	12,573	69.0%	25.9%	1.7%	3.4%	0.0%	13,205	86.3%	12.7%	1.0%	0.0%	0.0%
Jefferson County	9,707	85.8%	17,003	73.3%	25.4%	0.0%	0.6%	0.7%	26,185	80.9%	15.7%	1.6%	1.8%	0.0%
Platte County	3,846	73.8%	8,083	68.7%	22.4%	3.1%	5.8%	0.0%	12,428	59.8%	16.9%	13.7%	5.6%	3.9%
St. Charles County	15,995	88.5%	34,021	77.4%	18.3%	1.2%	2.6%	0.5%	43,865	70.9%	25.6%	3.4%	0.1%	0.0%
St. Louis County	40,499	88.6%	91,525	73.5%	20.7%	1.7%	2.6%	1.5%	110,930	77.4%	16.6%	2.1%	3.1%	0.7%
Montana														
Flathead County	3,906	90.6%	7,110	61.8%	16.8%	21.4%	0.0%	0.0%	8,899	66.7%	26.9%	3.7%	2.7%	0.0%
Gallatin County	3,825	83.1%	17,676	48.0%	40.2%	7.8%	3.7%	0.3%	13,205	69.8%	22.2%	0.0%	7.6%	0.3%
Missoula County	4,387	97.5%	14,743	51.9%	38.8%	5.3%	4.1%	0.0%	16,851	84.7%	7.7%	0.9%	6.7%	0.0%
Yellowstone County	4,798	93.5%	15,272	64.6%	27.8%	4.4%	3.0%	0.3%	18,802	71.0%	21.2%	5.2%	2.6%	0.0%
Nebraska														
Douglas County	21,857	85.5%	48,111	61.3%	30.1%	4.1%	2.9%	1.6%	79,252	72.7%	21.6%	3.0%	2.2%	0.5%
Lancaster County	9,211	93.7%	44,746	51.7%	42.4%	2.6%	2.3%	0.9%	40,689	73.8%	20.2%	0.4%	3.2%	2.3%
Sarpy County	7,461	89.7%	15,963	71.5%	22.1%	2.5%	3.9%	0.0%	21,981	84.3%	11.7%	0.8%	3.3%	0.0%
Nevada														
Clark County	80,669	80.9%	185,462	70.3%	22.5%	3.9%	2.7%	0.6%	282,745	70.4%	21.3%	5.0%	2.3%	1.0%
Washoe County	16,519	91.3%	40,531	62.7%	29.5%	5.1%	2.0%	0.6%	58,769	65.5%	26.2%	5.6%	2.0%	0.7%
New Hampshire														
Hillsborough County	16,014	89.0%	36,372	72.5%	19.5%	4.4%	2.4%	1.1%	44,349	72.1%	19.5%	4.9%	2.8%	0.7%
Merrimack County	6,225	90.6%	15,345	83.0%	13.1%	2.9%	0.4%	0.6%	14,153	70.9%	20.4%	1.8%	4.5%	2.5%
Rockingham County	11,728	93.9%	24,833	80.5%	15.1%	2.9%	1.3%	0.2%	29,641	74.9%	11.3%	9.4%	1.8%	2.6%
Strafford County	4,611	96.2%	20,330	53.8%	37.9%	6.8%	1.1%	0.4%	14,256	61.3%	16.4%	8.2%	8.9%	5.2%
New Jersey														
Atlantic County	10,031	86.2%	26,461	83.0%	15.0%	0.1%	0.8%	1.0%	30,078	74.9%	16.7%	2.4%	4.8%	1.2%

Table J-2: Counties—Mobility Status by Age—*Continued*

	15 to 17		18 to 24						25 to 33					
					Percent Living in a Different House							Percent Living in a Different House		
	Total Population	Percent Living in Same House	Total Population	Percent Living in Same House	Same State	Different State, Same Region	Different Region	Outside US	Total Population	Percent Living in Same House	Same State	Different State, Same Region	Different Region	Outside US
New Jersey—Cont.														
Bergen County	37,455	91.5%	76,394	92.9%	3.5%	1.7%	0.9%	0.9%	94,035	79.6%	14.6%	1.9%	1.3%	2.7%
Burlington County	18,067	88.3%	40,215	78.4%	15.9%	1.7%	3.4%	0.6%	49,139	79.1%	16.0%	2.5%	1.4%	1.0%
Camden County	19,864	93.4%	45,187	87.4%	8.1%	1.5%	1.7%	1.2%	63,339	79.5%	17.0%	1.1%	1.4%	1.1%
Cape May County	3,824	99.5%	6,462	79.4%	9.8%	1.3%	9.5%	0.0%	8,863	74.8%	17.2%	3.7%	3.0%	1.3%
Cumberland County	5,907	98.1%	12,525	80.8%	15.9%	1.7%	1.6%	0.0%	21,371	77.5%	21.4%	0.8%	0.2%	0.0%
Essex County	31,320	93.9%	73,719	85.2%	11.6%	1.3%	1.0%	1.0%	94,290	84.0%	12.9%	1.7%	0.5%	0.9%
Gloucester County	11,825	96.5%	25,009	79.2%	17.8%	2.2%	0.0%	0.9%	32,711	83.8%	14.2%	0.8%	1.0%	0.2%
Hudson County	20,002	86.7%	57,454	84.2%	7.8%	2.1%	2.4%	3.5%	126,934	76.2%	13.3%	5.5%	1.9%	3.0%
Hunterdon County	6,353	87.9%	11,277	82.0%	10.0%	4.2%	3.7%	0.0%	9,540	84.9%	13.8%	1.2%	0.0%	0.0%
Mercer County	14,182	88.6%	42,896	78.0%	16.0%	3.2%	2.4%	0.3%	39,044	78.2%	15.4%	3.7%	1.5%	1.2%
Middlesex County	31,955	96.4%	80,167	87.2%	9.9%	1.0%	0.2%	1.7%	102,594	81.2%	14.7%	1.5%	1.3%	1.3%
Monmouth County	26,652	94.0%	52,405	85.8%	11.1%	1.7%	0.7%	0.7%	61,769	77.8%	20.0%	1.2%	0.7%	0.2%
Morris County	21,633	98.8%	42,026	91.9%	5.7%	0.1%	1.2%	1.2%	50,784	83.4%	10.6%	1.2%	3.3%	1.5%
Ocean County	20,954	98.2%	42,927	86.4%	10.5%	1.9%	0.4%	0.9%	58,565	79.2%	17.3%	2.1%	0.8%	0.6%
Passaic County	20,397	96.5%	50,193	90.5%	8.2%	0.6%	0.6%	0.2%	61,390	90.3%	7.4%	0.2%	0.9%	1.3%
Somerset County	13,336	96.8%	26,813	88.8%	6.4%	2.0%	1.4%	1.4%	32,010	84.5%	13.2%	1.4%	0.4%	0.5%
Sussex County	6,130	98.6%	12,181	89.4%	8.5%	2.1%	0.0%	0.0%	12,390	79.7%	19.2%	0.8%	0.3%	0.0%
Union County	22,014	89.4%	49,137	83.7%	11.5%	0.5%	0.5%	3.8%	61,904	84.2%	13.0%	1.0%	0.4%	1.5%
Warren County	4,483	90.5%	8,731	77.7%	17.6%	0.8%	0.5%	3.5%	9,650	81.6%	15.8%	0.0%	2.7%	0.0%
New Mexico														
Bernalillo County	27,407	84.9%	65,746	65.6%	29.6%	0.7%	3.0%	1.1%	89,698	71.4%	22.4%	1.5%	2.8%	1.8%
Doña Ana County	8,988	89.7%	30,410	74.9%	20.0%	1.0%	4.1%	0.0%	24,696	83.4%	10.0%	3.3%	2.8%	0.5%
San Juan County	6,020	97.6%	10,605	81.8%	15.2%	1.9%	1.0%	0.0%	16,172	86.3%	9.7%	2.1%	1.9%	0.0%
Sandoval County	4,993	86.0%	11,608	80.3%	18.7%	0.7%	0.3%	0.0%	14,031	77.5%	16.4%	1.0%	4.2%	1.0%
Santa Fe County	4,909	97.2%	11,025	82.1%	11.6%	0.2%	6.1%	0.0%	15,060	77.7%	14.0%	3.2%	4.1%	0.9%
New York														
Albany County	10,630	91.7%	44,077	66.9%	28.4%	2.3%	0.9%	1.5%	35,898	74.8%	19.7%	1.8%	1.9%	1.8%
Bronx County	58,939	93.3%	158,547	90.0%	7.4%	0.9%	0.8%	0.9%	203,054	89.3%	9.0%	0.8%	0.2%	0.6%
Broome County	7,744	85.6%	28,337	68.4%	28.1%	0.3%	1.8%	1.3%	18,852	79.2%	19.0%	0.8%	1.0%	0.0%
Chautauqua County	5,229	83.0%	13,664	67.3%	29.1%	0.3%	1.0%	2.3%	12,863	82.9%	17.1%	0.0%	0.0%	0.0%
Dutchess County	11,448	94.0%	33,766	79.4%	11.8%	3.3%	3.5%	2.0%	30,439	77.7%	18.7%	1.6%	1.4%	0.6%
Erie County	33,991	91.9%	89,778	77.6%	20.2%	0.1%	0.7%	1.5%	116,105	78.2%	18.8%	0.6%	1.2%	1.2%
Jefferson County	4,181	92.8%	15,128	58.0%	19.2%	0.4%	16.3%	6.1%	16,116	64.5%	16.6%	1.3%	12.6%	5.0%
Kings County	90,537	95.1%	234,279	85.5%	9.8%	1.3%	1.7%	1.7%	428,199	81.6%	14.1%	0.8%	1.8%	1.7%
Monroe County	27,880	89.8%	79,736	59.6%	33.5%	2.3%	2.8%	1.9%	94,106	70.2%	24.3%	2.2%	1.4%	2.0%
Nassau County	55,111	95.7%	121,410	89.5%	6.7%	0.7%	1.8%	1.2%	138,159	86.3%	11.8%	0.3%	0.8%	0.8%
New York County	32,021	94.1%	148,981	61.0%	17.5%	6.2%	8.9%	6.3%	339,281	73.1%	17.5%	2.7%	4.1%	2.6%
Niagara County	7,822	88.6%	19,504	79.2%	19.0%	0.0%	1.1%	0.7%	22,101	81.7%	14.8%	0.0%	2.4%	1.1%
Oneida County	7,889	87.7%	22,344	77.8%	19.1%	1.9%	0.7%	0.5%	27,104	66.5%	29.2%	0.0%	3.7%	0.5%
Onondaga County	19,605	89.3%	48,374	66.7%	23.9%	3.5%	3.3%	2.5%	55,218	76.1%	21.5%	0.7%	0.6%	1.1%
Ontario County	4,273	94.8%	11,498	64.7%	24.5%	5.1%	2.0%	3.8%	10,546	83.4%	5.7%	6.1%	1.2%	0.0%
Orange County	17,935	97.6%	41,203	90.4%	7.3%	0.3%	1.4%	0.7%	37,039	85.6%	11.3%	0.8%	1.6%	0.8%
Oswego County	5,206	94.0%	13,878	57.8%	36.9%	0.9%	3.4%	1.0%	13,002	78.8%	19.3%	0.5%	0.7%	0.7%
Putnam County	4,496	87.5%	9,244	84.3%	13.6%	0.1%	0.0%	2.0%	7,803	91.4%	7.9%	0.0%	0.1%	0.6%
Queens County	73,248	94.4%	196,744	87.2%	8.8%	0.9%	1.1%	1.9%	338,427	85.7%	11.5%	0.6%	0.8%	1.4%
Rensselaer County	5,272	87.2%	17,497	71.5%	18.7%	5.6%	1.9%	2.2%	19,891	75.3%	21.6%	1.1%	1.0%	1.0%
Richmond County	19,035	94.4%	42,440	93.8%	5.5%	0.5%	0.0%	0.3%	57,132	89.6%	9.3%	0.0%	0.2%	0.9%
Rockland County	14,714	95.6%	31,709	91.2%	8.4%	0.4%	0.0%	0.0%	32,409	85.8%	12.5%	1.0%	0.4%	0.3%
Saratoga County	3,881	91.3%	15,881	61.9%	31.1%	3.8%	1.9%	1.3%	12,327	72.6%	25.5%	1.1%	0.8%	0.0%
Schenectady County	8,697	89.0%	17,709	70.8%	20.3%	2.6%	5.0%	1.3%	23,614	73.8%	20.4%	0.0%	4.3%	1.5%
St. Lawrence County	6,230	95.2%	13,854	74.9%	22.0%	0.0%	0.0%	3.0%	18,362	79.8%	17.7%	0.0%	0.5%	2.0%
Steuben County	4,443	92.8%	8,644	82.2%	13.5%	1.4%	2.9%	0.0%	9,588	77.9%	19.0%	1.5%	1.6%	0.0%
Suffolk County	60,924	94.6%	135,673	86.3%	11.1%	0.4%	0.8%	1.4%	154,323	87.0%	10.8%	0.4%	1.3%	0.6%
Tompkins County	2,564	94.0%	30,661	71.6%	19.6%	3.8%	5.1%	0.0%	11,325	56.9%	22.9%	3.8%	12.1%	4.3%
Ulster County	5,593	98.6%	19,614	82.9%	16.1%	0.4%	0.5%	0.0%	18,145	79.6%	19.0%	0.0%	0.5%	0.9%
Wayne County	3,794	93.8%	7,192	73.5%	23.7%	0.0%	1.3%	1.5%	9,606	78.6%	18.3%	1.5%	1.6%	0.0%
Westchester County	41,838	94.8%	88,759	84.2%	10.1%	2.3%	2.0%	1.4%	96,832	82.4%	14.1%	1.6%	0.9%	1.1%
North Carolina														
Alamance County	6,420	82.1%	14,754	77.3%	15.4%	2.7%	3.1%	1.5%	16,654	72.3%	23.7%	0.9%	2.0%	1.1%
Brunswick County	3,773	91.1%	8,370	77.0%	18.1%	2.7%	0.0%	2.2%	9,184	75.7%	19.7%	3.3%	1.3%	0.0%
Buncombe County	8,783	86.4%	21,142	76.5%	12.9%	5.0%	3.3%	2.2%	32,129	72.4%	19.8%	1.4%	6.2%	0.2%
Cabarrus County	8,592	74.6%	15,855	71.4%	25.2%	1.5%	1.9%	0.0%	20,760	71.1%	24.6%	0.0%	4.3%	0.0%
Catawba County	6,952	87.3%	13,521	76.3%	18.9%	3.7%	1.2%	0.0%	15,886	81.1%	16.1%	2.0%	0.8%	0.0%
Cleveland County	3,536	81.9%	9,470	89.3%	10.1%	0.6%	0.0%	0.0%	9,222	82.6%	16.2%	1.1%	0.1%	0.0%
Craven County	2,915	91.6%	12,867	57.3%	32.1%	7.2%	1.5%	1.9%	12,859	67.1%	22.7%	3.9%	4.3%	1.9%
Cumberland County	12,421	85.2%	40,795	57.1%	23.1%	10.6%	6.5%	2.7%	48,094	66.3%	19.0%	4.3%	7.5%	2.9%
Davidson County	7,031	79.6%	12,567	78.9%	19.4%	0.0%	1.5%	0.1%	16,728	56.4%	35.1%	4.9%	3.5%	0.1%
Durham County	9,831	88.1%	29,901	63.0%	22.6%	8.0%	5.2%	1.2%	50,048	64.1%	28.1%	2.5%	3.7%	1.6%
Forsyth County	14,264	89.3%	34,812	70.9%	20.6%	4.4%	3.3%	0.9%	43,345	73.3%	18.7%	5.2%	2.2%	0.6%
Gaston County	8,147	91.0%	17,543	77.1%	18.5%	2.9%	1.1%	0.4%	25,240	75.5%	19.2%	2.4%	1.5%	1.4%
Guilford County	20,720	90.8%	53,974	73.3%	22.2%	1.7%	2.3%	0.5%	62,889	77.6%	17.6%	2.3%	1.7%	0.8%
Harnett County	5,419	85.9%	13,395	54.0%	35.7%	2.6%	7.7%	0.0%	17,089	81.7%	13.9%	1.9%	2.5%	0.0%
Henderson County	2,993	89.3%	7,290	72.3%	13.7%	5.0%	8.9%	0.0%	10,238	79.7%	14.4%	3.2%	2.6%	0.0%

Table J-2: Counties—Mobility Status by Age—*Continued*

| | 15 to 17 | | 18 to 24 | | | | | | 25 to 33 | | | | | |
| | | | | | Percent Living in a Different House | | | | | | Percent Living in a Different House | | | |
	Total Population	Percent Living in Same House	Total Population	Percent Living in Same House	Same State	Different State, Same Region	Different Region	Outside US	Total Population	Percent Living in Same House	Same State	Different State, Same Region	Different Region	Outside US
North Carolina—Cont.														
Iredell County	8,299	89.0%	14,699	74.0%	20.9%	3.7%	1.4%	0.0%	16,137	72.7%	20.6%	2.4%	3.9%	0.4%
Johnston County	8,185	97.6%	14,762	81.8%	16.6%	1.5%	0.1%	0.0%	18,964	86.4%	11.9%	0.9%	0.9%	0.0%
Mecklenburg County	37,568	85.9%	95,025	62.2%	29.2%	4.8%	2.7%	1.0%	153,249	64.6%	25.0%	4.5%	4.9%	1.0%
Moore County	3,880	96.8%	6,442	85.3%	9.8%	2.7%	2.2%	0.0%	9,173	76.0%	18.8%	2.7%	2.6%	0.0%
Nash County	3,826	81.8%	7,992	75.7%	22.6%	0.6%	0.2%	0.8%	9,719	88.6%	11.4%	0.0%	0.0%	0.0%
New Hanover County	7,739	82.5%	28,270	57.5%	36.5%	4.3%	1.2%	0.4%	26,458	74.7%	19.6%	3.4%	1.8%	0.4%
Onslow County	5,861	80.1%	37,365	38.9%	34.5%	9.3%	10.8%	6.5%	33,337	58.9%	23.6%	8.5%	6.0%	3.1%
Orange County	4,940	85.6%	27,135	45.4%	42.6%	6.1%	5.2%	0.6%	17,241	64.1%	22.1%	2.4%	4.4%	7.1%
Pitt County	6,349	80.8%	32,609	48.4%	48.2%	1.6%	1.9%	0.0%	22,584	69.0%	27.5%	1.5%	1.7%	0.4%
Randolph County	5,468	86.9%	12,051	64.8%	35.2%	0.0%	0.0%	0.0%	14,689	76.7%	20.4%	1.9%	0.5%	0.5%
Robeson County	5,668	94.6%	15,277	78.9%	17.6%	2.6%	0.7%	0.2%	13,861	92.0%	6.8%	1.0%	0.0%	0.1%
Rockingham County	3,614	87.5%	6,545	88.1%	11.1%	0.0%	0.8%	0.0%	8,972	79.9%	17.1%	1.9%	1.1%	0.1%
Rowan County	5,287	90.1%	12,526	69.8%	23.7%	5.3%	1.2%	0.0%	14,692	68.5%	29.3%	0.5%	1.6%	0.0%
Union County	11,693	97.3%	20,842	77.3%	15.4%	5.1%	2.3%	0.0%	18,713	77.1%	17.3%	4.2%	1.5%	0.0%
Wake County	40,874	91.3%	92,700	68.8%	25.9%	1.3%	3.4%	0.5%	135,921	67.3%	25.8%	3.1%	2.6%	1.2%
Wayne County	4,258	74.5%	12,124	63.3%	26.4%	6.7%	1.4%	2.1%	16,422	76.2%	19.9%	0.6%	0.7%	2.5%
North Dakota														
Cass County	4,825	79.3%	28,541	42.2%	27.6%	26.7%	2.6%	0.8%	24,162	57.0%	30.7%	11.3%	1.0%	0.0%
Ohio														
Allen County	4,020	95.4%	9,702	64.7%	24.8%	4.3%	6.2%	0.0%	11,532	74.3%	18.7%	5.2%	1.8%	0.0%
Ashtabula County	4,992	89.5%	7,835	82.0%	15.0%	0.5%	2.5%	0.0%	9,787	77.3%	22.7%	0.0%	0.0%	0.0%
Butler County	15,977	84.1%	45,123	62.2%	25.2%	2.7%	7.9%	2.0%	39,877	70.1%	26.2%	0.0%	2.8%	0.9%
Clark County	5,603	82.7%	11,991	50.5%	45.5%	0.0%	2.3%	1.6%	13,749	70.5%	29.1%	0.0%	0.4%	0.0%
Clermont County	9,004	99.6%	15,117	80.3%	17.5%	0.0%	1.6%	0.6%	23,530	81.7%	14.4%	0.0%	3.5%	0.4%
Columbiana County	4,005	95.0%	7,504	76.5%	22.8%	0.0%	0.8%	0.0%	9,881	86.5%	10.6%	0.0%	2.9%	0.0%
Cuyahoga County	46,290	88.3%	113,117	68.8%	24.0%	2.2%	2.8%	2.2%	147,659	70.2%	25.7%	1.0%	2.1%	1.0%
Delaware County	9,153	93.4%	14,652	63.0%	32.4%	0.0%	4.1%	0.5%	16,882	78.7%	17.8%	0.0%	3.3%	0.2%
Fairfield County	6,608	89.1%	12,289	67.1%	28.2%	0.8%	3.9%	0.0%	14,860	74.0%	17.1%	1.3%	7.6%	0.0%
Franklin County	45,137	82.7%	120,906	56.1%	38.1%	0.8%	3.6%	1.4%	202,024	69.9%	24.9%	0.9%	3.0%	1.3%
Geauga County	4,337	94.1%	7,905	83.4%	14.8%	0.2%	1.6%	0.0%	6,927	88.3%	10.8%	0.0%	0.9%	0.0%
Greene County	5,937	87.3%	20,661	68.1%	24.2%	1.9%	3.7%	2.1%	19,019	63.0%	31.2%	0.3%	5.0%	0.5%
Hamilton County	30,908	89.1%	72,838	60.3%	33.1%	1.4%	4.1%	1.2%	107,089	72.8%	22.8%	1.9%	1.9%	0.7%
Lake County	9,398	85.3%	18,278	78.6%	18.6%	0.0%	2.7%	0.1%	21,640	76.7%	20.6%	0.0%	2.0%	0.7%
Licking County	7,293	89.0%	15,948	73.9%	22.7%	0.5%	2.9%	0.0%	17,374	68.9%	28.1%	0.0%	3.1%	0.0%
Lorain County	13,388	85.0%	26,112	68.3%	20.8%	1.6%	7.7%	1.6%	30,309	74.4%	23.1%	1.1%	1.0%	0.4%
Lucas County	16,806	81.2%	41,038	61.2%	31.1%	3.7%	2.6%	1.4%	54,283	67.7%	24.8%	1.3%	5.0%	1.2%
Mahoning County	8,365	96.0%	20,268	76.5%	21.9%	0.5%	0.7%	0.4%	25,603	77.4%	19.4%	0.0%	2.6%	0.6%
Medina County	7,493	94.2%	13,547	80.5%	17.3%	0.0%	2.1%	0.0%	17,648	79.4%	16.1%	0.0%	4.5%	0.0%
Miami County	4,948	100.0%	7,784	55.2%	41.7%	1.3%	1.7%	0.0%	10,561	66.3%	26.7%	3.8%	3.2%	0.0%
Montgomery County	19,440	88.3%	47,493	52.7%	40.4%	3.8%	2.3%	0.8%	64,115	67.0%	26.3%	3.3%	2.8%	0.6%
Portage County	6,294	78.0%	27,140	62.1%	34.6%	0.4%	2.7%	0.1%	16,223	76.3%	20.7%	0.0%	2.1%	0.8%
Richland County	4,664	97.2%	10,805	75.4%	24.6%	0.0%	0.0%	0.0%	12,484	63.9%	36.1%	0.0%	0.0%	0.0%
Stark County	14,912	84.6%	32,535	71.6%	23.1%	0.8%	3.3%	1.2%	40,681	74.8%	21.6%	0.1%	3.5%	0.0%
Summit County	19,791	91.1%	47,666	79.8%	18.2%	0.0%	2.0%	0.0%	61,441	79.8%	16.7%	0.2%	2.1%	1.2%
Trumbull County	8,438	96.0%	17,104	76.6%	23.2%	0.0%	0.3%	0.0%	18,634	76.5%	19.7%	0.0%	2.9%	0.8%
Tuscarawas County	4,220	91.1%	7,080	74.5%	18.5%	0.0%	7.0%	0.0%	9,522	77.0%	20.4%	1.4%	1.3%	0.0%
Warren County	11,507	91.4%	17,277	72.3%	25.1%	0.0%	2.6%	0.0%	21,167	79.5%	18.2%	0.0%	1.4%	0.9%
Wayne County	5,538	81.3%	11,242	62.4%	32.9%	0.2%	3.8%	0.7%	11,235	85.3%	12.6%	1.5%	0.0%	0.6%
Wood County	6,803	79.4%	17,983	53.8%	43.7%	2.1%	0.0%	0.4%	18,327	84.5%	13.7%	0.8%	0.1%	0.9%
Oklahoma														
Canadian County	4,902	79.1%	10,745	77.8%	20.8%	0.0%	1.4%	0.0%	16,997	67.9%	29.2%	0.0%	2.9%	0.0%
Cleveland County	10,792	89.2%	39,790	54.6%	30.1%	9.1%	3.0%	3.2%	37,668	76.2%	14.4%	3.2%	3.5%	2.6%
Comanche County	4,742	71.4%	14,998	56.3%	15.9%	8.2%	18.0%	1.7%	19,817	56.3%	28.0%	4.9%	9.6%	1.3%
Oklahoma County	26,652	87.8%	70,303	66.1%	28.1%	1.9%	2.4%	1.5%	111,707	71.4%	24.6%	1.3%	1.4%	1.3%
Tulsa County	26,366	80.2%	58,292	68.3%	22.9%	2.6%	4.3%	1.9%	81,376	70.6%	22.6%	2.0%	2.7%	2.1%
Oregon														
Clackamas County	17,870	85.2%	32,507	74.3%	19.6%	5.3%	0.8%	0.0%	41,000	72.4%	22.7%	3.1%	1.2%	0.6%
Deschutes County	5,366	86.3%	12,522	71.5%	16.4%	12.1%	0.0%	0.0%	19,618	61.7%	32.8%	4.3%	1.2%	0.0%
Douglas County	3,303	76.4%	7,578	76.1%	22.0%	1.9%	0.0%	0.0%	10,988	80.3%	19.4%	0.0%	0.0%	0.3%
Jackson County	7,333	86.2%	16,260	62.7%	27.6%	5.5%	3.7%	0.5%	24,414	71.1%	19.1%	7.3%	2.3%	0.3%
Lane County	12,849	89.5%	46,498	45.6%	40.0%	12.0%	1.7%	0.7%	42,066	71.3%	24.8%	0.9%	1.1%	1.9%
Linn County	4,217	79.8%	12,827	47.9%	43.1%	5.6%	1.0%	2.3%	11,296	59.8%	34.3%	4.8%	0.0%	1.1%
Marion County	14,733	83.4%	32,049	63.8%	30.7%	2.7%	0.6%	2.1%	38,868	79.1%	18.6%	0.4%	1.3%	0.5%
Multnomah County	22,350	91.3%	64,956	58.8%	23.5%	12.1%	3.5%	2.1%	130,045	66.6%	25.8%	3.7%	3.0%	1.0%
Washington County	23,839	87.1%	46,192	70.9%	22.7%	3.3%	2.5%	0.7%	78,390	64.7%	22.5%	6.0%	4.3%	2.5%
Yamhill County	4,387	94.4%	11,578	77.2%	21.0%	1.8%	0.0%	0.0%	10,384	61.9%	30.9%	7.2%	0.0%	0.0%
Pennsylvania														
Adams County	4,180	84.6%	8,558	69.5%	22.4%	6.1%	2.0%	0.0%	10,662	73.5%	22.3%	0.0%	3.8%	0.4%
Allegheny County	41,256	89.1%	110,343	64.8%	26.3%	2.2%	4.7%	2.0%	166,066	69.5%	23.1%	0.7%	5.0%	1.6%
Beaver County	6,300	93.2%	12,689	82.3%	17.7%	0.0%	0.0%	0.0%	18,443	84.8%	12.8%	0.0%	2.4%	0.0%
Berks County	16,614	87.2%	41,286	79.0%	18.5%	0.7%	0.9%	0.9%	44,483	78.6%	17.9%	2.1%	0.7%	0.7%
Blair County	5,226	98.2%	9,841	72.7%	25.5%	0.7%	0.3%	0.7%	13,578	83.8%	15.4%	0.0%	0.7%	0.0%

Table J-2: Counties—Mobility Status by Age—*Continued*

| | 15 to 17 | | 18 to 24 | | | | | | 25 to 33 | | | | | |
| | | | | | Percent Living in a Different House | | | | | | Percent Living in a Different House | | | |
	Total Population	Percent Living in Same House	Total Population	Percent Living in Same House	Same State	Different State, Same Region	Different Region	Outside US	Total Population	Percent Living in Same House	Same State	Different State, Same Region	Different Region	Outside US
Pennsylvania—Cont.														
Bucks County	25,062	94.2%	49,616	87.7%	8.7%	1.3%	1.9%	0.4%	59,844	73.4%	20.5%	2.1%	2.4%	1.6%
Butler County	7,222	92.5%	16,278	70.9%	24.0%	1.5%	3.7%	0.0%	19,823	78.9%	16.3%	0.4%	4.4%	0.0%
Cambria County	5,489	82.6%	12,403	71.2%	22.5%	2.2%	1.4%	2.7%	12,887	80.2%	17.7%	1.1%	1.0%	0.0%
Centre County	3,835	90.5%	41,020	48.1%	39.6%	8.0%	3.3%	1.0%	22,204	76.2%	16.9%	0.0%	4.4%	2.5%
Chester County	20,281	95.6%	46,694	76.8%	19.0%	1.5%	1.1%	1.5%	51,777	77.8%	15.7%	0.7%	4.2%	1.6%
Cumberland County	9,199	92.3%	24,633	74.1%	17.3%	3.9%	1.6%	3.2%	26,980	70.3%	23.6%	1.4%	3.9%	0.8%
Dauphin County	10,319	70.8%	26,451	66.1%	27.1%	0.2%	4.9%	1.8%	29,124	76.7%	21.4%	0.0%	1.6%	0.3%
Delaware County	22,183	91.9%	57,565	84.8%	10.2%	3.1%	1.3%	0.6%	63,379	83.7%	13.2%	1.2%	1.2%	0.7%
Erie County	11,465	90.2%	28,432	71.9%	19.9%	3.7%	3.7%	0.8%	31,135	76.9%	21.1%	0.0%	1.9%	0.2%
Fayette County	4,931	98.1%	9,656	87.7%	11.0%	0.0%	1.3%	0.0%	13,469	82.7%	17.3%	0.0%	0.0%	0.0%
Franklin County	5,437	90.6%	14,051	79.3%	15.7%	2.0%	2.5%	0.5%	15,211	82.9%	14.4%	0.0%	2.7%	0.0%
Lackawanna County	8,194	94.2%	19,620	77.3%	16.3%	5.6%	0.8%	0.0%	22,958	77.1%	16.8%	2.0%	2.2%	1.8%
Lancaster County	22,070	90.5%	49,519	77.7%	21.1%	0.0%	0.9%	0.3%	58,006	76.8%	19.7%	0.0%	2.9%	0.6%
Lebanon County	4,416	93.2%	12,415	64.2%	34.8%	0.0%	0.0%	1.0%	12,915	82.4%	17.6%	0.0%	0.0%	0.0%
Lehigh County	16,197	86.1%	33,016	76.9%	15.6%	5.3%	0.9%	1.2%	41,803	68.3%	22.9%	5.0%	2.1%	1.7%
Luzerne County	11,546	88.9%	31,241	72.2%	24.0%	2.3%	1.4%	0.0%	32,819	81.1%	17.2%	0.3%	0.2%	1.2%
Lycoming County	3,675	80.0%	12,018	79.8%	14.9%	0.5%	3.0%	1.9%	12,412	71.6%	26.2%	0.0%	1.9%	0.3%
Mercer County	5,096	73.7%	10,204	79.3%	12.5%	0.0%	6.9%	1.4%	10,723	83.8%	11.6%	0.0%	4.6%	0.0%
Monroe County	7,360	70.3%	18,241	76.8%	17.1%	4.6%	1.5%	0.0%	16,475	83.9%	9.5%	3.1%	3.5%	0.0%
Montgomery County	29,425	94.0%	65,670	81.7%	13.8%	1.4%	2.1%	1.0%	91,032	75.3%	21.4%	0.8%	1.3%	1.2%
Northampton County	11,123	94.2%	31,759	61.8%	25.2%	6.6%	4.2%	2.2%	29,745	73.5%	21.4%	3.1%	1.4%	0.6%
Northumberland County	3,106	93.4%	6,642	86.8%	13.2%	0.0%	0.0%	0.0%	10,582	73.6%	25.6%	0.8%	0.0%	0.0%
Philadelphia County	53,344	89.7%	165,336	75.0%	18.5%	3.3%	1.9%	1.3%	266,596	76.4%	16.7%	3.1%	2.7%	1.2%
Schuylkill County	5,347	97.0%	10,180	84.2%	15.0%	0.0%	0.5%	0.3%	14,846	77.6%	20.3%	0.5%	1.6%	0.0%
Washington County	6,857	93.0%	18,388	66.8%	27.6%	0.0%	4.1%	1.5%	20,742	72.7%	25.6%	0.2%	1.4%	0.0%
Westmoreland County	13,511	91.8%	28,973	77.2%	19.7%	0.5%	1.8%	0.7%	31,727	79.1%	18.6%	0.0%	2.3%	0.0%
York County	16,615	88.2%	34,225	76.5%	18.8%	0.9%	1.9%	1.8%	50,402	72.6%	21.1%	1.6%	4.5%	0.2%
Rhode Island														
Kent County	5,736	90.9%	11,627	90.0%	7.9%	0.0%	2.1%	0.0%	20,408	78.9%	14.9%	0.7%	5.5%	0.0%
Providence County	22,065	88.3%	70,500	69.4%	20.2%	4.3%	2.9%	3.3%	84,965	77.4%	17.4%	2.7%	1.9%	0.6%
Washington County	4,344	94.1%	17,643	69.6%	19.1%	11.3%	0.0%	0.0%	10,535	78.1%	15.9%	2.4%	3.6%	0.0%
South Carolina														
Aiken County	6,478	94.9%	14,965	77.3%	18.2%	3.8%	0.0%	0.7%	18,220	82.8%	12.9%	3.8%	0.5%	0.0%
Anderson County	8,898	84.9%	17,655	71.5%	21.2%	6.0%	1.2%	0.0%	17,931	74.7%	20.2%	5.0%	0.0%	0.0%
Beaufort County	4,910	81.9%	16,479	64.0%	23.3%	6.1%	5.5%	1.1%	20,810	63.2%	18.7%	15.7%	2.3%	0.0%
Berkeley County	8,654	84.4%	17,806	70.0%	20.5%	5.6%	3.7%	0.2%	28,825	75.3%	15.0%	6.5%	2.2%	1.0%
Charleston County	14,511	89.4%	38,878	73.0%	16.3%	3.8%	5.7%	1.2%	56,973	70.9%	19.6%	6.3%	2.1%	1.2%
Dorchester County	5,235	85.3%	12,198	75.7%	17.3%	5.2%	1.7%	0.0%	22,400	78.5%	18.3%	0.4%	2.8%	0.0%
Florence County	5,538	90.5%	13,112	73.0%	22.1%	2.3%	2.6%	0.0%	15,454	83.9%	10.0%	5.6%	0.5%	0.0%
Greenville County	19,624	94.1%	47,357	75.0%	19.1%	1.6%	3.9%	0.3%	60,082	74.0%	17.6%	2.4%	3.9%	2.0%
Horry County	10,824	91.0%	24,882	69.3%	19.9%	5.9%	4.6%	0.3%	33,554	70.8%	24.6%	1.5%	2.9%	0.2%
Lexington County	11,295	82.9%	23,719	74.1%	17.9%	3.8%	2.6%	1.6%	34,276	77.5%	19.4%	1.7%	1.2%	0.2%
Pickens County	4,994	80.8%	18,664	50.4%	44.7%	2.0%	2.8%	0.0%	15,557	74.1%	21.2%	3.7%	0.0%	0.9%
Richland County	16,757	89.5%	64,258	59.2%	20.2%	8.7%	11.2%	0.6%	52,538	68.6%	21.9%	6.9%	1.6%	1.0%
Spartanburg County	11,773	89.3%	28,689	74.0%	24.1%	0.6%	1.3%	0.0%	33,740	74.5%	23.8%	1.1%	0.1%	0.5%
Sumter County	4,406	89.1%	13,392	81.7%	14.0%	1.5%	1.9%	0.9%	12,191	64.5%	31.7%	1.8%	0.0%	1.9%
York County	10,926	89.1%	22,732	61.2%	33.2%	4.4%	1.3%	0.0%	27,355	80.4%	13.2%	4.6%	1.8%	0.0%
South Dakota														
Minnehaha County	6,496	95.8%	15,505	44.2%	48.0%	6.2%	1.3%	0.4%	29,060	74.0%	20.0%	1.0%	0.6%	4.3%
Pennington County	4,331	71.1%	8,522	48.0%	26.1%	12.0%	13.1%	0.7%	14,959	65.8%	23.3%	1.5%	9.4%	0.0%
Tennessee														
Blount County	4,936	94.0%	10,726	82.8%	9.2%	0.4%	7.6%	0.0%	12,700	78.0%	16.0%	6.0%	0.0%	0.0%
Bradley County	4,930	84.5%	10,032	66.0%	32.0%	0.3%	1.0%	0.7%	12,385	72.5%	22.1%	3.4%	2.0%	0.0%
Davidson County	20,832	84.5%	69,835	65.7%	23.8%	4.5%	5.3%	0.7%	116,613	68.4%	24.6%	2.8%	2.7%	1.5%
Hamilton County	12,276	93.4%	32,702	68.9%	24.1%	5.2%	1.1%	0.7%	44,034	81.4%	10.6%	6.1%	1.8%	0.1%
Knox County	17,800	88.3%	56,420	59.2%	34.2%	2.3%	3.7%	0.6%	52,327	70.8%	21.9%	2.7%	3.7%	0.9%
Madison County	3,796	98.3%	10,544	80.5%	17.5%	0.8%	1.3%	0.0%	10,779	90.1%	8.5%	1.5%	0.0%	0.0%
Montgomery County	7,374	81.8%	22,027	57.7%	28.3%	12.3%	1.5%	0.2%	35,085	67.1%	16.9%	14.4%	1.2%	0.4%
Rutherford County	12,608	82.6%	39,666	55.8%	38.9%	3.2%	1.0%	1.1%	37,880	66.6%	24.6%	2.1%	3.7%	2.9%
Sevier County	4,319	98.3%	8,480	59.0%	26.5%	10.3%	3.6%	0.6%	8,556	80.4%	19.6%	0.0%	0.0%	0.0%
Shelby County	40,130	86.2%	91,576	70.4%	22.3%	3.6%	2.2%	1.4%	123,261	73.9%	21.1%	3.3%	1.1%	0.6%
Sullivan County	7,445	85.8%	12,331	81.1%	16.3%	1.1%	1.5%	0.0%	14,272	70.1%	24.5%	1.8%	3.6%	0.0%
Sumner County	6,878	84.2%	14,595	69.4%	16.8%	11.6%	2.2%	0.0%	19,768	73.2%	23.1%	1.0%	2.6%	0.0%
Washington County	4,303	87.5%	15,505	51.1%	40.5%	3.8%	0.9%	3.7%	13,799	73.4%	18.3%	5.5%	2.8%	0.0%
Williamson County	11,788	91.1%	15,560	81.9%	10.7%	3.8%	2.9%	0.7%	14,755	59.9%	31.6%	3.7%	3.4%	1.4%
Wilson County	5,150	78.2%	10,983	82.5%	13.9%	2.8%	0.8%	0.0%	12,081	59.8%	25.7%	7.5%	7.0%	0.0%
Texas														
Bell County	13,872	83.8%	40,033	59.9%	28.0%	3.9%	4.5%	3.8%	51,420	65.5%	24.0%	3.4%	4.4%	2.6%
Bexar County	81,443	86.7%	195,287	70.4%	25.6%	1.5%	1.7%	0.9%	265,647	70.7%	24.3%	0.8%	3.3%	0.9%
Bowie County	3,541	71.4%	8,627	72.2%	20.7%	6.5%	0.7%	0.0%	10,857	79.2%	18.0%	2.0%	0.8%	0.0%

Table J-2: Counties—Mobility Status by Age—*Continued*

| | 15 to 17 | | 18 to 24 | | | | | | 25 to 33 | | | | | |
| | | | | | Percent Living in a Different House | | | | | | Percent Living in a Different House | | | |
	Total Population	Percent Living in Same House	Total Population	Percent Living in Same House	Same State	Different State, Same Region	Different Region	Outside US	Total Population	Percent Living in Same House	Same State	Different State, Same Region	Different Region	Outside US
Texas—Cont.														
Brazoria County	17,237	96.2%	29,299	87.8%	9.3%	0.8%	1.5%	0.6%	42,280	78.3%	17.6%	1.7%	1.9%	0.5%
Brazos County	6,520	87.9%	58,803	40.3%	56.1%	0.3%	1.3%	2.0%	31,962	60.7%	33.8%	1.0%	2.4%	2.1%
Cameron County	23,240	89.9%	44,967	91.7%	6.9%	0.0%	0.1%	1.3%	46,269	80.3%	17.8%	0.4%	0.2%	1.4%
Collin County	43,267	92.3%	71,235	79.7%	14.7%	1.8%	1.9%	1.8%	102,770	77.0%	17.0%	1.3%	3.3%	1.3%
Comal County	5,581	88.1%	10,469	81.9%	18.1%	0.0%	0.0%	0.0%	12,595	73.2%	22.5%	0.0%	2.2%	2.1%
Dallas County	103,457	88.4%	247,751	75.6%	20.1%	1.4%	1.5%	1.4%	361,996	72.5%	22.5%	1.2%	2.0%	1.8%
Denton County	33,504	84.0%	72,368	62.2%	33.9%	0.9%	2.4%	0.6%	104,559	69.0%	26.2%	0.5%	3.1%	1.2%
Ector County	7,443	84.2%	18,034	73.2%	25.1%	0.9%	0.6%	0.2%	24,031	70.7%	24.5%	1.8%	0.3%	2.6%
El Paso County	8,424	91.9%	14,510	76.4%	22.7%	0.5%	0.0%	0.5%	17,753	82.6%	15.9%	1.4%	0.0%	0.1%
Ellis County	38,124	84.8%	94,081	74.3%	19.9%	1.4%	2.5%	1.9%	110,389	75.8%	16.9%	0.7%	4.0%	2.6%
Fort Bend County	34,703	92.3%	60,267	86.4%	10.0%	0.8%	0.3%	2.5%	79,344	77.9%	17.6%	0.5%	1.8%	2.2%
Galveston County	13,541	86.6%	28,761	73.8%	22.3%	1.4%	1.8%	0.8%	36,906	75.5%	20.5%	1.5%	2.0%	0.5%
Grayson County	4,923	76.6%	12,296	66.2%	29.0%	0.6%	3.2%	1.0%	12,857	67.4%	28.4%	1.9%	2.3%	0.0%
Gregg County	4,911	95.9%	12,091	73.4%	24.3%	0.6%	0.1%	1.6%	14,705	64.1%	32.4%	2.6%	0.8%	0.0%
Guadalupe County	7,395	85.5%	12,985	82.2%	17.8%	0.0%	0.0%	0.0%	17,571	85.5%	11.8%	0.8%	0.5%	1.4%
Harris County	191,385	89.5%	431,721	74.3%	20.8%	1.7%	1.8%	1.4%	649,252	72.3%	22.0%	1.6%	1.9%	2.3%
Hays County	7,234	92.0%	34,323	64.1%	33.0%	0.0%	2.5%	0.3%	25,058	69.5%	28.0%	0.4%	2.1%	0.0%
Hidalgo County	44,577	94.7%	93,515	87.6%	11.6%	0.3%	0.1%	0.4%	98,073	88.2%	10.7%	0.3%	0.0%	0.7%
Jefferson County	10,267	79.8%	23,959	68.0%	26.9%	3.6%	0.6%	0.9%	33,763	68.8%	26.2%	2.2%	0.2%	2.6%
Johnson County	7,363	85.3%	14,217	84.4%	15.0%	0.0%	0.5%	0.2%	17,692	81.9%	15.2%	1.1%	1.0%	0.8%
Kaufman County	4,752	66.0%	9,480	76.7%	21.0%	1.3%	2.0%	0.0%	13,508	77.2%	21.3%	1.6%	0.0%	0.0%
Lubbock County	11,457	77.4%	50,728	49.4%	44.4%	0.8%	3.4%	2.0%	40,214	63.8%	33.3%	0.7%	1.0%	1.2%
McLennan County	10,718	85.3%	35,986	63.9%	33.0%	1.3%	1.7%	0.1%	28,137	76.9%	19.4%	0.7%	2.4%	0.6%
Midland County	7,423	93.2%	16,182	64.0%	31.1%	2.2%	2.4%	0.4%	25,270	68.4%	24.9%	0.4%	2.9%	3.5%
Montgomery County	23,918	96.7%	46,093	80.1%	15.3%	1.3%	0.2%	3.0%	58,593	78.9%	19.5%	0.2%	1.3%	0.1%
Nueces County	15,956	87.0%	36,530	67.2%	29.1%	1.9%	1.7%	0.2%	48,054	69.5%	28.3%	1.6%	0.5%	0.1%
Parker County	5,976	89.6%	10,442	88.6%	10.3%	0.0%	1.1%	0.0%	11,100	67.1%	29.5%	2.0%	1.5%	0.0%
Potter County	4,489	83.4%	11,257	70.9%	27.1%	0.0%	0.8%	1.2%	16,547	67.8%	30.0%	0.7%	0.3%	1.3%
Randall County	5,217	80.0%	13,490	69.6%	25.0%	0.8%	4.7%	0.0%	17,543	64.2%	33.6%	0.5%	1.5%	0.3%
Smith County	8,942	94.1%	23,359	67.9%	31.5%	0.3%	0.2%	0.0%	28,402	79.5%	19.7%	0.7%	0.2%	0.0%
Tarrant County	87,586	88.3%	183,333	73.3%	21.7%	1.2%	2.0%	1.8%	260,714	71.7%	23.3%	1.3%	2.1%	1.7%
Taylor County	5,383	88.3%	20,854	47.2%	50.5%	0.9%	1.4%	0.0%	17,073	75.9%	22.7%	1.5%	0.0%	0.0%
Tom Green County	4,482	91.4%	14,946	50.6%	32.1%	8.8%	8.5%	0.0%	16,337	84.8%	7.3%	1.8%	6.2%	0.0%
Travis County	39,547	90.0%	112,029	64.4%	29.2%	1.1%	4.0%	1.3%	212,482	69.0%	24.3%	1.9%	3.5%	1.3%
Webb County	14,816	95.9%	30,472	89.9%	7.8%	0.0%	0.0%	2.3%	30,918	86.3%	12.8%	0.0%	0.5%	0.5%
Wichita County	4,865	85.7%	19,000	53.5%	27.7%	9.6%	8.1%	1.2%	17,480	80.1%	17.0%	0.4%	2.6%	0.0%
Williamson County	23,089	89.3%	39,815	65.4%	30.1%	0.5%	3.0%	1.0%	59,894	74.6%	18.6%	1.5%	4.0%	1.4%
Utah														
Cache County	6,289	90.0%	21,031	67.9%	22.3%	2.1%	4.9%	2.8%	17,230	74.8%	21.4%	0.0%	1.6%	2.2%
Davis County	17,354	89.5%	32,376	72.6%	16.0%	1.9%	4.4%	5.0%	42,554	75.8%	16.3%	4.0%	2.6%	1.2%
Salt Lake County	49,421	92.8%	107,190	69.5%	23.6%	2.8%	3.1%	1.0%	159,139	72.9%	22.4%	2.5%	1.7%	0.6%
Utah County	30,240	87.4%	94,406	47.9%	32.9%	7.7%	4.2%	7.3%	72,255	69.3%	24.5%	3.9%	1.2%	1.1%
Washington County	7,485	89.4%	16,709	62.8%	29.7%	4.5%	2.0%	0.9%	15,243	61.1%	33.2%	2.8%	2.9%	0.0%
Weber County	11,020	92.2%	23,746	71.3%	23.2%	1.5%	0.8%	3.2%	33,518	70.8%	26.6%	0.8%	1.0%	0.7%
Vermont														
Chittenden County	6,437	97.6%	25,155	64.4%	16.5%	11.3%	5.6%	2.2%	19,823	68.3%	26.2%	3.2%	2.2%	0.0%
Virginia														
Albemarle County	2,381	81.6%	13,562	54.9%	34.3%	3.3%	4.7%	2.9%	13,254	63.2%	26.2%	1.4%	6.5%	2.7%
Arlington County	4,667	85.5%	17,377	45.5%	31.5%	7.2%	9.4%	6.3%	55,450	65.0%	21.8%	5.2%	6.6%	1.4%
Chesterfield County	15,836	84.6%	31,432	76.1%	19.2%	3.1%	0.9%	0.7%	33,832	74.9%	21.9%	1.1%	1.7%	0.4%
Fairfax County	44,237	89.4%	95,712	76.8%	14.7%	3.1%	3.9%	1.6%	142,057	70.3%	19.1%	3.4%	3.7%	3.4%
Hanover County	4,844	86.1%	9,818	84.4%	10.4%	4.3%	0.9%	0.0%	8,198	77.3%	17.8%	4.9%	0.0%	0.0%
Henrico County	12,260	94.7%	26,484	67.2%	27.8%	0.4%	3.6%	1.0%	40,556	68.1%	26.1%	2.7%	1.2%	2.0%
Loudoun County	16,911	91.2%	24,373	76.3%	18.9%	2.4%	1.9%	0.5%	43,326	74.9%	16.3%	5.3%	2.3%	1.3%
Montgomery County	2,557	95.3%	27,532	47.5%	43.2%	5.0%	1.7%	2.6%	12,992	67.3%	24.7%	2.0%	1.1%	4.9%
Prince William County	20,839	94.1%	40,126	82.2%	12.5%	2.6%	1.7%	1.0%	55,830	79.0%	16.4%	2.2%	0.9%	1.5%
Roanoke County	4,231	95.2%	7,175	60.0%	31.3%	0.3%	7.6%	0.8%	10,124	56.3%	36.6%	2.7%	0.0%	4.4%
Spotsylvania County	6,337	92.9%	12,088	83.0%	16.0%	0.9%	0.1%	0.0%	13,377	64.7%	27.6%	6.3%	0.7%	0.8%
Stafford County	6,019	83.4%	15,338	72.1%	16.9%	6.8%	4.2%	0.0%	16,712	70.5%	15.3%	6.9%	6.2%	1.2%
Washington														
Benton County	9,462	87.2%	17,372	66.1%	31.2%	2.8%	0.0%	0.0%	21,311	73.2%	22.4%	3.0%	1.4%	0.0%
Clark County	20,695	87.4%	39,349	67.5%	25.2%	6.0%	1.2%	0.2%	54,151	68.9%	20.0%	8.3%	2.2%	0.7%
Cowlitz County	3,440	88.0%	6,662	45.1%	51.2%	1.9%	0.0%	1.8%	12,951	69.5%	28.2%	1.7%	0.0%	0.6%
Grant County	3,102	89.4%	11,592	52.8%	39.8%	3.4%	1.4%	2.5%	10,034	64.5%	33.3%	1.6%	0.6%	0.0%
King County	68,176	88.2%	171,924	60.1%	28.6%	4.4%	4.8%	2.1%	327,984	65.5%	25.1%	2.7%	4.0%	2.7%
Kitsap County	9,762	91.4%	27,430	68.4%	19.7%	4.2%	6.9%	0.7%	32,727	66.9%	27.0%	2.8%	3.4%	0.0%
Pierce County	32,839	85.8%	78,851	69.2%	23.4%	3.0%	3.6%	0.9%	113,567	70.0%	22.7%	2.2%	2.8%	2.3%
Skagit County	4,657	94.2%	8,948	72.2%	20.9%	4.7%	2.2%	0.0%	13,682	65.9%	23.7%	3.7%	5.8%	1.0%
Snohomish County	30,570	81.7%	64,465	69.0%	26.3%	3.2%	0.5%	0.9%	97,289	69.9%	25.9%	2.5%	1.1%	0.5%
Spokane County	19,071	83.4%	48,491	52.1%	39.7%	6.1%	2.0%	0.2%	68,066	65.3%	26.2%	3.8%	2.7%	2.0%

Table J-2: Counties—Mobility Status by Age—*Continued*

	15 to 17		18 to 24						25 to 33					
					Percent Living in a Different House						Percent Living in a Different House			
	Total Population	Percent Living in Same House	Total Population	Percent Living in Same House	Same State	Different State, Same Region	Different Region	Outside US	Total Population	Percent Living in Same House	Same State	Different State, Same Region	Different Region	Outside US
Washington—Cont.														
Thurston County	9,282	84.1%	24,902	63.3%	24.6%	6.5%	3.1%	2.5%	33,146	71.1%	20.6%	3.4%	3.6%	1.2%
Whatcom County	7,277	84.5%	30,613	51.3%	44.1%	2.5%	2.1%	0.0%	26,325	68.3%	26.9%	0.8%	2.0%	2.1%
Yakima County	11,331	95.2%	25,431	78.7%	18.4%	1.5%	1.4%	0.0%	27,580	76.9%	17.7%	2.5%	1.9%	1.1%
West Virginia														
Berkeley County	4,078	88.0%	9,972	75.2%	15.8%	8.1%	0.9%	0.0%	12,772	85.3%	7.8%	6.4%	0.5%	0.0%
Cabell County	4,250	83.4%	11,420	70.1%	26.8%	2.8%	0.3%	0.0%	10,967	80.6%	13.6%	3.4%	2.5%	0.0%
Kanawha County	6,215	87.7%	14,130	68.8%	20.3%	5.3%	5.6%	0.0%	20,325	68.2%	29.7%	0.5%	1.5%	0.2%
Monongalia County	3,293	86.5%	21,629	68.4%	22.7%	5.3%	3.6%	0.0%	18,112	85.1%	12.5%	1.0%	1.4%	0.0%
Wisconsin														
Brown County	9,272	78.0%	23,305	70.1%	27.8%	0.0%	0.7%	1.4%	32,699	79.4%	18.8%	1.1%	0.6%	0.0%
Dane County	17,602	90.9%	67,409	41.6%	40.9%	7.4%	5.6%	4.5%	73,996	68.3%	23.2%	4.2%	2.7%	1.6%
Eau Claire County	4,486	79.9%	15,224	45.3%	46.2%	8.5%	0.0%	0.0%	12,710	71.1%	24.7%	2.7%	1.5%	0.0%
Fond du Lac County	5,121	90.2%	8,500	83.5%	15.3%	0.0%	0.2%	1.0%	10,541	84.0%	15.0%	0.0%	1.0%	0.0%
Kenosha County	7,132	98.7%	17,148	66.7%	20.4%	11.8%	1.1%	0.0%	17,742	66.6%	19.0%	10.6%	3.9%	0.0%
La Crosse County	4,026	94.5%	19,238	30.3%	60.9%	7.4%	1.4%	0.0%	12,539	78.7%	15.8%	1.9%	3.6%	0.0%
Marathon County	5,541	97.1%	9,696	73.3%	23.0%	0.0%	1.9%	1.8%	14,255	84.6%	13.8%	1.1%	0.5%	0.0%
Milwaukee County	35,510	83.7%	95,959	63.6%	29.4%	3.9%	1.4%	1.7%	136,081	73.8%	21.9%	1.5%	1.8%	0.9%
Outagamie County	7,237	91.9%	15,392	82.6%	17.4%	0.0%	0.0%	0.0%	23,277	84.5%	13.6%	0.6%	0.8%	0.5%
Racine County	8,017	93.3%	17,832	83.4%	15.9%	0.7%	0.0%	0.0%	19,655	75.9%	22.8%	0.8%	0.5%	0.0%
Rock County	6,618	84.8%	14,815	73.1%	20.2%	6.0%	0.8%	0.0%	15,271	64.4%	32.2%	0.2%	1.8%	1.3%
Sheboygan County	4,661	85.8%	8,517	63.0%	28.8%	8.2%	0.0%	0.0%	11,780	69.5%	27.4%	2.8%	0.0%	0.3%
Walworth County	3,868	76.2%	13,278	58.0%	32.6%	8.3%	0.0%	1.1%	10,055	73.7%	21.3%	1.1%	2.9%	1.2%
Washington County	4,784	97.1%	10,356	69.9%	27.4%	0.0%	0.8%	1.9%	12,465	71.4%	22.4%	4.2%	0.0%	2.1%
Waukesha County	17,531	89.2%	29,887	82.9%	13.2%	1.6%	1.4%	0.8%	35,375	75.2%	23.5%	0.5%	0.7%	0.0%
Winnebago County	6,316	97.7%	19,273	59.6%	37.0%	3.2%	0.2%	0.0%	21,198	84.2%	13.3%	2.5%	0.0%	0.0%
Wyoming														
Laramie County	3,281	100.0%	13,912	56.9%	22.6%	4.9%	12.2%	3.3%	9,429	68.1%	16.6%	8.0%	7.3%	0.0%

Table J-3: Places—Mobility Status by Age

| | 15 to 17 | | 18 to 24 | | | | | | 25 to 33 | | | | | |
| | | | | | Percent Living in a Different House | | | | | | Percent Living in a Different House | | | |
	Total Population	Percent Living in Same House	Total Population	Percent Living in Same House	Same State	Different State, Same Region	Different Region	Outside US	Total Population	Percent Living in Same House	Same State	Different State, Same Region	Different Region	Outside US
Alabama														
Birmingham city	7,925	93.5%	24,765	62.1%	28.0%	4.8%	4.1%	1.0%	32,586	73.5%	19.8%	3.1%	2.8%	0.8%
Huntsville city	6,976	91.6%	19,309	62.7%	32.7%	2.3%	1.5%	0.8%	24,297	68.3%	25.8%	4.6%	0.9%	0.3%
Mobile city	7,829	83.2%	20,136	71.5%	25.1%	3.0%	0.0%	0.5%	26,961	74.5%	21.3%	2.4%	0.0%	1.7%
Montgomery city	8,010	85.4%	21,793	61.3%	34.9%	2.3%	0.6%	0.9%	26,837	65.2%	32.1%	2.2%	0.5%	0.0%
Tuscaloosa city	3,709	79.4%	25,864	54.4%	30.0%	8.5%	7.1%	0.0%	13,727	76.6%	18.8%	2.3%	0.5%	1.8%
Alaska														
Anchorage municipality	11,771	77.9%	34,552	43.4%	42.8%	5.0%	5.9%	3.0%	46,126	67.0%	20.6%	5.5%	6.2%	0.8%
Arizona														
Chandler city	11,641	88.5%	21,152	74.7%	21.4%	2.8%	0.7%	0.4%	36,119	65.5%	25.5%	3.1%	4.8%	1.0%
Glendale city	11,712	76.9%	24,197	74.6%	16.7%	0.9%	6.6%	1.2%	31,617	70.1%	23.4%	2.9%	3.6%	0.0%
Mesa city	19,020	86.7%	45,282	59.5%	30.3%	5.4%	3.8%	1.0%	63,820	67.8%	27.3%	2.2%	2.4%	0.3%
Peoria city	7,196	88.5%	13,727	77.9%	18.8%	2.2%	0.0%	1.1%	21,111	72.3%	23.3%	1.4%	1.1%	2.0%
Phoenix city	65,047	88.4%	156,250	73.1%	21.9%	2.1%	1.8%	1.0%	211,638	73.3%	21.3%	1.8%	2.5%	1.1%
Scottsdale city	6,947	90.6%	15,416	58.7%	31.5%	2.5%	4.6%	2.7%	30,246	67.4%	18.4%	3.5%	9.7%	1.0%
Surprise city	5,937	81.7%	7,602	81.7%	14.3%	1.7%	2.3%	0.0%	13,542	80.2%	17.2%	0.7%	1.9%	0.0%
Tempe city	5,572	85.0%	44,340	48.1%	36.3%	7.5%	3.9%	4.2%	28,260	69.3%	20.6%	5.2%	3.4%	1.4%
Tucson city	20,366	80.0%	83,057	53.6%	36.0%	5.0%	3.5%	2.0%	66,272	67.6%	25.6%	2.4%	1.9%	2.6%
Yuma city	5,336	94.1%	11,281	76.5%	18.1%	1.6%	3.1%	0.7%	10,968	71.0%	22.7%	0.0%	4.8%	1.5%
Arkansas														
Little Rock city	6,883	87.7%	17,815	63.8%	33.9%	1.9%	0.4%	0.0%	28,900	65.0%	29.6%	3.9%	1.0%	0.5%
California														
Anaheim city	14,855	90.3%	38,451	83.7%	13.2%	0.5%	0.3%	2.3%	51,581	81.3%	16.4%	0.2%	0.1%	1.9%
Antioch city	5,261	83.9%	13,849	84.3%	15.7%	0.0%	0.0%	0.0%	12,047	71.1%	26.2%	0.0%	0.7%	2.0%
Bakersfield city	16,886	88.8%	45,417	77.9%	19.4%	0.4%	2.1%	0.2%	53,945	77.6%	21.3%	0.6%	0.4%	0.1%
Berkeley city	3,615	80.3%	25,791	39.3%	46.6%	2.3%	3.2%	8.6%	20,092	71.9%	15.1%	2.1%	3.8%	7.1%
Burbank city	3,997	90.5%	7,065	77.5%	12.6%	0.0%	3.7%	6.2%	16,868	81.0%	15.7%	0.0%	1.9%	1.4%
Carlsbad city	4,657	77.5%	8,757	82.5%	13.7%	2.9%	0.9%	0.0%	12,465	75.0%	22.9%	0.0%	1.1%	1.0%
Chico city	3,606	90.2%	20,214	51.9%	47.9%	0.0%	0.1%	0.0%	11,738	65.2%	33.8%	0.0%	0.0%	1.0%
Carson city	4,723	97.7%	9,998	88.7%	10.0%	0.0%	0.0%	1.3%	11,282	83.6%	10.0%	0.9%	2.3%	3.2%
Chula Vista city	11,333	94.4%	29,347	91.0%	7.8%	0.7%	0.0%	0.6%	32,687	85.0%	10.9%	0.0%	2.3%	1.8%
Clovis city	4,019	94.7%	8,292	89.2%	10.4%	0.0%	0.0%	0.4%	13,995	76.8%	20.7%	0.0%	0.4%	2.2%
Compton city	4,704	88.8%	13,133	89.3%	10.0%	0.0%	0.7%	0.0%	12,685	90.6%	8.9%	0.0%	0.0%	0.5%
Concord city	4,254	95.5%	10,042	87.7%	8.3%	1.5%	2.6%	0.0%	16,439	75.0%	19.3%	2.8%	1.5%	1.3%
Corona city	6,661	83.2%	11,781	76.0%	20.7%	0.0%	0.9%	1.6%	20,907	81.7%	16.5%	0.3%	0.6%	1.0%
Costa Mesa city	5,843	86.3%	10,854	86.7%	12.2%	1.1%	0.0%	0.0%	19,681	71.4%	23.2%	0.0%	4.8%	0.6%
Daly City city	2,037	96.8%	10,375	76.4%	21.1%	0.0%	1.8%	0.7%	17,192	81.4%	16.0%	0.4%	0.1%	2.1%
Downey city	4,610	88.4%	13,903	84.2%	15.0%	0.0%	0.0%	0.7%	15,220	77.7%	19.5%	0.0%	1.3%	1.5%
El Cajon city	3,902	88.1%	11,079	68.9%	28.7%	1.2%	1.2%	0.0%	15,091	74.7%	21.9%	0.0%	1.8%	1.7%
Elk Grove city	7,032	91.2%	17,398	83.0%	14.8%	0.0%	0.0%	2.2%	17,220	78.3%	21.7%	0.0%	0.0%	0.0%
El Monte city	5,200	96.3%	12,404	92.1%	7.9%	0.0%	0.0%	0.0%	15,964	90.3%	9.3%	0.0%	0.0%	0.4%
Escondido city	5,350	82.7%	17,660	70.7%	27.0%	0.5%	0.9%	0.8%	24,192	79.1%	16.1%	0.7%	1.5%	2.6%
Fairfield city	4,659	84.9%	10,589	79.1%	13.6%	4.2%	3.1%	0.0%	15,995	68.5%	22.4%	3.0%	5.9%	0.2%
Fontana city	8,977	92.4%	23,408	94.7%	4.4%	0.0%	0.1%	0.8%	31,601	90.8%	8.5%	0.0%	0.7%	0.0%
Fremont city	8,496	98.6%	19,330	93.9%	2.6%	0.0%	0.9%	2.6%	31,000	79.7%	13.3%	0.0%	3.2%	3.7%
Fresno city	24,032	86.5%	61,204	68.6%	27.5%	1.3%	1.2%	1.4%	75,584	71.3%	25.2%	1.0%	2.5%	0.0%
Fullerton city	6,182	91.4%	18,398	68.2%	25.3%	0.5%	3.1%	2.8%	19,400	73.3%	22.5%	0.0%	1.7%	2.5%
Garden Grove city	6,763	90.3%	17,516	85.5%	12.6%	0.0%	1.6%	0.4%	22,763	84.4%	13.3%	0.0%	1.6%	0.7%
Glendale city	5,276	95.5%	15,025	81.5%	11.3%	0.0%	3.8%	3.5%	28,888	80.3%	17.1%	0.0%	1.5%	1.1%
Hayward city	5,564	88.9%	15,039	84.5%	12.7%	0.4%	0.6%	1.7%	27,067	86.1%	11.3%	0.7%	1.4%	0.4%
Hesperia city	5,305	89.7%	8,864	81.1%	17.3%	0.8%	0.0%	0.8%	12,931	78.6%	15.6%	1.3%	4.6%	0.0%
Huntington Beach city	4,928	83.3%	14,445	74.5%	21.8%	0.0%	3.7%	0.0%	25,026	72.5%	24.0%	0.4%	1.2%	2.0%
Inglewood city	4,406	98.7%	11,548	90.1%	9.9%	0.0%	0.0%	0.0%	15,749	78.2%	21.1%	0.0%	0.7%	0.0%
Irvine city	10,459	84.0%	36,009	70.2%	22.7%	2.1%	1.8%	3.3%	36,640	59.1%	23.8%	4.3%	4.6%	8.1%
Jurupa Valley city	4,584	85.5%	12,342	90.4%	9.1%	0.0%	0.5%	0.0%	13,050	86.6%	11.5%	1.2%	0.0%	0.7%
Lancaster city	8,963	83.5%	14,851	89.0%	9.9%	0.5%	0.3%	0.4%	25,394	91.2%	8.2%	0.1%	0.5%	0.0%
Long Beach city	19,352	91.2%	47,955	85.2%	11.1%	0.5%	0.7%	2.5%	70,119	82.6%	15.7%	0.7%	0.8%	0.2%
Los Angeles city	143,058	91.3%	429,036	76.2%	18.2%	0.7%	2.5%	2.4%	636,484	79.7%	16.3%	0.4%	2.2%	1.3%
Mission Viejo city	3,523	97.8%	9,478	81.5%	7.9%	3.3%	3.8%	3.5%	9,308	73.9%	24.4%	0.0%	1.7%	0.0%
Modesto city	8,314	87.4%	23,005	76.1%	23.1%	0.2%	0.0%	0.6%	25,866	80.2%	15.7%	0.3%	1.4%	2.4%
Moreno Valley city	11,841	85.4%	27,021	86.1%	12.4%	0.0%	1.0%	0.5%	27,577	82.8%	14.8%	0.0%	0.6%	1.9%
Murrieta city	6,786	93.0%	9,635	79.3%	19.5%	0.0%	0.0%	1.1%	14,030	75.3%	23.8%	0.6%	0.2%	0.0%
Norwalk city	3,355	91.3%	13,714	91.1%	7.2%	0.0%	0.0%	1.7%	13,620	88.6%	10.1%	0.0%	0.0%	1.3%
Oakland city	13,374	87.2%	34,194	73.1%	22.6%	0.5%	2.3%	1.5%	74,769	73.5%	19.6%	0.4%	4.3%	2.1%
Oceanside city	4,874	82.4%	23,119	70.0%	15.5%	0.8%	10.6%	3.1%	17,362	68.6%	22.9%	0.6%	4.0%	3.8%
Ontario city	8,214	83.8%	18,889	83.5%	12.5%	1.2%	2.9%	0.0%	24,428	87.2%	11.7%	0.0%	0.8%	0.3%
Orange city	5,015	91.2%	17,383	72.6%	20.5%	2.8%	0.6%	3.6%	21,674	78.8%	17.2%	0.9%	1.0%	2.0%
Oxnard city	8,739	87.2%	21,543	87.6%	9.3%	0.3%	0.2%	2.6%	32,007	83.5%	15.1%	0.2%	0.9%	0.4%
Palmdale city	7,740	89.7%	16,298	85.5%	12.9%	0.6%	1.0%	0.0%	18,322	80.4%	17.2%	0.0%	1.4%	1.0%
Pasadena city	2,678	93.5%	11,802	77.2%	17.1%	0.5%	2.6%	2.6%	22,282	75.3%	18.3%	0.4%	3.7%	2.3%
Pomona city	6,661	84.9%	20,281	76.1%	19.0%	1.7%	1.9%	1.3%	21,771	82.8%	14.8%	0.4%	0.5%	1.5%
Rancho Cucamonga city	6,933	83.6%	21,193	68.0%	31.0%	0.0%	1.0%	0.0%	21,999	66.8%	30.8%	0.0%	0.4%	2.0%

Table J-3: Places—Mobility Status by Age—*Continued*

	15 to 17		18 to 24						25 to 33					
					Percent Living in a Different House						Percent Living in a Different House			
	Total Population	Percent Living in Same House	Total Population	Percent Living in Same House	Same State	Different State, Same Region	Different Region	Outside US	Total Population	Percent Living in Same House	Same State	Different State, Same Region	Different Region	Outside US
California—Cont.														
Redding city	4,610	83.7%	7,140	80.6%	15.6%	0.0%	0.0%	3.7%	13,090	72.2%	19.5%	0.2%	3.2%	4.9%
Rialto city	5,279	90.8%	12,693	93.7%	6.3%	0.0%	0.0%	0.0%	14,882	92.4%	7.6%	0.0%	0.0%	0.0%
Richmond city	2,574	97.6%	13,367	87.0%	11.3%	1.3%	0.0%	0.4%	16,605	83.2%	13.5%	1.1%	0.6%	1.7%
Riverside city	12,088	90.6%	47,199	79.0%	17.9%	0.7%	1.2%	1.2%	49,657	78.5%	17.4%	0.1%	2.4%	1.5%
Roseville city	5,797	91.6%	12,503	78.0%	15.3%	4.7%	1.0%	1.0%	14,296	68.4%	25.3%	1.8%	3.7%	0.9%
Sacramento city	19,543	85.0%	44,442	73.0%	23.5%	0.4%	1.6%	1.6%	78,271	76.4%	20.2%	0.2%	2.5%	0.7%
Salinas city	7,118	89.2%	16,341	88.7%	10.5%	0.4%	0.0%	0.3%	21,776	86.2%	13.4%	0.0%	0.4%	0.0%
San Bernardino city	10,249	85.7%	27,676	75.6%	19.3%	0.0%	1.6%	3.5%	30,586	81.4%	17.4%	0.4%	0.2%	0.6%
San Buenaventura (Ventura) city	3,800	99.8%	8,974	72.5%	26.8%	0.0%	0.7%	0.0%	14,855	74.0%	23.5%	0.0%	1.9%	0.7%
San Diego city	48,032	89.1%	163,607	68.1%	24.3%	1.3%	3.2%	3.1%	233,373	72.8%	18.9%	0.8%	4.6%	3.0%
San Francisco city	17,062	91.4%	63,520	62.3%	22.8%	2.7%	7.4%	4.8%	178,135	73.4%	17.0%	1.6%	5.6%	2.4%
San Jose city	37,124	93.7%	93,229	80.4%	16.7%	0.8%	1.4%	0.7%	139,521	77.1%	17.6%	0.9%	2.4%	2.0%
San Leandro city	3,246	94.8%	6,738	75.9%	22.7%	0.0%	0.0%	1.5%	12,776	85.1%	14.5%	0.5%	0.0%	0.0%
San Marcos city	3,908	93.0%	9,325	66.0%	33.0%	0.0%	1.1%	0.0%	11,169	72.8%	26.8%	0.0%	0.5%	0.0%
San Mateo city	4,395	89.6%	7,418	70.1%	20.5%	0.0%	4.1%	5.2%	12,624	66.4%	27.4%	0.0%	4.2%	2.1%
Santa Ana city	15,351	94.3%	34,544	89.9%	9.4%	0.0%	0.6%	0.1%	51,773	87.9%	12.0%	0.0%	0.1%	0.0%
Santa Clara city	2,783	85.0%	13,344	63.8%	26.5%	1.1%	8.3%	0.4%	23,466	58.3%	26.6%	0.3%	8.7%	6.1%
Santa Clarita city	6,978	91.4%	18,469	77.1%	19.8%	0.2%	1.5%	1.4%	22,326	67.8%	25.7%	0.9%	2.9%	2.7%
Santa Maria city	6,003	93.9%	12,496	76.6%	21.6%	0.0%	0.7%	1.1%	12,057	82.4%	16.3%	1.0%	0.3%	0.0%
Santa Monica city	2,793	82.0%	5,866	53.3%	35.7%	0.0%	5.5%	5.6%	16,013	68.9%	23.8%	0.8%	5.7%	0.8%
Santa Rosa city	5,788	87.9%	15,634	80.6%	17.8%	1.6%	0.0%	0.0%	23,024	78.6%	19.6%	0.3%	1.3%	0.2%
Simi Valley city	6,362	90.1%	12,530	89.7%	7.4%	1.9%	1.0%	0.0%	13,848	78.6%	18.8%	0.0%	1.3%	1.3%
South Gate city	4,348	82.0%	11,254	89.5%	8.8%	0.0%	0.0%	1.8%	12,675	81.5%	18.5%	0.0%	0.0%	0.0%
Stockton city	15,603	90.6%	34,010	77.0%	19.6%	1.9%	0.6%	0.8%	42,335	80.1%	17.7%	0.2%	1.6%	0.4%
Sunnyvale city	4,139	96.6%	8,863	65.2%	20.8%	1.0%	8.7%	4.2%	28,799	72.8%	18.8%	0.9%	3.9%	3.7%
Temecula city	6,828	95.2%	10,102	72.5%	27.5%	0.0%	0.0%	0.0%	13,346	83.1%	15.9%	0.0%	0.0%	1.0%
Thousand Oaks city	5,906	95.4%	10,437	88.6%	9.1%	1.2%	1.1%	0.0%	9,958	85.4%	10.7%	0.7%	3.2%	0.0%
Torrance city	4,539	93.8%	15,100	88.6%	9.0%	0.0%	0.0%	2.4%	15,611	75.4%	18.5%	0.4%	1.2%	4.5%
Vacaville city	4,170	90.8%	9,533	72.8%	24.2%	1.8%	0.0%	1.1%	12,759	69.8%	23.0%	1.8%	0.5%	5.0%
Vallejo city	4,350	92.6%	11,449	64.0%	27.9%	4.6%	2.4%	1.0%	17,933	76.9%	20.2%	1.1%	0.9%	1.0%
Victorville city	8,236	87.2%	11,547	70.2%	29.2%	0.0%	0.7%	0.0%	16,953	75.3%	21.4%	0.0%	2.7%	0.6%
Visalia city	4,868	92.2%	12,737	83.6%	16.4%	0.0%	0.0%	0.0%	16,358	82.1%	17.7%	0.2%	0.0%	0.0%
Vista city	3,531	74.1%	11,904	80.0%	16.0%	0.0%	1.2%	2.7%	16,140	70.8%	29.0%	0.0%	0.2%	0.0%
West Covina city	4,608	87.7%	9,485	90.3%	9.7%	0.0%	0.0%	0.0%	15,248	83.4%	15.3%	0.0%	0.0%	1.2%
Westminster city	2,846	91.4%	6,615	82.3%	15.4%	0.0%	0.0%	2.3%	12,305	92.8%	6.3%	0.0%	0.8%	0.0%
Colorado														
Arvada city	4,928	74.6%	7,135	73.3%	21.5%	3.3%	1.7%	0.3%	13,764	65.5%	27.7%	1.7%	4.5%	0.6%
Aurora city	16,434	82.5%	33,948	67.0%	24.1%	3.2%	2.8%	2.9%	51,712	69.7%	23.7%	2.0%	2.5%	2.1%
Boulder city	2,515	97.1%	32,366	34.6%	49.1%	3.1%	10.4%	2.8%	15,823	54.4%	29.8%	3.0%	12.0%	0.8%
Centennial city	5,451	97.7%	7,611	80.0%	19.0%	0.0%	1.0%	0.0%	11,724	59.2%	29.6%	5.6%	2.1%	3.4%
Colorado Springs city	17,229	89.7%	45,198	56.6%	32.4%	2.9%	6.7%	1.4%	69,650	62.4%	25.1%	1.4%	10.1%	1.0%
Denver city	16,768	91.4%	58,231	64.5%	24.2%	2.5%	7.2%	1.7%	142,282	64.3%	24.1%	2.7%	7.3%	1.5%
Fort Collins city	5,342	91.9%	32,030	43.3%	44.0%	5.6%	4.6%	2.5%	27,412	65.7%	27.2%	2.8%	3.1%	1.1%
Greeley city	5,241	92.8%	12,337	50.8%	42.1%	0.9%	3.6%	2.6%	14,747	71.7%	25.3%	0.2%	2.8%	0.0%
Lakewood city	6,096	91.4%	16,380	66.6%	20.1%	2.0%	11.3%	0.0%	21,541	71.1%	21.4%	1.2%	5.6%	0.7%
Longmont city	4,481	92.8%	7,630	68.4%	31.1%	0.0%	0.6%	0.0%	9,521	80.3%	17.9%	1.3%	0.5%	0.0%
Pueblo city	5,026	80.0%	10,047	68.2%	29.0%	1.5%	1.3%	0.0%	13,992	72.1%	24.4%	1.8%	1.7%	0.0%
Thornton city	6,397	86.8%	11,352	69.4%	25.7%	0.0%	3.9%	1.0%	17,167	70.4%	23.7%	3.2%	2.4%	0.3%
Westminster city	4,832	83.7%	9,356	74.3%	17.6%	1.1%	4.1%	2.9%	15,866	70.1%	21.5%	2.0%	6.4%	0.0%
Connecticut														
Bridgeport city	5,260	79.0%	17,826	75.3%	17.3%	6.2%	0.0%	1.1%	20,882	73.8%	16.9%	2.2%	4.3%	2.9%
Hartford city	5,079	82.0%	21,070	75.8%	13.3%	4.4%	3.0%	3.5%	17,959	73.0%	22.6%	0.6%	0.0%	3.8%
New Haven city	5,062	80.9%	21,920	78.2%	15.8%	2.0%	1.8%	2.2%	25,481	69.3%	20.4%	3.2%	3.4%	3.7%
Stamford city	5,078	81.6%	12,444	86.3%	8.1%	3.1%	0.6%	1.9%	20,672	68.4%	18.7%	9.7%	0.3%	2.9%
Waterbury city	4,419	76.8%	10,362	84.1%	14.5%	1.3%	0.2%	0.0%	13,325	85.5%	12.9%	0.0%	0.9%	0.7%
District of Columbia														
Washington city	15,198	89.9%	81,910	51.8%	17.3%	12.4%	15.7%	2.7%	139,024	67.4%	17.7%	8.2%	3.6%	3.1%
Florida														
Boca Raton city	3,722	74.4%	9,141	61.8%	34.5%	2.5%	0.5%	0.7%	8,790	63.9%	28.9%	2.7%	3.4%	1.1%
Cape Coral city	7,548	88.1%	10,150	93.9%	4.2%	0.0%	1.9%	0.0%	19,627	84.5%	14.8%	0.0%	0.0%	0.7%
Clearwater city	2,921	66.4%	7,867	79.7%	18.5%	0.0%	1.1%	0.7%	14,213	65.4%	24.6%	1.3%	8.7%	0.0%
Coral Springs city	8,390	95.0%	11,711	89.0%	7.1%	1.4%	0.0%	2.4%	12,738	79.6%	12.8%	0.0%	2.0%	5.6%
Fort Lauderdale city	5,657	80.0%	10,504	71.7%	24.0%	2.0%	2.3%	0.0%	24,714	67.0%	26.2%	3.3%	3.2%	0.3%
Gainesville city	3,533	77.3%	41,812	44.1%	48.8%	2.2%	3.7%	1.1%	20,893	61.5%	34.7%	1.0%	2.5%	0.3%
Hialeah city	7,047	89.9%	18,916	93.1%	5.0%	0.0%	0.0%	1.9%	28,617	91.5%	6.5%	1.0%	0.0%	1.0%
Hollywood city	2,825	84.6%	11,392	83.1%	15.6%	0.0%	0.5%	0.8%	18,482	67.5%	28.6%	1.3%	1.2%	1.4%
Jacksonville city	30,124	86.8%	82,935	64.1%	28.3%	2.6%	3.9%	1.1%	123,515	69.5%	25.1%	1.8%	2.1%	1.5%
Lakeland city	3,907	82.9%	10,492	73.2%	19.5%	2.0%	5.3%	0.0%	13,360	77.3%	21.9%	0.4%	0.0%	0.5%
Miami city	11,941	90.0%	33,513	80.6%	16.2%	1.4%	0.0%	1.8%	64,897	75.9%	17.4%	1.2%	2.0%	3.5%
Miami Beach city	2,617	87.7%	5,622	74.7%	13.0%	2.1%	1.8%	8.5%	13,576	72.6%	18.2%	2.8%	4.2%	2.3%
Miami Gardens city	4,341	81.9%	11,382	86.1%	12.9%	0.5%	0.6%	0.0%	15,208	89.3%	8.4%	2.3%	0.0%	0.0%

Table J-3: Places—Mobility Status by Age—*Continued*

| | 15 to 17 | | 18 to 24 | | | | | | 25 to 33 | | | | | |
| | | | | | Percent Living in a Different House | | | | | | Percent Living in a Different House | | | |
	Total Population	Percent Living in Same House	Total Population	Percent Living in Same House	Same State	Different State, Same Region	Different Region	Outside US	Total Population	Percent Living in Same House	Same State	Different State, Same Region	Different Region	Outside US
Florida—Cont.														
Miramar city	4,891	80.1%	12,731	83.1%	14.8%	0.0%	0.0%	2.2%	17,018	74.1%	21.1%	0.0%	0.0%	4.7%
Orlando city	9,660	78.8%	28,207	72.0%	20.7%	1.3%	2.1%	3.9%	54,102	68.7%	24.2%	0.7%	4.5%	1.8%
Palm Bay city	4,245	88.7%	9,453	77.5%	11.2%	1.4%	9.0%	1.0%	10,233	73.7%	10.7%	11.9%	2.9%	0.8%
Pembroke Pines city	6,575	92.3%	16,234	88.6%	10.0%	0.0%	0.0%	1.4%	18,884	73.2%	21.2%	0.3%	0.7%	4.6%
Plantation city	2,831	81.4%	6,199	78.5%	13.9%	2.0%	3.5%	2.1%	12,841	79.3%	12.5%	0.5%	2.8%	4.9%
Pompano Beach city	3,744	90.9%	8,856	61.2%	27.6%	5.3%	4.7%	1.2%	12,129	68.6%	27.1%	1.9%	2.1%	0.3%
Port St. Lucie city	6,234	79.1%	14,357	81.9%	12.8%	0.0%	5.2%	0.0%	18,502	75.6%	22.3%	2.1%	0.0%	0.0%
St. Petersburg city	9,050	77.6%	20,729	73.2%	20.5%	2.2%	1.7%	2.3%	32,599	73.4%	19.5%	2.5%	3.2%	1.5%
Sunrise city	3,246	83.8%	6,979	80.9%	12.4%	1.8%	3.1%	1.9%	14,792	79.6%	13.3%	0.4%	2.4%	4.3%
Tallahassee city	5,791	89.4%	57,815	45.9%	50.2%	2.2%	0.7%	1.0%	26,618	60.1%	34.1%	3.0%	1.8%	0.9%
Tampa city	13,115	88.1%	39,114	64.2%	23.5%	3.2%	7.6%	1.5%	57,156	71.6%	21.7%	2.5%	3.5%	0.8%
West Palm Beach city	4,037	76.7%	9,024	69.9%	22.0%	0.3%	6.1%	1.7%	14,859	81.4%	15.1%	0.3%	0.7%	2.4%
Georgia														
Athens-Clarke County unified govt (balance)	2,635	88.5%	36,399	44.2%	49.4%	3.3%	2.1%	1.0%	15,629	68.8%	25.6%	1.7%	1.3%	2.6%
Atlanta city	10,765	81.5%	59,522	58.6%	29.8%	5.5%	3.4%	2.7%	89,857	74.8%	20.1%	3.0%	1.6%	0.5%
Augusta-Richmond County consolidated govt (balance)	7,388	91.1%	23,296	78.3%	8.6%	10.2%	2.6%	0.3%	28,678	71.1%	21.6%	3.6%	2.2%	1.5%
Columbus city	6,999	85.8%	24,389	55.8%	22.8%	10.5%	10.5%	0.4%	29,720	58.4%	23.7%	9.4%	4.9%	3.6%
Macon-Bibb county	6,082	89.6%	16,246	68.7%	29.0%	0.8%	0.4%	1.1%	18,486	78.1%	19.9%	1.3%	0.7%	0.0%
Roswell city	4,937	92.2%	7,219	81.0%	14.8%	4.2%	0.0%	0.0%	8,771	62.6%	24.1%	9.6%	0.0%	3.7%
Sandy Springs city	4,514	93.8%	7,991	64.5%	16.7%	7.3%	10.0%	1.5%	17,561	71.4%	17.2%	7.5%	2.8%	1.0%
Savannah city	5,973	81.4%	24,692	51.8%	33.7%	7.7%	3.6%	3.2%	24,507	58.0%	27.4%	11.0%	2.8%	0.9%
Hawaii														
Urban Honolulu CDP	9,278	89.5%	30,770	77.1%	12.0%	4.8%	2.4%	3.6%	44,550	72.3%	14.6%	2.9%	7.5%	2.7%
Idaho														
Boise City city	9,105	85.8%	20,288	52.4%	36.0%	6.7%	1.2%	3.7%	32,766	68.4%	22.3%	6.4%	1.1%	1.7%
Meridian city	2,627	97.3%	5,891	67.2%	27.4%	2.8%	2.6%	0.0%	9,187	78.8%	18.5%	2.7%	0.0%	0.0%
Illinois														
Aurora city	8,412	85.0%	20,391	83.8%	13.3%	0.4%	0.7%	1.8%	26,219	76.9%	19.6%	1.4%	0.8%	1.3%
Chicago city	93,491	91.2%	284,971	70.2%	19.9%	3.4%	3.7%	2.8%	482.562	73.5%	20.7%	1.7%	2.5%	1.6%
Elgin city	3,346	91.8%	11,159	76.1%	19.1%	1.6%	0.0%	3.3%	11,983	82.5%	14.6%	1.3%	0.5%	1.1%
Joliet city	7,526	87.6%	16,026	90.1%	7.6%	2.4%	0.0%	0.0%	16,306	83.8%	15.6%	0.0%	0.7%	0.0%
Naperville city	6,360	99.7%	12,952	71.5%	22.6%	2.1%	3.7%	0.0%	14,606	73.6%	19.3%	4.6%	2.5%	0.0%
Peoria city	4,986	91.8%	11,731	58.0%	35.0%	3.4%	3.5%	0.0%	18,154	70.9%	26.3%	0.0%	1.5%	1.3%
Rockford city	6,451	95.3%	14,392	76.5%	19.0%	0.8%	3.8%	0.0%	19,169	76.3%	23.2%	0.0%	0.0%	0.5%
Springfield city	5,399	87.4%	11,083	69.9%	24.6%	0.0%	0.6%	4.8%	15,469	68.3%	27.4%	2.7%	1.7%	0.0%
Indiana														
Evansville city	4,094	82.0%	12,756	58.0%	30.0%	3.0%	8.7%	0.4%	15,885	71.2%	26.7%	0.0%	2.1%	0.0%
Fort Wayne city	9,722	90.1%	27,427	72.7%	22.6%	0.9%	2.1%	1.8%	33,623	69.3%	23.9%	2.9%	3.9%	0.0%
Indianapolis city (balance)	31,292	91.0%	80,525	70.4%	26.1%	1.6%	1.6%	0.3%	132,231	75.1%	20.9%	0.9%	2.6%	0.6%
South Bend city	3,566	98.3%	13,865	54.4%	29.5%	9.8%	3.0%	3.2%	12,052	72.6%	22.2%	2.1%	1.7%	1.3%
Iowa														
Cedar Rapids city	5,952	88.9%	12,970	61.2%	33.0%	0.5%	5.3%	0.0%	16,437	61.4%	17.0%	0.0%	5.8%	15.7%
Davenport city	4,284	93.1%	9,454	78.9%	9.8%	6.5%	3.5%	1.3%	14,051	87.5%	8.9%	3.3%	0.3%	0.0%
Des Moines city	7,504	74.9%	22,640	44.4%	46.7%	7.3%	1.5%	0.1%	32,683	63.3%	31.6%	0.0%	4.5%	0.6%
Kansas														
Kansas City city	6,296	99.2%	14,303	73.0%	19.7%	7.4%	0.0%	0.0%	19,764	68.8%	21.3%	7.0%	1.9%	0.9%
Olathe city	8,205	82.4%	11,229	77.3%	17.4%	1.7%	3.6%	0.0%	14,204	72.6%	22.5%	0.6%	3.3%	0.9%
Overland Park city	8,063	95.0%	12,995	74.9%	16.6%	3.6%	2.2%	2.6%	24,843	61.3%	25.3%	5.9%	4.3%	3.2%
Topeka city	5,658	85.2%	13,134	46.2%	46.4%	2.3%	3.8%	1.3%	14,998	66.9%	29.3%	0.2%	2.8%	0.9%
Wichita city	16,955	91.5%	32,837	67.7%	26.8%	2.3%	3.2%	0.0%	55,499	77.8%	19.6%	0.5%	1.3%	0.8%
Kentucky														
Lexington-Fayette urban county	9,984	84.4%	43,864	50.5%	37.9%	3.5%	7.1%	1.2%	45,356	66.0%	23.5%	4.5%	4.3%	1.7%
Louisville/Jefferson County metro govt (balance)	24,339	87.7%	56,727	72.6%	23.3%	0.7%	2.7%	0.7%	77,705	78.5%	17.3%	1.3%	2.8%	0.1%
Louisiana														
Baton Rouge city	8,509	92.1%	37,552	71.0%	23.7%	1.6%	2.2%	1.6%	35,081	73.0%	22.0%	3.6%	1.5%	0.0%
Lafayette city	6,834	67.4%	14,704	58.4%	40.0%	0.0%	1.1%	0.5%	22,933	68.8%	25.9%	3.2%	1.8%	0.3%
New Orleans city	12,156	88.5%	37,387	77.3%	15.1%	4.2%	3.1%	0.3%	66,489	75.4%	18.9%	2.2%	1.9%	1.7%
Shreveport city	9,120	82.6%	18,974	74.9%	22.0%	2.1%	0.9%	0.0%	26,743	88.3%	11.0%	0.8%	0.0%	0.0%
Maryland														
Baltimore city	19,693	85.8%	64,583	69.0%	23.5%	1.7%	4.5%	1.2%	107,588	74.2%	20.3%	1.6%	1.9%	2.1%
Massachusetts														
Boston city	17,511	88.3%	100,784	60.7%	21.1%	6.9%	7.3%	4.1%	148,487	70.6%	21.7%	2.1%	3.0%	2.7%
Brockton city	4,506	87.9%	11,101	76.3%	21.7%	0.0%	2.0%	0.0%	11,438	69.5%	21.4%	0.0%	5.8%	3.3%
Cambridge city	2,146	85.5%	20,489	61.8%	19.0%	6.6%	9.9%	2.7%	29,303	65.4%	13.0%	2.7%	9.7%	9.3%
Lowell city	2,964	97.0%	15,564	78.2%	18.4%	1.6%	0.8%	1.0%	16,486	74.4%	15.2%	5.5%	0.0%	4.9%
Lynn city	3,391	80.0%	8,414	70.9%	20.3%	1.9%	2.6%	4.3%	13,547	80.4%	18.4%	0.0%	0.0%	1.2%

Table J-3: Places—Mobility Status by Age—*Continued*

| | 15 to 17 | | 18 to 24 | | | | | | 25 to 33 | | | | | |
| | | | | | Percent Living in a Different House | | | | | | Percent Living in a Different House | | | |
	Total Population	Percent Living in Same House	Total Population	Percent Living in Same House	Same State	Different State, Same Region	Different Region	Outside US	Total Population	Percent Living in Same House	Same State	Different State, Same Region	Different Region	Outside US
Massachusetts—Cont.														
New Bedford city	3,127	90.5%	11,109	80.5%	15.6%	2.7%	0.0%	1.2%	11,068	70.7%	27.6%	0.3%	1.4%	0.0%
Quincy city	3,017	97.0%	7,210	77.2%	9.4%	5.3%	3.5%	4.6%	14,553	76.1%	10.5%	8.7%	2.1%	2.6%
Springfield city	6,944	82.7%	20,703	78.0%	14.7%	6.8%	0.5%	0.0%	19,325	81.4%	18.1%	0.0%	0.0%	0.5%
Worcester city	6,744	89.5%	27,597	71.2%	18.4%	4.9%	3.2%	2.3%	27,695	77.8%	18.4%	2.0%	0.3%	1.5%
Michigan														
Ann Arbor city	2,655	80.2%	36,381	23.1%	58.8%	5.2%	8.5%	4.4%	18,044	56.1%	29.1%	3.3%	9.2%	2.3%
Dearborn city	3,770	92.4%	10,993	92.8%	6.4%	0.0%	0.8%	0.0%	10,651	81.0%	14.8%	3.2%	1.1%	0.0%
Detroit city	29,159	81.8%	72,501	76.0%	22.6%	0.7%	0.7%	0.0%	87,500	77.1%	19.3%	0.8%	2.1%	0.7%
Flint city	3,995	91.7%	10,233	83.6%	16.4%	0.0%	0.0%	0.0%	11,405	77.3%	21.4%	0.0%	1.2%	0.0%
Grand Rapids city	5,500	80.2%	23,662	51.4%	45.3%	0.2%	1.8%	1.3%	34,970	67.1%	27.3%	0.0%	0.7%	4.8%
Lansing city	4,753	75.3%	14,440	59.5%	34.9%	0.9%	4.8%	0.0%	19,226	70.3%	25.6%	0.9%	3.1%	0.0%
Livonia city	3,284	92.7%	7,617	92.2%	5.5%	0.0%	2.3%	0.0%	9,580	78.6%	13.7%	5.3%	1.1%	1.2%
Sterling Heights city	2,768	100.0%	12,536	78.2%	16.5%	0.0%	4.3%	1.0%	17,324	73.0%	20.2%	0.0%	0.0%	6.9%
Warren city	6,260	97.1%	11,076	73.4%	25.5%	0.0%	1.1%	0.0%	14,106	84.6%	14.9%	0.0%	0.5%	0.0%
Minnesota														
Minneapolis city	12,450	82.3%	51,927	47.8%	41.5%	6.5%	2.8%	1.3%	83,500	69.4%	21.6%	1.8%	3.3%	4.0%
Rochester city	4,658	94.1%	10,947	70.0%	24.4%	5.6%	0.0%	0.0%	15,378	83.6%	12.3%	0.0%	2.3%	1.8%
St. Paul city	10,755	84.3%	36,831	61.9%	26.5%	5.0%	5.8%	0.9%	51,958	64.0%	25.9%	6.0%	3.6%	0.4%
Mississippi														
Jackson city	6,436	81.8%	20,753	75.8%	21.4%	1.9%	0.9%	0.0%	25,800	73.8%	23.9%	2.3%	0.0%	0.0%
Missouri														
Columbia city	5,270	77.7%	28,768	47.5%	40.6%	5.2%	5.0%	1.8%	21,450	64.6%	31.8%	0.0%	0.9%	2.6%
Independence city	3,777	89.5%	10,903	78.8%	21.2%	0.0%	0.0%	0.0%	13,982	85.9%	14.1%	0.0%	0.0%	0.0%
Kansas City city	17,336	82.5%	43,621	63.6%	25.8%	4.4%	4.7%	1.5%	67,268	67.0%	21.7%	6.3%	3.9%	1.1%
Lee's Summit city	4,379	89.2%	6,966	83.0%	17.0%	0.0%	0.0%	0.0%	10,667	79.5%	17.1%	0.5%	2.9%	0.0%
St. Louis city	9,510	82.9%	32,067	58.7%	28.5%	7.9%	2.5%	2.4%	56,718	67.9%	26.2%	2.1%	2.5%	1.3%
Springfield city	5,320	78.6%	29,221	44.8%	52.2%	0.5%	1.5%	0.9%	25,949	65.0%	32.1%	1.3%	1.2%	0.3%
Montana														
Billings city	3,531	91.7%	11,573	60.4%	30.0%	5.3%	4.0%	0.4%	14,982	67.5%	23.3%	6.3%	2.9%	0.0%
Nebraska														
Lincoln city	8,961	93.5%	43,889	50.8%	43.3%	2.7%	2.3%	0.9%	37,574	73.4%	20.2%	0.5%	3.4%	2.5%
Omaha city	18,185	83.0%	43,003	61.8%	29.5%	4.4%	2.7%	1.6%	68,472	72.0%	21.9%	3.1%	2.9%	0.2%
Nevada														
Henderson city	9,529	90.3%	19,103	75.0%	18.8%	4.8%	1.4%	0.0%	32,425	70.3%	18.7%	6.4%	3.6%	1.1%
Las Vegas city	23,875	77.7%	51,195	67.8%	25.8%	3.8%	2.3%	0.3%	83,225	68.6%	20.3%	7.0%	2.8%	1.3%
North Las Vegas city	12,834	76.8%	24,584	73.4%	18.8%	1.2%	4.4%	2.1%	29,623	77.4%	17.9%	1.3%	3.4%	0.0%
Reno city	8,710	85.8%	26,890	55.1%	35.7%	6.4%	2.1%	0.6%	33,201	59.6%	30.4%	7.5%	1.5%	1.0%
Sparks city	3,973	98.2%	8,371	81.4%	15.2%	0.8%	2.6%	0.0%	12,093	72.9%	20.0%	3.8%	2.6%	0.7%
New Hampshire														
Manchester city	2,790	81.1%	12,737	59.0%	34.7%	5.4%	0.9%	0.0%	14,766	56.4%	34.3%	5.4%	4.0%	0.0%
New Jersey														
Elizabeth city	4,828	73.8%	12,521	76.2%	18.4%	0.0%	0.5%	4.9%	17,452	86.4%	10.1%	0.0%	0.4%	3.2%
Jersey City city	8,066	90.8%	22,866	79.0%	10.0%	2.5%	4.1%	4.4%	52,020	69.5%	16.9%	6.3%	2.2%	5.1%
Newark city	9,931	87.8%	30,454	81.1%	14.7%	1.6%	1.6%	1.0%	39,268	85.5%	11.9%	1.2%	0.0%	1.3%
Paterson city	6,290	99.3%	15,741	97.5%	1.4%	1.1%	0.0%	0.0%	19,161	97.6%	2.4%	0.0%	0.0%	0.0%
New Mexico														
Albuquerque city	21,907	83.5%	52,676	65.5%	30.0%	0.8%	2.7%	0.9%	76,537	69.8%	23.9%	1.8%	2.4%	2.2%
Las Cruces city	2,309	82.6%	16,110	63.0%	30.1%	0.9%	6.0%	0.0%	12,066	86.3%	8.2%	4.0%	1.5%	0.0%
Rio Rancho city	4,635	96.9%	7,176	83.0%	12.6%	2.9%	1.5%	0.0%	11,744	87.7%	10.2%	0.7%	1.4%	0.0%
New York														
Albany city	2,732	77.6%	20,054	55.6%	39.9%	1.2%	2.0%	1.4%	14,733	72.4%	20.9%	2.1%	1.7%	2.9%
Buffalo city	9,138	90.1%	30,353	70.1%	27.6%	0.2%	0.3%	1.8%	41,937	74.3%	22.0%	1.0%	1.0%	1.7%
New York city	278,549	94.3%	794,431	82.5%	10.4%	2.0%	2.7%	2.4%	1,396,089	81.9%	13.5%	1.2%	1.8%	1.7%
Rochester city	7,207	75.0%	31,126	54.7%	38.6%	2.1%	3.6%	1.0%	33,485	63.4%	29.8%	2.7%	1.9%	2.2%
Syracuse city	5,491	84.3%	26,102	43.9%	39.7%	6.7%	5.7%	3.9%	21,880	72.0%	24.1%	1.1%	0.7%	2.2%
Yonkers city	8,135	93.3%	17,714	85.0%	13.5%	0.9%	0.6%	0.0%	25,135	88.5%	10.7%	0.8%	0.0%	0.0%
North Carolina														
Charlotte city	28,275	85.5%	80,539	59.4%	31.7%	5.4%	2.6%	1.0%	130,930	64.7%	25.2%	4.4%	4.8%	0.9%
Durham city	9,001	87.5%	26,426	62.7%	23.8%	8.0%	4.2%	1.3%	46,023	62.3%	29.4%	2.7%	3.8%	1.8%
Fayetteville city	9,411	86.9%	26,213	60.1%	25.7%	7.7%	4.8%	1.7%	33,692	67.0%	19.4%	3.6%	7.5%	2.5%
Greensboro city	11,226	92.7%	34,822	68.8%	26.6%	1.9%	2.2%	0.4%	37,660	80.4%	16.5%	2.6%	0.1%	0.4%
High Point city	5,491	81.1%	11,419	76.8%	19.1%	1.5%	2.6%	0.0%	12,920	68.3%	26.8%	1.9%	2.5%	0.5%
Raleigh city	16,199	93.5%	60,811	64.2%	29.9%	1.6%	3.6%	0.7%	72,032	67.1%	27.5%	2.7%	1.5%	1.3%
Wilmington city	4,024	85.5%	18,340	53.7%	39.6%	4.3%	1.7%	0.7%	15,528	75.1%	16.3%	5.6%	2.3%	0.7%
Winston-Salem city	9,000	84.6%	27,896	67.5%	23.4%	4.5%	3.5%	1.1%	32,107	75.5%	15.6%	6.7%	1.4%	0.8%
North Dakota														
Fargo city	3,266	80.0%	23,310	39.9%	29.9%	28.8%	0.5%	0.9%	18,285	60.0%	28.6%	10.0%	1.4%	0.0%

Table J-3: Places—Mobility Status by Age—*Continued*

	15 to 17		18 to 24						25 to 33					
					Percent Living in a Different House						Percent Living in a Different House			
	Total Population	Percent Living in Same House	Total Population	Percent Living in Same House	Same State	Different State, Same Region	Different Region	Outside US	Total Population	Percent Living in Same House	Same State	Different State, Same Region	Different Region	Outside US
Ohio														
Akron city	6,706	87.3%	21,704	77.8%	19.6%	0.0%	2.6%	0.0%	25,847	77.0%	20.2%	0.0%	1.9%	0.8%
Cincinnati city	11,568	84.0%	39,313	43.3%	48.8%	1.9%	4.9%	1.0%	51,501	71.7%	23.9%	1.6%	2.1%	0.7%
Cleveland city	16,100	83.9%	42,414	65.6%	26.2%	1.5%	2.1%	4.7%	52,322	69.5%	25.6%	1.8%	2.0%	1.1%
Columbus city	30,465	84.7%	102,832	53.8%	39.7%	0.9%	4.1%	1.6%	148,625	67.9%	26.2%	0.8%	3.7%	1.3%
Dayton city	5,329	78.5%	18,882	33.4%	56.0%	5.4%	4.2%	1.0%	21,241	63.0%	33.9%	1.3%	1.4%	0.4%
Toledo city	9,679	79.5%	31,522	57.5%	34.1%	3.8%	2.8%	1.8%	39,064	61.6%	29.9%	1.4%	5.6%	1.4%
Oklahoma														
Broken Arrow city	4,714	75.7%	8,531	69.1%	26.4%	1.2%	3.2%	0.0%	12,389	67.7%	25.5%	5.3%	1.5%	0.0%
Edmond city	3,774	98.3%	10,918	58.3%	32.3%	1.2%	2.4%	5.8%	12,496	79.8%	18.6%	0.0%	1.6%	0.0%
Lawton city	3,148	65.5%	11,092	48.7%	14.2%	11.1%	23.8%	2.2%	16,128	55.4%	29.2%	3.0%	10.8%	1.6%
Norman city	5,369	83.3%	20,878	55.9%	28.9%	8.5%	2.7%	3.9%	20,146	72.8%	13.5%	5.2%	6.6%	2.0%
Oklahoma City city	21,088	91.8%	58,633	65.9%	28.2%	2.2%	2.3%	1.4%	91,854	72.2%	23.3%	1.5%	1.1%	1.9%
Tulsa city	16,858	75.4%	39,469	67.9%	22.9%	2.7%	4.0%	2.5%	56,285	68.9%	23.1%	2.4%	3.3%	2.3%
Oregon														
Beaverton city	3,900	60.9%	8,713	76.8%	17.8%	1.7%	2.8%	0.8%	15,605	68.1%	22.4%	5.0%	0.9%	3.5%
Eugene city	6,130	95.2%	28,228	36.3%	46.7%	13.2%	2.5%	1.2%	23,017	69.6%	24.1%	0.9%	2.0%	3.3%
Gresham city	4,869	96.2%	8,610	75.3%	15.5%	4.9%	1.1%	3.2%	14,493	68.4%	13.8%	0.0%	1.0%	0.0%
Hillsboro city	4,363	79.0%	7,420	65.4%	21.9%	9.0%	3.0%	0.7%	15,643	68.4%	16.8%	7.3%	5.9%	1.6%
Portland city	16,496	89.0%	53,244	55.3%	25.5%	13.7%	3.6%	1.9%	110,931	63.5%	28.0%	3.9%	3.4%	1.2%
Salem city	6,919	94.4%	20,256	58.2%	37.2%	1.9%	1.0%	1.7%	18,923	73.2%	22.7%	1.5%	1.6%	1.1%
Pennsylvania														
Allentown city	5,383	71.0%	12,462	77.0%	14.8%	5.1%	1.1%	2.0%	17,006	55.6%	31.6%	9.9%	0.0%	2.8%
Erie city	4,110	84.2%	11,232	60.8%	25.6%	4.3%	7.6%	1.7%	13,416	77.0%	18.9%	0.0%	3.6%	0.5%
Philadelphia city	53,368	89.6%	165,390	75.0%	18.5%	3.3%	1.9%	1.3%	267,013	76.3%	16.7%	3.1%	2.7%	1.2%
Pittsburgh city	6,884	91.9%	54,164	48.1%	36.3%	3.7%	8.4%	3.5%	56,978	61.0%	28.9%	1.8%	5.1%	3.3%
Rhode Island														
Providence city	6,580	88.1%	30,753	52.7%	28.3%	7.4%	4.2%	7.5%	28,981	69.1%	23.1%	4.4%	1.4%	2.0%
South Carolina														
Charleston city	4,583	95.5%	17,312	74.2%	17.5%	1.5%	6.1%	0.7%	24,013	69.6%	21.7%	4.9%	2.8%	1.0%
Columbia city	4,730	80.5%	31,308	30.0%	28.2%	14.0%	16.7%	1.2%	23,959	64.4%	23.0%	7.3%	3.7%	1.0%
North Charleston city	4,033	83.2%	15,502	70.3%	13.6%	7.0%	6.5%	2.6%	16,951	75.4%	18.3%	3.8%	2.3%	0.2%
South Dakota														
Sioux Falls city	5,773	94.8%	15,217	46.8%	45.7%	3.6%	3.6%	0.4%	27,656	72.1%	22.3%	1.1%	0.0%	4.5%
Tennessee														
Chattanooga city	5,427	97.1%	20,231	61.7%	29.0%	7.3%	0.9%	1.1%	25,035	76.9%	13.7%	7.4%	1.7%	0.2%
Clarksville city	5,737	78.7%	18,369	57.9%	30.5%	10.4%	0.9%	0.3%	29,491	65.1%	17.5%	15.5%	1.4%	0.5%
Knoxville city	4,887	95.7%	35,254	46.3%	45.2%	2.6%	5.0%	1.0%	25,085	70.3%	21.7%	3.6%	3.2%	1.2%
Memphis city	25,478	89.3%	69,993	68.7%	24.1%	4.0%	1.8%	1.3%	92,279	74.1%	20.7%	3.7%	0.9%	0.5%
Murfreesboro city	4,888	73.0%	23,078	48.5%	46.6%	2.7%	0.3%	1.9%	17,931	58.7%	31.3%	2.7%	4.2%	3.0%
Nashville-Davidson metropolitan govt (balance)	20,461	84.3%	69,435	66.0%	23.5%	4.4%	5.4%	0.7%	114,997	68.5%	24.6%	2.6%	2.8%	1.5%
Texas														
Abilene city	5,597	88.7%	21,140	47.7%	50.0%	0.9%	1.4%	0.0%	16,864	76.2%	22.3%	1.5%	0.0%	0.0%
Allen city	5,367	97.0%	5,626	89.8%	1.9%	0.0%	0.0%	8.3%	10,327	84.8%	12.5%	0.0%	2.7%	0.0%
Amarillo city	8,179	82.9%	18,732	70.7%	24.7%	0.6%	3.3%	0.7%	26,111	65.5%	32.8%	0.4%	0.7%	0.7%
Arlington city	18,096	89.7%	43,654	76.5%	18.8%	0.8%	2.0%	1.9%	55,832	69.2%	26.3%	0.9%	1.4%	2.2%
Austin city	28,970	83.8%	104,338	61.7%	31.3%	1.1%	4.5%	1.4%	185,237	68.1%	24.8%	2.2%	3.9%	0.9%
Beaumont city	5,380	84.1%	13,486	67.0%	24.5%	6.4%	0.5%	1.6%	15,950	59.3%	34.1%	0.7%	0.5%	5.4%
Brownsville city	11,231	86.1%	21,099	92.1%	6.2%	0.0%	0.1%	1.6%	20,990	81.2%	17.2%	0.0%	0.0%	1.6%
Carrollton city	4,881	86.4%	11,583	66.5%	30.8%	2.2%	0.0%	0.5%	17,833	72.5%	20.7%	0.5%	2.9%	3.4%
College Station city	3,634	85.7%	37,239	38.4%	57.9%	0.3%	2.1%	1.3%	18,592	60.7%	33.1%	0.4%	3.5%	2.3%
Corpus Christi city	13,601	85.2%	34,598	67.0%	29.8%	2.0%	1.1%	0.2%	43,340	70.2%	28.2%	1.4%	0.3%	0.0%
Dallas city	48,617	89.3%	129,994	73.5%	21.5%	1.3%	2.2%	1.5%	205,380	72.8%	22.0%	1.5%	2.3%	1.4%
Denton city	4,468	78.2%	27,287	46.1%	51.9%	0.0%	0.7%	1.3%	21,384	67.9%	28.0%	0.4%	1.0%	2.8%
El Paso city	28,494	85.2%	76,155	75.7%	18.6%	1.2%	2.9%	1.6%	86,901	73.5%	17.7%	0.8%	4.9%	3.2%
Fort Worth city	33,297	86.9%	79,020	71.3%	23.6%	2.0%	1.9%	1.2%	121,870	73.8%	22.5%	1.2%	1.6%	1.0%
Frisco city	7,287	88.2%	7,961	73.1%	22.8%	0.0%	4.1%	0.0%	14,063	72.0%	20.7%	0.3%	6.7%	0.4%
Garland city	10,634	84.7%	21,680	73.7%	23.4%	0.9%	0.7%	1.3%	30,466	70.7%	26.1%	0.6%	1.7%	0.9%
Grand Prairie city	10,716	90.4%	20,178	90.2%	8.0%	0.0%	0.0%	1.8%	22,919	74.9%	21.6%	1.3%	0.4%	1.8%
Houston city	93,941	88.6%	240,690	73.4%	21.2%	1.5%	1.9%	2.1%	360,129	70.0%	23.5%	1.3%	2.1%	3.1%
Irving city	9,469	86.9%	25,563	68.6%	23.6%	2.8%	1.7%	3.4%	36,665	65.9%	25.8%	2.5%	2.4%	3.5%
Killeen city	6,374	79.8%	15,698	60.2%	24.8%	6.6%	4.4%	4.1%	25,678	65.8%	22.3%	2.6%	5.3%	4.0%
Laredo city	14,630	95.8%	29,370	90.3%	7.6%	0.0%	0.0%	2.1%	29,722	85.9%	13.1%	0.0%	0.5%	0.5%
Lewisville city	4,534	86.4%	8,657	66.0%	27.5%	2.6%	3.9%	0.0%	19,980	59.7%	34.6%	0.8%	4.9%	0.0%
Lubbock city	9,455	82.4%	46,318	49.7%	43.9%	1.1%	3.4%	1.8%	34,892	64.8%	32.0%	0.7%	1.1%	1.4%
McAllen city	6,846	95.2%	16,256	82.0%	17.6%	0.0%	0.0%	0.4%	16,732	78.1%	20.6%	0.0%	0.0%	1.4%
McKinney city	9,271	92.5%	12,154	78.2%	17.0%	0.7%	4.1%	0.0%	17,200	78.4%	14.8%	1.2%	5.5%	0.0%
Mesquite city	5,771	83.3%	13,465	78.0%	22.0%	0.0%	0.0%	0.0%	19,751	67.2%	29.8%	0.0%	0.4%	2.5%
Midland city	6,210	91.9%	13,875	68.5%	28.5%	2.5%	0.0%	0.5%	20,114	71.6%	22.0%	0.2%	3.2%	3.0%
Odessa city	5,341	83.2%	13,032	77.3%	21.8%	0.9%	0.0%	0.0%	18,578	77.1%	16.7%	2.3%	0.4%	3.4%

Table J-3: Places—Mobility Status by Age—*Continued*

| | 15 to 17 | | 18 to 24 | | | | | | 25 to 33 | | | | | |
| | | | | | Percent Living in a Different House | | | | | | Percent Living in a Different House | | | |
	Total Population	Percent Living in Same House	Total Population	Percent Living in Same House	Same State	Different State, Same Region	Different Region	Outside US	Total Population	Percent Living in Same House	Same State	Different State, Same Region	Different Region	Outside US
Texas—Cont.														
Pasadena city	6,315	74.4%	12,998	62.2%	27.8%	2.2%	4.9%	2.8%	22,286	71.0%	24.6%	2.4%	1.0%	1.0%
Pearland city	4,899	99.9%	8,269	92.4%	1.7%	2.3%	3.6%	0.0%	15,825	81.1%	16.9%	2.0%	0.0%	0.0%
Plano city	11,238	89.3%	22,643	85.3%	7.8%	2.5%	2.7%	1.6%	36,726	78.9%	15.9%	1.2%	2.1%	1.9%
Richardson city	2,899	93.0%	11,884	68.5%	21.2%	4.4%	4.7%	1.2%	17,044	75.6%	19.9%	0.7%	1.2%	2.7%
Round Rock City	6,601	89.3%	11,091	59.8%	38.1%	0.0%	2.1%	0.0%	13,486	67.0%	23.4%	0.9%	4.6%	4.1%
San Angelo city	4,068	90.6%	13,635	50.7%	31.8%	9.7%	7.8%	0.0%	14,415	82.7%	8.2%	2.0%	7.0%	0.0%
San Antonio city	61,440	87.0%	156,359	68.4%	27.3%	1.7%	1.7%	0.9%	217,816	70.3%	24.6%	0.6%	3.5%	0.9%
Tyler city	3,782	97.2%	13,986	66.6%	33.0%	0.4%	0.0%	0.0%	13,900	77.9%	20.8%	1.3%	0.0%	0.0%
Waco city	3,985	91.9%	24,361	56.0%	39.4%	1.9%	2.5%	0.2%	17,077	77.9%	17.6%	0.6%	3.3%	0.6%
Wichita Falls city	4,169	83.3%	14,773	51.7%	29.0%	10.2%	8.2%	0.9%	14,603	81.0%	15.9%	0.5%	2.6%	0.0%
Utah														
Orem city	5,042	92.6%	15,666	51.0%	31.2%	7.1%	4.2%	6.4%	14,174	70.1%	22.4%	3.8%	2.4%	1.3%
Provo city	3,590	79.2%	40,901	33.0%	40.3%	11.0%	5.4%	10.2%	18,730	64.6%	31.1%	4.0%	0.0%	0.4%
Salt Lake City city	6,540	90.8%	26,245	51.6%	35.7%	5.2%	5.4%	2.1%	38,151	62.1%	30.3%	2.1%	3.9%	1.7%
Sandy city	4,736	93.7%	7,641	72.7%	25.8%	0.0%	0.0%	1.5%	10,924	84.1%	15.1%	0.0%	0.0%	0.8%
West Jordan city	8,374	96.0%	8,837	77.2%	19.4%	2.4%	1.1%	0.0%	15,277	71.9%	24.7%	1.2%	2.1%	0.0%
West Valley City city	6,673	91.0%	15,698	72.8%	22.5%	4.7%	0.0%	0.0%	19,357	65.6%	31.2%	2.4%	0.4%	0.4%
Virginia														
Alexandria city	2,989	73.1%	7,083	55.3%	16.7%	4.7%	10.7%	12.7%	33,380	65.2%	22.0%	7.2%	3.6%	2.0%
Chesapeake city	9,636	98.0%	21,785	72.0%	18.2%	8.5%	1.3%	0.0%	31,728	67.9%	19.5%	6.0%	3.2%	3.4%
Hampton city	4,331	68.9%	16,083	57.0%	30.7%	8.6%	3.7%	0.0%	19,819	70.8%	24.6%	3.0%	1.2%	0.4%
Newport News city	6,474	80.8%	23,978	49.1%	31.1%	9.6%	8.4%	1.8%	28,073	65.0%	27.7%	3.5%	3.3%	0.4%
Norfolk city	6,550	72.4%	46,891	50.2%	29.4%	5.0%	14.9%	0.5%	42,408	64.7%	21.5%	4.1%	7.1%	2.6%
Portsmouth city	3,820	85.7%	10,240	62.9%	29.8%	1.2%	5.7%	0.4%	15,009	65.6%	28.1%	2.6%	3.8%	0.0%
Richmond city	5,033	88.0%	29,893	44.0%	46.5%	3.8%	4.0%	1.7%	41,924	59.4%	35.6%	1.8%	2.4%	0.8%
Roanoke city	2,205	74.5%	10,176	49.3%	44.8%	3.1%	1.6%	1.3%	13,759	67.4%	32.2%	0.4%	0.0%	0.0%
Virginia Beach city	17,334	84.5%	46,490	64.2%	20.3%	4.4%	8.2%	2.9%	69,123	65.4%	28.1%	2.1%	2.6%	1.9%
Washington														
Bellevue city	5,358	90.8%	10,338	67.5%	18.2%	1.9%	10.4%	2.0%	22,217	66.1%	20.2%	2.0%	1.1%	10.5%
Everett city	4,917	79.5%	10,760	55.1%	35.5%	8.7%	0.7%	0.0%	14,826	64.8%	32.2%	3.0%	0.0%	0.0%
Federal Way city	4,438	93.3%	6,788	63.5%	31.2%	3.2%	2.1%	0.0%	15,447	71.8%	23.0%	2.9%	0.6%	1.6%
Kent city	6,346	80.5%	12,389	68.7%	25.6%	2.3%	2.0%	1.3%	21,384	63.0%	28.3%	3.5%	2.9%	2.4%
Renton city	4,197	83.3%	5,919	64.7%	31.1%	4.1%	0.0%	0.0%	14,615	65.5%	29.0%	1.8%	3.8%	0.0%
Seattle city	13,730	88.0%	75,581	44.0%	37.1%	7.5%	7.9%	3.5%	147,020	63.1%	26.1%	3.4%	5.2%	2.2%
Spokane city	7,010	82.4%	21,782	51.2%	38.6%	8.4%	1.5%	0.2%	33,095	61.2%	26.3%	3.9%	5.0%	3.6%
Spokane Valley city	3,944	88.5%	7,006	56.4%	37.7%	5.9%	0.0%	0.0%	13,846	72.8%	22.9%	4.3%	0.0%	0.0%
Tacoma city	8,090	84.7%	19,387	64.7%	29.7%	4.4%	1.2%	0.0%	31,332	70.1%	22.7%	3.2%	2.9%	1.1%
Vancouver city	7,309	87.8%	15,490	69.9%	23.0%	6.4%	0.3%	0.4%	22,130	70.8%	18.6%	8.4%	0.6%	1.6%
Yakima city	3,524	87.9%	11,512	73.3%	22.7%	0.9%	3.2%	0.0%	10,350	70.3%	23.0%	3.9%	1.7%	1.0%
Wisconsin														
Green Bay city	2,817	89.2%	13,082	57.6%	40.3%	0.0%	1.3%	0.8%	14,708	79.8%	20.2%	0.0%	0.0%	0.0%
Kenosha city	3,809	99.5%	10,817	75.1%	17.3%	7.6%	0.0%	0.0%	10,402	64.9%	19.2%	12.9%	3.0%	0.0%
Madison city	9,540	84.9%	51,806	32.0%	47.9%	7.0%	7.3%	5.8%	39,715	66.2%	24.3%	3.5%	4.1%	2.0%
Milwaukee city	27,315	81.6%	69,180	67.5%	25.3%	4.0%	1.7%	1.5%	89,811	72.0%	22.3%	2.0%	2.4%	1.4%

Table J-4: Metropolitan/Micropolitan Statistical Areas—Mobility Status by Age

	15 to 17		18 to 24						25 to 33					
					Percent Living in a Different House						Percent Living in a Different House			
	Total Population	Percent Living in Same House	Total Population	Percent Living in Same House	Same State	Different State, Same Region	Different Region	Outside US	Total Population	Percent Living in Same House	Same State	Different State, Same Region	Different Region	Outside US
Abilene, TX	6,929	90.5%	23,544	49.8%	47.7%	1.1%	1.2%	0.2%	19,761	75.9%	22.6%	1.3%	0.2%	0.0%
Adrian, MI	3,649	67.1%	10,309	70.4%	21.0%	4.3%	2.9%	1.3%	8,941	70.9%	24.9%	0.4%	2.6%	1.2%
Akron, OH	26,085	88.0%	74,806	73.4%	24.2%	0.2%	2.2%	0.0%	77,664	79.1%	17.5%	0.2%	2.1%	1.1%
Albany, GA	6,505	89.2%	16,195	69.8%	25.5%	2.8%	1.7%	0.2%	16,784	68.3%	29.6%	0.6%	1.5%	0.0%
Albany, OR	4,217	79.8%	12,827	47.9%	43.1%	5.6%	1.0%	2.3%	11,441	59.1%	33.9%	6.0%	0.0%	1.1%
Albany-Schenectady-Troy, NY	32,357	91.3%	98,107	69.2%	24.9%	2.7%	1.6%	1.5%	102,488	75.4%	20.2%	0.9%	2.0%	1.5%
Albertville, AL	3,863	88.1%	8,881	64.4%	35.1%	0.6%	0.0%	0.0%	9,155	80.2%	18.5%	1.2%	0.1%	0.0%
Albuquerque, NM	35,349	87.8%	84,613	68.6%	26.7%	0.8%	2.6%	1.4%	113,245	74.1%	20.2%	1.5%	2.6%	1.6%
Alexandria, LA	6,747	92.8%	14,235	81.3%	11.3%	5.3%	0.8%	1.3%	17,893	78.4%	15.2%	3.2%	1.2%	2.0%
Allentown-Bethlehem-Easton, PA-NJ	33,424	89.5%	76,390	70.9%	19.8%	5.2%	2.3%	1.8%	84,989	71.4%	21.5%	3.6%	2.4%	1.0%
Altoona, PA	5,226	98.2%	10,242	73.8%	24.5%	0.7%	0.3%	0.6%	13,712	84.0%	15.3%	0.0%	0.7%	0.0%
Amarillo, TX	10,506	82.2%	25,578	70.8%	25.4%	0.4%	2.8%	0.5%	35,841	66.6%	31.3%	0.6%	0.9%	0.7%
Ames, IA	2,650	89.4%	30,643	31.2%	57.3%	10.0%	1.4%	0.0%	12,175	76.0%	15.0%	1.2%	2.4%	5.4%
Anchorage, AK	16,511	76.9%	45,782	52.3%	36.9%	4.6%	4.4%	1.9%	60,722	71.3%	17.8%	5.5%	4.7%	0.6%
Ann Arbor, MI	11,948	84.7%	65,988	42.1%	45.9%	3.8%	5.2%	3.0%	45,342	59.0%	28.2%	5.0%	6.4%	1.4%
Anniston-Oxford-Jacksonville, AL	4,735	90.0%	12,942	60.5%	29.5%	8.3%	1.7%	0.0%	12,913	75.0%	17.5%	4.4%	3.1%	0.0%
Appleton, WI	10,185	93.5%	19,110	81.7%	17.7%	0.0%	0.1%	0.5%	29,121	84.5%	14.0%	0.5%	0.6%	0.4%
Asheville, NC	14,327	86.1%	33,465	73.9%	17.7%	4.3%	2.8%	1.4%	44,992	76.6%	17.8%	1.4%	4.0%	0.2%
Ashtabula, OH	4,992	89.5%	7,835	82.0%	15.0%	0.5%	2.5%	0.0%	9,787	77.3%	22.7%	0.0%	0.0%	0.0%
Athens-Clarke County, GA	6,948	88.6%	40,739	52.0%	43.5%	2.3%	1.4%	0.9%	24,866	76.2%	19.5%	1.1%	2.0%	1.2%
Atlanta-Sandy Springs-Roswell, GA	248,760	88.5%	524,244	74.8%	19.9%	2.4%	2.0%	0.9%	691,741	74.7%	19.9%	2.8%	1.6%	1.1%
Atlantic City-Hammonton, NJ	9,931	86.1%	27,015	82.1%	14.6%	0.1%	2.3%	1.0%	29,552	74.4%	17.0%	2.4%	4.9%	1.2%
Auburn-Opelika, AL	5,316	97.9%	30,660	53.6%	35.1%	9.3%	1.1%	0.8%	18,813	71.6%	17.7%	8.3%	2.2%	0.2%
Augusta-Richmond County, GA-SC	24,023	93.0%	57,885	79.9%	12.5%	6.1%	1.2%	0.3%	77,257	78.0%	17.1%	3.2%	1.1%	0.6%
Augusta-Waterville, ME	4,104	96.2%	10,420	49.5%	41.5%	7.2%	0.1%	1.8%	11,402	71.2%	28.0%	0.7%	0.1%	0.0%
Austin-Round Rock, TX	77,358	90.1%	201,829	64.7%	30.1%	0.7%	3.5%	1.0%	307,346	70.3%	23.5%	1.6%	3.4%	1.2%
Bakersfield, CA	39,801	88.5%	96,404	79.5%	18.2%	0.5%	1.6%	0.2%	119,068	78.1%	19.0%	1.6%	0.7%	0.5%
Baltimore-Columbia-Towson, MD	101,865	90.4%	251,659	77.3%	16.0%	1.7%	4.3%	0.7%	360,376	75.9%	17.5%	2.6%	2.7%	1.2%
Bangor, ME	5,200	78.6%	17,405	58.6%	32.6%	8.8%	0.0%	0.0%	18,251	56.8%	37.9%	2.7%	2.7%	0.0%
Barnstable Town, MA	6,996	93.3%	14,201	82.3%	15.4%	1.1%	1.2%	0.0%	15,825	76.1%	15.8%	6.7%	1.4%	0.0%
Baton Rouge, LA	33,148	91.4%	98,596	71.5%	23.2%	2.0%	2.6%	0.6%	107,608	77.9%	17.9%	2.9%	1.3%	0.0%
Battle Creek, MI	5,674	89.2%	10,750	74.5%	23.3%	1.0%	0.5%	0.8%	15,498	74.4%	24.6%	0.8%	0.2%	0.0%
Bay City, MI	4,086	99.7%	8,750	77.1%	20.0%	0.1%	2.0%	0.0%	11,393	82.1%	15.1%	0.0%	0.0%	2.8%
Beaumont-Port Arthur, TX	17,406	79.5%	37,714	71.4%	24.9%	2.6%	0.5%	0.6%	52,493	69.9%	25.6%	2.7%	0.2%	1.6%
Beckley, WV	3,897	93.6%	9,532	73.2%	23.0%	1.3%	2.1%	0.3%	12,971	74.9%	18.7%	2.2%	2.0%	2.1%
Bellingham, WA	7,277	84.5%	30,613	51.3%	44.1%	2.5%	2.1%	0.0%	26,325	68.3%	26.9%	0.8%	2.0%	2.1%
Bend-Redmond, OR	5,366	86.3%	12,522	71.5%	16.4%	12.1%	0.0%	0.0%	19,618	61.7%	32.8%	4.3%	1.3%	0.0%
Billings, MT	4,423	90.0%	16,307	63.7%	27.0%	6.1%	2.8%	0.3%	19,898	70.7%	22.4%	4.7%	2.2%	0.0%
Binghamton, NY	9,502	87.8%	32,990	70.1%	26.0%	1.1%	1.7%	1.1%	24,016	78.6%	19.0%	0.6%	1.6%	0.3%
Birmingham-Hoover, AL	47,453	90.9%	99,509	71.6%	23.3%	3.2%	1.4%	0.6%	138,701	75.2%	19.4%	4.0%	1.1%	0.3%
Bismarck, ND	4,432	88.1%	10,971	53.8%	28.7%	14.3%	1.5%	1.8%	18,784	81.7%	16.4%	1.5%	0.4%	0.0%
Blacksburg-Christiansburg-Radford, VA	4,812	85.6%	40,796	46.2%	44.1%	5.0%	2.4%	2.4%	20,223	69.4%	24.5%	1.3%	0.7%	4.1%
Bloomington, IL	7,181	98.9%	32,433	57.6%	40.4%	0.8%	0.6%	0.6%	22,102	66.2%	30.7%	1.6%	0.8%	0.8%
Bloomington, IN	4,840	82.2%	41,299	30.0%	61.3%	2.0%	5.5%	1.2%	20,887	64.9%	23.9%	6.4%	4.5%	0.4%
Bloomsburg-Berwick, PA	2,251	79.2%	10,392	69.7%	28.6%	1.1%	0.5%	0.0%	10,893	77.9%	21.3%	0.0%	0.6%	0.2%
Boise City, ID	30,255	85.1%	58,208	65.1%	27.6%	3.8%	1.9%	1.6%	85,278	72.2%	20.4%	5.4%	1.2%	0.7%
Boston-Cambridge-Newton, MA-NH	172,606	93.4%	476,078	73.3%	17.2%	4.0%	3.3%	2.2%	621,558	74.0%	18.0%	2.8%	2.7%	2.5%
Boulder, CO	11,543	88.1%	49,567	44.0%	44.1%	2.6%	7.4%	2.0%	37,556	61.0%	29.2%	3.3%	5.8%	0.7%
Bowling Green, KY	6,726	72.6%	22,855	48.4%	40.9%	6.3%	2.8%	1.6%	18,892	68.1%	29.7%	0.7%	1.6%	0.0%
Bremerton-Silverdale, WA	9,762	91.4%	27,430	68.4%	19.7%	4.2%	6.9%	0.7%	32,727	66.9%	27.0%	2.8%	3.4%	0.0%
Bridgeport-Stamford-Norwalk, CT	40,383	90.2%	85,139	84.4%	9.4%	2.9%	1.2%	2.0%	97,867	73.8%	17.3%	6.4%	1.1%	1.5%
Brownsville-Harlingen, TX	23,240	89.9%	44,883	91.7%	6.9%	0.0%	0.1%	1.4%	45,622	80.0%	18.0%	0.4%	0.2%	1.4%
Brunswick, GA	4,512	82.5%	9,393	69.8%	24.3%	4.2%	1.8%	0.0%	12,722	73.3%	18.5%	8.2%	0.0%	0.0%
Buffalo-Cheektowaga-Niagara Falls, NY	41,259	91.4%	108,353	77.8%	20.1%	0.0%	0.8%	1.3%	137,249	78.8%	18.1%	0.5%	1.4%	1.2%
Burlington, NC	6,420	82.1%	14,754	77.3%	15.4%	2.7%	3.1%	1.5%	16,654	72.3%	23.7%	0.9%	2.0%	1.1%
Burlington-South Burlington, VT	7,394	97.8%	30,542	64.7%	16.9%	10.8%	5.4%	2.1%	26,095	66.0%	27.2%	4.7%	1.7%	0.3%
California-Lexington Park, MD	4,721	92.8%	11,172	84.1%	10.6%	0.5%	4.3%	0.5%	13,081	57.8%	34.5%	4.2%	2.3%	1.2%
Canton-Massillon, OH	16,276	83.8%	34,507	71.3%	23.3%	1.1%	3.2%	1.1%	42,794	75.4%	21.1%	0.1%	3.4%	0.0%
Cape Coral-Fort Myers, FL	22,116	85.0%	50,309	72.6%	22.5%	1.9%	2.7%	0.4%	69,819	77.1%	16.7%	1.6%	1.9%	2.8%
Cape Girardeau, MO-IL	3,293	74.3%	10,731	71.8%	24.1%	2.4%	1.2%	0.6%	11,904	80.2%	17.6%	0.0%	2.2%	0.0%
Carbondale-Marion, IL	5,731	98.0%	18,633	50.3%	47.4%	0.4%	1.6%	0.4%	14,854	72.4%	20.5%	0.0%	7.2%	0.0%
Carson City, NV	2,019	85.1%	5,225	66.8%	32.1%	1.1%	0.0%	0.0%	4,314	58.0%	20.8%	21.2%	0.0%	0.0%
Casper, WY	2,779	87.5%	7,113	62.0%	30.4%	2.9%	4.8%	0.0%	10,786	80.4%	13.3%	3.2%	3.1%	0.0%
Cedar Rapids, IA	10,560	88.3%	24,636	66.5%	28.4%	1.2%	3.9%	0.0%	30,774	73.2%	13.8%	0.9%	3.7%	8.4%
Chambersburg-Waynesboro, PA	5,730	92.3%	13,646	77.5%	17.4%	2.1%	2.4%	0.6%	15,478	84.3%	13.1%	0.0%	2.6%	0.0%
Champaign-Urbana, IL	7,284	94.3%	52,890	56.7%	35.8%	0.3%	4.2%	3.0%	28,892	68.8%	24.2%	0.5%	2.5%	3.9%
Charleston, WV	7,510	89.5%	15,789	71.3%	19.0%	4.8%	5.0%	0.0%	23,511	70.0%	27.1%	1.4%	1.3%	0.2%
Charleston-North Charleston, SC	26,310	85.2%	69,521	70.4%	18.7%	4.9%	4.5%	1.5%	108,893	73.7%	18.7%	4.8%	2.3%	0.6%
Charlotte-Concord-Gastonia, NC-SC	101,553	88.0%	213,700	70.2%	23.8%	3.7%	1.8%	0.5%	288,787	70.6%	21.7%	3.6%	3.4%	0.7%
Charlottesville, VA	7,040	89.5%	29,757	52.3%	37.1%	5.9%	3.1%	1.6%	30,260	69.7%	23.3%	1.4%	4.1%	1.5%
Chattanooga, TN-GA	20,908	91.6%	51,185	72.4%	21.8%	4.3%	1.1%	0.4%	65,730	78.3%	13.2%	7.2%	1.2%	0.2%
Cheyenne, WY	3,412	100.0%	14,476	56.1%	24.3%	4.7%	11.8%	3.1%	9,573	68.6%	16.4%	7.8%	7.2%	0.0%
Chicago-Naperville-Elgin, IL-IN-WI	389,155	91.3%	895,906	77.0%	16.9%	2.4%	2.5%	1.3%	1,219,063	76.6%	18.8%	1.5%	2.1%	1.1%

Table J-4: Metropolitan/Micropolitan Statistical Areas—Mobility Status by Age—*Continued*

| | 15 to 17 | | 18 to 24 | | | | | | 25 to 33 | | | | | |
| | | | | | Percent Living in a Different House | | | | | | Percent Living in a Different House | | | |
	Total Population	Percent Living in Same House	Total Population	Percent Living in Same House	Same State	Different State, Same Region	Different Region	Outside US	Total Population	Percent Living in Same House	Same State	Different State, Same Region	Different Region	Outside US
Chico, CA	7,589	91.1%	33,684	62.3%	36.9%	0.0%	0.1%	0.8%	25,312	69.6%	29.1%	0.0%	0.6%	0.7%
Cincinnati, OH-KY-IN	89,722	90.0%	198,140	66.1%	26.6%	1.4%	5.0%	0.9%	254,917	73.7%	21.2%	1.3%	3.2%	0.6%
Clarksburg, WV	3,332	89.7%	7,633	79.0%	17.6%	3.4%	0.0%	0.0%	8,720	69.4%	26.9%	0.4%	3.3%	0.0%
Clarksville, TN-KY	10,047	81.4%	32,686	60.3%	23.9%	11.2%	4.1%	0.4%	48,376	67.9%	15.6%	13.1%	2.7%	0.7%
Cleveland, TN	5,473	83.6%	12,021	64.9%	31.9%	0.9%	1.7%	0.6%	13,353	73.0%	22.0%	3.2%	1.9%	0.0%
Cleveland-Elyria, OH	80,973	88.2%	178,155	71.4%	21.9%	1.7%	3.4%	1.7%	225,453	72.6%	23.6%	1.0%	2.0%	0.8%
Coeur d'Alene, ID	5,612	87.3%	11,742	61.2%	34.8%	3.6%	0.2%	0.2%	17,751	69.3%	22.2%	6.7%	0.0%	1.8%
College Station-Bryan, TX	7,537	88.4%	59,179	42.8%	53.7%	0.2%	1.4%	1.9%	33,688	62.5%	32.0%	1.0%	2.6%	1.9%
Colorado Springs, CO	27,550	89.1%	75,550	59.0%	26.1%	3.9%	9.6%	1.4%	98,970	63.5%	23.3%	1.4%	10.1%	1.7%
Columbia, MO	5,971	77.0%	35,010	47.7%	39.3%	5.1%	5.2%	2.7%	24,966	64.6%	30.3%	0.6%	1.8%	2.7%
Columbia, SC	32,495	87.3%	99,606	63.4%	19.7%	7.2%	8.8%	0.9%	96,626	73.0%	20.7%	4.4%	1.3%	0.6%
Columbus, GA-AL	12,697	90.8%	36,082	59.6%	23.1%	8.5%	8.2%	0.6%	44,311	63.1%	21.0%	9.4%	4.1%	2.4%
Columbus, IN	3,580	97.2%	7,290	80.2%	13.5%	4.2%	2.1%	0.0%	9,971	80.3%	16.4%	0.0%	3.2%	0.0%
Columbus, OH	80,315	85.7%	185,106	61.4%	33.6%	0.7%	3.3%	1.0%	280,282	71.0%	24.4%	0.8%	3.2%	1.0%
Concord, NH	4,264	88.8%	10,518	82.2%	13.1%	3.2%	0.6%	0.9%	11,368	71.6%	20.3%	0.7%	4.3%	3.1%
Cookeville, TN	4,586	90.8%	14,332	71.0%	24.3%	1.4%	0.7%	2.6%	11,763	81.4%	11.9%	4.9%	1.0%	0.8%
Corpus Christi, TX	18,927	86.4%	44,738	67.7%	28.7%	2.1%	1.3%	0.1%	55,956	68.8%	28.9%	1.3%	0.8%	0.1%
Corvallis, OR	4,969	82.9%	15,283	49.1%	40.8%	6.5%	0.8%	2.8%	12,337	60.7%	31.4%	6.2%	0.7%	1.0%
Crestview-Fort Walton Beach-Destin, FL	7,454	83.0%	23,985	60.1%	24.9%	7.1%	5.8%	2.1%	37,896	64.3%	23.9%	5.6%	5.2%	1.0%
Cumberland, MD-WV	3,828	72.2%	11,906	70.6%	24.3%	4.6%	0.0%	0.5%	10,515	81.9%	10.9%	3.6%	2.2%	1.4%
Dallas-Fort Worth-Arlington, TX	308,719	88.3%	651,831	74.3%	21.5%	1.2%	1.6%	1.5%	913,935	72.8%	22.4%	1.2%	2.1%	1.5%
Dalton, GA	5,983	95.3%	13,690	79.4%	16.4%	2.4%	0.8%	1.0%	17,664	89.4%	7.7%	1.4%	1.5%	0.0%
Danville, IL	3,371	93.8%	5,300	69.8%	27.6%	0.4%	2.2%	0.0%	9,809	78.5%	20.7%	0.2%	0.6%	0.0%
Danville, VA	4,169	76.0%	7,826	83.7%	13.2%	1.4%	1.7%	0.0%	10,281	75.9%	21.5%	1.3%	1.4%	0.0%
Daphne-Fairhope-Foley, AL	7,453	97.5%	14,381	78.4%	17.0%	0.4%	4.2%	0.0%	20,047	73.9%	20.9%	4.1%	1.1%	0.0%
Davenport-Moline-Rock Island, IA-IL	13,302	90.6%	34,932	72.7%	18.8%	4.8%	3.3%	0.4%	42,931	78.4%	14.3%	3.5%	3.3%	0.5%
Dayton, OH	30,117	90.0%	74,740	56.9%	36.3%	3.1%	2.6%	1.1%	93,470	66.2%	27.2%	2.8%	3.3%	0.5%
Decatur, AL	6,237	91.6%	12,140	74.8%	21.7%	1.1%	2.2%	0.3%	17,056	81.6%	16.9%	0.8%	0.0%	0.7%
Decatur, IL	3,953	97.5%	10,188	78.8%	16.5%	3.2%	1.5%	0.0%	10,459	82.8%	17.2%	0.0%	0.0%	0.0%
Deltona-Daytona Beach-Ormond Beach, FL	20,948	88.6%	51,286	83.8%	10.4%	0.8%	2.4%	2.6%	60,527	80.2%	14.4%	2.0%	1.9%	1.5%
Denver-Aurora-Lakewood, CO	108,723	87.1%	234,203	69.9%	22.1%	2.5%	4.3%	1.2%	402,449	66.7%	24.2%	2.7%	5.2%	1.3%
Des Moines-West Des Moines, IA	26,423	76.6%	53,771	52.8%	43.3%	3.3%	0.6%	0.1%	84,680	66.3%	27.3%	1.0%	3.7%	1.6%
Detroit-Warren-Dearborn, MI	177,606	89.6%	368,804	76.7%	20.9%	0.6%	1.3%	0.5%	481,372	74.7%	21.1%	0.5%	2.3%	1.4%
Dothan, AL	6,001	92.4%	12,120	69.1%	24.0%	2.3%	4.1%	0.4%	16,153	77.0%	18.6%	3.5%	0.9%	0.0%
Dover, DE	6,870	84.0%	18,762	68.2%	25.6%	0.8%	4.9%	0.5%	20,537	76.8%	17.7%	2.8%	2.5%	0.2%
Dubuque, IA	4,498	79.7%	10,770	70.8%	16.0%	11.6%	1.3%	0.3%	10,320	77.0%	16.4%	4.0%	2.6%	0.0%
Duluth, MN-WI	9,153	84.2%	31,513	56.0%	34.8%	4.4%	4.2%	0.6%	32,043	81.9%	14.7%	2.9%	0.5%	0.1%
Dunn, NC	5,255	85.5%	13,083	54.1%	36.5%	2.7%	6.8%	0.0%	16,703	81.7%	14.2%	1.9%	2.1%	0.0%
Durham-Chapel Hill, NC	18,854	85.5%	65,360	56.1%	31.9%	6.3%	4.9%	0.8%	77,519	63.6%	28.2%	2.3%	3.4%	2.6%
East Stroudsburg, PA	7,360	70.3%	18,241	76.8%	17.1%	4.6%	1.5%	0.0%	16,475	83.9%	9.5%	3.1%	3.5%	0.0%
Eau Claire, WI	5,827	83.4%	22,132	48.0%	44.4%	7.6%	0.0%	0.0%	19,765	65.0%	31.7%	2.4%	1.0%	0.0%
El Centro, CA	8,239	88.3%	20,115	81.3%	15.6%	1.4%	1.3%	0.5%	21,437	78.1%	21.7%	0.1%	0.0%	0.0%
El Paso, TX	6,816	86.9%	13,120	66.1%	28.1%	1.7%	4.1%	0.0%	17,336	56.3%	29.5%	5.3%	8.2%	0.7%
Elizabethtown-Fort Knox, KY	9,847	91.3%	18,907	80.4%	19.1%	0.2%	0.3%	0.0%	22,639	83.3%	13.4%	2.3%	1.0%	0.0%
Elkhart-Goshen, IN	2,587	93.8%	7,341	79.3%	18.4%	0.4%	1.9%	0.0%	11,023	71.9%	23.0%	3.3%	1.9%	0.0%
Elmira, NY	38,189	84.8%	94,502	74.2%	20.0%	1.4%	2.5%	1.9%	110,937	75.7%	17.0%	0.7%	4.0%	2.6%
Erie, PA	11,465	90.2%	28,432	71.9%	19.9%	3.7%	3.7%	0.8%	31,135	76.9%	21.1%	0.0%	1.9%	0.2%
Eugene, OR	12,770	89.4%	46,350	45.7%	40.1%	11.7%	1.7%	0.7%	41,900	71.3%	24.8%	0.9%	1.1%	1.9%
Eureka-Arcata-Fortuna, CA	3,629	85.6%	18,225	42.3%	57.0%	0.6%	0.0%	0.1%	16,198	70.0%	28.3%	0.4%	1.0%	0.3%
Evansville, IN-KY	11,986	83.4%	28,292	62.2%	27.9%	2.8%	6.3%	0.7%	37,384	73.9%	24.2%	0.0%	1.9%	0.0%
Fairbanks, AK	4,177	90.7%	15,158	69.8%	12.0%	6.5%	11.6%	0.0%	15,499	69.4%	20.8%	3.6%	4.7%	1.6%
Fargo, ND-MN	7,350	84.9%	36,712	48.4%	27.4%	21.5%	2.1%	0.8%	32,049	62.6%	27.1%	9.3%	0.9%	0.1%
Farmington, NM	4,993	86.0%	11,608	80.3%	18.7%	0.7%	0.3%	0.0%	14,031	77.5%	16.4%	1.0%	4.2%	1.0%
Fayetteville, NC	14,516	86.7%	45,468	58.6%	23.7%	9.2%	6.2%	2.3%	54,810	65.6%	20.3%	3.8%	7.9%	2.4%
Fayetteville-Springdale-Rogers, AR-MO	20,389	87.7%	56,968	64.7%	26.6%	5.6%	2.0%	1.1%	67,776	75.7%	19.2%	2.0%	2.4%	0.8%
Flagstaff, AZ	4,964	85.7%	29,687	45.6%	36.7%	12.5%	3.7%	1.5%	17,120	74.1%	15.9%	5.6%	2.4%	2.0%
Flint, MI	16,466	91.7%	36,729	78.5%	20.1%	0.0%	0.8%	0.6%	43,078	76.8%	18.0%	0.0%	5.1%	0.1%
Florence, SC	8,423	92.2%	19,018	74.4%	21.5%	2.0%	2.2%	0.0%	21,857	82.6%	12.7%	4.4%	0.4%	0.0%
Florence-Muscle Shoals, AL	6,982	93.9%	13,870	67.3%	29.6%	2.3%	0.8%	0.0%	13,856	75.4%	21.3%	3.3%	0.0%	0.0%
Fond du Lac, WI	5,336	90.6%	8,500	83.5%	15.3%	0.0%	0.2%	1.0%	10,842	84.5%	14.6%	0.0%	1.0%	0.0%
Fort Collins, CO	11,319	93.3%	46,073	47.9%	40.4%	5.1%	4.8%	1.8%	46,242	69.1%	26.1%	2.3%	1.9%	0.7%
Fort Smith, AR-OK	10,280	88.1%	24,092	69.8%	23.1%	3.3%	2.9%	1.0%	34,033	75.5%	17.8%	0.8%	5.5%	0.5%
Fort Wayne, IN	18,479	91.2%	42,894	74.4%	19.9%	0.9%	3.5%	1.3%	49,413	71.5%	23.4%	2.2%	2.8%	0.1%
Fresno, CA	44,793	89.6%	106,206	74.9%	22.4%	0.9%	0.8%	1.0%	129,871	75.1%	21.9%	0.8%	1.7%	0.4%
Gadsden, AL	3,849	79.9%	9,075	70.3%	26.0%	1.8%	1.2%	0.6%	9,578	78.5%	20.2%	0.5%	0.7%	0.0%
Gainesville, FL	8,410	81.3%	56,926	51.7%	41.9%	1.9%	2.8%	1.7%	37,325	65.0%	30.6%	0.9%	2.2%	1.3%
Gainesville, GA	8,761	84.2%	18,304	71.6%	27.2%	0.9%	0.3%	0.0%	21,584	81.8%	17.3%	0.9%	0.0%	0.0%
Gettysburg, PA	4,180	84.6%	8,558	69.5%	22.4%	6.1%	2.0%	0.0%	10,662	73.5%	22.3%	0.0%	3.8%	0.4%
Glens Falls, NY	4,808	96.0%	9,770	77.9%	22.1%	0.0%	0.0%	0.0%	12,268	78.0%	14.3%	0.8%	6.3%	0.6%
Goldsboro, NC	4,258	74.5%	12,124	63.3%	26.4%	6.7%	1.4%	2.1%	16,422	76.2%	19.9%	0.6%	0.7%	2.5%
Grand Forks, ND-MN	3,660	88.8%	19,039	51.4%	28.3%	16.6%	3.1%	0.6%	13,706	73.6%	21.1%	3.0%	0.6%	1.7%
Grand Island, NE	3,594	81.9%	7,909	56.5%	42.8%	0.7%	0.0%	0.0%	9,116	70.8%	21.9%	1.5%	1.5%	4.3%
Grand Junction, CO	5,453	90.2%	15,516	63.5%	30.2%	5.2%	1.1%	0.0%	17,801	74.2%	13.3%	3.6%	8.9%	0.0%
Grand Rapids-Wyoming, MI	44,884	87.9%	108,123	64.2%	31.6%	0.9%	1.5%	1.9%	129,931	74.6%	21.9%	0.3%	1.2%	2.1%

Table J-4: Metropolitan/Micropolitan Statistical Areas—Mobility Status by Age—*Continued*

| | 15 to 17 | | 18 to 24 | | | | | | 25 to 33 | | | | | |
| | | | | | Percent Living in a Different House | | | | | | Percent Living in a Different House | | | |
	Total Population	Percent Living in Same House	Total Population	Percent Living in Same House	Same State	Different State, Same Region	Different Region	Outside US	Total Population	Percent Living in Same House	Same State	Different State, Same Region	Different Region	Outside US
Grants Pass, OR	3,979	71.9%	6,319	71.4%	16.2%	7.6%	0.0%	4.8%	6,561	76.4%	14.7%	0.2%	8.6%	0.0%
Great Falls, MT	2,295	99.1%	8,457	59.0%	40.0%	0.3%	0.7%	0.0%	9,734	75.3%	17.1%	3.5%	2.1%	2.0%
Greeley, CO	13,960	84.3%	29,769	55.1%	39.0%	2.0%	2.9%	1.1%	35,416	72.9%	22.9%	1.1%	2.5%	0.5%
Green Bay, WI	12,115	83.8%	27,413	71.8%	26.2%	0.0%	0.8%	1.2%	38,825	78.1%	20.4%	1.0%	0.5%	0.0%
Greensboro-High Point, NC	30,214	89.4%	71,418	74.4%	22.4%	1.3%	1.6%	0.3%	85,526	78.0%	17.8%	2.0%	1.5%	0.7%
Greenville, NC	6,240	81.6%	31,790	48.2%	48.3%	1.6%	1.9%	0.0%	22,438	68.8%	27.6%	1.5%	1.7%	0.4%
Greenville-Anderson-Mauldin, SC	34,925	89.7%	85,925	70.0%	23.8%	3.1%	3.0%	0.2%	99,564	74.3%	19.1%	2.6%	2.6%	1.4%
Greenwood, SC	3,615	90.7%	10,427	77.2%	22.8%	0.0%	0.0%	0.0%	8,790	87.4%	12.5%	0.1%	0.0%	0.0%
Gulfport-Biloxi-Pascagoula, MS	16,274	85.5%	36,927	67.7%	17.5%	5.6%	8.9%	0.3%	46,488	69.6%	22.9%	5.7%	0.4%	1.4%
Hagerstown-Martinsburg, MD-WV	9,406	88.3%	22,794	71.5%	20.9%	4.9%	0.5%	2.1%	29,667	74.2%	19.1%	3.2%	3.1%	0.4%
Hammond, LA	4,906	80.3%	14,495	59.2%	37.3%	2.4%	1.1%	0.0%	16,082	70.1%	27.6%	2.3%	0.0%	0.0%
Hanford-Corcoran, CA	6,293	84.4%	16,771	65.3%	26.4%	2.3%	5.2%	0.7%	23,428	74.1%	20.2%	0.3%	5.4%	0.0%
Harrisburg-Carlisle, PA	21,005	81.8%	54,749	69.4%	23.3%	2.1%	2.9%	2.4%	60,293	73.6%	22.7%	0.6%	2.5%	0.5%
Harrisonburg, VA	4,355	94.8%	25,737	56.7%	36.9%	2.1%	4.0%	0.4%	14,315	74.0%	25.0%	1.0%	0.0%	0.0%
Hartford-West Hartford-East Hartford, CT	44,663	89.9%	115,378	73.8%	19.3%	3.7%	2.0%	1.1%	127,732	73.8%	20.5%	1.9%	1.5%	2.3%
Hattiesburg, MS	5,118	79.5%	20,046	59.0%	29.0%	7.7%	3.0%	1.3%	16,974	79.0%	19.0%	1.4%	0.5%	0.2%
Hickory-Lenoir-Morganton, NC	14,991	88.3%	31,801	73.7%	23.7%	1.6%	1.0%	0.0%	35,052	80.5%	17.1%	1.9%	0.4%	0.0%
Ililo, Ill	6,367	86.3%	16,321	70.5%	13.1%	6.1%	0.0%	1.3%	21,668	72.3%	22.5%	4.2%	0.0%	1.0%
Hilton Head Island-Bluffton-Beaufort, SC	5,903	81.6%	18,348	65.0%	22.4%	6.6%	5.0%	1.0%	24,204	62.7%	16.9%	17.8%	2.5%	0.0%
Hinesville, GA	2,966	72.8%	13,060	62.2%	19.5%	8.8%	5.5%	4.0%	11,083	60.8%	28.7%	5.8%	4.2%	0.4%
Holland, MI	5,166	98.8%	9,792	73.9%	23.6%	0.4%	0.4%	1.7%	11,964	83.9%	16.1%	0.0%	0.0%	0.0%
Homosassa Springs, FL	3,920	94.5%	7,713	59.7%	39.0%	0.0%	1.3%	0.0%	8,986	72.0%	24.4%	0.0%	3.0%	0.6%
Hot Springs, AR	3,413	73.4%	8,016	43.5%	51.3%	4.0%	1.2%	0.0%	9,997	61.2%	26.1%	6.7%	6.0%	0.0%
Houma-Thibodaux, LA	8,204	89.8%	18,255	85.7%	9.8%	3.4%	1.1%	0.0%	27,684	80.4%	15.5%	2.3%	0.2%	1.6%
Houston-The Woodlands-Sugar Land, TX	291,005	90.8%	615,008	76.6%	18.9%	1.5%	1.5%	1.5%	889,477	73.7%	21.2%	1.4%	1.8%	1.9%
Huntington-Ashland, WV-KY-OH	14,789	90.3%	33,330	75.5%	22.6%	1.1%	0.7%	0.0%	36,570	76.5%	16.3%	2.8%	3.8%	0.6%
Huntsville, AL	18,099	94.1%	40,619	68.6%	28.2%	2.1%	0.7%	0.4%	57,381	70.9%	21.3%	6.1%	1.5%	0.1%
Idaho Falls, ID	6,345	84.4%	11,332	39.4%	48.0%	6.4%	2.1%	4.1%	17,251	67.7%	16.0%	6.1%	7.5%	2.8%
Indianapolis-Carmel-Anderson, IN	79,646	88.0%	174,852	70.7%	26.4%	1.2%	1.3%	0.4%	252,167	72.4%	23.1%	1.3%	2.7%	0.4%
Iowa City, IA	5,895	73.5%	31,586	45.9%	38.8%	8.5%	5.3%	1.6%	23,161	79.5%	13.9%	2.6%	3.1%	0.9%
Ithaca, NY	2,679	94.2%	30,987	71.9%	19.4%	3.7%	5.0%	0.0%	11,783	58.6%	22.1%	3.6%	11.6%	4.1%
Jackson, MI	5,934	90.9%	13,908	71.4%	24.4%	0.9%	2.9%	0.4%	18,624	78.8%	19.5%	0.7%	0.9%	0.0%
Jackson, MS	25,345	85.7%	54,327	74.9%	21.8%	2.1%	1.3%	0.0%	71,278	75.8%	20.3%	2.5%	1.2%	0.2%
Jackson, TN	4,733	97.2%	13,904	78.3%	18.9%	1.0%	1.8%	0.0%	15,287	90.4%	8.6%	1.0%	0.0%	0.0%
Jacksonville, FL	57,918	86.4%	130,435	67.6%	25.7%	2.2%	3.7%	0.8%	185,508	69.0%	25.1%	2.6%	2.2%	1.1%
Jacksonville, NC	5,861	80.1%	36,464	39.4%	34.2%	9.3%	10.7%	6.4%	32,983	58.6%	23.8%	8.4%	6.0%	3.1%
Jamestown-Dunkirk-Fredonia, NY	5,229	83.0%	13,664	67.3%	29.1%	0.3%	1.0%	2.3%	12,863	82.9%	17.1%	0.0%	0.0%	0.0%
Janesville-Beloit, WI	6,618	84.8%	14,815	73.1%	20.2%	6.0%	0.8%	0.0%	15,271	64.4%	32.2%	0.2%	1.8%	1.3%
Jefferson City, MO	6,315	91.3%	14,684	70.9%	23.1%	1.4%	4.6%	0.0%	17,313	61.4%	29.7%	0.0%	6.4%	2.5%
Johnson City, TN	6,659	85.3%	20,537	56.5%	34.0%	4.0%	1.1%	2.8%	21,051	75.3%	17.1%	4.3%	3.3%	0.0%
Johnstown, PA	5,489	82.6%	12,403	71.2%	22.5%	2.2%	1.4%	2.7%	12,887	80.2%	17.7%	1.1%	1.0%	0.0%
Jonesboro, AR	5,913	74.8%	15,635	64.6%	33.6%	0.7%	0.9%	0.2%	15,345	65.7%	30.6%	2.2%	0.7%	0.7%
Joplin, MO	7,806	93.4%	17,379	69.8%	25.0%	1.3%	3.8%	0.0%	18,676	87.6%	11.5%	0.9%	0.0%	0.0%
Kahului-Wailuku-Lahaina, HI	5,710	97.9%	12,607	84.3%	3.0%	5.9%	6.4%	0.5%	20,898	76.5%	17.2%	5.0%	0.9%	0.5%
Kalamazoo-Portage, MI	12,475	90.0%	48,185	57.1%	37.4%	2.9%	0.8%	1.8%	36,599	76.7%	21.2%	0.9%	1.1%	0.1%
Kalispell, MT	3,906	90.6%	7,110	61.8%	16.8%	21.4%	0.0%	0.0%	9,686	61.3%	32.9%	3.4%	2.5%	0.0%
Kankakee, IL	4,612	94.0%	11,549	78.0%	16.1%	4.8%	0.0%	1.1%	12,290	85.0%	8.5%	5.1%	0.0%	1.3%
Kansas City, MO-KS	84,123	88.5%	180,675	70.0%	22.3%	4.4%	2.3%	0.9%	258,765	70.4%	20.6%	4.3%	3.5%	1.2%
Kennewick-Richland, WA	13,135	86.6%	27,475	68.3%	29.4%	2.0%	0.4%	0.0%	35,262	74.6%	20.9%	2.2%	2.0%	0.3%
Killeen-Temple, TX	18,742	85.9%	53,911	61.9%	26.4%	3.9%	3.9%	3.8%	67,153	63.2%	27.0%	3.6%	3.9%	2.2%
Kingsport-Bristol-Bristol, TN-VA	12,611	89.7%	23,375	79.4%	18.3%	1.1%	0.8%	0.4%	30,784	77.2%	19.1%	1.9%	1.8%	0.0%
Kingston, NY	5,489	98.8%	19,374	82.7%	16.3%	0.4%	0.5%	0.0%	17,081	78.5%	20.0%	0.0%	0.6%	0.9%
Knoxville, TN	32,103	91.9%	88,102	70.1%	25.0%	1.7%	2.9%	0.4%	92,534	75.9%	18.1%	3.2%	2.3%	0.6%
Kokomo, IN	3,329	77.1%	6,039	77.7%	20.6%	0.0%	0.0%	1.7%	8,521	69.5%	27.8%	0.0%	0.0%	2.7%
La Crosse-Onalaska, WI-MN	4,668	93.3%	21,809	30.7%	61.1%	7.0%	1.3%	0.0%	14,177	78.7%	16.1%	2.0%	3.2%	0.0%
Lafayette, LA	21,756	80.9%	47,710	71.4%	27.4%	0.5%	0.5%	0.2%	64,879	73.4%	24.1%	1.5%	0.8%	0.3%
Lafayette-West Lafayette, IN	6,539	88.3%	48,319	43.7%	44.8%	3.6%	2.4%	5.5%	25,533	74.2%	21.2%	0.5%	1.1%	3.1%
Lake Charles, LA	8,364	88.9%	19,506	78.3%	16.4%	2.9%	1.8%	0.4%	27,030	75.9%	18.4%	3.2%	2.5%	0.0%
Lake Havasu City-Kingman, AZ	6,427	61.7%	12,700	56.4%	36.9%	4.2%	2.5%	0.0%	19,440	50.2%	38.8%	6.7%	2.5%	1.8%
Lakeland-Winter Haven, FL	25,335	87.8%	56,070	78.5%	15.8%	2.0%	2.8%	0.9%	76,330	76.5%	17.9%	2.8%	1.4%	1.3%
Lancaster, PA	22,072	90.4%	51,481	78.0%	20.2%	0.1%	0.9%	0.3%	59,762	76.1%	20.2%	0.0%	2.8%	0.9%
Lansing-East Lansing, MI	18,026	84.3%	71,250	52.6%	42.0%	0.7%	2.7%	2.0%	56,299	67.0%	28.1%	1.0%	2.9%	1.0%
Laredo, TX	14,816	95.9%	30,472	89.9%	7.8%	0.0%	0.0%	2.3%	30,918	86.3%	12.8%	0.0%	0.5%	0.5%
Las Cruces, NM	8,988	89.7%	30,410	74.9%	20.0%	1.0%	4.1%	0.0%	24,696	83.4%	10.0%	3.3%	2.8%	0.5%
Las Vegas-Henderson-Paradise, NV	80,966	80.8%	186,180	70.3%	22.4%	3.9%	2.7%	0.6%	284,231	70.4%	21.3%	5.0%	2.3%	1.0%
Lawrence, KS	2,982	68.5%	27,314	38.8%	40.6%	5.2%	8.1%	7.3%	16,467	78.0%	12.4%	1.2%	6.8%	1.6%
Lawton, OK	4,823	71.9%	15,217	56.9%	15.7%	8.1%	17.7%	1.6%	20,264	57.1%	27.6%	4.8%	9.4%	1.2%
Lebanon, PA	4,416	93.2%	12,415	64.2%	34.8%	0.0%	0.0%	1.0%	12,915	82.4%	17.6%	0.0%	0.0%	0.0%
Lewiston, ID-WA	1,867	75.9%	6,370	45.7%	43.2%	8.0%	0.7%	2.5%	6,197	61.5%	31.3%	7.3%	0.0%	0.0%
Lewiston-Auburn, ME	4,002	89.0%	9,422	53.2%	42.1%	2.8%	1.8%	0.0%	10,928	72.7%	27.3%	0.0%	0.0%	0.0%
Lexington-Fayette, KY	18,842	87.2%	58,755	60.0%	30.6%	3.4%	4.8%	1.3%	67,204	67.7%	23.4%	4.0%	3.9%	1.0%
Lima, OH	4,020	95.4%	9,702	64.7%	24.8%	4.3%	6.2%	0.0%	11,532	74.3%	18.7%	5.2%	1.8%	0.0%
Lincoln, NE	9,830	93.6%	46,333	51.9%	41.8%	3.2%	2.2%	0.9%	43,067	74.0%	20.4%	0.4%	3.0%	2.2%

Table J-4: Metropolitan/Micropolitan Statistical Areas—Mobility Status by Age—*Continued*

| | 15 to 17 | | 18 to 24 | | | | | | 25 to 33 | | | | | |
| | | | | | Percent Living in a Different House | | | | | | Percent Living in a Different House | | | |
	Total Population	Percent Living in Same House	Total Population	Percent Living in Same House	Same State	Different State, Same Region	Different Region	Outside US	Total Population	Percent Living in Same House	Same State	Different State, Same Region	Different Region	Outside US
Little Rock-North Little Rock-Conway, AR	28,782	85.1%	71,322	64.7%	30.7%	1.7%	2.3%	0.5%	97,350	74.3%	22.4%	1.7%	1.4%	0.2%
Logan, UT-ID	6,533	90.4%	22,240	67.7%	22.2%	2.6%	4.7%	2.9%	19,385	68.4%	22.7%	4.1%	1.8%	3.1%
Longview, TX	8,120	93.0%	19,837	76.5%	20.1%	2.3%	0.1%	1.0%	24,380	69.8%	28.1%	1.6%	0.5%	0.0%
Longview, WA	3,413	87.9%	6,540	44.1%	52.1%	2.0%	0.0%	1.8%	12,790	70.3%	27.4%	1.7%	0.0%	0.6%
Los Angeles-Long Beach-Anaheim, CA	510,482	90.6%	1,319,589	81.5%	14.6%	0.6%	1.6%	1.7%	1,818,998	80.5%	16.0%	0.5%	1.6%	1.4%
Louisville/Jefferson County, KY-IN	51,081	91.4%	108,623	75.4%	19.6%	2.0%	2.4%	0.7%	151,229	78.2%	18.0%	0.9%	2.8%	0.1%
Lubbock, TX	12,342	77.2%	53,067	49.4%	44.5%	1.0%	3.2%	1.9%	42,819	63.4%	33.8%	0.7%	0.9%	1.3%
Lumberton, NC	5,362	96.8%	13,854	83.8%	13.3%	1.9%	0.8%	0.2%	13,331	91.7%	7.1%	1.0%	0.0%	0.1%
Lynchburg, VA	10,793	90.3%	32,903	66.9%	21.3%	4.4%	5.7%	1.8%	27,594	75.3%	23.7%	0.9%	0.0%	0.0%
Macon, GA	8,744	91.1%	25,465	67.5%	30.9%	0.7%	0.3%	0.7%	23,089	76.7%	21.3%	1.1%	0.6%	0.4%
Madera, CA	6,628	95.2%	15,683	93.2%	6.8%	0.0%	0.0%	0.0%	19,229	87.4%	10.7%	1.9%	0.0%	0.0%
Madison, WI	23,576	90.8%	79,957	44.0%	40.2%	7.4%	4.7%	3.8%	88,503	70.4%	22.3%	3.7%	2.3%	1.3%
Manchester-Nashua, NH	16,014	89.0%	37,376	71.7%	20.5%	4.4%	2.4%	1.0%	45,577	71.2%	20.5%	4.9%	2.7%	0.7%
Manhattan, KS	3,864	82.8%	23,702	59.4%	19.5%	6.6%	6.9%	7.6%	16,967	67.3%	18.1%	0.0%	4.0%	10.6%
Mankato-North Mankato, MN	3,863	98.4%	18,713	70.0%	21.4%	5.6%	1.8%	1.2%	11,901	69.9%	23.2%	1.4%	5.6%	0.0%
Mansfield, OH	4,664	97.2%	10,805	75.4%	24.6%	0.0%	0.0%	0.0%	12,484	63.9%	36.1%	0.0%	0.0%	0.0%
McAllen-Edinburg-Mission, TX	43,446	94.6%	91,885	87.7%	11.4%	0.3%	0.2%	0.4%	96,344	88.1%	10.8%	0.3%	0.0%	0.7%
Medford, OR	7,333	86.2%	16,260	62.7%	27.6%	5.5%	3.7%	0.5%	24,414	71.1%	19.1%	7.3%	2.3%	0.3%
Memphis, TN-MS-AR	60,612	85.8%	128,977	72.5%	20.9%	3.8%	1.8%	1.0%	168,135	75.5%	19.6%	3.4%	0.9%	0.6%
Merced, CA	12,527	94.4%	32,689	72.9%	22.7%	1.1%	1.4%	1.9%	33,141	81.5%	18.0%	0.0%	0.5%	0.0%
Meridian, MS	4,691	95.4%	10,313	77.0%	17.5%	1.2%	4.2%	0.0%	12,320	77.2%	20.3%	1.4%	1.1%	0.0%
Miami-Fort Lauderdale-West Palm Beach, FL	215,129	86.8%	501,872	80.5%	15.2%	0.6%	1.5%	2.2%	724,010	77.6%	17.5%	1.0%	1.7%	2.2%
Michigan City-La Porte, IN	4,374	88.1%	8,713	65.5%	31.6%	1.9%	1.0%	0.0%	12,832	60.1%	35.1%	2.8%	2.0%	0.0%
Midland, MI	3,948	99.7%	6,706	76.1%	22.4%	0.1%	1.3%	0.0%	9,554	81.6%	16.2%	0.0%	0.0%	2.2%
Midland, TX	7,619	92.6%	17,003	62.9%	32.0%	2.1%	2.3%	0.8%	25,882	68.4%	25.1%	0.4%	2.8%	3.4%
Milwaukee-Waukesha-West Allis, WI	62,538	86.7%	143,449	69.2%	25.1%	2.9%	1.4%	1.4%	191,155	74.0%	22.3%	1.4%	1.5%	0.9%
Minneapolis-St. Paul-Bloomington, MN-WI	141,393	91.4%	291,586	68.5%	25.7%	3.2%	1.8%	0.9%	460,174	73.2%	20.7%	2.1%	2.3%	1.7%
Missoula, MT	4,696	97.7%	14,769	51.8%	38.9%	5.3%	4.1%	0.0%	17,127	84.2%	8.4%	0.9%	6.6%	0.0%
Mobile, AL	17,044	88.2%	37,483	75.6%	21.9%	2.0%	0.2%	0.3%	53,577	80.2%	17.4%	1.2%	0.2%	1.0%
Modesto, CA	20,440	88.5%	41,049	75.6%	23.2%	0.1%	0.4%	0.7%	52,079	81.2%	15.7%	0.2%	1.5%	1.4%
Monroe, LA	7,508	85.0%	17,986	80.0%	16.4%	3.2%	0.4%	0.0%	23,237	77.1%	17.8%	3.2%	1.4%	0.5%
Monroe, MI	6,328	97.0%	11,950	80.8%	18.0%	1.2%	0.0%	0.0%	15,224	78.3%	20.0%	1.6%	0.0%	0.0%
Montgomery, AL	15,184	82.4%	36,863	67.7%	29.5%	1.9%	0.4%	0.5%	46,764	71.5%	26.0%	1.7%	0.4%	0.5%
Morgantown, WV	3,909	86.2%	25,885	65.2%	25.1%	5.8%	3.9%	0.0%	21,424	84.4%	12.3%	0.8%	2.2%	0.3%
Morristown, TN	6,348	97.0%	9,800	75.3%	21.9%	0.0%	2.3%	0.5%	10,630	86.0%	12.6%	1.4%	0.0%	0.0%
Mount Vernon-Anacortes, WA	4,657	94.2%	8,948	72.2%	20.9%	4.7%	2.2%	0.0%	13,682	65.9%	23.7%	3.7%	5.8%	1.0%
Muncie, IN	3,898	82.9%	22,931	48.4%	44.5%	6.5%	0.7%	0.0%	10,355	65.8%	32.1%	0.6%	1.4%	0.0%
Muskegon, MI	6,611	80.5%	14,864	61.0%	38.0%	1.0%	0.0%	0.0%	20,232	74.2%	23.8%	0.5%	1.5%	0.0%
Myrtle Beach-Conway-North Myrtle Beach, SC-NC	14,597	91.1%	33,252	71.2%	19.5%	5.1%	3.5%	0.8%	42,738	71.9%	23.6%	1.9%	2.5%	0.1%
Napa, CA	5,350	80.8%	13,069	84.4%	12.8%	0.1%	2.0%	0.7%	14,989	63.4%	34.1%	0.2%	1.8%	0.6%
Naples-Immokalee-Marco Island, FL	11,293	84.5%	25,881	81.9%	11.8%	1.2%	4.2%	0.8%	30,802	73.6%	16.8%	3.0%	3.5%	3.0%
Nashville-Davidson-Murfreesboro-Franklin, TN	73,518	86.6%	175,465	69.2%	23.2%	3.9%	3.1%	0.6%	239,003	69.6%	23.7%	2.7%	2.7%	1.3%
New Bern, NC	4,030	84.7%	15,041	59.3%	30.8%	6.2%	2.1%	1.6%	15,525	67.9%	23.5%	3.4%	3.6%	1.6%
New Castle, PA	3,319	97.5%	6,676	78.1%	15.1%	0.9%	5.9%	0.0%	8,911	85.9%	7.8%	0.0%	6.3%	0.0%
New Haven-Milford, CT	33,493	90.4%	87,288	82.2%	13.8%	2.0%	1.1%	0.9%	99,958	78.8%	14.9%	1.6%	3.8%	0.9%
New Orleans-Metairie, LA	47,760	90.6%	107,238	80.0%	13.6%	4.3%	1.8%	0.3%	173,863	78.0%	16.7%	2.8%	1.6%	0.9%
New Philadelphia-Dover, OH	4,220	91.1%	7,080	74.5%	18.5%	0.0%	7.0%	0.0%	9,522	77.0%	20.4%	1.4%	1.3%	0.0%
New York-Newark-Jersey City, NY-NJ-PA	739,304	94.3%	1,823,529	85.3%	9.6%	1.6%	1.8%	1.8%	2,633,412	82.3%	13.4%	1.4%	1.5%	1.4%
Niles-Benton Harbor, MI	5,752	71.9%	12,450	63.1%	29.6%	2.5%	4.9%	0.0%	15,966	60.6%	31.1%	1.9%	5.1%	1.3%
North Port-Sarasota-Bradenton, FL	23,491	86.7%	49,953	74.1%	20.3%	2.0%	2.6%	1.1%	64,800	75.3%	19.7%	2.4%	1.8%	0.8%
Norwich-New London, CT	10,589	88.7%	28,636	72.4%	14.0%	3.1%	10.5%	0.0%	31,833	74.4%	17.2%	3.5%	3.2%	1.7%
Ocala, FL	11,395	93.5%	25,183	78.7%	15.9%	3.2%	2.2%	0.0%	33,781	71.4%	24.3%	2.1%	1.7%	0.5%
Ocean City, NJ	3,824	99.5%	6,265	78.7%	10.2%	1.4%	9.8%	0.0%	8,722	74.4%	17.5%	3.7%	3.1%	1.3%
Odessa, TX	7,443	84.2%	18,034	73.2%	25.1%	0.9%	0.6%	0.2%	24,031	70.7%	24.5%	1.8%	0.3%	2.6%
Ogden-Clearfield, UT	30,773	90.7%	61,568	71.6%	19.3%	1.8%	2.7%	4.6%	83,448	73.6%	20.9%	2.7%	1.8%	1.1%
Ogdensburg-Massena, NY	3,881	91.3%	15,881	61.9%	31.1%	3.8%	1.9%	1.3%	12,327	72.6%	25.5%	1.1%	0.8%	0.0%
Oklahoma City, OK	51,434	87.3%	139,317	64.6%	27.2%	4.0%	2.4%	1.7%	185,033	72.5%	22.8%	1.5%	1.9%	1.3%
Olympia-Tumwater, WA	9,282	84.1%	24,902	63.3%	24.6%	6.5%	3.1%	2.5%	33,146	71.1%	20.6%	3.4%	3.6%	1.2%
Omaha-Council Bluffs, NE-IA	37,769	87.1%	80,083	64.3%	27.0%	4.7%	3.0%	1.0%	120,657	75.0%	19.7%	2.7%	2.1%	0.5%
Orangeburg, SC	3,765	95.0%	7,609	94.5%	5.5%	0.0%	0.0%	0.0%	11,524	92.5%	6.8%	0.7%	0.0%	0.0%
Orlando-Kissimmee-Sanford, FL	95,185	86.7%	235,677	73.6%	20.0%	1.4%	3.1%	1.8%	317,056	71.1%	22.1%	1.6%	2.6%	2.7%
Oshkosh-Neenah, WI	6,316	97.7%	19,273	59.6%	37.0%	3.2%	0.2%	0.0%	21,198	84.2%	13.3%	2.5%	0.0%	0.0%
Ottawa-Peru, IL	4,432	89.4%	8,885	79.0%	13.7%	0.5%	6.9%	0.0%	11,899	75.3%	24.3%	0.1%	0.3%	0.0%
Owensboro, KY	4,641	78.6%	9,474	76.4%	23.1%	0.5%	0.0%	0.0%	13,140	77.2%	12.2%	1.2%	4.0%	5.3%
Oxnard-Thousand Oaks-Ventura, CA	34,640	91.0%	82,021	86.6%	11.5%	0.6%	0.6%	0.7%	100,843	79.3%	18.3%	0.4%	1.4%	0.7%
Palm Bay-Melbourne-Titusville, FL	20,157	79.5%	45,039	70.1%	19.9%	5.4%	3.9%	0.7%	55,168	72.1%	17.2%	5.2%	3.8%	1.7%
Panama City, FL	7,111	88.0%	16,270	77.5%	14.1%	4.0%	3.5%	0.9%	25,575	68.6%	24.4%	2.3%	4.4%	0.2%
Parkersburg-Vienna, WV	3,452	95.6%	7,321	68.6%	14.6%	0.9%	15.9%	0.0%	9,395	87.0%	13.0%	0.0%	0.0%	0.0%
Pensacola-Ferry Pass-Brent, FL	17,090	80.9%	53,366	61.9%	20.7%	8.7%	8.4%	0.3%	61,648	67.0%	23.6%	6.1%	2.6%	0.7%
Peoria, IL	14,472	88.2%	31,355	64.2%	31.2%	3.0%	1.6%	0.0%	44,780	76.8%	20.3%	0.3%	1.7%	0.9%

Table J-4: Metropolitan/Micropolitan Statistical Areas—Mobility Status by Age—*Continued*

| | 15 to 17 | | 18 to 24 | | | | | | 25 to 33 | | | | | |
| | | | | | Percent Living in a Different House | | | | | | Percent Living in a Different House | | | |
	Total Population	Percent Living in Same House	Total Population	Percent Living in Same House	Same State	Different State, Same Region	Different Region	Outside US	Total Population	Percent Living in Same House	Same State	Different State, Same Region	Different Region	Outside US
Philadelphia-Camden-Wilmington, PA-NJ-DE-MD	228,602	92.3%	558,640	79.7%	14.8%	2.2%	2.3%	0.9%	767,447	77.1%	17.1%	2.1%	2.6%	1.2%
Phoenix-Mesa-Scottsdale, AZ	190,301	86.5%	427,612	69.9%	22.8%	3.2%	2.8%	1.3%	573,047	72.6%	20.7%	2.5%	3.3%	0.9%
Pine Bluff, AR	3,536	81.3%	9,044	73.2%	25.1%	0.0%	1.6%	0.0%	9,911	80.0%	20.0%	0.0%	0.0%	0.0%
Pittsburgh, PA	82,813	91.0%	202,145	69.3%	24.4%	1.4%	3.5%	1.3%	274,703	73.7%	21.0%	0.5%	3.8%	0.9%
Pittsfield, MA	4,397	89.2%	13,210	65.2%	21.9%	8.9%	2.8%	1.3%	10,682	83.8%	8.2%	1.3%	5.0%	1.6%
Pocatello, ID	3,418	91.9%	9,910	57.6%	34.7%	6.9%	0.1%	0.7%	11,138	57.4%	28.0%	9.1%	3.6%	1.9%
Port St. Lucie, FL	19,311	92.0%	46,415	62.9%	27.8%	5.4%	3.2%	0.8%	56,267	68.3%	24.8%	4.8%	1.7%	0.5%
Portland-South Portland, ME	92,345	88.3%	201,224	66.9%	22.7%	7.3%	2.1%	0.9%	320,617	66.9%	23.9%	5.1%	2.9%	1.2%
Portland-Vancouver-Hillsboro, OR-WA	15,004	85.5%	33,555	76.2%	15.4%	0.2%	4.4%	3.8%	43,439	70.6%	25.2%	1.4%	1.1%	1.7%
Pottsville, PA	5,347	97.0%	10,180	84.2%	15.0%	0.0%	0.5%	0.3%	14,846	77.6%	20.3%	0.5%	1.6%	0.0%
Prescott, AZ	6,488	68.9%	15,292	59.9%	21.1%	13.3%	3.7%	2.0%	18,013	81.4%	16.6%	1.1%	0.8%	0.0%
Providence-Warwick, RI-MA	56,940	90.4%	165,357	74.7%	17.9%	4.1%	1.9%	1.4%	192,565	76.5%	17.5%	2.5%	2.9%	0.7%
Provo-Orem, UT	30,616	87.6%	94,597	48.6%	32.6%	7.5%	3.9%	7.3%	73,075	68.9%	25.0%	3.8%	1.2%	1.1%
Pueblo, CO	6,532	83.4%	15,000	67.7%	28.0%	1.3%	3.0%	0.0%	19,140	73.8%	22.6%	1.3%	2.3%	0.0%
Punta Gorda, FL	4,383	77.6%	9,538	89.1%	10.3%	0.7%	0.0%	0.0%	9,228	68.3%	24.8%	0.0%	6.9%	0.0%
Racine, WI	8,017	93.3%	17,832	83.4%	15.9%	0.7%	0.0%	0.0%	19,655	75.9%	22.8%	0.8%	0.5%	0.0%
Raleigh, NC	51,758	92.5%	113,029	70.6%	24.4%	1.4%	2.9%	0.6%	163,616	69.9%	23.8%	3.0%	2.4%	1.0%
Rapid City, SD	6,086	78.4%	11,262	48.1%	31.3%	9.1%	11.0%	0.5%	19,292	67.3%	23.8%	1.2%	7.8%	0.0%
Reading, PA	17,087	87.5%	41,421	79.1%	18.5%	0.7%	0.9%	0.9%	45,238	78.5%	17.6%	2.5%	0.7%	0.7%
Redding, CA	6,824	84.7%	12,988	75.7%	18.9%	3.3%	0.0%	2.0%	20,642	73.7%	21.1%	0.1%	2.1%	3.1%
Reno, NV	16,893	91.5%	40,446	62.9%	29.3%	5.2%	2.0%	0.6%	58,210	65.5%	26.4%	5.4%	2.0%	0.7%
Richmond, VA	49,670	89.7%	122,167	67.2%	27.1%	2.5%	2.3%	0.8%	159,399	67.6%	26.5%	2.7%	2.0%	1.2%
Riverside-San Bernardino-Ontario, CA	204,993	87.3%	473,053	79.3%	17.9%	0.6%	1.5%	0.8%	564,925	80.0%	17.7%	0.6%	0.9%	0.7%
Roanoke, VA	10,656	86.5%	27,298	61.6%	31.2%	2.1%	2.6%	2.5%	34,962	65.2%	31.7%	0.9%	0.3%	1.9%
Rochester, MN	7,236	92.5%	20,720	61.2%	33.6%	5.0%	0.2%	0.0%	23,747	80.6%	14.5%	0.3%	3.5%	1.2%
Rochester, NY	40,645	90.4%	110,492	62.8%	30.8%	2.1%	2.6%	1.8%	127,894	71.0%	24.1%	2.1%	1.4%	1.4%
Rockford, IL	14,502	92.1%	28,540	80.0%	16.8%	0.4%	2.8%	0.0%	37,019	81.0%	17.8%	0.4%	0.5%	0.3%
Rocky Mount, NC	6,288	87.2%	13,362	72.6%	26.1%	0.4%	0.1%	0.8%	14,191	89.0%	11.0%	0.0%	0.0%	0.0%
Rome, GA	3,826	82.5%	9,179	83.0%	15.1%	1.9%	0.0%	0.0%	11,680	69.4%	28.6%	1.8%	0.1%	0.0%
Roseburg, OR	3,303	76.4%	7,366	75.4%	22.6%	2.0%	0.0%	0.0%	10,908	80.1%	19.6%	0.0%	0.0%	0.3%
Sacramento-Roseville-Arden-Arcade, CA	88,053	88.1%	218,161	71.0%	25.3%	1.1%	0.9%	1.7%	204,903	72.6%	23.0%	1.1%	1.0%	1.2%
Saginaw, MI	6,999	79.9%	20,018	72.6%	25.9%	0.0%	1.1%	0.5%	21,353	73.6%	24.3%	0.0%	0.8%	1.2%
Salem, OH	8,303	92.8%	25,879	57.4%	38.2%	2.9%	0.2%	1.2%	23,951	64.3%	33.0%	1.7%	0.3%	0.7%
Salem, OR	7,485	89.4%	16,709	62.8%	29.7%	4.5%	2.0%	0.9%	15,243	61.1%	33.2%	2.8%	2.9%	0.0%
Salinas, CA	5,145	68.6%	11,288	66.4%	28.3%	0.7%	0.0%	4.6%	16,906	60.5%	33.9%	1.2%	2.0%	2.3%
Salisbury, MD-DE	110,903	88.5%	248,328	72.8%	21.5%	2.1%	2.5%	1.0%	335,801	75.7%	19.9%	2.0%	2.0%	0.5%
Salt Lake City, UT	4,005	95.0%	7,504	76.5%	22.8%	0.0%	0.8%	0.0%	9,881	86.5%	10.6%	0.0%	2.9%	0.0%
San Angelo, TX	18,605	85.5%	40,898	67.1%	28.4%	2.4%	0.5%	1.7%	46,862	77.5%	19.1%	1.9%	1.1%	0.4%
San Antonio-New Braunfels, TX	16,757	88.6%	45,593	75.2%	17.1%	2.5%	4.4%	0.8%	55,988	77.5%	16.8%	1.8%	1.8%	2.1%
San Diego-Carlsbad, CA	13,202	84.5%	39,103	70.2%	24.5%	2.9%	1.9%	0.6%	37,612	74.2%	23.1%	1.9%	0.8%	0.0%
San Francisco-Oakland-Hayward, CA	53,238	92.8%	114,848	69.5%	23.3%	2.9%	3.0%	1.3%	169,969	72.7%	22.7%	2.5%	1.6%	0.6%
San Jose-Sunnyvale-Santa Clara, CA	4,513	90.8%	15,384	49.8%	33.0%	8.6%	8.2%	0.4%	16,742	84.1%	8.1%	1.7%	6.0%	0.0%
San Luis Obispo-Paso Robles-Arroyo Grande, CA	104,960	87.4%	246,793	71.7%	24.9%	1.2%	1.3%	0.9%	322,810	71.7%	23.7%	0.7%	2.8%	1.1%
Santa Cruz-Watsonville, CA	117,600	88.3%	352,905	73.1%	20.7%	0.9%	3.0%	2.2%	473,892	73.7%	20.1%	0.5%	3.4%	2.3%
Santa Fe, NM	149,580	91.6%	375,073	73.9%	19.3%	1.2%	2.5%	3.1%	656,416	76.1%	17.5%	1.0%	3.2%	2.2%
Santa Maria-Santa Barbara, CA	69,917	92.0%	171,407	76.7%	17.3%	1.4%	3.0%	1.7%	267,421	73.5%	18.4%	0.8%	3.8%	3.5%
Santa Rosa, CA	8,526	92.1%	42,216	76.9%	17.8%	1.7%	3.2%	0.5%	30,829	72.0%	24.8%	0.7%	2.3%	0.3%
Savannah, GA	8,920	85.8%	42,214	67.6%	28.9%	0.7%	2.0%	0.9%	30,305	76.1%	20.0%	0.0%	3.1%	0.8%
Scranton–Wilkes-Barre–Hazleton, PA	4,909	97.2%	11,025	82.1%	11.6%	0.2%	6.1%	0.0%	15,060	77.7%	14.0%	3.2%	4.1%	0.9%
Seattle-Tacoma-Bellevue, WA	16,101	93.7%	71,192	51.7%	42.2%	1.3%	1.5%	3.3%	49,128	71.8%	20.9%	2.0%	4.2%	1.0%
Sebastian-Vero Beach, FL	17,598	87.8%	43,756	75.6%	21.9%	1.3%	0.5%	0.7%	57,264	77.6%	17.8%	0.7%	2.5%	1.4%
Sebring, FL	11,545	87.4%	47,166	55.9%	32.6%	6.1%	3.4%	2.0%	51,530	62.1%	24.3%	7.4%	5.5%	0.7%
Sheboygan, WI	20,854	91.1%	51,810	73.6%	21.2%	3.8%	1.3%	0.0%	58,176	79.6%	16.9%	1.0%	1.1%	1.4%
Sherman-Denison, TX	132,418	86.2%	317,404	64.0%	26.9%	3.8%	3.7%	1.6%	543,759	67.4%	24.6%	2.6%	3.2%	2.3%
Show Low, AZ	4,007	85.7%	11,503	82.8%	13.9%	2.1%	1.2%	0.0%	11,380	76.9%	15.5%	5.3%	2.0%	0.3%
Shreveport-Bossier City, LA	3,191	83.4%	6,255	72.1%	23.5%	2.8%	0.0%	1.5%	7,714	81.0%	14.8%	1.1%	0.6%	2.6%
Sierra Vista-Douglas, AZ	4,661	85.8%	8,517	63.0%	28.8%	8.2%	0.0%	0.0%	11,780	69.5%	27.4%	2.8%	0.0%	0.3%
Sioux City, IA-NE-SD	4,855	76.3%	12,228	66.0%	29.2%	0.6%	3.3%	1.0%	12,709	67.4%	28.4%	2.0%	2.3%	0.0%
Sioux Falls, SD	4,733	97.3%	9,752	79.8%	17.4%	1.4%	1.0%	0.4%	11,618	81.3%	17.5%	0.4%	0.6%	0.1%
South Bend-Mishawaka, IN-MI	17,025	84.4%	40,935	74.9%	18.9%	3.8%	1.7%	0.7%	57,754	81.2%	15.1%	1.7%	1.8%	0.1%
Spartanburg, SC	5,031	81.5%	9,550	60.8%	21.5%	1.3%	13.9%	2.5%	14,841	71.7%	18.7%	1.9%	6.9%	0.8%
Spokane-Spokane Valley, WA	7,620	84.4%	14,972	64.9%	28.0%	2.8%	4.0%	0.3%	18,340	87.7%	10.4%	1.0%	1.0%	0.0%
Springfield, IL	8,740	96.6%	22,812	42.4%	44.8%	10.1%	2.4%	0.2%	35,376	73.1%	22.0%	0.8%	0.5%	3.5%
Springfield, MA	14,300	89.3%	35,054	63.9%	26.2%	6.6%	1.7%	1.6%	34,788	74.2%	21.4%	2.1%	1.6%	0.7%
Springfield, MO	13,581	90.8%	31,299	75.3%	22.7%	0.8%	1.2%	0.0%	35,076	75.4%	23.0%	1.0%	0.0%	0.5%
Springfield, OH	20,669	85.1%	51,658	53.3%	39.0%	5.7%	1.8%	0.2%	71,816	65.1%	26.4%	3.9%	2.6%	1.9%
St. Cloud, MN	9,140	85.5%	18,486	73.6%	21.9%	1.0%	0.7%	2.9%	23,591	68.9%	26.8%	1.8%	2.5%	0.0%
St. George, UT	25,492	86.4%	81,426	67.9%	25.6%	4.3%	1.9%	0.3%	72,157	77.4%	20.3%	1.3%	0.6%	0.4%
St. Joseph, MO-KS	16,991	85.4%	54,905	56.1%	39.0%	1.6%	2.8%	0.5%	55,847	71.6%	25.0%	1.4%	1.6%	0.3%
St. Louis, MO-IL	5,603	82.7%	11,991	50.5%	45.5%	0.0%	2.3%	1.6%	13,749	70.5%	29.1%	0.0%	0.4%	0.0%

Table J-4: Metropolitan/Micropolitan Statistical Areas—Mobility Status by Age—*Continued*

	15 to 17		18 to 24						25 to 33					
					Percent Living in a Different House						Percent Living in a Different House			
	Total Population	Percent Living in Same House	Total Population	Percent Living in Same House	Same State	Different State, Same Region	Different Region	Outside US	Total Population	Percent Living in Same House	Same State	Different State, Same Region	Different Region	Outside US
State College, PA	3,835	90.5%	41,020	48.1%	39.6%	8.0%	3.3%	1.0%	22,204	76.2%	16.9%	0.0%	4.4%	2.5%
Staunton-Waynesboro, VA	3,536	89.8%	13,370	66.1%	27.2%	2.3%	4.2%	0.1%	11,802	80.7%	14.8%	4.5%	0.0%	0.0%
Stockton-Lodi, CA	33,581	90.7%	72,442	78.5%	18.4%	1.7%	0.9%	0.6%	88,953	79.1%	18.2%	1.1%	1.2%	0.5%
Sumter, SC	4,406	89.1%	13,392	81.7%	14.0%	1.5%	1.9%	0.9%	12,191	64.5%	31.7%	1.8%	0.0%	1.9%
Sunbury, PA	3,106	93.4%	6,642	86.8%	13.2%	0.0%	0.0%	0.0%	10,582	73.6%	25.6%	0.8%	0.0%	0.0%
Syracuse, NY	27,214	90.2%	71,499	66.4%	25.8%	2.4%	3.1%	2.3%	73,891	77.1%	20.6%	0.6%	0.9%	0.7%
Tallahassee, FL	12,444	88.4%	70,917	50.1%	46.0%	2.3%	0.6%	1.0%	47,845	65.6%	29.3%	2.7%	1.7%	0.7%
Tampa-St. Petersburg-Clearwater, FL	104,762	84.4%	239,308	74.7%	19.3%	1.5%	3.3%	1.2%	343,205	73.7%	20.5%	1.6%	3.3%	1.0%
Terre Haute, IN	7,338	91.0%	21,742	54.9%	37.1%	3.0%	4.4%	0.6%	18,309	72.3%	25.0%	0.0%	2.7%	0.0%
Texarkana, TX-AR	5,896	78.4%	13,517	71.4%	18.8%	9.4%	0.4%	0.0%	16,886	77.3%	17.2%	4.9%	0.5%	0.1%
The Villages, FL	2,181	88.1%	4,981	65.5%	32.4%	2.0%	0.0%	0.0%	3,847	60.6%	36.7%	0.0%	1.5%	1.2%
Toledo, OH	24,573	81.4%	67,145	55.9%	37.5%	3.3%	1.9%	1.4%	71,852	68.8%	25.3%	1.0%	3.8%	1.1%
Topeka, KS	9,187	88.3%	19,269	55.2%	38.2%	2.4%	3.3%	0.9%	25,917	67.9%	24.4%	1.7%	5.4%	0.5%
Torrington, CT	6,694	96.8%	13,568	75.6%	22.2%	1.4%	0.8%	0.0%	16,493	81.1%	17.5%	0.0%	0.9%	0.5%
Traverse City, MI	5,897	86.6%	11,620	66.4%	30.7%	1.2%	1.8%	0.0%	14,212	67.4%	27.0%	3.6%	2.1%	0.0%
Trenton, NJ	14,301	88.7%	42,985	77.9%	16.1%	3.2%	2.4%	0.3%	39,325	78.0%	15.7%	3.6%	1.5%	1.2%
Truckee-Grass Valley, CA	3,189	97.6%	6,149	77.1%	22.9%	0.0%	0.0%	0.0%	9,555	90.9%	7.7%	1.4%	0.0%	0.0%
Tucson, AZ	37,110	84.4%	118,139	56.3%	34.4%	4.9%	2.9%	1.5%	109,878	67.0%	26.2%	2.5%	2.5%	1.9%
Tullahoma-Manchester, TN	4,072	76.9%	9,870	77.8%	16.4%	1.2%	4.5%	0.0%	9,752	58.8%	17.8%	7.6%	15.9%	0.0%
Tulsa, OK	39,744	83.3%	90,037	68.7%	23.1%	3.1%	4.0%	1.2%	118,952	71.7%	22.6%	1.8%	2.2%	1.6%
Tupelo, MS	5,865	80.8%	13,296	60.1%	37.1%	0.5%	2.2%	0.0%	14,686	80.3%	18.2%	1.5%	0.0%	0.0%
Tuscaloosa, AL	8,900	88.2%	40,320	64.8%	23.9%	5.7%	5.4%	0.1%	31,163	81.8%	14.7%	2.5%	0.2%	0.8%
Tyler, TX	8,737	94.0%	22,578	67.3%	32.1%	0.3%	0.2%	0.0%	28,149	79.8%	19.4%	0.7%	0.2%	0.0%
Urban Honolulu, HI	30,847	91.9%	104,107	76.5%	12.7%	4.0%	4.5%	2.4%	138,456	73.2%	15.8%	3.0%	6.1%	1.9%
Utica-Rome, NY	10,563	89.0%	27,051	78.4%	17.7%	2.3%	1.2%	0.4%	31,574	71.0%	26.5%	0.0%	2.0%	0.5%
Valdosta, GA	5,450	88.2%	21,265	70.9%	25.2%	0.7%	1.3%	1.9%	19,484	65.4%	26.2%	2.7%	3.4%	2.4%
Vallejo-Fairfield, CA	16,430	89.9%	40,269	72.0%	22.0%	3.1%	1.8%	1.0%	55,432	73.0%	20.8%	1.7%	2.8%	1.7%
Victoria, TX	4,352	90.6%	9,641	79.3%	18.1%	0.7%	1.9%	0.0%	11,608	62.8%	30.4%	2.7%	0.0%	4.0%
Vineland-Bridgeton, NJ	6,209	98.2%	12,703	81.1%	15.6%	1.7%	1.6%	0.0%	21,889	78.0%	20.9%	0.8%	0.2%	0.0%
Virginia Beach-Norfolk-Newport News, VA-NC	65,605	86.1%	196,229	60.6%	24.5%	5.9%	7.6%	1.4%	246,051	67.9%	24.0%	3.1%	3.4%	1.5%
Visalia-Porterville, CA	23,180	91.2%	48,480	82.3%	17.0%	0.0%	0.1%	0.6%	59,578	84.8%	14.2%	0.3%	0.0%	0.7%
Waco, TX	11,522	86.3%	37,304	64.5%	32.5%	1.3%	1.6%	0.1%	29,407	76.8%	19.7%	0.7%	2.3%	0.5%
Walla Walla, WA	2,280	91.8%	6,587	76.9%	16.9%	6.2%	0.0%	0.0%	8,751	69.0%	26.2%	4.4%	0.0%	0.5%
Warner Robins, GA	7,432	83.1%	20,524	69.3%	27.4%	1.8%	1.5%	0.0%	21,473	74.0%	21.4%	2.3%	1.3%	1.1%
Washington-Arlington-Alexandria, DC-VA-MD-WV	226,857	89.5%	547,140	71.7%	16.8%	4.6%	5.1%	1.8%	831,802	71.9%	18.1%	4.8%	3.0%	2.1%
Waterloo-Cedar Falls, IA	5,818	96.9%	23,786	45.9%	42.9%	6.9%	3.9%	0.4%	21,302	76.2%	20.0%	2.7%	1.1%	0.0%
Watertown-Fort Drum, NY	4,197	92.9%	15,185	58.1%	19.3%	0.4%	16.2%	6.1%	16,496	64.1%	17.5%	1.2%	12.3%	4.9%
Wausau, WI	5,541	97.1%	9,696	73.3%	23.0%	0.0%	1.9%	1.8%	14,255	84.6%	13.8%	1.1%	0.5%	0.0%
Weirton-Steubenville, WV-OH	4,018	97.3%	11,083	87.6%	1.3%	0.0%	11.1%	0.0%	12,289	80.9%	8.9%	2.3%	7.5%	0.4%
Wenatchee, WA	4,331	91.1%	9,272	76.3%	22.6%	1.1%	0.0%	0.0%	12,335	79.6%	20.4%	0.0%	0.0%	0.0%
Wheeling, WV-OH	4,754	96.0%	13,727	85.5%	5.5%	0.0%	8.9%	0.0%	13,508	82.6%	8.1%	2.1%	6.8%	0.4%
Whitewater-Elkhorn, WI	3,868	76.2%	13,278	58.0%	32.6%	8.3%	0.0%	1.1%	10,055	73.7%	21.3%	1.1%	2.9%	1.2%
Wichita Falls, TX	29,379	89.4%	55,459	71.8%	22.9%	1.9%	3.2%	0.3%	85,074	76.8%	19.7%	0.9%	1.9%	0.6%
Wichita, KS	5,511	87.3%	20,494	55.4%	26.8%	9.0%	7.2%	1.5%	18,911	80.2%	17.1%	0.4%	2.4%	0.0%
Williamsport, PA	3,675	80.0%	12,018	79.8%	14.9%	0.5%	3.0%	1.9%	12,412	71.6%	26.2%	0.0%	1.9%	0.3%
Wilmington, NC	10,816	83.4%	32,247	61.1%	33.5%	3.8%	1.3%	0.4%	32,831	73.5%	21.9%	2.8%	1.5%	0.4%
Winchester, VA-WV	4,392	92.6%	12,202	85.6%	10.8%	3.2%	0.5%	0.0%	12,830	73.4%	20.5%	3.6%	0.8%	1.6%
Winston-Salem, NC	26,937	87.4%	59,671	76.4%	17.9%	2.7%	2.4%	0.6%	72,612	70.5%	22.0%	4.3%	2.8%	0.4%
Wooster, OH	5,538	81.3%	11,242	62.4%	32.9%	0.2%	3.8%	0.7%	11,235	85.3%	12.6%	1.5%	0.0%	0.6%
Worcester, MA-CT	39,211	91.7%	92,272	75.8%	17.7%	3.4%	1.9%	1.2%	100,837	80.1%	16.4%	1.0%	1.4%	1.1%
Yakima, WA	11,331	95.2%	25,431	78.7%	18.4%	1.5%	1.4%	0.0%	27,580	76.9%	17.7%	2.5%	1.9%	1.1%
York-Hanover, PA	16,774	88.3%	34,937	76.5%	18.9%	0.9%	1.9%	1.8%	50,766	72.6%	21.1%	1.6%	4.5%	0.2%
Youngstown-Warren-Boardman, OH-PA	21,208	90.7%	46,437	76.7%	20.6%	0.2%	2.0%	0.5%	53,069	78.6%	18.0%	0.0%	3.2%	0.3%
Yuba City, CA	6,570	88.9%	15,545	70.7%	25.7%	1.4%	2.0%	0.2%	23,344	63.3%	30.7%	0.6%	4.6%	0.8%
Yuma, AZ	9,130	95.2%	23,041	72.2%	19.4%	1.8%	5.2%	1.4%	25,579	72.3%	21.2%	0.5%	5.4%	0.6%

PART K

HOUSING SUMMARY

As the Baby Boom entered its household formation years in the late 1960s and 1970s, housing development grew to accommodate the growing adult population and their children. As the Millennials enter their household formation years, times have changed. The structure of living arrangements has shifted to more single person households or non-relatives living together. Millennials have delayed marriage and childbearing, and many more are living with other non-relative friends and have pushed home ownership until later in life. One thing that is almost universal, regardless of housing arrangements, is their access to the Internet and use of technology.

The tables presented here are for Millennial householders rather than all persons. The householder is the person who owns or rents the housing unit and other individuals in the household are defined in reference to the householder. This also means that Millennials who live in group quarters (primarily college housing) are excluded because they are not part of the household population and are not householders. While most of the tables in this book relate to the 83.5 million Millennials age 15 to 33, this section describes the housing characteristics for the 20.2 million householders age 18 to 33.

HOUSING STATUS

Nationwide, 78.3 percent of Millennial householders are age 25 to 33 compared to only 21.7 percent in the 18 to 24 age group. Among the 18 to 24 year olds, a little more than one-third (35.4 percent) are householders in North Dakota leaving 64.6 percent for older Millennials. In New Jersey only 13.0 percent of the 18 to 24 year olds are householders making it the highest percentage for the 25 to 33 age group at 87.0 percent.

Tenure describes whether a housing unit is owned or rented. As expected, Millennials in the older age group are more frequently owners compared to the younger ages. Among the 18 to 24 year olds, 87 percent are renters compared to 64.3 percent of the older age group.

Percent of Millennials Age 18 to 33 Who Are Home Owner Households

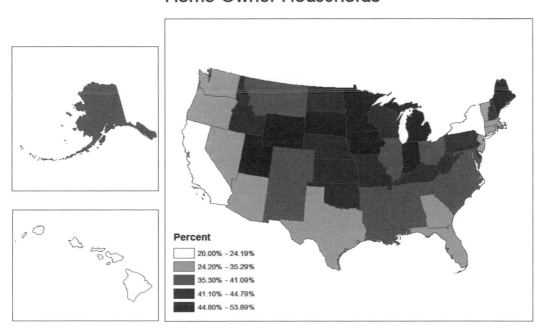

Percent
- 20.00% - 24.19%
- 24.20% - 35.29%
- 35.30% - 41.09%
- 41.10% - 44.79%
- 44.80% - 53.89%

The District of Columbia has the highest percentage of renters among 18 to 24 year old Millennials (98.9 percent) while Delaware is lowest at 73.3 percent. That means Delaware also has the highest percentage of home owners at 26.7 percent. For the older age group, more than half (53.8 percent) are home owners in South Dakota. The District of Columbia is lowest at only 20.4 percent. While home ownership is still a struggle, 30 percent of the nation's Millennials hold mortgage debt. The percentage ranges from a low of 18 percent in Hawaii to 46.4 percent in South Dakota.

Cape May County, NJ has the lowest percentage of young Millennial householders at 1.6 percent, while Clarke County, GA is highest with 54.7 percent and therefore the lowest percentage in the older age group. In most counties there is a much higher percentage of older Millennials as householders, but in 7 counties the reverse is true—there are more younger householders. The gap is largest in Clarke County, GA. In 266 of the 633 counties, more than 90 percent of householders age 18 to 24 are renters. In 31 counties the data shows that all (100 percent) young householders are renters while only two counties (Monroe County, MI and Cape May County, NJ) are above 75 percent owners. Among older Millennials, Scott County, MN has the highest percentage of homeowners at 84.4 percent while Bronx County, NY is lowest with 5.4 percent ownership.

Virtually all householders (98.5 percent) are age 25 to 33 in Norwalk, CA, and in 28 other cities the percentage is above 90 percent. Tallahassee, FL (home to Florida State University) has the lowest share of older householders at 43.5 percent. Renters are by far most common among the younger Millennials where 233 of 344 cities have renter rates above 90 percent. The ACS data shows that all householders (100 percent) are renters in 52 cities. Among the older age group, owners are more prevalent than renters in 31 cities. Elizabeth, NJ has the largest difference between owners and renters with 97.7 percent owning their homes. No other city has above 90 percent ownership. Carson, CA has the highest percentage of Millennials who hold mortgage debt at 70.2 percent. In 19 cities mortgages are held by less than 10 percent.

The 25- to 33-year-old Millennial householders are 98.4 percent of all householders in the Ocean City, NJ metropolitan area. In nine metro/micros they are more than 90 percent of the total. As with the other area types, the younger Millennials are mostly renters with renters being more than 90 percent of the total in 152 metro/micro areas. In the Ocean City, NJ metro area, the ACS reports that 100 percent of younger householders are home owners. Among the older ages, owners are more than 50 percent of the total in 64 metro/micros, and the highest level of ownership is in the Monroe, MI metro

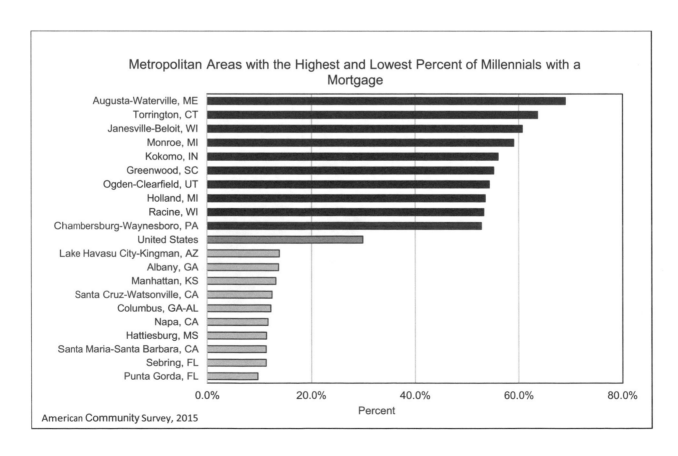

American Community Survey, 2015

area at 69.9 percent. Augusta-Waterville, ME has the highest percentage of Millennials with mortgage debt at 69.0 percent. The lowest level of ownership is in the Sebring, FL metro at 11.2 percent.

INTERNET ACCESS

The President's Council of Economic Advisors notes that the Millennials are the first generation to have grown up with access to the Internet. Technology is important to them, illustrated by the fact that 86.9 percent of Millennial householders age 25 to 33 have Internet access. Younger Millennials are only slightly behind at 80.2 percent. Among the older age group, residents of Mississippi have the lowest level of access at 74.6 percent compared to New Hampshire with 94.1 percent. Internet and phone access is carried with 42 percent of Millennials who have a mobile communications plan. Mississippi has the lowest level of access to a mobile plan at 31 percent, while Alaska is highest with 55.8 percent. Among older Millennials, in 258 counties, 90 percent or more of those age 25 to 33 have Internet access, but in Navajo County, AZ only 59.1 percent have access at home. Mobile communications plans are held by 86.3 percent in McHenry County, IL.

The Internet is accessible to more than 90 percent of younger Millennials in 89 cities and 155 cities for older Millennials. Mobile communications plans are held by 80.4 percent in Pasadena, TX but only 18.4 percent in Downey, CA. The Ogdensburg-Massena, NY micropolitan area has the lowest level of Internet access among the younger Millennials at 44.5 percent, while in 25 metro/micros access is greater than 90 percent. Among older Millennials, the Show Low, AZ micro has the lowest access at 59.1 percent, but 105 metro/micros are above 90 percent. At the metropolitan/micropolitan area level, mobile communications plans are held be 80.1 percent in the Carson City, NV micro but only 25.4 percent in the Sumter, SC metro area.

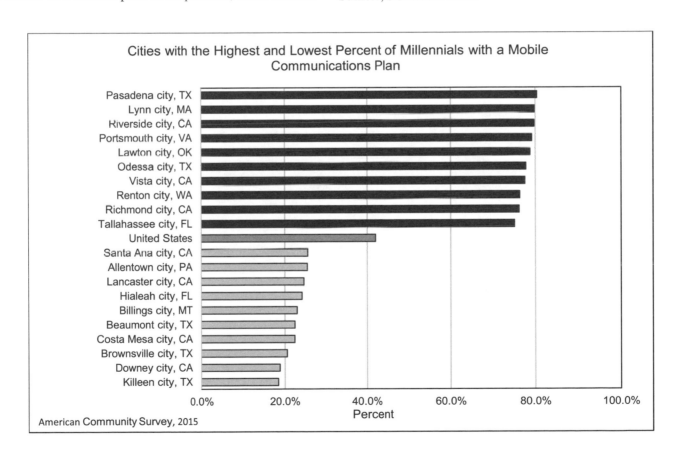

Cities with the Highest and Lowest Percent of Millennials with a Mobile Communications Plan

American Community Survey, 2015

Table K-1: States—Summary Housing Characteristics

	Millennial Householders	Age of Householders		18 to 24 Years Old		25 to 33 Years Old			Percent with Internet Access		Percent with Mobile Access Plan
		18 to 24	25 to 33	Owners	Renters	Owners	Renters	With Mortgage	18 to 24	25 to 33	
United States	20,236,604	21.7%	78.3%	13.0%	87.0%	35.7%	64.3%	30.0%	80.2%	86.9%	42.0%
Alabama	307,941	24.7%	75.3%	16.3%	83.7%	40.9%	59.1%	31.7%	76.7%	80.3%	39.5%
Alaska	60,141	25.4%	74.6%	16.6%	83.4%	38.6%	61.4%	34.3%	80.1%	88.6%	55.8%
Arizona	444,654	24.4%	75.6%	11.3%	88.7%	34.0%	66.0%	29.0%	81.0%	83.9%	44.6%
Arkansas	208,761	25.7%	74.3%	16.8%	83.2%	41.1%	58.9%	32.9%	75.6%	81.1%	35.3%
California	2,148,591	18.4%	81.6%	9.0%	91.0%	24.2%	75.8%	20.6%	84.7%	88.1%	46.0%
Colorado	427,918	23.2%	76.8%	11.7%	88.3%	38.0%	62.0%	33.5%	83.9%	90.6%	46.4%
Connecticut	183,706	16.5%	83.5%	10.4%	89.6%	35.3%	64.7%	32.9%	79.6%	90.5%	40.8%
Delaware	52,148	17.1%	82.9%	26.7%	73.3%	41.8%	58.2%	38.3%	77.7%	85.8%	35.0%
District of Columbia	75,493	15.9%	84.1%	1.1%	98.9%	20.4%	79.6%	18.1%	62.8%	91.4%	41.6%
Florida	1,052,016	19.8%	80.2%	13.3%	86.7%	30.5%	69.5%	24.8%	82.9%	85.3%	37.4%
Georgia	640,157	21.6%	78.4%	12.2%	87.8%	32.6%	67.4%	26.9%	77.5%	83.4%	38.9%
Hawaii	73,629	22.2%	77.8%	7.2%	92.8%	22.7%	77.3%	18.0%	81.9%	90.4%	54.1%
Idaho	112,847	24.5%	75.5%	16.3%	83.7%	44.3%	55.7%	38.1%	83.5%	86.3%	45.0%
Illinois	819,708	19.5%	80.5%	12.5%	87.5%	38.4%	61.6%	32.7%	82.7%	88.9%	47.9%
Indiana	450,981	26.4%	73.6%	17.7%	82.3%	45.8%	54.2%	40.0%	77.1%	83.4%	37.7%
Iowa	249,706	27.8%	72.2%	16.9%	83.1%	49.7%	50.3%	43.6%	76.4%	87.4%	40.0%
Kansas	219,589	26.6%	73.4%	12.5%	87.5%	44.7%	55.3%	37.1%	79.3%	86.6%	43.7%
Kentucky	297,025	25.6%	74.4%	16.2%	83.8%	42.7%	57.3%	34.4%	76.9%	85.6%	41.4%
Louisiana	328,047	22.2%	77.8%	15.2%	84.8%	39.3%	60.7%	29.9%	78.0%	79.6%	34.5%
Maine	74,620	21.6%	78.4%	17.0%	83.0%	46.3%	53.7%	40.7%	76.7%	89.1%	38.2%
Maryland	323,139	16.8%	83.2%	12.5%	87.5%	38.1%	61.9%	34.0%	82.3%	90.2%	43.7%
Massachusetts	398,291	16.6%	83.4%	8.0%	92.0%	30.7%	69.3%	27.1%	74.7%	92.2%	43.8%
Michigan	617,720	24.1%	75.9%	16.6%	83.4%	45.8%	54.2%	36.0%	81.8%	87.4%	41.3%
Minnesota	404,488	22.5%	77.5%	18.7%	81.3%	49.6%	50.4%	43.1%	81.9%	91.6%	46.7%
Mississippi	181,434	23.9%	76.1%	15.8%	84.2%	40.0%	60.0%	29.1%	70.1%	74.6%	31.0%
Missouri	441,625	25.7%	74.3%	15.7%	84.3%	42.5%	57.5%	36.8%	78.6%	84.8%	40.0%
Montana	69,136	32.1%	67.9%	11.6%	88.4%	39.0%	61.0%	32.4%	79.4%	85.5%	36.2%
Nebraska	166,781	29.3%	70.7%	17.4%	82.6%	43.6%	56.4%	39.5%	78.9%	91.1%	40.9%
Nevada	189,570	18.4%	81.6%	15.5%	84.5%	29.4%	70.6%	22.7%	86.0%	86.5%	43.4%
New Hampshire	73,464	21.1%	78.9%	18.0%	82.0%	43.2%	56.8%	38.2%	77.2%	94.1%	39.6%
New Jersey	405,437	13.0%	87.0%	12.5%	87.5%	29.3%	70.7%	25.8%	85.8%	90.7%	40.3%
New Mexico	130,761	24.2%	75.8%	17.7%	82.3%	38.4%	61.6%	29.7%	73.7%	78.7%	36.1%
New York	1,111,039	16.7%	83.3%	8.9%	91.1%	24.0%	76.0%	19.7%	79.7%	89.3%	36.1%
North Carolina	670,151	24.1%	75.9%	11.5%	88.5%	37.0%	63.0%	30.7%	76.6%	85.3%	39.9%
North Dakota	83,290	35.4%	64.6%	14.8%	85.2%	44.8%	55.2%	37.2%	82.7%	91.1%	47.7%
Ohio	799,404	24.0%	76.0%	11.6%	88.4%	40.0%	60.0%	34.0%	79.7%	88.6%	42.8%
Oklahoma	281,925	26.4%	73.6%	14.5%	85.5%	43.3%	56.7%	34.4%	75.0%	82.5%	45.0%
Oregon	261,663	23.3%	76.7%	10.1%	89.9%	30.9%	69.1%	27.4%	86.8%	91.2%	53.6%
Pennsylvania	739,881	18.8%	81.2%	13.6%	86.4%	41.7%	58.3%	34.8%	76.9%	88.4%	40.4%
Rhode Island	63,434	19.0%	81.0%	5.9%	94.1%	29.8%	70.2%	25.8%	69.7%	90.8%	44.0%
South Carolina	311,316	22.2%	77.8%	19.2%	80.8%	40.5%	59.5%	32.2%	74.6%	79.7%	36.2%
South Dakota	73,050	28.9%	71.1%	18.2%	81.8%	53.8%	46.2%	46.4%	75.0%	85.6%	35.3%
Tennessee	447,696	24.5%	75.5%	15.0%	85.0%	40.8%	59.2%	34.9%	78.2%	83.6%	40.4%
Texas	1,895,264	22.3%	77.7%	11.6%	88.4%	33.8%	66.2%	27.1%	79.1%	82.6%	40.8%
Utah	217,627	27.6%	72.4%	18.0%	82.0%	47.2%	52.8%	43.2%	88.5%	93.3%	48.2%
Vermont	37,338	28.6%	71.4%	16.8%	83.2%	33.5%	66.5%	27.3%	72.8%	87.8%	36.8%
Virginia	526,551	20.6%	79.4%	9.9%	90.1%	37.4%	62.6%	33.1%	77.6%	88.8%	44.2%
Washington	520,651	21.7%	78.3%	10.8%	89.2%	33.2%	66.8%	29.1%	86.2%	91.7%	52.5%
West Virginia	107,225	24.9%	75.1%	14.5%	85.5%	41.7%	58.3%	30.3%	80.6%	84.2%	39.5%
Wisconsin	413,898	24.4%	75.6%	12.8%	87.2%	43.0%	57.0%	38.4%	80.4%	89.8%	44.5%
Wyoming	45,677	26.8%	73.2%	16.2%	83.8%	47.3%	52.7%	40.6%	81.0%	88.6%	31.3%

Table K-2: Counties—Summary Housing Characteristics

	Millennial Householders	Age of Householders		18 to 24 Years Old		25 to 33 Years Old			Percent with Internet Access		Percent with Mobile Access Plan
		18 to 24	25 to 33	Owners	Renters	Owners	Renters	With Mortgage	18 to 24	25 to 33	
Alabama											
Baldwin County	7,995	21.4%	78.6%	42.2%	57.8%	31.1%	68.9%	24.1%	86.9%	80.8%	68.9%
Calhoun County	7,007	31.7%	68.3%	4.5%	95.5%	37.2%	62.8%	29.8%	80.0%	87.3%	49.4%
Etowah County	5,015	24.0%	76.0%	25.4%	74.6%	55.5%	44.5%	41.9%	79.6%	77.8%	36.9%
Houston County	5,651	30.6%	69.4%	23.8%	76.2%	31.0%	69.0%	27.6%	72.8%	76.5%	28.6%
Jefferson County	48,618	21.8%	78.2%	10.4%	89.6%	39.0%	61.0%	33.0%	76.9%	86.4%	41.6%
Lauderdale County	6,009	35.2%	64.8%	24.7%	75.3%	40.6%	59.4%	30.4%	80.4%	60.4%	36.3%
Lee County	15,160	50.0%	50.0%	16.2%	83.8%	42.1%	57.9%	26.0%	78.5%	82.3%	34.0%
Madison County	27,766	17.0%	83.0%	9.4%	90.6%	34.2%	65.8%	29.4%	79.0%	83.6%	58.9%
Marshall County	5,071	31.5%	68.5%	32.4%	67.6%	62.3%	37.7%	44.4%	94.6%	90.9%	68.3%
Mobile County	26,144	21.2%	78.8%	18.0%	82.0%	27.0%	73.0%	23.0%	74.0%	76.6%	39.5%
Montgomery County	19,970	27.8%	72.2%	4.4%	95.6%	27.0%	73.0%	17.8%	77.5%	82.4%	58.7%
Morgan County	7,150	13.1%	86.9%	31.5%	68.5%	44.8%	55.2%	33.6%	68.3%	78.7%	31.5%
Shelby County	11,398	18.0%	82.0%	16.2%	83.8%	59.6%	40.4%	48.7%	83.8%	91.2%	48.6%
Tuscaloosa County	17,049	39.8%	60.2%	11.4%	88.6%	32.1%	67.9%	26.9%	73.5%	84.5%	57.7%
Alaska											
Anchorage Municipality	28,378	27.5%	72.5%	22.8%	77.2%	37.7%	62.3%	36.6%	83.4%	92.5%	70.9%
Fairbanks North Star Borough	11,313	23.6%	76.4%	0.0%	100.0%	29.3%	70.7%	25.3%	76.9%	87.4%	56.8%
Matanuska-Susitna Borough	5,283	20.8%	79.2%	44.2%	55.8%	44.8%	55.2%	38.0%	90.4%	83.7%	59.3%
Arizona											
Cochise County	8,688	26.2%	73.8%	12.3%	87.7%	42.6%	57.4%	35.3%	70.3%	69.4%	40.3%
Coconino County	10,721	41.8%	58.2%	5.3%	94.7%	35.7%	64.3%	27.9%	54.0%	86.6%	39.1%
Maricopa County	280,393	21.8%	78.2%	10.3%	89.7%	31.9%	68.1%	27.9%	85.3%	87.1%	56.5%
Mohave County	9,690	19.6%	80.4%	25.4%	74.6%	21.9%	78.1%	14.4%	87.2%	77.1%	45.9%
Navajo County	3,341	16.7%	83.3%	17.2%	82.8%	39.9%	60.1%	26.4%	47.2%	59.1%	28.5%
Pima County	74,611	31.6%	68.4%	11.9%	88.1%	35.6%	64.4%	29.4%	83.8%	88.3%	60.5%
Pinal County	15,068	13.8%	86.2%	35.1%	64.9%	56.1%	43.9%	50.9%	78.9%	69.5%	35.9%
Yavapai County	11,063	28.1%	71.9%	13.3%	86.7%	48.9%	51.1%	45.9%	72.8%	79.3%	43.3%
Yuma County	14,514	31.3%	68.7%	12.3%	87.7%	37.1%	62.9%	29.8%	78.8%	79.3%	41.3%
Arkansas											
Benton County	17,718	16.7%	83.3%	28.0%	72.0%	45.9%	54.1%	41.3%	85.4%	81.3%	38.6%
Craighead County	8,521	42.8%	57.2%	19.9%	80.1%	21.1%	78.9%	21.1%	79.3%	84.1%	53.8%
Faulkner County	10,106	26.8%	73.2%	15.7%	84.3%	41.0%	59.0%	32.4%	72.4%	80.5%	28.1%
Garland County	4,178	4.4%	95.6%	0.0%	100.0%	32.5%	67.5%	23.1%	72.9%	82.1%	40.7%
Pulaski County	34,958	25.4%	74.6%	8.8%	91.2%	29.4%	70.6%	24.2%	88.3%	87.1%	44.6%
Saline County	6,169	23.1%	76.9%	35.3%	64.7%	57.9%	42.1%	52.6%	89.3%	95.9%	49.6%
Sebastian County	7,925	21.5%	78.5%	11.8%	88.2%	36.7%	63.3%	36.7%	72.9%	82.1%	34.5%
Washington County	24,022	37.5%	62.5%	3.9%	96.1%	31.4%	68.6%	24.5%	81.4%	85.8%	35.7%
California											
Alameda County	95,041	16.2%	83.8%	5.9%	94.1%	21.3%	78.7%	19.3%	85.7%	93.6%	63.9%
Butte County	18,081	37.6%	62.4%	3.0%	97.0%	29.5%	70.5%	21.9%	85.2%	85.4%	43.2%
Contra Costa County	47,760	14.6%	85.4%	14.1%	85.9%	30.8%	69.2%	26.1%	91.5%	94.4%	78.1%
El Dorado County	5,631	12.6%	87.4%	17.4%	82.6%	55.4%	44.6%	52.4%	92.2%	86.4%	57.2%
Fresno County	55,372	22.8%	77.2%	9.9%	90.1%	26.1%	73.9%	22.8%	83.4%	82.5%	53.3%
Humboldt County	10,785	38.4%	61.6%	9.9%	90.1%	27.9%	72.1%	19.6%	79.1%	80.8%	51.3%
Imperial County	5,994	7.1%	92.9%	13.2%	86.8%	45.5%	54.5%	39.4%	87.1%	71.8%	67.2%
Kern County	55,314	17.3%	82.7%	18.2%	81.8%	36.6%	63.4%	31.2%	78.2%	75.7%	44.5%
Kings County	11,389	16.2%	83.8%	0.0%	100.0%	21.8%	78.2%	18.1%	74.6%	61.3%	23.8%
Los Angeles County	534,286	16.5%	83.5%	7.9%	92.1%	17.6%	82.4%	14.8%	84.4%	86.9%	48.0%
Madera County	7,255	30.8%	69.2%	41.4%	58.6%	25.7%	74.3%	16.3%	79.3%	71.5%	58.2%
Marin County	9,616	16.0%	84.0%	6.9%	93.1%	15.7%	84.3%	15.7%	85.3%	84.9%	72.6%
Merced County	17,622	24.9%	75.1%	11.7%	88.3%	30.2%	69.8%	26.5%	83.8%	84.2%	54.5%
Monterey County	20,572	15.3%	84.7%	4.5%	95.5%	19.8%	80.2%	13.8%	74.0%	76.9%	44.7%
Napa County	5,947	13.0%	87.0%	0.0%	100.0%	18.6%	81.4%	11.6%	85.2%	94.5%	60.8%
Nevada County	4,381	9.8%	90.2%	17.0%	83.0%	52.4%	47.6%	47.6%	85.3%	88.1%	51.7%
Orange County	144,204	17.5%	82.5%	8.8%	91.2%	23.3%	76.7%	19.3%	90.4%	93.5%	54.4%
Placer County	15,236	11.8%	88.2%	4.4%	95.6%	40.0%	60.0%	34.7%	91.2%	89.4%	57.4%
Riverside County	102,079	17.2%	82.8%	17.0%	83.0%	40.5%	59.5%	36.2%	85.7%	86.5%	57.9%
Sacramento County	100,544	17.4%	82.6%	5.7%	94.3%	30.0%	70.0%	27.1%	89.0%	89.6%	56.9%
San Bernardino County	112,410	19.9%	80.1%	8.9%	91.1%	29.5%	70.5%	24.7%	86.5%	86.0%	45.6%
San Diego County	206,599	18.8%	81.2%	5.4%	94.6%	21.3%	78.7%	18.1%	82.5%	91.7%	56.6%
San Francisco County	80,073	11.8%	88.2%	5.1%	94.9%	13.2%	86.8%	9.2%	84.2%	95.7%	54.1%
San Joaquin County	37,260	18.6%	81.4%	10.4%	89.6%	32.0%	68.0%	25.2%	83.6%	85.5%	51.2%
San Luis Obispo County	18,454	33.8%	66.2%	5.9%	94.1%	24.2%	75.8%	24.2%	72.7%	90.8%	55.2%
San Mateo County	36,688	10.5%	89.5%	11.0%	89.0%	22.1%	77.9%	20.1%	95.0%	95.7%	66.8%
Santa Barbara County	25,668	43.0%	57.0%	11.3%	88.7%	13.1%	86.9%	11.2%	78.0%	87.1%	65.8%
Santa Clara County	98,998	15.8%	84.2%	7.5%	92.5%	21.9%	78.1%	19.6%	86.0%	94.0%	54.8%
Santa Cruz County	13,475	25.0%	75.0%	2.7%	97.3%	15.6%	84.4%	12.4%	71.5%	76.3%	51.4%
Shasta County	12,765	28.4%	71.6%	2.1%	97.9%	36.0%	64.0%	26.0%	81.7%	79.6%	27.4%
Solano County	22,354	18.8%	81.2%	12.2%	87.8%	22.8%	77.2%	21.0%	86.3%	91.1%	61.5%
Sonoma County	24,397	23.4%	76.6%	16.0%	84.0%	24.9%	75.1%	22.1%	90.8%	90.2%	59.9%
Stanislaus County	32,604	15.3%	84.7%	19.9%	80.1%	37.7%	62.3%	30.7%	92.8%	89.3%	76.0%
Sutter County	5,787	16.1%	83.9%	0.0%	100.0%	44.1%	55.9%	44.1%	93.4%	94.5%	74.2%
Tulare County	26,975	17.9%	82.1%	9.1%	90.9%	34.4%	65.6%	31.8%	80.9%	77.7%	55.3%
Ventura County	32,745	16.8%	83.2%	11.3%	88.7%	31.3%	68.7%	26.7%	85.3%	87.3%	52.7%
Yolo County	17,971	46.6%	53.4%	7.5%	92.5%	23.2%	76.8%	19.8%	84.8%	87.4%	52.3%

Table K-2: Counties—Summary Housing Characteristics—*Continued*

	Millennial Householders	Age of Householders		18 to 24 Years Old		25 to 33 Years Old			Percent with Internet Access		Percent with Mobile Access Plan
		18 to 24	25 to 33	Owners	Renters	Owners	Renters	With Mortgage	18 to 24	25 to 33	
Colorado											
Adams County	34,523	20.8%	79.2%	19.2%	80.8%	50.8%	49.2%	40.9%	84.4%	87.0%	50.2%
Arapahoe County	43,862	18.9%	81.1%	12.6%	87.4%	38.2%	61.8%	35.0%	91.5%	90.2%	53.5%
Boulder County	27,996	38.2%	61.8%	4.7%	95.3%	36.7%	63.3%	33.0%	81.2%	95.1%	38.5%
Denver County	79,885	14.5%	85.5%	4.4%	95.6%	26.3%	73.7%	23.6%	83.8%	91.5%	57.7%
Douglas County	17,118	25.3%	74.7%	33.4%	66.6%	53.9%	46.1%	52.1%	97.9%	96.6%	74.0%
El Paso County	59,044	23.2%	76.8%	17.0%	83.0%	34.5%	65.5%	30.4%	84.8%	96.0%	69.2%
Jefferson County	41,353	26.7%	73.3%	7.3%	92.7%	43.4%	56.6%	39.7%	91.0%	91.5%	57.0%
Larimer County	29,455	35.8%	64.2%	7.1%	92.9%	34.0%	66.0%	29.7%	86.1%	95.5%	49.0%
Mesa County	10,929	22.0%	78.0%	9.6%	90.4%	47.0%	53.0%	42.8%	82.1%	90.6%	60.9%
Pueblo County	10,777	21.6%	78.4%	8.4%	91.6%	45.0%	55.0%	42.5%	79.0%	86.3%	49.3%
Weld County	21,396	22.8%	77.2%	4.4%	95.6%	54.5%	45.5%	46.2%	84.5%	86.5%	45.5%
Connecticut											
Fairfield County	38,518	14.5%	85.5%	14.1%	85.9%	38.0%	62.0%	34.4%	87.7%	90.4%	49.9%
Hartford County	49,389	16.5%	83.5%	11.0%	89.0%	36.0%	64.0%	34.3%	81.9%	91.9%	50.6%
Litchfield County	7,089	14.0%	86.0%	5.1%	94.9%	65.5%	34.5%	63.7%	96.4%	88.6%	57.8%
Middlesex County	7,866	15.1%	84.9%	14.3%	85.7%	39.8%	60.2%	37.9%	70.8%	90.4%	44.6%
New Haven County	45,601	13.7%	86.3%	3.0%	97.0%	23.9%	76.1%	21.5%	77.8%	90.8%	46.1%
New London County	18,165	18.8%	81.2%	13.2%	86.8%	35.1%	64.9%	32.5%	74.4%	88.8%	44.4%
Tolland County	9,373	34.4%	65.6%	11.8%	88.2%	44.6%	55.4%	44.6%	57.9%	89.7%	39.5%
Windham County	6,587	20.3%	79.7%	18.5%	81.5%	50.5%	49.5%	45.2%	74.1%	90.0%	64.4%
Delaware											
Kent County	11,442	23.9%	76.1%	19.9%	80.1%	40.9%	59.1%	34.5%	71.9%	86.3%	56.3%
New Castle County	31,276	14.2%	85.8%	25.1%	74.9%	39.6%	60.4%	36.8%	77.4%	88.1%	38.8%
Sussex County	9,430	18.7%	81.3%	41.2%	58.8%	50.8%	49.2%	48.0%	84.8%	76.5%	32.2%
Florida											
Alachua County	26,612	37.9%	62.1%	10.4%	89.6%	19.7%	80.3%	14.5%	70.6%	85.1%	48.7%
Bay County	11,100	9.6%	90.4%	17.2%	82.8%	40.0%	60.0%	31.4%	83.8%	80.4%	55.6%
Brevard County	25,564	19.7%	80.3%	20.0%	80.0%	37.4%	62.6%	29.7%	92.4%	92.2%	57.2%
Broward County	88,518	14.9%	85.1%	8.6%	91.4%	29.8%	70.2%	24.3%	90.0%	88.6%	53.0%
Charlotte County	2,988	27.5%	72.5%	51.7%	48.3%	16.2%	83.8%	9.6%	86.4%	87.9%	59.5%
Citrus County	3,828	25.5%	74.5%	34.8%	65.2%	41.4%	58.6%	23.1%	77.4%	93.1%	29.1%
Clay County	9,846	20.7%	79.3%	9.5%	90.5%	43.9%	56.1%	37.3%	89.0%	89.3%	49.9%
Collier County	10,372	11.7%	88.3%	12.4%	87.6%	25.7%	74.3%	23.6%	77.3%	84.5%	54.1%
Duval County	67,749	24.1%	75.9%	3.8%	96.2%	29.3%	70.7%	27.5%	80.5%	88.9%	47.2%
Escambia County	21,747	21.1%	78.9%	11.0%	89.0%	30.8%	69.2%	26.4%	64.3%	85.7%	42.6%
Flagler County	3,525	25.9%	74.1%	45.7%	54.3%	39.7%	60.3%	38.8%	93.5%	92.2%	66.8%
Hernando County	5,547	5.2%	94.8%	12.8%	87.2%	49.9%	50.1%	46.4%	92.4%	86.7%	68.3%
Highlands County	3,381	25.4%	74.6%	39.7%	60.3%	11.2%	88.8%	11.2%	54.2%	60.7%	37.2%
Hillsborough County	98,507	18.7%	81.3%	5.7%	94.3%	29.2%	70.8%	25.0%	85.0%	88.4%	51.5%
Indian River County	3,756	15.1%	84.9%	24.2%	75.8%	48.1%	51.9%	39.4%	88.6%	82.9%	41.7%
Lake County	13,812	24.0%	76.0%	29.1%	70.9%	46.6%	53.4%	35.1%	88.5%	90.0%	55.6%
Lee County	24,256	16.6%	83.4%	14.5%	85.5%	31.5%	68.5%	24.7%	81.7%	84.3%	38.9%
Leon County	34,634	50.1%	49.9%	4.2%	95.8%	28.1%	71.9%	24.3%	83.1%	91.7%	65.2%
Manatee County	10,439	13.7%	86.3%	0.0%	100.0%	19.9%	80.1%	17.6%	82.9%	78.3%	42.5%
Marion County	9,634	12.1%	87.9%	21.7%	78.3%	53.6%	46.4%	49.0%	81.4%	76.3%	52.3%
Martin County	4,752	8.5%	91.5%	34.1%	65.9%	37.4%	62.6%	23.5%	89.2%	89.8%	63.1%
Miami-Dade County	119,912	12.5%	87.5%	13.7%	86.3%	23.0%	77.0%	16.6%	84.2%	81.8%	28.9%
Okaloosa County	17,494	26.8%	73.2%	21.2%	78.8%	34.1%	65.9%	31.9%	86.6%	88.3%	37.8%
Orange County	100,802	21.9%	78.1%	10.7%	89.3%	24.3%	75.7%	20.6%	81.5%	90.9%	40.8%
Osceola County	14,749	19.3%	80.7%	29.1%	70.9%	40.2%	59.8%	31.1%	75.7%	88.2%	42.7%
Palm Beach County	60,808	18.4%	81.6%	15.7%	84.3%	31.8%	68.2%	24.6%	87.7%	85.1%	46.9%
Pasco County	21,749	23.4%	76.6%	11.2%	88.8%	41.0%	59.0%	34.4%	83.9%	89.7%	39.7%
Pinellas County	44,124	14.2%	85.8%	21.3%	78.7%	25.8%	74.2%	20.7%	85.2%	87.6%	44.8%
Polk County	30,862	13.9%	86.1%	17.5%	82.5%	34.5%	65.5%	30.3%	74.6%	76.3%	25.4%
Santa Rosa County	9,487	23.7%	76.3%	31.7%	68.3%	48.7%	51.3%	35.9%	84.9%	91.7%	45.5%
Sarasota County	14,396	13.9%	86.1%	30.2%	69.8%	36.7%	63.3%	28.8%	90.9%	88.3%	48.8%
Seminole County	11,795	14.5%	85.5%	31.4%	68.6%	43.3%	56.7%	39.2%	84.2%	82.6%	51.4%
St. Johns County	14,982	19.5%	80.5%	32.3%	67.7%	34.8%	65.2%	30.1%	86.5%	89.1%	52.0%
St. Lucie County	26,678	17.4%	82.6%	11.3%	88.7%	32.8%	67.2%	24.5%	95.0%	94.4%	44.8%
Sumter County	1,713	19.0%	81.0%	0.0%	100.0%	27.0%	73.0%	24.2%	91.9%	75.3%	63.5%
Volusia County	25,907	22.9%	77.1%	16.7%	83.3%	37.0%	63.0%	28.6%	81.0%	85.7%	46.9%
Georgia											
Bartow County	5,583	26.8%	73.2%	1.9%	98.1%	46.7%	53.3%	42.3%	94.7%	86.8%	83.6%
Bibb County	10,969	24.3%	75.7%	0.0%	100.0%	26.3%	73.7%	23.9%	61.5%	76.9%	43.4%
Carroll County	9,447	37.2%	62.8%	20.2%	79.8%	38.0%	62.0%	32.9%	78.2%	92.8%	48.6%
Chatham County	24,508	22.4%	77.6%	4.2%	95.8%	24.6%	75.4%	21.6%	69.8%	87.1%	62.0%
Cherokee County	12,310	14.3%	85.7%	42.5%	57.5%	56.8%	43.2%	56.6%	96.1%	97.7%	69.4%
Clarke County	16,521	54.7%	45.3%	8.3%	91.7%	19.8%	80.2%	15.7%	70.8%	86.7%	39.8%
Clayton County	15,731	23.3%	76.7%	10.1%	89.9%	20.6%	79.4%	9.7%	74.6%	85.2%	57.0%
Cobb County	49,122	18.7%	81.3%	3.3%	96.7%	31.2%	68.8%	26.0%	85.3%	90.5%	38.6%
Columbia County	7,616	7.2%	92.8%	49.0%	51.0%	57.0%	43.0%	47.2%	72.4%	72.7%	47.5%
Coweta County	8,295	31.5%	68.5%	34.1%	65.9%	46.3%	53.7%	41.7%	96.3%	91.1%	64.4%
DeKalb County	53,714	15.9%	84.1%	7.9%	92.1%	20.0%	80.0%	17.2%	75.9%	89.1%	47.1%
Dougherty County	7,133	21.2%	78.8%	5.4%	94.6%	13.9%	86.1%	8.1%	67.4%	72.2%	54.4%
Douglas County	7,184	12.6%	87.4%	0.0%	100.0%	37.0%	63.0%	33.8%	90.0%	95.8%	41.0%

Table K-2: Counties—Summary Housing Characteristics—*Continued*

	Millennial Householders	Age of Householders		18 to 24 Years Old		25 to 33 Years Old			Percent with Internet Access		Percent with Mobile Access Plan
		18 to 24	25 to 33	Owners	Renters	Owners	Renters	With Mortgage	18 to 24	25 to 33	
Georgia—Cont.											
Fayette County	2,859	15.7%	84.3%	0.0%	100.0%	54.1%	45.9%	46.5%	98.1%	95.9%	75.2%
Floyd County	4,845	20.5%	79.5%	18.3%	81.7%	34.1%	65.9%	26.4%	80.9%	75.1%	47.8%
Forsyth County	7,620	9.9%	90.1%	59.3%	40.7%	68.9%	31.1%	63.5%	92.7%	93.4%	80.3%
Fulton County	86,348	19.0%	81.0%	3.6%	96.4%	21.3%	78.7%	17.9%	75.4%	91.4%	48.5%
Gwinnett County	44,803	17.8%	82.2%	7.1%	92.9%	33.9%	66.1%	28.2%	86.6%	87.1%	39.6%
Hall County	10,251	23.8%	76.2%	16.7%	83.3%	51.8%	48.2%	43.7%	74.8%	76.5%	43.3%
Henry County	9,550	14.7%	85.3%	24.1%	75.9%	56.4%	43.6%	48.6%	90.2%	94.7%	67.7%
Houston County	10,553	24.2%	75.8%	6.9%	93.1%	43.1%	56.9%	36.2%	81.0%	84.5%	45.2%
Lowndes County	8,907	37.9%	62.1%	6.7%	93.3%	26.0%	74.0%	25.7%	73.9%	72.6%	27.3%
Muscogee County	16,456	21.2%	78.8%	3.9%	96.1%	11.2%	88.8%	10.2%	77.1%	85.4%	24.9%
Newton County	5,529	25.4%	74.6%	54.3%	45.7%	30.7%	69.3%	25.3%	92.4%	86.1%	57.3%
Paulding County	6,941	6.2%	93.8%	2.6%	97.4%	57.3%	42.7%	46.6%	94.7%	79.0%	58.3%
Richmond County	15,327	21.1%	78.9%	6.2%	93.8%	23.6%	76.4%	19.4%	64.7%	76.8%	44.4%
Whitfield County	7,862	36.8%	63.2%	14.6%	85.4%	45.1%	54.9%	34.9%	82.7%	90.8%	54.2%
Hawaii											
Hawaii County	7,366	26.6%	73.4%	19.4%	80.6%	25.5%	74.5%	16.9%	89.0%	87.3%	46.0%
Honolulu County	56,312	24.0%	76.0%	5.8%	94.2%	21.6%	78.4%	17.3%	79.1%	90.5%	64.0%
Maui County	7,782	10.7%	89.3%	1.8%	98.2%	23.0%	77.0%	18.1%	91.6%	91.8%	63.5%
Idaho											
Ada County	31,952	19.7%	80.3%	22.4%	77.6%	43.5%	56.5%	40.0%	83.9%	81.2%	47.8%
Bonneville County	7,224	16.8%	83.2%	0.0%	100.0%	48.6%	51.4%	46.7%	88.4%	92.8%	68.3%
Canyon County	10,639	16.9%	83.1%	41.1%	58.9%	42.6%	57.4%	35.6%	80.2%	81.6%	42.6%
Kootenai County	9,393	17.5%	82.5%	0.0%	100.0%	44.1%	55.9%	36.0%	88.7%	95.4%	70.1%
Illinois											
Champaign County	23,553	45.1%	54.9%	7.6%	92.4%	27.6%	72.4%	19.8%	70.5%	86.8%	30.3%
Cook County	365,608	14.7%	85.3%	7.7%	92.3%	28.1%	71.9%	23.6%	83.8%	90.1%	52.8%
DeKalb County	10,816	50.5%	49.5%	9.1%	90.9%	37.8%	62.2%	34.7%	77.1%	95.6%	54.1%
DuPage County	46,016	18.0%	82.0%	15.6%	84.4%	39.0%	61.0%	34.5%	90.3%	94.2%	71.3%
Kane County	23,878	17.9%	82.1%	18.3%	81.7%	43.1%	56.9%	35.8%	93.6%	93.6%	83.4%
Kankakee County	6,321	18.6%	81.4%	25.2%	74.8%	38.6%	61.4%	28.4%	64.6%	83.5%	54.6%
Kendall County	8,483	6.4%	93.6%	0.0%	100.0%	74.7%	25.3%	70.5%	96.3%	97.5%	66.5%
Lake County	30,912	17.4%	82.6%	7.5%	92.5%	40.5%	59.5%	34.9%	85.0%	89.9%	68.9%
LaSalle County	7,286	19.8%	80.2%	25.6%	74.4%	37.8%	62.2%	32.5%	92.6%	86.9%	66.7%
Macon County	13,628	18.9%	81.1%	9.5%	90.5%	48.8%	51.2%	46.4%	96.3%	95.3%	86.3%
Madison County	18,229	38.8%	61.2%	5.1%	94.9%	42.1%	57.9%	39.3%	75.4%	89.4%	30.2%
McHenry County	6,853	28.9%	71.1%	4.2%	95.8%	47.5%	52.5%	39.3%	73.2%	76.0%	53.3%
McLean County	16,095	21.4%	78.6%	17.8%	82.2%	60.6%	39.4%	56.1%	74.7%	91.0%	69.4%
Peoria County	14,534	18.1%	81.9%	9.7%	90.3%	36.5%	63.5%	32.7%	72.0%	80.4%	41.2%
Rock Island County	9,376	16.3%	83.7%	10.0%	90.0%	49.2%	50.8%	44.7%	75.6%	82.1%	56.0%
Sangamon County	16,946	22.1%	77.9%	7.8%	92.2%	36.8%	63.2%	28.2%	82.5%	81.6%	45.5%
St. Clair County	12,754	18.7%	81.3%	11.4%	88.6%	39.0%	61.0%	29.0%	84.8%	87.9%	64.4%
Tazewell County	8,461	20.8%	79.2%	29.5%	70.5%	70.3%	29.7%	60.8%	88.6%	88.9%	65.5%
Will County	27,668	15.0%	85.0%	30.1%	69.9%	66.5%	33.5%	60.2%	93.5%	94.8%	60.6%
Winnebago County	16,885	25.2%	74.8%	13.8%	86.2%	52.9%	47.1%	45.1%	90.7%	85.4%	63.5%
Indiana											
Allen County	29,555	24.7%	75.3%	25.3%	74.7%	49.1%	50.9%	45.5%	86.3%	82.3%	54.6%
Clark County	6,399	13.8%	86.2%	13.6%	86.4%	69.3%	30.7%	68.1%	76.4%	84.2%	45.0%
Delaware County	10,987	53.4%	46.6%	3.4%	96.6%	51.1%	48.9%	36.8%	71.2%	87.7%	54.7%
Elkhart County	12,727	38.1%	61.9%	35.0%	65.0%	50.1%	49.9%	44.2%	86.2%	76.3%	31.1%
Hamilton County	18,849	21.7%	78.3%	9.9%	90.1%	57.9%	42.1%	52.5%	92.8%	92.7%	58.7%
Hendricks County	7,570	11.7%	88.3%	26.1%	73.9%	66.0%	34.0%	60.3%	93.7%	94.0%	58.9%
Johnson County	9,683	22.4%	77.6%	38.8%	61.2%	45.9%	54.1%	42.3%	87.5%	92.8%	46.1%
Lake County	23,791	18.8%	81.2%	5.0%	95.0%	39.3%	60.7%	34.8%	83.8%	88.0%	57.1%
LaPorte County	6,870	26.8%	73.2%	40.2%	59.8%	40.3%	59.7%	34.3%	79.8%	61.5%	33.1%
Madison County	8,022	24.2%	75.8%	9.7%	90.3%	45.7%	54.3%	39.6%	78.7%	84.5%	70.7%
Marion County	86,720	20.3%	79.7%	7.0%	93.0%	34.1%	65.9%	29.4%	80.3%	83.7%	45.2%
Monroe County	18,897	47.2%	52.8%	2.8%	97.2%	25.8%	74.2%	21.0%	63.4%	88.0%	52.8%
Porter County	8,168	21.7%	78.3%	28.5%	71.5%	57.8%	42.2%	40.1%	84.1%	91.2%	52.8%
St. Joseph County	16,326	18.1%	81.9%	24.9%	75.1%	40.0%	60.0%	34.6%	67.9%	84.6%	38.9%
Tippecanoe County	21,528	50.6%	49.4%	4.7%	95.3%	31.9%	68.1%	29.4%	64.7%	86.2%	29.7%
Vanderburgh County	15,657	28.0%	72.0%	6.9%	93.1%	49.8%	50.2%	42.5%	72.2%	81.2%	36.9%
Vigo County	7,772	45.4%	54.6%	5.3%	94.7%	30.6%	69.4%	23.5%	55.1%	67.5%	25.4%
Iowa											
Black Hawk County	13,558	37.5%	62.5%	16.3%	83.7%	50.3%	49.7%	43.8%	66.0%	81.9%	34.9%
Dubuque County	7,105	22.4%	77.6%	21.9%	78.1%	42.9%	57.1%	28.9%	71.2%	89.8%	59.4%
Johnson County	19,194	44.0%	56.0%	9.0%	91.0%	32.9%	67.1%	17.5%	78.0%	79.9%	36.9%
Linn County	16,951	27.8%	72.2%	0.9%	99.1%	54.4%	45.6%	49.0%	86.5%	94.3%	42.6%
Polk County	39,174	22.3%	77.7%	11.9%	88.1%	45.5%	54.5%	43.1%	81.1%	90.9%	54.3%
Pottawattamie County	7,282	22.6%	77.4%	39.1%	60.9%	52.9%	47.1%	46.2%	85.0%	85.3%	56.3%
Scott County	12,725	15.4%	84.6%	16.9%	83.1%	41.1%	58.9%	34.0%	81.1%	89.0%	42.4%
Story County	13,429	51.5%	48.5%	2.6%	97.4%	49.2%	50.8%	39.9%	67.5%	90.9%	24.3%
Woodbury County	8,952	18.7%	81.3%	19.7%	80.3%	46.8%	53.2%	44.7%	66.7%	78.7%	51.6%
Kansas											
Douglas County	12,639	45.5%	54.5%	0.0%	100.0%	29.0%	71.0%	25.3%	64.8%	82.7%	51.6%

Table K-2: Counties—Summary Housing Characteristics—*Continued*

	Millennial Householders	Age of Householders		18 to 24 Years Old		25 to 33 Years Old			Percent with Internet Access		Percent with Mobile Access Plan
		18 to 24	25 to 33	Owners	Renters	Owners	Renters	With Mortgage	18 to 24	25 to 33	
Kansas—Cont.											
Johnson County	41,652	16.9%	83.1%	14.5%	85.5%	44.9%	55.1%	39.9%	97.2%	96.8%	69.3%
Sedgwick County	41,303	22.9%	77.1%	8.5%	91.5%	38.4%	61.6%	30.9%	83.6%	82.2%	40.5%
Shawnee County	14,221	27.3%	72.7%	7.1%	92.9%	48.0%	52.0%	44.4%	84.8%	90.5%	50.6%
Wyandotte County	13,095	27.3%	72.7%	6.6%	93.4%	44.3%	55.7%	41.3%	82.0%	76.8%	60.4%
Kentucky											
Boone County	8,047	24.9%	75.1%	47.1%	52.9%	54.1%	45.9%	48.7%	87.6%	90.8%	64.7%
Campbell County	6,036	18.8%	81.2%	16.1%	83.9%	34.5%	65.5%	32.5%	69.7%	80.1%	30.6%
Daviess County	6,605	18.6%	81.4%	15.7%	84.3%	52.5%	47.5%	42.1%	75.1%	88.4%	60.1%
Fayette County	33,523	33.7%	66.3%	2.3%	97.7%	33.9%	66.1%	27.4%	77.8%	87.3%	58.8%
Hardin County	7,427	23.3%	76.7%	25.4%	74.6%	51.3%	48.7%	44.6%	79.2%	90.0%	65.3%
Jefferson County	57,397	21.7%	78.3%	8.0%	92.0%	36.3%	63.7%	31.9%	83.4%	92.2%	51.0%
Kenton County	12,928	19.2%	80.8%	8.2%	91.8%	35.9%	64.1%	33.0%	89.6%	88.6%	47.0%
Warren County	11,276	43.2%	56.8%	9.2%	90.8%	28.8%	71.2%	24.0%	69.6%	91.3%	58.3%
Louisiana											
Ascension Parish	7,837	12.0%	88.0%	51.2%	48.8%	70.2%	29.8%	62.4%	95.0%	96.4%	86.4%
Bossier Parish	11,245	19.8%	80.2%	31.9%	68.1%	36.5%	63.5%	33.4%	70.5%	82.8%	30.7%
Caddo Parish	17,225	20.9%	79.1%	13.5%	86.5%	28.7%	71.3%	23.2%	72.7%	84.2%	43.4%
Calcasieu Parish	16,598	21.4%	78.6%	12.6%	87.4%	49.4%	50.6%	34.0%	82.1%	80.8%	31.0%
East Baton Rouge Parish	42,243	34.6%	65.4%	8.5%	91.5%	31.5%	68.5%	26.0%	84.0%	93.1%	42.3%
Jefferson Parish	30,587	16.5%	83.5%	12.5%	87.5%	26.0%	74.0%	21.4%	80.5%	79.8%	33.5%
Lafayette Parish	20,984	22.4%	77.6%	8.9%	91.1%	40.5%	59.5%	34.2%	85.4%	90.7%	27.9%
Lafourche Parish	6,570	22.7%	77.3%	12.3%	87.7%	51.9%	48.1%	45.4%	76.9%	72.3%	31.3%
Livingston Parish	6,976	12.7%	87.3%	33.3%	66.7%	77.4%	22.6%	49.9%	93.3%	83.6%	35.9%
Orleans Parish	32,152	15.3%	84.7%	6.6%	93.4%	16.5%	83.5%	12.4%	62.7%	72.1%	33.5%
Ouachita Parish	11,051	27.5%	72.5%	12.3%	87.7%	42.6%	57.4%	25.4%	69.7%	80.4%	46.1%
Rapides Parish	9,607	22.6%	77.4%	12.7%	87.3%	27.7%	72.3%	20.0%	76.1%	78.0%	51.6%
St. Tammany Parish	11,201	17.0%	83.0%	11.4%	88.6%	61.0%	39.0%	52.1%	93.6%	92.1%	57.7%
Tangipahoa Parish	9,323	29.5%	70.5%	6.5%	93.5%	36.8%	63.2%	25.0%	56.8%	73.4%	40.8%
Terrebonne Parish	8,048	30.6%	69.4%	37.5%	62.5%	46.0%	54.0%	43.5%	91.9%	73.7%	36.2%
Maine											
Androscoggin County	8,067	21.7%	78.3%	38.0%	62.0%	49.7%	50.3%	39.7%	75.7%	89.7%	64.8%
Cumberland County	20,581	26.0%	74.0%	12.0%	88.0%	39.3%	60.7%	36.9%	78.4%	88.6%	42.8%
Kennebec County	7,085	32.8%	67.2%	12.4%	87.6%	69.0%	31.0%	69.0%	62.4%	92.1%	28.8%
Penobscot County	10,184	19.4%	80.6%	10.5%	89.5%	27.2%	72.8%	25.0%	64.0%	92.5%	48.5%
York County	9,320	20.7%	79.3%	33.4%	66.6%	72.3%	27.7%	70.1%	84.3%	90.3%	51.5%
Maryland											
Anne Arundel County	30,778	14.3%	85.7%	9.7%	90.3%	43.7%	56.3%	41.9%	80.7%	92.2%	56.2%
Baltimore County	45,367	18.2%	81.8%	12.5%	87.5%	37.6%	62.4%	32.1%	81.8%	91.4%	62.8%
Carroll County	6,630	10.3%	89.7%	47.9%	52.1%	62.6%	37.4%	57.8%	86.6%	94.7%	55.4%
Cecil County	6,283	18.3%	81.7%	38.9%	61.1%	43.6%	56.4%	33.1%	84.4%	85.4%	48.1%
Charles County	7,463	14.7%	85.3%	8.2%	91.8%	77.3%	22.7%	70.3%	89.5%	92.7%	32.8%
Frederick County	12,927	21.9%	78.1%	21.9%	78.1%	66.1%	33.9%	59.3%	87.9%	90.7%	42.3%
Harford County	12,141	14.3%	85.7%	42.3%	57.7%	54.8%	45.2%	49.7%	94.5%	91.1%	49.2%
Howard County	13,821	15.3%	84.7%	0.0%	100.0%	46.5%	53.5%	37.0%	99.1%	99.0%	78.5%
Montgomery County	50,852	14.5%	85.5%	3.7%	96.3%	31.8%	68.2%	27.8%	94.7%	94.5%	54.7%
Prince George's County	41,632	14.5%	85.5%	7.9%	92.1%	26.3%	73.7%	24.0%	78.1%	88.2%	38.6%
St. Mary's County	5,880	12.5%	87.5%	40.1%	59.9%	51.9%	48.1%	48.8%	84.7%	90.6%	48.7%
Washington County	7,446	32.7%	67.3%	30.0%	70.0%	40.4%	59.6%	36.7%	76.0%	81.1%	52.3%
Wicomico County	5,994	40.1%	59.9%	8.6%	91.4%	27.4%	72.6%	17.7%	73.6%	77.3%	29.8%
Massachusetts											
Barnstable County	6,875	8.3%	91.7%	11.9%	88.1%	41.5%	58.5%	38.7%	95.1%	90.0%	63.4%
Berkshire County	6,602	28.1%	71.9%	0.9%	99.1%	19.9%	80.1%	19.5%	63.0%	89.5%	45.8%
Bristol County	31,791	18.5%	81.5%	7.8%	92.2%	33.9%	66.1%	28.9%	81.0%	89.5%	46.5%
Essex County	37,753	15.3%	84.7%	12.8%	87.2%	34.9%	65.1%	32.0%	83.4%	89.0%	62.8%
Hampden County	25,722	21.3%	78.7%	12.5%	87.5%	40.0%	60.0%	35.3%	71.9%	88.1%	43.7%
Hampshire County	9,629	26.4%	73.6%	16.7%	83.3%	39.3%	60.7%	32.7%	57.2%	93.9%	30.3%
Middlesex County	91,538	14.3%	85.7%	9.8%	90.2%	28.7%	71.3%	24.9%	77.1%	93.6%	54.3%
Norfolk County	31,505	12.4%	87.6%	6.4%	93.6%	43.7%	56.3%	39.4%	78.5%	95.7%	60.9%
Plymouth County	16,546	12.3%	87.7%	2.8%	97.2%	46.9%	53.1%	41.8%	87.3%	94.2%	58.4%
Suffolk County	86,345	18.8%	81.2%	3.3%	96.7%	18.8%	81.2%	16.9%	65.2%	94.8%	38.9%
Worcester County	39,348	14.9%	85.1%	13.2%	86.8%	35.1%	64.9%	30.9%	78.1%	88.6%	51.2%
Michigan											
Allegan County	6,337	21.6%	78.4%	29.2%	70.8%	63.9%	36.1%	53.4%	91.5%	73.5%	49.7%
Bay County	7,389	26.6%	73.4%	27.6%	72.4%	62.5%	37.5%	42.1%	89.0%	87.3%	64.9%
Berrien County	10,272	20.4%	79.6%	15.5%	84.5%	38.4%	61.6%	33.2%	87.1%	85.0%	40.2%
Calhoun County	8,530	21.2%	78.8%	14.1%	85.9%	67.9%	32.1%	47.6%	78.6%	83.8%	60.0%
Eaton County	8,018	21.8%	78.2%	32.7%	67.3%	43.1%	56.9%	33.8%	90.5%	87.2%	53.3%
Genesee County	23,051	25.2%	74.8%	9.8%	90.2%	48.4%	51.6%	35.9%	75.8%	82.9%	35.8%
Ingham County	28,605	37.2%	62.8%	4.1%	95.9%	29.2%	70.8%	22.7%	69.5%	89.8%	46.6%
Jackson County	8,725	20.3%	79.7%	18.0%	82.0%	51.7%	48.3%	39.5%	77.8%	84.9%	61.0%
Kalamazoo County	21,755	37.4%	62.6%	4.3%	95.7%	48.7%	51.3%	42.6%	84.5%	97.8%	64.3%
Kent County	48,868	20.1%	79.9%	13.5%	86.5%	46.5%	53.5%	41.0%	86.5%	91.5%	67.4%
Lenawee County	5,431	30.7%	69.3%	4.6%	95.4%	53.3%	46.7%	48.0%	77.4%	81.2%	45.9%
Livingston County	7,402	21.2%	78.8%	52.3%	47.7%	72.6%	27.4%	62.7%	88.9%	95.4%	50.0%

Table K-2: Counties—Summary Housing Characteristics—*Continued*

	Millennial Householders	Age of Householders		18 to 24 Years Old		25 to 33 Years Old			Percent with Internet Access		Percent with Mobile Access Plan
		18 to 24	25 to 33	Owners	Renters	Owners	Renters	With Mortgage	18 to 24	25 to 33	
Michigan—Cont.											
Macomb County	49,700	18.6%	81.4%	14.8%	85.2%	47.6%	52.4%	35.9%	95.1%	93.1%	51.9%
Monroe County	6,709	24.0%	76.0%	79.0%	21.0%	69.9%	30.1%	59.0%	88.9%	89.8%	47.3%
Muskegon County	9,786	20.0%	80.0%	5.1%	94.9%	59.3%	40.7%	44.1%	75.9%	78.4%	30.4%
Oakland County	74,601	18.9%	81.1%	18.6%	81.4%	44.0%	56.0%	36.2%	90.1%	95.0%	65.0%
Ottawa County	16,768	31.5%	68.5%	15.4%	84.6%	63.7%	36.3%	50.7%	75.0%	91.7%	37.8%
Saginaw County	13,074	20.7%	79.3%	3.4%	96.6%	48.1%	51.9%	32.2%	72.7%	86.5%	53.9%
St. Clair County	8,955	28.7%	71.3%	35.5%	64.5%	50.5%	49.5%	38.8%	90.8%	92.1%	64.7%
Washtenaw County	37,602	39.5%	60.5%	5.0%	95.0%	27.7%	72.3%	26.0%	77.8%	90.3%	55.0%
Wayne County	101,949	17.4%	82.6%	22.9%	77.1%	36.6%	63.4%	23.4%	81.0%	83.4%	34.5%
Minnesota											
Anoka County	19,033	19.9%	80.1%	26.2%	73.8%	69.7%	30.3%	64.0%	96.1%	93.0%	61.1%
Carver County	4,970	11.8%	88.2%	7.5%	92.5%	77.7%	22.3%	64.0%	82.4%	94.0%	42.7%
Dakota County	25,362	18.3%	81.7%	20.6%	79.4%	58.1%	41.9%	48.5%	86.2%	92.2%	66.5%
Hennepin County	111,726	18.2%	81.8%	9.0%	91.0%	38.4%	61.6%	33.2%	86.5%	93.7%	57.4%
Olmsted County	11,087	26.1%	73.9%	16.1%	83.9%	57.4%	42.6%	50.8%	93.3%	94.0%	59.1%
Ramsey County	45,114	16.9%	83.1%	5.8%	94.2%	29.6%	70.4%	25.3%	76.4%	92.2%	60.1%
Scott County	15,443	26.5%	73.5%	26.1%	73.9%	57.4%	42.6%	49.1%	79.9%	88.2%	50.8%
St. Louis County	7,878	14.6%	85.4%	0.0%	100.0%	84.4%	15.6%	67.0%	85.0%	88.4%	56.2%
Stearns County	16,165	35.8%	64.2%	14.5%	85.5%	39.0%	61.0%	39.0%	69.1%	85.6%	36.5%
Washington County	11,041	10.0%	90.0%	20.3%	79.7%	55.1%	44.9%	62.2%	95.4%	94.3%	73.8%
Wright County	8,026	19.4%	80.6%	42.1%	57.9%	59.5%	40.5%	54.0%	95.5%	97.9%	46.8%
Mississippi											
DeSoto County	9,376	28.1%	71.9%	24.7%	75.3%	59.2%	40.8%	49.7%	93.8%	89.1%	44.3%
Harrison County	16,785	23.2%	76.8%	13.6%	86.4%	25.0%	75.0%	20.1%	70.7%	81.6%	53.3%
Hinds County	20,647	20.0%	80.0%	4.6%	95.4%	23.7%	76.3%	18.8%	63.1%	74.7%	27.5%
Jackson County	6,916	13.6%	86.4%	8.7%	91.3%	47.8%	52.2%	43.2%	80.9%	81.3%	35.0%
Madison County	5,181	23.9%	76.1%	0.0%	100.0%	55.5%	44.5%	42.6%	73.2%	82.5%	44.6%
Rankin County	8,953	11.9%	88.1%	0.0%	100.0%	61.8%	38.2%	51.9%	88.4%	81.0%	37.9%
Missouri											
Boone County	22,496	41.9%	58.1%	3.5%	96.5%	37.7%	62.3%	36.5%	72.1%	93.6%	33.3%
Cass County	6,317	19.0%	81.0%	13.2%	86.8%	61.0%	39.0%	58.0%	87.8%	91.6%	57.1%
Clay County	15,147	15.5%	84.5%	5.7%	94.3%	48.5%	51.5%	41.9%	93.0%	95.2%	63.2%
Franklin County	6,102	19.4%	80.6%	48.4%	51.6%	61.2%	38.8%	47.9%	87.9%	75.8%	50.6%
Greene County	30,088	38.8%	61.2%	12.6%	87.4%	40.1%	59.9%	34.6%	77.6%	86.9%	37.1%
Jackson County	58,428	23.4%	76.6%	14.1%	85.9%	36.6%	63.4%	30.0%	83.3%	84.9%	46.9%
Jasper County	7,923	27.6%	72.4%	23.7%	76.3%	45.0%	55.0%	40.5%	67.6%	82.7%	31.0%
Jefferson County	13,117	12.7%	87.3%	54.9%	45.1%	69.9%	30.1%	63.6%	91.1%	89.2%	34.8%
Platte County	7,393	26.1%	73.9%	1.8%	98.2%	33.5%	66.5%	31.6%	98.8%	91.3%	83.8%
St. Charles County	22,019	11.2%	88.8%	13.9%	86.1%	58.5%	41.5%	50.7%	79.4%	92.0%	48.7%
St. Louis County	62,382	19.7%	80.3%	14.5%	85.5%	42.7%	57.3%	38.7%	85.7%	92.6%	60.0%
Montana											
Flathead County	3,894	12.9%	87.1%	0.0%	100.0%	32.9%	67.1%	24.2%	89.6%	90.1%	40.5%
Gallatin County	11,016	39.6%	60.4%	11.7%	88.3%	43.7%	56.3%	40.9%	78.6%	90.9%	55.4%
Missoula County	11,686	30.4%	69.6%	13.9%	86.1%	39.2%	60.8%	28.1%	78.5%	85.6%	37.8%
Yellowstone County	10,252	34.5%	65.5%	17.4%	82.6%	36.7%	63.3%	34.4%	84.5%	87.0%	23.1%
Nebraska											
Douglas County	53,168	22.6%	77.4%	10.8%	89.2%	35.9%	64.1%	34.0%	83.2%	90.8%	49.9%
Lancaster County	33,223	38.0%	62.0%	6.4%	93.6%	39.9%	60.1%	36.9%	79.4%	91.2%	43.3%
Sarpy County	14,077	17.8%	82.2%	14.0%	86.0%	56.1%	43.9%	53.3%	92.6%	98.4%	61.3%
Nevada											
Clark County	137,446	16.7%	83.3%	13.5%	86.5%	28.1%	71.9%	22.6%	86.1%	86.0%	48.7%
Washoe County	33,204	21.7%	78.3%	7.5%	92.5%	34.5%	65.5%	26.9%	86.2%	89.9%	56.3%
New Hampshire											
Hillsborough County	24,458	18.4%	81.6%	6.5%	93.5%	46.7%	53.3%	42.9%	87.0%	94.6%	61.0%
Merrimack County	6,982	26.0%	74.0%	54.5%	45.5%	45.3%	54.7%	40.5%	72.8%	93.0%	33.5%
Rockingham County	14,768	12.4%	87.6%	43.7%	56.3%	50.1%	49.9%	46.7%	89.8%	95.6%	57.5%
Strafford County	9,005	35.2%	64.8%	10.7%	89.3%	36.8%	63.2%	31.3%	61.6%	95.5%	33.5%
New Jersey											
Atlantic County	14,511	16.4%	83.6%	15.1%	84.9%	35.8%	64.2%	26.4%	83.1%	90.4%	32.1%
Bergen County	34,405	13.6%	86.4%	22.3%	77.7%	28.6%	71.4%	27.5%	94.2%	92.9%	47.6%
Burlington County	19,035	13.1%	86.9%	13.4%	86.6%	34.3%	65.7%	28.5%	88.9%	90.1%	53.3%
Camden County	25,738	14.2%	85.8%	8.6%	91.4%	42.3%	57.7%	37.0%	90.8%	91.8%	63.4%
Cape May County	3,805	1.6%	98.4%	100.0%	0.0%	48.9%	51.1%	44.4%	88.0%	88.9%	40.7%
Cumberland County	7,253	14.9%	85.1%	5.1%	94.9%	33.2%	66.8%	26.4%	88.0%	71.5%	25.7%
Essex County	39,252	14.1%	85.9%	4.0%	96.0%	14.6%	85.4%	11.7%	81.2%	88.0%	51.3%
Gloucester County	12,908	13.7%	86.3%	36.2%	63.8%	50.3%	49.7%	45.3%	87.3%	95.5%	62.1%
Hudson County	61,005	11.8%	88.2%	3.7%	96.3%	14.9%	85.1%	12.4%	87.7%	94.0%	47.7%
Hunterdon County	3,253	31.3%	68.7%	19.1%	80.9%	47.9%	52.1%	47.9%	86.2%	92.7%	46.5%
Mercer County	15,640	9.5%	90.5%	20.0%	80.0%	24.7%	75.3%	15.3%	75.3%	87.7%	40.3%
Middlesex County	34,334	10.7%	89.3%	5.3%	94.7%	22.7%	77.3%	19.3%	71.8%	91.4%	50.7%
Monmouth County	24,284	10.0%	90.0%	15.9%	84.1%	36.3%	63.7%	34.5%	94.4%	95.7%	53.9%
Morris County	18,091	12.4%	87.6%	28.3%	71.7%	40.8%	59.2%	39.9%	91.9%	97.3%	45.9%
Ocean County	22,109	13.2%	86.8%	13.3%	86.7%	50.5%	49.5%	45.3%	86.3%	87.0%	37.2%
Passaic County	19,210	10.3%	89.7%	0.0%	100.0%	18.7%	81.3%	15.0%	76.3%	81.7%	47.5%

Table K-2: Counties—Summary Housing Characteristics—*Continued*

	Millennial Householders	Age of Householders		18 to 24 Years Old		25 to 33 Years Old		With Mortgage	Percent with Internet Access		Percent with Mobile Access Plan
		18 to 24	25 to 33	Owners	Renters	Owners	Renters		18 to 24	25 to 33	
New Jersey—Cont.											
Somerset County	11,299	16.5%	83.5%	13.1%	86.9%	39.9%	60.1%	37.8%	97.0%	97.8%	51.9%
Sussex County	5,036	18.6%	81.4%	44.1%	55.9%	59.8%	40.2%	57.4%	94.6%	94.6%	32.5%
Union County	24,353	15.1%	84.9%	12.7%	87.3%	25.8%	74.2%	24.1%	90.4%	90.9%	48.7%
Warren County	4,310	19.4%	80.6%	0.0%	100.0%	50.8%	49.2%	48.7%	89.7%	93.7%	34.0%
New Mexico											
Bernalillo County	50,234	19.3%	80.7%	12.9%	87.1%	33.1%	66.9%	27.9%	78.6%	84.8%	33.6%
Doña Ana County	15,136	36.6%	63.4%	18.7%	81.3%	27.2%	72.8%	15.1%	78.5%	77.6%	65.5%
San Juan County	5,399	4.4%	95.6%	4.2%	95.8%	57.4%	42.6%	54.7%	87.1%	92.3%	51.9%
Sandoval County	7,470	27.8%	72.2%	0.7%	99.3%	51.8%	48.2%	39.5%	68.4%	66.2%	34.8%
Santa Fe County	6,963	20.6%	79.4%	9.3%	90.7%	46.4%	53.6%	35.6%	69.2%	84.7%	52.0%
New York											
Albany County	21,821	30.5%	69.5%	2.5%	97.5%	18.9%	81.1%	12.5%	73.3%	88.6%	42.7%
Bronx County	79,965	15.8%	84.2%	5.9%	94.1%	5.3%	94.7%	3.5%	84.4%	86.9%	47.3%
Broome County	11,646	31.7%	68.3%	15.1%	84.9%	35.3%	64.7%	31.7%	73.4%	92.2%	42.7%
Chautauqua County	6,759	29.2%	70.8%	6.3%	93.7%	51.9%	48.1%	46.9%	71.1%	86.2%	36.3%
Dutchess County	12,117	13.7%	86.3%	0.0%	100.0%	34.7%	65.3%	30.9%	67.8%	92.0%	39.1%
Erie County	63,132	19.7%	80.3%	7.5%	92.5%	39.9%	60.1%	34.2%	78.1%	89.1%	36.0%
Jefferson County	10,431	29.2%	70.8%	5.3%	94.7%	28.5%	71.5%	24.6%	74.3%	87.9%	56.5%
Kings County	184,007	14.2%	85.8%	6.2%	93.8%	10.4%	89.6%	7.3%	85.9%	87.6%	38.3%
Monroe County	54,071	22.3%	77.7%	11.4%	88.6%	39.7%	60.3%	36.4%	75.5%	92.2%	51.7%
Nassau County	31,319	9.1%	90.9%	27.4%	72.6%	51.3%	48.7%	46.7%	91.1%	96.3%	40.0%
New York County	178,433	12.5%	87.5%	7.3%	92.7%	9.0%	91.0%	4.5%	71.9%	93.4%	44.5%
Niagara County	9,558	16.5%	83.5%	35.6%	64.4%	37.1%	62.9%	31.1%	90.4%	84.4%	45.0%
Oneida County	13,100	20.5%	79.5%	6.7%	93.3%	27.9%	72.1%	25.3%	70.2%	82.9%	32.0%
Onondaga County	29,799	19.9%	80.1%	6.4%	93.6%	33.9%	66.1%	30.2%	69.5%	84.7%	48.6%
Ontario County	6,352	21.2%	78.8%	14.4%	85.6%	57.3%	42.7%	51.1%	60.0%	85.6%	48.3%
Orange County	16,523	22.1%	77.9%	6.4%	93.6%	33.2%	66.8%	31.3%	78.9%	85.8%	44.2%
Oswego County	7,053	26.5%	73.5%	24.2%	75.8%	67.5%	32.5%	49.7%	65.9%	91.6%	53.3%
Putnam County	1,659	8.0%	92.0%	37.6%	62.4%	71.7%	28.3%	71.7%	95.6%	94.2%	70.1%
Queens County	114,190	13.6%	86.4%	5.6%	94.4%	17.9%	82.1%	13.4%	88.0%	90.9%	35.2%
Rensselaer County	9,950	15.9%	84.1%	8.1%	91.9%	34.9%	65.1%	32.1%	69.7%	91.0%	36.3%
Richmond County	18,525	12.5%	87.5%	21.0%	79.0%	35.6%	64.4%	31.8%	89.0%	89.1%	32.0%
Rockland County	11,454	10.5%	89.5%	0.0%	100.0%	32.3%	67.7%	30.8%	75.7%	79.3%	40.4%
Saratoga County	7,138	25.2%	74.8%	23.5%	76.5%	50.6%	49.4%	46.8%	44.5%	75.8%	45.5%
Schenectady County	13,045	14.5%	85.5%	9.4%	90.6%	37.9%	62.1%	33.0%	84.8%	98.8%	72.6%
St. Lawrence County	6,194	8.4%	91.6%	34.4%	65.6%	39.7%	60.3%	30.3%	69.1%	92.1%	36.7%
Steuben County	4,355	16.8%	83.2%	13.5%	86.5%	47.4%	52.6%	36.7%	82.3%	79.6%	45.0%
Suffolk County	35,152	11.1%	88.9%	17.9%	82.1%	52.5%	47.5%	46.8%	88.7%	92.2%	41.0%
Tompkins County	10,141	49.3%	50.7%	6.8%	93.2%	25.3%	74.7%	21.1%	54.0%	87.2%	18.1%
Ulster County	7,501	25.1%	74.9%	2.3%	97.7%	42.6%	57.4%	27.4%	78.4%	83.1%	38.2%
Wayne County	4,883	27.7%	72.3%	4.1%	95.9%	39.2%	60.8%	32.8%	74.1%	79.3%	40.9%
Westchester County	33,003	14.9%	85.1%	7.4%	92.6%	26.2%	73.8%	23.4%	82.7%	88.9%	61.4%
North Carolina											
Alamance County	9,123	27.4%	72.6%	8.5%	91.5%	52.2%	47.8%	39.5%	67.4%	88.4%	53.2%
Brunswick County	3,831	20.9%	79.1%	22.5%	77.5%	17.4%	82.6%	15.1%	83.3%	84.7%	41.8%
Buncombe County	17,761	23.0%	77.0%	8.4%	91.6%	33.2%	66.8%	28.0%	77.6%	82.8%	58.2%
Cabarrus County	10,479	20.5%	79.5%	38.5%	61.5%	47.4%	52.6%	40.0%	89.4%	91.5%	71.1%
Catawba County	8,368	18.9%	81.1%	11.3%	88.7%	35.6%	64.4%	33.9%	76.3%	90.7%	54.9%
Cleveland County	5,481	30.4%	69.6%	17.2%	82.8%	36.7%	63.3%	21.8%	75.3%	76.2%	41.9%
Craven County	8,731	35.1%	64.9%	26.2%	73.8%	26.8%	73.2%	19.0%	78.5%	89.3%	64.2%
Cumberland County	30,640	25.1%	74.9%	6.4%	93.6%	22.5%	77.5%	20.2%	74.3%	87.2%	41.5%
Davidson County	8,111	14.6%	85.4%	57.7%	42.3%	36.5%	63.5%	29.8%	87.7%	74.0%	34.5%
Durham County	30,462	25.7%	74.3%	3.6%	96.4%	32.6%	67.4%	30.7%	72.1%	93.0%	64.6%
Forsyth County	26,052	21.9%	78.1%	12.0%	88.0%	38.1%	61.9%	33.1%	74.7%	86.6%	36.8%
Gaston County	13,147	21.5%	78.5%	11.8%	88.2%	46.5%	53.5%	37.0%	83.4%	84.3%	56.3%
Guilford County	33,866	17.7%	82.3%	1.4%	98.6%	23.6%	76.4%	21.0%	67.9%	80.9%	32.0%
Harnett County	9,485	22.8%	77.2%	5.6%	94.4%	45.0%	55.0%	43.6%	73.4%	82.6%	24.6%
Henderson County	6,043	28.7%	71.3%	10.4%	89.6%	34.7%	65.3%	20.9%	82.5%	89.3%	71.9%
Iredell County	8,503	19.5%	80.5%	33.9%	66.1%	38.3%	61.7%	28.8%	92.0%	89.4%	35.3%
Johnston County	7,904	14.2%	85.8%	46.0%	54.0%	53.0%	47.0%	38.4%	78.6%	76.5%	26.7%
Mecklenburg County	89,021	19.9%	80.1%	7.6%	92.4%	31.6%	68.4%	29.0%	82.4%	90.4%	48.3%
Moore County	4,462	9.1%	90.9%	4.4%	95.6%	32.1%	67.9%	26.2%	87.3%	87.9%	65.7%
Nash County	4,339	5.5%	94.5%	0.0%	100.0%	18.0%	82.0%	14.9%	85.9%	74.5%	34.5%
New Hanover County	18,302	34.3%	65.7%	6.8%	93.2%	35.0%	65.0%	26.6%	75.0%	80.3%	50.0%
Onslow County	25,008	35.6%	64.4%	10.1%	89.9%	33.2%	66.8%	27.4%	60.7%	89.8%	54.8%
Orange County	12,251	38.9%	61.1%	3.5%	96.5%	28.7%	71.3%	21.7%	62.4%	91.7%	52.4%
Pitt County	20,100	38.5%	61.5%	4.3%	95.7%	36.8%	63.2%	25.1%	80.0%	90.9%	29.5%
Randolph County	7,730	25.5%	74.5%	6.3%	93.7%	55.1%	44.9%	46.7%	90.4%	94.4%	44.4%
Robeson County	6,089	20.1%	79.9%	10.2%	89.8%	27.2%	72.8%	13.6%	48.9%	62.7%	19.3%
Rockingham County	3,877	15.1%	84.9%	38.7%	61.3%	39.3%	60.7%	36.5%	84.6%	87.8%	46.3%
Rowan County	6,296	27.4%	72.6%	25.2%	74.8%	54.1%	45.9%	45.6%	81.0%	71.6%	48.0%
Union County	9,478	26.0%	74.0%	11.6%	88.4%	44.4%	55.6%	38.5%	88.9%	89.7%	85.4%
Wake County	79,381	22.0%	78.0%	3.2%	96.8%	39.7%	60.3%	36.0%	79.9%	91.4%	55.5%
Wayne County	8,110	21.7%	78.3%	42.6%	57.4%	33.5%	66.5%	32.9%	81.5%	92.9%	65.2%
North Dakota											
Cass County	23,451	42.6%	57.4%	13.3%	86.7%	30.4%	69.6%	23.9%	82.6%	95.6%	53.3%

Table K-2: Counties—Summary Housing Characteristics—*Continued*

	Millennial Householders	Age of Householders		18 to 24 Years Old		25 to 33 Years Old			Percent with Internet Access		Percent with Mobile Access Plan
		18 to 24	25 to 33	Owners	Renters	Owners	Renters	With Mortgage	18 to 24	25 to 33	
Ohio											
Allen County	6,332	31.1%	68.9%	16.3%	83.7%	32.3%	67.7%	21.6%	74.0%	93.6%	48.9%
Ashtabula County	4,201	27.5%	72.5%	4.2%	95.8%	48.3%	51.7%	40.2%	73.2%	80.9%	30.3%
Butler County	22,076	27.1%	72.9%	13.3%	86.7%	43.5%	56.5%	35.5%	83.0%	89.7%	53.3%
Clark County	8,439	27.5%	72.5%	8.1%	91.9%	37.7%	62.3%	33.0%	76.0%	81.2%	64.3%
Clermont County	11,704	15.1%	84.9%	6.3%	93.7%	50.3%	49.7%	40.2%	93.8%	94.1%	47.7%
Columbiana County	4,950	34.3%	65.7%	11.9%	88.1%	48.4%	51.6%	36.5%	81.4%	88.2%	58.3%
Cuyahoga County	87,961	22.1%	77.9%	4.0%	96.0%	32.4%	67.6%	26.8%	83.2%	90.7%	55.8%
Delaware County	8,044	19.3%	80.7%	3.8%	96.2%	72.5%	27.5%	69.4%	88.3%	91.1%	57.1%
Fairfield County	8,059	17.4%	82.6%	15.0%	85.0%	45.3%	54.7%	42.7%	94.8%	90.3%	60.7%
Franklin County	123,459	21.5%	78.5%	11.4%	88.6%	26.7%	73.3%	22.9%	77.2%	93.9%	51.9%
Geauga County	4,223	19.3%	80.7%	43.7%	56.3%	75.0%	25.0%	66.6%	76.1%	80.9%	46.1%
Greene County	14,280	30.6%	69.4%	4.3%	95.7%	36.8%	63.2%	33.2%	66.0%	92.8%	50.0%
Hamilton County	68,132	20.3%	79.7%	5.9%	94.1%	29.7%	70.3%	26.3%	83.1%	91.5%	53.7%
Lake County	13,434	20.5%	79.5%	23.7%	76.3%	45.9%	54.1%	42.4%	89.1%	88.1%	53.7%
Licking County	10,005	19.4%	80.6%	11.8%	88.2%	58.3%	41.7%	51.1%	75.7%	83.8%	56.3%
Lorain County	15,715	18.9%	81.1%	13.1%	86.9%	45.7%	54.3%	36.9%	83.4%	84.7%	47.9%
Lucas County	35,167	29.9%	70.1%	9.0%	91.0%	31.3%	68.7%	24.2%	81.1%	89.1%	51.9%
Mahoning County	15,500	23.6%	76.4%	21.8%	78.2%	40.3%	59.7%	33.9%	79.3%	90.0%	38.5%
Medina County	8,784	24.8%	75.2%	14.1%	85.9%	57.6%	42.4%	55.6%	96.3%	93.2%	68.9%
Miami County	6,508	27.6%	72.4%	26.6%	73.4%	58.9%	41.1%	57.3%	93.4%	88.9%	46.5%
Montgomery County	41,029	25.5%	74.5%	9.3%	90.7%	34.7%	65.3%	31.5%	72.9%	89.6%	63.9%
Portage County	12,177	43.4%	56.6%	9.4%	90.6%	44.2%	55.8%	38.3%	69.5%	82.9%	19.8%
Richland County	5,604	24.6%	75.4%	3.6%	96.4%	43.8%	56.2%	26.0%	76.8%	78.1%	37.1%
Stark County	23,653	19.5%	80.5%	14.3%	85.7%	48.1%	51.9%	41.3%	84.7%	91.3%	62.8%
Summit County	39,728	22.0%	78.0%	6.4%	93.6%	40.7%	59.3%	36.4%	88.2%	89.9%	52.0%
Trumbull County	12,905	33.8%	66.2%	14.9%	85.1%	49.7%	50.3%	40.9%	80.6%	79.8%	37.2%
Tuscarawas County	4,229	22.7%	77.3%	29.3%	70.7%	49.1%	50.9%	40.2%	90.7%	87.9%	52.2%
Warren County	10,662	19.3%	80.7%	13.8%	86.2%	60.7%	39.3%	57.8%	91.0%	87.0%	60.7%
Wayne County	5,560	19.7%	80.3%	18.6%	81.4%	53.4%	46.6%	43.2%	60.8%	84.4%	54.2%
Wood County	11,689	32.3%	67.7%	10.6%	89.4%	54.9%	45.1%	40.2%	80.7%	95.8%	38.1%
Oklahoma											
Canadian County	6,535	13.5%	86.5%	32.7%	67.3%	61.2%	38.8%	56.8%	89.9%	94.4%	55.6%
Cleveland County	23,619	30.7%	69.3%	15.7%	84.3%	49.2%	50.8%	35.6%	73.4%	90.4%	62.6%
Comanche County	9,115	23.9%	76.1%	20.9%	79.1%	38.7%	61.3%	25.8%	66.6%	83.8%	63.4%
Oklahoma County	65,851	21.1%	78.9%	12.3%	87.7%	35.4%	64.6%	30.4%	80.1%	83.8%	55.3%
Tulsa County	55,021	25.9%	74.1%	10.7%	89.3%	36.7%	63.3%	32.3%	84.1%	87.1%	56.9%
Oregon											
Clackamas County	18,367	15.2%	84.8%	1.6%	98.4%	46.2%	53.8%	41.3%	94.0%	94.3%	67.0%
Deschutes County	11,579	18.1%	81.9%	17.0%	83.0%	28.6%	71.4%	27.8%	86.7%	96.2%	64.6%
Douglas County	6,169	8.3%	91.7%	3.3%	96.7%	18.0%	82.0%	17.4%	93.0%	93.2%	66.8%
Jackson County	10,306	21.6%	78.4%	27.3%	72.7%	29.8%	70.2%	28.2%	90.1%	92.5%	52.0%
Lane County	28,697	36.5%	63.5%	5.0%	95.0%	26.1%	73.9%	24.5%	87.8%	94.6%	64.0%
Linn County	9,523	39.5%	60.5%	10.0%	90.0%	43.0%	57.0%	38.3%	80.4%	85.2%	51.4%
Marion County	18,573	21.1%	78.9%	2.9%	97.1%	37.8%	62.2%	34.4%	87.8%	86.4%	75.9%
Multnomah County	63,480	17.2%	82.8%	7.6%	92.4%	24.2%	75.8%	20.3%	83.5%	93.2%	65.2%
Washington County	37,874	17.9%	82.1%	8.7%	91.3%	33.7%	66.3%	29.2%	93.2%	93.7%	64.5%
Yamhill County	5,809	35.3%	64.7%	29.6%	70.4%	46.6%	53.4%	40.5%	88.0%	91.4%	65.5%
Pennsylvania											
Adams County	5,018	15.0%	85.0%	28.1%	71.9%	57.1%	42.9%	51.8%	66.8%	93.5%	43.4%
Allegheny County	98,795	20.9%	79.1%	11.5%	88.5%	35.6%	64.4%	30.3%	82.3%	92.9%	54.6%
Beaver County	7,864	14.7%	85.3%	7.8%	92.2%	53.0%	47.0%	42.8%	87.7%	96.6%	71.6%
Berks County	20,483	13.1%	86.9%	13.9%	86.1%	51.1%	48.9%	43.2%	77.0%	92.9%	58.8%
Blair County	6,151	17.8%	82.2%	12.6%	87.4%	53.7%	46.3%	40.9%	77.1%	86.1%	42.0%
Bucks County	23,313	9.9%	90.1%	13.4%	86.6%	53.4%	46.6%	48.0%	91.4%	94.3%	65.6%
Butler County	10,579	24.5%	75.5%	11.4%	88.6%	48.2%	51.8%	45.9%	78.7%	96.1%	63.1%
Cambria County	7,060	11.7%	88.3%	42.0%	58.0%	49.4%	50.6%	39.2%	65.5%	83.8%	52.7%
Centre County	16,872	41.2%	58.8%	0.7%	99.3%	31.5%	68.5%	29.8%	65.4%	86.4%	35.4%
Chester County	23,843	22.0%	78.0%	5.9%	94.1%	48.2%	51.8%	42.0%	78.0%	92.1%	50.0%
Cumberland County	12,404	7.7%	92.3%	6.9%	93.1%	44.3%	55.7%	42.7%	67.1%	91.6%	61.2%
Dauphin County	18,791	30.1%	69.9%	18.1%	81.9%	39.8%	60.2%	35.4%	88.1%	91.8%	53.1%
Delaware County	24,126	9.7%	90.3%	6.3%	93.7%	43.9%	56.1%	37.6%	70.1%	91.9%	41.9%
Erie County	17,419	25.9%	74.1%	8.3%	91.7%	38.4%	61.6%	25.6%	71.1%	86.7%	48.2%
Fayette County	7,048	20.4%	79.6%	22.3%	77.7%	53.8%	46.2%	37.0%	88.3%	79.4%	40.3%
Franklin County	7,801	21.2%	78.8%	9.8%	90.2%	55.4%	44.6%	54.0%	81.0%	91.7%	36.3%
Lackawanna County	10,035	20.8%	79.2%	10.5%	89.5%	47.2%	52.8%	31.5%	72.5%	90.4%	46.4%
Lancaster County	30,427	17.8%	82.2%	14.8%	85.2%	41.7%	58.3%	37.5%	74.0%	81.7%	35.0%
Lebanon County	7,886	29.8%	70.2%	9.1%	90.9%	58.3%	41.7%	51.1%	82.4%	90.5%	58.3%
Lehigh County	20,103	15.3%	84.7%	17.7%	82.3%	33.0%	67.0%	31.5%	81.3%	87.6%	33.7%
Luzerne County	17,097	18.3%	81.7%	9.5%	90.5%	45.5%	54.5%	39.8%	69.2%	86.6%	41.1%
Lycoming County	6,388	19.1%	80.9%	14.8%	85.2%	47.5%	52.5%	39.2%	65.5%	78.2%	23.3%
Mercer County	4,191	12.0%	88.0%	55.9%	44.1%	42.1%	57.9%	32.1%	58.7%	72.9%	48.4%
Monroe County	5,185	11.6%	88.4%	0.0%	100.0%	47.6%	52.4%	28.3%	90.3%	89.7%	45.6%
Montgomery County	38,061	10.9%	89.1%	16.4%	83.6%	44.1%	55.9%	39.1%	87.4%	92.3%	66.4%
Northampton County	14,618	22.4%	77.6%	19.1%	80.9%	38.5%	61.5%	34.3%	71.4%	91.9%	28.3%
Northumberland County	5,670	19.7%	80.3%	45.1%	54.9%	40.0%	60.0%	33.5%	76.2%	81.7%	26.0%
Philadelphia County	125,781	16.6%	83.4%	10.1%	89.9%	26.1%	73.9%	19.9%	74.9%	89.1%	46.2%

Table K-2: Counties—Summary Housing Characteristics—*Continued*

	Millennial Householders	Age of Householders		18 to 24 Years Old		25 to 33 Years Old			Percent with Internet Access		Percent with Mobile Access Plan
		18 to 24	25 to 33	Owners	Renters	Owners	Renters	With Mortgage	18 to 24	25 to 33	
Pennsylvania—Cont.											
Schuylkill County	7,441	16.2%	83.8%	16.5%	83.5%	56.3%	43.7%	36.3%	88.2%	80.1%	46.6%
Washington County	8,386	21.6%	78.4%	18.1%	81.9%	54.2%	45.8%	33.6%	70.5%	85.8%	54.2%
Westmoreland County	17,628	20.0%	80.0%	11.1%	88.9%	53.8%	46.2%	40.5%	81.3%	87.0%	45.8%
York County	23,411	9.0%	91.0%	46.5%	53.5%	52.4%	47.6%	45.2%	81.2%	84.4%	40.9%
Rhode Island											
Kent County	8,524	9.9%	90.1%	7.6%	92.4%	41.0%	59.0%	39.1%	93.3%	94.9%	57.0%
Providence County	41,664	18.9%	81.1%	7.0%	93.0%	27.9%	72.1%	24.4%	66.9%	89.2%	51.0%
Washington County	5,489	19.6%	80.4%	0.0%	100.0%	38.9%	61.1%	27.4%	71.1%	95.1%	35.8%
South Carolina											
Aiken County	9,929	17.6%	82.4%	6.7%	93.3%	39.3%	60.7%	19.2%	80.1%	67.9%	43.5%
Anderson County	10,992	25.2%	74.8%	28.0%	72.0%	41.2%	58.8%	36.3%	79.9%	83.3%	48.0%
Beaufort County	9,536	18.6%	81.4%	7.1%	92.9%	37.3%	62.7%	31.9%	71.9%	70.8%	27.9%
Berkeley County	13,706	14.5%	85.5%	30.6%	69.4%	41.6%	58.4%	38.0%	80.9%	83.0%	51.8%
Charleston County	31,094	16.7%	83.3%	15.4%	84.6%	36.0%	64.0%	32.5%	77.1%	83.7%	45.1%
Dorchester County	9,726	13.5%	86.5%	31.7%	68.3%	41.2%	58.8%	37.6%	85.6%	78.8%	52.3%
Florence County	7,557	22.9%	77.1%	15.4%	84.6%	28.7%	71.3%	22.5%	76.4%	84.1%	28.2%
Greenville County	33,569	21.4%	78.6%	18.3%	81.7%	40.1%	59.9%	35.0%	71.5%	83.8%	43.5%
Horry County	19,394	18.9%	81.1%	13.2%	86.8%	37.2%	62.8%	27.5%	84.8%	90.9%	74.7%
Lexington County	17,840	17.8%	82.2%	34.4%	65.6%	50.8%	49.2%	39.9%	80.8%	78.6%	33.7%
Pickens County	10,937	34.7%	65.3%	7.4%	92.6%	48.2%	51.8%	44.9%	65.8%	68.8%	41.5%
Richland County	31,911	25.7%	74.3%	12.8%	87.2%	32.4%	67.6%	29.3%	64.9%	82.2%	30.0%
Spartanburg County	17,932	23.9%	76.1%	36.5%	63.5%	39.9%	60.1%	31.4%	77.5%	83.6%	63.2%
Sumter County	5,820	21.8%	78.2%	30.1%	69.9%	35.1%	64.9%	28.7%	70.4%	68.0%	18.1%
York County	16,942	22.2%	77.8%	8.7%	91.3%	56.6%	43.4%	40.3%	85.0%	93.6%	66.5%
South Dakota											
Minnehaha County	18,675	20.1%	79.9%	16.2%	83.8%	52.6%	47.4%	49.7%	74.8%	84.2%	36.4%
Pennington County	9,245	24.5%	75.5%	28.4%	71.6%	63.0%	37.0%	48.4%	76.0%	91.2%	51.8%
Tennessee											
Blount County	5,927	21.1%	78.9%	4.8%	95.2%	42.1%	57.9%	35.9%	75.4%	87.2%	31.8%
Bradley County	5,926	41.0%	59.0%	11.9%	88.1%	44.2%	55.8%	39.2%	70.8%	77.5%	39.9%
Davidson County	74,140	22.9%	77.1%	11.8%	88.2%	32.0%	68.0%	29.8%	73.0%	92.2%	51.9%
Hamilton County	22,463	18.3%	81.7%	15.7%	84.3%	45.2%	54.8%	41.0%	76.8%	90.7%	41.8%
Knox County	37,758	29.7%	70.3%	13.7%	86.3%	36.9%	63.1%	28.3%	77.7%	85.8%	38.6%
Madison County	8,658	28.3%	71.7%	2.7%	97.3%	34.6%	65.4%	27.9%	68.2%	82.8%	61.1%
Montgomery County	25,109	27.2%	72.8%	13.9%	86.1%	37.6%	62.4%	34.8%	85.3%	93.5%	52.3%
Rutherford County	24,153	29.3%	70.7%	12.2%	87.8%	49.7%	50.3%	43.7%	91.0%	86.5%	51.9%
Sevier County	6,476	34.5%	65.5%	1.1%	98.9%	36.5%	63.5%	28.3%	85.7%	94.9%	65.7%
Shelby County	65,939	21.8%	78.2%	4.9%	95.1%	28.4%	71.6%	23.1%	73.5%	77.7%	46.2%
Sullivan County	6,304	18.0%	82.0%	33.7%	66.3%	53.7%	46.3%	46.6%	82.4%	90.1%	33.3%
Sumner County	9,225	23.0%	77.0%	29.5%	70.5%	61.2%	38.8%	59.1%	96.8%	85.2%	41.2%
Washington County	10,297	35.0%	65.0%	28.9%	71.1%	34.3%	65.7%	21.4%	81.6%	92.7%	64.1%
Williamson County	7,956	27.4%	72.6%	32.5%	67.5%	60.4%	39.6%	54.5%	92.3%	97.4%	73.3%
Wilson County	6,623	17.6%	82.4%	21.9%	78.1%	76.2%	23.8%	68.3%	96.2%	87.4%	52.7%
Texas											
Bell County	31,946	32.1%	67.9%	5.5%	94.5%	26.7%	73.3%	23.3%	71.9%	84.8%	25.9%
Bexar County	123,376	21.4%	78.6%	8.5%	91.5%	32.2%	67.8%	27.4%	82.4%	89.0%	45.6%
Bowie County	4,532	17.1%	82.9%	12.1%	87.9%	46.9%	53.1%	37.5%	73.0%	71.7%	31.2%
Brazoria County	18,382	12.0%	88.0%	36.3%	63.7%	38.0%	62.0%	28.4%	87.3%	86.0%	56.5%
Brazos County	31,784	48.5%	51.5%	7.0%	93.0%	22.7%	77.3%	17.4%	77.4%	86.2%	52.9%
Cameron County	19,816	15.3%	84.7%	19.6%	80.4%	38.0%	62.0%	30.2%	63.4%	68.5%	25.7%
Collin County	59,303	18.7%	81.3%	16.0%	84.0%	33.7%	66.3%	27.4%	90.7%	89.2%	44.9%
Comal County	6,589	14.5%	85.5%	4.1%	95.9%	43.1%	56.9%	30.9%	89.3%	86.6%	63.7%
Dallas County	198,665	20.5%	79.5%	6.3%	93.7%	20.6%	79.4%	16.5%	76.8%	78.8%	42.9%
Denton County	59,379	23.5%	76.5%	15.5%	84.5%	40.7%	59.3%	36.2%	84.2%	92.0%	51.2%
Ector County	13,925	27.3%	72.7%	36.3%	63.7%	60.3%	39.7%	47.0%	93.2%	90.5%	82.4%
El Paso County	7,307	27.1%	72.9%	11.4%	88.6%	57.3%	42.7%	50.8%	85.1%	84.6%	38.0%
Ellis County	52,462	21.5%	78.5%	20.0%	80.0%	31.9%	68.1%	27.1%	81.5%	85.2%	38.7%
Fort Bend County	31,563	8.4%	91.6%	19.1%	80.9%	48.5%	51.5%	38.4%	91.0%	92.3%	71.8%
Galveston County	18,653	20.2%	79.8%	1.1%	98.9%	46.1%	53.9%	42.6%	83.0%	91.5%	56.7%
Grayson County	6,778	18.2%	81.8%	28.3%	71.7%	47.8%	52.2%	41.6%	79.9%	72.0%	47.3%
Gregg County	8,827	32.2%	67.8%	2.3%	97.7%	35.6%	64.4%	25.3%	64.9%	86.4%	41.8%
Guadalupe County	7,533	13.5%	86.5%	28.7%	71.3%	42.0%	58.0%	35.1%	87.0%	93.0%	73.9%
Harris County	350,497	19.0%	81.0%	9.7%	90.3%	26.8%	73.2%	22.5%	81.9%	81.9%	53.5%
Hays County	18,154	42.0%	58.0%	10.8%	89.2%	45.4%	54.6%	36.0%	75.1%	81.1%	34.6%
Hidalgo County	36,184	15.7%	84.3%	40.3%	59.7%	42.5%	57.5%	26.8%	73.2%	73.2%	44.3%
Jefferson County	18,505	25.0%	75.0%	6.9%	93.1%	32.0%	68.0%	24.7%	70.5%	63.8%	18.8%
Johnson County	8,026	24.4%	75.6%	16.5%	83.5%	72.6%	27.4%	65.5%	86.8%	83.5%	49.6%
Kaufman County	4,230	14.0%	86.0%	0.0%	100.0%	51.2%	48.8%	50.0%	81.4%	86.5%	38.6%
Lubbock County	30,296	38.9%	61.1%	8.3%	91.7%	31.8%	68.2%	25.6%	75.4%	88.5%	31.4%
McLennan County	20,688	41.6%	58.4%	6.9%	93.1%	33.9%	66.1%	25.5%	78.7%	83.5%	27.9%
Midland County	14,810	23.3%	76.7%	29.7%	70.3%	58.6%	41.4%	49.1%	89.5%	90.1%	59.8%
Montgomery County	27,930	14.3%	85.7%	9.8%	90.2%	49.7%	50.3%	42.5%	92.6%	90.4%	70.5%
Nueces County	28,204	23.6%	76.4%	4.1%	95.9%	34.4%	65.6%	28.4%	76.1%	92.8%	55.9%
Parker County	5,466	19.7%	80.3%	38.5%	61.5%	61.8%	38.2%	58.1%	87.2%	91.0%	68.1%

Table K-2: Counties—Summary Housing Characteristics—*Continued*

	Millennial Householders	Age of Householders		18 to 24 Years Old		25 to 33 Years Old			Percent with Internet Access		Percent with Mobile Access Plan
		18 to 24	25 to 33	Owners	Renters	Owners	Renters	With Mortgage	18 to 24	25 to 33	
Texas—Cont.											
Potter County	11,384	18.4%	81.6%	20.1%	79.9%	30.4%	69.6%	22.1%	77.1%	82.0%	38.2%
Randall County	10,500	18.0%	82.0%	12.7%	87.3%	38.0%	62.0%	35.9%	84.9%	84.6%	55.0%
Smith County	15,413	33.6%	66.4%	13.8%	86.2%	38.5%	61.5%	30.0%	77.5%	82.7%	31.3%
Tarrant County	134,770	20.4%	79.6%	8.6%	91.4%	34.7%	65.3%	31.0%	87.7%	88.3%	50.7%
Taylor County	12,451	41.0%	59.0%	11.2%	88.8%	43.7%	56.3%	30.0%	63.6%	77.7%	49.3%
Tom Green County	10,056	25.1%	74.9%	6.0%	94.0%	43.3%	56.7%	41.3%	62.4%	75.6%	23.7%
Travis County	121,585	17.6%	82.4%	2.8%	97.2%	23.4%	76.6%	18.3%	78.5%	85.7%	51.0%
Webb County	11,745	19.5%	80.5%	0.0%	100.0%	35.6%	64.4%	27.6%	61.5%	65.3%	35.4%
Wichita County	10,762	38.7%	61.3%	4.3%	95.7%	35.2%	64.8%	28.2%	57.7%	78.4%	38.3%
Williamson County	28,064	21.1%	78.9%	4.9%	95.1%	48.2%	51.8%	42.6%	92.5%	93.2%	70.3%
Utah											
Cache County	13,154	38.5%	61.5%	15.6%	84.4%	42.4%	57.6%	35.8%	89.0%	97.9%	47.1%
Davis County	19,609	18.0%	82.0%	25.1%	74.9%	63.4%	36.6%	57.7%	94.3%	95.0%	55.7%
Salt Lake County	76,773	19.6%	80.4%	16.9%	83.1%	41.8%	58.2%	38.3%	90.8%	95.0%	61.2%
Utah County	46,596	37.8%	62.2%	16.2%	83.8%	48.1%	51.9%	44.4%	84.7%	92.8%	60.5%
Washington County	8,334	32.5%	67.5%	14.0%	86.0%	39.7%	60.3%	37.8%	86.2%	94.6%	38.4%
Weber County	19,881	27.8%	72.2%	22.9%	77.1%	50.1%	49.9%	48.6%	88.2%	88.4%	55.4%
Vermont											
Chittenden County	11,130	29.0%	71.0%	18.7%	81.3%	37.1%	62.9%	27.7%	67.8%	96.6%	63.5%
Virginia											
Albemarle County	7,746	13.4%	86.6%	7.4%	92.6%	31.4%	68.6%	28.6%	72.5%	88.1%	33.7%
Arlington County	32,016	13.1%	86.9%	0.0%	100.0%	21.3%	78.7%	18.9%	90.4%	96.7%	51.9%
Chesterfield County	15,680	19.0%	81.0%	15.3%	84.7%	52.2%	47.8%	48.1%	89.0%	95.0%	44.2%
Fairfax County	54,078	14.4%	85.6%	16.4%	83.6%	37.5%	62.5%	33.2%	93.7%	94.6%	70.2%
Hanover County	3,512	18.8%	81.2%	9.8%	90.2%	60.0%	40.0%	53.8%	72.2%	81.9%	48.9%
Henrico County	19,855	23.4%	76.6%	8.7%	91.3%	31.4%	68.6%	27.7%	94.5%	93.3%	77.5%
Loudoun County	18,094	12.9%	87.1%	12.9%	87.1%	54.5%	45.5%	51.9%	99.1%	94.5%	68.1%
Montgomery County	11,583	41.4%	58.6%	6.6%	93.4%	43.8%	56.2%	35.3%	69.2%	92.1%	54.7%
Prince William County	18,973	8.0%	92.0%	14.0%	86.0%	50.3%	49.7%	45.8%	92.0%	95.0%	61.4%
Roanoke County	4,097	13.2%	86.8%	49.5%	50.5%	33.1%	66.9%	31.1%	85.1%	90.7%	42.5%
Spotsylvania County	4,755	8.3%	91.7%	46.9%	53.1%	52.5%	47.5%	49.6%	90.6%	82.5%	41.2%
Stafford County	8,782	18.8%	81.2%	10.8%	89.2%	39.3%	60.7%	39.3%	72.7%	90.9%	41.6%
Washington											
Benton County	13,506	21.2%	78.8%	17.2%	82.8%	43.7%	56.3%	38.1%	86.9%	84.1%	32.7%
Clark County	26,233	23.7%	76.3%	22.8%	77.2%	34.7%	65.3%	32.5%	97.7%	92.9%	59.2%
Cowlitz County	6,886	25.6%	74.4%	26.6%	73.4%	34.1%	65.9%	31.4%	89.4%	87.3%	55.7%
Grant County	6,986	46.7%	53.3%	7.6%	92.4%	46.9%	53.1%	40.8%	75.4%	87.6%	45.3%
King County	179,453	15.9%	84.1%	5.5%	94.5%	26.4%	73.6%	23.1%	89.1%	96.1%	71.3%
Kitsap County	17,504	21.1%	78.9%	17.5%	82.5%	40.4%	59.6%	37.6%	86.9%	86.5%	69.1%
Pierce County	59,944	20.4%	79.6%	15.7%	84.3%	30.3%	69.7%	27.2%	81.6%	89.8%	58.1%
Skagit County	8,144	22.8%	77.2%	10.2%	89.8%	47.8%	52.2%	42.1%	88.8%	87.5%	66.8%
Snohomish County	47,926	20.5%	79.5%	11.7%	88.3%	48.0%	52.0%	44.5%	95.0%	94.9%	64.9%
Spokane County	39,856	25.8%	74.2%	7.6%	92.4%	33.7%	66.3%	32.4%	82.9%	90.2%	68.1%
Thurston County	18,627	25.9%	74.1%	4.0%	96.0%	40.6%	59.4%	31.6%	94.0%	93.5%	53.7%
Whatcom County	16,521	32.0%	68.0%	6.5%	93.5%	37.2%	62.8%	33.4%	85.1%	92.0%	57.5%
Yakima County	13,937	23.6%	76.4%	15.3%	84.7%	41.8%	58.2%	32.7%	83.2%	78.7%	38.3%
West Virginia											
Berkeley County	6,631	22.6%	77.4%	16.4%	83.6%	53.2%	46.8%	45.9%	81.4%	80.9%	52.2%
Cabell County	6,954	27.7%	72.3%	11.0%	89.0%	42.3%	57.7%	27.8%	82.9%	89.4%	58.3%
Kanawha County	12,827	23.9%	76.1%	13.4%	86.6%	33.9%	66.1%	27.0%	77.1%	84.5%	56.0%
Monongalia County	11,366	40.8%	59.2%	7.0%	93.0%	33.0%	67.0%	25.7%	83.1%	93.9%	37.4%
Wisconsin											
Brown County	21,150	17.6%	82.4%	18.8%	81.2%	42.0%	58.0%	37.0%	82.8%	87.5%	60.2%
Dane County	55,589	30.5%	69.5%	2.6%	97.4%	29.9%	70.1%	28.8%	84.5%	98.0%	37.5%
Eau Claire County	9,457	35.2%	64.8%	12.7%	87.3%	47.8%	52.2%	47.1%	77.1%	85.4%	59.3%
Fond du Lac County	5,136	13.6%	86.4%	31.1%	68.9%	39.5%	60.5%	35.2%	84.2%	86.7%	47.1%
Kenosha County	10,509	23.6%	76.4%	2.9%	97.1%	44.7%	55.3%	44.7%	79.4%	92.8%	67.8%
La Crosse County	10,249	40.4%	59.6%	7.3%	92.7%	37.9%	62.1%	28.1%	70.9%	97.8%	31.6%
Marathon County	8,359	20.1%	79.9%	9.5%	90.5%	56.8%	43.2%	47.9%	87.1%	96.6%	51.7%
Milwaukee County	86,797	21.3%	78.7%	6.0%	94.0%	25.6%	74.4%	21.8%	74.8%	86.1%	55.6%
Outagamie County	13,047	16.3%	83.7%	20.8%	79.2%	56.7%	43.3%	53.8%	90.2%	98.6%	62.3%
Racine County	11,585	14.8%	85.2%	20.1%	79.9%	55.3%	44.7%	53.1%	87.0%	85.0%	60.0%
Rock County	10,076	24.4%	75.6%	11.7%	88.3%	63.5%	36.5%	60.7%	84.0%	94.4%	42.4%
Sheboygan County	6,985	26.7%	73.3%	0.0%	100.0%	38.3%	61.7%	37.0%	80.5%	93.3%	64.0%
Walworth County	6,430	30.7%	69.3%	5.9%	94.1%	42.8%	57.2%	32.0%	76.8%	92.0%	47.5%
Washington County	5,943	8.0%	92.0%	22.9%	77.1%	51.4%	48.6%	45.0%	92.1%	93.1%	69.4%
Waukesha County	18,055	15.5%	84.5%	16.2%	83.8%	54.1%	45.9%	52.6%	88.3%	94.6%	74.0%
Winnebago County	14,919	29.9%	70.1%	12.4%	87.6%	42.1%	57.9%	36.6%	78.0%	89.6%	36.9%
Wyoming											
Laramie County	7,194	42.0%	58.0%	11.8%	88.2%	43.9%	56.1%	41.6%	77.3%	93.8%	39.8%

Table K-3: Places—Summary Housing Characteristics

	Millennial Householders	Age of Householders		18 to 24 Years Old		25 to 33 Years Old			Percent with Internet Access		Percent with Mobile Access Plan
		18 to 24	25 to 33	Owners	Renters	Owners	Renters	With Mortgage	18 to 24	25 to 33	
Alabama											
Birmingham city	20,059	29.4%	70.6%	8.5%	91.5%	16.6%	83.4%	12.9%	67.1%	82.2%	43.2%
Huntsville city	16,248	19.5%	80.5%	3.1%	96.9%	25.9%	74.1%	20.5%	80.8%	81.6%	59.0%
Mobile city	13,976	25.8%	74.2%	3.5%	96.5%	18.7%	81.3%	15.5%	72.9%	74.9%	49.6%
Montgomery city	17,344	26.2%	73.8%	0.9%	99.1%	24.8%	75.2%	15.3%	75.6%	82.0%	65.5%
Tuscaloosa city	11,344	50.1%	49.9%	9.1%	90.9%	20.2%	79.8%	15.1%	68.3%	85.6%	71.7%
Alaska											
Anchorage municipality	28,265	29.3%	70.7%	21.4%	78.6%	35.8%	64.2%	34.7%	83.3%	92.2%	69.5%
Arizona											
Chandler city	18,293	12.7%	87.3%	3.4%	96.6%	36.5%	63.5%	32.6%	96.3%	95.5%	54.3%
Glendale city	16,254	24.3%	75.7%	7.5%	92.5%	28.3%	71.7%	23.2%	77.7%	85.2%	52.8%
Mesa city	36,064	22.4%	77.6%	9.8%	90.2%	27.0%	73.0%	24.2%	89.8%	87.5%	58.5%
Peoria city	9,282	9.7%	90.3%	10.2%	89.8%	36.9%	63.1%	33.2%	87.9%	87.8%	54.0%
Phoenix city	116,199	23.3%	76.7%	10.5%	89.5%	26.3%	73.7%	22.4%	81.6%	81.2%	58.2%
Scottsdale city	16,002	16.7%	83.3%	9.4%	90.6%	31.6%	68.4%	24.5%	92.8%	96.8%	60.4%
Surprise city	5,850	11.5%	88.5%	19.7%	80.3%	52.9%	47.1%	48.8%	94.3%	90.7%	59.4%
Tempe city	23,163	45.0%	55.0%	6.1%	93.9%	29.4%	70.6%	23.1%	71.7%	91.9%	48.7%
Tucson city	48,208	34.1%	65.9%	7.7%	92.3%	33.9%	66.1%	26.6%	79.5%	87.8%	69.1%
Yuma city	6,724	38.7%	61.3%	20.0%	80.0%	40.4%	59.6%	35.4%	75.1%	81.4%	44.9%
Arkansas											
Little Rock city	18,789	33.0%	67.0%	10.0%	90.0%	29.2%	70.8%	22.2%	90.0%	88.3%	58.3%
California											
Anaheim city	16,577	19.0%	81.0%	11.9%	88.1%	24.2%	75.8%	21.5%	91.1%	92.9%	69.4%
Antioch city	5,589	15.1%	84.9%	0.0%	100.0%	29.7%	70.3%	26.5%	88.7%	87.9%	72.0%
Bakersfield city	28,023	16.0%	84.0%	15.0%	85.0%	40.6%	59.4%	35.7%	85.4%	86.1%	59.0%
Berkeley city	13,418	39.6%	60.4%	2.8%	97.2%	14.4%	85.6%	12.0%	63.3%	93.3%	66.6%
Burbank city	8,109	18.8%	81.2%	0.0%	100.0%	25.5%	74.5%	17.7%	98.5%	98.5%	63.2%
Carlsbad city	4,618	21.5%	78.5%	0.0%	100.0%	41.9%	58.1%	41.9%	99.5%	100.0%	70.9%
Chico city	9,639	50.8%	49.2%	1.7%	98.3%	27.3%	72.7%	18.7%	82.5%	90.0%	54.0%
Carson city	1,857	12.8%	87.2%	0.0%	100.0%	70.2%	29.8%	70.2%	99.5%	94.9%	58.9%
Chula Vista city	10,520	15.8%	84.2%	17.0%	83.0%	26.8%	73.2%	24.8%	90.6%	86.8%	45.9%
Clovis city	5,426	7.3%	92.7%	0.0%	100.0%	29.3%	70.7%	28.0%	98.3%	94.3%	40.1%
Compton city	4,071	16.0%	84.0%	33.4%	66.6%	22.3%	77.7%	19.6%	73.9%	74.5%	38.8%
Concord city	7,375	10.5%	89.5%	23.4%	76.6%	34.8%	65.2%	29.9%	97.7%	95.5%	69.5%
Corona city	9,092	17.2%	82.8%	31.1%	68.9%	46.8%	53.2%	41.6%	94.3%	87.9%	55.6%
Costa Mesa city	8,535	9.1%	90.9%	0.0%	100.0%	8.2%	91.8%	5.6%	95.3%	91.2%	22.4%
Daly City city	6,285	3.1%	96.9%	37.1%	62.9%	24.4%	75.6%	21.5%	95.6%	95.3%	71.9%
Downey city	4,637	10.1%	89.9%	0.0%	100.0%	33.0%	67.0%	26.1%	94.7%	89.3%	18.8%
El Cajon city	7,705	24.5%	75.5%	7.6%	92.4%	17.0%	83.0%	14.8%	88.7%	94.4%	74.4%
Elk Grove city	5,492	5.2%	94.8%	33.8%	66.2%	45.1%	54.9%	37.0%	97.7%	98.6%	68.2%
El Monte city	4,541	21.3%	78.7%	8.4%	91.6%	21.9%	78.1%	19.3%	88.8%	87.7%	51.0%
Escondido city	8,251	13.1%	86.9%	5.7%	94.3%	29.6%	70.4%	25.7%	87.3%	86.3%	30.5%
Fairfield city	6,370	16.0%	84.0%	0.0%	100.0%	22.7%	77.3%	19.0%	83.6%	86.1%	65.9%
Fontana city	8,813	13.0%	87.0%	12.0%	88.0%	37.9%	62.1%	34.0%	91.5%	94.0%	27.0%
Fremont city	9,025	4.6%	95.4%	0.0%	100.0%	21.7%	78.3%	18.4%	96.7%	98.9%	73.8%
Fresno city	32,755	24.6%	75.4%	8.1%	91.9%	21.5%	78.5%	18.1%	83.5%	86.1%	64.7%
Fullerton city	8,031	29.9%	70.1%	10.0%	90.0%	14.7%	85.3%	10.0%	90.6%	98.0%	69.7%
Garden Grove city	6,551	10.9%	89.1%	0.0%	100.0%	20.8%	79.2%	17.8%	88.6%	94.8%	31.9%
Glendale city	10,657	16.4%	83.6%	18.2%	81.8%	14.5%	85.5%	13.4%	96.2%	90.4%	55.8%
Hayward city	10,174	13.7%	86.3%	3.4%	96.6%	30.2%	69.8%	27.7%	91.8%	95.3%	52.1%
Hesperia city	6,382	20.4%	79.6%	20.9%	79.1%	31.3%	68.7%	28.2%	94.4%	93.3%	39.2%
Huntington Beach city	10,379	15.1%	84.9%	5.9%	94.1%	18.0%	82.0%	16.7%	92.9%	90.5%	38.1%
Inglewood city	5,204	5.5%	94.5%	0.0%	100.0%	12.4%	87.6%	6.9%	87.7%	89.7%	63.9%
Irvine city	19,768	29.7%	70.3%	6.1%	93.9%	18.6%	81.4%	15.6%	78.9%	98.3%	58.9%
Jurupa Valley city	4,405	26.4%	73.6%	58.1%	41.9%	52.4%	47.6%	42.0%	98.0%	98.3%	57.0%
Lancaster city	9,098	15.5%	84.5%	14.7%	85.3%	25.7%	74.3%	24.5%	75.4%	68.8%	24.6%
Long Beach city	34,316	13.9%	86.1%	5.1%	94.9%	13.9%	86.1%	11.7%	85.4%	88.4%	65.7%
Los Angeles city	281,849	18.8%	81.2%	5.4%	94.6%	11.9%	88.1%	10.0%	81.0%	86.0%	52.7%
Mission Viejo city	2,986	4.2%	95.8%	0.0%	100.0%	41.6%	58.4%	38.9%	96.9%	98.6%	60.0%
Modesto city	13,337	23.8%	76.2%	31.2%	68.8%	33.2%	66.8%	27.3%	91.4%	90.3%	71.4%
Moreno Valley city	8,437	15.2%	84.8%	16.4%	83.6%	46.0%	54.0%	42.1%	86.6%	89.9%	66.1%
Murrieta city	5,653	17.8%	82.2%	8.8%	91.2%	52.9%	47.1%	44.6%	87.0%	95.2%	62.2%
Norwalk city	2,977	1.5%	98.5%	0.0%	100.0%	22.6%	77.4%	22.6%	98.4%	81.1%	39.0%
Oakland city	33,098	16.3%	83.7%	4.8%	95.2%	13.2%	86.8%	11.3%	84.0%	86.7%	57.6%
Oceanside city	8,132	27.0%	73.0%	0.0%	100.0%	23.2%	76.8%	23.2%	49.1%	90.5%	60.0%
Ontario city	7,968	13.1%	86.9%	0.0%	100.0%	27.5%	72.5%	22.4%	84.7%	78.9%	50.1%
Orange city	6,188	16.0%	84.0%	6.0%	94.0%	31.7%	68.3%	22.9%	85.7%	98.6%	55.1%
Oxnard city	9,424	12.7%	87.3%	3.9%	96.1%	27.9%	72.1%	23.7%	81.5%	76.1%	35.4%
Palmdale city	6,697	18.6%	81.4%	19.9%	80.1%	58.2%	41.8%	52.1%	90.9%	82.3%	33.9%
Pasadena city	10,791	16.4%	83.6%	8.8%	91.2%	17.2%	82.8%	14.0%	78.9%	88.4%	42.2%
Pomona city	6,058	23.0%	77.0%	15.0%	85.0%	38.7%	61.3%	31.5%	75.8%	87.4%	55.4%
Rancho Cucamonga city	9,041	20.2%	79.8%	0.0%	100.0%	27.9%	72.1%	24.6%	92.4%	95.6%	56.6%
Redding city	7,613	22.0%	78.0%	1.1%	98.9%	26.8%	73.2%	26.1%	80.1%	81.5%	30.9%
Rialto city	3,439	10.7%	89.3%	0.0%	100.0%	62.6%	37.4%	55.4%	90.2%	92.9%	26.5%

Table K-3: Places—Summary Housing Characteristics—*Continued*

	Millennial Householders	Householders Percent		18 to 24 Percent		25 to 33 Percent		With Mortgage	Percent with Internet Access		Percent with Mobile Access Plan
		18 to 24	25 to 33	Owners	Renters	Owners	Renters		18 to 24	25 to 33	
California—Cont.											
Richmond city	5,831	19.7%	80.3%	4.8%	95.2%	26.9%	73.1%	17.6%	90.7%	93.5%	76.2%
Riverside city	19,172	23.9%	76.1%	11.3%	88.7%	23.1%	76.9%	21.7%	76.7%	93.1%	79.7%
Roseville city	6,602	13.7%	86.3%	8.7%	91.3%	52.0%	48.0%	49.0%	99.6%	95.7%	46.4%
Sacramento city	39,534	15.8%	84.2%	4.0%	96.0%	24.3%	75.7%	21.9%	87.3%	87.1%	51.8%
Salinas city	8,361	16.5%	83.5%	8.4%	91.6%	18.3%	81.7%	14.9%	80.7%	77.7%	45.4%
San Bernardino city	12,771	21.5%	78.5%	10.6%	89.4%	26.6%	73.4%	19.5%	82.1%	83.4%	37.9%
San Buenaventura (Ventura) city	6,369	8.6%	91.4%	0.0%	100.0%	31.0%	69.0%	31.0%	87.0%	91.8%	59.0%
San Diego city	117,211	20.2%	79.8%	4.9%	95.1%	18.0%	82.0%	15.1%	82.0%	92.3%	56.6%
San Francisco city	80,934	11.9%	88.1%	5.0%	95.0%	13.1%	86.9%	9.1%	84.4%	95.7%	55.3%
San Jose city	48,103	16.1%	83.9%	12.0%	88.0%	25.8%	74.2%	23.1%	89.5%	94.0%	51.0%
San Leandro city	4,970	19.5%	80.5%	32.4%	67.6%	18.9%	81.1%	15.4%	83.1%	97.5%	59.7%
San Marcos city	4,773	14.6%	85.4%	23.9%	76.1%	36.7%	63.3%	36.7%	88.7%	92.6%	44.0%
San Mateo city	5,299	12.9%	87.1%	12.6%	87.4%	19.6%	80.4%	15.9%	99.6%	95.4%	70.8%
Santa Ana city	11,634	15.9%	84.1%	13.3%	86.7%	17.7%	82.3%	14.5%	85.5%	84.2%	25.6%
Santa Clara city	9,915	11.1%	88.9%	0.0%	100.0%	13.2%	86.8%	11.2%	75.6%	97.6%	58.7%
Santa Clarita city	8,951	16.0%	84.0%	6.6%	93.4%	44.5%	55.5%	43.5%	86.2%	90.2%	56.0%
Santa Maria city	5,356	31.1%	68.9%	10.0%	90.0%	17.0%	83.0%	17.0%	84.8%	81.9%	73.5%
Santa Monica city	9,281	12.1%	87.9%	27.7%	72.3%	5.5%	94.5%	2.7%	91.7%	97.6%	63.7%
Santa Rosa city	9,429	21.7%	78.3%	24.5%	75.5%	24.6%	75.4%	20.4%	95.6%	89.6%	67.9%
Simi Valley city	5,016	19.9%	80.1%	17.4%	82.6%	44.6%	55.4%	43.2%	92.6%	92.0%	58.4%
South Gate city	2,782	18.4%	81.6%	0.0%	100.0%	20.4%	79.6%	20.4%	85.3%	79.7%	57.5%
Stockton city	19,209	23.4%	76.6%	11.0%	89.0%	25.6%	74.4%	20.9%	78.2%	82.7%	45.1%
Sunnyvale city	12,320	13.7%	86.3%	2.9%	97.1%	11.7%	88.3%	10.6%	94.3%	94.5%	50.1%
Temecula city	6,054	10.5%	89.5%	10.3%	89.7%	41.8%	58.2%	39.6%	94.0%	98.2%	66.0%
Thousand Oaks city	2,905	12.8%	87.2%	0.0%	100.0%	15.9%	84.1%	15.9%	85.7%	100.0%	57.9%
Torrance city	5,548	12.3%	87.7%	7.6%	92.4%	15.3%	84.7%	11.5%	96.9%	94.2%	53.2%
Vacaville city	5,468	26.3%	73.7%	18.3%	81.7%	25.1%	74.9%	25.1%	86.8%	92.8%	69.6%
Vallejo city	7,297	14.0%	86.0%	6.1%	93.9%	19.8%	80.2%	19.8%	88.8%	94.6%	48.2%
Victorville city	6,595	19.5%	80.5%	5.2%	94.8%	23.3%	76.7%	22.1%	87.4%	79.5%	70.9%
Visalia city	8,453	16.6%	83.4%	3.2%	96.8%	33.9%	66.1%	33.9%	85.3%	82.2%	66.3%
Vista city	7,077	9.8%	90.2%	0.0%	100.0%	17.6%	82.4%	17.1%	97.3%	89.6%	77.5%
West Covina city	2,958	7.4%	92.6%	0.0%	100.0%	33.9%	66.1%	27.0%	89.2%	90.4%	29.9%
Westminster city	3,134	14.0%	86.0%	9.3%	90.7%	14.4%	85.6%	7.4%	96.5%	86.5%	32.6%
Colorado											
Arvada city	7,355	14.7%	85.3%	7.4%	92.6%	37.6%	62.4%	33.2%	96.7%	82.8%	47.1%
Aurora city	27,090	19.0%	81.0%	17.8%	82.2%	43.4%	56.6%	39.1%	87.7%	86.5%	43.9%
Boulder city	16,008	52.9%	47.1%	5.9%	94.1%	12.7%	87.3%	11.0%	74.9%	95.3%	36.6%
Centennial city	3,909	17.4%	82.6%	7.8%	92.2%	33.6%	66.4%	33.6%	96.7%	89.9%	59.8%
Colorado Springs city	44,065	23.2%	76.8%	14.2%	85.8%	33.0%	67.0%	29.4%	90.2%	96.3%	66.2%
Denver city	81,984	14.6%	85.4%	6.2%	93.8%	27.0%	73.0%	24.3%	81.4%	91.5%	62.1%
Fort Collins city	20,471	42.4%	57.6%	7.5%	92.5%	32.4%	67.6%	28.6%	85.2%	96.2%	57.4%
Greeley city	9,916	21.1%	70.9%	10.3%	89.7%	51.7%	48.3%	47.8%	77.1%	87.6%	46.6%
Lakewood city	13,593	28.9%	71.1%	3.2%	96.8%	44.8%	55.2%	41.1%	85.8%	95.9%	61.6%
Longmont city	4,621	10.8%	89.2%	0.0%	100.0%	56.7%	43.3%	52.4%	95.5%	98.8%	44.1%
Pueblo city	7,878	22.0%	78.0%	7.3%	92.7%	43.5%	56.5%	40.1%	78.7%	89.0%	57.4%
Thornton city	10,464	24.1%	75.9%	14.5%	85.5%	35.3%	64.7%	29.1%	75.7%	87.3%	47.6%
Westminster city	8,523	26.3%	73.7%	6.0%	94.0%	48.8%	51.2%	41.4%	90.0%	95.3%	41.9%
Connecticut											
Bridgeport city	9,420	22.3%	77.7%	12.4%	87.6%	14.7%	85.3%	10.1%	75.4%	86.5%	26.5%
Hartford city	11,175	27.6%	72.4%	7.0%	93.0%	15.3%	84.7%	15.3%	59.0%	81.4%	36.0%
New Haven city	14,469	19.6%	80.4%	0.0%	100.0%	6.4%	93.6%	4.4%	56.8%	83.5%	45.5%
Stamford city	7,944	12.3%	87.7%	4.1%	95.9%	27.8%	72.2%	26.4%	93.6%	91.5%	55.1%
Waterbury city	6,974	13.9%	86.1%	6.9%	93.1%	17.9%	82.1%	16.3%	83.2%	81.7%	34.6%
District of Columbia											
Washington city	75,493	15.9%	84.1%	1.1%	98.9%	20.4%	79.6%	18.1%	62.8%	91.4%	55.8%
Florida											
Boca Raton city	6,187	32.6%	67.4%	7.1%	92.9%	19.3%	80.7%	13.4%	77.4%	93.7%	67.0%
Cape Coral city	5,281	6.6%	93.4%	17.3%	82.7%	34.3%	65.7%	30.3%	98.2%	90.5%	30.8%
Clearwater city	5,698	8.8%	91.2%	12.0%	88.0%	24.2%	75.8%	17.8%	88.2%	78.8%	37.6%
Coral Springs city	4,279	9.7%	90.3%	11.1%	88.9%	28.0%	72.0%	24.8%	99.1%	95.2%	64.2%
Fort Lauderdale city	11,966	13.1%	86.9%	0.0%	100.0%	24.9%	75.1%	21.2%	82.6%	81.0%	65.9%
Gainesville city	18,066	43.1%	56.9%	10.8%	89.2%	17.2%	82.8%	10.5%	65.1%	86.1%	61.3%
Hialeah city	7,616	12.6%	87.4%	16.9%	83.1%	28.5%	71.5%	25.0%	88.8%	81.2%	24.2%
Hollywood city	7,575	14.7%	85.3%	9.3%	90.7%	14.4%	85.6%	11.5%	85.2%	96.1%	54.4%
Jacksonville city	65,664	24.2%	75.8%	3.9%	96.1%	28.4%	71.6%	26.6%	80.2%	88.3%	49.0%
Lakeland city	5,970	19.5%	80.5%	17.1%	82.9%	16.4%	83.6%	15.8%	73.8%	80.5%	39.9%
Miami city	31,048	15.7%	84.3%	16.6%	83.4%	14.0%	86.0%	8.7%	81.2%	74.3%	36.7%
Miami Beach city	5,876	10.8%	89.2%	0.0%	100.0%	10.5%	89.5%	5.5%	84.1%	87.8%	34.9%
Miami Gardens city	2,233	8.3%	91.7%	0.0%	100.0%	20.8%	79.2%	18.4%	73.9%	88.5%	31.8%
Miramar city	5,881	12.7%	87.3%	29.3%	70.7%	52.1%	47.9%	38.7%	92.7%	91.7%	41.0%
Orlando city	30,008	21.9%	78.1%	9.7%	90.3%	16.3%	83.7%	13.4%	85.9%	88.7%	41.5%
Palm Bay city	5,306	17.2%	82.8%	37.1%	62.9%	42.7%	57.3%	29.0%	96.4%	93.4%	46.2%
Pembroke Pines city	5,957	6.8%	93.2%	79.2%	20.8%	42.5%	57.5%	34.5%	94.4%	97.6%	50.0%
Plantation city	4,530	12.2%	87.8%	0.0%	100.0%	25.5%	74.5%	22.3%	94.2%	86.7%	41.6%

Table K-3: Places—Summary Housing Characteristics—*Continued*

	Millennial Householders	Householders Percent		18 to 24 Percent		25 to 33 Percent			Percent with Internet Access		Percent with Mobile Access Plan
		18 to 24	25 to 33	Owners	Renters	Owners	Renters	With Mortgage	18 to 24	25 to 33	
Florida—Cont.											
Pompano Beach city	6,075	29.5%	70.5%	0.0%	100.0%	22.6%	77.4%	11.4%	82.2%	76.5%	58.7%
Port St. Lucie city	7,316	8.4%	91.6%	42.2%	57.8%	53.4%	46.6%	45.4%	99.4%	97.4%	49.3%
St. Petersburg city	14,408	15.5%	84.5%	6.4%	93.6%	17.2%	82.8%	14.0%	77.0%	87.7%	58.2%
Sunrise city	4,648	11.9%	88.1%	0.0%	100.0%	27.6%	72.4%	24.1%	95.1%	86.3%	43.3%
Tallahassee city	28,798	56.5%	43.5%	3.7%	96.3%	15.3%	84.7%	10.5%	81.5%	90.9%	75.1%
Tampa city	34,933	21.4%	78.6%	4.3%	95.7%	20.7%	79.3%	16.7%	79.4%	86.2%	51.7%
West Palm Beach city	7,173	13.7%	86.3%	13.1%	86.9%	22.1%	77.9%	17.3%	82.9%	75.6%	40.9%
Georgia											
Athens-Clarke County unified govt (balance)	16,475	54.9%	45.1%	8.3%	91.7%	20.0%	80.0%	15.8%	71.0%	86.1%	54.0%
Atlanta city	61,423	21.6%	78.4%	4.6%	95.4%	18.6%	81.4%	16.4%	60.8%	89.9%	55.6%
Augusta-Richmond County consolidated govt (balance)	14,260	21.5%	78.5%	6.5%	93.5%	22.2%	77.8%	17.7%	64.9%	76.9%	56.6%
Columbus city	16,456	21.2%	78.8%	3.9%	96.1%	11.2%	88.8%	10.2%	77.0%	85.4%	30.5%
Macon-Bibb county	10,910	24.4%	75.6%	0.0%	100.0%	26.5%	73.5%	24.1%	61.5%	76.8%	57.1%
Roswell city	3,566	8.7%	91.3%	7.7%	92.3%	26.7%	73.3%	23.5%	84.8%	90.0%	59.7%
Sandy Springs city	10,580	19.5%	80.5%	0.0%	100.0%	23.9%	76.1%	20.6%	94.8%	92.7%	39.8%
Savannah city	14,588	29.0%	71.0%	4.4%	95.6%	12.4%	87.6%	11.3%	67.7%	87.7%	69.9%
Hawaii											
Urban Honolulu CDP	16,577	23.2%	76.8%	6.1%	93.9%	16.3%	83.7%	13.4%	75.9%	89.5%	60.5%
Idaho											
Boise City city	19,224	25.6%	74.4%	20.0%	80.0%	38.1%	61.9%	35.2%	85.3%	81.9%	48.4%
Meridian city	4,300	1.8%	98.2%	0.0%	100.0%	54.9%	45.1%	48.3%	77.8%	81.7%	47.6%
Illinois											
Aurora city	10,959	19.2%	80.8%	32.6%	67.4%	27.1%	72.9%	23.1%	92.5%	92.3%	75.0%
Chicago city	262,459	16.7%	83.3%	6.4%	93.6%	21.1%	78.9%	17.6%	79.5%	90.4%	56.6%
Elgin city	4,643	32.0%	68.0%	3.6%	96.4%	47.7%	52.3%	44.9%	84.2%	90.2%	64.6%
Joliet city	8,776	15.2%	84.8%	15.7%	84.3%	54.7%	45.3%	49.2%	88.4%	91.3%	46.1%
Naperville city	7,556	30.3%	69.7%	9.9%	90.1%	36.0%	64.0%	36.0%	88.9%	94.4%	64.7%
Peoria city	10,384	18.9%	81.1%	8.1%	91.9%	38.2%	61.8%	34.3%	72.0%	86.7%	44.1%
Rockford city	11,319	23.3%	76.7%	11.7%	88.3%	49.2%	50.8%	45.6%	92.4%	87.2%	63.8%
Springfield city	9,575	19.4%	80.6%	11.0%	89.0%	42.9%	57.1%	32.1%	86.9%	85.1%	66.0%
Indiana											
Evansville city	10,974	29.1%	70.9%	5.6%	94.4%	48.6%	51.4%	41.5%	70.5%	81.1%	36.8%
Fort Wayne city	23,974	23.4%	76.6%	26.1%	73.9%	45.0%	55.0%	41.9%	84.1%	80.1%	55.6%
Indianapolis city (balance)	80,053	20.5%	79.5%	7.1%	92.9%	32.8%	67.2%	27.8%	81.0%	83.3%	50.9%
South Bend city	6,324	14.3%	85.7%	16.7%	83.3%	36.8%	63.2%	26.2%	51.9%	76.7%	38.7%
Iowa											
Cedar Rapids city	8,894	17.9%	82.1%	2.6%	97.4%	51.5%	48.5%	48.8%	85.7%	95.6%	44.6%
Davenport city	8,030	16.9%	83.1%	24.4%	75.6%	44.1%	55.9%	40.2%	74.7%	92.8%	42.4%
Des Moines city	21,776	23.8%	76.2%	6.7%	93.3%	39.4%	60.6%	35.8%	69.8%	88.4%	60.4%
Kansas											
Kansas City city	11,801	25.2%	74.8%	7.9%	92.1%	45.5%	54.5%	42.3%	82.5%	76.3%	64.1%
Olathe city	8,661	20.5%	79.5%	23.3%	76.7%	60.5%	39.5%	59.6%	95.7%	96.8%	65.6%
Overland Park city	12,306	15.7%	84.3%	19.6%	80.4%	48.7%	51.3%	42.9%	97.9%	97.9%	58.6%
Topeka city	11,175	32.0%	68.0%	2.4%	97.6%	42.8%	57.2%	38.4%	81.6%	88.9%	48.3%
Wichita city	33,653	24.8%	75.2%	7.5%	92.5%	37.1%	62.9%	29.8%	80.8%	83.0%	42.7%
Kentucky											
Lexington-Fayette urban county	33,986	33.7%	66.3%	2.3%	97.7%	34.5%	65.5%	28.1%	77.6%	87.4%	68.3%
Louisville/Jefferson County metro govt (balance)	45,180	23.2%	76.8%	8.7%	91.3%	37.1%	62.9%	31.9%	85.4%	91.1%	54.3%
Louisiana											
Baton Rouge city	24,859	34.3%	65.7%	4.9%	95.1%	34.2%	65.8%	27.4%	79.0%	92.5%	42.7%
Lafayette city	13,260	14.6%	85.4%	4.6%	95.4%	44.7%	55.3%	41.8%	86.3%	93.2%	30.2%
New Orleans city	32,980	15.2%	84.8%	6.5%	93.5%	16.3%	83.7%	12.4%	62.8%	72.6%	46.3%
Shreveport city	14,905	23.3%	76.7%	13.9%	86.1%	25.7%	74.3%	21.9%	70.9%	85.5%	48.8%
Maryland											
Baltimore city	51,134	16.6%	83.4%	3.7%	96.3%	24.3%	75.7%	21.3%	65.3%	85.5%	58.5%
Massachusetts											
Boston city	80,718	19.2%	80.8%	3.4%	96.6%	19.0%	81.0%	17.3%	62.6%	95.2%	40.7%
Brockton city	4,785	21.9%	78.1%	5.5%	94.5%	39.9%	60.1%	34.7%	97.8%	96.3%	60.9%
Cambridge city	14,459	15.7%	84.3%	5.4%	94.6%	17.2%	82.8%	12.8%	39.7%	88.9%	60.6%
Lowell city	7,331	19.7%	80.3%	0.0%	100.0%	14.5%	85.5%	14.5%	70.2%	87.5%	27.0%
Lynn city	6,597	14.9%	85.1%	14.8%	85.2%	33.9%	66.1%	31.0%	89.9%	87.3%	79.8%
New Bedford city	6,530	29.5%	70.5%	4.8%	95.2%	22.7%	77.3%	21.6%	86.9%	83.6%	60.8%
Quincy city	6,431	9.9%	90.1%	0.0%	100.0%	31.8%	68.2%	22.1%	75.3%	95.8%	47.2%
Springfield city	10,260	27.2%	72.8%	12.7%	87.3%	28.2%	71.8%	23.1%	71.3%	91.0%	35.9%
Worcester city	17,138	19.1%	80.9%	8.9%	91.1%	15.9%	84.1%	9.7%	59.5%	83.4%	45.4%
Michigan											
Ann Arbor city	18,446	51.8%	48.2%	1.3%	98.7%	17.4%	82.6%	14.2%	72.2%	93.9%	65.9%
Dearborn city	4,613	18.7%	81.3%	8.6%	91.4%	43.3%	56.7%	40.8%	99.6%	98.6%	26.9%

Table K-3: Places—Summary Housing Characteristics—*Continued*

	Millennial Householders	Householders Percent		18 to 24 Percent		25 to 33 Percent			Percent with Internet Access		Percent with Mobile Access Plan
		18 to 24	25 to 33	Owners	Renters	Owners	Renters	With Mortgage	18 to 24	25 to 33	
Michigan—Cont.											
Detroit city	45,849	21.0%	79.0%	16.8%	83.2%	21.2%	78.8%	5.1%	68.2%	69.9%	32.4%
Flint city	7,136	28.6%	71.4%	0.0%	100.0%	37.8%	62.2%	11.5%	64.4%	78.1%	26.1%
Grand Rapids city	22,308	26.7%	73.3%	9.8%	90.2%	40.2%	59.8%	37.9%	84.6%	90.2%	71.7%
Lansing city	12,015	22.3%	77.7%	4.0%	96.0%	31.3%	68.7%	25.2%	87.1%	87.7%	62.7%
Livonia city	3,684	4.5%	95.5%	100.0%	0.0%	73.0%	27.0%	58.9%	90.5%	96.4%	51.2%
Sterling Heights city	7,749	23.6%	76.4%	28.0%	72.0%	44.1%	55.9%	36.8%	98.2%	93.2%	27.3%
Warren city	7,341	15.3%	84.7%	8.1%	91.9%	46.1%	53.9%	34.1%	94.4%	82.8%	60.4%
Minnesota											
Minneapolis city	56,329	22.5%	77.5%	7.7%	92.3%	25.4%	74.6%	22.0%	77.2%	90.8%	59.3%
Rochester city	9,091	24.4%	75.6%	9.3%	90.7%	65.0%	35.0%	57.7%	94.7%	94.7%	53.4%
St. Paul city	29,604	18.5%	81.5%	3.3%	96.7%	23.0%	77.0%	20.8%	74.6%	90.8%	61.5%
Mississippi											
Jackson city	15,321	20.9%	79.1%	6.0%	94.0%	20.1%	79.9%	15.0%	63.8%	73.8%	32.7%
Missouri											
Columbia city	17,792	39.3%	60.7%	2.5%	97.5%	36.5%	63.5%	35.1%	72.3%	94.4%	39.1%
Independence city	7,194	34.3%	65.7%	11.5%	88.5%	57.1%	42.9%	38.9%	85.7%	78.0%	38.6%
Kansas City city	44,506	25.5%	74.5%	9.1%	90.9%	28.7%	71.3%	22.4%	83.5%	88.1%	55.6%
Lee's Summit city	5,691	14.3%	85.7%	9.7%	90.3%	75.3%	24.7%	62.4%	97.4%	99.3%	56.5%
St. Louis city	39,369	18.9%	81.1%	4.6%	95.4%	22.6%	77.4%	18.6%	65.9%	05.1%	58.3%
Springfield city	21,729	40.0%	60.0%	5.5%	94.5%	34.6%	65.4%	30.3%	71.7%	86.1%	41.2%
Montana											
Billings city	8,010	37.4%	62.6%	20.6%	79.4%	32.9%	67.1%	32.0%	87.2%	07.0%	23.0%
Nebraska											
Lincoln city	31,603	39.9%	60.1%	6.4%	93.6%	38.3%	61.7%	35.1%	79.0%	92.6%	46.2%
Omaha city	46,205	24.3%	75.7%	11.6%	88.4%	36.5%	63.5%	34.6%	78.8%	88.6%	52.8%
Nevada											
Henderson city	14,299	8.9%	91.1%	16.2%	83.8%	31.8%	68.2%	27.7%	95.0%	93.7%	41.8%
Las Vegas city	39,623	15.6%	84.4%	15.8%	84.2%	24.2%	75.8%	20.5%	81.0%	82.6%	54.9%
North Las Vegas city	11,811	18.9%	81.1%	14.3%	85.7%	41.7%	58.3%	34.1%	87.9%	84.8%	50.2%
Reno city	20,898	27.3%	72.7%	1.6%	98.4%	26.0%	74.0%	20.7%	85.6%	90.2%	56.6%
Sparks city	6,657	15.3%	84.7%	37.5%	62.5%	39.8%	60.2%	27.9%	89.6%	91.4%	62.6%
New Hampshire											
Manchester city	9,980	29.3%	70.7%	3.4%	96.6%	26.7%	73.3%	22.9%	87.3%	89.5%	71.1%
New Jersey											
Elizabeth city	8,059	21.4%	78.6%	10.7%	89.3%	2.3%	97.7%	2.3%	81.5%	79.1%	46.8%
Jersey City city	26,524	12.9%	87.1%	0.0%	100.0%	13.3%	86.7%	10.4%	86.7%	95.3%	55.9%
Newark city	16,215	14.7%	85.3%	0.0%	100.0%	4.4%	95.6%	3.1%	71.3%	86.2%	47.4%
Paterson city	8,119	8.0%	92.0%	0.0%	100.0%	10.1%	89.9%	5.6%	75.0%	70.2%	50.6%
New Mexico											
Albuquerque city	44,843	20.5%	79.5%	11.8%	88.2%	31.6%	68.4%	26.7%	80.0%	85.4%	38.4%
Las Cruces city	9,791	44.1%	55.9%	12.3%	87.7%	22.2%	77.8%	9.3%	81.1%	76.1%	71.9%
Rio Rancho city	3,948	4.7%	95.3%	5.4%	94.6%	53.4%	46.6%	49.6%	91.1%	93.4%	47.7%
New York											
Albany city	11,649	36.6%	63.4%	0.0%	100.0%	10.5%	89.5%	9.2%	62.4%	86.9%	35.0%
Buffalo city	26,891	20.3%	79.7%	5.8%	94.2%	17.9%	82.1%	12.8%	66.4%	82.7%	29.9%
New York city	590,981	13.9%	86.1%	6.5%	93.5%	11.4%	88.6%	7.8%	83.5%	89.8%	42.4%
Rochester city	23,338	27.6%	72.4%	3.5%	96.5%	18.8%	81.2%	15.3%	71.7%	85.2%	62.9%
Syracuse city	13,768	29.6%	70.4%	6.6%	93.4%	13.7%	86.3%	9.4%	48.1%	70.4%	55.5%
Yonkers city	8,223	24.1%	75.9%	7.6%	92.4%	16.9%	83.1%	16.9%	78.3%	91.8%	45.9%
North Carolina											
Charlotte city	77,812	20.8%	79.2%	7.5%	92.5%	31.1%	68.9%	28.5%	81.0%	89.2%	49.2%
Durham city	28,725	26.1%	73.9%	3.8%	96.2%	31.6%	68.4%	29.6%	73.6%	93.5%	70.0%
Fayetteville city	22,539	25.6%	74.4%	2.5%	97.5%	25.8%	74.2%	23.5%	78.1%	86.9%	47.3%
Greensboro city	23,590	19.6%	80.4%	0.7%	99.3%	13.9%	86.1%	13.9%	60.9%	74.6%	43.8%
High Point city	6,363	16.8%	83.2%	4.5%	95.5%	27.5%	72.5%	17.1%	74.9%	84.2%	44.5%
Raleigh city	45,074	27.5%	72.5%	1.6%	98.4%	34.1%	65.9%	31.3%	71.4%	90.0%	52.0%
Wilmington city	11,670	34.3%	65.7%	7.3%	92.7%	25.6%	74.4%	18.7%	69.7%	84.6%	63.8%
Winston-Salem city	20,516	25.2%	74.8%	6.5%	93.5%	36.1%	63.9%	33.0%	71.6%	86.3%	38.1%
North Dakota											
Fargo city	17,180	44.7%	55.3%	17.4%	82.6%	27.9%	72.1%	22.8%	82.9%	95.6%	55.6%
Ohio											
Akron city	19,387	26.0%	74.0%	3.3%	96.7%	25.1%	74.9%	19.2%	79.6%	87.3%	53.1%
Cincinnati city	41,547	25.7%	74.3%	2.3%	97.7%	17.5%	82.5%	14.8%	74.2%	89.2%	54.9%
Cleveland city	35,011	21.6%	78.4%	0.5%	99.5%	16.3%	83.7%	11.6%	79.4%	82.7%	55.2%
Columbus city	93,403	24.5%	75.5%	10.1%	89.9%	24.0%	76.0%	19.5%	76.0%	93.1%	52.2%
Dayton city	13,261	24.4%	75.6%	15.6%	84.4%	32.8%	67.2%	26.5%	51.0%	87.5%	73.1%
Toledo city	26,970	30.4%	69.6%	8.2%	91.8%	26.3%	73.7%	20.6%	77.2%	86.4%	62.2%
Oklahoma											
Broken Arrow city	8,573	27.8%	72.2%	4.2%	95.8%	52.7%	47.3%	47.1%	84.6%	93.5%	67.1%

Table K-3: Places—Summary Housing Characteristics—*Continued*

	Millennial Householders	Householders Percent		18 to 24 Percent		25 to 33 Percent		With Mortgage	Percent with Internet Access		Percent with Mobile Access Plan
		18 to 24	25 to 33	Owners	Renters	Owners	Renters		18 to 24	25 to 33	
Oklahoma—Cont.											
Edmond city	7,709	40.1%	59.9%	7.9%	92.1%	51.5%	48.5%	44.4%	88.2%	91.7%	64.2%
Lawton city	7,497	25.9%	74.1%	14.8%	85.2%	33.9%	66.1%	28.4%	57.2%	84.4%	78.7%
Norman city	12,387	31.1%	68.9%	7.7%	92.3%	53.2%	46.8%	39.5%	72.6%	87.1%	73.4%
Oklahoma City city	52,774	22.9%	77.1%	14.0%	86.0%	34.6%	65.4%	31.1%	80.8%	84.7%	64.1%
Tulsa city	37,957	26.9%	73.1%	9.3%	90.7%	34.6%	65.4%	31.2%	83.3%	90.2%	57.8%
Oregon											
Beaverton city	8,961	20.7%	79.3%	2.6%	97.4%	44.6%	55.4%	40.9%	98.1%	92.3%	67.2%
Eugene city	16,970	37.2%	62.8%	1.4%	98.6%	23.9%	76.1%	22.2%	86.0%	92.6%	67.0%
Gresham city	6,941	16.6%	83.4%	6.2%	93.8%	26.3%	73.7%	19.2%	78.8%	83.4%	70.5%
Hillsboro city	7,697	13.8%	86.2%	5.7%	94.3%	19.3%	80.7%	16.4%	94.3%	93.1%	58.4%
Portland city	54,665	17.5%	82.5%	7.9%	92.1%	25.0%	75.0%	21.2%	83.9%	94.3%	66.7%
Salem city	10,557	32.9%	67.1%	2.1%	97.9%	33.6%	66.4%	33.0%	85.8%	82.2%	71.9%
Pennsylvania											
Allentown city	8,624	15.8%	84.2%	7.7%	92.3%	10.3%	89.7%	9.4%	68.9%	77.3%	25.5%
Erie city	7,629	26.1%	73.9%	5.6%	94.4%	38.0%	62.0%	23.6%	68.1%	81.1%	47.8%
Philadelphia city	125,993	16.5%	83.5%	10.1%	89.9%	26.1%	73.9%	19.9%	74.9%	89.1%	51.5%
Pittsburgh city	41,244	30.1%	69.9%	7.3%	92.7%	23.7%	76.3%	19.7%	69.2%	87.4%	48.2%
Rhode Island											
Providence city	16,199	23.7%	76.3%	4.2%	95.8%	17.2%	82.8%	14.4%	49.3%	84.3%	59.0%
South Carolina											
Charleston city	12,781	23.0%	77.0%	15.4%	84.6%	36.6%	63.4%	33.2%	75.6%	89.7%	56.9%
Columbia city	17,144	26.0%	74.0%	8.6%	91.4%	21.7%	78.3%	16.3%	47.2%	76.1%	39.2%
North Charleston city	9,766	16.9%	83.1%	10.5%	89.5%	29.8%	70.2%	24.6%	78.6%	68.1%	49.8%
South Dakota											
Sioux Falls city	18,911	22.1%	77.9%	7.4%	92.6%	50.2%	49.8%	47.9%	70.9%	84.8%	42.3%
Tennessee											
Chattanooga city	13,991	21.7%	78.3%	12.6%	87.4%	33.7%	66.3%	32.4%	77.8%	88.1%	43.8%
Clarksville city	21,989	26.6%	73.4%	13.1%	86.9%	37.4%	62.6%	34.2%	87.1%	93.6%	55.2%
Knoxville city	21,618	35.3%	64.7%	7.1%	92.9%	25.6%	74.4%	19.9%	74.1%	80.8%	39.6%
Memphis city	52,327	23.6%	76.4%	5.8%	94.2%	25.5%	74.5%	19.1%	68.4%	74.8%	55.2%
Murfreesboro city	13,082	31.1%	68.9%	4.2%	95.8%	48.9%	51.1%	43.3%	89.9%	85.5%	54.3%
Nashville-Davidson metropolitan govt (balance)	72,788	22.8%	77.2%	12.9%	87.1%	32.3%	67.7%	30.2%	72.5%	92.2%	61.9%
Texas											
Abilene city	12,377	41.3%	58.7%	11.4%	88.6%	44.6%	55.4%	30.3%	64.5%	77.6%	63.3%
Allen city	5,488	12.4%	87.6%	32.8%	67.2%	46.3%	53.7%	37.5%	95.5%	78.6%	45.7%
Amarillo city	16,575	18.0%	82.0%	20.4%	79.6%	36.5%	63.5%	31.2%	84.2%	83.0%	49.9%
Arlington city	29,508	20.4%	79.6%	12.9%	87.1%	24.0%	76.0%	21.1%	88.5%	92.1%	44.1%
Austin city	108,235	19.7%	80.3%	2.7%	97.3%	19.6%	80.4%	15.0%	77.1%	86.1%	57.4%
Beaumont city	11,297	29.0%	71.0%	5.9%	94.1%	23.9%	76.1%	18.8%	63.2%	67.2%	22.4%
Brownsville city	8,522	15.6%	84.4%	36.1%	63.9%	39.1%	60.9%	31.1%	61.9%	70.7%	20.6%
Carrollton city	12,028	19.9%	80.1%	0.0%	100.0%	20.1%	79.9%	18.5%	87.3%	86.0%	33.0%
College Station city	19,600	50.7%	49.3%	7.0%	93.0%	17.4%	82.6%	14.7%	75.9%	87.0%	68.6%
Corpus Christi city	25,805	25.6%	74.4%	3.7%	96.3%	32.8%	67.2%	28.2%	75.6%	92.5%	58.2%
Dallas city	124,820	23.1%	76.9%	5.6%	94.4%	18.5%	81.5%	15.1%	72.2%	75.7%	52.9%
Denton city	15,507	43.2%	56.8%	9.8%	90.2%	36.2%	63.8%	33.2%	70.2%	91.8%	48.5%
El Paso city	42,709	21.0%	79.0%	13.9%	86.1%	26.0%	74.0%	22.4%	83.2%	86.6%	44.1%
Fort Worth city	62,723	20.6%	79.4%	8.1%	91.9%	40.9%	59.1%	35.7%	82.8%	82.2%	51.5%
Frisco city	6,166	6.2%	93.8%	0.0%	100.0%	61.6%	38.4%	55.1%	90.4%	98.9%	50.0%
Garland city	12,899	15.7%	84.3%	23.0%	77.0%	31.5%	68.5%	28.8%	90.8%	90.2%	56.0%
Grand Prairie city	11,161	17.7%	82.3%	28.3%	71.7%	24.4%	75.6%	20.2%	75.4%	74.2%	47.5%
Houston city	205,747	19.5%	80.5%	7.1%	92.9%	19.2%	80.8%	15.0%	75.7%	77.9%	62.2%
Irving city	21,807	19.2%	80.8%	1.1%	98.9%	14.5%	85.5%	13.7%	82.7%	77.5%	27.9%
Killeen city	15,889	28.3%	71.7%	1.6%	98.4%	25.0%	75.0%	22.4%	92.6%	91.0%	18.4%
Laredo city	11,607	19.0%	81.0%	0.0%	100.0%	35.2%	64.8%	27.8%	61.1%	64.8%	49.8%
Lewisville city	11,262	14.4%	85.6%	0.0%	100.0%	19.7%	80.3%	18.2%	91.9%	93.2%	68.1%
Lubbock city	28,268	40.1%	59.9%	8.5%	91.5%	30.9%	69.1%	24.5%	73.7%	87.6%	38.7%
McAllen city	7,081	18.3%	81.7%	56.0%	44.0%	33.4%	66.6%	24.6%	94.1%	94.3%	67.1%
McKinney city	8,830	23.7%	76.3%	4.3%	95.7%	44.0%	56.0%	35.1%	78.0%	85.2%	43.9%
Mesquite city	8,612	20.6%	79.4%	10.0%	90.0%	23.4%	76.6%	15.2%	80.8%	84.1%	69.9%
Midland city	12,399	23.7%	76.3%	33.6%	66.4%	61.9%	38.1%	52.6%	88.0%	93.6%	60.3%
Odessa city	11,904	28.4%	71.6%	37.8%	62.2%	60.3%	39.7%	44.8%	93.6%	90.7%	77.8%
Pasadena city	12,673	15.6%	84.4%	10.8%	89.2%	32.4%	67.6%	26.1%	91.8%	89.7%	80.4%
Pearland city	6,037	3.0%	97.0%	0.0%	100.0%	38.1%	61.9%	31.0%	85.1%	93.8%	65.7%
Plano city	21,727	16.7%	83.3%	12.4%	87.6%	21.5%	78.5%	16.7%	93.8%	92.7%	39.2%
Richardson city	10,526	16.0%	84.0%	0.0%	100.0%	17.1%	82.9%	13.9%	86.2%	89.3%	37.1%
Round Rock City	7,962	34.3%	65.7%	1.5%	98.5%	38.4%	61.6%	34.1%	99.2%	98.3%	64.8%
San Angelo city	9,389	25.2%	74.8%	6.4%	93.6%	41.5%	58.5%	40.6%	63.1%	73.5%	31.4%
San Antonio city	105,406	22.0%	78.0%	5.9%	94.1%	27.2%	72.8%	22.8%	81.2%	87.9%	48.5%
Tyler city	9,390	41.5%	58.5%	5.2%	94.8%	29.8%	70.2%	25.6%	76.7%	80.7%	32.9%
Waco city	14,071	47.8%	52.2%	8.5%	91.5%	29.9%	70.1%	19.9%	75.5%	84.0%	28.1%
Wichita Falls city	8,952	38.6%	61.4%	5.2%	94.8%	34.3%	65.7%	26.4%	58.6%	77.1%	56.8%

Table K-3: Places—Summary Housing Characteristics—*Continued*

	Millennial Householders	Householders Percent		18 to 24 Percent		25 to 33 Percent			Percent with Internet Access		Percent with Mobile Access Plan
		18 to 24	25 to 33	Owners	Renters	Owners	Renters	With Mortgage	18 to 24	25 to 33	
Utah											
Orem city	8,081	36.8%	63.2%	16.5%	83.5%	39.1%	60.9%	37.8%	85.8%	88.9%	68.2%
Provo city	16,827	54.1%	45.9%	2.5%	97.5%	21.6%	78.4%	20.2%	77.4%	94.1%	70.2%
Salt Lake City city	24,344	22.9%	77.1%	10.0%	90.0%	22.2%	77.8%	20.1%	83.4%	95.0%	62.9%
Sandy city	5,646	12.1%	87.9%	0.0%	100.0%	53.1%	46.9%	40.7%	96.1%	92.0%	49.0%
West Jordan city	7,678	14.0%	86.0%	22.3%	77.7%	58.9%	41.1%	53.4%	94.9%	97.9%	56.7%
West Valley City city	8,875	22.5%	77.5%	32.6%	67.4%	46.8%	53.2%	45.8%	90.2%	91.9%	67.9%
Virginia											
Alexandria city	16,154	10.6%	89.4%	1.3%	98.7%	17.9%	82.1%	15.7%	72.8%	92.4%	65.4%
Chesapeake city	15,382	18.5%	81.5%	16.0%	84.0%	50.3%	49.7%	49.3%	84.7%	91.5%	59.5%
Hampton city	11,014	25.7%	74.3%	6.9%	93.1%	37.9%	62.1%	37.9%	75.7%	90.4%	54.8%
Newport News city	18,760	29.8%	70.2%	0.4%	99.6%	28.4%	71.6%	23.3%	66.6%	83.7%	61.2%
Norfolk city	23,980	28.8%	71.2%	8.3%	91.7%	22.3%	77.7%	21.0%	53.7%	87.4%	70.4%
Portsmouth city	8,126	27.2%	72.8%	3.9%	96.1%	28.8%	71.2%	27.0%	68.3%	83.2%	79.2%
Richmond city	25,558	23.7%	76.3%	2.2%	97.8%	21.7%	78.3%	20.0%	66.3%	90.5%	62.3%
Roanoke city	10,454	27.0%	73.0%	0.0%	100.0%	27.1%	72.9%	27.1%	61.9%	79.6%	43.4%
Virginia Beach city	37,129	20.0%	80.0%	3.9%	96.1%	36.9%	63.1%	33.6%	78.9%	93.2%	54.1%
Washington											
Bellevue city	11,213	16.3%	83.7%	3.8%	96.2%	14.1%	85.9%	12.1%	92.0%	97.1%	70.9%
Everett city	8,171	21.8%	78.2%	18.0%	82.0%	32.0%	68.0%	27.2%	93.2%	91.2%	58.1%
Federal Way city	7,094	10.4%	89.6%	0.0%	100.0%	30.3%	69.7%	28.0%	96.7%	96.2%	65.6%
Kent city	8,820	15.5%	84.5%	7.0%	93.0%	32.0%	68.0%	22.9%	94.9%	91.0%	74.1%
Renton city	6,917	8.6%	91.4%	0.0%	100.0%	31.9%	68.1%	23.5%	97.3%	92.3%	76.3%
Seattle city	92,473	18.9%	81.1%	3.6%	96.4%	18.2%	81.8%	16.1%	82.3%	97.1%	66.3%
Spokane city	19,156	23.1%	76.9%	4.8%	95.2%	35.9%	64.1%	35.9%	80.5%	90.7%	68.8%
Spokane Valley city	8,713	22.4%	77.6%	4.5%	95.5%	39.6%	60.4%	38.5%	93.7%	92.2%	62.5%
Tacoma city	16,492	20.6%	79.4%	11.9%	88.1%	24.1%	75.9%	19.8%	77.2%	86.3%	60.4%
Vancouver city	12,070	18.1%	81.9%	6.6%	93.4%	25.5%	74.5%	24.3%	96.7%	93.0%	62.1%
Yakima city	6,523	35.5%	64.5%	7.8%	92.2%	33.9%	66.1%	29.0%	77.5%	84.7%	33.0%
Wisconsin											
Green Bay city	11,410	27.8%	72.2%	18.1%	81.9%	38.9%	61.1%	28.3%	84.3%	95.4%	62.0%
Kenosha city	5,229	22.0%	78.0%	0.0%	100.0%	58.9%	41.1%	58.9%	84.6%	92.2%	64.4%
Madison city	33,149	39.1%	60.9%	1.9%	98.1%	21.4%	78.6%	19.6%	82.7%	97.7%	41.1%
Milwaukee city	56,783	21.8%	78.2%	6.1%	93.9%	19.2%	80.8%	15.5%	69.5%	82.7%	62.7%

Table K-4: Metropolitan/Micropolitan Statistical Areas—Summary Housing Characteristics

	Millennial Householders	Age of Householders		18 to 24 Years Old		25 to 33 Years Old			Percent with Internet Access		Percent with Mobile Access Plan
		18 to 24	25 to 33	Owners	Renters	Owners	Renters	With Mortgage	18 to 24	25 to 33	
Abilene, TX	13,711	38.5%	61.5%	11.7%	88.3%	44.0%	56.0%	29.8%	64.2%	75.2%	50.1%
Adrian, MI	5,431	30.7%	69.3%	4.6%	95.4%	53.3%	43.8%	48.0%	78.9%	81.2%	46.4%
Akron, OH	51,905	27.0%	73.0%	7.5%	92.5%	41.4%	56.7%	36.8%	81.4%	88.5%	42.9%
Albany, GA	9,852	19.6%	80.4%	6.6%	93.4%	17.9%	80.7%	13.7%	71.0%	72.9%	56.0%
Albany, OR	9,523	39.5%	60.5%	10.0%	90.0%	43.0%	57.0%	38.3%	80.4%	85.4%	51.1%
Albany-Schenectady-Troy, NY	52,888	20.4%	79.6%	6.5%	93.5%	29.9%	68.3%	24.1%	73.0%	92.4%	45.5%
Albertville, AL	5,071	31.5%	68.5%	32.4%	67.6%	62.3%	36.4%	44.4%	94.6%	90.9%	68.3%
Albuquerque, NM	60,297	18.7%	81.3%	15.8%	84.2%	37.8%	61.5%	31.8%	79.6%	85.5%	36.6%
Alexandria, LA	10,443	23.2%	76.8%	14.4%	85.6%	33.0%	62.2%	20.5%	77.0%	69.7%	47.9%
Allentown-Bethlehem-Easton, PA-NJ	41,187	17.6%	82.4%	17.3%	82.7%	39.2%	57.5%	36.9%	77.5%	90.3%	32.3%
Altoona, PA	6,285	17.4%	82.6%	12.6%	87.4%	52.3%	45.0%	39.8%	78.0%	86.3%	42.8%
Amarillo, TX	22,440	18.0%	82.0%	16.4%	83.6%	33.3%	65.2%	28.1%	79.9%	83.3%	46.8%
Ames, IA	13,573	52.0%	48.0%	2.5%	97.5%	49.2%	46.9%	39.9%	67.6%	91.0%	24.2%
Anchorage, AK	34,657	24.8%	74.3%	20.7%	79.3%	40.1%	54.5%	38.0%	84.9%	90.9%	68.0%
Ann Arbor, MI	37,602	39.5%	60.5%	5.0%	95.0%	27.7%	71.4%	26.0%	77.8%	90.3%	55.0%
Anniston-Oxford-Jacksonville, AL	7,081	31.3%	67.6%	4.5%	95.5%	37.2%	55.1%	29.8%	80.0%	87.3%	49.4%
Appleton, WI	15,700	17.2%	82.8%	24.5%	75.5%	54.2%	44.6%	51.1%	89.9%	95.4%	59.3%
Asheville, NC	25,810	25.9%	73.9%	11.8%	88.2%	38.0%	59.1%	29.8%	78.2%	82.1%	57.8%
Ashtabula, OH	4,201	27.5%	72.5%	4.2%	95.8%	48.3%	45.4%	40.2%	73.2%	80.9%	30.3%
Athens-Clarke County, GA	20,836	45.6%	54.4%	13.1%	86.9%	26.0%	69.5%	23.0%	71.7%	77.2%	45.6%
Atlanta-Sandy Springs-Roswell, GA	343,298	18.0%	81.9%	11.6%	88.4%	32.1%	66.7%	27.1%	83.8%	88.8%	49.9%
Atlantic City-Hammonton, NJ	14,342	16.6%	83.4%	15.1%	84.9%	38.6%	58.6%	29.1%	82.1%	90.5%	32.2%
Auburn-Opelika, AL	15,160	50.0%	50.0%	16.2%	83.8%	42.1%	53.4%	26.0%	78.5%	82.3%	34.0%
Augusta-Richmond County, GA-SC	34,833	16.1%	83.8%	12.0%	88.0%	35.4%	62.5%	25.8%	69.6%	70.0%	43.5%
Augusta-Waterville, ME	7,085	32.8%	67.2%	12.4%	87.6%	69.0%	31.0%	69.0%	62.4%	92.1%	28.8%
Austin-Round Rock, TX	173,095	21.4%	78.5%	6.4%	93.6%	29.7%	69.4%	24.0%	79.6%	86.0%	53.3%
Bakersfield, CA	55,388	17.3%	82.6%	18.2%	81.8%	36.6%	60.5%	31.2%	78.2%	75.7%	44.5%
Baltimore-Columbia-Towson, MD	159,520	16.1%	83.9%	10.6%	89.4%	37.8%	60.3%	33.5%	81.1%	90.7%	57.7%
Bangor, ME	10,184	19.4%	80.6%	10.5%	89.5%	27.2%	72.1%	25.0%	64.0%	92.5%	48.5%
Barnstable Town, MA	6,254	9.1%	90.9%	11.9%	88.1%	41.9%	49.0%	38.8%	95.0%	89.6%	63.2%
Baton Rouge, LA	62,823	28.8%	71.2%	16.2%	83.8%	46.1%	48.4%	37.0%	86.3%	88.9%	48.1%
Battle Creek, MI	8,530	21.2%	78.8%	14.1%	85.9%	67.9%	30.8%	47.6%	78.6%	83.8%	60.0%
Bay City, MI	7,389	26.6%	73.4%	27.6%	72.4%	62.5%	37.5%	42.1%	89.0%	87.3%	64.9%
Beaumont-Port Arthur, TX	29,229	23.2%	76.8%	19.5%	80.5%	43.2%	56.8%	28.0%	77.7%	73.4%	32.4%
Beckley, WV	5,935	26.4%	73.6%	24.6%	75.4%	41.0%	58.6%	23.6%	87.1%	81.3%	50.6%
Bellingham, WA	16,521	32.0%	68.0%	6.5%	93.5%	37.2%	56.1%	33.4%	85.1%	92.0%	57.5%
Bend-Redmond, OR	11,579	18.1%	81.9%	17.0%	83.0%	28.6%	69.7%	27.8%	86.7%	96.2%	64.6%
Billings, MT	10,359	35.3%	64.7%	16.9%	83.1%	34.7%	63.9%	32.4%	84.3%	88.5%	24.3%
Binghamton, NY	15,127	28.9%	70.3%	16.2%	83.8%	38.5%	61.2%	35.1%	75.5%	91.1%	45.5%
Birmingham-Hoover, AL	72,178	19.1%	80.8%	14.5%	85.5%	47.1%	51.1%	37.6%	76.1%	86.8%	46.9%
Bismarck, ND	13,320	17.5%	82.5%	32.8%	67.2%	58.6%	39.9%	51.7%	87.6%	83.6%	50.1%
Blacksburg-Christiansburg-Radford, VA	18,860	46.3%	53.6%	6.2%	93.8%	37.3%	58.0%	29.2%	68.6%	92.4%	54.7%
Bloomington, IL	19,159	37.2%	62.8%	5.0%	95.0%	45.1%	53.8%	42.4%	75.5%	89.9%	33.0%
Bloomington, IN	19,574	47.0%	53.0%	3.3%	96.7%	27.2%	69.9%	22.0%	63.6%	88.0%	52.5%
Bloomsburg-Berwick, PA	5,672	21.1%	78.9%	1.3%	98.7%	42.1%	50.5%	38.1%	60.4%	89.4%	39.9%
Boise City, ID	46,902	18.0%	82.0%	25.7%	74.3%	45.5%	51.3%	40.1%	83.6%	81.3%	47.7%
Boston-Cambridge-Newton, MA-NH	285,272	16.4%	83.4%	8.2%	91.8%	31.0%	67.5%	27.8%	76.7%	93.8%	53.1%
Boulder, CO	27,569	39.1%	60.9%	4.7%	95.3%	33.9%	66.1%	31.7%	81.4%	95.5%	38.2%
Bowling Green, KY	14,671	37.6%	62.4%	14.0%	86.0%	37.6%	62.4%	31.6%	71.0%	91.2%	53.5%
Bremerton-Silverdale, WA	17,504	21.1%	78.9%	17.5%	82.5%	40.4%	58.7%	37.6%	86.9%	86.5%	69.1%
Bridgeport-Stamford-Norwalk, CT	38,608	14.5%	85.3%	14.1%	85.9%	38.0%	61.0%	34.4%	87.7%	90.4%	49.9%
Brownsville-Harlingen, TX	19,809	15.3%	84.4%	19.6%	80.4%	37.8%	58.3%	30.3%	63.3%	68.3%	25.9%
Brunswick, GA	7,621	21.5%	78.5%	26.1%	73.9%	46.7%	53.3%	28.7%	67.3%	80.0%	31.7%
Buffalo-Cheektowaga-Niagara Falls, NY	72,178	19.4%	80.5%	10.7%	89.3%	39.4%	59.3%	33.6%	80.8%	88.3%	37.6%
Burlington, NC	9,123	27.4%	72.6%	8.5%	91.5%	52.2%	47.6%	39.5%	67.4%	88.4%	53.2%
Burlington-South Burlington, VT	16,188	28.6%	71.4%	13.0%	87.0%	30.4%	65.4%	23.9%	69.6%	91.7%	59.8%
California-Lexington Park, MD	6,217	11.8%	88.2%	40.1%	59.9%	54.9%	45.1%	52.0%	84.7%	90.4%	49.4%
Canton-Massillon, OH	24,789	19.4%	80.6%	14.4%	85.6%	48.2%	51.8%	41.8%	84.1%	90.8%	62.4%
Cape Coral-Fort Myers, FL	25,514	16.4%	83.6%	14.0%	86.0%	34.2%	65.2%	24.0%	81.6%	84.3%	39.6%
Cape Girardeau, MO-IL	6,933	29.8%	70.2%	28.3%	71.7%	32.6%	66.3%	26.3%	77.4%	83.7%	63.4%
Carbondale-Marion, IL	11,272	33.9%	66.1%	5.5%	94.5%	39.1%	53.6%	30.8%	72.1%	71.9%	32.9%
Carson City, NV	2,655	30.5%	68.9%	23.6%	76.4%	25.4%	74.6%	25.4%	86.2%	91.1%	84.1%
Casper, WY	6,443	30.3%	69.7%	23.0%	77.0%	47.6%	50.7%	47.1%	88.4%	88.7%	25.4%
Cedar Rapids, IA	20,380	29.0%	68.3%	6.4%	93.6%	54.3%	45.7%	47.8%	86.5%	92.0%	42.3%
Chambersburg-Waynesboro, PA	7,982	21.0%	79.0%	9.7%	90.3%	54.0%	46.0%	52.7%	79.9%	91.8%	35.5%
Champaign-Urbana, IL	26,033	41.5%	58.5%	7.5%	92.5%	34.2%	64.6%	25.8%	70.7%	86.0%	31.9%
Charleston, WV	13,684	22.4%	77.6%	13.4%	86.6%	38.7%	59.5%	31.0%	79.5%	85.3%	54.3%
Charleston-North Charleston, SC	54,533	16.3%	83.5%	17.9%	82.1%	36.3%	61.3%	32.6%	78.4%	83.9%	45.6%
Charlotte-Concord-Gastonia, NC-SC	159,482	22.2%	77.8%	16.0%	84.0%	40.7%	57.5%	33.7%	84.5%	87.8%	53.6%
Charlottesville, VA	16,676	22.1%	77.7%	12.0%	88.0%	37.2%	58.3%	30.5%	69.0%	83.9%	31.8%
Chattanooga, TN-GA	33,375	23.5%	76.5%	28.9%	71.1%	47.2%	48.9%	40.9%	78.2%	90.5%	43.5%
Cheyenne, WY	7,565	44.9%	55.1%	10.5%	89.5%	43.9%	48.9%	41.6%	78.2%	93.9%	40.9%
Chicago-Naperville-Elgin, IL-IN-WI	584,586	16.3%	83.5%	10.2%	89.8%	34.8%	63.8%	30.0%	85.9%	91.1%	58.7%
Chico, CA	18,081	37.6%	62.4%	3.0%	97.0%	29.5%	69.6%	21.9%	85.0%	85.5%	43.0%
Cincinnati, OH-KY-IN	149,208	21.5%	78.4%	13.9%	86.1%	38.9%	59.3%	34.1%	84.6%	89.7%	51.6%

Table K-4: Metropolitan/Micropolitan Statistical Areas—Summary Housing Characteristics—*Continued*

	Millennial Householders	Age of Householders		18 to 24 Years Old		25 to 33 Years Old			Percent with Internet Access		Percent with Mobile Access Plan
		18 to 24	25 to 33	Owners	Renters	Owners	Renters	With Mortgage	18 to 24	25 to 33	
Clarksburg, WV	5,305	23.5%	76.5%	3.7%	96.3%	49.0%	49.3%	37.6%	86.1%	89.5%	50.4%
Clarksville, TN-KY	34,140	29.4%	70.6%	17.6%	82.4%	33.7%	63.2%	30.7%	77.7%	87.9%	44.7%
Cleveland, TN	6,444	39.2%	60.8%	11.4%	88.6%	39.5%	57.3%	34.9%	73.4%	77.0%	40.4%
Cleveland-Elyria, OH	130,621	21.5%	78.3%	7.4%	92.6%	37.7%	60.4%	32.1%	84.1%	89.4%	54.8%
Coeur d'Alene, ID	9,393	17.5%	82.5%	0.0%	100.0%	44.1%	55.9%	36.0%	88.7%	95.4%	70.1%
College Station-Bryan, TX	31,101	46.9%	53.1%	6.9%	93.1%	21.5%	76.8%	16.5%	76.4%	87.5%	55.1%
Colorado Springs, CO	59,970	22.9%	77.0%	17.0%	83.0%	34.5%	64.5%	30.5%	83.7%	96.0%	69.1%
Columbia, MO	22,496	41.9%	58.1%	3.5%	96.5%	37.7%	59.8%	36.5%	72.1%	93.6%	33.3%
Columbia, SC	55,844	23.1%	76.1%	18.7%	81.3%	39.2%	58.4%	33.0%	68.7%	79.1%	30.5%
Columbus, GA-AL	23,802	20.0%	80.0%	7.3%	92.7%	15.4%	81.9%	12.1%	71.6%	82.3%	30.5%
Columbus, IN	5,971	24.6%	75.4%	52.4%	47.6%	46.9%	44.4%	39.7%	86.1%	86.5%	37.0%
Columbus, OH	164,667	21.1%	78.8%	13.2%	86.8%	33.7%	65.3%	29.6%	79.9%	91.4%	53.9%
Concord, NH	5,142	21.7%	78.3%	25.9%	74.1%	38.4%	59.2%	32.2%	70.9%	91.6%	33.7%
Cookeville, TN	8,871	39.0%	61.0%	5.0%	95.0%	36.0%	63.0%	26.1%	68.8%	85.0%	27.4%
Corpus Christi, TX	31,638	24.0%	76.0%	5.2%	94.8%	35.6%	60.7%	29.7%	74.4%	87.4%	53.2%
Corvallis, OR	11,212	42.2%	57.8%	8.0%	92.0%	42.5%	57.5%	38.3%	80.1%	86.4%	54.3%
Crestview-Fort Walton Beach-Destin, FL	21,657	24.2%	75.5%	18.9%	81.1%	31.8%	65.8%	28.5%	84.2%	85.2%	42.5%
Cumberland, MD-WV	5,561	20.4%	78.0%	30.7%	69.3%	40.9%	47.7%	38.4%	74.6%	87.9%	55.8%
Dallas-Fort Worth-Arlington, TX	488,640	21.0%	78.7%	10.4%	89.6%	31.9%	67.0%	27.3%	82.9%	85.0%	46.6%
Dalton, GA	9,278	32.6%	67.1%	14.9%	85.1%	48.9%	48.9%	32.6%	83.1%	91.4%	58.1%
Danville, IL	5,702	20.9%	79.1%	10.6%	89.4%	58.9%	37.1%	49.7%	77.6%	80.3%	64.5%
Danville, VA	6,517	24.3%	75.7%	16.9%	83.1%	28.3%	69.5%	18.3%	89.2%	69.3%	44.3%
Daphne-Fairhope-Foley, AL	7,995	21.4%	78.6%	42.2%	57.8%	31.1%	66.7%	24.1%	86.9%	80.8%	68.9%
Davenport-Moline-Rock Island, IA-IL	26,493	16.3%	83.7%	24.6%	75.4%	48.2%	49.5%	38.9%	76.0%	85.4%	48.8%
Dayton, OH	61,664	26.6%	73.1%	10.0%	90.0%	37.6%	60.9%	34.5%	73.0%	90.1%	58.8%
Decatur, AL	10,030	13.2%	86.6%	41.2%	58.8%	49.0%	42.2%	41.0%	73.4%	79.8%	32.0%
Decatur, IL	6,853	28.9%	71.1%	4.2%	95.8%	47.5%	52.5%	39.3%	73.2%	76.0%	53.3%
Deltona-Daytona Beach-Ormond Beach, FL	29,623	23.4%	76.0%	22.4%	77.6%	36.6%	59.5%	28.7%	83.3%	85.9%	48.8%
Denver-Aurora-Lakewood, CO	215,594	18.8%	81.2%	12.7%	87.3%	38.1%	61.2%	34.0%	88.7%	90.6%	56.9%
Des Moines-West Des Moines, IA	51,261	21.1%	78.7%	16.2%	83.8%	50.0%	48.2%	45.5%	80.6%	89.7%	58.4%
Detroit-Warren-Dearborn, MI	244,302	19.0%	80.9%	20.6%	79.4%	43.0%	54.5%	32.0%	87.2%	89.6%	48.0%
Dothan, AL	7,912	31.0%	69.0%	19.2%	80.8%	34.1%	62.6%	31.3%	71.0%	77.7%	29.1%
Dover, DE	11,442	23.9%	76.1%	19.9%	80.1%	40.9%	56.6%	34.5%	71.9%	86.3%	56.3%
Dubuque, IA	7,280	23.4%	76.6%	20.4%	79.6%	43.5%	55.0%	28.6%	71.5%	89.4%	58.9%
Duluth, MN-WI	21,188	28.1%	71.9%	24.8%	75.2%	60.6%	36.7%	50.6%	79.1%	88.3%	46.8%
Dunn, NC	9,215	22.2%	77.8%	5.9%	94.1%	45.0%	53.6%	43.5%	72.8%	82.1%	24.1%
Durham-Chapel Hill, NC	46,518	28.4%	71.6%	4.4%	95.6%	32.1%	66.7%	28.5%	69.7%	92.0%	59.9%
East Stroudsburg, PA	5,185	11.6%	88.4%	0.0%	100.0%	47.6%	46.6%	28.3%	90.3%	89.7%	45.6%
Eau Claire, WI	13,055	38.2%	61.8%	14.6%	85.4%	52.0%	47.8%	43.2%	77.2%	87.8%	56.1%
El Centro, CA	6,053	7.0%	92.0%	13.2%	86.8%	45.5%	53.8%	39.4%	87.2%	71.8%	67.3%
El Paso, TX	10,597	27.2%	72.8%	17.1%	82.9%	45.3%	53.0%	39.8%	78.7%	84.7%	63.6%
Elizabethtown-Fort Knox, KY	12,945	37.4%	60.9%	35.0%	65.0%	50.1%	45.2%	44.2%	86.2%	76.3%	31.1%
Elkhart-Goshen, IN	5,302	23.7%	76.3%	6.8%	93.2%	36.4%	63.6%	32.1%	78.7%	81.9%	31.9%
Elmira, NY	52,737	21.4%	78.3%	20.0%	80.0%	31.9%	66.3%	27.1%	81.4%	85.3%	38.8%
Erie, PA	17,419	25.9%	74.1%	8.3%	91.7%	38.4%	57.3%	25.6%	71.1%	86.7%	48.2%
Eugene, OR	28,697	36.5%	63.5%	5.0%	95.0%	26.1%	73.6%	24.5%	87.9%	94.6%	64.2%
Eureka-Arcata-Fortuna, CA	10,785	38.4%	61.6%	9.9%	90.1%	27.9%	63.8%	19.6%	79.1%	80.8%	51.3%
Evansville, IN-KY	23,520	25.2%	74.8%	14.1%	85.9%	50.1%	48.9%	42.1%	74.6%	85.2%	40.3%
Fairbanks, AK	11,313	23.6%	76.4%	0.0%	100.0%	29.3%	69.0%	25.3%	76.9%	87.4%	56.8%
Fargo, ND-MN	28,986	39.3%	60.7%	14.8%	85.2%	37.2%	61.7%	31.4%	79.5%	91.8%	50.9%
Farmington, NM	7,470	27.8%	72.2%	0.7%	99.3%	51.8%	39.0%	39.5%	68.4%	66.2%	34.8%
Fayetteville, NC	34,510	24.5%	75.5%	7.8%	92.2%	24.1%	73.9%	22.3%	73.6%	85.0%	41.0%
Fayetteville-Springdale-Rogers, AR-MO	45,716	30.8%	69.2%	14.7%	85.3%	37.9%	57.3%	31.6%	84.0%	83.1%	37.9%
Flagstaff, AZ	10,848	41.3%	57.5%	5.3%	94.7%	35.7%	53.8%	27.9%	54.0%	86.6%	39.1%
Flint, MI	22,632	25.7%	74.3%	9.8%	90.2%	48.3%	50.9%	35.5%	75.6%	82.4%	35.2%
Florence, SC	11,446	21.4%	78.3%	10.9%	89.1%	37.3%	60.7%	27.9%	79.5%	84.2%	31.3%
Florence-Muscle Shoals, AL	8,620	33.7%	66.0%	18.0%	82.0%	47.3%	42.7%	34.1%	82.6%	67.2%	44.7%
Fond du Lac, WI	5,213	13.4%	86.6%	31.1%	68.9%	40.6%	59.4%	36.3%	84.2%	87.1%	46.7%
Fort Collins, CO	30,115	36.1%	63.9%	6.9%	93.1%	33.8%	65.5%	29.5%	85.9%	95.6%	49.0%
Fort Smith, AR-OK	18,703	19.1%	80.9%	6.7%	93.3%	47.4%	50.9%	44.1%	75.2%	81.1%	39.0%
Fort Wayne, IN	32,873	23.5%	76.5%	26.9%	73.1%	50.7%	47.7%	46.2%	83.8%	83.5%	52.7%
Fresno, CA	55,418	22.8%	77.1%	9.9%	90.1%	26.1%	72.1%	22.8%	83.4%	82.5%	53.3%
Gadsden, AL	5,015	24.0%	76.0%	25.4%	74.6%	55.5%	40.9%	41.9%	79.6%	77.8%	36.9%
Gainesville, FL	26,833	37.8%	62.2%	10.5%	89.5%	20.6%	78.4%	14.9%	70.4%	84.2%	48.0%
Gainesville, GA	10,251	23.8%	76.2%	16.7%	83.3%	51.8%	43.0%	43.7%	74.8%	76.5%	43.3%
Gettysburg, PA	5,018	15.0%	85.0%	28.1%	71.9%	57.1%	41.9%	51.8%	66.8%	93.5%	43.4%
Glens Falls, NY	5,163	17.3%	82.7%	3.7%	96.3%	48.2%	42.8%	40.0%	93.0%	85.2%	57.6%
Goldsboro, NC	8,110	21.7%	78.3%	42.6%	57.4%	33.5%	66.5%	32.9%	81.5%	92.9%	65.2%
Grand Forks, ND-MN	13,427	41.9%	58.1%	4.7%	95.3%	48.9%	48.8%	45.3%	75.9%	81.5%	41.9%
Grand Island, NE	7,179	31.4%	68.6%	36.8%	63.2%	53.1%	46.6%	48.5%	87.0%	91.2%	32.9%
Grand Junction, CO	10,989	22.9%	77.1%	9.1%	90.9%	47.3%	52.7%	43.1%	81.9%	91.5%	61.0%
Grand Rapids-Wyoming, MI	73,232	22.1%	77.9%	15.0%	85.0%	50.2%	49.3%	42.9%	80.7%	89.8%	56.2%
Grants Pass, OR	3,888	30.0%	69.2%	0.0%	100.0%	34.9%	65.1%	24.9%	93.8%	83.4%	51.8%
Great Falls, MT	5,666	24.1%	75.9%	0.0%	100.0%	30.6%	64.8%	28.8%	68.9%	71.8%	32.0%
Greeley, CO	21,511	22.7%	77.0%	4.4%	95.6%	54.2%	42.7%	45.9%	84.1%	85.8%	45.1%

Table K-4: Metropolitan/Micropolitan Statistical Areas—Summary Housing Characteristics—*Continued*

	Millennial Householders	Age of Householders		18 to 24 Years Old		25 to 33 Years Old			Percent with Internet Access		Percent with Mobile Access Plan
		18 to 24	25 to 33	Owners	Renters	Owners	Renters	With Mortgage	18 to 24	25 to 33	
Green Bay, WI	24,711	17.7%	82.3%	16.0%	84.0%	45.3%	52.1%	40.5%	84.0%	86.2%	59.9%
Greensboro-High Point, NC	44,271	17.8%	81.9%	8.5%	91.5%	32.2%	65.1%	28.5%	73.9%	84.1%	37.0%
Greenville, NC	19,954	38.8%	61.2%	4.3%	95.7%	37.2%	61.5%	25.4%	80.9%	91.5%	30.0%
Greenville-Anderson-Mauldin, SC	57,578	24.0%	76.0%	17.4%	82.6%	42.1%	55.3%	36.8%	72.0%	80.8%	44.0%
Greenwood, SC	4,177	37.2%	61.3%	30.2%	69.8%	56.1%	41.4%	55.1%	77.5%	78.5%	40.3%
Gulfport-Biloxi-Pascagoula, MS	26,493	18.9%	78.7%	14.7%	85.3%	35.8%	62.7%	29.6%	74.9%	79.7%	46.7%
Hagerstown-Martinsburg, MD-WV	13,690	28.7%	71.3%	24.8%	75.2%	48.6%	48.6%	43.0%	78.5%	82.1%	52.9%
Hammond, LA	9,323	29.5%	70.5%	6.5%	93.5%	36.8%	61.2%	25.0%	55.0%	73.4%	41.7%
Hanford-Corcoran, CA	11,389	16.2%	83.8%	0.0%	100.0%	21.8%	72.8%	18.1%	74.6%	61.3%	23.8%
Harrisburg-Carlisle, PA	34,305	21.4%	78.6%	16.0%	84.0%	41.6%	57.0%	38.7%	76.2%	91.3%	56.6%
Harrisonburg, VA	11,104	45.2%	54.8%	9.8%	90.2%	45.3%	54.7%	45.3%	60.6%	87.4%	24.7%
Hartford-West Hartford-East Hartford, CT	63,409	18.6%	81.4%	11.0%	89.0%	37.9%	61.8%	36.4%	77.2%	91.7%	49.0%
Hattiesburg, MS	9,756	23.4%	76.6%	17.6%	82.4%	29.1%	68.0%	11.2%	80.9%	83.7%	37.8%
Hickory-Lenoir-Morganton, NC	17,262	16.2%	83.8%	13.4%	86.6%	47.2%	49.0%	43.6%	77.5%	85.4%	45.2%
Hilo, HI	7,366	26.6%	73.4%	19.4%	80.6%	25.5%	71.9%	16.9%	89.0%	87.3%	46.0%
Hilton Head Island-Bluffton-Beaufort, SC	10,548	19.3%	79.9%	17.1%	82.9%	35.8%	62.6%	30.8%	72.5%	71.9%	28.4%
Hinesville, GA	8,325	35.8%	64.2%	0.0%	100.0%	23.4%	72.2%	19.8%	81.7%	85.2%	43.0%
Holland, MI	6,337	21.6%	78.4%	29.2%	70.8%	63.9%	28.5%	53.4%	91.5%	73.5%	49.7%
Homosassa Springs, FL	3,828	25.5%	74.5%	34.8%	65.2%	41.4%	48.7%	23.1%	77.4%	93.1%	29.1%
Hot Springs, AR	4,352	4.2%	95.8%	0.0%	100.0%	35.4%	59.4%	24.8%	72.7%	81.2%	39.9%
Houma-Thibodaux, LA	15,008	27.2%	72.8%	27.2%	72.8%	49.3%	46.3%	45.0%	84.6%	72.7%	33.7%
Houston-The Woodlands-Sugar Land, TX	459,870	17.9%	82.1%	10.1%	89.9%	31.9%	66.4%	26.4%	83.5%	83.5%	56.7%
Huntington-Ashland, WV-KY-OH	17,907	22.7%	77.3%	24.8%	75.2%	48.4%	43.5%	31.5%	78.0%	81.4%	44.0%
Huntsville, AL	33,777	16.5%	83.5%	9.2%	90.8%	41.9%	57.4%	34.8%	79.7%	81.0%	57.6%
Idaho Falls, ID	8,874	20.8%	79.2%	11.7%	88.3%	49.7%	47.1%	47.1%	89.3%	93.8%	69.5%
Indianapolis-Carmel-Anderson, IN	146,848	20.9%	78.7%	11.6%	88.4%	42.9%	55.8%	37.9%	83.6%	86.4%	49.3%
Iowa City, IA	21,416	42.2%	57.7%	10.7%	89.3%	37.9%	53.7%	24.5%	77.7%	80.4%	38.3%
Ithaca, NY	10,470	47.7%	52.3%	6.8%	93.2%	23.7%	75.7%	19.9%	54.2%	84.7%	18.3%
Jackson, MI	8,977	19.7%	80.3%	18.0%	82.0%	49.9%	49.3%	38.1%	77.9%	84.7%	60.5%
Jackson, MS	38,219	18.6%	81.3%	6.3%	93.7%	38.8%	56.0%	31.2%	68.5%	78.9%	33.8%
Jackson, TN	10,328	28.2%	71.8%	2.2%	97.8%	38.5%	60.0%	30.0%	64.5%	81.5%	58.8%
Jacksonville, FL	91,875	23.2%	76.7%	8.1%	91.9%	34.6%	63.8%	31.0%	82.1%	88.7%	46.1%
Jacksonville, NC	24,973	35.6%	64.1%	10.1%	89.9%	33.4%	65.6%	27.6%	61.9%	89.8%	55.4%
Jamestown-Dunkirk-Fredonia, NY	6,759	29.2%	70.8%	6.3%	93.7%	51.9%	45.3%	46.9%	71.1%	86.2%	36.3%
Janesville-Beloit, WI	11,074	22.2%	68.7%	11.7%	88.3%	63.5%	35.8%	60.7%	84.0%	94.4%	42.4%
Jefferson City, MO	9,039	17.9%	82.1%	19.4%	80.6%	43.9%	55.4%	37.7%	75.9%	78.0%	37.1%
Johnson City, TN	14,128	32.3%	67.0%	25.5%	74.5%	42.1%	56.7%	25.8%	80.5%	84.4%	56.9%
Johnstown, PA	7,060	11.7%	88.3%	42.0%	58.0%	49.4%	49.1%	39.2%	65.5%	83.8%	52.7%
Jonesboro, AR	9,773	38.6%	61.4%	19.2%	80.8%	30.4%	65.8%	25.7%	77.5%	78.3%	50.9%
Joplin, MO	11,807	30.4%	67.8%	26.0%	74.0%	44.5%	54.8%	40.0%	73.1%	83.1%	28.4%
Kahului-Wailuku-Lahaina, HI	7,782	10.7%	89.3%	1.8%	98.2%	23.0%	77.0%	18.1%	91.6%	91.8%	63.5%
Kalamazoo-Portage, MI	25,607	36.6%	63.0%	6.7%	93.3%	52.0%	47.2%	44.5%	84.5%	95.5%	63.1%
Kalispell, MT	3,894	12.9%	87.1%	0.0%	100.0%	32.9%	62.6%	24.2%	89.6%	90.9%	43.3%
Kankakee, IL	6,321	18.6%	81.4%	25.2%	74.8%	38.6%	58.4%	28.4%	64.6%	83.5%	54.6%
Kansas City, MO-KS	156,819	21.8%	78.0%	11.6%	88.4%	41.7%	57.3%	35.5%	86.8%	89.1%	58.2%
Kennewick-Richland, WA	22,833	18.2%	81.3%	17.8%	82.2%	38.6%	60.5%	33.8%	86.2%	82.2%	30.5%
Killeen-Temple, TX	40,240	32.3%	67.7%	6.7%	93.3%	27.6%	69.5%	23.8%	68.1%	82.3%	30.6%
Kingsport-Bristol-Bristol, TN-VA	15,085	17.0%	83.0%	25.1%	74.9%	50.5%	38.1%	43.8%	82.4%	81.1%	35.0%
Kingston, NY	7,288	25.8%	74.2%	2.3%	97.7%	42.9%	56.4%	27.1%	78.8%	82.6%	37.9%
Knoxville, TN	55,807	27.8%	72.1%	16.2%	83.8%	37.8%	58.6%	28.4%	78.7%	81.7%	40.4%
Kokomo, IN	5,235	17.3%	82.7%	16.9%	83.1%	57.8%	36.3%	55.9%	78.5%	90.9%	47.0%
La Crosse-Onalaska, WI-MN	11,264	39.3%	60.7%	7.2%	92.8%	38.9%	60.8%	30.1%	70.4%	97.4%	33.2%
Lafayette, LA	36,234	18.3%	81.7%	9.9%	90.1%	45.4%	48.1%	33.5%	85.1%	85.9%	30.1%
Lafayette-West Lafayette, IN	23,028	50.4%	49.4%	5.3%	94.7%	32.4%	63.9%	30.0%	67.4%	85.7%	30.3%
Lake Charles, LA	16,933	21.3%	78.6%	11.8%	88.2%	47.4%	49.6%	32.3%	81.3%	81.2%	31.6%
Lake Havasu City-Kingman, AZ	9,322	20.4%	79.6%	25.4%	74.6%	21.7%	75.6%	13.9%	87.1%	78.3%	45.8%
Lakeland-Winter Haven, FL	30,889	13.9%	86.0%	17.5%	82.5%	34.5%	63.4%	30.3%	74.6%	76.3%	25.4%
Lancaster, PA	32,129	19.5%	80.5%	12.9%	87.1%	41.3%	57.8%	37.2%	74.6%	81.8%	35.3%
Lansing-East Lansing, MI	40,424	32.0%	68.0%	8.6%	91.4%	36.2%	62.9%	29.2%	74.3%	88.8%	49.1%
Laredo, TX	11,745	19.5%	80.5%	0.0%	100.0%	35.6%	62.5%	27.6%	61.5%	65.3%	35.4%
Las Cruces, NM	15,136	36.6%	63.4%	18.7%	81.3%	27.2%	71.2%	15.1%	78.5%	77.6%	65.5%
Las Vegas-Henderson-Paradise, NV	138,642	16.6%	83.4%	13.4%	86.6%	28.0%	70.7%	22.4%	86.1%	86.0%	48.6%
Lawrence, KS	12,639	45.5%	54.5%	0.0%	100.0%	29.0%	71.0%	25.3%	64.8%	82.7%	51.6%
Lawton, OK	9,372	23.2%	76.7%	20.9%	79.1%	38.0%	61.7%	25.5%	67.1%	83.8%	62.8%
Lebanon, PA	7,909	29.7%	70.0%	9.1%	90.9%	58.3%	41.7%	51.1%	82.4%	90.5%	58.3%
Lewiston, ID-WA	3,677	40.7%	59.3%	2.5%	97.5%	46.4%	50.6%	46.4%	65.7%	90.1%	51.6%
Lewiston-Auburn, ME	8,067	21.7%	78.3%	38.0%	62.0%	49.7%	50.3%	39.7%	75.7%	89.7%	64.8%
Lexington-Fayette, KY	42,348	26.7%	73.3%	6.2%	93.8%	36.6%	58.5%	29.7%	76.3%	87.1%	57.5%
Lima, OH	6,332	31.1%	68.9%	16.3%	83.7%	32.3%	65.8%	21.6%	74.0%	93.6%	48.9%
Lincoln, NE	34,763	38.4%	61.6%	7.0%	93.0%	40.4%	59.2%	37.2%	79.2%	91.3%	43.3%
Little Rock-North Little Rock-Conway, AR	57,869	24.8%	74.7%	15.0%	85.0%	36.3%	61.9%	29.2%	79.7%	86.1%	40.1%
Logan, UT-ID	14,686	37.2%	62.8%	14.2%	85.8%	43.9%	53.0%	38.1%	88.3%	97.2%	48.8%
Longview, TX	13,602	26.2%	73.8%	5.2%	94.8%	40.6%	55.8%	28.8%	68.4%	80.1%	41.4%
Longview, WA	6,733	26.2%	73.8%	26.6%	73.4%	35.1%	64.2%	32.4%	89.2%	88.3%	56.2%
Los Angeles-Long Beach-Anaheim, CA	681,766	16.7%	83.2%	7.9%	92.1%	18.8%	79.9%	15.7%	85.6%	88.3%	49.4%
Louisville/Jefferson County, KY-IN	80,301	19.7%	80.3%	13.6%	86.4%	44.3%	52.9%	39.4%	83.4%	89.6%	49.4%

Table K-4: Metropolitan/Micropolitan Statistical Areas—Summary Housing Characteristics—*Continued*

	Millennial Householders	Age of Householders		18 to 24 Years Old		25 to 33 Years Old		With Mortgage	Percent with Internet Access		Percent with Mobile Access Plan
		18 to 24	25 to 33	Owners	Renters	Owners	Renters		18 to 24	25 to 33	
Lubbock, TX	31,945	38.3%	61.6%	8.9%	91.1%	31.5%	64.9%	25.4%	74.8%	87.4%	31.8%
Lumberton, NC	5,588	17.3%	82.7%	10.3%	89.7%	28.2%	69.4%	14.3%	50.5%	61.5%	19.4%
Lynchburg, VA	17,155	28.6%	71.4%	18.8%	81.2%	39.2%	56.0%	32.3%	57.3%	79.2%	32.5%
Macon, GA	13,971	29.1%	70.5%	0.0%	100.0%	33.4%	64.0%	29.0%	62.7%	77.6%	41.9%
Madera, CA	7,255	30.8%	69.2%	41.4%	58.6%	25.7%	66.2%	16.3%	79.3%	71.5%	58.2%
Madison, WI	64,252	28.2%	71.8%	4.8%	95.2%	33.2%	64.9%	31.1%	82.8%	95.0%	39.3%
Manchester-Nashua, NH	25,020	18.7%	81.3%	6.3%	93.7%	45.8%	51.1%	42.1%	86.9%	94.7%	60.7%
Manhattan, KS	13,250	42.8%	57.2%	9.2%	90.8%	16.9%	81.8%	13.2%	63.0%	94.8%	47.5%
Mankato-North Mankato, MN	11,070	42.6%	57.4%	3.1%	96.9%	61.4%	38.6%	46.5%	74.7%	84.9%	33.7%
Mansfield, OH	5,604	24.6%	75.4%	3.6%	96.4%	43.8%	52.3%	26.0%	76.8%	78.1%	37.1%
McAllen-Edinburg-Mission, TX	36,119	15.3%	84.4%	38.4%	61.6%	42.5%	56.8%	26.8%	73.2%	72.8%	44.3%
Medford, OR	10,306	21.6%	78.4%	27.3%	72.7%	29.8%	65.5%	28.2%	90.1%	92.5%	52.0%
Memphis, TN-MS-AR	87,444	22.4%	77.4%	9.7%	90.3%	34.3%	64.8%	28.5%	75.1%	77.3%	46.1%
Merced, CA	17,712	24.8%	74.7%	11.7%	88.3%	30.2%	66.5%	26.5%	83.8%	84.2%	54.5%
Meridian, MS	7,327	14.5%	85.5%	25.8%	74.2%	30.9%	65.9%	15.7%	72.9%	85.9%	31.5%
Miami-Fort Lauderdale-West Palm Beach, FL	270,416	14.5%	85.3%	12.6%	87.4%	27.1%	71.6%	20.9%	86.7%	84.7%	40.2%
Michigan City-La Porte, IN	6,922	26.6%	72.6%	40.2%	59.8%	40.3%	55.2%	34.3%	79.8%	61.5%	33.1%
Midland, MI	5,752	15.2%	84.8%	24.9%	75.1%	60.7%	39.3%	38.4%	90.1%	84.8%	67.8%
Midland, TX	15,206	23.4%	76.6%	32.0%	68.0%	58.1%	41.9%	48.4%	89.6%	89.9%	59.1%
Milwaukee-Waukesha-West Allis, WI	114,719	19.4%	80.6%	7.5%	92.5%	34.1%	64.3%	30.5%	79.7%	88.5%	60.9%
Minneapolis-St. Paul-Bloomington, MN-WI	254,703	18.1%	81.8%	17.0%	83.0%	48.6%	50.8%	42.9%	85.9%	92.4%	59.5%
Missoula, MT	11,988	29.9%	70.1%	13.8%	86.2%	37.9%	60.2%	27.2%	78.6%	85.8%	38.3%
Mobile, AL	26,211	21.2%	78.6%	18.0%	82.0%	27.0%	72.3%	23.0%	74.0%	76.6%	39.5%
Modesto, CA	26,300	16.3%	83.7%	23.2%	76.8%	38.2%	59.3%	30.7%	91.7%	89.2%	77.0%
Monroe, LA	11,849	28.3%	71.7%	11.2%	88.8%	44.4%	54.0%	25.3%	67.3%	76.2%	41.3%
Monroe, MI	6,761	23.8%	75.4%	79.0%	21.0%	69.9%	26.9%	59.0%	88.9%	89.8%	47.3%
Montgomery, AL	26,446	26.5%	73.4%	7.2%	92.8%	33.7%	61.8%	25.8%	81.1%	80.3%	56.2%
Morgantown, WV	13,920	36.9%	62.8%	9.5%	90.5%	31.0%	68.9%	24.2%	80.9%	94.4%	38.7%
Morristown, TN	5,532	19.5%	80.5%	19.9%	80.1%	32.7%	67.3%	30.2%	83.7%	89.0%	43.8%
Mount Vernon-Anacortes, WA	8,144	22.8%	77.2%	10.2%	89.8%	47.8%	52.2%	42.1%	88.8%	87.5%	66.8%
Muncie, IN	10,987	53.4%	46.6%	3.4%	96.6%	51.1%	41.4%	36.8%	71.2%	87.7%	54.7%
Muskegon, MI	9,786	20.0%	80.0%	5.1%	94.9%	59.3%	40.7%	44.1%	75.9%	78.4%	30.4%
Myrtle Beach-Conway-North Myrtle Beach, SC-NC	23,225	19.2%	80.8%	14.8%	85.2%	34.0%	63.6%	25.5%	84.4%	89.6%	67.1%
Napa, CA	5,947	13.0%	87.0%	0.0%	100.0%	18.6%	81.0%	11.6%	85.2%	84.6%	60.8%
Naples-Immokalee-Marco Island, FL	10,388	11.7%	88.1%	12.4%	87.6%	25.7%	73.1%	23.6%	77.3%	84.5%	54.1%
Nashville-Davidson—Murfreesboro—Franklin, TN	138,894	22.2%	77.7%	16.8%	83.2%	43.5%	54.8%	38.8%	83.9%	88.7%	53.6%
New Bern, NC	11,131	33.6%	65.0%	21.5%	78.5%	32.2%	67.8%	26.0%	77.6%	88.8%	64.8%
New Castle, PA	4,328	19.4%	80.6%	15.0%	85.0%	53.9%	43.9%	31.3%	77.9%	89.4%	40.7%
New Haven-Milford, CT	45,855	13.7%	86.2%	3.0%	97.0%	23.9%	73.2%	21.5%	77.8%	90.6%	46.1%
New Orleans-Metairie, LA	83,049	16.1%	83.9%	12.9%	87.1%	30.7%	67.0%	24.6%	76.5%	80.3%	39.7%
New Philadelphia-Dover, OH	4,229	22.7%	77.3%	29.3%	70.7%	49.1%	41.4%	40.2%	90.7%	87.9%	52.2%
New York-Newark-Jersey City, NY-NJ-PA	1,018,202	13.4%	86.5%	8.9%	91.1%	20.3%	78.1%	16.9%	84.7%	90.5%	43.6%
Niles-Benton Harbor, MI	10,272	20.4%	79.6%	15.5%	84.5%	38.4%	60.4%	33.2%	87.1%	85.0%	40.2%
North Port-Sarasota-Bradenton, FL	25,421	17.1%	82.9%	21.7%	78.3%	28.4%	71.6%	24.7%	84.7%	83.6%	47.3%
Norwich-New London, CT	18,165	18.8%	81.2%	13.2%	86.8%	35.1%	63.6%	32.5%	74.4%	88.8%	44.4%
Ocala, FL	9,634	12.1%	87.9%	21.7%	78.3%	53.6%	45.4%	49.0%	81.4%	76.3%	52.3%
Ocean City, NJ	3,805	1.6%	98.4%	100.0%	0.0%	48.9%	47.1%	44.4%	87.6%	88.7%	40.5%
Odessa, TX	13,925	27.3%	72.7%	36.3%	63.7%	60.3%	39.7%	47.0%	93.2%	90.5%	82.4%
Ogden-Clearfield, UT	42,723	23.0%	77.0%	23.5%	76.5%	58.8%	40.2%	54.2%	91.4%	92.5%	56.1%
Ogdensburg-Massena, NY	7,138	25.2%	74.8%	23.5%	76.5%	50.6%	48.0%	46.8%	44.5%	75.8%	45.5%
Oklahoma City, OK	105,910	22.6%	77.4%	14.1%	85.9%	42.1%	53.6%	35.5%	77.8%	86.4%	55.7%
Olympia-Tumwater, WA	18,699	25.8%	73.8%	4.0%	96.0%	40.6%	58.7%	31.6%	94.0%	93.5%	53.7%
Omaha-Council Bluffs, NE-IA	79,846	21.6%	78.4%	15.0%	85.0%	42.7%	56.2%	39.8%	84.9%	91.9%	53.1%
Orangeburg, SC	6,130	22.7%	77.3%	24.7%	75.3%	35.6%	54.1%	14.5%	66.3%	73.6%	40.0%
Orlando-Kissimmee-Sanford, FL	157,160	20.7%	79.3%	13.9%	86.1%	29.3%	69.8%	23.4%	84.0%	90.8%	43.1%
Oshkosh-Neenah, WI	14,919	29.9%	70.1%	12.4%	87.6%	42.1%	57.9%	36.6%	78.0%	89.6%	36.9%
Ottawa-Peru, IL	7,286	19.8%	80.2%	25.6%	74.4%	37.8%	60.0%	32.5%	92.6%	86.9%	66.7%
Owensboro, KY	7,992	17.5%	82.5%	25.7%	74.3%	52.4%	44.3%	43.3%	73.7%	87.9%	53.6%
Oxnard-Thousand Oaks-Ventura, CA	32,209	16.3%	83.7%	11.8%	88.2%	31.4%	67.4%	26.7%	85.3%	87.3%	53.0%
Palm Bay-Melbourne-Titusville, FL	25,564	19.7%	80.3%	20.0%	80.0%	37.4%	60.2%	29.7%	92.4%	92.2%	57.2%
Panama City, FL	11,717	9.7%	89.8%	22.4%	77.6%	38.6%	58.6%	30.1%	83.3%	78.7%	54.2%
Parkersburg-Vienna, WV	5,380	23.9%	76.1%	21.4%	78.6%	50.0%	47.9%	33.7%	82.3%	90.7%	57.3%
Pensacola-Ferry Pass-Brent, FL	33,327	18.9%	81.1%	16.5%	83.5%	35.7%	60.8%	31.4%	69.3%	84.6%	45.3%
Peoria, IL	26,239	20.6%	79.4%	17.7%	82.3%	46.4%	51.2%	39.9%	76.1%	86.6%	51.1%
Philadelphia-Camden-Wilmington, PA-NJ-DE-MD	331,832	14.6%	85.2%	12.9%	87.1%	37.3%	61.6%	31.6%	81.1%	90.5%	52.0%
Phoenix-Mesa-Scottsdale, AZ	298,491	21.6%	78.3%	11.2%	88.8%	33.1%	65.3%	29.0%	84.4%	85.6%	54.7%
Pine Bluff, AR	6,187	17.5%	82.5%	26.5%	73.5%	34.3%	62.7%	29.7%	57.3%	60.9%	38.0%
Pittsburgh, PA	152,881	20.7%	78.9%	11.8%	88.2%	42.0%	55.1%	34.2%	81.0%	91.3%	54.4%
Pittsfield, MA	6,500	28.6%	71.4%	0.9%	99.1%	20.4%	79.6%	19.9%	62.7%	90.4%	45.5%
Pocatello, ID	7,258	31.1%	68.9%	3.0%	97.0%	54.1%	42.0%	42.1%	79.7%	90.8%	61.4%
Port St. Lucie, FL	30,769	21.0%	79.0%	10.0%	90.0%	45.6%	53.4%	41.9%	82.1%	90.2%	44.6%
Portland-South Portland, ME	156,194	19.0%	81.0%	13.0%	87.0%	31.8%	66.8%	27.8%	90.8%	93.1%	64.1%

Table K-4: Metropolitan/Micropolitan Statistical Areas—Summary Housing Characteristics—*Continued*

	Millennial Householders	Age of Householders		18 to 24 Years Old		25 to 33 Years Old			Percent with Internet Access		Percent with Mobile Access Plan
		18 to 24	25 to 33	Owners	Renters	Owners	Renters	With Mortgage	18 to 24	25 to 33	
Portland-Vancouver-Hillsboro, OR-WA	19,163	12.6%	87.4%	30.8%	69.2%	36.9%	62.9%	27.4%	90.3%	88.7%	53.1%
Pottsville, PA	7,441	16.2%	83.8%	16.5%	83.5%	56.3%	41.8%	36.3%	88.2%	80.1%	46.6%
Prescott, AZ	11,063	28.1%	71.9%	13.3%	86.7%	48.9%	50.7%	45.9%	72.8%	79.3%	43.3%
Providence-Warwick, RI-MA	94,956	18.9%	81.1%	6.5%	93.5%	31.5%	66.6%	27.2%	73.8%	90.3%	49.6%
Provo-Orem, UT	47,051	38.8%	61.2%	17.8%	82.2%	48.9%	48.5%	45.1%	85.0%	92.7%	60.4%
Pueblo, CO	10,716	21.7%	78.3%	8.4%	91.6%	47.2%	52.3%	44.7%	80.1%	86.9%	49.4%
Punta Gorda, FL	2,988	27.5%	72.5%	51.7%	48.3%	16.2%	68.2%	9.6%	86.4%	87.9%	59.5%
Racine, WI	11,585	14.8%	85.2%	20.1%	79.9%	55.3%	43.0%	53.1%	87.0%	85.0%	60.0%
Raleigh, NC	90,669	21.1%	78.9%	5.9%	94.1%	40.5%	56.9%	35.8%	78.6%	88.5%	51.2%
Rapid City, SD	12,091	23.1%	76.9%	25.0%	75.0%	55.8%	42.4%	44.8%	77.9%	89.6%	51.1%
Reading, PA	20,697	13.0%	86.8%	13.9%	86.1%	51.5%	46.4%	43.2%	77.0%	93.1%	59.1%
Redding, CA	12,277	27.2%	72.8%	2.2%	97.8%	36.0%	62.1%	25.7%	82.9%	79.7%	27.5%
Reno, NV	32,457	20.9%	79.1%	8.0%	92.0%	34.7%	62.6%	27.0%	86.1%	90.1%	57.3%
Richmond, VA	77,799	20.8%	79.2%	9.7%	90.3%	35.2%	63.2%	32.0%	81.0%	88.3%	53.0%
Riverside-San Bernardino-Ontario, CA	213,999	18.3%	81.5%	12.3%	87.7%	35.0%	63.7%	30.4%	86.1%	86.3%	51.9%
Roanoke, VA	21,048	19.8%	80.2%	7.9%	92.1%	34.1%	63.2%	30.3%	73.1%	83.3%	39.4%
Rochester, MN	14,903	29.8%	70.2%	21.8%	78.2%	56.3%	41.7%	50.6%	86.7%	92.7%	55.3%
Rochester, NY	70,513	22.2%	77.8%	11.6%	88.4%	43.2%	55.1%	39.0%	73.4%	89.1%	48.2%
Rockford, IL	19,909	24.3%	74.7%	12.1%	87.9%	51.9%	45.0%	44.8%	91.6%	86.8%	64.1%
Rocky Mount, NC	7,568	18.6%	81.4%	8.4%	91.6%	23.5%	73.8%	21.1%	84.1%	76.8%	34.5%
Rome, GA	5,078	19.6%	80.4%	18.3%	81.7%	32.1%	61.9%	24.9%	80.9%	73.7%	47.4%
Roseburg, OR	6,136	7.8%	92.2%	3.6%	96.4%	18.0%	77.5%	17.4%	92.8%	93.1%	66.5%
Sacramento–Roseville–Arden-Arcade, CA	139,240	20.3%	79.6%	6.4%	93.6%	31.7%	66.3%	28.4%	88.8%	89.2%	56.4%
Saginaw, MI	13,074	20.7%	79.3%	3.4%	96.6%	48.1%	50.1%	32.2%	72.7%	86.5%	53.9%
Salem, OH	18,470	31.5%	68.5%	15.0%	85.0%	40.8%	58.1%	40.8%	72.7%	85.0%	42.2%
Salem, OR	8,334	32.5%	67.5%	14.0%	86.0%	39.7%	56.0%	37.8%	86.2%	94.6%	38.4%
Salinas, CA	8,527	21.8%	78.2%	17.8%	82.2%	33.5%	65.3%	27.5%	76.2%	68.2%	48.6%
Salisbury, MD-DE	187,509	18.2%	81.6%	15.4%	84.6%	47.1%	51.5%	41.2%	80.8%	88.0%	53.0%
Salt Lake City, UT	5,001	34.0%	65.0%	11.9%	88.1%	48.4%	46.2%	36.5%	81.4%	88.2%	58.3%
San Angelo, TX	23,239	23.4%	76.6%	7.6%	92.4%	40.2%	57.5%	36.9%	87.5%	87.8%	73.4%
San Antonio-New Braunfels, TX	20,242	15.5%	84.5%	4.5%	95.5%	20.5%	77.8%	14.4%	73.8%	76.9%	44.2%
San Diego-Carlsbad, CA	19,791	26.3%	73.7%	19.0%	81.0%	42.7%	52.4%	38.5%	76.8%	78.6%	30.0%
San Francisco-Oakland-Hayward, CA	81,821	19.5%	80.5%	17.8%	82.2%	42.8%	56.1%	39.0%	90.6%	94.9%	61.5%
San Jose-Sunnyvale-Santa Clara, CA	10,394	25.4%	74.6%	10.2%	89.8%	42.7%	55.2%	40.1%	63.1%	75.5%	23.9%
San Luis Obispo-Paso Robles-Arroyo Grande, CA	148,162	20.8%	79.2%	9.7%	90.3%	33.9%	63.5%	28.2%	82.6%	88.8%	49.8%
Santa Cruz-Watsonville, CA	208,190	19.1%	80.8%	5.4%	94.6%	21.5%	76.3%	18.0%	82.8%	91.7%	56.6%
Santa Fe, NM	270,170	13.9%	86.1%	7.4%	92.6%	20.5%	78.4%	17.5%	88.2%	94.4%	65.3%
Santa Maria-Santa Barbara, CA	100,766	15.8%	84.1%	8.6%	91.4%	22.0%	77.5%	19.6%	85.7%	92.9%	54.7%
Santa Rosa, CA	18,454	33.8%	66.2%	5.9%	94.1%	24.2%	75.8%	24.2%	72.7%	90.8%	55.2%
Savannah, GA	13,475	25.0%	75.0%	2.7%	97.3%	15.6%	79.4%	12.4%	71.5%	76.3%	51.4%
Scranton–Wilkes-Barre–Hazleton, PA	6,963	20.6%	79.4%	9.3%	90.7%	46.4%	51.1%	35.6%	69.2%	84.7%	52.0%
Seattle-Tacoma-Bellevue, WA	25,668	43.0%	57.0%	11.3%	88.7%	13.1%	84.8%	11.2%	78.0%	87.1%	65.8%
Sebastian-Vero Beach, FL	24,397	23.4%	76.6%	16.0%	84.0%	24.9%	74.3%	22.1%	90.8%	90.2%	59.9%
Sebring, FL	32,283	27.7%	72.2%	4.7%	95.3%	24.3%	74.4%	20.9%	71.6%	85.8%	56.5%
Sheboygan, WI	27,955	19.0%	81.0%	9.5%	90.5%	45.6%	51.6%	36.6%	71.2%	88.4%	44.0%
Sherman-Denison, TX	289,653	17.5%	82.4%	9.3%	90.7%	30.6%	68.0%	27.3%	88.2%	94.6%	66.8%
Show Low, AZ	3,784	15.0%	84.3%	24.2%	75.8%	48.1%	49.0%	39.4%	88.6%	82.9%	41.7%
Shreveport-Bossier City, LA	3,381	25.4%	74.6%	39.7%	60.3%	11.2%	88.8%	11.2%	53.9%	61.6%	36.4%
Sierra Vista-Douglas, AZ	6,985	26.7%	73.3%	0.0%	100.0%	38.3%	60.5%	37.0%	80.5%	93.3%	64.0%
Sioux City, IA-NE-SD	6,778	18.2%	81.8%	28.3%	71.7%	47.8%	49.8%	41.6%	79.8%	72.1%	47.0%
Sioux Falls, SD	3,404	16.4%	81.8%	17.2%	82.8%	39.9%	48.7%	26.4%	47.2%	59.1%	28.5%
South Bend-Mishawaka, IN-MI	31,910	20.6%	79.4%	18.4%	81.6%	33.4%	62.4%	27.8%	72.6%	83.4%	38.8%
Spartanburg, SC	8,688	26.2%	73.8%	12.3%	87.7%	42.6%	51.0%	35.3%	70.3%	69.4%	40.3%
Spokane-Spokane Valley, WA	11,874	17.6%	82.4%	24.0%	76.0%	51.8%	46.5%	46.3%	72.2%	81.1%	52.5%
Springfield, IL	25,163	26.8%	73.2%	10.8%	89.2%	54.7%	38.5%	51.0%	75.8%	86.9%	38.1%
Springfield, MA	19,245	20.8%	78.7%	25.3%	74.7%	45.8%	52.2%	38.6%	70.2%	84.4%	41.6%
Springfield, MO	18,850	23.3%	76.7%	36.3%	63.7%	43.1%	52.7%	34.2%	75.6%	83.2%	61.1%
Springfield, OH	41,304	25.4%	74.6%	8.4%	91.6%	34.7%	65.2%	32.8%	80.8%	89.3%	67.0%
St. Cloud, MN	13,474	18.1%	81.9%	11.2%	88.8%	42.5%	57.5%	33.1%	84.3%	88.4%	63.9%
St. George, UT	35,157	22.0%	78.0%	14.3%	85.7%	38.3%	61.2%	34.1%	65.5%	89.4%	38.5%
St. Joseph, MO-KS	39,592	34.2%	65.8%	13.9%	86.1%	41.0%	56.2%	36.6%	74.3%	83.8%	37.9%
St. Louis, MO-IL	8,439	27.5%	72.5%	8.1%	91.9%	37.7%	59.6%	33.0%	76.0%	81.2%	64.3%
State College, PA	16,872	41.2%	58.8%	0.7%	99.3%	31.5%	68.5%	29.8%	65.4%	86.4%	35.4%
Staunton-Waynesboro, VA	7,517	19.1%	80.9%	15.4%	84.6%	45.9%	49.8%	37.9%	50.6%	67.4%	32.9%
Stockton-Lodi, CA	37,310	18.6%	81.3%	10.4%	89.6%	32.0%	63.5%	25.2%	83.6%	85.5%	51.2%
Sumter, SC	5,820	21.8%	78.2%	30.1%	69.9%	35.1%	63.9%	28.7%	70.4%	68.0%	18.1%
Sunbury, PA	5,670	19.7%	80.3%	45.1%	54.9%	40.0%	52.1%	33.5%	76.2%	81.7%	26.0%
Syracuse, NY	39,679	20.5%	79.5%	10.5%	89.5%	39.3%	59.5%	33.2%	66.2%	86.4%	49.8%
Tallahassee, FL	38,874	46.7%	52.7%	6.0%	94.0%	29.9%	68.3%	24.4%	82.2%	84.4%	59.9%
Tampa-St. Petersburg-Clearwater, FL	170,755	18.1%	81.8%	9.7%	90.3%	30.3%	68.4%	25.7%	85.4%	88.3%	48.6%
Terre Haute, IN	11,344	36.2%	63.2%	17.2%	82.8%	38.4%	58.0%	30.8%	57.8%	66.7%	30.3%
Texarkana, TX-AR	9,001	20.6%	79.4%	5.1%	94.9%	48.0%	48.8%	32.7%	78.8%	75.3%	45.9%
The Villages, FL	1,713	19.0%	81.0%	0.0%	100.0%	27.0%	73.0%	24.2%	92.3%	75.0%	62.0%
Toledo, OH	49,577	32.2%	67.6%	8.7%	91.3%	37.5%	62.1%	30.1%	79.2%	90.9%	49.3%
Topeka, KS	16,684	24.6%	75.4%	9.6%	90.4%	46.9%	52.0%	41.9%	85.9%	90.2%	51.9%

Table K-4: Metropolitan/Micropolitan Statistical Areas—Summary Housing Characteristics—*Continued*

	Millennial Householders	Age of Householders		18 to 24 Years Old		25 to 33 Years Old			Percent with Internet Access		Percent with Mobile Access Plan
		18 to 24	25 to 33	Owners	Renters	Owners	Renters	With Mortgage	18 to 24	25 to 33	
Torrington, CT	7,089	14.0%	86.0%	5.1%	94.9%	65.5%	31.9%	63.7%	96.4%	88.6%	57.8%
Traverse City, MI	6,564	13.4%	86.6%	21.3%	78.7%	52.2%	47.5%	46.4%	81.7%	85.2%	60.8%
Trenton, NJ	15,755	9.5%	90.5%	20.0%	80.0%	24.5%	72.6%	15.1%	75.3%	87.5%	40.3%
Truckee-Grass Valley, CA	4,381	9.8%	90.2%	17.0%	83.0%	52.4%	47.6%	47.6%	85.3%	88.1%	51.7%
Tucson, AZ	74,308	31.5%	68.2%	12.0%	88.0%	35.8%	61.8%	29.6%	84.0%	88.2%	60.7%
Tullahoma-Manchester, TN	5,792	28.4%	71.6%	19.6%	80.4%	45.7%	54.3%	40.3%	59.6%	76.4%	37.9%
Tulsa, OK	76,289	25.2%	74.8%	11.0%	89.0%	39.0%	57.3%	33.1%	82.8%	85.8%	55.7%
Tupelo, MS	9,514	35.1%	64.9%	28.0%	72.0%	33.1%	61.8%	28.2%	86.7%	80.9%	57.7%
Tuscaloosa, AL	18,227	37.3%	62.7%	11.4%	88.6%	32.3%	64.3%	24.6%	71.6%	84.5%	56.7%
Tyler, TX	15,344	33.8%	66.2%	13.8%	86.2%	38.1%	60.0%	30.2%	76.9%	82.5%	31.3%
Urban Honolulu, HI	56,312	24.0%	76.0%	5.8%	94.2%	21.6%	77.5%	17.3%	79.1%	90.5%	64.0%
Utica-Rome, NY	14,746	19.3%	79.6%	6.3%	93.7%	30.1%	67.1%	25.3%	73.0%	83.7%	31.6%
Valdosta, GA	10,930	35.0%	65.0%	14.6%	85.4%	32.8%	63.0%	24.9%	75.5%	68.2%	25.7%
Vallejo-Fairfield, CA	22,389	18.8%	81.1%	12.2%	87.8%	22.8%	75.6%	21.0%	86.3%	91.1%	61.5%
Victoria, TX	6,372	27.5%	72.2%	0.0%	100.0%	47.8%	52.2%	46.7%	82.0%	73.7%	42.3%
Vineland-Bridgeton, NJ	7,384	14.6%	85.4%	5.1%	94.9%	34.6%	64.7%	27.9%	88.1%	71.1%	26.0%
Virginia Beach-Norfolk-Newport News, VA-NC	133,457	22.3%	77.6%	6.1%	93.9%	36.4%	62.7%	32.9%	71.7%	90.0%	53.9%
Visalia-Porterville, CA	27,040	17.9%	81.9%	9.1%	90.9%	34.4%	64.4%	31.8%	80.9%	77.7%	55.3%
Waco, TX	20,994	41.6%	58.3%	6.8%	93.2%	34.4%	61.6%	26.1%	78.6%	82.0%	28.4%
Walla Walla, WA	4,660	13.2%	86.8%	0.0%	100.0%	51.9%	43.8%	47.1%	73.1%	86.3%	36.5%
Warner Robins, GA	13,601	28.2%	71.8%	4.6%	95.4%	47.9%	49.9%	39.7%	77.7%	84.9%	42.9%
Washington-Arlington-Alexandria, DC-VA-MD-WV	361,813	14.6%	85.3%	8.6%	91.4%	34.4%	64.5%	31.1%	84.9%	92.1%	52.3%
Waterloo-Cedar Falls, IA	16,736	33.3%	66.7%	20.1%	79.9%	56.0%	44.0%	49.4%	65.5%	83.5%	39.7%
Watertown-Fort Drum, NY	10,566	28.8%	71.2%	5.3%	94.7%	28.8%	53.9%	25.0%	74.4%	86.9%	56.2%
Wausau, WI	8,359	20.1%	79.9%	9.5%	90.5%	56.8%	42.1%	47.9%	87.1%	96.6%	51.7%
Weirton-Steubenville, WV-OH	6,042	15.0%	85.0%	35.2%	64.8%	47.4%	50.7%	30.7%	72.4%	86.8%	44.7%
Wenatchee, WA	4,572	22.1%	77.9%	42.5%	57.5%	32.7%	63.4%	17.1%	76.4%	84.1%	33.9%
Wheeling, WV-OH	6,972	23.2%	76.8%	19.8%	80.2%	49.4%	48.9%	33.2%	73.4%	83.9%	42.1%
Whitewater-Elkhorn, WI	6,430	30.7%	69.3%	5.9%	94.1%	42.8%	56.0%	32.0%	76.8%	92.0%	47.5%
Wichita Falls, TX	51,577	23.9%	76.0%	11.9%	88.1%	40.4%	58.9%	33.3%	84.3%	82.7%	44.4%
Wichita, KS	11,137	38.9%	61.1%	4.2%	95.8%	36.9%	60.1%	30.1%	59.6%	78.4%	38.5%
Williamsport, PA	6,388	19.1%	80.9%	14.8%	85.2%	47.5%	50.9%	39.2%	65.5%	78.2%	23.3%
Wilmington, NC	21,490	31.9%	68.1%	6.6%	93.4%	37.3%	58.2%	29.4%	75.2%	80.7%	49.0%
Winchester, VA-WV	4,492	10.2%	89.8%	0.0%	100.0%	56.3%	39.7%	51.8%	86.4%	82.4%	34.2%
Winston-Salem, NC	40,330	21.4%	78.1%	21.8%	78.2%	41.9%	56.3%	35.1%	81.5%	82.8%	34.8%
Wooster, OH	5,560	19.7%	80.3%	18.6%	81.4%	53.4%	44.4%	43.2%	60.8%	84.4%	54.2%
Worcester, MA-CT	46,710	15.7%	84.2%	14.0%	86.0%	37.0%	61.5%	32.7%	77.3%	88.9%	52.8%
Yakima, WA	13,937	23.6%	76.4%	15.3%	84.7%	41.8%	67.2%	30.7%	63.2%	78.7%	38.3%
York-Hanover, PA	23,775	8.8%	91.2%	46.5%	53.5%	52.2%	46.6%	45.1%	81.4%	84.5%	41.3%
Youngstown-Warren-Boardman, OH-PA	30,747	26.1%	73.9%	18.2%	81.8%	42.0%	54.4%	34.5%	75.9%	81.6%	39.8%
Yuba City, CA	10,651	20.0%	78.6%	12.6%	87.4%	36.5%	63.5%	33.6%	91.0%	88.1%	70.7%
Yuma, AZ	14,514	31.3%	68.7%	12.3%	87.7%	37.1%	59.7%	29.8%	78.8%	79.3%	41.3%

APPENDIXES

Metropolitan and Micropolitan Areas and Components (as defined February 2013)

Metropolitan and Micropolitan Area Code	State/County FIPS code	Title and Geographic Components
10180		Abilene, TX Metro area
	48059	Callahan County, TX
	48253	Jones County, TX
	48441	Taylor County, TX
10300		Adrian, MI Micro area
	26091	Lenawee County, MI
10420		Akron, OH Metro area
	39133	Portage County, OH
	39153	Summit County, OH
10500		Albany, GA Metro area
	13007	Baker County, GA
	13095	Dougherty County, GA
	13177	Lee County, GA
	13273	Terrell County, GA
	13321	Worth County, GA
10540		Albany, OR Metro area
	41043	Linn County, OR
10580		Albany-Schenectady-Troy, NY Metro area
	36001	Albany County, NY
	36083	Rensselaer County, NY
	36091	Saratoga County, NY
	36093	Schenectady County, NY
	36095	Schoharie County, NY
10700		Albertville, AL Micro area
	01095	Marshall County, AL
10740		Albuquerque, NM Metro area
	35001	Bernalillo County, NM
	35043	Sandoval County, NM
	35057	Torrance County, NM
	35061	Valencia County, NM
10780		Alexandria, LA Metro area
	22043	Grant Parish, LA
	22079	Rapides Parish, LA
10900		Allentown-Bethlehem-Easton, PA-NJ Metro area
	34041	Warren County, NJ
	42025	Carbon County, PA
	42077	Lehigh County, PA
	42095	Northampton County, PA
11020		Altoona, PA Metro area
	42013	Blair County, PA
11100		Amarillo, TX Metro area
	48011	Armstrong County, TX
	48065	Carson County, TX
	48359	Oldham County, TX
	48375	Potter County, TX
	48381	Randall County, TX
11180		Ames, IA Metro area
	19169	Story County, IA
11260		Anchorage, AK Metro area
	02020	Anchorage Municipality, AK
	02170	Matanuska-Susitna Borough, AK
11460		Ann Arbor, MI Metro area
	26161	Washtenaw County, MI
11500		Anniston-Oxford-Jacksonville, AL Metro area
	01015	Calhoun County, AL
11540		Appleton, WI Metro area
	55015	Calumet County, WI
	55087	Outagamie County, WI
11700		Asheville, NC Metro area
	37021	Buncombe County, NC
	37087	Haywood County, NC
	37089	Henderson County, NC
	37115	Madison County, NC
11780		Astabula, OH Micro area
	39007	Astabula County, OH
12020		Athens-Clarke County, GA Metro area
	13059	Clarke County, GA
	13195	Madison County, GA
	13219	Oconee County, GA
	13221	Oglethorpe County, GA
12060		Atlanta-Sandy Springs-Roswell, GA Metro area
	13013	Barrow County, GA
	13015	Bartow County, GA
	13035	Butts County, GA
	13045	Carroll County, GA
	13057	Cherokee County, GA
	13063	Clayton County, GA

Metropolitan and Micropolitan Areas and Components (as defined February 2013)

Metropolitan and Micropolitan Area Code	State/County FIPS code	Title and Geographic Components
	13067	Cobb County, GA
	13077	Coweta County, GA
	13085	Dawson County, GA
	13089	DeKalb County, GA
	13097	Douglas County, GA
	13113	Fayette County, GA
	13117	Forsyth County, GA
	13121	Fulton County, GA
	13135	Gwinnett County, GA
	13143	Haralson County, GA
	13149	Heard County, GA
	13151	Henry County, GA
	13159	Jasper County, GA
	13171	Lamar County, GA
	13199	Meriwether County, GA
	13211	Morgan County, GA
	13217	Newton County, GA
	13223	Paulding County, GA
	13227	Pickens County, GA
	13231	Pike County, GA
	13247	Rockdale County, GA
	13255	Spalding County, GA
	13297	Walton County, GA
12100		Atlantic City-Hammonton, NJ Metro area
	34001	Atlantic County, NJ
12220		Auburn-Opelika, AL Metro area
	01081	Lee County, AL
12260		Augusta-Richmond County, GA-SC Metro area
	13033	Burke County, GA
	13073	Columbia County, GA
	13181	Lincoln County, GA
	13189	McDuffie County, GA
	13245	Richmond County, GA
	45003	Aiken County, SC
	45037	Edgefield County, SC
12300		Augusta-Waterville, ME Micro area
	23011	Kennebec County, ME
12420		Austin-Round Rock, TX Metro area
	48021	Bastrop County, TX
	48055	Caldwell County, TX
	48209	Hays County, TX
	48453	Travis County, TX
	48491	Williamson County, TX
12540		Bakersfield, CA Metro area
	06029	Kern County, CA
12580		Baltimore-Columbia-Towson, MD Metro area
	24003	Anne Arundel County, MD
	24005	Baltimore County, MD
	24013	Carroll County, MD
	24025	Harford County, MD
	24027	Howard County, MD
	24035	Queen Anne's County, MD
	24510	Baltimore city, MD
12620		Bangor, ME Metro area
	23019	Penobscot County, ME
12700		Barnstable Town, MA Metro area
	25001	Barnstable County, MA
12940		Baton Rouge, LA Metro area
	22005	Ascension Parish, LA
	22033	East Baton Rouge Parish, LA
	22037	East Feliciana Parish, LA
	22047	Iberville Parish, LA
	22063	Livingston Parish, LA
	22077	Pointe Coupee Parish, LA
	22091	St. Helena Parish, LA
	22121	West Baton Rouge Parish, LA
	22125	West Feliciana Parish, LA
12980		Battle Creek, MI Metro area
	26025	Calhoun County, MI
13020		Bay City, MI Metro area
	26017	Bay County, MI
13140		Beaumont-Port Arthur, TX Metro area
	48199	Hardin County, TX
	48245	Jefferson County, TX
	48351	Newton County, TX
	48361	Orange County, TX
13220		Beckley, WV Metro area
	54019	Fayette County, WV

Metropolitan and Micropolitan Areas and Components (as defined February 2013)

Metropolitan and Micropolitan Area Code	State/County FIPS code	Title and Geographic Components
	54081	Raleigh County, WV
13380		Bellingham, WA Metro area
	53073	Whatcom County, WA
13460		Bend-Redmond, OR Metro area
	41017	Deschutes County, OR
13740		Billings, MT Metro area
	30009	Carbon County, MT
	30037	Golden Valley County, MT
	30111	Yellowstone County, MT
13780		Binghamton, NY Metro area
	36007	Broome County, NY
	36107	Tioga County, NY
13820		Birmingham-Hoover, AL Metro area
	01007	Bibb County, AL
	01009	Blount County, AL
	01021	Chilton County, AL
	01073	Jefferson County, AL
	01115	St. Clair County, AL
	01117	Shelby County, AL
	01127	Walker County, AL
13900		Bismarck, ND Metro area
	38015	Burleigh County, ND
	38059	Morton County, ND
	38065	Oliver County, ND
	38085	Sioux County, ND
13980		Blacksburg-Christiansburg-Radford, VA Metro area
	51063	Floyd County, VA
	51071	Giles County, VA
	51121	Montgomery County, VA
	51155	Pulaski County, VA
	51750	Radford city, VA
14010		Bloomington, IL Metro area
	17039	De Witt County, IL
	17113	McLean County, IL
14020		Bloomington, IN Metro area
	18105	Monroe County, IN
	18119	Owen County, IN
14100		Bloomsburg-Berwick, PA Metro area
	42037	Columbia County, PA
	42093	Montour County, PA
14260		Boise City, ID Metro area
	16001	Ada County, ID
	16015	Boise County, ID
	16027	Canyon County, ID
	16045	Gem County, ID
	16073	Owyhee County, ID
14460		Boston-Cambridge Newton, MA-NH Metro area
14460		Boston, MA Metro Div 14454
	25021	Norfolk County, MA
	25023	Plymouth County, MA
	25025	Suffolk County, MA
14460		Cambridge-Newton-Framingham, MA Metro Div 15764
	25009	Essex County, MA
	25017	Middlesex County, MA
14460		Rockingham County-Strafford County-NH Metro Div 40484
	33015	Rockingham County, NH
	33017	Strafford County, NH
14500		Boulder, CO Metro area
	08013	Boulder County, CO
14540		Bowling Green, KY Metro area
	21003	Allen County, KY
	21031	Butler County, KY
	21061	Edmonson County, KY
	21227	Warren County, KY
14740		Bremerton-Silverdale, WA Metro area
	53035	Kitsap County, WA
14860		Bridgeport-Stamford-Norwalk, CT Metro area
	09001	Fairfield County, CT
15180		Brownsville-Harlingen, TX Metro area
	48061	Cameron County, TX
15260		Brunswick, GA Metro area
	13025	Brantley County, GA
	13127	Glynn County, GA
	13191	McIntosh County, GA
15380		Buffalo-Cheektowaga-Niagara Falls, NY Metro area
	36029	Erie County, NY
	36063	Niagara County, NY
15500		Burlington, NC Metro area
	37001	Alamance County, NC
15540		Burlington-South Burlington, VT Metro area
	50007	Chittenden County, VT
	50011	Franklin County, VT
	50013	Grand Isle County, VT
15680		California-Lexington Park, MD Metro area
	24037	St. Mary's County, MD

Metropolitan and Micropolitan Areas and Components (as defined February 2013)

Metropolitan and Micropolitan Area Code	State/County FIPS code	Title and Geographic Components
15940		Canton-Massillon, OH Metro area
	39019	Carroll County, OH
	39151	Stark County, OH
15980		Cape Coral-Fort Myers, FL Metro area
	12071	Lee County, FL
16020		Cape Girardeau, MO-IL Metro area
	17003	Alexander County, IL
	29017	Bollinger County, MO
	29031	Cape Girardeau County, MO
16060		Carbondale-Marion, IL Metro area
	17077	Jackson County, IL
	17199	Williamson County, IL
16180		Carson City, NV Metro area
	32510	Carson City, NV
16220		Casper, WY Metro area
	56025	Natrona County, WY
16300		Cedar Rapids, IA Metro area
	19011	Benton County, IA
	19105	Jones County, IA
	19113	Linn County, IA
16540		Chambersburg-Waynesboro, PA Metro area
	42055	Franklin County, PA
16580		Champaign-Urbana, IL Metro area
	17019	Champaign County, IL
	17053	Ford County, IL
	17147	Piatt County, IL
16620		Charleston, WV Metro area
	54005	Boone County, WV
	54015	Clay County, WV
	54039	Kanawha County, WV
16700		Charleston-North Charleston, SC Metro area
	45015	Berkeley County, SC
	45019	Charleston County, SC
	45035	Dorchester County, SC
16740		Charlotte-Concord-Gastonia, NC-SC Metro area
	37025	Cabarrus County, NC
	37071	Gaston County, NC
	37097	Iredell County, NC
	37109	Lincoln County, NC
	37119	Mecklenburg County, NC
	37159	Rowan County, NC
	37179	Union County, NC
	45023	Chester County, SC
	45057	Lancaster County, SC
	45091	York County, SC
16820		Charlottesville, VA Metro area
	51003	Albemarle County, VA
	51029	Buckingham County, VA
	51065	Fluvanna County, VA
	51079	Greene County, VA
	51125	Nelson County, VA
	51540	Charlottesville city, VA
16860		Chattanooga, TN-GA Metro area
	13047	Catoosa County, GA
	13083	Dade County, GA
	13295	Walker County, GA
	47065	Hamilton County, TN
	47115	Marion County, TN
	47153	Sequatchie County, TN
16940		Cheyenne, WY Metro area
	56021	Laramie County, WY
16980		Chicago-Naperville-Elgin, IL-IN-WI Metro area
16980		Chicago-Naperville-Arlington Heights, IL Metro Div 16974
	17031	Cook County, IL
	17043	DuPage County, IL
	17063	Grundy County, IL
	17093	Kendall County, IL
	17111	McHenry County, IL
	17197	Will County, IL
16980		Gary, IN Metro Div 23844
	18073	Jasper County, IN
	18089	Lake County, IN
	18111	Newton County, IN
	18127	Porter County, IN
16980		Lake County-Kenosha County, IL-WI Metro Div 29404
	17097	Lake County, IL
	55059	Kenosha County, WI
17020		Chico, CA Metro area
	06007	Butte County, CA
17140		Cincinnati, OH-KY-IN Metro area
	18029	Dearborn County, IN
	18115	Ohio County, IN
	18161	Union County, IN
	21015	Boone County, KY
	21023	Bracken County, KY

Metropolitan and Micropolitan Area Code	State/County FIPS code	Title and Geographic Components
	21037	Campbell County, KY
	21077	Gallatin County, KY
	21081	Grant County, KY
	21117	Kenton County, KY
	21191	Pendleton County, KY
	39015	Brown County, OH
	39017	Butler County, OH
	39025	Clermont County, OH
	39061	Hamilton County, OH
	39165	Warren County, OH
17220		Clarksburg, WV Micro area
	54017	Doddridge County, WV
	54033	Harrison County, WV
	54091	Taylor County, WV
17300		Clarksville, TN-KY Metro area
	21047	Christian County, KY
	21221	Trigg County, KY
	47125	Montgomery County, TN
17420		Cleveland, TN Metro area
	47011	Bradley County, TN
	47139	Polk County, TN
17460		Cleveland-Elyria, OH Metro area
	39035	Cuyahoga County, OH
	39055	Geauga County, OH
	39085	Lake County, OH
	39093	Lorain County, OH
	39103	Medina County, OH
17660		Coeur d'Alene, ID Metro area
	16055	Kootenai County, ID
17780		College Station-Bryan, TX Metro area
	48041	Brazos County, TX
	48051	Burleson County, TX
	48395	Robertson County, TX
17820		Colorado Springs, CO Metro area
	08041	El Paso County, CO
	08119	Teller County, CO
17860		Columbia, MO Metro area
	29019	Boone County, MO
17900		Columbia, SC Metro area
	45017	Calhoun County, SC
	45039	Fairfield County, SC
	45055	Kershaw County, SC
	45063	Lexington County, SC
	45079	Richland County, SC
	45081	Saluda County, SC
17980		Columbus, GA-AL Metro area
	01113	Russell County, AL
	13053	Chattahoochee County, GA
	13145	Harris County, GA
	13197	Marion County, GA
	13215	Muscogee County, GA
18020		Columbus, IN Metro area
	18005	Bartholomew County, IN
18140		Columbus, OH Metro area
	39041	Delaware County, OH
	39045	Fairfield County, OH
	39049	Franklin County, OH
	39073	Hocking County, OH
	39089	Licking County, OH
	39097	Madison County, OH
	39117	Morrow County, OH
	39127	Perry County, OH
	39129	Pickaway County, OH
	39159	Union County, OH
18180		Concord, NH Micro area
	33013	Merrimack County, NH
18260		Cookeville, TN Micro area
	47087	Jackson County, TN
	47133	Overton County, TN
	47141	Putnam County, TN
18580		Corpus Christi, TX Metro area
	48007	Aransas County, TX
	48355	Nueces County, TX
	48409	San Patricio County, TX
18700		Corvallis, OR Metro area
	41003	Benton County, OR
18880		Crestview-Fort Walton Beach-Destin, FL Metro area
	12091	Okaloosa County, FL
	12131	Walton County, FL
19060		Cumberland, MD-WV Metro area
	24001	Allegany County, MD
	54057	Mineral County, WV
19100		Dallas-Fort Worth-Arlington, TX Metro area
19100		Dallas-Plano-Irving, TX Metro Div 19124
	48085	Collin County, TX

Metropolitan and Micropolitan Area Code	State/County FIPS code	Title and Geographic Components
	48113	Dallas County, TX
	48121	Denton County, TX
	48139	Ellis County, TX
	48231	Hunt County, TX
	48257	Kaufman County, TX
	48397	Rockwall County, TX
19100		Fort Worth-Arlington, TX Metro Div 23104
	48221	Hood County, TX
	48251	Johnson County, TX
	48367	Parker County, TX
	48425	Somervell County, TX
	48439	Tarrant County, TX
	48497	Wise County, TX
19140		Dalton, GA Metro area
	13213	Murray County, GA
	13313	Whitfield County, GA
19180		Danville, IL Metro area
	17183	Vermilion County, IL
19260		Danville, VA Micro area
	51143	Pittsylvania County, VA
	51590	Danville city, VA
19300		Daphne-Fairhope-Foley, AL Metro area
	01003	Baldwin County, AL
19340		Davenport-Moline-Rock Island, IA-IL Metro area
	17073	Henry County, IL
	17131	Mercer County, IL
	17161	Rock Island County, IL
	19163	Scott County, IA
19380		Dayton, OH Metro area
	39057	Greene County, OH
	39109	Miami County, OH
	39113	Montgomery County, OH
19460		Decatur, AL Metro area
	01079	Lawrence County, AL
	01103	Morgan County, AL
19500		Decatur, IL Metro area
	17115	Macon County, IL
19660		Deltona-Daytona Beach-Ormond Beach, FL Metro area
	12035	Flagler County, FL
	12127	Volusia County, FL
19740		Denver-Aurora-Lakewood, CO Metro area
	08001	Adams County, CO
	08005	Arapahoe County, CO
	08014	Broomfield County, CO
	08019	Clear Creek County, CO
	08031	Denver County, CO
	08035	Douglas County, CO
	08039	Elbert County, CO
	08047	Gilpin County, CO
	08059	Jefferson County, CO
	08093	Park County, CO
19780		Des Moines-West Des Moines, IA Metro area
	19049	Dallas County, IA
	19077	Guthrie County, IA
	19121	Madison County, IA
	19153	Polk County, IA
	19181	Warren County, IA
19820		Detroit-Warren-Dearborn, MI Metro area
19820		Detroit-Dearborn-Livonia, MI Metro Div 19804
	26163	Wayne County, MI
19820		Warren-Troy-Farmington Hills, MI Metro Div 47664
	26087	Lapeer County, MI
	26093	Livingston County, MI
	26099	Macomb County, MI
	26125	Oakland County, MI
	26147	St. Clair County, MI
20020		Dothan, AL Metro area
	01061	Geneva County, AL
	01067	Henry County, AL
	01069	Houston County, AL
20100		Dover, DE Metro area
	10001	Kent County, Delaware
20220		Dubuque, IA Metro area
	19061	Dubuque County, IA
20260		Duluth, MN-WI Metro area
	27017	Carlton County, MN
	27137	St. Louis County, MN
	55031	Douglas County, WI
20380		Dunn, NC Micro area
	37085	Harnett County, NC
20500		Durham-Chapel Hill, NC Metro area
	37037	Chatham County, NC
	37063	Durham County, NC
	37135	Orange County, NC
	37145	Person County, NC

Metropolitan and Micropolitan Areas and Components (as defined February 2013)		
Metropolitan and Micropolitan Area Code	State/County FIPS code	Title and Geographic Components
20700		East Stroudsburg, PA Metro area
	42089	Monroe County, PA
20740		Eau Claire, WI Metro area
	55017	Chippewa County, WI
	55035	Eau Claire County, WI
20940		El Centro, CA Metro area
	06025	Imperial County, CA
21340		El Paso, TX Metro area
	48141	El Paso County, TX
	48229	Hudspeth County, TX
21060		Elizabethtown-Fort Knox, KY Metro area
	21093	Hardin County, KY
	21123	Larue County, KY
	21163	Meade County, KY
21140		Elkhart-Goshen, IN Metro area
	18039	Elkhart County, IN
21300		Elmira, NY Metro area
	36015	Chemung County, NY
21500		Erie, PA Metro area
	42049	Erie County, PA
21660		Eugene, OR Metro area
	41039	Lane County, OR
21700		Eureka-Arcata-Fortuna, CA Micro area
	06023	Humboldt County, CA
21780		Evansville, IN-KY Metro area
	18129	Posey County, IN
	18163	Vanderburgh County, IN
	18173	Warrick County, IN
	21101	Henderson County, KY
21820		Fairbanks, AK Metro area
	02090	Fairbanks North Star Borough, AK
22020		Fargo, ND-MN Metro area
	27027	Clay County, MN
	38017	Cass County, ND
22140		Farmington, NM Metro area
	35045	San Juan County, NM
22180		Fayetteville, NC Metro area
	37051	Cumberland County, NC
	37093	Hoke County, NC
22220		Fayetteville-Springdale-Rogers, AR-MO Metro area
	05007	Benton County, AR
	05087	Madison County, AR
	05143	Washington County, AR
	29119	McDonald County, MO
22380		Flagstaff, AZ Metro area
	04005	Coconino County, AZ
22420		Flint, MI Metro area
	26049	Genesee County, MI
22500		Florence, SC Metro area
	45031	Darlington County, SC
	45041	Florence County, SC
22520		Florence-Muscle Shoals, AL Metro area
	01033	Colbert County, AL
	01077	Lauderdale County, AL
22540		Fond du Lac, WI Metro area
	55039	Fond du Lac County, WI
22660		Fort Collins, CO Metro area
	08069	Larimer County, CO
22900		Fort Smith, AR-OK Metro area
	05033	Crawford County, AR
	05131	Sebastian County, AR
	40079	Le Flore County, OK
	40135	Sequoyah County, OK
23060		Fort Wayne, IN Metro area
	18003	Allen County, IN
	18179	Wells County, IN
	18183	Whitley County, IN
23420		Fresno, CA Metro area
	06019	Fresno County, CA
23460		Gadsden, AL Metro area
	01055	Etowah County, AL
23540		Gainesville, FL Metro area
	12001	Alachua County, FL
	12041	Gilchrist County, FL
23580		Gainesville, GA Metro area
	13139	Hall County, GA
		Gettysburg, PA Metro area
	42001	Adams County, PA
24020		Glens Falls, NY Metro area
	36113	Warren County, NY
	36115	Washington County, NY
24140		Goldsboro, NC Metro area
	37191	Wayne County, NC
24220		Grand Forks, ND-MN Metro area
	27119	Polk County, MN

Metropolitan and Micropolitan Areas and Components (as defined February 2013)		
Metropolitan and Micropolitan Area Code	State/County FIPS code	Title and Geographic Components
	38035	Grand Forks County, ND
24260		Grand Island, NE Metro area
	31079	Hall County, NE
	31081	Hamilton County, NE
	31093	Howard County, NE
	31121	Merrick County, NE
24300		Grand Junction, CO Metro area
	08077	Mesa County, CO
24340		Grand Rapids-Wyoming, MI Metro area
	26015	Barry County, MI
	26081	Kent County, MI
	26117	Montcalm County, MI
	26139	Ottawa County, MI
24420		Grants Pass, OR Metro area
	41033	Josephine County, OR
24500		Great Falls, MT Metro area
	30013	Cascade County, MT
24540		Greeley, CO Metro area
	08123	Weld County, CO
24580		Green Bay, WI Metro area
	55009	Brown County, WI
	55061	Kewaunee County, WI
	55083	Oconto County, WI
24660		Greensboro-High Point, NC Metro area
	37081	Guilford County, NC
	37151	Randolph County, NC
	37157	Rockingham County, NC
24780		Greenville, NC Metro area
	37147	Pitt County, NC
24860		Greenville-Anderson-Mauldin, SC Metro area
	45007	Anderson County, SC
	45045	Greenville County, SC
	45059	Laurens County, SC
	45077	Pickens County, SC
29940		Greenwood, SC Micro area
	45001	Abeville County, SC
	45045	Greenwood County, SC
25060		Gulfport-Biloxi-Pascagoula, MS Metro area
	28045	Hancock County, MS
	28047	Harrison County, MS
	28059	Jackson County, MS
25180		Hagerstown-Martinsburg, MD-WV Metro area
	24043	Washington County, MD
	54003	Berkeley County, WV
25220		Hammond, LA Metro area
	22105	Tangipahoa Parish, LA
25260		Hanford-Corcoran, CA Metro area
	06031	Kings County, CA
25420		Harrisburg-Carlisle, PA Metro area
	42041	Cumberland County, PA
	42043	Dauphin County, PA
	42099	Perry County, PA
25500		Harrisonburg, VA Metro area
	51165	Rockingham County, VA
	51660	Harrisonburg city, VA
25540		Hartford-West Hartford-East Hartford, CT Metro area
	09003	Hartford County, CT
	09007	Middlesex County, CT
	09013	Tolland County, CT
25620		Hattiesburg, MS Metro area
	28035	Forrest County, MS
	28073	Lamar County, MS
	28111	Perry County, MS
25860		Hickory-Lenoir-Morganton, NC Metro area
	37003	Alexander County, NC
	37023	Burke County, NC
	37027	Caldwell County, NC
	37035	Catawba County, NC
25900		Hilo, HI Micro area
	15001	Hawaii County, HI
25940		Hilton Head Island-Bluffton-Beaufort, SC Metro area
	45013	Beaufort County, SC
	45053	Jasper County, SC
25980		Hinesville, GA Metro area
	13179	Liberty County, GA
	13183	Long County, GA
26090		Holland, MI Micro area
	26005	Allegan County, MI
26140		Homosassa Springs, FL Metro area
	12017	Citrus County, FL
26300		Hot Springs, AR Metro area
	05051	Garland County, AR
26380		Houma-Thibodaux, LA Metro area
	22057	Lafourche Parish, LA
	22109	Terrebonne Parish, LA

Metropolitan and Micropolitan Area Code	State/County FIPS code	Title and Geographic Components
26420		Houston-The Woodlands-Sugar Land, TX Metro area
	48015	Austin County, TX
	48039	Brazoria County, TX
	48071	Chambers County, TX
	48157	Fort Bend County, TX
	48167	Galveston County, TX
	48201	Harris County, TX
	48291	Liberty County, TX
	48339	Montgomery County, TX
	48473	Waller County, TX
26580		Huntington-Ashland, WV-KY-OH Metro area
	21019	Boyd County, KY
	21089	Greenup County, KY
	39087	Lawrence County, OH
	54011	Cabell County, WV
	54043	Lincoln County, WV
	54079	Putnam County, WV
	54099	Wayne County, WV
26620		Huntsville, AL Metro area
	01083	Limestone County, AL
	01089	Madison County, AL
26820		Idaho Falls, ID Metro area
	16019	Bonneville County, ID
	16023	Butte County, ID
	16051	Jefferson County, ID
26900		Indianapolis-Carmel-Anderson, IN Metro area
	18011	Boone County, IN
	18013	Brown County, IN
	18057	Hamilton County, IN
	18059	Hancock County, IN
	18063	Hendricks County, IN
	18081	Johnson County, IN
	18095	Madison County, IN
	18097	Marion County, IN
	18109	Morgan County, IN
	18133	Putnam County, IN
	18145	Shelby County, IN
26980		Iowa City, IA Metro area
	19103	Johnson County, IA
	19183	Washington County, IA
27060		Ithaca, NY Metro area
	36109	Tompkins County, NY
27100		Jackson, MI Metro area
	26075	Jackson County, MI
27140		Jackson, MS Metro area
	28029	Copiah County, MS
	28049	Hinds County, MS
	28089	Madison County, MS
	28121	Rankin County, MS
	28127	Simpson County, MS
	28163	Yazoo County, MS
27180		Jackson, TN Metro area
	47023	Chester County, TN
	47033	Crockett County, TN
	47113	Madison County, TN
27260		Jacksonville, FL Metro area
	12003	Baker County, FL
	12019	Clay County, FL
	12031	Duval County, FL
	12089	Nassau County, FL
	12109	St. Johns County, FL
27340		Jacksonville, NC Metro area
	37133	Onslow County, NC
27460		Jamestown-Dunkirk-Fredonia, NY Micro area
	36013	Chautauqua County, NY
27500		Janesville-Beloit, WI Metro area
	55105	Rock County, WI
27620		Jefferson City, MO Metro area
	29027	Callaway County, MO
	29051	Cole County, MO
	29135	Moniteau County, MO
	29151	Osage County, MO
27740		Johnson City, TN Metro area
	47019	Carter County, TN
	47171	Unicoi County, TN
	47179	Washington County, TN
27780		Johnstown, PA Metro area
	42021	Cambria County, PA
27860		Jonesboro, AR Metro area
	05031	Craighead County, AR
	05111	Poinsett County, AR
27900		Joplin, MO Metro area
	29097	Jasper County, MO
	29145	Newton County, MO
27980		Kahului-Wailuku-Lahaina, HI Metro area

Metropolitan and Micropolitan Area Code	State/County FIPS code	Title and Geographic Components
	15005	Kalawao County, HI
	15009	Maui County, HI
28020		Kalamazoo-Portage, MI Metro area
	26077	Kalamazoo County, MI
	26159	Van Buren County, MI
28060		Kalispell, MT Micro area
	30029	Flathead County, MT
28100		Kankakee, IL Metro area
	17091	Kankakee County, IL
28140		Kansas City, MO-KS Metro area
	20091	Johnson County, KS
	20103	Leavenworth County, KS
	20107	Linn County, KS
	20121	Miami County, KS
	20209	Wyandotte County, KS
	29013	Bates County, MO
	29025	Caldwell County, MO
	29037	Cass County, MO
	29047	Clay County, MO
	29049	Clinton County, MO
	29095	Jackson County, MO
	29107	Lafayette County, MO
	29165	Platte County, MO
	29177	Ray County, MO
28420		Kennewick-Richland, WA Metro area
	53005	Benton County, WA
	53021	Franklin County, WA
28660		Killeen-Temple, TX Metro area
	48027	Bell County, TX
	48099	Coryell County, TX
	48281	Lampasas County, TX
28700		Kingsport-Bristol-Bristol, TN-VA Metro area
	47073	Hawkins County, TN
	47163	Sullivan County, TN
	51169	Scott County, VA
	51191	Washington County, VA
	51520	Bristol city, VA
28740		Kingston, NY Metro area
	36111	Ulster County, NY
28940		Knoxville, TN Metro area
	47001	Anderson County, TN
	47009	Blount County, TN
	47013	Campbell County, TN
	47057	Grainger County, TN
	47093	Knox County, TN
	47105	Loudon County, TN
	47129	Morgan County, TN
	47145	Roane County, TN
	47173	Union County, TN
29020		Kokomo, IN Metro area
	18067	Howard County, IN
29100		La Crosse-Onalaska, WI-MN Metro area
	27055	Houston County, MN
	55063	La Crosse County, WI
29180		Lafayette, LA Metro area
	22001	Acadia Parish, LA
	22045	Iberia Parish, LA
	22055	Lafayette Parish, LA
	22099	St. Martin Parish, LA
	22113	Vermilion Parish, LA
29200		Lafayette-West Lafayette, IN Metro area
	18007	Benton County, IN
	18015	Carroll County, IN
	18157	Tippecanoe County, IN
29340		Lake Charles, LA Metro area
	22019	Calcasieu Parish, LA
	22023	Cameron Parish, LA
29420		Lake Havasu City-Kingman, AZ Metro area
	04015	Mohave County, AZ
29460		Lakeland-Winter Haven, FL Metro area
	12105	Polk County, FL
29540		Lancaster, PA Metro area
	42071	Lancaster County, PA
29620		Lansing-East Lansing, MI Metro area
	26037	Clinton County, MI
	26045	Eaton County, MI
	26065	Ingham County, MI
29700		Laredo, TX Metro area
	48479	Webb County, TX
29740		Las Cruces, NM Metro area
	35013	Doña Ana County, NM
29820		Las Vegas-Henderson-Paradise, NV Metro area
	32003	Clark County, NV
29940		Lawrence, KS Metro area
	20045	Douglas County, KS

Metropolitan and Micropolitan Area Code	State/County FIPS code	Title and Geographic Components
30020		Lawton, OK Metro area
	40031	Comanche County, OK
	40033	Cotton County, OK
30340		Lewiston-Auburn, ME Metro area
	23001	Androscoggin County, ME
30300		Lewiston, ID-WA Metro area
	16069	Nez Perce County, ID
	53003	Asotin County, WA
30460		Lexington-Fayette, KY Metro area
	21017	Bourbon County, KY
	21049	Clark County, KY
	21067	Fayette County, KY
	21113	Jessamine County, KY
	21209	Scott County, KY
	21239	Woodford County, KY
30620		Lima, OH Metro area
	39003	Allen County, OH
30780		Little Rock-North Little Rock-Conway, AR Metro area
	05045	Faulkner County, AR
	05053	Grant County, AR
	05085	Lonoke County, AR
	05105	Perry County, AR
	05119	Pulaski County, AR
	05125	Saline County, AR
30860		Logan, UT-ID Metro area
	16041	Franklin County, ID
	49005	Cache County, UT
30980		Longview, TX Metro area
	48183	Gregg County, TX
	48401	Rusk County, TX
	48459	Upshur County, TX
31020		Longview, WA Metro area
	53015	Cowlitz County, WA
31080		Los Angeles-Long Beach-Anaheim, CA Metro area
31080		Anaheim-Santa Ana-Irvine, CA Metro Div 11244
	06059	Orange County, CA
31080		Los Angeles-Long Beach-Glendale, CA Metro Div 31084
	06037	Los Angeles County, CA
31140		Louisville/Jefferson County, KY-IN Metro area
	18019	Clark County, IN
	18043	Floyd County, IN
	18061	Harrison County, IN
	18143	Scott County, IN
	18175	Washington County, IN
	21029	Bullitt County, KY
	21103	Henry County, KY
	21111	Jefferson County, KY
	21185	Oldham County, KY
	21211	Shelby County, KY
	21215	Spencer County, KY
	21223	Trimble County, KY
31180		Lubbock, TX Metro area
	48107	Crosby County, TX
	48303	Lubbock County, TX
	48305	Lynn County, TX
31300		Lumberton, NC Micro area
	37155	Robeson County, NC
31340		Lynchburg, VA Metro area
	51009	Amherst County, VA
	51011	Appomattox County, VA
	51019	Bedford County, VA
	51031	Campbell County, VA
	51515	Bedford city, VA
	51680	Lynchburg city, VA
31420		Macon, GA Metro area
	13021	Bibb County, GA
	13079	Crawford County, GA
	13169	Jones County, GA
	13207	Monroe County, GA
	13289	Twiggs County, GA
31460		Madera, CA Metro area
	06039	Madera County, CA
31540		Madison, WI Metro area
	55021	Columbia County, WI
	55025	Dane County, WI
	55045	Green County, WI
	55049	Iowa County, WI
31700		Manchester-Nashua, NH Metro area
	33011	Hillsborough County, NH
31740		Manhattan, KS Metro area
	20149	Pottawatomie County, KS
	20161	Riley County, KS
31860		Mankato-North Mankato, MN Metro area
	27013	Blue Earth County, MN
	27103	Nicollet County, MN

Metropolitan and Micropolitan Area Code	State/County FIPS code	Title and Geographic Components
31900		Mansfield, OH Metro area
	39139	Richland County, OH
32580		McAllen-Edinburg-Mission, TX Metro area
	48215	Hidalgo County, TX
32780		Medford, OR Metro area
	41029	Jackson County, OR
32820		Memphis, TN-MS-AR Metro area
	05035	Crittenden County, AR
	28009	Benton County, MS
	28033	DeSoto County, MS
	28093	Marshall County, MS
	28137	Tate County, MS
	28143	Tunica County, MS
	47047	Fayette County, TN
	47157	Shelby County, TN
	47167	Tipton County, TN
32900		Merced, CA Metro area
	06047	Merced County, CA
32940		Meridian, MS Micro area
	28023	Clarke County, MS
	28069	Kemper County, MS
	28075	Lauderdale County, MS
33100		Miami-Fort Lauderdale-West Palm Beach, FL Metro area
33100		Fort Lauderdale-Pompano Beach-Deerfield Beach, FL Metro Div 22744
	12011	Broward County, FL
33100		Miami-Miami Beach-Kendall, FL Metro Div 33124
	12086	Miami-Dade County, FL
33100		West Palm Beach-Boca Raton-Delray Beach, FL Metro Div 48424
	12099	Palm Beach County, FL
33140		Michigan City-La Porte, IN Metro area
	18091	LaPorte County, IN
33220		Midland, MI Metro area
	26111	Midland County, MI
33260		Midland, TX Metro area
	48317	Martin County, TX
	48329	Midland County, TX
33340		Milwaukee-Waukesha-West Allis, WI Metro area
	55079	Milwaukee County, WI
	55089	Ozaukee County, WI
	55131	Washington County, WI
	55133	Waukesha County, WI
33460		Minneapolis-St. Paul-Bloomington, MN Metro area
	27003	Anoka County, MN
	27019	Carver County, MN
	27025	Chisago County, MN
	27037	Dakota County, MN
	27053	Hennepin County, MN
	27059	Isanti County, MN
	27079	Le Sueur County, MN
	27095	Mille Lacs County, MN
	27123	Ramsey County, MN
	27139	Scott County, MN
	27141	Sherburne County, MN
	27143	Sibley County, MN
	27163	Washington County, MN
	27171	Wright County, MN
	55093	Pierce County, WI
	55109	St. Croix County, WI
33540		Missoula, MT Metro area
	30063	Missoula County, MT
33660		Mobile, AL Metro area
	01097	Mobile County, AL
33700		Modesto, CA Metro area
	06099	Stanislaus County, CA
33740		Monroe, LA Metro area
	22073	Ouachita Parish, LA
	22111	Union Parish, LA
33780		Monroe, MI Metro area
	26115	Monroe County, MI
33860		Montgomery, AL Metro area
	01001	Autauga County, AL
	01051	Elmore County, AL
	01085	Lowndes County, AL
	01101	Montgomery County, AL
34060		Morgantown, WV Metro area
	54061	Monongalia County, WV
	54077	Preston County, WV
34100		Morristown, TN Metro area
	47063	Hamblen County, TN
	47089	Jefferson County, TN
34540		Mount Vernon, OH Micro area
	39083	Knox County, OH
34620		Muncie, IN Metro area

Metropolitan and Micropolitan Area Code	State/County FIPS code	Title and Geographic Components
		Metropolitan and Micropolitan Areas and Components (as defined February 2013)
	18035	Delaware County, IN
34740		Muskegon, MI Metro area
	26121	Muskegon County, MI
34820		Myrtle Beach-Conway-North Myrtle Beach, NC-SC Metro area
	37019	Brunswick County, NC
	45051	Horry County, SC
34900		Napa, CA Metro area
	06055	Napa County, CA
34940		Naples-Immokalee-Marco Island, FL Metro area
	12021	Collier County, FL
34980		Nashville-Davidson–Murfreesboro–Franklin, TN Metro area
	47015	Cannon County, TN
	47021	Cheatham County, TN
	47037	Davidson County, TN
	47043	Dickson County, TN
	47081	Hickman County, TN
	47111	Macon County, TN
	47119	Maury County, TN
	47147	Robertson County, TN
	47149	Rutherford County, TN
	47159	Smith County, TN
	47165	Sumner County, TN
	47169	Trousdale County, TN
	47187	Williamson County, TN
	47189	Wilson County, TN
35100		New Bern, NC Metro area
	37049	Craven County, NC
	37103	Jones County, NC
	37137	Pamlico County, NC
35260		New Castle, PA Micro area
	42073	Lawrence County, PA
35300		New Haven-Milford, CT Metro area
	09009	New Haven County, CT
35380		New Orleans-Metairie, LA Metro area
	22051	Jefferson Parish, LA
	22071	Orleans Parish, LA
	22075	Plaquemines Parish, LA
	22087	St. Bernard Parish, LA
	22089	St. Charles Parish, LA
	22093	St. James Parish, LA
	22095	St. John the Baptist Parish, LA
	22103	St. Tammany Parish, LA
35420		New Philadelphia-Dover, OH Micro area
	39157	Tuscarawas County, OH
35620		New York-Newark-Jersey City, NY-NJ-PA Metro area
35620		Dutchess County-Putnam County, NY Metro Div 20524
	36027	Dutchess County, NY
	36079	Putnam County, NY
35620		Nassau County-Suffolk County, NY Metro Div 35004
	36059	Nassau County, NY
	36103	Suffolk County, NY
35620		Newark, NJ-PA Metro Div 35084
	34013	Essex County, NJ
	34019	Hunterdon County, NJ
	34027	Morris County, NJ
	34035	Somerset County, NJ
	34037	Sussex County, NJ
	34039	Union County, NJ
	42103	Pike County, PA
35620		New York-Jersey City-White Plains, NY-NJ Metro Div 35614
	34003	Bergen County, NJ
	34017	Hudson County, NJ
	34023	Middlesex County, NJ
	34025	Monmouth County, NJ
	34029	Ocean County, NJ
	34031	Passaic County, NJ
	36005	Bronx County, NY
	36047	Kings County, NY
	36061	New York County, NY
	36071	Orange County, NY
	36081	Queens County, NY
	36085	Richmond County, NY
	36087	Rockland County, NY
	36119	Westchester County, NY
35660		Niles-Benton Harbor, MI Metro area
	26021	Berrien County, MI
35840		North Port-Sarasota-Bradenton, FL Metro area
	12081	Manatee County, FL
	12115	Sarasota County, FL
35980		Norwich-New London, CT Metro area
	09011	New London County, CT
36100		Ocala, FL Metro area
	12083	Marion County, FL
36140		Ocean City, NJ Metro area
	34009	Cape May County, NJ

Metropolitan and Micropolitan Area Code	State/County FIPS code	Title and Geographic Components
		Metropolitan and Micropolitan Areas and Components (as defined February 2013)
36220		Odessa, TX Metro area
	48135	Ector County, TX
36260		Ogden-Clearfield, UT Metro area
	49003	Box Elder County, UT
	49011	Davis County, UT
	49029	Morgan County, UT
	49057	Weber County, UT
36300		Ogdensburg-Massena, NY Micro area
	36089	St. Lawrence County, NY
36420		Oklahoma City, OK Metro area
	40017	Canadian County, OK
	40027	Cleveland County, OK
	40051	Grady County, OK
	40081	Lincoln County, OK
	40083	Logan County, OK
	40087	McClain County, OK
	40109	Oklahoma County, OK
36500		Olympia-Tumwater, WA Metro area
	53067	Thurston County, WA
36540		Omaha-Council Bluffs, NE-IA Metro area
	19085	Harrison County, IA
	19129	Mills County, IA
	19155	Pottawattamie County, IA
	31025	Cass County, NE
	31055	Douglas County, NE
	31153	Sarpy County, NE
	31155	Saunders County, NE
	31177	Washington County, NE
36700		Orangeburg,SC Micro area
	45075	Orangeburg County, SC
36740		Orlando-Kissimmee-Sanford, FL Metro
	12069	Lake County, FL
	12095	Orange County, FL
	12097	Osceola County, FL
	12117	Seminole County, FL
36780		Oshkosh-Neenah, WI Metro area
	55139	Winnebago County, WI
36860		Ottaw-Peru, IL Micro area
	17011	Bureau County, IL
	17099	LaSalle County, Il
	17155	Putnam County, IL
36980		Owensboro, KY Metro area
	21059	Daviess County, KY
	21091	Hancock County, KY
	21149	McLean County, KY
37100		Oxnard-Thousand Oaks-Ventura, CA Metro area
	06111	Ventura County, CA
37340		Palm Bay-Melbourne-Titusville, FL Metro area
	12009	Brevard County, FL
37460		Panama City, FL Metro area
	12005	Bay County, FL
	12045	Gulf County, FL
37620		Parkersburg-Vienna, WV Metro area
	54105	Wirt County, WV
	54107	Wood County, WV
37860		Pensacola-Ferry Pass-Brent, FL Metro area
	12033	Escambia County, FL
	12113	Santa Rosa County, FL
37900		Peoria, IL Metro area
	17123	Marshall County, IL
	17143	Peoria County, IL
	17175	Stark County, IL
	17179	Tazewell County, IL
	17203	Woodford County, IL
37980		Philadelphia-Camden-Wilmington, PA-NJ-DE-MD Metro area
37980		Camden, NJ Metro Div 15804
	34005	Burlington County, NJ
	34007	Camden County, NJ
	34015	Gloucester County, NJ
37980		Montgomery County-Bucks County-Chester County, PA Metro Div 33874
	42017	Bucks County, PA
	42029	Chester County, PA
	42091	Montgomery County, PA
37980		Philadelphia, PA Metro Div 37964
	42045	Delaware County, PA
	42101	Philadelphia County, PA
37980		Wilmington, DE-MD-NJ Metro Div 48864
	10003	New Castle County, Delaware
	24015	Cecil County, MD
	34033	Salem County, NJ
38060		Phoenix-Mesa-Scottsdale, AZ Metro area
	04013	Maricopa County, AZ
	04021	Pinal County, AZ
38220		Pine Bluff, AR Metro area

Metropolitan and Micropolitan Area Code	State/County FIPS code	Title and Geographic Components
	05025	Cleveland County, AR
	05069	Jefferson County, AR
	05079	Lincoln County, AR
38300		Pittsburgh, PA Metro area
	42003	Allegheny County, PA
	42005	Armstrong County, PA
	42007	Beaver County, PA
	42019	Butler County, PA
	42051	Fayette County, PA
	42125	Washington County, PA
	42129	Westmoreland County, PA
38340		Pittsfield, MA Metro area
	25003	Berkshire County, MA
38540		Pocatello, ID Metro area
	16005	Bannock County, ID
38860		Portland-South Portland, ME Metro area
	23005	Cumberland County, ME
	23023	Sagadahoc County, ME
	23031	York County, ME
38900		Portland-Vancouver-Hillsboro, OR-WA Metro area
	41005	Clackamas County, OR
	41009	Columbia County, OR
	41051	Multnomah County, OR
	41067	Washington County, OR
	41071	Yamhill County, OR
	53011	Clark County, WA
	53059	Skamania County, WA
38940		Port St. Lucie, FL Metro area
	12085	Martin County, FL
	12111	St. Lucie County, FL
39060		Pottsville, PA Micro area
	42107	Schuylkill County, PA
39140		Prescott, AZ Metro area
	04025	Yavapai County, AZ
39300		Providence-Warwick, RI-MA Metro area
	25005	Bristol County, MA
	44001	Bristol County, RI
	44003	Kent County, RI
	44005	Newport County, RI
	44007	Providence County, RI
	44009	Washington County, RI
39340		Provo-Orem, UT Metro area
	49023	Juab County, UT
	49049	Utah County, UT
39380		Pueblo, CO Metro area
	08101	Pueblo County, CO
39460		Punta Gorda, FL Metro area
	12015	Charlotte County, FL
39540		Racine, WI Metro area
	55101	Racine County, WI
39580		Raleigh, NC Metro area
	37069	Franklin County, NC
	37101	Johnston County, NC
	37183	Wake County, NC
39660		Rapid City, SD Metro area
	46033	Custer County, SD
	46093	Meade County, SD
	46103	Pennington County, SD
39740		Reading, PA Metro area
	42011	Berks County, PA
39820		Redding, CA Metro area
	06089	Shasta County, CA
39900		Reno, NV Metro area
	32029	Storey County, NV
	32031	Washoe County, NV
40060		Richmond, VA Metro area
	51007	Amelia County, VA
	51033	Caroline County, VA
	51036	Charles City County, VA
	51041	Chesterfield County, VA
	51053	Dinwiddie County, VA
	51075	Goochland County, VA
	51085	Hanover County, VA
	51087	Henrico County, VA
	51101	King William County, VA
	51127	New Kent County, VA
	51145	Powhatan County, VA
	51149	Prince George County, VA
	51183	Sussex County, VA
	51570	Colonial Heights city, VA
	51670	Hopewell city, VA
	51730	Petersburg city, VA
	51760	Richmond city, VA
40140		Riverside-San Bernardino-Ontario, CA
	06065	Riverside County, CA
	06071	San Bernardino County, CA
40220		Roanoke, VA Metro area
	51023	Botetourt County, VA
	51045	Craig County, VA
	51067	Franklin County, VA
	51161	Roanoke County, VA
	51770	Roanoke city, VA
	51775	Salem city, VA
40340		Rochester, MN Metro area
	27039	Dodge County, MN
	27045	Fillmore County, MN
	27109	Olmsted County, MN
	27157	Wabasha County, MN
40380		Rochester, NY Metro area
	36051	Livingston County, NY
	36055	Monroe County, NY
	36069	Ontario County, NY
	36073	Orleans County, NY
	36117	Wayne County, NY
	36123	Yates County, NY
40420		Rockford, IL Metro area
	17007	Boone County, IL
	17201	Winnebago County, IL
40580		Rocky Mount, NC Metro area
	37065	Edgecombe County, NC
	37127	Nash County, NC
40660		Rome, GA Metro area
	13115	Floyd County, GA
40700		Roseburg, OR Micro area
	41019	Douglas County, OR
40900		Sacramento-Roseville-Arden-Arcade, CA Metro area
	06017	El Dorado County, CA
	06061	Placer County, CA
	06067	Sacramento County, CA
	06113	Yolo County, CA
40980		Saginaw, MI Metro area
	26145	Saginaw County, MI
41400		Salem, OH Micro area
	39029	Columbiana County, OH
41420		Salem, OR Metro area
	41047	Marion County, OR
	41053	Polk County, OR
41500		Salinas, CA Metro area
	06053	Monterey County, CA
41540		Salisbury, MD-DE Metro area
	10005	Sussex County, DE
	24039	Somerset County, MD
	24045	Wicomico County, MD
	24047	Worcester County, MD
41620		Salt Lake City, UT Metro area
	49035	Salt Lake County, UT
	49045	Tooele County, UT
41660		San Angelo, TX Metro area
	48235	Irion County, TX
	48451	Tom Green County, TX
41700		San Antonio-New Braunfels, TX Metro
	48013	Atascosa County, TX
	48019	Bandera County, TX
	48029	Bexar County, TX
	48091	Comal County, TX
	48187	Guadalupe County, TX
	48259	Kendall County, TX
	48325	Medina County, TX
	48493	Wilson County, TX
41740		San Diego-Carlsbad, CA Metro area
	06073	San Diego County, CA
41860		San Francisco-Oakland-Hayward, CA Metro area
41860		Oakland-Hayward-Berkeley, CA Metro Div 36084
	06001	Alameda County, CA
	06013	Contra Costa County, CA
41860		San Francisco-Redwood City-South San Francisco, CA Metro Div 41884
	06075	San Francisco County, CA
	06081	San Mateo County, CA
41860		San Rafael, CA Metropolitan Div 42034
	06041	Marin County, CA
41940		San Jose-Sunnyvale-Santa Clara, CA Metro area
	06069	San Benito County, CA
	06085	Santa Clara County, CA
42020		San Luis Obispo-Paso Robles-Arroyo Grande, CA Metro area
	06079	San Luis Obispo County, CA
42100		Santa Cruz-Watsonville, CA Metro area
	06087	Santa Cruz County, CA
42140		Santa Fe, NM Metro area
	35049	Santa Fe County, NM

Metropolitan and Micropolitan Area Code	State/County FIPS code	Title and Geographic Components
42200		Santa Maria-Santa Barbara, CA Metro
	06083	Santa Barbara County, CA
42220		Santa Rosa, CA Metro area
	00097	Sonoma County, CA
42340		Savannah, GA Metro area
	13029	Bryan County, GA
	13051	Chatham County, GA
	13103	Effingham County, GA
42540		Scranton–Wilkes-Barre–Hazleton, PA Metro area
	42069	Lackawanna County, PA
	42079	Luzerne County, PA
	42131	Wyoming County, PA
42660		Seattle-Tacoma-Bellevue, WA Metro area
42660		Seattle-Bellevue-Everett, WA Metro Div 42644
	53033	King County, WA
	53061	Snohomish County, WA
42660		Tacoma-Lakewood, WA Metro Div 45104
	53053	Pierce County, WA
42680		Sebastian-Vero Beach, FL Metro area
	12061	Indian River County, FL
42700		Sebring, FL Metro area
	12055	Highlands County, FL
43100		Sheboygan, WI Metro area
	55117	Sheboygan County, WI
43300		Sherman-Denison, TX Metro area
	48181	Grayson County, TX
43320		Show Low, AZ Micro area
	04017	Navajo County, AZ
43340		Shreveport-Bossier City, LA Metro area
	22015	Bossier Parish, LA
	22017	Caddo Parish, LA
	22031	De Soto Parish, LA
	22119	Webster Parish, LA
43420		Sierra Vista-Douglas, AZ Metro area
	04003	Cochise County, AZ
43580		Sioux City, IA-NE-SD Metro area
	19149	Plymouth County, IA
	19193	Woodbury County, IA
	31043	Dakota County, NE
	31051	Dixon County, NE
	46127	Union County, SD
43620		Sioux Falls, SD Metro area
	46083	Lincoln County, SD
	46087	McCook County, SD
	46099	Minnehaha County, SD
	46125	Turner County, SD
43780		South Bend-Mishawaka, IN-MI Metro area
	18141	St. Joseph County, IN
	26027	Cass County, MI
43900		Spartanburg, SC Metro area
	45083	Spartanburg County, SC
	45087	Union County, SC
44060		Spokane-Spokane Valley, WA Metro area
	53051	Pend Oreille County, WA
	53063	Spokane County, WA
	53065	Stevens County, WA
44100		Springfield, IL Metro area
	17129	Menard County, IL
	17167	Sangamon County, IL
44140		Springfield, MA Metro area
	25013	Hampden County, MA
	25015	Hampshire County, MA
44180		Springfield, MO Metro area
	29043	Christian County, MO
	29059	Dallas County, MO
	29077	Greene County, MO
	29167	Polk County, MO
	29225	Webster County, MO
44220		Springfield, OH Metro area
	39023	Clark County, OH
41060		St. Cloud, MN Metro area
	27009	Benton County, MN
	27145	Stearns County, MN
41100		St. George, UT Metro area
	49053	Washington County, UT
41140		St. Joseph, MO-KS Metro area
	20043	Doniphan County, KS
	29003	Andrew County, MO
	29021	Buchanan County, MO
	29063	DeKalb County, MO
41180		St. Louis, MO-IL Metro area
	17005	Bond County, IL
	17013	Calhoun County, IL
	17027	Clinton County, IL
	17083	Jersey County, IL

Metropolitan and Micropolitan Area Code	State/County FIPS code	Title and Geographic Components
	17117	Macoupin County, IL
	17119	Madison County, IL
	17133	Monroe County, IL
	17163	St. Clair County, IL
	29071	Franklin County, MO
	29099	Jefferson County, MO
	29113	Lincoln County, MO
	29183	St. Charles County, MO
	29189	St. Louis County, MO
	29219	Warren County, MO
	29510	St. Louis city, MO
44300		State College, PA Metro area
	42027	Centre County, PA
44420		Staunton-Waynesboro, VA Metro area
	51015	Augusta County, VA
	51790	Staunton City, VA
	51820	Waynesboro City, VA
44700		Stockton-Lodi, CA Metro area
	06077	San Joaquin County, CA
44940		Sumter, SC Metro area
	45085	Sumter County, SC
44980		Sunbury, PA Micro area
	42097	Northumberland County, PA
45060		Syracuse, NY Metro area
	36053	Madison County, NY
	36067	Onondaga County, NY
	36075	Oswego County, NY
45220		Tallahassee, FL Metro area
	12039	Gadsden County, FL
	12065	Jefferson County, FL
	12073	Leon County, FL
	12129	Wakulla County, FL
45300		Tampa-St. Petersburg-Clearwater, FL Metro area
	12053	Hernando County, FL
	12057	Hillsborough County, FL
	12101	Pasco County, FL
	12103	Pinellas County, FL
45460		Terre Haute, IN Metro area
	18021	Clay County, IN
	18153	Sullivan County, IN
	18165	Vermillion County, IN
	18167	Vigo County, IN
45500		Texarkana, TX-AR Metro area
	05081	Little River County, AR
	05091	Miller County, AR
	48037	Bowie County, TX
45540		The Villages, FL Metro area
	12119	Sumter County, FL
45780		Toledo, OH Metro area
	39051	Fulton County, OH
	39095	Lucas County, OH
	39173	Wood County, OH
45820		Topeka, KS Metro area
	20085	Jackson County, KS
	20087	Jefferson County, KS
	20139	Osage County, KS
	20177	Shawnee County, KS
	20197	Wabaunsee County, KS
45860		Torrington, CT Micro area
	09005	Litchfield County, CT
45900		Traverse City, MI Micro area
	26019	Benzie County, MI
	26055	Grand Traverse County, MI
	26079	Kalkaska County, MI
	26089	Leelanau County, MI
45940		Trenton, NJ Metro area
	34021	Mercer County, NJ
46020		Truckee-Grass Valley, CA Micro area
	06057	Nevada County, CA
46060		Tucson, AZ Metro area
	04019	Pima County, AZ
46100		Tullahoma-Manchester, TN Micro area
	47031	Coffee County, TN
	47051	Franklin County, TN
	47127	Moore County, TN
46140		Tulsa, OK Metro area
	40037	Creek County, OK
	40111	Okmulgee County, OK
	40113	Osage County, OK
	40117	Pawnee County, OK
	40131	Rogers County, OK
	40143	Tulsa County, OK
	40145	Wagoner County, OK
46180		Tupelo, MS Micro area
	28057	Itawamba County, MS

Metropolitan and Micropolitan Areas and Components (as defined February 2013)

Metropolitan and Micropolitan Area Code	State/County FIPS code	Title and Geographic Components
	28081	Lee County, MS
	28115	Pontotoc County, MS
46220		Tuscaloosa, AL Metro area
	01065	Hale County, AL
	01107	Pickens County, AL
	01125	Tuscaloosa County, AL
46340		Tyler, TX Metro area
	48423	Smith County, TX
46520		Urban Honolulu, HI Metro area
	15003	Honolulu County, HI
46540		Utica-Rome, NY Metro area
	36043	Herkimer County, NY
	36065	Oneida County, NY
46660		Valdosta, GA Metro area
	13027	Brooks County, GA
	13101	Echols County, GA
	13173	Lanier County, GA
	13185	Lowndes County, GA
46700		Vallejo-Fairfield, CA Metro area
	06095	Solano County, CA
47020		Victoria, TX Metro area
	48175	Goliad County, TX
	48469	Victoria County, TX
47220		Vineland-Bridgeton, NJ Metro area
	34011	Cumberland County, NJ
47260		Virginia Beach-Norfolk-Newport News, VA-NC Metro area
	37053	Currituck County, NC
	37073	Gates County, NC
	51073	Gloucester County, VA
	51093	Isle of Wight County, VA
	51095	James City County, VA
	51115	Mathews County, VA
	51199	York County, VA
	51550	Chesapeake city, VA
	51650	Hampton city, VA
	51700	Newport News city, VA
	51710	Norfolk city, VA
	51735	Poquoson city, VA
	51740	Portsmouth city, VA
	51800	Suffolk city, VA
	51810	Virginia Beach city, VA
	51830	Williamsburg city, VA
47300		Visalia-Porterville, CA Metro area
	06107	Tulare County, CA
47380		Waco, TX Metro area
	48145	Falls County, TX
	48309	McLennan County, TX
47460		Walla Walla, WA Metro area
	53013	Columbia County, WA
	53071	Walla Walla County, WA
47580		Warner Robins, GA Metro area
	13153	Houston County, GA
	13225	Peach County, GA
	13235	Pulaski County, GA
47900		Washington-Arlington-Alexandria, DC-VA-MD-WV Metro area
47900		Silver Spring-Frederick-Rockville, MD Metro Div 43524
	24021	Frederick County, MD
	24031	Montgomery County, MD
47900		Washington-Arlington-Alexandria, DC-VA-MD-WV Metro Div 47894
	11001	District of Columbia, DC
	24009	Calvert County, MD
	24017	Charles County, MD
	24033	Prince George's County, MD
	51013	Arlington County, VA
	51043	Clarke County, VA
	51047	Culpeper County, VA
	51059	Fairfax County, VA
	51061	Fauquier County, VA
	51107	Loudoun County, VA
	51153	Prince William County, VA
	51157	Rappahannock County, VA
	51177	Spotsylvania County, VA
	51179	Stafford County, VA
	51187	Warren County, VA
	51510	Alexandria city, VA
	51600	Fairfax city, VA
	51610	Falls Church city, VA
	51630	Fredericksburg city, VA
	51683	Manassas city, VA
	51685	Manassas Park city, VA
	54037	Jefferson County, WV
47940		Waterloo-Cedar Falls, IA Metro area
	19013	Black Hawk County, IA
	19017	Bremer County, IA
	19075	Grundy County, IA
48060		Watertown-Fort Drum, NY Metro area
	36045	Jefferson County, NY
48140		Wausau, WI Metro area
	55073	Marathon County, WI
48260		Weirton-Steubenville, WV-OH Metro area
	39081	Jefferson County, OH
	54009	Brooke County, WV
	54029	Hancock County, WV
48300		Wenatchee, WA Metro area
	53007	Chelan County, WA
	53017	Douglas County, WA
48540		Wheeling, WV-OH Metro area
	39013	Belmont County, OH
	54051	Marshall County, WV
	54069	Ohio County, WV
48580		Whitewater-Elkhorn, WI Micro area
	55127	Walworth County, WI
48620		Wichita, KS Metro area
	20015	Butler County, KS
	20079	Harvey County, KS
	20095	Kingman County, KS
	20173	Sedgwick County, KS
	20191	Sumner County, KS
48660		Wichita Falls, TX Metro area
	48009	Archer County, TX
	48077	Clay County, TX
	48485	Wichita County, TX
48700		Williamsport, PA Metro area
	42081	Lycoming County, PA
48900		Wilmington, NC Metro area
	37129	New Hanover County, NC
	37141	Pender County, NC
49020		Winchester, VA-WV Metro area
	51069	Frederick County, VA
	51840	Winchester city, VA
	54027	Hampshire County, WV
49180		Winston-Salem, NC Metro area
	37057	Davidson County, NC
	37059	Davie County, NC
	37067	Forsyth County, NC
	37169	Stokes County, NC
	37197	Yadkin County, NC
49300		Wooster, OH Micro area
	39169	Wayne County, OH
49340		Worcester, MA-CT Metro area
	09015	Windham County, CT
	25027	Worcester County, MA
49420		Yakima, WA Metro area
	53077	Yakima County, WA
49620		York-Hanover, PA Metro area
	42133	York County, PA
49660		Youngstown-Warren-Boardman, OH-PA Metro area
	39099	Mahoning County, OH
	39155	Trumbull County, OH
	42085	Mercer County, PA
49700		Yuba City, CA Metro area
	06101	Sutter County, CA
	06115	Yuba County, CA
49740		Yuma, AZ Metro area
	04027	Yuma County, AZ

APPENDIX B. CITIES BY COUNTY

The following table is arranged alphabetically by state. Under each state heading are listed all cities identifiable based on the PUMA allocation procedure, along with their component counties. The population in each city and component reflects the 2010 Census population, which in some cases is less than the 100,000 PUMA threshold.

State code	County Code	Place Code	Geographic Area Name	2010 census population
01			**ALABAMA**	4,779,736
01		07000	Birmingham city	212,237
01	073		Jefferson County	210,609
01	117		Shelby County	1,628
01		37000	Huntsville city	180,105
01	083		Limestone County	1,521
01	089		Madison County	178,584
01		50000	Mobile city	195,111
01	097		Mobile County	195,111
01		51000	Montgomery city	205,764
01	101		Montgomery County	205,764
01		77256	Tuscaloosa city	90,468
01	125		Tuscaloosa County	90,468
02			**ALASKA**	710,231
02		03000	Anchorage municipality	291,826
02	020		Anchorage Municipality	291,826
04			**ARIZONA**	6,392,017
04		12000	Chandler city	236,123
04	013		Maricopa County	236,123
04		27820	Glendale city	226,721
04	013		Maricopa County	226,721
04		46000	Mesa city	439,041
04	013		Maricopa County	439,041
04		54050	Peoria city	154,065
04	013		Maricopa County	154,058
04	025		Yavapai County	7
04		55000	Phoenix city	1,445,632
04	013		Maricopa County	1,445,632
04		65000	Scottsdale city	217,385
04	013		Maricopa County	217,385
04		71510	Surprise city	117,517
04	013		Maricopa County	117,517
04		73000	Tempe city	161,719
04	013		Maricopa County	161,719
04		77000	Tucson city	520,116
04	019		Pima County	520,116
04		85540	Yuma city	93,064
04	027		Yuma County	93,064
05			**ARKANSAS**	2,915,918
05		41000	Little Rock city	193,524
05	119		Pulaski County	193,524
06			**CALIFORNIA**	37,253,956
06		02000	Anaheim city	336,265
06	059		Orange County	336,265
06		02252	Antioch city	102,372
06	013		Contra Costa County	102,372
06		03526	Bakersfield city	347,483
06	029		Kern County	347,483
06		06000	Berkeley city	112,580
06	001		Alameda County	112,580
06		08954	Burbank city	103,340

State code	County Code	Place Code	Geographic Area Name	2010 census population
06	037		Los Angeles County	103,340
06		11194	Carlsbad city	105,328
06	073		San Diego County	105,328
06		11530	Carson city	91,714
06	037		Los Angeles County	91,714
06		13014	Chico city	86,187
06	007		Butte County	86,187
06		13392	Chula Vista city	243,916
06	073		San Diego County	243,916
06		14218	Clovis city	95,631
06	019		Fresno County	95,631
06		15044	Compton city	96,455
06	037		Los Angeles County	96,455
06		16000	Concord city	122,067
06	013		Contra Costa County	122,067
06		16350	Corona city	152,374
06	065		Riverside County	152,374
06		16532	Costa Mesa city	109,960
06	059		Orange County	109,960
06		17918	Daly City city	101,123
06	081		San Mateo County	101,123
06		19766	Downey city	111,772
06	037		Los Angeles County	111,772
06		21712	El Cajon city	99,478
06	073		San Diego County	99,478
06		22230	El Monte city	113,475
06	037		Los Angeles County	113,475
06		22020	Elk Grove city	153,015
06	067		Sacramento County	153,015
06		22804	Escondido city	143,911
06	073		San Diego County	143,911
06		23182	Fairfield city	105,321
06	095		Solano County	105,321
06		24680	Fontana city	196,069
06	071		San Bernardino County	196,069
06		26000	Fremont city	214,089
06	001		Alameda County	214,089
06		27000	Fresno city	494,665
06	019		Fresno County	494,665
06		28000	Fullerton city	135,161
06	059		Orange County	135,161
06		29000	Garden Grove city	170,883
06	059		Orange County	170,883
06		30000	Glendale city	191,719
06	037		Los Angeles County	191,719
06		33000	Hayward city	144,186
06	001		Alameda County	144,186
06		33434	Hesperia city	90,173
06	071		San Bernardino County	90,173
06		36000	Huntington Beach city	189,992
06	059		Orange County	189,992
06		36546	Inglewood city	109,673

State code	County Code	Place Code	Geographic Area Name	2010 census population
06	037		Los Angeles County	109,673
06		36770	Irvine city	212,375
06	059		Orange County	212,375
06		40130	Lancaster city	156,633
06	037		Los Angeles County	156,633
06		43000	Long Beach city	462,257
06	037		Los Angeles County	462,257
06		44000	Los Angeles city	3,792,621
06	037		Los Angeles County	3,792,621
06		48256	Mission Viejo city	93,305
06	059		Orange County	93,305
06		48354	Modesto city	201,165
06	099		Stanislaus County	201,165
06		49270	Moreno Valley city	193,365
06	065		Riverside County	193,365
06		50076	Murrieta city	103,466
06	065		Riverside County	103,466
06		52526	Norwalk city	105,549
06	037		Los Angeles County	105,549
06		53000	Oakland city	390,724
06	001		Alameda County	390,724
06		53322	Oceanside city	167,086
06	073		San Diego County	167,086
06		53896	Ontario city	163,924
06	071		San Bernardino County	163,924
06		53980	Orange city	136,416
06	059		Orange County	136,416
06		54652	Oxnard city	197,899
06	111		Ventura County	197,899
06		55156	Palmdale city	152,750
06	037		Los Angeles County	152,750
06		56000	Pasadena city	137,122
06	037		Los Angeles County	137,122
06		58072	Pomona city	149,058
06	037		Los Angeles County	149,058
06		59451	Rancho Cucamonga city	165,269
06	071		San Bernardino County	165,269
06		59920	Redding city	89,861
06	089		Shasta County	89,861
06		60466	Rialto city	99,171
06	071		San Bernardino County	99,171
06		60620	Richmond city	103,701
06	013		Contra Costa County	103,701
06		62000	Riverside city	303,871
06	065		Riverside County	303,871
06		62938	Roseville city	118,788
06	061		Placer County	118,788
06		64000	Sacramento city	466,488
06	067		Sacramento County	466,488
06		64224	Salinas city	150,441
06	053		Monterey County	150,441
06		65000	San Bernardino city	209,924
06	071		San Bernardino County	209,924
06		65042	San Buenaventura (Ventura) city	106,433
06	111		Ventura County	106,433
06		66000	San Diego city	1,307,402
06	073		San Diego County	1,307,402
06		67000	San Francisco city	805,235
06	075		San Francisco County	805,235
06		68000	San Jose city	945,942
06	085		Santa Clara County	945,942
06		68196	San Marcos city	83,781
06	073		San Diego County	83,781
06		68252	San Mateo city	97,207
06	081		San Mateo County	97,207
06		69000	Santa Ana city	324,528
06	059		Orange County	324,528
06		69084	Santa Clara city	116,468
06	085		Santa Clara County	116,468
06		69088	Santa Clarita city	176,320
06	037		Los Angeles County	176,320
06		69196	Santa Maria city	99,553
06	083		Santa Barbara County	99,553
06		70000	Santa Monica city	89,736
06	037		Los Angeles County	89,736
06		70098	Santa Rosa city	167,815
06	097		Sonoma County	167,815
06		72016	Simi Valley city	124,237
06	111		Ventura County	124,237
06		73080	South Gate city	94,396
06	037		Los Angeles County	94,396
06		75000	Stockton city	291,707
06	077		San Joaquin County	291,707
06		77000	Sunnyvale city	140,081
06	085		Santa Clara County	140,081
06		78120	Temecula city	100,097
06	065		Riverside County	100,097
06		78582	Thousand Oaks city	126,683
06	111		Ventura County	126,683
06		80000	Torrance city	145,438
06	037		Los Angeles County	145,438
06		81554	Vacaville city	92,428
06	095		Solano County	92,428
06		81666	Vallejo city	115,942
06	095		Solano County	115,942
06		82590	Victorville city	115,903
06	071		San Bernardino County	115,903
06		82954	Visalia city	124,442
06	107		Tulare County	124,442
06		82996	Vista city	93,834
06	073		San Diego County	93,834
06		84200	West Covina city	106,098
06	037		Los Angeles County	106,098
06		84550	Westminster city	89,701
06	059		Orange County	89,701
08			**COLORADO**	5,029,196
08		03455	Arvada city	106,433
08	001		Adams County	2,849
08	059		Jefferson County	103,584
08		04000	Aurora city	325,078
08	001		Adams County	39,871
08	005		Arapahoe County	285,090
08	035		Douglas County	117
08		07850	Boulder city	97,385
08	013		Boulder County	97,385
08		12815	Centennial city	100,377
08	005		Arapahoe County	100,377
08		16000	Colorado Springs city	416,427
08	041		El Paso County	416,427

State code	County Code	Place Code	Geographic Area Name	2010 census population
08		20000	Denver city	600,158
08	031		Denver County	600,158
08		27425	Fort Collins city	143,986
08	069		Larimer County	143,986
08		32155	Greeley city	92,889
08	123		Weld County	92,889
08		43000	Lakewood city	142,980
08	059		Jefferson County	142,980
08		45970	Longmont City	86,270
08	013		Boulder County	86,240
08	123		Weld County	30
08		62000	Pueblo city	106,595
08	101		Pueblo County	106,595
08		77290	Thornton city	118,772
08	001		Adams County	118,772
08	123		Weld County	0
08		83835	Westminster city	106,114
08	001		Adams County	63,696
08	059		Jefferson County	42,418
09			**CONNECTICUT**	3,574,097
09		08000	Bridgeport city	144,229
09	001		Fairfield County	144,229
09		37000	Hartford city	124,775
09	003		Hartford County	124,775
09		52000	New Haven city	129,779
09	009		New Haven County	129,779
09		73000	Stamford city	122,643
09	001		Fairfield County	122,643
09		80000	Waterbury city	110,366
09	009		New Haven County	110,366
11			**DISTRICT OF COLUMBIA**	601,723
11		50000	Washington city	601,723
11	001		District of Columbia	601,723
12			**FLORIDA**	18,801,310
12		07300	Boca Raton city	84,392
12	099		Palm Beach County	84,392
12		10275	Cape Coral city	154,305
12	071		Lee County	154,305
12		12875	Clearwater city	107,685
12	103		Pinellas County	107,685
12		14400	Coral Springs city	121,096
12	011		Broward County	121,096
12		24000	Fort Lauderdale city	165,521
12	011		Broward County	165,521
12		25175	Gainesville city	124,354
12	001		Alachua County	124,354
12		30000	Hialeah city	224,669
12	086		Miami-Dade County	224,669
12		32000	Hollywood city	140,768
12	011		Broward County	140,768
12		35000	Jacksonville city	821,784
12	031		Duval County	821,784
12		38250	Lakeland city	97,422
12	105		Polk County	97,422
12		45000	Miami city	399,457
12	086		Miami-Dade County	399,457
12		45025	Miami Beach city	87,779
12	086		Miami-Dade County	87,779
12		45060	Miami Gardens city	107,167
12	086		Miami-Dade County	107,167
12		45975	Miramar city	122,041
12	011		Broward County	122,041
12		53000	Orlando city	238,300
12	095		Orange County	238,300
12		54000	Palm Bay city	103,190
12	009		Brevard County	103,190
12		55775	Pembroke Pines city	154,750
12	011		Broward County	154,750
12		57425	Plantation city	84,955
12	011		Broward County	84,955
12		58050	Pompano Beach city	99,845
12	011		Broward County	99,845
12		58715	Port St. Lucie city	164,603
12	111		St. Lucie County	164,603
12		63000	St. Petersburg city	244,769
12	103		Pinellas County	244,769
12		69700	Sunrise city	84,439
12	011		Broward County	84,439
12		70600	Tallahassee city	181,376
12	073		Leon County	181,376
12		71000	Tampa city	335,709
12	057		Hillsborough County	335,709
12		76600	West Palm Beach city	99,919
12	099		Palm Beach County	99,919
13			**GEORGIA**	9,687,653
13		04000	Atlanta city	420,003
13	089		DeKalb County	28,292
13	121		Fulton County	391,711
13		19000	Columbus city	189,885
13	215		Muscogee County	189,885
13		67284	Roswell city	88,346
13	121		Fulton County	88,346
13		68516	Sandy Springs city	93,853
13	121		Fulton County	93,853
13		69000	Savannah city	136,286
13	051		Chatham County	136,286
15			**HAWAII**	1,360,301
15		71550	Urban Honolulu CDP	337,256
15	003		Honolulu County	337,256
16			**IDAHO**	1,567,582
16		08830	Boise City city	205,671
16	001		Ada County	205,671
16		52120	Meridian city	75,092
16	001		Ada County	75,092
17			**ILLINOIS**	12,830,632
17		03012	Aurora city	197,899
17	043		DuPage County	49,433
17	089		Kane County	130,976
17	093		Kendall County	6,019
17	197		Will County	11,471
17		14000	Chicago city	2,695,598
17	031		Cook County	2,695,598
17	043		DuPage County	0
17		23074	Elgin city	108,188
17	031		Cook County	24,032
17	089		Kane County	84,156
17		38570	Joliet city	147,433
17	093		Kendall County	9,749
17	197		Will County	137,684
17		51622	Naperville city	141,853

State code	County Code	Place Code	Geographic Area Name	2010 census population
17	043		DuPage County	94,533
17	197		Will County	47,320
17		59000	Peoria city	115,007
17	143		Peoria County	115,007
17		65000	Rockford city	152,871
17	201		Winnebago County	152,871
17		72000	Springfield city	116,250
17	167		Sangamon County	116,250
18			**INDIANA**	6,483,802
18		22000	Evansville city	117,429
18	163		Vanderburgh County	117,429
18		25000	Fort Wayne city	253,691
18	003		Allen County	253,691
18		71000	South Bend city	101,168
18	141		St. Joseph County	101,168
19			**IOWA**	3,046,355
19		12000	Cedar Rapids city	126,326
19	113		Linn County	126,326
19		19000	Davenport city	99,685
19	163		Scott County	99,685
19		21000	Des Moines city	203,433
19	153		Polk County	203,419
19	181		Warren County	14
20			**KANSAS**	2,853,118
20		36000	Kansas City city	145,786
20	209		Wyandotte County	145,786
20		52575	Olathe city	125,872
20	091		Johnson County	125,872
20		53775	Overland Park city	173,372
20	091		Johnson County	173,372
20		71000	Topeka city	127,473
20	177		Shawnee County	127,473
20		79000	Wichita city	382,368
20	173		Sedgwick County	382,368
21			**KENTUCKY**	4,339,367
21		46027	Lexington-Fayette urban county	295,803
21	067		Fayette County	295,803
22			**LOUISIANA**	4,533,372
22		05000	Baton Rouge city	229,493
22	033		East Baton Rouge Parish	229,493
22		40735	Lafayette city	120,623
22	055		Lafayette Parish	120,623
22		55000	New Orleans city	343,829
22	071		Orleans Parish	343,829
22		70000	Shreveport city	199,311
22	015		Bossier Parish	2,702
22	017		Caddo Parish	196,609
24			**MARYLAND**	5,773,552
24		04000	Baltimore city	620,961
24	510		Baltimore city	620,961
25			**MASSACHUSETTS**	6,547,629
25		07000	Boston city	617,594
25	025		Suffolk County	617,594
25		09000	Brockton city	93,810
25	023		Plymouth County	93,810
25		11000	Cambridge city	105,162
25	017		Middlesex County	105,162
25		37000	Lowell city	106,519
25	017		Middlesex County	106,519
25		37490	Lynn city	90,329
25	009		Essex County	90,329
25		45000	New Bedford city	95,072
25	005		Bristol County	95,072
25		55745	Quincy city	92,271
25	021		Norfolk County	92,271
25		67000	Springfield city	153,060
25	013		Hampden County	153,060
25		82000	Worcester city	181,045
25	027		Worcester County	181,045
26			**MICHIGAN**	9,883,640
26		03000	Ann Arbor city	113,934
26	161		Washtenaw County	113,934
26		21000	Dearborn city	98,153
26	163		Wayne County	98,153
26		22000	Detroit city	713,777
26	163		Wayne County	713,777
26		29000	Flint city	102,434
26	049		Genesee County	102,434
26		34000	Grand Rapids city	188,040
26	081		Kent County	188,040
26		46000	Lansing city	114,297
26	045		Eaton County	4,734
26	065		Ingham County	109,563
26		49000	Livonia city	96,942
26	163		Wayne County	96,942
26		76460	Sterling Heights city	129,699
26	099		Macomb County	129,699
26		84000	Warren city	134,056
26	099		Macomb County	134,056
27			**MINNESOTA**	5,303,925
27		43000	Minneapolis city	382,578
27	053		Hennepin County	382,578
27		54880	Rochester city	106,769
27	109		Olmsted County	106,769
27		58000	St. Paul city	285,068
27	123		Ramsey County	285,068
28			**MISSISSIPPI**	2,967,297
28		36000	Jackson city	173,514
28	049		Hinds County	172,891
28	089		Madison County	622
28	121		Rankin County	1
29			**MISSOURI**	5,988,927
29		15670	Columbia city	108,500
29	019		Boone County	108,500
29		35000	Independence city	116,830
29	047		Clay County	0
29	095		Jackson County	116,830
29		38000	Kansas City city	459,787
29	037		Cass County	197
29	047		Clay County	113,415
29	095		Jackson County	302,499
29	165		Platte County	43,676
29		41348	Lee's Summit city	91,364
29	037		Cass County	1,917
29	095		Jackson County	89,447
29		65000	St. Louis city	319,294
29	510		St. Louis city	319,294
29		70000	Springfield city	159,498
29	043		Christian County	2

State code	County Code	Place Code	Geographic Area Name	2010 census population
29	077		Greene County	159,496
30			**MONTANA**	989,415
30		06550	Billings city	104,170
30	111		Yellowstone County	104,170
31			**NEBRASKA**	1,826,341
31		28000	Lincoln city	258,379
31	109		Lancaster County	258,379
31		37000	Omaha city	408,958
31	055		Douglas County	408,958
32			**NEVADA**	2,700,551
32		31900	Henderson city	257,729
32	003		Clark County	257,729
32		40000	Las Vegas city	583,756
32	003		Clark County	583,756
32		51800	North Las Vegas city	216,961
32	003		Clark County	216,961
32		60600	Reno city	225,221
32	031		Washoe County	225,221
32		68400	Sparks city	90,264
32	031		Washoe County	90,264
33			**NEW HAMPSHIRE**	1,316,470
33		45140	Manchester city	109,565
33	011		Hillsborough County	109,565
34			**NEW JERSEY**	8,791,894
34		21000	Elizabeth city	124,969
34	039		Union County	124,969
34		36000	Jersey City city	247,597
34	017		Hudson County	247,597
34		51000	Newark city	277,140
34	013		Essex County	277,140
34		57000	Paterson city	146,199
34	031		Passaic County	146,199
35			**NEW MEXICO**	2,059,179
35		02000	Albuquerque city	545,852
35	001		Bernalillo County	545,852
35		39380	Las Cruces city	97,618
35	013		Doña Ana County	97,618
35		63460	Rio Rancho city	87,521
35	001		Bernalillo County	130
35	043		Sandoval County	87,391
36			**NEW YORK**	19,378,102
36		01000	Albany city	97,856
36	001		Albany County	97,856
36		11000	Buffalo city	261,310
36	029		Erie County	261,310
36		51000	New York city	8,175,133
36	005		Bronx County	1,385,108
36	047		Kings County	2,504,700
36	061		New York County	1,585,873
36	081		Queens County	2,230,722
36	085		Richmond County	468,730
36		63000	Rochester city	210,565
36	055		Monroe County	210,565
36		73000	Syracuse city	145,170
36	067		Onondaga County	145,170
36		84000	Yonkers	195,976
36	119		Westchester County	195,976
37			**NORTH CAROLINA**	9,535,483

State code	County Code	Place Code	Geographic Area Name	2010 census population
37		12000	Charlotte city	731,424
37	119		Mecklenburg County	731,424
37		19000	Durham city	228,330
37	063		Durham County	228,300
37	135		Orange County	30
37		22920	Fayetteville city	200,564
37	051		Cumberland County	200,564
37		28000	Greensboro city	269,666
37	081		Guilford County	269,666
37		31400	High Point city	104,371
37	057		Davidson County	5,310
37	067		Forsyth County	8
37	081		Guilford County	99,042
37	151		Randolph County	11
37		55000	Raleigh city	403,892
37	063		Durham County	1,067
37	183		Wake County	402,825
37		74440	Wilmington city	106,476
37	129		New Hanover County	106,476
37		75000	Winston-Salem city	229,617
37	067		Forsyth County	229,617
38			**NORTH DAKOTA**	672,591
38		25700	Fargo city	105,549
38	017		Cass County	105,549
39			**OHIO**	11,536,504
39		01000	Akron city	199,110
39	153		Summit County	199,110
39		15000	Cincinnati city	296,943
39	061		Hamilton County	296,943
39		16000	Cleveland city	396,815
39	035		Cuyahoga County	396,815
39		18000	Columbus city	787,033
39	041		Delaware County	7,245
39	045		Fairfield County	9,666
30	040		Franklin County	770,122
39		21000	Dayton city	141,527
39	113		Montgomery County	141,527
39		77000	Toledo city	287,208
39	095		Lucas County	287,208
40			**OKLAHOMA**	3,751,351
40		09050	Broken Arrow city	98,850
40	143		Tulsa County	80,634
40	145		Wagoner County	18,216
40		23200	Edmond city	81,405
40	109		Oklahoma County	81,405
40		41850	Lawton city	96,867
40	031		Comanche County	96,867
40		52500	Norman city	110,925
40	027		Cleveland County	110,925
40		55000	Oklahoma City city	579,999
40	017		Canadian County	44,541
40	027		Cleveland County	63,723
40	109		Oklahoma County	471,671
40	125		Pottawatomie County	64
40		75000	Tulsa city	391,906
40	113		Osage County	6,136
40	131		Rogers County	0
40	143		Tulsa County	385,613
40	145		Wagoner County	157
41			**OREGON**	3,831,074
41		05350	Beaverton city	89,803
41	067		Washington County	89,803
41		23850	Eugene city	156,185

State code	County Code	Place Code	Geographic Area Name	2010 census population
41	039		Lane County	156,185
41		31250	Gresham city	105,594
41	051		Multnomah County	105,594
41		34100	Hillsboro city	91,611
41	067		Washington County	91,611
41		59000	Portland city	583,776
41	005		Clackamas County	744
41	051		Multnomah County	581,485
41	067		Washington County	1,547
41		64900	Salem city	154,637
41	047		Marion County	130,398
41	053		Polk County	24,239
42			**PENNSYLVANIA**	12,702,379
42		02000	Allentown city	118,032
42	077		Lehigh County	118,032
42		24000	Erie city	101,786
42	049		Erie County	101,786
42		60000	Philadelphia city	1,526,006
42	101		Philadelphia County	1,526,006
42		61000	Pittsburgh city	305,704
42	003		Allegheny County	305,704
44			**RHODE ISLAND**	1,052,567
44		59000	Providence city	178,042
44	007		Providence County	178,042
45			**SOUTH CAROLINA**	4,625,364
45		13330	Charleston city	120,083
45	015		Berkeley County	8,095
45	019		Charleston County	111,988
45		16000	Columbia city	129,272
45	063		Lexington County	559
45	079		Richland County	128,713
45		50875	North Charleston city	97,471
45	015		Berkeley County	0
45	019		Charleston County	78,393
45	035		Dorchester County	19,078
46			**SOUTH DAKOTA**	814,180
46		59020	Sioux Falls city	153,888
46	083		Lincoln County	21,095
46	099		Minnehaha County	132,793
47			**TENNESSEE**	6,346,105
47		14000	Chattanooga city	167,674
47	065		Hamilton County	167,674
47		15160	Clarksville city	132,929
47	125		Montgomery County	132,929
47		40000	Knoxville city	178,874
47	093		Knox County	178,874
47		48000	Memphis city	646,889
47	157		Shelby County	646,889
47		51560	Murfreesboro city	108,755
47	149		Rutherford County	108,755
48			**TEXAS**	25,145,561
48		01000	Abilene city	117,063
48	253		Jones County	5,145
48	441		Taylor County	111,918
48		01924	Allen city	84,246
48	085		Collin County	84,246
48		03000	Amarillo city	190,695
48	375		Potter County	105,486
48	381		Randall County	85,209
48		04000	Arlington city	365,438
48	439		Tarrant County	365,438
48		05000	Austin city	790,390
48	209		Hays County	2
48	453		Travis County	754,691
48	491		Williamson County	35,697
48		07000	Beaumont city	118,296
48	245		Jefferson County	118,296
48		10768	Brownsville city	175,023
48	061		Cameron County	175,023
48		13024	Carrollton city	119,097
48	085		Collin County	2
48	113		Dallas County	49,352
48	121		Denton County	69,743
48		15976	College Station city	93,857
48	041		Brazos County	93,857
48		17000	Corpus Christi city	305,215
48	007		Aransas County	0
48	273		Kleberg County	0
48	355		Nueces County	305,215
48	409		San Patricio County	0
48		19000	Dallas city	1,197,816
48	085		Collin County	46,885
48	113		Dallas County	1,124,296
48	121		Denton County	26,579
48	257		Kaufman County	0
48	397		Rockwall County	56
48		19972	Denton city	113,383
48	121		Denton County	113,383
48		24000	El Paso city	649,121
48	141		El Paso County	649,121
48		27000	Fort Worth city	741,206
48	121		Denton County	7,813
48	367		Parker County	7
48	439		Tarrant County	733,386
48	497		Wise County	0
48		27684	Frisco city	116,989
48	085		Collin County	72,489
48	121		Denton County	44,500
48		29000	Garland city	226,876
48	085		Collin County	266
48	113		Dallas County	226,608
48	397		Rockwall County	2
48		30464	Grand Prairie city	175,396
48	113		Dallas County	123,487
48	139		Ellis County	45
48	439		Tarrant County	51,864
48		35000	Houston city	2,099,451
48	157		Fort Bend County	38,124
48	201		Harris County	2,057,280
48	339		Montgomery County	4,047
48		37000	Irving city	216,290
48	113		Dallas County	216,290
48		39148	Killeen city	127,921
48	027		Bell County	127,921
48		41464	Laredo city	236,091
48	479		Webb County	236,091
48		42508	Lewisville city	95,290
48	113		Dallas County	841
48	121		Denton County	94,449
48		45000	Lubbock city	229,573
48	303		Lubbock County	229,573
48		45384	McAllen city	129,877
48	215		Hidalgo County	129,877
48		45744	McKinney city	131,117
48	085		Collin County	131,117
48		47892	Mesquite city	139,824
241	113		Dallas County	139,824

State code	County Code	Place Code	Geographic Area Name	2010 census population
48		48072	Midland city	111,147
48	317		Martin County	0
48	329		Midland County	111,147
48		53388	Odessa city	99,940
48	135		Ector County	98,270
48	329		Midland County	1,670
48		56000	Pasadena city	149,043
48	201		Harris County	149,043
48		56348	Pearland city	91,252
48	039		Brazoria County	86,706
48	157		Fort Bend County	721
48	201		Harris County	3,825
48		58016	Plano city	259,841
48	085		Collin County	254,525
48	121		Denton County	5,316
48		61796	Richardson city	99,223
48	085		Collin County	28,569
48	113		Dallas County	70,654
48		63500	Round Rock city	99,887
48	453		Travis County	1,362
48	491		Williamson County	98,525
48		64472	San Angelo city	93,200
48	451		Tom Green County	93,200
48		65000	San Antonio city	1,327,407
48	029		Bexar County	1,327,381
48	091		Comal County	0
48	325		Medina County	26
48		74144	Tyler city	96,900
48	423		Smith County	96,900
48		76000	Waco city	124,805
48	309		McLennan County	124,805
48		79000	Wichita Falls city	104,553
48	485		Wichita County	104,553
49			**UTAH**	2,763,885
49		57300	Orem city	88,328
49	049		Utah County	88,328
49		62470	Provo city	112,488
49	049		Utah County	112,488
49		67000	Salt Lake City city	186,440
49	035		Salt Lake County	186,440
49		67440	Sandy city	87,461
49	035		Salt Lake County	87,461
49		82950	West Jordan city	103,712
49	035		Salt Lake County	103,712
49		83470	West Valley City city	129,480
49	035		Salt Lake County	129,480
51			**VIRGINIA**	8,001,024
51		01000	Alexandria city	139,966
51	510		Alexandria city	139,966
51		16000	Chesapeake city	222,209
51	550		Chesapeake city	222,209
51		35000	Hampton city	137,436
51	650		Hampton city	137,436
51		56000	Newport News city	180,719
51	700		Newport News city	180,719
51		57000	Norfolk city	242,803
51	710		Norfolk city	242,803
51		64000	Portsmouth city	95,535
51	740		Portsmouth city	95,535
51		67000	Richmond city	204,214
51	760		Richmond city	204,214
51		68000	Roanoke city	97,032

State code	County Code	Place Code	Geographic Area Name	2010 census population
51	770		Roanoke city	97,032
51		82000	Virginia Beach city	437,994
51	810		Virginia Beach city	437,994
53			**WASHINGTON**	6,724,540
53		05210	Bellevue city	122,363
53	033		King County	122,363
53		22640	Everett city	103,019
53	061		Snohomish County	103,019
53		23515	Federal Way city	89,306
53	033		King County	89,306
53		35415	Kent city	92,411
53	033		King County	92,411
53		57745	Renton city	90,927
53	033		King County	90,927
53		63000	Seattle city	608,660
53	033		King County	608,660
53		67000	Spokane city	208,916
53	063		Spokane County	208,916
53		67167	Spokane Valley city	89,755
53	063		Spokane County	89,755
53		70000	Tacoma city	198,397
53	053		Pierce County	198,397
53		74060	Vancouver city	161,791
53	011		Clark County	161,791
53		80010	Yakima city	91,067
53	077		Yakima County	91,067
55			**WISCONSIN**	5,686,986
55		31000	Green Bay city	104,057
55	009		Brown County	104,057
55		39225	Kenosha city	99,218
55	059		Kenosha County	99,218
55		48000	Madison city	233,209
55	025		Dane County	233,209
55		53000	Milwaukee city	594,833
55	079		Milwaukee County	594,833
55	131		Washington County	0
55	133		Waukesha County	0

The following consolidated cities are included here. They are listed here with their 2010 census populations, followed by the separate entities that make up the consolidated city. Data from the American Community Survey include only the "balance," the major city of each consolidated city.

13			**GEORGIA**	9,687,653
13		03436	Athens-Clark county	116,714
13		03440	Athens-Clark county (balance)	115,452
13		09068	Bogart town	140
13		83728	Winterville city	1,122
13		04200	Augusta-Richmond county	200,549
13		04204	Augusta-Richmond county (balance)	195,844
13		09040	Blythe city	694
13		38040	Hephzibah city	4,011
18			**INDIANA**	6,483,802
18		36000	Indianapolis city	829,718
18		04204	Beech Grove city	0
18		13492	Clermont town	1,356
18		16156	Crows Nest town	73
18		16336	Cumberland town	2,597
18		34420	Homecroft town	722
18		36003	Indianapolis city (balance)	820,445
18		42426	Lawrence city	42
18		48456	Meridian Hills town	1,616
18		54612	North Crows Nest town	45

State code	County Code	Place Code	Geographic Area Name	2010 census population
18		65556	Rocky Ripple town	606
18		72232	Spring Hill town	98
18		80234	Warren Park town	1,480
18		84374	Williams Creek town	407
18		85742	Wynnedale town	231
21			**KENTUCKY**	4,339,367
21		46003	Louisville/Jefferson County	741,096
21		01504	Anchorage city	2,348
21		02656	Audubon Park city	1,473
21		03376	Bancroft city	494
21		03556	Barbourmeade city	1,218
21		05068	Beechwood Village city	1,324
21		05392	Bellemeade city	865
21		05464	Bellewood city	321
21		07858	Blue Ridge Manor city	767
21		09532	Briarwood city	435
21		09847	Broeck Pointe city	272
21		10162	Brownsboro Farm city	648
21		10198	Brownsboro Village city	319
21		12066	Cambridge city	175
21		16395	Coldstream city	1,100
21		18270	Creekside city	305
21		18766	Crossgate city	225
21		22204	Douglass Hills city	5,484
21		22474	Druid Hills city	308
21		27262	Fincastle city	817
21		28342	Forest Hills city	444
21		31348	Glenview city	531
21		31402	Glenview Hills city	319
21		31420	Glenview Manor city	191
21		31870	Goose Creek city	294
21		32523	Graymoor-Devondale city	2,870
21		32986	Green Spring city	715
21		36102	Heritage Creek city	1,076
21		36374	Hickory Hill city	114
21		36865	Hills and Dales city	142
21		37576	Hollow Creek city	783
21		37630	Hollyvilla city	537
21		38170	Houston Acres city	507
21		38814	Hurstbourne city	4,216
21		38818	Hurstbourne Acres city	1,811
21		39304	Indian Hills city	2,868
21		40222	Jeffersontown city	26,595
21		42598	Kingsley city	381
21		43900	Langdon Place city	936
21		46540	Lincolnshire city	148
21		48006	Louisville/Jefferson County (balance)	597,337
21		48558	Lyndon city	11,002
21		48648	Lynnview city	914
21		49800	Manor Creek city	140
21		50412	Maryhill Estates city	179

State code	County Code	Place Code	Geographic Area Name	2010 census population
21		51193	Meadowbrook Farm city	136
21		51258	Meadow Vale city	736
21		51294	Meadowview Estates city	363
21		51978	Middletown city	7,218
21		52842	Mockingbird Valley city	167
21		53328	Moorland city	431
21		54660	Murray Hill city	582
21		56550	Norbourne Estates city	441
21		56730	Northfield city	1,020
21		56928	Norwood city	370
21		57658	Old Brownsboro Place city	353
21		59322	Parkway Village city	650
21		61554	Plantation city	832
21		62370	Poplar Hills city	362
21		63264	Prospect city	4,636
21		65208	Richlawn city	405
21		65766	Riverwood city	446
21		66486	Rolling Fields city	646
21		66504	Rolling Hills city	959
21		67944	St. Matthews city	17,472
21		67998	St. Regis Park city	1,454
21		69384	Seneca Gardens city	696
21		70284	Shively city	15,264
21		72138	South Park View city	7
21		72770	Spring Mill city	287
21		72790	Spring Valley city	654
21		74064	Strathmoor Manor city	337
21		74082	Strathmoor Village city	648
21		75190	Sycamore city	160
21		75963	Ten Broeck city	103
21		76380	Thornhill city	178
21		80913	Watterson Park city	976
21		81372	Wellington city	565
21		81624	West Buechel city	1,230
21		82164	Westwood city	634
21		83208	Wildwood city	261
21		83784	Windy Hills city	2,385
21		84486	Woodland Hills city	696
21		84756	Woodlawn Park city	942
21		84891	Worthington Hills city	1,446
47			**TENNESSEE**	6,346,105
47		52004	Nashville-Davidson	626,681
47		04620	Belle Meade city	2,912
47		05140	Berry Hill city	537
47		27020	Forest Hills city	4,812
47		29920	Goodlettsville city	10,319
47		40720	Lakewood city	2,302
47		52006	Nashville-Davidson (balance)	601,222
47		54780	Oak Hill city	4,529
47		63140	Ridgetop city	48

INDEX

INDEX